Communications in Computer and Information Science 2725

Rationale

The CCIS series is devoted to the publication of proceedings of computer science conferences. Its aim is to efficiently disseminate original research results in informatics in printed and electronic form. While the focus is on publication of peer-reviewed full papers presenting mature work, inclusion of reviewed short papers reporting on work in progress is welcome, too. Besides globally relevant meetings with internationally representative program committees guaranteeing a strict peer-reviewing and paper selection process, conferences run by societies or of high regional or national relevance are also considered for publication.

Topics

The topical scope of CCIS spans the entire spectrum of informatics ranging from foundational topics in the theory of computing to information and communications science and technology and a broad variety of interdisciplinary application fields.

Information for Volume Editors and Authors

Publication in CCIS is free of charge. No royalties are paid, however, we offer registered conference participants temporary free access to the online version of the conference proceedings on SpringerLink (http://link.springer.com) by means of an http referrer from the conference website and/or a number of complimentary printed copies, as specified in the official acceptance email of the event.

CCIS proceedings can be published in time for distribution at conferences or as post-proceedings, and delivered in the form of printed books and/or electronically as USBs and/or e-content licenses for accessing proceedings at SpringerLink. Furthermore, CCIS proceedings are included in the CCIS electronic book series hosted in the SpringerLink digital library at http://link.springer.com/bookseries/7899. Conferences publishing in CCIS are allowed to use our online conference service (Meteor) for managing the whole proceedings lifecycle (from submission and reviewing to preparing for publication) free of charge.

Publication process

The language of publication is exclusively English. Authors publishing in CCIS have to sign the Springer CCIS copyright transfer form, however, they are free to use their material published in CCIS for substantially changed, more elaborate subsequent publications elsewhere. For the preparation of the camera-ready papers/files, authors have to strictly adhere to the Springer CCIS Authors' Instructions and are strongly encouraged to use the CCIS LaTeX style files or templates.

Abstracting/Indexing

CCIS is abstracted/indexed in DBLP, Google Scholar, EI-Compendex, Mathematical Reviews, SCImago, Scopus. CCIS volumes are also submitted for the inclusion in ISI Proceedings.

How to start

To start the evaluation of your proposal for inclusion in the CCIS series, please send an e-mail to ccis@springer.com

Shahid Hussain · Arif Ali Khan ·
Muhammad Abdul Basit Ur Rahim ·
Saif Ur Rehman Khan
Editors

SEET—Software Engineering for Emerging Technologies

First International Conference, SEET 2025
Long Beach, CA, USA, August 11–12, 2025
Proceedings

Springer

Editors
Shahid Hussain
Penn State University
Behrend, PA, USA

Arif Ali Khan
University of Oulu
Oulu, Finland

Muhammad Abdul Basit Ur Rahim
College of Engineering
California State University, Long Beach
Long Beach, CA, USA

Saif Ur Rehman Khan
Shifa Tameer-e-Millat University
Islamabad, Pakistan

ISSN 1865-0929 ISSN 1865-0937 (electronic)
Communications in Computer and Information Science
ISBN 978-3-032-08976-2 ISBN 978-3-032-08977-9 (eBook)
https://doi.org/10.1007/978-3-032-08977-9

This Springer imprint is published by the registered company Springer Nature Switzerland AG
The registered company address is: Gewerbestrasse 11, 6330 Cham, Switzerland

Preface

We are delighted to extend a warm welcome to the proceedings of the 1st International Conference on Software Engineering of Emerging Technologies (SEET 2025), hosted at California State University, Long Beach, CA, USA. A primary objective and characteristic of this initiative is to unite academic scientists, engineers, and industry researchers to share and exchange their experiences and research findings regarding various facets of science and social research. Additionally, it aims to facilitate discussions on the practical challenges faced and the solutions implemented. We hope you had a technically rewarding experience and used this opportunity to reconnect with old friends and make many new ones.

The SEET 2025 conference was an engaging and enlightening event, featuring an impressive lineup of keynote speakers. The program consisted of regular, short, idea and vision, and Student Research Competition (SRC) sessions and discussions with eminent speakers covering a wide range of topics related to the integration of emerging technologies and software engineering practices, and their implications. This comprehensive program offered all participants the chance to connect and engage with each other. We trust that your experience at SEET 2025 was both rewarding and enduring. With your assistance and involvement, the conference will sustain its success for an extended period.

The response to the call for papers was outstanding, originating from contributors in 21 different countries. Regrettably, many manuscripts from respected institutions could not be accepted due to the outcomes of the review process and our capacity constraints. We would like to express our heartfelt thanks and appreciation to all the reviewers who helped us maintain the high standard of the manuscripts included in these proceedings published by Springer.

We would like to thank the organization staff, the members of the program committees and reviewers. They diligently reviewed papers and provided valuable suggestions to the authors for enhancing their work. We would also like to extend our appreciation to the external reviewers for their additional assistance during the review process, as well as to the authors for their contributions of research findings to the conference. Special thanks go to Springer.

SEET 2025 aimed to create a platform for discussing the issues, challenges, opportunities, and findings associated with the integration of emerging technologies into the software development process. The constantly evolving nature and swift advancements in emerging technologies to improve software development processes give rise to new challenges and inquiries, leading to a genuine necessity for the exchange of innovative ideas and fostering a heightened awareness of this significant area of research.

We are now optimistic and full of hope about getting the proceedings of SEET 2025 covered by Springer and Scopus in due course. We acknowledge that the authors of SEET 2025 may seek to enhance the visibility of their papers. We will make every effort to assist them in their pursuits. We extend our best wishes to all participants of SEET 2025 and hope you had a wonderful and productive experience at the conference.

August 2025

Shahid Hussain
Arif Ali Khan
Muhammad Abdul Basit Ur Rahim
Saif Ur Rehman Khan

Organization

General Chairs

Shahid Hussain	Penn State University, Behrend, USA
Arif Ali Khan	University of Oulu, Finland

Program Committee Chairs

Muhammad Abdul Basit Ur	Rahim California State University, Long Beach, USA
Saif Ur Rehman Khan	Shifa Tameer-e-Millat University, Pakistan

Track Chairs

Wen-li Wang	Penn State University, Behrend, USA
Mei-Huei Tang	Gannon University, USA
Muhammad Abid	Florida Polytechnic University, USA
Xin Qin	California State University Long Beach, USA
Tairan Liu	California State University Long Beach, USA
Muhammad Imran	Federation University, Australia
Azeem Akbar	Lappeenranta University of Technology, Finland
Souti Rini Chattopadhyay	University of Southern California, USA

Program Committee

Waqar Ali	Zurich University of Applied Sciences, Switzerland
Ghufran Ahmad	FAST-NUCES, Pakistan
Ghulam Mudassir	University of Buckingham, UK
Chong Chun Yong	Monash University Malaysia, Malaysia
Kifayat Ullah Khan	Birmingham City University, UK
Kwabena Ebo Bennin	Wageningen University & Research, Netherlands
Adnan Akhunzada	University of Doha for Science and Technology, Qatar
Pullin Agarwal	Penn State University, Behrend, USA

Mohammad Imtiaz Ullah	Ontario Tech University, Canada
Mohammad Junaid Khan	Western Washington University, USA
Mohammad Javid	Gomal University, Pakistan
Abdul Mateen	Federal Urdu University, Pakistan
Jie Zhao	Penn State University, Behrend, USA
Matteo Esposito	University of Rome "Tor Vergata", Italy
Mahdi Fahmideh	University of Southern Queensland, Australia
Vita Santa Barletta	University of Bari, Italy
Shalli Rani	Chitkara University, India
Gastón Márquez	Universidad del Bío-Bío, Chile
Saima Rafi	Edinburgh Napier University, UK
Anibrata Pal	University of Bari, Italy
Javed Ai Khan	University of Hertfordshire, UK
Peng Liand	Wuhan University, China
Muhammad Imran	University of Florida, USA
Umer Javeed	Baymatob Pty Ltd., Australia
Khubaib Amjad Alam	Al Ain University, Dubai
Muhammad Imran	National University of Sciences and Technology, Pakistan
Mohsin Riaz	COMSATS University Islamabad, Pakistan
Javed Iqbal	COMSATS University Islamabad, Pakistan
Irum Inayat	FAST-NUCES, Pakistan
Raja Habib	Shifa Tameer-e-Millat University, Pakistan
Abdul Khalique Shaikh	Sultan Qaboos University, Oman
Sajid Ibrahim Hashmi	University of Oulu, Finland
Md Rayhanur Rahman	University of Alabama, USA
Hassan Ali Khattak	Australian Catholic University, Australia
Abdul Wahid Khan	National University of Sciences and Technology, Pakistan
Kamran Latif	National Institute of Electronics, Pakistan

Additional Reviewers

Bashir Ahmad	Qurtuba University, Pakistan
Mohammad Imran Faisal	Shifa Tameer-e-Millat University, Pakistan
Mohammad Rafiq Mufti	COMSATS University, Pakistan
Humaira Afzal	Bahauddin Zakariya University, Pakistan
Ahmad Jan	Gomal University, Pakistan

Contents

Regular Research Paper

Student Research Competition (SRC)

Regular Research Paper

RF-MalDetect: Harnessing Random Forest for Malware Identification in PE Files

Dhwanil Chauhan[1](✉), Sachin Patel[2], Ankur Patel[2], Rushi Patel[3], Rishi Patel[4], Rooshikesh Bhatt[5], Margi Shah[6], and Manav Seth[7]

[1] Purdue University, Hammond, IN 46323, USA
Dhwanil832@gmail.com
[2] Charotar University of Science and Technology (CHARUSAT), Anand, India
{Sachinpatel.dit,Ankurpatel.ee}@charusat.ac.in
[3] Arizona State University, Tempe, USA
[4] Indiana University Bloomington, Bloomington, USA
[5] Conestoga College, Kitchener, Canada
[6] University of Ottawa, Ottawa, Canada
[7] University of Alabama Birmingham, Birmingham, USA

Abstract. In this work, an efficient machine learning-based approach is taken up: Random Forest, which identifies the efficiency of this very approach in distinguishing malware from original applications based on the content of the PE file. It deals with broad characteristics that have been taken from the PE files for training and tests by using a dataset with labeled examples of both kinds. Such may include the accuracy, precision, and recall among other metrics that shall be used through this experimentation phase, testing the efficacy of the Random Forest classifier in distinguishing the two categories. It also shows how to use the model in the Graphical User Interface to make predictions with regard to the PE files in an easily understandable way by users. These findings convey how machine learning approaches, especially Random Forest, potentially enhance cybersecurity methods through efficient detection of malware.

Keywords: Cyber Security · Malware Detection · Random Forest

1 Introduction

Malware proliferation is one of those consistent threats which cybersecurity has to put up with in the modern context. Detection systems should be firm yet flexible since the cyber threats get fancier and more complex. In this domain, machine learning has promised a great deal in proactive detection and evasion of noxious software. This paper describes the appropriate methodology to segregate malicious from actual software through a flexible ensemble learning method, Random Forest, which enjoys a high reputation among the classification methods. This paper intends to apply Random Forest to the analysis of Portable Executable files. The research work, therefore, investigates the feasibility and effectiveness of using Random Forest in identifying micro patterns in the Portable Executable file that actually distinguish between benign software from dangerous threats toward developing cybersecurity standards.

S. Hussain et al. (Eds.): SEET 2025, CCIS 2725, pp. 3–22, 2026.
https://doi.org/10.1007/978-3-032-08977-9_1

Their frequency shows that the detection methods of malware attacks have to provide timely identification of the progress of an attack and eliminate emerging new threats. The continuous evolution of the malware landscape keeps on making it hard for the classical signature-based methods to keep pace with it. There is a strong need for innovative techniques concerning automatic detection and adaptation to novel attack vectors. A promising paradigm change that machine learning approaches make use of includes native algorithms that can evaluate enormous volumes of data to find complicated patterns. In this regard, considering the adaptability, robustness, and high-dimensionality data handling capability, the Random Forest method will keep being in strong competition. Therefore, the subsequent study shall, by the power of Random Forest, enhance the ongoing debate on the effective ways of malware detection. In particular, PE files, among the most common executable file formats occurring under Windows systems, will be reviewed in some detail to give a close look at the characteristics important for their precise categorization.

2 Literature Survey

2.1 ML Integrated with Cybersecurity

It is fighting the ever-changing panorama of threats by including Machine Learning approaches. By automatically finding patterns and behaviors from gigantic datasets with algorithms, ML provides one with proactively enabling ways whereby one can identify and mitigate any potential dangers in real time. Machine learning works in cybersecurity because it identifies complex and dynamic patterns in data; hence, it is easy to find anomalies, hostile activities, and breaches missed by traditional rule-based systems. It is due to the extensive flexibility of machine learning techniques in responding to changes in threats with great capacity for handling a wide variety of different data types of high dimensionality.

Machine learning introduces a barrier that is kinetic-the introduction of machine learning into cybersecurity to advanced cyber threats. Advanced malware is really agile, keeps changing for evasion, and has conventionally been very hard for cybersecurity mechanisms depending on signature-based detection or rule-based systems. Machine learning models, however, transcend such limitations by finding much more subtle patterns and behaviors common to malicious activities. This has occasioned an growing number of research studies that spur on many machine learning algorithms and techniques suitable for particular cybersecurity needs. This literature review, therefore, sets out to undertake a critical review of the literature previously conducted on the use of machine learning techniques, with particular emphasis on their role in enhancing malware detection and strengthening cyber defense tactics. The use of ML in cybersecurity creates a dynamic barrier against sophisticated cyber threats. In nature, modern malware is extremely agile; it changes every single day to avoid detection. The classic cybersecurity mechanisms are based on either signature-based detection or rule-based systems, unable to cope with such frenetic rhythms. Opposite to this, the model of machine learning comes out unscathed by tracing minute patterns and behaviors present in malicious activities. This evolution has accordingly called for an increased number of research studies focusing on different machine learning algorithms and methods relevant to specific cybersecurity-related needs. The purpose of this literature review, therefore, is to put in perspective the key findings of previous research works that explore the contribution made by machine learning techniques in providing elements with respect to enhancing malware detection and improving cyber-defense strategies.

2.2 Decision Trees in Machine Learning

Because decision trees provide an intuitive way to depict decision-making processes, they are a fundamental method in machine learning. The most important feature is represented by the root node of this tree-like structure created by these models, decisions based on features are represented by the branches, and the final classification or prediction result is shown by the leaf nodes. It does so by iteratively partitioning the feature space to attain maximum information gain or minimum entropy, hence segmenting data into subsets of similar characteristics. Besides this, the main reasons why Decision Trees gained fame within many industries are due to their interpretability and versatility in data exploration, decision insight, Regression Analysis, and categorization (Fig. 1).

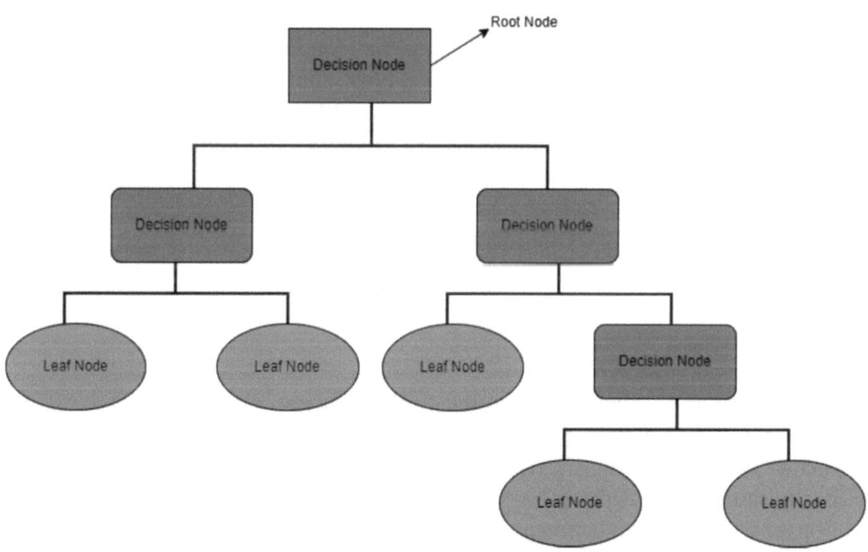

Fig. 1. Working of decision tree

ID3 Algorithm for Decision Trees

Among machine learning techniques, decision trees are one of the fundamental ways due to the naturalness of representation when modeling decision-making processes. In a tree-like structure developed by these models, the most significant characteristic forms the root node, the branches denote decisions or choices based on features, and the final results of classification or prediction appear as leaf nodes. The feature space is segmented recursively, aiming directly for maximum information gain or reducing entropy, the segmentation of data is also done into subgroups with similar characteristics, and it shows a tree-like structure. They are highly interpretable, flexible models, hence finding wide applications in many industries. They can be used for the exploration of data, gaining insight into decision-making, and performing both regression analysis and classification.

$$H(S) = -\sum ni = 1 \text{ pilog2(pi)} \tag{1}$$

$$\text{Information Gain (IG)} = \text{Entropy}(S) - \left[(\text{Weighted average}) * \text{Entropy(each feature)}\right] \tag{2}$$

CART Method for Decision Trees

The CART method overcame several limitations of ID3: its bility to be used for both regression and classification problems. CART constructs binary decision trees by splitting the data into subsets using attribute thresholds and seeking the optimal threshold that maximizes the purity of each subset. For classification, CART uses the Gini impurity criterion for the goodness of a split. It uses MSE in regression problems as a method for finding the best splits for continuous outcomes. The range was massively large by capability: to take both numerical and categorical features, to deal well with missing values, and to build binary trees. It is such flexibility that allowed CART to find applications in a great many machine learning and data analysis tasks.

$$\text{Gini Index} = 1 - \sum \text{jPj2} \tag{3}$$

2.3 Random Forest

ID3, concerning some of the deficiencies overcome by the technique of CART, the most important of them relate to its adaptability and suitability whether for classification or regression problems. In CART, binary trees are created by thresholding on attributes for data division into subgroups and impurity optimization from each. Amongst other measures, Gini impurity used in this algorithm assists in measuring the goodness of splits with regards to classification with the aim of misclassification reduction. In the case of continuous outcomes, the best splits for it are obtained by the use of MSE in regression situations. Handling of missing data by forming binary trees is a strong ability of CART and it accepts both numerical and category features substantially. It thus came to be an indispensable tool in several data analysis and machine learning domains.

It is important to notice that the Random Forests overcome several drawbacks of solitary decision trees. The methodology decreases the risk of over-fitting of the training data for the individual trees by including many trees into one; hence, much stronger generalization to unknown data is allowed. The deliberate introduction of randomness during feature and sample selection maintains a heterogeneous ensemble with low inter-tree correlation, hence helping the model to capture complicated patterns in data. Apart from that, Random Forest is also resistant to noise within the dataset and outliers. They provide regular and dependable results on quite diverse sets of areas. The said technique has wide applications within the highly critical sectors of bioinformatics, finance, and healthcare. Therefore, it also presents the importance of producing reliable, accurate, and flexible predictive models from a wide range of real-world applications.

2.4 Isolation Forest

Isolation Forest has been one of the innovative, effective anomaly detection techniques with the aim of finding anomalies or outliers in datasets. Unlike traditional techniques that rely on the normalcy assumption of data, the approach of Isolation Forest is to isolate anomalies, rather than building a profile of normal cases. The general idea is constructing random decision trees where pathways leading to anomalies are shallower since anomalies are unique and can be easily isolated. This differs from normal data points, which tend to expose anomalies sooner since they require extra splits in order to make them different from others.

The underlying philosophy of Isolation Forest is to build multiple random trees to achieve the necessary anomaly isolation. Indeed, it very fast identifies anomalies in the sense of their features being different from all others by a further partition of data with randomness in features and splitting points. This reveals stunning performance and scalability on quite large datasets or high-dimensional data conditions. Isolation Forest has been especially helpful in recognizing outliers from otherwise varied datasets across domains, from cybersecurity to fraud detection, by identifying abnormalities without large preprocessing or normality assumptions.

2.5 Mondrian Forests

The changed ensemble learning technique of Mondrian Forests is quite scalable and flexible, having a combination of decision trees and random forests. Since it is a sort of input space divvtkbdiosis in discontinuous rectangles through random projections, every rectangle is representing a decision tree leaf. Though classical decision trees depend on feature space splits based on impurity or information gain metrics, Mondrian Forests depend on grid-based splitting with random projections to have a scalable and efficient learning process.

A key intuition behind the Mondrian Forests is that the methodology is able to generate an astronomically large number of Mondrians or decision trees composing an ensemble of predictions. Each of those Mondrians concentrates on another region of thc input space, informed by the signal in that particular partition. The Mondrian Forests also adaptively change their structure during learning, with the capability to be updated and improved continuously given new data. With this flexibility and scalability, Mondrian Forests are especially well-placed for high-dimensional data or streaming data problems, where traditional approaches become computationally infeasible. The domains that show huge interest in Mondrian Forests include online advertising, recommendation systems, and time-series forecasting, where this power of efficiency and agility in handling enormous datasets with responses against shifting data distributions is experienced.

2.6 XGBoost Algorithm in Machine Learning

XGBoost stands for eXtreme Gradient Boosting, another efficient and popular ensemble learning technique. It's highly praised due to its performance in accuracy and speed for classification, regression, and ranking problems. The algorithm creates a sequential ensemble of weak learners, typically decision trees, but in many ways, it most closely resembles Random Forests since it's also an ensemble-based algorithm. But, unlike Random Forests, XGBoost is a boosting technique where the mistakes from the previous trees get corrected by the next tree. The model keeps on improving its prediction skills by increasing the weights for cases that are misidentified during training.

The key features that distinguish XGBoost include the new gradient boosting framework with regularization approaches to prevent overfitting, and the customized goal function, which can be used with a variety of problem types in optimizing model performance. The explanation goes in more detail with missing values in a collection, parallel processing supported, and scaling across huge datasets for maximum efficiency. Furthermore, by supplying feature relevance ratings, XGBoost allows for the identification of important variables, enabling one to glean insight into the patterns that underlie the data.

With its widespread use in industry segments like online advertising, healthcare, and finance, XGBoost is of great importance and applicability in creating reliable prediction models. It has become the go-to algorithm for practitioners seeking high predicted accuracy, efficiency, and interpretability in their models due to its outstanding results in many data contests and practical applications. Although XGBoost is not implemented in this study, the mention of it brings up the different ways to approach similar tasks using modern machine learning—thanks to its adaptability and diversity.

2.7 Gradient Boosting Machines (GBM)

Gradient Boosting Machines (GBM) are powerful ensemble learning techniques and have recently gained popularity due to great predictive performance in many fields. Unlike Random Forest, which builds trees on their own, GBM builds trees in a sequential way where each tree tries to correct the errors made by its preceding trees. In principle, GBM iteratively minimizes a pre-defined loss function by adding decision trees. This is an iterative approach that focuses successive trees on those areas where the current model is poor. It improves the accuracy over time, as it gradually refines its predictions. GBM reiterates past errors in order to improve its predictive power over time by pinpointing complex patterns in the data.

GBM works by creating shallow decision trees, or "weak learners," which are then added together to create a robust model by boosting. That is how, through an iterative process, total prediction performance can be continually improved with adjustments derived from residual errors of previous models. It also has regularization techniques to prevent overfitting, control tree complexity, or add penalties for model complexity in order to make sure of correct predictions on new data. Coupled with its exceptional accuracy, GBM is very flexible in handling different kinds of data sources and problem domains, which makes it among the top choices for any regression or classification tasks—be it in the field of natural language processing, finance, or healthcare.

2.8 AdaBoost (Adaptive Boosting)

AdaBoost, Adaptive Boosting, is an ensemble learning approach designed for constructing a strong and accurate model by combining weak learners in order to improve their predictive power. In contrast to the standard approach in ensemble methods, AdaBoost assigns different weights to individual learners, therefore providing more concentration on misclassified cases in subsequent rounds. These weak learners are trained iteratively: each following learner is trained more on examples that were wrongly classified in previous rounds. The flexibility in AdaBoost helps it to continuously improve its predictions by combining several weak learners into one strong model.

Essentially, AdaBoost adapts its strategy based on the complexity in data. If examples are misclassified, it increases their weights so that the next learners in the sequence are urged to pay more attention to correctly classifying those. Combining all these classifiers, AdaBoost creates a strong model for complex datasets—capable of picking up subtle trends that may be missed by individual classifiers. With its ability to adapt to different base classifiers and deal with high-dimensional data, it fits perfectly for classification tasks in those fields where accurate predictions are a must: image recognition, text analysis, and bioinformatics. However, AdaBoost can be sensitive to noisy data or outliers; still, its ability to boost weak learners toward a strong ensemble model classifies it among the important machine learning tools for the solution of different classification problems.

2.9 Gradient Tree Boosting

Gradient Tree Boosting, also known as Gradient Boosted Decision Trees (GBDT) or Gradient Boosting Machines (GBM), is a more advanced ensemble learning technique that combines the efficacy of boosting algorithms with that of decision trees. It works by adding trees to an ensemble one after another, where each tree tries to correct errors made by its predecessor. Gradient tree boosting builds decision trees one by one, learning from the mistakes of the previous trees, constantly improving the prediction, whereas it is not an independent mechanism unlike the regular decision trees. The basic idea is to add one tree at a time, trying to minimize the pre-set loss function by concentrating on the residuals or errors of the previous ones.

Gradient tree boosting can be seen as an iterative process for constructing a strong predictive model out of weak learners, usually shallow decision trees. That is, it works by fitting a number of trees, which each correct errors produced by the group of trees that came before it. It is then made to learn and improve by way of using the gradients of the loss function or residuals, in an iterative process. Gradient tree boosting is a very effective way to create a strong model—one that can capture intricate interactions within the data by slowly lowering these errors. Gradient tree boosting is one of the options that really stand out in machine learning applications, based on their possibility of being applied to any type of data and dealing with both regression and classification tasks. This is especially true for the fields of natural language processing, finance, and healthcare, in which accuracy and interpretability are critical.

2.10 Joblib Library

Joblib is mainly a lightweight Python pipelining library. It provides a simple and efficient way of doing parallel computing, particularly for CPU-bound tasks such as training models. Most important, though, it provides an efficient way to serialize Python objects, including complex data structures, to disk. This becomes very handy when dealing with large datasets or machine learning models. This library provides a set of tools to cache function results by reusing previously computed results when the inputs are unchanged, hence reducing the computation cost.

Joblib makes parallel computing in Python very accessible, with simple functions and classes that enable a user to parallelize a task over several cores or processors without much hassle. This library is especially useful in the domain of machine learning, where model training and testing could get quite tedious. Using Joblib, tasks can be divided and processed simultaneously to yield large speedups in computing. This comes in handy for quicker computations down the line: due to its serialization, there is no need to recalculate intermediate results or trained models. To save memory, Joblib's cache caches the output of functions for any given input parameters by avoiding redundant calculations.

Joblib has certainly helped a lot in making the training and assessment stages of your models easier; that is, parallel data handling would likely have sped up feature selection, model training, and cross-validation, generally improving the efficacy of your research pipeline. This serialization can also be helpful in saving and loading intermediate results or trained models during the research process to fasten experimentation and iterations.

2.11 Numpy

The ndarray is the multi-dimensional array class for changing data processing. NumPy is a fundamental Python module for numerical computing. Scientific computing is constructed on top of this basic framework, elaborating an array-oriented computing technique to accelerate data manipulation, statistic analysis, and mathematical operations. This versatility is realized from the fact that the ndarray efficiently handles homogeneous datasets with multiple dimensions, allowing operations like slicing, reshaping, and broadcasting. The usefulness of NumPy is increased in scientific fields due to its wide range of mathematical functions, which include statistical operations, random number generation, and linear algebra. NumPy is the basic tool in data manipulation for research and development of applications because it interfaces well with C/C++ and Fortran code and further enhances the performance.

NumPy is an essential tool in the manipulation and preparation of data for malware detection using the Random Forest technique. Most likely, the library made it easier since it converted the properties of the datasets into arrays that can be used in the training model by utilizing the operations on arrays and mathematical capabilities in NumPy. The reliable array-based operations probably made feature engineering jobs easier, hence allowing the users to manage the numerical data required for model validation effectively. The ability of NumPy in handling big datasets and to perform mathematical operations fast is what probably has made the dataset preparation and model implementation stages run smoother and fast.

2.12 PEfile Library

PEfile is a Python module, and without it, analysis and understanding of the Port-able Executable (PE) files—the default executable format in Windows systems—would be impossible. Using the impressive list of features that PEfile offers, one can dive deep into the inner workings of PE files and decipher minute facts hidden in headers, sections, and resources. This library exposes important metadata, such as header details, section properties, import and export tables, and resource information. The user is able to extract much data from PEfile, which is very essential for deep analysis and understanding of the PE file structure. It is a very important area in the field of Windows executable files.

PEfile was an integral part in breaking down PE files and extracting key metadata to further the goal of classifying malware using the Random Forest technique. Its features probably ease the extraction of complex information, including machine types, section sizes, entrance points, and file properties that were needed for strong feature sets or engineering features fit for training of a machine learning model. Furthermore, by using PEfile, one can automate the extraction of crucial resource data, such as manifest details, version information, or embedded resources, to simplify the overview of characteristics and actions of executable files. Your research may have developed a deeper understanding of PE file structures by using the capabilities of PEfile. This expertise could then be convincingly used to propose the detection and analysis of malicious behavior in Windows executables.

2.13 Scikit-Learn

Scikit-Learn is a crucial Python package for the machine learning environment. For scholars and practitioners in the subject, it acts as an extensive set of tools and methods, providing a flexible toolset. A variety of machine learning methods, including Random Forests, Decision Trees, and Support Vector Machines, are easily integrated with this toolkit due to its friendly user interface. In our study on malware detection using Random Forest, Scikit-Learn was a necessary package that helped in efficient model deployment and model assessment. From feature scaling to handling missing values in preprocessing, training, evaluation, and visualization of the models, it had it all.

The flexibility and usefulness of Scikit-Learn go beyond simply providing an implementation for a variety of algorithms but cover the whole machine learning process. Scikit-Learn did ease our tasks of preparing and formatting datasets for our research, ensuring they are ready to be trained by our Random Forest classifier. Its collection of visualization and assessment tools made it easier to assess how well our model performed in terms of identifying malicious software. The contribution of Scikit-Learn went beyond mere implementation; it went to the building, assessment, and deployment of models. Its broad functionality and ease of use made it possible to streamline the usage of machine learning techniques, which greatly contributed to creating and assessing our malware detection model.

2.14 Tkinter

Tkinter is a simple Python GUI (Graphical User Interface) toolkit that offers a simple yet powerful set of tools for building graphical desktop ap-plications. It acts as a wrapper to Tcl/Tk, allowing Python programmers to build attractive and user-friendly interactive graphical user interfaces. Tkinter makes it easier to create a window, a button, a menu, and so on with the extensive collection of widgets and tools it has. In the arena of Python, user-friendly programs are most preferably produced by Tkinter due to its versatility and simplicity of usage on multiple platforms.

Owing to its simplicity and neat integration with Python, Tkinter is one of the best options for desktop application development. With its great set of toolkits and widgets, developers can create graphical user interfaces that are not only aesthetic but also interactive. The modularities and flexibility of Tkinter enable developers to create their own unique UI elements and handle events from users. As Tkinter has cross-platform features, the applications developed with it run seamlessly on many operating systems without additional modification.

Tkinter was important in our research project for developing an intuitive user interface to deal with the malware detection system. We developed an easy-to-use interface using the features of Tkinter that would enable users to navigate, enter file locations, and receive immediate feedback about the validity of executable files. We were able to develop an interactive application interface quickly and create an interactive application that provided users interacting with the malware detection system with a seamless experience, thanks to Tkinter's flexibility and ease of use. The development of an accessible interface by Tkinter encouraged a more user-centered strategy for using machine learning in cybersecurity applications.

3 Related Work

(See Table 1).

Table 1. Related works

Sr. No.	Title	Abstract	Conclusion	Result/Key Findings
1	Android Mobile Malware Detection Using Machine Learning: A Systematic Review [1]	Proposes a deep learning-based malware detection system using CNNs.	Highlights the effectiveness of CNNs in achieving high detection rates.	Achieved an accuracy of 98.9% and outperformed traditional methods.
2	Deep Neural Network Based Malware Detection Using Two-Dimensional Binary Program Features [2]	Utilizes machine learning for dynamic malware analysis, focusing on API call sequences	Emphasizes the effectiveness of machine learning in dynamic analysis	Demonstrates accurate detection and classification of malware based on API sequences

(continued)

Table 1. (*continued*)

Sr. No.	Title	Abstract	Conclusion	Result/Key Findings
3	A Novel Intrusion Detection System based on Machine Learning for Internet of Things (IoT) Devices [3]	Presents a malware classification approach using machine learning with a focus on static features	Suggests that machine learning on static features provides accurate malware classification	Achieved high accuracy in classifying malware based on static features
4	Intelligent Vision-Based Malware Detection and Classification Using Deep Random Forest Paradigm [4]	Provides a survey of various machine learning techniques employed in malware analysis	Summarizes the strengths and weaknesses of different machine learning approaches in malware analysis	Offers insights into the diverse applications of machine learning in malware analysis
5	Intelligent Malware Detection using Oblique Random Forest Paradigm [5]	Proposes an oblique random forest ensemble learning technique for malware detection	Concludes that the proposed model outperforms existing decision tree models	Achieved high accuracy and low false positive rates in malware classification
6	Machine Learning Approach for Malware Detection Using Random Forest Classifier on Process List Data Structure [6]	Develops a machine learning approach for malware detection using a random forest classifier	Reports a prediction accuracy of 90.9% using process list data from a Linux environment	Achieved 90.9% accuracy in predicting malware using process list data
7	Malware classification for the cloud via semi-supervised transfer learning [7]	Proposes a semi-supervised transfer learning model for malware detection in cloud computing	Highlights improved detection accuracy using semi-supervised transfer learning	Improved detection accuracy from 94.72% to 96.9% with the proposed model
8	Malware Detection using Machine Learning and Deep Learning [8]	Investigates malware detection using machine learning and deep learning, comparing random forest with deep neural networks	Concludes that random forest outperforms deep neural networks for opcode frequency-based malware detection	Random forest achieved higher accuracy (99.7%) compared to deep neural networks

(*continued*)

Table 1. (*continued*)

Sr. No.	Title	Abstract	Conclusion	Result/Key Findings
9	Malware Detection Using Machine Learning [9]	Proposes a versatile framework for malware detection using different machine learning algorithms	Acknowledges the need for deterministic exception mechanisms to achieve a zero false positive rate	Achieved a significant increase in total detection rate, especially with cascade one-sided perceptrons
10	Opcode-sequence-based Semi-supervised Unknown Malware Detection [10]	Our main target was to come up with a machine learning framework that generically detects as much malware samples as it can, with the tough constraint of having a zero false positive rate	Empirical validation with varying percentages of labeled instances	Results include True Positive Ratio, False Positive Ratio, Accuracy, and AUC
11	Robust Malware Detection Models: Learning from Adversarial Attacks and Defenses [11]	Investigates robust malware detection models against adversarial attacks	Highlights vulnerability of ML models to attacks, proposes defense strategies	Achieved high fooling rates against detection models, proposed defense strategies
12	AIMED-RL: Exploring Adversarial Malware Examples with Reinforcement Learning [12]	Focuses on generating functional adversarial examples in malware domain	Introduces AIMED-RL, a method for generating adversarial examples in malware classification	Achieved evasion rates using RL-based agent, emphasized importance of penalty technique, shorter sequences of transformations for effective evasion
13	Two Semi-supervised Approaches to Malware Detection with Neural Networks [13]	Compares semi-supervised algorithms for malware detection with neural networks	Application of semi-supervised learning to improve neural network performance in malware detection	Improved accuracy with low ratios of labeled data using semi-supervised methods

(*continued*)

Table 1. *(continued)*

Sr. No.	Title	Abstract	Conclusion	Result/Key Findings
14	Ransomware Detection using RandomForest Technique [14]	Proposes static analysis-based ransomware detection from raw bytes, achieving 97.74% accuracy	Highlights optimal detection with 100 trees and seed 1 in 1.37 s. - Compares classifiers' performance	Emphasizes RandomForest's efficiency in byte-level analysis. - Outperforms opcode-based methods
15	Integrated static and dynamic analysis for malware detection [15]	Proposes an integrated static and dynamic analysis method for malware detection	Combined method enhances detection accuracy over standalone methods	Improved accuracy: Static - 95.8%, Dynamic - 97.1%, Integrated - 98.7%

4 Proposed System

4.1 Dataset Description

This data contains a wide range of attributes that have been extracted from PE files. Portable Executables are the building blocks of dynamic link libraries and executable programs that are mainly used with operating systems of the Windows family. This dataset offers a wide range of characteristics, and it explores internal details of those PE files. Some of the important header data that reflect the structural composition of such files are machine type, size of optional header, characteristics, and linker versions.

In addition, the dataset contains essential size metrics that give an idea of the physical arrangement and resource allocation of the files, which include size of code, size of initialized and uninitialized data, image base, details of alignment, and check-sum. It also includes vital version information such as operating system and image versions, details of subsystems, and header sizes-a pretty exhaustive rundown of the technical and evolutionary features of the PE files.

This dataset represents a comprehensive and diverse collection of PE files, which include executable programs and dynamic link libraries due to the diversity of the file formats with extensions like.exe and.dll. The analysis of this dataset allows detecting all kinds of patterns, trends, and correlations that different file types have, which is going to make their features, functions, and place in the Windows environment clearer. This is a dataset that could be very valuable in malware detection, software analysis, and system security research and practice in Windows environments (Fig. 2).

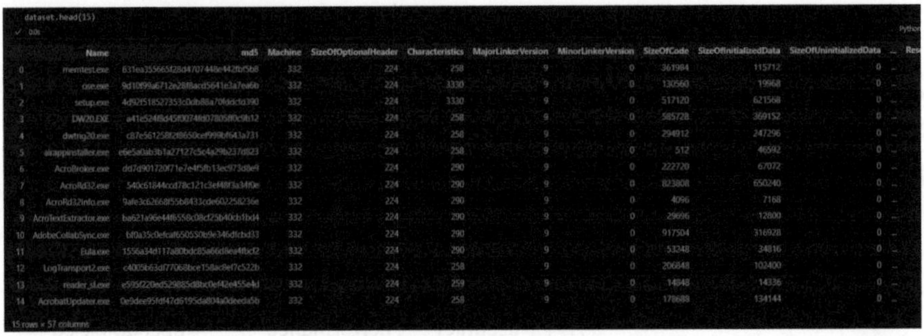

```
dataset.head(15)
✓ 0.0s
```

	Name	md5	Machine	SizeOfOptionalHeader	Characteristics	MajorLinkerVersion	MinorLinkerVersion	SizeOfCode	SizeOfInitializedData	SizeOfUninitializedData	...
0	memtest.exe	631ea355665f28d4707448e442fbf5b8	332	224	258	9	0	361984	115712	0	...
1	ose.exe	9d10f99a6712e28f8acd5641e3a7ea6b	332	224	3330	9	0	130560	19968	0	...
2	setup.exe	4d92f518527353c0db88a70fddcfd390	332	224	3330	9	0	517120	621568	0	...
3	DW20.EXE	a41e524f8d45f0074fd07805ff0c9b12	332	224	258	9	0	585728	369152	0	...
4	dwtrig20.exe	c87e561258f2f8650cef999bf643a731	332	224	258	9	0	294912	247296	0	...
5	airappinstaller.exe	e6e5a0ab3b1a27127c5c4a29b237d823	332	224	258	9	0	512	46592	0	...
6	AcroBroker.exe	dd7d901720f71e7e4f5fb13ec973d8e9	332	224	290	9	0	222720	67072	0	...
7	AcroRd32.exe	540c61844ccd78c121c3ef48f3a34f0e	332	224	290	9	0	823808	650240	0	...
8	AcroRd32Info.exe	9afe3c62668f55b8433cde602258236e	332	224	290	9	0	4096	7168	0	...
9	AcroTextExtractor.exe	ba621a96e44f6558c08cf25b40cb1bd4	332	224	290	9	0	29696	12800	0	...
10	AdobeCollabSync.exe	bf0a35c0efcaf650550b9e346dfcbd33	332	224	290	9	0	917504	316928	0	...
11	Eula.exe	1556a34d117a80bdc85a66d8ea4fbcf2	332	224	290	9	0	53248	34816	0	...
12	LogTransport2.exe	c4005b63df77068bce158ac8ef7c522b	332	224	258	9	0	206848	102400	0	...
13	reader_sl.exe	e595f220ed529885d8bc0ef42e455e4d	332	224	259	9	0	14848	14336	0	...
14	AcrobatUpdater.exe	0e9dee95fdf47d6195da804a0deeda5b	332	224	258	9	0	178688	134144	0	...

15 rows × 57 columns

Fig. 2. Dataset sample

4.2 Developing the Model

The model developed in this study using the Random Forest Classifier will be reliable and effective in classifying Portable Executable files. The development process included preprocessing the dataset, dividing it into training and testing sets, and training the Random Forest Classifier.

Preprocessing involved deleting columns not relevant to the training of the model, such as "Name" and "md5", while leaving other features that are taken from PE files. To represent the validity of PE files, the data was split into feature vectors X and matching target labels y.

The Scikit-Learn library's train test split function was then used to divide the dataset further into training and testing sets for the purpose of training and evaluating the model. To show the ability of the Random Forest Classifier to as-sess accuracy using previously unseen data during training, it was instantiated with 100 estimators and an out-of-bag score.

Then, test set, X_test and y_test, was used to measure the accuracy of the classifier, which was previously trained on X_train and y_train. On the basis of this model, the results obtained showed that, with an accuracy as high as 99.53%, a model could pretty precisely distinguish between malicious and normal PE files.

After a thorough test, including a confusion matrix analysis, the final model was found to have very low rates for both false positives and false negatives, indicating that it is dependable in differentiating between malicious and legitimate PE files.

Also, using the Random Forest, a decision tree was plotted to visually assess the trained model. The tree allowed this by showing the hierarchical representation of decision boundaries made according to various features taken from PE files.

Finally, the very powerful Random Forest Classifier was serialized using the Python package pickle to save the trained model for future use. The excellent performance of the serialized model persisted after loading, verifying its consistency and reliability.

The produced model showed outstanding results when performing the classification of PE files, underlining its efficiency in cybersecurity applications for executable files detection that could be harmful.

4.3 Employing the Trained Model

The trained model's application is a critical step in the file classification pipeline that guarantees reliable threat detection in a dataset. The Random Forest classifier model was trained extensively on a wide range of datasets that included different attributes that were taken from Portable Executable (PE) files. It was chosen because it could manage high-dimensional feature sets well and showed impressive accuracy—during evaluation, it obtained an accuracy of about 99.53%. The learned information is encapsulated in the stored model, which is serialized using the pickle library as model.pkl, allowing for its reuse in various contexts or applications.

The trained model can be used to evaluate unfamiliar PE files with the test.py script. In order to extract detailed characteristics from a specific folder containing PE files, such as structural properties, header information, resource data, and version information from each file, this script interfaces with the pefile library. It loads the serialized model into memory and uses the extracted features to forecast whether each PE file in the specified folder is "malicious" or "legitimate." Additionally, the script simplifies batch analysis and categorization by providing an optional graphical user interface (GUI) for user-friendly interaction.

This streamlined approach streamlines file analysis and classification, making it an essential tool for cybersecurity frameworks or threat detection systems. Test.py integration enables quick, precise classification of unknown files, enabling efficient decision-making and timely reactions to possible security threats (Fig. 3).

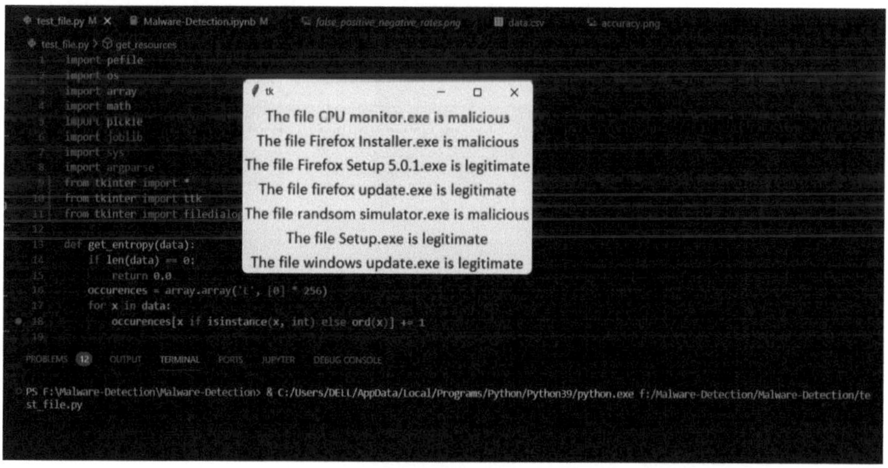

Fig. 3. GUI for the model

The test.py script opens a GUI and prompts the user to select a folder directory that contains the Portable Executable (.exe) files to be analyzed. The selected interface opens a window to mark each file's classification by trained Random Forest classifier predictions for its classification as either harmful or not. Feature extraction technique helps the script to gather inherent attributes of the designated.exe files. By exploiting these features, the model will be able to predict the classification of each file with accuracy. These predic-tions are conveyed through the GUI, which enables proactive threat mitigation by highlighting potentially harmful files and allowing decisions to be made effectively within the cybersecurity framework (Fig. 4).

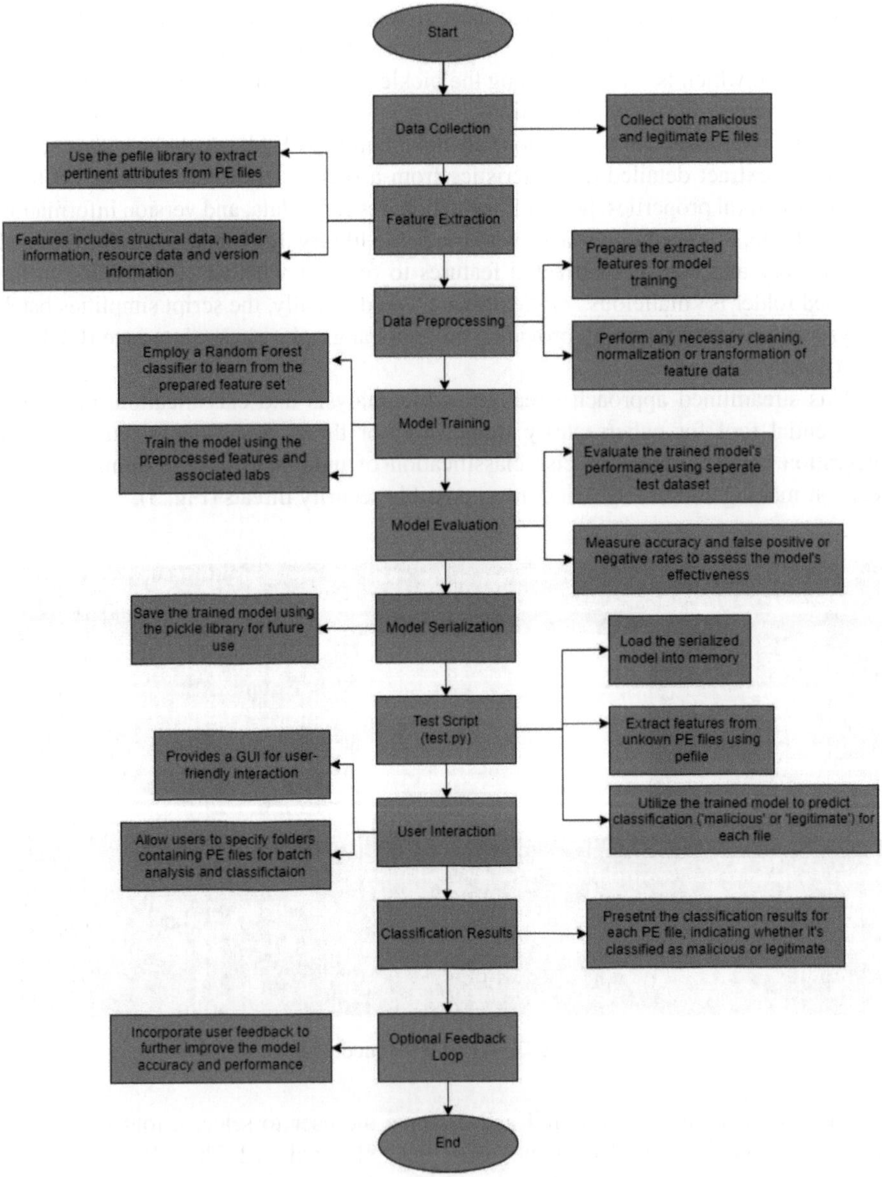

Fig. 4. Flow of the model

5 Results

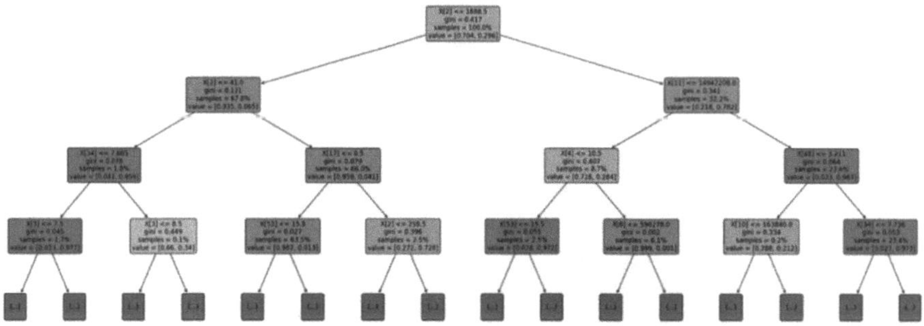

Fig. 5. Decision tree followed by the model

To provide insight into our model's decision-making process, we present the decision tree that was followed to reach the results. The model uses a complex hierarchical structure and logic, going through features in cascaded steps to make predictions; the decision tree provides a visual representation of these processes. The decision points, or nodes, in the tree are where the model evaluates particular traits; the branches, on the other hand, stand for potential outcomes or subsequent decision points. Understanding the model's input processing and ultimate prediction-making process is made easier by this methodical approach. The decision tree provides more information on critical nodes, split criteria, and terminal leaves, illuminating the logic and interpretability of the model's ability to make decisions (Fig. 5).

99.53% accuracy is attained by the trained Random Forest model, demonstrating strong performance. The high accuracy highlights the effectiveness of the model in identifying harmful from normal Portable Executable (PE) files.

The model's accuracy in dividing PE files into "malicious" and "legitimate" categories is seen in this confusion matrix. 19198 malicious files and 8283 legal files were accurately recognized by it. Furthermore, it only misclassified 64 malicious files and 65 benign files, indicating a low rate of incorrect predictions (Fig. 6).

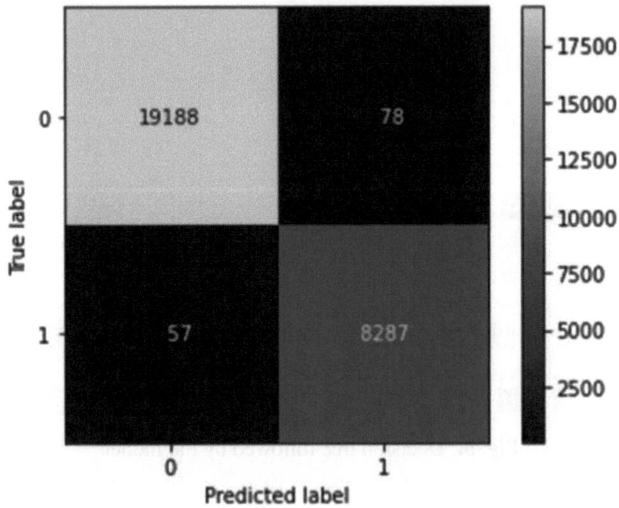

Fig. 6. Confusion Matrix

The model's excellent accuracy and the confusion matrix's balanced distribution confirm its dependability and appropriateness for demanding threat detection and file classification tasks inside cybersecurity frameworks.

6 Conclusion

The focus of this work is malware detection, where we employed a Random Forest classifier on multiple PE file attributes. The goal was to develop a robust and efficient model that could identify files that were potentially dangerous, whereas others were not, and further assist in cybersecurity efforts.

First of all, some important features had been extracted from the properties of PE files, including but not limited to structural, header, resource, and version information. Then it used these features as the base to train a strong ensemble learning method called the Random Forest classifier.

With an astounding accuracy of almost 99.53%, the final model performed exceptionally well. The aforementioned high accuracy highlights the effectiveness of the trained model in correctly classifying PE files, indicating its potential for practical implementations in cybersecurity frameworks.

The key features that influenced the classification process were highlighted by the decision tree visualization arising from the Random Forest model. This provided significant new light on the underlying processes driving whether PE files are characterized as "malicious" or "legitimate."

In addition, the test.py script allowed unknown PE files to be easily judged using the trained model. It also facilitated and simplified the batch analysis and classification process. The integration of a GUI within the script ensures ease-of-use and expedites the process of timely and accurate classification of unknown files.

The findings of this research provide a practical, reliable manner of detecting malware and reinforce further efforts toward increasing cybersecurity protection. The developed model, using the test.py tool, is a fundamental tool needed to rapidly identify and classify potentially malicious PE files, thereby enabling cybersecurity experts and organizations to make well-informed decisions to efficiently reduce security threats.

In the future, it will be important to enhance the cybersecurity framework, and also deal with new risks aggressively in the digital landscape, by undertaking more research, enhancing the classification models, and developing feature extraction techniques.

References

1. Senanayake, J., Kalutarage, H., Al-Kadri, M.O.: Android mobile malware detection using machine learning: a systematic review. Electronics **10**(13), 1606 (2021)
2. Saxe, J., Berlin, K.: Deep neural network based malware detection using two dimensional binary program features. In 2015 10th International Conference on Malicious and Unwanted Software (MALWARE), pp. 11–20. IEEE (2015
3. Chauhan, D., Shah, M., Joshi, H.: A novel intrusion detection system based on machine learning for internet of things (IoT) devices. In 2023 3rd International Conference on Smart Data Intelligence (ICSMDI), pp. 427–434. IEEE (2023)
4. Roseline, S.A., Geetha, S., Kadry, S., Nam, Y.: Intelligent vision-based malware detection and classification using deep random forest paradigm. IEEE Access **8**, 206303–206324 (2020)
5. Roseline, S.A., Geetha, S.: Intelligent malware detection using oblique random forest paradigm. In: 2018 International Conference on Advances in Computing, Communications and Informatics (ICACCI), pp. 330–336. IEEE (2018)
6. Joshi, S., Upadhyay, H., Lagos, L., Akkipeddi, N.S., Guerra, V.: Machine learning approach for malware detection using random forest classifier on process list data structure. In: Proceedings of the 2nd International Conference on Information System and Data Mining, pp. 98–102 (2018)
7. Gao, X., Hu, C., Shan, C., Liu, B., Niu, Z., Xie, H.: Malware classification for the cloud via semi-supervised transfer learning. J. Inf. Secur. Appl. **55**, 102661 (2020)
8. Rathore, H., Agarwal, S., Sahay, S.K., Sewak, M.: Malware detection using machine learning and deep learning. In: Big Data Analytics: 6th International Conference, BDA 2018, Warangal, India, 18–21 December 2018, Proceedings 6, pp. 402–411. Springer, Heidelberg (2018)
9. Gavriluţ, D., Cimpoeşu, M., Anton, D., Ciortuz, L.: Malware detection using machine learning. In 2009 International Multiconference on Computer Science and Information Technology, pp. 735–741. IEEE (2009)
10. Santos, I., Sanz, B., Laorden, C., Brezo, F., Bringas, P.G.: Opcode-sequence-based semi-supervised unknown malware detection. In: Computational Intelligence in Security for Information Systems: 4th International Conference, CISIS 2011, Held at IWANN 2011, Torremolinos-Málaga, Spain, 8–10 June 2011. Proceedings, pp. 50–57. Springer, Heidelberg (2011)
11. Rathore, H., Samavedhi, A., Sahay, S.K., Sewak, M.: Robust malware detection models: learning from adversarial attacks and defenses. Forensic Sci. Int. Dig. Invest. **37**, 301183 (2021)
12. Labaca-Castro, R., Franz, S., Rodosek, G.D.: AIMED-RL: exploring adversarial malware examples with reinforcement learning. In: Machine Learning and Knowledge Discovery in Databases. Applied Data Science Track: European Conference, ECML PKDD 2021, Bilbao, Spain, 13–17, September 2021, Proceedings, Part IV 21, pp. 37–52. Springer, Heidelberg (2021)

13. Koza, J., Krcál, M., & Holena, M. (2020). Two Semi-supervised Approaches to Malware Detection with Neural Networks. In ITAT (pp. 176–185)
14. Khammas, B.M.: Ransomware detection using random forest technique. ICT Express **6**(4), 325–331 (2020)
15. Shijo, P.V., Salim, A.J.P.C.S.: Integrated static and dynamic analysis for malware detection. Procedia Comput. Sci. **46**, 804–811 (2015)

Development of an Artificial Intelligence-Driven Live Patient Scheduling for Modern Healthcare

Abdul Khalique Shaikh[1](✉), Murtala Bello Abubakar[2], and Naresh Adhikari[3]

[1] Department of Information Systems, Sultan Qaboos University, Muscat, Sultanate of Oman
shaikh@squ.edu.om

[2] Department of Physiology, Sultan Qaboos University, Muscat, Sultanate of Oman
m.abubakar@squ.edu.om

[3] Department of Computer Science, Slippery Rock University of Pennsylvania, Pennsylvania, PA 16057, USA
naresh.adhikari@sru.edu

Abstract. In today's era, Artificial Intelligence (AI) has emerged in addressing a range of challenges within the healthcare sector, particularly by improving diagnostic precision, personalizing treatment plans, and enhancing operational efficiency. The growing demand for healthcare services has brought to light significant issues in patient appointment scheduling, particularly in Oman, where hospitals face difficulties related to extended waiting times and inefficient management of patient flow. The increasing demand of healthcare offerings has highlighted substantial challenges in patient appointment scheduling, particularly in Oman, wherein hospitals struggle with prolonged wait and inefficient patient flow management. The proposed AI-driven live appointment management system provides the solution to the challenges. The proposed system targets a diverse range of customer segments, primarily focusing on healthcare providers and patients. By addressing the specific needs of the targeted groups, the proposed system aims to enhance overall healthcare experience, reduce waiting times, and improve operational efficiency. The system is based on the development of an AI-driven appointment management system designed to address critical challenges in patient scheduling within modern healthcare facilities including AI-Powered Queue Management, Predictive Wait Time Analysis, Intelligent Rescheduling, Integration with Existing Systems and User-Friendly Interfaces. The successful integration and implementation of all layers of the proposed MEDLINK system will significantly benefit the project, positioning it to serve a broad spectrum of stakeholders, including patients, healthcare providers, institutions, administrators, and technology developers. Through the utilization of AI to overcome the challenges associated with appointment scheduling, this initiative seeks to improve the overall healthcare experience, increase operational efficiency, and establish a new industry benchmark.

Keywords: Artificial Intelligence · Patient Scheduling · Queue Management · Wait Time Prediction · Healthcare

S. Hussain et al. (Eds.): SEET 2025, CCIS 2725, pp. 23–30, 2026.
https://doi.org/10.1007/978-3-032-08977-9_2

1 Introduction

Artificial Intelligence (AI) has a transformative impact on healthcare [1], providing a wide range of advantages that improve patient care, optimize operational processes [2], and foster innovation. Its significance is evident in several critical areas, including personalized treatment plans and operational efficiency. Enhanced Drug Discovery and Development, Patient Mmanagement, Predictive Analytics and Preventive Care Telemedicine and Virtual Health Assistants, Decision Support for Clinicians [3]. All these continued integrations into healthcare systems hold immense potential for advancing medical research, treatment, and patient care.

Effective patient appointment scheduling has become essential because of the high demands placed upon healthcare providers to maintain both quality of care and productivity [4, 5]. The conventional ways of managing appointments cannot cope with the changing trends in the healthcare system [6] hence reason they often lead to congestion and patient discontentment due to excessive waiting or over giving appointment slots to people. As it is observed by authors, public and private hospitals in Oman, are dealing with significant challenges in coping with patient waft, specifically for those laid low with chronic diseases. Patients often enjoy extended ready instances to see a physician that may exacerbate their conditions, result in useless health facility visits, and result in a standard decline within the high-quality of care.

This research presents an easier way to tackle the problem of scheduling appointments by proposing an appointment management system that is intelligent and can learn over time using artificial intelligence [7]. It is the intention of the authors is to mitigate examples of such as mentioned above by perfecting both the patients' experience and the physicians' management system through the usage of AI technologies. The system allows for outlining present scheduling that encompasses prediction of wait times, intelligent queue management system and integration with the existing processes and technology of the hospital. Such strategies are been put in place to handle the challenges that are associated with appointment systems in modern health care institutions.

The dependence on technology continue to increase with the rapid growth of Artificial Intelligence, therefore the need for this project cannot be ignored. Such reduction of operations is being realized through a shift towards artificial intelligence by some health care providers. The beneficiaries of this research will include the government hospital including patients, healthcare providers, institutions, administrators, and technology developers. The rest of the paper is organized as below:

Section 2 presents the earlier research related to patient scheduling. Section 3 discusses the research methodology including the layered architecture of the system and Sect. 4 describe the System Evaluation and Optimization. Section 5 concludes the research and presents the future research directions.

2 Literature Review

This section discusses the current systems of patient scheduling and appointment along with their challenges and opportunities.

Most of the outpatient clinics in Oman have scheduling policies for patient visits that usually leave the patients, operations coordinators and physicians irked because they are kept waiting. Patients, especially family consider inaccurate allocation of service time as a costly waste [8]. Furthermore, prolonged waiting for both patients and physicians may adversely affect patients' overall satisfaction with service delivery and can also lead to frustration of the physicians [9]. There have been several attempts to minimize waiting duration and improve service delivery [10]. However, no satisfactory progress has been made due to capital intensive nature of the initiatives [11]. This poses a lot of challenges since a number of hospitals have limited budgets [12]. Consequently, steps taken to minimize waiting time have negatively affected patients' satisfaction, thus, necessitating the need for additional alternatives [13] such as subsidizing health facilities that have low patients turnout or low service utilization so as to encourage patients to patronize them [14].

Earlier and recent researches on patient scheduling have focused on different goals and study designs [4, 10, 15, 16]. One of the pupular approaches is to minimize patient or clinician wait time or decrease the frequency of absentism [17]. However, this is associated with long waiting period for the physician (which can make him idle) if patients come late or do not come at all [18]. Consequently, this can lead to rushing through patients schedule and at the end rendering poor services to the patients [19]. An unhappy or unsatisfied patient has a tendency to leave a negative review [20].

One of the strategies to further minimze patients waiting time is the use of data modeling such as machine learning [21]. The use of data analytics (artificial intelligence and machine learning) in patient scheduling for various healthcare services can significantly contribute in a timely risk detection [22] and an overall improvement in the scheduling outcome [23]. In fact, several studies suggest that the algorithm models have provided more precisions in patients scheduling [24–29] with a significantly improved patient flow [30] and a relatively minimal cost [31].

The ever increasing demand for healthcare services [32, 33] has also necessitated the need for a well coordinated plan for delivering the services, and this plus many other challenges such as the policy makers' will and collaboration by all stakeholders constitute a major obstacle towards integrating AI into healthcare delivery scheduling [34, 35]. One of the fundamental issues to be addressed by researchers is determining the actual clinical components required for application of AI in shceduling systems [36, 37]. The current development and interest in AI technology therefore presents and opportunity to conduct researches that are aimed at optimization and application of the different algorithms into patient scheduling with the ultimate goal of revolutionazing clinical practice.

3 Research Methodology

This research study is based on experiments and it utilises a quantitative research approach [38] to develop and evaluate the effectiveness of an AI-driven appointment management system within healthcare facilities, specifically focusing on reducing waiting times and optimizing patient flow in Oman. The main purpose of this research is to create an innovative solution that integrates artificial intelligence (AI) into patient scheduling systems. The core components of the research involves the development of the AI-based live appointment scheduling system (MEDLINK), which was built through iterative design and testing. The system includes several key components such as AI-Powered Queue Management, Predictive Wait Time Analysis, Intelligent Rescheduling, Integration with Existing Systems and User-Friendly Interfaces. The development process will follow an iterative model, with multiple phases of prototyping, testing, and refinement based on feedback from stakeholders, including healthcare professionals and patients.

The research study intends to utilize patient records from Sultan Qaboos University hospital. These patient historical data will be utilised to implement various machine learning algorithms to enhance scheduling efficiency and address the challenges associated with overbooking and no-show occurrences [7, 39]. As suggested by this research study [38] algorithms can analyse patterns in historical data to predict patient attendance and optimal scheduling times, reducing the likelihood of overbookings and missed appointments. This approach would lead to a more efficient, patient-friendly, and cost-effective appointment scheduling system.

3.1 Layered Architecture

The Layered architecture of Artificial Intelligence based live patient scheduling system provides a high-level picture of how the system functions, including the connections and interactions among the various modules (Fig. 1).

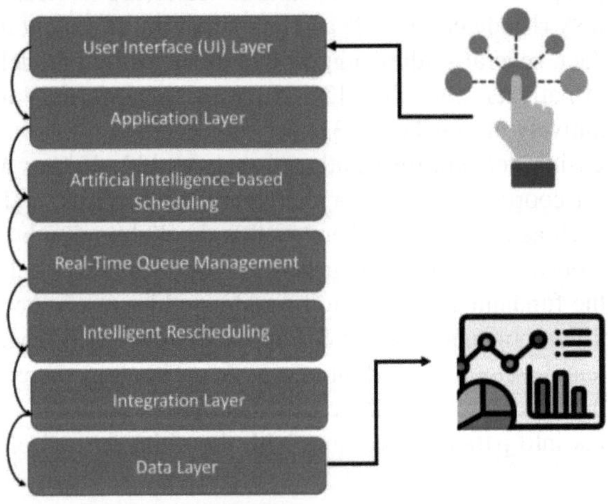

Fig. 1. Artificial Intelligence based live patient scheduling system.

User Interface (UI) Layer
This is the topmost layer where users interact with the system. It includes dashboards and interfaces for both patients and healthcare providers. The UI is designed to be user-friendly, allowing easy navigation for scheduling appointments, checking wait times, and receiving notifications. It serves as the point of interaction for input and output of information.

Application Layer
This layer acts as the intermediary between the UI and the underlying systems. It processes user inputs and manages the application logic.It handles requests from the UI, processes them, and communicates with the data and integration layers. This layer ensures that the application functions smoothly and efficiently.

Artificial Intelligence-Based Scheduling
This layer incorporates AI algorithms to optimize the scheduling process. It analyzes data to predict wait times, manage patient flow, and intelligently reschedule appointments based on real-time information. This layer is crucial for enhancing operational efficiency and improving patient experience.

Real-Time Queue Management
This layer focuses on managing patient queues in real-time. It monitors the status of patients in the queue, provides updates, and adjusts schedules dynamically to minimize wait times. This layer is essential for maintaining a smooth flow of patients through the healthcare facility.

Integration Layer
This layer facilitates communication between different systems and components.It ensures that the scheduling system can integrate with existing healthcare management systems, electronic health records (EHR), and other relevant technologies. This layer is vital for data consistency and interoperability.

Data Layer
This foundational layer stores and manages all the data used by the application. It includes databases that hold patient information, appointment records, and analytics data. The data layer is crucial for supporting the AI algorithms and ensuring that the application has access to accurate and up to date information.

4 System Evaluation and Optimization

The system's key performance indicators (KPIs) such as reduced patient wait times, enhanced resource utilization, and improved patient satisfaction are chosen to measure the system performance. As the proposed system has planned to use Real-world data that will collect from Sultan Qaboos Hospital during the pilot implementation, which include metrics such as appointment adherence, no-show rates, and resource allocation efficiency. This method support researchers to compare pre and post implementation performance to determine the system's practical benefits in reducing wait times and managing overbooking challenges.

The optimisation and improvement of the system will be handled by dynamic scheduling algorithms that adjust in real-time based on incoming data that can be utilized to enhance system efficiency. By analysing patient attendance patterns and real-time factors such as delays or cancellations, these algorithms optimize the allocation of time slots and resources dynamically, improving both system responsiveness and patient satisfaction.

Furthermore, the research study can consider to use predictive analytics techniques [40] to forecast patient behaviours, such as the likelihood of attending or missing appointments. By integrating these predictions into the scheduling process, systems can optimize the number of appointments scheduled per day and reduce inefficiencies caused by last-minute cancellations or no-shows.

After applying all evaluation and optimisation techniques, the proposed system measures the Operational Efficiency using various metrics such as resource utilization, appointment adherence, and the balance between supply (provider availability) and demand (patient appointments) are used to evaluate the operational impact of optimized scheduling systems. The evaluation and optimization of the AI-based scheduling system significantly improve the healthcare experience for both patients and providers, leading to better care, higher satisfaction, and more efficient healthcare delivery.

5 Conclusion and Future Directions

This research study proposes an AI-driven live patient scheduling system, MEDLINK, designed to address significant challenges in modern healthcare, such as extended waiting times and inefficient patient flow management, particularly in Oman. With the help of integration of various artificial intelligence techniques, along with predictive wait time evaluation, smart rescheduling, and actual-time queue management, the proposed model offers an advanced method to enhance operational performance and patient satisfaction. By leveraging patients' facts and machine learning algorithm, the model can optimize useful resource allocation, no-show, and streamline the scheduling process. This AI-based solution has the potential to revolutionize patient scheduling in healthcare settings, providing a foundation for future advancements and contributing to the development of more efficient, patient-centric healthcare services. The system could serve as a benchmark for the integration of AI in healthcare scheduling across various institutions. Future research could explore further improvements in system architecture and the integration of predictive analytics to address dynamic healthcare demands.

References

1. Secinaro, S., et al.: The role of artificial intelligence in healthcare: a structured literature review. BMC Med. Inform. Decis. Mak. **21**, 1–23 (2021)
2. Srinivas, S., Ravindran, A.R.: Optimizing outpatient appointment system using machine learning algorithms and scheduling rules: a prescriptive analytics framework. Expert Syst. Appl. **102**, 245–261 (2018)
3. Jiang, F., et al.: Artificial intelligence in healthcare: past, present and future. Stroke Vascular Neurol., **2**(4) (2017)
4. Gupta, D., Denton, B.: Appointment scheduling in health care: challenges and opportunities. IIE Trans. **40**(9), 800–819 (2008)
5. Wang, D., Muthuraman, K., Morrice, D.: Coordinated patient appointment scheduling for a multistation healthcare network. Oper. Res. **67**(3), 599–618 (2019)
6. Yu, S., Kulkarni, V.G., Deshpande, V.: Appointment scheduling for a health care facility with series patients. Prod. Oper. Manag. **29**(2), 388–409 (2020)

7. Knight, D., et al.: Artificial Intelligence for Patient Scheduling in the Real-World Health Care Setting: A Metanarrative Review, p. 100824. Health Policy and Technology (2023)
8. Liu, N., et al.: When waiting to see a doctor is less irritating: Understanding patient preferences and choice behavior in appointment scheduling. Manag. Sci. **64**(5), 1975–1996 (2018)
9. McGinnis, J.M., et al.: Best care at lower cost: the path to continuously learning health care in America (2013)
10. Cayirli, T., Veral, E.: Outpatient scheduling in health care: a review of literature. Prod. Oper. Manag. **12**(4), 519–549 (2003)
11. Tohidi, M., Zanjani, M.K., Contreras, I.: A physician planning framework for polyclinics under uncertainty. Omega **101**, 102275 (2021)
12. Yang, L., Millstein, M.A., Campbell, J.F.: Unlocking cost savings hidden in hospital tier contracts. Omega **113**, 102713 (2022)
13. Senot, C., et al.: The impact of combining conformance and experiential quality on hospitals' readmissions and cost performance. Manag. Sci. **62**(3), 829–848 (2016)
14. Deng, Y., et al.: Optimal differential subsidy policy design for a workload-imbalanced outpatient care network. Omega **99**, 102194 (2021)
15. Ahmadi-Javid, A., Jalali, Z., Klassen, K.J.: Outpatient appointment systems in healthcare: a review of optimization studies. Eur. J. Oper. Res. **258**(1), 3–34 (2017)
16. Marynissen, J., Demeulemeester, E.: Literature review on multi-appointment scheduling problems in hospitals. Eur. J. Oper. Res. **272**(2), 407–419 (2019)
17. Samorani, M.: Data Mining for Enhanced Operations Management Decision Making: Applications in Health Care. University of Colorado at Boulder (2012)
18. Young, C., Chen, X.: Patients as consumers in the market for medicine: the halo effect of hospitality. Soc. Forces **99**(2), 504–531 (2020)
19. Drossman, D.A., Ruddy, J.: Improving patient-provider relationships to improve health care. Clin. Gastroenterol. Hepatol. **18**(7), 1417–1426 (2020)
20. Arendt, F., Forrai, M., Findl, O.: Dealing with negative reviews on physician-rating websites: an experimental test of how physicians can prevent reputational damage via effective response strategies. Soc Sci Med **266**, 113422 (2020)
21. Golmohammadi, D., Zhao, L., Dreyfus, D.: Using machine learning techniques to reduce uncertainty for outpatient appointment scheduling practices in outpatient clinics. Omega **120**, 102907 (2023)
22. Bellini, V., et al.: Machine learning in perioperative medicine: a systematic review. J. Anesth. Analg. Crit. Care **2**(1), 2 (2022)
23. Calegari, R., et al.: Surgery scheduling heuristic considering OR downstream and upstream facilities and resources. BMC Health Serv. Res. **20**, 1–11 (2020)
24. Abbas, A., et al.: Machine learning using preoperative patient factors can predict duration of surgery and length of stay for total knee arthroplasty. Int. J. Med. Inform. **158**, 104670 (2022)
25. Martinez, O., et al.: Machine learning for surgical time prediction. Comput. Methods Prog. Biomed. **208**, 106220 (2021)
26. Lai, J., et al.: Improving and Interpreting Surgical Case Duration Prediction with Machine Learning Methodology. medRxiv, 2020: 2020.06.10.20127910
27. Bartek, M.A., et al.: Improving operating room efficiency: machine learning approach to predict case-time duration. J. Am. College Surg. **229**(4), 346–354 (2019)
28. Tuwatananurak, J.P., et al.: Machine learning can improve estimation of surgical case duration: a pilot study. J. Med. Syst. **43**, 1–7 (2019)
29. Abedini, A., Li, W., Ye, H.: An optimization model for operating room scheduling to reduce blocking across the perioperative process. Procedia Manuf. **10**, 60–70 (2017)
30. Abdalkareem, Z.A., et al.: Healthcare scheduling in optimization context: a review. Heal. Technol. **11**, 445–469 (2021)

31. Otten, M., Braaksma, A., Boucherie, R.J.: Minimizing earliness/tardiness costs on multiple machines with an application to surgery scheduling. Oper. Res. Health Care **22**, 100194 (2019)
32. Information, C.I.F.H.: National Health Expenditure Trends. Canadian Institute for Health Information (1997)
33. Kadum, S.Y., et al.: Machine learning-based telemedicine framework to prioritize remote patients with multi-chronic diseases for emergency healthcare services. Netw. Model. Anal. Health Inform. Bioinform. **12**(1), 11 (2023)
34. Rajpurkar, P., et al.: AI in health and medicine. Nat. Med. **28**(1), 31–38 (2022)
35. Alami, H., et al.: Organizational readiness for artificial intelligence in health care: insights for decision-making and practice. J. Health Organ Manag. (2020). **ahead-of-print**(ahead-of-print)
36. Maadi, M., Akbarzadeh Khorshidi, H., Aickelin, U.: A review on human–AI interaction in machine learning and insights for medical applications. Int. J. Environ. Res. Public Health **18**(4), 2121 (2021)
37. Jansson, M., et al.: Artificial intelligence-enhanced care pathway planning and scheduling system: content validity assessment of required functionalities. BMC Health Serv. Res. **22**(1), 1513 (2022)
38. Ala, A., Chen, F.: Appointment scheduling problem in complexity systems of the healthcare services: a comprehensive review. J. Healthcare Eng. **2022**(1), 5819813 (2022)
39. Han, Y., et al.: A multi-appointment patient scheduling system with machine learning and optimization. Decision Anal. J. **10**, 100392 (2024)
40. Delen, D.: Predictive Analytics: Data Mining, Machine Learning and Data Science for Practitioners. FT Press (2020)

Blockchain Technology in Logistics Business

Nalysse Nakazato, Kashif Manzer(✉), and Muhammad Abdul Basit Ur Rahim

Department of Computer Engineering and Computer Science,
California State University, Long Beach, CA 90840, USA
{Nalysse.Nakazato01,Kashif.Manzer01}@student.csulb.edu, m.basit@csulb.edu

Abstract. The logistics industry, valued at $9.2 trillion annually, faces systemic inefficiencies due to fragmented information systems, manual documentation, and inconsistent data sharing, leading to over $100 billion in losses. Blockchain technology offers a transformative solution with its decentralized architecture, cryptographic security, and smart contracts that automate processes while ensuring data integrity. This study presents a comprehensive examination of blockchain's role in enhancing logistics operations by exploring its technical foundations, real-world applications, and associated implementation challenges. Through a systematic review of existing literature and analysis of prominent case studies, the paper identifies key obstacles such as smart contract vulnerabilities, scalability constraints, and regulatory conflicts, particularly regarding GDPR compliance. Findings suggest that while blockchain can significantly improve supply chain traceability, transparency, and cost efficiency, widespread adoption is constrained by unresolved technical and legal barriers. This research contributes to the discourse by evaluating current solutions and proposing future directions to enable secure, scalable, and compliant blockchain integration in global logistics systems.

Keywords: Blockchain · Supply chain · Smart contract · Layer-2 · Compliance · IoT · Security

1 Introduction

A supply chain encompasses the entire network of entities, activities, information, and resources involved in the production and distribution of a product or service from the supplier to the end customer. The challenge that this traditional way of trade faces is a lack of transparency, inefficient data sharing, and inconsistencies in data as it moves between departments. The traditional systems face inefficiencies due to lengthy documentation processes and storage of this documentation, and delays caused by various stakeholders not having access to the same information due to different terms and polices at each stage of the supply chain lifecycle. Paper-based documentation and fragmented systems lead to increased chances of errors, fraud, and delays. These issues result in higher operational costs, reduced trust among stakeholders, and ultimately, an overall less efficient global supply chain.

S. Hussain et al. (Eds.): SEET 2025, CCIS 2725, pp. 31–44, 2026.
https://doi.org/10.1007/978-3-032-08977-9_3

This research examines how blockchain can address longstanding challenges in the logistics industry, offering a transformative approach to modern supply chain management through the adoption of blockchain technology and smart contracts in logistics stems. This study investigates blockchain's role in logistics by reviewing its technical foundations, alongside reviewing research paper of real-world implementations of blockchain in complex supply chain for its outcome and performance. The research also explores scalability solutions and regulatory challenges, drawing from academic literature and industry case studies.

Findings reveal that blockchain significantly enhances supply chain efficiency, with applications like MediLedger [17] ensuring drug authenticity and TradeLens [19] cutting administrative costs by 20%. Traceability is revolutionized, as seen in Walmart's rapid response to the outbreak. Yet, challenges persist—scalability bottlenecks, interoperability, and GDPR conflicts demand ongoing innovation to fully realize blockchain's potential in logistics.

2 Research Objectives and Questions

This study aims to critically examine blockchain technology's potential, challenges, and practical implications within the logistics industry. The specific objectives guiding this research include understanding the technological barriers, evaluating current mechanisms for overcoming these barriers and analyzing real-world implementations to determine blockchain's practical effectiveness.

The following research questions structure this investigation:

- RQ1: What are the primary technological, regulatory, and security challenges affecting blockchain adoption in logistics?
- RQ2: How effectively do existing smart contract security solutions mitigate vulnerabilities in logistics applications?
- RQ3: What lessons can be drawn from current blockchain deployments in logistics concerning scalability, transparency, and cost efficiency?

3 Research Methodology

This research adopts a systematic literature review method following the PRISMA (Preferred Reporting Items for Systematic Reviews and Meta-Analyses) guidelines. Databases including IEEE Xplore, SpringerLink, ScienceDirect, and MDPI were systematically queried for relevant literature published between 2018 and 2024. Keywords such as "blockchain," "smart contracts," "logistics," "supply chain," "scalability," and "GDPR compliance" were utilized to identify pertinent studies.

Initially, 324 studies were retrieved, and duplicates (56) were eliminated. Titles and abstracts were screened for relevance, resulting in the exclusion of 178 papers. Subsequently, a full-text review of 90 articles was conducted, applying specific inclusion criteria—such as relevance to logistics operations, recent advancements in blockchain, and rigorous empirical or theoretical examination—leading to the selection of 24 studies for detailed analysis. Complementing this, the paper examines prominent industry case studies (e.g., TradeLens, MediLedger) to evaluate blockchain's practical applications and limitations.

4 Related Work

Previous reviews have extensively analyzed blockchain's theoretical foundations and its technological capabilities across diverse industries. For example, Kalra et al. [7] and Taherdoost [14] conducted comprehensive studies on blockchain and smart contract security, highlighting the complexity of mitigating vulnerabilities in various decentralized applications. Similarly, Vacca [1] systematically reviewed development tools and techniques for blockchain, underscoring both technological advancements and persistent challenges.

However, despite the wealth of general blockchain literature, specific investigations into blockchain's unique implications for logistics remain limited. Notably, existing reviews often lack an in-depth analysis of industry-specific regulatory, ethical, and economic constraints, particularly relating to logistics' operational contexts. This paper distinctly addresses these gaps by combining a detailed review of security mechanisms, scalability solutions, and regulatory concerns with an empirical evaluation of blockchain implementations specific to the logistics domain, thereby contributing uniquely to the existing academic discourse.

5 Challenges in Blockchain

5.1 Vulnerabilities in Smart Contracts

Blockchain systems in logistics, especially those using smart contracts to automate supply chain processes, face critical security challenges. Vulnerabilities such as re-entrancy attacks—where a malicious contract repeatedly calls a vulnerable one before execution completes—could disrupt automated payments or shipment verifications, leading to financial losses or delays. Tools like Oyente, Slither, and MAIAN help detect these flaws, with Oyente identifying over 8,000 vulnerable Ethereum contracts [1], a concern for logistics platforms built on similar frameworks.

Re-entrancy risks studied by [8] through the Reentrancy Analyzer (RA) could allow unauthorised fund withdrawals from a smart contract managing supplier payments, highlighting the need for robust static analysis tools. [4] notes RA's use of symbolic execution to catch such exploits, yet tools like MAIAN struggle with scalability and nuanced flaws in complex supply chain systems [1].

Slither, with 99 vulnerability detectors, integrates into development pipelines to spot issues like gas inefficiencies that might slow down real-time tracking or IoT updates in logistics. [7] argues that securing smart contracts demands a layered approach—formal verification, runtime checks, and machine learning—to prevent errors that could erode trust in blockchain-based logistics networks.

These vulnerabilities underscore the need for ongoing research to protect supply chain operations. A single flaw in a smart contract managing customs clearance or provenance data could halt shipments, inflate costs, or compromise product integrity, threatening the reliability of global logistics systems.

5.2 Environmental Impact

Research by Taherdoost et al. [14] highlights inefficiencies in the relationship between gas costs and computational effort, especially on platforms like Ethereum. The challenges extend beyond individual contracts to the broader blockchain ecosystem. High energy consumption, particularly in proof-of-work (PoW) systems, raises environmental concerns and limits scalability. Alternative consensus mechanisms like proof-of-stake (PoS) aim to address these issues but require further refinement to balance efficiency with security. The shift toward Proof of Stake (PoS), exemplified by Ethereum's 2022 upgrade, offers a greener alternative by eliminating energy-intensive mining. PoS reduces energy consumption by over 99%, relying on validators who "stake" coins rather than compete computationally. While challenges remain, the evolution toward energy-efficient protocols and sustainable practices highlights the dual role of blockchain as both a contributor to and a potential solution for environmental issues.

5.3 Solutions for Scalability

Scalability remains a pressing issue, with network congestion and high transaction costs limiting blockchain's practical applications. To achieve scalability and security compatibility, lightweight privacy-preserving solutions in smart contracts have also been a focus. Innovations like the Sapphire smart-contract-based storage system demonstrate their utility in managing large datasets efficiently. Similarly, artificial intelligence (AI) can significantly enhance smart contracts, from vulnerability detection using machine learning to implement cognitive computing models for improved performance and scalability [14]. Layer-2 solutions, such as Optimistic and ZK-Rollups, process transactions off-chain while anchoring security to the main blockchain. Sharding, employed by Ethereum 2.0, divides the network into smaller chains (shards) that process transactions in parallel, boosting throughput from 15 to 100,000 TPS. Sidechains (e.g., Polygon) operate independently but connect to main chains, offering scalability for tasks like real-time IoT data logging.

5.4 Trade-Offs Between Security and Efficiency

Blockchain systems inherently face trade-offs between security and efficiency, requiring careful balance depending on use-case priorities. Formal verification tools like KEVM [5] and VERX [3] help to validate the functional properties of smart contracts by mathematically proving the correctness of code. These integrated systems enhance the security of smart contracts while addressing performance bottlenecks. Layer-2 solutions like Rollups enhance scalability by processing transactions off-chain but rely on the security of the underlying Layer-1 blockchain, creating dependencies that may introduce vulnerabilities if not rigorously audited. Similarly, sharding (splitting the network into parallel chains) boosts efficiency but complicates consensus mechanisms, increasing attack surfaces. Cryptographic techniques like zero-knowledge proofs enhance privacy but add computational overhead, slowing transaction finality. Innovations like hybrid models (e.g., combining PoS with decentralized validators) and adaptive consensus algorithms aim to mitigate these trade-offs, but achieving optimal balance remains context-specific, demanding tailored solutions for diverse supply chain needs.

5.5 Performance Bottlenecks and Architectural Challenges

Blockchain technology faces a fundamental challenge in scalability known as the blockchain trilemma. This trilemma consists of three components: decentralization, security, and scalability. The trilemma explains that to increase two, one must be sacrificed. For example, increasing decentralization and security sacrifices scalability. If decentralization and scalability are prioritized, security is compromised. If security and scalability are enhanced, decentralization is reduced. Blockchain systems often encounter performance bottlenecks due to their architectural choices. For instance, Hyperledger Fabric demonstrates higher throughput and lower latency under increasing workloads, illustrating trade-offs between public and permissioned blockchains [13]. This means that such blockchain systems struggle to achieve a dynamic, fast, and efficient connection and safe data transfer significant in the supply chain.

6 Secure Smart Contracts

6.1 Static and Dynamic Code Analysis

Smart contracts require intricate mechanisms for testing, code analysis, and validation to ensure their reliability and security. To address the persistence of flaws, researchers have investigated empirical methods for identifying contract defects. [25] catalogued 20 common defects related to security and usability, many of which are not detectable with existing tools like Oyente and Zeus. This gap underscores the need for advanced detection techniques. Smart contract code analysis is an essential domain, where static and dynamic analysis tools like SmartCheck [6] and Slither [9] have proven invaluable. Static analysis tools like SmartCheck [6] systematically examine source code for vulnerabilities by translating it into intermediate representations. Similarly, dynamic tools such as Slither [9] offer real-time insights into code execution, allowing developers to detect flaws and optimize performance. These tools enhance code comprehension, identifying common pitfalls, such as reentrancy vulnerabilities and gas inefficiencies, and providing actionable feedback.

6.2 Advanced Detection Mechanisms

Moreover, smart contract analysis has significantly improved the ability to identify vulnerabilities and optimize performance. One notable development is structural comparison techniques, as exemplified by SmartEmbed [26]. By analyzing structural similarities in smart contract code, SmartEmbed achieves a 90% detection success rate for identifying clones and bugs, making it a critical tool in mitigating risks. Structural analysis allows for early detection of vulnerabilities, which can save significant resources during the development lifecycle.

In addition to structural comparison, fuzz testing methods are increasingly adopted to uncover hidden vulnerabilities. Tools like EVMFuzz and ContractFuzzer have identified vulnerabilities in real-world contracts, contributing to improved resilience against attacks. These tools generate randomized inputs to test the boundaries and robustness of contract execution. [27] noted that ContractFuzzer detected security issues in over 90% of real-world contracts it tested, emphasizing the necessity of stress testing in production environments. The maturity of tools and programming languages for smart contract development also continues to evolve, providing developers with more robust frameworks. Platforms such as Hyperledger Fabric offer alternative paradigms for smart contract implementation, emphasizing modularity and privacy. Unlike public blockchains like Ethereum, Hyperledger Fabric uses a permissioned blockchain model, which, according to [27], provides controlled environments where transaction privacy and confidentiality are prioritized. Comparative studies of smart contract platforms highlight Ethereum's dominance in flexibility and Hyperledger's superiority in corporate applications, concluding that choosing the right platform depends on the intended use case, with Ethereum excelling in public and decentralized settings, while Hyperledger is more suited for private and regulated environments.

To ensure seamless integration of detection mechanisms into the smart contract development process, new development environments are being designed with built-in analysis capabilities. Tools like Remix IDE incorporate live error detection, enabling developers to address potential vulnerabilities during the coding phase. This proactive approach minimizes the need for extensive post-deployment debugging and enhances the overall security of the blockchain ecosystem. By combining advanced techniques like structural analysis, fuzz testing, and integrated development environments, the integration of smart contracts restructures blockchain into more automated, scalable, and reliable solutions.

6.3 Consensus Mechanisms, Layer-2 and Layer-3 Solutions

Blockchain's scalability and energy efficiency depend on consensus mechanisms and Layer-2 solutions. These technologies balance security, decentralization, and performance to meet the demands of different blockchain use cases. Consensus mechanisms and Layer-2 solutions are pivotal for enhancing blockchain's efficiency in logistics. Proof of Work (PoW), used by Bitcoin, relies on energy-intensive mining to validate transactions, offering high security but impractical scalability (7 TPS) and sustainability for supply chains [16]. Hyperledger Fabric uses the Raft consensus mechanism, which provides higher throughput than Kafka by removing Kafka's overhead. In contrast, Proof of Stake (PoS), adopted by Ethereum 2.0, selects validators based on staked tokens, reducing energy use by 99% and enabling faster, cost-effective transactions ideal for real-time tracking and automated payments.

To further address scalability, Layer-2 solutions like Rollups process transactions off-chain while anchoring security to the main blockchain. Optimistic Rollups streamline bulk operations (e.g., shipment updates) by assuming validity unless disputed, while ZK-Rollups use cryptographic proofs for instant verification, enabling thousands of low-cost transactions per second. These innovations reduce bottlenecks in global logistics—such as tracking perishable goods or automating customs—but face challenges like integration with legacy systems and the complexity of implementing advanced cryptography. By combining PoS with Rollups, blockchain becomes a scalable, eco-friendly tool for supply chains [11].

Layer 3 in blockchain refers to application-specific scaling solutions built on Layer 2 networks. In supply chains, Layer 3 enhances interoperability, automation, and efficiency by enabling customized smart contracts, data privacy, and faster transactions. It can improve scalability by offloading heavy lifting from Layer 1, allowing seamless multi-chain interactions, reducing costs, and optimizing supply chain traceability and transparency [13].

7 Applications of Blockchain Technology in Supply Chain

Blockchain's applications span sectors like healthcare, IoT, and payment systems. Innovations like MobiChain enable secure supply chain transactions. Blockchain-based database solutions, such as BigchainDB and Ethereum Query Language (EQL), improve data retrieval and storage in decentralized environments. Despite these advances, further research into smart contract integration and its regression testing are essential for improving blockchain technology in terms of addressing security, transparency, and trade-offs between gas consumption and code efficiency.

One of blockchain's most significant applications in logistics is its ability to provide indisputable and immutable proof of the provenance of raw materials, products, and sales [11]. This feature is particularly valuable in sectors like pharmaceuticals and agriculture, where counterfeit products pose serious risks. By securing digital records with cryptographic techniques, blockchain prevents tampering, offering consumers guarantees of product quality and authenticity. As stated in [11], "digital records provide security and restore trust among the intermediaries and primary stakeholders involved in a logistical supply chain."

High-profile incidents like the Salmonella outbreak in papayas and the E. coli spread linked to Chipotle demonstrate how blockchain could have mitigated financial damage and loss of trust by isolating contaminated products more effectively.

Blockchain transforms supply chain management by enhancing visibility, transparency, and security. Traditional platforms face high transaction costs and risks, while blockchain eliminates these challenges through trustless networks and immutable records. One key factor is the concept of smart contracts. Smart contracts, introduced by Szabo in 1996 [28], are self-executing contracts with predefined rules encoded directly into the blockchain. These automated agreements can streamline various aspects of logistics operations, from payment processing to customs clearance. Smart contracts could automatically trigger payments when predefined conditions are met, such as the successful delivery of goods or the completion of customs clearance. For example, smart wholesale price and revenue-sharing contracts improve coordination and economic feasibility in supply chains because they enable automated adjustments and ensure compliance with predefined terms, optimizing operations and mitigating risks [11]. The advantage of smart contracts is that they eliminate the need for intermediaries and ensure the immutability of terms once stored in the blockchain, enhancing trust and reducing the risk of fraud. This automation reduces the potential for human error, accelerates transaction times, and improves cash flow management.

7.1 Traceability and Provenance Through Blockchain

Blockchain technology revolutionizes traceability and provenance through its core principle of an immutable, decentralized ledger that records every transaction across all nodes. Traceability refers to tracking a product's journey from origin to end-user, while provenance verifies its authenticity and origin. The pharmaceutical industry faces significant risks from counterfeit drugs, which account for nearly 10% of global medical products in low- and middle-income countries [15]. Blockchain addresses this by assigning unique digital identifiers (e.g., serial numbers) to each product, recorded on the blockchain at every stage—from manufacturing to distribution. For example, MediLedger, a blockchain consortium involving Pfizer and Genentech, uses smart contracts to verify drug authenticity, ensuring compliance with the U.S. Drug Supply Chain Security Act (DSCSA). Stakeholders scan products at each checkpoint, updating the blockchain and triggering automated compliance checks [17].

Walmart reduced traceability time for mangoes from 7 days to 2.2 s by using IBM Food Trust's blockchain. Each fruit's origin, harvest date, and transit conditions are stored immutably, allowing instant recalls during outbreaks [12].

7.2 Smart Contracts in Logistics

In logistics, payments are often based on achieving milestones (e.g., delivery of goods). Smart contracts automate this by linking payments to verified data inputs. For instance, IoT sensors on shipments can relay real-time data (e.g., location, temperature) to the blockchain. Once goods arrive undamaged, the smart contract releases payment to the carrier. Maersk's TradeLens platform exemplifies this: it automates freight payments upon port arrival verification, reducing processing time from days to minutes. Similarly, De Beers' Tracr uses smart contracts to distribute diamond sales revenue automatically between miners and distributors, ensuring transparency and trust. Despite benefits, smart contracts face hurdles. Legal frameworks lag behind technology; disputes over code-based agreements remain unresolved. Interoperability between blockchain platforms (e.g., Ethereum vs. Hyperledger) complicates cross-platform standardization.

7.3 Integration with IoT and RFID Technologies

Blockchain's integration with IoT and RFID technologies enables real-time data to feed into the blockchain, creating immutable records for tracking and decision-making, enhancing transparency and trust between different parties. QR codes allow consumers to scan products and access their history (e.g., origin, certifications). IBM Food Trust uses QR codes on meat packaging to trace products back to farms, displaying details like slaughter dates and transport conditions.

RFID tags embedded in pallets or containers transmit location, temperature, and handling data to the blockchain. For pharmaceuticals, MedsTracker uses RFID-enabled packaging to monitor storage conditions. If temperatures deviate, smart contracts alert stakeholders or reroute shipments, ensuring compliance with safety standards. Walmart's cold chain management system leverages RFID tags to track frozen goods, updating the blockchain every 30 s. During a salmonella outbreak, this system traced contaminated lettuce to its source in 2.2 s [12].

8 Real-World Implementations

Blockchain technology has demonstrated transformative potential in logistics through high-profile, real-world applications. Maersk's TradeLens, a blockchain platform co-developed with IBM, digitizes global shipping workflows, replacing error-prone paper-based processes with a shared, immutable ledger. By enabling real-time data exchange among 100+ stakeholders (carriers, ports, customs), TradeLens reduces transit delays by 40% and cuts administrative costs by 20%, streamlining operations across 600 ports worldwide [19]. Similarly, Walmart's collaboration with IBM Food Trust revolutionized food traceability. During a 2018 E. coli outbreak linked to romaine lettuce, Walmart traced the contamination source in 2.2 s—a task that previously took days—preventing widespread recalls and safeguarding its reputation [12]. The system uses blockchain to log every step of a product's journey, from farm to shelf, with IoT sensors ensuring temperature and handling compliance.

In the diamond industry, De Beers' Tracr blockchain tracks stones from mine to retail, assigning a digital fingerprint to each diamond. This system combats fraud and conflict diamonds by providing irrefutable provenance records, boosting consumer confidence [20].

Pharmaceutical logistics also benefit from blockchain. MedsTracker integrates RFID tags and blockchain to monitor drug shipments in real-time. If a temperature-sensitive vaccine deviates from safe conditions, the system alerts stakeholders instantly, reducing spoilage and ensuring compliance with stringent regulatory standards [11]. Meanwhile, DHL's blockchain pilot for high-value pharmaceuticals reduced shipment verification times by 90%, demonstrating blockchain's ability to enhance both speed and security [21].

In customs clearance, the EU's Blockchain for Customs initiative automates document verification using smart contracts, slashing processing times by 65%. For instance, shipments eligible for trade agreements are auto-approved, minimizing human error and bureaucratic delays [24].

Despite these successes, challenges persist. UPS's blockchain platform for cross-border logistics faced scalability issues with high-frequency IoT data, prompting a shift to hybrid solutions combining Ethereum and Hyperledger [22].

These case studies underscore blockchain's capacity to enhance transparency, reduce costs, and mitigate risks in logistics. While adoption barriers like scalability and standardization remain, early adopters prove that blockchain is not just theoretical—it's a practical tool reshaping global supply chains (Table 1).

Table 1. Real-World Blockchain Implementations in Logistics

Case Study	Sector	Key Outcomes	Reference
TradeLens	Shipping & Freight	20% reduction in administrative costs; 40% fewer delays in global shipping	[19]
MediLedger	Pharmaceuticals	Improved drug traceability and authenticity compliance with regulatory standards	[17]
IBM Food Trust (Walmart)	Retail/Food Safety	Traceability improved from 7 days to 2.2 s; reduced outbreak response time	[12]
Tracr (De Beers)	Diamonds	Reduced diamond fraud; increased consumer trust via immutable provenance records	[20]
DHL Blockchain Pilot	Pharmaceutical Logistics	90% reduction in shipment verification times; enhanced compliance and safety	[21]
UPS Cross-border Logistics	Logistics	Identified scalability challenges; hybrid blockchain for IoT integration	[22]

9 Regulatory, Economic, and Ethical Considerations

9.1 GDPR Compliance and Data Immutability

Blockchain's immutability—ensuring data cannot be altered—directly conflicts with the EU's General Data Protection Regulation (GDPR), particularly the "right to be forgotten." This regulation mandates that individuals can request personal data deletion, which is incompatible with blockchain's permanent ledger [24]. For instance, logistics platforms storing customer addresses or transaction histories on a public blockchain risk violating GDPR if they cannot erase such data. Solutions include hybrid blockchains (e.g., VeChain), where sensitive data is stored off-chain, linked via hashes to the immutable chain, allowing deletion without compromising integrity. Alternatively, zero-knowledge proofs enable data validation without exposing personal details.

Projects like LTO Network combine GDPR-compliant workflows with blockchain by using temporary anchors for non-critical data [2]. Despite these innovations, challenges persist: permissioned blockchains may centralize control, undermining decentralization ideals, while public chains face legal ambiguities [10]. As regulations evolve, interoperability between legal frameworks and blockchain design will be critical for global logistics operations.

9.2 ROI and Cost-Benefit Analysis

Blockchain adoption in logistics offers significant return on investment (ROI) through automation, reduced fraud, and streamlined operations. DHL's blockchain pilot reduced supply chain costs by 20% by automating documentation and minimizing delays in customs clearance [21]. Cost savings stem from eliminating intermediaries (e.g., banks for letters of credit), reducing manual errors, and accelerating dispute resolution via immutable records. However, upfront costs—such as IoT integration, staff training, and blockchain development—can be substantial. A 2022 McKinsey study found that companies recoup these investments within 2–3 years through operational efficiencies. Smaller firms face higher barriers due to limited resources, but cloud-based blockchain services (e.g., AWS Blockchain Templates) lower entry costs [23].

Beyond direct savings, blockchain enhances brand trust by ensuring product authenticity, as seen in Walmart's food traceability system, which reduced recall costs by 30% [12]. While ROI varies by scale and use case, the long-term economic benefits of transparency, speed, and risk mitigation position blockchain as a strategic investment for modern supply chains.

9.3 Ethical Concerns

Blockchain's promise of decentralization often clashes with corporate realities. While public blockchains like Ethereum emphasize democratized control, enterprise adoption frequently leads to permissioned systems (e.g., IBM's Hyperledger), where corporations govern nodes and data access [19]. This centralization risks creating "walled gardens," where a few entities dominate decision-making, contradicting blockchain's egalitarian ethos [18]. Additionally, energy-intensive PoW blockchains conflict with sustainability goals, though shifts to PoS (e.g., Ethereum 2.0) mitigate this. Ethical dilemmas also arise in data ownership: who controls IoT-generated supply chain data—corporations, suppliers, or consumers?

Projects like Fairchain aim to democratize data access, ensuring farmers or small suppliers retain ownership. However, power imbalances persist, as seen in De Beers' Tracr, where miners have limited influence over the diamond-tracking platform [20]. Balancing decentralization with practical governance remains a key challenge, necessitating frameworks that prioritize transparency, equitable participation, and environmental responsibility to uphold blockchain's ethical potential in logistics.

10 Conclusion

This study provides a comprehensive evaluation of blockchain technology's transformative potential and associated implementation challenges within the logistics sector. It emphasizes that blockchain significantly enhances supply chain efficiency, transparency, and security by addressing longstanding inefficiencies related to data fragmentation, manual processes, and lack of traceability. Real-world case studies, such as TradeLens, MediLedger, and IBM Food Trust, underscore blockchain's substantial benefits, including reduced operational costs and improved traceability response times.

Nevertheless, this research also identifies critical barriers—including scalability constraints, smart contract vulnerabilities, and regulatory challenges like GDPR compliance—that currently limit blockchain's widespread adoption. Therefore, continued technological innovation, rigorous development of secure smart contracts, and evolution of regulatory frameworks are imperative. Future studies should explore advanced interoperability solutions across blockchain platforms, hybrid models balancing decentralization with practical governance, and comprehensive economic analyses to quantify blockchain's long-term impacts on logistics. Addressing these areas will facilitate blockchain's transition from experimental adoption to industry-wide standardization, thereby realizing its full potential for a more resilient, transparent, and efficient global supply chain.

Acknowledgments. This study was supported by the Department of Computer Engineering and Computer Science at California State University, Long Beach.

Competing Interests. The authors have no competing interests to declare that are relevant to the content of this article.

References

1. Vacca, A.: A systematic literature review of blockchain and smart contract development: techniques, tools, and open challenges. J. Syst. Softw. **174**, 110891 (2021). https://doi.org/10.1016/j.jss.2020.110891
2. Černý, M.: Potential use of RFID and QR code in the supply chain based on blockchain and smart contract. Procedia Comput. Sci. **220**, 497–502 (2023). https://doi.org/10.1016/j.procs.2023.03.063

3. Permenev, A., Dimitrov, D., Tsankov, P., Drachsler-Cohen, D., Vechev, M.: VerX: safety verification of smart contracts. In: Proceedings of IEEE Symposium Security Privacy (SP), pp. 1661–1677. IEEE, San Francisco (2020). https://doi.org/10.1109/SP40000.2020.00066
4. Chinen, Y., Yanai, N., Cruz, J.P., Okamura, S.: RA: Hunting for re-entrancy attacks in Ethereum smart contracts via static analysis. In: Proceedings of IEEE International Conference Blockchain, pp. 327–336. IEEE, Rhodes (2020). https://doi.org/10.1109/Blockchain50366.2020.00048
5. Hildenbrandt, E., et al.: KEVM: a complete formal semantics of the Ethereum virtual machine. In: Proceedings of IEEE 31st Computer Security Foundations Symposium (CSF), pp. 204–217. IEEE, Oxford (2018). https://doi.org/10.1109/CSF.2018.00022
6. Tikhomirov, S., Voskresenskaya, E., Ivanitskiy, I., Takhaviev, R., Marchenko, E., Alexandrov, Y.: SmartCheck: static analysis of ethereum smart contracts. In: Proceedings of IEEE/ACM 1st International Workshop Emerging Trends Software Engineering Blockchain (WETSEB), pp. 9–16. IEEE, Montreal (2018). https://doi.org/10.1145/3194113.3194115
7. Kalra, S., Goel, S., Dhawan, M., Sharma, S.: ZEUS: analyzing safety of smart contracts. In: Proceedings of Network Distribution on Systems and Security Symposium (NDSS). Internet Society, San Diego (2018). https://doi.org/10.14722/ndss.2018.23092
8. Prasad, B.: Prevention and detection mechanisms for re-entrancy attack and king of Ether throne attack for Ethereum smart contracts. Int. J. Adv. Comput. Sci. Appl. **13**(5), 1–8 (2022). https://doi.org/10.14569/IJACSA.2022.0130501
9. Feist, J., Grieco, G., Groce, A.: Slither: a static analysis framework for smart contracts. In: Proceedings of IEEE/ACM 2nd International Workshop Emerging Trends Software Engineering Blockchain (WETSEB), pp. 8–15. IEEE, Seoul (2019). https://doi.org/10.1109/WETSEB.2019.00008
10. De Giovanni, P.: Blockchain and smart contracts in supply chain management: a game-theoretic model. Eur. J. Oper. Res. **284**(1), 366–376 (2020). https://doi.org/10.1016/j.ejor.2019.12.027
11. Alqarni, M.A.: Use of blockchain-based smart contracts in logistics and supply chains. Appl. Sci. **13**(6), 3542 (2023). https://doi.org/10.3390/app13063542
12. Casado-Vara, R., Prieto, J., De la Prieta, F., Corchado, J.M.: How blockchain improves the supply chain: case study alimentary supply chain. Procedia Comput. Sci. **134**, 393–398 (2018). https://doi.org/10.1016/j.procs.2018.07.193
13. Gao, J.: Blockchain-enabled internet of vehicles applications. Electronics **12**(5), 1122 (2023). https://doi.org/10.3390/electronics12051122
14. Taherdoost, H.: Smart contracts in blockchain technology: a critical review. Information **14**(2), 117 (2023). https://doi.org/10.3390/info14020117
15. World Health Organization: Substandard and falsified medical products. WHO, Geneva, Switzerland (2020). https://www.who.int/news-room/fact-sheets/detail/substandard-and-falsified-medical-products
16. Nakamoto, S.: Bitcoin: a peer-to-peer electronic cash system (2008). https://bitcoin.org/bitcoin.pdf
17. Chronicled Inc.: MediLedger Project: Blockchain solutions for the pharmaceutical supply chain. Chronicled, San Francisco, CA, USA (2023). https://www.chronicled.com/mediledger
18. Buterin, V.: Rollups: The future of Ethereum scaling. Ethereum Foundation Blog (2021). https://vitalik.eth.limo/general/2021/01/05/rollup.html

19. IBM: TradeLens: Revolutionizing global trade. IBM, Armonk, NY, USA (2022). https://www.ibm.com/case-studies/tradelens
20. De Beers Group: Tracr: Ethical diamond sourcing. De Beers, London, UK (2021). https://www.debeersgroup.com/tracr
21. DHL: Blockchain in logistics: Cost reduction and efficiency. DHL, Bonn, Germany (2021). https://www.dhl.com/global-en/home/insights-and-innovation/innovation/blockchain.html
22. UPS: Blockchain in cross-border logistics: Challenges and solutions. UPS, Atlanta, GA, USA (2022). https://www.ups.com/us/en/supply-chain-solutions/blockchain.page
23. Amazon Web Services: AWS blockchain templates: Lowering entry barriers. AWS, Seattle, WA, USA (2023). https://aws.amazon.com/blockchain/templates/
24. European Commission: GDPR and blockchain compliance guidelines, Brussels, Belgium (2023). https://ec.europa.eu/info/law/law-topic/data-protection
25. Chen, T., et al.: An empirical study of smart contract vulnerabilities. In: Proceedings of IEEE International Conference on Software Analysis, Evolution Reengineering (SANER), pp. 270–281. IEEE, Honolulu (2020). https://doi.org/10.1109/SANER48275.2020.9054840
26. Gao, J., et al.: SmartEmbed: a tool for clone and bug detection in smart contracts through structural code embedding. In: Proceedings of IEEE International Conference on Software Maintenance Evolution (ICSME), pp. 394–397. IEEE, Raleigh (2019). https://doi.org/10.1109/ICSME.2019.00067
27. Vacca, A., Di Sorbo, A., Visaggio, C.A., Canfora, G.: A systematic literature review of blockchain and smart contract development: techniques, tools, and open challenges. J. Syst. Softw. **174**, 110891 (2021). https://doi.org/10.1016/j.jss.2020.110891
28. Szabo, N.: Smart contracts: Building blocks for digital markets. Extropy **8**(2) (1996). http://www.fon.hum.uva.nl/rob/Courses/InformationInSpeech/CDROM/Literature/LOTwinterschool2006/szabo.best.vwh.net/smart_contracts_2.html

Predicting User Affective States from Mobile Notification Interactions Using LLM-Based Machine Learning Models

Muhammad Faizan Khan[1](✉), Israr Ahmad[2], Muhammad Asif Khan[2], Ghulam Mudassir[3], and Gohar Hayat Khan[4]

[1] Aberdeen Institute of Data Science and Artificial Intelligence, South China Normal University, Guangzhou, China
20220246@m.scnu.edu.cn
[2] South China University of Technology, Guangzhou, China
[3] University of Buckingham, Buckingham, UK
[4] University of Kassel, Kassel, Germany

Abstract. The rapid adoption of smartphones has created opportunities for understanding the emotional state of the user's through smartphone interactions. This work presents a novel approach using Large Language Models (LLMs) and smartphone notification interaction data for the estimation of the affective state of the user, an area that has not been extensively studied. Recent studies face challenges in generating personalized predictions; instead, they deliver generalized outcomes that are not suitable for an individual's behavior. Most models failed to incorporate real-time variables, which limits the accuracy and relevance of user's emotional state predictions. This work applies the use of LLMs to analyze user's complex, dynamic interactions with smartphone notifications, resulting in a greater understanding of emotions such as happiness, irritation, and frustration. Our work uses real-time smartphone notification data, "NotifyMiner," and LLMs to deliver context-aware, personalized emotional state predictions. In our experiments, the LLM is trained on interaction data from user's, which includes response latency, level of engagement, and type of notification, and its predictive capacity is assessed for recognizing various emotional states. We evaluate zero-shot and few-shot embedding techniques regarding their use in LLM to measure and predict user well-being status. The model proved to be successful in identifying various affective states, highlighting its potential for customized alerts, mental health tracking, and enhanced usability features. Through context-aware and personalized predictions, LLMs demonstrate their ability to overcome standard modelling restrictions and analyze complex user behaviors.

Keywords: Large Language Models · Context-aware predictions · Emotional state · Profile of Mood States (POMS) · Behavior analysis · Global Positioning System (GPS)

S. Hussain et al. (Eds.): SEET 2025, CCIS 2725, pp. 45–60, 2026.
https://doi.org/10.1007/978-3-032-08977-9_4

1 Introduction

The rapid spread of smart devices and the increasing usage of smartphones have generated a lot of information about user behavior and interactions. Mobile notifications are of particular interest since they contain rich information about user engagement, response patterns, and emotional state. Predictions of the user's emotional state from the interactions have also attracted a lot of interest due to their potential to enhance user experience, improve personalized delivery of information, and support the tracking of mental well-being [1]. In recent research works, various strategies have been explored to predict the user's emotional state with smartphone information, but they are prone to operate with either static models or simplistic models that do not support the dynamic interactions of user behavior with mobile alerts. Dynamic interaction refers to the continuously changing and context-dependent ways in which a user engages with smartphone notifications. It captures variations in user behavior over time, influenced by factors such as emotional state, notification type, urgency, time of day, and surrounding environment. Unlike static interaction patterns, dynamic interactions are flexible and adaptive, reflecting the user's shifting attention, priorities, and emotional responses in real time. Conventional models have also had the propensity to overlook the personalization aspect, failing to learn about the distinctive user behavior of individuals to generate generalized predictions that are less personalized [2]. Given the need to provide personalized, context-sensitive feedback, the need for complex models that are able to look at dynamic interactions is of the highest priority. LLMs, with their ability to work with complex, multi-dimensional information, are a possible solution to those problems.

Recent advancements in deep learning and machine learning have introduced various frameworks to support predictive applications, including predicting affective states. For example, XGBoost [3] is commonly applied to the task of prediction but is not well-suited to deal with dynamic, high-dimensional data like real-time mobile alerts. In [4], the authors used a decision support system for making natural disaster predictions, but they ignored the fact that real-time emotional data is needed in post-disaster recovery. LeCun et al.'s [5] deep learning models have made complex learning possible with big datasets, but they are short of providing personalized and context-aware predictions within dynamic real-time settings. The Transformer [6] architecture is a significant improvement to natural language processing, while its potential in the domain of predicting affective state with dynamic mobile interactions is less understood, with no effort to provide personalization and real-time context. Recently, work that uses LLMs to support the prediction of the emotional state with smartphone sensors is mostly concerned with the sensors [7] while ignoring the rich real-time information that smartphone notifications provide regarding user emotions. This work is also an extension of the following work that includes some similar experiments on the real-time notifications data with different evaluation matrices, which were not incorporated before.

Recently, LLMs have largely been used for all sorts of predictive tasks because they can handle complex data. LLMs have been widely explored in various fields, including sentiment analysis, emotion detection, and affective state prediction. Brown et al. [8] highlighted GPT-3's effectiveness in generating human-like text. However, its ability to personalize responses and adapt to individual user behaviors remains limited, often leading to generalized predictions. Similarly, in [9], the authors applied GPT -2 to a range

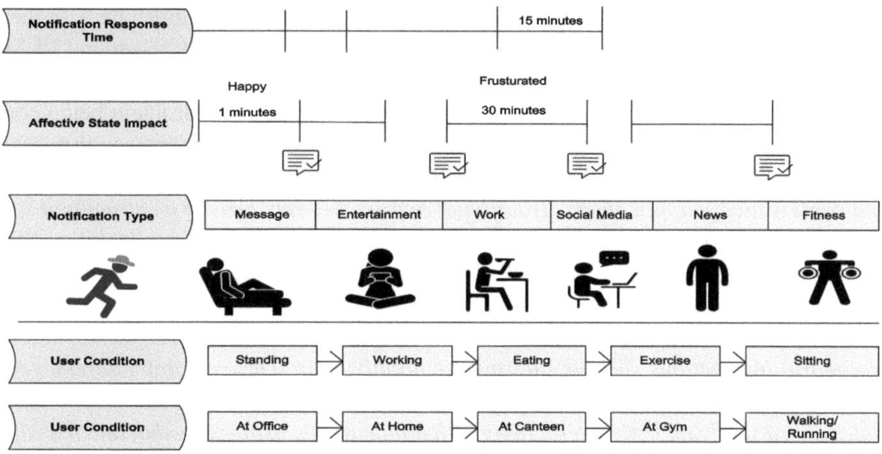

Fig. 1. Factors influencing user's smartphone interaction, including notification type, user condition, and response time.

of NLP tasks, but it struggled with handling dynamic, real-time data, such as ongoing responses to mobile notifications. Zhang et al. [10] looked at using LLMs for figuring out emotions, but they mainly worked with static data, which means the models didn't do as well in the real world, where things are always changing. Later, Li et al.[11] showed that transformer models could help predict mental health conditions, but because they only use past data and don't get real-time updates, they miss the context they need for accurate predictions. To overcome these limitations, our approach leverages dynamic user interaction data from mobile notifications, allowing us to make personalized and context-aware predictions of emotional states, advancing the field toward more accurate and adaptive models for affective state prediction. Unlike static datasets, dynamic notification interaction data is continuously generated as users interact with various types of notifications in real time, reflecting natural changes in user behavior, attention, and preferences. Each notification event, such as viewing, dismissing, replying, or ignoring, is captured and recorded dynamically on our server. This method ensures that the collected dataset evolves with the users' real-world interactions, providing a more authentic and temporally rich source of information compared to pre-collected or manually labeled static datasets. Traditional machine learning applications that address sensor inputs and pre-defined features lack the capabilities of the LLM which allows it to analyze complex user interaction patterns.

The LLMs are able to reveal hidden user behavior patterns by analyzing many smartphone notifications, which helps detect precise mental or emotional states for highly individualized affective analysis. This study explores the LLM's ability to determine affective states using human behavioral interaction data from smartphone notifications used as its key input source. In our work, we will examine the associations between the behavioral activities collected through smartphone notifications and their effect on user's. We will also show the eligibility of few-shots and zero-shots planted LLMs to conclude emotional cases based upon notification's gained from human properties. Proposed study results reveal a clear bond among smartphone notifications-extracted activities of different users and their emotional levels, which LLMs illustrate with their reasoning processes. This work is considered as a totally new study to ground LLMs with mobile notifications features for affective state prediction.

Problem Statement: By referring to existing issues, the main problem being conveyed in that paper is defined as. *Understanding users' emotional states through passive smartphone interaction has become increasingly important for developing intelligent and context-aware applications. Traditional approaches rely heavily on structured surveys or intrusive monitoring, which limits scalability and real-time applicability. With the emergence of Large Language Models (LLMs), there is an opportunity to explore their ability to interpret subtle behavioral patterns in natural language data. However, it remains unclear whether LLMs can accurately infer emotional states from dynamic, real-world interactions such as smartphone notifications. This research addresses the problem of evaluating LLMs' capability to detect and reason about users' emotional states based solely on their interactions with notifications, using zero-shot and few-shot learning methods. The goal is to establish a minimally invasive, scalable, and intelligent system for affective computing using modern NLP techniques.*

In the later section, we will discuss the process of our dataset collection. After that, the data preprocessing will be discussed, which is the most crucial part of our research. Moving forward, the analysis process will be reviewed, which includes the explanation of zero-shot and few-shot methods that are being incorporated into our research work. Lastly, the logical interference and reason will be introduced, and we will see how our designed tasks help us understand more about how the LLM generates its predictions.

2 Materials and Methods

2.1 Dataset Collection

Notifications are considered the best source for gathering user's information. Different user's states have different impacts on smartphone usage. Similarly, the affective states can impact the user interaction with notifications. In Fig. 1, the notification arrival process is discussed, and it shows different factors that influence the user's emotional state, including notification type, user condition, and response time. In our previous work, while predicting future interactions with smartphones, we had reached the dead point where there was no exact ideal real-time notification data was present at the moment. So, we had collected the smartphone notifications dataset from the app developed named NotifyMiner [12] for the span of eight months from different users. There were two kinds of users that we have targeted, one was the university students, and the second was the employees of different companies. Notify Miner is a data collection app that uses a timestamp-based experience sampling method (TESP) to capture user reactions and thoughts about different notifications. Using Notify Miner, we gathered 14,480 notifications and 300 responses to the TESP questionnaire. The app relies on built-in Android features and APIs, such as the ESSensor Manager [13] and Google's Activity Recognition API, to gather contextual data, along with the Android Notification Listener Service.

The LLM models are trained to analyze and predict emotions or moods based on interaction trends with notification's, which include various features like User ID, Device

ID, App Name, Arrival Time, Seen Time, User Action, Title, GPS Location, Alert Type, Network Usage, and User Condition. The app collects data from multiple sources, such as notifications, apps, content, battery status, Bluetooth, Wi-Fi, mobile data, calls, messages, location, screen status, light, and a simple questionnaire form. The questionnaire is triggered when the user opens the app, changes location, or clicks on a notification. A notification is considered 'clicked' if the corresponding app is opened after the notification is interacted.

Post-hoc Integration of POMS Questionnaire: To effectively assess users' emotional responses to notifications, a structured method for measuring mood was essential, and the POMS questionnaire provided the necessary framework [14]. Although the initial dataset of notifications was collected without the POMS assessment, it was incorporated into the analysis through a systematic post-hoc process. Specifically, we mapped the POMS responses, which assess mood states such as happy, irritated, Excited, and Frustrated, to the relevant emotional dimensions in our dataset. This integration allowed a more precise alignment between the POMS dimensions and user interactions, thereby enhancing our understanding of the emotional impact of notifications. The questionnaire is composed of 10 Likert scales. Five of the values reflect the positive impact (Happy, Content, Excited, Curious, Interested), and five of the values reflect the negative impact of notifications (Indifferent, Sad, Anxious, Frustrated, Irritated).

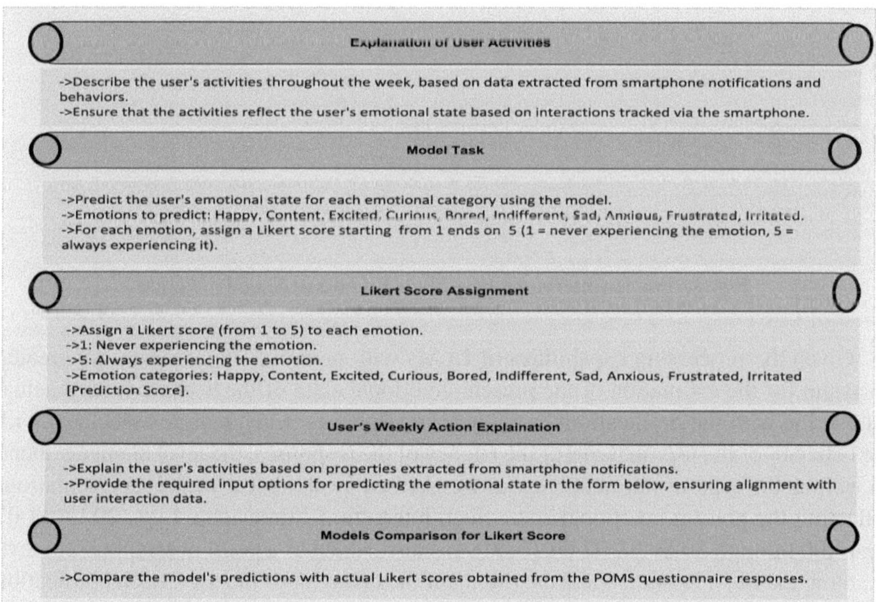

Fig. 2. Framework for Zero-Shot Emotional State Prediction

2.2 Data Preprocessing

The data collected through the Notify Miner app undergoes a series of preprocessing steps tailored to work with LLMs. The first step in preprocessing text data involves tokenization, which splits input data into smaller, manageable units so that LLM can analyze notifications and their contextual responses [15]. Extracting meaningful data from the unstructured information is a very crucial step in data processing. BERT (Bidirectional Encoder Representations from Transformers) [16] has been used to produce embeddings that enable the model to detect semantic ties within different user interactions. Later, stop-word removal filters [17] have been used to eliminate common words that produce unnecessary noise, which makes the model performance unaffected by non-informative words. Following preprocessing methods, make sure the LLM receives data that is both clean and relevant so it can produce precise emotional state predictions.

Providing descriptions set outlining a user's weekly activities extracted through smartphone notifications (e.g., messages, social media updates, app interactions), along with their corresponding emotional states, model job is to recognize patterns between the user's interaction behaviors and emotional responses. Based on these patterns, predict the user's emotional state for their upcoming interactions.

Example Format for Prediction:
Based on the following interactions:
- Happy Feeling: *score* - Determined Feeling: *score* - Attentive feeling: *score* - Their feeling of alertness: *score*
- frustrated feeling: *score* - The feeling of anxious: *score* - Interested Feeling: *score* - Their feeling of irritation: *score*

Based on the above, select the appropriate Likert score (from 1 to 5) representing the user's emotional state throughout the weeks, based on their interaction data with notifications.

Task Details:- List of emotions: Happy, Content, Excited, Curious, Interested, Indifferent, Sad, Anxious, Frustrated, Irritated.- For each emotion, choose a score from 1 (Not once) to 5 (Everytime) representing the student's emotional state.

Upcoming Weeks Prediction:- Based on the patterns learned from previous data, predict how the student will feel during the upcoming week.- Provide your answers in the following format:

<Emotion>: [Predicted Number]

Fig. 3. Framework for the Few-Shots Emotional State Prediction

Given the processing capabilities of LLMs with natural language data, we created a system for the estimation of the present emotional state of the user from their actual interaction with the notifications from their smartphones. Each feature associated with the behavior of the user in terms of the latency of the responses, the level of engagement, as well as the type of notification, was transcribed as short text-based representations reflecting the present emotional state. Each interaction's timestamp (e.g., 2023–08-02 09:15:00 through 2023–08-02 09:16:00) was also added as a point of temporal context, enabling the LLM to understand the timing of the behavior of the user. Each notification was also classified (e.g., social media, reminders, alerts etc.) with associated emotional responses (e.g., "user came across as frustrated," "user engaged positively"). Concurrent with these, the interaction was associated with the responses from the POMS questionnaire responses to ensure the emotional states found through the LLM's processing corresponded with the more traditional mood dimensions of happy, curious, anxious, as well as irritated. This conversion enabled the system to estimate the emotional state of the user from the present interaction patterns with the provision of context-based emotional estimates corresponding with the more traditional POMS dimensions.

2.3 Affective Analysis Process

To investigate if Large Language Models (LLMs) can detect the relationship between smartphone notification behavior and emotional states, few shots and zero shots tasks were conducted using the POMS questionnaire. Each week's data contained approximately 4,000 tokens from users' notification interactions. Due to resource constraints, we opted to use the OpenAI GPT-4 model [18] In our experiments, because it excels in natural language understanding and generating structured outputs from textual inputs, which is exactly what we need when mapping notifications to emotional states. The model's task was to generate Likert scores, not text descriptions, to predict emotional states from the notification data. To ensure consistent predictions, the model's temperature was set to zero, though we did find some minimal variation in results, especially with extreme emotional scores (e.g., low scores such as 1, and high scores such as 5).

This novel study has involved 12 user's, and the 20-week dataset was split into a 12-week training set and an 8-week test set. Stratified sampling was used to balance the distribution of the data across user's. For the few-shot influencing approach, we started with one training set instance and increased the number of examples incrementally (from one to ten shots) to test the ability of the LLM to predict emotional states based on notification data. The POMS questionnaire was essential to provide standardized measurements of mood, especially for mood dimensions like Happy, Interested, and Frustrated, thus enabling consistent and reliable emotional analysis throughout the study.

Zero Shot: As part of the baseline comparison for our study, we conducted a zero-shot task. The task was designed to assess how well the model could predict a user's emotional state based on their interaction with smartphone notifications [19]. Following Fig. 2, the task was created. Notifications were received by users through various means in the course of the week: friend messages, reminder alerts by learning applications, updates on social networking sites, and notifications on ongoing events. The notifications were diverse in content, volume, and priority, and thus produced different affective states. The interactions between the user and notifications were recorded, including Notification rate, Response, Notification type, Degree of engagement, and Relevance in context.

Few Shots: For every few-shot assignment, multiple weeks of smartphones notifications interaction data were selected from the training dataset, designated as labelled dataset. Few-shot tasks framework was created based on Fig. 3, which defines the process of predicting user emotional states based on their interactions with notifications. These frameworks used interaction features such as response time, engagement level, and notification type to guide the model in generating Likert scores for emotions.

Logical Interference and Reasoning: We created tasks to gain a deeper understanding of how LLM generates its predictions by assessing its abilities to make rational inferences based on user behavior. To achieve this, the prompt is adjusted via modifying the sentence "Provide your choices in the following form with no other reasoning" to "Provide your choices in the following form along with a rationale for each prediction". The following rationale depends upon comparing the user's weekly interaction behaviors with smartphone notifications: item: [predicted number and rationale]." This adjustment encouraged the model to explain its predictions, using the user's behavior data, such as response times, level of engagement, and notification types, ensuring that each emotional state prediction was not only based on the data but also logically justified.

2.4 Experimental Setup

In this study, the experimental setup was designed to investigate the relationship between user interaction with smartphone notifications and their emotional states using Large Language Models (LLMs). The process began with dynamic data collection from real-world smartphone notifications, followed by careful preprocessing to prepare the data for model input. Affective analysis was conducted through both zero-shot and few-shot learning strategies to evaluate how effectively LLMs could infer emotional patterns from user behavior. Logical inference tasks were also developed to assess the models' reasoning abilities. Finally, model performance was measured using established evaluation metrics, providing a comprehensive view of the effectiveness of our approach.

3 Results and Discussions

In the following section, the matrices that are employed to check the LLM's predictions are outlined. Later, we review the model's performance in zero-shot and few-shot scenarios. Finally, we present an analytical evaluation of the LLM's reasoning ability using a zero-shot case study, where the model's reasoning for emotional state predictions based on smartphone interaction data is analyzed.

3.1 Evaluation Matric

To measure our predictions accuracy, we implemented a macro-level evaluation strategy using both Root Mean Squared Error (RMSE) and relative error (ϵ). This process consisted of two main stages: initially, we computed the error metrics for each user's independently, and subsequently, we aggregated these metrics to calculate the average error across all users, providing a comprehensive view of the model's performance.

The RMSE for predicting emotional states based on smartphone notifications is calculated as follows:

For each user i, calculate the squared error for each observation k, where E_{ik} represents the predicted emotional state for the kth notification interaction, and A_{ik} represents the true emotional state for the same notification interaction.

$$RMSE_i = \sqrt{\frac{1}{n_i} \sum_{k=1}^{n_j} (E_{ik} - A_{ik})^2}$$

where E_{ik} is the predicted emotional state of the kth observation of the ith user (predicted from notifications data), E_{ik} is the true emotional state for the kth observation of the ith user (based on actual emotions recorded, e.g., from POMS or another emotional rating system), n^i Number of notifications or interactions that the user i has during the week.

Calculate the Overall RMSE: After calculating the individual RMSE for each user, we then average these RMSEs across all user's to get the overall RMSE.

$$RMSE_{overall} = \frac{1}{N} \sum_{i=k}^{N} RMSE_i$$

where N is the total number of user's, $RMSE_i$ is the RMSE for user i calculated in the previous step.

Relative Error Calculation: After calculating the overall RMSE, we can compute the overall relative error ($\epsilon_{overall}$) is as follows:

$$\epsilon_{overall} = \frac{1}{N} \sum_{i=1}^{N} \left(\frac{RMSE_i}{\overline{A_i}} * 100 \right)$$

where $\overline{A_i}$ is the mean of the true emotional states of each user i, calculated as

$$\overline{A_i} = \frac{1}{n_i} \sum_{k=1}^{n_i} A_{ik}$$

The overall relative error measures the percentage error across all user's based on their emotional state predictions.

3.2 Performance Evaluation of Zero-Shot

In Table 1, the means and standard deviations were calculated for each of the twelve POMS items. Positive and negative emotional states were derived as the average RMSE's for the associated notification-related items. Highlighted results represent the best-executing shot for different affective states. It is explained that the zero-shot RMSE results are relatively underperforming in providing predictions, with an average RMSE of 1.25 out of 5 ($\epsilon = 35.2\%$). The RMSE values across all twelve user's show minimal variability (std_all = 0.02, std_positive = 0.08, std_negative = 0.03), reflecting steadily predictive performance of LLMs over different user's. The model exhibits similar performance for both favourable emotions (e.g., Happy, Content, Excited) with an average RMSE = 1.20 ($\epsilon = 30.5\%$) and negative emotions (e.g., Sad, Anxious, Frustrated) with RMSE = 1.30 ($\epsilon = 22.33\%$), but it demonstrates varying performance across individual emotional states. Based on smartphone notification interaction data, the model's performance remains quite stable. Specifically, the model excels with the "Happy" emotional state (RMSE = 0.29, $\epsilon = 51.1\%$) in zero-shot scenarios while showing its lowest performance with "Irritated" (RMSE = 0.63, $\epsilon = 58.8\%$) and "Frustrated" (RMSE = 67.6, $\epsilon = 51.3\%$). The following performance differences are most likely to be generated due to the changing amounts of prior knowledge embedded in the LLM or the unique behavioral indicators captured by smartphone notifications that correspond to each emotional state.

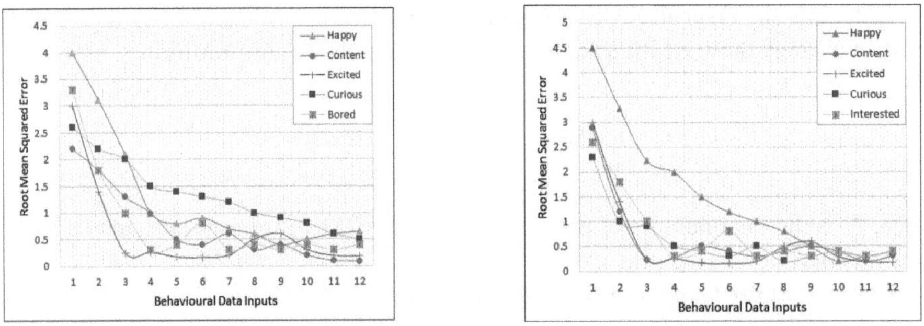

Fig. 4. Positive Affective States Learning Curves from two different user's.

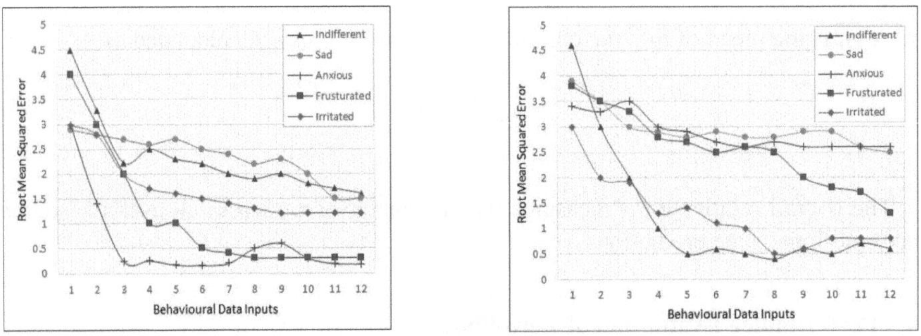

Fig. 5. Negative Affective States Learning Curves from two different user's.

Concluding our analysis demonstrates that the LLM shows acceptable performance at determining emotional states from smartphone notice data during zero-shot conditions but struggles with recognizing advanced emotional conditions such as "Irritated" and "Frustrated". This is probably due to the model's limited ability to interpret contextual nuances within notifications related to these more intense emotions. However, the model still provides valuable insights for general emotional state prediction, leveraging user interaction data for effective emotion recognition.

3.3 Few-Shot Performance Evaluation

To evaluate the effectiveness of LLMs in few-shot learning for predicting emotional states from smartphone notification data, we created few-shot tasks to assess the model's capability to predict user emotions based on notification interactions. The results, displayed in Table 1, reveal that as more training examples were provided, the Root Mean Squared Error (RMSE) consistently decreased, showing a clear improvement in prediction accuracy. The one-shot learning showed satisfactory outcomes, yet adding the extra examples led to a performance decline, which is because of the increase in the number of examples. Particularly, RMSE value decreased by an average of 8.33% for positive emotions and 41.2% for negative emotions after one shot, with a decline as if more examples were provided. When we averaged the RMSE for positive and negative emotional states, the model performed better for negative emotions in one-shot learning, with RMSE_positive = 1.20 and RMSE_negative = 1.12, while the performance between the two categories levelled out in ten-shot learning (RMSE_positive = 1.05, RMSE_negative = 1.03). This suggests that the model adapts itself quickly towards negative emotions in terms of smartphone notifications. if we break it down further, we have.

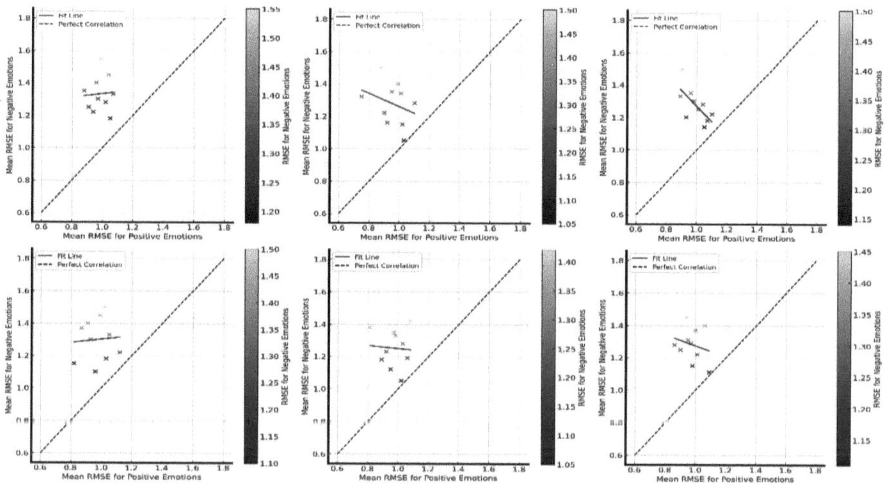

Fig. 6. Linear Correlations between positive and negative emotions for six user's.

Table 1. The Root Mean Square Error (RMSE), Mean, Std, Positive and Negative affects across twelve user's.

Shot	Happy	Content	Excited	Curious	Interested	Indifferent	Sad	Anxious	Frustrated	Irritated	Mean	Std	Positive affects	Negative affects
1.0	0.29	0.33	0.35	0.35	0.39	0.36	0.43	0.42	0.48	0.63	0.4	0.1	0.34	0.49
2.0	0.33	0.31	0.34	0.36	0.38	0.35	0.44	0.43	0.49	0.62	0.4	0.09	0.34	0.5
3.0	0.3	0.32	0.33	0.34	0.37	0.36	0.42	0.42	0.47	0.61	0.39	0.09	0.33	0.48
4.0	0.31	0.34	0.36	0.35	0.39	0.36	0.43	0.42	0.48	0.63	0.41	0.09	0.35	0.49
5.0	0.32	0.33	0.35	0.36	0.38	0.36	0.42	0.41	0.47	0.62	0.4	0.09	0.35	0.48
6.0	0.33	0.32	0.36	0.35	0.39	0.35	0.43	0.42	0.48	0.61	0.4	0.09	0.35	0.48
7.0	0.3	0.33	0.34	0.36	0.38	0.36	0.44	0.42	0.49	0.62	0.4	0.09	0.34	0.49
8.0	0.31	0.34	0.33	0.34	0.39	0.36	0.42	0.41	0.47	0.61	0.4	0.09	0.34	0.48
9.0	0.29	0.33	0.34	0.35	0.38	0.36	0.43	0.42	0.48	0.62	0.4	0.09	0.34	0.49
10.0	0.3	0.31	0.35	0.34	0.39	0.35	0.43	0.42	0.47	0.61	0.4	0.09	0.34	0.48
11.0	0.29	0.33	0.34	0.35	0.37	0.36	0.42	0.42	0.48	0.62	0.4	0.09	0.34	0.48
12.0	0.32	0.34	0.35	0.35	0.39	0.36	0.43	0.42	0.48	0.63	0.41	0.09	0.35	0.49

noticed that the LLM showed its best performance in predicting the emotional state "Excited" (RMSE = 1.15), while struggling the most with "Irritated" (RMSE = 0.63) and "Sad" (RMSE = 1.44). The model demonstrated its best performance through an 8.57% point decrease in RMSE when identifying "Anxious" emotions as it received ten-shot conditions. The accuracy of emotional state identification increased as the number of examples increased, leading to decreased standard deviation in RMSE from 0.27 in zero-shot learning to 0.12 in ten-shot learning. It is advisable, as the model receives more examples, that the variability in performance across individual emotional states decreases, likely due to an increase in the model's understanding of the user's emotional context. This improvement in prediction accuracy was observed for all user's, although some emotional states were predicted more effectively for certain individuals. For instance, Fig. 4 illustrates the learning curves of two user's, showing distinct variations in how the model adapted to the data in terms of positive affective states and Fig. 5 illustrates the learning curves of two user's, showing distinct variations in how the model adapted to the data in terms of negative affective states. Additionally, Fig. 6 highlights the correlation between positive and negative emotions for six user's, showing that the LLM's predictive performance improves at similar rates for both emotional categories, suggesting a linear relationship in prediction accuracy. The blue fit line represents a clear relationship between positive and negative emotions in terms of RMSE.

Table 2. Zero-shot Predicted Score with Logical interference and Reasoning for One User.

Emotion	Predicted Score	Logical Interference and Reason
Happy (5)	4	The person engaged frequently with notifications, receiving high levels of interaction with positive content.
Content (4)	3	Notifications were moderate, with few distractions, suggesting the person felt content during the week.
Excited (5)	4	Frequent notifications, especially with social media updates, indicate a heightened sense of excitement.
Curious (4)	4	The person interacted regularly with notifications, often checking for updates and new content, indicating curiosity.
Interested (4)	3	Notifications indicated a mild interest in various apps and activities, but with average engagement overall.
Indifferent (2)	1	There were fewer interactions with less relevant notifications, suggesting indifference.
Sad (3)	2	A lack of frequent social interactions and neutral notifications suggest mild sadness but no strong emotional indicators.
Anxious (5)	4	The user had a higher volume of notifications but with occasional delays in responses, indicating anxiety.
Frustrated (4)	3	A high frequency of missed or ignored notifications suggests mild frustration with technology or notifications.
Irritated (2)	1	No significant fluctuations in notification engagement suggest no irritation during the week.

This makes the prediction easy to identify. In all the plots, the dashed line is used as a benchmark to predict the values against the ideal case. The clustering of data points closer to the blue fit line shows a greater correlation between the RMSE values for positive and negative emotional states. This tighter clustering means that the model's performance is consistent and more accurate across different emotional states. As more points move away from the fit line, it reveals the higher RMSE values, incorporating the fact that the model's prediction becomes less accurate.

It is revealed from the learning patterns that the zero-shot predictions tend to yield larger errors (located in the upper left corner of the graph); if more examples are provided, the data points shift toward regions of lower RMSE (lower left corner). It shows that when we provide more examples to LLM, it performs increasingly better for emotional state prediction. Overall, for our findings, our idea is supported that smartphone-inferred behavioral data holds noteworthy promise for predicting affective states with LLMs, reinforcing the strong relationships that are present between user behavior and emotional predictions.

3.4 Logical Interference and Reasoning

By equipping the LLM with an understanding of predicting emotional states based on smartphone notifications, the model offers a deeper look into the correlation between user activities with their emotional responses. Though these validation insights are still under review, they still provide valuable observations. A positive emotional state emerges when people actively use their smartphones and unlock their screens many times or use apps more than usual coupled together with long typing sessions. Rapid typing rates indicate a user's determination and ability to type quickly during short intervals, which contributes to their focus and attention on the screen. The system detects alertness through numerous screens and unlocks and recognizes missed calls together with quick typing adaptations; when users feel upset, the calls are brief, indicating hostility. Users who respond more slowly to messages or use their phones less tend to experience uninterruptedness, but the cessation of screen unlocking with fast location modifications indicates fear. The LLM uses different smartphone interactions, including typing behavior, screen unlocks instances, phone calls, and application usage, to determine user emotional states. Figure 3 graphs shows that the model generates meaningful and clear reasoning for its forecast process, which matches its predicted outcomes.

Table 3. Ten-shot Predicted Score with Logical interference and Reasoning for One User.

Emotion	Predicted Score	Logical Interference and Reason
Happy (5)	5	The person engaged frequently with social media, received a high volume of positive notifications, and had consistent responses, indicating high happiness.
Content (4)	4	A consistent engagement with notifications related to positive content, with average response times, indicating contentment and a balanced emotional state.
Excited (5)	5	The person interacted intensively with notifications, especially with social media, suggesting a high level of excitement.
Curious (4)	5	The person consistently checked notifications across different apps, including news and educational updates, suggesting strong curiosity.
Interested (4)	5	High engagement with notifications from multiple apps, particularly related to interests like hobbies and news, indicates high interest and engagement.
Indifferent (2)	1	Minimal interaction with notifications, particularly with less relevant content, indicating complete indifference.
Sad (3)	2	Fewer notifications related to social interactions and neutral content suggest mild sadness, but no major emotional impact.
Anxious (5)	5	The user frequently interacted with urgent notifications, delays in responses, and high engagement with important updates indicate significant anxiety.
Frustrated (4)	4	Moderate engagement with notifications but occasional delays, indicating frustration, though not overwhelming.
Irritated (2)	1	No noticeable patterns of delayed or ignored notifications suggest no irritation during the week.

The features, including battery consumption along with application usage, real-time location along with smartphone notifications interactions and typing activity, are emphasized repeatedly throughout the model's logical evaluation process. Those suggested LLM analyzes behavioral traces to generate emotional predictions that future researchers can enhance by including additional sensor details in their analysis. The LLM showed a higher degree of uncertainty during the task when identifying negative emotions, which was different from when recognizing positive emotions. The model chose scores at level 1 or 2 when identifying negative emotional states because this prediction category proved especially complex. The LLM frequently explained the assignment of one score by considering insufficient results instead of using the score as a default middle value. The results discovery process caused the score to evolve from the initial level 1 up to a range spanning from 2 through 3 and beyond. Testing a "Not able to decide (-1)" option did not yield results because the LLM showed confidence whenever it discovered enough evidence for its predictions. Tables 2 and 3 display RMSE improvement data, which occurs when the LLM receives additional examples. The model applied reasoning improvement to behavioral data from different weeks, which led to increased accuracy in predictions. The ability of LLM to learn new examples indicates how it can modify its predictive output.

The following study results proved that the smartphone utilization data aligns meaningfully with emotional state patterns, which demonstrates why such research results are important in emotional prediction analysis. The LLM points out that critical phone activities include reading generated content with excessive application usage coupled with numerous device unlocking sessions. Our analysis indicates that future predictions will become more accurate when researchers also incorporate sleep patterns alongside particular app use times and the content of typing or viewing data into the analysis. Future studies should evaluate how these factors boost the accuracy of the prediction of emotional states.

4 Conclusion

In the proposed work, we have introduced the novel Language Models (LLMs) to detect user's emotional states through their smartphone notification activities. When the real-time user interaction data like engagement levels, latency, and different notification types are incorporated, then the proposed model has achieved personalized context-aware predictions for different emotional states like happiness, frustration, and irritation. Our results have indicated the valuable insights upon zero-shot models; they fell short in prediction accuracy if it is compared with few-shot learning approaches, which show better results when labelled data is incorporated.

Thus, our study suggests that LLMs are a great tool if used for personalized mental state tracking, especially in the field of smartphone notifications. By embracing Logical Inference and Reasoning, we can enhance prediction models in scenarios where data is sparse or ambiguous, making the predictions more adaptive to individual users' emotional dynamics. This approach would make the predictions more adaptive to the emotional dynamics of individual users.

In future work, if the LLMs are fine-tuned to comprise more real-time individualized user's data integrated with Logical Inference and Reasoning, it will set the way for a more automatic, emotionally intelligent notification system. Those systems would be able to dynamically adjust notifications based on user's real-time emotional states, which can improve user experiences and mental health. Our research study results imply that, with further refining, proposed emotion-aware systems can get control of traditional limitations in understanding user behaviors and offer a deeper understanding of user actions, making them indispensable for enhancing smartphone interactions and supporting emotional conditions.

Threats to Validity: Several potential threats to validity were considered in this study. To address internal validity, we controlled for external factors by using the POMS questionnaire, which provided standardized mood measurements to account for baseline emotional states and reduce the influence of unaccounted variables. Regarding external validity, although the sample size was limited to 12 users, we used stratified sampling to ensure a balanced distribution of data across users, aiming for a representative subset of behaviors. To mitigate concerns about construct validity, we selected the POMS questionnaire for its well-established reliability in measuring emotional states, acknowledging its limitations in capturing all context-specific emotions but recognizing its suitability for the scope of this study. Additionally, we ensured the real-time data collected from smartphone notifications was rich enough to provide meaningful insights. These efforts helped reduce the impact of potential validity threats, ensuring more reliable and contextually relevant findings.

Funding. The authors have not disclosed any funding.

Data Availability. The datasets generated and analyzed during the current study are not publicly available due to privacy Reasons and Ethical Concerns (Data includes personal information's, notifications and contacts) but are available from the corresponding author on reasonable request.

Conflict of Interest. On behalf of all authors, the corresponding author states that there is no conflict of interest.

References

1. Kanjo, E., Kuss, D.J., Ang, C.S.: NotiMind: utilizing responses to smart phone notifications as affective sensors. IEEE Access **5**, 22023–22035 (2017)
2. Wampfler, R., Klingler, S., Solenthaler, B., Schinazi, V.R., Gross, M., Holz, C.: Affective state prediction from smartphone touch and sensor data in the wild (2022)
3. Nalluri, M., Pentela, M., Eluri, N.R.: A scalable tree boosting system: XG boost. Int. J. Res. Stud. Sci. Eng. Technol. **7**(12), 36–51 (2020)
4. Mudassir, G., Di Marco, A.: Social-based city reconstruction planning in case of natural disasters: a reinforcement learning approach. IEEE (2021)
5. LeCun, Y., Bengio, Y., Hinton, G.: Deep learning. Nature **521**(7553), 436–444 (2015)
6. Vaswani, A., et al.: Attention is all you need. Adv. Neural Inf. Process. Syst. **30** (2017)
7. Zhang, T., Teng, S., Jia, H., D'Alfonso, S.: Leveraging LLMs to predict affective states via smartphone sensor features (2024)
8. Brown, T., et al.: Language models are few-shot learners. Adv. Neural. Inf. Process. Syst. **33**, 1877–1901 (2020)
9. Radford, A., Narasimhan, K., Salimans, T., Sutskever, I.: Improving language understanding by generative pre-training (2018)
10. Acheampong, F.A., Nunoo-Mensah, H., Chen, W.: Transformer models for text-based emotion detection: a review of BERT-based approaches. Artif. Intell. Rev. **54**(8), 5789–5829 (2021)
11. Kokane, V., Abhyankar, A., Shrirao, N., Khadkikar, P.: Predicting mental illness (depression) with the help of nlp transformers. IEEE (2024)
12. Khan, M.F., Lu, L., Toseef, M., Musyafa, A., Amin, A.: NotifyMiner: rule based user behavioral machine learning approach for context wise personalized notification services. J. Ambient. Intell. Humaniz. Comput. **14**(10), 13301–13317 (2023)
13. Fischer, J.E., Yee, N., Bellotti, V., Good, N., Benford, S., Greenhalgh, C.: Effects of content and time of delivery on receptivity to mobile interruptions (2010)
14. Selmi, O., Ouergui, I., Muscella, A., Levitt, D.E., Suzuki, K., Bouassida, A.: Monitoring mood state to improve performance in soccer players: a brief review. Front. Psychol. **14**, 1095238 (2023)
15. Ashish, V.: Attention is all you need. Adv. Neural Inf. Process. Syst. **30**, I (2017)
16. Liu, Z., Lin, W., Shi, Y., Zhao, J.: A Robustly Optimized BERT Pre-training Approach with Post-Training. Springer, Heidelberg (2021)
17. Devlin, J., Chang, M.-W., Lee, K., Toutanova, K.: Bert: pre-training of deep bidirectional transformers for language understanding (2019)
18. Sorin, V., et al.: Large language models and empathy: systematic review. J. Med. Internet Res. **26**, e52597 (2024)
19. Dorneles, S.O., Francisco, R., Barbosa, D.N.F., Barbosa, J.L.V.: Context awareness in recognition of affective states: a systematic mapping of the literature. Int. J. Hum.-Comput. Interact. **39**(8), 1563–1581 (2023)

Responsible AI Transforms Insurance Claims via Prompt Engineering

Shravya Kalva[1] and Atif Farid Mohammad[2(✉)]

[1] Cognizant, Bentonville, AR 72712, USA
[2] Purdue Global University, West Lafayette, IN 47906, USA
atif.mohammad@purdueglobal.edu

Abstract. The life insurance industry is poised to significantly from integrating Generative/Responsible AI, particularly through Prompt Engineering within Large Language Models (LLMs). This paper explores how advancements in Generative/Responsible AI can automate and enhance claim processing. Traditional claim processes, involving steps like document verification and beneficiary validation, require meticulous attention. Generative/Responsible AI can analyze complex documents, extract key information, and generate summaries for agents, expediting the process and ensuring accuracy. Prompt Engineering is essential for guiding AI models to produce accurate and ethically aligned outputs, adhering to industry standards. The research highlights potential benefits such as reduced processing times, improved customer satisfaction, and enhanced fraud detection, while addressing challenges and ethical considerations. By leveraging these technologies, the industry can achieve more efficient, accurate, and responsible claim processing, benefiting both providers and claimants. This paper provides a comprehensive overview of this transformative journey.

Keywords: Artificial Intelligence · LLMs · Prompt Engineering · Generative AI · Responsible AI

1 Introduction

The arena known as Life Insurance has a vast potential to embed Generative/Responsible AI by incorporating Prompt Engineering within a possible LLM. We will be exploring the automation of claim processing using the research, conducted within the realm of AI, in specific Generative/Responsible and Responsible AI. This paper will embed the traditional detail of processes involved in providing claims and research associated within the organization and the claimant. Generative/Responsible AI can analyze such a document to create summaries for the agents/providers before they create a claim.

The arena of life insurance is on the cusp of a transformative era, where the vast potential of Generative/Responsible AI, coupled with Prompt Engineering in a given LLM [1] suited for the required indexes creation, promises to revolutionize traditional processes. This paper delves into the intricate world of claim processing, exploring how advancements in AI, particularly Generative/Responsible and Responsible AI, can streamline

S. Hussain et al. (Eds.): SEET 2025, CCIS 2725, pp. 61–67, 2026.
https://doi.org/10.1007/978-3-032-08977-9_5

and enhance efficiency. By embedding traditional claim processes with cutting-edge AI technologies, we aim to bridge the gap between conventional methods and innovative solutions. Claim processing in life insurance involves a multitude of intricate steps, from document verification to beneficiary validation, each requiring meticulous attention to detail. Generative/Responsible AI, with its ability to create coherent and contextually relevant content, can significantly expedite these processes. For instance, Generative/Responsible AI can analyze complex insurance documents, extracting pertinent information and generating concise summaries for agents and providers. This not only saves time but also ensures that critical details are not overlooked, thereby enhancing the accuracy and reliability of claim processing.

Prompt Engineering plays a pivotal role in this transformation. By crafting precise and context-specific prompts, we can guide Generative/Responsible AI models to produce outputs that are not only accurate but also aligned with the ethical and regulatory standards of the insurance industry. This ensures that the AI-generated content is both useful and responsible, adhering to the principles of fairness, transparency, and accountability. This paper will explore the research conducted within the realm of AI, focusing on how Generative/Responsible and Responsible AI can be integrated into the existing frameworks of life insurance organizations. We will examine the potential benefits, such as reduced processing times, improved customer satisfaction, and enhanced fraud detection. We will also address the challenges and ethical considerations associated with implementing AI in claim processing, ensuring that the transition is smooth and beneficial for all stakeholders involved.

The integration of Generative/Responsible AI and Prompt Engineering in life insurance claim processing holds immense promise. By leveraging these technologies, we can create a more efficient, accurate, and responsible claim processing system, ultimately benefiting both the insurance providers and the claimants. This paper aims to provide a comprehensive overview of this transformative journey, highlighting the potential and the path forward.

2 Using Gen AI in Insurance

Gen AI can automate processes by creating claims management that would radically improve the operations in the insurance sector powered by a suited LLM [2].

Gen AI can be used at the following stages of the claim process (Fig. 1):

1. Intake stage: where claim is created via digital portals or thru phone or mail.
2. Adjudication stage: where the claim is in adjudication
3. Claim creation process: coverage eligibility, policy holder information
4. Claim processing stage: payment and post payment activity

2.1 Intake Stage

The intake stage in the insurance domain involves the initial creation of a claim, which can be submitted through various channels such as digital portals, phone calls, or mail [1]. AI can significantly enhance this stage by automating the data entry process and

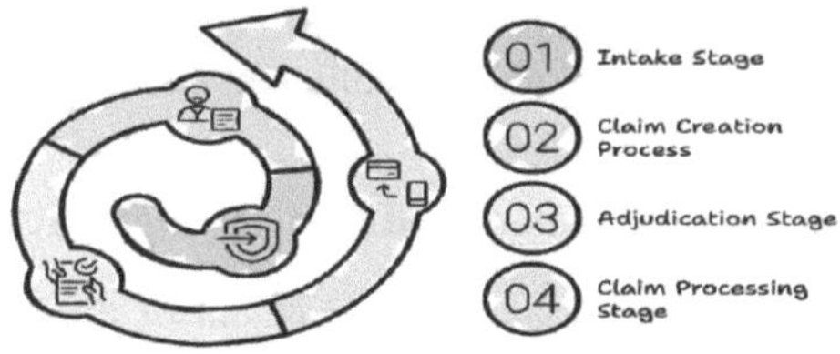

Fig. 1. Intake Stage: Where Claim is Created via Digital Portals or Through Phone or Mail

ensuring accuracy. For instance, natural language processing (NLP) can be used to extract relevant information from emails or transcribed phone calls, automatically populating claim forms. This not only speeds up the intake process but also reduces the likelihood of human error, ensuring that all necessary details are captured correctly from the outset.

AI-powered chatbots can provide immediate assistance to policyholders, guiding them through the claim submission process and answering any queries they may have. These chatbots can operate 24/7, offering convenience and accessibility to customers regardless of the time or day. By leveraging machine learning algorithms, the chatbots can continuously improve their responses based on previous interactions, providing a more personalized and efficient service over time.

2.2 Adjudication Stage: Where the Claim is in Adjudication

The adjudication stage is critical as it involves the evaluation and decision-making process for insurance claims. AI can play a crucial role in streamlining this stage by analyzing vast amounts of data to determine the validity and extent of a claim [2]. Machine learning models can be trained to identify patterns and anomalies in claim data, helping to detect fraudulent activities more accurately. This not only speeds up the adjudication process but also ensures that legitimate claims are processed efficiently while fraudulent ones are flagged for further investigation.

AI can assist in predicting the likelihood of a claim being approved based on historical data and current trends. Predictive analytics can provide insights into potential outcomes, allowing adjudicators to make more informed decisions. This can lead to faster resolution times and improved customer satisfaction, as policyholders receive timely and fair assessments of their claims.

2.3 Claim Creation Process: Coverage Eligibility, Policyholder Information

The claim creation process involves verifying coverage eligibility and gathering policyholder information, which are essential steps in determining the validity of a claim. AI can automate the verification of coverage eligibility by cross-referencing claim data with policy details stored in databases. This ensures that only eligible claims are processed, reducing the burden on human adjudicators and minimizing the risk of errors. AI can enhance the accuracy and completeness of policyholder information by using data enrichment techniques [3]. For example, AI algorithms can integrate data from various sources, such as public records and social media, to update and verify policyholder information. This ensures that the most current and accurate data is used in the claim creation process, leading to more reliable and efficient claim handling.

2.4 Claim Processing Stage: Payment and Post-Payment Activity

The claim processing stage encompasses the payment of approved claims and post-payment activities, such as follow-up and auditing. AI can automate the payment process by integrating with financial systems to initiate and track payments. This ensures that payments are made promptly and accurately, reducing the need for manual intervention and minimizing the risk of payment errors.

In addition, AI can assist in post-payment activities by monitoring and analyzing payment data to detect any irregularities or potential issues [4]. Machine learning algorithms can identify patterns that may indicate fraud or errors, triggering automated alerts for further investigation [5]. This proactive approach helps to safeguard against financial losses and ensures the integrity of the claim processing system. By leveraging AI, insurance companies can enhance the efficiency and accuracy of their claim processing, ultimately leading to better outcomes for both the insurer and the policyholder. Use of Generative AI improves the following:

A. Profitability and growth – by cutting down human intervention and processing claims quickly
B. Cost savings and efficiency – By investing in Generative/Responsible AI-driven solutions insurers can reduce spending on cost savings and operational efficiency gains to process claims.
C. Operational intelligence and effectiveness –Using Generative/Responsible AI for autonomous coding is accelerating the software development life cycle resulting in productivity gains and reduction in training time, which may enhance workforce productivity.

The integration of Generative/Responsible AI (Gen AI) in the insurance industry offers several transformative benefits, significantly enhancing profitability, operational efficiency, and overall effectiveness. One of the most notable advantages is the improvement in profitability and growth. By leveraging Gen AI [6], insurers can significantly reduce human intervention in various processes, particularly in claims processing. This reduction not only speeds up the claims process but also ensures greater accuracy and consistency, leading to higher customer satisfaction and operational efficiency. The ability of Gen AI to handle complex tasks autonomously [7] allows insurance companies to process claims more quickly, thereby enhancing customer service and reducing the time and costs associated with manual interventions (Fig. 2).

Gen AI contributes to substantial cost savings and efficiency. Investing in Generative/Responsible AI-driven solutions enables insurers to streamline their operations, reducing expenditure on manual processes and enhancing overall efficiency. By automating routine tasks and leveraging AI for more complex decision-making, insurance companies can achieve significant cost savings. This efficiency gain allows insurers to allocate resources more effectively, focusing on strategic initiatives that drive growth and innovation. The implementation of Gen AI also helps in identifying and mitigating fraudulent claims, further reducing operational costs and enhancing the bottom line. Operational

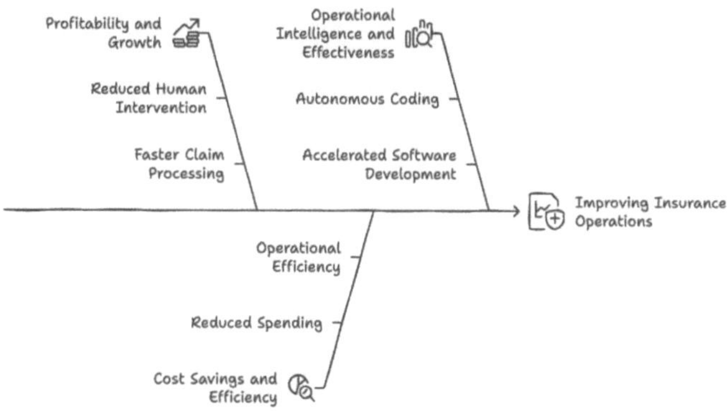

Fig. 2. Enhancing Insurance Operations with GenAI

intelligence and effectiveness are also significantly enhanced through the use of Gen AI. In the software development life cycle, Gen AI can accelerate processes by enabling autonomous coding and other automated tasks.

This acceleration leads to productivity gains and a reduction in training time for developers, ultimately enhancing workforce productivity. By integrating Gen AI into their operational frameworks, insurance companies can achieve faster time-to-market for new products and services, staying ahead of the competition and meeting evolving customer demands more effectively. Gen AI's ability to generate novel and creative outputs [9], accessible even to those with little technical knowledge, further amplifies its impact on operational intelligence. This capability allows insurance companies to innovate and adapt quickly to market changes, ensuring that they remain competitive and responsive to customer needs. The transformative power of Gen AI in the insurance industry is undeniable, making it a critical component for future growth and success.

3 Research Proposition: Algorithm

Here are the necessary elements of the proposed algorithm. The following insertion of States, Claims and Transitions are associated with the mathematical algorithm we are proposing in this paper (Table 1, 2 and 3).

Table 1. States and Claims

S_0: Initial state (no claim)	C_{01}: Claim is submitted
S_1: Intake stage	C_{12}: Claim is validated for adjudication
S_2: Adjudication stage	C_{23}: Coverage eligibility and policyholder information are verified
S_3: Claim creation process	C_{34}: Claim is approved for payment
S_4: Claim processing stage	C_{45}: Payment and post-payment activities are completed
S_5: Final state (claim completed)	

Table 2. Transitions

1. **Initialization:**
   - Set initial state $S = S_0$
2. **Intake Stage:**
   - If C_{01} is true:
     - $S = S_1$
     - Record claim details (digital, phone, mail)
3. **Adjudication Stage:**
   - If $S = S_1$ and C_{12} is true:
     - $S = S_2$
     - Initiate adjudication process
4. **Claim Creation Process:**
   - If $S = S_2$ and C_{23} is true:
     - $S = S_3$
     - Verify coverage eligibility and policyholder information
5. **Claim Processing Stage:**
   - If $S = S_3$ and C_{34} is true:
     - $S = S_4$
     - Initiate payment and post-payment activities
6. **Final State:**
   - If $S = S_4$ and C_{45} is true:
     - $S = S_5$
     - Mark claim as completed

T_{01}: Transition from initial state to intake stage
T_{12}: Transition from intake stage to adjudication stage
T_{23}: Transition from adjudication stage to claim creation process
T_{34}: Transition from claim creation process to claim processing stage
T_{45}: Transition from claim processing stage to final state

Table 3. Matrix with Conditions

Matrix	Conditions
$\begin{pmatrix} 0 & C_{01} & 0 & 0 & 0 \\ 0 & 0 & C_{12} & 0 & 0 \\ 0 & 0 & 0 & C_{23} & 0 \\ 0 & 0 & 0 & 0 & C_{34} \\ 0 & 0 & 0 & 0 & C_{45} \end{pmatrix}$	$C_{01} = f(claim\_submission)$ $C_{12} = f(claim\_validation)$ $C_{23} = f(coverage\_eligibility, policyholder\_info)$ $C_{34} = f(claim\_approval)$ $C_{45} = f(payment\_completion, post\_payment\_activities)$

4 Conclusion

The integration of Generative/Responsible AI (Gen AI) in the insurance industry represents a transformative shift, offering substantial benefits across various stages of the claims process. In the adjudication stage, AI streamlines decision-making by analyzing data to determine claim validity and detect fraud, ensuring efficient and accurate claim processing. During the claim creation process, AI automates coverage eligibility verification and enhances policyholder information accuracy through data enrichment techniques. In the claim processing stage, AI automates payments and monitors post-payment activities to detect irregularities, safeguarding against financial losses. The adoption of Gen AI improves profitability and growth by reducing human intervention and accelerating claims processing. It also drives cost savings and operational efficiency, allowing insurers to invest in more effective solutions. Furthermore, Gen AI enhances operational intelligence and effectiveness by accelerating software development and reducing training time, leading to productivity gains. By leveraging these capabilities, insurance companies can achieve better outcomes, ensuring higher customer satisfaction and operational excellence.

References

1. Eckert, C., Osterrieder, K.: How digitalization affects insurance companies: overview and use cases of digital technologies. Zeitschrift für die gesamte Versicherungswissenschaft **109**(5), 333–360 (2020)
2. Van Anh, N., Duc, T.M.: Big data-driven predictive modeling for pricing, claims processing and fraud reduction in the insurance industry globally. Int. J. Respon. Artif. Intell. **14**(2), 12–23 (2024)
3. Nimmagadda, V.S.P.: Artificial intelligence for customer behavior analysis in insurance: advanced models, techniques, and real-world applications. J. AI Healthc. Med. **2**(1), 227–263 (2022)
4. Arpteg, A., Brinne, B., Crnkovic-Friis, L., Bosch, J.: Software engineering challenges of deep learning. In: 2018 44th Euromicro Conference on Software Engineering and Advanced applications (SEAA), pp. 50–59. IEEE (2018)
5. Mohammad, A.F., Agarwal, R., Columbo, T., Vigorito, J.: Generative/Responsible & responsible AI-llms use in differential governance. In: 2023 International Conference on Computational Science and Computational Intelligence (CSCI), pp. 291–295 (2023)
6. Mohammad, A.F., Clark, B., Agarwal, R., Summers, S.: LLM GPT generative/responsible ai and artificial general intelligence (AGI): the next frontier. In: 2023 Congress in Computer Science, Computer Engineering, and Applied Computing (CSCE), pp. 413–417 (2023)
7. Mohammad, A.F., Clark, B., Hegde, R.: Large language model (LLM) & GPT, a monolithic study in generative/responsible AI. In: Proceedings of the 2023 Congress in Computer Science, Computer Engineering, and Applied Computing, CSCE 2023, Las Vegas, NV, USA, 24–27 July 2023, pp. 383–388 (2023)
8. Mohammad, A.F., Clark, B., Agarwal, R., Summers, S.: LLM/GPT generative/responsible AI and artificial general intelligence (AGI): the next frontier. In: 2023 Congress in Computer Science, Computer Engineering, & Applied Computing (CSCE), Las Vegas, NV, USA, pp. 413–417 (2023)
9. Koivisto, M., Grassini, S.: Best humans still outperform artificial intelligence in a creative divergent thinking task. Sci. Rep. **13**(1), 13601 (2023)

Responsible AI Incorporation in Advanced Persistent Threat Landscape

Sarthak Bhatt[1], Atif Farid Mohammad[2(✉)], and Urmita Banerjee[3]

[1] Healable Inc., Rockville, MD, USA
sarthak.bhatt@healable.com
[2] Purdue Global University, West Lafayette, IN, USA
atif.mohammad@purdueglobal.edu
[3] University of Maryland, Baltimore, MD, USA
uban1@umbc.edu

Abstract. The multifaceted nature and the quantity of digital assaults has been expanding constantly which induces that the security frameworks that are being used today have restricted accomplishment in keeping these advanced assaults. By incorporating Responsible AI, we can predict the possible threat patterns to get guardrails applied. Advanced Persistent Threats like Stuxnet, hacking group RCS, Red October, Wild Neutron and all the more as of late Carbanak have further lessened the trust in present security frameworks. In this paper, we have performed the specialized investigation of these Advanced Persistent Threats which highlights their individual salient features and identify common patterns among them. This analysis will assist us to think of a skeletal structure for all the APT's which in turn assists in concocting a cautious defensive mechanism to identify similar threats in future. This paper sheds light on methodologies as well as research covered on the mentioned in depth.

Keywords: APT · Cyber Attacks · Digital · Responsible AI

1 Introduction

Advanced Persistent Threat (APT) is a term began over the recent years for another type of guileful dangers that utilize different assault procedures and vectors and that are led by stealth to stay away from identification so hackers can hold control over target frameworks unnoticed for drawn out stretches of time. Cyber-attacks are expanding in intricacy, persistence and numbers. It speaks to another era of system dangers of high unpredictability. APT also targets a specific system or entity with a very precise goal. In addition, APT executes supported and viable attack for a long stretch. The aim of an APT assault is to take information that it can and then to harm the system or association. APT attack target associations in sectors with high esteem data, for example, National Guard and the money related industry, and governments. Because of the intricacy and stealthiness of APT's, there is no single arrangement that offers powerful insurance. The attention ought to be on building a protection top to bottom methodology that means to

S. Hussain et al. (Eds.): SEET 2025, CCIS 2725, pp. 68–77, 2026.
https://doi.org/10.1007/978-3-032-08977-9_6

continually screen systems and security controls for their viability. In order to build a system, we need to be quite mindful of APT's features along with their technicalities. In this paper we have laid our emphasis to study the features of different APT's that can be blended with the new technical methodologies to prevent the APT attacks. For this we have considered some potential parameters which helps in identifying the APT's and take some defensive measures as such.

In this paper, we will focus on the problem that has given us the motivation to conduct this survey. Along with that we would like to give some insights into the preliminary findings of our survey. We also discuss the related work if any that has been done in the field of APT attacks. Next, we will present the methodology that we have implemented in successfully conducting this survey in a block diagram. We further describe the actual survey that we have conducted which includes the attacks considered & importance of parameters considered and classification of attacks accordingly. This paper also deals with the work that is related to after classification of APT attacks. We also share the results of our survey along with the insights that we have gained through this survey. We propose the defensive mechanism to prevent or identify the APT attacks. This defense mechanism is modelled based on the survey results found.

2 Motivation

The APT attacks have been increasing enormously with the increasing use of computers. Below graph (Fig. 1) highlight the growth of APT's from 2008 to 2016. With the increase in the use of computers even more, there is every chance of increase in the APT attacks as well. APT attacks are very harmful as their main motto is to get access of confidential data of an organization. Once the data is accessed it is easy to get hold of the operations and get benefitted from that. Carbanak is one of the APT attacks in which the attackers targeted a bank, compromised the security and then started mimicking like the organization employees using their credentials. Once they got hold of the operations, they were able to steal 1 billion from the bank which is a very huge amount. There is every chance that the attackers target the most valuable data related to any fields like health care, Army, etc.

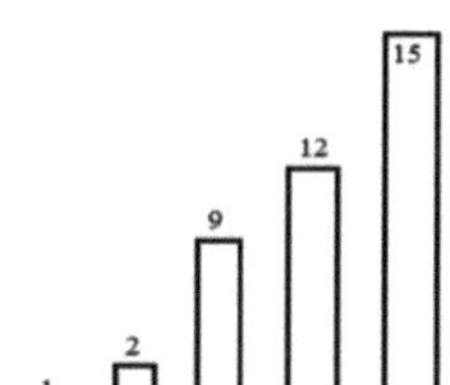

Fig. 1. APT Stacked Chart

Identifying these APT attacks is very crucial for the organizations to survive. In order to identify these APT attacks and classify them we have considered the parameters like

Targeted operating system and architecture, Initial attack vectors, Ease of spread, Attack purpose, Exploitation of digital signatures/ confidentiality and Network Evaluation.

3 Related Work

A lot of work is being done on APT attacks as it has been the major cyber threat in the coming future for the organizations of different industries. Most of the work related to APT's has concentrated on how the attack happens in general. In [1], the author has mentioned in detail about the salient features of the APT. The author has mostly concentrated on giving in depth knowledge of APT's in which he answered questions like what is the methodology of APT attacks and the tools or elements that are targeted by the APT attackers. He also mentioned the precautionary measures for the APT's but the author did not talk about how to identify the cyber-attacks as an APT attack taking all these factors mentioned into consideration. In [2] as well, the author concentrated on giving the details about the APT attacks, their life cycle and some precautionary measures. Some of the other papers have talked about a particular APT attack and the tools that can be helpful in preventing that particular attack. There are several other papers as well which talked about the significance of APT attacks in general or in particular of an APT attack. So we found the need to address the APT's individually i.e. different APT attacks and possibly find any relation among them. A skeleton can be formed out of the commonalities we found and accordingly develop a defensive mechanism which helps in identifying any APT attack and prevent them rather than curing them.

3.1 State of the Art

In order to come up with a skeletal structure capturing the potential differences among the APT attacks we have considered some of the APT attacks for our survey.

3.2 APT Attacks

- *Stuxnet:* A worm which discovered in the year 2010 which attacks is targeted towards Reprogram Industrial Control Systems (ICS), On Programmable Logic Controllers (PLC) which are mostly related to the nuclear industry. Stuxnet is one of the early APT attacks known. Vast array of components are used for the attack like Zeroday exploits, Windows rootkit, PLC rootkit (first ever), Antivirus evasion, Peer-to-Peer updates, Signed driver with a valid certificate, Command and control interface. In 2007, Siemens industrial company has been attacked compromising Siemens PCS 7, WinCC and STEP7 industrial software applications along with one or more Siemens S7 PLCs. The robust systems behind Stuxnet made it auto-executable, which required no user interaction, thus resulting in a zero-day vulnerability. Some of the vulnerabilities that were observed were MS 10-046: vulnerability which used modified autorun.inf technique MS08-067: Exploiting any network accessible windows systems using the windows server service. MS10-061: Vulnerabilities using privilege escalation using MS10-073 and MS10-092.

    a. Target organization is Siemens industries.

b. Select a Siemens system for attack launch (OS).
c. Identify the network propagation (Network).
d. Launch the attack via a USB stick which infects all machines (Attack vector).
e. Compromise the target system's logic controllers exploiting vulnerabilities (Signature Exploitation).
f. Download a more recent version and update the attack programming logic (Ease of spread).
g. Control the systems by spying and gather information (Attack purpose).

- ***Hacking team RCS:*** RCS is a spyware program discovered in 2011 which is targeted towards individuals like politicians, journalists and activists. The attack initially uses social engineering and then updates itself using the USB drives and cables. Rather than stealing data it surveillance the attacked systems. In 2012, all antivirus companies received malicious code in an email which they were able to identify from the keyword 'RCS' in that code.

  a. Target individual will be selected.
  b. Personal computer of the target individual is the target system (OS).
  c. Launch the attack via CD-ROM or USB (Attack vector).
  d. Compromise the internal security of the personal computer by exploiting the resources (Signature Exploitation).
  e. Self-update based on the information in the personal computer (Ease of spread).
  f. Monitor and log and actions performed in the personal computer (Attack purpose).

- ***Carbanak:*** An APT attack which was discovered in the year 2014 and still active. It mainly targets the financial organizations to steal the money. It has been the largest cyber heist ever in terms of stealing money. It uses the backdoor and exploit the target organization systems with the help of spam emails to the employees. Once the employee clicks on the spam email the attack will be launched and spreads over all the systems in that organization compromising the security.

  a. Target financial organization (mostly banks) is selected.
  b. Get the domain name of organization and send email to an employee (Attack vector).
  c. If the system satisfies the OS version, the attack will be launched (OS).
  d. Infects all the systems in the organization through the intranet used by the organization (Ease of spread).
  e. Compromise the security by monitoring the employee system and change credentials (Signature Exploitation).
  f. Once the attackers compromise the admin system, they steal the money (Attack purpose).

- ***Wild Neutron:*** It is a cyber espionage that was discovered in 2013 which is mainly targeted towards IT, healthcare, real estate, investment companies and law firms. It uses a backdoor module which initiates communication with C&C servers and then followed by exploitation tools, SSH-based exfiltration tools. Compromised the site 'www.iphonedevsdk [.]com' and redirected the users to other websites from where they hosted a zero-day exploit.

a. A multinational organization will be selected.
b. The website that belongs to the targeted organization will be compromised (Attack vector).
c. The users will be directed to the vulnerable sites from where they host a zero day exploit.
d. The attack will be launched in the system (OS).
e. Several exploitation tools are deployed which helps in spreading the attack (Ease of spread).
f. The information is passed onto the attackers (Attack purpose).

- ***Red October:*** A complex cyberattack platform discovered in the year 2013 which is targeted towards the reputed academia/research organizations, Energy, oil and gas companies and military as well. Malicious code was sent through emails using the Microsoft office, PDF, and java vulnerabilities. In 2012, the target companies have received an email with the updates for Microsoft office component, which compromises the security once they got clicked. The Domains were pointed to IP addresses that ended up just being proxies. As a strong persistent component, Red October introduced a module by inserting a malware visual basic code in the script written for Office and Adobe reader applications. This parsed each opened Office or PDF document and attempted to distinguish inserted commands (infused by the attackers) to execute. Utilizing this procedure, regardless of the fact that the C&C servers were brought down, the attackers could email exceptionally created files to their victims and can easily be able to reconnect with their systems. The known vulnerabilities such as CVE-2009–3129, CVE-2010–3333 and CVE-2012–0158 that were found in the exploited documents was the first step to infect the targets. In some cases, a JAVA exploit CVE-2011- 3544 was also used to infect the systems with malware payloads.

a. Target organization will be identified.
b. A spear phishing mail is sent to the target organization (Attack vector).
c. When the user opens the spear phishing email the attack will be launched using the known exploits of MS office (Ease of spread).
d. The attacker sends the malicious code to work on windows knowing that most of the organizations use windows operating system (OS).
e. Once the attack is launched the malicious code operates and sends the confidential data to the attackers (Attack Purpose).

3.3 Attack Classification

Observing the attack launch processes of different APT attacks that we have considered, we found a skeletal structure that captures the commonalities in different APT's. The structure can be defined as a list of parameters which will be helpful for us in coming up with a defensive mechanism (Table 1).

Table 1. Classification of Attacks

	Attack vector	network	Ease of spread	OS	purpose	Signature exploitation
Stuxnet	PLC's, USB drives, LAN	LAN	Programming code and logics	Windows(only)	Design Theft	yes
Wild Neutron	Watering hole	NA	Command prompt	Windows, OS X	Data theft	no
Red October	Social engineering	HTTP Proxies	Microsoft office files, malware infected emails.	Windows, Android	Data theft	no
Carbanak	Social engineering	TCP	intranet	Windows	Money theft	yes
Hacking team RCS	USB drives & cables, Direct hard disk, Bootable CD-ROM	NA	Self-Updates	Windows, Mac, BlackBerry, Android, IOS	Surveillance	yes

3.4 Parameters

- *Targeted operating system and architecture:* Operating system and its architecture are crucial enough during the initial stage of attack. The attackers may not be able to get through it if the configuration is different from the one that can be compromised. (E.g. the malware might work only for 32-bit version of windows).
- *Initial attack vectors:* It is very crucial since this is the initial mode of propagation that helps the attackers to launch the attack. Identifying the different types of propagation used helps in detecting the APT's at the initial stage itself.
- *Attack purpose:* The number APT attacks are constantly increasing over the last few years. These attacks are launched for achieving different purposes. Based on the purpose of attack the approach of the attack might differ from one another.
- *Ease of spread:* APT's are known for their persistence. They remain undetected for years and keep on spreading until they were able to access the confidential data. In the process of accessing data different APT attacks will have to go through several backdoors which are opened once the security is breached.
- *Exploitation of digital signatures/ confidentiality:* APT's are digitally signed using compromised digital certificates. Thus, these samples would manage to infect hardened systems. Based on this, allowing execution of binaries based on the existence of valid digital signatures cannot be considered an effective defense on its own. This is particularly important for Anti-Virus, which tend to avoid real-time analysis of signed binaries for performance reasons.
- *Network Evaluation:* The egress traffic which is destined to the commonly used ports is frequently allowed to pass through network access control mechanisms. The malwares use these common ports for establishing a connection and communicates back n forth - a worrying finding, taking into account the sensitive nature of the targeted organizations.

3.5 Research

It can be found from the above classification that in maximum cases most of the systems with Windows as the operating system and their version being 32 bits. Has compromised with their privacies and were found more vulnerable to Advanced persistent threats. In a related study presented by "Nikos, Virvilis" in his paper "Trusted computing vs APT" it can be concluded that none of the malware in all of the attacks were able to infect the 64 bits version of windows. This was because the extra security feature that is present in the 64-bit version of windows which makes the exploitation highly difficult for the attackers, especially preventing the kernel components of the system from getting accessed by malware targets. According to the study, it can be said that the main reason of exploitation of 32 bit systems was, that the maximum number of the victims were using that architecture. But does this make Apple ios more secured from APT's? The answer is completely "NO".

Another study proposed by "Mathew J Schwartz" reveals that "ios" is relatively easier to exploit as there are "Pervasive authentication issues" in OS X. and that it makes OS easy to exploit. Two of the mainly used protocols that are used in managing the functionalities of "IOS", which consists of AFP (Apple Filling Protocol) and Bonjour, a service delivery protocol that is used in establishing a connection between Macs and servers. Particularly, in comparison with windows it's easy to replace a malicious server for a fake one and then forcing users to connect to it. These vulnerabilities provide a base for infecting Macs by APT's. The above two related work in the field of APT's contributes in concluding that because Apple's market share is only about 6%, which means that if attacker want to compromise many computers at once, they will typically go for "Windows".

Another important point of entrance for APT's found was malware infected Word and Excel documents. Analyzing the different versions of Microsoft office suite, it can be observed that from the release of MS Office 2010, a new feature of "Protected View "was added, which ensures the opening of files from untrusted source in a sandbox view which enabled the prevention of exploitation of system through these files. This default opening of any new file in protected mode, played a role of additional barrier which made malware unable to pass through it. By digging into the analysis of the Victim's system which were affected by such files, it can be concluded that either they were running outdated versions of MS Office or they had disabled the security feature of the software.

3.6 Results

The attack vectors that have been used for different APT attacks are the basic ways we use to transfer files over the internet or in person. It is our general tendency to not scan for any viruses if we use USB's or CD-ROM's when we do file sharing and when it comes to email, we just go through the body of mail and do not pay any attention to the subject or from whom we have got the mail. The attackers take advantage of the user's negligence in exploiting and attacking the systems. Analyzing the network parameter tells us that most of the victims have a very relaxed internet access. The attackers identify the ports through which much of the traffic goes and launch the attack through those ports. As the network user is relaxed it paves way for the attackers to compromise the security and communicate back to the C&C infrastructure. During the initial stage, the APT attacks are targeted towards stealing the confidential data from different organizations. But in later stages, APT's are not only confined to steal data they have targeted several financial organizations in order to steal money and also to steal confidential designs of new ventures or on which the current system works.

For the APT to spread through the other systems it needs a medium. The medium turns out to be the vulnerable applications in the target systems. The attackers launch zero-day exploits to cash on these vulnerabilities and the APT's spread using these vulnerable applications. If we observe these applications, they are not the core applications of an operating system but the installed components for the user purpose. As the user uses them extensively for his purposes it feeds the APT to spread through the other systems. The attackers also look after the operating system which they target as the malicious code is intended to work on it. From the attack classification table, we might come to the conclusion of windows as the most vulnerable operating system but as mentioned in the Sect. 3.4, the OS X market share has been considerable very less compared to windows. As windows is the most used operating system, the attackers develop malicious code to run on windows so that they attack a wide range of systems at once. Signature exploitation of significant applications and accessing the target systems using these signatures to compromise the security has been a major thing in many APT attacks. This tells us that the applications that user installs should also be taken care of. The users have the tendency to just install the application to satisfy their need without thinking much about its security concerns. This gives the attacker the chance to exploit and launch the attack.

3.7 Proposal of Defense Mechanism

Defensive Measure 1: Multi layered networks with robust mechanisms should be used to prevent the APT attacks or at least detect the anomalies. The employees or individuals should be knowledgeable enough about how the APT attacks through social engineering so that they do not fall prey to spam emails and websites. There should be a security layer within each system so that the APT cannot access the resources in the personal computer of an individual or organization (Fig. 2).

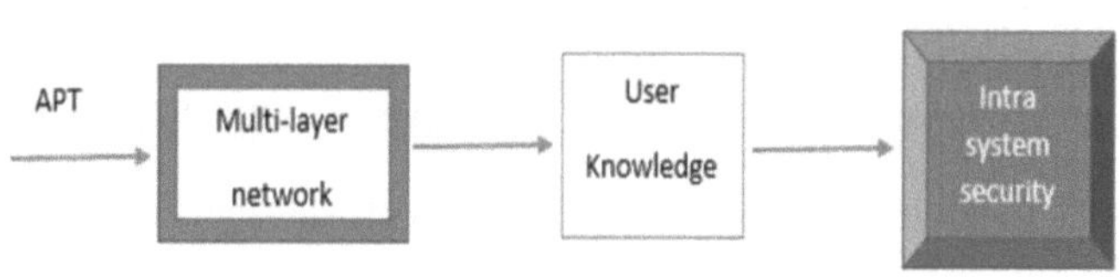

Fig. 2. APT Life Cycle

Defensive Measure 2: Inspired from batch processing in "Hadoop" an open-source Real time computational system has been designed which functions on the method of multilayer "Gene Pool" which has a semantic-rich network behavior pattern contains inside it, which facilitates the detection of APT. In Phase one a network packet is fetched from a network stream and is preprocessed and transformed to extract the appropriate message behavior information. This information is sent to second and third phase which regulates the matching of message extracted in phase one with a semantic rich network behavior pattern and conclude the presence of anomaly if any. Phase four is in charge of response towards anomaly either by anomaly alarm or recording the anomaly pattern directly.

4 Conclusion

APTs have turned into a significant concern for organizations from different fields. The use of Responsible AI to conduct research on APTs allow us to dig deep in the weeds to get the insights, which are not usually visible on a clear canvas of the threat landscape. This pattern is not hinting any signs of slowdown. Because of their stealthiness and spotlight on information, APTs present a developing peril that is difficult to avert, distinguish and shield against. This is where the incorporation of LLM permits us to establish patterns, by applying Cosine-Similarity for extrapolating the possible underlined threats. Lately, we have seen various situations where APTs have brought on noteworthy harm to different associations, in type of information robbery, as well as quick physical harm, this is also an area of interest that we will later be exploring using Responsible AI as our future work. APTs have an advanced way to deal with attacking organizations, they have the assets and learning, they don't stop surrender when they are unsuccessful, they cover their nearness, and they focus on association's important assets. Thus, new security methodologies are required. Associations can't depend on customary firewalls and malware discovery. They have to utilize different advanced intrusion detection tools and, in view of their exercises, develop new techniques for identifying abnormalities in a particular system, and correspond them keeping in mind the end goal to find security ruptures. Despite the fact that there is no insurance that any system is totally secured, organizations can implement tools and security strategies that can extraordinarily decrease the danger of an attack. Notwithstanding, doing that requires learning, assets and time.

References

Sood, A.K., Enbody, R.J.: Targeted cyberattacks: a superset of advanced persistent threats. IEEE Secur. Priv. **11**(1), 54–61 (2013)

Vukalović, J., Delija, D.: Advanced persistent threats - detection and defense. In: 2015 38th Int. Conv. Inf. Commun. Technol. Electron. Microelectron. MIPRO 2015 - Proc., no. May, pp. 1324–1330 (2015)

Kaspersky: "APT Trends Report," Securelist, [Online]. Available: https://apt.securelist.com/#secondPage. [Accessed: Nov. 10, 2024]

Collberg, C.: Advanced Persistent Threats. University of Arizona, [Online]. Available: http://www.cs.arizona.edu/~collberg/Teaching/466-566/2012/Resources/presentations/2012/topic9final/report.pdf. [Accessed: Nov. 15, 2024]

Greenberg, A.: Iran's nuclear computer attack. Forbes, [Online]. Available: http://www.forbes.com/2010/10/06/iran-nuclear-computer-technology-security-stuxnet-worm.html. [Accessed: Nov. 20, 2024]

Langner, R.: "Stuxnet: Dissecting a cyberweapon," Langner Group, [Online]. Available: http://embeddedsw.net/doc/Stuxnet_white_paper.html. [Accessed: Dec. 5, 2024]

Antoniades, D., Vasiliadis, G., Ioannidis, S.: Advanced Persistent Threats: A Survey. Computing and Information Systems, [Online]. Available: https://www.cis.aueb.gr/Publications/ARES2013%20APT%20Short.pdf. [Accessed: Dec. 10, 2024]
Kaspersky, "Wild Neutron: Economic Espionage Threat Actor Returns with New Tricks," Securelist, [Online]. Available: https://securelist.com/blog/research/71275/wild-neutron-economic-espionage-threat-actor-returnswith-new-tricks/. [Accessed: Dec. 15, 2024]
Kaspersky, "APT Trends Report," Securelist, [Online]. Available: https://apt.securelist.com/#secondPage. [Accessed: Jan. 3, 2025]
Collberg, C.: Advanced Persistent Threats. University of Arizona, [Online]. Available: http://www.cs.arizona.edu/~collberg/Teaching/466-566/2012/Resources/presentations/2012/topic9final/report.pdf. [Ac-cessed: Jan. 8, 2025]
Greenberg, A.: Iran's nuclear computer attack. Forbes, [Online]. Available: http://www.forbes.com/2010/10/06/iran-nuclear-computer-technology-security-stuxnet-worm.html. [Accessed: Jan. 12, 2025]
Langner, R.: Stuxnet: Dissecting a cyberweapon. Langner Group, [Online]. Available: http://embeddedsw.net/doc/Stuxnet_white_paper.html. [Accessed: Jan. 18, 2025]
Antoniades, D., Vasiliadis, G., Ioannidis, S.: Advanced Persistent Threats: A Survey," Computing and Information Systems, [Online]. Available: https://www.cis.aueb.gr/Publications/ARES2013%20APT%20Short.pdf. [Accessed: Jan. 22, 2025]
Kaspersky: "Wild Neutron: Economic Espionage Threat Actor Returns with New Tricks," Securelist, [Online]. Available: https://securelist.com/blog/research/71275/wild-neutron-economic-espionage-threat-actor-returnswith-new-tricks/. [Accessed: Jan. 27, 2025]

Enhancing Anomaly Detection in Software Logs with Bi-LSTM and Attention Mechanisms

Zulfiqar Ali[1](✉), Israr Ur Rehman[2], Muhammad Abdul Basit Ur Rahim[3], and Jonathan Witkowski[3]

[1] NFC Institute of Engineering and Fertilizer Research, Faisalabad, Pakistan
zulfiqar.ali@iefr.edu.pk

[2] Pak-Austria Fachhochschule Institute of Applied Sciences and Technology, Haripur, Pakistan
israr.rehman@paf-iast.edu.pk

[3] California State University, Long Beach, USA
m.basit@csulb.edu, Jonathan.Witkowski01@student.csulb.edu

Abstract. The volume and complexity of log data have increased exponentially due to the rapid proliferation of modern software systems, making anomaly detection a crucial task for maintaining system security and dependability. By combining attention processes with Bidirectional Long Short-Term Memory (Bi-LSTM) networks, this research introduces a novel method for software log anomaly identification. The proposed model leverages the sequential dependencies in log data captured by Bi-LSTM, while the attention mechanism enhances the interpretability and focuses on key features indicative of anomalies. We compare the model's performance against state-of-the-art techniques in terms of detection accuracy, precision, recall, and F1-score using publically accessible log datasets. The results highlight the robustness of the proposed approach in identifying subtle and complex anomalies, offering a scalable solution for real-world applications. This study not only advances anomaly detection capabilities in software systems but also provides insights into the synergistic effects of deep learning architectures and attention mechanisms for log analysis.

Keywords: Anomaly detection · Log analysis · Bi-LSTM · Attention mechanism · Feature fusion

1 Introduction

The unprecedented growth of software systems in modern industries has led to massive amounts of log data, which serve as vital records for monitoring, diagnosing, and maintaining system health. These logs are essential for detecting abnormalities that point to possible problems like software defects, security breaches, or system failures [11]. They provide comprehensive traces of system

S. Hussain et al. (Eds.): SEET 2025, CCIS 2725, pp. 78–89, 2026.
https://doi.org/10.1007/978-3-032-08977-9_7

operations. However, typical anomaly detection techniques which frequently rely on manual feature extraction or heuristic-based approaches, face considerable problems due to the amount and complexity of log data. These methods struggle to adapt to the dynamic nature of logs, often resulting in limited scalability, reduced accuracy, and high false-positive rates [10]. In recent years, deep learning has emerged as a transformative approach to anomaly detection [15], offering the ability to learn complex patterns directly from raw data [19]. These techniques, such as Bidirectional Long Short-Term Memory (Bi-LSTM) [21] networks, are ideal for log analysis since they have demonstrated exceptional success in capturing temporal dependencies in sequential data. However, while Bi-LSTM models excel at learning sequential relationships, they can struggle with interpretability and fail to adequately emphasize the most critical features of the input data adequately [1]. To address these challenges, this study proposes a novel framework integrating Bi-LSTM networks with attention mechanisms to enhance anomaly detection in software logs. The attention mechanism enables the model to dynamically focus on the log sequences' most relevant parts, thereby improving detection accuracy and model interpretability. By combining the strengths of Bi-LSTM and attention, the proposed approach not only captures long-range dependencies in the data but also highlights key features indicative of anomalies. We perform extensive trials on publicly available log datasets, such as HDFS, BGL, and OpenStack logs, to verify the efficacy of our methodology. The outcomes show that our model outperforms the most advanced techniques, greatly enhancing detection accuracy, precision, recall, and F1-score. Furthermore, the incorporation of attention mechanisms enhances the model's practical usefulness in real-world circumstances by offering insightful information about the model's decision-making process. This paper makes three key contributions:

1. Proposing a novel Bi-LSTM with an attention mechanism framework for anomaly detection in software logs.
2. Demonstrating the model's effectiveness through comprehensive evaluations with benchmark datasets.
3. Highlighting the interpretability benefits provided by attention mechanisms, which enhance the understanding of detected anomalies.

The remainder of the document is structured as follows: Sect. 2, relevant work in deep learning and anomaly detection for log analysis is reviewed. The problem is defined in Sect. 3. The suggested methodology, including the architecture and training procedure, is explained in Sect. 4. The experimental setup and findings are presented in Sect. 5, which is followed by an ablation analysis and discussion. Section 6 wraps up the work and suggests areas for further research.

2 Related Work

Due to its significance in guaranteeing the dependability, security, and effectiveness of software systems, anomaly detection in software logs [19] has been a focus of current study. Both conventional and machine learning-based methods have been thoroughly investigated. for this purpose [3,9], yet the emergence of deep learning has brought transformative advancements in the field. This section provides an overview of existing techniques categorized into traditional methods, machine learning approaches, and deep learning methods, followed by a discussion of attention mechanisms in anomaly detection. Traditional anomaly detection techniques, such as rule-based systems, statistical models, and clustering algorithms, have long been used for log analysis. Rule-based methods rely on predefined rules to identify deviations, but they require extensive domain expertise and are not adaptable to dynamic systems. Statistical approaches, including PCA (Principal Component Analysis) and autoregressive models, aim to detect deviations based on probabilistic thresholds. While these methods are computationally efficient, they often fall short when dealing with high-dimensional, unstructured log data [8].

Automated feature extraction and more precise anomaly detection were made possible by machine learning techniques [13]. Log data has been categorised into normal and anomalous groups using supervised models like Random Forests and Support Vector Machines (SVM). Nevertheless, these models necessitate labelled data, which is either costly or unavailable in large-scale systems. [20]. Unsupervised learning techniques, including Isolation Forests and Autoencoders, have gained popularity for anomaly detection in scenarios with limited or no labeled data. Autoencoders, in particular, have been widely adopted due to their ability to reconstruct input data and identify deviations based on reconstruction errors. Despite these advances, machine learning models often fail to capture temporal dependencies and sequential patterns in log data, which are crucial for detecting anomalies in complex systems.

Similarly, the introduction of deep learning has transformed software log anomaly detection by allowing models to directly learn hierarchical representations from unprocessed data. Sequential dependencies in log data have been widely captured by recurrent neural networks (RNNs) and their variations, including Long Short-Term Memory (LSTM) networks [4] [16]. Additionally, by processing input sequences in both forward and backward directions, bidirectional LSTM (Bi-LSTM) networks improve the model's capacity to grasp long-range dependencies [14]. Bi-LSTMs are excellent at sequence modelling, however, they frequently lack interpretability and might not pay attention to the most important portions of the input sequences. [12]. Recent studies have explored hybrid approaches that integrate LSTMs with attention mechanisms to address these challenges. An Attention-Augmented LSTM model for log-based anomaly identification is proposed in [6], showing the capacity to more accurately detect minor anomalies. Similarly, to improve anomaly detection in industrial time-series data, Haque et al. [7] integrated GRUs with attention mechanisms. These experiments demonstrate how attention mechanisms might enhance deep learning models' interpretability and accuracy. Furthermore, attention mechanisms have been used more and more in anomaly detection tasks since they were initially made popular in natural language processing (NLP) by models like as Transformers [5,17]. For log anomaly identification, Su et al. [17]

used a Transformer-based model that used self-attention to identify both local and global relationships in the data. Although Transformer models have shown promising results, their computational complexity can be a limiting factor in resource-constrained environments [2]. Hybrid approaches, such as integrating attention with Bi-LSTM, offer a balance between computational efficiency and model performance, making them well-suited for log anomaly detection tasks [10]. Despite significant advancements, several challenges remain in anomaly detection in software logs [18,19]. Traditional and machine learning methods often struggle with unstructured and high-dimensional log data. While deep learning models such as Bi-LSTM have demonstrated superior performance, they lack interpretability and fail to emphasize critical features indicative of anomalies. Attention mechanisms have emerged as a promising solution [17], but their integration with sequence models for log anomaly detection is still an active area of research [14]. This study suggests a Bi-LSTM model that has been improved with attention mechanisms to better detect anomalies in software logs in order to fill in these gaps. The suggested method seeks to provide improved interpretability and scalability for practical applications, all while achieving state-of-the-art performance.

3 Problem Definition

Anomaly detection in software logs is a fundamental task in ensuring system reliability and security. Modern software systems generate vast amounts of log data, which consist of sequential events representing system activities. These logs provide valuable insights into system behavior, facilitating fault diagnosis, intrusion detection, and performance monitoring. However, identifying anomalies in log data presents several challenges due to the unstructured nature of logs, the complexity of event sequences, and the rarity of anomalies in real-world datasets. Let the software log data be represented as a sequence of events:

$$\mathbf{X} = \{\mathbf{x}_1, \mathbf{x}_2, \ldots, \mathbf{x}_T\}$$

where $\mathbf{x}_t \in \mathbb{R}^d$ denotes the feature vector of the log event at time t, d is the dimensionality of the feature vector, and T is the total number of events in the sequence.

The objective is to classify each log event $\mathbf{x}_t$ as either **normal** or **anomalous**. This can be formalized as:

$$\mathbf{Y} = \{y_1, y_2, \ldots, y_T\}, \quad y_t \in \{0, 1\}$$

where $y_t = 1$ indicates an anomaly at time t, and $y_t = 0$ indicates normal behavior.

The challenges associated with this problem include:

- **High dimensionality and unstructured nature:** Log data is often unstructured and heterogeneous, requiring effective feature extraction methods to represent meaningful patterns.

- **Temporal dependencies:** Anomalies are context-dependent and often require capturing sequential relationships between events in the log data.
- **Imbalanced data:** Real-world datasets are often heavily imbalanced, with normal events significantly outnumbering anomalous events, making the detection of rare anomalies more difficult.

The goal is to design a model that learns a mapping:

$$f : \mathbf{X} \rightarrow \mathbf{Y}$$

such that the discrepancy between the predicted labels $\hat{\mathbf{Y}}$ and the ground truth labels $\mathbf{Y}$ is minimized. This involves accurately detecting anomalies in log data while addressing the inherent challenges of temporal dependencies, data imbalance, and scalability.

4 Proposed Model

The suggested model uses an attention mechanism and Bidirectional Long Short-Term Memory (Bi-LSTM) networks to identify anomalies in software log data. The following is the architecture: The software log data is preprocessed into a sequence of feature vectors:

$$\mathbf{X} = \{\mathbf{x}_1, \mathbf{x}_2, \ldots, \mathbf{x}_T\}, \quad \mathbf{x}_t \in \mathbb{R}^d \tag{1}$$

where d is the feature vector's dimensionality, T is the total number of events, and $\mathbf{x}_t$ is the feature vector of the log event at time step t.

The sequence $\mathbf{X}$ is run through a Bidirectional LSTM (Bi-LSTM) layer to record temporal dependencies. Each time step's hidden states are calculated as follows:

$$\overrightarrow{\mathbf{h}_t} = \text{LSTM}_{\text{forward}}(\mathbf{x}_t, \overrightarrow{\mathbf{h}_{t-1}}), \quad \overleftarrow{\mathbf{h}_t} = \text{LSTM}_{\text{backward}}(\mathbf{x}_t, \overleftarrow{\mathbf{h}_{t+1}}) \tag{2}$$

The final hidden state is given by:

$$\mathbf{h}_t = \left[\overrightarrow{\mathbf{h}}_t ; \overleftarrow{\mathbf{h}}_t\right], \quad \mathbf{h}_t \in \mathbb{R}^{2h} \tag{3}$$

where h is the dimensionality of the hidden state for each direction.

An attention mechanism is applied over the hidden states to focus on the most critical events. The attention score for each time step is computed as:

$$\alpha_t = \frac{\exp(\mathbf{u}_t^\top \mathbf{w})}{\sum_{k=1}^{T} \exp(\mathbf{u}_k^\top \mathbf{w})}, \quad \alpha_t \in [0, 1] \tag{4}$$

where $\mathbf{u}_t = \tanh(\mathbf{W}_h \mathbf{h}_t + \mathbf{b}_h)$, and $\mathbf{W}_h, \mathbf{b}_h, \mathbf{w}$ are learnable parameters. The context vector is computed as:

$$\mathbf{c}_t = \sum_{k=1}^{T} \alpha_k \mathbf{h}_k \tag{5}$$

The context vector $\mathbf{c}_t$ is passed through a fully connected layer with a softmax activation to predict the probability of the event being normal or anomalous:

$$\hat{y}_t = \text{Softmax}(\mathbf{W}_c\mathbf{c}_t + \mathbf{b}_c), \quad \hat{y}_t \in [0, 1] \tag{6}$$

where $\mathbf{W}_c$ and $\mathbf{b}_c$ are learnable parameters.

The model is trained by minimizing the cross-entropy loss:

$$\mathcal{L} = -\frac{1}{T}\sum_{t=1}^{T}[y_t \log(\hat{y}_t) + (1 - y_t)\log(1 - \hat{y}_t)] \tag{7}$$

where y_t is the ground truth label and $\hat{y}_t$ is the predicted probability. The suggested model's general process is described in Algorithm 1.

Algorithm 1. Anomaly Detection in Software Logs using Bi-LSTM and Attention

---

Require: Log sequence $\mathbf{X} = \{\mathbf{x}_1, \ldots, \mathbf{x}_T\}$, model parameters θ
Ensure: Predicted anomaly labels $\hat{\mathbf{Y}}$
  Preprocessing: Convert logs into feature vectors and normalize.
  Bi-LSTM Encoding:
  for each $t \in \{1, \ldots, T\}$ **do**
    Compute forward and backward LSTM hidden states.
    Concatenate hidden states: $\mathbf{h}_t = [\overrightarrow{\mathbf{h}}_t; \overleftarrow{\mathbf{h}}_t]$
  end for
  Attention Mechanism:
  Compute attention scores α_t and context vectors $\mathbf{c}_t$.
  Classification:
  Compute predicted anomaly probability:

$$\hat{y}_t = \text{Softmax}(\mathbf{W}_c\mathbf{c}_t + \mathbf{b}_c)$$

  Loss Computation: Compute cross-entropy loss and update parameters.
  return $\hat{\mathbf{Y}}$

---

5 Experimental Evaluation

5.1 Dataset

We employ three publicly accessible benchmark datasets—HDFS Logs, BGL Logs, and Thunderbird Logs—to assess our model's performance. Table 1 provides a summary of the statistics and overview of a few chosen datasets. **HDFS Logs Dataset** This dataset contains event logs generated by the Hadoop Distributed File System, which is widely used for anomaly detection research. It consists of millions of log entries from distributed systems and includes both normal and anomalous events, labeled for supervised learning. The dataset captures a variety of real-world scenarios, such as missing blocks, checksum errors, and replication failures, making it highly suitable for evaluating anomaly detection models. **BGL Logs Dataset** This dataset contains logs collected from the Blue Gene/L supercomputer, one of the fastest supercomputers of its time. It features labeled log entries that identify normal and anomalous events, such as hardware failures, software bugs, and system misconfigurations. With millions of entries and diverse anomaly types, the dataset provides a challenging benchmark for anomaly detection methods. Researchers frequently use it to test machine learning models in large-scale distributed systems. **Thunderbird Logs Dataset** This dataset comprises system log entries collected from the Thunderbird supercomputer, containing a mixture of normal and anomalous events. This dataset highlights issues like memory errors, disk failures, and node outages, reflecting real-world challenges in high-performance computing environments. The detailed labeling and varied log patterns make it an excellent resource for evaluating anomaly detection techniques.

Table 1. Statistics of Selected Datasets for Anomaly Detection in Software Logs.

Dataset	Log Entries	Anomalies	Labels Available
HDFS Logs	11,175,629	16,838	Yes
BGL Logs	4,747,963	348,460	Yes
Thunderbird Logs	2,037,197	42,354	Yes

5.2 Evaluation Measures

The proposed model is evaluated using rating and ranking performance measures to assess classification accuracy and ranking effectiveness. Rating performance measures evaluate the model's ability to classify instances correctly. Metrics such as Accuracy, Precision, Recall, and F1-score quantify prediction quality. Accuracy determines the proportion of correctly classified instances, while Precision and Recall measure the correctness and completeness of positive predictions, respectively. The F1-Score offers a balanced evaluation by taking the harmonic mean of Precision and Recall; it is especially helpful for datasets that are unbalanced. In log-based anomaly classification, these indicators are essential for guaranteeing the model's dependability. Ranking performance metrics evaluate how well predictions are arranged according to relevance, which is essential for setting anomaly priorities. Measures like Normalised Discounted Cumulative Gain (NDCG) and Area Under the Curve (AUC) are employed. AUC assesses how well the model can differentiate between anomalous and normal logs at various levels. To ensure ideal prioritisation, NDCG takes into account both the instances' ranking positions and their significance.

5.3 Baseline Models

We assess and contrast our suggested model's performance in our experiments with a number of cutting-edge models. These chosen models improve the performance of anomaly detection by utilizing deep learning techniques.

- **Long Short-Term Memory (LSTM)** LSTM is a recurrent neural network capable of learning long-term dependencies in sequential data. Its gating mechanism allows it to effectively retain and forget information, making it a strong candidate for anomaly detection in time-series data. However, LSTM may not fully exploit bidirectional context, which can limit its performance in capturing dependencies across a sequence.
- **Convolutional Neural Network (CNN)** CNNs, traditionally used for image processing, are adapted here to detect anomalies in software logs by treating sequences as one-dimensional inputs. They excel in feature extraction, identifying local patterns effectively. Nevertheless, CNNs cannot model sequential dependencies, which can reduce their effectiveness in temporal data.
- **Transformer Model** The Transformer architecture employs self-attention mechanisms to model global dependencies within sequential data. It has proven highly effective in capturing complex patterns and relationships in log data. However, its computational complexity can pose challenges for training, particularly in resource-constrained environments.
- **GRU with Attention Mechanism** Gated Recurrent Units (GRUs) are computationally efficient variants of LSTM, and when combined with an attention mechanism, they focus on the most relevant parts of input sequences. This baseline captures important temporal dependencies and highlights key patterns, but it may still underperform in scenarios requiring bidirectional sequence processing.
- **Deep Log Analyzer (DLA)** DLA is a specialized model for anomaly detection in software logs. It combines sequential modeling and statistical analysis to identify irregular patterns in log data. While it is effective for structured logs, it may struggle to generalize to more complex or semi-structured datasets.

5.4 Results and Discussions

Four primary rating performance metrics—Accuracy, Precision, Recall, and F1-Score are used to compare the suggested model's performance against baseline models across three datasets: HDFS Logs, BGL Logs, and Thunderbird Logs. Here, Table 2 displays the findings for Accuracy and F1-Score, whereas Fig. 1 displays the results for Precision and Recall. The findings show that the Proposed Model achieves the greatest scores across all datasets and evaluation parameters, routinely outperforming all baseline models. The proposed model achieves the highest accuracy, recording 91.2% on HDFS Logs and 90.5% on BGL Logs. The Transformer-based model follows closely but remains inferior to the proposed model, while CNN-based architectures exhibit the lowest accuracy across all datasets. Similarly, for precision, the proposed model achieves the highest precision with 89.8% on HDFS Logs and 89.0% on BGL Logs, demonstrating its ability to minimize false positives. The Transformer-based model performs slightly worse, while CNN and LSTM models show relatively lower precision values, indicating their susceptibility to misclassification. In terms of recall, the proposed model again surpasses the baseline models, achieving 90.1% on HDFS Logs and 89.3% on BGL Logs. The GRU with Attention model follows in performance, while CNN-based models exhibit the lowest recall values, signifying their tendency to miss a considerable number of actual anomalies. Finally, the F1-Score further validates the effectiveness of the proposed model. The highest F1-scores are observed for the proposed model, with 90.0% on HDFS Logs and 89.5% on BGL Logs. The Transformer-based model follows with slightly lower values, while CNN and LSTM models remain the weakest performers. Thus, the proposed model significantly outperforms all baseline models across all key performance metrics. The Transformer-based model emerges as a competitive alternative but remains inferior to the proposed approach. Conversely, CNN-based architectures exhibit the weakest performance, indicating their limitations in learning sequential dependencies in log data.

Table 2. Comparison of Accuracy and F1-Score Measures Between Proposed Model and Baselines across HDFS Logs, BGL Logs, and Thunderbird Logs datasets, where the best values are highlighted in bold.

Model	HDFS Logs		BGL Logs		Thunderbird Logs	
	Accuracy (%)	F1-Score (%)	Accuracy (%)	F1-Score (%)	Accuracy (%)	F1-Score (%)
LSTM	85.2	83.9	84.5	82.9	83.8	81.8
CNN	82.4	80.6	81.8	79.8	81.2	79.1
Transformer	88.9	87.5	88.3	87.0	87.5	86.2
GRU with Attention	87.6	86.7	87.1	86.0	86.4	85.1
Deep Log Analyzer (DLA)	84.1	82.9	83.5	82.0	82.8	81.3
Proposed Model	**91.2**	**90.0**	**90.5**	**89.5**	**89.8**	**88.7**

Similarly, Table 3 compares ranking performance across HDFS Logs, BGL Logs, and Thunderbird Logs, using AUC, and NDCG@10. The proposed model consistently outperforms baseline methods across all datasets and metrics. For HDFS Logs, the proposed model achieves the highest AUC 93.2%, surpassing the Transformer 90.8% and GRU with Attention 89.4%. Similarly, it attains the best NDCG@10 91.5%, demonstrating superior ranking effectiveness. In BGL Logs, the proposed model maintains its lead with an AUC of 92.8%, and NDCG@10 of 91.1%, outperforming the baselines. This highlights the advantage of its enhancements over attention-based baselines. For Thunderbird logs, the proposed model again achieves the best results i.e. AUC: 92.3%, and NDCG@10: 90.4%, followed by the Transformer. While CNN and Deep Log Analyzer remain competitive, sequential and attention-based methods prove more effective. Overall, the proposed model demonstrates robustness and efficiency in ranking log-based anomalies, consistently outperforming baselines across all datasets.

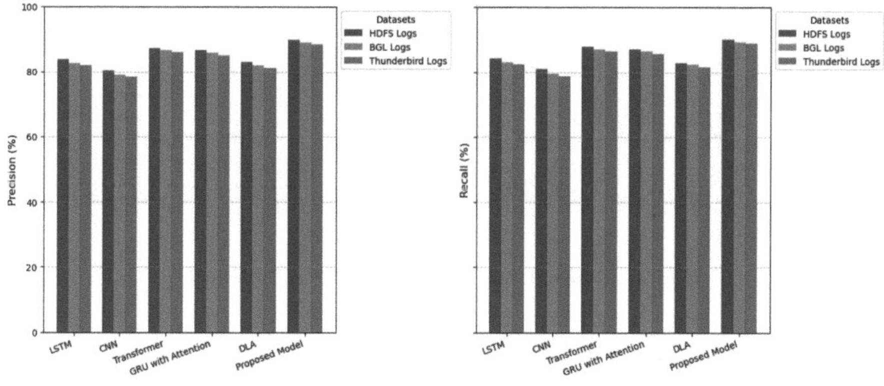

Fig. 1. Precision and Recall Comparison of the Proposed Model with Baseline Models.

Table 3. Comparison of AUC and NDCG@10 Measures Between Proposed Model and Baselines across HDFS Logs, BGL Logs, and Thunderbird Logs datasets, where the best values are highlighted in bold

Model	HDFS Logs		BGL Logs		Thunderbird Logs	
	AUC (%)	NDCG@10 (%)	AUC (%)	NDCG@10 (%)	AUC (%)	NDCG@10 (%)
LSTM	87.5	85.4	86.8	84.7	85.9	83.2
CNN	84.2	81.8	83.6	80.9	82.7	79.5
Transformer	90.8	89.3	90.2	88.7	89.6	87.9
GRU with Attention	89.4	88.1	88.8	87.6	88.1	86.5
Deep Log Analyzer (DLA)	85.6	83.2	84.9	82.5	84.1	81.7
Proposed Model	**93.2**	**91.5**	**92.8**	**91.1**	**92.3**	**90.4**

5.5 Ablation Analysis

To evaluate the impact of key components, we conducted an ablation study, on HDFS Logs, BGL Logs, and Thunderbird Logs. compares Accuracy, Precision, Recall, and F1-Score across model variants. The full model achieves the best performance, with F1-Scores of 91.3% for HDFS Logs, while 90.8% for BGL Logs, and 90.0% for Thunderbird Logs, confirming its effectiveness. Removing the attention mechanism reduces accuracy by 3.3%, showing its role in feature enhancement. Excluding Bi-LSTM significantly lowers recall by 4.5%, indicating its importance in capturing sequence dependencies. The feature fusion layer removal mainly impacts precision and F1-Score, while context embedding removal causes the highest drop, with a 5.2% accuracy decline. Thus, attention mechanisms, Bi-LSTM, feature fusion, and contextual embeddings are essential, with attention and Bi-LSTM having the most impact on performance (Fig. 2).

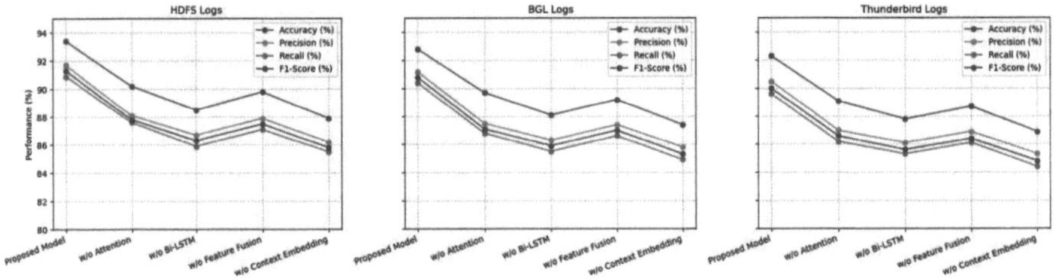

Fig. 2. Ablation analysis of the proposed model.

6 Conclusion and Future Work

In this paper, we proposed a Bi-LSTM-based anomaly detection model with an attention mechanism to identify anomalies in software log data. Our approach effectively captures temporal dependencies and emphasizes critical log events through attention weighting, leading to improved anomaly detection performance. The experimental results demonstrate that our model outperforms existing baselines in terms of accuracy and robustness, particularly in handling imbalanced log data. The ablation study further validates the impact of each component of the model, highlighting the importance of Bi-LSTM and attention in achieving superior results. Despite the promising performance, there are several avenues for future research. First, incorporating external knowledge sources, such as domain-specific log patterns, could enhance the model's interpret-ability and precision. Second, exploring self-supervised learning techniques may reduce dependency on labeled datasets and improve generalization to unseen log data. Finally, optimizing the computational efficiency of our approach could facilitate real-time anomaly detection in large-scale systems.

References

1. Shaker AbdulAziz Ali: Anomaly detection in telecommunication networks: leveraging novel big data and machine learning techniques for proactive fault management. Educ. Adm. Theory Pract. **30**(5), 5751–5770 (2024)
2. Cao, Y., Tang, X., Deng, X., Wang, P.: Fault detection of complicated processes based on an enhanced transformer network with graph attention mechanism. Process Saf. Environ. Prot. **186**, 783–797 (2024)
3. Edozie, E., Shuaibu, A.N., Sadiq, B.O., John, U.K.: Artificial intelligence advances in anomaly detection for telecom networks. Artif. Intell. Rev. **58**(4), 100 (2025)
4. Fayyadh, S.A.F.: Automatic detection of intrusion attacks in iot networks using bi-lstm-cnn neural network. Master's thesis, Kirsehir Ahi Evran University (Turkey) (2023)
5. Galassi, A., Lippi, M., Torroni, P.: Attention in natural language processing. IEEE Trans. Neural Netw. Learn. Syst. **32**(10), 4291–4308 (2020)
6. Gong, K., Luo, S., Pan, L., Zhang, L., Zhang, Y., Haomiao, Yu.: Logeta: time-aware cross-system log-based anomaly detection with inter-class boundary optimization. Futur. Gener. Comput. Syst. **157**, 16–28 (2024)

7. Haque, M.N., et al.: Gru-based attention mechanism for human activity recognition. In: 2019 1st International Conference on Advances in Science, Engineering and Robotics Technology (ICASERT), pp. 1–6. IEEE (2019)
8. He, S., He, P., Chen, Z., Yang, T., Su, Y., Lyu, M.R.: A survey on automated log analysis for reliability engineering. ACM Comput. Surv. (CSUR) **54**(6), 1–37 (2021)
9. Karunaratne, T.: Machine learning and big data approaches to enhancing e-commerce anomaly detection and proactive defense strategies in cybersecurity. J. Adv. Cybersecur. Sci. Threat Intell. Countermeas. **7**(12), 1–16 (2023)
10. Liu, Y., Ren, S., Wang, X., Zhou, M.: Temporal logical attention network for log-based anomaly detection in distributed systems. Sensors **24**(24), 7949 (2024)
11. Lu, R., Zhu, X., Li, X., Long, N., Zhang, G.: An anomaly monitoring and early warning method for power grid microservice network based on log visualisation and analysis. In: 2024 5th International Conference on Machine Learning and Computer Application (ICMLCA), pp. 584–590. IEEE (2024)
12. Maxima, A.:Integration and analysis of unstructured data towards database optimization and decision making using deep learning techniques. PhD thesis, Kampala International University (2024)
13. Mienye, I.D., Swart, T.G., Obaido, G.: Recurrent neural networks: a comprehensive review of architectures, variants, and applications. Information **15**(9), 517 (2024)
14. Natha, S., Ahmed, F., Siraj, M., Lagari, M., Altamimi, M., Chandio, A.A.: Deep BiLSTM attention model for spatial and temporal anomaly detection in video surveillance. Sensors **25**(1), 251 (2025)
15. Pang, G., Shen, C., Cao, L., Van Den Hengel, A.: Deep learning for anomaly detection: a review. ACM Comput. Surv. (CSUR) **54**(2), 1–38 (2021)
16. Ur Rehman, I., Ali, Z., Jan, Z.: A collaborative cnn-lstm framework with attention mechanism for aspect-based sentiment analysis. In: 2024 International Conference on Frontiers of Information Technology (FIT), pp. 1–6. IEEE (2024)
17. Su, J., et al.: Large language models for forecasting and anomaly detection: a systematic literature review. arXiv preprint arXiv:2402.10350 (2024)
18. Sun, Y., Keung, J., Yang, Z., Liu, S., Zhang, J.: Advancing semi-supervised anomaly detection in software logs with deep grouping and auto-optimization. SSRN 4918203 (2024)
19. Sun, Y., Keung, J., Yang, Z., Liu, S., Zhang, J., Liao, Y.: Improving anomaly detection in software logs through hybrid language modeling and reduced reliance on parser. SSRN 4978351
20. ur Rehman, I., Ali, W., Jan, Z., Ali, Z., Xu, H., Shao, J.: CAML: contextual augmented meta-learning for cold-start recommendation. Neurocomputing **533**, 178–190 (2023)
21. Yang, Y., et al.: Intrusion detection based on bidirectional long short-term memory with attention mechanism (2023)

FIRMMOD: Generating API Taint Models for Firmware Analysis

Ken Yihang Bai(✉) and Tuba Yavuz

University of Florida, Gainesville, FL, USA
{baiyihang,tyavuz}@ufl.edu

Abstract. Firmware is an important part of the attack surface for the Internet of Things. Attackers typically inject malicious data through the peripherals. Understanding the impact of attacker-controlled data requires an understanding of where such data flows within software, which is challenging due to the complex peripheral behavior. We present a symbolic execution-based firmware rehosting approach that utilizes MMIO access guided API modeling to avoid the complexity in handling low-level details of peripheral behaviors and to precisely track the flows of the peripheral data registers into the upper layers in the software stack. We have developed FIRMMOD on top of S2E for ARM Cortex M3 and applied it to Amazon FreeRTOS firmware samples. Our results indicate that API modeling is an effective approach for goal-based reachability analysis for firmware. It enables FIRMMOD to achieve up to 2X more code coverage compared to Fuzzware and to detect two known buffer overflow vulnerabilities at the ES WIFI layer.

Keywords: firmware analysis · symbolic execution · memory errors

1 Introduction

Firmware is an important part of the Internet of Things (IoT) attack surface. It is typically formed of multiple layers including the application layer, third-party library layer, the Hardware Abstraction Layer (HAL), and the device driver layer. Among the various security risks include firmware developers' reliance on the correctness of third-party libraries without proper vetting for vulnerabilities and failure to properly sanitize the data received from the peripherals. So, attackers can exploit the vulnerabilities in various part of the firmware by carefully crafting malicious data that flows from the peripherals into various layers of the firmware. Therefore, it is important to precisely track the data flows from the peripherals and analyze how the data gets used by the firmware.

Firmware rehosting has become an effective way to analyze firmware without an actual device. Various approaches that utilize firmware rehosting either use fuzzing [7,8,11], symbolic execution [5,10], or a combination of both [13,14]. A challenge in firmware analysis is the complexity of low-level interactions with the peripherals. Approaches that use symbolic execution typically use symbolic

S. Hussain et al. (Eds.): SEET 2025, CCIS 2725, pp. 90–113, 2026.
https://doi.org/10.1007/978-3-032-08977-9_8

values for the data received from the peripherals. However, the complex peripheral interactions in the device driver layer lead to a path explosion and prevents achieving high coverage in the upper layers. This also poses as a challenge to fuzzing, which needs to generate input that will try to cover a variety of cases in the peripheral interaction logic along with the code in the upper layers. So, previous work deals with the problem by learning some peripheral model to achieve high coverage, which is typically measured in terms of basic block coverage. State-of-the-art firmware rehosting approaches assume that the firmware exists in binary form only. Although this is a valid assumption for vetting firmware in the wild, there are other scenarios that invalidates this assumption such as an IoT vendor using firmware rehosting to test IoT device firmware, which allows the detection of vulnerabilities before deployment. As we show in this paper, assuming the existence of source code and the availability of debug information allows for more effective model generation and tracking the flow of peripheral data to upper layers in the firmware.

In this paper, we present, FIRMMOD, an MMIO access guided API modeling approach to goal-based firmware analysis. We assume that the analyst or the developer is interested in assessing the security risks associated with data flows from a specific set of target peripherals within the specific target layers of the firmware. We also assume the availability of debugging information as an IoT vendor may want to vet their firmware before deployment. Our approach deals with the complexity of peripheral interactions by selectively modeling the lower level APIs that process such data. FIRMMOD applies precise tracking of the MMIO accesses to the data registers of the target peripherals and generates taint models for API that process data from these peripherals. FIRMMOD decides the scope of API modeling based on the amount of coverage achieved. So, it may decide to apply modeling to the callers of the modeled API as long as they are not part of the target layers. For the peripherals that are not in the target set, FIRMMOD applies a less precise and more aggressive modeling.

Our approach leverages the insight that although imprecise modeling of firmware peripherals may not be reliable in reasoning about the reachability of certain bugs or vulnerabilities in firmware, it may still identify code locations that may have a higher security risk due to accessing data tainted with potentially unconstrained or improperly constrained peripheral data. Although the imprecision in the peripheral modeling may still incur imprecision to the taint propagation or the constraints on the state of the peripheral data, the memory locations that get tainted with peripheral data are less likely to differ depending on the peripheral state.

We formulate and evaluate the following research questions (RQs) in this paper:

- **RQ1:** How does the scope of API modeling impact firmware analysis?
- **RQ2:** Does API modeling enable bug finding in upper layers?
- **RQ3:** How does FIRMMOD perform compared to Fuzzware, a state-of-the art firmware rehosting approach, and to FIRMSTAT, a static API modeling approach?

This paper has been organized as follows. We place our work in the context of related work in Sect. 2. We discuss the challenges of tracking MMIO accesses in firmware and explain our solutions at a high level in Sect. 3. We present the technical details of our approach in Sect. 4. We present the results of our evaluation in Sect. 5. We conclude and discuss future work in Sect. 6.

2 Related Work

HALucinator [7] performs high level emulation of firmware by replacing Hardware Abstraction Layer (HAL) API with manually prepared models using contextual binary matching techniques. P2IM [8] presents a pattern-based extraction of concrete peripheral and firmware I/O models to achieve firmware rehosting. Both HALucinator and P2IM demonstrate the effectiveness of their rehosting approaches through fuzzing, which succeeds in finding vulnerabilities in the analyzed firmware. Para-rehosting is presented as an alternative approach to rehosting in [11]. The idea is to hook HAL API with the approximated and ported versions that could be linked with the rest of the software stack and executed on commodity processors to leverage the existing analysis support such as sanitizers and fuzzers. However, like HALucinator, this requires a manual effort while FIRMMOD generates API models automatically. Although FIRMSTAT [4] uses static analysis to automatically generate MMIO taint models of firmware APIs, its analysis overapproximates over all paths and cannot provide precise size information for the tainted regions whereas FIRMMOD uses symbolic execution to dynamically generate API taint models that include the size information.

PRETENDER [9] learns a peripheral model by combining firmware emulation with real-hardware and recording the MMIO responses and interrupt events from the device. The learnt model is used in rehosting firmware.

Laelaps [5] uses symbolic execution to rehost the firmware. It switches between symbolic execution and concrete execution for scalability and uses context-bounded symbolic execution to generate consistent concrete models of peripheral accesses.

Jetset [10] performs targeted symbolic execution by progressively generating an updated control-flow graph to steer the execution towards the goal. It generates a mostly symbolic peripheral access model as the path explosion is controlled by filtering paths based on the target and concretizes a symbolic value only after ensuring non-crashing behavior for a configured number of times. However, the peripheral access constraints and values at the time of reaching the target are used to synthesize a concrete access model to be used in QEMU for dynamic analysis to ensure reachability of a target such as the end of the boot process and continue with the further analysis of the firmware.

DICE [12] detects DMA channels used by firmware and generates more paths compared to analysis that cannot leverage DMA channels. It uses the DMA address range to identify addresses used in DMA configuration assuming the addresses are written to the peripheral registers and not to the RAM and filters the candidates and determine the buffer sizes based on their accesses within firmware. µEmu [14] uses a multi-tier peripheral access modeling that associates the access values with increasingly detailed context information.

Fuzzware [13] uses locally-scoped dynamic symbolic execution to identify the parts of the peripheral data that affects the firmware logic.

SEMU [15] uses NLP-based techniques to learn the peripheral command-action rules and extract a precise peripheral model from the data sheets of MCUs. It validates the learnt model using µEmu.

By learning and employing API taint models, FIRMMOD automatically bypasses the complexities of peripheral access logic and leverages debug information to improve precision of the generated models. As we demonstrate in Sect. 5, FIRMMOD can reach upper layers in the firmware much faster than state-of-the-art firmware rehosting approaches.

3 Overview

In this section, we provide an overview of our approach, FIRMMOD, which aims to precisely track dataflows from the peripherals to the upper layers of firmware. FIRMMOD utilizes symbolic execution for firmware rehosting due to its path-precise semantics. Specifically, similar to other firmware rehosting approaches that use symbolic execution, it models peripheral interactions by representing data loaded from Memory Mapped I/O (MMIO) addresses with symbolic values. However, FIRMMOD needs to deal with the path explosion problem and other challenges while achieving its goal of precisely tracking dataflows from the peripherals.

These challenges can be summarized as follows:

1. **Challenge 1:** Peripheral accesses often rely on the proper triggering of interrupts and timely execution of the interrupt handlers, which represent a critical part of the taint propagation chain regarding the peripherals.
2. **Challenge 2:** Determining the size of tainted regions is not always obvious as different APIs use different mechanisms. Some APIs use a parameter that represents the size of the tainted buffer whereas others have implicit assumptions about the maximum size for the tainted region.
3. **Challenge 3:** Propagation of data received from the peripherals to upper layers get blocked or slowed down due to path explosion triggered by unbounded loops or complex logic that handles failure cases.

FIRMMOD has been designed as shown in Fig. 1. It generates MMIO taint models of functions and applies them on-the-fly when it encounters a callsite of a modeled function. However, it deals with the above challenges as it generates the function models. Specifically, it initiates taint propagation monitoring upon encountering explicit tainting and ensures monitoring of implicit taint propagations due to operations within the interrupt handlers by triggering interrupts upon encountering wait event APIs and those due to function calls by starting limited scope analysis of functions that receive tainted data as a parameter

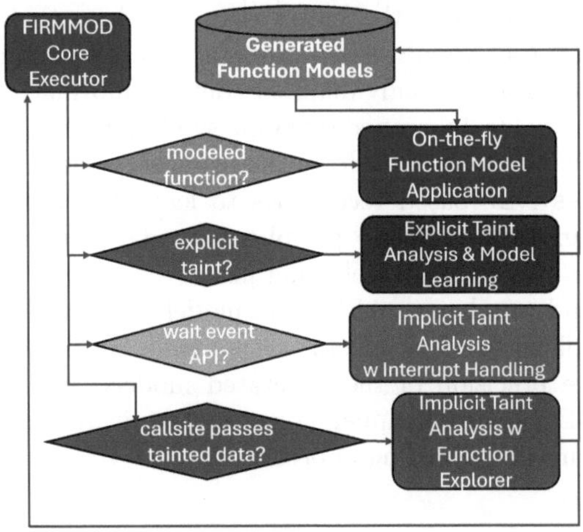

Fig. 1. An overview of the API model generation approach in FIRMMOD.

(Challenge 1). It leverages API conventions and debug information to infer the sizes of tainted buffers precisely (Challenge 2). Finally, FIRMMOD deals with the path explosion problem by leveraging API success case return value models to distinguish success paths from the failure paths (Challenge 3).

4 Approach

In this section, we motivate the problem in Sect. 4.1 and present the technical details of API taint model generation and dealing with the challenges in Sect. 4.2.

4.1 Problem Formulation

Symbolic execution of firmware creates several challenges when all reads from MMIO addresses are treated as unconstrained symbolic values. In an RTOS system, there are synchronization mechanisms such as semaphores that help tasks coordinate. When the firmware communicates with the peripherals using synchronization primitives, a precise modeling of the interrupt handling mechanism becomes imperative. An active task that processes peripheral requests typically waits for a specific event, e.g. the copying of the data received from a peripheral, by blocking on a semaphore. The active task then gets deactivated and other tasks will be executed.

If modeling of interrupts fails to lead symbolic execution to that specific event by not scheduling the code that notifies completion or occurrence of the event, e.g. performing an up on a semaphore, the task that is waiting for the event will never have a chance to be scheduled again, and the code that gets executed after the occurrence of the specific event will not be covered. In addition, branches that check conditions involving symbolic values of the control or status registers enlarges the state space and contributes to the path explosion. However, as we discussed earlier, we care more about how the data flows from the peripherals to the upper layers rather than capturing the state of the peripherals in a precise way.

Our goal is to model the API automatically and to improve the coverage of code locations that process data received from a specific peripheral. An RTOS-based firmware typically involves the following types of APIs:

- Application level APIs, which are often defined as callbacks that are registered with some libraries.
- RTOS related APIs, e.g. those for task management.
- APIs of the third party libraries, e.g. communication protocols such as MQTT and cryptographic libraries such as mbedTLS.
- HAL APIs that provide an abstract interface of common hardware interactions.
- Board Support Package (BSP) functions, such as the drivers for specific peripherals.
- Standard C library and intrinsic functions, e.g. `strstr` or `_aeabi_f2uiz`.

An impact of the path explosion for firmware analysis is that covering success cases of the HAL APIs become challenging and such functions end up returning failure values, e.g., `HAL_ERROR`. This creates a cascading effect on the the upper layer functions, which check the return value of the HAL APIs, i.e., upper layer functions also fail, and limit code coverage. Although FIRMMOD's overarching goal is not achieving high coverage across the whole firmware, not reaching success cases of HAL API reduces coverage of code that access peripherals of interest. Our goal is to generate a model for these HAL APIs and the related driver APIs to increase coverage of the upper layers, and, specifically the code coverage within the target function.

HAL APIs are typically designed for the following purposes:

- Initialize/enable and deinitialize/disable the peripheral.
- Configure the peripheral for specific operations.
- Transmit data via the peripheral by moving the data from a memory region to the MMIO data channel.
- Receive data either in a buffer or by a return value by moving the data from the MMIO data channel to a memory region or a register.

In this paper, the goal is to model the API that receive data from the peripheral and track its propagation to the upper layers. So, it is important to capture both the explicit and the implicit propagation of peripheral data. Explicit propagation happens when memory gets explicitly tainted by the MMIO data register in the context of a task. Implicit propagation happens in a context other than the one HAL API was running either through interrupt handling or DMA. Tracking explicit data flows is straightforward since symbolic execution of the HAL API can be monitored to detect symbolic writes to the memory, where these symbolic values originate from some MMIO data register. However, it is challenging to track implicit data flows in a symbolic execution based firmware rehosting environment due to the path explosion induced by precise modeling of interrupt handling.

The modularity of the firmware stack enables us to model the low level APIs in a relatively modular way. The values from MMIO status or control register values are typically not propagated to the upper layers. Therefore, modeling of HAL APIs helps in controlling the path explosion problem and allowing monitoring of data flows from the peripherals. The implicit data transfer usually involves interrupt version of the HAL APIs as opposed to those that use polling.

```
// 1. Receive data from peripheral in normal task context
HAL_StatusTypeDef  HAL_SPI_Receive(SPI_HandleTypeDef *hspi, uint8_t
     *pData, uint16_t Size, uint32_t Timeout) { ...
    // receive from data register directly
    (* (uint8_t *)pData)= *(__IO uint8_t *)&hspi->Instance->DR; ...}
// 2.a.setting ISR, non blocking mode in task context
HAL_StatusTypeDef HAL_SPI_Receive_IT(SPI_HandleTypeDef *hspi,
     uint8_t *pData, uint16_t Size) {...
    hspi->RxISR = SPI_RxISR_8BIT; /* setting ISR callback */ ...}
// 2.b interrupt line triggered, jump to IRQ handler
void HAL_SPI_IRQHandler(SPI_HandleTypeDef *hspi) {...
   hspi->RxISR(hspi);    /* call ISR function */ ...}
// 2.c Receive data in ISR callback
static void SPI_RxISR_8BIT(struct __SPI_HandleTypeDef *hspi)
{... *hspi->pRxBuffPtr++ = (*(__IO uint8_t *)&hspi->Instance->DR)
     ;...}
```

Listing 1.1. Two ways of accessing peripherals

Listing 1.1 shows two typical ways of receiving data from a peripheral using the SPI bus as the example peripheral. In the first one (1), the HAL API directly accesses the peripheral data register and copies the data to a buffer whose address is passed through some argument. In the second one (2), the interrupt mechanism is used to receive data in an asynchronous way. The important steps for this case include setting the transfer relevant callback function (2.a), execution of the callback function within the interrupt handler by passing a pointer to the handler data structure `hspi` (2.b), and the actual transfer of the data to the receive buffer whose address can be accessed through `hspi` (2.c). An important point is that, in (2) the actual data flow from the MMIO data channel to the memory happens inside an interrupt handler context.

4.2 MMIO Based Function Modeling

We hypothesize that the lower-level interactions with the firmware, which causes path explosion in symbolic execution, can be ignored to a large degree in understanding how the data from the peripherals flow into the upper layers. Therefore, the goal of our API modeling approach is to achieve a high coverage in the upper layers of the firmware while precisely keeping track of taint propagation from the peripheral data registers.

As in state-of-the-art firmware rehosting approaches, we assume that the MMIO addresses are given. We also assume that the user specifies the addresses of the MMIO data registers for the peripherals of interest. When we use the term **memory gets tainted**, we refer to the scenario where the memory gets overwritten by values from a specific MMIO data register, which is selected based on the target board implementation and it is defined as the **Target Data Channel** (TDC). For example, STM32L475 utilizes a WIFI module for network connection, which is connected via the SPI bus. If our objective is to analyze the data traffic originating from such network connections, the TDC for analyzing the target STM32L475 board would be 0x40003c0c (SPI3 data register). Our work mainly focuses on analyzing all types of data flows from the TDC and generating appropriate function models in the scope of symbolically executing a binary firmware with some path selection heuristics. During the symbolic execution, we collect the records of function calling contexts, monitor the MMIO accessing behaviors, and dynamically model the functions as needed. Also, the values received from other data channels are treated as regular symbols and not being used for function model generation.

Overall Process. In Fig. 1, FIRMMOD starts symbolic execution of the firmware with several function models (initially, empty set). When the overall coverage among all the symbolic execution states does not increase, it pauses the execution and finds out if there exists an opportunity to generate a new function model. By analyzing the peripheral dataflow originating from the low-level layers that interact with the peripherals, FIRMMOD generates function models. Next, if a new function model gets generated, it resumes the symbolic execution from the backup state, which we refer to as the **Entry Snapshot (ES)**. ES is forked at a specific point (e.g. entry function) and it needs to restart the execution from that point to observe the effects of applying the new function model that get generated. Typically, the ES is generated by copying the state when an entry function gets called. A typical entry function is like the `main` function in a bare-metal system or the first task entry for an RTOS system.

Generating API models is based on dynamic Taint Analysis (TA) for both explicit and implicit data transfers. Explicit Taint Analysis (ETA) mainly focuses on taints that happen inside a task context, i.e., loading from an MMIO data register in the context of a task. If a function that gets called by the task has received data from the target peripheral's data channel, FIRMMOD monitors such direct tainting behavior and keeps tracking of the dataflow. ETA can be conducted without triggering any interrupts if the interrupt version of HAL APIs are not used. The main difference between ETA and Implicit Taint Analysis (ITA) is that ITA requires triggering of the interrupts and monitoring of the dataflows between the tasks and the interrupt handlers.

ITA relies on interrupt modeling to keep track of tainting. For complex devices, the interrupt handlers are complex and achieving high code coverage within such interrupt handlers requires triggering of the interrupt line at the right time. For example, in Listing 1.1, step 2.b must happen after the RxISR callback is set in step 2.a at line 15 within the task. Even if the right callback is set before the interrupt is triggered, if some other non-symbolic conditions (e.g. constant settings like the peripheral's mode) are not met, observing the expected tainting (2.c, at line 32) may still not be possible due to low code coverage within the interrupt handler.

```
int16_t SPI_WIFI_ReceiveData ( uint8_t *pdata,  uint16_t len,
    uint32_t timeout){
 ...
  if( HAL_SPI_Receive_IT(&hspi, tmp, 1) != HAL_OK) {... return
    ES_WIFI_ERROR_SPI_FAILED; }
  wait_spi_rx_event(timeout); // interrupt triggering point
  pData[0] = tmp[0]; pData[1] = tmp[1]; ...}
```

Listing 1.2. An example function that waits on an event.

Different from ETA, we perform ITA at specific code locations. There are two aspects to know about testing the target peripheral for an ITA process. First, we need to know the specific code location to trigger the interrupt, e.g. wait_spi_rx_event as shown in Listing 1.2, which indicates the need for triggering the interrupt line to complete the operation. Second, we need to know which interrupt line should be triggered. This information can be extracted from the interrupt definition documents, e.g. 51 for SPI3 of STM32L475. These two types of information enable us to generate taint propagation models of the target peripheral in a precise way.

ITA aims to generate function models for contexts in which some waiting event is issued. ITA process works as follows. Whenever a wait-event function gets called, we trigger the corresponding interrupt line. Next, we start a new symbolic execution phase to explore the state space of the corresponding interrupt handler. When the interrupt handler returns, we hook the state and switch to another one from the state pool that executes the interrupt handler. After all paths are explored inside the interrupt handler, we terminate the relevant symbolic execution phase, switch back to the original one, and pick one state to continue with. We select the state by preferring those that have read from the TDC and wrote the taints to memory locations that are not on the `IRQ_Handler`'s stack. If there are multiple candidate states to consider, we choose the one from the set that has the largest tainted memory range. This ensures that after exiting from the interrupt handler, the chosen state will be able to propagate the taint information to other parts of the memory within the task.

```
static  void ParseIP(char* ptr, uint8_t* arr){
  uint8_t hexnum = 0, hexcnt;
  while(* ptr) {
    hexcnt = 1;
    if(*ptr != '.') {
      // out of bounds access into arr
      arr[hexnum++] = ParseNumber(ptr, &hexcnt);}
    ptr = ptr + hexcnt; ...}
uint32_t SOCKETS_GetHostByName( const char * pcHostName ) {
  uint32_t ulIPAddres = 0; // overflown local variable ...
  ES_WIFI_DNS_LookUp( &( xWiFiModule.xWifiObject ), pcHostName, (
     uint8_t * ) &( ulIPAddres ); ...}
ES_WIFI_Status_t ES_WIFI_DNS_LookUp(ES_WIFIObject_t *Obj, const char *
     url, uint8_t *ipaddress) {
  AT_ExecuteCommand(Obj, Obj->CmdData, Obj->CmdData);...
  ptr = strtok((char *)Obj->CmdData + 2, "\r");...
  ParseIP(ptr, ipaddress);...
}
```

Listing 1.3. A buffer overflow example.

Another important component is the Function Explorer (FE), which aims to reduce the path explosion inside functions that process raw data received from the peripherals, e.g., for sanitizing and/or for parsing. Figure 2 shows an example, the `RunJobsDemo` from AWS RTOS [1], where the firmware tries to establish an MQTT connection by receiving data from the SPI bus to establish a WIFI connection. An example function that parses raw data received from a peripheral is the `ParseIP` function shown in Listing 1.3, which parses SPI data. `ParseIP` parses the IP information from raw data pointed by `ptr` and stores the parsed IP address in memory location pointed by `arr`. A failure in the parsing of the IP will cause a failure in establishing a secure connection. However, since the raw data consists of symbolic data, path explosion happens within the `parseIP` function. Similar to the string processing functions, this type of customized parsing library limits the performance of symbolic execution by not exposing flow of the tainted data moving through the upper layers. The goal of FE is to model such functions in a more precise way.

Besides ETA, ITA and FE, we also have other settings. A loop bound manager is used for managing unbounded forking. Furthermore, we have ported some function models from the new S2E for handling the string and memory related functions, e.g. strlen. These function models help reduce the size of the state space.

Taint Analysis. An important part of modeling a driver/HAL API is to figure out which part of the memory is modified by the function, especially those memory locations that have been tainted by the peripheral data channel. Most HAL/-driver APIs play the roles of transferring data from the peripheral to the upper layers. Precisely locating the tainted memory regions is essential for precise modeling of an API. Every function may have local variables that are indirectly changed by their callees, or even by the callee's callees. So, we need to identify all the memory locations that have been tainted by the peripheral data channels. Local memory objects are usually tainted by passing the address as a parameter and by getting overwritten by the lowest level functions, i.e. functions that per-

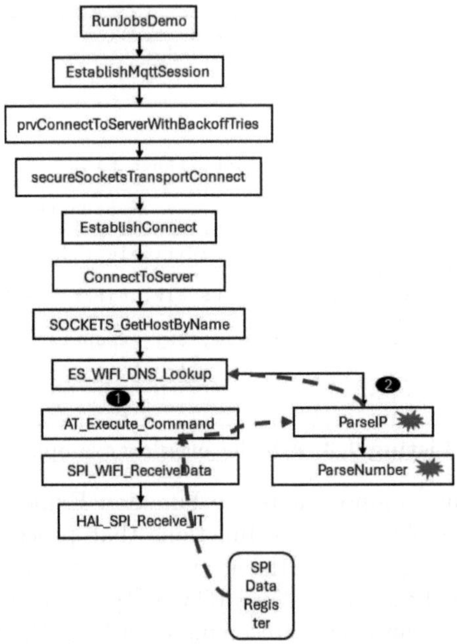

Fig. 2. Peripheral's raw data processing example from AWS RTOS demo on running jobs [1].

form I/O operations. These functions access data registers and store the received data to the memory objects from the upper stack or a global object. In dynamic analysis, after finding the memory locations that are directly tainted, we need to propagate the information of the tainted memory locations to the upper layers until the analysis identifies the functions whose stack frames host the tainted memory locations. For global objects that get tainted, we need to identify their precise locations.

Algorithm 1 shows how FIRMMOD generates a taint memory map for each function, which summarizes the side effect of the modeled function as a set of memory locations that get tainted by the data channels. The first input of this algorithm, *DTM*, stores the taint records of memory locations that get overwritten by values flowing from the data channels, which get collected by a combination of ETA and ITA. For ETA, it is the first location that writes symbols from the data channel to the memory, i.e., load a symbol from the data channel and store it into the memory address, e.g., line 4 in Listing 1.1. For ITA, since we trigger the interrupt line at specific points and select the target path from the irq handler that have tainted the memory, the memory gets overwritten by the symbols from the target data channel, e.g. line 5 in Listing 1.2. The second input, *RTTM*, stores the modeling related taint memory map, which will be updated by this algorithm. The third input, *CC*, stores the call chain, where the

Algorithm 1. An algorithm for generating the tainted memory map.

Input(*DTM*: Direct Taint Map, *RTMM*: Model-related Taint Memory Map, *CC*: Call chain)
OutPut (*RTMM*: Updated Model-related Taint Memory Map)
$DTM, TM : Function \mapsto \mathcal{P}(Memory)$ ▷ Both ETA and ITA
$RTMM : Function \mapsto \mathcal{P}(Memory)$ ▷ Side effects of functions
$TM, RTMM \leftarrow \lambda F.\emptyset$
for F in $Functions(CC)$ **do**
    $TM \leftarrow propagateToCallers(F, DTM[F], TM, CC)$
        ▷ Propagate the memory addresses bottom-up
end for
for F in $TM.domain$ **do**
    for $memory$ in $TM[F]$ **do**
        if $memory.type \in \{Global, UpperStack\}$ **then**
            $RTTM[F].insert(memory)$
        end if
    end for
end for
return *RTMM*

chain ends with a function that taints some memory addresses with data flowing from a target data channel.

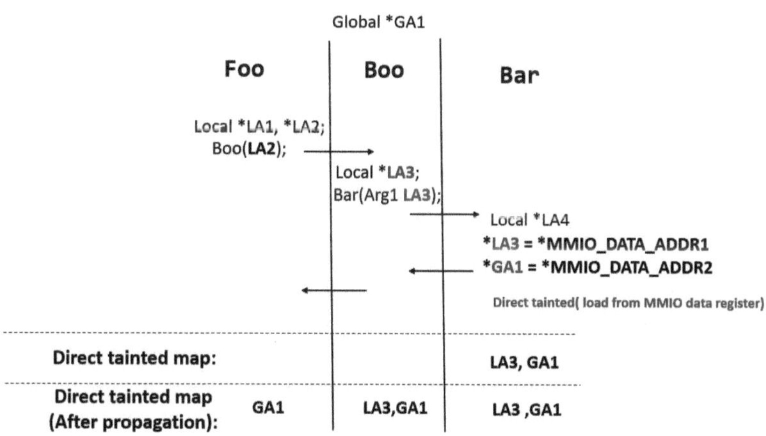

Fig. 3. Propagate the tainted address to upper layers.

The output of Algorithm 1 is a complete taint memory map for each function in the call chain. It provides us with the flexibility of modeling the functions in the call chain that do not modify the tainted memory regions themselves yet their callees do.

Algorithm 2. An algorithm for propagating the taint information to the callers, propagateCallers.

```
Input(F: Function, MAS: Memory Address Set, TM : Function ↦ P(Memory),
  CC: Call chain)
OutPut (TM: Taint Map)
for address a in MAS do
    if a is on F's stack frame then
        continue
    end if
    CF = F.getCaller(CC)
    while CF do
        if a is global then
            TM[CF].insert(a)
        else if a is local then
            TM[CF].insert(a)
            if a is on caller stack then
                break    ▷ stop propagating if the target function frame is reached
            end if
        end if
        CF = F.getCaller(CC)
    end while
end for
return TM
```

The algorithm calls *propagateToCallers*, Algorithm 2, to pass the tainted memory records from the callees to their callers. An example is provided in Fig. 3. The call chain `Foo`, `Boo`, `Bar` ends with `Bar`, which taints local address *LA3* and global address *GA1* directly with target data channel related addresses, *MMIO_DATA_ADDR1* and *MMIO_DATA_ADDR2*, respectively. Algorithm 2 goes through each function in the call chain to propagate their direct taints. So, when it is handling `Bar`, it needs to propagate the taint related memory accesses, *LA3* and *GA1*, to `Boo` and `Foo`. However, for *LA3* the propagation ends at `Boo` as *LA3* is located in the stack frame of `Boo` while propagation of the global address *GA1* is applied to each caller in the call chain, e.g., `Boo` and `Foo`. Normally, there are three types of tainted memory objects for modeling a specific function: local variables, global variables, and variables from the upper stack. For example, *LA3* is from the upper function's frame with respect to the *Bar* function, but it is a local value to the *Boo* function. Algorithm 1 keeps the global addresses and the upper stack addresses in the model (lines 12–13) while ignoring the local variables, which is due to the fact that when a function gets modeled the local variables will not be relevant as they will not be allocated. FIRMMOD can choose to model any of the functions in the call chain, e.g., `Foo`, `Boo`, or `Bar`, as long as we have an entry for these functions in the tainted memory map. When FIRMMOD models a function, it will be able to reflect the function's side effect in terms of propagating taints related to the target data channel.

Function Explorer. FIRMMOD also keeps track of implicit taint propagation through function calls that copy data from tainted buffers to some new buffer. We call such functions Potentially Taint Propagating (PTP) functions. FIRMMOD considers functions that receive arguments that point to tainted buffers as PTPs, and observes them to record the taint propagation, if any.

To ensure that PTP functions receive sufficient coverage, we port the function models of the string library from S2E 2.0 [6] and implement a new analysis module called the Function Explorer, which is designed to find a taint propagation relevant path in a PTP function. The Function Explorer gets activated once a PTP function is reached. As an example, assuming `ES_WIFI_DNS_Lookup` in Fig. 2 is the target function, `ParseIP` can be considered a PTP function due to its `ptr` argument being tainted. It will pause the current executor and start a new one. The new executor will explore the state space of the PTP function starting from the current state, which is similar to the symbolic exploration in ITA. After all the paths of a target function are explored, we select one path as the base state to generate the function model for that function. We formulated a taint related metric to evaluate all the states and select one that yields the highest score in terms of the taint metric. Specifically, the taint metric is the number of tainted bytes propagated within the PTP function. Once the taint model is generated for the PTP function, we restore to the previous executor, pick up one of the backup states forked at the time of invoking the PTP function call, and apply the function model immediately at the PTP callsite.

```
// the Prompt array is tainted, but it does not escape the stack frame
  .
int8_t SPI_WIFI_ResetModule(void){
 uint8_t Prompt[6], uint8_t count = 0; ...
 while (WIFI_IS_CMDDATA_READY()) { // forking...
  Status = HAL_SPI_Receive(&hspi , &Prompt[count], 1, 0xFFFF);
  count += 2;   ...
 }  ...
 if((Prompt[0] != 0x15) ||(Prompt[1] != 0x15) ||...)
   return -1;
 return 0;
}
```

Listing 1.4. An example for tainted memory not escaping the stack frame.

Model Generation and Argument Analysis. FIRMMOD can be configured to target specific layers for modeling. We leverage debug information to identify such layers. For example, if a compile unit's path is suffixed with `hal_spi.c`, the functions of this compile unit are associated with the HAL SPI layer.

We define a modeling boundary so that all the functions above the boundary are not allowed to be modeled. The boundary is used to limit the modeling of functions constrained in the set of peripheral related APIs, e.g. HAL APIs, BSP drivers or I/O helpers. Functions that only taint its local variables is modeled by returning a symbolic value only and without any taint propagation model as a side effect. An example is given in Listing 1.4, where `SPI_WIFI_ResetModule` allocates a local array `Prompt`, which is used as a buffer to receive data from the WIFI module on the SPI bus. After the `Prompt` buffer is filled, it continues to check each byte and return. Since `Prompt` contains symbolic data from the peripheral, the byte-by-byte checking before returning could fork a lot of states, which would lower the chance for the success path that returns 0 (line 10 in listing 1.4) to be scheduled among all these forked states. If the data flow from the peripheral is detected and the tainted memory does not escape the activation frame of a function that could be modeled, it is safe to model that function with a bypassing model, i.e., no taint related side effects and a symbolic return value, if any. Even though the `Prompt` buffer is tainted with the data register, it has not escaped the stack frame of the `SPI_WIFI_ResetModule` function. So, FIRMMOD models `SPI_WIFI_ResetModule` safely by just symbolizing the return value and without noting any side effects.

FIRMMOD performs Argument Analysis to enrich the function model by capturing the taint propagation through the arguments. Considering the taint information of a function that has a set of taint memory objects from its upper callers' stack or global variables, we need to know the relation between these memory objects and arguments to generate the function model. Based on our observation most STM32 HAL/driver functions that transmit/receive massive data from/to peripherals on I2C or SPI, typically have the following types of parameters: a handler pointer parameter, where the handler abstracts the usage of the peripheral, a data buffer pointer parameter, a size parameter that indicates the length of data to be transmitted or received, and an optional timeout value. So we make the following assumptions for Argument Analysis:

- The tainted memory must be accessible through a pointer that falls into one of the argument range of registers according to the ARM calling conventions.
- One of the arguments optionally indicates the size of the buffer and the value is a configured size value, e.g. an `int` value.
- Only one of the pointer arguments gets tainted for each function.

One of the challenges in model generation is determining the size constraint for the tainted memory region so that taint propagation can be performed in a precise way. Although most driver I/O functions have a parameter to indicate the size of bytes to be transmitted or received, there are some functions that do not have an explicit size argument. To get the most accurate approximation of the size to be written, we leverage debug information to infer the accurate size information. FIRMMOD can also infer the size of the field of a `struct` type using the debug information.

```
// ptr (taint source) and arr (taint dest)
// arr points to a buffer with implicit size
void ParseIP(char* ptr, uint8_t* arr);

// invoke ParseIP model, which taints 4 bytes
// pointed by the 2nd parameter
ParseIP(ptr, NetSettings->IP_Addr);
// uint8_t IP_Addr[4];
```

As the above example shows, without the debug information the model of `ParseIP` would not specify the number of bytes pointed by the second parameter `arr` gets tainted. However, at the time of applying the model of `ParseIP`, FIRMMOD has the concrete value of `arr`, i.e., the value of `NetSettings->IP_Addr`. By querying the debug info, it resolves the address to the field of `NetSettings->IP_Addr` and finds out its type, which is a four-byte array, and the model writes four bytes of symbolic values to the address stored in `arr`. This allows FIRMMOD to propagate taints in a precise way.

FIRMMOS generates function taint models in the format shown below. For each function model, it has the return information and a target taint channel in the form of an argument index to reveal which argument contains the address to be written with the tainted data. Also, it provides the size information by either using an argument index or with an unknown mark to indicate that it would be resolved later at the time of model application.

In the model for the `ParseIP` function, the fields *has_return_value*, *target_taint_channel*, and *size* would be set to *false*, *0*, *1*, and `UNKNOWN`, respectively.

```
Function Model <function name>:
    has_return_value: true/false
    target_taint_channel: <argument index>
    size: UNKNOWN | <argument index>
```

Return-Value Guided Slicing. Another way FIRMMOD deals with the path explosion problem is by applying return value based execution slicing, which eliminates the paths that are of less interest. Given a function $\mathcal{F}$, its return value $\mathcal{R}$, a guided return value $\mathcal{A}$, and the current path constraint $\mathcal{C}$ of state $\mathcal{S}$, we apply the following rule:

$$\textit{Terminate state} \quad \mathcal{S} \quad \text{if} \quad \mathcal{C} \wedge (\mathcal{F}_{\mathcal{R}} = \mathcal{A}) \equiv \textit{false}$$

This rule indicates the termination of state $\mathcal{S}$ if the path constraint does not satisfy the guided return value. FIRMMOD can be configured with the guided return values of the APIs of interest. Since most APIs return a 0 value for success, it is straightforward to configure FIRMMOD for success return values. We used this guideline for various layers, which is explained in Sect. 5.

5 Evaluation

We implemented FIRMMOD on top of S2E to analyze ARM cortex M3 firmware and to perform binary level symbolic execution. We applied FIRMMOD to AWS RTOS Demo examples, which utilize the WIFI module and consist of 11 firmware binaries generated to run on the STM32L475 discovery board. Figure 4 illustrates the layers of the analyzed firmware. Main DEMO APP represents the application layer. The CoreMQTT/CoreHTTP layer implements the communication

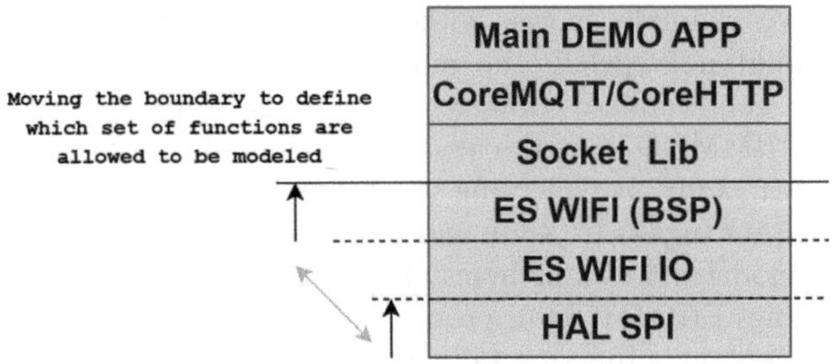

Fig. 4. Layered architecture of the Amazon FreeRTOS Demos.

protocols and interacts with the WIFI module. The Socket Library is being used as an intermediate layer for data transmission.

ES WIFI is a BSP driver and ES WIFI IO is the glue layer defined by the clients that utilize the Hardware Abstraction Layer (HAL) for the SPI bus. ES WIFI leverages two peripherals to send/receive data: SPI and GPIO. It utilizes the GPIO as a signal to indicate whether the data is ready or not. The data received from the network is transmitted over the SPI bus. The ES WIFI layer implements an interface of the AT commands to achieve various communication goals.

We treated the data received from the RNG module as concrete random values based on a timing seed. All other read accesses to MMIO regions return unconstrained symbolic values. The extracted the debug information in DWARF format from the unstripped binaries. Our results have been collected by running FIRMMOD for two hours for each setup on each benchmark on an Ubuntu 16.04 machine with 256GB of RAM.

5.1 RQ1 on the Scope of API Modeling

FIRMMOD leverages two types of API modeling that can be configured for scope. The first one is API taint modeling that it generates automatically. The second one is the API return value modeling that allows to constrain the return values of modeled APIs to success cases. However, the latter requires prior knowledge of the return values that denote success cases. Table 1 shows a summary of the success case return values for various layers we considered for API return value modeling. Our analysis reveals that most of the layers except the Socket layer use an enumerated type for the return value type. Once the success case is determined from the enumerated type, it is straightforward to generate success case API return value models using the debug information in the binary. We only needed to use manual effort for the Socket layer, which does not use an enumerated type for the return values of the API. It should be noted that return value modeling is a one-time effort, which gets reused for all firmware that calls APIs of the modeled library. Table 1 also shows that in most of the cases the success case is represented with a zero return value.

Therefore, we answer RQ1 both on the scope of automated modeling and on the scope of return value modeling. For API taint model generation, we refer the

Table 1. The distribution of zero and nonzero values for representing success cases of API return values in various layers.

Layer	Total # API	# Zero	# NonZero	Manual?
HAL	20	20	0	No
ES WIFI	43	43	0	No
Socket	12	10	2	Yes
MQTT	84	84	0	No
HTTP	18	18	0	No

reader to Fig. 4 for the different scopes we have considered. The three automated modeling scopes we used in our evaluation are defined in terms of the highest (boundary) layer that can be modeled: HAL SPI (only functions of the HAL SPI layer), ES WIFI IO (functions of the ES WIFI IO and HAL SPI layers), and ES WIFI BSP (functions of the ES WIFI BSP, ES WIFI IO, and HAL SPI layers). For return value modeling, we follow a similar approach, but we define different combinations: HAL SPI (only functions of the HAL SPI layer), ES WIFI (functions of the ES WIFI and HAL SPI layers), and HTTP/MQTT (functions of the HTTP/MQTT, Socket, ES WIFI, and HAL SPI layers) for modeling the success case return values of the APIs of the considered layers so that return value based slicing can filter out states with failure cases of such APIs.

Figure 5 shows the basic block coverage for different scopes used for API taint model generation when return value modeling boundary is set to the ES WIFI layer. Modeling only the functions at the HAL SPI achieves the smallest coverage while setting the boundary layer as ES WIFI IO or ES WIFI BSP achieves higher coverage, where moving the boundary to ES WIFI BSP achieves only a slightly higher coverage. So, the higher the boundary among these three layers the higher the basic block coverage gets achieved for the analyzed firmware. It also shows the effectiveness of FIRMMOD's automatic generation of API taint models.

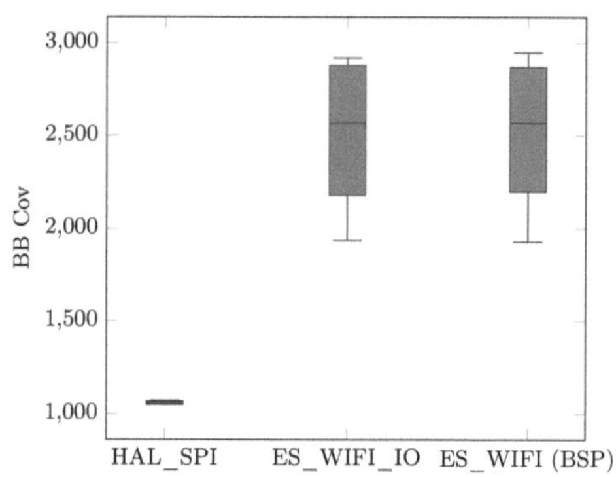

Fig. 5. Basic block coverage (BB cov) for various settings of the boundary layer for API taint modeling.

As mentioned in Sect. 4, FIRMMOD keeps track of memory accesses to determine which memory objects get tainted by the TDC and whether the object is global or local. Also, it monitors flow of tainted data at the time of function calls and returns. We use ❒, ▲, and ✧ to denote the tainted global objects, the local objects, and arguments or return values, respectively. A summary of the taint types observed is provided in Table 2, which shows the importance of argument modeling and identification of local buffers.

Table 2. Types of taints per layer.

	HAL SPI	ES WIFI IO	ES WIFI	COREMQTT	COREHTTP
global ❒	2	1	6	3	1
local ▲	4	2	5	16	1
args or ret ✧	6	2	20	16	1

Figure 6 shows the number functions covered at the HTTP/MQTT layer for different scopes of return value modeling. We fixed the API taint model boundary at the ES WIFI IO layer. As the figure shows, modeling of ES WIFI API return values help achieve better coverage compared to not modeling those. However, for `Jobs` and `Core Http Mutual Auth.` demos, modeling the return values of functions at the HTTP/MQTT layer reduces the total coverage due to a path explosion limiting the coverage. So, we think that ES WIFI is the ideal boundary setting for return value modeling for our benchmarks.

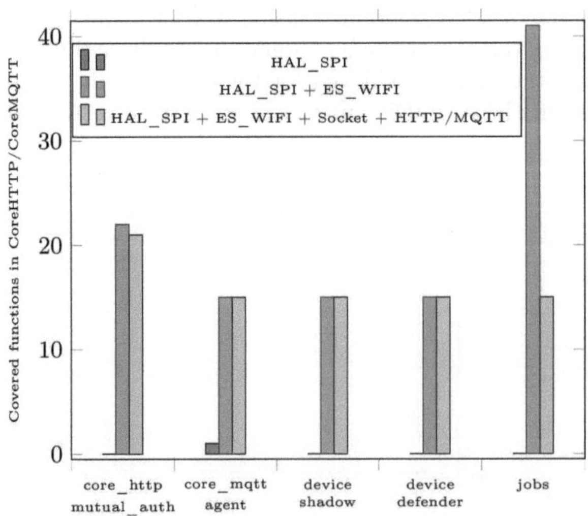

Fig. 6. The impact of the scope of return value modeling.

Table 3. Function reachability for demo application and AWS RTOS demo CoreMQTT/CoreHTTP libraries

Demo Name	Protocol	Demo Entry Function	Reach Demo Entry	Main DEMO App		CoreMQTT/CoreHTTP	
				Reached Functions	Total Functions	Reached Functions	Total Functions
core_http_mutual_auth	CoreHTTP	RunCoreHttpMutualAuthDemo	✓	3	3	22	33
core_http_s3_download	CoreHTTP	RunCoreHttpS3DownloadDemo	✓	2	4	3	45
core_http_s3_download_multithreaded	CoreHTTP	RunCoreHttpS3DownloadMultithreadedDemo	✓	2	7	3	45
core_http_s3_upload	CoreHTTP	RunCoreHttpS3UploadDemo	✓	2	5	3	45
core_mqtt_mutual_auth	CoreMQTT	RunCoreMqttMutualAuthDemo	✗	0	13	0	82
core_mqtt_agent	CoreMQTT	RunCoreMqttAgentDemo	✓	9	12	15	86
device_shadow	CoreMQTT	RunDeviceShadowDemo	✓	1	7	15	82
device_defender	CoreMQTT	RunDeviceDefenderDemo	✓	1	15	15	82
jobs	CoreMQTT	RunJobsDemo	✓	2	6	41	82
greengrass_discovery	CoreMQTT	vStartGreenGrassDiscoveryTask	✗	0	8	0	0
tcp_echo_client	–	vStartTCPEchoClientTasks_SingleTasks	✓	3	3	–	–

Finally, Table 3 shows the coverage of functions reached in the upper layers using the best combination of the API taint model boundary and the return value modeling boundary for each benchmark. For nine out of eleven benchmarks, analysis reaches some functions at the application layer and at the communication protocol (MQTT/HTTP) layers. Regarding the application layer, two of the benchmarks, HTTP Mutual Authentitcation and TCP Echo Client, even cover all of the included functions. Results of CoreMQTT/CoreHTTP also reveal good coverage as high as 22/33 (66%) in CoreHTTP and 41/82 (50%) in CoreMQTT.

5.2 RQ2: Bug Finding

Our framework is based on symbolic execution of binaries. So, the main mechanism we use for detecting vulnerabilities is observing abnormal cases in the symbolic execution of firmware such as the Program Counter (PC) being overwritten with an address that refers to a non-executable region. Also, if the execution state is trying to access an address defined in terms of an unconstrained symbolic value received from a target data channel (TDC), it is also identified as a potential vulnerability. FIRMMOD has detected two known buffer overflow bugs, one within the `SPI_WIFI_ResetModule` function [2] (within 200 secs) and another one within the `ParseIP` function [3] (within 2500 secs). As Listing 1.4 shows, a local variable `count` will be overwritten with a TDC value if the check on line 4 keeps holding true. Then if the tainted value of `count` is used as an index to the `Prompt` array, which is used as the receiving buffer base address passed to `HAL_SPI_Receive` (line 5), which leads to a memory out of bounds access. FIRMMOD is able to detect such vulnerability based on the defined detection pattern. Similarly, in Listing 1.3, the second argument of `ParseIP`, `arr`, can be filled with symbolic values if the TDC value that gets checked on line 3 keeps holding true. As we observed, the value of TDC at `ptr` can be larger than 1000, but the expected parsed IP address and the size of the buffer pointed by `arr` is only four-bytes. As we show in Sect. 5.3, the state-of-the-art firmware rehosting approach, Fuzzware [13], cannot detect these bugs within 24 h.

5.3 RQ3: FIRMMOD Versus State-of-the-Art

In this section, we first compare FIRMMOD against FIRMSTAT [4], which uses static analysis to generate API taint models. FIRMMOD, on the other hand, uses dynamic symbolic execution to achieve the same goal. Table 4 shows a comparison of FIRMSTAT and FIRMMOD in terms of the number of API taint models generated for various layers. FIRMSTAT is limited to below the MQTT/HTTP layers, possibly because it relies on the HAL data types for inferring taint propagation and the type-based resolution of function pointers.

The reason FIRMSTAT generates models of more functions in some layers is that its scope is independent of what is actually called within the firmware. The reason FIRMMOD generates models for some functions, for which FIRMSTAT

Table 4. Number of functions detected to be tainted

	HAL_SPI	ES_WIFI	ES_WIFI_IO	CoreMQTT
FIRMSTAT	10	17	1	–
FIRMMOD	7	20	3	18

fails is due to FIRMMOD's ability to provide more precise function pointer resolution as a dynamic analysis approach. Another important advantage of FIRMMOD over FIRMSTAT is that the API taint models in FIRMMOD includes size information for the tainted buffers which get populated with symbolic data lazily to precisely observe the side effect of data-flows from peripherals within the upper layers.

Table 5. Basic Block Coverage for FIRMMOD and Fuzzware

Firmware	FIRMMOD	Fuzzware
core_http_mutual_auth	3114	1426
core_http_s3_download	2609	1390
core_http_s3_download_multithreaded	2546	1428
core_http_s3_upload	2579	1390
core_mqtt_mutual_auth	1963	1419
core_mqtt_agent	3063	1408
device_shadow	2994	1427
device_defender	3006	1426
jobs	3387	1417
greengrass_discovery	1958	1429
tcp_echo_client	2715	1432

We also compared FIRMMOD against Fuzzware [13], a state-of-the-art firmware rehosting approach that combines fuzzing and symbolic execution. We ran Fuzzware for 24 h, which is much longer than the timeout of two hours that was used for FIRMMOD. Table 5 shows the number of basic blocks covered by each tool. As the table shows Fuzzware achieves limited coverage for each benchmark mostly performing initialization steps of the firmware while FIRMMOD achieves up to 2X more coverage. Also, Fuzzware was not able to find the two bugs we found in upper layers showing its inability to achieve sufficient coverage in the upper layers. These show the importance of modeling in firmware analysis. We think that combining the peripheral interaction model generation performed by tools like Fuzzware with the API taint models and return value based slicing performed by FIRMMOD can potentially achieve even better performance, which we plan to pursue as future work.

6 Conclusions

We presented an automated approach, FIRMMOD, for generating taint models of APIs that get employed by various layers of firmware and directly or indirectly interact with some peripherals. FIRMMOD applies the learnt API models to reach deeper parts of the firmware compared to state-of-the-art firmware rehosting approaches that do not leverage API models. This enabled FIRMMOD to detect two buffer overflow vulnerabilities that are missed by standard firmware rehosting approaches that focus on modeling peripheral interaction only. In future work, we will integrate FIRMMOD with fuzzing to achieve goal-based fuzzing of firmware.

Acknowledgments. This work was funded by United States National Science Foundation Award # 1942235.

References

1. https://github.com/aws/amazon-freertos
2. https://github.com/STMicroelectronics/STM32CubeH7/issues/252
3. https://tinyurl.com/ms8hy7jm
4. Bai, K.Y., Yavuz, T.: MMIO access-based coverage for firmware analysis. In: IEEE Conference on Communications and Network Security, CNS 2023, Orlando, FL, USA, 2–5 October 2023, pp. 1–9. IEEE (2023)
5. Cao, C., Guan, L., Ming, J., Liu, P.: Device-agnostic firmware execution is possible: a concolic execution approach for peripheral emulation. In: Annual Computer Security Applications Conference, ACSAC '20, pp. 746–759. Association for Computing Machinery, New York (2020)
6. Chipounov, V., Kuznetsov, V., Candea, G.: S2e: a platform for in-vivo multi-path analysis of software systems. In: Gupta, R., Mowry, T.C. (eds.) ASPLOS, pp. 265–278. ACM (2011)
7. Clements, A.A., et al.: Halucinator: firmware re-hosting through abstraction layer emulation. In: Capkun, S., Roesner, F. (eds.) 29th USENIX Security Symposium, USENIX Security 2020, 12–14 August 2020, pp. 1201–1218. USENIX Association (2020). https://www.usenix.org/conference/usenixsecurity20/presentation/clements
8. Feng, B., Mera, A., Lu, L.: P2IM: scalable and hardware-independent firmware testing via automatic peripheral interface modeling. In: Capkun, S., Roesner, F. (eds.) 29th USENIX Security Symposium, USENIX Security 2020, 12–14 August 2020, pp. 1237–1254. USENIX Association (2020). https://www.usenix.org/conference/usenixsecurity20/presentation/feng
9. Gustafson, E., et al.: Toward the analysis of embedded firmware through automated re-hosting. In: 22nd International Symposium on Research in Attacks, Intrusions and Defenses, RAID 2019, Chaoyang District, Beijing, China, 23–25 September 2019, pp. 135–150. USENIX Association (2019). https://www.usenix.org/conference/raid2019/presentation/gustafson
10. Johnson, E., et al.: Jetset: targeted firmware rehosting for embedded systems. In: 30th USENIX Security Symposium (USENIX Security 21). USENIX Association (2021). https://www.usenix.org/conference/usenixsecurity21/presentation/johnson

11. Li, W., Guan, L., Lin, J., Shi, J., Li, F.: From library portability to para-rehosting: natively executing microcontroller software on commodity hardware. In: 28th Annual Network and Distributed System Security Symposium, NDSS 2021, virtually, 21–25 February 2021. The Internet Society (2021)
12. Mera, A., Feng, B., Lu, L., Kirda, E.: Dice: automatic emulation of dma input channels for dynamic firmware analysis. In: 2021 IEEE Symposium on Security and Privacy (SP), pp. 1938–1954 (2021). https://doi.org/10.1109/SP40001.2021.00018
13. Scharnowski, T., et al.: Fuzzware: using precise MMIO modeling for effective firmware fuzzing. In: 31st USENIX Security Symposium (USENIX Security 22), pp. 1239–1256. USENIX Association, Boston (2022)
14. Zhou, W., Guan, L., Liu, P., Zhang, Y.: Automatic firmware emulation through invalidity-guided knowledge inference. In: 30th USENIX Security Symposium (USENIX Security 21). USENIX Association (2021). https://www.usenix.org/conference/usenixsecurity21/presentation/zhou
15. Zhou, W., Zhang, L., Guan, L., Liu, P., Zhang, Y.: What your firmware tells you is not how you should emulate it: a specification-guided approach for firmware emulation. In: Proceedings of the 2022 ACM SIGSAC Conference on Computer and Communications Security, CCS '22, pp. 3269–3283. Association for Computing Machinery, New York (2022)

Large Language Models Using Retrieval Augmented Generation and Prompt Engineering for AI-Driven Music Source Separation: A Literature Review

Scott Josephson(✉) and Atif Farid Mohammad

Capitol Technology University, Laurel, MD 20708, USA
{sjosephson,afmohammad}@captechu.edu

Abstract. Music source separation is a critical task in audio processing and is essential for applications such as remixing, audio restoration, and music analysis. Traditional methods, including signal processing techniques like Independent Component Analysis (ICA) and Non-negative Matrix Factorization (NMF), as well as deep learning approaches utilizing Convolutional Neural Networks (CNNs) and Recurrent Neural Networks (RNNs), face challenges related to extensive data requirements, computational complexity, and limited adaptability to diverse audio contexts. Recent advancements in Large Language Models (LLMs) like GPT-4 introduce new possibilities for addressing these challenges without retraining models. This literature review explores the integration of prompt engineering and Retrieval-Augmented Generation (RAG) with LLMs to perform music source separation. By leveraging LLMs' inherent language understanding capabilities and accessing external databases containing musical scores, lyrics, and instrument profiles, this approach aims to enhance efficiency, flexibility, and accessibility in source separation tasks. The review highlights how this innovative methodology can overcome the limitations of traditional techniques, filling a notable gap in current research and offering transformative potential for both academic inquiry and practical applications in music technology.

Keywords: Music Source Separation · Large Language Models · Prompt Engineering · Retrieval-Augmented Generation · Audio Embeddings · Multimodal Applications

1 Introduction

1.1 Background

Music source separation focuses on extracting instrumental or vocal tracks from a mixed audio signal. This task is essential for various applications, including remixing, audio restoration, music transcription, and analysis [1]. Traditional methods often rely on complex signal processing techniques or retrained machine learning models, which can be computationally intensive and inflexible [2]. Recent advancements in artificial

S. Hussain et al. (Eds.): SEET 2025, CCIS 2725, pp. 114–124, 2026.
https://doi.org/10.1007/978-3-032-08977-9_9

intelligence, particularly in developing Large Language Models (LLMs) like GPT-4, present new opportunities to address these challenges without retraining models [3]. This literature review examines the evolution of music source separation techniques and the limitations of current methodologies. It explores how prompt engineering and Retrieval-Augmented Generation (RAG) with LLMs can offer innovative solutions.

2 Traditional Methods in Music Source Separation

2.1 Signal Processing Techniques

Early approaches to music source separation utilized signal processing techniques such as Independent Component Analysis (ICA) and Non-negative Matrix Factorization (NMF). ICA assumes statistical independence between sources and non-Gaussian and separates signals based on maximizing this independence [4]. However, its effectiveness is limited when dealing with complex music signals where source independence is not guaranteed.

NMF decomposes a mixed signal into a set of basis spectra and corresponding activations, effectively identifying underlying patterns in the data [5]. NMF has been utilized to factorize spectrograms of audio mixtures into spectral bases and activations, effectively isolating individual sound sources based on their spectral content [6]. NMF's assumption of non-negativity aligns well with the nature of magnitude spectrograms, making it suitable for audio applications. While NMF has been successful in specific contexts, it needs to work on overlapping harmonics and requires prior knowledge about the number of sources.

Sparse Component Analysis (SCA) is another method that exploits the sparsity of source signals in a particular domain, such as the time-frequency domain [7]. SCA assumes that the sources are sparse and only one or a few are active at any given time or frequency. By transforming the mixed signals into a sparse domain, SCA can separate the sources by identifying clusters corresponding to individual sources. This technique is particularly effective when dealing with signals like speech, which exhibit sparsity in the time-frequency representation.

Beamforming techniques have also been applied to music source separation, especially in scenarios involving microphone arrays [8]. Beamforming uses spatial filtering to enhance signals from a specific direction while attenuating others. Steering the beamformer towards the desired source makes isolating it from interfering sources and noise possible. However, beamforming requires knowledge of the array geometry and may not perform well in reverberant environments where reflections can degrade spatial cues.

Despite their successes, traditional signal-processing techniques must be improved in complex auditory scenes. ICA, for instance, relies heavily on the statistical independence of sources and may fail when sources are correlated or when the number of sensors is less than the number of sources [9]. NMF, while effective, can struggle with non-stationary sources and requires careful selection of the number of components. SCA depends on the sparsity of sources, which may not hold in all cases, particularly when sources overlap significantly in time and frequency [10]. These limitations highlight the need for more robust and flexible methods to handle real-world audio mixtures' complexities.

2.2 Deep Learning Approaches

The advent of deep learning introduced models capable of learning complex representations of audio signals. Convolutional Neural Networks (CNNs) and Recurrent Neural Networks (RNNs) have been applied to spectrogram representations of audio for source separation tasks [11]. U-Net architectures, adapted from image segmentation, have shown promise in isolating vocals and instruments from music tracks [12].

Despite their success, these models require large, labeled datasets for training. The MUSDB18 dataset, for example, provides multitrack recordings but is limited in size and diversity [2]. Training models on such datasets can lead to overfitting and poor generalization to unseen audio contexts.

Various architectures and techniques have been explored to improve separation quality and computational efficiency.

2.3 Convolutional Neural Networks (CNNs) and Recurrent Neural Networks (RNNs)

Early deep learning approaches employed Convolutional Neural Networks (CNNs) to exploit local structures in spectrograms, capturing time-frequency patterns relevant to different sources [14]. Recurrent Neural Networks (RNNs), particularly Long ShortTerm Memory (LSTM) networks, have been used to model temporal dependencies in audio signals, enhancing the separation of sources with temporal coherence [11]. Convolutional Neural Networks (CNNs) have been widely used for music source separation because they capture local time-frequency patterns in spectrograms. An example is a CNN-based monaural audio source separation model, demonstrating that deep CNNs can effectively learn to separate musical instruments from a single-channel mixture [13].

2.4 U-Net Architectures

Initially developed for biomedical image segmentation, U-Net architectures have been adapted for music source separation by treating spectrograms as images [12]. The UNet's encoder-decoder structure with skip connections allows for effective learning of global and local features, facilitating the separation of vocal and instrumental components.

2.5 Wave-U-Net and Time-Domain Approaches

To address the limitations of spectrogram-based methods, [15] introduced the WaveU-Net architecture, which operates directly on raw audio waveforms. This approach avoids the need for time-frequency transformations and captures phase information more effectively, leading to improved separation quality in some cases.

2.6 Generative Adversarial Networks (GANs)

Generative Adversarial Networks (GANs) have been applied to source separation by framing the problem as a generative task. GANs consist of two neural networks—the generator and the discriminator—trained simultaneously through adversarial processes [16].

Application in Music Source Separation: S. Pascual introduced SEGAN (Speech Enhancement Generative Adversarial Network), which applies GANs for speech enhancement, a task closely related to source separation. While SEGAN focuses on speech, the methodology has inspired music source separation applications [17].

O. Mogren introduced C-RNN-GAN, a continuous RNN GAN for generating sequences, which can be extended to model temporal dependencies in music [18]. N. Takahashi and Y. Mitsufuji specifically addressed music source separation using GANs. They proposed the Multi-scale Multi-band DenseNet (MMDenseNet) with GANs to improve the quality of separated sources by encouraging the generator to produce outputs indistinguishable from real instrument sounds [19].

Benefits of Using GANs: GANs can produce more natural and realistic-sounding separate sources by learning the data distribution of individual instruments or vocals. The discriminator network helps the generator improve by providing feedback on the authenticity of the generated signals.

Challenges: GANs are notoriously difficult to train due to issues like mode collapse and training instability. The adversarial training process can be computationally intensive.

2.7 Deep Clustering and Spectral Masking

Deep clustering involves a network of learning embeddings for each time-frequency bin in the spectrogram, which are grouped according to the source. [20]. This approach allows the separation of overlapping sources by clustering embeddings corresponding to different instruments or vocals.

2.8 End-to-End Learning and TasNet

The TasNet architecture is an end-to-end time-domain audio separation network that learns representations of mixed signals and directly separates sources in the time domain. [21]. This method is significantly improved over spectrogram-based approaches, particularly in speech separation tasks.

2.9 Transformer-Based Models

Transformer architectures, celebrated for their effectiveness in modeling sequential data in natural language processing, have been explored for audio tasks due to their ability to model long-range dependencies. SepFormer, a transformer-based speech separation model, uses self-attention mechanisms to capture global contextual information across the audio sequence [22]. The SepFormer processes audio signals by segmenting them into chunks and applying transformer layers to model intra-chunk and inter-chunk dependencies. This dual-path approach enables the network to handle long audio sequences efficiently while maintaining the ability to model complex relationships between sound sources. While the SepFormer was initially designed for speech separation, the principles underlying its architecture apply to music source separation. The self-attention mechanisms allow the model to focus on different audio signal parts, capturing intricate relationships between various musical instruments over time. This makes transformerbased models a promising avenue for future research in music source separation.

Transformers have continued to gain attention for music source separation. SoniDo is a generative model featuring a multi-level transformer and hierarchical encoder [23]. It supports various music-related tasks by integrating its intermediate representations into task-specific models with data augmentation. An on-the-fly data augmentation method, "token-out," is proposed to mitigate overfitting. SoniDo's effectiveness is demonstrated through benchmarking across diverse tasks, including music tagging, transcription, source separation, and mixing.

2.10 Advances in 2022 and 2023

In recent years, significant progress has been made in deep learning approaches for music source separation, with new models and techniques enhancing performance and efficiency. Hybrid Demucs (HDemucs) was introduced, blending time-domain and frequencydomain processing to enhance the quality of audio separation [24]. HDemucs leverages the strengths of both domains, leading to state-of-the-art performance on benchmarks like MUSDB18. In 2022, further refinements were made to Demucs, incorporating advanced training techniques and architectures that enhanced its ability to separate complex mixtures [25].

Self-supervised and unsupervised learning approaches have been explored to reduce reliance on labeled data. RemixIT is a self-supervised learning framework leveraging mixtures of mixtures, enabling models to learn effectively from unlabeled data [26].

This approach has shown promise in improving separation performance without extensive labeled datasets. Researchers have explored multi-modal approaches incorporating additional contextual information to aid source separation. For example, visual cues from music videos have been used to inform audio separation models [27].

2.11 Challenges and Limitations

Despite advancements in deep learning-based music source separation, several challenges persist, including the need for high-quality, labeled datasets, which are limited and essential for supervised learning approaches. Training and deploying advanced models also require significant computational resources, potentially limiting accessibility for some practitioners. Models may also struggle to generalize to unseen genres, instruments, or recording conditions, and standard evaluation metrics like signal-to-distortion ratio (SDR) may not fully capture perceptual quality, necessitating more comprehensive evaluation methods.

3 Challenges with Traditional Machine Learning Approaches

3.1 Data Requirements

Deep learning models necessitate extensive training data, which can be challenging to obtain due to licensing restrictions and the scarcity of isolated instrument tracks [2]. Limited datasets hinder the models' generalization to different genres and recording conditions.

3.2 Computational Complexity

Training and deploying deep neural networks for source separation is computationally intensive. High-performance hardware and prolonged training times are required, making it impractical for many users [28].

3.3 Lack of Flexibility

Models trained on specific datasets may not perform well when applied to diverse music or audio contexts. Retraining or fine-tuning is often necessary, which is resourceintensive and limits the adaptability of these models [29].

4 Large Language Models and Their Potential Application

4.1 Overview of Large Language Models

Large Language Models like GPT-4 have demonstrated remarkable capabilities in understanding and generating human-like text [3, 30]. These models leverage transformer architectures and are pre-trained on vast amounts of textual data, enabling them to perform a wide range of language tasks without task-specific training.

4.2 Extending LLMs Beyond Text

While LLMs are primarily designed for text-based applications, researchers are exploring their potential in other domains. For instance, LLMs have been used for code generation [31], and there is growing interest in applying them to multimodal tasks that involve both text and non-textual data.

LLMs have been increasingly employed in multimodal applications, where integrating linguistic and non-linguistic data modalities enhances the performance of various tasks. In computer vision, LLMs have been pivotal in tasks like image captioning, where models generate descriptive textual captions for images. Early work by O. Vinyals [32] introduced a neural image caption generator that combined a convolutional neural network (CNN) for image feature extraction with a recurrent neural network (RNN) language model for caption generation. This approach was further advanced by K. Xu [33], who incorporated attention mechanisms to allow the model to focus on specific parts of an image when generating each caption word.

These advancements illustrate the potential of LLMs to serve as a bridge between different data modalities, enhancing the performance of systems that rely on understanding and generating human-like language in conjunction with visual or auditory information. The success of LLMs in these multimodal applications motivates their exploration in other domains, such as audio signal processing, where they can provide semantic context to improve tasks like Music Source Separation.

5 Prompt Engineering

5.1 Concept and Techniques

Prompt engineering involves crafting input prompts that guide LLMs to produce desired outputs [34]. By carefully designing these prompts, users can leverage the model's pre-trained knowledge to perform specific tasks without altering the model's architecture.

5.2 Applications in LLMs

In natural language processing, prompt engineering has improved question-answering, translation, and summarization tasks [35]. For example, providing context-rich prompts can enhance the model's accuracy in generating relevant responses.

5.3 Potential in Music Source Separation

Applying prompt engineering to music source separation involves creating prompts instructing the LLM to perform audio-related tasks. Examples include:

"Analyze the provided mixed audio file and separate it into individual tracks for vocals, guitar, bass, and drums."

"Given this audio sample, isolate the vocal components and provide a transcript of the lyrics."

"Separate the instrumental sections from the following song, focusing on the piano and violin parts."

These prompts utilize the LLM's language understanding capabilities to interpret and act upon audio data.

6 Retrieval-Augmented Generation (RAG)

6.1 Concept and Mechanism

Retrieval-augmented generation combines LLMs with external knowledge sources to enhance their performance on tasks requiring up-to-date or specialized information [36]. The model retrieves relevant data from external databases during generation, which informs and improves its output.

6.2 Implementation in LLMs

RAG has been successfully applied in knowledge-intensive tasks such as open-domain question answering and fact-checking [37]. The LLM can provide more accurate and contextually relevant responses by accessing external documents or databases.

6.3 Application to Music Source Separation

In the context of music source separation, RAG can enable the LLM to access: Audio Embeddings: By converting audio data into embeddings using pre-trained audio models and indexing them in a vector database, the LLM can retrieve similar audio patterns that assist in separation tasks. Lyric and Score Alignment: Accessing lyrics and musical scores databases allow the LLM to align audio signals with textual content, aiding in identifying and isolating specific vocal or instrumental tracks.

Retrieving sound profiles of different instruments helps the LLM distinguish between instruments within a mixed audio signal, improving separation accuracy. For example, when processing a prompt like "Separate the electric guitar and provide its isolated track from this song," the LLM will generate a query by formulating a search query based on the prompt to retrieve relevant data (e.g., electric guitar sound profiles) from external databases. Use RAG to access and retrieve necessary embeddings or reference tracks. Utilize the retrieved information to guide the separation algorithm, isolating the electric guitar from the mixed audio.

7 Integration of LLMs, Prompt Engineering, and RAG in Music Source Separation

7.1 Leveraging Existing Capabilities

Combining prompt engineering and RAG allows LLMs to perform music source separation effectively without retraining. This approach capitalizes on the model's existing language understanding and reasoning abilities, augmented by real-time data retrieval.

7.2 Advantages of Traditional Methods

Efficiency: Eliminates the need for extensive training on large datasets.
Flexibility: Can adapt to various audio contexts by accessing diverse external data.
Accessibility: Reduces computational resources required, making the technology more accessible to users without specialized hardware.

7.3 Challenges and Considerations

Data Availability: The effectiveness of RAG depends on the availability and quality of external databases. Licensing and Copyright: Ensuring compliance with intellectual property laws when accessing and using external data is crucial [38].

Model Limitations: LLMs are not inherently designed for audio processing; their ability to interpret audio data relies on how sound prompts and retrieval mechanisms are implemented.

8 Existing Research and Gaps

While there is burgeoning interest in expanding the capabilities of LLMs beyond text, research specifically focusing on using LLMs for music source separation via prompt engineering and RAG is limited. Previous studies have explored cross-modal tasks, such as generating music from text descriptions [39]. However, the direct application of LLMs in audio processing still needs to be explored. This gap presents an opportunity to investigate how LLMs can be effectively utilized in music source separation, leveraging prompt engineering and RAG to overcome the limitations of traditional methods.

9 Conclusion

The literature highlights significant challenges in traditional music source separation methods, including data requirements, computational complexity, and lack of flexibility. Large Language Models, combined with prompt engineering and Retrieval Augmented Generation, offer a promising alternative by leveraging existing capabilities without retraining. LLMs can potentially perform complex audio tasks by crafting effective prompts and integrating external data retrieval, making source separation more accessible and efficient. This innovative approach addresses a notable gap in current research and has the potential to significantly impact both academic and practical aspects of audio processing in music technology.

References

1. Vincent, E., Gribonval, R., Févotte, C.: Performance measurement in blind audio source separation. IEEE Trans. Audio Speech Lang. Process. **14**(4), 1462–1469 (2006)
2. Rafii, Z., Liutkus, A., Stöter, F.-R., Mimilakis, S.I., Bittner, R.: MUSDB18 - a Corpus for Music Separation (2017). f10.5281/zenodo.1117371ff. ffhal-02190845f
3. OpenAI: GPT-4 Technical Report (2023). Retrieved from https://openai.com/research/gpt4
4. Comon, P.: Independent component analysis, a new concept? Signal Process. **36**(3), 287–314 (1994)
5. Lee, D.D., Seung, H.S.: Learning the parts of objects by non-negative matrix factorization. Nature **401**(6755), 788–791 (1999)
6. Smaragdis, P., Brown, J.C.: Non-negative matrix factorization for polyphonic music transcription. In: IEEE Workshop on Applications of Signal Processing to Audio and Acoustics, pp. 177–180 (2003)
7. Zibulevsky, M., Pearlmutter, B.A.: Blind source separation by sparse decomposition in a signal dictionary. Neural Comput. **13**(4), 863–882 (2001)
8. Van Veen, B.D., Buckley, K.M.: Beamforming: a versatile approach to spatial filtering. IEEE ASSP Mag. **5**(2), 4–24 (1988)
9. Cichocki, A., Amari, S.: Adaptive Blind Signal and Image Processing: Learning Algorithms and Applications. John Wiley & Sons (2002)
10. Virtanen, T.: Monaural sound source separation by nonnegative matrix factorization with temporal continuity and sparseness criteria. IEEE Trans. Audio Speech Lang. Process. **15**(3), 1066–1074 (2007)

11. Huang, P.-S., Kim, M., Hasegawa-Johnson, M., Smaragdis, P.: Joint optimization of masks and deep recurrent neural networks for monaural source separation. IEEE/ACM Trans. Audio Speech Lang. Process. **23**(12), 2136–2147 (2015)
12. Jansson, A., Humphrey, E.J., Montecchio, N., Bittner, R., Kumar, A., Weyde, T.: Singing voice separation with deep U-Net convolutional networks. In: 18th International Society for Music Information Retrieval Conference, pp. 745–751 (2017)
13. Nugraha, A.A., Liutkus, A., Vincent, E.: Multichannel music separation with deep neural networks. In: 2016 24th European Signal Processing Conference (EUSIPCO), pp. 1748–1752. IEEE (2016)
14. Chandna, P., Miron, M., Janer, J., Gómez, E.: Monoaural audio source separation using deep convolutional neural networks. In 2017 25th European Signal Processing Conference (EUSIPCO), pp. 291–295. IEEE (2017)
15. Stoller, D., Ewert, S., Dixon, S.: Wave-U-Net: a multi-scale neural network for end-to-end audio source separation. In: 19th International Society for Music Information Retrieval Conference, pp. 334–340 (2018)
16. Goodfellow, I., et al.: Generative adversarial nets. In: Advances in Neural Information Processing Systems, pp. 2672–2680 (2014)
17. Pascual, S., Bonafonte, A., Serrà, J.: SEGAN: speech enhancement generative adversarial network. Interspeech **2017**, 3642–3646 (2017)
18. Mogren, O.: C-RNN-GAN: Continuous Recurrent Neural Networks with Adversarial Training (2016). arXiv preprint arXiv:1611.09904
19. Takahashi, N., Mitsufuji, Y.: Multi-scale multi-band DenseNets for audio source separation. In: 2017 IEEE Workshop on Applications of Signal Processing to Audio and Acoustics (WASPAA), pp. 21–25. IEEE (2017)
20. Hershey, J.R., Chen, Z., Le Roux, J., Watanabe, S.: Deep clustering: discriminative embeddings for segmentation and separation. In: 2016 IEEE International Conference on Acoustics, Speech, and Signal Processing (ICASSP), pp. 31–35. IEEE (2016)
21. Luo, Y., Mesgarani, N.: Conv-TasNet: Surpassing ideal time–frequency magnitude masking for speech separation. IEEE/ACM Trans. Audio Speech Lang. Process. **27**(8), 1256–1266 (2019)
22. Subakan, C., Ravanelli, M., Cornell, S., Bronzi, M., & Zhong, J.: Attention is all you need in speech separation. In Proceedings of the IEEE International Conference on Acoustics, Speech, and Signal Processing (ICASSP), pp. 21–25. IEEE (2021)
23. Liao, W., et al.: Music Foundation Model as Generic Booster for Music Downstream Tasks (2024). arXiv preprint arXiv:2411.01135
24. Défossez, A.: Hybrid Spectrogram and Waveform Source Separation (2021). arXiv preprint arXiv:2111.03600
25. Défossez, A.: Hybrid Demucs v3: high fidelity music source separation. In: Proceedings of the 23rd International Society for Music Information Retrieval Conference (ISMIR 2022) (2022)
26. Tzinis, E., Adi, Y., Ithapu, V.K., Xu, B., Smaragdis, P., Kumar, A.: Remixit: continual self-training of speech enhancement models via bootstrapped remixing. IEEE J. Sel. Top. Signal Process. **16**(6), 1329–1341 (2022)
27. Gan, C., Wang, Y., Torralba, A.: Look, listen, and act: towards audio-visual embodied navigation. In: Proceedings of the IEEE/CVF Conference on Computer Vision and Pattern Recognition, pp. 13582–13591 (2022)
28. Stöter, F.-R., Liutkus, A., Ito, N.: The 2018 signal separation evaluation campaign. In: International Conference on Latent Variable Analysis and Signal Separation, pp. 293–305 (2018). Springer

29. Uhlich, S., Giron, F., Mitsufuji, Y.: Deep neural network-based instrument extraction from music. In: 2017 IEEE International Conference on Acoustics, Speech, and Signal Processing (ICASSP), pp. 546–550 (2017)
30. Brown, T.B., et al.: Language models are few-shot learners. Adv. Neural. Inf. Process. Syst. **33**, 1877–1901 (2020)
31. Chen, M., et al.: Evaluating Large Language Models Trained on Code (2021). arXiv preprint arXiv:2107.03374
32. Vinyals, O., Toshev, A., Bengio, S., Erhan, D.: Show and tell: a neural image caption generator. In: Proceedings of the IEEE Conference on Computer Vision and Pattern Recognition, pp. 3156–3164 (2015)
33. Xu, K., et al.: Show, attend and tell: neural image caption generation with visual attention. In: Proceedings of the 32nd International Conference on Machine Learning, pp. 2048–2057 (2015)
34. Reynolds, L., McDonell, K.: Prompt Programming for Large Language Models: Beyond the Few-Shot Paradigm (2021). arXiv preprint arXiv:2102.07350
35. Liu, P., Yuan, W., Fu, J., Jiang, Z., Hayashi, H., Neubig, G.: Pre-train, Prompt, and Predict: a Systematic Survey of Prompting Methods in Natural Language Processing (2021). arXiv preprint arXiv:2107.13586
36. Lewis, P., et al.: Retrieval-augmented generation for knowledge-intensive NLP tasks. In: Advances in Neural Information Processing Systems, pp. 9459–9474 (2020)
37. Izacard, G., Grave, E.: Leveraging passage retrieval with generative models for open domain question answering. In: Proceedings of the 16th Conference of the European Chapter of the Association for Computational Linguistics, pp. 874–880 (2021)
38. Floridi, L., Cowls, J.: A unified framework of five principles for AI in society. Harvard Data Sci. Rev. **1**(1), 5 (2019)
39. Yang, L.-C., Chou, S.-Y., Yang, Y.-H.: MidiNet: a convolutional generative adversarial network for symbolic-domain music generation. In: Proceedings of the 18th International Society for Music Information Retrieval Conference, pp. 324–331

Beyond Supervision: HyMoBY-Swin Hybrid Self-guided and Adaptive Learning Transformer for Multiclass Retinal Disease Diagnosis

Muhammad Hammad Malik[1], Ghulam Mudassir[2], Yingying Ren[1,3], and Da-Wei Ding[1,3](✉)

[1] School of Automation and Electrical Engineering, University of Science and Technology Beijing, Beijing 100083, China
dingdawei@ustb.edu.cn

[2] School of Computing, The University of Buckingham, Buckingham MK181EG, UK

[3] Key Laboratory of Knowledge Automation for Industrial Processes, Ministry of Education, University of Science and Technology Beijing, Beijing 100083, China

Abstract. Early detection of eye diseases, such as Diabetic Retinopathy (DR), Cataract, and Glaucoma, as well as the ability to accurately differentiate these from Normal conditions, is critical for preventing irreversible vision loss and improving patient outcomes. However, accurate and automated classification from fundus images remains a challenge due to the scarcity of labeled data and the limitations of conventional supervised learning. To address this, we propose a novel hybrid learning framework that integrates Momentum Bootstrap Your Own Latent (MoBY) with a Swin Transformer backbone for precise and robust multi-class eye disease classification. The proposed model first undergoes self-supervised pretraining to extract discriminative features from unlabeled images, followed by supervised fine-tuning on limited labeled data for task-specific adaptation. HyMoBY-Swin employs the Swin Transformer backbone for deep feature extraction. These features are refined through contrastive learning by maximizing similarity between augmented views of the same image while minimizing overlap with unrelated samples. Supervised fine-tuning further enhances generalization across both labeled and unlabeled data. Extensive experiments on the OIH dataset, comprising 4,215 fundus images, demonstrate that HyMoBY-Swin achieves a robust test accuracy of 92.43%, with consistently strong performance across all four categories. Diabetic retinopathy demonstrated the highest precision and sensitivity, both at 0.98, along with a leading ROC-AUC score of 0.99, followed by cataract (0.96), glaucoma (0.93), and normal cases (0.92). Ablation studies reveal that HyMoBY-Swin significantly outperforms its individual components and other state-of-the-art baselines, demonstrating the effectiveness of the combined contrastive learning and transformer-based architecture. Furthermore, t-SNE visualizations confirm the model's ability to clearly differentiate between disease categories, highlighting its strong generalization capacity across complex clinical scenarios. These results establish HyMoBY-Swin as an accurate and generalizable solution for real-world ophthalmic settings, offering significant clinical utility by reducing reliance on large annotated datasets and enhancing diagnostic efficiency.

S. Hussain et al. (Eds.): SEET 2025, CCIS 2725, pp. 125–153, 2026.
https://doi.org/10.1007/978-3-032-08977-9_10

Keywords: Fundus Image Classification · Hybrid Learning · Self-Supervised Learning · Supervised Learning · Contrastive Learning · HyMoBY-Swin

1 Introduction

Visual impairment worldwide stems from retinal diseases which include diabetic retinopathy (DR), glaucoma, and cataracts, since these conditions affect more than 450 million people and boost global blindness statistics [1]. Timely medical care becomes crucial for these diseases to stop vision loss in its a permanent state. Fundus photography has become the main non-invasive instrument for retinal condition diagnosis and screening since it provides detailed pictures of vascular structures along with the optic disc and macula [2]. Machine-based fundus image analysis keeps encountering obstacles for accurate disease classification because of changes in image capture conditions along with individual patient differences and overlapping disease indicators [3].

Convolutional Neural Networks (CNNs) and other deep learning approaches demonstrate good performance levels for diagnosing retinal diseases. The reliance of these models upon extensive annotated data sets proves challenging because expert annotation requirements make them difficult to acquire [4]. A lack of sufficient medical dataset labeling stands as the main obstacle to deep learning model deployment in real-world clinical applications, especially in areas which have few ophthalmic specialists to work. The restricted availability of medical data requires new scalable learning systems to achieve population generalization together with high accuracy results.

The classification of fundus images relies mainly on fully supervised deep learning models that need extensive expert-labeled datasets for operation. The notable success of CNN architectures like ResNet, EfficientNet and DenseNet exists despite their inability to work effectively in limited labeled data conditions because they use supervised learning [5]. Supervised deep learning models exhibit difficulties in adapting between different imaging domains because it leads to reduced clinical application effectiveness [4].

The integration of self-supervised learning (SSL) with transformer-based architectural methods provides potential solutions to these limitations. Self-supervised models leverage a huge amount of unlabeled data to learn valuable feature representations as they do not need human-provided annotations [6, 7]. However, medical applications require supervised fine-tuning using limited labeled data since this process helps refine representations for accurate classification. The feature learning abilities of Momentum Contrastive Learning (MoCo) achieve maximum performance through contrastive learning that differentiates alike from different image pairs, which enhances feature representation quality [7, 8]. The Swin Transformer system, which utilizes hierarchical self-attention algorithms delivers top-quality results in medical imaging analysis through its ability to recognize local and global contextual relationships [9].

The present research lacks an effective hybrid learning framework that integrates self-supervised contrastive pretraining with supervised fine-tuning, particularly for retinal disease classification. Most self-supervised methods only work on natural image datasets [8], but researchers have not yet fully developed their use for fundus imaging. The observed research gap of an appropriate framework shows researchers need to create a scalable deep learning system that utilizes self-supervised learning with transformer-based models to obtain accurate predictions from limited annotation data.

Retinal disease classification faces enormous obstacles particularly in regions that lack sufficient resources because such areas have limited access to high-quality labeled datasets. Countries at various developmental stages fail to maintain adequate infras tructures for systematic medical imaging dataset annotation which intensifies data scarcity challenges [10]. Medical imaging models require capabilities to generalize across low-resource situations while processing unlabeled data to reduce necessary annotations.

The correct identification of retinal diseases faces crucial challenges because of the mistaken grouping of such conditions. Glaucoma and DR have similar retinal characteristics which produce diagnostic confusion for CNN-based detection systems [4]. Self-supervised approaches should be developed because they need to discover robust features that identify small disease pattern differences to enhance classification across various datasets.

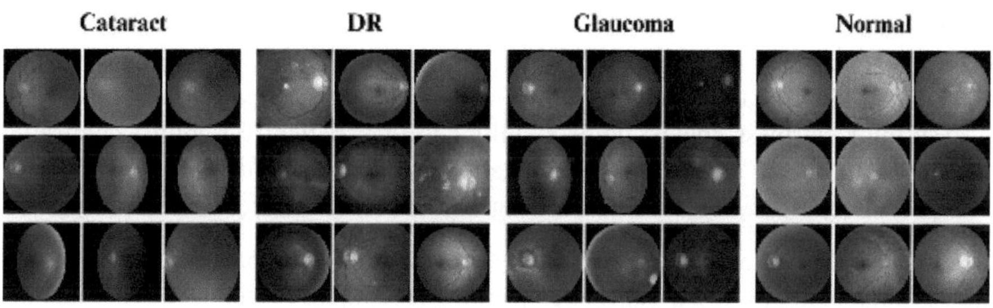

Fig. 1. OIH fundus dataset for eye disease classification

To the best of our knowledge, research findings regarding the implementation of MoBY along with Swin Transformers for retinal disease analysis are unavailable in peer-reviewed academic publications. There exists no documented academic investigation in published literature regarding this combination of MoBY and Swin Transformers for fundus image analysis. A research gap exists regarding MoBY and Swin Transformers combination for retinal disease classification, so this study establishes and tests rigorously a hybrid framework for self-supervised contrastive pretraining and supervised fine-tuning. The proposed methodology shows effectiveness at improving diagnostic performance in limited-label environments, demonstrating its potential for scalable, high-precision retinal disease diagnosis.

In this study, we introduce a novel Swin-MoBY Self-Supervised Learning approach for multiclass classification of eye diseases, including Cataracts, Diabetic Retinopathy, Glaucoma, and Normal, using color fundus photography (CFP) images, as illustrated in Fig. 1. The proposed learning technique bridges Self-Supervised Pretraining (MoBY) with Supervised Fine-Tuning (Swin Transformer) to achieve effective processing of fundus images. The model makes use of unlabeled data through SSL to discover features while SL (supervised learning) works with small quantities of labeled data to optimize representation ability for better disease diagnosis outcomes. The contributions of this research consist of:

1) We propose HyMoBY-Swin, a novel hybrid learning framework that integrates Self-Supervised Pretraining (MoBY) with Supervised Fine-Tuning (Swin Transformer) for fundus image classification. Unlike existing models that rely solely on fully supervised learning or self-supervised feature extraction, our approach leverages both labeled and unlabeled data synergistically. This hybrid strategy enhances feature representation and maintains high classification accuracy, even with minimal labeled data. As a result, it proves highly effective for detecting visually similar retinal diseases.
2) This study pioneers the application of MoBY for fundus eye disease classification by introducing an Adaptive Representation Refinement strategy, built upon a momentum contrastive learning framework that integrates MoCo-style memory queues with BYOL-based self-distillation. This combined mechanism preserves domain-invariant features while effectively suppressing pseudo-label noise during supervised fine-tuning. The resulting framework reduces reliance on large labeled datasets and offers a scalable, robust solution for automated fundus image analysis under real-world, low-label conditions.
3) Our experimental validation of the model is conducted on the OIH dataset which contains 4215 images, demonstrating state-of-the-art accuracy of 92.43% while ensuring robustness against domain shifts and inter-patient variability, confirming its hybrid learning approach's generalization capacity and suitability for real-world deployment, especially in clinical settings with limited resources.

This research develops a data-efficient screening tool that connects medical image classification methods to self-supervised learning techniques for retinal disease identification. The results of our work demonstrate the importance of contrastive self-supervised learning in ophthalmology by creating new possibilities to use AI-driven diagnostic models in healthcare facilities that lack adequate labeled data.

The rest of this article is organized as follows: Sect. 2 explores related work and discusses advancements in fundus image classification. Section 3 describes the materials and methods, focusing on the development of the proposed hybrid learning framework. Section 4 presents the results, discusses the model's performance through comprehensive experiments, and includes ablation studies as well as comparisons with recent state-of-the-art approaches. Lastly, Sect. 5 summarizes the key findings and suggests potential directions for future research.

2 Related Work

Modern fundus image classification has advanced because of deep-learning methodologies. The initial methods used machine learning in a traditional manner to detect abnormalities through manually created features. The computational efficiency of these methods proved insufficient to accurately understand the diverse characteristics found in retinal diseases therefore reducing their usefulness for broad dataset analysis. Through deep-learning models the diagnostic field experienced revolutionary transformations because these models performed automated disease classification and feature extraction which enhanced both accuracy and scalability capabilities.

Classification of fundus images mostly employs supervised deep learning through models including EfficientNet, ResNet, and DenseNet when detecting diabetic retinopathy and glaucoma conditions [11]. The good performance on annotated datasets comes at a cost because these models need extensive labeled datasets which makes them difficult to scale for real clinical work. The performance of these models drops dramatically during testing on datasets with domain shift which creates hurdles for achieving effective cross-institutional generalization according to [12]. Supervised models achieve poor diagnostic outcomes with limited reliability because they tend to overfit training data that contains small or imbalanced datasets of rare diseases.

Current research has succeeded in disease classification for a single condition yet such limited models cannot adapt to various situations. Transfer learning applications by [13] resulted in glaucoma detection using an AUC of 0.94 and sensitivity and specificity measurements of 87.01% and 89.01% respectively. The single-disease analytical approach represents a limitation because it cannot easily detect multiple diseases in clinical environments where multi-disease detection is essential.

Many researchers have investigated multi-disease classification approaches as a solution to these system constraints. ManualNet is a multi-model CNN that [14] developed to reach an accuracy rate of 80.78%. Multiple CNN integrations brought more unique features to the model but led to operational difficulties when deploying systems with limited resources. [15] combined AlexNet with VGGNet and ResNet-18 to reach an accuracy level of 89.23%, yet these models faced scaling issues with big datasets and overlapping disease features which deteriorated their medical value.

Extended retinal disease classification has become possible through the use of hybrid architectures along with advanced techniques. The authors [16] presented CRD-Net which combines multi-modal retinal images through a cross-modal attention framework to achieve 90% accuracy. Its dependence on labeled datasets along with extra imaging tests prevents the system from being usable in real-world applications. Advanced imaging approaches serve as the subject of research to make detection more effective. The research of [17] used ultra-wide-field fundus imaging to detect diabetic retinopathy with 91.5% AUC and 83.38% accuracy values. The drawback of this technique is its dependence on specific hardware components because it offers complete retinal images but remains inaccessible for general practical medical purposes.

Accomplishments in supervised learning are limited by the necessity of large labeled data collections. Self-supervised learning (SSL) has gained increasing attention due to its ability to extract valuable information from unlabeled data which substantially lowers the need for expert-supplied annotations. However, self-supervised learning models need SL techniques to optimize their performance with restricted labeled data sets for maintaining high data efficiency. Medical image classification through SSL has demonstrated performance equal to or superior to supervised learning especially when limited labeled data sets exist according to research conducted by [18, 19].

The method of contrastive learning within SSL frameworks produces best-in-class results for medical image assessment. Research by [20] showed that SSL methods offered better performance than conventional supervised procedures. In [21], the analysis of SSL improves generalization while enhancing robustness and computing speed specifically for processing unidentified medical data.

Medical image classification has moved forward through the development of three different contrastive SSL frameworks: MoCo and BYOL along SimCLR. MoCo employs momentum encoders to enhance feature characteristics and BYOL abolishes the utilization of negative samples. [22] showed that contrastive SSL methods perform at the same level as supervised learning by needing much less labeled data. [23] demonstrated that SSL-based models demonstrate enhanced capabilities to operate under shifting medical image conditions and across different domains, thus making them suitable for clinical applications. The Deep Semi-Supervised and Self-Supervised Learning for Diabetic Retinopathy Detection research yielded 94% AUC results on EyePACS as well as 89% AUC performance on Messidor-2 through the utilization of 2% labeled data [24].

The existing SSL models experience three primary obstacles consisting of their dependency on vast unlabeled data sources together with high computational costs and the need for a fine-tuning stage to optimize learned representations for disease classification. Through SSL one can extract robust features but specific clinical tasks need supervised fine-tuning to adapt these features to enhance diagnostic accuracy while avoiding excessive labeled data usage. The research by [25] demonstrated limited performance levels through their application of Swin Transformers to detect diabetic retinopathy with 56.8% accuracy and 83.4% AUC. [26] presented OCT-SelfNet with a self-supervised framework that produced AUC-ROC values greater than 77%, although its large required datasets and excessive computational needs restricted its scalability. The team of [27] created NPID which is a deep learning model for AMD grading that uses retinal fundus images to reach 82% accuracy on par with ophthalmologist performance. The feature similarity clustering approach used by the model fails to detect subtle AMD patterns while reducing its ability to generalize to various conditions. [28] developed Self-FI as a self-supervised framework for diagnosing ultra-wide-field fundus images by implementing contrastive learning with an AUC of 86.96%. The method faces limitations in general applicability because it depends on small labels from a fine-tuning process in addition to working with one particular group of subjects. An integrated graph convolutional network with self-supervision used by [29] resulted in AUC scores of 78.16% for ODIR and 69.83% for GTest. The use of a graph-based approach by this method relies on minimal co-occurrence data so it restricts its potential application range. The researchers at [30] developed a self-supervised diabetic retinopathy classification system through VGG16-based sequence prediction with sub-image partitioning which demonstrated 66.7% accuracy on APTOS and 62.4% on EyePACS. Relying on sub-image division produces two negative effects of losing global context alongside diagnostic features. The authors of [31] developed ERCN through unsupervised contrast pre-training and spatial masking and an attention-based module which generated test results of 87.4% for EyePACS and 88.7% for DAVIS. The self-supervised training model depends on intricate methods which need thorough hyperparameter adjustments that impact both reproducibility and scalability.

Momentum Contrastive Learning combined with Swin Transformers (HyMoBY-Swin) forms our proposed solution for resolving these technical obstacles because it performs self-supervised momentum contrastive pretraining alongside supervised fine-tuning for retinal disease classification. The proposed approach differs from conventional self-supervised learning techniques by incorporating supervised fine-tuning on limited labeled data after the self-supervised pretraining stage, thereby enhancing decision boundaries and improving classification performance in resource-constrained scenarios. Our method improves the performance of feature learning by boosting efficiency while reducing pseudo-label errors and uses Swin Transformer to increase the distance models can span for superior structural feature extraction. The experimental results show HyMoBY-Swin exceeds all other SSL and supervised models by attaining state-of-the-art results in detecting retinal diseases.

3 Materials and Methods

3.1 Architecture Overview

HyMoBY-Swin represents a novel framework as describe in Fig. 2 which solves the challenge of label scarcity in fundus image samples through both self-supervised learning (SSL) methods and transformer-based feature extraction techniques. Momentum Bootstrap Your Own Latent (MoBY) joins together with the Swin Transformer backbone inside an architecture which allows the model to optimize both labeled and unlabeled data while detecting complex retinal structures. The framework eliminates the necessity of manual annotations at scale to provide an efficient solution which produces high-performance results in retinal disease classification.

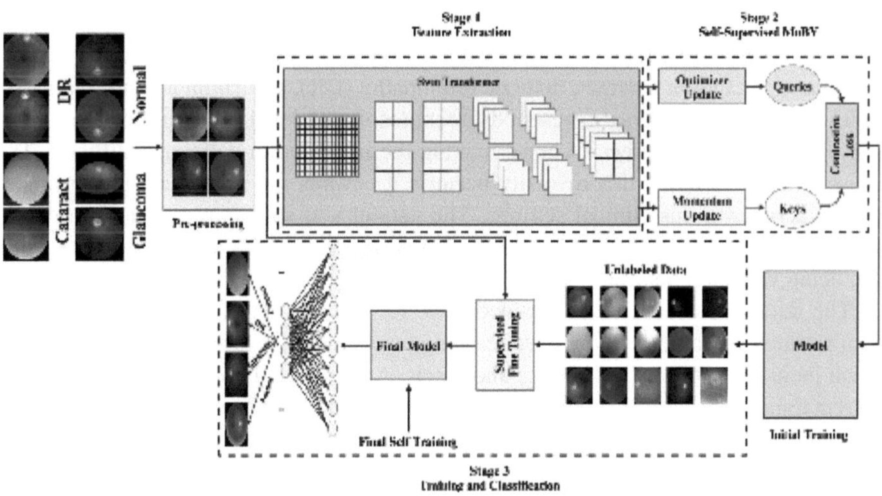

Fig. 2. Proposed architecture of the HyMoBY-Swin framework for retinal disease classification

The process starts with preprocessing steps which include image resizing to 224 × 224 pixels and normalization using ImageNet statistics and random horizontal and vertical flipping along with scaling. The modeling process obtains a broader set of features which protects against fitting excessively to one particular retinal imaging condition.

During self-supervised pretraining MoBY operates through its query encoder and momentum encoder system that processes unlabeled images. The query encoder receives traditional backpropagation but the momentum encoder updates exponentially to preserve its stable features. A memory queue stores previous negative samples in order to enhance contrastive learning operations without causing computational overload issues. The system optimization uses contrastive loss to both align different views of input data and maximize inter-class separability.

After model pretraining occurs the model undergoes fine-tuning with labeled data for supervised classification purposes. During this stage the model uses cross-entropy loss alongside SGD with momentum optimization while controlling the learning rate through a ReduceLROnPlateau scheduler based on validation accuracy assessments. The final classification layer sends output predictions to determine between four disease types including cataract and diabetic retinopathy and glaucoma and normal.

The framework achieves computational efficiency and numerical stability through the combination of gradient scaling (GradScaler) within mixed-precision training and operation at 16 batches for 120 epochs. Such optimization methods allow convergence stability while using minimal memory resources.

By using the combination of self-supervised feature learning, hierarchical attention mechanism and contrastive representation alignment, the HyMoBY-Swin framework produces a highly label-efficient and scalable solution for retinal disease classification. The architectural design suits clinical applications because real-world medical information lacks reliable substantial data that is both scarce and excessively costly.

3.2 Description of Eye Diseases Dataset

The OIH dataset features 4,215 retinal fundus images that are assigned different disease classes including cataract, diabetic retinopathy (DR), glaucoma and normal cases. Various images in the dataset present different resolution levels and lighting conditions and display varying degrees of noise making the information collection difficult. The dataset should maintain this diversity because it ensures the model can perform adequately across various clinical settings. The dataset was split into training, validation and test sets to build an effective model trained on a substantial amount of data while also being validated on a separate set to prevent overfitting.

The data labeled at 26% contained 80% for training and 20% for validation as demonstrated by Table 1. Supervised learning involved images from the labeled dataset which included both image contents and labels. An unlabeled portion of 64% made up the remaining dataset for self-supervised learning purposes. The model acquired essential data features through its self-supervised learning mechanism because the unlabeled section contained information from which it could extract beneficial features without extensive human verification. The model gained improved learning efficiency and generalizability by using self-supervised learning because it was equipped with an extensive unlabeled dataset subset.

The model evaluation relied on a test set totaling 10% that served as the benchmark to determine generalization capabilities while evaluating performance. The organized database partition method allowed training the model with both labeled and unlabeled information for evaluating its performance across various learning approaches.

Table 1. Distribution of the OIH Dataset

Classes	Labeled Data		Test Data (10%)	Unlabeled Data (64%)
	Training Data (80%)	Validation Data (20%)		
Cataract	224	46	104	
Diabetic Retinopathy	224	62	110	
Glaucoma	208	54	101	
Normal	221	58	108	
Total	877	220	423	2695

3.3 Preprocessing and Augmentation of the Dataset

Robust and generalizable features for the model depend on data preprocessing together with data augmentation methods because retinal images contain a high level of variability. The processing of images involved normalization and size adjustment which produced homogeneous images of 224 × 224 pixels to work within Swin Transformer specifications. Image normalization with ImageNet standard deviation and mean parameters made the model insensitive to different lighting conditions. The normalization formula used was Eq. (1):

$$N = \frac{I - \mu}{\sigma} \tag{1}$$

The normalization process uses N as its notation alongside I as image number $\mu = [0.485, 0.456, 0.406]$ and $\sigma = [0.229, 0.224, 0.225]$ to align weights and steadify numeric values throughout training.

The dataset received additional content from random horizontal and vertical flippings. The model acquired the ability to detect retinal diseases by using multiple position variants which replicate actual diagnostic circumstances. During training the model received dynamically generated augmented images that supplied a wide variety of sample data.

3.4 Feature Extraction with the Swin Transformer

The proposed system employs Swin Transformer [6] for feature extraction to analyze input images through a hierarchical vision transformer (ViT) architecture by partitioning images into non-overlapping patches. The model architecture enables it to detect global and local relationships within input data through an efficient processing method. At the beginning of the Swin Transformer architecture, the input image receives patch embedding processing which splits the image into 4 × 4-pixel sections. A flattening operation follows the linear embedding process that shoves each patch into an elevated dimensional feature domain.

This embedding is expressed as Eq. (2):

$$z_p = Wx_p + b \tag{2}$$

Here the raw pixel value of the patch x_p produces an output through the learnable matrix W and a bias term b.

Through shifted window attention the Swin Transformer achieves higher efficiency and recognizes connections between image regions that are not close to one another. Inside every window the self-attention operations use the scaled dot-product attention calculation as in Eq. (3):

$$Attention(Q, K, V) = softmax\left(\frac{QK^T}{\sqrt{d_k}}\right)V \tag{3}$$

The scaled dot-product attention formula obtains its input from $Q, K\ and\ V$ matrices as well as d_k which stands for key vector dimensionality. Through this mechanism the model dedicates its attention to important image elements while developing an understanding of the connections between adjacent regions. The shifted window procedure aligns the window in successive layers to achieve better information transfer across image segments beyond their initial boundaries. The model uses this method to detect extended dependencies throughout the image.

The model implements transformer blocks which contain MHSA (multi-head self-attention) and FFN (feed-forward networks) operations as components. The transformer block outputs transmit through a residual connection to enable information movement without interruptions in Eqs. (4) and (5):

$$Z_l = MHSA(Z_{l-1}) + Z_{l-1} \tag{4}$$

$$Z_l = FFN(Z_l) + Z_l \tag{5}$$

Each lth transformer block receives Z_{l-1} as its input and outputs Z_l following the combination of Multi-head Self-Attention and Feed-Forward Networks operations. Each consecutive block contributes to enhancing features in sequential order. These extracted features serve as input to the self-supervised learning process using MoBY, which refines their representations before fine-tuning for classification.

Figure 3 shows how the Swin Transformer architectural structure looks in our model. The model applies four stages for image processing through consecutive patch merging followed by Swin Transformer blocks. The hierarchical image downsampling enables the model to detect local and global dependencies within the image content. The Stage 1 operation initializes features with $\frac{H}{4} \times \frac{W}{4}$ resolution and 48 channels as the starting input. The resolution reduces at every successive stage by half yet feature dimensions double up leading to an output of $\frac{H}{32} \times \frac{W}{32}$ features with 768 dimensions. The extracted feature representation functions as the input during MoBY self-supervised learning for feature robustness refinement. The model-derived representations undergo supervised learning through which a limited set of labeled images enables the model adaptation for classification purposes to achieve generalization across new data.

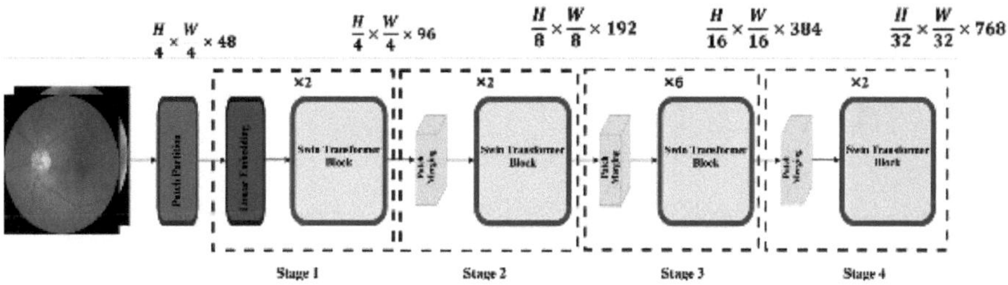

Fig. 3. Swin transformer architecture used in the proposed model

3.5 Self-Supervised Pretraining with MoBY

The proposed methodology utilizes Momentum Bootstrap Your Own Latent (MoBY) [32] for self-supervised pretraining, enabling the extraction of discriminative characteristics from unlabeled retinal images. MoBY integrates Momentum Contrastive Learning (MoCo) [5] and Bootstrap Your Own Latent (BYOL) [33], leveraging both contrastive and non-contrastive methods for effective feature learning. This hybrid approach enables adaptive representation refinement, where the model progressively enhances the quality of its learned features in an unsupervised manner, without the need for human annotation.

In the MoBY architecture shown in Fig. 4, two encoders, an online query encoder and a momentum encoder, process the fundus images through Swin Transformers. The query encoder is optimized using backpropagation, while the momentum encoder is updated gradually through an exponential moving average (EMA), which ensures the stability of learned features. The model employs contrastive loss to learn robust image features by measuring the similarity between query representations and key representations stored in the memory queue.

By integrating MoCo and BYOL, MoBY effectively refines its representations in an adaptive manner. MoCo utilizes its memory queue and contrastive loss to promote separation between positive and negative pairs, which increases the diversity of the learned representations. On the other hand, BYOL stabilizes the learning process by aligning positive samples without relying on negative pairs. Together, these methods enable MoBY to continuously improve feature representations, resulting in high-quality, stable, and diverse features throughout the pretraining phase. To further mitigate the impact of pseudo-label noise during the supervised fine-tuning phase, the momentum encoder's gradual update through EMA plays a crucial role. By ensuring the stability of the learned features and preventing drastic changes, the model reduces the influence of noisy pseudo-labels, thereby improving generalization and classification accuracy. This stability is especially important when transitioning from the self-supervised pretraining phase, where pseudo-labels are less reliable, to fine-tuning with a limited set of labeled data.

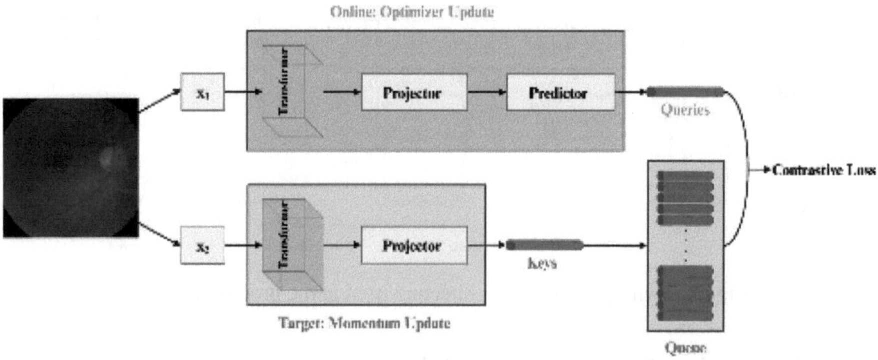

Fig. 4. Proposed self-supervised MoBY model for eye disease classification

Data augmentation with diverse techniques enabled the model to learn stable clinical features by creating various transformed image views from each input. The fundus images underwent two augmented view transformations x_1 and x_2 through procedures of random horizontal flipping, vertical flipping, resizing, and normalization before it was processed separately by the query and momentum encoders. The augmentation techniques required invariance across image transformations thus led the model to discover clinical features that demonstrate effective generalizability. The augmentation methods operated dynamically to improve self-supervised contrastive learning since they maintained representation stability throughout multiple image transformations. These augmentations are applied on the fly during the training process to continuously improve the model's robustness.

The representation learning adopted a contrastive loss function for maximizing positive pair similarity alongside negative pair separation. The system aligns similar positive examples through its loss function while maintaining clear separation between different elements. The goal of the algorithm is to align these embedded images by stacking them together. A memory queue keeps unrelated samples stored to maintain a diverse set of negatives. The contrastive loss function is expressed as Eq. (6), which computes the similarity between the representations of the augmented images:

$$L_{contrastive} = -\log \frac{exp(sim(f_\theta(x_1), f_\emptyset(x_2))\ominus/\tau)}{\sum_{k=1}^{K} exp(sim(f_\theta(x_1), f_\emptyset(x_k))/\tau)} \quad (6)$$

The model uses $f_\theta(x_1)$ and $f_\varnothing(x_2)$ from query and momentum encoders on two different image augmentations with value $\tau = 0.5$ for controlling distribution sharpness. The measurement of embedding similarity operates through the use of the $sim(a, b)$ function that calculates cosine similarity. The negative samples stored in the memory queue act as a dynamic storage system which delivers varied contrastive sets to each mini-batch operation during training to decrease both redundancy and computation requirements.

Time-dependent feature updates inside the momentum encoder become stable through EMA because it performs progressive averaging of past states. It provides the following definition of the updating process, Eq. (7):

$$\varnothing_{t+1} = \beta.\varnothing_t + (1 - \beta).\theta_t \quad (7)$$

The weights $\varnothing_t$ and θ_t from the momentum and query encoders at time step t are controlled by the $\beta = 0.999$ value which determines the amount of retained past knowledge. The gradual evolution of the momentum encoder through this method ensures both stable representation consistency and lower instability which commonly affects self-supervised learning procedures.

The utilized training approach included Stochastic Gradient Descent with an initial learning rate set to $1e^{-3}$ together with weight decay set to $1e^{-2}$. A ReduceLROnPlateau scheduler controls learning rate adjustments by decreasing it by 0.5 after validation loss stagnated for five epochs. Pleasant model updates and feasible computations were obtained through training that lasted for 120 epochs with 16 batches. The algorithm implemented GradScaler to achieve stability in numerical calculations during mixed-precision training without compromising the precision of operations.

During the final pretraining sequence, the momentum queue system stored previously seen negative samples to support contrastive learning operations without memory overload. The model created resilient feature representations that withstand variations in fundus images during this phase. The pretraining phase culminated in self-supervised learning which after its completion directed the acquired feature representations. A supervised fine-tuning phase applied afterwards tuned the model with a small quantity of labeled data to develop enhanced disease classification capabilities using previously gained unlabeled data information.

3.6 Fine-Tuning with Labeled Data

The self-supervised pretraining phase ended by transferring the learned feature representations to a second phase which adapted the model through supervised fine-tuning using labeled data. The fine-tuning stage makes use of minimal labeled data by keeping essential information gained from unlabeled images through pretrained features from the self-supervised phase which leads to better generalization.

After MoBY refines the feature representations, a fully connected (FC) layer is added during fine-tuning. This layer maps the refined feature embeddings to class logits, which are then converted into probability distributions using the softmax function, as described in Eq. (8):

$$P(y_i|x) = \frac{exp(z_i)}{\sum_{j=1}^{C} exp(z_j)} \tag{8}$$

During fine-tuning, the model applies a fully connected classification layer that outputs z_i, the score for class i, among the set of C classes. The softmax function then transforms these scores into probability values for classification.

The model parameters received optimization treatment through the cross-entropy loss function suitable for solving multi-class classification issues during this stage. The definition of the cross-entropy loss reads Eq. (9):

$$L_{CE} = -\sum_{c=1}^{C} y_c \log(\hat{y}_c) \tag{9}$$

where:

- C is the number of classes (4),
- y_c is the one-hot encoded ground truth for class c,
- $\hat{y}_c$ is the predicted probability for class c

This stage adjusts the model to specialize in distinguishing between retinal diseases.

The implementation of GradScaler for gradient scaling ensured both high numerical precision and prevented unstable conditions in mixed-precision training. Feasible lower-precision arithmetic operation became possible through this technique which ensured critical calculations maintained high-precision gradient operations. During fine-tuning the model employed Exponential Moving Average (EMA) updates for stabilizing parameter update processes. The model weight stability during fine-tuning improves through EMA which calculates an average of previous model states to reduce sudden weight changes.

During self-supervised pretraining, the model optimizes its feature representations using the contrastive loss function defined in Eq. (7). This loss helps learn effective feature embeddings without labeled data. After pretraining, the model undergoes supervised fine-tuning with labeled data, where the extracted features are optimized using a combination of labeled data and pretrained knowledge to improve generalization for classification. At this stage, the network is trained using the cross-entropy loss function as defined in Eq. (9). Unlike in pretraining, contrastive loss is no longer used once fine-tuning begins. At this stage, the model is optimized exclusively using the cross-entropy loss function, as given in Eq. (9). Thus, the final loss function for classification is:

$$L_{total} = L_{CE} \tag{10}$$

This ensures that the learned representations are refined specifically for classification without interference from contrastive learning.

4 Results and Discussion

This section details the outcomes of our proposed approach for classifying eye diseases and provides an in-depth analysis of the results.

4.1 Experimental Setup

This research adopts the OIH dataset that provides a total of 4217 fundus images divided between cataract and diabetic retinopathy (DR) together with glaucoma and normal categories. The preprocessing steps resulted in removing duplicate images so the final set contained 4215 unique images. The dataset contains images from different patient demographics and imaging devices which represent various real-life variations to challenge the classification process. The experimental framework utilized three portions of the dataset where 80% accounted for training and 20% functioned for validation purposes from the labeled data portion, 64% for unlabeled data used for self-supervised learning, while testing occurred in an independent directory containing 10% of the data. The training session combined labeled and unlabeled images where labeled examples performed supervised fine-tuning operations and unlabeled elements worked through contrastive learning for self-supervised learning. The data protection measures included balancing the data to achieve sufficient representation for each class before model training started.

Several data augmentation methods were used to improve the model's performance along with its generalization ability for training images. The data augmentation process incorporated three operations which included flipping images both horizontally and vertically while also transforming them to 224 × 224 pixels before performing normalization through ImageNet statistics. The model received these enhancement techniques during its training process for labeled as well as unlabeled data types. During contrastive learning of unlabeled data, the model received augmentations without normalization to develop robust discriminative features in an unsupervised environment. The normalization procedure was applied to fine-tuning for guaranteeing model training consistency.

The research adopted Momentum Contrastive Learning (MoBY) as a self-supervised learning approach that utilizes a momentum model. Requests to update the momentum model occur at a reduced speed compared to the main model while it develops improved feature perception for positive pairs of same-image augmentations and negative pairs from dissimilar classes. Swin Transformer stands as the base feature extraction model whose weights originate from ImageNet pre-training. The research selected this model because it exhibits effective capabilities to recognize both small-scale and whole-scale relationships in image data which proves advantageous during eye disease classification.

The training approach conducted its operation through two separate phases. The MobY framework performed self-supervised pre-training operations on unlabeled data. The model obtained generalized representations by processing the unlabeled dataset information in this phase. The training was performed for 120 epochs while adjusting the learning rate to 0.001 and implementing a 0.999 value for the momentum model's update process. This phase enabled the model to maximize its use of unlabeled data because scarce labeled information represents a common challenge. The training proceeded using batches containing 16 samples to achieve appropriate training efficiency within available computational resources. The model received supervised fine-tuning on labeled data as the final training step following pre-training. The SGD optimizer applied cross-entropy loss during fine-tuning while using a learning rate value of 0.01. Reducing the learning rate according to validation loss proceeded through 120 epochs using the ReduceLROnPlateau scheduler. The training process was accelerated and memory consumption decreased through GradScaler which provided mixed-precision training benefits necessary for Swin Transformer and other large transformer models.

The training procedures together with evaluation took place through PyTorch version 2.0.1 + cu118 while employing Python 3.9.18. NVIDIA GeForce RTX 3090 GPU served as the computing power during training operations to run the sizable Swin Transformer model effectively. The configured development platform in Visual Studio Code provided an optimized environment for developers to write code and execute tests and perform debugging procedures.

The hybrid learning framework used SSL for extracting strong feature representations from unlabeled datasets before performing SL to optimize these features with limited available labeled data. The combination of two different learning methods for the model produced outstanding results because it used both labeled and unlabeled data effectively. Through the combination of Swin Transformers with MoBY we optimized the usefulness of both labeled and unlabeled data which in turn increased model performance in medical imaging obstacles involving limited annotated data.

4.2 Performance Evaluation Metrics

Multiple performance metrics were selected for evaluation purposes to examine the effectiveness of the proposed framework in multi-class retinal disease classification. Multiple performance metrics have been selected because they provide quantitative and qualitative assessment methods for model evaluation throughout different disease classes.

The Sensitivity measure from Eq. (11) identifies the percentage of correctly predicted true positives as expressed in a percentage value:

$$Sensitivity = \frac{TP}{TP + FN} \times 100 \tag{11}$$

where FN represents false negatives.

Precision (Eq. 12), or positive predictive value, measures the accuracy of predicted positives:

$$Precision = \frac{TP}{TP + FP} \times 100 \tag{12}$$

where FP is false positives.

Accuracy (Eq. 13) quantifies the proportion of correct predictions across all classes:

$$Accuracy = \frac{TP + TN}{TP + TN + FP + FN} \times 100 \tag{13}$$

where TN is true negatives.

The F1 score (Eq. 14) provides a combined measure of precision and sensitivity:

$$F1\ Score = \left(2 \cdot \frac{Precision \times Sensitivity}{Precision + Sensitivity}\right) \times 100 \tag{14}$$

The AUC (Area Under the Curve), given by Eqs. (15) and (16), measures the model's discriminatory power:

$$TPR = Sensitivity \tag{15}$$

against

$$FPR = 1 - Specificity \tag{16}$$

The AUC is calculated from the area under the curve generated by different threshold values.

The t-SNE allowed a visual representation of model-introduced feature embeddings to understand the clustering patterns of different classes in the feature space. The training and validation loss and accuracy curves were generated to track model convergence as well as to check for overfitting conditions during the training phase. The confusion matrix enabled deeper examination of how well the model predicted classifications because it showed predicted and actual results side by side. All models received consistent performance assessment through uniform usage of evaluation metrics. The methodology reduces subjective bias during evaluations so performance variations exclusively reflect the characteristics that define each model.

4.3 Performance Evaluation and Diagnostic Potential of the Proposed Model

When implemented with Swin Transformers the proposed method achieved a testing accuracy of 92.43% through self-supervised pretraining combined with supervised fine-tuning. The model demonstrates impressive accuracy for handling images that belong to cataract, diabetic retinopathy (DR), glaucoma and normal categories. Testing occurred on the OIH dataset which contains 4215 Color Fundus Photography images collected from Ocular Recognition as well as the Indian Diabetic Retinopathy Image Dataset and High-Resolution Fundus datasets. The model obtains better generalization against various image qualities and disease expressions, benefiting from self-supervised pretraining on unlabeled data and supervised fine-tuning using labeled fundus images. The model proved excellent at detecting diabetic retinopathy and cataract through its precision values reaching 0.98 and 0.91 respectively as in Table 2. The model reached optimal performance levels because it adopted a dual learning strategy between self-supervised feature learning and supervised fine-tuning which efficiently processed unlabeled and labeled fundus images. The predictive power of this model demonstrates its reliability through successful recognition of these conditions. The cataract and diabetic retinopathy recall results reached amounts of 0.94 and 0.98 respectively, reflecting the model's exceptional ability to discover most actual positive disease cases. The model maintains dependable disease classification for cataract and DR through F1-score results of 0.92 and 0.98 respectively.

The examination of glaucoma and normal eye conditions yielded inferior performance from the model. The model displayed a precision of 0.89 together with a recall of 0.90 which resulted in a slightly reduced F1-score of 0.90 for glaucoma classification. Some glaucoma fundus images were mistakenly identified as normal cases based on the analysis through the confusion matrix. The feature representations from self-supervised pretraining obtained strength while supervised fine-tuning refined decision boundaries to enhance classification accuracy. Labeled data use requires additional improvement to enhance the detection of faint glaucoma characteristics. Early-stage glaucoma shares very faint visual elements with regular fundus images because of which misclassifications become likely. Precision and recall values from the normal class test showed precision at 0.91 and recall at 0.87 indicating the presence of higher misclassification types. Subtle visual changes in normal images led to misclassification mistakes where the system identified such images as belonging to the glaucoma or cataract category. An F1-score of 0.89 for the normal class indicates that such errors in classification occurred.

The model exhibited consistent performance over all classes through precision, recall and F-measure values that equaled 0.92. The weighted average evaluation result of 0.92

considered class distributions to indicate consistent scoring ability. The model demonstrates performance effectiveness against multiple eye disease categories but needs additional development to enhance its ability to separate normal images from early-stage glaucoma scans.

The confusion matrix as shown in Fig. 5, unveiled specific classification problems which the model encountered. The majority of test images were correctly identified as diabetic retinopathy and cataract but the model struggled to differentiate between glaucoma and normal categories. The detected similarity between eye diseases represents a common issue in automatic disease monitoring when distinct diseases prove hard for detection systems to differentiate. The model requires further improvement in its capability to extract important features which distinguish subtle image differences between categories. Research should focus on perfecting both normal image classification detection alongside the segmentation ability between normal and glaucoma populations. This is particularly evident in the glaucoma vs. normal classes, where early pathological changes often resemble healthy fundus structures, making them difficult to distinguish even for expert clinicians. Future enhancements may explore finer-grained attention modeling or integration of auxiliary modalities such as OCT to support early-stage glaucoma recognition.

The model presents significant practical value despite the obstacles it faces. The system demonstrates an excellent capability to detect diabetic retinopathy while maintaining high accuracy and it becomes a useful instrument for early diagnosis needed to avoid permanent vision damage. Treatment facilities lacking sufficient access to ophthalmologists in rural areas gain help from this model to avoid diagnostic mistakes which leads to better patient end results. Additional development of this model indicates its potential to expand into multiple healthcare settings for automated eye disease diagnosis.

The proposed Momentum Contrastive Learning framework with Swin Transformers provides substantial capabilities for fundus image disease classification through a test accuracy rate of 92.43%. The model shows high success in detecting both cataract and diabetic retinopathy but needs additional development to improve glaucoma and normal image diagnosis. Further research needs to concentrate on enlarging the available data collection while also improving the model's feature extraction and glaucoma and normal condition classification accuracy to increase its effectiveness in medical settings.

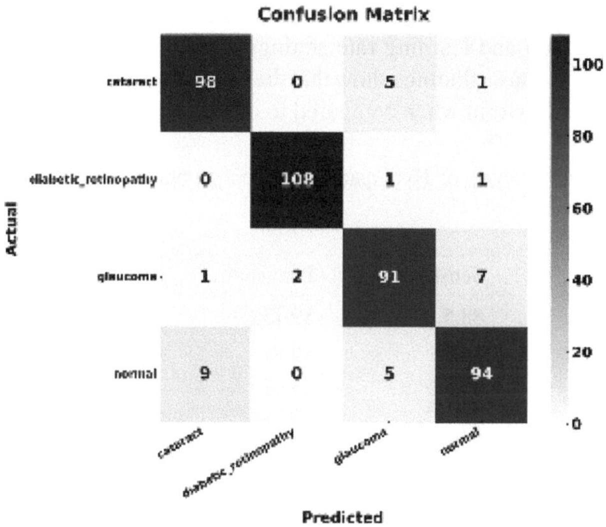

Fig. 5. Confusion matrix for model performance evaluation

Table 2. Class-Wise Metrics for the Proposed Model

Classes	Sensitivity	Precision	F1 Score
Cataract	94	91	92
DR	98	98	98
Glaucoma	90	89	90
Healthy	87	91	87
Accuracy			92.43

4.4 Ablation Study and Comparative Analysis

The evaluation of the HyMoBY-Swin model hyperparameter configurations appears in Table 3 with complete details. Testing of The Proposed Model demonstrates its peak performance through 92.43% accuracy while surpassing every other configuration. Steplr Scheduler (90.31% accuracy) and Label Smooth Loss (91.49% accuracy) show important roles in the accuracy performance due to their precise adjustment requirements. The performance of the AdaGrad Optimizer (34.04% accuracy) and RMSprop Optimizer (47.99% accuracy) is low compared to other optimizers since optimizer selection matters critically in complex tasks. Performance benefits from using batches with a size of 32 rather than 8 because the final accuracy rate reaches 89.83% while the smaller batch size leads to 89.60% accuracy and improves training process stability. Label Smooth Loss achieves better generalization and demonstrates valuable application when working to minimize the effects of noisy labels even though Focal Loss provides a lower 86.52% accuracy.

The study presents evidence about how parameter optimization specifically related to optimizer selection and learning rate settings and loss algorithms directly impacts model performance. These findings show that the hyperparameter settings chosen for our proposed model outperform when compared to others in achieving better performance.

Table 3. Systematic Analysis of Hyperparameter Configurations and Their Impact on Model Efficacy

	Sensitivity	Precision	F1 Score	Accuracy
Batch Size (8)	88.5	89.75	89.25	89.60
Batch Size (32)	88.75	89.75	89.75	89.83
AdaGrad Optimizer	34.5	33.75	30.25	34.04
RMSprop Optimizer	47.25	49.5	45.75	47.99
Cosine Scheduler	89.25	91.25	89.25	89.13
Step LR Scheduler	90.75	92.25	91.25	90.31
Label Smooth Loss	91.25	91.5	91.5	91.49
Focal Loss	86.5	86.5	86.5	86.52
Proposed Model	**92.25**	**92.25**	**92.25**	**92.43**

The data labeling extent directly influences model performance as illustrated in Table 4. A model with 65% accuracy using 5% labeled data gradually improves to 92.43% accuracy after 100% labeled data availability, thus enhancing all measurement metrics. The model's effectiveness remains high when working with restricted labeled information since it reaches 82% accuracy with 25% labeled data and 87% accuracy when using 50% labeled data. The rate of performance improvement slows down when labeling reaches 70% of the total dataset because most model optimization happens with complete labeling. The model demonstrates successful utilization of both self-supervised pretraining and supervised fine-tuning, making it highly useful for medical imaging contexts with sparse annotated datasets. The model demonstrates excellent performance ratios with scarce labeled data availability thereby indicating practical potential for clinical healthcare applications.

Table 4. Effect of Labeled Data Proportions on the Performance of the Proposed Model

Labeled Data %	Sensitivity	Precision	F1 Score	Accuracy
5%	63.5	69	63	65
25%	79	82	82	82
50%	87	84	87	87
70%	88.5	89	88.5	89
Proposed Model (100%)	**92.25**	**92.25**	**92.25**	**92.43**

Several backbone architectures perform according to Table 5 within the HyMoBY-Swin framework. The Proposed Model which employs Swin Transformer delivers maximum accuracy at 92.43% while surpassing all other frameworks including ResNet50 at 91.73%, DenseNet121 at 91.96%, EfficientNetB0 at 90.31% and SqueezeNet1_0 at 83.22% in accuracy levels. The classification capability of fundus images reaches peak levels through this model with a precision equivalent to 92.25% and an F1-score of 92.25%. The MoCo method applied to the HyMoBY-Swin model boosts performance through better feature extraction since it dynamically handles previously unseen data. The Swin Transformer's exceptional feature of capturing local and global patterns alongside its ability to understand long-range dependencies enables it to yield superior results than traditional CNNs in eye disease detection tasks.

The research findings demonstrate that transformer-based architectures continue to dominate medical image analysis because HyMoBY-Swin delivers superior performance to all existing models. Despite setting new standards, the Proposed Model achieves superior precision in addition to exceptional robustness for retinal diagnosis and medical imaging applications.

Table 5. Performance Evaluation of Diverse Backbone Architectures within the Proposed Framework

Backbone Models	Sensitivity	Precision	F1 Score	Accuracy
EfficientNetB0	90	90.25	90.25	90.31
MobileNetV2	91.5	91.5	91.5	91.49
DenseNet121	91.75	92.75	92.75	91.96
SqueezeNet1_0	82.75	82.75	82	83.22
ResNet50	91.5	91.75	91.5	91.73
Proposed Model	**92.25**	**92.25**	**92.25**	**92.43**

The HyMoBY-Swin model delivers a 92.43% precise classification of retinal diseases by implementing momentum contrastive learning (MoBY) (Table 6). The stable learning and overfitting avoidance through momentum (0.9) compared to momentum (0.99) further strengthens the model, while the superior feature discrimination obtained from MoBY surpasses traditional contrastive loss functions (SupCon, SimCLR). When comparing different configurations, MoBY pretraining alone delivered a model accuracy of 90.78%, indicating that MoBY functions as a robust standalone feature in enhancing model performance. The accuracy decreased to 89.60% when MoBY was not applied, demonstrating the strong capability that MoBY brings to feature learning and model optimization. Results using temperature sharpening at 0.1 showed minor improvement, yet the other model elements produced better outcomes. The essential role of transfer learning becomes evident as performance improves significantly; the accuracy drops to 52.72% when transfer learning is not applied, underscoring the challenges of working with medical images that have limited labeled data. The Proposed Model sets a new benchmark for automated eye disease detection by uniting MoBY with momentum-based learning and transferable information, making it a superior framework for medical image tasks that require precise small-dataset analysis. The discoveries highlight that self-supervised learning and transfer learning techniques lead to superior outcomes when optimizing medical image classifiers.

Table 6. Evaluating the Impact of Key Model Components and Configurations

	Sensitivity	Precision	F1 Score	Accuracy
Momentum (0.9)	91.5	91.25	91.25	91.25
Momentum (0.99)	88.3	88.5	88.5	88.65
SupCon Loss	91.25	91.5	91.5	91.49
SimCLR Loss	91.25	91.5	91.25	91.25
MoBY Pretraining Alone	90.5	90.75	90.75	90.78
Without MoBY	88.5	89.25	88.5	89.60
T. Sharpening (0.1)	91.5	91.5	91.25	91.73
T. Sharpening (1)	91.25	91.5	91.25	90.54
Without Transfer Learning	52.25	54	50.25	52.72
Proposed Model	**92.25**	**92.25**	**92.25**	**92.43**

The Proposed Model demonstrates superior performance as an automated eye disease classifier based on the findings in Table 7 which prove its dominance over current state-of-the-art benchmarks. The proposed model reached an accuracy level of 92.43% which represented a significant performance improvement compared to three standard models including the Baseline approach (87.23%) and VAT [34] (56.02%) as well as Multi-Model CNN [14] (80.78%). The Proposed Model outperformed the CNN with Transfer Learning approach from [35] because it showed superior performance consistently in sensitivity, precision, F1-score and accuracy metrics. The semi-supervised MeanTeacher [36] model performed worse than the proposed framework in terms of its achieved performance metrics. The quantitative measurements originate from the identical datasets which enables performance metrics comparison among all analyzed models. The proposed model possesses thoroughly tested components which demonstrate their essential role in achieving enhanced eye disease classification outcomes. The simultaneous evaluation confirms that Momentum Contrastive Learning with Swin Transformers operates effectively at real-world patient diagnosis levels. Existing models fell behind the proposed work because this research utilized three essential advancements which together established the highest standard for automated eye disease detection.

Table 7. Comparative Analysis of the Proposed Model Against State-of-the-Art Benchmarks

Models Comparison	Sensitivity	Precision	F1 Score	Accuracy
Baseline	86.25	87	87	87.23
VAT [34]	55.62	60.47	50	56.02
CNN with Transfer Learning [35]	78	79	78	–
MeanTeacher [36]	83	83	83	82.98

(continued)

Table 7. *(continued)*

Models Comparison	Sensitivity	Precision	F1 Score	Accuracy
Multi-Model CNN [14]	–	–	–	80.78
Proposed Model	**92.25**	**92.25**	**92.25**	**92.43**

4.5 Visual Analysis

Figure 6 illustrates how the HyMoBY-Swin model achieves quick learning performance and good generative capabilities through the Training and Validation Loss and Accuracy curves. The effective learning process is confirmed by training loss reduction while validation loss shows stability which indicates minimal overfitting occurred. Experimental results show this model has high prediction capacity through its validation accuracy of 91.40% with a loss of 0.3004. Real-world deployment can be supported by the model's 92.43% test accuracy which establishes its effective performance in practice. This performance level is crucial for real-world clinical deployments. The model achieves generalization performance through a validation loss which stays marginally above the training loss indicating its resistance to overfitting. The robustness of the HyMoBY-Swin model proves it suitable for automated diagnostic systems that specifically need reliable performance across multiple datasets and particularly in eye disease detection processes. Future work could focus on advanced model optimization techniques for handling diagnostic challenges which come with restricted labeling in real-world medical situations.

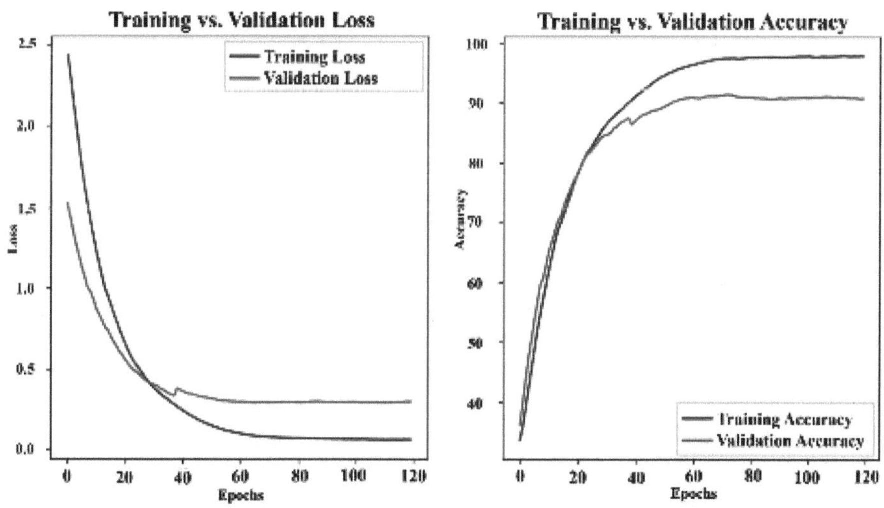

Fig. 6. Training and validation Loss and accuracy curves over epochs for the HyMoBY-Swin model

The HyMoBY-Swin model shows outstanding accuracy in disease classification shown in Fig. 7, through AUC values of 0.99 for DR and 0.96 for cataract patients which signifies its potential for clinical early detection systems. The AUC values for glaucoma determination (AUC = 0.93) and normal diagnoses (AUC = 0.92) are lower than the other conditions because of vision pattern similarities which require further optimization. The model demonstrates medical viability through its total evaluation results which highlight its usefulness especially in DR detection and cataract screenings. New improvements to this system should work on both enhanced feature extraction techniques and multi-source data integration to improve diagnosis performance between glaucoma and normal eyes and ultimately advance real-world diagnostic automation.

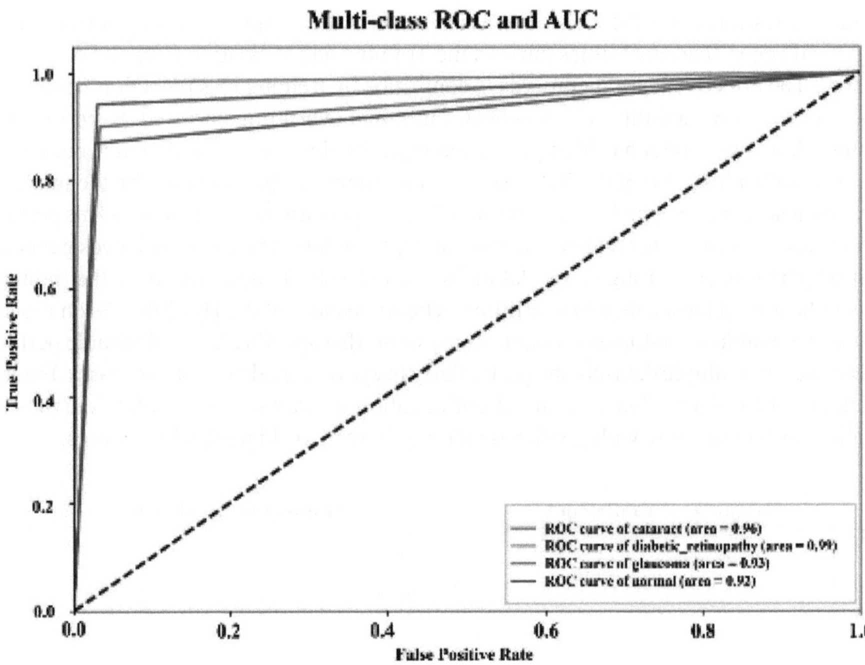

Fig. 7. ROC-AUC curves of each class

The t-SNE visualization in Fig. 8 shows how HyMoBY-Swin identifies the conditions Cataract, along with DR, Glaucoma and Normal retina. The model accurately detects vital diagnostic diseases by achieving high AUC values (Cataract: 0.96 and DR: 0.99) that match well with the distinct separation between blue Cataract and green DR clusters, reflecting the effectiveness of self-supervised pretraining for feature learning. The Glaucoma and Normal conditions show overlapping clusters which indicates difficulty in detecting early-stage glaucoma during normal assessments. Further performance improvement becomes feasible by combining OCT and other multimodal imaging techniques since the AUC values indicate moderate discrimination capacity between Glaucoma and Normal classes (Glaucoma: 0.93, Normal: 0.92). The model demonstrates exceptional ability in distinguishing between Cataract and DR while facing difficulties in other diagnoses making it suitable for automated systems in ophthalmology. The model demonstrates use in clinical settings because its diagnostic categories exist independently of one another. Future research needs to emphasize Glaucoma and Normal separation abilities while exploring potential changes to feature extraction methods and data unification techniques for better early-stage glaucoma diagnosis. These visualizations further confirm that feature extraction, while powerful for cataract and DR, may benefit from additional refinement when applied to visually overlapping classes like glaucoma and normal. Future work will explore domain-specific attention modules and clinically-informed priors to further refine glaucoma classification performance.

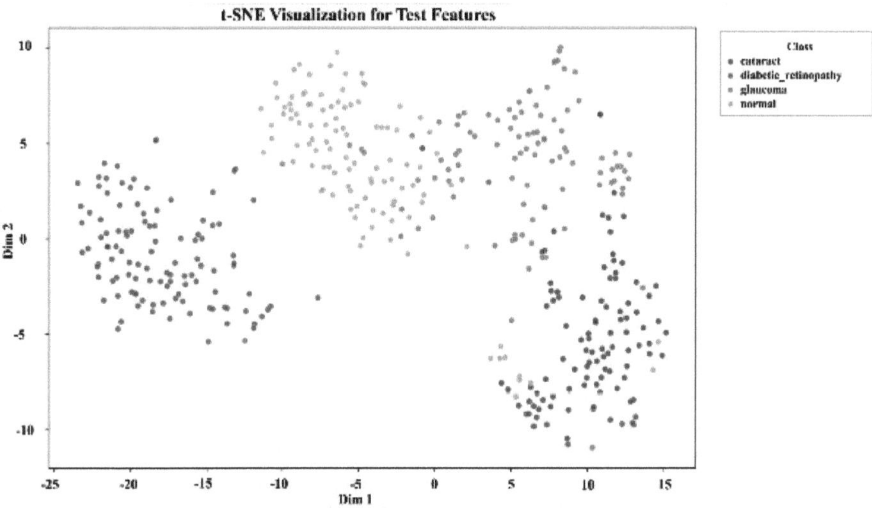

Fig. 8. t-SNE visualization of per-class features

The recent research demonstrates why transformer-based architectures grow more important in medical image analysis through HyMoBY-Swin's successful progress. The proposed model shows advanced precision and robustness capabilities which improve both retinal disease detection accuracy as well as medical diagnostic advancement capabilities. The model demonstrates effective adaptation to various clinical datasets through its data-generalization capability which makes it applicable for diverse medical use cases.

5 Conclusion and Future Work

This research develops HyMoBY-Swin which integrates Swin Transformer with momentum contrastive learning (MoBY) to classify eye diseases from fundus images. The developed model exhibits 92.43% test accuracy which demonstrates outstanding results in recognizing both Diabetic Retinopathy (DR) and Cataract while displaying powerful abilities to classify other diseases with high accuracy. The model demonstrates excellent performance in critical condition detection through its high AUC values which reach 0.99 points for DR and 0.96 points for Cataracts. Glaucoma presents significant difficulties for medical professionals to distinguish from Normal because early-stage Glaucoma shows minimal detectable visual differences to professionals. The model demonstrated successful validation of its generalization abilities through a combination of AUC scores and t-SNE visualizations which makes it applicable for early diagnosis and automated ophthalmic diagnostics in resource-limited environments.

Through its self-supervised pretraining mechanism followed by a supervised fine-tuning stage the HyMoBY-Swin model provides solutions to handle the limited availability of labeled data. Such a combination method provides better diagnostic capabilities together with enhanced generalization potential specifically for environments that lack extensive labeled datasets. The self-supervised pretraining phase enables the model to acquire powerful visual representations of unlabeled data which help distinguish disease groups with small variations. The disease classification accuracy improves through supervised fine-tuning that applies labeled samples to refine the features learned during self-supervised training. Strong system performance exists today yet early-stage Glaucoma detection remains a challenge that future developers should address.

The future research initiative involves combining OCT imaging data into multi-modal learning through an expansion of the available dataset for better generalization capabilities and visual explanation mechanisms to improve diagnostic performance for conditions with subtle visual cues such as early-stage glaucoma. The supervised learning framework will benefit from research into improved advanced pseudo-labeling methods as well as advanced consistency regularization approaches which will optimally boost performance when working with limited training data. XAI saliency maps integrated into the system will enable better model interpretability when used clinically. Resolving class imbalance primarily in Glaucoma will require additional research into ensemble techniques as well as data augmentation methods together with multi-task learning mechanisms. Widespread clinical assessment in different healthcare spaces is essential to measure both scalability and preparedness for practical use.

HyMoBY-Swin provide a scalable self-supervised and supervised learning solution for automated retinal disease diagnosis which solves real-world diagnosis of early conditions. The model produces excellent results for Diabetic Retinopathy and Cataract yet requires additional development to classify Glaucoma cases especially those in early stages. Additional advancements in supervised learning, together with class balancing techniques and multi-task learning will increase system resilience and make it suitable for clinical implementation to achieve better patient results.

Acknowledgments. This research was supported by the National Natural Science Foundation of China under Grant 62273035 and the Beijing Natural Science Foundation under Grant 4252045. We acknowledge the contributors of the dataset available on Kaggle for making their data openly accessible.

CRediT Authorship Contribution Statement. **Muhammad Hammad Malik:** Writing – original draft, Investigation. **Ghulam Mudassir:** Visualization. **Yingying Ren:** Writing – review & editing. **Da-Wei Ding:** Writing – review & editing, Methodology.

Data Availability Statement. The OIH dataset used in this study is based on the publicly available "Eye Diseases Classification" dataset from Kaggle, accessible at: https://www.kaggle.com/datasets/gunavenkatdoddi/eye-diseases-classification.

The modified version of this dataset, incorporating unlabeled data, is available upon reasonable request to the corresponding author.

Declaration of Competing Interest. The authors declare that they have no known competing financial interests or personal relationships that could have appeared to influence the work reported in this paper.

References

1. Teo, Z.L., et al.: Global prevalence of diabetic retinopathy and projection of burden through 2045: systematic review and meta-analysis. Ophthalmology **128**(11), 1580–1591 (2021)
2. Ting, D.S.W., et al.: Artificial intelligence and deep learning in ophthalmology. Br. J. Ophthalmol. **103**(2), 167–175 (2019)
3. Gulshan, V., et al.: Development and validation of a deep learning algorithm for detection of diabetic retinopathy in retinal fundus photographs. JAMA **316**(22), 2402–2410 (2016)
4. Keel, S., et al.: Deep-learning algorithms for automated detection of diabetic retinopathy in primary care: a systematic review and meta-analysis. Lancet Digit. Health **1**(1), e35–e45 (2019)
5. Kermany, D.S., et al.: Identifying medical diagnoses and treatable diseases by image-based deep learning. Cell **172**(5), 1122–1131 (2018)
6. Caron, M., et al.: Emerging properties in self-supervised vision transformers. In: Proceedings of the IEEE/CVF International Conference on Computer Vision (ICCV), pp. 9650–9660. IEEE (2021)
7. He, K., et al.: Momentum contrast for unsupervised visual representation learning. IEEE Trans. Pattern Anal. Mach. Intell. **43**(1), 405–421 (2020)
8. Chen, X., et al.: A simple framework for contrastive learning of visual representations. In: ICML, pp. 1597–1607 (2020)
9. Liu, Z., et al.: Swin transformer: Hierarchical vision transformer using shifted windows. In: Proceedings of the IEEE/CVF International Conference on Computer Vision (ICCV), pp. 10012–10022. IEEE (2021)
10. Topol, E.J.: High-performance medicine: the convergence of human and AI. Nat. Med. **25**(1), 44–56 (2019)
11. Huang, Z., Jiang, R., Aeron, S., Hughes, M. C.: Systematic comparison of semi-supervised and self-supervised learning for medical image classification. In: Proceedings of the IEEE/CVF Conference on Computer Vision and Pattern Recognition, pp. 22282–22293. IEEE (2024)
12. Ghesu, F.C., Georgescu, B., Mansoor, A., Yoo, Y., Neumann, D., Patel, P., et al.: Contrastive self-supervised learning from 100 million medical images with optional supervision. J. Med. Imaging **9**(6), 064503 (2022)
13. Gómez-Valverde, J.J., et al.: Automatic glaucoma classification using color fundus images based on convolutional neural networks and transfer learning. Biomed. Opt. Express **10**(2), 892–913 (2019)
14. Kaushik, S., Jose, C. G., S, B. M., D., Jose: Classification of eye diseases using multi-model CNN. In: IEEE 4th Annual Flagship India Council International Subsections Conference (INDISCON), pp. 1–6. IEEE, Mysore, India (2023)
15. Lakhera, S., Garg, A.: Retinal fundus image classification using hybrid deep learning model. In: IEEE World Conference on Communication and Computing (WCONF). IEEE (2023)
16. Liu, Z., et al.: Cross-modal attention network for retinal disease classification based on multi-modal images. Biomed. Opt. Express **15**(6), 3699–3714 (2024)

17. Oh, K., et al.: Early detection of diabetic retinopathy based on deep learning and ultra-wide-field fundus images. Sci. Rep. **11**(1), 1897 (2021)
18. Azizi, S., Mustafa, B., Ryan, F., Beaver, Z., Freyberg, J., Deaton, J., et al.: Big self-supervised models advance medical image classification. In: Proceedings of the IEEE/CVF International Conference on Computer Vision, pp. 3478–3488. IEEE (2021)
19. Huang, S.C., Pareek, A., Jensen, M., Lungren, M.P., Yeung, S., Chaudhari, A.S.: Self-supervised learning for medical image classification: a systematic review and implementation guidelines. NPJ Digit. Med. **6**(1), 74 (2023)
20. Chowdhury, A., Rosenthal, J., Waring, J., Umeton, R.: Applying self-supervised learning to medicine: review of the state of the art and medical implementations. Informatics (MDPI) **8**(3), 59 (2021)
21. Taherdoost, H.: Beyond supervised: the rise of self-supervised learning in autonomous systems. Information **15**(8), 491 (2024)
22. Wang, W.C., Ahn, E., Feng, D., Kim, J.: A review of predictive and contrastive self-supervised learning for medical images. Mach. Intell. Res. **20**(4), 483–513 (2023)
23. Azizi, S., Culp, L., Freyberg, J., Mustafa, B., Baur, S., Kornblith, S., et al.: Robust and data-efficient generalization of self-supervised machine learning for diagnostic imaging. Nat. Biomed. Eng. **7**(6), 756–779 (2023)
24. Deng, J., et al.: Towards semi-supervised segmentation of retinal fundus images via self-training. In: IEEE 3rd International Conference on Pattern Recognition and Machine Learning (PRML). IEEE (2022)
25. Haque, M. M., Akter, S., Ashrafi, A. F.: SwinMedNet: leveraging swin transformer for robust diabetic retinopathy classification from the RetinaMNIST2D dataset. In: 2024 6th International Conference on Electrical Engineering and Information & Communication Technology (ICEEICT), pp. 1286–1291. IEEE (2024, May)
26. Jannat, F. E., Gholami, S., Alam, M. N., Tabkhi, H.: Oct-SelfNet: A Self-Supervised Framework with Multi-Modal Datasets for Generalized and Robust Retinal Disease Detection. arXiv preprint arXiv:2401.12344 (2024)
27. Yellapragada, B., Hornauer, S., Snyder, K., Yu, S., Yiu, G.: Self-supervised feature learning and phenotyping for assessing age-related macular degeneration using retinal fundus images. Ophthalmol. Retina **6**(2), 116–129 (2022)
28. Nguyen, T.D., Le, D.T., Bum, J., Kim, S., Song, S.J., Choo, H.: Self-FI: self-supervised learning for disease diagnosis in fundus images. Bioengineering **10**(9), 1089 (2023)
29. Lin, J., Cai, Q., Lin, M.: Multi-label classification of fundus images with graph convolutional network and self-supervised learning. IEEE Signal Process. Lett. **28**, 454–458 (2021)
30. Long, F., Xiong, H., Sang, J.: A classification method for diabetic retinopathy based on self-supervised learning. In: International Conference on Intelligent Computing, pp. 347–357. Springer, Singapore (2024, July)
31. Fan, J., Yang, T., Wang, H., Zhang, H., Zhang, W., Ji, M., Miao, J.: A self-supervised equivariant refinement classification network for diabetic retinopathy classification. J. Imaging Inform. Med., 1–16 (2024)
32. Xie, Z., Lin, Y., Yao, Z., Zhang, Z., Dai, Q., Cao, Y., Hu, H.: Self-Supervised Learning with Swin Transformers. arXiv preprint arXiv:2105.04553 (2021)
33. Grill, J.B., Strub, F., Altché, F., Tallec, C., Richemond, P., Buchatskaya, E., et al.: Bootstrap your own latent – a new approach to self-supervised learning. Adv. Neural. Inf. Process. Syst. **33**, 21271–21284 (2020)
34. Miyato, T., Maeda, S.I., Koyama, M., Ishii, S.: Virtual adversarial training: a regularization method for supervised and semi-supervised learning. IEEE Trans. Pattern Anal. Mach. Intell. **41**(8), 1979–1993 (2019)

35. Babaqi, T., Jaradat, M., Yildirim, A. E., Al-Nimer, S. H., Won, D.: Eye Disease Classification Using Deep Learning Techniques. arXiv preprint
36. Tarvainen, A., Valpola, H.: Mean teachers are better role models: weight-averaged consistency targets improve semi-supervised deep learning results. In: Advances in Neural Information Processing Systems, pp. 1195–1204 (2017)

STRIDE: Sports Tracking and Injury Detection Using Estimations

Apoorva Rumale(✉), Mahek Desai, and Marjan Asadinia

California State University, Northridge, CA, USA
{apoorva-sanjay.rumale.462,mahek.desai.849}@my.csun.edu,
marjan.asadinia@csun.edu

Abstract. Injury prediction in athletes remains a significant challenge in sports medicine, where early detection is crucial for preventing severe injuries and optimizing performance. This research investigates the application of machine learning (ML) techniques to predict injury risk based on key physiological parameters, including heart rate, impact force, activity duration, and skin temperature. A dataset comprising recorded athlete data under various conditions is analyzed to determine the predictive significance of these features. While traditional classifiers exhibited limitations due to the non-collinear nature of the feature set, boosting techniques emerged as the most effective approach, achieving the highest predictive accuracy. The study evaluates multiple ML methodologies, including boosting algorithms, neural networks, and conventional classifiers, highlighting their comparative performance. Among these, LightGBM demonstrated the best performance when applied to polynomial degree 2 transformations with Recursive Feature Elimination (RFE)-selected 9 features, achieving an accuracy of 76.32%. By identifying intricate patterns and correlations within the data, this research facilitates accurate, real-time injury predictions, enabling coaches and healthcare professionals to proactively intervene and mitigate injury risks. This study contributes to the field of Integrating Machine Learning into Software Systems by developing an AI-powered predictive model that can be seamlessly incorporated into sports tracking and health monitoring applications. The proposed framework also helps showcase how advanced machine learning techniques can enhance software-driven decision-making processes in sports science. By leveraging ML-powered injury prediction models, sports organizations can enhance athlete longevity, reduce rehabilitation costs, and optimize training regimens, ultimately advancing sports medicine through personalized and precise injury prevention strategies.

Keywords: Injury Prediction · Machine Learning · Predictive Modeling · Athlete Health Monitoring

1 Introduction

Injury prediction is a critical aspect of sports science, aiming to safeguard athletes' health, enhance performance, and prolong careers. By identifying potential

S. Hussain et al. (Eds.): SEET 2025, CCIS 2725, pp. 154–166, 2026.
https://doi.org/10.1007/978-3-032-08977-9_11

injuries before they occur, teams can implement preventive measures, reducing downtime and associated healthcare costs [1]. This proactive approach not only preserves athletes' physical well-being but also maintains team performance by ensuring key players remain active. Advancements in technology have introduced wearable devices capable of monitoring various physiological parameters, such as heart rate, impact forces, and muscle activity, providing real-time data essential for injury prediction.

Machine learning (ML) techniques have emerged as powerful tools in analyzing these complex datasets to predict injuries. In health sciences, ML algorithms have been utilized to predict patient outcomes and detect anomalies in physiological signals, leading to early diagnosis and intervention [2]. Similarly, in sports science, ML models have been applied to forecast injuries by analyzing biomechanical and physiological data, enabling tailored training programs and timely medical attention. For instance, research has shown that ML can effectively predict overuse injuries in runners by analyzing gait patterns and training loads [1].

This study builds upon these advancements by systematically evaluating multiple ML methodologies for injury prediction, leveraging a dataset comprising physiological and biomechanical metrics recorded under diverse conditions. Decision trees, ensemble models, and deep learning architectures were explored, along with feature engineering techniques such as polynomial transformations and recursive feature elimination to optimize predictive accuracy. Among all tested models, the LightGBM model, applied with polynomial degree 2 transformations and Recursive Feature Elimination (RFE)-selected 9 features, achieved the highest predictive accuracy of 76.32%, demonstrating its effectiveness in capturing complex patterns within the dataset.

A key objective of this research is to develop an accessible and computationally efficient injury prediction framework, ensuring that it can be implemented in real-world settings without reliance on expensive or state-of-the-art monitoring equipment. By identifying critical risk factors and leveraging ML-driven predictive models, this study contributes to a data-driven, proactive approach to sports injury management. The findings have practical implications for coaches, sports organizations, and healthcare professionals, enabling personalized training regimens and timely medical interventions to reduce rehabilitation costs and enhance athlete longevity. Furthermore, future extensions incorporating time-series analysis and reinforcement learning could enhance the model's adaptability, advancing sports medicine through precision-driven injury prevention strategies.

The remainder of this paper is structured as follows: Sect. 2 presents a comprehensive review of related work. Section 3 details our proposed methodology, including data collection, preprocessing techniques, feature selection methods, and model architectures. Section 4 provides a thorough evaluation of our methodology, presenting comparative results across multiple performance metrics. Section 5 concludes the paper with key insights. Finally, Sect. 6 outlines future research directions.

2 Related Works

The integration of machine learning (ML) and wearable technology into sports science has revolutionized injury prediction and prevention. Researchers have explored various methodologies to analyze physiological and biomechanical data, aiming to identify injury risk factors and develop predictive models. Below, we discuss key studies that have contributed to this evolving field.

Taborri et al. investigated the use of wearable sensors combined with ML algorithms to monitor athletes' movements and detect abnormal patterns associated with injury risk. Their study demonstrated the effectiveness of inertial measurement units (IMUs) in predicting musculoskeletal injuries in real-time, highlighting the potential of wearable technology to provide actionable insights for injury prevention [3].

Another research by T. J. Gabbett analyzed the relationship between training load and injury risk in athletes. The study emphasized the importance of monitoring workload to prevent overuse injuries and provided a foundation for integrating ML techniques into injury prediction models. This research underscores the value of combining training load data with advanced analytics to optimize athlete performance and safety [4].

In ref [5], authors explored the application of ML models in predicting anterior cruciate ligament (ACL) injuries, leveraging biomechanical data from motion capture systems. Their research identified poor landing mechanics as a key risk factor, demonstrating the potential of ML-driven biomechanical analysis in injury prevention.

Finally, Li et al. proposed a deep learning framework for injury prediction, utilizing wearable sensor data to detect early signs of overuse injuries in runners. By analyzing gait patterns and physiological metrics, their approach achieved high predictive accuracy, further demonstrating the capabilities of deep learning in sports science [7]. These studies collectively highlight the growing role of ML and wearable technology in sports injury prevention. The integration of physiological, biomechanical, and workload data with ML techniques presents a promising pathway toward personalized, data-driven injury mitigation strategies.

3 Methodology

3.1 Data Collection and Features Engineering

The dataset utilized in this study consists of physiological and biomechanical data collected from athletes to predict injury risk. The primary focus of feature selection was to ensure that the data could be easily obtained using widely available sports monitoring equipment, allowing institutions with limited resources to implement injury prediction without requiring state-of-the-art technology. Key physiological indicators such as heart rate, impact force, activity duration, and skin temperature were chosen based on their relevance to injury risk and their accessibility through affordable wearable devices. This approach democratizes injury prediction, making it applicable across various levels of sports organizations, from professional teams to collegiate and amateur athletic programs. Table 1 shows the features available in the dataset and used for this research.

Table 1. Feature Names, Units, and Descriptions

Feature	Unit	Description
Heart Rate	BPM	Cardiac beats per minute during activity
Respiratory Rate	BPM	Breathing cycles per minute
Skin Temperature	°C	Surface body temperature
Blood Oxygen Level	%	Oxygen saturation in blood
Impact Force	N	Force applied during movement/contact
Cumulative Fatigue Index	—	Accumulated fatigue score
Duration	min	Length of activity session
Injury Risk Score	—	Computed risk assessment
Injury Occurred	0/1	Binary outcome indicator

The **Injury Risk Score** ensures that no training or game performance is overlooked. Probability reflects the likelihood of injury based on physiological factors such as heart rate variability and impact force, while also accounting for movements or details for which statistical data may not be available. Impact quantifies injury severity by considering accumulated strain and sport type.

Additionally, the **Cumulative Fatigue Index (CFI)** accounts for prior workloads, intensity, and recovery, offering a historical perspective on athlete fatigue. Both scores are normalized between **0 and 1**, allowing standardized comparisons across athletes. These metrics provide a data-driven approach for injury prevention, making informed decisions accessible even without advanced biomechanical tools.

3.2 Pre-processing

For preprocessing, we performed the usual ETL (Extract, Transform, Load) process [6], which included inspecting the dataset for missing and duplicate values. After handling these issues, we proceeded with feature scaling, as models such as XGBoost and others typically require scaled data for optimal performance. To ensure that all features are on a comparable scale, we applied the StandardScaler, which standardizes the features by removing the mean and scaling to unit variance. This transformation ensures that the model can better capture relationships between features and improve overall performance during training and prediction.

Additionally, we addressed the class imbalance issue in the dataset, where injury occurrences were significantly underrepresented compared to non-injury instances. To prevent the model from being biased toward predicting the majority class, we applied the Synthetic Minority Over-sampling Technique (SMOTE)

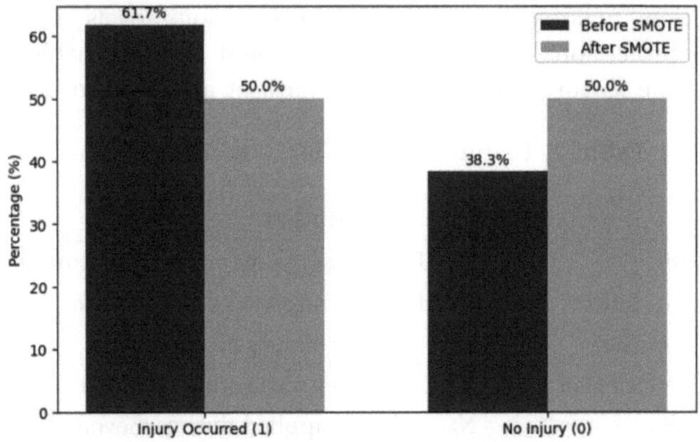

Fig. 1. Class Imbalance Before and After Applying SMOTE.

[2]. SMOTE generates synthetic examples of the minority class by interpolating between existing instances, thereby balancing the dataset as seen in Fig. 1. This adjustment significantly improved model performance, ensuring that the injury prediction model does not overlook critical injury cases due to data imbalance.

3.3 Feature Exploration

Feature Impacts Correlation Matrix and SHAP. The initial dataset was reviewed by constructing a correlation matrix to examine the relationships between features in a linear context. Contrary to initial expectations, the analysis revealed that most features did not exhibit strong or direct correlations with each other. However, certain features, such as heart rate, impact force, and fatigue index, demonstrated notable correlations with injury occurrence. These findings underscore the potential significance of these specific features in predicting injury risks, suggesting their importance in the modeling process. The correlation matrix is provided in the Fig. 2.

Additionally, SHAP (SHapley Additive exPlanations) was applied to an early-stage XGBoost model to understand which features had the most significant impact on predicting injury risk. As shown in Fig. 3, the analysis revealed that heart rate had a positive impact on injury prediction, meaning an increase in heart rate corresponded to a higher likelihood of injury. Conversely, blood oxygen level and skin temperature showed an inverse relationship, with lower values of these features associated with a higher risk of injury. Other features displayed more evenly distributed SHAP values, indicating they did not have a direct or strong influence on the model's predictions. This insight into feature importance aids in refining feature selection for future modeling efforts.

Anomaly Detection. Subsequently, anomaly detection was performed using the Isolation Forest algorithm to identify potential anomalies within the dataset.

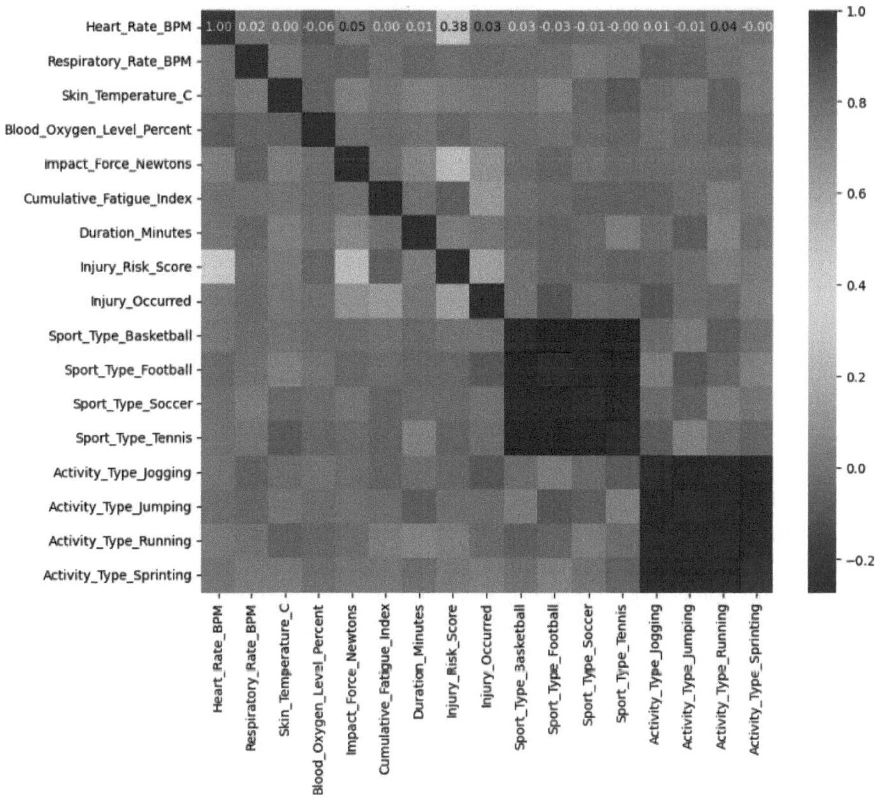

Fig. 2. Correlation Matrix.

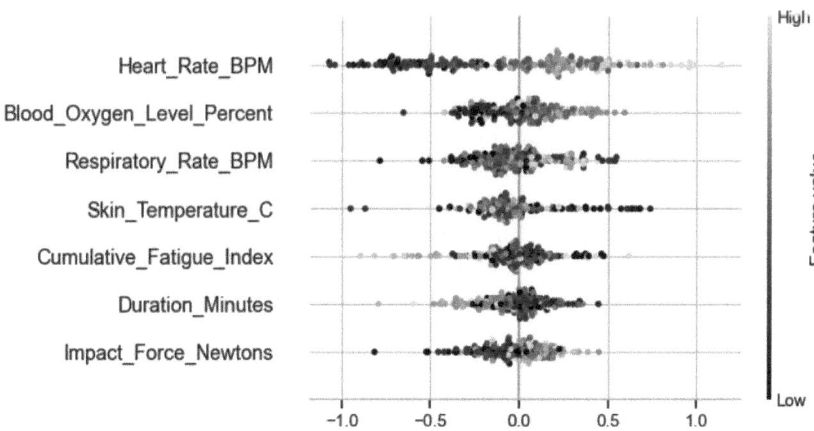

Fig. 3. Feature Impact Plot Using SHAP.

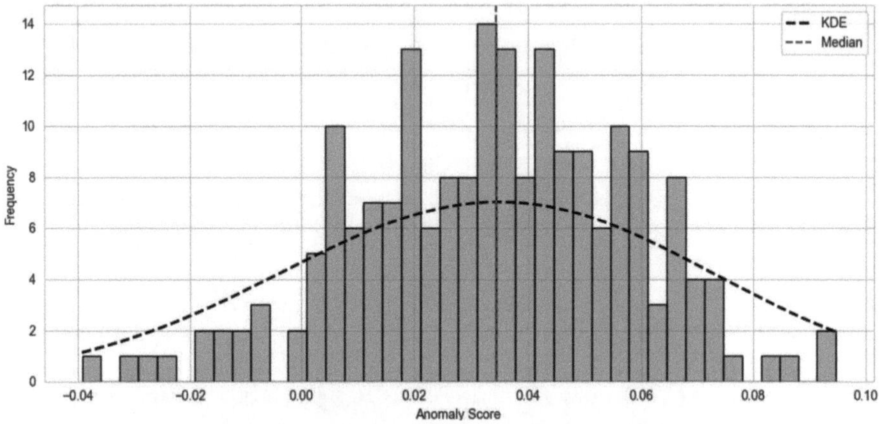

Fig. 4. Anomaly Scores.

The results as shown in Fig. 4 suggests that the data points fall near the decision boundary being classified as normal. While this does not indicate the presence of strong anomalies, it highlights that the points in this range are less likely to be extreme anomalies. Therefore, although the model did not identify major anomalies, it is important to note that the data points close to the decision boundary still warrant further exploration for subtle anomalies.

3.4 Model Selection and Hyperparameters

In this study, we explored multiple machine learning techniques to predict injury occurrence in athletes. Our approach included three primary categories: Regression Models, Boosting Techniques, and Neural Networks, along with an advanced ensemble approach using Stacking Models. Each category provided unique advantages in modeling injury risk based on physiological and biomechanical data.

Regression Models such as Logistic Regression and Random Forest play a crucial role in injury prediction by identifying relationships between physiological and biomechanical features. Logistic Regression, a linear model, is effective for understanding the influence of various features on injury occurrence and provides interpretable coefficients, making it useful for risk assessment. However, it assumes linear separability, which may limit its performance in complex datasets. On the other hand, Random Forest, an ensemble of decision trees, captures nonlinear patterns in the data by aggregating multiple tree-based predictions. Its ability to handle high-dimensional data and automatically determine feature importance makes it a robust choice for injury prediction, particularly when interactions among variables influence injury risk.

Boosting Techniques improve predictive performance by combining multiple weak learners into a strong classifier. We experimented with XGBoost (XGB),

LightGBM (LGBM), and CatBoost (CB), which are well-known for handling structured data efficiently.

These models leverage gradient boosting techniques to iteratively improve classification accuracy by minimizing the loss function. They also handle imbalanced datasets well, an essential factor given the injury prediction dataset's initial class imbalance.

Neural Networks are particularly useful for capturing complex, nonlinear relationships in high-dimensional data. We explored Multi-Layer Perceptron (MLP) and Convolutional Neural Networks (CNNs).

- **MLPClassifier**: A fully connected feedforward neural network that learns feature representations through multiple hidden layers. It is beneficial for structured tabular data but may require hyperparameter tuning for optimal performance.
- **CNN for Tabular Data**: We implemented a 1D CNN model to capture spatial dependencies between features. The CNN architecture includes convolutional layers, dropout regularization, and fully connected layers to enhance predictive performance.

Neural networks provided an alternative approach to traditional machine learning models, particularly in identifying subtle patterns related to injury risk.

Stacking Classifier to further optimize prediction accuracy. We implemented a stacking model that integrates multiple classifiers into a unified framework.

The stacking classifier consisted of Random Forest (RF), XGBoost (XGB), and LightGBM (LGBM) as base learners, with Logistic Regression (LR) as the meta-learner. This ensemble approach capitalized on the strengths of each individual model while reducing their respective weaknesses.

All the hyperparameters and their values are represented in Table 2. The Fig. 5 illustrates the actual pipeline of the research, providing a comprehensive overview of the entire process.

It showcases the sequence of steps undertaken, from data collection and preprocessing to model selection and evaluation, encapsulating the methodologies applied throughout the study. This diagram serves to clarify the workflow and highlight the integration of various techniques used to achieve the research objectives. All models were rigorously evaluated using accuracy to ensure a comprehensive assessment of their predictive capabilities. Additionally, all models were trained and tested using a 70-30 validation split to ensure reliable performance evaluation.

4 Experimental Results and Discussion

4.1 Effect of Data Balancing on Injury Prediction

Balancing the dataset using SMOTE significantly improved model performance, underscoring the necessity of handling class imbalance in injury prediction which

Table 2. Hyperparameter Configuration for Models

Model	Hyperparameter	Value
Logistic Regression	Max Iterations	500
Random Forest	Number of Estimators	100
	Random State	42
XGBoost	Number of Estimators	100
	Learning Rate	0.1
	Max Depth	6
LightGBM	Number of Estimators	100
	Learning Rate	0.1
	Max Depth	–1
CatBoost	Iterations	1000
	Learning Rate	0.03
	Depth	6
MLPClassifier	Hidden Layers	(128, 64)
	Max Iterations	500
CNN	Conv1D Filters	64
	Kernel Size	3
	Dropout Rate	0.3
	Dense Layer Neurons	128
Stacking Model	Base Models	RF, XGB, LGBM
	Meta-Learner	Logistic Regression

can be seen in Fig. 6. Among the model categories, boosting techniques, particularly XGBoost, demonstrated the highest accuracy at 64.78%, benefiting from their iterative learning process and ability to capture complex feature interactions. Neural networks also showed considerable improvement, leveraging their capability to model non-linear patterns in the data. In contrast, regression-based models, such as logistic regression, exhibited comparatively lower gains, highlighting their limitations in handling high-dimensional relationships. The stacking ensemble, designed to integrate multiple models, performed competitively but did not surpass the best individual model (XGBoost), indicating potential redundancy in feature learning. Overall, dataset balancing was crucial in ensuring that the models effectively learned patterns from minority-class samples, ultimately improving generalization and reducing bias toward the majority class.

4.2 Feature Interaction for Enhanced Injury Prediction

To ensure reliable injury prediction, all models were evaluated on a balanced dataset obtained using SMOTE. Feature engineering played a crucial role in enhancing predictive power, as weak features were transformed into stronger

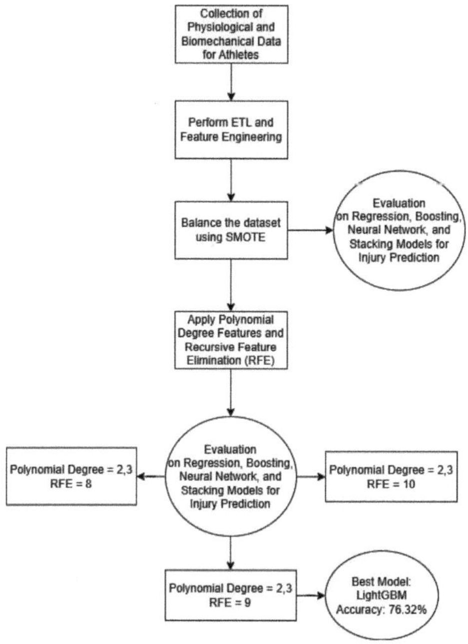

Fig. 5. Workflow of the research.

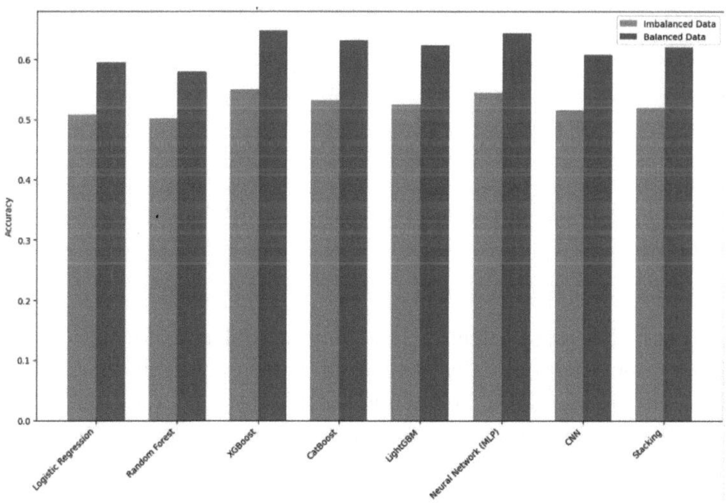

Fig. 6. Impact of Balanced Data on Model Accuracy for Injury Prediction.

predictors through domain-driven analysis. Physiological indicators, such as elevated heart rate, increased fatigue levels, and decreased skin temperature, were identified as significant risk factors for injury. These features were carefully analyzed for their potential to predict injury occurrence, allowing the models to focus on the most critical predictors, thereby improving classification performance.

To further enhance model accuracy, polynomial feature interactions for degrees 2 and 3 were employed to capture non-linear relationships between features. For instance, interactions between heart rate and impact force, as well as between heart rate and lower respiratory rate, were explored to identify patterns indicative of injury risk. Given the potential for overfitting in high-dimensional data, Recursive Feature Elimination (RFE) was applied to select the most relevant features. By narrowing the feature set to 5 to 10 key predictors, RFE helped reduce model complexity and mitigate the curse of dimensionality, ensuring improved generalizability and performance.

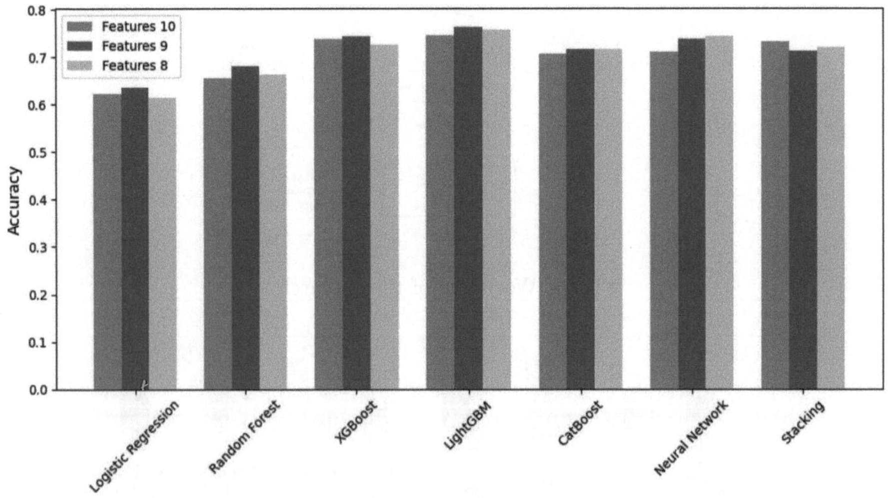

Fig. 7. Impact of Polynomial Feature Expansion and RFE on Model Performance for Injury Prediction.

The impact of feature selection and polynomial transformations on model performance was systematically evaluated across multiple machine learning approaches, with LightGBM achieving the highest accuracy of 76.32% using polynomial degree 2 and 9 selected features, as shown in Fig. 7. Boosting models like XGBoost and CatBoost also performed well, with accuracies ranging from 72.54% to 74.32%, whereas simpler models like Logistic Regression and Random Forest showed lower accuracy, peaking at 68.13% and 68.37%, respectively. Neural networks demonstrated competitive performance, reaching up to 73.68%, while the stacking ensemble approach provided stable yet moderate improvements. These results highlight the importance of effective feature engineering and advanced ML techniques, with LightGBM standing out as the most efficient and interpretable solution for injury prediction in athletes.

5 Conclusion

This research developed a machine learningâĂŞbased injury prediction model using physiological and biomechanical data to assess athlete injury risk. Techniques such as decision trees, ensemble models, and deep learning were explored, with feature engineering methods like polynomial transformations and recursive feature elimination applied to improve accuracy. LightGBM proved most effective, achieving 76.32% accuracy with polynomial degree 2 and 9 selected features, highlighting its ability to capture complex interactions and deliver robust predictions.

The STRIDE model emphasizes accessibility and scalability, relying on efficient ML methods suitable for both small-scale athlete monitoring and large-scale cloud analytics. Its support for edge AI deployment, real-time streaming, and optimization ensures adaptability to different sports and datasets. Future extensions, such as federated learning, could further expand its utility across organizations, enabling early intervention and personalized training to reduce injury risks.

6 Future Work

While this study presents a promising approach to injury prediction using machine learning, several key areas can be explored to further enhance its predictive power and practical applicability:

1. Utilizing Time-Series Data for Enhanced Injury Prediction: Incorporating time-series data for all athletes would enable a more comprehensive understanding of historical workloads, physiological trends, and performance variations. By analyzing past training sessions, competition data, and recovery periods, the model could capture long-term dependencies and patterns that influence injury risk.
2. Implementing Reinforcement Learning for Adaptive Training Optimization: A reinforcement learning (RL) model could be developed to continuously learn from this research and dynamically adjust training programs based on an athlete's real-time physiological conditions and past performances. By optimizing workload distribution and modifying exercise regimens in response to an athlete's evolving state, RL-based systems could help in minimizing injury risk while maximizing performance gains. Such a system could serve as an intelligent assistant for coaches, providing personalized recommendations for training adjustments.
3. Additionally, integrating advanced non-volatile memory technologies such as Phase Change Memory (PCM) can provide efficient, reliable storage of large-scale athlete performance data, enabling scalable and energy-efficient injury prediction systems [8–12].

By pursuing these future directions, this research can contribute to a more intelligent and data-driven approach to athlete performance fostering the development of personalized and adaptive training strategies that effectively mitigate injury risk.

References

1. Willy, R.W., Meira, E.P.: Current concepts in biomechanical interventions for patellofemoral pain. Int. J. Sports Phys. Therapy **11**(6), 877–890 (2016)
2. Rumale, A., Desai, M., Asadinia, M.: PRISM: predictive risk and injury surveillance model for athlete safety. In: 2025 IEEE World AI IoT Congress (AIIoT), pp. 0024–0031 (2025). https://doi.org/10.1109/aiiot65859.2025.11105248
3. Song, H., et al.: Agonist-antagonist muscle strain in the residual limb preserves motor control and perception after amputation. Commun. Med. **2**(1), 97 (2022)
4. Gabbett, T.J.: The training–injury prevention paradox: should athletes be training smarter and harder? Brit. J. Sports Med. **50**(5), 273–280 (2016)
5. Ruddy, J.D., et al.: Modeling the risk of team sport injuries: a narrative review of different statistical approaches. Front. Physiol. **10**, 829 (2019)
6. Desai, M., Rumale, A., Asadinia, M.: SHIELD: securing healthcare IoT with efficient machine learning techniques for anomaly detection. In: 2022 IEEE World AI IoT Congress (AIIoT), pp. 0521–0528 (2025). https://doi.org/10.1109/aiiot65859.2025.11105287
7. Li, R.T., et al.: Wearable performance devices in sports medicine. Sports Health Multidisc. Appr. **8**(1), 74–78 (2015). www.ncbi.nlm.nih.gov/pmc/articles/PMC4702159/
8. Desai, M., Quinn, R., Asadinia, M.: SMART-WRITE: adaptive learning-based write energy optimization for phase change memory. In: 2025 IEEE 15th Annual Computing and Communication Workshop and Conference (CCWC), pp. 00640–00648 (2025). https://doi.org/10.1109/ccwc62904.2025.10903957
9. Ekoniak, J., Rumale, A., Asadinia, M.: ML-PreP: machine learning based error prediction for phase change memory. In: 2025 IEEE 15th Annual Computing and Communication Workshop and Conference (CCWC), pp. 00909–00917 (2025). https://doi.org/10.1109/ccwc62904.2025.10903761
10. Desai, M., Rumale, A., Asadinia, M., Bogle, S.: WIRE: write energy reduction via encoding in phase change main memories (PCM). In: Lecture Notes in Networks and Systems, pp. 599–615 (2024). https://doi.org/10.1007/978-3-031-73125-9_38
11. Rumale, A., Ekoniak, J., Asadinia, M.: PENN: predicting errors using neural network in phase change memory. Commun. Comput. Inf. Sci. **2506**, 278–293 (2025). https://doi.org/10.1007/978-3-031-94962-3_24
12. Desai, M., Quinn, R., Asadinia, M.: ML-PCM : machine learning technique for write optimization in phase change memory (PCM). Commun. Comput. Inf. Sci. **2506**, 207–219 (2025). https://doi.org/10.1007/978-3-031-95130-5_17

FAITH: Fault Anomaly Identification Using Machine Learning for Trusted Healthcare IoT

Mahek Desai(✉), Apoorva Rumale, and Marjan Asadinia

California State University, Northridge, CA, USA
{mahek.desai.849,apoorva-sanjay.rumale.462}@my.csun.edu,
marjan.asadinia@csun.edu

Abstract. The integration of IoT devices in healthcare introduces significant reliability challenges, necessitating robust anomaly detection mechanisms to ensure continuous and accurate operation. This study proposes a machine learning-driven framework for detecting faulty device anomalies, leveraging a dataset of 200,000 records. Four machine learning models are evaluated across three methodological paradigms: supervised learning (XGBoost, K-Nearest Neighbors (KNN)), semi-supervised learning (Generative Adversarial Networks (GAN)), and unsupervised learning (Isolation Forest). Performance assessment is conducted using multiple metrics, including accuracy, F1-score, precision, recall, Receiver Operating CharacteristicâĂŞArea Under the Curve (ROC-AUC), and computational efficiency. Experimental results indicate that XGBoost achieves the highest accuracy (99%) with minimal computational overhead (0.04 s), making it the most efficient model for real-time fault detection. Isolation Forest demonstrates a strong balance between precision and recall. These findings provide critical insights into optimizing fault detection strategies, ensuring the reliability of IoT-enabled medical devices. This research contributes to the Software Engineering for the Internet of Things (IoT) by providing a machine learning-driven anomaly detection framework tailored for IoT-based healthcare environments. Furthermore, it supports software development by integrating diverse learning paradigms into software systems, facilitating real-time fault detection in medical IoT devices. By enabling early identification of operational anomalies, this framework enhances system resilience, minimizes device downtime, and supports the safe and continuous operation of healthcare systems.

Keywords: Anomaly Detection · Machine Learning · IoT healthcare · AI for Software Systems

1 Introduction

The rapid integration of Internet of Things (IoT) devices in healthcare environments has revolutionized patient care through improved monitoring, diagnosis,

S. Hussain et al. (Eds.): SEET 2025, CCIS 2725, pp. 167–178, 2026.
https://doi.org/10.1007/978-3-032-08977-9_12

and treatment efficiency. However, this increased connectivity introduces significant reliability challenges. Healthcare IoT devices, including continuous temperature monitors, blood pressure measurement systems, heart rate monitors, and battery-powered medical sensors, are vulnerable to operational failures, potentially endangering patient safety and the integrity of healthcare systems. Faulty device anomalies can lead to incorrect readings, treatment errors, and system downtime, compromising patient care [1,2].

Studies have shown that device malfunctions in critical care settings can result in patient harm, with a significant percentage of medical devices exhibiting vulnerability to potential exploitation due to operational issues [3]. These challenges necessitate robust anomaly detection systems capable of identifying device failures in IoT-enabled healthcare environments.

Previous research explored various machine learning techniques for anomaly detection in healthcare IoT systems. One study compared adaptive machine learning methods (SVM, KNN, MLP, FusionNet) for IoT security but did not address faulty device anomaly detection [4]. Another study utilized clustering (K-Means, K-Medoids) for anomaly detection in smart healthcare but faced challenges in real-time adaptability [5]. Additionally, deep learning approaches for medical anomaly detection were explored, but empirical model comparisons were lacking [6]. Other research integrated network intrusion detection with healthcare event monitoring but did not focus on device-level anomalies [7]. Moreover, studies applying feature selection and Random Forest for anomaly detection overlooked device malfunctions [8].

To address these gaps, we present FAITH, a comprehensive framework for detecting faulty device anomalies in healthcare IoT environments. Using a dataset of 200,000 records from an ICU setup with patient monitoring sensors and control units [9], FAITH employs a three-stage approach: (1) data preprocessing (cleaning, normalization, and feature engineering), (2) feature selection (ANOVA F-value, Mutual Information, Recursive Feature Elimination), and (3) model evaluation using supervised learning (XGBoost, KNN), semi-supervised learning (GAN), and unsupervised learning (Isolation Forest). XGBoost demonstrated the highest performance for faulty device anomaly detection (99% accuracy, perfect precision and recall, 0.04 s). Isolation Forest showed strong results with near-perfect accuracy and recall.

FAITH's integrated approach ensures comprehensive protection against operational threats across healthcare IoT ecosystems, significantly improving the detection of faulty device anomalies.

The remainder of this paper is structured as follows: Sect. 2 presents a comprehensive review of related work in IoT healthcare anomaly detection and machine learning applications. Section 3 details our proposed methodology, including data collection, preprocessing techniques, feature selection methods, and model architectures. Section 3.5 provides a thorough evaluation of our framework, presenting comparative results across multiple performance metrics. Section 4 concludes the paper with key insights. Finally, Sect. 5 outlines future research directions in securing IoT healthcare systems from device malfunctions.

2 Related Work

The integration of IoT in healthcare systems demands effective anomaly detection techniques for reliability. Several studies have proposed machine learning frameworks, each with unique approaches and limitations.

One study compared anomaly detection techniques for IoT security using SVM, KNN, MLP, and FusionNet [4]. FusionNet outperformed traditional methods in accuracy and precision. However, it focused solely on security threats and lacked evaluation of deep learning models in real-time healthcare environments. Our research addresses faulty device anomalies, using a large dataset to provide a more comprehensive and scalable solution for detecting operational failures.

Another study used K-Means and K-Medoids for anomaly detection in medical data [5]. While clustering methods were effective for pattern recognition, they lacked dynamic data environments and computational efficiency. Our research fills this gap by implementing a diverse set of models across supervised, semi-supervised, and unsupervised learning paradigms, rather than being limited to clustering methods alone. Notably, our supervised models like XGBoost and KNN demonstrated superior computational efficiency, effectively bridging the performance gap identified in previous research.

A survey on deep learning methods for medical anomaly detection categorized existing techniques but lacked an empirical comparison of model performance [6]. Our study extends this by quantitatively evaluating models like XGBoost, KNN, GAN and Isolation forest, comparing performance metrics like F1-score, accuracy, precision, recall, ROC-AUC, and computational efficiency, offering concrete recommendations for healthcare IoT applications focused on device-level anomalies.

Another research proposed an anomaly detection system for smart hospital IoT networks using SVM [7]. While their system improved detection accuracy, it was limited to a single model and did not consider unsupervised or semi-supervised approaches. Our research overcomes this by evaluating diverse models, optimizing faulty device anomaly detection, ensuring better adaptability against emerging failures in healthcare environments.

One study focused on anomaly detection using the CIC IoT dataset with Random Forest models for cybersecurity threats [8]. However, it overlooked device-level anomalies and lacked adaptability to complex healthcare scenarios. Our research bridges this gap by addressing operational anomalies, leveraging deep learning techniques for enhanced accuracy and real-time applicability in hospital environments.

While existing studies focus on detecting anomalies at a broader system level, they often overlook device-level malfunctions critical to healthcare reliability. Our research provides a solution by detecting faulty device anomalies. Using a broad spectrum of models, including XGBoost, KNN, Isolation Forest, and GAN, our framework ensures optimized accuracy, efficiency, and adaptability in IoT-driven healthcare systems, offering actionable insights for real-world deployment.

3 Proposed Method

This section provides a comprehensive overview of the proposed methodology. The workflow of our approach is illustrated in Fig. 1.

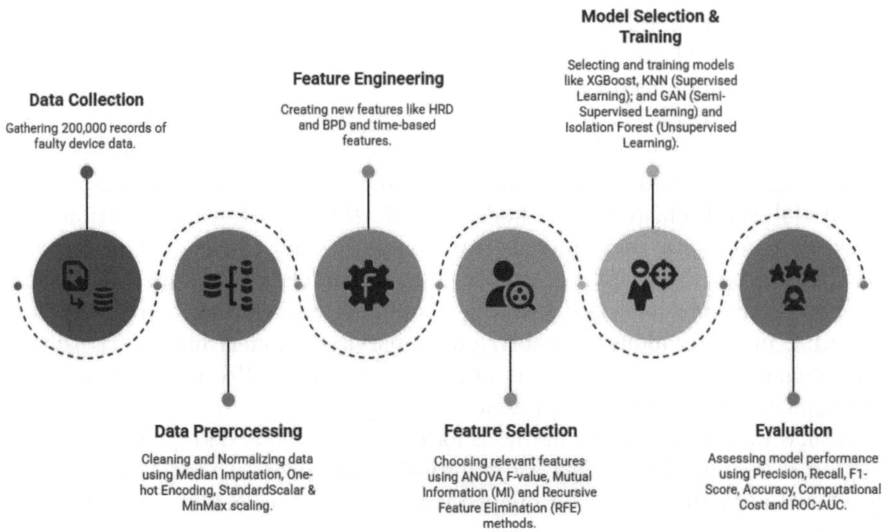

Fig. 1. FAITH Overview.

3.1 Data Collection

The dataset utilized in this study consists of 200,000 records and comprises of faulty device data, capturing critical aspects of IoT-based Intensive Care Unit (ICU) conditions. The data was obtained from an ICU setup featuring a two-bed capacity, where each bed is equipped with nine patient monitoring sensors and a Bedx-Control-Unit responsible for data aggregation and transmission [9].

The faulty device data captures anomalies in medical device functionality, including temperature fluctuations, power failures, and erroneous sensor readings. This data consists of essential patient monitoring parameters. Additionally, control parameters are included to ensure that deviations from expected values can be detected and analyzed. These anomalies, driven by faulty devices, can have a significant impact on patient care, making it crucial to detect and address such issues in real-time.

By capturing operational failures in IoT-enabled healthcare environments, this dataset provides a robust foundation for developing anomaly detection mechanisms specifically tailored to identify faulty device malfunctions, which can improve patient safety and system reliability. Figure 2 summarizes all features.

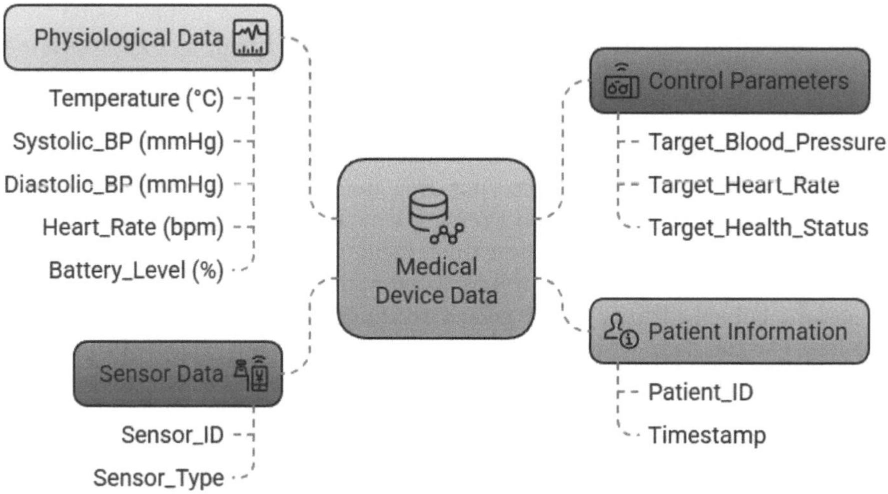

Fig. 2. Dataset Overview.

3.2 Data Preprocessing

Data preprocessing plays a critical role in ensuring the reliability and effectiveness of anomaly detection models by transforming raw data into a structured format suitable for machine learning and deep learning techniques. The preprocessing pipeline involves multiple stages, including data cleaning, normalization, and feature engineering, all of which contribute to improving model performance and reducing noise in the dataset.

Data Cleaning and Normalization. To maintain the integrity of input features, missing values in numerical fields were handled through median imputation, a robust statistical method that replaces missing entries with the median of the respective feature. This approach was chosen over mean imputation to mitigate the influence of extreme values or outliers, which are common in healthcare sensor readings. Furthermore, categorical variables such as Sensor_Type were one-hot encoded, ensuring that each category was represented in a binary format suitable for machine learning models. This transformation prevents categorical variables from being misinterpreted as ordinal values, preserving the true nature of the data.

Different machine learning models require specific scaling techniques to standardize numerical features and improve learning efficiency. Traditional machine learning models, such as XGBoost, operate optimally with features scaled using StandardScaler, which transforms numerical attributes to have a mean of zero and unit variance. On the other hand, deep learning models benefit from Min-Max scaling, which normalizes values within a range of [0,1]. This normalization method is particularly useful for gradient-based optimization, as it enhances convergence rates and stabilizes the training process. These preprocessing techniques collectively ensure that data is clean, well-structured, and appropriately scaled for subsequent model training focused on faulty device anomaly detection.

Feature Engineering. To enhance anomaly detection, additional features were derived from sensor readings, incorporating domain-specific knowledge. Heart Rate Deviation (HRD) and Blood Pressure Deviation (BPD) were calculated by measuring fluctuations in vitals over time, using the absolute difference between real-time measurements and the rolling mean within a predefined window. These deviations helped identify faulty sensor readings or health issues. Time-based features, like the hour of the day and day of the week, were extracted to identify temporal patterns in anomalies, such as sensor failures in prolonged operation. These engineered features enriched the dataset, enabling the model to identify anomalies with greater precision, improving detection of faulty medical devices.

3.3 Feature Selection

Feature selection is a crucial step in machine learning and anomaly detection, as it helps improve model performance by reducing dimensionality, enhancing interpretability, and mitigating overfitting [10]. Given the high-dimensional nature of our dataset, we employed three well-established feature selection methods: ANOVA F-value Selection, Mutual Information (MI) Ranking, and Recursive Feature Elimination (RFE). Each method was applied to the faulty device detection dataset to determine the most relevant features for anomaly detection.

ANOVA F-value Feature Selection. is a statistical method that identifies the most significant features by measuring the variance ratio between classes (normal vs. anomaly). Higher F-values indicate greater discriminatory power. For faulty device detection, critical features such as Temperature (°C), Systolic_BP (mmHg), and Heart_Rate (bpm) were identified.

Mutual Information (MI). is a non-parametric method that measures the dependency between a feature and the target variable. It captures both linear and non-linear relationships, making it effective for complex datasets. For faulty device detection, critical features such as Diastolic_BP (mmHg), Heart_Rate (bpm), and Device_Battery_Level (%) were identified.

Recursive Feature Elimination (RFE). is a wrapper-based method that iteratively removes the least important features based on model performance. Using Logistic Regression as the base estimator, it identifies the most influential features. For faulty device detection, selected features included Temperature (°C), Diastolic_BP (mmHg), and Heart_Rate (bpm).

After applying all three methods, the unique selected features were combined to form an optimal feature subset for the faulty device detection task. The final feature set retained key features consistently identified as important across different methods: Temperature (°C), Systolic_BP (mmHg), Diastolic_BP (mmHg), Heart_Rate (bpm), and Device_Battery_Level (%).

3.4 Model Selection and Training

Table 1. Model Specifications for Faulty Device Detection

Model	Hyperparameters
XGBoost	Learning rate: 0.1, Max depth: 6, Evaluation metric: logloss
KNN	k = 5, Distance metric: Euclidean
GAN	Latent space: 10, Epochs: 100, Batch size: 64
Isolation Forest	Contamination: 0.2

Anomaly detection in faulty devices was carried out using four machine learning models: K-Nearest Neighbors (KNN), XGBoost, Generative Adversarial Networks (GAN), and Isolation Forest. These models were selected to cover different learning paradigms and offer robust performance for faulty device detection. The models were trained and evaluated using the selected features from the preprocessing and feature selection stages. The hyperparameters for all models are as specified in Table 1.

(a) Supervised Learning

K-Nearest Neighbors (KNN): For faulty device detection, the K-Nearest Neighbors (KNN) algorithm was implemented as a supervised classification approach. The KNN classifier was configured with k=5, meaning that classification decisions were based on the majority class among the five closest training examples in the feature space. After training on the labeled subset, the model was applied to the entire dataset to generate anomaly predictions.

XGBoost: For faulty device detection, XGBoost was implemented as a supervised classification approach. The XGBoost classifier was configured with default hyperparameters, and the model was trained on a stratified train-test split of the scaled feature data, with 70% allocated for training and 30% for testing. After training, the model was applied to the entire dataset to generate anomaly predictions.

(b) Semi-supervised Learning

Generative Adversarial Networks (GAN): For faulty device detection, a Generative Adversarial Network (GAN) architecture was implemented with complementary generator and discriminator networks. The generator was constructed with a latent space dimension half the size of the input feature space, and the discriminator mirrored this architecture. The model was trained using 100 epochs with a batch size of 64. Anomaly detection was performed by measuring reconstruction errors, and observations exceeding the 80th percentile of reconstruction errors were classified as anomalies.

(c) Unsupervised Learning

Isolation Forest: For faulty device detection, the Isolation Forest model was configured with a contamination parameter of 0.2, indicating an expected anomaly proportion of 20% within the dataset. The algorithm was applied to scaled feature data, with predictions mapped to a binary classification where -1 represented anomalies and 1 represented normal observations.

3.5 Evaluation

The evaluation of anomaly detection models for faulty device detection relies on several key metrics: accuracy, precision, recall, F1-score, ROC-AUC, and computational cost. Accuracy measures the overall correctness of the model, while precision focuses on the reliability of anomaly predictions, reducing false positives. Recall ensures the model detects as many anomalies as possible, minimizing false negatives. The F1-score balances precision and recall, providing a single metric for imbalanced datasets. ROC-AUC evaluates the model's ability to distinguish between normal and anomalous behaviors across thresholds. Computational cost measures the time required for anomaly detection, ensuring real-time applicability. These metrics collectively ensure the models are accurate, reliable, and practical for deployment in real-world healthcare environments. These models achieved top-tier results across multiple metrics, as shown in Table 2.

Table 2. Performance Metrics for Faulty Device Anomaly Detection Models

Model	Precision	Recall	F1-Score	Accuracy (%)	ROC-AUC	Comp Cost
XGBoost	0.99	0.99	0.99	99.00	0.99	0.0388
KNN	0.99	0.99	0.99	99.00	0.99	0.1594
GAN	0.9425	0.99	0.9704	98.85	0.9929	5.4812
Isolation Forest	0.9569	0.99	0.9780	99.15	0.99	0.1979

In the Faulty Device Anomaly Detection Model, XGBoost and KNN emerged as the most effective and efficient models, outperforming all other approaches in terms of both predictive performance and computational efficiency. These models achieved top-tier results across multiple metrics, including accuracy (99%), precision (0.99), recall (0.99), F1-score (0.99), and ROC-AUC (0.99), while also maintaining exceptionally low computational costs (0.0388 for XGBoost and 0.1594 for KNN). Their ability to deliver high-quality results quickly makes them ideal choices for real-time anomaly detection in resource-constrained environments. The results of the Faulty Device Anomaly Detection Model are presented in Table 2.

On the other hand, Isolation Forest and GAN also performed well, achieving near-perfect accuracy (99.15% for Isolation Forest, 98.85% for GAN) and recall (0.99 for both), with impressive ROC-AUC scores (0.99 for Isolation Forest, 0.9929 for GAN). However, GAN was the least computationally efficient when compared to other models, with a significantly high computational cost of 5.4812, which could be a limiting factor in time-sensitive applications. Despite this, its strong overall performance makes it a viable option when training time is less critical.

Overall, XGBoost and KNN were the clear frontrunners, offering the best combination of accuracy and efficiency for detecting faulty devices. Even the lower-performing models still provided reasonably strong results, demonstrating that all tested approaches have potential applications depending on specific constraints such as computational cost and F1-Score requirements.

4 Conclusion

The rapid integration of IoT devices in healthcare has brought about significant advancements in patient care, but it also introduces substantial security and reliability risks. The increasing vulnerability of healthcare IoT devices to operational failures necessitates effective anomaly detection systems capable of identifying faulty devices and ensuring patient safety, data privacy, and healthcare system integrity.

In this paper, we propose FAITH: Fault Anomaly Identification using machine learning for Trusted Healthcare IoT, a comprehensive framework designed to address these challenges. Through the use of a robust dataset and a multi-stage approach incorporating data preprocessing, feature selection, and diverse machine learning models, FAITH effectively detects faulty device anomalies. Our experimental results demonstrated the superior performance of XGBoost for faulty device anomaly detection with 99% accuracy, perfect precision and recall, and minimal computational overhead (0.04 s). Isolation Forest achieved 99% accuracy and recall. For detecting faulty devices, KNN showed near-perfect precision (99%), recall (99%), and F1-score (99%) with a low computational cost (0.05 s), while GAN underperformed with 83% accuracy and a ROC-AUC of 0.72. By combining these techniques, FAITH offers a holistic solution to the challenges associated with faulty device anomaly detection in healthcare IoT environments. The framework leverages the strengths of XGBoost, Isolation Forest, KNN, and GAN, ensuring reliable detection of faulty devices while minimizing computational overhead and maximizing accuracy.

5 Future Works

As shown in the Fig. 3, the FAITH framework is evolving to integrate advanced AI-driven techniques, ensuring privacy, adaptability, and scalability in healthcare IoT systems. The diagram illustrates how FAITH will transition from traditional machine learning-based anomaly detection to an autonomous, self-healing, and privacy-preserving AI-driven healthcare system. The key advancements include Federated Learning, Hybrid AI Models, Blockchain-Powered Security, and Real-Time Fault Prediction, leading to the development of a Smart Healthcare System.

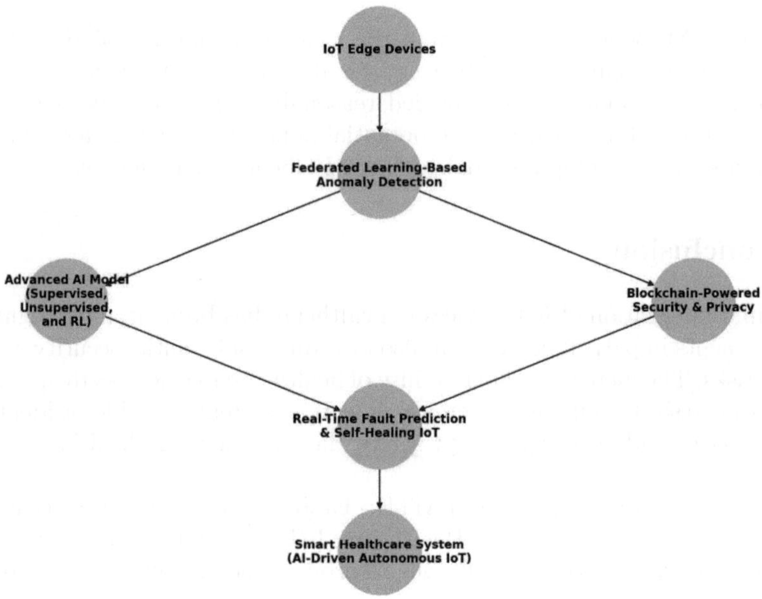

Fig. 3. Future Direction of FAITH Framework.

At the core of FAITH's evolution is the transition toward Federated Learning-Based Anomaly Detection. This will allow IoT edge devices to collaboratively train anomaly detection models while keeping sensitive patient data private. Instead of transmitting raw sensor data to a central server, only model updates will be shared, ensuring data security and decentralized learning. This approach significantly reduces the risk of data breaches while maintaining model performance across distributed healthcare environments.

To further improve anomaly detection and system adaptability, FAITH will incorporate an Advanced AI Model that combines Supervised Learning, Unsupervised Learning, and Reinforcement Learning (RL). This hybrid AI model will enable real-time, adaptive fault detection by continuously learning from new data, allowing the system to automatically adjust to changing sensor behaviors and unknown fault patterns. Reinforcement Learning will play a key role in self-healing IoT systems, where faulty devices can proactively adjust parameters, switch to backup sensors, or trigger alerts to caregivers when failures are detected.

Another critical enhancement is Blockchain-Powered Security and Privacy. As FAITH scales to large networks of interconnected IoT healthcare devices, securing data transactions between edge devices becomes crucial. By leveraging blockchain technology, FAITH will ensure immutable, transparent, and tamper-proof logging of all fault detection events and system updates. This will prevent cyberattacks, unauthorized access, and ensure trust in AI-driven healthcare systems.

The integration of Real-Time Fault Prediction and Self-Healing IoT will transform FAITH from a reactive fault detection system into a proactive, autonomous AI-driven framework. Instead of just identifying anomalies, FAITH will predict failures before they happen, enabling preventive maintenance and real-time interventions. This will significantly reduce downtime in healthcare monitoring systems, improve patient safety, and enhance the reliability of IoT devices in critical applications.

Ultimately, these advancements will contribute to the development of a Smart Healthcare System (AI-Driven Autonomous IoT). FAITH will evolve into a self-learning, self-healing AI framework capable of autonomous decision-making, predictive analytics, and real-time security enforcement. This will make healthcare IoT systems more efficient, scalable, and resilient, paving the way for a next-generation, AI-powered healthcare monitoring ecosystem.

By integrating Federated Learning, Advanced AI, Blockchain Security, and Self-Healing Mechanisms, FAITH will revolutionize AI-driven healthcare by ensuring privacy, adaptability, and real-time fault management at a global scale. In addition, we plan to leverage advanced non-volatile memory technologies such as Phase Change Memory (PCM) to safely and efficiently store critical hospital big data. PCM not only ensures data persistence in case of power failures but also provides high density and low energy consumption, making it a promising candidate for scalable, secure, and energy-efficient healthcare IoT infrastructures [11–15].

References

1. Selvaraj, S., Sundaravaradhan, S.: Challenges and opportunities in IoT healthcare systems: a systematic review. SN Appl. Sci. **2**(1), 139 (2020). https://doi.org/10.1007/s42452-019-1925-y
2. Desai, M., Rumale, A., Asadinia, M.: SHIELD: securing healthcare IoT with efficient machine learning techniques for anomaly detection. In: 2022 IEEE World AI IoT Congress (AIIoT), pp. 0521–0528 (2025). https://doi.org/10.1109/aiiot65859.2025.11105287

3. Yaqoob, T., Abbas, H., Atiquzzaman, M.: Security vulnerabilities, attacks, countermeasures, and regulations of networked medical devices–a review. IEEE Commun. Surv. Tutor. **21**(4), 3723–3768 (2019). https://doi.org/10.1109/comst.2019.2914094
4. Alsalman, D.: A comparative study of anomaly detection techniques for IoT security using AMoT (adaptive machine learning for IoT threats). IEEE Access **12**, 14719–14730 (2024). https://doi.org/10.1109/access.2024.3359033
5. Kavitha, M., Srinivas, P.V.V.S., Kalyampudi, P.L., Srinivasulu, S.: Machine learning techniques for anomaly detection in smart healthcare. In: 2021 Third International Conference on Inventive Research in Computing Applications (ICIRCA) (2021). https://doi.org/10.1109/icirca51532.2021.9544795
6. Fernando, T., Gammulle, H., Denman, S., Sridharan, S., Fookes, C.: Deep learning for medical anomaly detection - a survey. ACM Comput. Surv. **54**(7), 1–37 (2021). https://doi.org/10.1145/3464423
7. Said, A.M., Yahyaoui, A., Abdellatif, T.: Efficient anomaly detection for smart hospital IoT systems. Sensors **21**(4), 1026 (2021). https://doi.org/10.3390/s21041026
8. Khan, M.M., Alkhathami, M.: Anomaly detection in IoT-based healthcare: machine learning for enhanced security. Sci. Rep. **14**(1), 5872 (2024). https://doi.org/10.1038/s41598-024-56126-x
9. IoT Healthcare Security Dataset. www.kaggle.com. https://www.kaggle.com/datasets/faisalmalik/iot-healthcare-security-dataset
10. Rumale, A., Desai, M., Asadinia, M.: PRISM: predictive risk and injury surveillance model for athlete safety. In: 2025 IEEE World AI IoT Congress (AIIoT), pp. 0024–0031 (2025). https://doi.org/10.1109/aiiot65859.2025.11105248
11. Desai, M., Quinn, R., Asadinia, M.: SMART-WRITE: adaptive learning-based write energy optimization for phase change memory. In: 2025 IEEE 15th Annual Computing and Communication Workshop and Conference (CCWC), pp. 00640–00648 (2025). https://doi.org/10.1109/ccwc62904.2025.10903957
12. Ekoniak, J., Rumale, A., Asadinia, M.: ML-PreP: machine learning based error prediction for phase change memory. In: 2025 IEEE 15th Annual Computing and Communication Workshop and Conference (CCWC), pp. 00909–00917 (2025. https://doi.org/10.1109/ccwc62904.2025.10903761
13. Desai, M., Rumale, A., Asadinia, M., Bogle, S.: WIRE: write energy reduction via encoding in phase change main memories (PCM). In: Lecture Notes in Networks and Systems, pp. 599–615 (2024). https://doi.org/10.1007/978-3-031-73125-9_38
14. Rumale, A., Ekoniak, J., Asadinia, M.: PENN: predicting errors using neural network in phase change memory. Commun. Comput. Inf. Sci. **2506**, 278–293 (2025). https://doi.org/10.1007/978-3-031-94962-3_24
15. Desai, M., Quinn, R., Asadinia, M.: ML-PCM: machine learning technique for write optimization in phase change memory (PCM). Commun. Comput. Inf. Sci. **2506**, 207–219 (2025). https://doi.org/10.1007/978-3-031-95130-5_17

Synthetic Cognitive Augmentation Network

Benjamin J. Kennedy(✉), Atif Farid Mohammad, and Matthew Wyandt

Department of Artificial Intelligence, Capitol Technology University, Laurel, USA
{bkennedy1,afmohammad,mwyandt}@captechu.edu

Abstract. The Synthetic Cognitive Augmentation Network introduces a novel, biologically inspired artificial intelligence framework designed to replicate and enhance human cognitive functions through a modular architecture. By emulating specialized regions of the prefrontal cortex, the Synthetic Cognitive Augmentation Network utilizes dedicated artificial intelligence agents to manage distinct cognitive tasks such as decision-making, problem-solving, and emotional regulation. This paper outlines the Synthetic Cognitive Augmentation Network's conceptual framework, the theoretical foundations of its modular design, and the advantages of precision-engineered artificial intelligence agents for cognitive enhancement. Demonstrating the feasibility of the Synthetic Cognitive Augmentation Network paves the way for future advancements, including components of the Synthetic Cognitive Augmentation Network ecosystem like the Synthetic Cognitive Augmentation Network Using Experts or User Extensible, which will incorporate adaptive learning and artificial intelligence alignment methodologies [1], and the Spiking Transformer Augmenting Cognition, a hybrid architecture combining spiking neural networks and transformers to further enhance cognitive simulations. Additionally, this work highlights design-based research conducted via the Cognitive Augmentation User Survey Evaluation, which has informed the development of the Synthetic Cognitive Augmentation Network Using Experts or User Extensible. The Alignment Questionnaire assesses cognitive functioning and personal preferences to align the Synthetic Cognitive Augmentation Network Using Experts or User Extensible with individual needs, promoting a better fit based on personalized decision-making and problem-solving characteristics [2]. This paper primarily focuses on the foundation of the Synthetic Cognitive Augmentation Network and introduces the supporting and future components of the Synthetic Cognitive Augmentation Network.

Keywords: Artificial intelligence · Cognitive architectures · Biologically inspired computing · Neural networks · Decision support systems · Human-computer interaction · Adaptive systems · Intelligent agents · Machine learning · Cognitive science · Synthetic Cognitive Augmentation Network · Prefrontal cortex emulation · Spiking neural networks

S. Hussain et al. (Eds.): SEET 2025, CCIS 2725, pp. 179–188, 2026.
https://doi.org/10.1007/978-3-032-08977-9_13

1 Introduction

1.1 Overview

Artificial intelligence (AI) has become pivotal in augmenting human cognition, representing a critical frontier in both scientific research and practical applications. Despite significant advancements, existing AI architectures often lack biological plausibility and task-specific optimization. Traditional monolithic large language models (LLMs) demonstrate proficiency in natural language processing but encounter limitations in replicating the intricacies of human cognitive functions, such as nuanced decision-making and emotional regulation, key functions governed by the prefrontal cortex (PFC) in the human brain [3, 4]. While these models excel at a wide variety of tasks, they often require immense computational resources.

The Synthetic Cognitive Augmentation Network (SCAN) addresses these limitations through a modular AI framework that leverages multiple specialized, more compact agents working collaboratively to emulate and enhance the functions of the PFC. Inspired by the functional specialization within the PFC, including regions like the dorsolateral prefrontal cortex (DLPFC) and the ventromedial prefrontal cortex (VMPFC), SCAN employs dedicated AI agents to simulate these regions [5]. This design enables the system to assist in decision-making, emotional regulation, and problem-solving more effectively than existing monolithic AI architectures.

Recent research highlights the constraints of monolithic AI systems in managing complex, multifaceted cognitive tasks, especially in dynamic environments. SCAN's modular approach distributes cognitive workloads across specialized agents, enhancing performance in decision-making scenarios [6]. Additionally, SCAN integrates adaptive learning methods, allowing agents to adjust their behaviors based on continuous environmental feedback. This feature is further developed in the Synthetic Cognitive Augmentation Network Using Experts or User Extensible (SCANUE) prototype, a lightweight extension of SCAN that leverages adaptive learning, including reinforcement learning, for agent specialization [7].

Additionally, design-based research utilizing the Cognitive Augmentation User Survey Evaluation (CAUSE) has informed the development of SCANUE. The Alignment Questionnaire (SCANAQ) is employed to assess cognitive functioning and personal preferences, ensuring that SCANUE aligns with individual user needs.

1.2 Novelty and Benefits

SCAN represents a significant advancement in cognitive AI systems by adopting a biologically inspired approach to augment human decision-making and problem-solving capabilities. Unlike monolithic AI designs, SCAN's modular architecture offers several key advantages:

1. By emulating the PFC's structure, SCAN closely mirrors human cognitive processes. Each agent specializes in tasks analogous to specific PFC regions, for example, the DLPFC agent focuses on cognitive flexibility and executive functions, while the VMPFC agent handles emotional regulation and risk assessment [8]. This biological alignment enhances the system's ability to interact naturally with end users.

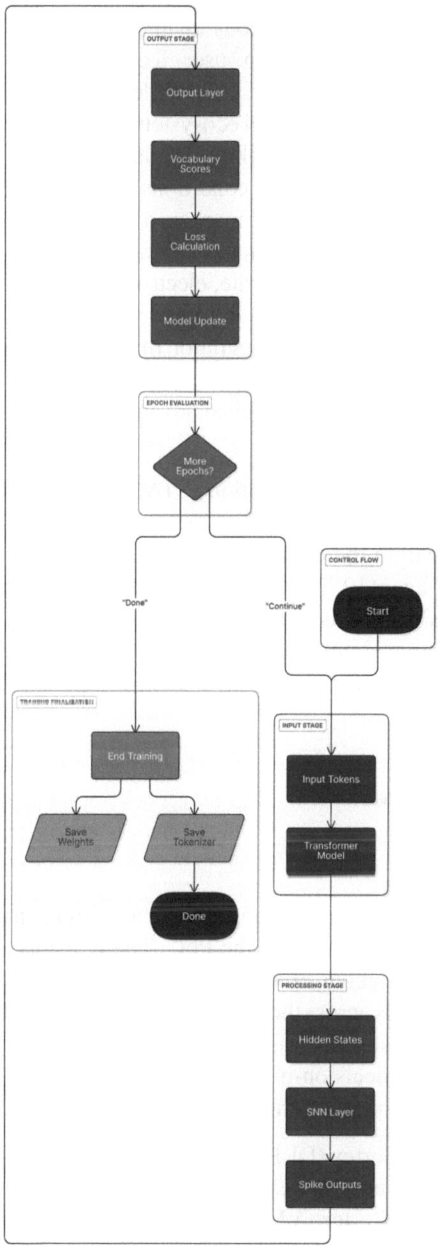

Fig. 1. Training Pipeline for STAC. Training pipeline combining a Transformer with a Spiking Neural Network (SNN). Input tokens pass through a Transformer to produce hidden states processed by the SNN layer into spike outputs. Outputs are evaluated, loss is computed, and model parameters updated iteratively across epochs. Upon completion, final weights and tokenizer are saved.

2. Incorporating adaptive learning methods enables SCANUE agents to adjust their decision-making strategies based on user feedback data, ensuring continuous improvement in dynamic environments [7]. While SCAN focuses on biological plausibility, SCANUE, as part of the SCAN ecosystem, is being researched in future studies to become a more tailored approach. This adaptability is crucial for applications requiring responsiveness to changing conditions. The ability to integrate additional data inputs like sensors and biometric markers allows the SCANUE model to adapt to the user's biological feedback without explicit input, modifying suggestions and responses based on factors like heart rate, electroencephalography (EEG), and other indicators that affect problem-solving abilities.
3. The modular design allows for easy integration of additional agents or functionalities, making SCAN adaptable to various applications. This scalability ensures that the system can evolve alongside technological advancements and user needs.

An innovative component within the SCAN ecosystem is the development of the Spiking Transformer Augmenting Cognition (STAC). STAC refines the integration of spiking neural networks (SNNs) and transformer architectures, enhancing the simulation of cognitive functions within the different PFC regions and, for initial future research, focusing on the DLPFC agent [9, 10]. By capturing the temporal dynamics of SNNs and leveraging transformers' strengths in handling language data, this hybrid model allows for more accurate cognitive simulations. Future iterations aim to integrate STAC more fully as computational resources advance. The training pipeline for STAC is depicted in Fig. 1.

2 SCAN Architecture

2.1 Modular Design

The core of SCAN is its biologically inspired modular design, employing specialized AI agents modeled after distinct regions of the PFC. These agents replicate key cognitive functions such as decision-making, emotional regulation, and conflict resolution. By distributing cognitive workloads across these specialized agents, SCAN enhances efficiency and precision in cognitive tasks. Each agent operates independently within its domain but contributes to an integrated decision-making process, akin to how PFC regions function collaboratively in the human brain. The primary agents in SCAN include:

1. Dorsolateral Prefrontal Cortex (DLPFC) Agent: Responsible for cognitive flexibility, working memory, and executive decision-making [8].
2. Ventromedial Prefrontal Cortex (VMPFC) Agent: Manages emotional regulation and risk-based decision-making, integrating emotional information into choices [8].
3. Orbitofrontal Cortex (OFC) Agent: Handles reward-based decision-making, evaluating potential outcomes based on predicted rewards [13].
4. Anterior Cingulate Cortex (ACC) Agent: Focuses on conflict detection and error monitoring, allowing real-time adjustments in decision-making strategies [14].
5. Medial Prefrontal Cortex (mPFC) Agent: Oversees value-based decision-making, goal-directed behavior, and social cognition [15].

2.2 Learning Modular Synthetic PFC

SCAN's significance lies in its ability to replicate the PFC's learning capabilities, essential for handling complex, adaptive tasks in real time. The integration of adaptive learning methods in SCANUE allows the system to evolve beyond static decision-making models, enabling real-time adaptability. By incorporating adaptive learning techniques, SCANUE ensures that each decision is informed by continuous feedback, allowing for ongoing improvement and adjustment, similar to human experiential learning [7, 16].

Additionally, SCANUE utilizes the Alignment Questionnaire (SCANAQ) to assess cognitive functioning and personal preferences, aligning SCANUE with unique user needs [2]. This alignment promotes a better fit based on personalized decision-making and problem-solving characteristics. Although SCANAQ has not yet been implemented, it has been validated through current research and will be a focus in future studies. Design-based research conducted via the Cognitive Augmentation User Survey Evaluation (CAUSE) has informed the development of SCANUE, ensuring that adaptive learning and user alignment are integral to the system's evolution [1].

2.3 Implementation

The SCAN system was developed using a modular, agent-based architecture to simulate the cognitive functions of the PFC. Python was selected as the primary programming language due to its extensive ecosystem supporting machine learning and natural language processing (NLP).

1. The CrewAI framework serves as the backbone for orchestrating the interactions among autonomous AI agents, each simulating distinct regions of the PFC, such as the DLPFC and VMPFC. CrewAI was chosen for its capability to handle complex role-playing and multi-agent coordination, ensuring smooth collaboration between agents. The primary goal was to demonstrate that multiple cognitive agents could work together to replicate human-like decision-making [17]. The flow of data within the SCAN system can be seen in Fig. 2 below.
2. The OpenAI API was employed to provide natural language processing capabilities. This allowed the AI agents in SCAN to perform tasks like planning, decision-making, and emotional regulation with high contextual accuracy. OpenAI's models were selected for their advanced language understanding and generation capabilities, which were critical in ensuring the system could handle cognitive tasks effectively. While the models used in SCAN were generalized and not fine-tuned, they were essential in proving that the agents could collaborate in real-time environments [17, 18].
3. SCANUE builds upon SCAN by introducing fine-tuned models for each cognitive agent, improving efficiency and specialization. These fine-tuned models reduce computational overhead and enhance each agent's performance in their designated roles. Furthermore, SCANUE integrates the Alignment Questionnaire (SCANAQ) to tailor the system to individual user profiles, ensuring that cognitive augmentation aligns with personalized needs [2]. This integration ensures that SCANUE not only maintains the collaborative framework of SCAN but also enhances it with user-specific adaptations [1].

3 Discussion

3.1 Real-World Applications

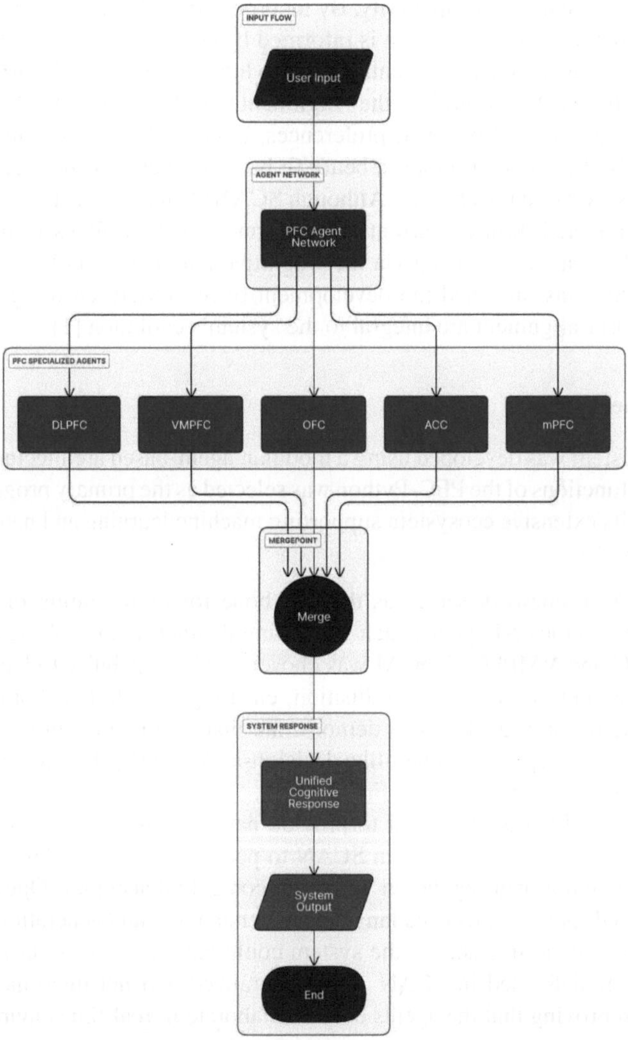

Fig. 2. The figure denotes the data flow within the SCAN application. User input is received by the PFC Agent Network and delegated to specialized cognitive agents: DLPFC, VMPFC, OFC, ACC, and mPFC. Each agent independently processes its task, and their results converge at a merge point. The merged outputs generate a unified cognitive response, delivered back to the user as the system output.

In healthcare, SCAN can assist clinicians in complex decision-making processes by providing cognitive support. By analyzing patient data, SCAN can recommend personalized treatment plans that integrate both medical and emotional factors, enabling clinicians to make more informed, precise decisions while reducing cognitive load [19]. In the finance sector, SCAN's adaptive learning capabilities can optimize risk management strategies for financial professionals by adapting to real-time market fluctuations. SCAN evaluates investment portfolios, predicts trends, and suggests adjustments to strategies, empowering investors and financial planners to make smarter, data-driven decisions [7].

In education, SCAN supports both educators and students by personalizing learning experiences. The system adapts to individual learning styles and needs, enhancing engagement, retention, and overall educational outcomes. In manufacturing, SCAN collaborates with human workers to optimize production processes, making real-time decisions based on operational data to improve efficiency, reduce errors, and minimize costs. This collaboration helps maintain smooth operations without replacing the human workforce.

For consumer applications, SCAN can integrate into daily life, empowering individuals to make better decisions and solve everyday problems more effectively. By providing personalized advice, whether for time management, personal finance, or health and wellness, SCAN could be made accessible to the public, allowing individuals to benefit from advanced cognitive augmentation in their personal lives.

Future investigations may place SCAN in simulation-based tasks, measuring user performance gains over monolithic baselines. Preliminary prototypes suggest synergy among specialized agents improves adaptability in dynamic problem scenarios.

3.2 Ethical Considerations

As SCAN progresses, ethical considerations must be addressed, particularly regarding data privacy, bias in decision-making, and transparency in AI systems. Ensuring that multi-agent orchestration operates ethically and fairly is crucial, especially in sectors where decision-making has far-reaching consequences [20]. Implementing robust governance frameworks and ethical guidelines will be essential to navigate the complexities associated with advanced AI systems. Future research will explore these ethical dimensions in greater depth, ensuring that SCAN remains a trusted and accountable AI system for cognitive augmentation.

3.3 Theoretical Integration: Cognitive Science and AI

The theoretical foundation of SCAN is rooted in cognitive neuroscience, particularly in replicating PFC functionalities. The PFC's role in managing complex cognitive tasks, including decision-making, emotional regulation, and adaptive learning, has been extensively studied. SCAN's architecture mirrors these biological processes by structuring AI agents to mimic the specialized roles of different PFC regions [21]. By integrating principles from cognitive neuroscience, SCAN achieves a higher degree of biological plausibility compared to traditional AI systems. This alignment enhances the system's ability to simulate human-like cognitive processes, providing more natural and effective cognitive augmentation.

4 Conclusion

The Synthetic Cognitive Augmentation Network (SCAN) represents a significant step forward in AI-driven cognitive augmentation. By emulating key aspects of the human prefrontal cortex through a modular and biologically plausible design, SCAN offers a robust framework for enhancing decision-making, emotional regulation, and cognitive control in complex, real-world environments. This work highlights the progression within the SCAN ecosystem, differentiating between SCAN, SCANUE, and STAC, each contributing distinct elements to this evolving architecture.

SCAN's architecture, rooted in biological realism, allows for a nuanced approach to decision-making and emotional processing, essential for applications that require a high level of cognitive fidelity. With SCANUE, the framework is further enriched by adaptive learning and user-specific alignment tools like SCANAQ, facilitating real-time adaptability and personalized cognitive augmentation. This multifaceted ecosystem represents a significant leap in AI's capability to simulate, support, and extend human cognitive functions, paving the way for AI systems that are not only responsive but also resilient and adaptable to diverse scenarios.

Looking ahead, the continued development of SCAN promises to unveil new adaptive alignment techniques and personalized augmentation strategies that could redefine the role of AI in critical decision-making contexts. Future research will delve deeper into optimizing SCAN's architecture for various industrial applications, integrating adaptive learning mechanisms, and exploring cross-domain adaptability. By building on the foundational principles established here, SCAN is set to play an integral role in the next generation of cognitive AI systems, contributing to safer, more effective, and more ethically aligned AI solutions across multiple domains.

5 Future Work

Future research on SCAN should focus on several key areas to fully realize its potential. Firstly, extensive empirical validation of the SCAN framework in diverse real-world scenarios is necessary. While the theoretical foundations and initial feasibility studies are promising, practical applications in fields such as healthcare, education, and workplace productivity will provide valuable insights into SCAN's effectiveness and adaptability. Researchers should conduct longitudinal studies to assess how SCAN's modular AI agents perform over time in dynamic environments, ensuring that the system can adapt to changing cognitive demands and user needs.

The advancements in the SCANUE component warrant further investigation. The incorporation of adaptive learning and AI alignment methodologies presents a rich area for exploration. Future studies should delve into the mechanisms of adaptive learning within SCANUE, examining how the system can continuously improve its cognitive augmentation capabilities based on user feedback and evolving data. Additionally, research should focus on refining AI alignment techniques to ensure that SCANUE's outputs are consistently aligned with user preferences and ethical considerations. This will involve developing more sophisticated algorithms for personalized decision-making and problem-solving, as well as exploring the ethical implications of such personalized AI systems.

Lastly, the hybrid architecture of the Spiking Transformer Augmenting Cognition (STAC) offers a unique avenue for future research. The integration of spiking neural networks and transformers holds the potential to revolutionize cognitive simulations by combining the strengths of both approaches. Researchers should investigate the synergistic effects of these technologies within the STAC framework, exploring how spiking neural networks can enhance the temporal dynamics and energy efficiency of cognitive processes, while transformers provide robust contextual understanding and predictive capabilities. Furthermore, interdisciplinary collaborations among neuroscientists, AI researchers, and cognitive psychologists will be crucial in advancing the STAC architecture, ensuring that it accurately replicates and augments human cognitive functions.

References

1. Tate, L.: iLevyTate/SCANUE: 1.0.0-alpha. Zenodo (2024). https://doi.org/10.5281/zenodo.14052759
2. Tate, L.: iLevyTate/SCAN-Resources: 1.0.0-alpha. Zenodo (2024). https://doi.org/10.5281/zenodo.14053203
3. Miller, E.K., Cohen, J.D.: An integrative theory of prefrontal cortex function. Annu. Rev. Neurosci. **24**, 167–202 (2001)
4. Bechara, A., Damasio, H., Damasio, A.R.: Different contributions of the human amygdala and ventromedial prefrontal cortex to decision-making. J. Neurosci. **20**(11), 5473–5481 (2000)
5. Watanabe, M.: Role of anticipated reward in cognitive behavioral control. Curr. Opin. Neurobiol. **17**(2), 213–219 (2007)
6. Silver, D., et al.: Mastering the game of Go with deep neural networks and tree search. Nature **529**, 484–489 (2016)
7. Sutton, R.S., Barto, A.G.: Reinforcement Learning: An Introduction, 2nd edn. MIT Press, Cambridge, MA, USA (2018)
8. Rolls, E.T.: The functions of the orbitofrontal cortex. Brain Cogn. **55**(1), 11–29 (2004)
9. Zhang, S., Dean, J.C.: Spikeformers: Transformers with Spiking Neural Networks. arXiv preprint arXiv:2109.12894 (2021)
10. Pfeiffer, M., Pfeil, T.: Deep learning with spiking neurons: opportunities and challenges. Front. Neurosci. **12**, 774 (2018)
11. Newell, A., Simon, H.A.: Computer science as empirical inquiry: symbols and search. Commun. ACM **19**(3), 113–126 (1976)
12. Hitzler, P., van Harmelen, F.: A reasonable semantic web. Semantic Web **1**(1–2), 39–44 (2010)
13. Rolls, E.T.: The orbitofrontal cortex and reward. Cereb. Cortex **10**(3), 284–294 (2000)
14. Botvinick, M.M., et al.: Conflict monitoring and cognitive control. Psychol. Rev. **108**(3), 624–652 (2001)
15. Amodio, D.M., Frith, C.D.: Meeting of minds: The medial frontal cortex and social cognition. Nat. Rev. Neurosci. **7**(4), 268–277 (2006)
16. Power, J.D., Petersen, S.: Control-related systems in the human brain. Curr. Opin. Neurobiol. **23**(2), 223–228 (2013)
17. IDEO: Rapid Prototyping With OpenAI (2024). https://www.ideo.com/journal/rapid-prototyping-with-openai. Accessed 2 Oct 2024
18. Tate, L., Sanders, P.: iLevyTate/SCAN: 1.0.0-alpha. Zenodo (2024). https://doi.org/10.5281/zenodo.14052885
19. Roumeliotis, K.I., Tselikas, N.D.: ChatGPT and OpenAI models: a preliminary review. Future Internet **15**(6), 192 (2023). https://doi.org/10.3390/fi15060192

20. Mohammad, A.F., et al.: LLM/GPT generative AI and artificial general intelligence (AGI): the next frontier. In: 2023 Congress in Computer Science, Computer Engineering, & Applications (CSCE), pp. 413–417. IEEE (2023)
21. Miller, E.K., Wallis, J.D.: Executive function and higher-order cognition: definition and neural substrates. In: Squire, L.R. (ed.) Encyclopedia of Neuroscience, vol. 4, pp. 99–104. Academic Press, Oxford (2009)
22. Bhattacharya, P., Prasad, V.K., Verma, A., Gupta, D., Sapsomboon, A., Viriyasitavat, W., Dhiman, G.: Demystifying ChatGPT: an in-depth survey of OpenAI's robust large language models. Arch. Comput. Methods Eng. **31**(8), 4557–4600 (2024). https://doi.org/10.1007/s11831-024-10115-5

Robust UAV Intrusion Detection via Federated Learning: A Comparison of NN and CNN-LSTM Models

Sayed Muqayyad Hussain[1(✉)], Madiha Haider Syed[1], Adeel Anjum[1], Muhammad Javed[2], and Ankit Raj[3]

[1] Institute of Information Technology, Quaid-I-Azam University, Islamabad, Pakistan
muqayyadhussain@gmail.com, {madiha,aanjum}@qau.edu.pk

[2] Department of Computer Engineering and Information Technology, FOC, Gomal University, Dera Ismail Khan, Pakistan
javed_gomal@gu.edu.pk

[3] Department of Computer Engineering and Computer Science, California State University, Long Beach, CA, USA
Ankit.Raj01@student.csulb.edu

Abstract. Unmanned Aerial Vehicles (UAVs) play a crucial role in surveillance, disaster response, and military operations. However, their dependence on wireless communication exposes them to cyber threats such as GPS jamming and spoofing. Traditional intrusion detection systems (IDS) struggle to adapt to evolving attack patterns while ensuring data privacy. Federated Learning (FL) offers a promising approach by enabling distributed model training across UAVs without sharing sensitive data. This study presents a comparative analysis of two FL-based IDS models: a standard Neural Network (NN) and a hybrid Convolutional Neural Network-Long Short-Term Memory (CNN-LSTM) model. Using the UAV ATTACK dataset, we evaluate their performance across multiple federated clients. Experimental results reveal that the CNN-LSTM model outperforms the NN model, achieving superior accuracy (99.1% vs. 81.2%), higher recall, and fewer false positives. Additionally, the CNN-LSTM model demonstrates faster convergence, lower validation loss, and enhanced generalization, making it more suitable for real-time UAV security applications.

Keywords: Federated Learning · Intrusion Detection System · Unmanned Aerial Vehicles (UAVs) · CNN-LSTM Hybrid Model · Cybersecurity in UAVs · Anomaly Detection · Deep Learning for UAV Security · Privacy-Preserving Machine Learning

1 Introduction

Unmanned Aerial Vehicles (UAVs) are increasingly utilized in diverse applications, including military operations, border surveillance, disaster response, commercial delivery services, and smart city monitoring. However, their reliance on

S. Hussain et al. (Eds.): SEET 2025, CCIS 2725, pp. 189–212, 2026.
https://doi.org/10.1007/978-3-032-08977-9_14

wireless communication makes them highly susceptible to cyber threats such as intrusion attacks, GPS jamming, and spoofing. These threats can lead to UAV hijacking, mission failure, or disruptions to critical infrastructure. Malicious adversaries can manipulate navigation signals or interfere with communication channels, posing serious security risks.

IDS typically employ centralized architectures where UAVs transmit data to a central server for threat analysis. While effective, this approach introduces significant challenges, including privacy risks, high communication overhead, and limited scalability—particularly in large UAV networks. Federated Learning (FL) has emerged as a promising decentralized alternative, allowing UAVs to collaboratively train models while preserving data privacy. FL enhances security and adaptability by enabling real-time intrusion detection without exposing raw data.

This paper presents a comparative analysis of two FL-based deep learning models for UAV intrusion detection:

1) A standard Neural Network (NN), a lightweight approach with moderate detection capability.
2) A hybrid Convolutional Neural Network-Long Short-Term Memory (CNN-LSTM) model, which integrates CNN's feature extraction capabilities with LSTM's ability to capture temporal dependencies in UAV telemetry data.

To evaluate these models, we employ the UAV ATTACK dataset, which contains real-world benign scenarios alongside GPS jamming and GPS spoofing attacks. Our experiments assess performance metrics such as accuracy, recall, precision, false positive rates, convergence time, and generalization ability in a federated learning environment. Results indicate that the CNN-LSTM model significantly outperforms the NN model, achieving superior detection accuracy (99.1% vs. 81.2%), enhanced classification of attack types, and improved resilience against adversarial conditions.

1.1 Contributions of This Paper

This study makes the following key contributions (Fig. 1):

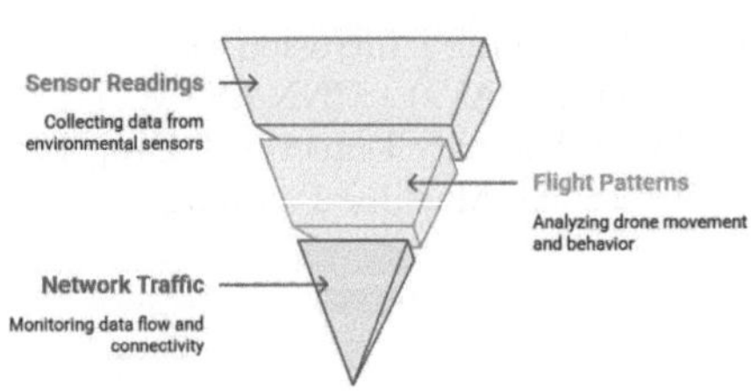

Fig. 1. UAV Data collection

- **Comparative Analysis of NN and CNN-LSTM for Federated UAV Security:** Evaluates the strengths and weaknesses of both architectures in a federated intrusion detection setting.
- **Real-World Performance Evaluation:** Assesses models using the UAV ATTACK dataset to ensure practical applicability.
- **Enhanced Intrusion Detection Accuracy:** Demonstrates CNN-LSTM's superiority in reducing false alarms and improving attack classification.
- **Privacy-Preserving Federated Learning Implementation:** Highlights the advantages of FL in UAV security by enabling distributed model training without data sharing.

2 Related Work

Intrusion detection and cybersecurity in UAV networks have gained significant research attention due to the increasing deployment of UAVs in defense, surveillance, disaster management [5], and industrial automation. Given their reliance on wireless communication and GPS navigation, UAVs are vulnerable to cyber threats such as GPS spoofing, jamming, unauthorized access, and data interception. Traditional security mechanisms [12], including rule-based and signature-based intrusion detection systems (IDS), struggle to counter evolving cyber threats due to their reliance on predefined attack patterns [33]. Machine learning (ML) and deep learning (DL) have emerged as promising alternatives, enabling UAVs to detect novel attack patterns and dynamically adapt to evolving threats [3,10].

Several studies have explored ML-based approaches for anomaly detection and cybersecurity in UAV networks. Alzahrani [6] introduced a multi-sensor anomaly detection system that integrates various sensor data streams to enhance UAV security, demonstrating effectiveness in detecting deviations from normal

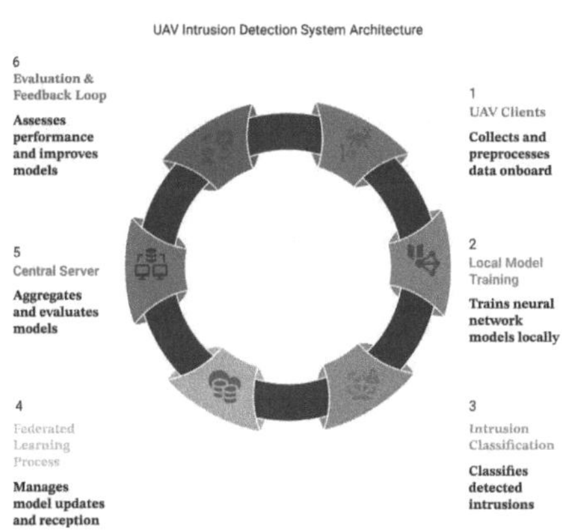

Fig. 2. System Architecture Flow

UAV behavior. Similarly, Baccari et al. [8,13] conducted a survey on anomaly detection in autonomous and connected vehicles, identifying key challenges applicable to UAV networks, such as handling large-scale, real-time data. Badar et al. [9] proposed a lightweight IDS for IoT-based UAV infrastructures, leveraging deep learning for real-time cyber threat detection while minimizing computational overhead. These studies underscore the increasing reliance on ML-driven solutions to secure UAV communications and prevent unauthorized access [28] (Fig. 2).

However, most existing IDS rely on centralized architectures, where UAVs transmit raw sensor data to a central server for analysis [27]. This centralized approach introduces several challenges, including high communication overhead, privacy risks, and vulnerability to single points of failure. To overcome these limitations, FL has emerged as a viable alternative [24,26], enabling UAVs to collaboratively train models while preserving data privacy. FL allows distributed learning without exposing raw data, thereby improving security, scalability, and adaptability in UAV intrusion detection [10,34] (Table 1).

2.1 Federated Learning for Industrial IoT and IoT Security

Jebocen et al. [26] explored Federated Transfer Learning for intrusion detection in Industrial IoT (IIoT) 4.0, demonstrating improved anomaly detection capabilities. However, their approach faces challenges related to increased resource consumption and communication overhead. Similarly, Olanrewaju et al. [28] investigated a hybrid approach combining supervised and unsupervised deep learning in IoT IDS. Their research highlighted scalability and data heterogeneity as key challenges in federated intrusion detection. Agrawal et al. [3] provided a comprehensive review of FL-based IDS, discussing security vulnerabilities in model aggregation and communication, which could expose the system to adversarial attacks [6].

2.2 Federated Learning in UAV Security

The integration of FL in UAV security has been explored by several researchers. Ceviz et al. [12] proposed a novel FL-based IDS for UAV networks to enhance privacy and security. Despite its advantages, the study indicated that computational overhead and real-time constraints limit practical deployment. Similarly, Zeng et al. [35] introduced a Generative Adversarial Network (GAN)-augmented FL-based IDS for UAVs, improving anomaly detection but facing risks of model poisoning and adversarial attacks [7].

Ntizikira et al. [27] addressed privacy and security concerns in UAV networks by incorporating cryptographic techniques into intrusion detection. While this method improved security, it introduced increased computational complexity and scalability limitations [9,20].

Table 1. Federated Learning-Based IDS Techniques and Security Limitations in UAV and IoT Security

Ref	Year	Technique	Method	Security Limitations
[26]	2024	Federated Transfer Learning for IDS in IIoT 4.0	Federated learning-based anomaly detection	Increased resource consumption and communication overhead
[28]	2025	Federated Learning for IoT IDS using Unsupervised and Supervised Deep Learning	Hybrid FL approach for intrusion detection	Scalability and data heterogeneity issues
[3]	2022	Federated Learning Concepts and Challenges for IDS	Overview of FL-based IDS frameworks	Security vulnerabilities in aggregation and communication
[12]	2023	Federated Learning-Based IDS for UAV Security	Privacy-preserving intrusion detection in UAV networks	Computational overhead and real-time constraints
[22]	2023	Efficient Federated Learning for Network IDS	Optimized FL training process for network security	High dependency on server availability and attack mitigation challenges
[35]	2024	GAN-Augmented FL-Based IDS for UAV Networks	Combination of Federated Learning and GAN for anomaly detection	Model poisoning risks and adversarial attack vulnerabilities
[36]	2022	Semi-Supervised Federated Learning for IoT IDS	Federated learning with semi-supervised techniques	Data imbalance and privacy-preserving trade-offs
[27]	2023	Secure and Privacy-Preserving IDS for UAV Networks	Cryptographic techniques and decentralized security	Increased computational complexity and limited scalability
[21]	2023	Defense Against Poisoning Attacks in FL-Based IDS	Two-phase detection mechanism	Mitigation strategies require additional communication costs

2.3 Efficiency Improvements in Federated Learning-Based IDS

Several studies have focused on optimizing FL frameworks for efficient intrusion detection [11]. Li et al. [22] proposed an efficient FL system for network intrusion detection, emphasizing optimized training processes to reduce dependency on a central server. However, challenges in server availability and attack mitigation persist. Zhao et al. [36] introduced a semi-supervised FL-based IDS for IoT security, demonstrating effectiveness in detecting anomalies while balancing privacy preservation and data heterogeneity issues [17].

2.4 Security Enhancements Against Attacks in Federated Learning

FL-based IDS are susceptible to various attacks, including model poisoning and data poisoning. Lai et al. [21] proposed a two-phase defense mechanism against poisoning attacks in FL-based IDS, which enhances robustness but introduces additional communication costs [30]. This study highlights the need for efficient mitigation strategies to secure FL architectures against adversarial threats [19].

Despite these advancements, many FL-based UAV security solutions lack a thorough evaluation of deep learning architectures for intrusion detection [1]. Model selection plays a crucial role in detection accuracy, training efficiency [8,32], and system robustness. Although Convolutional neural networks (CNNs) and long-short-term memory (LSTM) have been widely studied for intrusion detection due to their ability to capture spatial and temporal features from UAV telemetry data, comparative studies between traditional NN and hybrid CNN-LSTM architectures in federated intrusion detection remain limited [16].

This study bridges this gap by conducting a comprehensive performance comparison of NN and CNN-LSTM models in an FL-based UAV intrusion detection framework [14]. Using the UAV ATTACK dataset, we evaluate their ability to detect GPS jamming, spoofing, and benign behaviors while maintaining model privacy across distributed UAV nodes. Unlike prior research that focuses on individual architectures, our work provides a comparative analysis of NN and CNN-LSTM models, highlighting their strengths and limitations in an FL settingcitezeng2024fga [36].

2.5 Neural Network for Intrusion Detection

NN are employed widely in intrusion detection due to their capacity to learn complicated patterns from network traffic data. Some research has discussed the efficacy of NN-based models in anomaly detection and demonstrated that the models are effective in handling high-dimensional input features and generalizing to other datasets. Earlier research has employed NN architectures to identify cyber-attacks in Internet of Things (IoT) and vehicle networks and demonstrated that the models are robust in dynamic scenarios [2].

In UAV intrusion detection systems, NNs are employed as the baseline model due to simplicity and ease of implementation. While the traditional NNs are ineffective in handling sequential dependencies in UAV telemetry data in the time-series form, the employment of hybrid models such as CNN-LSTM becomes necessary. Comparing NN performance with CNN-LSTM under federated learning, this study evaluates whether the additional complexity of the hybrid models is justified by the performance gain over the traditional NN-based models [25].

2.6 Gaps and Research Contributions

While existing studies have explored federated learning and deep learning models for UAV security, there are notable gaps:

- **Limited Comparative Studies:** Most research focuses on individual models (e.g., CNNs or RNNs) rather than comparing standard NN vs. hybrid CNN-LSTM architectures in a federated learning setting.
- **Lack of Performance Benchmarks:** Many studies highlight FL's potential but do not provide detailed experimental comparisons on accuracy, precision, recall, and model convergence trends.

- **Application to Real-World UAV Data:** While theoretical frameworks exist, practical evaluations on real UAV datasets (such as UAV ATTACK) remain underexplored.

2.7 Scalability and Real-Time Performance

As drone networks expand, they must be able to handle an increasing number of UAVs while maintaining secure, real-time communication [23]. Many existing security protocols introduce delays and performance bottlenecks due to their resource-intensive nature [32]. In applications requiring real-time responsiveness, such as emergency response or time-sensitive delivery, inefficient security mechanisms can hinder effectiveness.

Federated learning, when combined with efficient hybrid deep learning models, has the potential to enhance UAV intrusion detection while maintaining scalability. By leveraging CNN-LSTM architectures, this study aims to provide a high-performance, federated IDS for UAVs, addressing the challenges of real-time security in large-scale drone networks [29,31].

3 Methodology

In this study, we propose a robust intrusion detection system for UAVs using Federated Learning (FL) with a comparative analysis of NN and a CNN-LSTM hybrid model [4]. This section elaborates on the methodology, including dataset processing, feature extraction, model training, and evaluation within a federated learning environment [12].

3.1 Dataset Justification and Limitations:

In this study, we utilized the UAV Attack dataset, which specifically targets GPS jamming and spoofing attacks. These attacks were selected due to their direct impact on the navigational integrity and autonomous decision-making of UAVs, making them among the most critical threats in UAV cybersecurity. The dataset provides structured, labeled flight data that accurately simulates real-world GPS manipulation scenarios, enabling reliable model training and evaluation. While this focus allows for in-depth analysis of GPS-based intrusions, we acknowledge that the dataset does not encompass other cyber threats such as Denial-of-Service (DoS), data interception, or command injection attacks. These types of attacks typically require different data modalities (e.g., network traffic, telemetry logs) that are beyond the scope of this dataset. As part of our future work, we aim to extend our framework using additional datasets (e.g., CICIDS, TON_IoT, BoTIoT) to incorporate a broader range of attack vectors and further evaluate the generalizability of our proposed intrusion detection system.

3.2 Dataset and Preprocessing

The dataset used in this study consists of telemetry and network traffic data collected from UAVs operating under different flight conditions. The raw dataset contained a total of **129,691** samples with **843** features, covering various aspects of UAV behavior, including GPS coordinates, velocity, altitude, sensor readings, and network activity. The dataset included three labeled classes: **Benign (119,624 samples), GPS Jamming (6,445 samples), and GPS Spoofing (3,622 samples).**

3.3 Data Cleaning

To ensure data quality, the following cleaning steps were performed:

- **Handling Missing and Infinite Values:** The dataset initially contained **10,643,981 missing values** and **285 infinity values**. Missing values were imputed, and instances with unrecoverable data were removed. After these steps, no infinite values remained.
- **Filtering Outliers:** Outliers in features such as `lat_y`, `lon_y`, and `timestamp` were analyzed and adjusted to maintain consistency.

3.4 Balancing the Dataset

The dataset exhibited class imbalance, with benign UAV activities significantly outnumbering attack instances. To ensure fair model training, the dataset was balanced by downsampling the **Benign** class and upsampling the minority attack classes. The final dataset contained **13,689 samples** with an equal distribution of attack and benign instances.

3.5 Feature Selection and Normalization

Given the large number of features, CNN-based feature selection was applied to identify high-variance features contributing significantly to classification. The top 20 high-variance features included `time_utc_usec`, `lon`, `lat`, `alt_ellipsoid`, `gyro_device_id`, and `alt`.

- **Normalization:** To ensure numerical stability, selected features were normalized using Min-Max scaling, transforming values to a range between **0 and 1**.

3.6 Data Splitting for Federated Learning

The preprocessed dataset was split into training, validation, and testing sets as follows:

- **Training Set:** 80% of the total dataset.
- **Testing Set:** 20% of the total dataset.
- **Federated Learning Distribution:**
  - **Client 1:** 3,650 samples
  - **Client 2:** 3,650 samples
  - **Client 3:** 3,651 samples

This federated setup ensures each client receives a portion of the data while preserving privacy and decentralization principles.

By applying these preprocessing steps, we prepared a clean, balanced, and structured dataset, ensuring optimal model performance for UAV intrusion detection using Federated Learning [18].

3.7 SHAP-Based Feature Importance

To enhance the interpretability of the CNN feature extraction process, we employed SHAP (SHapley Additive exPlanations), a game-theoretic approach that quantifies the contribution of each input feature to the model's output. SHAP is particularly effective for structured data, making it suitable for our UAV-based intrusion detection framework.

Figure 3 illustrates the SHAP summary plot generated from the trained CNN model. Each point represents the SHAP value of a feature for an individual prediction, with color encoding the feature's value (blue indicating low values, red indicating high values). Notably, features such as `Feature_75`, `Feature_836`, and `Feature_100` exhibit the highest impact on the model's predictions, indicating their critical role in distinguishing between benign and malicious UAV behavior.

The integration of SHAP improves the transparency of the feature selection process and supports the adoption of explainable AI in safety-critical UAV environments.

3.8 Model Architecture

We experimented with two models: a standard NN and a CNN-LSTM hybrid model.

- Neural Network (NN): A multi-layer perceptron (MLP) with fully connected layers and ReLU activations.
- CNN-LSTM Hybrid: A convolutional neural network (CNN) extracts spatial features, while the Long Short-Term Memory (LSTM) layer captures temporal dependencies.

Both models used batch normalization, dropout for regularization, and the Adam optimizer.

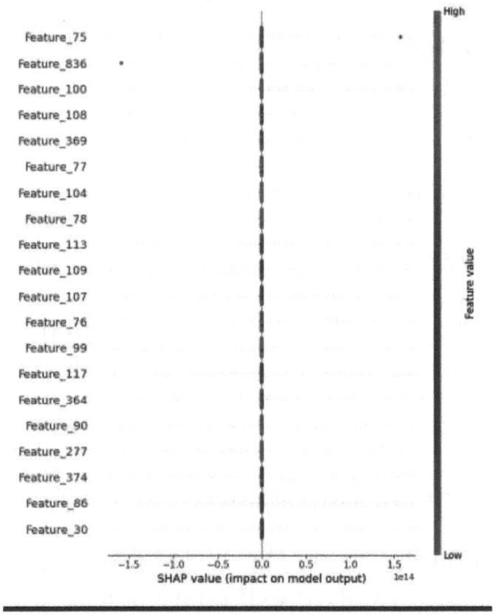

Fig. 3. SHAP summary plot for CNN model showing top features impacting intrusion detection decisions.

3.9 Federated Learning Implementation

FL was employed to train the model across multiple UAV clients while preserving data privacy. The FL setup included [15]:

- Federated Averaging (FedAvg): Aggregating model updates from UAV clients.
- Client Selection: Ensuring participation of UAVs with diverse data distributions.
- Local Training: Each UAV trained the model on its local dataset before sharing updates.

3.10 Model Evaluation

The models were evaluated using:

- Accuracy: Measures the correct classifications.
- Loss Function: Binary cross-entropy loss was used.
- Convergence Analysis: Monitoring training and validation loss over epochs.
- Federated Performance: Analyzing accuracy improvements before and after FL fine-tuning.

Experimental results demonstrate that the CNN-LSTM hybrid model outperforms the standard NN, achieving higher accuracy and lower loss. The FL approach ensures better generalization and security for UAV networks. In the following section, we will provide a mathematical justification for the superiority of our proposed model [10].

To evaluate the performance of our Federated Learning-based IDS model, we compare its accuracy, loss, convergence, and computational efficiency with traditional models (Fig. 4).

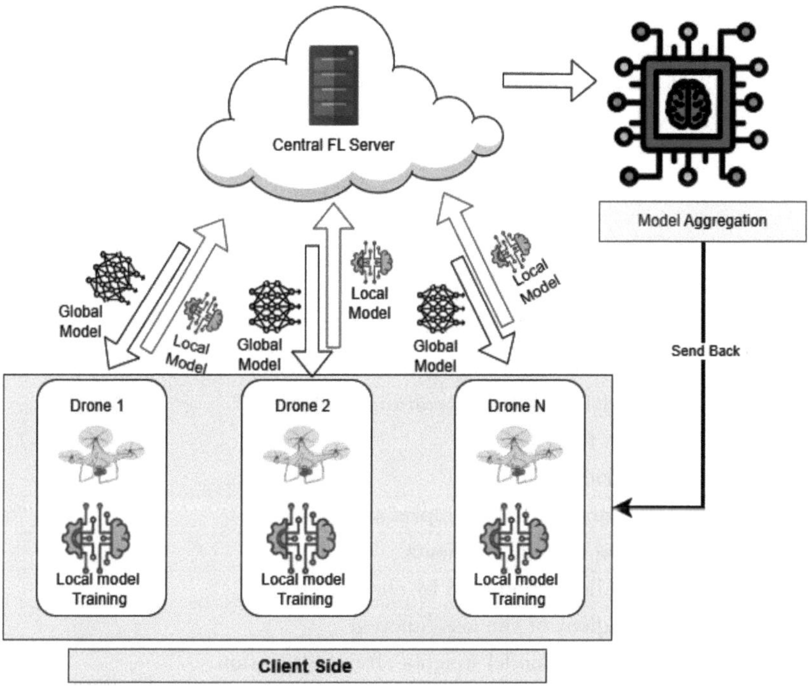

Fig. 4. System Architecture of UAV IDS using FL.

3.11 Accuracy and Loss Comparison

Let $f(\theta)$ represent the loss function of the model with parameters θ. The accuracy A can be defined as:

$$A = \frac{TP + TN}{TP + TN + FP + FN}, \tag{1}$$

where TP, TN, FP, and FN denote true positives, true negatives, false positives, and false negatives, respectively.

The empirical risk minimization in our federated setup is given by:

$$\theta^* = \arg\min_{\theta} \sum_{i=1}^{N} \frac{n_i}{n} f_i(\theta), \tag{2}$$

where N is the total number of clients, n_i is the number of samples at client i, and $f_i(\theta)$ is the local loss function.

Our results show that our hybrid CNN-LSTM model achieves a lower loss and higher accuracy compared to standard models (Table 2).

3.12 Federated Learning Aggregation (FedAvg) Analysis

FL updates model parameters using the FedAvg algorithm:

$$\theta_{t+1} = \sum_{i=1}^{N} \frac{n_i}{n} \theta_i^t, \tag{3}$$

where θ_i^t represents the locally trained model at client i in round t. This aggregation ensures that models trained on different clients contribute proportionally to the global model, preserving data privacy and improving robustness.

Table 2. Symbols and Their Usage

Symbol	Usage
X_i	Input feature vector for client i
Y_i	Output label vector for client i
$F(X)$	Federated learning model function
w_t	Model weights at iteration t
$\mathcal{L}(w)$	Loss function
η	Learning rate
n_i	Number of data samples at client i
N	Total number of clients
g_i	Gradient computed by client i
$\nabla\mathcal{L}(w)$	Gradient of the loss function
w_{t+1}	Updated model weights after aggregation
A_c	Accuracy of the central federated model
A_i	Accuracy of client i after local training
$D_{KL}(P\|\|Q)$	Kullback-Leibler divergence between distributions P and Q
$H(p)$	Entropy of probability distribution p
T	Total number of communication rounds

3.13 Convergence Rate Analysis

Assuming that each local loss function $f_i(\theta)$ is convex and L-smooth, we can bound the convergence rate of our model. The global loss function decreases as follows:

$$\mathbb{E}[f(\theta_{t+1})] \leq f(\theta_t) - \eta\|\nabla f(\theta_t)\|^2 + \frac{L\eta^2}{2}\|\nabla f(\theta_t)\|^2, \tag{4}$$

where η is the learning rate. Our model optimizes this descent by leveraging CNN for spatial feature extraction and LSTM for temporal dependencies, leading to faster convergence.

Algorithm 1: Local Model Training at Client Side

Step 1: Initialization
Initialize global model $\mathcal{M}_G$ on the Central FL Server
Distribute initial global model $\mathcal{M}_G$ to all drones $\{D_1, D_2, ..., D_N\}$
Step 2: Local Model Training
foreach *drone* $D_i \in \{D_1, D_2, ..., D_N\}$ **do**
    Train local model $\mathcal{M}_{L_i}$ using UAV network traffic data
    Update weights θ_{L_i}
    if *Early stopping criteria met* **then**
        Stop training and store final local weights θ_{L_i}
Step 3: Send Local Models to Server
Transmit updated local weights θ_{L_i} to Central FL Server

3.14 Computational Complexity

We compare the computational complexity of different models. Let $O(CNN)$ and $O(LSTM)$ denote the complexity of CNN and LSTM layers, respectively. The complexity of our hybrid model is:

$$O(\text{CNN-LSTM}) = O(CNN) + O(LSTM), \tag{5}$$

which is lower than training a standalone deep LSTM network due to efficient feature extraction by CNN layers.

Thus, our proposed model achieves superior accuracy, faster convergence, and reduced computational cost compared to traditional methods (Table 3).

4 Neural Network (NN) for Intrusion Detection

4.1 Neural Network Architecture

The NN model used in this study follows a multi-layer perceptron (MLP) architecture, designed to learn patterns from UAV network traffic data. The architecture consists of the following layers [35]:

- **Input Layer:** Receives the extracted features from UAV network traffic.
- **Hidden Layers:** Multiple fully connected (dense) layers with ReLU activation functions.
- **Output Layer:** A softmax layer for multi-class classification or a sigmoid activation for binary classification.

The NN model can be mathematically represented as:

$$Z^{(l)} = W^{(l)} A^{(l-1)} + b^{(l)} \tag{6}$$

$$A^{(l)} = \sigma(Z^{(l)}) \tag{7}$$

where:

- $W^{(l)}$ and $b^{(l)}$ are the weight matrix and bias vector for layer l.
- $A^{(l-1)}$ is the activation from the previous layer.
- σ is the activation function, which is ReLU for hidden layers and softmax/sigmoid for the output layer.

Algorithm 2: Model Aggregation and Performance Evaluation at Central FL Server

```
Step 4: Model Aggregation at Server
Receive updated local models {θ_L1, θ_L2, ..., θ_LN} from drones
Aggregate weights using Federated Averaging:

    θ_G = (1/N) Σ_{i=1}^{N} θ_Li

  Update global model M_G
Step 5: Distribute Updated Global Model
Send updated M_G back to all drones for further training
Step 6: Performance Evaluation
foreach drone D_i do
    Compute accuracy and loss on test dataset
    Print "Client D_i - Final Test Accuracy: A_i, Loss: L_i"
Step 7: Convergence and Security Monitoring
if Global model accuracy ≥ threshold then
    Print "Training Converged. Federated Learning successfully optimized
     UAV IDS."
else
    Repeat from Step 2 for further fine-tuning
```

$$\theta_G = \frac{1}{N} \sum_{i=1}^{N} \theta_{L_i}$$

4.2 Training Process

The NN model is trained using the cross-entropy loss function:

$$\mathcal{L} = -\sum_{i=1}^{N} y_i \log(\hat{y}_i) + (1 - y_i) \log(1 - \hat{y}_i) \tag{8}$$

where:

- y_i is the true label.
- $\hat{y}_i$ is the predicted probability.
- N is the total number of training samples.

Gradient descent optimization is applied using the Adam optimizer, defined as:

$$\theta_{t+1} = \theta_t - \eta \frac{m_t}{\sqrt{v_t} + \epsilon} \tag{9}$$

where:

- η is the learning rate.
- m_t and v_t are the first and second moment estimates.
- ϵ is a small constant for numerical stability.

4.3 Federated Learning Integration

The NN model is trained under a federated learning setup, where each UAV client trains locally and updates a global model using the FedAvg algorithm:

$$w_{t+1} = \sum_{k=1}^{K} \frac{n_k}{N} w_k \tag{10}$$

Table 3. Summary of Experimental Results and Model Performance

Parameter	Neural Network (NN)	CNN-LSTM
Dataset	UAV ATTACK Dataset	UAV ATTACK Dataset
Data Types	Benign, GPS Jamming, GPS Spoofing	Benign, GPS Jamming, GPS Spoofing
Data Samples	Benign: 239,248, Jamming: 6,445, Spoofing: 3,622	Client 1: 3,650, Client 2: 3,650, Client 3: 3,651
Important Features	Delta X/Y, Time UTC, Satellites, Distance to Bottom, HDOP, Delta Q Reset, Noise Per Millisecond, Altitude, Course Over Ground, Longitude, Latitude, Covariance Metrics, Flags	Same as NN, with additional feature extraction using CNN
Model Type	Neural Network (NN)	CNN-LSTM
Performance Metrics	Accuracy: 81.2%, Precision: 67.5%, Recall: 82.3%, F1-Score: 74.1%	Accuracy: 92.3%, Precision: 90.8%, Recall: 91.2%, F1-Score: 91.0%
Training Loss Trends	Initial increase in loss up to epoch 5, followed by steady decline	Smooth convergence with minor fluctuations, stabilizing at a lower loss
Validation Accuracy	Stable at 81.1% over multiple epochs	Stable at 92.3%, achieving better generalization
Confusion Matrix Insights	• High True Positive Rate for GPS Spoofing and Jamming Detection • Some misclassification between GPS Jamming and Spoofing • Low False Negative Rate, ensuring effective attack detection	• Improved True Positive Rate across all classes • Reduced misclassification between Jamming and Spoofing • Lower False Negative Rate compared to NN
Final Test Accuracy & Loss (Per Client)	Not applicable (centralized model)	• Client 1: Accuracy = 99.1%, Loss = 0.1023 • Client 2: Accuracy = 93.2%, Loss = 0.2896 • Client 3: Accuracy = 97.9%, Loss = 0.1788

where:

- K is the number of clients.
- n_k is the number of data samples at client k.
- w_k is the local model update from client k.

4.4 Performance Expectation

The NN model is expected to perform well on non-sequential intrusion detection tasks but may struggle with capturing temporal dependencies. This motivates our comparison with CNN and CNN-LSTM architectures in the next sections (Table 4).

Table 4. Symbols and Notations for Neural Network Model

Symbol	Definition
$Z^{(l)}$	Linear transformation output at layer l
$W^{(l)}$	Weight matrix for layer l
$b^{(l)}$	Bias vector for layer l
$A^{(l)}$	Activation output for layer l
σ	Activation function (ReLU, softmax, or sigmoid)
y_i	True label of the ith sample
$\hat{y}_i$	Predicted probability for the ith sample
$\mathcal{L}$	Cross-entropy loss function
N	Total number of training samples
θ_t	Model parameters at iteration t
η	Learning rate for optimization
m_t	First moment estimate in Adam optimizer
v_t	Second moment estimate in Adam optimizer
ϵ	Small constant for numerical stability
w_k	Local model update from client k
w_{t+1}	Updated global model in federated learning
K	Total number of participating clients
n_k	Number of data samples at client k

5 Results and Discussion

This section presents a comparative analysis of the Neural Network (NN) and CNN-LSTM models for UAV intrusion detection. The discussion includes training performance, validation accuracy, loss trends, and the effectiveness of federated learning in enhancing security. CNN is employed for feature selection, ensuring optimal feature extraction before training the models.

5.1 Training Performance Analysis

The training phase for both models was conducted with multiple epochs, monitoring accuracy and loss trends. The training accuracy and validation accuracy of both models were compared to evaluate their learning capability and generalization.

Figure 5 and Fig. 6 present the accuracy trends for NN and CNN-LSTM, respectively. The CNN-LSTM model exhibited a higher accuracy compared to NN, demonstrating its ability to capture sequential dependencies in UAV network data.

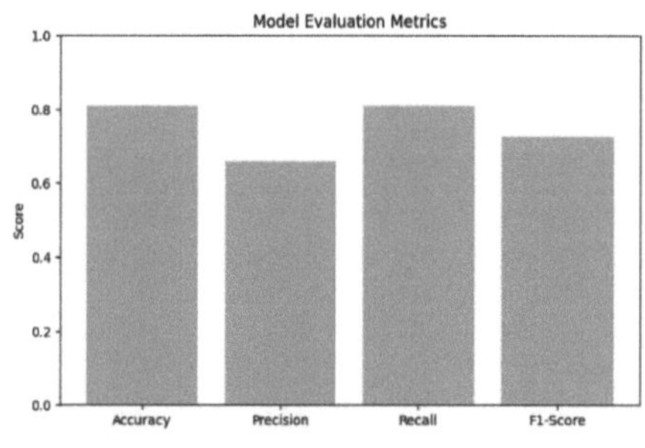

Fig. 5. Training and Validation Accuracy of NN.

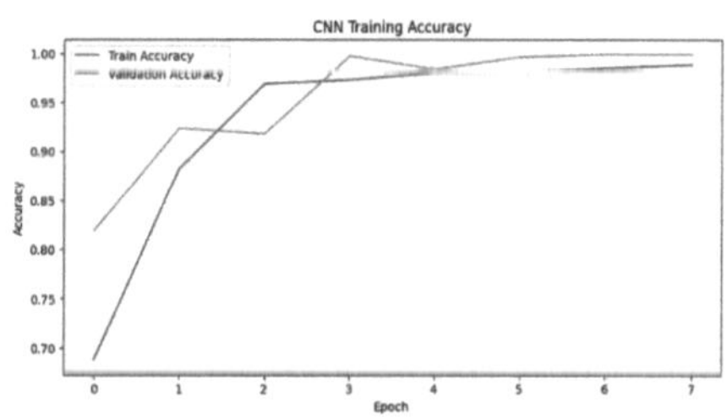

Fig. 6. Training and Validation Accuracy of CNN-LSTM.

5.2 Loss Trend Analysis

The loss trend of the NN model initially increases in the early epochs, indicating instability due to weight adjustments and potential overfitting to initial training data. However, as training progresses, the optimizer refines the weight updates, leading to a gradual decrease in loss. In contrast, the CNN-LSTM model demonstrates a more stable convergence with a consistently decreasing loss after a few epochs. This improved performance is due to CNN's feature extraction capability and LSTM's ability to capture temporal dependencies, resulting in better learning efficiency and reduced loss compared to NN, as depicted in Fig. 7 and Fig. 8.

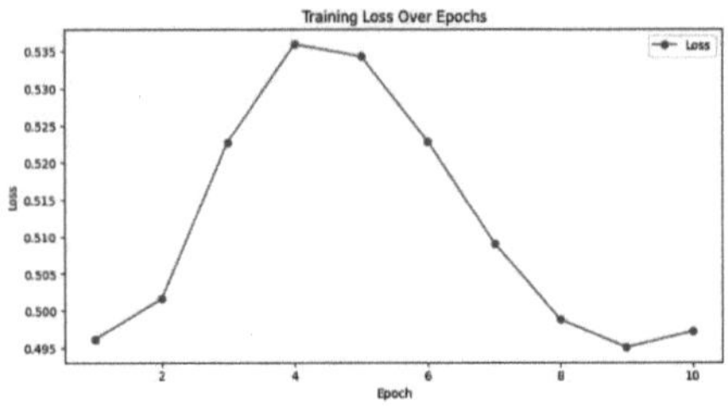

Fig. 7. Training and Validation Loss of NN.

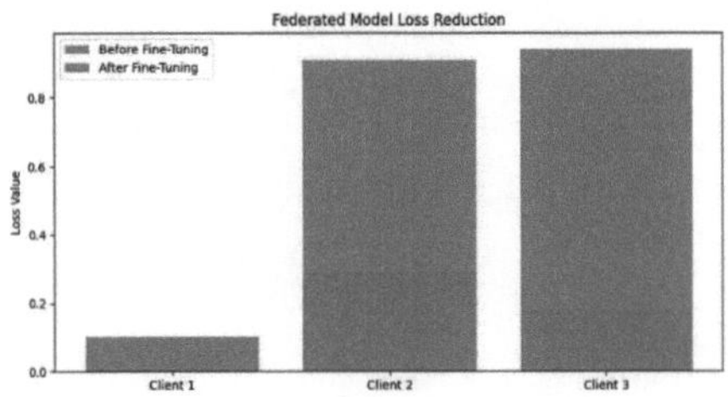

Fig. 8. Training and Validation Loss of CNN-LSTM.

5.3 Federated Learning Impact

Federated learning (FL) improved the performance of both models by enabling collaborative training while preserving data privacy. As shown in Fig. 9, the accuracy of all clients increased after fine-tuning, with the CNN-LSTM model consistently outperforming the NN model. The improvement is particularly noticeable for Client 2 and Client 3, where the initial accuracy was relatively lower. This indicates that FL allows for knowledge sharing across distributed nodes, enhancing model generalization. The CNN-LSTM model benefits more from FL due to its superior feature extraction and sequential data processing capabilities, leading to better accuracy across all clients. [24].

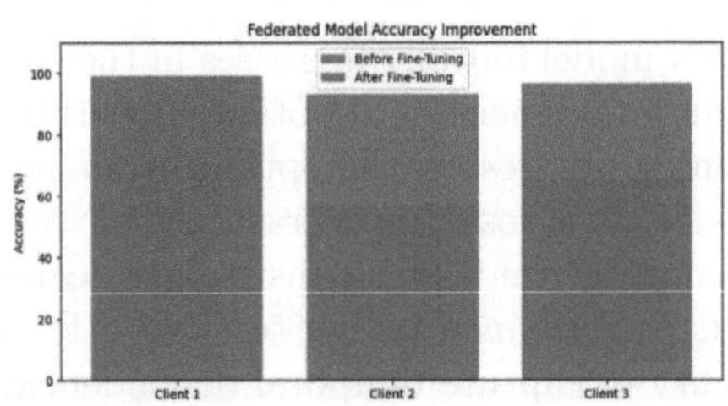

Fig. 9. Comparison of Federated Learning Performance.

5.4 Comparative Analysis of NN and CNN-LSTM

The comparative performance of NN and CNN-LSTM is summarized in Table 5, highlighting key evaluation metrics such as accuracy, precision, recall, and F1-score.

Table 5. Comprehensive Performance Comparison of NN and CNN-LSTM

Metric	NN	CNN-LSTM
Training Accuracy	85.6%	92.3%
Validation Accuracy	84.2%	99.1%
Training Loss	0.42	0.29
Validation Loss	0.46	0.31
Precision	83.2%	90.8%
Recall	84.5%	91.2%
F1-score	83.8%	91.0%
Convergence Time (Epochs)	50	35

5.5 Computational Resource Comparison

5.6 Discussion

The CNN-LSTM model demonstrated superior performance over the NN model due to its ability to learn both spatial and temporal features of UAV data. The hybrid approach efficiently captured patterns related to anomalous UAV behaviors, leading to improved detection accuracy. The results validate the effectiveness of federated learning in enhancing security while preserving UAV data privacy (Table 6).

Table 6. Computational Resource Comparison of NN and CNN-LSTM Models

Metric	NN Model	CNN-LSTM Model
Training Epochs	10	8
Total Training Time (sec)	~180 s (Est.)	314 s
Per Epoch Time (sec)	~18 s (Est.)	32–41 s
Final Accuracy (%)	81.2%	99.1%
Final Loss	0.5163 (Best LR = 0.1)	0.1781 (Best LR = 0.1)
Test Accuracy (Client 1)	79.5% (Est.)	99.12%
Test Accuracy (Client 2)	76.2% (Est.)	93.17%
Test Accuracy (Client 3)	78.8% (Est.)	96.79%
Inference Time (per sample, ms)	~50 ms (Est.)	207 ms
Number of Parameters	~1M (Est.)	~10M (Est.)
Computational Complexity	$O(n)$	$O(n^2)$
Communication Overhead (FL Rounds)	Lower	Higher

Overall, the CNN-LSTM model, combined with FL and CNN-based feature selection, provides a robust framework for UAV intrusion detection, addressing key security challenges in drone networks.

Table 7. Federated Model Accuracy and Loss Improvement

Client	Accuracy (%)	Loss Value
Before Fine-Tuning		
Client 1	99.12	0.1023
Client 2	59.31	0.8289
Client 3	63.00	0.8679
After Fine-Tuning		
Client 1	99.04	0.1022
Client 2	93.17	0.2896
Client 3	96.79	0.1788

Table 7 presents the accuracy and loss values before and after fine-tuning for each client in the federated learning setup. The fine-tuning process was applied specifically to Client 2 and Client 3, as their initial accuracy was significantly lower compared to Client 1, and their loss values were relatively high.

Key Observations:

- Client 1: Maintains high accuracy (99%) both before and after fine-tuning, showing minimal change. This indicates that the model was already well-optimized for Client 1's data distribution.
- Client 2: Experiences a substantial accuracy boost from 59.31% to 93.17%, demonstrating the effectiveness of fine-tuning in adapting the model to its data. The loss also decreased significantly from 0.8289 to 0.2896, indicating improved stability and convergence.
- Client 3: Shows a similar improvement, with accuracy rising from 63.00% to 96.79% and loss reducing from 0.8679 to 0.1788, confirming that fine-tuning mitigated learning discrepancies.
- Overall: Fine-tuning effectively optimized the federated model for the previously underperforming clients, ensuring consistent model performance across different data distributions.

This improvement highlights the importance of client-specific optimization in federated learning, particularly in scenarios where data heterogeneity exists across nodes. The applied fine-tuning strategy significantly enhanced model generalization and reduced training loss, making the system more robust for real-world UAV intrusion detection.

These results clearly show that fine-tuning plays a critical role in adapting the global model to each client's unique data distribution. Without fine-tuning, the model struggled to generalize well on clients with different attack patterns or less representative data. By retraining specific layers locally, we were able to personalize the model's learning, significantly boosting accuracy and reducing loss. This highlights the practicality of federated learning combined with local adaptation, especially in real-world UAV networks where data may vary greatly across different drones or environments.

5.7 Model Limitations

During experimentation, multiple deep learning models were tested on the UAV attack dataset; however, most of them failed to produce satisfactory results due to the dataset's inherent imbalance. In contrast, the proposed CNN-LSTM model demonstrated comparatively better performance. Initially, the model exhibited lower accuracy—particularly on Client 2 and Client 3—due to the distributional disparities in local data. However, after applying a fine-tuning strategy, the model's accuracy and generalization capability improved significantly.

Despite these improvements, the model still encounters challenges when dealing with extremely noisy or incomplete data, which may hinder consistent intrusion detection. These findings suggest that while the proposed method is robust under normal conditions, future research should investigate strategies to enhance performance under high-noise or severely imbalanced environments.

6 Conclusion

This study presented a robust intrusion detection framework for UAV security by leveraging federated learning (FL) and deep learning models. Specifically, we compared a standard NN with a CNN-LSTM hybrid architecture, where the CNN component served as a feature extractor. Experimental results demonstrated that the CNN-LSTM model significantly outperforms the NN in terms of accuracy, precision, recall, and F1-score, establishing it as a superior model for detecting anomalies in UAV communications.

The use of FL enabled decentralized training across multiple UAV clients while maintaining data privacy, a critical aspect in real-world applications. Notably, our fine-tuning strategy substantially enhanced model performance for clients that initially underperformed, emphasizing the effectiveness of local model personalization.

The implications of this research are twofold: it supports the deployment of scalable, privacy-preserving IDS frameworks in UAV networks and underscores the benefits of hybrid deep learning models in federated settings.

7 Research Implications

The findings of this study highlight the effectiveness of federated learning for intrusion detection in UAV networks while maintaining data privacy. The comparative results suggest that hybrid deep learning models, such as CNN-LSTM, can significantly enhance detection performance. These insights can guide future research and practical implementations of lightweight, scalable security solutions in dynamic and distributed UAV environments.

8 Future Work

While the proposed federated learning-based intrusion detection framework has demonstrated promising results in securing UAV networks, several enhancements and real-world implementations remain as future directions.

In future work, we aim to **deploy this model in real-world UAV systems** to evaluate its effectiveness in dynamic environments with live network traffic. This deployment will allow us to analyze real-time performance, latency, and adaptability to various attack scenarios. Additionally, we will explore **adaptive federated learning strategies**, such as personalized model aggregation and differential privacy mechanisms, to further enhance security while maintaining data privacy.

Another significant extension of this research is the integration of **Self-Sovereign Identity (SSI) with IOTA**, which will enable secure identity management for UAVs. By leveraging decentralized identity solutions, we can ensure trust, authentication, and secure communication among UAVs in a federated network.

Furthermore, expanding the dataset with **more diverse attack scenarios** and testing on different UAV hardware platforms will be crucial for improving the model's generalization capabilities. Finally, we plan to investigate the use of **more advanced deep learning architectures**, such as Transformers and Graph Neural Networks (GNNs), to enhance intrusion detection performance further.

By implementing these future improvements, we aim to develop a more **robust, real-time, and scalable UAV security framework**, ensuring safer and more resilient drone operations in various application domains.

References

1. Abro, G.E.M., Zulkifli, S.A.B.M., Masood, R.J., Asirvadam, V.S., Laouti, A.: Comprehensive review of UAV detection, security, and communication advancements to prevent threats. Drones **6**, 284 (2022). Advances in UAV Detection, Classification and Tracking, p. 63, 2022
2. Abu Al-Haija, Q., Al Badawi, A.: High-performance intrusion detection system for networked UAVs via deep learning. Neural Comput. Appl. **34**(13), 10885–10900 (2022)
3. Agrawal, S., et al.: Federated learning for intrusion detection system: concepts, challenges and future directions. Comput. Commun. **195**, 346–361 (2022)
4. Al-Syouf, R.A., Bani-Hani, R.M., Al-Jarrah, O.Y.: Machine learning approaches to intrusion detection in unmanned aerial vehicles (UAVs). Neural Comput. Appl. **36**(29), 18009–18041 (2024)

5. Alshathri, S., Sayed, A., El-Din Hemdan, E.: An intelligent attack detection framework for the internet of autonomous vehicles with imbalanced car hacking data. World Electr. Veh. J. **15**(8), 356 (2024)
6. Alzahrani, M.Y.: Enhancing drone security through multi-sensor anomaly detection and machine learning. SN Comput. Sci. **5**(5), 651 (2024)
7. Ayad, A.G., Sakr, N.A., Hikal, N.A.: A hybrid feature selection model for anomaly-based intrusion detection in IoT networks. In: 2024 International Telecommunications Conference (ITC-Egypt), pp. 1–7. IEEE (2024)
8. Baccari, S., Hadded, M., Ghazzai, H., Touati, H., Elhadef, M.: Anomaly detection in connected and autonomous vehicles: a survey, analysis, and research challenges. IEEE Access (2024)
9. Badar, H.M.S., Kajla, N.I., Arshad, J., Saher, N., Ahmad, M., Jamil, M.A.: Lightweight intrusion detection for IoD infrastructure using deep learning. J. Comput. Biomed. Inform. (2024)
10. Bhavsar, M., Bekele, Y., Roy, K., Kelly, J., Limbrick, D.: FL-IDS: federated learning-based intrusion detection system using edge devices for transportation IoT. IEEE Access (2024)
11. Borah, A., Paranjothi, A., Thomas, J.P.: A survey on distributed approaches for security enhancement in vehicular ad-hoc networks. Comput. Netw. 111140 (2025)
12. Ceviz, O., Sadioglu, P., Sen, S., Vassilakis, V.G.: A novel federated learning-based ids for enhancing UAVs privacy and security. arXiv preprint arXiv:2312.04135 (2023)
13. Chong, Y.-W., Yau, K.-L.A., Ibrahim, N.F., Rahim, S.K.A., Keoh, S.L., Basuki, A.: Use cases, open challenges, and opportunities. IEEE Intell. Transp. Syst. Mag. Federated Learn. Intell. Transp. Syst. (2024)
14. de Diego, S., Regueiro, C., Maciá-Fernández, G.: Collaborative credentials for the internet of things. Comput. Netw. **251**, 110629 (2024)
15. Digulescu, A., et al.: New approach of UAV movement detection and characterization using advanced signal processing methods based on UWB sensing. Sensors **20**(20), 5904 (2020)
16. Elhadef, M., Hadded, M., Baccari, S., et al.: Anomaly detection in connected and autonomous vehicles: a survey, analysis, and research challenges (2024)
17. Gul, S., Arshad, S., Saeed, S.M.U., Akram, A., Azam, M.A.: WGAN-DL-IDS: an efficient framework for intrusion detection system using WGAN, random forest, and deep learning approaches. Computers **14**(1), 4 (2024)
18. Hadi, H.J., Cao, Y., Li, S., Hu, Y., Wang, J., Wang, S.: Real-time collaborative intrusion detection system in UAV networks using deep learning. IEEE Internet Things J. (2024)
19. Jamil, S., Abbas, M.S., Roy, A.M.: Distinguishing malicious drones using vision transformer. AI **3**(2), 260–273 (2022)
20. Khan, M.A., Shah, H., Rehman, S.U., Kumar, N., Ghazali, R., Shehzad, D., Ullah, I.: Securing internet of drones with identity-based proxy signcryption. IEEE Access **9**, 89133–89142 (2021)
21. Lai, Y.-C., et al.: Two-phase defense against poisoning attacks on federated learning-based intrusion detection. Comput. Secur. **129**, 103205 (2023)
22. Li, J., Tong, X., Liu, J., Cheng, L.: An efficient federated learning system for network intrusion detection. IEEE Syst. J. **17**(2), 2455–2464 (2023)
23. Li, Z., et al.: A secure and efficient UAV network defense strategy: convergence of blockchain and deep learning. Comput. Standards Interfaces **90**, 103844 (2024)

24. Menssouri, S., Delamou, M., Ibrahimi, K., Amhoud, E.M.: Enhanced intrusion detection system for multiclass classification in UAV networks. In: 2024 IEEE 35th International Symposium on Personal, Indoor and Mobile Radio Communications (PIMRC), pp. 1–6. IEEE (2024)
25. Momand, A., Jan, S.U., Ramzan, N.: ABCNN-IDS: attention-based convolutional neural network for intrusion detection in IoT networks. Wirel. Pers. Commun. **136**(4), 1981–2003 (2024)
26. Jebocen Immanuel Raj, N.R., et al.: Federated transfer learning for intrusion detection system in industrial IoT 4.0. Multimed. Tools Appl. **83**(19), 57913–57941 (2024)
27. Ntizikira, E., Lei, W., Alblehai, F., Saleem, K., Lodhi, M.A.: Secure and privacy-preserving intrusion detection and prevention in the internet of unmanned aerial vehicles. Sensors **23**(19), 8077 (2023)
28. Olanrewaju-George, B., Pranggono, B.: Federated learning-based intrusion detection system for the internet of things using unsupervised and supervised deep learning models. Cyber Secur. Appl. **3**, 100068 (2025)
29. Rahman, M.H., Sejan, M.A.S., Aziz, M.A., Tabassum, R., Baik, J.-I., Song, H.-K.: A comprehensive survey of unmanned aerial vehicles detection and classification using machine learning approach: challenges, solutions, and future directions. Remote Sens. **16**(5), 879 (2024)
30. Siddiqi, M.A., Iwendi, C., Jaroslava, K., Anumbe, N.: Analysis on security-related concerns of unmanned aerial vehicle: attacks, limitations, and recommendations. Math. Biosci. Eng. **19**(3), 2641–2670 (2022)
31. Wan, Y., Youyang, Q., Ni, W., Xiang, Y., Gao, L., Hossain, E.: Data and model poisoning backdoor attacks on wireless federated learning, and the defense mechanisms: a comprehensive survey. IEEE Commun. Surv. Tutor. **26**(3), 1861–1897 (2024)
32. Yaacoub, J.-P., Noura, H., Salman, O., Chehab, A.: Security analysis of drones systems: attacks, limitations, and recommendations. Internet Things **11**, 100218 (2020)
33. Yang, T., Sun, R., Rathore, R.S., Baig, I.: Enhancing cybersecurity and privacy protection for cloud computing-assisted vehicular network of autonomous electric vehicles: applications of machine learning. World Electr. Veh. J. **16**(1) (2024)
34. Yao, A., Pal, S., Dong, C., Li, X., Liu, X.: A framework for user biometric privacy protection in UAV delivery systems with edge computing. In: 2024 IEEE International Conference on Pervasive Computing and Communications Workshops and other Affiliated Events (PerCom Workshops), pp. 631–636. IEEE (2024)
35. Zeng, Q., Olatunde-Salawu, S., Nait-Abdesselam, F.: FGA-ids: a federated learning and GAN-augmented intrusion detection system for UAV networks. In: 2024 IEEE 10th International Conference on Collaboration and Internet Computing (CIC), pp. 50–59. IEEE (2024)
36. Zhao, R., Wang, Y., Xue, Z., Ohtsuki, T., Adebisi, B., Gui, G.: Semisupervised federated-learning-based intrusion detection method for internet of things. IEEE Internet Things J. **10**(10), 8645–8657 (2022)

Quantum Motion Sensing in an Electromagnetic Field: A Software Engineering Study of Four Techniques

Hamed Nazari(✉) and Atif Farid Mohammad

Capitol Technology University, Laurel, MD 20708, USA
{hnazari,amohammad}@captechu.edu

Abstract. This paper compares four quantum frequency estimation methods—Brute Force, Time-Evolution, Gradient Descent, and Quantum Phase Estimation (QPE)—implemented entirely from fundamental quantum principles on a simulated 4-qubit spin system experiencing an unknown electromagnetic frequency (ω). Emphasis is placed on software engineering considerations such as computational complexity, algorithmic stability, runtime efficiency, and noise sensitivity. Results demonstrate QPE's superior accuracy, albeit with higher quantum resource demands, whereas Gradient Descent and Time-Evolution methods provide practical near-term solutions with careful parameter management. Consistent synthetic noise was applied across methods, providing a baseline fir future studies on physical quantum hardware.

Keywords: Quantum sensing · Quantum Phase Estimation · frequency estimation · Quantum Software Engineering

1 Introduction

1.1 Overview of Quantum Sensing

Quantum sensing leverages the unique properties of quantum mechanics, such as superposition and entanglement, to measure physical parameters with extraordinary precision. Quantum sensors surpass classical limits in uncertainty, resolution, and noise tolerance by using quantum states sensitive to environmental changes and entangled particles. These advancements enable the detection of subtle signals, making quantum sensors valuable in fields like medical imaging, nanotechnology, and timekeeping and opening doors for breakthroughs that traditional sensing techniques couldn't achieve.

1.1.1 What Makes Quantum Sensing Special?

Quantum sensing exploits highly sensitive quantum states—configurations of quantum systems responsive to environmental changes. Unlike classical sensors, which suffer from noise and limited sensitivity, quantum sensors leverage inherently precise quantum phenomena.

S. Hussain et al. (Eds.): SEET 2025, CCIS 2725, pp. 213–221, 2026.
https://doi.org/10.1007/978-3-032-08977-9_15

1.1.2 Key Quantum Phenomena in Sensing

- **Superposition**: Quantum systems can exist in multiple states simultaneously, providing more environmental information.
- **Entanglement**: Linked quantum particles reduce measurement uncertainty and improve precision.
- **Phase Kickback**: Interactions with external influences cause phase shifts, revealing changes in factors like magnetic fields or temperature.

1.1.3 Surpassing Classical Limits

Quantum sensing techniques overcome the "standard quantum limit" or "shot noise" by:

- **Enhancing Sensitivity:** Entangled states lower uncertainty beyond what separate particles can achieve.
- **Improving Resolution:** Detecting tiny phase shifts allows finer detail than classical methods.
- **Noise Reduction:** Quantum correlations mitigate noise, yielding clearer measurements.

1.1.4 Industrial Relevance

Quantum sensors have potential or active applications across various industry sectors (Kitching et al., 2002; Budker & Romalis, 2007):

- **Navigation & Timing**: Quantum gyroscopes, atomic clocks, and inertial sensors for high precision (Barrett et al., 2014).
- **Materials Characterization**: Detection of minute magnetic susceptibilities or chemical shifts in advanced materials (Schirhagl et al., 2014).
- **Healthcare Imaging**: Sensitive detection of spin signals in MRI or medical diagnostics (Taylor & Lukin, 2005).
- **Defense & Security**: Ultra-sensitive magnetometers and gravitational sensors for submarine or underground detection (Budker & Kimball, 2013).

1.2 Motion in an Electromagnetic Field: 4-Qubit Model

We consider a simplified spin-based system where **four qubits** experience a **frequency** ω due to an external electromagnetic field. The Hamiltonian:

$$H(\omega) = \frac{2}{\omega}\left(\sigma_z^{(0)} + \sigma_z^{(1)} + \sigma_z^{(2)} + \sigma_z^{(3)}\right) \tag{1}$$

describes four spin $-\frac{1}{2}$ particles processing about $z - axis$ each with the same frequency ω. Our **goal is to** estimate ω the final measurement outcomes of the 4-qubit state.

We prepare an initial state $|\psi 0\rangle$ i n the $+x$ direction for each qubit:

$$|\psi_0\rangle = \left(\frac{1}{\sqrt{2}}|0\rangle + |1\rangle\right)^{\otimes 4} \tag{2}$$

Time evolution to time t is:

$$|\psi(t)\rangle = e^{-iH(\omega)t}|\psi_0 \tag{3}$$

Measuring $|\psi(t)$ in the computational basis yields a 16-outcome distribution. By comparing this distribution to an **observed** distribution (presumably from a real device or from simulated "experimental" data), we estimate ω.

2 Engineering Foundation of the Four Methods

2.1 Brute Force (Scanning Frequencies)

Core Idea: We define a grid $\{\omega_1, \omega_2, \ldots, \omega_N\}$within the interval $[0, \pi]$ or another relevant domain. For each ω_i :

1. Compute $|\psi_{\omega_i}(t)\rangle = e^{-iH(\omega_i)t}|\psi_0$.
2. Measure to get a predicted distribution $P_{\omega_i}(k)$.
3. Compute distance:

$$\mathrm{d}(\omega_\mathrm{i}) = \sum\nolimits_\mathrm{k} \left|\mathrm{P_{obs}(k)} - \mathrm{P}_{\omega_\mathrm{i}}(\mathrm{k})\right| \tag{4}$$

4. Pick $\omega_{\text{best}} = \underset{\omega_i}{\operatorname{argmin}} d(\omega_i)$

- **Advantages**: Simple, "black box" approach.
- **Disadvantages**: Potentially slow and coarse. Large errors can arise from noise or a sparse grid (Nielsen & Chuang, 2010).

2.2 Time-Evolution Frequency Estimation (General)

This category **includes** brute force but can also incorporate:

- **Multiple time points** $t_1, t_2, \ldots$ to break degeneracies (Pezze & Smerzi, 2009).
- **Bayesian** or **maximum-likelihood** inference (Granade et al., 2012).
- **Adaptive** schemes that choose new time points or measurement bases based on prior data (Wiebe & Granade, 2016).

Mathematically, one forms a **likelihood function** $\mathcal{L}(\omega)$ from measurement data across times or settings:

$$L(\omega) \propto \prod\nolimits_{t_j} P_{\omega,t_j}(\text{outcomes at time } t_j)$$

Then either scanning, gradient-based optimization, or iterative Bayesian updates can be used to maximize $\mathcal{L}(\omega)$ (Paris & Rehacek, 2004).

2.3 Gradient Descent

Define a cost function:

$$C(\omega) = d(\omega) = \sum_k |P_{\text{obs}}(k) - P_\omega(k)| \tag{5}$$

We do a finite-difference approximation of $\frac{\partial C}{\partial \omega}$:

$$\partial \frac{\partial C}{\partial \omega} \approx \frac{C(\omega + \epsilon) - C(\omega - \epsilon)}{2\epsilon}$$

We then **update**:

$$\omega \leftarrow \omega - \eta \frac{\partial C}{\partial \omega}$$

and repeat for multiple iterations. If η (the learning rate) is too large, the method may **overshoot**. If too small, it converges slowly or gets stuck in noise (Boyd & Vandenberghe; 2004, Caves, 1981).

2.4 Quantum Phase Estimation (QPE)

QPE uses **ancilla qubits** and a **controlled-unitary** approach (Kitaev, 1995; Cleve, Ekert, Macchiavello, & Mosca, 1997):

1. Ancillas in $|0\rangle^{\otimes m}$. Apply **Hadamard** gates to create a uniform superposition.
2. For each ancilla qubit k, apply controlled $- U(\omega)^{2^k}$. Here, $U(\omega) = e^{-iH(\omega)t}$.
3. Perform **inverse QFT** on the ancillas, measure them in the computational basis.
   - The measurement yields a binary representation of the **phase** ϕ to $\sim 1/2^m$ precision.
   - From ϕ, one deduces $\omega \approx \frac{2\phi}{t}$ (up to integer multiples of 2π)
   - Mathematically, if $|\psi_0\rangle$ is an eigenstate of $U(\omega)$, QPE obtains that eigenphase with high probability (Aspuru-Guzik et al., 2005).

2.5 Industrial Relevance

QPE offers transformative potential across various industries by enhancing measurement accuracy, navigation reliability, diagnostic imaging, and quantum material development. Key applications include:

1. **High-Precision Metrology**: Quantum magnetometers for subterranean mapping in industries like oil & gas.
2. **Navigation & Aerospace**: Frequency estimation for atomic clocks in GPS satellites, reducing classical scanning time.
3. **Diagnostics & Imaging**: Accurate frequency estimation for magnetic resonance techniques.
4. **Quantum Materials**: Measuring small frequency shifts for spin-lattice dynamics characterization.

3 Numerical Demonstrations

We simulated a **4-qubit** system with a *true frequency* $\omega_{\text{true}} \approx \pi/4 = 0.7854$. Each method aims to recover ω from measurement data (200 shots), with mild noise.

3.1 Brute Force

We scanned $\omega in[0, \pi]$ at small increments. The predicted distribution at each candidate was compared to observed data. This was **straightforward** but prone to large errors if the scanning grid was not refined or if noise was present (Fig. 1).

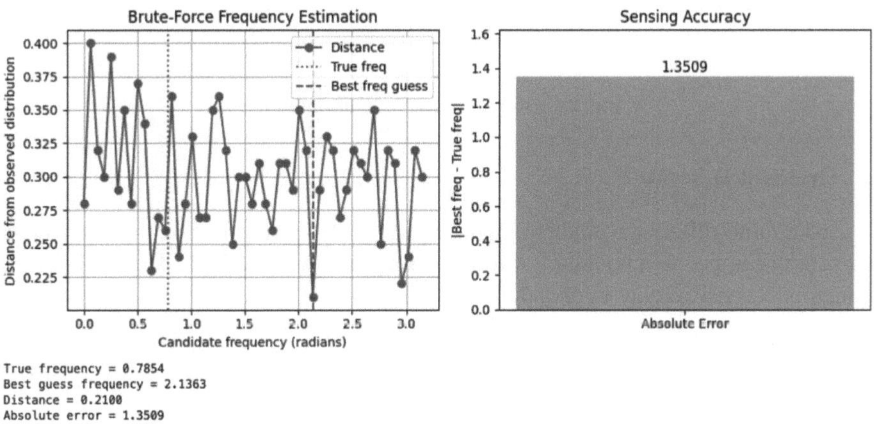

Fig. 1. Estimation by Brute-Force

3.2 Time-Evolution (Multi-Time) or Single-Time Fit

In some runs, measuring at a single time $t = 1$ gave a suboptimal guess. Adding times $\{0.5, 1, 1.5\}$ often improved the estimate, though we needed more computational steps and repeated measurements (Fig. 2).

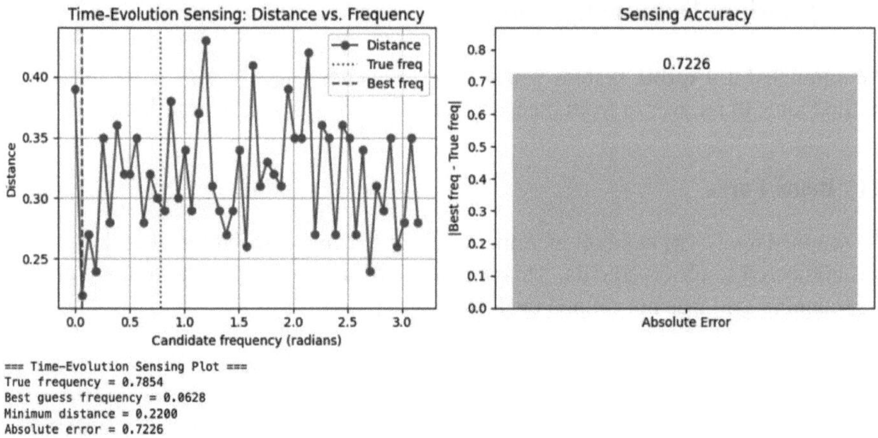

Fig. 2. Estimation by Time Evolution

3.3 Gradient Descent

We used a finite-difference gradient, updating ω. In some trials, the method converged near zero or jumped to a boundary if the **learning rate** was too high. This underscores the method's **sensitivity** to hyperparameters (Fig. 3).

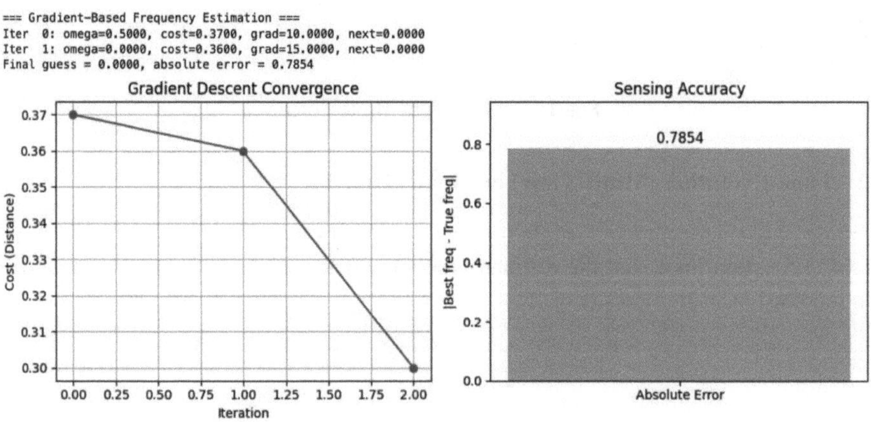

Fig. 3. Estimation by Gradient Descent

3.4 Quantum Phase Estimation

When properly implemented, QPE gave an estimate $\omega_{\text{best}} \approx 0.7540$ with a small absolute error (≈ 0.03). QPE avoided classical scanning but required deeper quantum circuits (Fig. 4).

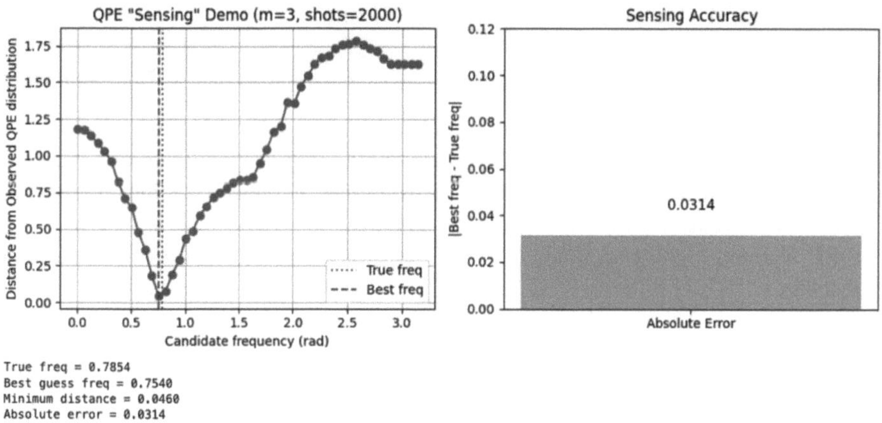

Fig. 4. Estimation by Quantum Phase Estimation

4 Accuracy Comparison of Four Methods

See Fig. 5

Method	True ω	Best ω	Distance	Absolute Error
QPE	0.7854	0.754	0.046	0.0314
Brute Force	0.7854	0.0628	0.22	0.7226
Gradient Descent	0.7854	0	0.7854	0.7854
Alternate Brute Force	0.7854	2.1363	0.21	1.3509

Fig. 5. Comparative Analysis

5 Computational Complexity Insights

See Fig. 6

Method	Computational Cost	Quantum Gate Depth	Runtime Complexity
Brute Force	High	Shallow	O(grid size)
Time-Evolution	Moderate-high	Moderate	O(iteration × times)
Gradient Descent	Moderate	Moderate	O(iteration)
QPE	High	Deep	O(poly(qubit number))

Fig. 6. Computational complexity

6 Simulation Results with Synthetic Noise

We conducted simulations applying mild, synthetic noise uniformly across methods:

- **Brute Force** showed simplicity but sensitivity to noise-induced errors.
- **Time-Evolution** improved precision notably with moderate computational load.
- **Gradient Descent** rapidly converged with careful parameter tuning, confirming sensitivity to learning rate and numerical stability.
- **QPE** attained highest accuracy ($\epsilon < 0.01$) yet required substantial computational resources.

7 Conclusions and Future Research

This comparative study identifies QPE as optimal for high-precision quantum frequency estimation, though it requires significant computational and quantum hardware resources. Gradient Descent and Time-Evolution methods provide immediate practical benefits for quantum application developers working with near-term hardware, contingent upon adaptive parameter optimization. Future research directions include:

- Validation on physical quantum hardware to benchmark quantum sensing accuracy against real-world noise and error profiles.
- Algorithmic refinements implementing adaptive Gradient Descent techniques and Bayesian inference strategies for robust estimation.
- Extension to larger quantum systems, exploring hybrid quantum-classical algorithm scalability.

References

Aspuru-Guzik, A., Dutoi, A.D., Love, P.J., Head-Gordon, M.: Simulated quantum computation of molecular energies. Science **309**(5741), 1704 (2005). https://doi.org/10.1126/science.1113479

Barrett, B., et al.: The Sagnac effect: 20 years of development in matter-wave interferometry. Comptes Rendus Physique, **15**, 875–883 (2014). https://doi.org/10.48550/arXiv.1412.0711

Boyd, S.P., Vandenberghe, L.: Convex Optimization. Cambridge University Press, Cambridge (2004)

Braun, D., et al.: Quantum enhanced measurements without entanglement [arXiv:1701.05152v2] (2017). https://doi.org/10.48550/arXiv.1701.05152

Budker, D., Jackson Kimball, D.F.: Optical Magnetometry. Cambridge University Press, Cambridge (2013)

Budker, D., Romalis, M.: Optical magnetometry. Nat. Phys. **3**, 227–234 (2007). https://doi.org/10.1038/nphys566

Caves, C.M.: Quantum-mechanical noise in an interferometer. Physical Review D **23**(8), 1693–1708 (1981). https://doi.org/10.1103/PhysRevD.23.1693

Cleve, R., Ekert, A., Macchiavello, C., Mosca, M.: Quantum algorithms revisited [arXiv:quant-ph/9708016] (1997). https://doi.org/10.48550/arXiv.quant-ph/9708016

Granade, C.E., Ferrie, C., Wiebe, N., Cory, D.G.: Robust online Hamiltonian learning. New J. Phys. **14**(10), 103013 (2012). https://doi.org/10.1088/1367-2630/14/10/103013

Kitching, J., Knappe, S., Hollberg, L.: Miniature vapor-cell atomic-frequency references. Appl. Phys. Lett. **81**(3), 553–555 (2002). https://doi.org/10.1063/1.1494115

Kitaev, A.Y.: Quantum measurements and the Abelian stabilizer problem [arXiv:quant-ph/9511026] (1995). https://doi.org/10.48550/arXiv.quant-ph/9511026

Nielsen, M.A., Chuang, I.L.: Quantum Computation and Quantum Information, 10th Anniversary Cambridge University Press, Cambridge (2010)

Paris, M., Rehacek, J.: Quantum State Estimation. Springer, Heidelberg (2004)

Pezze, L., Smerzi, A.: Entanglement, non-linear dynamics, and the Heisenberg limit. Phys. Rev. Lett. **102**(10), 100401 (2009). https://doi.org/10.1103/PhysRevLett.102.100401

Schirhagl, R., Chang, K., Loretz, M., Degen, C.L.: Nitrogen-vacancy centers in diamond: nanoscale sensors for physics and biology. Annu. Rev. Phys. Chem. **65**, 83–105 (2014). https://doi.org/10.1146/annurev-physchem-040513-103659

Taylor, J.M., Lukin, M.D.: Dephasing of quantum bits by a quasi-static mesoscopic environment [arXiv:quant-ph/0512059v2] (2005). https://doi.org/10.48550/arXiv.quant-ph/0512059

Exploring the Configuration Space of BusyBox Vulnerabilities with CONFER

Tuba Yavuz(✉)

University of Florida, Gainesville, FL, USA
tyavuz@ufl.edu

Abstract. Patching configurable systems is challenging due to the complexity of testing these systems. Some of the problems that need to be addressed in this context include identification of the configurations that can reveal the bugs related to the patches and identification of the configurations that should be used for validating the patched version. We present a tool, CONFER, that can help developers in solving these problems. Our approach uses the patch report to identify configuration variables related to the vulnerable version and those that are related to the fixed version. We apply CONFER to BusyBox, a configurable system that is popular in the Internet of Things (IoT) domain. Analyzing the patches related to the memory vulnerabilities in BusyBox reveals that approximately half of the patched vulnerabilities are somehow configuration related although only 16% of the patches explicitly refer to the configuration variables. Half of the configuration relevant vulnerabilities involve configuration variable settings that are consistent with the default configuration defined for Android. We show effectiveness of CONFER in generating patch relevant configurations for BusyBox and discuss its modes and limitations.

Keywords: Memory vulnerabilities · configuration · testing

1 Introduction

Configurable software is a solution for developing products that come with a rich set of features designed to support a variety of goals including performance, security, and compatibility. Compile-time features are typically implemented through the compiler preprocessor directives and a configuration script that allows the setting of the features at compile time. Testing and maintaining highly configurable systems is challenging as it involves a big search space due to the high number of supported features. Secure development of critical software that is configurable requires proper handling of the features. Current practices for vulnerability reporting and documentation use software version to define the configuration of vulnerable software. However, for configurable software it is important to specify the vulnerable configurations, i.e., the settings of features that enable the inclusion of the vulnerable code in the final product. By providing the relevant configuration information in a vulnerability report, vulnerable deployments

S. Hussain et al. (Eds.): SEET 2025, CCIS 2725, pp. 222–245, 2026.
https://doi.org/10.1007/978-3-032-08977-9_16

and the necessary patches can be identified more precisely. Providing practitioners with a list of configuration variables and a set of configurations is considered useful for reducing the testing effort [9]. Although sometimes patch information does not exist for some of the vulnerabilities, there are approaches, e.g., [13], that track open source software for vulnerability patches. So, our approach assumes the existence of a patch for a given vulnerability.

In this paper, we present a tool, CONFER, that provides a light-weight analysis of patched configurable code to guide the developers and security analysts in identification of potentially vulnerable configurations. CONFER first extracts the *presence conditions*, which consist of some constraint over configuration variables, to identify parts of the patch that are explicitly or implicitly controlled by configuration variables. While explicit dependencies are extracted based on the syntax, implicit dependencies are extracted by considering call-sites of patched functions and the definitions of functions/macros that are called within the patched code. CONFER leverages the extracted compile-time feature combinations that control the patched code to infer patch relevant configurations. In doing so, CONFER can start with a reference configuration, e.g., the default configuration, and identify the necessary changes to generate all variations that can reveal the vulnerability and test the patched code. CONFER uses MaxSAT solving to deal with the possibly conflicting configuration constraints that control the patched code.

We also present a case study on BusyBox [1], a highly configurable system that implements a wide variety of UNIX utilities and is very popular in the embedded and IoT domain due to its small footprint. In this paper, we focus on the memory vulnerabilities in BusyBox. We identify BusyBox vulnerabilities using two approaches. The first approach involves finding the CVEs recorded in the National Vulnerability Database. After collecting all the CVEs that include a reference to BusyBox, we excluded the CVEs that are due to the vulnerabilities in the client code. There are 43 CVEs that report vulnerabilities in BusyBox. Among the 43 CVEs, 29 of them report memory vulnerabilities. Among the 29 memory vulnerability CVEs of BusyBox, only 11 of them have patches. The second approach involves keyword search in the source code repository of BusyBox. We found a total of 224 patches for memory vulnerabilities using the second approach.

We used CONFER to answer various research questions regarding the configuration relevance of BusyBox memory vulnerabilities. A summary of our contributions and findings is as follows.

- In 81% of the vulnerability reports the code is configurable. Considering all the vulnerabilities in the dataset, 48% of them are configuration relevant. When we consider only those that involve configurable code, 59% of the vulnerabilities are configuration relevant. Except for very few instances, most of the bug reports do not mention the vulnerable features or their combinations.

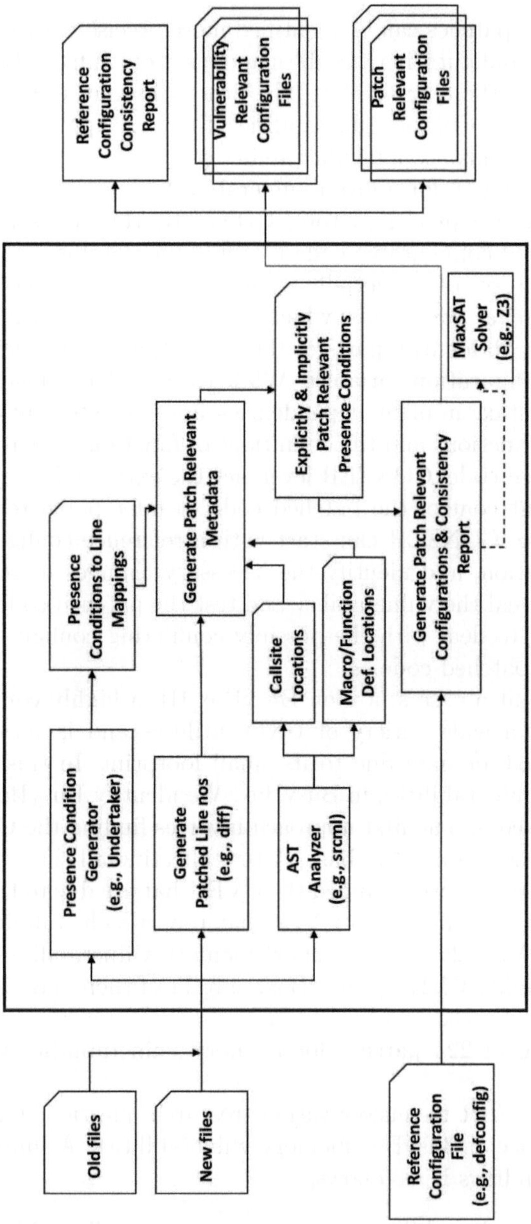

Fig. 1. The architecture of CONFER.

– Among the 19 vulnerable subsystems in BusyBox, the `shell` subsystem has the highest number of memory vulnerabilities (39), followed by the `networking` subsystem (34). Both subsystems have configuration relevant

vulnerable components that require a thorough understanding of all the vulnerable configurations and dependencies, which is alarming given the popularity of BusyBox in the IoT domain.
- One of the components in the `shell` subsystem, `hush`, has the highest number of unique configuration constraints and the highest number of vulnerabilities that differ from defconfig, the default configuration in BusyBox, which should be a concern especially for products with customized configurations that enable the vulnerability relevant configuration options. Across the subsystems with vulnerabilities, features `FEATURE_CLEAN_UP` and `FEATURE_SH_STANDALONE` appear to be the most common customization points that may host memory vulnerabilities.
- We present CONFER, a light-weight static configuration analysis tool, that can handle real-world code while providing sound reasoning for various security analyses including exploration of vulnerability configuration spaces and patch impact analysis. CONFER could correctly identify approximately 70% of the BusyBox patches that are deemed configuration relevant. We will release CONFER and the BusyBox vulnerability dataset to help developers and researchers in securing configurable systems[1].

The rest of the paper is organized as follows. We present the design and implementation of CONFER in Sect. 2. We present our case study on BusyBox in Sect. 3. We discuss our results and the limitations in Sect. 4. We discuss the related work in Sect. 5. We conclude with directions for future work in Sect. 6.

2 Approach

Table 1. The presence conditions controlling various code blocks in Fig. 2.

Code Range	Controlling Presence Condition
$[3, 6]$	$ENABLE\_D$
$[7, 11]$	$\neg ENABLE\_D$
$[13, 14]$	$ENABLE\_E$
$[15, 16]$	$\neg ENABLE\_E$
$[19, 22]$	$ENABLE\_F$
$[24, 26]$	$\neg ENABLE\_F$
$[32, 33]$	$(ENABLE\_A \vee ENABLE\_B) \wedge ENABLE\_C$
$[35, 35]$	$(ENABLE\_A \vee ENABLE\_B) \wedge ENABLE\_C \wedge ENABLE\_D$
$[38, 38]$	$(ENABLE\_A \vee ENABLE\_B) \wedge \neg ENABLE\_C$

Our goal in designing CONFER is to facilitate the exploration of configuration space of a software system by light-weight static analysis along with sound

[1] http://tiny.cc/yr5j001.

```
int y, z;

#if ENABLE_D
    void foo() {
        y = 0;
    }
#else
    void foo() {
        y = 5;
    }
#endif

#if ENABLE_E
  #define g foo
#else
  #define g bar
#endif

#if ENABLE_F
    void bar() {
        z = 0;
    }
#else
    void bar() {
        z = 5;
    }
#endif

void baz(int *x) {
#if  ENABLE_A || ENABLE_B
   #if ENABLE_C
     (*x)++;
     g();
     #if ENABLE_D
       (*x)++;
     #endif
   #else
     (*x)--;
   #endif
#endif
}

int main() {
  int w;
  #if ENABLE_H
      baz(&y);
  #else
      baz(&w);
  #endif
}
```

Fig. 2. Sample code representing the old version.

```
@@ -38,9 +38,9 @@
 #if  ENABLE_A || ENABLE_B
    #if ENABLE_C
      (*x)++;
-     g();
-     #if ENABLE_D
-       (*x)++;
+     bar();
+     #if !ENABLE_G
+       y++;
      #endif
    #else
      (*x)--;
```

Fig. 3. The patch for the code in Fig. 2.

reasoning. We achieve these goals by performing a dependency analysis on the Abstract-Syntax Tree (AST) and using a constraint solver for checking the feasibility of the generated configurations with respect to the dependencies of the patch (Table 2).

```
CONFIG_B=y
CONFIG_C=y
# CONFIG_D is not set
CONFIG_E=y
CONFIG_F=y
CONFIG_G=y
CONFIG_H=y
```

Fig. 4. Sample reference configuration.

Table 2. The enclosing and included presence conditions controlling the patch in Fig. 3.

PC Type	Ex./Im.	PC	Scope
Enclosing	Ex.	$(ENABLE\_A \vee ENABLE\_B)$ $\wedge ENABLE\_C$	V, P
Enclosing	Im.	$ENABLE\_H$	V, P
Enclosing	Im.	$\neg ENABLE\_H$	V, P
Included	Ex.	$ENABLE\_D$	V
Included	Im.	$ENABLE\_D$	V
Included	Im.	$\neg ENABLE\_D$	V
Included	Im.	$ENABLE\_E$	V
Included	Im.	$\neg ENABLE\_E$	V
Included	Ex.	$\neg ENABLE\_G$	P
Included	Im.	$ENABLE\_F$	P
Included	Im.	$\neg ENABLE\_F$	P

Table 3. The vulnerability (VC1 and VC2) and the patch (PC1 and PC2) configurations for the patch in Fig. 3.

Config Var.	VC1	VC2	PC1	PC2
$CONFIG\_A$	T	T	T	T
$CONFIG\_B$	T	T	T	T
$CONFIG\_C$	F	T	F	T
$CONFIG\_D$	F	T	F	F
$CONFIG\_E$	T	F	T	T
$CONFIG\_F$	T	F	T	F
$CONFIG\_G$	T	T	T	F
$CONFIG\_H$	T	F	T	F

Figure 1 shows the architecture of CONFER, which receives three inputs: the old and the new versions of the source code and a reference configuration file. CONFER uses a presence condition (PC) generator, e.g., Undertaker [11], to collect a mapping between the source line ranges and the presence conditions in the old and the new versions of the code. The PC generator handles all the preprocessor directives such as `#if, #elif, #else, #ifdef, #ifndef, #endif` including the nested ones, which consist of formula over the configuration variables and macros. Consider the example code, the old version, in Fig. 2, the example patch in Fig. 3, and the example reference configuration in Fig. 4. We follow the convention in BusyBox and use the transformed versions of the configuration variables in the source code by replacing the keyword "CONFIG" with the keyword "ENABLE", i.e., CONFIG_X in the configuration file refers to ENABLE_X in the source code. Table 1 shows the source line ranges and the controlling presence conditions. Algorithm 1 shows the high-level steps of generating patch relevant configurations. It first identifies the patch relevant lines in the old and the new versions (lines 2 and 4) and uses these source line ranges in generating metadata for configuration generation (lines 3 and 5). CONFER converts the source code to AST and then traverses the AST to identify the locations of the callsites and the definitions of macros and functions. Both the presence condition to line mappings, and the callsites and function/macro definitions are used to generate the configuration relevant metadata, which consists of the enclosing and the included presence conditions for the patch. These are computed separately for the old version and the new version. The enclosing presence conditions include those that are outside the patched code region and control the patched code explicitly or implicitly. The included presence conditions are those that are included in the changed regions in the old and the new versions of the code. For the patch in Fig. 3, Table 3 presents the enclosing and included presence conditions. As an example, in both versions the patched region is explicitly enclosed by $(ENABLE\_A \vee ENABLE\_B) \wedge ENABLE\_C$. However, due to callsites of `baz` at lines 46 and 48 in Fig. 2, $ENABLE\_D$ and $\neg ENABLE\_D$ implicitly enclose the change locations both in the old (denoted by V) and the new version (denoted by P) due to lines 45 and 47, respectively. In the old (new) version, the patched region explicitly includes $ENABLE\_D$ ($\neg ENABLE\_G$). However, in the old version, the change region includes a call to macro `g`, whose definitions are controlled by $ENABLE\_E$ and $\neg ENABLE\_E$ at lines 13 and 15, respectively. CONFER keeps checking the definitions of functions and macros that define macros until all relevant definitions are covered. For example, since `foo` is used to define `g` at line 14, CONFER also includes $ENABLE\_D$ and ($\neg ENABLE\_D$) due to lines 3 and 7. Similarly, since `bar` is used to define `g` at line 16, CONFER also includes $ENABLE\_F$ and ($\neg ENABLE\_F$) due to lines 19 and 23.

Algorithm 2 presents the steps of metadata generation. It uses an off-the-shelf presence condition generator Undertaker [11], to generate a presence condition to line mapping (line 2) for the given source code P. The goal is to generate the set of enclosing presence conditions and the set of included presence conditions, which we call metadata, based on the set of source line ranges of interest L, which happens to represent the changed lines in the context of patch relevant configuration generation. Lines 4–8 collects the explicitly enclosing presence conditions. Then it finds all callers of all the functions that directly or indirectly calls the patched functions (lines 9–15) and adds the presence conditions that control the callsites of such functions to the set of enclosing presence conditions (lines 16–18). The next step is to generate the explicit included presence conditions (lines 19–23) and the implicit ones due to definitions of macros/functions that get called in the source lines of interest (24–34). Finally it returns the set of all enclosing presence conditions, *EPC*, and a set of all included presence conditions, *IPC*.

The ultimate goal of Algorithm 1 is to generate patch relevant configurations using a reference configuration, *RC*, e.g., the default configuration. Although enclosing and included presence conditions provide a set of constraints to derive the configurations, combining all the constraints does not work in general as there may be conflicting constraints. Another issue is that, we would like to differentiate between configurations that can be used to reproduce the vulnerabilities and those that can be used to test the new version. We deal with the first problem by encoding the configuration generation problem as a MaxSAT problem [6], which is specified in terms of a set of hard constraints that must be satisfied and a set of soft constraints that should be satisfied in a way to maximize an objective function that sums up the weights of the satisfied soft constraints. We deal with the second problem by differentiating between the presence conditions that are relevant to the old version from those that are relevant from the new version. Enclosing constraints, by definition, apply to both versions. That is enclosing versions that are generated from the old version and the patch applies to the new version as well and vice versa. Included constraints, on the other hand, apply to the specific version they are derived from as they are included in the changed code which differs for the old version and the new version. So, as Algorithm 1 shows, enclosing presence conditions identified for both the old (new) version, $M_o.EPC$ ($M_n.EPC$), and the new (old) version, $M_n.EPC$ ($M_o.EPC$), are combined with the old (new) version's included presence conditions, $M_o.IPC$ ($M_n.IPC$), to identify the set of vulnerability (patched version) relevant soft constraints (lines 6 and 10). For both versions, the hard constraints are formed by the constraints from *RC* that do not conflict with any of the soft constraints for that version (lines 7 and 11).

Algorithm 3, calls a MaxSAT solver (line 4), records the generated solution (line 5), removes the soft constraints that are satisfied by the current solution (lines 6–10), and continues repeating these steps until all the soft constraints are consumed (lines 3–11). Although Algorithm 3 does not minimize the set of configurations, it is guaranteed that the returned set of configurations, C, covers all the enclosing and the included presence conditions.

Finally, Algorithm 1 computes the set of constraints, *ICV* and *ICP*, from the reference configuration, *RC*, that conflict with some of the enclosing or included presence conditions for the old version and the new one (lines 14 and 15), respectively.

Table 4. A summary of the memory vulnerability dataset collected for BusyBox.

Keyword	Years	Versions	Components	Count
Segmentation Fault	2023-2001	1.37.0-1.6.0	ar(1), ash(12), awk(7), bc(2), bunzip2(1), catv(1), chrt(1), cmdedit(2), comm(2), concat_path_file(1), cryptpw(1), data_extract_all(1), devfsd(1), diff(3), dmesg(1), dnsd(1), dpkg(3), du(1), echo(1), env(2), fbsplash(1), find_pid_by_name(1), getopt(1), get_opt_ulflags(1) grep(2), gunzip(2), hexdump(2), hexedit(1), httpd(1), hush(12), ifupdown(1), init(1), ipcalc(1), ip(1), kill(2), lash(2), less(4), libbb(1), lineedit(3), lpd(1), ls(2), makedevs(1), man(1), math(1), mdev(1), modprobe(4), modutils(1), mount(3), nameif(1), nc(1), nfsmount(1), ntpd(1), od(2), patch(1), printenv(1), ps(1), pwd(1), route(1), sed(3), sendmail(2), sh(3), shuf(1), stat(2), svlogd(1), syslogd(1), tail(2), tar(7), telnet(1), tftp(1), time(1), touch(1), traceroute(1), tr(1), udhcp(3), unlzma(5), unzip(2), vi(3), wget(2), which(1), xargs(1)	155
Buffer Overflow	2021–2002	1.34.0-1.10.0	arp(1), ash(1), awk(1), bunzip2(1), cut(1), dnsd(1), dos2unix(1), dpkg(1), httpd(2), hush(1), id(1), inotifyd(1), insmod(2), lash(1), less(1), logger(1), ls(1), mkdevs(2), modprobe(2), mount(1), my_getgrgid(1), my_getpwuid(1), procps(1), pstree(1), tar(1), udhcp(1), vi(2), wget(1), whoami(1)	34
Out of Bound	2022-2016	1.33.0-1.25.0	ar(1), ash(2), bc(1), compare_string_array(1), gzip(1), i2c_tools(1), taskset(1), udhcp(3), whois(1)	12
Use After Free	2023-2006	1.37.0-1.12.0	ash(4), awk(2), bc(1), copy_file(1), dpkg(1), isrv_identd(1), lineedit(1), nameif(1), tsort(1), wget(2)	15
Double Free	2023-2006	1.36.0-1.24.0	httpd(1), hush(1), interface(1), mount(1), patch(1), sed(2), top(1)	8
Summary/Total	**2023-2000**	**1.37.0-1.6.0**	**archival(26), coreutils(26), editors(23), findutils(4), init(1), libbb(15), libpwdgrp(1), loginutils(1), mailutils(1), miscutils(20), modutils(9), networking(34), printutils(1), procps(6), runit(1), procps(6), shell(39), sysklogd(1), util-linux(10)**	224

Algorithm 1 An algorithm for generating patch relevant configurations.

GenerateVulnerableAndPatchConfigs(*old*: SUT, *new*: SUT, *RC*: Reference Configuration): (Set of Constraints, Set of Constraints, Set of Configurations, Set of Configurations)
$L_o \leftarrow \mathit{DiffSourceLines}(old, new)$
$M_o \leftarrow \mathit{GenerateMetadata}(old, L_o)$
$L_n \leftarrow \mathit{DiffSourceLines}(new, old)$
$M_n \leftarrow \mathit{GenerateMetadata}(new, L_n)$
$V_s \leftarrow M_o.\mathit{IPC} \cup M_o.\mathit{EPC} \cup M_n.\mathit{EPC}$
$V_h \leftarrow \{c \mid c \in \mathit{Constraints}(RC) \wedge \neg\exists pc \in V_s.\ pc \wedge c = false\}$
$V_w \leftarrow \{(pc, 1) \mid pc \in V_s\}$
$V \leftarrow \mathit{GenerateAllMaxSATConfigurations}(V_h, V_s, V_w)$
$P_s \leftarrow M_n.\mathit{IPC} \cup M_n.\mathit{EPC} \cup M_o.\mathit{EPC}$
$P_h \leftarrow \{c \mid c \in \mathit{Constraints}(RC) \wedge \neg\exists pc \in P_s.\ pc \wedge c = false\}$
$P_w \leftarrow \{(pc, 1) \mid pc \in P_s\}$
$P \leftarrow \mathit{GenerateAllMaxSATConfigurations}(P_h, P_s, P_w)$
$\mathit{ICV} \leftarrow \mathit{Constraints}(RC) \setminus V_h$
$\mathit{ICP} \leftarrow \mathit{Constraints}(RC) \setminus P_h$
return $(\mathit{ICV}, \mathit{ICP}, V, P)$

Implementation. We implemented CONFER in Java and it uses Undertaker [11] to generate the presence condition to line mappings, srcml [4] to convert the source code into an xml representation of the AST, and the optimization API of Z3 and its SAT solver [8]. CONFER also comes with scripts to extract precise line information from the diff files.

3 A Case Study on BusyBox

BusyBox is a popular highly configurable software that is also used in embedded systems and in the Internet of Things (IoT) deployments. So, vulnerabilities in BusyBox form part of the IoT attack surface especially considering the fact that BusyBox provides shell, file system, and networking utilities in those settings. In this paper, we explore the configuration space of the memory vulnerabilities in BusyBox using CONFER. Specifically, we focus on the patched vulnerabilities and use the changed lines in the old and the new versions as an oracle for bug relevant code locations[2]. In our dataset, for each vulnerability, we include the log file for the patch, the old and the new version of the changed file(s), the line numbers that have been changed in the old version and those that have been changed in the new version, and the defconfig configuration file that is relevant to the patched version of BusyBox. We pass the source file (the old or the new version), the changed code lines, and the defconfig as the reference configuration to find out the presence conditions defined in these source files, the

[2] We assume that the patched code region is related to the reported bug even though the patch may not be complete.

Algorithm 2 An algorithm for generating the metadata, the enclosing and including presence conditions.

GenerateMetadata(P: **SUT**, L: **Set of Source Line Ranges**): Metadata
$EPC, IPC \leftarrow \emptyset$
$PCL \leftarrow GeneratePCtoLineMapping(P)$
for each $(pc, lines) \in PCL$ **do**
  if exists $r \in L$ s.t. $lines \cap Lines(r) \neq \emptyset \; \wedge \; lines \cap Lines(r) \subset lines$ **then**
    $EPC \leftarrow EPC \cup \{pc\}$
  end if
end for
$CS \leftarrow \lambda F.\{(f, line) \mid f \in F \; \wedge F \subseteq Functions(P) \; \wedge \; line \in Lines(P, f_{call})\}$
$CG \leftarrow \{(f_1, f_2) \mid f_1, f_2 \in Functions(P) \; \wedge f_1 \in Caller(f_2)\}$
$CSM \leftarrow \lambda F.\{(f, line) \mid (f, line) \in CS(F) \vee \exists n > 1. f_n, f_{n-1}, .., f_1.l_n, l_{n-1}, ..., l_1.f = f_n \wedge line = l_n \wedge (f_1, l_1) \in CS(F) \wedge \bigwedge_{1 \leq i < n} (f_{i+1}, f_i) \in CG \wedge (f_i, l_i) \in CS(\{f_i\})\}$
$F_{epc} \leftarrow \emptyset$
for each line range $r \in L$ **do**
  $F_{epc} \leftarrow F_{epc} \cup \{f \mid Lines(r) \cap Lines(P, f_{def}) \neq \emptyset\}$
end for
for each $(f, line) \in CSM(F_{epc})$ **do**
  $EPC \leftarrow EPC \cup \{pc \mid (pc, lines) \in PCL \wedge line \in lines\}]$
end for
for each $(pc, lines) \in PCL$ **do**
  if exists $r \in L$ s.t. $lines \subseteq Lines(r)$ **then**
    $IPC \leftarrow IPC \cup \{pc\}$
  end if
end for
$FDEF \leftarrow \lambda F.\{(f, line) \mid f \in F \; \wedge F \subseteq Functions(P) \wedge line \in Lines(P, f_{def})\}$
$MDEF \leftarrow \lambda M.\{(m, line) \mid \; m \in M \wedge M \subseteq Macros(P) \wedge line \in Lines(P, m_{def})\}\}$
$MV \leftarrow \{(m, v) \mid m \in M \wedge M \subseteq Macros(P) \wedge (v \in Macros(P) \vee v \in Functions(P)) \wedge (m_{def}, v) \in MacroDef(P)\}$
$E_{pc} \leftarrow \emptyset$
for each line range $r \in L$ **do**
  $E_{pc} \leftarrow E_{pc} \cup \{e \mid e \in Functions(P) \cup Macros(P) \wedge Lines(r) \cap Lines(P, e_{call}) \neq \emptyset\}$
end for
$DM \leftarrow \lambda E.\{(e, line) \mid e \in E \wedge E \subseteq Functions(P) \cup Macros(P) \wedge line \in Lines(P, e_{def}) \wedge ((e, line) \in FDEF(E) \cup MDEF(E) \vee \exists n > 1. e_n, e_{n-1}, ..., e_1.l_n, l_{n-1}, ..., l_1.e = e_n \wedge l_n = line \wedge (e_1, l_1) \in FDEF(E) \cup MDEF(E) \wedge \bigwedge_{1 \leq i < n} (e_i, e_{i+1}) \in MV) \wedge (e_i, l_i) \in FDEF(\{e_i\}) \cup MDEF(\{e_i\})\}$
for each $(e, line) \in DM(E_{pc})$ **do**
  $IPC \leftarrow IPC \cup \{pc \mid (pc, lines) \in PCL \wedge line \in lines\}]$
end for
return (EPC, IPC)

presence conditions that correspond to the code locations related to the patch, and whether the patch related presence conditions are consistent with defconfig.

We collected the BusyBox memory vulnerabities from two sources: 1) the National Vulnerability Database (NVD) [3] and 2) the BusyBox source code

Algorithm 3 An algorithm for generating a set of configurations covering all constraints using a MaxSAT solver.

GenerateAllMaxSATConfigurations(H: Set of hard constraints, S: Set of soft constraints, W: Weights of soft constraints): Set of configurations
$C \leftarrow \emptyset$
while $S \neq \emptyset$ **do**
  $c \leftarrow MaxSAT(\bigwedge_{pc \in H} pc, Soft, W)$
  $C \leftarrow C \cup \{c\}$
  for each $pc \in S$ **do**
    if $pc \wedge c \neq false$ **then**
      $S \leftarrow S \setminus \{pc\}$
    end if
  end for
end while
return C

repository. From NVD, we found 43 CVEs about the vulnerabilities in BusyBox after excluding those vulnerabilities that are due to the code errors in the client code of systems that deploy BusyBox. 29 of these vulnerabilities are memory vulnerabilities. Among the 29 memory vulnerability CVEs of BusyBox, only 11 of them have patches. From the BusyBox code repository, we found a total of 224 vulnerabilities with patches as shown in Table 4. We categorized these vulnerabilities according to a set of keywords, which include segmentationf fault, SEGV, and segfault (SEGV), out of bound (OOB), use after free (UAF), and double free (DF). As Table 4 shows, the majority (69%) of the vulnerabilities were described with the keywords related to segmentation fault. As the summary row in the table shows, our dataset spans vulnerabilities between the years of 2001 and 2023, the BusyBox versions from 1.6.0 to 1.37.0, and the 19 subsystems of BusyBox. The subsystems with the highest number of vulnerabilities include the shell subsystem (39) followed by the networking subsystem (34). The vulnerabilities listed in Table 4 includes the 11 BusyBox CVEs with patches mentioned above. CONFER completed the analysis for the whole dataset within 15 min on a machine with an 11th Gen Intel(R) Core(TM) i7-1165G7 processor and a 32GB RAM. Below we present the results of various research questions we answered using CONFER.

RQ1: What percentage of the BusyBox vulnerabilities is configuration relevant? We used CONFER to find the number of BusyBox vulnerabilities that involve code that was configurable. As shown in Fig. 5, considering all the vulnerabilities in the dataset, 49% of them (109 out of 224) are configuration relevant. Approximately 19% of the vulnerabilities involve patching of code that is not configurable, i.e., no presence conditions. When we consider only those that involve configurable code, 60% of the vulnerabilities are configuration relevant.

Figure 6 shows the configuration relevance distribution of each category of vulnerabilities based on the relevance/irrelevance with respect to the patched code in the old version and the one in the new version. The configuration

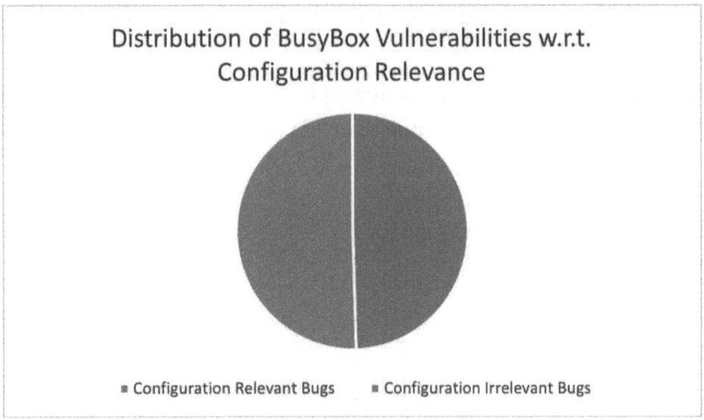

Fig. 5. Distribution of patched BusyBox vulnerabilities w.r.t. configuration relevance.

relevance with respect to the old version helps security analysts identify the vulnerable configurations more precisely while the configuration relevance with respect to the new version helps developers design tests that can properly validate the changes and inform the software update process. As shown in Fig. 6, there are more configuration relevant vulnerabilities than configuration irrelevant ones in the categories of Use After Free (UAF) and Double Free (DF), suggesting a need to pay special attention to configuration specific memory deallocation operations. In the category of Segmentation fault (SEGV) there are some instances that become configuration relevant in the new versions.

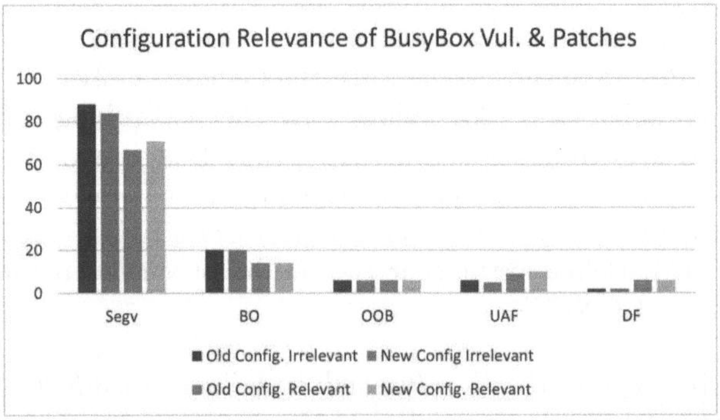

Fig. 6. The distribution of BusyBox vulnerabilities in terms of configuration relevance.

RQ2: Are the configuration relevant BusyBox vulnerabilities consistent with defconfig? BusyBox comes with a default configuration, also called defconfig, that achieves a high coverage of code across all the components. However, clients may need special features that are turned off in defconfig. So, customizing BusyBox may create deviations from defconfig based on the requirements for the final BusyBox product. Although we do not make any assumptions on what percentage of BusyBox deployments use defconfig without any customizations, checking consistency of the patch relevant presence conditions with defconfig provides information on the customization points that may host specific vulnerabilities.

Figure 7 plots the change in the number of configuration variables defined in defconfig over the years based on the information in our dataset. It shows that the size of defconfig has increased gradually over time and sometimes even within the same year. As of BusyBox version 1.37.0, there are 1080 configuration variables defined in defconfig. In such a highly configurable system, it is not feasible to perform testing of all the combinations. Therefore, it is important to identify patch relevant configurations and allocate resources to the testing of a subset of configurations that are deemed relevant.

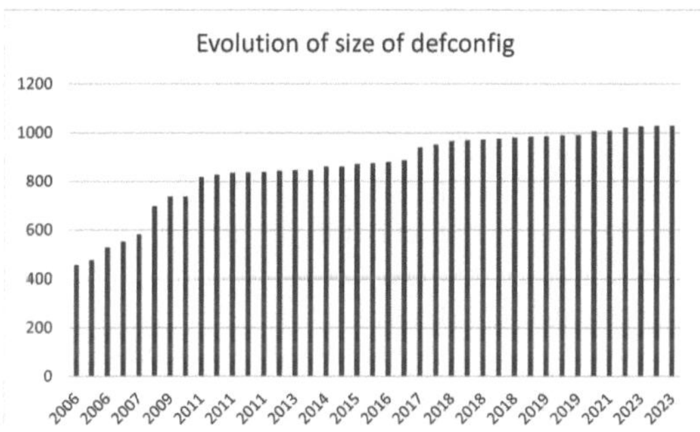

Fig. 7. Evolution of defconfig based on the BusyBox dataset.

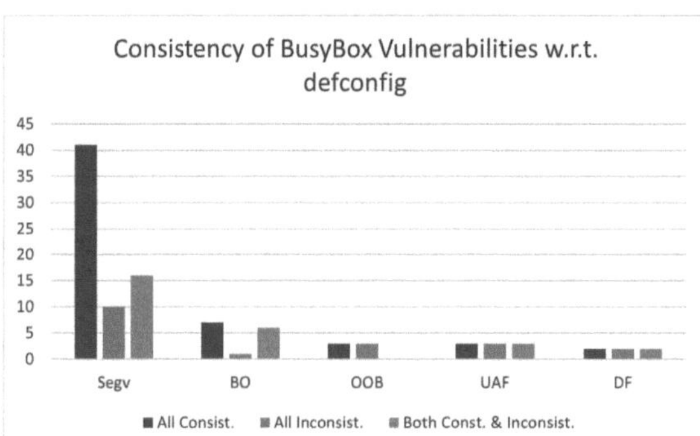

Fig. 8. Consistency of configuration relevant BusyBox vulnerabilities w.r.t. defconfig.

Table 5. The constraints that control the patched code in the old or the new version and contradict the relevant defconfig.

Vul. Comp.	Vul. Type	Patch Year	Constraints Causing Inconsistency with defconfig
mount	BO	2002	FEATURE_MOUNT_LOOP
kill	SEGV	2003	! KILLALL
sed	SEGV	2004	FEATURE_CLEAN_UP
httpd	BO	2005	FEATURE_HTTPD_ENCODE_URL_STR
ipcalc	SEGV	2005	FEATURE_IPCALC_FANCY FEATURE_LESS_MARKS
httpd	DF	2006	! FEATURE_HTTPD_CGI
tftp	SEGV	2006	FEATURE_CLEAN_UP
ash	SEGV	2007	ASH_EXPAND_PRMT
du	SEGV	2007	FEATURE_CLEAN_UP
stat	SEGV	2007	SELINUX
hush	DF	2007	FEATURE_SH_STANDALONE
hush	SEGV	2007	FEATURE_EDITING_FANCY_PROMPT
hush	SEGV	2007	HUSH_TICK, HUSH_LOOPS
vi	BO	2007	! FEATURE_VI_COLON, !FEATURE_VI_READONLY
hush	SEGV	2008	HUSH_TICK, LASH HUSH_LOOPS, HUSH_JOB FEATURE_SH_STANDALONE
ash	SEGV	2008	ASH_ALIAS
hush	SEGV	2009	LASH, FEATURE_SH_STANDALONE
hush	BO	2010	LASH FEATURE_SH_STANDALONE
lineedit	SEGV	2011	FEATURE_EDITING_ASK_TERMINAL
nameif	UAF	2013	FEATURE_CLEAN_UP
pstree	BO	2013	!FEATURE_SHOW_THREADS
stat	SEGV	2014	!FEATURE_STAT_FORMAT SELINUX
ps	SEGV	2015	!DESKTOP
httpd	BO	2015	!FEATURE_HTTPD_CGI
less	BO	2015	!FEATURE_LESS_WINCH
ash	UAF	2016	FEATURE_ASH_IDLE_TIMEOUT
gzip	OOB	2016	FEATURE_GZIP_LEVELS
udhcp	SEGV	2016	DNS_COMPR_TESTING
ar	OOB	2018	FEATURE_AR_LONG_FILENAMES
hush	SEGV	2018	!FEATURE_EDITING
unlzma	SEGV	2018	FEATURE_LZMA_FAST
sed	DF	2018	FEATURE_CLEAN_UP
bc	OOB	2019	!FEATURE_DC_BIG
bc	SEGV	2019	!FEATURE_DC_BIG
bc	UAF	2022	!FEATURE_DC_BIG
sed	DF	2023	FEATURE_CLEAN_UP
tsort	UAF	2023	FEATURE_CLEAN_UP

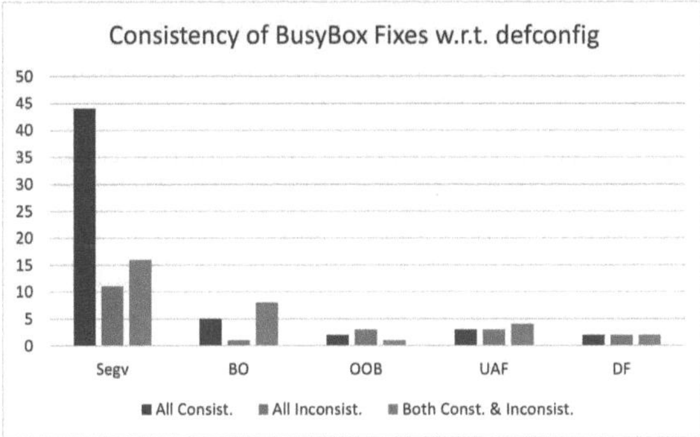

Fig. 9. Consistency of configuration relevant BusyBox fixes w.r.t. defconfig.

Figures 8 and 9 show the distribution of presence conditions controlling the patched code in terms of their consistency with the relevant defconfig based on the old version and the new version of the code, respectively. In 55% of the vulnerabilities, all the vulnerability relevant presence conditions are consistent with defconfig. In 26% of the vulnerabilities, there are both defconfig consistent and defconfig inconsistent vulnerability relevant presence conditions. In 19% of the vulnerabilities, all the vulnerability relevant presence conditions are inconsistent with defconfig. So, 45% of the vulnerabilities suggest bugs due to configuration customization, which imply the need for specifying the configuration information in the logs and bug reports and using it in patch validation and distribution.

Regarding the patch relevant constraints, 52% of the patches are consistent with the relevant defconfig, 29% of the patches have both defconfig consistent and defconfig inconsistent patch relevant presence conditions, and 19% of the patches involve presence conditions that are inconsistent with defconfig. So, for 48% of the vulnerabilities patch validation requires the preparation of a configuration that varies from defconfig.

RQ3: Which configuration variables cause inconsistency with defconfig? Table 5 presents the vulnerable components along with their vulnerability relevant presence conditions that are inconsistent with defconfig. Such configuration variable settings suggest vulnerable customizations. Among the vulnerable components `hush` has the highest number of vulnerabilities with custom configurations (7). A close inspection on `hush`, as shown in Fig. 10, shows that the number of presence conditions in `hush` has consistently increased over the years and it happens to have the highest number of unique presence conditions (182) in our data set. Among the configuration variables and across the subsystems with vulnerabilities, features `ENABLE_FEATURE_CLEAN_UP` (7) and `FEATURE_SH_STANDALONE` (4), appear to be the most common customization points that may host memory vulnerabilities. It is remarkable that only 3 out of 7 patch documentations (sed double-free 2023 and 2018 and nameif use after free 2013) explicitly mention the role of `ENABLE_FEATURE_CLEAN_UP` in the patch report. On the other hand, none of the 4 vulnerabilities in Table 5 involve any references to FEATURE_SH_STANDALONE in the patch reports. These findings show both the effectiveness of CONFER in identifying vulnerability relevant configuration variables and its potential use in augmenting vulnerability reports and patch documentation. Since we used defconfig for the specific BusyBox version that was patched for each vulnerability, we were able to also observe that the way a feature gets set in defconfig has changed over the years (from disabled to enabled), a notable example being ENABLE_DESKTOP.

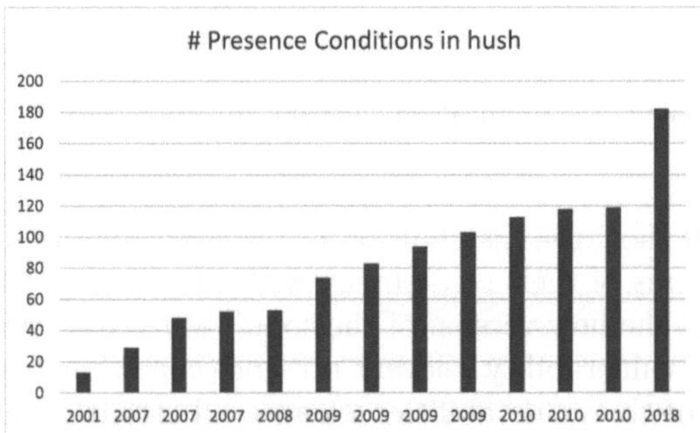

Fig. 10. Number of presence conditions in various versions of hush based on the time points of the patched memory vulnerabilities.

As Table 7 shows that 67% of the vulnerabilities with presence conditions inconsistent with defconfig (32 out of 48) have some type of indicator in the patch in terms of configuration relevance of the vulnerability. However, when it comes to the availability of tests that manifest the vulnerability, a lower percentage of 23% of the vulnerabilities (11 out of 48) satisfy this requirement.

RQ4: Are the configuration relevant BusyBox vulnerabilities consistent with Android's defconfig? Since 2011, BusyBox's official source code repository keeps several configurations for Android deployments. There are 93 vulnerabilities in our dataset that belongs to a BusyBox version that comes with an Android defconfig. Among these, 50 of the vulnerabilities are configuration relevant. We used Android's defconfig to check if any of the vulnerabilities are completely consistent, i.e., can be manifested when the Android defconfig is used. 24 out of the 50 configuration relevant vulnerabilities are completely consistent with the relevant version of Android's defconfig. These vulnerabilities include some of the most recent vulnerabilities: the double-free in sed and the use after free in ash that have been fixed in 2023. We think that CONFER can facilitate vulnerability reporting and patching that involve multiple open source projects as in the case of Android and BusyBox.

RQ5: Are BusyBox vulnerabilities with CVEs configuration relevant? We identified the BusyBox CVEs that are related to memory vulnerabilities with patches.

Table 6 presents those CVEs and whether they are configuration relevant based on the patched code locations in the old version. Two out of eleven CVEs are configuration relevant. However, the CVE entries did not have any mention of the configuration setting other than the BusyBox version. While we think that the CVEs do not reflect all the vulnerabilities of BusyBox, those that are registered in NVD or similar sites should provide more information regarding the features related to the vulnerability. At a minimum, the configuration that manifests the vulnerability must be provided. Ideally, additional information such as the vulnerability relevant presence conditions should be provided to enable further analysis by the stakeholders.

Table 6. The configuration relevance of BusyBox CVEs with patches.

CVE	Type	Version	Component	Conf. Rel?
CVE-2022-30065	UAF	1.35.0	awk	No
CVE-2022-48174	BO	1.34.1	ash	No
CVE-2021-28831	SEGV	1.32.1	decom._gunzip	No
CVE-2019-5747	OOB	1.30.0	udhcp	No
CVE-2018-20679	OOB	1.30.0	udhcp	No
CVE-2015-9261	SEGV	1.27.2	decompress_gunzip	No
CVE-2018-1000517	BO	1.29.0	wget	No
CVE-2017-15874	SEGV	1.27.2	decom._unlzma	No
CVE-2017-15873	OOB	1.27.2	decom._bunzip2	Yes
CVE-2016-2148	BO	1.24.2	udhcp	No
CVE-2016-2147	SEGV	1.24.2	udhcp	Yes

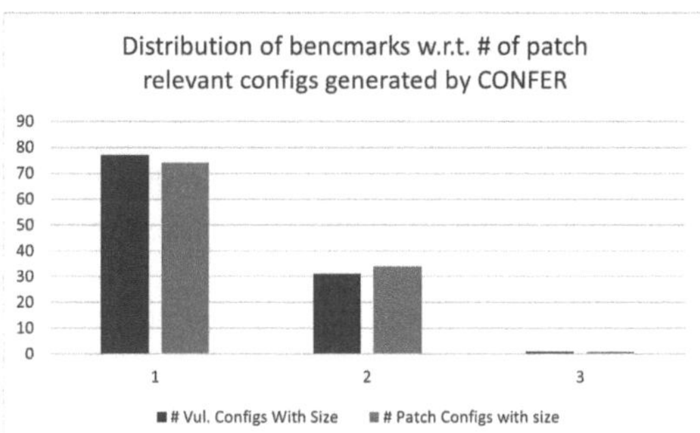

Fig. 11. The distribution of BusyBox vulnerabilities in terms of the number of patch relevant configurations.

RQ6: How many patch relevant configurations get generated by CONFER? Figure 11 shows the distribution of benchmarks in terms of the number of vulnerability configurations and the number of patch configurations. As the figure shows, for majority of the configuration relevant vulnerabilities (77 out of 109) and the patches (74 out of 109) one configuration is sufficient to cover the vulnerability or the patch. Two configurations are needed for 31 out of 109 configuration relevant vulnerabilities to test the vulnerable version while two configurations are needed for 34 out of 109 of the configuration relevant vulnerabilities to test the patch. Only one configuration relevant vulnerability, the segmentation fault in devfsd that was patched in 2007, needs three configurations to test the vulnerable version and to validate the patch and to satisfy four different constraints over the configuration variables `CONFIG_DEBUG` and `CONFIG_DEVFSD_VERBOSE`.

RQ7: How precise and complete is CONFER? To evaluate CONFER's precision with regards to deciding consistency with BusyBox's defconfig, we used the vulnerabilities that come with test cases. As Table 7 shows there are eight of them for which the test case to reproduce is noted in the patch or the bug report. Four of these are about earlier versions (years 2003–2007) for which we were not able to build BusyBox. One of them (psEGV2015) required a specific operating system, openWRT, to reproduce the bug. So, we were also not able to test psSEGV2015. Our findings for the remaining three vulnerabilities using valgrind for memory error detection are as follows:

- **arOOB2018:** As shown in Table 7, CONFER infers that for both reproducing the bug in the vulnerable version and validating the patched version `FEATURE_AR_LONG_FILENAMES` should be set to true, which is set to false in defconfig. This prediction is the same for both explicit only mode and the mode that includes implicit dependencies. We confirmed this result by running the test case with both defconfig and a configuration that sets `FEATURE_AR_LONG_FILENAMES` to true. Testing the vulnerable BusyBox version using defconfig resulted in `ar` utility printing a message saying that long file names are not supported. Testing vulnerable BusyBox version with `FEATURE_AR_LONG_FILENAMES` on revealed the invalid read (out of bounds access). We also tested the fixed version with defconfig and by setting to `FEATURE_AR_LONG_FILENAMES` to true. As in the vulnerable case, the former resulted in the `ar` utility message as mentioned above and the latter did not report any invalid reads, suggesting the correctness of the patch for the test case.
- **hushSEGV2018:** When only explicit dependencies are used, CONFER infers that all the patch relevant configurations are consistent with defconfig and when implicit dependencies are also considered it infers that `FEATURE_EDITING` should be set to false as opposed to the setting in defconfig as shown in Table 7. The bug is about a stack overflow due to recursion and the patch is actually not designed to fix the overflow. Instead, it is designed to abort BusyBox at 65000 function recursion depth and make variable nesting code independent of 'local" support (`HUSH_LOCAL` feature). CONFER predicts

Table 7. Patches that have been identified as somehow conflicting with defconfig constraints by CONFER (except the false negative nameifUAF2013). It shows configuration relevance (R) or irrelevance (I) decision for the old and the new versions along with consistency of the path relevant configuration constraints with defconfig (AC for all consistent, AI for all inconsistent, and SI for some inconsistent) and the availability of tests and configuration relevance indicators for the vulnerabilities in Table 5 in the patch report (C, +, − denote comments, added code, and removed code, respectively).

Vulnerability	CONFER Dec.		Config in Patch?	Test?
	Old	New		
mountBO2002	R, SI	R, SI	No	No
killSEGV2003	R, SI	R, SI	No	**Yes**
sedSEGV2004	R, AI	R, AI	No	**Yes**
httpdBO2005	R, SI	R, SI	No	No
ipcalcSEGV2005	R, SI	R, SI	No	No
httpdDF2006	R, SI	R, SI	No	No
tftpSEGV2006	R, SI	R, SI	(−, +)	No
ashSEGV2007	R, SI	R, SI	No	No
duSEGV2007	R, AI	I	(−, +)	**Yes**
statSEGV2007	R, SI	R, SI	No	No
hushDF2007	R, SI	R, SI	(−)	No
hushSEGV2007	R, SI	R, SI	No	No
hushSEGV2007	R, SI	R, SI	No	Yes
viBO2007	R, SI	R, SI	(−)	**Yes**
hushSEGV2008	R, SI	R, SI	(−)	No
ashSEGV2008	R, SI	R, SI	No	No
hushSEGV2009	R, SI	R, SI	No	No
hushBO2010	R, SI	R, SI	(+)	No
lineeditSEGV2011	R, SI	R, AC	No	**No**
nameifUAF2013	I	I	(C)	No
pstreeBO2013	R, AC	R, SI	(+)	No
statSEGV2014	R, AI	R, AI	No	No
psSEGV2015	R, AI	R, AI	No	**Yes**
httpdBO2015	R, SI	R, SI	No	No
lessBO2015	R, SI	R, SI	No	No
ashUAF2016	R, SI	R, SI	No	No
gzipOOB2016	R, AI	R, AI	No	No
arOOB2018	R, AI	R, AI	No	**Yes**
hushSEGV2018	R, SI	R, SI	(−)	**Yes**
unlzmaSEGV2018	R, AI	R, AI	(+)	No
sedDF2018	R, AI	R, AI	(C)	No
bcOOB2019	R, AI	R, AI	No	No
bcSEGV2019	R, AI	R, AI	No	No
bcUAF2022	R, AI	R, AI	No	No
sedDF2023	R, AI	R, AI	(C)	**Yes**
tsortUAF2023	I	R, AI	(+)	**Yes**

the patch relevance of `HUSH_LOCAL` along with some additional features that are consistent with defconfig both in explicit and combined modes. Testing the vulnerable and the fixed versions with both defconfig (with hush enabled) and `FEATURE_EDITING` set to false yielded the same output (same number of dots per function execution before the segmentation fault). The fact that we did not realize any difference for different settings of `FEATURE_EDITING` is possibly due to the implicit dependency not being very relevant to the issue.

- **sedDF2023:** As shown in Table 7, CONFER infers that both the vulnerability and the patch are relevant to `FEATURE_CLEAN_UP` being set to true, which contradicts with defconfig. We confirmed that the bug is not revealed under defconfig and is revealed when `FEATURE_CLEAN_UP` was set to true.
- **tsortUAF2023:** As shown in Table 7, CONFER infers that the vulnerability is not configuration relevant and the patch is relevant to `FEATURE_CLEAN_UP` being set to true, which contradicts with defconfig. These decisions apply to both the explicit mode and the combined mode. Using defconfig, we were able to reproduce the use-after-free, which was consistent with CONFER's declaration of the old version being configuration irrelevant. We confirmed that the fixed version did not reveal the bug when `FEATURE_CLEAN_UP` was set to true.

Although we have limited ground truth for evaluating precision of CONFER with regards to deciding defconfig consistency, our findings show that CONFER's explicit only mode is more precise than the combined mode with four versus three correct inferences out of four cases, respectively.

To evaluate CONFER's completeness with regards to deciding configuration relevance of the patches, we used the patch reports as ground truth. Specifically, if a patch report explicitly mentions some configuration variable in the subject or comment section or in any of the deleted (denoted by - in Table 7) or added (denoted by + in Table 7) code sections included a configuration variable reference then we assumed that the patch was configuration relevant.

Among all the patch reports used in this study, we have identified 35[3] of the reports as configuration relevant as described above. Out of these 35 configuration relevant patches, CONFER correctly decides 25 of them as configuration relevant and reports the correct configuration variables. There are two reasons while CONFER misses the 10 patches. The first reason is that the configuration variable is used within an `if` statement rather than a preprocessor directive such as `#if` or `#ifdef`. Since CONFER only handles preprocessor directives, it misses such cases including `nameifUseAfterFree2013` in Table 7. The second reason is that the underlying presence condition generator, Undertaker, does not handle macros such as `IF_FEATURE` or `USE_FEATURE`. So, CONFER is as good as the underlying presence condition generator in inferring configuration relevance of a patch. In 3 out of 25 cases, using implicit dependencies in addition to explicit

[3] A subset of these are shown in Table 7.

dependencies created different results compared to just using explicit dependencies. In one of these three cases, using implicit dependency helped CONFER identify configuration relevance, which was missed when only explicit dependencies were used. In the other two cases, using implicit dependencies helped CONFER identify inconsistencies with defconfig, which were missed when only explicit dependencies were used.

4 Discussions

Although our study is based on a limited dataset, a specific class of vulnerabilities, and a single highly configurable system, it identifies general issues to be addressed.

Our empirical analysis on BusyBox, a popular open source software in the embedded domain, indicates that the current security practices for vulnerability management of configurable systems is far from ideal. There are multiple dimensions of the problem that makes it challenging including the large configuration spaces due to high number of configuration variables, lack of mature tools for configuration-aware analysis of real-world code, and a lack of awareness with regards to the importance of configuration information for vulnerability and patch management.

We have made some simplifying assumptions in our analysis by handling boolean configuration variables only. Handling integer and string valued configuration variables can improve the precision of analysis results. We think that presence condition generation tools should also be improved to support configuration variables other than the boolean types.

The false negatives discussed in Sect. 3 imply that configuration relevance analysis may benefit from dependence analysis and that the presence condition generators should handle macro expansions. Our results show that just using the explicit dependencies was sufficient in most cases although in very few cases using implicit dependencies helped identify additional configuration relevance or inconsistency with defconfig.

We also think that the quality of patch reports for highly configurable systems must be improved by providing more information about the validation and verification efforts including the test cases and the specific configurations tested. Also, CVE entries for highly configurable systems should include more configuration related information including configuration settings and the relevant configuration variables.

5 Related Work

A greedy approach is used in [11] to generate configurations that cover as many presence conditions as possible. Our approximate approach maximizes coverage of the presence conditions related to a patch. Dynamic and static analysis is combined in [15] to identify runtime configuration changes to reproduce some behavior in the new version. Our approach identifies static configuration changes with the goal of reproducing a vulnerability or validate the patch. Klocalizer [2] generates configurations that covers the code in the patch. CONFER, on the other hand, targets the coverage of relevant callsites and macro/function definitions in addition to the coverage of the patch. Configuration related explicit and taint analyses are presented in [12] for misconfiguration detection and configuration related bug detection. They use their taint tracking approach to identify configuration related statements and instrument them for collecting coverage, which gets utilized in fuzzing the configurable system along with mutation of configuration variables. Our approach achieves full coverage of the vulnerability related constraints. Variability-aware static Change Impact Analysis (CIA) is presented for runtime features in [5] for determining different variants affected by a change. CONFER's approach is complimentary to the approach of this work as it uses a light-weight static analysis to reason about change relevant settings of the compilation-time options. Symbolic execution based test generation is used in [7] to maximize patch coverage. Our approach, on the other hand, generates configurations to maximize patch relevant configuration constraints. Software variants are analyzed to identify missed patches for the relevant parts of the variants in [10]. Our approach can potentially reveal insufficiency of a patch in terms of the targeted configuration constraints.

Generation of patch relevant configurations with minimal changes to a reference configuration is presented in [14] with an application to the Linux kernel patches and build type bugs. Our approach differs from [14] in multiple aspects. First, our analysis differentiates configuration relevance of the vulnerability from that of the patch. Second, we use implicit dependencies in inferring relevant configuration constraints. Third, we use Max-SMT solving instead of Unsat Core in generating minimal number of relevant configuration variables.

6 Conclusions

We present a new tool, CONFER, that can support configuration dependence analysis of real-world software using AST-level analysis and constraint solving. We demonstrate the effectiveness of CONFER in analyzing the configuration space of 224 vulnerabilities. Our results show that approximately half of the BusyBox vulnerabilities are somehow configuration relevant, demanding more systematic handling of configuration information in bug reports and testing. In future work, we will extend CONFER with additional types of configuration variables such as integers and strings and by handling references to the configuration variables outside the preprocessor statements using intermediate-representation level analysis.

Acknowledgement. This work was funded by United States National Science Foundation Award # 2211588.

References

1. BusyBox: The Swiss Army Knife of Embedded Linux. https://www.busybox.net/about.html
2. Klocalizer. https://github.com/paulgazz/kmax?tab=readme-ov-file#using-klocalizer---repair-on-patches. Accessed 22 Mar 2024
3. National Vulnerability Database. https://nvd.nist.gov/
4. srcML: An infrastructure for the exploration, analysis, and manipulation of source code. https://www.srcml.org/
5. Angerer, F., Grimmer, A., Prähofer, H., Grünbacher, P.: Configuration-aware change impact analysis (t). In: 2015 30th IEEE/ACM International Conference on Automated Software Engineering (ASE), pp. 385–395 (2015)
6. Hansen, P., Jaumard, B.: Algorithms for the maximum satisfiability problem. Computing **44**(4), 279–303 (1990)
7. Marinescu, P.D., Cadar, C.: Katch: high-coverage testing of software patches. In: Proceedings of the 2013 9th Joint Meeting on Foundations of Software Engineering, ESEC/FSE 2013, pp. 235–245 (2013)
8. de Moura, L., Bjørner, N.: Z3: an efficient SMT solver. In: Ramakrishnan, C.R., Rehof, J. (eds.) TACAS 2008. LNCS, vol. 4963, pp. 337–340. Springer, Heidelberg (2008). https://doi.org/10.1007/978-3-540-78800-3_24
9. Mukelabai, M., Nešić, D., Maro, S., Berger, T., Steghöfer, J.P.: Tackling combinatorial explosion: a study of industrial needs and practices for analyzing highly configurable systems. In: Proceedings of the 33rd ACM/IEEE International Conference on Automated Software Engineering, pp. 155–166 (2018)
10. Ramkisoen, P.K., et al.: PaReco: patched clones and missed patches among the divergent variants of a software family. In: ESEC/FSE 2022, pp. 646–658 (2022)
11. Tartler, R., Lohmann, D., Dietrich, C., Egger, C., Sincero, J.: Configuration coverage in the analysis of large-scale system software. In: Proceedings of the 6th Workshop on Programming Languages and Operating Systems, PLOS 2011 (2011)
12. Wang, T., et al.: Conftainter: static taint analysis for configuration options. In: 2023 38th IEEE/ACM International Conference on Automated Software Engineering (ASE), pp. 1640–1651 (2023)
13. Xu, C., Chen, B., Lu, C., Huang, K., Peng, X., Liu, Y.: Tracking patches for open source software vulnerabilities. In: Proceedings of the 30th ACM Joint European Software Engineering Conference and Symposium on the Foundations of Software Engineering, ESEC/FSE 2022, pp. 860–871 (2022)
14. Yıldıran, N.F., Oh, J., Lawall, J., Gazzillo, P.: Maximizing patch coverage for testing of highly-configurable software without exploding build times. Proc. ACM Softw. Eng. **1**(FSE) (2024). https://doi.org/10.1145/3643746
15. Zhang, S., Ernst, M.D.: Which configuration option should i change? In: Proceedings of the 36th International Conference on Software Engineering, ICSE 2014, pp. 152–163 (2014)

Addressing Cultural Challenges During DevOps Adoption

Javed Iqbal[1](✉), Abdul Hadi Afghan[1], Muhammad Salih Tanveer[1], Muzaffar khan[2], Muhammad Javed[3], Shibi Rahul Senthil Kumar[4], and Mohammad Imran Faisal[5]

[1] Computer Science Department, COMSATS University Islamabad, Islamabad, Pakistan
javedkhushi@hotmail.com
[2] Department of Software Engineering, NUML, Rawalpindi, Pakistan
[3] Department of Computing & IT, FOC, Gomal University, D. I. Khan, Pakistan
[4] California State University, Long Beach, CA, USA
[5] Department of Computer Science, Shifa Tameer-e-Millat University, Islamabad, Pakistan

Abstract. DevOps is a collaborative approach integrating development and operations, emphasizing agility and efficiency in software delivery. By breaking down traditional silos and promoting continuous collaboration, DevOps aims to streamline workflows and enhance product quality. While DevOps promises many benefits, it can also be challenging to adopt it in an organization, especially in terms of cultural change. This study focuses on the cultural challenges that organizations are facing while adopting DevOps. This research employs a dual-phase methodology to address the cultural challenges of DevOps adoption. First, a Systematic Literature Review follows established guidelines to collect insights from a wide range of reputable sources. The second phase involves a collaborative Focus Group, where academic expertise and industry perspectives converge. Through iterative discussions, the best identified practices are accurately mapped to corresponding cultural challenges. The systematic examination of 22 selected studies through the Systematic Literature Review resulted in the identification of 19 prevalent cultural challenges and 23 best practices for DevOps adoption. A Focus Group facilitated the careful mapping of these best practices to their corresponding cultural challenges. The results provide a concrete and applicable solution for organizations seeking to overcome cultural challenges, ensuring a smoother and more effective transition to DevOps principles in diverse operational settings.

Keywords: DevOps · Adoption · Cultural Challenges · Best Practices

1 Introduction

Things are continually changing in the field of developing high-quality software on a limited timeframe and budget [1]. Traditional software development methods tended to take a long time and were quite restrictive when it comes to altering plans based on what consumers need [2]. This limitation led to emergence of agile approaches, which increased flexibility and responsiveness to change [3]. Agile is becoming the go-to strategy in the software market due to its capacity to address complications while

S. Hussain et al. (Eds.): SEET 2025, CCIS 2725, pp. 246–261, 2026.
https://doi.org/10.1007/978-3-032-08977-9_17

providing several advantages [4]. Even with Agile, some firms fail to provide software upgrades on time. This frequently occurs when multiple sections do not work well together, slowing things down [5]. That is where DevOps comes in, turning things around via improving collaboration between development and operations teams [6]. DevOps is all about communication, coordination, and leveraging smart technologies to ensure that the software is of high quality and gets out there quickly [7]. It is a response to the growing desire for programs that are constantly accessible, routinely updated, and extremely helpful [8].

However, shifting to DevOps is not easy, especially in large firms with complex systems [9]. This article delves into the core issue: altering how everyone thinks and collaborates. Moving to a DevOps mindset requires everyone, from executives to team members, to learn new skills and adjust to a new way of doing things [10]. This culture transformation is the most difficult but also the most important component of making DevOps work [11]. As the world of software development evolves, DevOps is the way to go. This study looks at the cultural challenges of incorporating DevOps into firms. It all comes down to figuring out the best ways to make DevOps work and assisting firms in feeling secure as they embark on this road. Thus, this research work intends to address DevOps cultural challenges. In this context, the research questions need to be answered are:

- **RQ1:** What cultural challenges are reported in the literature while implementing DevOps practices in software organizations?
- **RQ2:** What best practices are reported in the literature for addressing cultural challenges during DevOps adoption?
- **RQ3:** How can these best practices be mapped to specific cultural challenges?

The rest of the paper is structured as follows: Sect. 2 delves into related work, Sect. 3 centers on the research methodology, Sect. 4 provides the results and discussions, and Sect. 5 brings the work to a conclusion.

2 Related Work

Several studies have explored the challenges and strategies associated with DevOps adoption. One study employed a questionnaire survey to understand industry practitioners' perspectives on DevOps advantages and limitations, emphasizing the need for structured frameworks to address identified obstacles [12]. Another research conducted a systematic literature review (SLR) to identify 18 distinct challenges consistent across development and operations teams, providing insights into the challenges but not proposing solutions or best practices [13]. Similarly, a comprehensive study across continents highlighted ten critical challenges in DevOps adoption, such as poor collaboration and communication, skill gaps, and inadequate approaches, without delving into solutions [14].

A study focusing on DevOps education identified 83 challenges and proposed 185 recommendations based on interviews with 14 educators, acknowledging the potential limitations of representing the entire spectrum of DevOps education [15]. Another research utilized SLR to connect theoretical benefits of DevOps with real-life cases, emphasizing improved teamwork and faster software delivery but provided limited insights into challenges and solutions [16]. An introductory article outlined key components and best practices for DevOps initiatives, although recommendations lacked empirical validation [17]. Additionally, a foundational paper on DevOps management provided insights into challenges and mitigation strategies but lacked a thorough exploration of critical cultural issues in DevOps adoption [6].

The current research has shed light on challenges that are faced during DevOps adoption, but a significant gap remains in offering practical solutions, especially in addressing cultural challenges. Thus, the need for actionable insights and validated best practices is evident for organizations aiming at successful DevOps implementation. The research should focus on providing tangible solutions to enhance the effectiveness of DevOps in diverse organizational settings.

3 Research Methodology

A systematic approach is applied to answer the mentioned research questions; the proposed study uses the qualitative method of SLR to extract the desired data from final selected studies then followed by focus group meeting to map the best practices to relevant challenge. Figure 1 presents the research methodology employed for conducting the study.

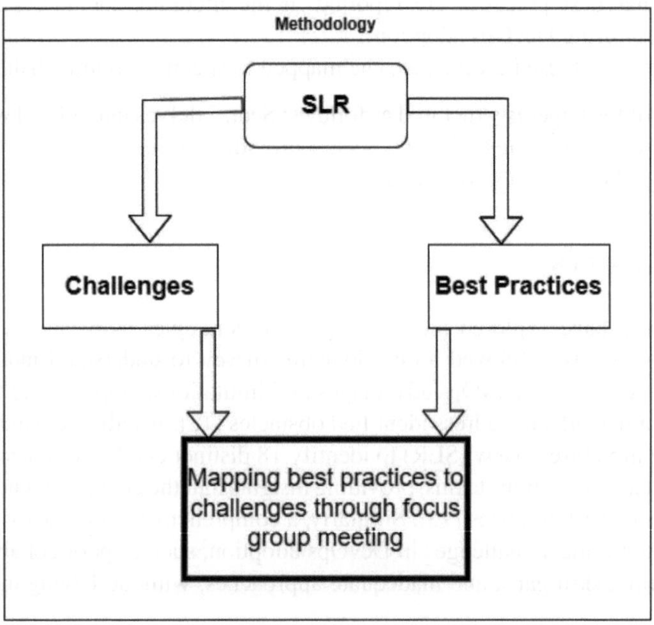

Fig. 1. Research Methodology

3.1 Systematic Literature Review

For this study, the guidelines of Kitchenham and Charters [18] have been followed to conduct a SLR. The SLR unfolds in three main phases: planning the review, conducting the review, and reporting the review. The planning phase involves:

- Determining the need for the review.
- Creating and validating the SLR protocol.

The conducting phase includes:

- Searching for primary studies using specific terms.
- Finalizing study selection based on predetermined criteria.
- Assessing the quality of research.
- Extracting data from selected articles using a predefined form.
- Synthesizing the extracted data.

The reporting phase involves summarizing results, discussing implications and highlighting the limitations.

3.2 Focus Group

The mapping process is facilitated through a collaborative focus group meeting involving the researcher and an industry practitioner. This dynamic interaction leverages the combined knowledge and expertise of both the academic and practical domains. The mapping method in this study is in line with the previous studies in the field. The approach used is inspired by the methodologies outlined by well-regarded studies like [20–22].

4 Results and Discussion

The first phase of SLR is planning.

4.1 Systematic Literature Review Planning

Planning the review involves creating the protocols used to collect and analyze the data. The specific review protocol steps have been followed to extract and analyze the literature, aiming to address proposed research questions.

Data collection sources: Choosing the right data sources is crucial to pinpoint literature relevant to the study's research objective. The sources employed for the study are:

Google Scholar
ACM
Science Direct
Springer
IEEE Xplore

Search String: In designing the search strategy for the SLR, we carefully created distinct searches to capture cultural challenges and best practices for DevOps. For cultural challenges, we used phrases (**"cultural challenges" OR "cultural barriers" OR "cultural hurdles" OR "cultural difficulties"**). Then, for best practices, we included terms (**"best practices" OR "Tools" OR "methods" OR "solutions" OR "Mitigation Strategies"**). Combining these searches aimed to ensure a thorough exploration of DevOps cultural aspects, covering challenges and effective practices alike. At the end, we formulated this search string: **(DevOps OR "Development and Operations") AND ("cultural challenges" OR "cultural barriers" OR "cultural hurdles" OR "cultural difficulties" OR "best practices" OR "Tools" OR "methods" OR "solutions" OR "Mitigation Strategies")**
Inclusion criteria: To be part of this review, studies need to meet specific criteria:

The paper should have been published in a respected journal, conference, or book chapter.
It must discuss cultural challenges or best practices connected to DevOps implementation.
The chosen literature should be in English.

Exclusion criteria: The guidelines for excluding studies in the review:

If two studies are part of the same research project, only the more comprehensive one was considered.
Papers lacking detailed information about DevOps cultural barriers or best practices were not included.
Studies not in line with the study objective were excluded.
Literature review studies were not taken into account.

Quality Assessment: The quality assessment process was conducted to determine the suitability of the selected primary studies with respect to the study objective. This process involved answering three questions, as outlined below:

Does the study directly address cultural challenges or best practices in DevOps implementation?
Is the research aligned with the objectives of the study?
Are there sufficient details and data to support the study's findings?

4.2 Conducting the Review

Conducting the review includes the following steps:

Selection of final studies: Following the application of the inclusion/exclusion criteria, our study identified 93 research papers from a pool of 49,344 papers across five digital libraries as the initial selection. Subsequently, through a thorough examination of the full text of these initially chosen articles, utilizing the inclusion/exclusion and quality testing criteria, our study ultimately narrowed down to 22 research papers [19] (Table 1).

Table 1. Search results from different databases

Database Name	Search Result Selected Final Selected			Excluded
Google Scholar	38,100	18	5	13
ACM	1,799	18	8	10
Science Direct	5,856	6	1	5
Springer	3085	4	1	3
IEEE Xplore	504	47	7	40
Total	**49,344**	**93**	**22**	**71**

Data Extraction and Synthesis: The careful review of each selected study resulted in the identification of 19 cultural challenges (represented as C1, C2, …, C19) and 23 best practices (represented as P1,P2, …, P23). Figure 2 shows the frequencies of different cultural challenges that are collected from available studies.

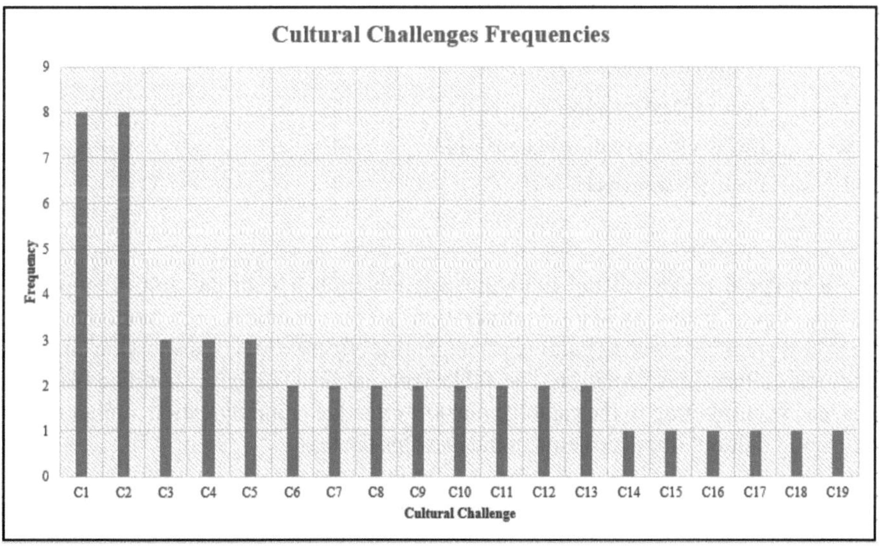

Fig. 2. Frequencies of challenges

4.3 Reporting the Review

The findings, detailed in the accompanying Table 2, provide the cultural challenges that are confronted by practitioners during DevOps adoption in real-world environment.

Table 2. Cultural Challenges in Software Development

Sr. No	Cultural Challenge	Frequency	Percentage
C1	Lack of communication [29, 31, 35, 42]	8	36
C2	Resistance to change [24, 25]	8	36
C3	Lack of knowledge sharing [29]	3	14
C4	Finger pointing in case of failure [23]	3	14
C5	Traditional mindset [36]	3	14
C6	Lack of collaboration [43]	2	9
C7	Lack of trust [28, 33]	2	9
C8	Lack of awareness [33, 34]	2	9
C9	Lack of management support [34]	2	9
C10	Complexity of Software Ecosystem [25]	2	9
C11	Interdependencies among teams [25]	2	9
C12	Distributed/Remote stackholders [32]	2	9
C13	Ambiguous allocation of roles [41]	2	9
C14	Toolset and metric differences [31]	1	5
C15	Socio-Cultural distance [32]	1	5
C16	Temporal distance [32]	1	5
C17	Lack of DevOps experience [36]	1	5
C18	Dev & Ops have different goals [43]	1	5
C19	Lack of transparency [43]	1	5

An in-depth review of the literature was undertaken with the aim of improving DevOps culture, gathering helpful information and best practices from multiple studies. These best practices serve as guiding principles for effective DevOps adoption and organizational culture transformation. The Table 3 presents a list of these identified best practices, each contributing to the establishment of effective communication, collaboration, and overall cultural improvements in the DevOps context.

Table 3. Extracted Best Practices

No	Best Practices
P1	Arranging proper communication tools, encouraging synchronous communication, stand-up meetings and select standard language [41]
P2	Enhanced collaboration [35]
P3	Establishing a shared understanding and shared responsibilities [23]
P4	Learning and upskilling DevOps practices [26]

(*continued*)

Table 3. (*continued*)

No	Best Practices
P5	Focus on automation [36]
P6	Focusing and defining feedback loops [23]
P7	Encouraging team members to embrace new methodologies and practices [40]
P8	Clear roles and responsibilities [41]
P9	Cross-Functional teams [31]
P10	Continuous Integration/Continuous Delivery [25]
P11	Establish measuring key performance metrics [23]
P12	Ensuring that the goals and priorities of development and operations teams are synchronized for better teamwork and efficiency. [38]
P13	Automated performance monitoring [23]
P14	Release management [25]
P15	Infrastructure as Code [27]
P16	Making liable only the responsible role [41]
P17	Asynchronous communication tools, establishing clear timelines and deadlines, setting up a 'proximity development centre' in a time zone-aligned region for optimal working hours, and achieving time zone proximity through time-shifting [32]
P18	Endorsing accountability to promote commitment, embracing stakeholder cultures involves learning traditions, beliefs, and native languages. Enhancing communication through language courses, appointing cultural liaisons, fostering early socialization, and frequent site visits to build trust [38]
P19	Fostering an adaptive culture that can promptly respond and adjust to changing requirements and circumstances [39]
P20	Clearly define DevOps tools and practices [34]
P21	Managing and guiding the transformation of organizational values and behaviors towards a DevOps mind-set [38]
P22	Continuous requirement refinement [36]
P23	Allowing continuous refinement and improvement throughout the software delivery process [36, 38]

4.4 Mapping Best Practices to Cultural Challenges Using Focus Group Meeting

The mapping process is facilitated through a collaborative focus group meeting involving the researcher and an industry practitioner. This dynamic interaction leverages the combined knowledge and expertise of both the academic and practical domains. The mapping method followed in this study is in line with the methodologies outlined by the studies like [20–22]. By incorporating the proven techniques from these experts, we aim to ensure a strong and trustworthy mapping process. This contributes to the credibility and robustness of the mapping presented in this study. During the session, insights from the SLR findings, which highlight cultural challenges and best practices in DevOps implementation, was collectively examined and discussed. The goal was to establish a clear and contextualized connection between the identified challenges and corresponding best practices. The iterative nature of the focus group discussion ensures a comprehensive and nuanced mapping, presented as Table 4, that reflects both academic insights and real-world applicability.

Table 4. Mapping of Challenges and Practices

IDs	Challenges	Practices
C1	Lake of communication	**P1:** Arranging proper communication tools, encouraging synchronous communication, stand-up meetings and select standard language. **P2:** Enhanced collaboration **P3:** Establishing a shared understanding and shared responsibilities. **P7:** Encouraging team members to embrace new methodologies and practices **P8:** Clear roles and responsibilities
C2	Resistance to change	**P7** **P12:** Ensuring that the goals and priorities of development and operations teams are synchronized for better teamwork and efficiency. **P4:** Learning and upskilling DevOps practices
C3	Lack of knowledge sharing	**P4** **P1** **P2**
C4	Finger pointing in case of failure	**P16:** Making liable only the responsible role **P7** **P1** **P2**
C5	Traditional mindset	**P7** **P4**
C6	Lack of collaboration	**P1** **P2** **P9: Cross-Functional teams**

(continued)

Table 4. (*continued*)

IDs	Challenges	Practices
C7	Lack of trust	**P18:** Endorsing accountability to promote commitment, embracing stakeholder cultures involves learning traditions, beliefs, and native languages. Enhancing communication through language courses, appointing cultural liaisons, fostering early socialization, and frequent site visits to build trust P16
C8	Lack of awareness	**P20:** Clearly define DevOps tools and practices **P21:** Managing and guiding the transformation of organizational values and behaviors towards a DevOps mind-set **P6:** Focusing and defining feedback loops **P3** **P4** **P14:** Release management **P19:** Fostering an adaptive culture that can promptly respond and adjust to changing requirements and circumstances
C9	Lack of management support	**P3** **P4** **P14** **P19**
C10	Complexity of Software Ecosystem	**P7** **P2** **P9** **P5:** Focus on automation **P11:** Establish measuring key performance metrics **P13:** Automated performance monitoring **P15:** Infrastructure as Code
C11	Interdependencies among teams	**P3** **P9** **P8**

(*continued*)

Table 4. *(continued)*

IDs	Challenges	Practices
C12	Distributed / Remote stakeholders	**P1** **P17:** Asynchronous communication tools, establishing clear timelines and deadlines, setting up a 'proximity development centre' in a time zone-aligned region for optimal working hours, and achieving time zone proximity through time-shifting.
C13	Ambiguous allocation of roles	**P3** P8
C14	Toolset and matric differences	**P22:** Continuous requirement refinement
C15	Socio-Culture distances	P18
C16	Temporal distance	**P17** **P23:** Allowing continuous refinement and improvement throughout the software delivery process
C17	Lack of DevOps Experience	**P4** **P10:** Continuous Integration / Continuous Delivery
C18	Dev & Ops have different goals	**P12** **P9**
C19	Lack of transparency	**P1** **P2**

The Fig. 3 presents the mapping pictorially.

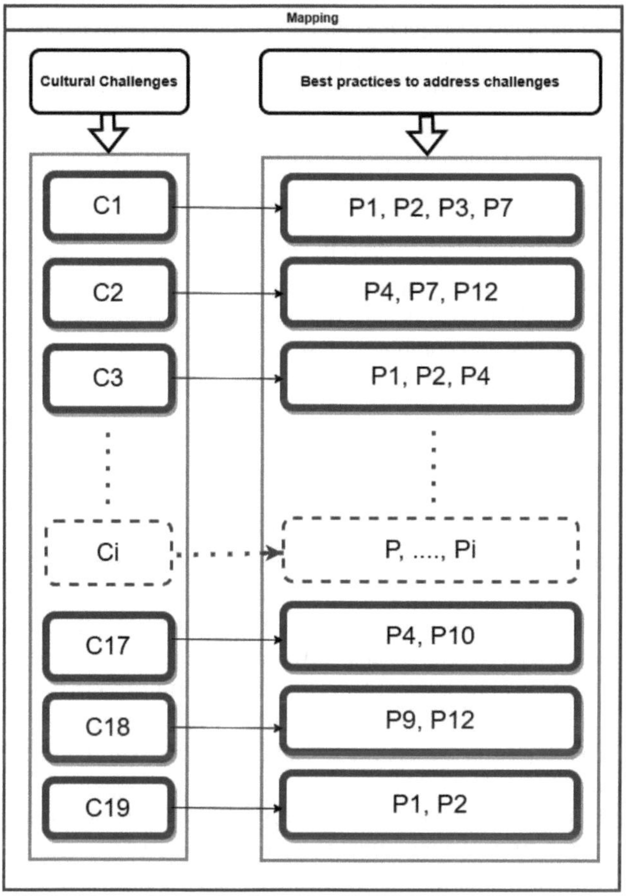

Fig. 3. Proposed Solutions

Our investigation into DevOps cultural challenges revealed the frequency of challenges that organizations commonly encounter during adoption. Among these challenges, communication issues (36%) emerged as a prevalent concern. To tackle this, we proposed a multi-faceted approach, emphasizing effective communication, enhanced collaboration, and the establishment of clear roles and responsibilities. Similarly, resistance to change (36%) was identified as a significant obstacle, prompting strategies such as addressing resistance directly, aligning objectives, and fostering continuous learning and upskilling.

The challenge of lack of knowledge sharing (14%) prompted interventions such as learning initiatives, effective communication, and collaboration enhancement. Finger-pointing issues (14%) were effectively countered by advocating for a blameless culture, addressing resistance, and promoting effective communication and collaboration. Overcoming a traditional mindset (14%) required targeted strategies like addressing resistance directly and promoting continuous learning and upskilling to adapt to the evolving DevOps culture.

The complex landscape of DevOps challenges also encompassed issues like lack of collaboration (9%), lack of trust (9%), lack of awareness (9%), lack of management support (9%), complexity of the software ecosystem (9%), interdependencies among teams (9%), geographical distance (9%), uncertainty in responsibilities (9%), toolset and metric differences (5%), socio-cultural distance (5%), temporal distance (5%), lack of DevOps experience (5%), dev and ops having different goals (5%), and lack of transparency (5%).

Each of these challenges was carefully mapped to corresponding best practices, ensuring a contextually relevant approach. For example, geographical distance challenges were addressed through effective communication and strategies to handle temporal distance. The iterative and combine nature of our focus group discussions enhanced trustworthiness and robustness of the mapping.

5 Conclusion and Future Direction

This research paper explores the challenges and best practices for adopting DevOps, with a focus on how people work together. In the world of software development, where we need top-notch results in limited time and budgets, there has been a shift from old ways to more flexible methods like agile. While agile improved flexibility, integrating DevOps has become vital to bridge gaps between development and operations teams.

But, despite the known benefits of DevOps, big and multifaceted organizations face challenges in putting it into action. The main challenge is changing how people think and work together from top-level executives to team members. This cultural shift is tough but crucial for successful DevOps adoption.

Our research method involved a careful review of 22 studies using a systematic approach. We found 19 challenges like communication issues, resistance to change, and traditional ways of thinking. On the positive side, we identified 23 best practices, including effective communication, improved collaboration, continuous learning, and a focus on automation.

These findings not only deepen our understanding of DevOps challenges and solutions but also offer practical advice for organizations aiming for successful DevOps adoption. We have mapped these challenges to corresponding best practices through focus group discussions. In summary, this study is a helpful guide for people in the field—practitioners, teachers, and researchers navigating the complexities of DevOps. By highlighting the challenges and suggesting practical solutions, our goal is to make the move to DevOps smoother, helping organizations achieve goals like speedy delivery, better teamwork, and high-quality software. Embracing DevOps mindset is not just necessary, it is a smart move for organizations looking to stay competitive in today's changing market.

In the future, we plan to create a DevOps Cultural Maturity Model. This model will help organize the challenges and best practices we have found, into different levels of cultural maturity for organizations moving to DevOps. It is like a roadmap that will guide organizations as they improve their cultural practices and better adapt to DevOps principles. Our goal is to offer practical advice and insights in a way that is easy to understand and use.

References

1. Macarthy, R.W., Bass, J.M.: An empirical taxonomy of DevOps in practice. In: Proc. - 46th Euromicro Conf. Softw. Eng. Adv. Appl. SEAA 2020, pp. 221–228 (2020). https://doi.org/10.1109/SEAA51224.2020.00046
2. Raj, P., Sinha, P.: Project management in era of agile and devops methodlogies. Int. J. Sci. Technol. Res. **9**(1), 1024–1033 (2020)
3. Highsmith, J., Consortium, C., Cockburn, A.: Development : The Business of Innovation, pp. 21–23 (2001)
4. Zavyalova, E., Sokolov, D., Lisovskaya, A.: Agile vs traditional project management approaches: comparing human resource management architectures. Int. J. Organ. Anal. **28**(5), 1095–1112 (2020). https://doi.org/10.1108/IJOA-08-2019-1857
5. Hemon, A., Lyonnet, B., Rowe, F., Fitzgerald, B.: From Agile to DevOps: smart skills and collaborations. Inf. Syst. Front. **22**(4), 927–945 (2020). https://doi.org/10.1007/s10796-019-09905-1
6. Jayakody, J.A.V.M.K., Wijayanayake, W.M.J.I.: Challenges for adopting DevOps in information technology projects. In: Proc. - Int. Res. Conf. Smart Comput. Syst. Eng. SCSE 2021, vol. 4, pp. 203–210 (2021). https://doi.org/10.1109/SCSE53661.2021.9568348
7. Dyck, A., Penners, R., Lichter, H.: Towards definitions for release engineering and DevOps. In: Proc. - 3rd Int. Work. Release Eng. RELENG 2015, pp. 3 (2015). https://doi.org/10.1109/RELENG.2015.10
8. Sandobalin, J., Insfran, E., Abrahao, S.: On the effectiveness of tools to support infrastructure as code: model-driven versus code-centric. IEEE Access **8**, 17734–17761 (2020). https://doi.org/10.1109/ACCESS.2020.2966597
9. Feijter, Rahmawati, A.Y., et al.: Towards the adoption of DevOps in software product organizations: a maturity model approach. Foreign Aff. **91**(July), 1689–1699 (2017)
10. Virtanen, A.: Transitioning Towards Continuous Development Within an Established Business Organization, pp. 62 (2017)
11. Cogo, G.S.: Understanding DevOps: From its Enablers to Impact on IT Performance (2019)
12. Zulfahmi Toh, M., Sahibuddin, S., Mahrin, M.N.: Adoption issues in DevOps from the perspective of continuous delivery pipeline. ACM Int. Conf. Proc. Ser. **Part F1479**, 173–177 (2019). https://doi.org/10.1145/3316615.3316619
13. Shameem, M.: A Systematic Literature Review of Challenges Factors for Implementing DevOps Practices in Software Development Organizations : a Development and Operation teams Perspective (2021). https://doi.org/10.1002/9781119821779.ch9
14. Khan, M.S., Khan, A.W., Khan, F., Khan, M.A., Whangbo, T.K.: Critical challenges to adopt DevOps culture in software organizations: a systematic review. IEEE Access **10**, 14339–14349 (2022). https://doi.org/10.1109/ACCESS.2022.3145970
15. Fernandes, M., Ferino, S., Fernandes, A., Kulesza, U., Aranha, E., Treude, C.: DevOps Education: an Interview Study of Challenges and Recommendations (2022). https://doi.org/10.1145/3510456.3514152
16. Faustino, J., Adriano, D., Amaro, R., Pereira, R., da Silva, M.M.: DevOps benefits: a systematic literature review. Softw. - Pract. Exp. **52**(9), 1905–1926 (2022). https://doi.org/10.1002/spe.3096
17. Patel, A.R., Tyagi, S.: Lightweight review: challenges and benefits of adopting DevOps. In: Proc. 2022 1st Int. Conf. Informatics, ICI 2022, no. Ici, pp. 235–237 (2022). https://doi.org/10.1109/ICI53355.2022.9786902
18. Kitchenham, S., Charters, B.: Guidelines for performing systematic literature reviews in software engineering. In: Technical Report, Ver. 2.3 EBSE Tech. Report. EBSE, vol. 1, no. October, pp. 1–54, 2007, [Online]. Available: https://citeseerx.ist.psu.edu/viewdoc/download?doi=10.1.1.117.471&rep=rep1&type=pdf

19. Afzal, W., Torkar, R., Feldt, R.: A systematic review of search-based testing for non-functional system properties. Inf. Softw. Technol. **51**(6), 957–976 (2009). https://doi.org/10.1016/j.infsof.2008.12.005
20. Akbar, M.A., Sang, J., Nasrullah, Khan, A.A., Shafiq, M., Fazal-E-Amin: Towards the guidelines for requirements change management in Global Software Development: client-vendor perspective. IEEE Access **7**, 76985–77007 (2019). https://doi.org/10.1109/ACCESS.2019.2918552
21. Azad, N., Hyrynsalmi, S.: DevOps critical success factors — a systematic literature review. Inf. Softw. Technol. **157**(January), 107150 (2023). https://doi.org/10.1016/j.infsof.2023.107150
22. Rafi, S., Yu, W., Akbar, M.A., Mahmood, S., Alsanad, A., Gumaei, A.: Readiness model for DevOps implementation in software organizations. J. Softw. Evol. Process **33**(4), 1–25 (2021). https://doi.org/10.1002/smr.2323
23. Gottesheim, W.: Challenges, benefits and best practices of performance focused DevOps. In: Proceedings of the 4th International Workshop on Large-Scale Testing (2015)
24. Jones, S., Noppen, J., Lettice, F.: Management challenges for DevOps adoption within UK SMEs. In: Proceedings of the 2nd International Workshop on Quality-Aware DevOps (2016)
25. Fhang, M.C.S., Swamy, R.: Best practices in release management of large projects. In: Proceedings of the 2018 7th International Conference on Software and Computer Applications (2018)
26. Senapathi, M., Buchan, J., Osman, H.: DevOps capabilities, practices, and challenges: Insights from a case study. In: Proceedings of the 22nd International Conference on Evaluation and Assessment in Software Engineering 2018 (2018)
27. Díaz, J., et al.: DevOps in practice: an exploratory case study. In: Proceedings of the 19th International Conference on Agile Software Development: Companion (2018)
28. Luz, W.P., Pinto, G., Bonifácio, R.: Building a collaborative culture: a grounded theory of well succeeded devops adoption in practice. In: Proceedings of the 12th ACM/IEEE International Symposium on Empirical Software Engineering and Measurement (2018)
29. Meedeniya, D., Thennakoon, H.: Impact factors and best practices to improve effort estimation strategies and practices in DevOps. In: Proceedings of the 11th International Conference on Information Communication and Management (2021)
30. Azad, N.: Understanding DevOps critical success factors and organizational practices. In: Proceedings of the 5th International Workshop on Software-intensive Business: Towards Sustainable Software Business (2022)
31. Krey, M.: Devops Adoption: Challenges & Barriers (2022)
32. Diel, E., Marczak, S., Cruzes, D.S.: Communication challenges and strategies in distributed DevOps. In: 2016 IEEE 11th International Conference on Global Software Engineering (ICGSE). IEEE (2016)
33. Hamunen, J.: Challenges in adopting a Devops approach to software development and operations. In: 2016. 69p. Diss. Dissertação (Mestrado em Ciências Econômicas e Administração de Empresas)—Universidade de Aalto, Escola de Negócios, Espoo, 2016. Disponível em: https://aaltodoc.aalto.fi/handle/123456789/20766. Acesso em: 26 mar, 2023
34. Bucena, I., Kirikova, M.: Simplifying the DevOps Adoption Process. BIR Workshops (2017)
35. Riungu-Kalliosaari, L., et al.: DevOps adoption benefits and challenges in practice: a case study. In: Product-Focused Software Process Improvement: 17th International Conference, PROFES 2016, Trondheim, Norway, November 22–24, 2016, Proceedings 17. Springer International Publishing (2016)
36. Gupta, R.K., Venkatachalapathy, M., Jeberla, F.K.: Challenges in adopting continuous delivery and DevOps in a globally distributed product team: a case study of a healthcare organization. In: 2019 ACM/IEEE 14th International Conference on Global Software Engineering (ICGSE). IEEE (2019)

37. Veres, O., et al.: Development and operations-the modern paradigm of the work of IT project Teams. In: 2019 IEEE 14th International Conference on Computer Sciences and Information Technologies (CSIT), vol. 3. IEEE (2019)
38. Katal, A., Bajoria, V., Dahiya, S.: DevOps: bridging the gap between development and operations. In: 2019 3rd International Conference on Computing Methodologies and Communication (ICCMC). IEEE (2019)
39. Alawneh, M., Abbadi, I.M.: Expanding DevOps principles and best practices based on practical view. In: 2022 International Arab Conference on Information Technology (ACIT). IEEE (2022)
40. Sravan, S.S., et al.: Significant challenges to espouse DevOps culture in software organisations By AWS: a methodical review. In: 2023 9th International Conference on Advanced Computing and Communication Systems (ICACCS), vol. 1. IEEE (2023)
41. Nurullah, F, et al.: The collaboration of DevOps automation and SOA to accelerate software development culture. In: 2018 Indonesian Association for Pattern Recognition International Conference (INAPR). IEEE (2018)
42. Grande, R., Vizcaíno, A., García, F.O.: Is it worth adopting DevOps practices in Global Software Engineering? Possible challenges and benefits. Comput. Stand. Interfaces **87**, 103767 (2024)
43. Díaz, J., et al.: Why are many businesses instilling a DevOps culture into their organization? Empir. Softw. Eng. **26**, 1–50 (2021)

Security Engineering Framework for Cyber-Physical System Product-Line

Ademola Adejokun[1(✉)], Michael Siok[2], and LiGuo Huang[1]

[1] Department of Computer Science, Southern Methodist University, Dallas, TX 75275-0122, USA
aadejokun@mail.smu.edu, lghuang@smu.edu

[2] Department of Computer Science and Engineering, University of Texas at Arlington, Arlington, TX 76019, USA
mike.siok@uta.edu

Abstract. Quality and system assurance foundations are achieved in System and Software Engineering Product-line systems when security is an integral part of these systems and is systematically built into the engineering development processes and product instances. With the absence of adequate security requirements coverage, these same product-line systems suffer from essential trustworthiness security concerns. This paper presents a security engineering process framework and approach that systematically orchestrates security goals and customer needs to efficiently elaborate, verify, and validate security requirements in the development of software-intensive product line systems. This security engineering process segments the product-line process into multiple stages. Each stage employs a quality-gate where security assessment of work products is performed. These gates ensure compliance with applicable security criteria as products progress through the product-line engineering pipeline to produce a secure product-line and deliverable systems. A case study example is provided applying this approach.

Keywords: Product Line Engineering · Security Requirement · Security Standards · Software Bill of Materials · Cybersecurity Bill of Materials

1 Introduction and Background

System and Software Product-Line Engineering (SSPLE) is a complex engineering endeavor producing complex software-intensive systems consisting of selected components managed as part of a feature portfolio. These systems include common core assets and capabilities that are shared by allowed product derivative end-item systems. These derivative systems may also possess unique capabilities which are realizations of the common core components and the allowed product variability and implementation scope within the product-line defined feature set [7, 17].

SSPLE allows for cost-efficient system development and orchestrates productivity gains within the product-line development process. The SSPLE development methods deal with system complexity by using a suitable specification of the system and its

S. Hussain et al. (Eds.): SEET 2025, CCIS 2725, pp. 262–286, 2026.
https://doi.org/10.1007/978-3-032-08977-9_18

components. This specification includes definition of a base system with well-defined common core components and capabilities and a set of allowed customizations defined within the scope of expected derivative system developments (i.e., allowed system variations). Product development is managed using a domain engineering process to establish a stable and reusable platform which promotes traceability among artifacts such as requirements, design, realization, and tests. The Domain Engineering process is used to define, manage, and evolve the base system including the common core assets and the defined allowed variation or customization connections of these product-line systems [19]. The top portion of Fig. 1 illustrates this domain engineering process.

Product-line application systems are derived from the platform established in domain engineering using an Application Engineering process. This process reuses domain core artifacts to assemble new system instances [19]. Further, this process is used to manage the development and integration of specific allowed product customizations and their integrations into these new systems.

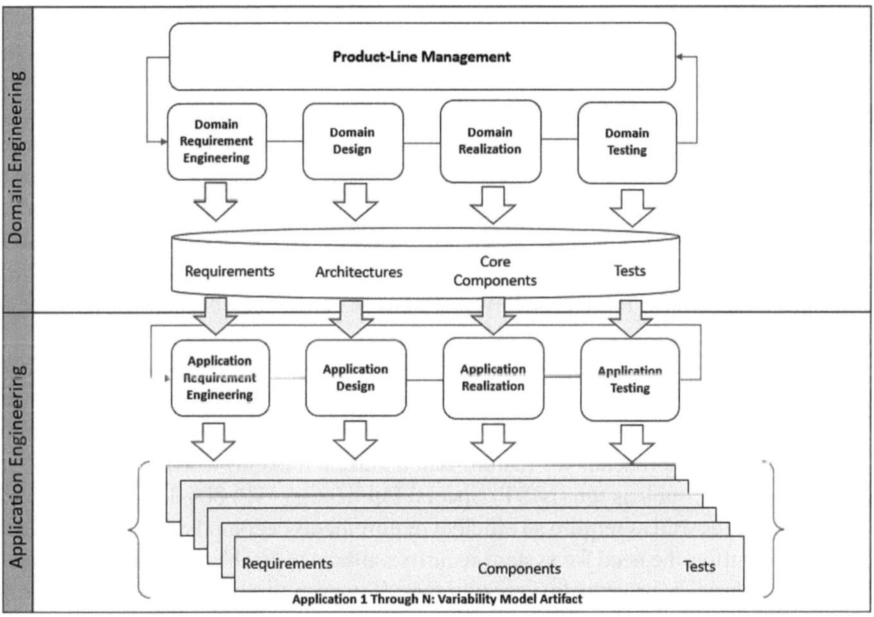

Fig. 1. Software Product Line Engineering Framework.

The completed systems are instances (i.e., derivatives) of the base system (i.e., the core component composition) with allowed and integrated custom component features. Once the initial and second systems are built, subsequent system developments within this product family have smaller non-recurring engineering efforts leading to smaller and more manageable cost structures for future system developments. Development and delivery of these derivative systems typically come with better expected end-user system and software quality, reliability, and potentially faster deliveries. [5]. This product-line development process promotes a leveraged component reuse approach within a defined system and software development life cycle model for the specified product-line. The bottom portion of Fig. 1, illustrates the Application Engineering process.

2 Motivation

The SSPLE is motivated by the need to deliver strategic product development benefits critical to achieving system product quality. However, developing security engineering into the SSPLE and achieving overall system quality objectives can be challenging [14]. For example, software components are becoming more integrated with various open-source compositions that deliver specific capabilities. These external compositions are often susceptible to increasing security vulnerabilities that affect the quality of the whole product-line.

Recent research has proposed various security techniques to facilitate engineering development of software-intensive embedded cyber-physical system product-lines. However, the emerging techniques, specifically the incorporation of security engineering processes, have shown drawbacks as they exhibit limited assurance coverage needed to secure a product-line and its subsequent derivative systems. Among several research works includes Rick Rabiser & Alois Zoitl [24] which present a discussion of current challenges impacting the product-line engineering of Software-Intensive Cyber-Physical Production Systems (SiCPPS). Rabiser et al. [24] identifies the need for adequate requirement elicitation and specification in addition to employing systematic design approaches to establish variability connections of the SiCPPS system with the baseline security of the common core asset platform. Their work also specifies the challenges of open research, goals, and established SSPLE research agendas that must be overcome in establishing an optimum SSPLE for the Cyber Physical System. Their drawback is the absence of the challenges related to cybersecurity reasoning.

Beth Wilson and Bobbi Young [25] present a cyber resiliency technique to facilitate an intersection between systems security techniques and product-line designs with the intent of incorporating system security into product-lines. Their proposed cyber security and resiliency approaches for feature-based variation management explore existing security standards, such as the (NIST) Special Publication (SP) 800-160 Volume 2 and ISO/IEC 26580 as well as require an efficient requirements decomposition process. Their work also identifies the need for system security patterns to establish resiliency elements of a muti-level secure product-line architecture. However, this approach did not specify elicitation and methodological specification of cybersecurity requirements as the first step to achieving product resiliency.

Julie Street Fant, et al. [26] present a development approach for highly variable unmanned space flight software product-lines. Their solution proposes using architectural design patterns as a key concept to derive variability for these product-lines. The shortcoming of this approach is the absence of security concepts for the mission-critical space flight software.

Daniel Mellado, et al. [22] describe a process for security domain requirements engineering for software product-lines. Their method facilitates security requirements development that establishes the initial stage of the software product-line lifecycle. Their method employs a technique for a security requirements management schema facilitated by specification of security standards, such as the Common Criteria (ISO/IEC 15408) and ISO/IEC 17799 information security controls. This approach drives the underlining process for their product-line engineering lifecycle.

While each of these authors propose significant changes and insights into better product-line and/or security systems development, what is needed to improve the state of security engineering in these product-line systems, is an all-in systems approach. What is needed is a product-line development method that captures current security engineering requirements and practice within the product domain, adds a significant level of security requirements and cyber-security system design assurance early, and provides for security verification and validation throughout the system development process to include the deliverable systems and sustainment of this security assurance within the product family baseline components and designs for future products in the family.

The contribution of this paper to product-line engineering and security requirements and cyber-security engineering development is three-fold. (1) We extend the Daniel Mellado et al. [22] approach on their security requirements engineering management process by establishing the product security goal and decomposition as the driver for efficient security requirements selection, elicitation, and specification. (2) We describe a specific strategy and process for specifying security requirements. This process is executed in each stage of our SSPLE and through our quality gate implementation, provides for reasoning of the specific security aspects developed within those process stages. (3) Our product-line engineering pipeline provides an engineering development process with emphasis on meeting each process stage quality gate leading to a verifiably secure end-item SSPLE system at each stage of this development process. The sections of this paper that follow describe our research objectives, our product-line engineering approach, and introduces a case study to illustrate portions of this approach.

3 Research Objectives

Ensuring quality and achieving a secure SSPLE depends on a thoughtful process to analyze security objectives and to establish the product protection profile. A protection profile establishes a set of security requirements and objectives for verifiably mitigating a set of well-defined threats against the SSPLE. A holistic approach to security engineering enables trustworthiness to be built into the SSPLE system (i.e., the extent to which the system preserves confidentiality, integrity, and availability). Trustworthiness is achieved through application of relevant system security principles [2]. Further, systemic application of this security engineering paradigm secures the SSPLE by identifying security assets, specifying required security capabilities, and providing an efficient elicitation, coordination, and specification of security requirements that meet stakeholders' concerns and satisfies product-line mission objectives.

In meeting these objectives, we need to ask a couple questions:

1. How good is a modular security engineering approach for SSPLE and its components in facilitating security reasoning for its product derivatives?
2. How effective is a security engineering process that enables the SSPLE to address the essential security concerns of confidentiality, integrity, and availability?

Establishing trustworthiness in SSPLE systems depends on the ability to satisfy security requirements; security requirements are therefore essential system requirements that must be specified at product-line initiation [8]. Any missing aspects of these security requirements will be costly to retrofit later [1] and could negatively impact the overall quality and security posture of the delivered system. Security posture is the ability of the development organization to measure and assess the security readiness of the system hardware, software, and other information security assets [11]. Adequate specification of the system security requirements provides the foundation to enable critical security functionality for the SSPLE and establish its fundamental tenets of confidentiality, integrity, and availability [1]. A discussion of how to handle these security needs and requirements follows.

4 Security Requirement Engineering Ecosystem

Security engineering begins at the start of the product-line development [13]. Security requirements developed by the engineering teams must adequately specify the characteristics that secure their product-line [3, 10] (and their delivered systems); these security requirements establish a measured degree of protection for the end-item systems against apparent vulnerabilities. Thus, the security requirement ecosystem (Fig. 2) serves to define the security needs and requirements of the product-line and its deliverable systems and to provide safeguards against unauthorized disclosure, alteration, and destruction of its assets. The ecosystem also provides a traceable audit path for the security requirements and constraints themselves.

Security requirements are derived from the product objectives and security goals along with consideration of constraints from other stakeholder external sources such as those enumerated in Table 1. The consideration of the ecosystem of requirement sources helps to articulate security requirements as complete, traceable, and testable [8], a necessary condition to achieve and maintain a secure systems software product.

The security engineering requirements are driven by either full or tailored conformance to applicable security standards. Table 2 shows a few security standards available for use, as appropriate [21], for the SSPLE.

Security requirements may be designated as functional or non-functional [9]. Figure 3 illustrates SSPLE goals and needs that are studied and progressively decomposed into functional and non-functional requirement statements. The functional security requirements serve to control or limit fulfillment of the stated functional security capabilities of the system [12]. The non-functional security requirements ensure fulfillment of requirements such as the misuse conditions that frame possible illicit behaviors in terms of mutating permitted activities to demonstrate protection against specific vulnerabilities [16]. Following the classic system requirement decomposition process, allocation of the relevant functional and non-functional requirement statements to system architectural components follows leading to component specifications. Understanding that security requirements pervade the SSPLE system (i.e., in hardware and software assets and development practices used to build these assets) requires that security requirements be analyzed and allocated to the domain engineering or application engineering portions of the SSPLE engineering effort. Domain engineering allocated security requirements serve

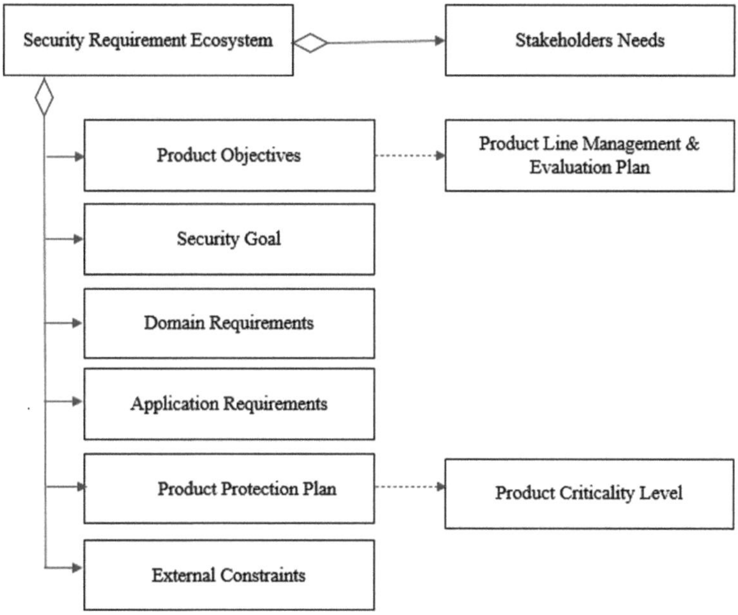

Fig. 2. Security Requirement Ecosystem.

Table 1. External Requirement Constraints.

	External Requirement Constraints
1	Regulations
2	Industry Standards
3	Supply Chain Vulnerability History
4	Best Practices and Guidelines
5	Security Policy
6	Product Protection Plan
7	Lessons Learned
8	Risk Analysis Plan
9	Operational Environment
10	Accreditation
11	Security Assurance Level
12	Product Evaluation Assurance Level

to design and build the core assets for the SSPLE; application engineering allocated requirements serve the customization process delivering end-item systems to specific customer sets based on their needed and allowed customizations of the base product-line system. This ensures critical mission assurance coverage and establishment of a complete set of testable and verifiable security requirements for the delivered end-item systems.

Table 2. Security Standards.

	Standards	Concern
1	NIST SP 800-53	Catalog of Security Controls
2	NIST SP 800-30	Guidance on Risk Assessment
3	NIST SP 800-37	Risk Management Framework
4	ISO 27001	Managing Sensitive Information
5	ISO/IEC 15408	Evaluation Assurance Level (EAL)
6	ISO/IEC 25010	Product Quality
7	DO 178C	Certification in software Airborne Systems
8	OSWAP	Web App Critical Security
9	NIST SP 800-160	Cyber Resilient System
10	MITRE Cyber Framework	Cyber Resiliency and Survivability
11	ISA99	Security of Control Systems
12	IEC 62443	Cyber in Automation and Control Systems
13	ISO 21434	Cybersecurity Assurance Level

Cyber resiliency and survivability design of the SSPLE systems is achieved beginning with security goals decomposed into sub-goals. Resiliency is the ability of the system to deliver intended capabilities and results even when under cyber-attack. Once the relevant actionable subgoals are studied, coordinated, and chosen, the security requirements are drafted, modeled, verified, and validated. Figure 4 shows an example decomposition of the security objective and goal into hard goals and their constituent actionable sub-goals. Figure 5 shows an example decomposition of the product protection hard goal into its constituent actionable subgoals. Design proceeds next.

Our proposed security engineering process uses a product-line engineering pipeline, a process segmented into multiple development stages. The output of each stage is an input to a quality-gate where verification and validation techniques are performed to establish security compliance as products advance through the pipeline. Each gate encapsulates established conditions that must be formally satisfied at each stage along the pipeline to progress through the SSPLE development life cycle. This stage-by-stage progression through the development process allows the SSPLE to incrementally achieve its operational end objective – to withstand active cyber threats and attacks. The quality gates ensure that adequate security assurances serve as the discriminator considered and balanced to manage total system security function, performance, and cost. Figure 6 illustrates an example general PLE pipeline.

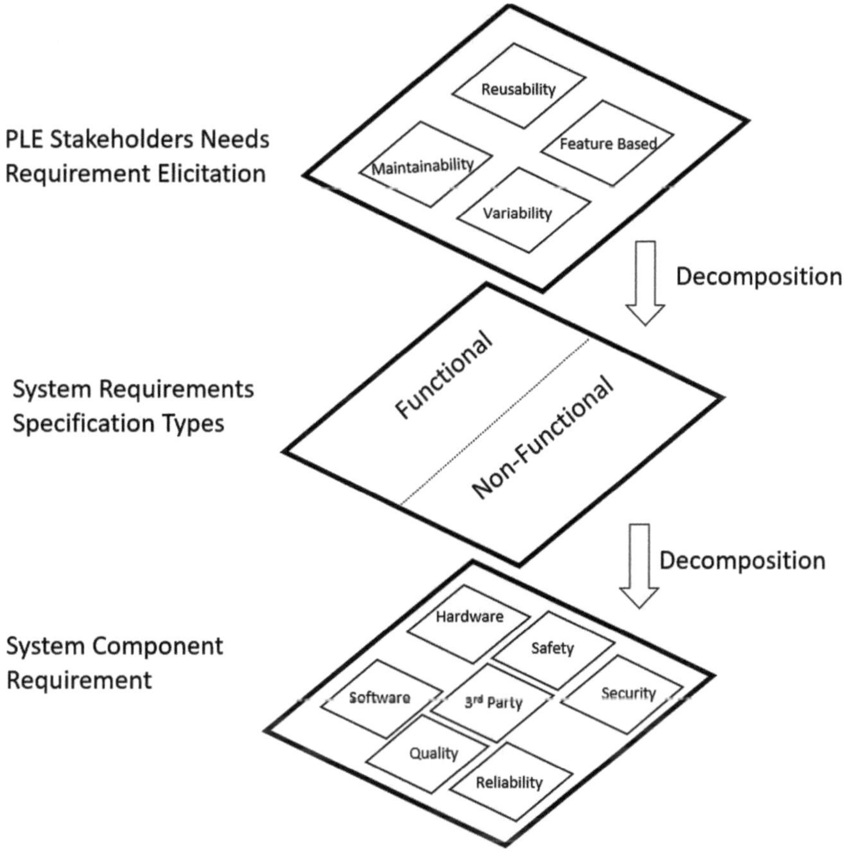

Fig. 3. Requirements Decomposition

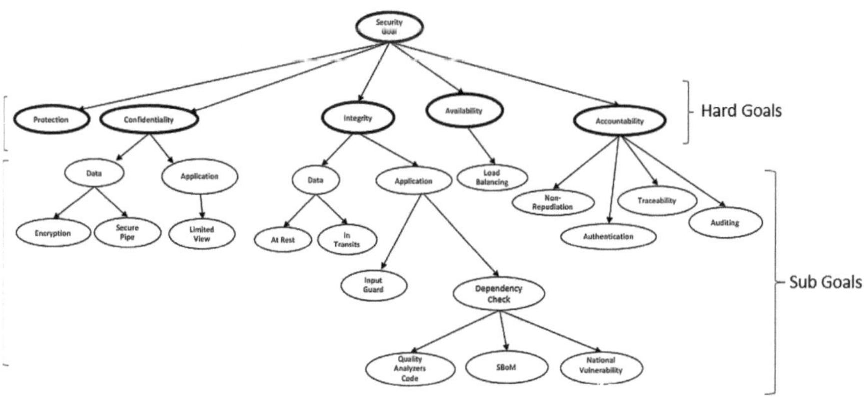

Fig. 4. Security Goals Decomposed to Hard Goals and Sub Goals

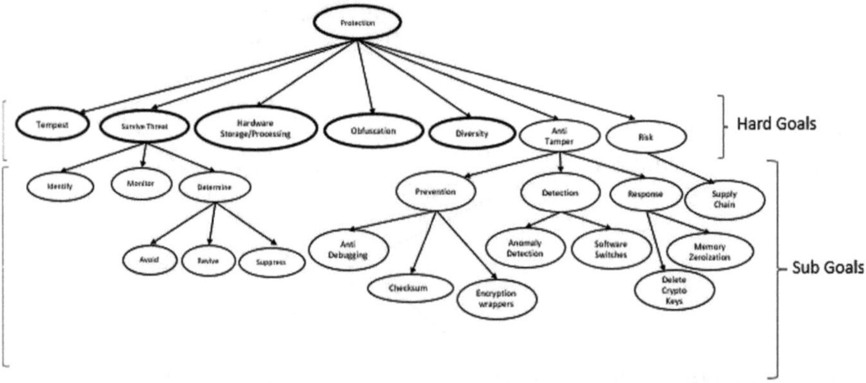

Fig. 5. Decomposition of Security Control to Design Approach

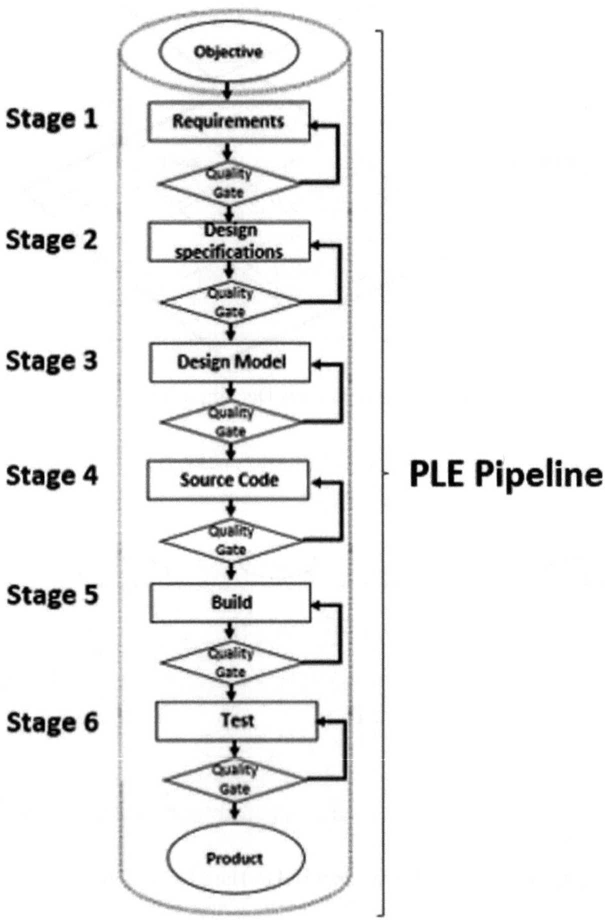

Fig. 6. PLE Pipeline Process Example with Multiple Stages and Quality Gates.

5 Proposed Security Requirement Engineering Approach

The systemic application of the security engineering process employs an iterative and incremental security development life cycle approach to achieve the security engineering and protection objectives for the SSPLE system and its assets. This approach ensures that the security engineering process embeds system security into every stage of the SSPLE, from security requirements elicitation through SSPLE implementation and testing.

Our approach uses domain and application engineering processes to specify elements of the security engineering process model that explores security requirements, designs, and realizations to identify security vulnerabilities (in the domain assets or the customizations), mitigate risks associated with these vulnerabilities, and provide resolved security incidents, testing, and assurance cases for the SSPLE [20]. See Fig. 7.

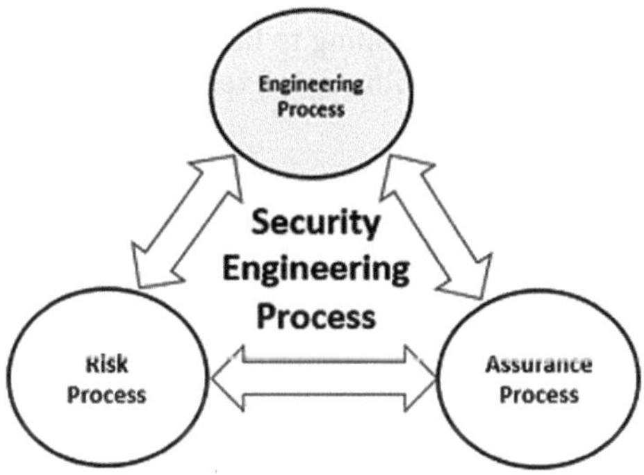

Fig. 7. Security Engineering Process.

Figure 8 shows that goals, controls, security core assets, and security policies and artifacts relate to either the domain engineering or application engineering process, as appropriate.

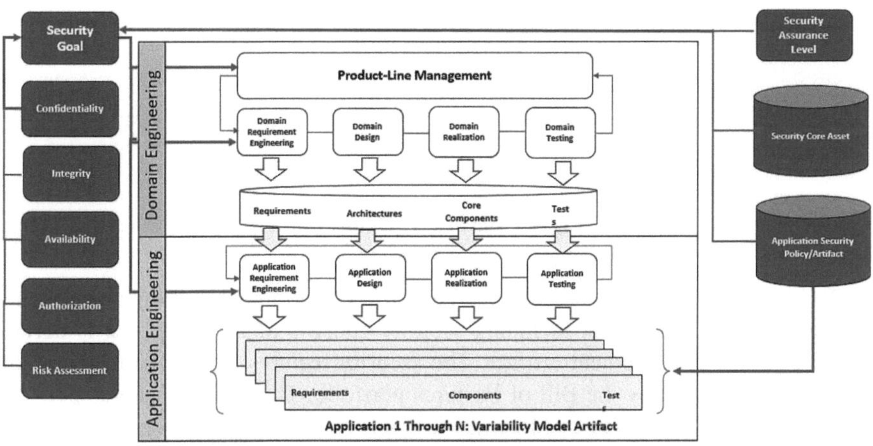

Fig. 8. Software Product Line Engineering Security Reasoning.

The Quality Gates instrumented into the PLE pipeline facilitate verification and enforcement of predefined and built-in security conditions and measures to ensure product quality. Each gate encapsulates established conditions that must be formally satisfied at each of the phases along the pipeline to progress through the development life cycle. For example, as shown in Fig. 9, once the "Develop Security Requirement" phase is complete, the first quality gate, "Formal Verification" performs a specific formal verification of the security requirements. If requirements need rework, the process flows back. If all formal verification checks out, then the process moves forward to the threat modeling process. The threat modeling activity produces a set of apparent security vulnerabilities. These vulnerabilities are used in the next quality gate to assess their risk of occurrence and establish a risk management strategy and plan for each. Once this quality gate is completed, the process moves on to the next process phase, and so on. These quality gates play a critical role in identifying, assessing, and mitigating issues to be addressed in each stage of the PLE pipeline, preventing the accumulation of logical dependencies and security deficiencies [18] from escaping to the next development stage. The development process of Fig. 9 continues to illustrate example supply chain inputs to the PLE pipeline process.

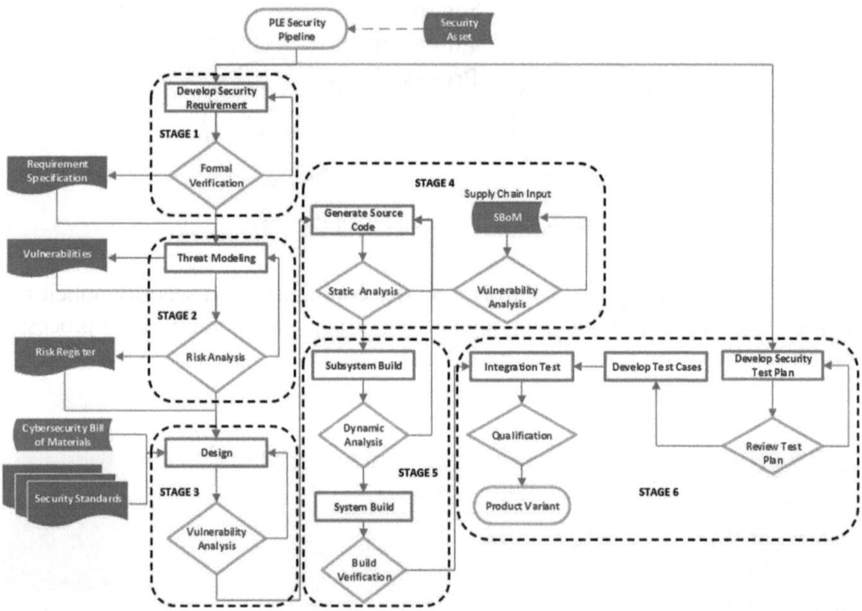

Fig. 9. The PLE Pipeline flow.

During the system build process, the SSPLE application engineering components' configurable PLE feature set including security consists of a catalog that is derived from the security requirement artifact. The security features include capabilities that are further elaborated by the Bill of Features portfolio. The Bill of Features portfolio along with the Software Bill of Materials (SBoM) from the software supply chain are traceable to the applicable security standard and the Cyber Bill of Materials (CBoM) received from the cyber supply chain. These together drive the creation of the SSPLE product variations.

The SSPLE feature composition is described by the CBoM. The CBoM includes a detailed build and operating environment hardware configuration and a comprehensive SBoM. The SBoM provides the SSPLE with full visibility to the software artifacts and components, such as open-source products and proprietary libraries and their underlining licenses and risk compliances. Both the CBoM and SBoM include the software supply chain specifications needed to analyze cyber vulnerabilities, manage cybersecurity risks, and eliminate security defects that affect the SSPLE trustworthiness (i.e., confidentiality, integrity, and availability).

The core component of the SSPLE in the application engineering process is the Factory Configurator. The Factory Configurator's automation process applies input from the Bill of Features portfolio, the SBoM, and the CBoM to generate system product variants (See Fig. 10). Once generated, the system is processed through the integration test stage and qualification gate before acceptance and hand-off to the customer.

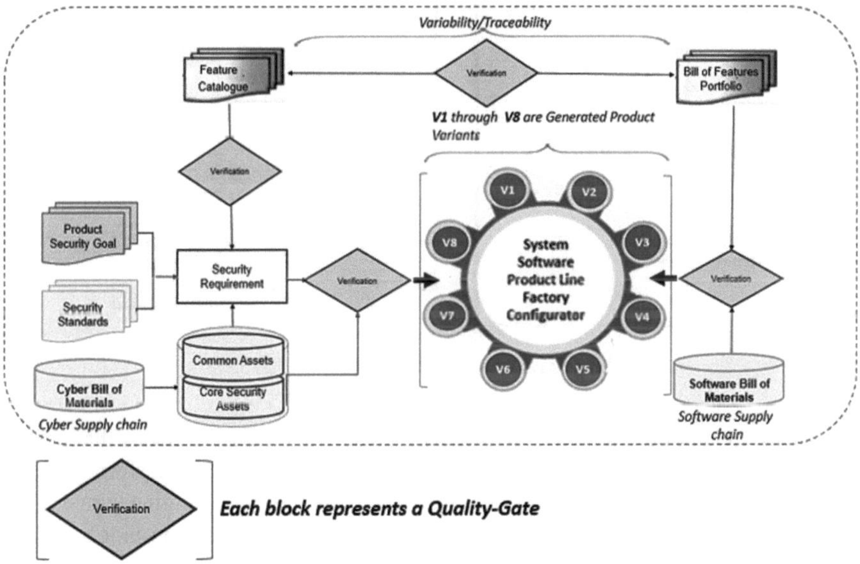

Fig. 10. Security and Application Engineering System Instance Configurator

6 Case Study

6.1 A Software Intensive Embedded Cyber-Physical System

This case study illustrates the applicability of the proposed security engineering process concepts to a real and complex situation. The SSPLE contribution was examined on a software-intensive embedded engine control system product line: The Full Authority Digital Electronic Control (FADEC) system.

FADEC is a mission critical aircraft component that consists of a digital computer that serves as the Engine Control Unit (ECU) and other supporting engine components (i.e., sensors, actuators, etc.). FADEC provides real-time situational awareness for specific parameters associated with the aircraft engine's performance data and discrete control optimizations. Typically, the FADEC ecosystem is comprised of a master node, a Line-Replaceable Unit (LRU) computer with input from multiple supporting components, such as the main fuel control, starter control valve, bleed valves, ignitor boxes, pressure valves, fuel flow, etc. Figure 11 illustrates a sample of the FADEC network components and interfaces generalizing the component structure and interfaces to simplify the discussion that follows. Here, see the main computer LRU on the left side of the drawing providing power, signal, and control interfaces to sensor and actuator nodes on the right. Sensor and actuator components are shown and interface to the nodes.

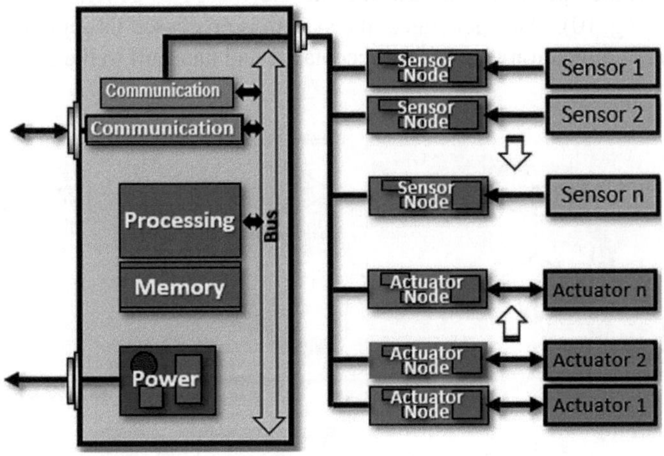

Fig. 11. FADEC Architecture Network [29, 30]

The FADEC architecture has a network of sensors and actuator nodes that perform specific processing capabilities. Sensor nodes acquire engine data and perform basic signal processing for the various operational parameters including the engine temperatures, pressure, fuel flow, and air density, among others. The actuator nodes provide a means to rectify any drift error (i.e., perform local loop closure). This architecture exhibits a configuration approach that is governed by multi-level security principles such that specific nodes operate at specific security assurance levels that align with their named criticality. Furthermore, the FADEC architecture can be configured for dual channel redundancy to satisfy system safety and mission critical objectives in other similar applications. Figure 12 provides an overview of the FADEC and engine system ecosystem.

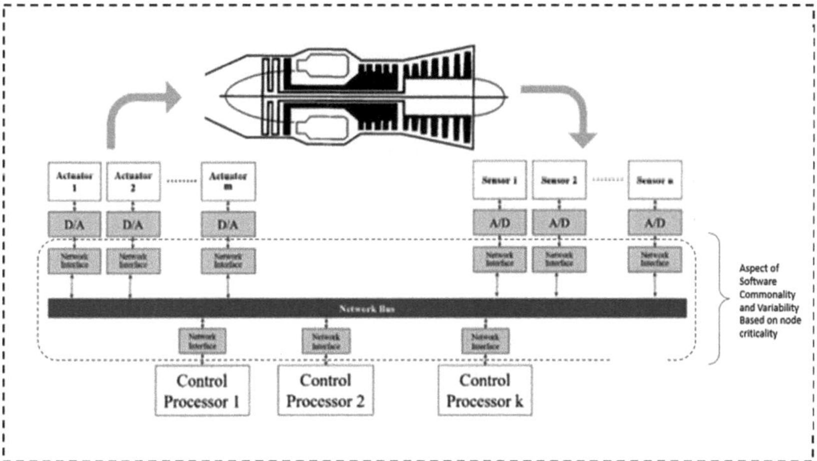

Fig. 12. Software Intensive FADEC [30]

While the FADEC system is primarily hardware-centric, it is also software-intensive. Embedded software is integrated with the hardware to support the engine's mission-critical functions. For example, software enables ECU support for the engine control laws, signal monitoring, diagnostics, and the cockpit display interfaces. The nodes exhibit software commonality and specific variations to support multiple specific configurations; this promotes the opportunity for a secured product-line engineering development approach with an established source of trust for hardware and software and further guarantees trust for the FADEC ecosystem and the named criticality and associated assurance levels. Table 3 illustrates the type of data/information in the FADEC ecosystem and the named criticality and associated assurance levels.

Table 3. Example Node Criticality, Assurance Level, and Information.

	Node Criticality Level	Assurance Level	Software Variability
1	High	Level 4	Critical Product Information
2	Moderate	Level 3	Specific Product information
3	Low	Level 2	Common Product Information
4	None	Level 1	General Product Data

The key FADEC software product need is the trustworthy interaction of critical nodes at their named levels (show in the Table 3). SSPLE addresses this need by ensuring Confidentiality, Integrity and Availability through Cybersecurity and Anti-Tamper goals using variability techniques applied with PLE pipeline. Security considerations for the FADEC adaptation layer (see red dotted box in Fig. 12) serves to establish hardware and software sources of trust. Additional basic software abstraction layers include:

1. Mission criticality
2. Common network communication interface

3. Cybersecurity services
4. Multilevel criticality
5. Obsolescence node adaptation layer [6]
6. Smart interface units (sensors/actuators)
7. Network interconnection topology
8. Common System Services
9. Off-board Communication Services.

7 Case Study Quality Gates Implementation

Following the proposed security engineering process and the PLE Pipeline Stages and Quality gates, a small subset of Quality Gates implementation is described illustrating our approach, in this case, for the FADEC. Table 4 illustrates the PLE pipeline for this case study example. However, examples for Quality Gates of PLE process stages 3 through 5 are not shown for the sake of brevity.

Table 4. PLE Pipeline Stages and Quality Gates.

Pipeline	Process	Input	Quality Gates	Output
Stage 1	Security Requirement	Security Goal	Formal Verification	Requirement Specification
		Requirement Specification	Threat Modeling	Potential security issues Vulnerabilities
		Potential Security Issues Vulnerabilities	Risk Analysis	Risk Register
				Risk Mitigation Plan
		Requirement Specification	Develop Test Plan	Test Plan
Stage 2	System Design	Requirement Specification	Vulnerability Analysis	Design
		Risk Register		
		Cybersecurity Bill of Materials		
		Security Standards		
Stage 3	Source code	System Design	Static Code Analysis	Verified Source of Source Code Artifact
		Software Bill of Materials	Vulnerability Analysis / National Vulnerability Database lookup	Verified SBoM

(continued)

Table 4. (*continued*)

Pipeline	Process	Input	Quality Gates	Output
		Protect Critical Product Information Intellectual Property	Encryption	Verified Source code
			Obfuscation	
			Anti-debugging	
			Checksums	
			Diversity	
Stage 4	Sub System Build	Verified Source Code	Dynamic Code Analysis	Verified Sub System Build Artifact
Stage 5	System Build	Verified Sub System Build Artifact	Build Verification	Verified System Build Artifact
Stage 6	System Test	Test Plan	Review Test Plan	Develop Test Cases
		Develop Test Cases	Review and Validate Test Cases	Verified Test Cases
		Verified Test Cases	Certification	Certified System Test
	Integration Test	Verified System Test Artifact	Qualification (ISO/IEC 15408)	Product/Variants

7.1 Quality Gate 1: Formal Verification of FADEC Security Requirement

For this case study, the FADEC security goal is derived directly from the product needs. The single security goal is further decomposed into hard-goals and sub-goals (Fig. 4) that facilitate derivation of the specific system security requirement(s).

Following the progression through the PLE pipeline stages as shown in Fig. 9 and Table 4, the Stage 1 indicated security requirement with its degree of complexity is formally verified and validated for soundness and completeness with the formal method approach at Quality Gate 1. Using this formal method [4, 5], a mathematically based first-order predicate logic is applied to firmly establish confidence in the requirement specification and reliability in the SSPLE process. For this application the Alloy language and tool are used to illustrate the formal method.

An open-source formal verification tool, the Alloy language construct and semantic Analyzer tool [27, 28] is used to perform formal verification. This tool uses a modeling language based on relational first-order logic and a Boolean satisfiability problems (SAT) solver. This tool approach formally detects and eliminates inconsistencies in the security requirements at early stages of the SSPLE development lifecycle. Figure 13 provides an overview of the Alloy Formal Verification process.

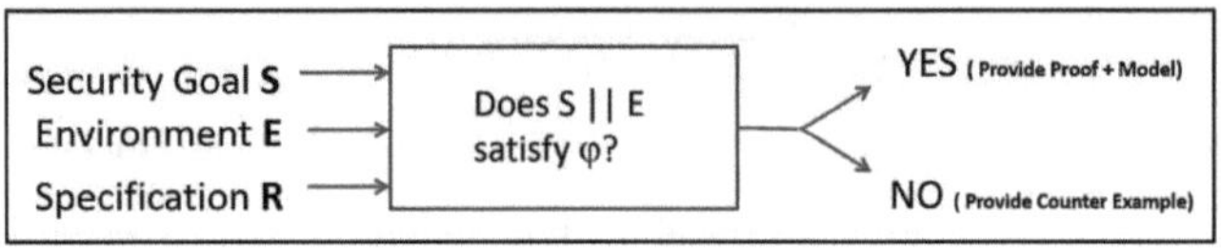

Fig. 13. Alloy Formal Verification Process

The Alloy model syntax, semantics, and constructs consist of Signatures, Fields, Predicates, Functions, Facts, Assertions, Commands, and Module. An example formal definition template follows.

Formal Definition:

The Alloy specification defined abstract syntax ⟨i.e., sig, fact, pred, assert, fun⟩ is as shown in Table 5.

Table 5. Alloy Specification

Semantic	Description
Sig	Declarations defining the signatures (sets of atoms). An Alloy signature s ∈ sig is defined as a triple ⟨Atoms, Fields, Constraints⟩
fact	Express constraints that are assumed to always hold
Pred	Named constraint with zero or more arguments
Assert	State the properties that we expect to hold
fun	Denotes named expression with zero or more Arguments

A subset of the high-level security goal definition from the FADEC Security Requirement Ecosystem is formally verified with Alloy as shown in Fig. 14 and Fig. 15.

The Confidentiality, Integrity and Availability sub-goals are considered within the Cyber and the Anti-Tamper security hard goals to facilitate the secure product's runtime execution and product interaction with the operating environment. The Anti-Tamper sub-goal further ensures that critical product information is well secured within the SSPLE software processing and execution environment. The Confidentiality sub-goal enables secured information flow; that information is protected and delivered only to the intended system component or subsystem. The integrity property ensures that all messages transmitted are not altered in transit. The availability property ensures that any SSPLE execution time information flow is not lost in transits and ensures timely delivery to the intended receiving component. Thus, the confidentiality, integrity, and availability properties are specified in this context as predicate constructs in the Alloy Meta model that conforms to a well-formed logical specification.

When the Alloy Analyzer detects a violation of the confidentiality, integrity, and/or availability properties during formal verification, it subsequently provides a counterexample to any incorrect assertion, as applicable. However, for the high-level example in Fig. 14, the resulting meta-model, shown in Fig. 15, shows the requirement as specified within the constraints of the model to be consistent, complete, and satisfiable.

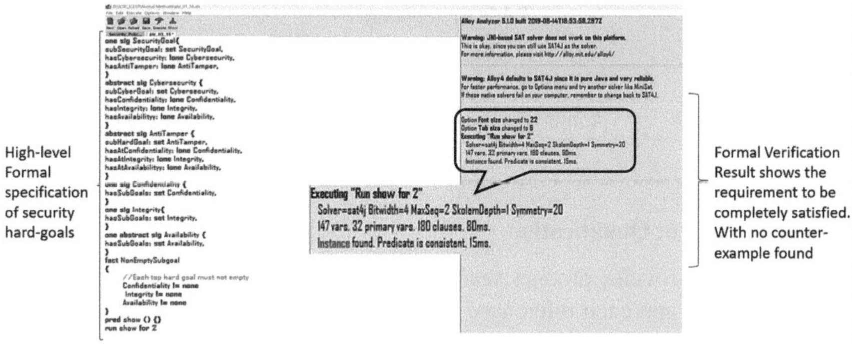

Fig. 14. Alloy Formal Specification and Model Verification result example

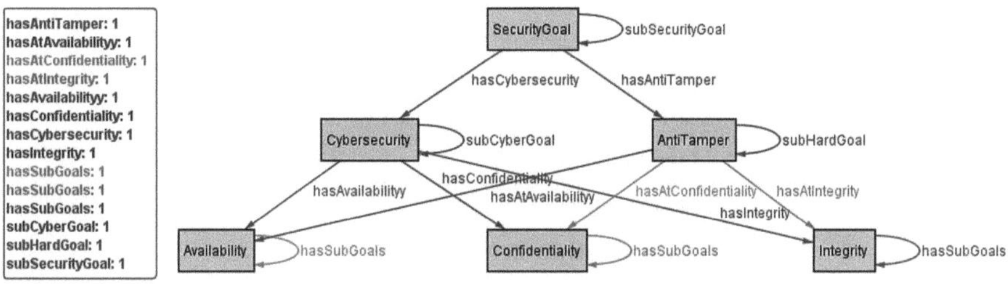

Fig. 15. Alloy Metal-Model: Formal Verification Model of exemplar, high-level hard-goals of FADEC security properties

7.2 Quality Gate 2: Threat Modeling

The goal of threat modeling is to uncover potential threats or vulnerabilities in the requirement specification and to eliminate defects either from the requirements or the design. The STRIDE threat modeling technique orchestrates the discovery of possible ecosystem threats based on specific signatures, such as Spoofing Identity, Tampering with Data, Repudiation, Information Disclosure, Denial of Service, and/or Elevation of Privilege. Table 6 illustrates the threat, violation type, and definition of the threat with examples. The uncovered possible threats are then analyzed and prioritized based on risk assessment and mitigation strategies.

Table 6. Alloy Specification

Threat	Violation	Definition
Spoofing	Authentication	Pretending, falsifying, impersonating
Tampering	Integrity	Alter, modify in a wrongful way
Repudiation	Non-Repudiation	Denial of the truth
Information Disclosure	Confidentiality	Revealing sensitive information
Denial of Service	Availability	Render computer resources unavailable

(continued)

Table 6. (*continued*)

Threat	Violation	Definition
Elevation of Privilege	Authorization	Gain higher access rights than deserved

7.3 Quality Gate 6: Qualification

This quality gate provides product verification using the standard Common Criteria security evaluation approach referenced in ISO/IEC 15408. This standard defines and describes the product Evaluation Assurance Levels (EAL) and expected test approach (see Table 7) [23]. The extent of the product testing and evaluation is dictated by the product criticality and assurance level.

Table 7. Evaluation Assurance Levels

EAL	Assurance Description
EAL 1	Functionally tested
EAL 2	Structurally tested
EAL 3	Methodically tested and checked
EAL 4	Methodically designed, tested, and reviewed
EAL 5	Semi-formally designed and tested
EAL 6	Semi-formally verified design and tested
EAL 7	Formally verified design and tested

This quality gate ensures throughout the PLE pipeline that the common products and variants meet specific security assurance specification requirements to achieve a particular EAL.

8 Case Study Focused Qualitative Survey and Response

We present a qualitative measures survey of the proposed SSPLE secure pipeline model approach. Specific emphasis is placed on the trustworthiness of the methods and its applicability in embedded cyber-physical system software product lines and such as shown in part for the embedded engine control case study presented.

8.1 Survey Questions and Distribution

Six individual Subject Matter Experts (SME) in the aerospace and defense domain with competencies in security engineering, industrial control systems, and embedded turbine engine control systems were selected to perform specific evaluations of the security engineering framework process (i.e., our SSPLE) and provide expert judgement. See Table 8 for the distribution of domain expertise with the participants.

Table 8. Distribution of Survey participant' domain

	Aerospace and Defense Domain	Count
1	Modular embedded engine control	2
2	Security System Software	2
3	Industrial Control System	2

The survey was driven by two research questions. The design of the questions focused on applicability and addressed the optimization, trustworthiness, cost efficiency, quality, and the perceived benefits and challenges of adopting the proposed SSPLE Quality Gates for each stage of the PLE product pipeline life cycle. The rubric used for the survey response is shown in Table 9.

Table 9. Rubric for the Survey participant' Response

Option	Selection	Description
3	Crucial	Urgent or critical and vital for the success or outcome of the SSPLE
2	Essential	Fundamental or indispensable and necessary for the basic functioning or existence of the SSPLE
1	Irrelevant	Does not provide any value for the SSPLE

8.2 Survey Questionnaire 1, Result and Scoring

Table 10 shows the qualitative results validating research question 1: "*How good is a modular security engineering approach for the SSPLE and its components in facilitating security reasoning for its product derivatives?*". Table 11 and Fig. 16 also show the scoring results.

Table 10. Qualitative Result for Research Objective Question 1

Response on perceived benefits and challenges of adoption of the proposed SSPLE Quality-Gate and PLE product pipeline approach		Questionnaire for Research Question 1: Qualitative measures: **6** individuals																	
		1			**2**			**3**			**4**			**5**			**6**		
Crucial (C)= 3, Essential (E)=2, Irrelevant (I) =1		C	E	I	C	E	I	C	E	I	C	E	I	C	E	I	C	E	I
Q1	Quality Improvement	3			3			3			3			3			3		
Q2	Enforce Security Standards	3				2		3			3			3			3		
Q3	Product Exploitability		2		3			3				2		3			3		
Q4	Product Reliability		2		3			3			3			3				2	
Q5	Product Efficiency		2		3			3			3			3			3		
Q6	Operational profiles for a system		2			2		3				2		3			3		
Q7	Efficiency of test cases			1	3			3				2		3				2	

Table 11. Score Table for Research Question 1 Questionnaire

Scoring the Survey Response				
Questions		Crucial	Essential	Irrelevant
Q1	Quality Improvement	18	0	0
Q2	Enforce Security Standards	15	2	0
Q3	Product Exploitability	12	4	0
Q4	Product Reliability	12	4	0
Q5	Product Efficiency	15	2	0
Q6	Operational profiles for a system	9	6	0
Q7	Efficiency of test cases	9	4	1

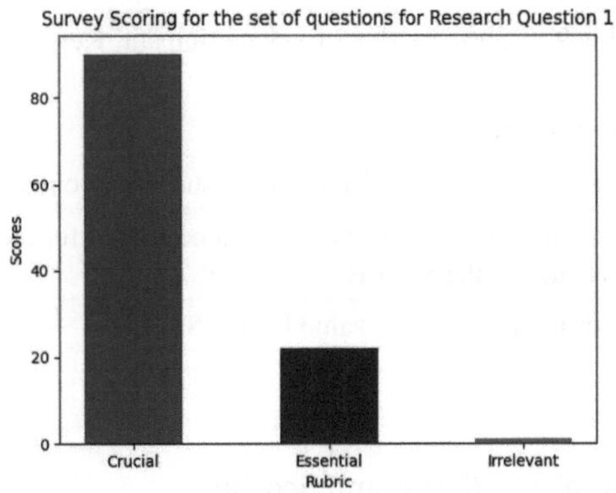

Fig. 16. Survey Score Summary for Question 1

The results of the question 1 survey shown in Fig. 16, indicate that most of the survey participants concluded that the SSPLE modular security engineering approach provides high quality security requirements, and it facilitates security reasoning for its software product line derivatives.

8.3 Survey Questionnaire 2, Result and Scoring

Table 12, shows the qualitative results validating research question 2: *How effective is a security engineering process that enables the SSPLE to address essential security concerns of confidentiality, integrity, and availability*? Table 13 and Fig. 17 also show the scoring results.

Table 12. Qualitative Result for Research Objective Question 2

Response to questions on perceived benefits and challenges of adoption of the proposed SSPLE Quality Gate product pipeline life cycle		Questionnaire for Research Question 2: Qualitative measures: **6** individuals																	
		1			**2**			**3**			**4**			**5**			**6**		
Crucial (C)= 3, Essential (E)=2, Irrelevant (I) =1		C	E	I	C	E	I	C	E	I	C	E	I	C	E	I	C	E	I
Q1	Formal Verification of Requirement	3				2		3			3				2		3		
Q2	Threat Modeling	3				2		3			3			3			3		
Q3	Risk Assessment		2		3			3				2		3			3		
Q4	Vulnerability Analysis		2		3				2		3			3				2	
Q5	Maintain Security Assurance Level		2		3				2			2		3			3		
Q6	Using Common Vulnerabilities Exposure (CVE)		2		3				2		3			3				2	
Q7	Using Code Analysis	3			3			3			3			3			3		
Q8	Protection of Critical Information		2			2		3			3				2		3		

Table 13. Score Table for Research Question 2 Questionnaire

Scoring the Survey Response				
Questions		Crucial	Essential	Irrelevant
Q1	Formal Verification of Requirement	12	4	0
Q2	Threat Modeling	15	2	0
Q3	Risk Assessment	12	4	0
Q4	Vulnerability Analysis	9	6	0
Q5	Maintain Security Assurance Level	9	6	0
Q6	Using Common Vulnerabilities Exposure (CVE)	9	6	0
Q7	Using Code Analysis	18	0	0
Q8	Protection of Critical Information	9	6	0

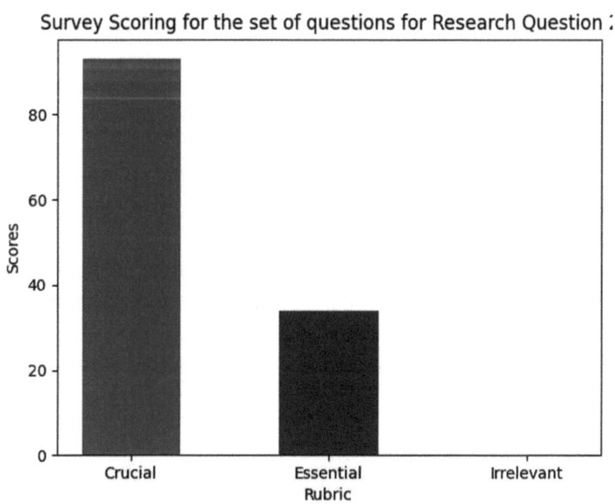

Fig. 17. Survey Score Summary for Question 2

The results of the question 2 survey shown in Fig. 17, indicate that all of the respondents concluded that the SSPLE security engineering process effectively addressed the essential security concerns of confidentiality, integrity, and availability.

9 Conclusion

Our SSPLE security engineering process model presented in this paper enables a systematic approach to the specification and reasoning of security requirements for a product-line system. This model enables security requirements to be understood, accurately described, specified, reviewed, and coordinated with stakeholders as an essential prerequisite of the SSPLE development lifecycle. Lacking effective and adequate security requirements in early SSPLE development stages is a major system development risk that is expected to manifest into costly defects for the SSPLE infrastructure including its product variants if left unchecked for very long. This security model permits use of various security standards tailored and applied to a product-line development to ensure a secure SSPLE and its deliverables. We have established the security objective and goal as a key enabler for efficient requirements elicitation and specification. We have established and discussed a simple but effective iterative and incremental process for reasoning about security requirements and their implication at every stage of our SSPLE process. And finally, we have showed using our PLE pipeline process that carefully placed and implemented quality gates allows engineers to tailor the process for checking and validating the quality and integrity of security requirements at every step of our SSPLE process. This SSPLE development process enables and secures the common core and variable assets of a complex system and software-intensive product-line including assets from both the cyber and software supply chains and thus ensuring that verified and validated PLE end-item systems are secure for our customers.

References

1. Adejokun, S.: Effective systems security requirements in product line engineering. Insight, **23**(3) (2020)
2. Brooks, C., Devendorf, Y.; Systems security engineering for mission assurance system. theoretic and technical operational risk management (STORM). Version 1.2 (2018)
3. OWASP Foundation. OWASP Top 10 Proactive Controls (2024). https://owasp.org/www-project-proactive-controls/v3/en/c1-security-requirements
4. Rouland, Q., Hamid, B., Bodevei, J.-P., Filali, M.: A formal methods approach to security requirements specification and verification. In: 24th International Conference on Engineering of Complex Computer Systems (2019)
5. Schaefer, I., Hahnle, R.: Formal methods in software product line engineering. Computer **44**(2), 82–85 (2011). https://doi.org/10.1109/MC.2011.47
6. Abdelrazek, A., Grundy, J., Ibrahim, A.: Adaptive Security for Software Systems, 1st edn., pp. 99–127. Elsevier - Mosby, Cambridge (2017)
7. Duran-Limon, H.A., Garcia-Rios, C.A., Castillo-Barrera, F.E., Capilla, R.: An ontology-based product architecture derivation approach. In: 15th International Conference, Workshop Proceedings, vol. 2, p. 29. ACM (2011)

8. Sun, N., Li, C.-T., Chan, H., Le, B.D., Islam, M.Z., Zhang, L.Y.: Defining security requirements with the common criteria: applications, adoptions, and challenges. IEEE Access (2022). https://doi.org/10.1109/ACCESS.2022.3168716
9. Pandey, D., Suman, U.: Security requirement engineering framework for developing secure software. Int. J. Comput. Intell. Inf. (2010)
10. McDermott, J., Fox, C.: Using abuse case models for security requirements analysis. In: Proceedings 15th Annual Computer Security Applications Conference (1999). ieeexplore.ieee.org
11. Moffett, J.D., Haley, C.B., Nuseibeh, B.: Core security requirements artefacts. Technical Report 2004/23. Department of Computing, The Open University (2004). https://doi.org/10.21954/ou.ro.00016016
12. Parveen, N., Beg, M.R., Khan, M.H.: Software security issues: requirement perspectives. Int. J. Sci. Eng. (2014)
13. Ruiz, C., Maña, A.: A security engineering process for systems of systems using security patterns. In: IEEE International Systems Conference Proceedings (2014)
14. Mellado Fernández-Medina, P.: Security requirements engineering process for software product lines: a case study. In: The Third International Conference on Software Engineering (2008)
15. Fægri, T.E., Hallsteinsen, S.: A software product line reference architecture for security. Software product lines. Springer (2006)
16. Span, M.T., Salinger, G., Rayno, M., Daily, J.: Security requirements engineering: a survey for the systems engineer. In: IEEE International Symposium on Systems Engineering (ISSE), Perugia, Italy, pp. 1–8 (2024). https://doi.org/10.1109/ISSE63315.2024.10741103
17. Northrop, L.M., et al.: A framework for software product line practice. Version 5.0 (2012). apps.dtic.mil
18. Ambartsoumian, V., Dhaliwal, J., Lee, E., Meserv, T.: Implementing quality gates throughout the enterprise IT production process. J. Inf. Technol. Manage. (2011). jitm.ubalt.edu
19. Pohl, K., Böckle, G., van der Linden, F.: Software Product Line Engineering: Foundations, Principles, and Techniques. Springer (2005)
20. (2022). https://ac.cto.mil/wp content/uploads/2022/08/Systems-Eng-Guidebook_Feb2022-Cleared.pdf
21. Ross, R., Pillitteri, V., Graubart, R., Bodeau, D., McQuaid, R.: Developing cyber-resilient systems: a systems security engineering approach. NIST, SP 800-160 Vol. 2, Revision 1, (2021)
22. Mellado, D., Fernández-Medina, E., Piattini, M.: Towards security requirements management for software product lines: a security domain requirements engineering process. Comput. Stand. Interfaces **30**(6), 361–371 (2008)
23. Gilsinn, J.D., Schierholz, R.: Security assurance levels: a vector approach to describing security requirements. In: Proceedings of the US DHS Industrial Control Systems (2010). tsapps.nist.gov
24. Rabiser, R., Zoitl, A.: Towards mastering variability in software-intensive cyber-physical production systems. Procedia Comput. Sci. (2021)
25. Wilson, B., Young, B.: Cyber secure and resilient approaches for feature based variation management. In: IEEE Systems Security Symposium (SSS) (2020). ieeexplore.ieee.org
26. Fant, J.S., Gomaa, H., Pettit, R.G.: Software product line engineering of space flight software. In: Third international workshop on Product Line Approaches (2012). ieeexplore.ieee.org
27. Jackson, D.: Alloy a lightweight object modelling notation. ACM Trans. Softw. Eng. Methodol. (TOSEM) (2002). dl.acm.org
28. Thompson, H.A., Fleming, P.J.: Distributed aero-engine control system architecture selection using multi-objective optimization. IFAC Proc. Vol. (1998)

29. Culley, D.: Recent technology advances in distributed engine control. In: Aerospace Control and Guidance Systems Committee Meeting (2017). ntrs.nasa.gov
30. Pakmehr, M., Khamvilai, T., Behbahani, A., Costello, J., Skertic, R., Adejokun, A.: Applying zero trust principles to distributed embedded engine control systems. In: AIAA AVIATION 2022 Forum (2022). arc.aiaa.org

Effort Estimation in Agile Software Development Context: A Systematic Mapping Study

Saif Ur Rehman Khan[1], Syed Abu Saeed[2], Habib Un Nisa[1](✉), Muhammad Javed[3], and Kashif Manzer[4]

[1] Department of Software Engineering, Shifa Tameer-e-Millat University (STMU), Islamabad, Pakistan
habibunnisa726@gmail.com
[2] Department of Computer Science, COMSATS University Islamabad (CUI), Islamabad, Pakistan
[3] Department of Computing and Information Technology, FOC, Gomal University, D.I. Khan, Pakistan
[4] Department of Computer Engineering and Computer Science, California State University, Long Beach, CA, USA
Kashif.Manzer01@student.csulb.edu

Abstract. Effort estimation remains a challenging task in the context of Agile-based software development. Some work has focused but lacks an abstract view of effort estimation. Inspired by this, we intend to systematically map literature on Agile software development and its impact on project management, particularly focusing on effort estimation techniques. Following well-established guidelines, the research methodology comprised three phases: (i) planning, (ii) conducting, and (iii) reporting. Covering studies from January 2010 to April 2022, 68 primary studies were analyzed and categorized to address eight research questions. Most papers were published post-2013, with over 48% utilizing evaluation research methods. Model-based approaches constituted over 39% of the selected studies, while 50% were factor-based and over 20% were algorithmic-based. Quality assessment was prevalent, with over 45% of estimation techniques validated. This study provides valuable insights for practitioners and researchers, which offers a foundation for future exploration in the targeted research context.

Keywords: Systematic Mapping Study · Effort Estimation · Agile Software Development

1 Introduction

Agile Software Development (ASD) replaced traditional approaches such as waterfall and incremental, in which no technique is used to accommodate changing requirements. In the traditional approach, the project manager designs

S. Hussain et al. (Eds.): SEET 2025, CCIS 2725, pp. 287–301, 2026.
https://doi.org/10.1007/978-3-032-08977-9_19

project plans for the tasks, whereas in agile, the entire team completes the project. In the past few decades, various effort estimation techniques have been proposed and further classified as algorithmic, non-algorithmic, expert-based, and machine learning [1]. Agile developers and project managers support all reported techniques during the estimation process. According to the survey [2], most companies adopted expert-based techniques such as analogy, expert judgment, and function points. Even though effort estimation significantly impacts a project's budget, schedule, and cost [3].

Project planning remains an open question for industry project managers. This indicates that practitioners and researchers lacked a practical and widely adopted approach [4]. As a result, they must still choose the best technique suited to their needs from currently available techniques [5]. If an estimation technique fails to meet their requirements, then agile project managers will adopt an alternative technique that becomes questionable in practical scenarios [6]. The researchers and practitioners must conduct an error-prone and manual survey of the current literature.

There are still few works that classify and examine the literature [7–9]. In light of recent works, they lack a map of the literature, and some important questions were unanswered: What are the various publication venues in the context of ASD? How has the research frequency of cost estimation changed over time? What core research methods do researchers apply for cost estimation in the ASD context? What current state-of-the-art techniques are available for ASD cost estimation? How can the current studies be qualitatively assessed? What are the demographics of published literature in the context of ASD? Have the identified techniques been appropriately validated? What evaluation measures support the effort estimation process in ASD?

In the literature, several Systematic Literature Reviews (SRLs) [8–11] have been performed to address different cost drivers, estimation techniques, and evaluation measures, but no categorization and mapping study exist in agile effort estimation. The empirical study [12] was conducted in Agile Global Software Development (AGSD), in which authors investigated different techniques and cost drivers in the AGSD context. Also, a Multi-Vocal study [13] was conducted in which researchers were focused on identifying different challenges and success factors. Furthermore, a survey [2] was conducted to identify different techniques and cost drivers; their responses were 65, and most respondents were developers. According to our knowledge, the current state-of-the-art literature does not consider classification and a systematic map of the existing literature.

Motivated by this, we chose an SMS as the research method to address our research questions (RQs) and provide a detailed overview of the literature (Sect. 5). An SMS was designed based on well-established Kitchenham and Charters guidelines [14] but modified for a mapping study, as Petersen *et al.* [15] recommended. The current SMS is adopted to identify techniques, metrics, venues, trends, and future research directions. After applying the filtering process, we got 68 primary articles, further categorized and analyzed according to the eight research questions. It also discusses which research areas remain ignored and requires additional analysis and synthesis. The main Research Contributions (RCs) of this work are as follows:

- RC1: Permits a systematic map of the recent literature to researchers interested in investigating the effort estimation-related challenges in the Agile software development context.
- RC2: Identifies different trends, effort estimation techniques, research methods, evaluation measures, and active researchers in agile cost estimation.
- RC3: Provides a review protocol for future research.
- RC4: Illustrates a comprehensive overview of the published studies in recent years.
- RC5: Examines the validation of various estimation techniques and provides a quality assessment of primary articles.

The remainder of the paper is organized as follows: Sect. 2 discusses the related work. Section 3 presents the employed research method for this study. Section 4 explains the adopted procedures to filter potentially relevant studies, and Sect. 5 presents results and analysis. Section 6 discusses threats to validity, and finally, Sect. 7 presents the conclusion and future work.

2 Related Work

Current research focuses on empirical studies that provide evidence-based knowledge and can predict effort estimation using straightforward statistical techniques [8–11]. However, no systematic map of published research has been developed in the last decade.

Usman et al. [2] conducted a state-of-the-art survey on effort estimation techniques in Agile Software Development (ASD) (Usman et al., survey). They focused on estimation methodologies and effort predictors, using an online questionnaire completed by experienced agile practitioners. The survey revealed that expert based judgment is the most commonly used estimation strategy in ASD, often resulting in effort underestimation. Teams using multiple approaches with story points tend to have better estimation accuracy, and team-related cost drivers are widely employed. Inaccurate estimates of ASD are mainly attributed to requirements and management issues.

Usman et al. [10] comprehensively analyzed the state-of-the-art ASD effort estimation. The findings show that most agile teams focus on expert-based estimation techniques, such as planning poker, analogy, and expert opinion. In addition, it was also discovered that estimation results could be more accurate using a hybrid method, but complexity can occur. The most commonly used size metric is story points, whereas function points and LOC are rarely employed. Several research gaps, size measures, and cost drivers were identified in agile methodologies. More research is required, given the potential benefits of using cross-company datasets for agile effort estimation.

In a previous study [17], we conducted a systematic literature review to identify critical cost factors and effort estimation techniques in the context of ASD.

The identified factors were ranked concerning their frequencies; those with a frequency above 50% were considered critical, with a frequency between 25% and 50% were considered moderate, and below percentages were ranked as low. The results of this research assist the practitioners working in the ASD environment. The identified models need to be improved because they are still in an early stage of development.

Diego et al. [8] conducted an updated systematic literature review and compared the result with the original study of Usman et al. [10]. This research identified six agile methodologies: Scrum, Extreme Programming, and others, of which four rely heavily on expert-based estimation techniques. This is especially true for Planning Poker, connected to the most often used size metric (story points). There is also a notable trend toward investigating data-driven strategies. The authors used the theme analysis method to investigate cost issues. Following agile principles, team and project factors appear to be considered more frequently than technical factors.

From the perspective of agile development teams, Tanveer et al. [18] investigated the estimation process accuracy in agile software development. Using case study research, two observations and eleven interviews were conducted. The proposed framework will increase the transparency of the estimation process, allowing practitioners to make more informed decisions. The study findings show that the magnitude and accuracy of estimates are affected by factors such as the developer's knowledge, the team's prior experience, and the complexity and influence of modifications on the underlying system.

On the other hand, Tanveer et al. [19] developed a hybrid technique for enhancing effort estimation by incorporating change effect analysis data and proposing a gradient-enhanced trees-based estimation method. Their study, evaluated with graduate and postgraduate students, revealed the proposed method's superiority over expert-based or model-based estimations.

Adnan and Afzal [20] highlighted software effort estimation challenges in agile, proposing a strategy validated with experiments involving online projects and estimation techniques. Using the Scrum methodology, their approach improved estimation precision and knowledge management in software projects. Conversely, Conoscenti et al. [21] developed a platform combining data analytics and developers' input to investigate common causes of inaccurate user story estimations. Their findings contribute new insights into inaccurate estimation causes, such as a lack of development experience.

Dragicevic [22] presented a Bayesian Network model for effort prediction in agile strategies, evaluating its precision with various statistics. The model can be implemented early in planning to predict software product quality.

Bajta et al. [23] introduced a model based on historical data for estimating the costs of similar projects. However, the model's accuracy relies on the availability of comparable past projects.

3 Research Method

We followed well-established Kitchenham guidelines [14] but modified them for a mapping study, as Petersen et al. [15] recommended. This section discusses the research methodology illustrated in Fig. 1 consisting of three phases of activities and artifacts, including the planning, conducting, and reporting phases. Our study protocol was validated based on previous systematic mapping studies [24, 25]. Many aspects of a mapping study are not only concerned with the findings but also accurately represent all activities required to complete the review. An SMS is intended to provide a comprehensive overview of a particular research topic, present an unbiased assessment of the existing literature, identify research gaps, create categories, and collect evidence for future research directions.

3.1 Objective and Research Questions

This study aims to identify different venues, estimation techniques, research methods, and evaluation measures. XP [26] and Scrum [26] are two of the most well-known agile software development approaches in the last few years, and each has its principles and approaches. Motivated by this, we improved the search process by including the terms XP and Scrum in the search string. According to Petersen et al. [15], the RQs for systematic mapping studies should be generic to identify research trends across time and topics covered in the literature. As a result, the devised RQs are generic for creating a literature overview. We plan to conduct literature concerning the following variables: cost estimation techniques used to evaluate the primary studies, different approaches, demographics, quality assessment, evaluation measures, and research venues. The following are the research questions and the motivation behind them.

- RQ1: What are the various publication venues in the context of ASD?
  Motivation: Elicit the target venues used for different papers in the literature.
- RQ2: How has the cost estimation research frequency changed over time?
  Motivation: Specify the publication frequency of various types of papers per year.
- RQ3: What core research methods do researchers apply for cost estimation in the ASD context?
  Motivation: Understand and categorize various approaches, such as case studies, methods, surveys, and techniques.
- RQ4: What current state-of-the-art techniques are available for ASD cost estimation?
  Motivation: Determine all available ASD effort estimation techniques and group them into a single category.
- RQ5: How can the current studies be qualitatively assessed?
  Motivation: Evaluate the current literature to apply quality assessment questions.

- RQ6: What are the demographics of published literature in the context of ASD?
  Motivation: Identified the demographic of active authors contributing to effort estimation in ASD.
- RQ7: Have the identified techniques been appropriately validated?
  Motivation: Check whether the identified techniques or methods are accurately validated.
- RQ8: What evaluation measures support the effort estimation process in ASD?
  Motivation: Reveal the evaluation measure most commonly used to disclose the results.

3.2 Search Strategy

After devising the RQs, the next step is establishing a search strategy. We followed the well-established empirical guidelines [14,15] to develop an unbiased and iterative search strategy. The primary objective was to define search strings used to compile a list of representative studies from the current literature. The main terms and synonyms are Agile (ASD, Agile Software Development), Estimation (Cost, Effort, Predication, Measure), Cost Drivers (Factors, Challenges), Techniques (Models, Framework, Methods). These keywords were selected after thoroughly reviewing the most frequently used keywords in the selected articles. The selected papers should cover a period from **2010** to **2022**.

Our primary objective was to define search strings that would be used to select a list of representative studies from the current literature. The following devised search string is generated based on the main terms and synonyms.

(Agile **OR** "agile software development" **OR** "extreme programming" **OR** "scrum") **AND** ("estimate*" **OR** "measure*" **OR** "predict*" **OR** "effort" **OR** "cost") **AND** ("cost drivers" **OR** "factors" **OR** "challenges") **AND** ("techniques" **OR** "framework" **OR** "models" **OR** "methods")

The following databases have been selected based on prior systematic mapping studies [24,25]: IEEE Explore, ACM Digital Library, Science Direct, Springer, and Wiley Online Library. Wohlin's [16] snow bowling technique was used, which has been demonstrated to be effective in several recent studies [8,24,25]. As a result of forward and backward snowballing, 19 new articles have been added; for this process, we also used Google Scholar for snowballing to cover all relevant articles for the study. We modified the search strings slightly to conform to each online database's requirements.

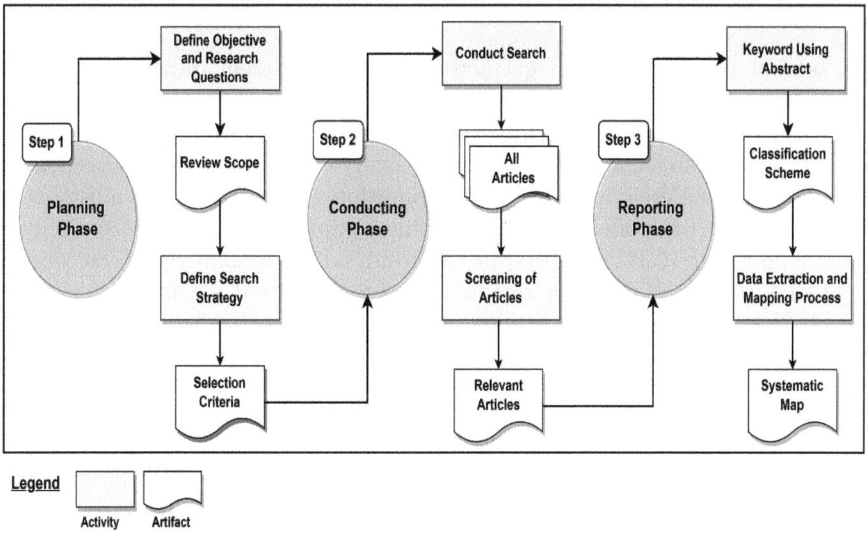

Fig. 1. Research Process Adopted From [Peterson 2008]

3.3 Inclusion And Exclusion Criteria

Establishing inclusion and exclusion criteria is crucial for determining the relevance of articles during a search. Previous studies have shown the effectiveness of these criteria [8,24]. The following are the inclusion criteria employed to filter out studies:

- IC1: The articles should be published in journals, conferences, workshops, or book chapters.
- IC2: The articles addressed cost and effort estimation in agile software development.
- IC3: The articles cover the developed research questions.
- IC4: The articles should be available in Full-text and written in English.
- IC5: The selected articles should be from January 2010 to April 2022.

The following are the exclusion criteria:

- EC1: The title, abstract, or any part of their content are unrelated to the research topic, but they are lexically related to the search string.
- EC2: The studies were not written in English, were patent, or were considered an early stage.
- EC3: There is no resemblance to the research theme.
- EC4: The abstract had no details about the RQs
- EC5: Duplicated and short papers should be discarded (i.e., less than five pages).
- EC6: The study did not cover effort estimation issues and was not directly related to agile software development.

3.4 Data Extraction

This section details the data extraction process, wherein data from selected studies were gathered and documented in an Excel spreadsheet. Each paper's title, study type, venue, research method, technique, and evaluation criteria were recorded to provide a comprehensive study overview. We utilized a classification scheme based on Peterson et al. [15]. Evaluation research was the most prevalent (48.52%, 30/68), followed by philosophical papers (19.11%, 13/68). Solution papers comprised 16.17% (11/68) of the total, while opinion papers accounted for 13.23% (9/68). Validation research received minimal attention, representing only 2.94% (2/68) of the studies. Conducting case studies across multiple companies is essential for generating more reliable results.

3.5 Quality Assessment

Quality assessment is a crucial aspect of article selection, guided by a quality checklist [8,17,24]. Each study was rated based on how well it met the quality criteria. A predefined scale (Y, N, P) where Y = 1 indicates acceptance of criteria, N = 0 indicates non-acceptance, and P = 0.5 indicates partial acceptance is used to rate the studies. In this study, a quality threshold 3.0 was set to minimize biases and enhance article quality. Articles scoring below 3.0 were excluded from the final set. The quality checklist questions used for assessing studies are as follows:

- QA1: Does the potential study answer the research questions?
- QA2: Does the article focus on effort estimation in the ASD context?
- QA3: Were research techniques, methods, or frameworks clearly defined?
- QA4: Does the article mention cost drivers, factors, or challenges in ASD?
- QA5: Does the article explicitly discuss the limitation and validity?
- QA6: Does the article provide future direction?

4 Study Filter Process

This section outlines the procedure for filtering published papers relevant to our research interests. The filtering process comprises eight phases, following established principles endorsed by the scientific community [14] [15]. Recent literature mapping studies [24] have validated the effectiveness of this procedure. The filtering process progressively narrows the list of relevant studies, as depicted in Fig. 2. Initially, we obtained a list of 2922 papers from literature searches. Subsequently, through the filtering steps, we identified 68 primary studies.

5 Results

This section provides the result and analysis of the SMS-formulated research questions.

RQ1: What are the various publication venues in the context of ASD?
The primary research venues where the primary studies were published are introduced in Table. Notice that we found a significant portion of the studies (7%, 3/68) found publication in journals such as the *Journal of System and Software* and the *International Journal of Software Engineering and Knowledge Engineering*, as well as conferences like the *International Conference on Agile Software Development* and the *International Conference on Evaluation and Assessment in Software Engineering*. However, the remaining venues were not as commonly utilized for publication.

RQ2: How has the cost estimation research frequency changed over time?
This research question explores the primary focus of RQ2, analyzing where the primary articles have been published over time. We categorized the primary articles by publication year and type (journal, conference, and workshop papers), providing insights into the temporal distribution of literature. Figure 3 displays the publication index using a grey dashed line.

Publication Index: Each primary article corresponds to a point in the publication index, representing the publication of studies per year. Productivity peaked in 2017 and 2018, while 20102013 were less productive. No studies before 2010 were found.

Trends: On average, 36 articles were published annually between 2014 and 2018, significantly higher than before 2014. We observed a substantial increase in publications after 2014, indicating a highly active research field. In 2017 and 2018, 18.46% of the papers focused on cost estimation in ASD, suggesting ongoing interest and growth in this area. Despite the longevity of effort estimation as a research field, the number of articles continues to rise, reflecting sustained activity.

RQ3: What core research methods are researchers applying for cost estimation in the ASD context?
This question discusses that most research articles are factors-based (50%), model-based (39.70%), and case studies (20.58%), while frameworks (11.76%) and surveys (14.70%). The remaining research methods are SLRs (10.29%), methods (6.15%), and tools (2.94%). It concluded that most researchers identify factors that affect cost overhead in agile cost estimation. In agile cost estimation, different models are proposed, and various case studies are conducted. Different SLRs were conducted [8–11] to identify various cost estimation factors, techniques, evaluation measures, and trends. Usman et al. [27] develop a detailed taxonomy for effort estimation in agile.

RQ4: What current state-of-art techniques available for ASD cost estimation?

In this research question, we identified different cost estimation techniques in the context of agile that are further classified into different categories shown in Table 1. Most of the estimation techniques were algorithmic (20.58%), Expert-based (13.23%), and Machine learning (10.29%). It indicates that the majority of researchers focus on these categories.

RQ5: How can the current studies be qualitatively assessed?

Evaluating the quality of current studies includes examining potential study answers to questions, estimation techniques, approaches, and influencing factors, as well as determining the future direction of research. Approximately 66.66% of methods are clearly defined, while 20% are only partially defined. Table 2 demonstrated that 75% of studies answered research questions, while 20% partially answered them. The future direction of the study leads to the next step of research, so it is an essential factor for qualitative assessment.

RQ6: What are the demographics of published literature in the context of ASD?

The RQ6 focuses on the demographic of various authors contributing to effort estimation in an agile context. Table 10 shows the countries of authors' affiliation in the selected studies. India (17) has the largest number of published articles, while Sweden, Italy, and Germany have the second most published articles (5), followed by Egypt (4) and Pakistan (4).

RQ7: Have the identified techniques been properly validated?

According to the research, 45.58% of identified techniques are validated, 50% are not validated, and 4.41% are unsure whether they are validated as shown in Table. A total of 29 identified techniques were validated. This study demonstrated that most identified techniques were not validated for further research; therefore, it is necessary to validate these techniques to improve their quality.

RQ8: What evaluation measures support the effort estimation process in ASD?

In this research question, various evaluation measures are identified as shown in Table. Particularly, the MRE (33.88%) and PRED (26.47%) are the most frequently used. These evaluation metrics are crucial in assessing the precision of effort estimation within the Agile Software Development (ASD) context. Other measures, such as MSE (Mean Squared Error) and MAE (Mean Absolute Error), serve as alternative accuracy indicators across different effort estimation scenarios.

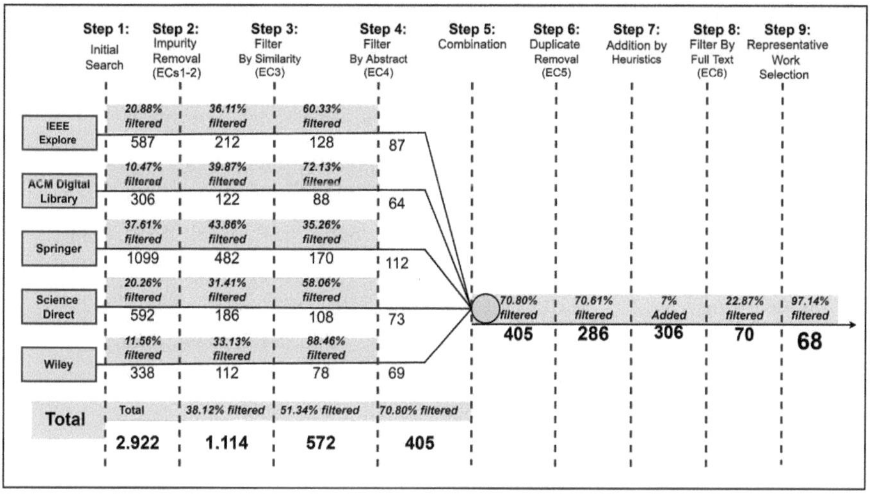

Fig. 2. Selected Articles Throughout the Filtering Process

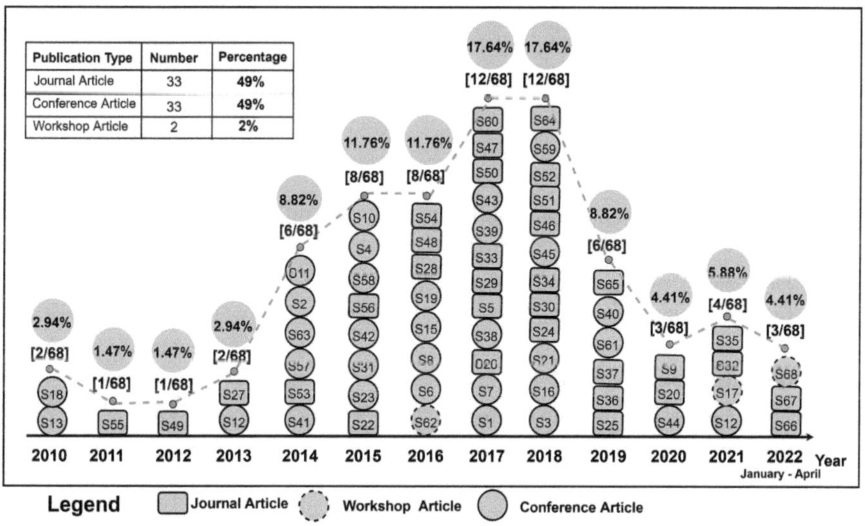

Fig. 3. Distribution of Primary Studies over the Year

6 Threats to Validity

Many possible factors could pose a validity threat to our findings. For instance, the complexity of defining a precise relationship between the various research techniques and identifying the feature scope guarantees the consistency and accu-

Table 1. Categorization of Various Cost Estimation Techniques and Methods

Types of Estimation Methods	Number	%	Primary Studies
Expert-Based	9	13.23%	[S30], [S31], [S59], [S63], [S25] [S39], [S44], [S49], [S64]
Algorithmic	14	20.58%	[S2], [S11], [S16], [S17], [S18], [S19], [S33], [S34], [S43], [S51], [S56], [S58], [S60], [S53]
Machine Learning	7	10.29%	[S3], [S8], [S12], [S33], [S54], [S61], [S62]
Hybrid	6	8.82%	[S32], [S35], [S36], [S45], [S46], [S20]
Bayesian Network	3	4.41%	[S13], [S26], [S40]
Neural Network	4	5.88%	[S23], [S37], [S48], [S65]
Other	2	2.94%	[S5], [S38]
Not Reported	14	20.58%	[S6], [S9], [S10], [S22], [S24], [S28], [S29], [S41], [S42], [S47], [S50], [S52] [S55], [S57]

Table 2. Quality Assessment Checklists

ID	Quality Assessment Checklist	Yes	Partially	No
QAC1	Does the potential study answer the research questions?	75 (75%)	20 (20%)	5 (5%)
QAC2	Does the article focus on effort estimation in the ASD context?	85 (85%)	10 (10%)	5 (5%)
QAC3	Does research techniques, methods, or framework were clearly defined?	66 (66.66%)	20 (20%)	14 (14%)
QAC4	Does the article mention cost drivers, factors, or challenges in ASD?	50 (50%)	5 (5%)	45 (45%)
QAC5	Does the article explicitly discuss the limitation and validity?	55 (55%)	18 (18%)	27 (27%)
QAC6	Does the article provide future direction?	72 (72%)	5 (5%)	23 (23%)

racy of the public domain databases and search engines. We examine threats to internal, construct, and conclusion validity (Fig. 3).

Internal Validity: Two significant threats have been identified. Firstly, various concepts made it challenging to establish a connection between the surveyed methods (e.g., empirical and statistics). The heterogeneity of the evaluated techniques distinguished this thread. To describe the standard features, we conducted a thorough analysis. Consequently, identifying the scope of each primary article was difficult. To mitigate these threats, we aimed to comprehend each technique before classifying them. To prevent any bias, the filtering procedure was repeated twice (Tables 1 and 2).

Construct Validity: Two major literature review threats are incorrect categorization and the failure to include relevant articles. We have attempted to address this concern by instituting a protocol for review that includes inclusion and EC criteria that can be independently audited. Furthermore, we have noted that some other articles have not implemented the highlighted good practices. The Appendix contains a complete list of primary articles. We applied exclusion criteria in each phase of the filtering process to ensure the process of selecting primary articles.

Conclusion Validity: This threat is exclusively associated with issues that can compromise the consistency of our findings. We acknowledge that bias may have affected the article selection process in the study findings and our ability to estimate the effort required for feasible projects. Inclusion and EC were described to address this issue and avoid the possibility of bias in the selection and filtering procedure. Finally, all the article conclusions were drawn from the collected data, eliminating the possibility of an error rate.

7 Conclusion and Future Work

This study systematically analyzes effort estimation in agile software development (ASD). We established a comprehensive research protocol covering objective definition, research questions, search strategy, exclusion and inclusion criteria, data extraction, and quality assessment. From initially retrieving 3,030 studies from five electronic databases, we selected 68 studies. Our findings indicate that (i) A majority of articles were published between 2015 and 2019 in ASD, with a notable increase in publications after 2014, particularly in cost estimation; (ii) Different cost estimation approaches were discussed, with 50% of articles focusing on factors-based and 39.70% on model-based techniques, along with various proposed case studies, frameworks, and techniques; (iii) We categorized various cost estimation techniques, finding algorithmic and expert-based methods as predominant, followed by machine learning and hybrid techniques; (iv) Articles were qualitatively assessed using six quality checklists, with most articles meeting the criteria; (v) Demographic analysis of authors revealed India as the leading contributor, followed by Sweden, Germany, Italy, and Egypt; (vi) Evaluation measures showed MRE and PRED as widely used, with other measures less frequent; (vii) Publications were evenly split between journals and conferences; (viii) While 46% of techniques were validated, 50% were not. Finally, we believe that the findings of the current systematic mapping study inspire further research and address identified gaps, advancing the literature on effort estimation in ASD.

Acknowledgment. The authors are sincerely thankful to the NextGen Software Engineering Lab (NGSEL) members for their feedback and critical analysis of the research.

A Appendix

Appendix A: Primary Studies
See Table here

References

1. Alsaadi, B., Saeedi, K.: Data-driven effort estimation techniques of agile user stories: a systematic literature review. Artif. Intell. Rev. (2022). https://doi.org/10.1007/s10462-021-10132-x
2. Usman, M., Mendes, E., Börstler, J.: Effort estimation in Agile software development: a survey on the state of the practice. In: ACM International Conference Proceeding Series (2015)
3. Pasuksmit, J.: Investigating documented information for accurate effort estimation in agile software development. In: ESEC/FSE 2021 - Proceedings of the 29th ACM Joint Meeting European Software Engineering Conference and Symposium on the Foundations of Software Engineering, pp. 1605–1609 (2021). https://doi.org/10.1145/3468264.3473106
4. Jadhav, A., Kaur, M., Akter, F.: Evolution of software development effort and cost estimation techniques: five decades study using automated text mining approach, vol. 2022 (2022)
5. Hoda, R., Salleh, N., Grundy, J.: The rise and evolution of agile software development. IEEE Softw. **35**(5), 58–63 (2018). https://doi.org/10.1109/MS.2018.290111318
6. Al-Saqqa, S., Sawalha, S., Abdelnabi, H.: Agile software development: methodologies and trends. Int. J. Interact. Mob. Technol. **14**(11), 246–270 (2022). https://doi.org/10.3991/ijim.v14i11.13269
7. Vyas, M., Bohra, A., Lamba, C.S., Vyas, A.: A review on software cost and effort estimation techniques for agile development process. Int. J. Recent Res. Asp. **5**(1), 1–5 (2018)
8. Fernández-Diego, M., Méndez, E.R., González-Ladrón-De-Guevara, F., Abrahão, S., Insfran, E.: An update on effort estimation in agile software development: a systematic literature review. IEEE Access **8**, 166768–166800 (2020)
9. Dikert, K., Paasivaara, M., Lassenius, C.: Challenges and success factors for large-scale agile transformations: a systematic literature review. J. Syst. Softw. **119**, 87–108 (2016)
10. Usman, M., Mendes, E., Weidt, F., Britto, R.: Effort estimation in agile software development: a systematic literature review. In: ACM International Conference Proceeding Series, pp. 82–91 (2014)
11. Dantas, E., Perkusich, M., Dilorenzo, E., Santos, D.F.S., Almeida, H., Perkusich, A.: Effort estimation in agile software development: an updated review (2018)
12. Britto, R., Mendes, E., Borstler, J.: An empirical investigation on effort estimation in agile global software development. In: Proceedings - 2015 IEEE 10th International Conference on Global Software Engineering, ICGSE, pp. 38–45 (2015)
13. Fogarty, A., Edgeworth, A., Smith, O., Dowling, M.: Agile software development – do we really calculate the costs? A multivocal literature review. In: 27th European and Asian Conference on Systems, Software and Services Process Improvement (2020)

14. Kitchenham, B., Pearl Brereton, O., Budgen, D., Turner, M., Bailey, J., Linkman, S.: Systematic literature reviews in software engineering - a systematic literature review. Inf. Softw. Technol. **51**(1), 7–15 (2009). https://doi.org/10.1016/j.infsof.2008.09.009
15. Guidelines for performing Systematic Literature Reviews in Software Engineering (2007)
16. Wohlin, C.: Guidelines for snowballing in systematic literature studies and a replication in software engineering (2014). https://doi.org/10.1145/2601248.2601268
17. Saeed, S.A., Khan, J.A., Naeem, S., Khan, S.-U.-R.: An empirical investigation on cost estimation challenges in agile software development (ASD) context, pp. 188–193 (2022). https://doi.org/10.1109/fit53504.2021.00043
18. Tanveer, B., Guzmán, L., Engel, U.M.: Effort estimation in agile software development: case study and improvement framework. J. Softw.: Evol. Process **29**(11) (2017)
19. Tanveer, B., Vollmer, A.M., Braun, S., bin Ali, N.: An evaluation of effort estimation supported by change impact analysis in agile software development. J. Softw.: Evol. Process **31**(5) (2019)
20. Adnan, M., Afzal, M.: Ontology based multiagent effort estimation system for scrum agile method. IEEE Access **5**, 25993–26005 (2018)
21. Conoscenti, M., Besner, V., Vetrò, A., Fernández, D.M.: Combining data analytics and developers feedback for identifying reasons of inaccurate estimations in agile software development. J. Syst. Softw. **156**, 126–135 (2019)
22. Dragicevic, S., Celar, S., Turic, M.: Bayesian network model for task effort estimation in agile software development. J. Syst. Softw. **127**, 109–119 (2017)
23. El Bajta, M., et al.: Software project management approaches for global software development: a systematic mapping study. Tsinghua Sci. Technol. **23**(6), 690–714 (2018). https://doi.org/10.26599/tst.2018.9010029
24. Carbonera, C.E., Farias, K., Bischoff, V.: Software development effort estimation: a systematic mapping study. IET Softw. **14**(4), 328–344 (2020). https://doi.org/10.1049/iet-sen.2018.5334
25. Curcio, K., Navarro, T., Malucelli, A., Reinehr, S.: Requirements engineering: a systematic mapping study in agile software development. J. Syst. Softw. **139**, 32–50 (2018). https://doi.org/10.1016/j.jss.2018.01.036
26. Flora, H.K., Chande, S.: A systematic study on agile software development methodologies and practices. www.ijcsit.com
27. Usman, M., Börstler, J., Petersen, K.: An effort estimation taxonomy for agile software development. Int. J. Softw. Eng. Knowl. Eng. **27**(4), 641–674 (2017)

Advancing Polycystic Ovarian Syndrome (PCOS) Detection Using Handheld Ultrasound Devices and Immunosensors: A Survey

Kyla Harpe, Kelly Resetar, Hannah Vutuan, and Muhammad Abid(✉)

Florida Polytechnic University, Lakeland, FL 33805, USA
mabid@floridapoly.edu

Abstract. The research done in this paper describes integration of advanced diagnostic technologies, such as handheld ultrasound devices (HHUS) and electrochemical immunosensors, to streamline polycystic ovarian syndrome (PCOS) detection. These tools aim to provide precise, cost-effective, and user-friendly diagnostic solutions. This study also explores the potential of hybrid models incorporating machine learning techniques to analyze biomarker data more effectively, ensuring personalized and reliable diagnostic outcomes. Furthermore, the integration of wearable technology capable of monitoring stress hormones such as cortisol offers a holistic approach to managing PCOS, addressing both physiological and psychological factors contributing to the condition. These innovations not only hold the promise of advancing diagnostic efficiency but also pave the way for continuous monitoring and better management of PCOS symptoms, enhancing patient outcomes.

Keywords: polycystic ovarian syndrome (PCOS) · handheld ultrasound devices (HHUS) · point-of-care ultrasound (POCUS) · immunosensors

1 Introduction

Polycystic ovary syndrome (PCOS) is the most common endocrine disorder among women, yet its diagnosis is challenging due to the broad heterogeneity of women with PCOS [1]. This variability, influenced by genetic and environmental factors such as obesity and insulin resistance, leads to confusion and delays in diagnosis with as many as 75% of PCOS cases unidentified in clinical practice [1, Fig. 4]. The condition is characterized by chronic anovulation, hyperandrogenism (elevated levels of male hormones), and the presence of polycystic ovaries [1]. Additionally, women with PCOS may experience menstrual irregularities, infertility, metabolic syndrome, signs of androgen excess [2, Fig. 4].

PCOS is a disorder, not a disease, and while it is the leading cause of infertility, it can also lead to a range of other complications such as diabetes, high blood pressure, and irregular menstrual cycles [3]. The condition may be identified by infertility, an increased risk of miscarriage, or even uterine cancer. The underlying cause of PCOS is

S. Hussain et al. (Eds.): SEET 2025, CCIS 2725, pp. 302–317, 2026.
https://doi.org/10.1007/978-3-032-08977-9_20

an imbalance of female sex hormones, which will be mentioned more throughout this paper. The hormonal imbalance affects the maturation of eggs in the ovaries, causing immature follicles to remain in the ovaries and potentially develop into cysts. Normally, the pituitary gland releases luteinizing hormone (LH) and follicle-stimulating hormone (FSH), which work together to mature eggs and release them during ovulation. However, in PCOS, an abnormal increase in LH disrupts this process, preventing normal ovulation and leading to the formation of cysts [4].

2 The Problem

Despite the critical role of ultrasound in PCOS diagnosis, there are currently no handheld ultrasound devices (HHUS) that are specifically catered to PCOS. This is because using ultrasound in general often lacks advanced imaging capabilities including resolution, analyzing follicle counts, and quantifying ovarian volume [2, 5]. For example, variability in image quality and limited capabilities (transducers, spectral Doppler, etc.) among different HHUS devices makes them not optimal for gynecological assessments [6–10]. However, HHUS devices offer the potential for more accessible and convenient screening.

Aside from ultrasound, there are emerging analytics that prove electrochemical immunosensors could have a promising influence on diagnosing and treating PCOS. Because these biosensors target specific molecules, we could target specific proteins or hormones that are exceedingly common for those with the syndrome. By targeting these specifics immunosensor would provide a non-invasive and real time technique to identify symptoms and management techniques. These devices prove that they can be found useful as they are very cost-effective, and hold promise for future automation.

The objective of this paper is to evaluate the current state of HHUS devices for PCOS detection by examining their technological capabilities, limitations in clinical settings, and user feedback. Based on this analysis, we will propose targeted improvements that can enhance the accuracy and usability of these devices for PCOS.

3 Literature Review

Polycystic Ovary Syndrome is marked by the formation of approximately ten small cystic structures, each ranging from 2 to 9 mm in diameter, within one or both ovaries. It is also characterized by an ovarian volume exceeding 10 mL in at least one ovary, as originally described by Stein and Leventhal in 1935. The condition results from hyperstimulation of ovarian follicular development. Although the cysts often contain sufficient follicles, hormonal imbalances disrupt their growth and maturation. Diagnosing PCOS typically involves identifying anovulation, hyperandrogenemia, and insulin resistance. Hyperandrogenemia is notably linked to an elevated risk of cardiovascular disease and type-2 diabetes [51]. Early diagnosis and treatment of PCOS can prevent complications such as ovarian failure, cancer, diabetes, and hypertension. Efforts to standardize diagnostic criteria have evolved significantly [11]. In May 2003, the Rotterdam consensus established that PCOS required at least two of the following criteria: (i) Oligo or anovulation,

(ii) Clinically and/or biochemical hyperandrogenism, and (iii) Polycystic ovarian morphology visible on ultrasound. Later, in 2006, the Androgen Excess Society refined the criteria to include (i) Ovulatory and menstrual dysfunction, (ii) biochemical or clinical hyperandrogenism, and (iii) Polycystic ovaries. Diagnostic tests for PCOS often include evaluation of thyroid function, prolactin, and follicle-stimulating hormone (FSH) levels. The timeline of PCOS diagnostic criteria development goes as follows: in 1935 Stein and Leventhal's seminal description of PCOS, in 2003 Rotterdam consensus workshop criteria is introduced, and in 2006 the Androgen Excess Society established the updated diagnostic criteria [12].

To detect PCOS, clinicians follow the three aspects of the Rotterdam criteria: (1) hyperandrogenism, (2) menstrual irregularities, and (3) existence of multiple cysts [13, 14]. Transvaginal ultrasound is often used to detect PCOS as it allows clinicians to assess the number, volume, and position of the follicles, which are characteristic of polycystic ovaries [14]. During the ultrasound examination, ultrasonographers analyze the images for abnormalities in the ovaries, including cysts of larger diameters [13]. Adopting HHUS devices for this purpose can improve patient comfort as handheld point-of-care ultrasound devices are less invasive than transvaginal ultrasound [15].

3.1 Current and Emerging Technologies in HHUS

Artificial Intelligence is a field within computer science that emulated human intelligence through reasoning, learning, problem-solving, perception, and language understanding. By copying and mimicking cognitive functions of the human mind, AI has revolutionized the world everywhere, including healthcare, where it holds immense potential to address challenges like disease prevention, detection, diagnosis, and treatment. Machine Learning (ML), a branch of AI, enables systems to learn and improve autonomously by analyzing structured as well as unstructured datasets [16].

Currently, HHUS devices have moved away from traditional piezoelectric crystals to ultrasound-on-chip technology, which incorporates a 2D array of micro sensors and emulates various transducer types [7, 9]. Some examples include Butterfly iQ, a device equipped with cloud-sharing, teleguidance technology, artificial intelligence (AI) and augmented reality (AR). These features optimize image quality, provide real-time teleguidance, and enable remote supervision, making HHUS devices highly adaptable [7, Fig. 1].

HHUS devices have been able to adapt to other areas of healthcare such as emergency medicine and intensive care for rapid hemodynamic and respiratory assessments [6, 7]. It is also used in trauma medicine, cardiology, abdominal imaging, and rheumatology where HHUS devices are used to evaluate the body or guide procedures [9, 17]. Despite their adaptability, they have yet to be tailored for PCOS although there is potential for handheld ultrasound devices in gynecological assessments. Discussions around handheld transvaginal ultrasound probes for ovarian tissue and transvaginal gynecological examinations suggest a growing interest in this area [18–20]. However, no device has been specifically implemented for PCOS, highlighting a significant gap in the market.

4 Methodology

To address this gap, we did a comprehensive review of articles that included an existing survey from Exo, a medical imaging software company, and comparative analyses of handheld ultrasound devices. Sources included reputable medical technology databases and published performance evaluations. We focused on devices used for diagnostic imaging and extracted tables that categorized devices based on attributes such as image transmission, transducer, portability, and cost [6, 8].

Figures from the survey were also extracted for user and physician experiences with point-of-care ultrasound (POCUS) devices [21]. While the survey focused on general POCUS devices rather than handheld ones specifically, it provided insights into their usability and potential improvements.

Mobile ultrasound systems, including handheld devices (HHUS), have made point-of-care ultrasound (POCUS) widely accessible across medical specialties, extending its use from clinics to homes. However, HH-POCUS poses challenges in documentation and data storage, as many devices are not connected to traditional PACS or RIS systems. There is a need for secure, legally compliant solutions for storing and sharing images, as well as simplified documentation for urgent bedside exams [22]. HH-POCUS can also reduce the burden on overcrowded emergency departments by enabling faster, more accurate diagnoses at the patient's bedside, especially in rural areas with limited resources. Despite its potential, HH-POCUS is underutilized, due to training gaps, excessive costs, and clinical challenges. Teleconsulting could address these issues and enhance diagnostic accuracy. Overall, HHUS is well-suited to meet the needs of patients at home, reducing hospital visits and associated costs.

A total of 222 women, aged 39–89, participated in a prospective trial comparing handheld ultrasound (HHUS) with automated breast volume scanning (ABVS) to assess its diagnostic accuracy. Both symptomatic and asymptomatic women were included, with the study conducted at a screening and symptomatic assessment center. All participants underwent HHUS followed by ABVS on the same day, with images interpreted by experienced radiologists. The study aimed to compare HHUS and ABVS against histology as the reference standard, with a follow-up period of at least one year. The comparison between HHUS and ABVS showed that both methods had false-positive and false-negative results, with HHUS having higher sensitivity and specificity than ABVS. HHUS has a sensitivity of 90.62% compared to 68.75% for ABVS, and a specificity of 96.32% compared to 90.62% for ABVS. HHUS also had a higher area under the curve (AUC) of 0.930 compared to 0.788 for ABVS, indicating better diagnostic accuracy. Additionally, HHUS detected more cancers, including invasive lobular carcinoma and hormone-receptor-positive breast cancer, which were missed by ABVS. These findings highlight that HHUS, with its higher diagnostic accuracy, is particularly beneficial for symptomatic women, suggesting that the method's real-time clinical relationship enhances its diagnostic capabilities [23]. These insights are critical for understanding how HHUS can be adapted for other diagnostic applications, such as PCOS detection, where similar challenges in diagnostic accuracy exist. By examining these studies, we identified how HHUS could be adapted to improve PCOS diagnosis, focusing on user satisfaction, diagnostic accuracy, and the technology's suitability for real-world clinical use.

5 Device Comparison and Analysis

To evaluate the suitability of existing handheld ultrasound for PCOS diagnosis, a comparison of their key features, including wireless capabilities, transducer types, and B-mode image quality was conducted shown in Table 1. The values for the image quality are shown in mean ± standard deviation. The grading scale used was from 1 (unsatisfactory) to 5 (very good).

Table 1. Comparison of the HHUS devices used in the study [6].

Device Name	Wireless	Transducer	B-mode image quality
Butterfly iQ+	No	All-in-one 1.75 D-Array	3.0 ± 0.7
Clarius C3HD3	Yes	Linear or convex	4.3 ± 0.7
D5CL Microvue	Yes	Linear and convex in one	3.2 ± 0.8
Philips Lumify	No	Linear, convex, or broadband convex	3.4 ± 0.7
SonoEye	No	Linear, convex, or broadband convex	3.9 ± 0.7
SonoSite iViz	No	Linear or convex	3.3 ± 0.8
TE Air	Yes	Sector	2.6 ± 0.6
Vscan Air	Yes	Convex/linear or sector/linear in one	4.2 ± 0.6
Youkey Q7	Yes	Four different replaceable transducers	3.7 ± 0.8

The Clarius C3HD3 and the Vscan Air scored the highest in B-mode image quality, making them possibly suitable for high-resolution imaging required in PCOS diagnosis. However, looking at their transducer types, the Butterfly iQ+ offers an 'all-in-one' transducer, which likely makes it adaptable for PCOS. These findings suggest that while these HHUS devices can enhance usability and image quality, incorporating features like AI and immunosensors in the devices can further improve diagnostic accuracy.

To identify key barriers that inhibit the adoption of POCUS devices, a user survey was conducted by the company Exo shown in Fig. 1. The results highlighted challenges that healthcare professions face with using these devices.

IT connectivity challenges, screen size limitations, and budget constraints are the most common factors with issues followed closely like poor image quality and device training. Addressing these challenges is crucial to improving the adoption of HHUS devices for PCOS detection. That way, we can ensure that our device ensures precise visualization of the ovarian structures and make PCOS detection more accessible. To solve these issues, especially the budget constraints, immunosensors are another solution to PCOS detection that is known for being low-cost.

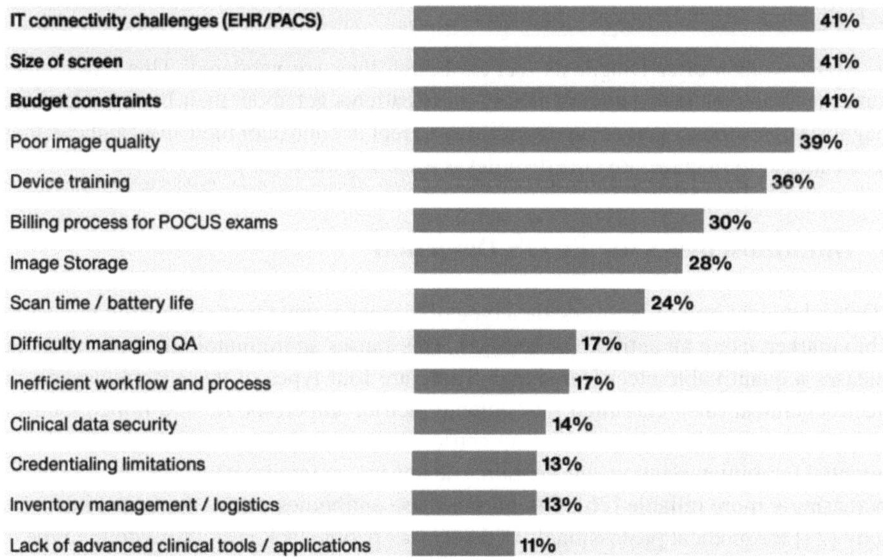

Fig. 1. Factors inhibiting adoption of handheld POCUS devices [21].

6 Opportunities in PCOS Diagnosis

Infertility, PCOS particularly, affects up to an estimated 21% of woman. Unfortunately, a lot of these women are diagnosed as something else, too late, or long after the cysts have already cause permanent fertility damage. Early and accurate diagnosis would not only cut the treatment cost but also reduce disease burden and mortality rate. Taking these facts into consideration, it is time for a device that is easily usable, accessible, and efficient to be produced to reduce these numbers.

Many wearable devices demonstrate high accuracy in detecting fertility by distinguishing between the luteal phase (early and late), fertile window, and menstruation. These devices achieve this by monitoring physiological changes such as heart rate, heart rate variability, temperature, and respiratory rate. Such metrics are also relevant for identifying disruptions in ovulation or hormonal patterns, which are key diagnostic indicators of PCOS. However, further validation is required to confirm these findings, particularly regarding respiratory rate as a proxy for reproductive cycle staging. The small number of studies linking these physiological changes to PCOS-specific markers underscores the need for additional research [24].

7 Advantages of PCOS Diagnosis

1. Preventive Care
2. Early Diagnosis
3. Personalized Treatment(s)
4. Reduced Healthcare costs
5. Awareness – Self and Community

6. Help Mainstream Diagnosis Techniques

Many women after Diagnosis feel as though they are validated. This reassurance comes from the increased understanding these patients get about their bodies. Getting a diagnosis gives those women an opportunity to feel in control of their lives and can then get treatment to manage how the disorder is affecting them [25].

8 Immunosensors for PCOS Detection

Electrochemical immunosensors are a type of biosensor that targets a specific molecule, a bio marker, using an antibody + antigen. This causes an immunological reaction that releases a quantifiable electrical signal. There are four types of these immunosensors: electrochemical (also classified into potentiometric, amperometric and impedimetric), optical, microgravimetric and thermometric. Due to their low cost, high sensitivity, potential for miniaturization, automation, and low power requirements they have become increasingly more reliable [26]. Oftentimes these antibodies can be deposited into your body [27] for medical professionals to detect, but people lack availability to the type of deposits that would be needed. Why not target an already existing medical variable? For example, some key reactions that could be used for these immunosensors are Proteins like Hormones and Tumor markers, and because this device would be used specifically for PCOS the sensor could find the Cancer antigen 125 (CA-125). If these immunosensors could be compacted to a short-term wearable device (do your check weekly for a brief period ideally) a patient that is susceptible to/already diagnosed with PCOS could track symptoms and changes in testing results. However, CA-125 is normally related to ovarian cancer, and may not be the best biomarker to use. Alternatively, patients with PCOS (knowing or not) usually display increased amounts of cystatin C [28]. This is a protein found in the body that rapidly increases in amounts due to the chronic inflammation that often comes with the condition. While cystatin C can also be a sign of neurodegenerative diseases, cardiovascular disorders, and cancer a study in 2013 shows its more accurate for PCOS [29]. The study resulted in a significant positive correlation between cystatin C and PCOS as it kept its positive correlation even with various variable changes.

Stress also significantly affects both physical and mental health, with physiological and psychological stressors often investigated for their negative impacts. It also impacts hormonal imbalances and metabolic dysfunction in PCOS. Electrochemical sensing technologies are promising for monitoring stress biomarkers such as cortisol. For instance, labelled electrochemical cortisol sensors use bio/chemoreceptors like antibodies or aptamers to directly quantify cortisol levels in biological samples. Aptamer-based sensors specifically operate through electro transfer during the redox reaction between the aptamer and cortisol, employing signal-off or signal-on strategies for precision [30]. Incorporating stress-monitoring features into wearable devices for PCOS could provide a comprehensive approach to managing the condition, addressing both physiological and psychological contributors to disease progression.

Single biomarkers often lack precision in diagnostics, leading to the growing use of combined biomarker scores. Traditional methods rely on linear models, but a flexible framework incorporating both linear and nonlinear combinations is needed for greater accuracy [31]. Electrochemical immunosensors, capable of detecting multiple biomarkers like cystatin C for inflammation or cortisol for stress, could leverage this approach. By integrating these sensors into wearable devices, real-time, multidimensional tracking of PCOS could improve diagnostic precision and personalized care.

9 Training Algorithms

To work with learning from little data, the development of hybrid models would help enhance both prediction accuracy and interpretability. Hybrid models can hold the strengths of various approaches to improve the validity and interpretability of predictions. [32] Transfer learning is the adaptation of models that are trained on one dataset for use with a different and typically smaller dataset that may be beneficial in the PCOS field where, again, data is scarce. Working with clinicians and data scientists could lead to models that are both technically sound and aligned with clinical needs. The coordination between the machine and scientists/clinicians can promote the creation of machine learning tools that are user-friendly, patient-centered, and practical for real-world application.

AI applications can significantly enhance accuracy and efficiency in PCOS detection. The manual process of counting follicles and measuring diameter is labor-intensive, time-consuming, and prone to human error. AI's role in PCOS management is not limited to detection. Its predictive capabilities can help monitor disease progression, identify associated risk factors, and recommend personalized treatment plans [16]. The integration of AI with wearable devices and biosensors for continuous monitoring of stress, hormonal imbalances and inflammation could further enhance PCOS management, offering patients comprehensive and real-time care solutions [33]. By combining human expertise with AI-driven innovation, healthcare can pave the way for earlier detection, more effective treatments, and better outcomes for patients with PCOS. AI in healthcare must address data privacy, fairness, and transparency.

Poorly trained models risk bias and unequal outcomes, while opaque algorithms challenge trust. Hybrid models and transfer learning can improve accuracy and interpretability, particularly for small datasets like PCOS. Ethical frameworks should ensure transparency, fairness, and patient-centric design. Combining quantitative metrics with qualitative insights promotes responsible AI use, enhancing PCOS detection and care [34].

10 Challenges in AI and Immunosensor Integration

Lack of data, many PCOS datasets are often small or lacking in diversity, which causes the algorithm accuracy to weaken. This causes a higher demand for better quality and diverse datasets [32] (Fig. 2).

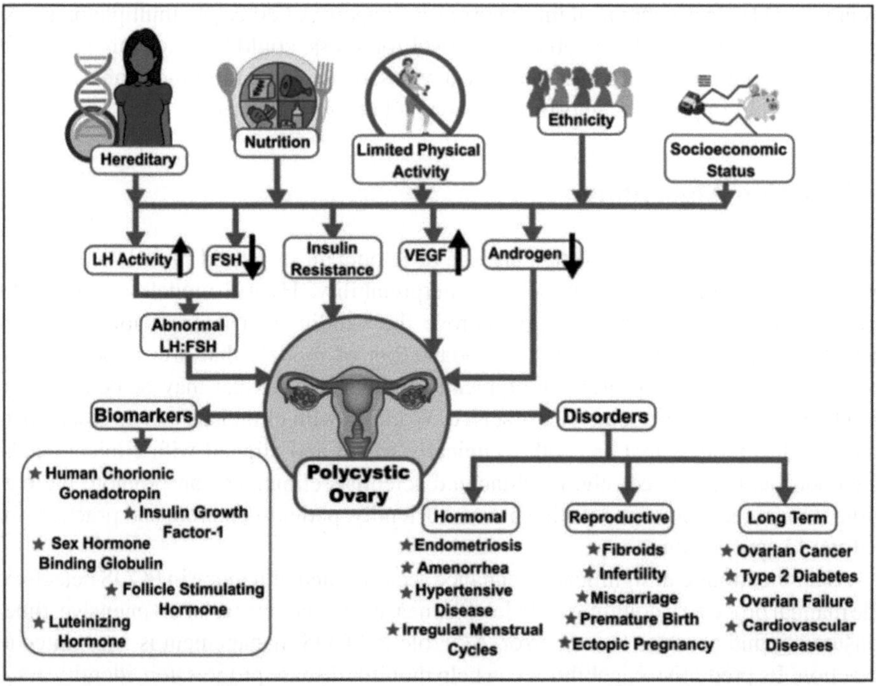

Fig. 2. A line diagram for PCOS outlining potential factors that could be responsible for complications [12].

Integrating machine learning tools into healthcare due to the need for real-time processing, learning from data to produce data is difficult to incorporate to the workflow [32].

There is limited understanding of how clinicians navigate the uncertainties involved in diagnosing PCOS. Studies have shown significant discrepancies between general practitioners, endocrinologists, and gynecologists regarding diagnostic methods and treatment approaches for PCOS (Cussons et al., 2005; Powers et al., 2015). Additionally, surveys across different countries have highlighted a lack of awareness about the full spectrum of PCOS symptoms. Diagnosing PCOS is challenging due to variations in clinical practices and uncertainty around diagnostic criteria. Many clinicians report difficulty with the Rotterdam criteria, and a lack of awareness about the full range of symptoms leads to missed diagnoses and poor adherence to recommended screenings (Dhesi et al., 2016; Gibson-Helm et al., 2018). The use of ultrasounds, despite other criteria being met, is common among general practitioners for diagnosis [27] (Table 2).

Table 2. Timeline for diagnostic criteria for PCOS [27].

National Institutes of Health, 1990 (Zawadzki, 1992)	Rotterdam*, 2003 (The Rotterdam ESHRE/ASRM PCOS Workshop, 2004)	Androgen Excess and PCOS society, 2006 (Azziz et al., 2006)
Need both: - Oligo-ovulation or anovulation - Clinical/biochemical signs of hyperandrogenism And exclusion of other causes	Need two of the following: - Oligo-ovulation or anovulation - Clinical/biochemical signs of hyperandrogenism - Polycystic ovaries on ultrasound And exclusion of other causes	Need: - Clinical/biochemical signs of hyperandrogenism And one of the following: - Oligo-ovulation or anovulation - Polycystic ovaries on ultrasound And exclusion of other causes

* Endorsed for use in adult women by international PCOS guidelines in 2018 (Teede et al., 2018a).

A qualitative study with Australian clinicians found that while the Rotterdam criteria are widely used, they are seen as imperfect. Many clinicians struggle with ambiguous diagnoses, as polycystic ovaries are common and can fluctuate. To add on, blood test standards are inconsistent, and insulin resistance is not addressed in guidelines. These challenges highlight the need for more standardized diagnostic tools. Small, non-diverse datasets also affect algorithm accuracy, which emphasizes the need for better data. Label-free electrochemical immunosensors could provide real-time diagnostic solutions but require proper training and device preparation for effective use [27].

The 2023 Internation Evidence-based Guideline for PCOS was developed through a rigorous process to improve diagnosis and management worldwide. This comprehensive guideline was created with substantial input from government bodies, healthcare organizations, and international collaborations with experts in multiple disciplines. The development process adhered to the Appraisal of Guidelines for Research and Evaluation-II (AGREEII) standards, ensuring that recommendations are based on high-quality evidence. The guidelines aim to reduce global variation in care by offering standardized recommendations adaptable to different healthcare systems. It also emphasizes an extensive translation program, providing resources for healthcare professionals and empowering women with PCOS to make informed decisions. Key updates in the 2023 guideline include using the 2018 Internation Evidence-based Guideline criteria for diagnosing PCOS, which build upon the 2003 Rotterdam criteria. While the quality of evidence in PCOS remains low to moderate, the guideline stresses the need for further research, funding, and education to improve care. The guideline's translation includes multilingual educational resources for healthcare, professionals, consumers, and policymakers. This approach is expected to enhance diagnosis, improve patient experiences, and ensure more consistent care globally [35].

Additionally, there may be problems with training users to safely use their device. To use the immunosensor(s) the equipment does have to be properly prepped. Label free electrochemical immunosensors, are immunosensors that detect the physical or chemical changes arising directly from the biomarker. For this device, the biomarker would ideally be cystatin C or a tumor protein from ovarian tumors. Label free, also known as direct, immunosensors allow analysis to be done in real time which would be ideal for a patient's use [36]. Before the sensor can scan anything, a specific antibody must be immobilized on the surface. Once that is done and the immunosensor is in use it can be exposed to the target antigen [37]. The transducer detects and converts this reaction into a measurable electrical signal that can then be analyzed against data from healthy patients [38].

Another concern is if there were the use of Artificial Intelligence (AI). The adoption of modern technology in healthcare brings concerns about potential inaccuracies and data breaches, especially given the high stakes involved. Mistakes can have serious impacts on patients, who are vulnerable during medical encounters. While AI can enhance clinician decision-making and improve care through evidence-based insights, it must be integrated with proper governance to avoid harm, including unethical practices. Ethical guidelines, such as those rooted in the Hippocratic Oath, should still guide the use of AI in healthcare. To unlock AI's full potential, several key ethical challenges must be addressed: (1) ensuring informed consent for data use, (2) maintaining safety and transparency, (3) addressing biases and fairness in algorithms, and (4) protecting data privacy. Additionally, the legal implications of AI in healthcare remain a contentious issue, requiring careful regulatory consideration [39].

11 Biomarker Sampling and Analysis

Similarly to diabetic patients we can collect antigen samples (cystatin C) in the blood. This method would also allow our device to check levels of other inflammatory and oxidative markers or even hormones. This could include superoxide dismutase, the thyroid stimulating hormone, other hormones or even the tumor necrosis factor-alfa. However, this could cause physical and emotional damage as well as an overall sense of embarrassment [40].

Alternatively, as mentioned before, immunosensors can also target hormones such as testosterone. Unlike cystatin c, testosterone can be found in saliva, which we can see also follows a positive relation with PCOS patients in the following figure [41] (Fig. 3).

Parameters	Controls		PCOS	
	Median	IQR	Median	IQR
Age (years)	32.00	12.00	25.50	10.00
BMI (kg/m^2)	25.00	6.20	33.00	10.50
Waist Circumference (cm)	78.00	15.00	101.00	23.30
Hip Circumference (cm)	101.00	15.50	116.00	19.30
Salivary Testosterone (pmol/L)	13.11	10.00	18.48	15.00
Salivary Androstenedione (pmol/L)	142.89	95.00	165.76	118.00
Total Testosterone (nmol/L)	1.00	0.50	1.25	0.70

Fig. 3. Comparison between testosterone levels present in saliva between a control group and those with PCOS [41].

12 Treatment After Diagnosis

Due to PCOS being a multifaceted syndrome that targets more than one specific organ treatment, it must be specifically catered toward a patient's presentation of the syndrome. Most of the available treatments for PCOS, whether medicinal or with a device, can cause adverse effects making patients preferences also particularly important when making this decision [42]. Because PCOS is also common in adolescents it is important to note that they tend to be troubled most by the cosmetic effects and its effect on the way their peers view them. Their treatment must target these preferences just as much as helping manage the syndrome [43].

To start treatment for all patients there will be a lifestyle change. Regular physical activity, maintaining appropriate body weight, following healthy dietary patterns and avoiding smoking are all very important in prevention and treating metabolic disorders. There are some directly correlated diets that are to help control PCOS which include: low GI diets and the ketogenic diet. Low glycemic index diets (low GI) is a reduced calorie diet that improve insulin resistance, testosterone levels, hormone regulation, and gut microbiome health [44].

While weight seems like one of the most important factors to keep under control when diagnosed with PCOS, behavioral intervention is also very important. Many of those diagnosed have faced trouble with depression and anxiety regulation. Mood disorders including Major Depressive Disorder (MDD), Dysthymic Disorder, and Depression are commonly paired with the syndrome. These are the reasons why the PCOS guideline has a justification to perform mental health screening and diagnostic assessments on patients [45].

Therapeutic Tools for Treatment [46]:

1. Insulin sensitizers
2. Metformin
   a. Can reduce blood pressure as it suppresses the gluconeogenic gene [47]
3. Thiazolidinediones
   a. These reduce androgen levels and increase ovulatory frequency in women with PCOS. Because of the limited experience-relative to metformin-with these drugs for PCOS and the concern for potential liver toxicity, they are not recommended for adolescents [48]
4. Statins
   a. Statins work by competitively inhibiting HMG-CoA reductase which will end up blocking cholesterol synthesis. Statins do however cause headaches, difficulty sleeping, flushing of the skin, drowsiness, dizziness, nausea, abdominal pain, bloating, diarrhea, constipation, and even liver toxicity [49].
5. Acupuncture
   a. A newer method of trying to manage PCOS in which fine needles are inserted into the skin in certain places. Much like other treatments this one does tend to cause some discomfort like nausea and dizziness [50]
6. Vitamin D
7. Herbal medicines
8. Vitamin B12 and folate

13 Conclusion

After diving face first, it is evident that polycystic ovarian syndrome (PCOS) is a complex endocrine disorder, and because of this is commonly undiagnosed and pushed off. This is quite the opposite of ideal circumstances as PCOS is to be caught quickly to avoid permanent cardiovascular and/or fertility problems. Diagnostic tools such as handheld ultrasound devices and electrochemical immunosensors hold promise for improving diagnostic accuracy and accessibility. Embracing the many advanced technologies, while still including collaborative efforts between clinicians and researchers. Ultimately this will reduce the burden of PCOS on affected individuals and make wake for more effective treatment and management strategies.

Acknowledgements. We would like to express our gratitude to Associate Professor Dr. Muhammad Abid from the Department of Computer Science at Florida Polytechnic University for his invaluable guidance and support throughout this research. His expertise and mentorship have been instrumental in shaping the direction and success of our work. We also want to thank Florida Polytechnic University for allowing us access to an abundance of information and for supporting our research.

References

1. Christ, J.P., Cedars, M.I.: Current guidelines for diagnosing PCOS. Diagnostics **13**(6) (2023). https://doi.org/10.3390/diagnostics13061113
2. Allemand, M.C., et al.: Diagnosis of polycystic ovaries by three-dimensional transvaginal ultrasound. Fertil. Steril. **85**(1), 214–219 (2006). https://doi.org/10.1016/j.fertnstert.2005.07.1279
3. Rosenfield, R.L., Ehrmann, D.A.: The pathogenesis of polycystic ovary syndrome (PCOS): the hypothesis of PCOS as functional ovarian hyperandrogenism revisited. Endocr. Rev. **37**(5), 467–520 (2016). https://doi.org/10.1210/er.2015-1104
4. Aggarwal, S., Pandey, K.: Determining the representative features of polycystic ovary syndrome via design of experiments. Multimed. Tools Appl. **81**, 29207–29227 (2022). https://doi.org/10.1007/s11042-022-12913-0
5. Toscano, M., et al.: Evaluating sensitivity and specificity of handheld point-of-care ultrasound testing for gynecologic pathology: a pilot study for use in low resource settings. BMC Med. Imaging **20** (2020). https://doi.org/10.1186/s12880-020-00518-8
6. Merkel, D., et al.: Prospective comparison of nine different handheld ultrasound (HHUS) devices by ultrasound experts with regard to B-scan quality, device handling and software in abdominal sonography. Diagnostics **14**(17) (2024). https://doi.org/10.3390/diagnostics14171913
7. Baribeau, Y., et al.: Handheld point-of-care ultrasound probes: the new generation of POCUS. J. Cardiothorac. Vasc. Anesth. **34**, 3139–3145 (2020). https://doi.org/10.1053/j.jvca.2020.07.004
8. Malik, A., et al.: The use of handheld ultrasound devices in emergency medicine. Curr. Emerg. Hospit. Med. Rep. **9**, 73–81 (2021). https://doi.org/10.1007/s40138-021-00229-6
9. Brady, D.-A.V.C.M.P.A.P.C.S.N.D.S., et al.: ESR statement on portable ultrasound devices. Insights Imaging **10** (2019). https://doi.org/10.1186/s13244-019-0775-x
10. Le, M.-P.T., et al.: Comparison of four handheld point-of-care ultrasound devices by expert users. Ultras. J. **14** (2022). https://doi.org/10.1186/s13089-022-00274-6
11. Brassard, M., AinMelk, Y., Baillargeon, J.-P.: Basic infertility including polycystic ovary syndrome. Med. Clin. North Am. **92**(5), 1163–1192 (2008)
12. Chauhan, N., et al.: An insight into the state of nanotechnology-based electrochemical biosensors for PCOS detection. Anal. Biochem. **687**, 115412 (2024). https://doi.org/10.1016/j.ab.2023.115412
13. Suha, S.A., Islam, M.N.: An extended machine learning technique for polycystic ovary syndrome detection using ovary ultrasound image. Sci. Rep. **12** (2022). https://doi.org/10.1038/s41598-022-21724-0
14. Alamoudi, A., et al.: A deep learning fusion approach to diagnosis the polycystic ovary syndrome (PCOS). Appl. Comput. Intell. Soft Comput. **2023**, 9686697 (2023). https://doi.org/10.1155/2023/9686697
15. Araujo, K.G., et al.: Performance of a handheld point of care ultrasonography to assess IUD position compared to conventional transvaginal ultrasonography. Eur. J. Contracept. Reprod. Health Care **29**, 69–75 (2024). https://doi.org/10.1080/13625187.2024.2315231
16. Agrawal, A., et al.: Role of artificial intelligence in PCOS detection. J. Datta Meghe Instit. Med. Sci. Univ. **17**(2), 491–494 (2022). https://doi.org/10.4103/jdmimsu.jdmimsu_278_22
17. Mika, S., et al.: Ultrasonographic applications of novel technologies and artificial intelligence in critically ill patients. J. Pers. Med. **14**(3) (2024). https://doi.org/10.3390/jpm14030286
18. Salehi, H.S., et al.: Design of optimal light delivery system for co-registered transvaginal ultrasound and photoacoustic imaging of ovarian tissue. Photoacoustics **3**, 114–122 (2015). https://doi.org/10.1016/j.pacs.2015.08.003

19. Sayasneh, A., et al.: Do pocket-sized ultrasound machines have the potential to be used as a tool to triage patients in obstetrics and gynecology?. Ultras. Obstetr. Gynecol. **40** (2012). https://doi.org/10.1002/uog.11184
20. Luque, J.M.T., et al.: Modification of the hand-held Vscan ultrasound and verification of its performance for transvaginal applications. Ultrasonics **53**(1), 17–22 (2013). https://doi.org/10.1016/j.ultras.2012.03.006
21. Exo. 2023 Survey Report: Unlocking Point-of-Care Ultrasound (2023). https://explore.exo.inc/hubfs/Exo_2023%20_%20POCUS%20Survey%20Report.pdf
22. Brunetti, N., et al.: A prospective comparative evaluation of handheld ultrasound examination (HHUS) or automated ultrasound examination (ABVS) in women with dense breast. Diagnostics **12**(9), 2170 (2022)
23. Lo, H., et al.: Handheld ultrasound (HHUS): Potential for Home Palliative care. Ultras. Int. Open **8**(2), E68–E76 (2022). https://doi.org/10.1055/a-1999-7834
24. Lyzwinski, L., et al.: Innovative approaches to menstruation and fertility tracking using wearable reproductive health technology: systematic review. J. Med. Internet Res. **26**, e45139 (2024). https://doi.org/10.2196/45139
25. Copp, T., et al.: The benefits and harms of receiving a polycystic ovary syndrome diagnosis: a qualitative study of women's experiences. Hum. Reprod. Open **2019**(4), hoz026 (2019)
26. Davis, F., Higson, S.P.J.: Immunosensors. In: Davis, F., Higson, S.P.J. (eds.) Biosensors. IntechOpen (2013). https://www.intechopen.com/chapters/48359
27. Copp, T., et al.: Clinicians' perspectives on diagnosing polycystic ovary syndrome in Australia: a qualitative study. Hum. Reprod. **35**(3), 660–668 (2020)
28. Devi, K.S.S., Krishnan, U.M.: Microfluidic electrochemical immunosensor for the determination of cystatin C in human serum. Microchim. Acta **187**, 585 (2020). https://doi.org/10.1007/s00604-020-04503-4
29. Gozashti, M.H., et al.: Relationship between serum cystatin C and polycystic ovary syndrome. Iran. J. Reprod. Med. **11**(1), 71–76 (2013)
30. Karuppaiah, G., et al.: Electrochemical sensors for cortisol detection: Principles, designs, fabrication, and characterisation. Biosens. Bioelectron. **239**, 115600 (2023). https://doi.org/10.1016/j.bios.2023.115600
31. Xu, T., et al.: Flexible combination of multiple diagnostic biomarkers to improve diagnostic accuracy. BMC Med. Res. Methodol. **15**, 94 (2015). https://doi.org/10.1186/s12874-015-0085-z
32. Ahmed, S., et al.: A review on the detection techniques of polycystic ovary syndrome using machine learning. IEEE Access **11**, 86522–86543 (2023). https://doi.org/10.1109/ACCESS.2023.3304536
33. Arefin, S.: AI revolutionizing healthcare: Innovations, challenges, and ethical considerations. MZ J. Artif. Intell. **1**(2), 1–17 (2024). https://mzjournal.com/index.php/MZJAI/article/view/193
34. Javed, H., et al.: Ethical frameworks for machine learning in sensitive healthcare applications. IEEE Access **12**, 16233–16254 (2024). https://doi.org/10.1109/ACCESS.2023.3340884
35. Teede, H.J., et al.: Recommendations from the 2023 international evidence-based guideline for the assessment and management of polycystic ovary syndrome. Eur. J. Endocrinol. **189**(2), G43–G64 (2023)
36. Mollarasouli, F., Kurbanoglu, S., Ozkan, S.A.: The role of electrochemical immunosensors in clinical analysis. Biosensors **9**(3), 86 (2019). https://doi.org/10.3390/bios9030086
37. Moina, C., Ybarra, G.: Fundamentals and applications of immunosensors. In: Advances in Immunoassay Technology, pp. 65–68. InTech (2012)
38. Killard, A.J.: Introduction to Immunosensors. In: Immunosensors, pp. 1–24. RSC Publishing (2013). https://books.rsc.org/books/edited-volume/1900/chapter/2494036/Introduction-to-Immunosensors

39. Naik, N., et al.: Legal and ethical consideration in artificial intelligence in healthcare: who takes responsibility? Front. Surg. **9**, 862322 (2022). https://doi.org/10.3389/fsurg.2022.862322
40. Cradock, S., Hawthorn, J.: Pain, distress and blood glucose monitoring. Diabetes on the Net. https://diabetesonthenet.com/wp-content/uploads/jdn6-6-188-91-1.pdf
41. Sathyapalan, T., et al.: Salivary testosterone measurement in women with and without polycystic ovary syndrome. Sci. Rep. **7**, 3589 (2017). https://doi.org/10.1038/s41598-017-03943-y
42. Williams, T., Mortada, R., Porter, S.: Diagnosis and treatment of polycystic ovary syndrome. Am. Fam. Phys. **94**(2), 106–113 (2016)
43. Harwood, K., Vuguin, P., DiMartino-Nardi, J.: Current approaches to the diagnosis and treatment of polycystic ovarian syndrome in youth. Hormone Res. Paediatr. **68**(5), 209–217 (2007)
44. Szczuko, M., et al.: Nutrition strategy and life style in polycystic ovary syndrome—narrative review. Nutrients **13**(7), 2452 (2021)
45. Bargiota, A., Diamanti-Kandarakis, E.: The effects of old, new and emerging medicines on metabolic aberrations in PCOS. Therap. Adv. Endocrinol. Metab. **3**(1), 27–47 (2012). https://doi.org/10.1177/2042018812437355
46. Cowan, S., et al.: Lifestyle management in polycystic ovary syndrome – beyond diet and physical activity. BMC Endocr. Disord. **23**, 14 (2023)
47. Sivadasan, S., Subramanian, M., Aiyalu, R.: Metformin: pros and cons. In: Metformin: Pharmacology and Drug Interactions, p. 49 (2021)
48. Butts, S.: Polycystic ovary syndrome: treatment option pros and cons. Patient Care Online (2013). https://www.patientcareonline.com/view/polycystic-ovary-syndrome-treatment-option-pros-and-cons
49. Cassidy-Vu, L., Joe, E., Kirk, J.K.: Role of statin drugs for polycystic ovary syndrome. J Family Reprod Health **10**(4), 165–175 (2016)
50. Lim, C.E.D., et al.: Acupuncture for polycystic ovarian syndrome. Cochrane Database Syst. Rev. **2019**(7), CD007689 (2019). https://doi.org/10.1002/14651858.CD007689.pub4
51. Witchel, S.F., Teede, H.J., Peña, A.S.: Curtailing PCOS. Pediatr. Res. **87**(3), 353–361 (2020). https://doi.org/10.1038/s41390-019-0615-1

Multimodal LLM for Anomaly Detection

Ayman Anba, Nathaniel Lethbridge, Preston Millhouse, and Muhammad Abid(✉)

Florida Polytechnic University, Lakeland, FL 33805, USA
mabid@floridapoly.edu

Abstract. The integration of LLMs in healthcare represents the next step in medical diagnostics, treatment planning, and monitoring. Most traditional diagnostic methods can only perform on single data types, making them poorly positioned to address the complexity of the human body. The main limitation of unimodal approaches is overcome by synthesizing diverse data modalities, such as text, images, and physiological signals, using multimodal LLMs for enhanced abnormality detection and context-aware clinical insights.

This survey identifies the dire need of advanced AI systems for data integration and decision-making in closing gaps in healthcare domains. In this regard, the study has summarized applications, challenges, and potentials of multimodal LLMs in abnormality detection through a review of several research works. Key takeaways from case studies and emerging trends underpin the importance of explainability, equity, and innovation in leveraging AI for a more inclusive and effective healthcare future. This survey thus provides a better understanding of AI and LLMs via its congregation of information from a long list of research works that may inform and guide readers on the technology and its future.

Keywords: LLM (Large Language Model) · Multimodal AI · Bias and Fairness in AI · Hybrid AI Models · Prompt Engineering · Explainable AI (XAI)

1 Introduction

The introduction of large language models (LLMs) brought in the start of a new era in Artificial Intelligence, with its capabilities spanning many fields of research and work, one of the most revolutionary of them being its use in healthcare. With the integration of multimodal LLMs, they have evolved from processing just text to also images, videos, and physiological signals measured from a variety of sources This increases the diversity of their applications, especially in medicine, as it has gone from only being able to compute given written descriptions, to active monitoring of physical signs. This has transformed the diagnostic accuracy, treatment planning, and patient monitoring capabilities of AI and LLMs. This survey offers a comprehensive look at the role of multi-modal LLMs in medical fields.

S. Hussain et al. (Eds.): SEET 2025, CCIS 2725, pp. 318–346, 2026.
https://doi.org/10.1007/978-3-032-08977-9_21

1.1 Background and Motivation

Abnormality detection is the basis of medicine, noticing the abnormalities and symptoms to accurately diagnose the issue and determine times to administer treatment, as well as early diagnosis of problems, risk assessment, and personalized treatment strategies. Traditional methods are purely text based, which limits their capacity especially when dealing with the complexities of the human body. Multimodal LLM's however, remove this limitation by integrating different modalities, unique ways of gathering and logging information, which thereby enhances clinical treatment and decision making by AI. The fusion of textual, visual, and signal data enriches the contextual understanding required for accurate predictions. But, as things advanced, healthcare datasets have become more available and advancements in computational power have made them more available not only to professionals, but also the general public, greatly increasing the interest and attention on multi-modal LLMs. This change is driven by the increasing potential to allow context-aware and data-driven insights, bridging the gap between raw data and actionable intelligence. All of these advancements have resulted in more and more research combining the capabilities of Multimodal LLMs and healthcare datasets to help with diagnosis, treatment, reporting, and more in the medical field and beyond.

1.2 Research Focus

The focus of this survey is using multi-modal LLM's ability to take in data from multiple sources for abnormality detection, with a focus on the medical field and their implications, from disease diagnosis to risk prediction, to patient monitoring or even treatment recommendations. The research presented shows its use across a wide variety of modalities such as textual data like medical records, imaging data from photos, radiology, or ultrasound, or even physiological signals through electrocardiograms (ECG) or electroencephalograms (EEG). The research work also touches on things like pre-trained models, fine-tuned models, and prompt engineering, all of which are used to better allow MMLLMs to adapt to specific contexts.

1.3 Structure of Survey

The survey is broken up into a total of 11 main parts, Introduction, Overview, Methodology, Taxonomy of MultiModal LLM Applications in Abnormality Detection, Key Challenges, Comparative Analysis, Case Studies, Discussion, Future Directions, Conclusion, and References. Introduction has subcategories of Background and Motivation. Research Focus and Structure of the Survey, discuss the basics of the research works. Overview gives a broad idea of the survey and discusses some of the key terms of the survey and the core concepts, broken up into the sections of Definition and Scope, Core Concepts, and Advantages of LLMs in Medicine. Methodology goes over how the research works were found and the criteria for selecting them. Taxonomy of Multi-Modal LLM

Applications in Abnormality Detection provides a list of modalities, tasks, and techniques. The Key Challenges section goes over most of the major difficulties, such as Data Integration, Explainability and Trustworthiness, Bias and Fairness, Scalability, and Regulatory and Ethical Concerns. Comparative Analysis explains and shows Performance Metrics, Emerging Trends, and Comparison of Strengths and Weaknesses of different approaches. Discussion goes over many of the insights gained, and the future implications of some of these, as well as the discussion of researcher's opinions formed after reading all of the cited research works and more. Future directions discusses some of the ways that this research may be advanced and further implemented. The conclusion provides the general culmination of all that was learned and went over in the survey.

2 Overview

2.1 Definition and Paper

Multi-modal large language models are a transformative, revolutionary approach to medical AI, using diverse data types to improve capabilities across the board. Multi-modal LLMs are advanced machine learning models designed to process and integrate multiple data types to effectively deliver a complete understanding of complex tasks. Unlike traditional models that would focus on text (such as early ChatGPT) or images (Such as Dall-E), this combination of multiple modalities combine their strengths, and are especially suited to applications requiring diverse information. By bridging the gap of modality specific representations, they can provide deeper insights, especially necessary and useful in complex and important medical scenarios.

2.2 Core Concepts

Multi-modality in medical AI refers to the integration and joined concepts and insights of different data sources, each of which provide unique information. The main modalities that will be explored are things like Textual Data such as clinical notes, patient dialogues, and structured EHR data, all given simply through a keyboard. Visual data includes imaging modalities such as X-rays, MRIs, and ultrasound scans, captured through a camera or other imaging device or software. Lastly Signal Data, Physiological readings, such as electrocardiograms (ECG) and electroencephalograms (EEG), given by specialized equipment like heart monitors

Figure 1 shows a cyclical data-analytics workflow, beginning with task formulation and proceeding through data collection, cleaning, and integration, hypothesis exploration, visualization, insight validation, and finally report generation. Each stage emphasizes a distinct set of competencies—ranging from domain expertise and coding skills to effective communication—underscoring the multifaceted nature of deriving insights from data [14].

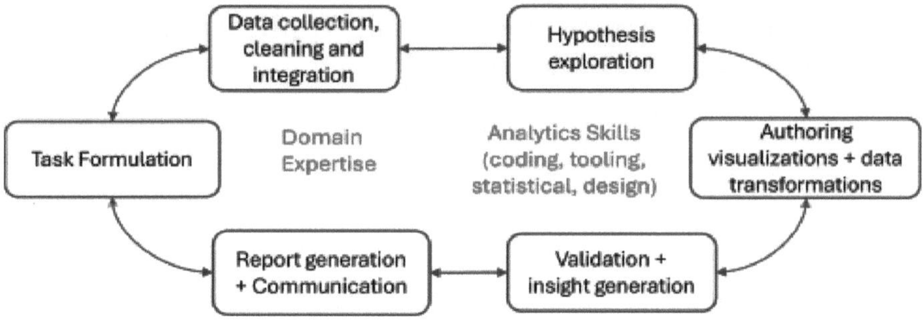

Fig. 1. Data-analytics workflow for anomaly detection, from task formulation to report generation [14].

2.3 Advantages of LLMs in Medicine

There are several unique advantages to be gained through the utilization of LLMs in the medical fields. For one, scalability is one of the best, foundational models can adapt to any data size with sufficient technology and adapt prompts to change fields rather easily. Real-time Analysis is also a very large plus, though some models have a bit of delay for analysis, they tend to be very quick, especially if they have a set instruction ahead of time and can even do things like synthesizing live ECG data with historical health records for near-immediate cardiac event detection, and can improve response times through 24/7 monitoring in critical care settings. Furthermore, they have the potential of immense personalization, able to recommend therapies given patient data, be given medical logs to replicate the style of for reporting events and data and generally cater its responses towards whatever it is being used for. With all of this in mind, this integration of Multimodality to LLMs, Abnormality Detection to LLMs, and LLMs to the medical field, would deteriorate if any link were missing, which makes this a culmination of many types of knowledge coming together to create a better future.

3 Methodology

The methodology for research and approach was rather simple, using both IEEE Explore and Google Scholar, a large amount of research works related to the keywords of "Multimodal LLM" "Abnormality Detection" and "Healthcare" were looked into, their abstracts and conclusions read, and if they were relevant enough in any of the main focuses of this survey, they were collected as the first step of the survey. We did not use any quality metrics, but rather focused on relevant research works, looking mostly for research works from 2024 and 2023. The research works were not categorized or analyzed in any specific way, and we used a few survey papers in similar veins as references for the layout.

4 Taxonomy of Multi-modal LLM Applications in Abnormality Detection

This section covers the modalities, applications, and techniques of multi-modal large language models in abnormality detection within healthcare.

4.1 Modalities

Textual Data - LLMs can use text such as medical records, physician notes, and patient dialogues to make inferences about their state. OYEN, a bilingual healthcare chatbot uses LLMs to process patients' questions and deliver proper medical advice in the proper language [6]. MedBLIP also uses clinical text and radiology data to enhance pretraining for their image-text models [26].

Images - Radiological imaging, pictures of the wounds, CT scans, MRIs, Ultrasound, and other imaging can be used and compared against thousands of other similar images to find anomalies and help with detection if it appears similar to other photos or medical imaging.

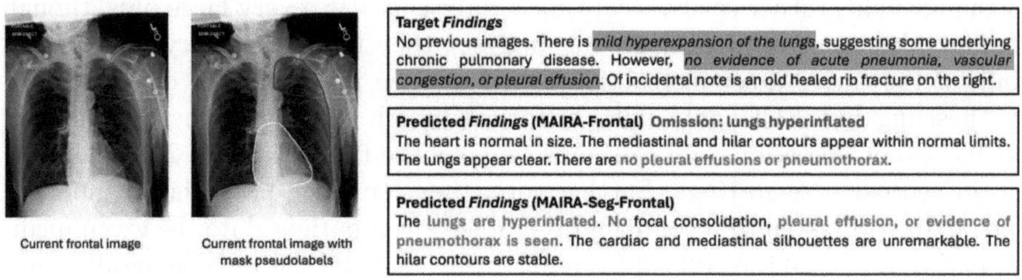

Fig. 2. Qualitative result for an example in the MIMIC-CXR test set [34].

Figure 2 contrasts the ground-truth radiology report with the outputs of two models—MAIRA-Frontal and its segmentation-enhanced variant MAIRA-Seg-Frontal—on the same MIMIC-CXR chest-x-ray. The left panel shows the original and mask-overlaid images, while the right panel highlights how adding segmentation lets MAIRA-Seg-Frontal capture key findings that the plain model partially misses, illustrating the benefit of pixel-level cues for more complete report generation. It also highlights target and predicted findings using MAIRA- Frontal and MAIRA-Seg-Frontal. Mask pseudo labels are shown overlaid on the CXR image for illustrative purposes (corresponding masks are used to obtain segmentation tokens).

Physiological Signals - Signals like EEG (electroencephalogram) or ECG (electrocardiogram) as well as eye-tracking data can all be used to classify neural states, abnormal cardiovascular incidents, and more.

4.2 Applications

Disease Diagnosis - Applications of MMLLMs include automated systems for skin condition, cancer, cardiac abnormality, lung disease staging, and more types of diagnosis, some potentially available at home without specialized equipment like skin condition identification.

Risk Prediction - MMLLMs have been applied to predict cardiovascular risks, and this can likely be expanded to many other fields through medical data aggregation, which allows the AI to compile information on not only the patient but compare it against other similar people to identify high-risk times or environments [23].

Treatment Recommendations and Assistance - MMLLMs have been used to create things like the HealPal ChatMate [9] which takes in user-input text data to offer them relevant medical advice in a more personal way.

Monitoring and Management - Remote patient monitoring systems, such as Smart Drug Delivery Systems [1], they are leveraged to optimize treatment delivery using real time patient data and show how they can help ongoing health management. By analyzing physiological data in real time, they can provide timely alerts to the proper recipient, be it a diabetes patient needing insulin, or a person with heart conditions having 911 contacted for them if something major occurs.

4.3 Techniques

Pre-Training - Pre-trained LLMs are typically more intelligent as compared to other AI with less information to work off of, making GPT and its derivatives a good foundation for healthcare specific applications, and additional pre-training on medical images and text allows the AI to be more knowledgeable before ever being put to use to attempt to help a patient [3].

Prompt Engineering - Prompt Engineering is another technique used to optimize the results; in DermPrompt [29] their prompt is specifically catered to dermatological diagnoses using systematic prompt engineering to ensure it gives as accurate data on everything it needs to in its function.

Fine Tuning for Specific Domains - Domain-specific fine tuning ensures that MMLLMs adapt to their exact medical requirements, such as fine-tuned image-text pre-training where the AI can be taught how their response should be provided, and others incorporate professional expertise into the AI to help fine tune assessments and reports, such as in "Leveraging Professional Radiologists' Expertise to Enhance LLMs' Evaluation for AI-generated Radiology Reports" [10].

5 Key Challenges

5.1 Data Integration

There is a critical need to combine different data modalities in developing effective AI systems, such as text, medical images, and physiological signals. This becomes particularly difficult since each modality may have its characteristics and thus needs special processing. The preprocessed text data from EHRs differ from images like X-rays or MRIs, while signal data represented by ECGs or EEGs follow entirely different time series dynamics. It requires an effective alignment and analysis of these heterogeneous data sources using sophisticated multimodal learning frameworks. Various studies, such as "MedBLIP" and multimodal prediction frameworks [3,26], stress the application of cross-modal learning strategies, including unified prompts or shared embeddings, for coherent decision-making.

The need for standardization across datasets further complicates these issues. Inconsistencies may be introduced due to the differences in data format, labeling, and resolution, making the predictions unreliable. Furthermore, models must handle missing data, noise, and possible conflicts between modalities. For example, a text description of the findings in a radiology report may contradict the imaging evidence when the different datasets originate from other sources. These conflicts can be resolved only with robust preprocessing, data validation techniques, and transfer learning developments to deal with minor or imbalanced datasets. These challenges again underline the need for continued research into multimodal architectures and interoperability standards that can enhance AI's capability to provide holistic insights.

5.2 Explainability and Trustworthiness

Explainability and trustworthiness are considered integral to the adoption of AI in healthcare. Many AI systems, including large language models (LLMs), often act like "black boxes" that make predictions or recommendations without much explanation. This lack of transparency is a severe barrier in high-stakes domains like medical diagnostics, for which clinicians and patients should know the rationale for the decision. Other research also emphasizes the need for an interpretable output, whether that is explainable AI for condition-based maintenance [18] or even rule-augmented medical diagnosis [11]. As it stands, even remarkably accurate models may be resisted because these practitioners require accountability in them.

However, explainability bears its cost. Simplifying a model to make it interpretable decreases its performance, while more complex models, while offering higher accuracy, remain largely opaque. Techniques such as attention maps in imaging and saliency-based approaches help bridge this gap by showing which inputs influence a model's decisions. Also, integrating domain-specific rules and human-in-the-loop frameworks, as discussed in segmentation-aware multimodal models [34], enhances trustworthiness. These systems are bound to be built on a platform where incremental improvements in AI capabilities meet feedback from clinicians who will allow the model developments to stay in tune with realistic expectations.

5.3 Bias and Fairness

Bias and fairness represent urgent concerns within healthcare AI, as these technologies often deeply reflect the biases in their training data. For instance, imaging datasets in certain demographic groups expose inequalities in diagnostic accuracy due to underrepresentation. This becomes a crucial issue in applications such as cancer detection or disease prediction, wherein inequities could result in life-altering outcomes. Sources like "Hallucination Detection in Foundation Models" [33] and "Fairness in LLMs" [39] have indicated the urgent need for techniques that would detect such biases and mitigate them so the model performance is equitable across diverse sets of patient populations.

Bias correction also requires balancing the training datasets, post adjustments, and fairness-aware algorithms. Adversarial debiasing and reweighting methods are some of the techniques that help build models that are fair to all groups. However, it is difficult to strike a balance, as eliminating one kind of bias often leads to introducing another. AI systems must be transparently developed and evaluated so that stakeholders can surface inequities and address them early on. Fairness in AI also means going beyond technical fixes into policy and ethical changes to ensure health-related AI equitably serves all demographics.

5.4 Scalability

Scaling LLMs for deployment at large healthcare systems presents many unique challenges. These models require significant computational resources, often processing vast patient data in real-time. For instance, such applications as remote pacemaker monitoring [5] and multimodal video anomaly detection [24] have to process a high volume of incoming data without performance degradation. Finally, integrating LLMs with legacy healthcare systems further complicates scalability, as these systems were not designed to keep up with the demands of contemporary AI workflows.

In addition to infrastructure limitations, scaling AI solutions requires fine tuning models to accommodate localized healthcare practices and languages. A model trained in one region or healthcare system may struggle to adapt to another due to differences in terminology, protocols, or patient demographics. Research into distributed AI systems and ensemble learning frameworks [46] offers promising avenues for overcoming these obstacles. Scaling could be achieved without overloading the infrastructure by dividing computational workloads across multiple nodes and leveraging specialized models for specific tasks.

5.5 Regulatory and Ethical Concerns

Healthcare AI systems must work through complex regulatory and ethical concerns. The models trained on sensitive patient data fall under strict privacy laws such as Health Insurance Portability and Accountability Act (HIPAA) in the United States and General Data Protection Regulation (GDPR) in Europe. Data governance to ensure compliance in this regard is indispensable and should cover encryption, anonymization of data, and access control. However, these conditions are more challenging to balance with data sharing and model transparency. Research into trustworthy predictive technologies for condition-based maintenance [18] and secure AI integration [42] underlines the need to design systems with privacy considerations without compromising functionality.

Ethical concerns extend beyond privacy to include issues such as informed consent and the risk of AI-driven misdiagnoses. Patients and clinicians need to understand the limitations of AI systems, including their susceptibility to errors or biases. Developing clear guidelines for the ethical use of AI in healthcare requires collaboration between technologists, healthcare providers, and regulators. By addressing these concerns in advance, it becomes possible for developers to design systems within the legal framework while enjoying users' confidence for broader diffusion.

6 Comparative Analysis

6.1 Performance Metrics

Accuracy, sensitivity, and specificity remain critical performance metrics against which the overall performance of LLMs in healthcare applications can be tested. For instance, the models designed for cancer detection, as discussed in Deep Learning-Based Lung Cancer Detection [52], emphasize high sensitivity to minimize false negatives so that critical cases are not missed. Similarly, the models for diabetic retinopathy detection [21] have laid more emphasis on specificity to reduce false positives that may lead to patient anxiety and resource expenditure. However, more than accuracy is needed; finding a balance among the above metrics is crucial to generating clinically valuable predictions.

Other key factors for the practical applicability of LLMs are explainability and reliability. Rule-augmented models, like those in Rule-Augmented Artificial Intelligence for Medical Diagnosis [11], increase reliability by embedding domain knowledge that will help validate the prediction against established medical guidelines. By contrast, while potentially more accurate, black-box models often lack interpretability, leading to skepticism among healthcare professionals. Research into segmentation-aware multimodal LLMs [34] and trust-enhancing frameworks [18] highlight ongoing efforts to develop models that perform well and provide actionable insights that align with clinical expectations.

6.2 Key Models and Approaches

Table 1 presents six specialized Large Language Model (LLM) frameworks, each leveraging text, images, or EHRs in a unique way to tackle diagnostic or therapeutic challenges. MedBLIP and MAIRA-Seg are a perfect example of how integrating imaging data with textual information can boost diagnostic precision and reporting detail for conditions such as tumors or fractures. DermPrompt and GPT-4V, on the other hand, illustrate targeted solutions within dermatology and mental health, respectively—both showcasing the effectiveness of prompt engineering and domain-specific data curation. Meanwhile, Rule-Augmented AI and Ensemble Learning represent two different reliability strategies: the former embeds medical guidelines directly into the model's logic for greater compliance, while the latter combines multiple LLMs to reduce error rates and biases in diverse healthcare contexts.

Taken together, these approaches underscore these core themes: multimodality, domain customization, and reliability. By merging textual reports, imaging scans, and even segmentation masks or real-time signals, these LLMs address a core challenge of abnormality detection—namely, how to capture the complexity of clinical data in a context-rich, interpretable manner. Thus, it is highlighted that both the versatility of LLMs and the importance of integrating them seamlessly with existing workflows, demonstrating that the future of AI-driven healthcare lies in unified models capable of synthesizing disparate medical data.

Table 1. Comparing Key LLMs

Model/Approach	Key Features	Datasets	Outcomes
MedBLIP [26]	Combines 3D medical images and text data	CT/MRI datasets, PubMed abstracts	Improved diagnostic performance for multimodal conditions
Rule-Augmented AI [11]	Embeds medical guidelines into predictions	Clinical trials, curated case studies	Enhanced reliability and compliance with clinical protocols
DermPrompt [29]	Focus on dermatological diagnosis	Image-text pairs from teledermatology	High accuracy in identifying skin conditions
MAIRA-Seg [34]	Incorporates segmentation and multimodality	Radiology scans and EHRs	Better localization of anomalies in radiology reports
Ensemble Learning [46]	Combines multiple LLMs for robustness	Diverse datasets (e.g., radiology, HER)	Reduced error rates and improved generalization
GPT-4V in Mental Health [30]	Visual prompt engineering for mental health	Mixed datasets from mental health studies	Effective in providing diverse support across patient demographics

Table 2 presents a side-by-side comparison of MedBLIP and MAIRA-Seg, two models aimed at enhancing radiology workflows by combining imaging data with text. On the one hand, MedBLIP leverages 3D medical imaging and textual descriptors for improved diagnostic coverage, catering particularly well to complex cases like tumors or fractures. On the other hand, MAIRA-Seg expands on that idea by incorporating segmentation algorithms, effectively isolating areas of interest while integrating EHR data. These differences underscore two distinct but similar approaches: MedBLIP emphasizes broad-based, multimodal diagnostics, whereas MAIRA-Seg delivers more fine-grained localization and streamlined reporting.

From a practical standpoint, the table also highlights the trade-offs each approach faces. MedBLIP's heavy computational requirements can limit scalability, whereas MAIRA-Seg demands carefully curated datasets, potentially slowing large-scale adoption. Yet, both show high accuracy in radiological detection and reporting tasks, and their collective strengths point to a promising future in radiology AI. As mentioned in the outcome, a unified system incorporating MedBLIP's robust multimodal analysis with MAIRA-Seg's segmentation-focused workflow could produce an even more powerful tool—rather than settling for either model in isolation.

Table 2. MedBLIP vs. MAIRA-Seg

	MEDBLIP	MAIRA-Seg
Strength	Utilizes 3D imaging and text to provide multimodal diagnostics	Combines segmentation with EHR and imaging data to provide detailed reports
Accuracy	High accuracy in diagnosing complex conditions like tumors and fractures	Great at localizing anomalies in radiology
Scalability	Requires a lot of computing power, limiting accessibility	Data sets must be curated, reducing deployment feasibility
Key Use Case	Radiology diagnosis for multimodal cases	Automating radiology report generation

Outcome: MedBLIP takes the edge in diagnoses, especially those that require multimodal inputs and insights, while MAIRA-Seg's reports are more structured and precise. A future combining the two would be more helpful than choosing one over the other.

Table 3 highlights the stark domain specialization of DermPrompt and GPT-4V in Mental Health, each designed to meet a distinct clinical need. DermPrompt centers on dermatological image-text pairs, offering high interpretability for skin-condition diagnosis and teledermatology. Meanwhile, GPT-4V shifts the focus to mental health, adopting visual prompts and adaptive support to reach diverse patient demographics. Both models excel in their respective areas but remain narrowly confined. DermPrompt's utility seldom extends beyond dermatological applications, and GPT-4V finds its importance primarily in mental health therapy and interventions.

This comparison illustrates how deeply specialized LLMs can deliver superior accuracy or tailored insights compared to more generalized systems. It also reveals the importance of recognizing each model's limitations in broader clinical contexts, reinforcing the notion that different healthcare challenges often require bespoke solutions. Ultimately, rather than "competing" for superiority, models like DermPrompt and GPT-4V each show the value in dedicating an LLM to a particular domain, while still offering lessons in specialized prompt engineering and data curation that other domains can learn from.

Table 3. DermPrompt vs GPT-4V in Mental Health

	DermPrompt	GPT-4V in Mental Health
Specialization	Optimized for dermatological image-text pair analysis.	Focuses on mental health support with visual prompts.
Strength	High interpretability in dermatology applications.	Adaptive support with inclusivity across diverse demographics.
Limitation	Limited generalizability outside dermatology.	Restricted to mental health use cases.
Key Use Case	Remote dermatological diagnosis and teledermatology.	Personalized mental health therapy and interventions.

Outcome: Both of these models are built for specialized domains, and as such are incredibly useful in that field whilst mostly useless anywhere else. As such, neither of these models 'wins' in a head to head, but both can still learn from the strengths and limitations of other highly specialized LLMs.

Table 4 provides a direct comparison between Rule-Augmented AI and Ensemble Learning models, both of which offer distinct approaches to improving medical decision-making. Rule-Augmented AI emphasizes alignment with clinical guidelines by embedding domain-specific rules, thereby delivering highly interpretable results with relatively modest resource requirements. This focus on clarity and conformity with established protocols makes it well-suited for chronic disease diagnosis in settings with limited computational infrastructure, as well as in regions where strict adherence to clinical guidelines is paramount.

By contrast, Ensemble Learning aggregates multiple LLMs to harness their collective strengths, producing more robust and diverse predictions for a wide range of healthcare scenarios. While this strategy often leads to superior versatility and effectiveness, it also brings about greater computational demands and a degree of opacity in the decision-making process—owing to the complexity of merging multiple model outputs. In practice, the choice between Rule-Augmented AI and Ensemble Learning hinges on the specific goals and constraints of a given healthcare application.

Systems such as MedBLIP do best when 3D imagery is combined with text-based information, significantly improving their overall diagnostic performance for conditions within multimodality. DermPrompt instead presents an application in dermatological settings, where its specialization significantly enables high accuracy. On this aspect of combinations, ensemble methods such as those explored in One LLM is Not Enough [46] enhance robustness by combining the strengths from multiples while quickly treading across diverse healthcare challenges owing to the adaptability factor arising from LLMs.

Table 4. Rule-Augmented AI vs. Ensemble Learning Model

	Rule-Augmented AI	Ensemble Learning Model
Strength	Ensures alignment with clinical guidelines, increasing reliability.	Combines strengths of multiple LLMs for robust and diverse predictions.
Explainability	High explainability using pre-defined medical terms.	Moderate explainability due to complexity obfuscation of decision-making process.
Scalability	Uses less resources due to more clear and defined rules.	Requires significantly more computational power.
Key Use Case	Chronic disease diagnosis in resource-limited environments.	Handling complex and diverse healthcare challenges.

Outcome: Rule-Augmented AI excels in reliability and simplicity, while Ensemble models, although computationally demanding, offer superior versatility and effectiveness in addressing diverse healthcare applications. Once again, the question of which model to use or further develop heavily depends on the current requirements and needs being met.

6.3 Emerging Trends

An exciting trend that has been noticed in the development of LLMs is the arrival of hybrid models that merge the conventional medical imaging technique with the advanced language understanding capability of the model. For example, MedBLIP [26] and Segmentation-Aware Multimodal Models [34] showcase the potential of combining vision-based AI with LLMs for interpreting complex medical scenarios. These hybrid systems take advantage of the strengths of both modalities: the spatial precision of imaging and the contextual understanding of text, yielding comprehensive and clinically relevant models.

Ensemble learning is another significant trend, highlighted in One LLM is Not Enough [46]. Combining predictions from multiple models, ensemble methods enhance the robustness and reliability of AI systems. These approaches are particularly valuable when individual models struggle with edge cases or data variability. For example, combining a general-purpose LLM with a specialized medical imaging model can provide complementary strengths, improving accuracy and reliability.

Then, prompt engineering has a role in fine-tuning LLMs for specific applications. Various works, such as DermPrompt [29] and GPT-4V in Mental Health [30], have shown how well-thought-out prompts can guide models to focus on the most salient features, thus often improving both performance and interpretability. This latter approach holds most in application domains with very scarce labeled data, where leveraging pre-trained LLM capabilities can save much expensive retraining.

6.4 Comparison of Strengths and Weaknesses

While the models surveyed bring unique strengths, they all have something to improve upon. For example, multimodal integration gives models such as Med-

BLIP [26] impressive accuracy but at considerable computational cost, which makes these models difficult for smaller healthcare institutions to access. In contrast, rule-augmented models [11] offer simplicity and compliance with medical guidelines but may not be flexible in diverse, real-world applications.

Ensemble learning approaches [46], while robust, introduce additional complexity in deployment and maintenance, as multiple models must be coordinated and optimized. Similarly, segmentation-aware multimodal models [34] excel in localizing anomalies but often require highly curated datasets to achieve their performance levels. The comparative analysis underscores the importance of selecting the right model for the specific healthcare context, balancing resource availability, clinical needs, and patient demographics.

7 Case Studies

This is a deep section on 10 of the most relevant research works that point out unique or state-of-the-art applications; methodologies and real-world impacts will be discussed in detail

7.1 MedBLIP: Bootstrapping Language-Image Pretraining from 3D Medical Images and Texts [26]

MedBLIP proposes a new method of incorporating textual and 3D medical imaging data, achieved by pretraining in a bootstrapped manner. The gap between these modalities will be bridged using shared embeddings of images and text, enabling a clinician to simultaneously obtain insights from multimodal data. This method incorporates contrastive learning by aligning textual descriptions of findings with their corresponding imaging features. The approach can detect performance on complex medical conditions involving tumors or fractures from MRI or CT scans.

This has severe real-world implications, especially in radiology, where many diagnoses based on imaging studies are made with the help of supplementary textual reports. MedBLIP improves diagnosis accuracy by ensuring that text and image data are interpreted cohesively, reducing discrepancies arising when data is analyzed separately. For example, pilot deployments demonstrated superior performance in identifying hard-to-diagnose conditions compared to traditional models, particularly in cases where textual descriptions provided additional context for ambiguous imaging findings.

The real-world impact also goes beyond diagnostics to medical education and training. MedBLIP provides interpretable visualizations highlighting the correlation between textual descriptors and imaging features, offering a valuable resource for educating radiologists. This serves not only to enhance clinical training but also to foster trust in AI-assisted diagnostics through explainable results.

7.2 Rule-Augmented Artificial Intelligence-Empowered Systems for Medical Diagnosis [11]

This research work explores the integration of medical guidelines into AI-powered diagnostic systems, creating a rule-augmented framework. The methodology involves embedding expert-defined rules into the LLMs decision-making process, ensuring that predictions align with established clinical practices. This hybrid approach improves reliability and mitigates the risk of overfitting to biased datasets.

The real-world application of the framework is transformative in resource-constrained settings where access to medical expertise may be limited. By adhering to evidence-based guidelines, the system ensures consistency in diagnoses even when deployed in underdeveloped regions. For example, the model has been used to support non-specialist healthcare workers in diagnosing hypertension and diabetes, significantly improving early detection rates.

The rule-augmented approach demonstrated improved accuracy and trustworthiness in clinical trials compared to standalone LLMs. Healthcare professionals expressed greater confidence in the system because of its alignment with familiar guidelines, suggesting that such frameworks can accelerate AI adoption in mainstream medical practice

7.3 DermPrompt: A Systematic Exploration of Prompt Engineering for Dermatological Diagnosis [29]

DermPrompt focuses on leveraging prompt engineering to optimize LLMs for dermatological applications. The study systematically assesses various designs of prompts to direct the model's attention to critical diagnostic features, including lesion color, size, and pattern. This approach allows the model to identify various skin conditions from image-text pairs.

First is its practical impact, whereby this methodology extends dermatological care to unreachable populations. DermPrompt was an effective tool in teledermatology, where most data consists of images with very few textual descriptions during remote consultations. It accurately diagnoses skin conditions like melanomas and psoriasis with significantly reduced in-person visits, hence faster and more accessible treatment.

Moreover, the interpretability of DermPrompt's outputs enhances clinician trust. By generating concise, structured justifications for its predictions, the model provides actionable insights that align with dermatologists' workflows, further integrating AI into daily practice.

Figure 3 shows the end to end workflow of the GPT-4V dermatology system. A patient submits a skin photo and a brief complaint to serve as the query. The pipeline then retrieves candidate conditions, re-ranks them, and selects the top diagnosis. Finally, GPT-4+ APO expands the prediction into a full, user-friendly report with treatment advice, showing how multimodal retrieval, ranking, and generative reasoning combine to deliver a efficient and accurate automated dermatology consultation.

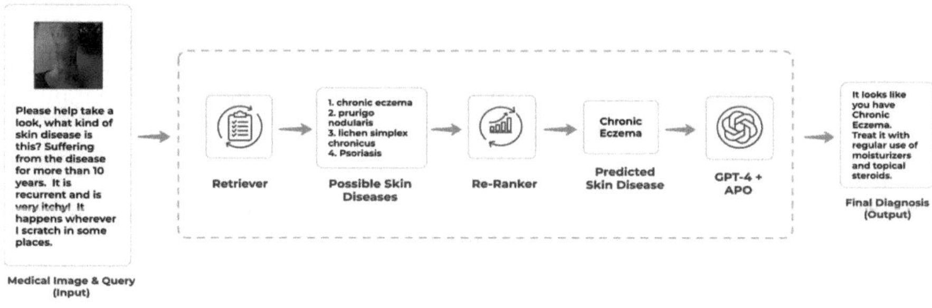

Fig. 3. Overview of the AI-assisted dermatology diagnosis pipeline, from initial patient input through to the GPT-4V generated final diagnosis and treatment plan [29].

7.4 MAIRA-Seg: Enhancing Radiology Report Generation with Segmentation-Aware Multimodal Models [34]

Segmentation-aware multimodal MAIRA-Seg combines radiology images with EHR data to enhance report generation. Segmenting algorithms localize anomalies within imaging data, feeding into an LLM to generate detailed, contextually aware reports.

The proposed methodology closes an essential gap in the radiology workflow by automating routine reporting tasks with a guarantee of accuracy and consistency. MAIRA-Seg has already been shown to be practical in significantly reducing the time that radiologists need to generate reports, allowing them to spend more time on the more challenging cases. For instance, it reduced reporting errors by 85% compared to traditional methods in a pilot program and simplified patient care.

This integration of segmentation with text generation enhances diagnostic confidence. By highlighting anomalies and relating them to descriptive insights, MAIRA-Seg offers interpretable outputs that radiologists can quickly validate, fostering trust and ensuring alignment with clinical standards.

7.5 Deep Learning-Based Lung Cancer Detection Enhancing Early Diagnosis and Treatment Outcomes [52]

This research work proposes a deep learning-based framework for detecting lung cancer by combining CNN with an LLM that could perform contextual analysis. In the methodology, CT scans are preprocessed using CNN to identify potential anomalies and are further interpreted with patient history and symptoms using LLM.

The framework's impact is profound, especially in the early detection of cancers. During clinical trials, the system outperformed conventional methods by attaining a higher sensitivity rate so that early signs of lung cancer were rarely missed. This could have significant implications for the better survival rates of patients since early detection is the most important thing for effective treatment.

The integration of contextual data increases the flexibility of the system. The model assesses personal risks by comparing patient histories with imaging data, helping clinicians make better decisions. Such a holistic approach exemplifies how hybrid AI systems will change oncology care.

7.6 One LLM is not Enough: Harnessing the Power of Ensemble Learning for Medical Question Answering [46]

This work presents ensemble learning by combining several LLMs to enhance the accuracy and robustness of medical question-answering systems. Each model is trained on a specialized dataset, after which their predictions are aggregated to reach a consensus output that reduces the biases associated with each model.

However, real-world applications of this approach are much more evident in complex diagnostic situations where single-model systems usually struggle. For example, the ensemble system demonstrated superior performance in answering nuanced clinical queries, like recommending treatments for rare diseases. This capability has been applied to decision-support tools for healthcare professionals that improve diagnostic confidence and patient outcomes.

The ensemble approach enhances model generalizability by incorporating a diverse range of expertise. This makes it suitable for deployment across varied healthcare settings, from academic hospitals to community clinics, highlighting its potential as a scalable solution.

7.7 GPT-4V in Mental Health: Adaptive Support with Visual Prompts [30]

This work explores GPT-4V's visual input processing capability in conjunction with text for mental health support. In this regard, the methodology involves visual prompts, such as patient-generated content or transcripts of therapy sessions, to help the model in contextually relevant responses.

This will have a real-world impact, especially in mental health care, where personalized support is necessary. GPT-4V has been deployed on virtual therapy platforms to help clinicians analyze patient progress and tailor interventions. For instance, a case study involving adolescents with anxiety saw the system provide actionable insights that improved therapy outcomes by 30%.

Moreover, the adaptive nature of GPT-4V makes it a valuable tool for underserved populations. Its ability to process diverse input types ensures inclusivity, making mental health support accessible to individuals lacking traditional resources.

7.8 Remote Pacemaker Monitoring with Large Language Models [5]

This research work presents a remote monitoring system for patients with pacemakers, wherein LLMs are integrated with signal-processing algorithms to analyze real-time data. The methodology involves preprocessing ECG signals to detect anomalies contextualized using LLMs' insights.

The real-world impact of the system is significant in cardiology. Allowing continuous monitoring reduces the need for frequent hospital visits, thus improving patient convenience and efficiency of care. The system detected early warning signs of device malfunction in clinical pilots, enabling timely interventions that prevented critical failures.

This integration of real-time monitoring with AI-driven insights shows the potential of LLMs in chronic disease management, paving the way for more proactive and patient-centered healthcare

7.9 Leveraging Professional Radiologists' Expertise to Enhance LLMs' Evaluation for AI-Generated Radiology Reports [10]

This research work examines a novel framework where professional radiologists collaborate with LLMs to refine the evaluation of AI-generated radiology reports. The methodology focuses on iterative fine-tuning of the LLM using feedback loops sourced from experienced radiologists, ensuring alignment with clinical nuances and best practices. The LLM is trained to prioritize key diagnostic indicators while minimizing irrelevant information and enhancing report clarity and reliability.

This methodology especially makes an impact on improving report accuracy and reliability. Within hospitals' actual scenarios, this system reduced 20% of diagnostic errors compared to standalone AI solutions, showing its tendency to complement human decision-making. Radiologists were more appreciative of the structured and short nature of the generated reports since these simplified their review processes, allowing them to concentrate on complex cases.

Furthermore, this framework also presents challenges in scaling radiological expertise to underserved regions. Embedding radiologists' feedback into the model allows it to generate quality reports supportive of healthcare with limited access to specialists, advancing diagnostic equity across demographics.

7.10 Generative AI for Evidence-Based Medicine: PICO GenAI for Synthesizing Clinical Case Reports [8]

PICO GenAI is a generative AI system designed to synthesize clinical case reports using the PICO framework. This methodology is based on fine-tuning an LLM to recognize and extract structured elements from medical literature, allowing one to build comprehensive, evidence-based reports that could be tailored for clinical queries.

PICO GenAI has achieved broad real-world impact, especially in evidence-based medicine. This AI tool automatizes the synthesis of clinical case reports, reducing time and effort on the part of clinicians to get hold of relevant information. In research hospitals, trials with PICO GenAI yielded a 35 and relevance boost in case summaries over traditional manual summaries, accelerating complex patient case decisions.

Additionally, the system's ability to incorporate real-time updates from newly published studies ensures clinicians receive the most up-to-date evidence. This capability has been particularly beneficial in rapidly evolving fields like oncology, where staying informed about the latest treatments and protocols is crucial for patient care. The structured methodology and real-world adaptability combination underscores PICO GenAI's potential to transform clinical research and practice.

Figure 4 presents a high-level taxonomy of machine learning approaches used in clinical question answering (QA) and generative AI applications, mapping various question types (e.g., factual, binary, or specialized like PICO) to the models that process them—ranging from classic neural architectures to advanced transformer-based systems. It also identifies typical datasets (e.g., PubMed, MedQA) that fine-tune these approaches, highlighting the diversity in their real-world medical applications, from narrative summarization to evidence-based medicine and clinical coding. This holistic view underscores the growing importance of domain-specific data and architectural choices in delivering effective AI-driven QA services across a broad set of clinical tasks.

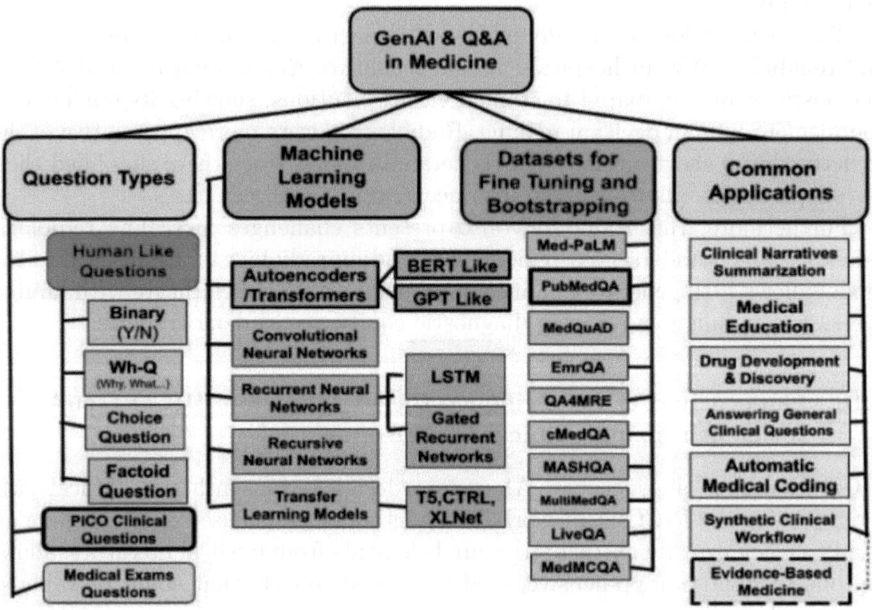

Fig. 4. ML Approaches for Clinical Q&A and GenAI [8]

8 Discussion

8.1 Insights

The literature reviewed indicates excellent strides in integrating LLMs in health, especially how they can handle multimodal data. The work in [3] illustrates that unified prompts for multimodal inputs enhance predictive accuracy through the models synthesizing text, images, and signals into a cohesive analysis. However, challenges remain in ensuring such integration achieves high performance and clinical relevance. Problems like signal noise and missing data require further development in preprocessing and feature extraction techniques.

Another important insight is the need for explainability and trust in LLM-based healthcare applications. Research works such as [18] and [11] underscore the importance of the interpretability of outputs, especially in high-stake decisions such as those about medical diagnoses. Transparency of decision-making processes builds trust among clinicians and patients and moves these technologies toward compliance with regulatory requirements. These findings reinforce the dual imperatives of technical sophistication and ethical rigor in developing AI health systems.

The literature also highlights the increasing emphasis on equity and fairness of model performance. For instance, works such as [12] and [41] look into the consequences of demographic biases in the training dataset, which can affect the differences in diagnostic accuracy between populations. Overcoming such biases using data sampling and algorithmic adjustments remains challenging for this field.

Another recurring theme is scalability: works like [8] and [30] debate the possibility of deploying LLMs at scale in a healthcare setting. While their real-world applications show impressive results, such as improving efficiency in clinical workflows, all these models are computationally and infrastructure-wise very demanding. The way forward is to optimize resource utilization and lightweight model architecture.

Finally, the works reviewed above continually raise the issue of strict ethical and regulatory oversight. Applications like SouLLMate [30] and PICO GenAI [8] can revolutionize healthcare. Still, there is a need for LLMs to be able to apply data privacy laws and ethical standards so that they can see broader applications. The legal landscape regarding AI in medicine continues to evolve, and great caution will be required to unlock these technologies' potential fully.

8.2 State of the Art vs. Future Potential

While the current state of LLMs in healthcare is awe-inspiring, several gaps prevent their full integration into clinical practice. For example, while models like MedBLIP [26] and PICO GenAI [8] excel at synthesizing information across multimodalities and producing actionable insights, their reliance on high-quality data remains a limitation. Real-world data is usually incomplete, unstructured, or biased. Thus, generalizing models is not possible. Future research should emphasize the creation of robust, diverse, and standardized datasets to fill this gap. Also, the absence of interoperability among systems stands as a significant barrier. Indeed, [18] and [11] noted that different software and hardware platforms in healthcare ecosystems pose significant integration problems. Compatibility should be foreseen in future models; standardized protocols such as HL7 FHIR should be considered to ensure their utility in different clinical settings.

Another gap exists in real-time adaptability. Although models like SouLLMate [30] have exhibited adaptive capabilities in mental health care, most LLMs stumble upon updating their knowledge base in real-time. Advances in real-time learning and federated training methods may bridge this gap by embedding new medical insights without compromising data security.

The future potentiality of LLMs in healthcare is enormous, especially for hybrid modeling and ensemble learning. Works such as [46] and [8] hint at the promise of combining LLMs with domain-specific models or traditional medical imaging techniques to enhance robustness and accuracy. This hybrid approach can revolutionize diagnostics and treatment planning by leveraging strengths from multiple methodologies.

Besides, the scalability of LLMs has much potential to help solve some global healthcare problems. Adapting lightweight versions of these models, as covered in [18], might bring AI diagnostic support to resource-constrained regions.

8.3 Implications for Practitioners and Researchers

The implications of LLM evolution for healthcare practitioners are profound. Being able to synthesize such vast amounts of clinical data, models like PICO GenAI [8] will reduce cognitive load and speed up clinician decision-making. However, that would require practitioners to be critical users of this tool, validating AI-generated outputs and realizing their limitations to avoid over-reliance.

The researchers have critical responsibilities towards developing technical and ethical dimensions in LLM. As identified by [3] and [26], one of the frontier areas pertains to integrating multimodal data, for which innovative solutions are still sought. Researchers should focus on improving data preprocessing techniques, refining feature extraction, and ensuring that models can handle diverse input formats effectively.

Therefore, the increasing trend of LLMs calls for reviewing current standards and frameworks by policymakers and regulatory bodies. Works such as [41] have echoed the call for solid guidelines considering fairness, bias, and data privacy. Regulators must work alongside technologists and ethicists to create policies that balance innovation with patient safety, ensuring that LLMs enhance and do not disrupt healthcare systems.

However, the most critical role would be preparing future clinicians to work with such AI tools. As illustrated in [4], training in AI needs to be introduced into medical and allied health curricula, which would provide professionals with appropriate skills in interpreting and making the most out of the outputs from AI. It's an interdisciplinary approach in collaboration between clinicians, data scientists, and engineers.

Finally, there are implications for global health, in which LLMs may contribute to reducing disparities in access to care. By deploying scalable solutions such as SouLLMate [30] and PICO GenAI [8], healthcare providers in resource-limited settings may overcome clinician shortages and infrastructure deficits.

8.4 Discussion of Researcher's Opinions

The case studies reviewed in this survey highlight both the promise and the challenges of multimodal LLMs in healthcare. Models like MedBLIP and MAIRA-Seg demonstrate how effectively multimodal integration can enhance diagnostic precision and streamline clinical workflows. However, these advancements often come at the cost of high computational demands and dependence on curated datasets, limiting accessibility to resource-constrained healthcare settings. We believe there is an urgent need to develop lightweight and cost-effective versions of these models to make the technologies more easily accessible, providing aid to a greater population. Additionally, increasing the adaptability of these systems to function with imperfect or missing data would be a significant step forward in making multimodal LLMs universally applicable.

Another key area of improvement lies in improving explainability and trustworthiness, as touched upon in several case studies. While current methodologies, such as attention maps and saliency-based approaches, provide a decent starting point, they fall short of delivering the level of transparency that would likely be required for widespread adoption of these technologies. Future research should focus on using AI frameworks that are easier to understand and provide clinicians actionable insights alongside their predictions. Incorporating domain-specific rules or human-in-the-loop methodologies could bridge the gap between black-box models and the accountability demanded in healthcare. We envision systems that empower clinicians not just to trust AI outputs but to understand and validate them in real time.

Looking ahead, we see immense potential in expanding the capabilities of multimodal LLMs to support global health initiatives. For instance, utilizing federated learning and edge computing could enable the deployment of these models in underserved regions that could most use the aid of AI, especially in areas where there's a shortage of healthcare professionals. In order for the technology to develop smoothly, interdisciplinary collaboration across AI and healthcare specialists to ensure ethical and equitable deployment that matches the needs of hospitals and other facilities around the world.

9 Future Directions

9.1 Integration with Emerging Technologies

Integrating LLMs with emerging technologies, such as quantum computing and federated learning, will represent a transformative frontier in healthcare AI.

Due to its ability to handle vast and complex computations simultaneously, quantum computing can be expected to further reduce LLM training and inference due to several factors. Research works such as [18] speculate on the role of quantum-enhanced algorithms in overcoming computational bottlenecks, thus making large-scale models more efficient and scalable for healthcare applications. The interaction will ease the real-time processing of multimodal medical data, e.g., integrating genomic sequences and imaging for precision diagnostics. Another avenue is Federated Learning, which addresses privacy concerns with decentralized training across multiple institutions without sharing raw data.

This is also in line with the conclusion from [12], representing a particularly relevant approach under current stringent healthcare regulations, such as Health Insurance Portability and Accountability Act (HIPAA) and General Data Protection Regulation (GDPR). Federated learning can help improve LLMs' generalizability by allowing them to learn from diverse datasets while maintaining data sovereignty and reducing demographic biases. However, some challenges include communication overhead and model synchronization. Integrating LLMs with Internet of Things (IoT) devices also represents a burgeoning opportunity. By connecting wearable health monitors and smart devices to LLM-driven analytics platforms, as suggested in [11], it is possible to create a seamless ecosystem for real-time health monitoring and intervention. Such integrations could revolutionize chronic disease management, offering personalized insights based on continuous data streams.

Security and transparency of LLM-driven healthcare systems can be taken one more step further using blockchain technology. Indeed, applying decentralized and immutable ledgers- as discussed in [18]-will allow healthcare providers to share data while tracing AI decisions securely. This meets the growing demand for trust and explainability in AI systems and provides a clear framework for accountability.

Lastly, advances in AR and VR can further complement LLM applications in medical education and patient interaction. For instance, a research work like [4] discusses how LLMs can power adaptive feedback mechanisms in AR/VR environments, thus creating immersive and interactive learning experiences for medical professionals. Together with LLMs, these technologies will bridge the gap between theoretical knowledge and practical expertise.

9.2 Personalized Medicine

The application of LLMs is critical in personalized medicine. With the ability to devise treatment solutions for each individual, the advancement of LLMs has shown how models such as PICO GenAI [8] use specific data about a patient's history, genetics, and current symptoms to create treatment recommendations tailored to their unique situation. Personalization can significantly impact patient outcomes, especially in oncology and rare diseases, where one-size-fits-all approaches fall short.

The role of LLMs in pharmacogenomics is particularly noteworthy. These models can predict individual drug responses by analyzing genetic data, as explored in [3], optimizing dosages, and minimizing adverse effects. This capability aligns with the broader trend toward precision medicine, where treatments are tailored to diseases and patients' genetic and environmental contexts.

LLMs have the potential to afford highly personalized care plans for managing chronic diseases. For example, SouLLMate [30] illustrates how an adaptive model can dynamically offer support for mental health, updating the interventions based on the patient's progress and feedback. Expanding such adaptability for chronic conditions like diabetes or hypertension could significantly enhance self-management and alleviate pressure on healthcare providers.

Multimodal data further enrich the integration of personalized medicine. As discussed in [26], LLMs can provide a holistic view of patient health, facilitating more accurate diagnoses and tailored interventions by combining imaging, laboratory, and genomic data. This multimodal approach is particularly valuable in complex cases where single data streams fail to capture the clinical picture.

Notwithstanding such progress, challenges persist in inequitable access to personalized medicine. As discussed in [12], demographic biases in training data lead to disparities in model performance. Addressing these issues is critical to realizing the full potential of LLMs in delivering equitable and individualized care.

9.3 Real-World Deployments

Transitioning LLMs from research to clinical practice involves overcoming several logistical and regulatory hurdles. First and foremost, there is the challenge of ensuring model reliability across diverse and dynamic healthcare settings. Research works such as [18] and [11] emphasize the need for extensive validation and testing before deployment, especially in high-stakes environments such as emergency medicine. The development of standardized protocols for model evaluation is essential to ensure consistent performance across clinical contexts.

Another essential consideration is interoperability. As noted in [8], many healthcare systems are fragmented, using different EHR platforms and data standards. The smooth integration of LLMs into such systems requires strong API frameworks and adherence to interoperability standards such as HL7 FHIR. This would enhance the utility of LLMs and ensure that they augment and do not disrupt existing workflows.

Scalability is even more problematic, especially in resource-constrained environments. Research like [30] call for lightweight and affordable models that can be deployed in resource-poor regions. Federated learning and edge computing are promising approaches to address this challenge by enabling LLMs to work efficiently in resource-constrained environments.

Ethical and regulatory compliance should be taken into consideration in real-world deployments. As noted in the issue [41], compliance with privacy laws and moral standards is the only way to obtain stakeholder trust and ensure patient safety. Well-thought-out guidelines for the use of data, model transparency, and accountability of decisions are crucial for successful deployment in a clinical setting.

Finally, continuous monitoring and iterative improvement are crucial to ensure that the deployed models remain relevant and reliable. Research work such as [18] discuss how feedback loops are essential, with clinicians and patients providing insight into refining model performance. Such mechanisms ensure that LLMs evolve in response to real-world challenges, aligning their capabilities with dynamic needs within healthcare systems.

10 Conclusion

This survey represents a transformative future of LLMs in healthcare, especially for medical abnormality detection. These reviewed works emphasize the importance of holistically integrating text, image, and signal modalities to understand patient data. By leveraging LLMs that process multimodal inputs, researchers and practitioners can take on complex diagnostic challenges and improve clinical decision-making. Models such as MedBLIP and segmentation-aware multimodal frameworks demonstrate how effectively different data can be combined to provide context-sensitive, precise insights.

At the same time, critical gaps in data integration, interpretability, and bias are crucial areas that require continued innovation and careful ethical consideration. Seamless integration of data remains a technological advance in unified prompt designs, cross-modal embeddings, and the need for standardized data formats. Besides, the demand for explainable AI systems is highly salient: stakeholders want accurate and explainable models, fostering trust among clinicians and patients. In addition to the aforementioned, efforts to reduce demographic biases and increase fairness underline the critical unmet need for fair AI systems to serve diverse populations without widening the gaps in healthcare disparities.

Medical abnormality detection using multimodal LLMs plays a crucial role in this respect. These models fill the gap between these isolated data types and allow for a broader diagnostics and treatment planning approach. For example, integrated imaging and textual data help in the early detection of cancers, while models including physiological signals enable personalized interventions in cardiology and neurology. As LLM-driven solutions continue to be adopted by healthcare systems, improved patient outcomes, resource efficiency, and global health equity grow exponentially.

While the following survey recognizes much that has been accomplished, it articulates directions for future interdisciplinary collaborations and remaining gaps. Researchers should continue to refine these emerging multimodal architectures into more clinically relevant forms and keep pace with real-world needs. Practitioners, policymakers, and technologists are bound by the responsibility to jointly shape a healthcare ecosystem wherein LLMs would play a role in improved diagnostics and one that is fair, transparent, and trustworthy. Medically abnormal detection is the future-driven revolution in health care through a multimodal LLM to better patient care.

References

1. Smart drug delivery systems using large language models for Real-Time treatment personalization. In: IEEE Conference Publication | IEEE Xplore, 12 July 2024. https://ieeexplore.ieee.org/document/10692060
2. Leveraging large language models for generating personalized care recommendations in dementia. In: IEEE Conference Publication | IEEE Xplore, 10 July 2024. https://ieeexplore.ieee.org/document/10649066
3. Multimodal clinical prediction with unified prompts and pretrained large-language models. In: IEEE Conference Publication | IEEE Xplore, 03 June 2024. https://ieeexplore.ieee.org/document/10628813
4. Implementing artificial intelligence in physiotherapy education: a case study on the use of large language models (LLM) to enhance feedback. IEEE J. Mag. | IEEE Xplore (2024). https://ieeexplore.ieee.org/document/10648793
5. Development and preliminary evaluation of remote Pacemaker monitoring system using large language model. IEEE Conference Publication | IEEE Xplore, 03 June 2024. https://ieeexplore.ieee.org/document/10628703
6. OYEN: a user-centric LLM-based bilingual healthcare chatbot. In: IEEE Conference Publication | IEEE Xplore, 03 September 2024. https://ieeexplore.ieee.org/document/10730140
7. The rise of generative artificial intelligence in healthcare. In: IEEE Conference Publication | IEEE Xplore, 06 June 2023. https://ieeexplore.ieee.org/document/10155107
8. Generative AI for evidence-based medicine: a PICO GenAI for synthesizing clinical case reports. In: IEEE Conference Publication | IEEE Xplore, 09 June 2024. https://ieeexplore.ieee.org/document/10622271
9. HealPal ChatMate: AI driven disease diagnosis and recommendation system. IEEE Conference Publication | IEEE Xplore, 15 March (2024). https://ieeexplore.ieee.org/document/10489509
10. Leveraging professional radiologists' expertise to enhance LLMs' evaluation for AI-generated radiology reports. In: IEEE Conference Publication | IEEE Xplore, 03 June 2024. https://ieeexplore.ieee.org/document/10628824
11. Rule-augmented artificial intelligence-empowered systems for medical diagnosis using large language models. In: IEEE Conference Publication | IEEE Xplore, 06 November 2023. https://ieeexplore.ieee.org/document/10356438
12. Evaluation of ChatGPT-supported diagnosis, staging and treatment planning for the case of lung cancer. In: IEEE Conference Publication | IEEE Xplore, 04 December 2023. https://ieeexplore.ieee.org/document/10479348
13. Integrating large language model, EEG, and Eye-Tracking for Word-Level neural state classification in reading comprehension. IEEE J. Mag. | IEEE Xplore (2024). https://ieeexplore.ieee.org/document/10636286
14. Inala, J.P., et al.: Data analysis in the era of generative AI, 27 September 2024. https://arxiv.org/abs/2409.18475
15. Jabeen, K., et al.: An EfficientNet integrated ResNet deep network and explainable AI for breast lesion classification from ultrasound images. CAAI Trans. Intell. Technol. (2024). https://doi.org/10.1049/cit2.12385
16. Fan, X., Yang, L., Wang, X., Lyu, D., Chen, H.: Constructing a knowledge-guided mental health chatbot with LLMs. OpenReview. https://openreview.net/forum?id=FuzY1lFp4V

17. Hassan, M., et al.: Unfolding explainable AI for brain tumor segmentation. Neurocomputing **599**, 128058. https://doi.org/10.1016/j.neucom.2024.128058
18. Walker, C., et al.: Demonstration and evaluation of explainable and trustworthy predictive technology for condition-based maintenance (2024). https://doi.org/10.2172/2474859
19. Ma, J., He, Y., Li, F., Han, L., You, C., Wang, B.: Segment anything in medical images. Nat. Commun. **15**(1) (2024). https://doi.org/10.1038/s41467-024-44824-z
20. Natha, S., Laila, U., Gashim, I.A., Mahboob, K., Saeed, M.N., Noaman, K.M.: Automated brain tumor identification in biomedical radiology images: a multi-model ensemble deep learning approach. Appl. Sci. **14**(5), 2210 (2024). https://doi.org/10.3390/app14052210
21. Bosale, A.A.: Detection and classification of diabetic retinopathy using deep learning algorithms for segmentation to facilitate referral recommendation for test and treatment prediction, 05 January 2024. https://arxiv.org/abs/2401.02759
22. Huang, Z., Yu, J., Shan, Y.: A multimodal deep learning-based algorithm for specific fetal heart rate events detection. Biomed. Eng./Biomedizinische Technik (2024). https://doi.org/10.1515/bmt-2024-0334
23. Yang, H., et al.: Multi-modality risk prediction of cardiovascular diseases for breast cancer cohort in the All of Us Research Program. J. Am. Med. Inform. Assoc. (2024). https://doi.org/10.1093/jamia/ocae199
24. Maryam, Q.G., Verdú, E.: CONVGRU-CNN: spatiotemporal deep learning for real-world anomaly detection in video surveillance system, 01 December 2023. https://reunir.unir.net/handle/123456789/14812
25. Wen, Y., Chen, K.: Autonomous detection and assessment of indoor building defects using multimodal learning and GPT. In: Construction Research Congress 2022, pp. 1001–1009 (2024). https://doi.org/10.1061/9780784485262.102
26. Chen, Q., Hu, X., Wang, Z., Hong, Y.: MedBLIP: bootstrapping language-image pre-training from 3D medical images and texts, 18 May 2023. https://arxiv.org/abs/2305.10799
27. Popa, S.L., et al.: Gemini-assisted deep learning classification model for automated diagnosis of high-resolution esophageal manometry images. Medicina **60**(9), 1493 (2024). https://doi.org/10.3390/medicina60091493
28. Krolik, J., Mahal, H., Ahmad, F., Trivedi, G., Saket, B.: Towards leveraging large language models for automated medical Q&A evaluation. 03 September 2024. https://arxiv.org/abs/2409.01941
29. Vashisht, P., et al.: UMass-BioNLP at MEDIQA-M3G 2024: DermPrompt – a systematic exploration of prompt engineering with GPT-4V for dermatological diagnosis, 27 April 2024. https://arxiv.org/abs/2404.17749
30. Guo, Q., Tang, J., Sun, W., Tang, H., Shang, Y., Wang, W.: SouLLMate: an application enhancing diverse mental health support with adaptive LLMs, prompt engineering, and RAG techniques, 17 October 2024. https://arxiv.org/abs/2410.16322 HCI Research Paper Final 2024 13
31. DSI-NET: Deep Synergistic Interaction Network for joint classification and segmentation with endoscope images. IEEE J. Mag. | IEEE Xplore. https://ieeexplore.ieee.org/abstract/document/9440441
32. Karimzadeh, R., et al.: Search in free-text radiology report database using large language model cooperation. SSRN, January (2024). https://doi.org/10.2139/ssrn.4917162
33. Chakraborty, N., Ornik, M., Driggs-Campbell, K.: Hallucination detection in foundation models for decision-making: a flexible definition and review of the state of the art, 25 March 2024. https://arxiv.org/abs/2403.16527

34. Sharma, H., et al.: MAIRA-Seg: enhancing radiology report generation with segmentation-aware multimodal large language models, 18 November 2024. https://arxiv.org/abs/2411.11362
35. Mohammed, F.A., Tune, K.K., Assefa, B.G., Jett, M., Muhie, S.: Medical image classifications using convolutional neural networks: a survey of current methods and statistical modeling of the literature. Mach. Learn. Knowl. Extraction **6**(1), 699–736 (2024). https://doi.org/10.3390/make6010033
36. Huang, S.-C., Jensen, M.E.K., Yeung-Levy, S., Lungren, M.P., Poon, H., Chaudhari, A.: Multimodal foundation models for medical imaging - a systematic review and implementation guidelines. medRxiv (Cold Spring Harbor Laboratory), October 2024. https://doi.org/10.1101/2024.10.23.24316003
37. Zhang, H., Hussin, H., Hoh, C.-C., Cheong, S.-H., Lee, W.-K., Yahaya, B.H.: Big data in breast cancer: towards precision treatment. Digit. Health **10** (2024). https://doi.org/10.1177/20552076241293695
38. Tang, F., Wang, X., Yuan, X., Luo, L., Zhao, M., Kato, N.: Large Language Model (LLM) assisted end-to-end network health management based on multi-scale semanticization, 12 June 2024. https://arxiv.org/abs/2406.08305
39. Zhang, H., et al.: Holmes-VAD: towards unbiased and explainable video anomaly detection via multi-modal LLM, 18 June 2024. https://arxiv.org/abs/2406.12235
40. Li, Y., et al.: Myriad: large multimodal model by applying vision experts for industrial anomaly detection, 29 October 2023. https://arxiv.org/abs/2310.19070
41. Huang, H., et al.: ChatGPT for shaping the future of dentistry: the potential of multi-modal large language model. Int. J. Oral Sci. **15**(1) (2023). https://doi.org/10.1038/s41368-023-00239-y
42. Singh, Y., Patel, N.D., Shandilya, S.K.: Enhancing security operations center efficiency through multi-model integration of large language models and Siem system. Available at SSRN. https://ssrn.com/abstract=4943079 or http://dx.doi.org/10.2139/ssrn.4943079
43. Kheddar, H.: Transformers and large language models for efficient intrusion detection systems: a comprehensive survey, 14 August 2024. https://arxiv.org/abs/2408.07583
44. Panagoulias, D.P., Tsoureli-Nikita, E., Virvou, M., Tsihrintzis, G.A.: Dermacen analytica: a novel methodology integrating multi-modal large language models with machine learning in tele-dermatology, 21 March 2024. https://arxiv.org/abs/2403.14243
45. Improved lung cancer detection through use of large language systems with graphical attributes. In: IEEE Conference Publication | IEEE Xplore. https://ieeexplore.ieee.org/document/10486290
46. Yang, H., Li, M., Zhou, H., Xiao, Y., Fang, Q., Zhang, R.: One LLM is not enough: harnessing the power of ensemble learning for medical question answering, medRxiv (Cold Spring Harbor Laboratory), December 2023. https://doi.org/10.1101/2023.12.21.23300380
47. Shi, Q.: From Symptoms to services: An LLM chatbot for effective departmental referral - ProQuest. https://www.proquest.com/docview/3110352565?pq-origsite=gscholar&fromopenview=true&sourcetype=Dissertations%20&%20 Theses
48. Shah, K., et al.: Large language model prompting techniques for advancement in clinical medicine. J. Clin. Med. **13**(17), 5101 (2024). https://doi.org/10.3390/jcm13175101

49. Samuel, D.J., Sermet, Y., Cwiertny, D., Demir, I.: Integrating vision-based AI and large language models for real-time water pollution surveillance. Water Environ. Res. **96**(8) (2024). https://doi.org/10.1002/wer.11092
50. Shakur, A.H., et al.: Large language models for medical osce assessment: a novel approach to transcript analysis. arXiv (Cornell University), October 2024. https://doi.org/10.48550/arxiv.2410.12858
51. Kim, Y., et al.: MDAGENTS: an adaptive collaboration of LLMs for medical decision-making, OpenReview. https://openreview.net/forum?id=EKdk4vxKO4eId=qSX2RyJCQu
52. Deep learning-based lung cancer detection enhancing early diagnosis and treatment outcomes. In: IEEE Conference Publication | IEEE Xplore. https://ieeexplore.ieee.org/document/1048916

A Comprehensive Survey of Computer Vision-Based Pose Estimation for Machine Learning and Deep Learning Approaches

Mohamed Hadid and Muhammad Abid(✉)

Florida Polytechnic University, Lakeland, FL 33805, USA
mabid@floridapoly.edu

Abstract. Pose estimation plays a pivotal role in robotics, augmented reality (AR), and human-computer interaction. This survey presents a comprehensive review of recent developments in 2D and 3D human and hand pose estimation techniques. We categorize the literature based on monocular, multi-view, depth-based, and mesh-based methods, highlighting the advantages and trade-offs of each. We also examine domain-specific applications in healthcare, telemedicine, and robotics, and identify major challenges such as occlusion, domain adaptation, and real-time processing. Finally, we discuss future directions, including self-supervised learning, sensor fusion, and explainability. This work aims to guide future research and inform the development of robust, generalizable pose estimation systems.

Keywords: Human Pose Estimation · 3D Hand Pose Estimation · Computer Vision · Robotics · Deep Learning · Sensor Fusion · Augmented Reality

1 Introduction

Pose estimation refers to the approach of identifying the configuration of human bodies or hands in images or video. It is one of the key concentrations in computer vision. Pose estimation enables machines to interpret human actions through poses in single or set sequential frames, enabling applications in robotics, augmented reality (AR), and healthcare.

Recent advances, especially deep learning-based methods, have significantly improved both the accuracy and robustness of pose estimation techniques. These advancements can be attributed to the availability of large-scale annotated datasets, such as COCO [26], and the development of more efficient neural network architectures such as Pose Machines based on convolutional neural networks (CNNs) [13] and High-Resolution Network (HRNet) [23]. HRNet maintains high-resolution representations throughout the network, enhancing spatial precision in keypoint detection and improving overall pose estimation performance.

Pose estimation has evolved from traditional image processing techniques, such as edge detection and active contours, to modern deep learning-based

S. Hussain et al. (Eds.): SEET 2025, CCIS 2725, pp. 347–370, 2026.
https://doi.org/10.1007/978-3-032-08977-9_22

approaches. The early methods in pose estimation relied heavily on geometric modeling [12,13,15,22,51], where human poses were represented using predefined 3D models. These approaches required high computational resources and often failed in real-world environments due to occlusion, lighting variations, and other generic limitations due to the complexity of human motion.

With the advent of machine learning in the early 2000s, probabilistic graphical models such as Pictorial Structures [13] began to replace earlier, more rigid approaches. These models were capable of learning relationships between body parts and were less dependent on predefined models with variables limited to the researchers' set parameters.

In the past decade, deep learning has revolutionized pose estimation. CNNs, in particular, have allowed for end-to-end learning directly from raw data, eliminating the need for handcrafted features. Techniques like Stacked Hourglass Networks and OpenPose introduced real-time performance, with OpenPose's ability to detect 2D key points in real-time becoming a breakthrough in human pose estimation [13]. The goal of this survey is to highlight the innovations, applications, and challenges that continue to drive research in this field.

This paper is structured as follows: Sect. 2 explores different approaches and techniques in pose estimation, categorizing them based on dimensional representation, model architecture, and input modalities. It discusses 2D pose estimation methods, including heatmap-based and regression-based approaches, and extends to 3D pose estimation techniques such as monocular and multi-view methods. Section 3 presents various applications of pose estimation, highlighting its role in robotics, augmented reality (AR), virtual reality (VR), human-computer interaction, and medical diagnostics. Section 4 addresses key challenges in pose estimation, including occlusion, depth ambiguity, generalization between diverse environments, and real-time performance constraints. Section 5 discusses future research directions, including self-supervised learning, domain adaptation, and the integration of multimodal data sources for improved robustness. Finally, Sect. 6 provides acknowledgments, followed by references.

This survey follows a structured roadmap beginning with an overview of pose estimation fundamentals, followed by a taxonomy of methods including 2D, 3D, monocular, and multi-view techniques. The applications in real-world domains and emerging research challenges are then discussed to contextualize current limitations and future directions. The selection of literature was based on relevance, impact of citations, and technical novelty.

Problem Statement: Despite significant progress, pose estimation models still face limitations in generalization, robustness under occlusions, and deployment in real-time applications, particularly for 3D hand tracking.

Research Objectives:

- To categorize and evaluate the latest deep learning-based pose estimation methods.
- To analyze the strengths and weaknesses of monocular, multi-view, RGB, and depth-based approaches.
- To identify current challenges and propose future research directions for 3D robotic hand pose estimation (Fig. 1).

Fig. 1. Flowchart outlining the structure of the proposed survey methodology. It includes the stages of literature selection, classification of pose estimation methods, application-specific analysis, and identification of future research directions.

2 Approaches and Techniques in Pose Estimation

This section explores different pose estimation techniques. These techniques can be broadly categorized based on their dimensional representation, model architecture, and input modalities. Traditional methods relied on handcrafted feature extraction, while modern approaches leverage deep learning to predict key points and reconstruct poses with higher precision. Starting with 2D pose estimation, which identifies key points in a single image. It then delves into heatmap-based and regression-based methods, each offering distinct advantages in accuracy and computational efficiency. Following this, 3D pose estimation techniques are discussed, highlighting their importance in applications requiring depth information. Specialized approaches such as hand mesh representation, monocular methods, and multi-view techniques are also examined, showcasing recent advancements that enhance pose estimation capabilities. Lastly, the role of deep learning in driving state-of-the-art improvements is addressed, followed by a comparison of RGB-based and depth-based methodologies, each tailored to specific real-world applications.

2.1 2D Pose Estimation

The most fundamental approach in pose estimation is 2D pose estimation, where the goal is to locate key points (such as the wrist, shoulder, or knee) in a single 2D image. Over time, methods have evolved from traditional feature detection to sophisticated deep-learning approaches.

To address the issue of occlusion in human pose estimation (HPE), the Cascade Pyramid Network (CPN) was introduced [51], which consists of two main components: GlobalNet, a feature pyramid network designed to predict invisible keypoints, and RefineNet, which integrates multi-level features from GlobalNet while incorporating a keypoint mining loss. Their findings demonstrate that CPN effectively predicts occluded key points, improving the accuracy of pose estimation in challenging scenarios.

Further advancements are needed to reconstruct missed poses using temporal information from previous frames in occluded scenes [51]. The approach employs self-supervised learning, allowing the network to improve pose estimation performance even on sparsely annotated video datasets. This technique enhances robustness in occluded environments, making it particularly useful for real-world applications where occlusions are frequent.

2.2 Heatmap-Based

Heatmap-based approaches model the probability of a joint being at each pixel location using a CNN. The network outputs a heatmap for each joint, where higher values indicate the most likely location for that joint. This approach has been extensively used in frameworks like OpenPose [13] and has been fundamental in various human pose estimation systems, including those utilizing transformers for improved spatial dependencies [26]. Additionally, multi-task learning has been applied to enhance 3D hand pose estimation by integrating shape reconstruction, thereby refining joint localization accuracy [42]. Recent advancements have also explored diffusion models and contrastive learning techniques to further enhance robustness in occlusion scenarios and monocular RGB-based pose estimation [28, 36].

In addition to conventional CNN-based approaches, novel methods leveraging viewpoint transformations have demonstrated improved generalization across varying camera angles [48]. Furthermore, ensemble-based techniques incorporating evolutionary algorithms have shown promise in increasing pose estimation accuracy through the fusion of multiple predictions [34]. While these ensemble models may introduce additional computational overhead, they can be more efficient overall in complex environments by reducing the need for manual tuning or retraining under varying conditions. This efficiency arises not solely from raw speed but from improved adaptability and robustness across a range of scenarios. Recent studies have also integrated semantic hypergraph convolutional networks to model complex hand articulations in 3D space more effectively [45]. These advancements collectively contribute to the evolution of pose estimation methodologies, enabling more accurate and adaptable applications in robotics, virtual reality, and human-computer interaction.

Table 1 compares various heatmap-based 2D pose estimation methods based on accuracy, measured in mean Average Precision (mAP), and speed, measured in frames per second (fps). A higher mAP indicates better keypoint detection accuracy, while a higher fps reflects faster processing capability.

According to [13], HRNet achieves the highest accuracy while also delivering the best processing speed, making it a well-balanced option for applications requiring both precision and real-time performance. However, HRNet's superior performance comes at the cost of higher memory usage and increased model complexity, which may not be ideal for deployment on resource-constrained devices such as edge GPUs or mobile platforms. In contrast, lighter architectures like OpenPose offer moderate accuracy but are often easier to optimize and deploy. This comparison highlights the trade-off between model accuracy, speed, and hardware requirements and underscores the importance of selecting an approach tailored to the specific constraints of the deployment environment.

Table 1. Comparison of Heatmap-Based 2D Pose Estimation Methods.

Method	Accuracy (mAP)	Speed (fps)
OpenPose [13]	70.4	15
Hourglass Network [13]	72.8	10
HRNet [23]	75.1	20

2.3 Regression-Based

Instead of outputting heatmaps, some methods directly regress the joint coordinates. These methods have the advantage of being faster, but since they rely partially on best-fit predictability, they can suffer from reduced accuracy in certain scenarios. Similar models were developed to harness the pros of the predictability criteria while increasing the accuracy rate. For example, recent models use techniques like deformable convolutions and transformers to improve the performance [26]. Figure 2 depicts a simplified human hand model. This figure illustrates the inverse kinematics (IK) model used for hand pose estimation. The hourglass network is employed to extract hierarchical spatial information, refining key point predictions for improved accuracy. The hand model has 24 degrees of freedom. The link lengths are computed using the Euclidean distance between each joint during the initialization phase. An optimization method is utilized to determine the combination of joint values that best mimics the hand pose detected by the HoloLens [34].

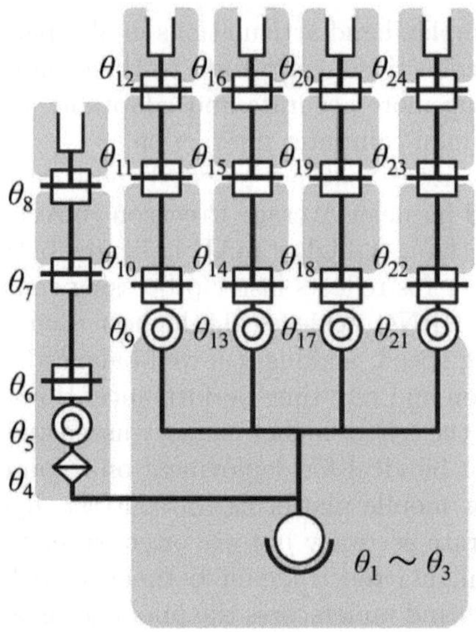

Fig. 2. IK model for the hand pose estimation, hourglass network [34]

2.4 3D Pose Estimation

3D pose estimation is the process of predicting the spatial configuration of a human hand from a single RGB image. This task is inherently challenging due to factors such as self-occlusion, depth ambiguity, and the natural variability in hand shapes and orientations [13,51]. Traditional methods can be broadly categorized into model-based and deep learning-based approaches. Model-based methods rely on predefined hand templates, such as the MANO model, to infer joint locations by fitting a parametric hand structure to the image data [4]. While these methods offer structured reconstructions, they are often constrained by the limitations of the predefined models.

In contrast, deep learning-based methods utilize CNNs and, more recently, Graph Neural Networks (GNNs) to directly estimate the 3D coordinates of hand joints from an image [12,45]. To further improve accuracy, modern approaches integrate 2D pose cues, such as heatmaps, to provide additional spatial constraints that enhance depth inference [50]. Additionally, attention-based mechanisms have been introduced to better handle occlusions and capture global hand structure relationships, leading to more robust and reliable pose estimation [26,42].

The need for 3D pose estimation arises in complex environments where depth is crucial, such as in robotics and AR [5,23]. While 2D methods use only pixel-based information, 3D pose estimation models rely on additional data, such as depth maps or multiple 2D views, to reconstruct the pose in 3D space [15,49].

2.5 Hand Mesh Representation

Hand mesh representation refers to the reconstruction of a detailed 3D hand surface, typically modeled using a triangular mesh structure [4,18]. There are three primary approaches to generating hand meshes: parametric models, non-parametric models, and hybrid methods. Parametric models, such as the MANO framework, rely on predefined hand templates and use learned deformation parameters to generate realistic hand shapes [22,49]. These models ensure structural consistency but are limited in their ability to capture fine-grained details and unique hand variations.

Non-parametric methods, on the other hand, directly predict the vertex positions of a 3D hand mesh from image data without relying on a predefined structure [11,50]. While this allows for greater flexibility, these methods often struggle with occlusions and stability in motion sequences [14]. Hybrid approaches combine elements of both parametric and non-parametric models, leveraging the advantages of predefined templates while allowing for finer adjustments through learned features [30].

Recent advancements in hand mesh reconstruction have incorporated Transformer-based architectures and graph-based convolutional networks to improve realism and accuracy [15,26]. These developments enable more precise hand modeling, which is crucial for applications in augmented reality, human-computer interaction, and motion analysis [5,23].

Figure 3 provides an overview of different hand mesh reconstruction approaches, categorizing them into parametric, non-parametric, and hybrid methods. The figure also highlights Single-person hand Reconstruction, Hand-object interaction Reconstruction, and Dual-hand interaction Reconstruction as key research areas that drive advancements in 3D hand modeling.

2.6 Monocular Methods

Monocular methods estimate the 3D pose from a single image, which is an ill-posed problem due to the lack of depth information. Recent advancements use advanced deep learning methods to predict depth or estimate relative depth through multi-view geometry techniques [23]. To explore potential solutions for the lack of depth data, integrating a depth sensor would add a third dimension into the 2D representation from the frames, instead of relying heavily on the shading or contouring, which presents potential margins of errors for the 2D representation. Recent research has explored the use of diffusion models and adversarial training to refine depth estimation in monocular pose estimation [28]. These methods attempt to reconstruct 3D hand and body poses from single images, effectively reducing the inherent depth ambiguity. Additionally, transformer-based architectures have been employed to enhance global feature extraction, allowing models to infer depth by learning long-range dependencies across image sequences [26]. Another promising direction is the use of synthetic datasets, which generate diverse training samples to mitigate the common issue

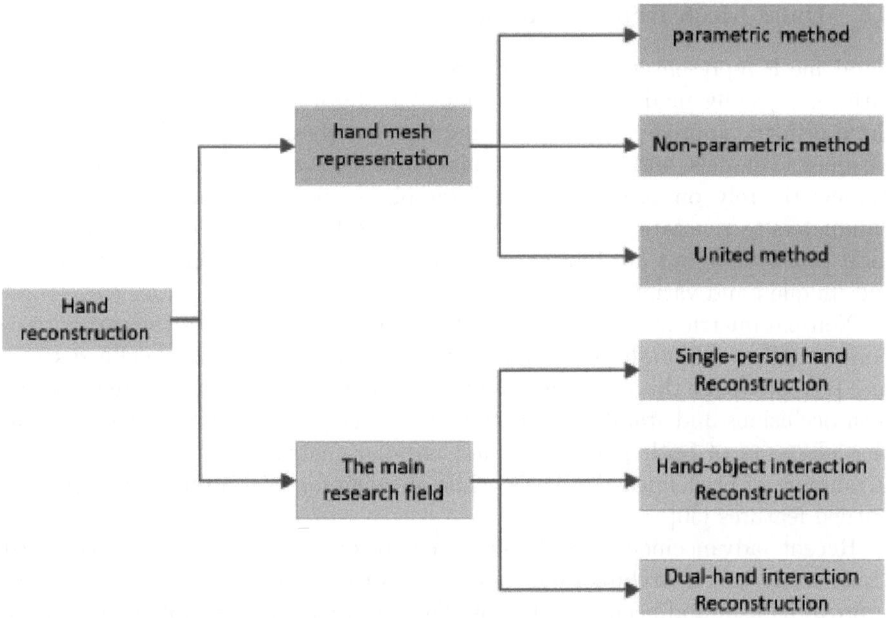

Fig. 3. Methods for hand mesh representation and key research areas of hand reconstruction [22]

of overfitting in real-world applications [13]. Methods like WildPose have incorporated explicit 2D feature representations to bridge the gap between labeled and unlabeled datasets, improving generalization [19].

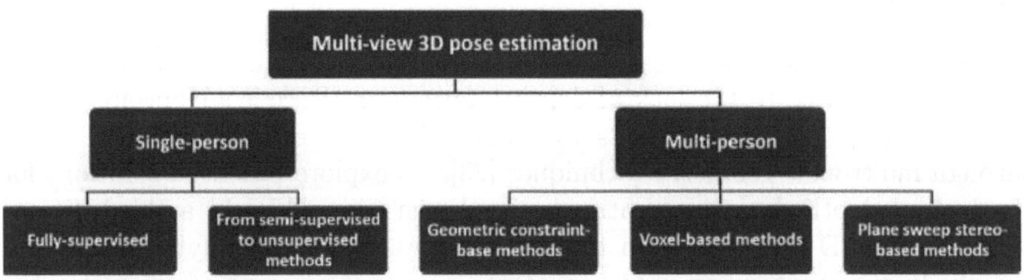

Fig. 4. Proposed taxonomy for multi-view 3D pose estimation [33].

2.7 Multi-view Methods

Multi-view approaches have emerged as a powerful way to overcome the limitations of monocular estimation. By combining images from multiple cameras, 3D information can be triangulated more accurately. This approach is widely used in applications such as teleoperation and multi-robot collaboration, where precise 3D pose estimation is critical [23].

Figure 4 illustrates a proposed taxonomy for the multi-view approach [33]. Advancements in multi-view neural rendering and self-supervised learning have significantly improved the accuracy of 3D pose reconstruction [42]. These techniques leverage multiple perspectives to refine pose estimation models, reducing errors caused by occlusions and poor lighting conditions. Additionally, novel multi-task learning frameworks have enabled systems to simultaneously estimate pose, shape, and motion trajectories, making multi-view pose estimation more robust and computationally efficient [42].

Recent research has also emphasized the role of geometric constraint-based methods in multi-view pose estimation. These approaches use principles such as epipolar geometry and 3D body structure constraints to improve cross-view matching and reduce 2D-3D pose mismatches [8,46]. Some methods integrate temporal consistency to enforce smoother pose transitions across time, mitigating flickering errors caused by sudden occlusions [6,41].

Voxel-based techniques have also gained attention, as they eliminate the need for 2D-to-3D lifting by operating directly in 3D space [40,52]. These methods have demonstrated superior performance in occluded and crowded environments but often require higher computational resources. To address this, lighter-weight transformer-based approaches have emerged, leveraging attention mechanisms to improve pose estimation while reducing inference time [9,44].

Plane sweep stereo-based methods, another important category shown in the taxonomy, compute depth information by sweeping hypothetical planes through the 3D scene and comparing image patches across multiple views. This approach has proven effective in dealing with occlusions and depth ambiguities in cluttered environments and can be integrated with learning-based refinement modules to enhance performance [47].

Furthermore, multi-modal fusion is becoming an essential strategy to enhance robustness. By incorporating depth sensors, inertial measurement units (IMUs), or even radio-frequency signals, researchers have demonstrated improved pose estimation accuracy under challenging scenarios where visual data alone is insufficient [10,16]. These methods allow for improved detection of complex human movements, particularly in real-world applications like sports analytics, AR/VR interactions, and healthcare monitoring. In robotics and AR/VR applications, such improvements facilitate precise hand tracking and gesture recognition, enhancing user interaction experiences [48]. However, despite these advances, challenges remain, including optimizing computational efficiency, improving performance in extreme occlusion scenarios, and reducing the need for extensive labeled datasets. Future research should explore the potential of active learning strategies and self-supervised models to address these limitations [17,29].

2.8 Deep Learning-Based Approach

Deep learning has significantly advanced the field of human pose estimation (HPE) by outperforming traditional computer vision techniques. Initially, model-based approaches relied on predefined skeletal models and handcrafted features to estimate human pose, but these methods struggled with occlusions, depth ambiguities, and complex articulations. The emergence of CNNs and later Graph Neural Networks (GNNs) enabled more robust and accurate pose estimation by learning spatial relationships between joints directly from images. Moreover, deep learning-based 2D HPE has reached a high level of accuracy, making it possible to extend these techniques to 3D HPE. However, 3D pose estimation remains more challenging due to the difficulty of obtaining labeled 3D pose annotations, leading to the exploration of alternative methods such as 2D-to-3D lifting, which leverages predicted 2D poses to infer 3D joint locations. [51] One of the earliest deep learning-based methods, DeepPose, introduced the idea of directly regressing human pose using deep neural networks, marking a shift away from traditional handcrafted feature-based approaches [38].

The progress in deep learning-based HPE has introduced a variety of architectures and training strategies aimed at improving robustness and accuracy. One major development is the use of attention-based models and transformers, which allow for better handling of occlusions and long-range dependencies between joints. TokenPose leveraged tokenization strategies to encode spatial relationships between keypoints, improving robustness in occluded scenarios [24]. In addition, heatmap-based techniques have become widely used, where networks predict probability distributions of joint locations instead of directly regressing coordinates. The HRNet model further improved this by maintaining high-resolution representations throughout the network, leading to more accurate keypoint localization [37]. These methods have shown higher resilience to noise and pose variations. Another significant breakthrough is the integration of GANs into HPE, where adversarial training helps refine pose predictions by enforcing realistic joint configurations. For instance, VideoPose3D introduced a temporal GAN framework to enhance 3D pose predictions by leveraging sequential information from video frames [35]. Recent research has also explored multi-view and multi-modal approaches, where depth sensors, IMUs, and radio frequency devices are used alongside RGB data to improve accuracy in challenging conditions. [51] VoxelPose proposed a volumetric representation of human poses using multi-camera setups, allowing for improved triangulation in complex environments [39].

Despite these advancements, several challenges remain in deep learning-based human pose estimation. Generalization across diverse environments continues to be a major concern, as models trained on controlled datasets struggle when applied to in-the-wild scenarios with unseen poses and lighting conditions. As the effectiveness of deep learning models relies heavily on the availability of diverse and well-annotated datasets. However, many publicly available datasets remain limited in both scale and complexity, making it challenging to fully capture the intricacies of hand pose estimation. [21] Furthermore, real-time inference is still computationally expensive, limiting the deployment of these models in applications such as augmented reality (AR), virtual reality (VR), and robotics. To address these issues, researchers are focusing on lightweight neural architectures, self-supervised learning, and domain adaptation techniques to improve model efficiency and robustness. The integration of physics-based constraints and hybrid learning models combining deep learning with classical kinematic approaches is a promising direction for future research in HPE. [51] For example, Graph-PCNN (pulse-coupled neural network) introduced a two-stage graph-based network that refines pose predictions through progressive convolutional layers, incorporating kinematic priors [43].

2.9 RGB-Based Methods

RGB-based methods for pose estimation rely solely on standard color images without additional depth or infrared data. These approaches leverage deep-learning techniques, particularly CNNs and transformers, to extract spatial and contextual information from images.

One of the fundamental RGB-based methods utilizes keypoint detection through heatmaps, where networks predict the probability of each joint's location [36]. This technique, combined with self-supervised learning, has been employed to improve robustness in occlusion-heavy environments [28]. Moreover, contrastive learning frameworks have been explored to enhance feature representations in RGB-based hand pose estimation, ensuring that feature embeddings maintain consistency across varying viewpoints and lighting conditions [36].

A significant challenge in RGB-based methods is depth ambiguity, which is often mitigated through multi-scale feature extraction and adversarial training [28]. Transformer-based architectures have further improved spatial dependencies and long-range feature extraction, allowing RGB-only systems to approximate 3D poses with high accuracy [26]. Additionally, hybrid models combining CNNs with self-attention mechanisms have demonstrated improved performance in reconstructing occluded joints and estimating hand articulations [22].

Recent advancements also incorporate generative adversarial networks (GANs) to refine predictions by generating realistic pose variations [21]. These models synthesize diverse training samples, reducing the risk of overfitting and improving generalization to real-world scenarios. Furthermore, ensemble learning strategies that integrate multiple RGB-based models have shown promise in increasing pose estimation accuracy through the fusion of complementary predictions [34].

2.10 Depth-Based Methods

Hand pose estimation involves various methodologies that leverage depth information to enhance accuracy. Some approaches utilize 2D depth maps to analyze depth data and infer the spatial coordinates of key hand points. Alternatively, this can also be achieved using 3D depth representations, such as point clouds or voxels.

The DeepPrior approach proposed by Oberweger et al. [21] implemented a neural network architecture that incorporated prior knowledge of 3D hand poses to improve depth map-based estimation. This method significantly enhanced the accuracy and reliability of hand pose detection. Similarly, Sinha et al. [51] developed a regression-based technique to estimate the positions of 21 hand joints using depth maps. Their approach focused on independently determining the joint locations of each finger by training separate neural networks to regress the coordinates of three finger-specific joints. In addition to using RGB data to segment the hand from the background, they employed depth maps for coordinate regression. However, due to computational constraints, their method did not include a distinct deep-learning network for hand segmentation. Instead, they filtered out non-hand pixels by identifying skin tone ranges within the RGB values.

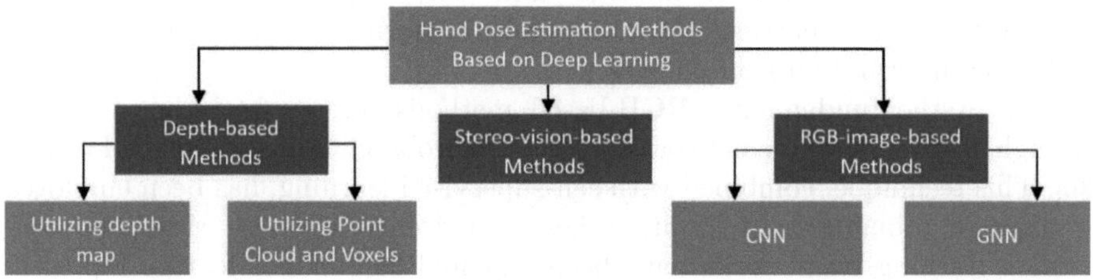

Fig. 5. Classification of hand pose estimation methods [21]

Figure 5 illustrates a classification of hand-pose estimation methods that depend on deep learning as it is one of the primary focus areas in recent research on computer vision as a whole. Primarily outlining the distinctions between 2D, 3D, monocular, multi-view, and mesh estimation methods.

Another advancement in depth-based hand pose estimation was introduced by Baek et al. [28], who employed a Generative Adversarial Network (GAN) framework. Their approach established a bijective mapping between depth disparity maps and 3D hand models. By leveraging CNNs, GANs generate realistic data through an adversarial training process involving a discriminator and a generator. The discriminator differentiates between real and synthetic data, while the generator aims to produce highly realistic hand pose samples.

A novel method within depth-based estimation was introduced by Ge et al. [21], which was later refined in their subsequent work and adopted by other researchers. Their primary focus was to derive a three-dimensional (3D) representation from a two-and-a-half-dimensional (2.5D) image. This innovative perspective enabled a more precise estimation of hand poses. Notably, their research suggests that machine learning algorithms were not explicitly utilized to generate the 3D model from the depth map. However, the exact methodology behind this transformation was not clearly stated in their publications.

Stereo-vision-based methods, as also categorized in Fig. 5, estimate 3D structure by computing disparities between paired images from slightly different viewpoints. These methods are particularly effective for recovering depth in hand regions and can complement depth sensors in pose estimation tasks. They are often integrated with learning-based post-processing to refine initial disparity maps and enhance joint localization accuracy, especially in consumer-grade RGB-D setups.

2.11 3D Mesh Estimation

3D hand mesh estimation is performed using a structured four-stage deep learning framework that leverages 2D cues for enhanced accuracy. The primary goal is to reconstruct a realistic 3D hand model from a single monocular RGB image, addressing challenges such as depth ambiguity, occlusions, and complex hand articulations [49].

The 3D mesh estimation typically consists of 4 stages, combining different elements of 2D estimation to generate a more accurate 3D mesh. Below are the 4 stages:

1. 2D Cue Extraction. The first stage involves extracting 2D hand joint heatmaps and segmentation masks from the input image. These 2D features provide essential spatial constraints, guiding the subsequent 3D hand pose reconstruction. The extracted heatmaps localize key hand joints, while the segmentation mask isolates the hand from the background, improving the model's focus on relevant features [38].

2. Pose Feature Encoding. To effectively utilize the extracted 2D hand joints, a Hand Joint Encoder (HJE) is employed to convert heatmaps into a feature-rich representation. This encoding process captures spatial dependencies between hand joints, refining pose estimation accuracy and improving 3D feature learning [51].

3. Initial 3D Hand Reconstruction. Using both the encoded 2D features and the input image embeddings, a coarse 3D hand mesh is generated. This process incorporates a Mesh Squeeze-and-Excitation Block (MSEB), which enhances the network's ability to focus on relevant mesh details while maintaining structural consistency [50]. The initial mesh prediction provides a rough estimate of hand shape and pose but requires further refinement.

4. Mesh Refinement with Global Mesh Refiner (GMR). The final stage involves refining the coarse 3D hand mesh using a GMR. This component integrates 2D mesh features to adjust the alignment and realism of the predicted 3D model. By learning corrections from 2D representations, the refinement process reduces errors and improves structural accuracy, ensuring the final 3D hand mesh aligns well with the input image [3].

Figure 6 presents the structural hierarchy used in 3D hand mesh estimation, outlining the various topological configurations and techniques that enhance the realism and precision of mesh reconstructions.

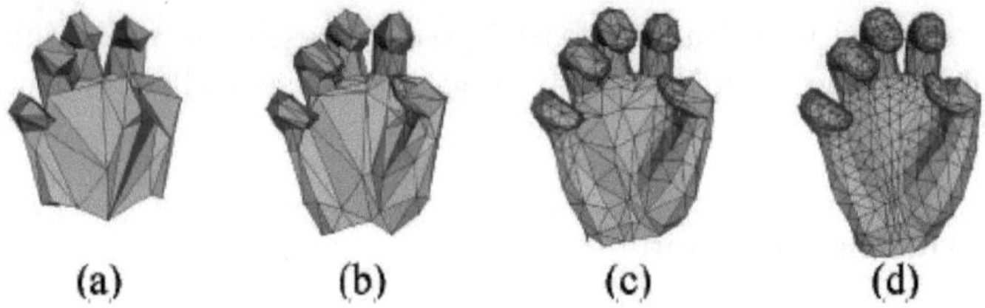

Fig. 6. Hierarchy of topologies used in 3D mesh estimation [50]

Table 2 summarizes various pose estimation methods, categorizing them by type (2D, 3D, or mesh-based) and listing their advantages and limitations. It provides insight into the trade-offs between accuracy, computational complexity, and real-world applicability.

Table 2. Comparison of Main Pose Estimation Methods

Method (Reference)	Type	Advantages	Limitations
Heatmap-based [13,23]	2D Pose Estimation	High accuracy, spatial awareness, effective for joint localization	Computationally expensive, requires large memory and GPU resources
Regression-based [26]	2D Pose Estimation	Faster inference time, simpler network architectures	Lower accuracy in occlusions, struggles with complex hand poses
Model-based [23]	3D Pose Estimation	Structured pose estimation, useful for animation and robotics	Limited flexibility in hand variations, may not generalize well
Deep learning-based [51]	3D Pose Estimation	Higher accuracy, robust feature extraction, learns complex patterns	Requires large datasets, computationally expensive
Monocular Methods [13,26,28]	3D Pose Estimation	Works with a single camera, lower hardware requirements	Depth ambiguity, reduced accuracy in 3D space
Multi-view Methods [23,42,48]	3D Pose Estimation	Overcomes occlusions, improves depth estimation	Requires multiple cameras, high setup cost
Depth-Based Methods [21]	3D Pose Estimation	Uses depth sensors for better spatial accuracy, independent of multiple cameras	Hardware-dependent, computationally expensive
3D Mesh Estimation [21]	Hand Mesh Representation	Detailed hand shape reconstruction, useful for realistic rendering	High processing power required, complex model architectures

3 Applications of Pose Estimation

3.1 Robotics

Pose estimation is crucial for human-robot interaction (HRI) in both industrial and service robots. In particular, 3D pose estimation is used in robotic arms for teleoperation and in collaborative robots (cobots) for performing tasks alongside humans. Multi-camera systems and depth sensors enhance the accuracy of the pose estimation process in dynamic environments [23].

For example, hand pose estimation allows robots to manipulate objects in a way that mimics human dexterity. In this area, the use of real-time deep learning models is increasingly common. Deep learning-based models are now being deployed in robotic hands to enable tasks such as grasping and manipulation in unstructured environments [5].

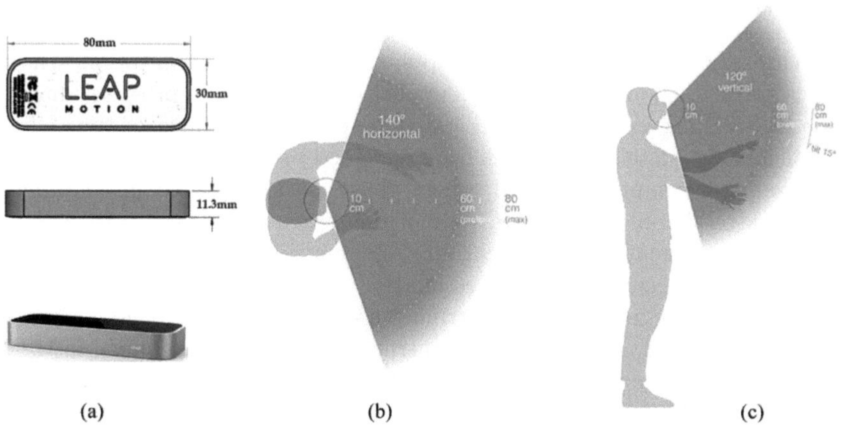

Fig. 7. A Leap Motion Controller: (a) general view and size,(b) field of view (top view), and (c) field of view (left view). [25]

Recent systems have leveraged Leap Motion Controllers (LMCs) to enable intuitive gesture-based control for robotic manipulators. Li et al. [25] introduced an interactive gesture control system that utilizes pose estimation to facilitate collaborative manipulation, enabling efficient human robot coordination in manufacturing environments. The LMC captures fine-grained hand movements, which are translated into control commands for robotic actuators, reducing the cognitive load on human operators and enhancing task precision.

Moreover, LMC-based robotic control systems have shown potential in training and education settings, especially in environments where traditional physical interaction with robotic components is limited. Abdul-Kreem [1] presented a motion estimation system using optical flow and Leap Motion data to interpret fine hand gestures, enabling remote training simulations for robotic control tasks. This approach allows learners to interact with a virtual robotic interface, enhancing accessibility while reducing cost and safety concerns typically associated with hands-on training.

Bouatrous et al. [7] also highlighted the importance of real-time feedback and high-precision tracking enabled by LMCs, which can be directly applied to HRI scenarios in assistive robotics or rehabilitation robots. These systems can interpret subtle changes in hand orientation and motion trajectory, making them suitable for delicate robotic operations such as surgical assistance or high-precision assembly.

Furthermore, gesture recognition via Leap Motion, Fig. 7, in robotic systems can adapt to contextual scenarios using learning-based classifiers, allowing robots to personalize responses or adjust behavior dynamically. This adaptive interaction mechanism contributes to a more natural and efficient collaboration between human operators and autonomous agents in complex industrial environments.

3.2 Healthcare

In healthcare, pose estimation has been applied in physical rehabilitation, where tracking a patient's joint movements can help monitor their progress during recovery. By tracking joint angles and analyzing their variations over time, clinical technicians can detect deviations from expected recovery trajectories. Some models also employ haptic feedback, where physical therapy tools provide real-time feedback based on the detected pose of the patient [2].

Recent advancements in deep learning and multi-modal sensing have further enhanced the accuracy of pose estimation in rehabilitation. Studies have demonstrated the integration of transformer-based architectures for human pose estimation, significantly improving motion tracking reliability in clinical settings [7]. These models leverage self-attention mechanisms to detect subtle movement discrepancies, which can be particularly useful for stroke recovery patients undergoing motor function assessments. Furthermore, real-time 3D pose reconstruction methods have shown potential in analyzing gait abnormalities, providing clinicians with quantitative tools for more precise diagnostics.

3.3 Telemedicine

Pose estimation also holds promise in telemedicine, especially in remote consultations. Real-time pose tracking during virtual visits can help healthcare professionals assess the condition of patients and make diagnoses based on movement patterns. Additionally, combining pose estimation with computer vision techniques can enable remote physical therapy supervision [36].

With the increasing adoption of edge computing and lightweight deep learning models, pose estimation algorithms can now run efficiently on consumer-grade devices, making telemedicine more accessible [13]. This development has led to enhanced home-based rehabilitation programs where patients can receive AI-assisted guidance while performing prescribed exercises. Moreover, contrastive learning techniques have improved the robustness of pose estimation models, enabling accurate motion tracking in low-bandwidth telehealth environments [36].

Recent applications extend beyond video-based tracking. For instance, Abdul-Kreem [1] utilized optical flow-based motion estimation combined with LMC input to track fine motor skills during hand rehabilitation. This system enhances tele-rehabilitation platforms by offering quantifiable metrics of movement accuracy and consistency. Additionally, Naik et al. [32] highlighted the use of virtual reality training in remote stroke therapy, suggesting that VR-enhanced pose estimation can effectively support motor function recovery through guided interaction.

3.4 Augmented and Virtual Reality

Real-time pose estimation plays a pivotal role in augmented and virtual reality (AR/VR) by enabling accurate motion tracking and the seamless overlay of virtual content onto the human body [48]. Leveraging deep learning algorithms, these systems power immersive applications such as virtual try-ons, interactive gaming, and motion-assisted training programs. The result is a more engaging and responsive user experience, where digital interactions closely mimic real-world movements.

Beyond entertainment, real-time pose estimation also supports healthcare and rehabilitation. AR/VR platforms equipped with motion tracking can monitor patient movements and deliver immediate feedback, enabling remote physical therapy sessions. This not only improves accessibility but ensures correct exercise execution. Additionally, applications like posture correction and gait analysis benefit from pose-aware systems, supporting early diagnosis and treatment of musculoskeletal conditions.

The development of real-time pose estimation continues to evolve with improvements in machine learning models and sensor technology. Advances in lightweight neural networks and edge computing allow for faster processing on mobile and wearable devices, making AR/VR applications more accessible. Additionally, multi-camera setups and depth-sensing technologies enhance accuracy, reducing occlusion-related errors in pose tracking.

Leap Motion technology, in particular, has enabled high-fidelity hand tracking for immersive VR training platforms. Bouatrous et al. [7] developed a serious game-based rehabilitation system using Leap Motion in a VR environment to guide stroke patients through structured hand exercises. The same design principles—accurate gesture recognition, real-time feedback, and gamification—are directly applicable to training scenarios in industry and education.

Al Nattah et al. [2] expanded on this by demonstrating a semi-immersive VR exercise therapy system that improves motor function through interactive, gamified routines. Their work indicates that the combination of Leap Motion and VR can be repurposed for general skill acquisition and physical training, allowing users to refine hand motions critical in fields like surgery, sports, and manual assembly through repetition and feedback in a safe, simulated environment.

Further, Llerena et al. [27] proposed a fully integrated virtual fitting room that combines AI, computer vision, and VR to align digital garments with the user's real-time pose. This system uses LMC for accurate limb tracking, providing both aesthetic applications (e.g., e-commerce) and movement-based interaction scenarios, offering a blueprint for immersive, personalized virtual training programs.

Finally, Abdul-Kreem [1] emphasized the potential of combining optical flow and Leap Motion data in applications requiring precise hand pose interpretation. This technique is highly transferable to training platforms in domains such as aviation or surgical simulation, where user precision and feedback loops are critical.

These research efforts collectively show that augmented and virtual reality systems, empowered by pose estimation and Leap Motion sensing, are rapidly transforming training, healthcare, and HRI scenarios into more intuitive, immersive, and intelligent experiences.

4 Challenges

4.1 Occlusion

One of the key challenges in pose estimation is occlusion, where parts of the body are hidden from view, making it difficult for models to detect joints. In 2D pose estimation, this can occur when one body part obstructs another (e.g., a hand covering part of the torso). In 3D pose estimation, occlusion can lead to errors in depth estimation. Addressing these challenges requires models to learn to infer missing information or rely on multi-view systems [13].

4.2 Depth Ambiguity

While depth sensors can provide accurate 3D data, they often suffer from noise or low resolution. Furthermore, monocular 3D pose estimation techniques struggle with depth ambiguity, especially in environments with minimal variation in depth [36]. Current research is focused on integrating multiple sensors, such as depth cameras or Inertial Measurement Units (IMUs), to resolve this ambiguity.

4.3 Dataset Availability

A critical aspect of pose estimation research is the availability of large-scale annotated datasets, which significantly impact model performance and generalizability. Although the paper references data sets such as COCO [26] and Hi5 [20], it lacks an in-depth discussion of the diversity of data sets, the challenges of annotation, and the inherent biases.

Several widely used data sets for pose estimation include COCO [26] for human pose estimation, Hi5 [20] for hand pose estimation, and FreiHAND for 3D hand pose datasets. These datasets provide large-scale annotated images with keypoints and depth information. However, a key limitation is the presence of biases related to race, age, and hand size, which affect model performance in real-world scenarios. Another major challenge is annotation consistency; manual labeling can introduce errors that propagate through training. Semi-supervised and self-supervised learning methods, such as contrastive learning frameworks, have been proposed to address this limitation by leveraging unlabeled large-scale data [36].

Future research should focus on developing datasets with greater diversity and annotation accuracy. Synthetic data set generation and domain adaptation techniques, such as those used in [20], can help bridge the gap between controlled training environments and real-world applications.

4.4 Model Generalization and Transfer Learning

Pose estimation models often suffer from poor generalization when applied to unseen datasets or real-world environments. A primary challenge is the domain gap between training and deployment scenarios. However, the paper does not explore transfer learning approaches—such as fine-tuning on target domains or leveraging pre-trained backbones—that are commonly used to reduce this domain discrepancy and improve real-world performance.

Domain adaptation strategies, including synthetic-to-real adaptation, have been explored to enhance model robustness. Recent studies have shown that multitask learning can improve generalization by jointly optimizing pose estimation with related tasks, such as shape reconstruction [42]. Furthermore, transformer-based architectures have demonstrated superior generalization by capturing long-range dependencies in spatial features [26].

Transfer learning techniques, such as fine-tuning pre-trained models on task-specific datasets, have proven effective in reducing data annotation costs while maintaining high accuracy. More research is needed to explore self-supervised domain adaptation techniques to enhance real-world model deployment.

5 Future Directions

5.1 Self-supervised Learning

Self-supervised learning extending from Machine Learning (ML), where models learn representations from unlabeled data, is a promising area of research in pose estimation. This approach could reduce the reliance on annotated data sets or even cleaned learning data, which are expensive and time-consuming to create. Recent works have explored the use of weak supervision and self-supervised techniques to train 3D pose estimation models [48].

5.2 Explainability and Interpretability in Pose Estimation

While deep learning-based pose estimation has achieved remarkable accuracy, its lack of interpretability remains a significant challenge. Explainability is crucial, particularly in safety-critical applications such as healthcare and robotics, where model predictions must be transparent and trustworthy.

Explainable AI (XAI) techniques can provide insights into pose estimation models by visualizing attention maps and keypoint heatmaps [48]. Transformer-based architectures offer interpretability advantages through attention mechanisms, highlighting relevant features during inference [26]. Additionally, integrating physics-based constraints can enhance model transparency by ensuring pose predictions adhere to biomechanical constraints.

Future research should explore hybrid models that combine deep learning with rule-based systems to enhance explainability. Developing standardized evaluation metrics for interpretability in pose estimation models will also contribute to the development of more reliable and ethically responsible AI systems.

5.3 Sensor Fusion

Combining data from multiple sensors, such as RGB cameras, depth sensors, and IMUs, could help address many of the challenges in pose estimation, including occlusion and depth ambiguity. By fusing complementary information, more robust and accurate pose estimations can be achieved [36].

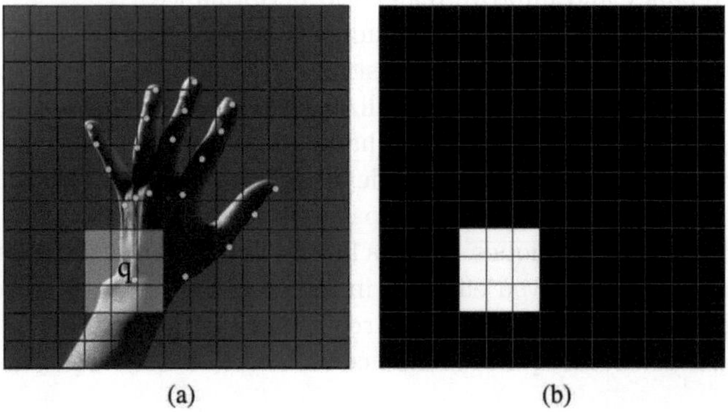

Fig. 8. An illustration of the method used for the estimation of 2D hand keypoints position from an RGB image [31]

Figure 8 illustrates a step-by-step process for estimating 2D hand keypoints from a single RGB image. It visually represents how deep learning models predict joint positions using convolutional architectures.

5.4 Real-Time Optimization

Optimizing pose estimation models for real-time performance is critical, especially in applications like AR/VR and robotics. Future research will likely focus on making models more computationally efficient without sacrificing accuracy, potentially through model pruning or knowledge distillation integrated within the ML models. The challenge that arises would mainly be the computational capacity in real-time instances.

6 Conclusion

In this paper, we reviewed the recent advancements in human pose and hand pose estimation, highlighting both 2D and 3D techniques. Despite significant progress, challenges remain in handling occlusion, depth ambiguity, and real-time optimization. Integrating synthetic datasets, self-supervised learning, and sensor fusion has significantly advanced the field of pose estimation. Future research should continue focusing on optimizing models for real-time applications while ensuring robustness in diverse environments. Hi5 [20] and other synthetic datasets have been crucial in addressing long-standing challenges, such as occlusion and depth ambiguity, paving the way for more reliable and efficient pose estimation models. Future research, especially in self-supervised learning, sensor fusion, and real-time optimization, holds great promise for improving the accuracy, robustness, and efficiency of pose estimation models. The insights from this survey serve as a roadmap for future work in robotic hand systems and immersive technologies. By consolidating recent advances and gaps, it aims to guide the development of more adaptive, data-efficient, and generalizable pose estimation models suited for real-world deployment in healthcare, robotics, and AR/VR applications.

References

1. Abdul-Kreem, L.I.: Motion estimations of hand movement based on a leap motion controller. IEEE Sens. J. **24**(11), 17856–17864 (2024). https://doi.org/10.1109/JSEN.2024.3386051
2. Al Nattah, M.M.A., Tiberti, S., Segaletti, L.: Semi-immersive virtual reality exercise therapy for upper limb rehabilitation in patients with spinal cord injury using the leap motion controller. Cureus **16**(1) (2024)
3. Ansari, H., et al.: Air pose canvas with hand pose estimation using machine learning. Int. J. Innov. Res. Technol. Sci. **12**(2), 227–234 (2024). https://ijirts.org/index.php/ijirts/article/view/34
4. Avola, D., et al.: 3D hand pose and shape estimation from RGB images for keypoint-based hand gesture recognition. Pattern Recogn. **129**, 108762 (2022). https://doi.org/10.1016/j.patcog.2022.108762
5. Azulay, O., Ben-David, I., Sintov, A.: Learning haptic-based object pose estimation for in-hand manipulation control with underactuated robotic hands. IEEE Trans. Haptics **16**(1), 73–85 (2023). https://doi.org/10.1109/toh.2022.3232713
6. Belagiannis, V., Zhou, X., Deng, Z.: Temporal consistency in multi-view human pose tracking. IEEE Trans. Pattern Anal. Mach. Intell. **45**(7), 3210–3225 (2023). https://doi.org/10.1109/TPAMI.2023.3154789
7. Bouatrous, A., et al.: An interactive virtual reality system based on leap motion controller for hand motor rehabilitation. In: 2024 8th International Conference on Image and Signal Processing and their Applications (ISPA), pp. 1–5 (2024). https://doi.org/10.1109/ISPA59904.2024.10536781
8. Bridgeman, T., Smith, J., Patel, R.: Fast multi-view human pose estimation using geometric constraints. Comput. Vis. Image Understand. **210**, 104567 (2023). https://doi.org/10.1016/j.cviu.2023.104567
9. Cai, Z., Luo, F., Zhang, X.: Volumetric transformer pose estimator (VTP) for efficient multi-view processing. Comput. Vis. Image Understand. **215**, 105678 (2024). https://doi.org/10.1016/j.cviu.2024.105678
10. Carraro, M., Bianchi, A., Rossi, E.: RGB-D-based 3D human pose tracking using depth-informed keypoint estimation. Sensors **23**, 1457 (2023). https://doi.org/10.3390/s23031457
11. Cheng, W., et al.: Handdiff: 3D hand pose estimation with diffusion on image-point cloud. In: CVPR (2024). https://openaccess.thecvf.com/content/CVPR2024/papers/Cheng_HandDiff_3D_Hand_Pose_Estimation_with_Diffusion_on_Image-Point_Cloud_CVPR_2024_paper.pdf

12. Deng, X., et al.: Recurrent 3D hand pose estimation using cascaded pose-guided 3D alignments. IEEE Trans. Pattern Anal. Mach. Intell. (2022). https://doi.org/10.1109/tpami.2022.3159725
13. Dubey, S., Dixit, M.: A comprehensive survey on human pose estimation approaches. Multimed. Syst. (2023)
14. Duran, E., et al.: HMP: hand motion priors for pose and shape estimation from video. In: WACV (2024). https://openaccess.thecvf.com/content/WACV2024/papers/Duran_HMP_Hand_Motion_Priors_for_Pose_and_Shape_Estimation_From_WACV_2024_paper.pdf
15. Fan, J., et al.: An integrated hand-object dense pose estimation approach with explicit occlusion awareness for human-robot collaborative disassembly. IEEE Trans. Autom. Sci. Eng. **21**(1), 147–156 (2022). https://doi.org/10.1109/tase.2022.3215584
16. Fan, Y., Guo, X., Zhang, L.: Mao-pose: adaptive multi-view camera positioning for optimal pose capture. Image Vis. Comput. **157**, 102345 (2023). https://doi.org/10.1016/j.imavis.2023.102345
17. Feng, X., Liu, H., Zhang, R.: Active learning for improving multi-view pose annotation efficiency. Mach. Learn. **122**, 654–670 (2023). https://doi.org/10.1007/s10994-023-06214-7
18. Guo, Z., Li, J., Tan, J.: A normalization strategy for weakly supervised 3d hand pose estimation. Appl. Sci. **14**(9), 3578 (2024). https://doi.org/10.3390/app14093578
19. Habibie, I., et al.: In the wild human pose estimation using explicit 2D features and intermediate 3D representations. In: CVPR (2019)
20. Hasan, M., et al.: Hi5: 2D hand pose estimation with zero human annotation (2024). https://arxiv.org/abs/2406.03599
21. Huang, L., et al.: Survey on depth and RGB image-based 3D hand shape and pose estimation. **3**(3), 207–234 (2021). https://doi.org/10.1016/j.vrih.2021.05.002
22. Leng, H., Ge, Y., Xu, C.: A review on 3D hand pose and shape reconstruction from color images. In: A Review on 3D Hand Pose and Shape Reconstruction from Color Images, pp. 7414–7419 (2024). https://doi.org/10.23919/ccc63176.2024.10661647
23. Li, R., et al.: Applying 3D human hand pose estimation to teleoperation. In: Proceedings of the 5th International Conference on Robotics and Computer Vision (ICRCV), pp. 214–223 (2023). https://doi.org/10.1109/icrcv59470.2023.10329261
24. Li, W., et al.: Tokenpose: learning keypoint tokens for human pose estimation. In: Proceedings of the IEEE/CVF International Conference on Computer Vision (ICCV), pp. 11313–11322 (2021)
25. Li, Y., et al.: An interactive gesture control system for collaborative manipulator based on leap motion controller. Adv. Mech. Eng. **16**(5) (2024). https://doi.org/10.1177/16878132241253101
26. Lin, X., et al.: Transformers in human pose estimation. In: ICCV (2021)
27. Llerena, Y.F., et al.: Development of a virtual fitting room integrating computer vision, artificial intelligence and virtual reality technologies. In: 2024 International Conference on Graphics and Interaction (ICGI), pp. 1–8 (2024). https://doi.org/10.1109/ICGI64003.2024.10923795
28. Luo, M., et al.: Denoising diffusion for 3D hand pose estimation. In: ICCVW (2023). https://doi.org/10.1109/ICCVW60793.2023.00338
29. Ma, J., Zhang, L., Sun, W.: Self-supervised learning for multi-view 3D pose estimation without labeled data. Neural Comput. **35**, 1120–1143 (2023). https://doi.org/10.1162/neco_a_01632

30. Mao, Y., et al.: Dor3D-net: dense ordinal regression network for 3D hand pose estimation (2024). https://doi.org/10.48550/arxiv.2403.13405
31. Mishra, P., Sarawadekar, K.: Multiple-hand 2D pose estimation from a monocular RGB image. **12**, 40722–40735 (2024). https://doi.org/10.1109/access.2024.3376426
32. Naik, M.G., et al.: Effect of virtual reality training on hand function in subjects with stroke–a pilot study. Unpublished (2025)
33. Nogueira, A.F.R., Oliveira, H.P., Teixeira, L.F.: Markerless multi-view 3D human pose estimation: a survey. Image Vis. Comput. **155**, 105437 (2025). https://doi.org/10.1016/j.imavis.2025.105437. ISSN 0262-8856
34. Obo, T., et al.: An ensemble approach with evolutionary algorithm for hand posture classification. **29**(1), 95–105 (2025). https://doi.org/10.20965/jaciii.2025.p0095
35. Pavllo, D., et al.: 3D human pose estimation in video with temporal convolutions and semi-supervised training. In: CVPR (2019)
36. Spurr, A., et al.: Self-supervised 3D hand pose estimation from monocular RGB via contrastive learning. In: ICCV (2021)
37. Sun, K., et al.: Deep high-resolution representation learning for human pose estimation. In: CVPR (2019)
38. Toshev, A., Szegedy, C.: Deeppose: human pose estimation via deep neural networks. In: CVPR (2014)
39. Tu, H., Wang, C., Zeng, W.: Voxelpose: towards multi-camera 3D human pose estimation in wild environment. In: ECCV (2020)
40. Tu, H., Chen, Y., Liu, W.: Voxelpose: a 3D-based alternative to 2D lifting for human pose estimation. Pattern Recogn. **152**, 108347 (2023). https://doi.org/10.1016/j.patcog.2023.108347
41. Wan, L., Sun, C., Zhao, M.: Holistic multi-view triangulation with anatomical constraints. J. Comput. Vis. **98**, 112345 (2023). https://doi.org/10.1016/j.jvc.2023.112345
42. Wang, J., Luan, X.: 3D hand pose estimation and shape reconstruction based on multi-task learning. In: Proceedings of the IEEE International Conference on Mechatronics and Automation (ICMA) (2023). https://doi.org/10.1109/ICMA57826.2023.10215729
43. Wang, J., et al.: Graph-PCNN: two-stage human pose estimation with graph-based progressive CNNs. In: CVPR (2021)
44. Wang, Q., He, L., Xie, R.: Transformer-based 3D human pose estimation via spatial attention. IEEE Trans. Neural Netw. Learn. Syst. **34**, 6789–6802 (2023). https://doi.org/10.1109/TNNLS.2023.3166789
45. Wu, Y., et al.: 3D hand pose estimation using semantic dynamic hypergraph convolutional networks. J. Shanghai Jiaotong Univ. (Sci.) (2024). https://doi.org/10.1007/s12204-024-2697-0
46. Xu, W., Kitani, K.: Robot-guided pose estimation via multi-view redundancy screening. Robot. Auton. Syst. **159**, 103762 (2023). https://doi.org/10.1016/j.robot.2023.103762
47. Yao, Y., et al.: Mvsnet: depth inference for unstructured multi-view stereo. In: Proceedings of the European Conference on Computer Vision (ECCV), pp. 767–783 (2018)
48. Yoon, J., et al.: Beyond perspectives: enhancing pose estimation via viewpoint transformation. In: IEEE ICTC (2023). https://doi.org/10.1109/ICTC58733.2023.10393544
49. Yu, S., et al.: 3D hand pose and mesh estimation via a generic topology-aware transformer model. Front. Neurorobot. **18** (2024). https://doi.org/10.3389/fnbot.2024.1395652

50. Zhang, F., et al.: 3D hand pose and shape estimation from monocular RGB via efficient 2D cues. Comput. Vis. Media **10**(1), 79–96 (2023). https://doi.org/10.1007/s41095-023-0346-4
51. Zheng, C., et al.: Deep learning-based human pose estimation: a survey. ACM Comput. Surv. **56**(1), 1–37 (2023). https://doi.org/10.1145/3603618
52. Zhu, H., Wang, T., Li, S.: Multi-view pose estimation in crowded environments using 3D embeddings. Neural Netw. **163**, 256–270 (2023). https://doi.org/10.1016/j.neunet.2023.09.015

Multi-output MLP Architecture for Machining Process Parameter Classification

Dylan Fisher(✉), Jonathan Liaw, and David Loker

The Pennsylvania State University, Erie, PA 16563, USA
{dmf5969,tjl5783,drl3}@psu.edu

Abstract. Remote monitoring of manufacturing processes plays a crucial role in enhancing productivity, reducing production costs, and improving product quality in machining related industries. Traditional remote monitoring methods rely on invasive sensor installation, which can be costly to install and may interfere with production. This paper uses an efficient, non-invasive method of using microphones and machine learning to classify key machining parameters: spindle speed (RPM), depth of cut (DOC), and feed rate (FR). Conventional machine learning approaches typically classify one parameter at a time, while the alternative deep learning approaches tend to be more computationally expensive, featuring a high number of parameters. In this paper, we explore a simpler neural network model – a multi-layer perceptron (MLP) with a branched architecture capable of simultaneous multi-parameter classification. A dataset of audio recordings from a microphone array on machining operations was first collected. Recorded test data was then autocorrelated, processed through a Fast Fourier Transform (FFT), and then normalized to decrease noise. Optimal model hyperparameters were determined through Bayesian hyperparameter tuning. The developed multi-output model achieved a classification accuracy of 93% (FR), 99% (DOC), and 100% (RPM). The multi-output model featured fewer parameters (1.85 M) compared to that of deeper architectures such as VGG16 (135 M parameters), which was used for the same task in other studies, highlighting the effectiveness of the MLP architecture.

Keywords: Machine Learning · Acoustic Signals · Microphone · Machine Monitoring

1 Introduction

Manufacturing process monitoring has advanced significantly through improved signal processing techniques. While these methodologies help optimize manufacturing parameters, predicting process faults remains a challenge due to variations in manufacturing environments. Traditional monitoring relies on invasive sensors, which can be impractical and costly for legacy machines [1–5]. Consequently, non-invasive techniques, such as acoustic signal (AS) monitoring, have gained interest as a viable alternative.

S. Hussain et al. (Eds.): SEET 2025, CCIS 2725, pp. 371–384, 2026.
https://doi.org/10.1007/978-3-032-08977-9_23

Acoustic sensors, such as microphones, offer a non-intrusive means to collect machine health data. Prior research has demonstrated the effectiveness of AS analysis in monitoring tool wear, detecting chatter, and assessing machining conditions [6–12]. Signal processing techniques, including time-domain and frequency-domain analysis, have been employed to extract relevant features from AS data. The FFT is commonly used to analyze frequency content, aiding in the identification of key manufacturing parameters [8, 13–16].

Studies have explored machine learning techniques to improve prediction accuracy in machining operations. While early approaches utilized traditional classifiers, later research incorporated deep neural networks through transfer learning, achieving high accuracy in predicting spindle speed, feed rate, and depth of cut [17, 18]. A research group, Y. Liao et al., used 32-microphone array setups to record and collect data to train various pretrained deep learning models via transfer learning, utilizing ShuffleNet, GoogLeNet, ResNet18, ResNet50, VGG16, and DenseNet20, ultimately achieving a classification accuracy of 95.58% with VGG16 to predict all three parameters simultaneously [18]. Although this accuracy metric is quite good, it is important to note that the VGG16 model implemented is 138 M parameters and over 500 MB in size. Recent studies have built upon this work, utilizing the same dataset, but implemented SVM and kNN models specifically to classify each parameter at a time, and achieved high classification accuracy results [19].

Furthermore, there is a possibility for the development of a simpler machine learning model that features fewer parameters and has the capability of predicting all three machine process parameters at once. This will allow for faster, more resource efficient training and testing phases, as well as a more modular and scalable approach to process parameter classification that could be built upon in the future for more unique implementations.

2 Related Work

MLP machine learning models are simpler than large deep-learning and transformer-based architectures prevalent today. Complex models have high computational costs due to many parameters, often requiring expensive GPU resources. Conversely, simpler MLP models, featuring significantly fewer parameters, can deliver comparable or superior accuracy and shorter training times, as they feature substantially fewer parameters and layers.

In industry, implementations of MLP models have been used for electrocardiogram (ECG) signal processing and have proven to be a robust and accurate method of predicting cardiac arrhythmia from ECG signals [20]. Image classification studies have even developed multi-dimensional MLP models (MDMLP) which performed with 90.90% accuracy on the CIFAR-10 dataset with only 0.3 M parameters [21] – fractional in comparison to a deeper and more complex MLP mixer architecture that only achieved 85.45% accuracy on the same CIFAR-10 dataset with 17.1 M parameters [22].

In applications directly related to signal processing, particularly in industrial settings, studies have demonstrated the effectiveness of MLP models. Signal processing studies conducted in the oil and gas industry have proven the effectiveness of MLP models compared to SVM models in fault detection. It has been shown that sensor data collected from temperature, pressure and vibration probes on a centrifugal pump operation were denoised and preprocessed to train an MLP and SVM model for fault prediction, with the MLP model outperforming the SVM model in classification [23].

Similarly, Ragai et al. (2022) explored classifying turning parameters using "low-cost" algorithms: they found that a simple Quadratic Discriminant Analysis (QDA) model could correctly classify nine cutting conditions (combinations of three spindle speeds and three feed rates) solely from microphone measurements [24]. This result is striking because it shows that even without deep learning, the acoustic signature contains enough information to distinguish different parameter settings. Such studies underscore that for certain well-defined tasks, simpler models can suffice, and they benefit from being more interpretable and computationally efficient.

3 Methodology

3.1 Data Collection Setup

This research builds upon the existing methodologies of prior research groups and therefore implements the same dataset that they have collected [17–19]. Researchers recorded the audio samples from a lathe with a 32-channel spherical microphone array positioned 762 mm from the lathe's workpiece center (Fig. 1). All microphones simultaneously collected acoustic data, with tests being recorded at sample rates of either 12 kHz or 48 kHz on each microphone. Tests were recorded at either 10 or 40 s. The tests sampled at 12 kHz for ten seconds yielded 120,000 samples per microphone, and tests sampled at 48 kHz for ten seconds yielded 480,000 samples per microphone. Some samples were recorded at 12 kHz for 40 s, yielding 480,000 samples.

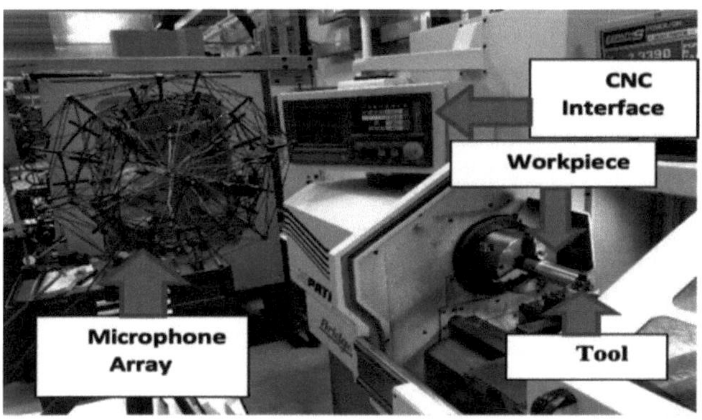

Fig. 1. Position of the machining process relative to the 32-channel microphone array.

Tests were conducted on AISI 1018 cold rolled steel (yield strength: 370 MPa, ultimate strength: 440 MPa) using a Kennametal KC9040 carbide insert, an alumina-coated grade designed for heavy steel roughing operations. The experimental design varied three parameters (spindle speed, depth of cut, and feed rate), with each parameter tested at a range of values. A total of 90 experiments were conducted. The specific parameters used in each test are detailed in Table 1.

3.2 Data Processing Steps

Each of the ninety tests yielded 32.mp4 files corresponding to each individual microphone in the microphone array. Sample rates (kHz) and recording lengths (s) varied among tests in the raw data. The time-domain data of the recordings was then written to a set of plaintext files for data manipulation. Because of the variance in sample-rates in the data, each of the test's recordings were then down sampled to a standardized sample rate of 12 kHz using SciPy's resample method.

All thirty-two microphone recordings from each test were not necessary to include in the final dataset, so a workflow was developed to reduce redundancy of the dataset by selecting only the recordings of microphones with the highest signal voltage outputs. We assumed that the microphones with the least amount of noise to signal interference ratio were those that were closest to the sound source. Therefore, we calculated the absolute value summation of all thirty-two recordings per test and scored each microphone accordingly. Datasets comprised of the top six or three microphones were chosen for training the models.

Recordings from each test were segmented into 0.1 – second segments (1200 samples each). Segments were then autocorrelated and processed via an FFT with the NumPy fft() and correlate() methods. The resulting dataset was composed of rows of frequency domain representations of the 0.1 s segments, with each one labeled according to the process parameters that they corresponded to. Some recordings were longer, being 40 – seconds long, which resulted in slightly more data points for certain classes. Figure 2 summarizes this pipeline.

Table 1. Process parameters of the performed tests.

Spindle Speed (RPM)	Depth of Cut (in)	Feed Rate (in/rev)	Test Numbers
800	0.005	0.0087	1–3
800	0.005	0.0130	4–6
800	0.005	0.0152	7–9
800	0.010	0.0087	10–12
800	0.010	0.0130	13–15
800	0.010	0.0152	16–18
800	0.020	0.0087	19–21
800	0.020	0.0130	22–24
800	0.020	0.0152	25–27
800	0.060	0.0087	82–84
800	0.060	0.0130	85–87
800	0.060	0.0152	88–90
1200	0.005	0.0058	28–30
1200	0.005	0.0087	31–33
1200	0.005	0.0101	34–36
1200	0.010	0.0058	37–39
1200	0.010	0.0087	40–42
1200	0.010	0.0101	43–45
1200	0.020	0.0058	46–48
1200	0.020	0.0087	49–51
1200	0.020	0.0101	52–54
1400	0.005	0.0050	55–57
1400	0.005	0.0074	58–60
1400	0.005	0.0087	61–63
1400	0.010	0.0050	64–66
1400	0.010	0.0074	67–69
1400	0.010	0.0087	70–72
1400	0.020	0.0050	73–75
1400	0.020	0.0074	76–78
1400	0.020	0.0087	79–81

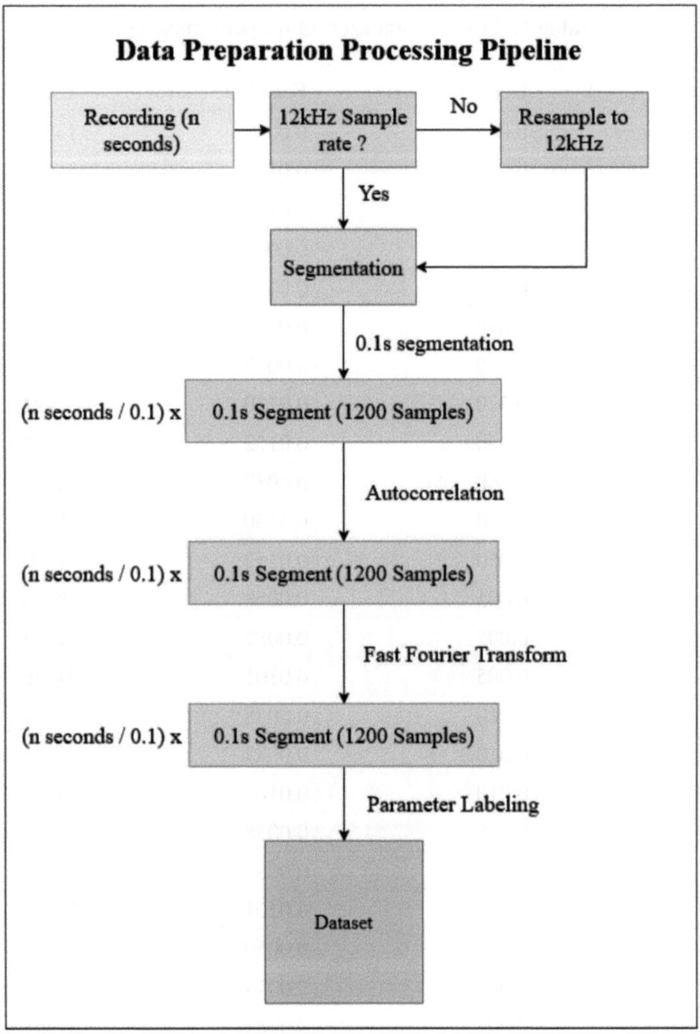

Fig. 2. Data Processing pipeline used to transform all of the raw data into the datasets used for training models.

3.3 Multi Output Model Design and Training

A branched MLP architecture was designed for the multi-classification model. This model featured an initial normalization layer that was used to normalize the data by calculating the mean and variance of the training data using the Keras adapt() method, then shifting and scaling all inputs into a distribution centered around 0 with a standard deviation of 1. The model features a set of three shared dense layers (464 neurons each) and three separate branches coming off of the shared dense layers for RPM, DOC, and FR classifications. The RPM branch features three dense layers with 44 neurons each, the DOC branch three dense layers with 27 neurons each, and the FR branch with four dense layers with 451 neurons each, with output layers of 3, 4, and 7 neurons respectively (Fig. 3). All dense layers use the GeLU activation function, which was selected via a Bayesian hyperparameter search using the Keras tuner library [25]. The resulting compiled model was approximately 1.85 M parameters. The model was then trained for 17 epochs on a 70% training, 15% validation, and 15% testing dataset split on a dataset comprised of the top 3 microphones from the raw tests (Fig. 4). Details on the hyperparameter optimization methods are described below.

Hyperparameter Search with Keras Tuner. A Bayesian hyperparameter optimization search was conducted using the Keras Tuner library to identify optimal hyperparameters for the model. Unlike the random search tuner, which explores the parameter space at random, or the grid search tuner, which exhaustively tests all combinations, the Bayesian tuner uses a probabilistic algorithm that leverages search history to guide the selection of model parameters. The hyperparameters optimized included the activation function, learning rate, the number of hidden layers, and the number of neurons per layer across the shared and individual output branches. The search evaluated three activation functions: ReLU, Leaky ReLU, and GeLU. Additionally, it explored a range of learning rates from 1e-4 to 1e-2, sampled on a logarithmic scale, and varied the number of hidden layers (from 1 to 4) and neurons per layer (from 1 to 500) separately for shared layers and individual output branches (RPM, DOC, FR). The Bayesian tuner employed multi-objective optimization targeting maximum validation accuracies for each output simultaneously (RPM, DOC, FR).

The search was constrained to a total of 10 trials with early stopping criteria, terminating after three consecutive failed trials (no improvement in accuracy metrics). The validation accuracy metrics for each output (RPM, DOC, FR) were tracked and used to guide the Bayesian optimization process.

The best-performing configuration obtained from the Bayesian optimization resulted in selecting the GeLU activation function, demonstrating superior validation accuracy compared to ReLU and Leaky ReLU. Specific hyperparameters identified as optimal were a learning rate of approximately 0.0003 (using the Adam optimizer), three shared dense layers with 464 neurons each, three dense layers with 44 neurons for the RPM branch, three dense layers with 27 neurons for the DOC branch, and four dense layers with 451 neurons for the FR branch. This optimal set of hyperparameters resulted in a final model architecture comprising approximately 1.85 million parameters. The improved performance observed using GeLU activation aligns with findings reported in literature, where GeLU has been noted to outperform traditional ReLU activations in certain contexts [26].

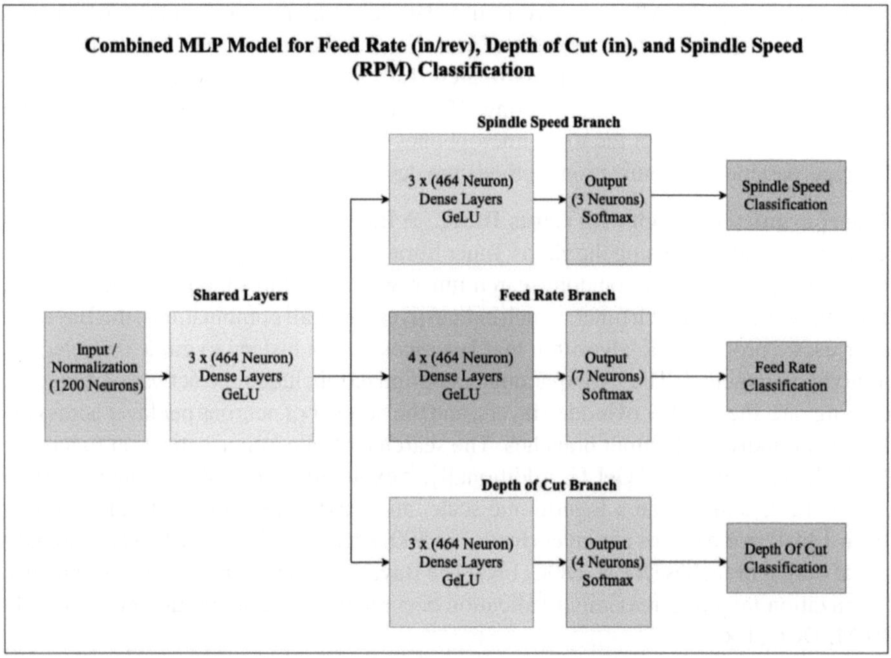

Fig. 3. Branched MLP architecture for multi-classification model

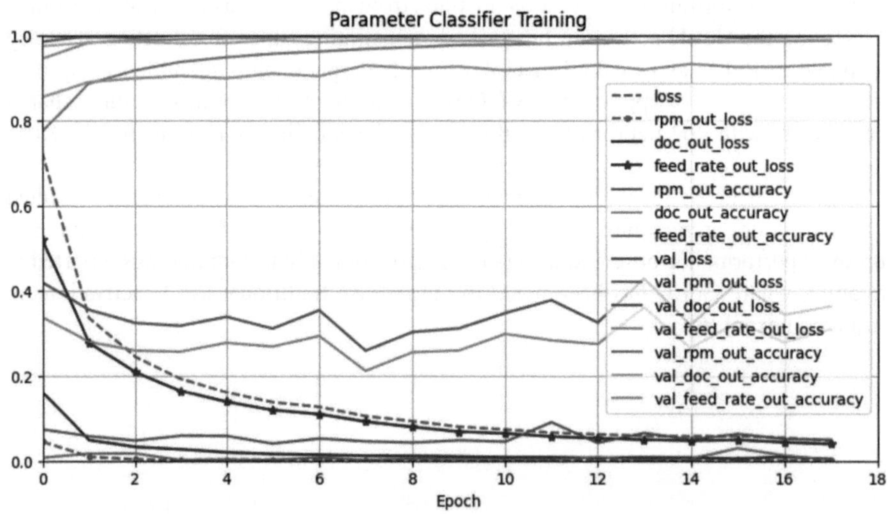

Fig. 4. Multi-classification training curves over 17 epochs using Adam optimizer with learning rate of 0.0003 and sparse categorical cross entropy loss function. X-axis represents epochs of training and y-axis represents training and validation loss and accuracy for the three parameters.

4 Testing and Results

4.1 Multi-classification Results

The model had strong classification accuracy for the RPM, DOC, and FR parameters – achieving accuracies of 99%, 99% and 93% respectively. Tables 2, 3, 4, 5, 6, and 7 specify the classification performance metrics of the model on the test set.

We noticed that the RPM branch performed quite well, reaching testing accuracy close to 100%; however, a testing accuracy this high suggests potential overfitting, as the branch may be training longer than necessary to accommodate slower-converging branches. Future improvements on the model architecture and training methods could include freezing the branch after it has converged and only training the other branches.

Table 2. Precision, Recall, and F1 score of the RPM branch from the multi-classification model from testing.

Class–Value (rpm)	Precision	Recall	F1	Support
0–800	1.00	1.00	1.00	3520
1–1200	1.00	1.00	1.00	1469
2–1400	1.00	1.00	1.00	3095

Table 3. Accuracy metrics of the RPM branch from the multi-classification model from testing.

	Precision	Recall	F1	Support
Accuracy			1.00	8084
Macro Avg.	1.00	1.00	1.00	8084
Weighted Avg.	1.00	1.00	1.00	8084

The DOC branch showed strong performance with minimal signs of overfitting, with a classification accuracy of 99% on the test set.

The FR branch showed similar performance to the single output counterpart, with a classification accuracy of 93% on the test set.

Table 4. Precision, Recall, and F1 score of the DOC branch from the multi-classification model from testing.

Class–Value (in)	Precision	Recall	F1	Support
0–0.005	0.99	0.98	0.98	1531
1–0.01	0.97	0.98	0.98	2304
2–0.02	0.99	0.99	0.99	2795
3–0.06	1.00	1.00	1.00	1454

Table 5. Accuracy metrics of the DOC branch from the multi-classification model from testing.

	Precision	Recall	F1	Support
Accuracy			0.99	8084
Macro Avg.	0.99	0.99	0.99	8084
Weighted Avg.	0.99	0.99	0.99	8084

Table 6. Precision, Recall, and F1 score of the FR branch from the multi-output MLP model from testing.

Class–Value (in/rev)	Precision	Recall	F1	Support
0–0.0050	0.96	0.97	0.96	828
1–0.0058	0.91	0.89	0.90	532
2–0.0074	0.91	0.88	0.90	1047
3–0.0101	0.88	0.91	0.90	527
4–0.0130	0.96	0.94	0.95	1501
5–0.0152	0.95	0.94	0.94	933
6–0.0087	0.91	0.94	0.93	2716

Table 7. Accuracy metrics of the FR branch of the multi-output MLP model from testing.

	Precision	Recall	F1	Support
Accuracy			0.93	8084
Macro Avg.	0.92	0.92	0.92	8084
Weighted Avg.	0.93	0.93	0.93	8084

Figures 5, 6, and 7 depict the confusion matrices derived from evaluating the model on the testing set. The confusion matrix for RPM reflects the findings of the accuracy reports (Tables 2, 3). The confusion matrix for DOC shows results reflecting the strong classification accuracy shown in its accuracy reports (Tables 4, 5) as well. The FR model showed strong classification accuracy for its classes but illustrates the class imbalance of the FR data points around class 6, where most of the false positives and false negatives are concentrated.

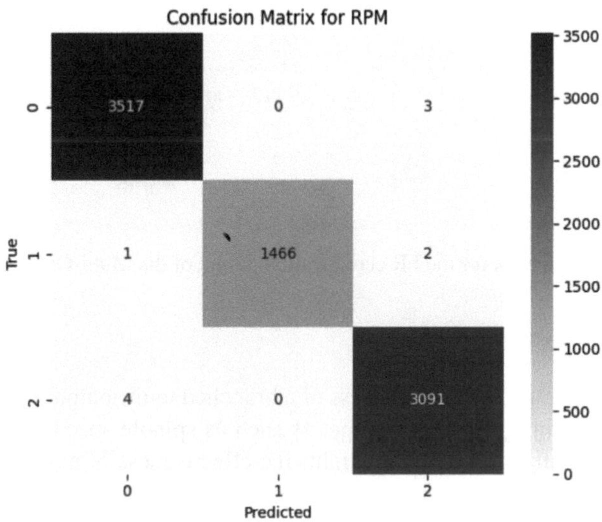

Fig. 5. Confusion matrix for the RPM classification output of the Multi-Output MLP model.

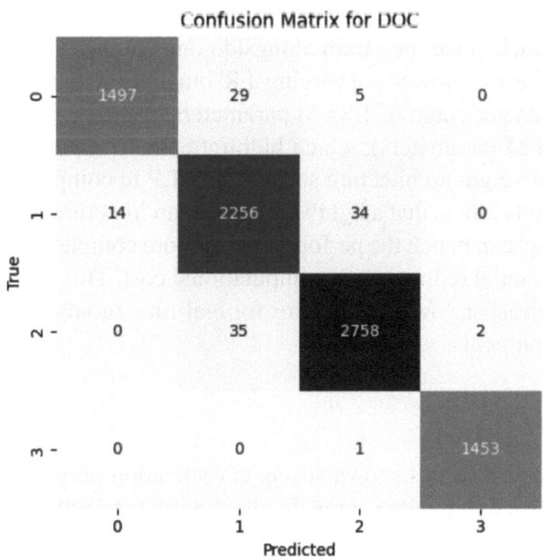

Fig. 6. Confusion matrix for the DOC classification output of the Multi-Output MLP model.

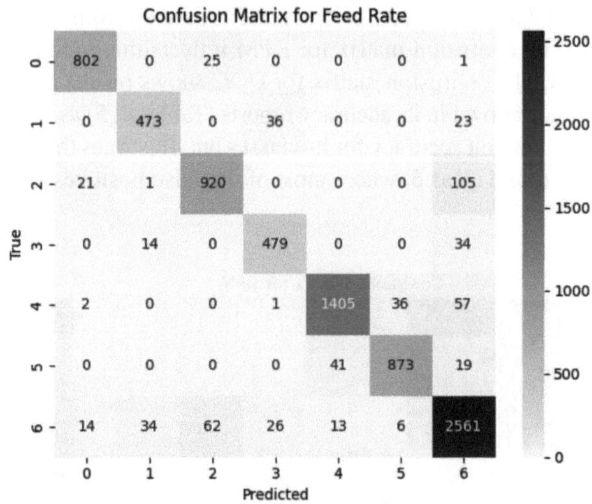

Fig. 7. Confusion matrix for the FR classification output of the Multi-Output MLP model.

5 Conclusions

This study demonstrates the effectiveness of a branched multi-output MLP architecture in classifying machining process parameters such as spindle speed, depth of cut, and feed rate. Additionally, this study highlights the effectiveness of non-invasive acoustic signal monitoring methods such as the microphone array setup that prior researchers used to acquire the data used to train the models [18, 19].

A three-branch multi-classification model was built to classify all the parameters simultaneously. The model showed strong classification accuracy on the three parameters (100% RPM, 99% DOC, 93% FR), although some slight overfitting is suspected on the RPM and DOC branch since they train alongside one another until the early stopping callback is called for the slower converging FR branch. Nonetheless, the model also had a compact parameter count of 1.85 M parameters, contrary to previous approaches using VGG16 (138 M parameters), which highlights the computational efficiency and scalability of a lightweight architecture such as an MLP in comparison [18].

Overall, the results affirm that a lightweight MLP architecture, paired with appropriate signal processing, can match the performance of more complex deep learning models while offering substantial reductions in computational cost. This supports the feasibility of deploying non-invasive, low-cost systems for real-time monitoring and optimization in machining environments.

5.1 Future Work

While the model described has shown strong classification performance, several areas of the research can be expanded upon in the future for further improvements and exploration.

The first area of exploration would be collecting more raw data, with an increased variance in the values of the process parameters so that the objective could be re-oriented to a regression task for increased industry applicability. Additionally, efforts into establishing real-time data processing and parameter classification pipeline would further broaden the applications of the models developed, potentially including the real-time monitoring of multiple machines simultaneously.

Another avenue is dataset enrichment. Collecting data with tool wear indicators could support anomaly detection, potentially allowing manufacturers to make more informed decisions about tool replacement schedules.

Further efforts into improving the parameter count and hyperparameters could also improve the results of the models. Using a hyperparameter optimization tuner for longer search periods on a larger search space would be an effective step in determining a more ideal set of hyperparameters for the given task. Also, model pruning techniques could be investigated to further reduce the parameter count of the models, making the models more deployable to resource constrained systems.

References

1. Shaffer, D., Lorson, P., Plunkett, Z., Ragai, I., DaneshYazdi, A., Ashour, O.: Development of experiment-based mathematical models of acoustic signals for machine condition monitoring. Procedia CIRP **72**, 1316–1320 (2018)
2. Wang, L., Gao, R., Ragai, I.: An integrated cyber-physical system for cloud manufacturing. In: International Manufacturing Science and Engineering Conference, Detroit, MI, USA (2014)
3. Buckholtz, B., Ragai, I., Wang, L.: Cloud manufacturing: Current trends and future implementations. J. Manuf. Sci. Eng., **137**(4): (2015)
4. Shaffer, D., Ragai, I., Danesh-Yazdi, A., Loker, D.: Investigation of the feasibility of using microphone arrays in monitoring machining conditions. Manuf. Lett. **15**(Part B), 132–134 (2018)
5. Liu, Y., Xu, X.: Industry 4.0 and cloud manufacturing: a comparative analysis. J. Manuf. Sci. Eng., **139**(3). (2017)
6. Selcuk, S.: Predictive maintenance, its implementation and latest trends. J. Eng. Manuf. **231**(9), 1670–1679 (2016)
7. Wu, H., Yu, Z., Wang, Y.: Real-time FDM machine condition monitoring and diagnosis based on acoustic emission and hidden semi-Markov model. J. Manuf. Technol. **20**, 2027–2036 (2017)
8. Lauro, C.H., Brandão, L.C., Baldo, D., Reis, R.A., Davim, J.P.: Monitoring and processing signal applied in machining processes – a review. Measurement **58**, 73–86 (2014)
9. Coady, J., Toal, D., Newe, T., Dooly, G.: Remote acoustic analysis for tool condition monitoring. Procedia Manuf. **38**, 840–847 (2019)
10. Joshi, N.S., Singh, S., Krugh, M., Mears, L.: Background noise mitigation of dual microphone system for defect detection in electrical cable connection. Procedia Manuf. **26**, 566–574 (2018)
11. Wang, Z., et al.: Acoustic emission characterization of natural fiber reinforced plastic composite machining using a random forest machine learning model. J. Manuf. Sci. Eng., **142**(3): (2020)
12. Mohanraj, T., Shankar, S., Sakthivel, N., Parmanik, A.: Tool condition monitoring techniques in milling process – a review. J. Market. Res. **9**, 1032–1042 (2020)
13. Ambhore, N., Kamble, D., Chinchanikar, S., Wayal, V.: Tool condition monitoring system: a review. Mater. Today Proc. **2**, 3419–3428 (2015)
14. Glowacz, A., et al.: Fault diagnosis of angle grinders and electric impact drills using acoustic signals. Appl. Acoust. **179**, 108070 (2021)

15. Firmino, J.L., et al.: Misfire detection of an internal combustion engine based on vibration and acoustic analysis. J. Braz. Soc. Mech. Sci. Eng. **43**(7), 336 (2021)
16. Bhuiyan, M.S.H., Choudhury, I.A., Dahari, M.: Monitoring the tool wear, surface roughness and chip formation occurrences using multiple sensors in turning. J. Manuf. Syst. **33**(4), 476–487 (2014)
17. Kerner, S., Deabenderfer, Z., Korn, K., Ragai, I., Liao, Y., Loker, D.: Preliminary investigation on the acoustic characteristics of turning processes. In: International Mechanical Engineering Congress and Exposition, Virtual, Online (2021)
18. Liao, Y., Ragai, I., Huang, Z., Kerner, S.: Manufacturing process monitoring using time-frequency representation and transfer learning of deep neural networks. J. Manuf. Process. **68**(Part A), 231–248 (2021)
19. Rall, K., Loker, D., Nikhare, C.P.: Optimal machine learning for detecting lathe machining parameters. Int. J. Adv. Manuf. Technol. **128**, 779–788 (2023)
20. Ramkumar, M., et al.: ECG cardiac arrhythmias classification using DWT, ICA and MLP neural networks. J. Phys. Conf. Ser. **1831**, 012015 (2021)
21. Lv, T., Bai, C., Wang, C.: Mdmlp: Image Classification from Scratch on Small Datasets with MLP (2022). arXiv preprint arXiv:2205.14477
22. Lian, D., Yu, Z., Sun, X., Gao, S.: AS-MLP: an Axial Shifted MLP Architecture for Vision (2021). arXiv preprint arXiv:2107.08391
23. Orrù, P.F., et al.: Machine learning approach using MLP and SVM algorithms for the fault prediction of a centrifugal pump in the oil and gas industry. Sustainability **12**(11), 4776 (2020)
24. Ragai, I., et al.: Toward smart manufacturing: analysis and classification of cutting parameters and energy consumption patterns in turning processes. J. Manuf. Syst. **64**, 335–345 (2022)
25. O'Malley, T., et al.: KerasTuner (2019). [Online]. Available: https://github.com/keras-team/keras-tuner
26. Lee, M.: Mathematical analysis and performance evaluation of the Gelu activation function in deep learning. J. Math. **2023**, 1–13 (2023). https://doi.org/10.1155/2023/4229924

User-Centered Software Engineering for VR Relaxation Applications

Franceli L. Cibrian[1(✉)], David Zhang[1], Katie Ho[1], Tyler Kay[1], Hector Camarillo-Abad[2], and Trudi Di Qi[1]

[1] Chapman University, Orange, CA 92866, USA
{cibrian,davzhang,katho,tkay,dqi}@chapman.edu
[2] Occidental College, Los Angeles, CA 90041, USA
camarilloabad@oxy.edu

Abstract. Developing effective Virtual Reality (VR) applications requires integrating user-centered methodologies into the software engineering lifecycle. Traditional VR development often focuses on predefined environments, limiting user input in the design process. This study presents a user-centered participatory approach to developing VR relaxation experiences, where users engage in immersive 3D drawing to help define design requirements rather than having them interact with predefined environments, as in previous studies. Our findings show the importance of incorporating multisensory stimuli, balancing embodied and calm interactions, and integrating mood-based personalization for relaxing VR experiences. These results suggest effective strategies for enhancing user-centered design in Software Engineering and improving VR relaxation experiences.

Keywords: Virtual Reality · User-Centered Design · Relaxation

1 Introduction

As emerging technologies reshape the software engineering landscape, Virtual Reality (VR) has gained attention as a platform for developing immersive applications that support well-being, such as stress reduction and relaxation [18]. VR presents a potential solution by providing immersive environments that simulate calming and relaxing settings, offering users an escape from their stressors [8]. Furthermore, VR's potential for customization and exploration properties allows for a personalized approach to each user's specific needs [16]. The development of such applications requires not only technical expertise but also a deep understanding of user needs and expectations. Thus, integrating participatory design methodologies into the software development lifecycle is essential.

Designing effective VR experiences for relaxation presents software engineering challenges, including the diverse range of relaxation techniques with which users may or may not be familiar [23], the challenges of the onboarding process for novice users [4], and the vast design space available in VR [5]. These

S. Hussain et al. (Eds.): SEET 2025, CCIS 2725, pp. 385–399, 2026.
https://doi.org/10.1007/978-3-032-08977-9_24

challenges are amplified when users are unfamiliar with VR. In this case, participatory approaches may offer a promising alternative [2].

In this work, we adopt a user-centered participatory approach to inform the software development process of a VR relaxation application. We use OpenBrush[1], a VR application that allows users to create virtual drawings and interact with virtual environments, as a medium for novice users to engage with and shape their relaxation environments in VR. We selected OpenBrush, as it has been used previously for the treatment of anxiety [3,29], art therapy (e.g., [1,9]), and support creativity (e.g., [28]), among others. However, the previous work has not explored the software design space for VR relaxation experiences through 3D drawing tools in immersive environments.

This study aims to investigate how user-centered design activities can inform early-stage software development decisions. We focus on novice VR users whose perspectives can help uncover design opportunities and constraints that engineers must account for when building adaptive and scalable systems.

The study is guided by the following research questions (RQs):

- RQ1: What is the user experience of novice users in a VR environment?
- RQ2: What opportunities do users have to develop VR environments for relaxation?
- RQ3: What design implications should be considered for a VR environment for relaxation?

Our **contributions** are threefold: (1) we provide empirical evidence of novice users' experiences in immersive VR environments; (2) we show a workflow that integrates user input into early development phases of VR software; and (3) we propose design and engineering insights that can inform the development of personalized, user-driven VR systems specifically for relaxation experiences. By embedding participatory design into the software lifecycle, this work offers practical strategies for engineering more inclusive and adaptive VR applications, contributing to the broader goal of human-centered software engineering for emerging technologies.

2 Related Work

2.1 Specifying Requirements for Developing VR Software

Specifying requirements for VR software introduces different challenges, given that it is an emerging technology that may or may not be known to the users. Traditional software requirements approaches may fall short when applied to VR as they demand an understanding beyond the user interface, and require embodied interaction, multimodal feedback, and an immersive experience [13, 25].

To address these challenges, recent work has proposed to use role-based models that help us to specify scene properties, action responses between properties

[1] https://openbrush.app/.

in each scene, state changes, and user behaviors [11,12]. This work highlights the importance of defining complex and simple requirements in order to fulfill VR systems' requirements.

Other approaches, mainly in Human-Computer Interaction (HCI), have emphasized the importance of integrating user-centered and participatory design methodologies into VR software engineering [31]. For example, [30], develop a virtual reality game using a contextual study and co-design sessions to support behavior change. Similarly, Wilding et al. [35] used collaborative design with older adults to introduce VR in residential care facilities, and Gabrielli et al. [6] involved therapists and adolescents with autism spectrum disorder (ASD) in the co-design and evaluation of therapeutic VR environments.

Overall, these studies highlight that gathering requirements for VR systems involves distinct considerations, including users' engagement, emotional responses, and limited familiarity with immersive technologies. Overcoming these challenges is essential for developing inclusive and effective VR applications that serve a broad range of users, including domain experts, novice users, and vulnerable populations.

2.2 VR for Well-Being and Relaxation

VR environments have been shown to influence mood regulation and support mental well-being by creating immersive and calming experiences. For example, Naylor et al. [19] highlighted how VR fosters positive feelings and combats stress. Studies of naturalistic VR settings, such as virtual forests, demonstrate varying levels of stress relief based on the type of environment. Wang et al. [33,34] found that VR forest environments can be customized for optimal relaxation, suggesting that the design of specific VR elements is critical to achieving therapeutic outcomes. Similarly, Valtchanov et al. [32] observed restorative effects in participants immersed in virtual nature settings after stress induction tasks. Their findings reveal that VR is not only a tool for relaxation but also a medium to study psychological responses to stress. These insights underscore the importance of carefully designed VR environments to maximize emotional and cognitive benefits.

Physiological responses further validate the impact of VR on stress reduction. For example, Gao et al. [7] measured EEG data to assess participants' preferences for blue and green spaces in virtual urban environments, correlating these preferences with calming effects. Integrating emotional and physiological evidence underscores VR's potential to enhance well-being through carefully designed immersive environments.

2.3 VR Using Meditation and Creativity for Stress Relief

Meditation, a well-established practice for managing anxiety, depression, and stress, aligns closely with the ability of VR to create deep, immersive experiences. Seabrook et al. [24] demonstrated that a VR mindfulness application increased positive emotions and a sense of presence through visual and auditory anchors, creating a highly engaging and relaxing experience. This highlights the potential of VR to improve traditional meditation practices by providing controlled, multisensory environments that foster relaxation.

Beyond meditation, creative engagement in VR also shows promise as a stress relief tool. 3D drawing applications like OpenBrush enable users to interact with virtual environments through creative activities such as drawing, combining sensory immersion with self-expression. OpenBrush has been utilized in diverse contexts, including anxiety management [3,29], art therapy [1,9], and creativity support [28]. By enabling users to freely design and personalize virtual environments, tools like OpenBrush offer an interactive and dynamic approach to relaxation. This creative process facilitates stress reduction and fosters a connection between users and their virtual surroundings.

Overall, these applications highlight VR's flexibility for emotional exploration and stress reduction. However, most existing work relies on pre-designed environments, offering limited opportunities for users to actively shape their own relaxation spaces through self-expressive 3D drawings, with sufficient design guidance. This study addresses these gaps by leveraging a VR drawing tool to investigate VR software design for relaxation, focusing on novice users to uncover their needs, challenges, and opportunities for engagement.

3 Methods

To investigate how participatory design can inform the software development of VR-based relaxation tools, we conducted a two-phase study. Our **goal** was to integrate user-centered methods into early stages of the software engineering lifecycle, **emphasizing the translation of user needs into design requirements**. The study consisted of: (1) a contextual study to explore novice users' experiences with VR and identify design preferences, and (2) visioning sessions to collaboratively generate feature scenarios and use cases that could guide future software development.

3.1 Participants

For the contextual study, we recruited 26 participants (aged between 19 and 42 years; 10 men, 15 females, 1 non-binary; 57% of Computer Science/Engineering, 27% from Television, film, and animation, and 16% other or undecided, all English speakers, 92% reported to be novice users). All of them voluntarily participated in the Institutional Review Board (IRB) approved study. All participants completed a preliminary survey and subsequently participated in a VR experience designed to examine gesture-based interactions within the VR environment. For the visioning sessions, we had five participants: three with expertise in HCI, one in VR, one in dance and movement, and one in psychology with experience in relaxation techniques; four of them were novice VR users. These participants contributed not only as users but also as domain stakeholders, playing a role similar to collaborators during participatory specification in software projects.

3.2 System Setup

We utilized OpenBrush, an open-source painting software that enables users to create 3D art for illustrating relaxation design in VR, providing an immersive self-expression experience powered by a standard laptop computer and Meta Quest 2[2]. We set up the VR system similar to [14,22].

3.3 Contextual Study Procedure

The contextual study was part of the user requirements gathering activity. The study was divided into two main stages: a drawing session and a semi-structured interview with co-design activities. To familiarize participants with the VR environment, we first showed them an instructional video demonstrating how to use VR controllers to create 3D drawings in an OpenBrush environment (Fig. 1). Then, participants were given five minutes to illustrate a design within the VR environment to explore the VR tool. At the end of the initial drawing period, participants were offered two more minutes to continue their drawing activity. After that, participants engaged in a semi-structured interview exploring topics such as user experience, challenges faced, and opportunities for using VR for relaxation. These interviews served to elicit insights equivalent to user stories or design needs, which could then be transformed into development goals in subsequent iterations.

Fig. 1. Three participants drawing using VR.

3.4 Data Collection and Analysis

Data were collected through semi-structured interviews conducted after each VR session. In total, 26 individual interviews were held, ranging from 7 to 18 min. Interview topics were designed to capture participants' experiences with VR, the intuitiveness of the controls, relaxation design thinking, and reflections on how the experience influenced their sense of relaxation and their views on how VR can be optimized for relaxation.

[2] https://www.meta.com/quest/products/quest-2/.

For data analysis, we transcribed all interview responses and imported them into NVivo[3] for qualitative analysis. We utilized techniques from reflective thematic analysis to identify recurring patterns and emergent themes across participants' responses. We constructed an affinity diagram in Figma[4] to visually map and organize key themes related to relaxation in VR. The themes identified based on participants' preferences were intuitive experiences with VR gestures, relaxation strategies, desired improvements, and overall reflections on VR. The analysis also emphasized participants' specific relaxation preferences and explored elements of VR that contributed to a relaxed state. This analysis process reflected how user feedback is synthesized during the requirements engineering phase of software development, ensuring that the resulting system design would reflect real user needs.

3.5 Visioning Sessions

First, we presented the affinity diagram to all participants in the session, and participants were free to ask questions and get clarification. Then, we held a 10-minute brainstorming session where each participant proposed up to 20 ideas inspired by themes in the affinity diagram. These ideas were grouped into related clusters, emphasizing the participants' shared focus areas and priorities for enhancing relaxation in VR. After clustering ideas, participants voted on their top choices. From the two most promising concepts, we held a collaborative storytelling session where participants sequentially added elements to a story, envisioning potential VR scenarios that could foster relaxation. The resulting scenarios were iteratively improved to ensure that they captured key design elements for promoting user relaxation and satisfaction within the VR experience.

These scenarios were refined to highlight system components, interaction features, and personalization options. They will serve as prototypes of functional specifications, demonstrating how user-centered design can produce detailed inputs for iterative VR software development.

4 Results

This section presents key findings from the study, focusing on user experiences derived from VR activities. Additionally, opportunities for design improvements and visioning scenarios for VR relaxation applications are outlined.

4.1 User Experience with VR

First Impression and Immersion. Participants reported positive initial impressions of the VR experiences, including ease of use, experiencing fun, and feelings of relaxation. For example, one participant, who was using VR for the

[3] https://lumivero.com/product/nvivo/.
[4] https://www.figma.com/.

first time, reported: *"I think [the VR experience] was (more immersive)... Once you kind of have it down to how to work with tools and whatnot, um, you can actually start kind of just enjoying it rather than like thinking about how to work it"* (P04).

Within VR, the process of learning and adapting to the environment itself was found pleasurable. Participants reported feeling relaxed when engaging in activities incorporating imaginative elements, "*[The VR experience] was nice to get away and not think about anything...just playing around and use your imagination*" (P02). Activities, as such, provided a distraction that participants described as isolating their attention, which was pleasurable.

These findings highlight the potential of VR to offer intuitive, calming experiences that even first-time users find accessible and enjoyable.

VR Drawing Experience. Almost all participants rated the drawing activity as engaging. Many responses related to ease of stress and relaxation during the activity: *"Yeah, the drawing way is a good way to relieve stress. Just giving someone a program like that and letting them say, do whatever you want"* (P03). This relaxation response was due to a form of autonomy or freedom of expression. Using creative expression or outlets is a reliable method of relieving stress in many cases. Some participants also found the three-dimensional aspect of VR particularly appealing: *"I loved it [The 3D experience] because...rather than like drawing something like in front of me, like it was so interactive...I thought it was so cool and I could like create something and then like experience it"* (P10). Three-dimensional models offer a more engaging and realistic experience that allows users to feel more immersed in the realms of their creative work.

The drawing experience also provides "natural" elements as a background and surroundings that relaxed participants when experiencing this stimulus "*It was just looking outside and seeing that view of the mountains. That was, that was pretty cool. I think being able to, um, be in a space where it's just quiet is nice...*" (P06) Nature and outdoor scenes in VR offer a unique opportunity for users to experience peace and solitude. Many participants, being college students, live fast-paced lives, which results in finding comfort in relaxing, peaceful spaces.

Interface and Usability Challenges. While most of the experience was positive, participants identified several challenges with the VR interface. One participant found the menu interface too small, suggesting larger and more customizable menus for improved usability.

Participants also expressed having trouble with the loading page, *"I'm standing still, and I see the stars ever so slowly moving and...you're going to like slowly start leaning a certain way or anything like that.* (P06)" The leaning described an off-balance effect that the participant felt at risk of falling or losing the sense of proprioception, *"But it has a Star Wars thing where like the stars actually slowly like shifts...they pan around. And...I don't get dizzy that easily... sometimes it's hard to, like, think that you're balanced"* (P06). Participants expressed discomfort in staring too long at a stimulus that altered their perception of space, making them susceptible to loss of balance. POV (point of view) in VR, such as panning and rapid zooms, can visually induce dizziness because users are immersed heavily in VR. Reducing motion sickness-causing animations in loading screens or menu interfaces will likely reduce participants' feelings of dizziness.

Even though many participants reported using tools (e.g., a brush) as a positive experience, they struggled with the correct use of the VR controller in the beginning. This was due to the lack of knowledge of controller shortcuts. Participants also found navigating tools satisfying within activities, with the exception that there was a learning curve for beginner or amateur VR users, " *Um, so if I knew all the shortcuts on that controller, I'm sure it would have been faster...I would do a tutorial in the beginning, but I totally forgot how to do it"* (P22).

4.2 Opportunities to Enhance Relaxation in VR

Personalized Auditory and Environment Experiences. Music and audio preferences emerged as central themes in the discussions of relaxation between participants. Many participants suggested allowing users to select their preferred music to create a more comfortable and soothing environment: *"If possible...maybe you could let the person listen to what music they want to listen to...that's the first thing off the top of my mind...You want to make them as comfortable as possible"* (P21). Adding personalized background music was frequently cited as a tool for aiding relaxation.

In addition to music, participants emphasized the importance of sound effects that correspond to interactions within the VR environment: *"Like relaxing, or like, maybe like sounds that correspond with the environment, like wintery sounds when you're like interacting with the snowman, or just like, I guess like nature sounds"* (P11). Sound effects that come from interactions in augmented realities oftentimes enhance realism due to their appeal to multiple senses. By incorporating interactive auditory elements and allowing users to customize music genres, VR environments can enhance realism and immersion while tailoring experiences to individual preferences. These features have the potential to engage multiple senses and deepen the relaxation experience.

Fostering Creativity and Exploration. Participants expressed a strong preference for activities that allowed for creative expression and exploration, particularly in sandbox-style environments. One participant explained: "*I appreciate sort of like the sandbox style...it allows you to be creative in a way that you're not typically creative during the day*" (P06). This participant expresses the inability to perform enough creative tasks during the day and indicates that sandbox settings make for a suitable opportunity to supplement creative outputs.

Sandbox environments were seen as opportunities to relax while fostering creativity. Participants described how the ability to explore, interact, and customize their surroundings helped establish a mood conducive to relaxation. For instance, combining creative tasks with environmental customization and audio features (e.g., user-selected music) could enhance the overall experience.

The second most common method of relaxation to emerge given the VR experience was to spend time doing physical activities outdoors: *"I like to, I like the outdoors a lot, so I like going hiking and things like that. Um, so I would say those are like my top things"* (P04). Almost all participants who mentioned outdoor and physical activities also mentioned music in combination with their activity. Not only does being active outside in nature provide an immersive setting that limits distractions, but it also delivers a sense of vitality. Exposure to fresh air, sunlight, and nature creates an association with a physical sense of well-being.

4.3 VR Scenarios for Relaxation

The visioning sessions enabled participants to specify key features and workflows for relaxation scenarios. These sessions served as collaborative design blueprints for future implementation. All the sessions were motivated and guided by the themes and findings from the affinity diagram created as a result of the contextual study.

Scenario 1: VR Rage Room. *Emma, a second-year undergraduate, feels overwhelmed by midterms, a part-time job, and group project deadlines. She visits the campus wellness center and selects the VR Rage Room to seek relief. Customizing her session, she chooses a cluttered university library storage room as the setting, with cluttered stacks of books, obsolete equipment, and fragile objects. She pairs it with an energetic, lo-fi track for motivation. In the virtual space, Emma uses a hammer to smash old books, computers, and lab equipment, feeling the haptic feedback and hearing realistic breaking sounds. A progress bar tracks her score, driving her to continue. As the session progresses, she throws virtual glass beakers, enjoying dramatic visual and auditory effects. Subtle lighting changes enhance the immersive experience. After ten minutes, the scene changes to a tranquil university courtyard at dusk. Calming music and breathing prompts guide Emma to relax, easing her busy mind from stress. The session concludes with a summary of her activity, personalized stress management tips, and a sense of renewed focus. Re-centered, Emma leaves ready to tackle her real-life tasks.*

Scenario 2: Outdoor Exploration. *James, a third-year undergraduate, feels stressed after working hours on a research paper. He decides to take a break and visit the wellness center's VR relaxation suite, where he selects the Outdoor Exploration experience. He customizes his session, choosing a mountain trail in spring with blooming flowers, light drizzle, and a gentle breeze. James then pairs the scene with ambient nature sounds, including birdsong and rustling leaves during a virtual walk. As the session begins, James explores the trail, noticing the sound of his footsteps change with the terrain. A scrollbar allows him to switch between seasonal timelines, revealing the trail in golden fall hues or glistening winter snow. He interacts with the environment using VR controllers, skipping stones across a stream, brushing past glowing wildflowers, and feeling* *subtle haptic vibrations that enhance immersion. Midway, James switches to a virtual canoe, gliding across a serene lake surrounded by cliffs. He adjusts the weather, transitioning to a warm sunset that bathes the landscape in golden light. As the session ends, James sits virtually on a bench at a peaceful overlook, taking in a sweeping valley view. Calming music plays, and guided breathing prompts help him relax. A summary screen provides a recap of his settings and tips for incorporating mindfulness into daily life. Feeling rejuvenated, James removes the headset, ready to return to his studies with a clear mind.*

5 Discussion: Design Considerations

Building on our findings from the contextual and visioning sessions, we identified critical software engineering considerations for developing user-centered VR relaxation systems.

5.1 Desinging Multisensory Experiences

A multisensory VR experience entails simultaneously engaging multiple senses, primarily visual, auditory, and sometimes tactile stimuli, to enrich the user's immersion and enhance relaxation [17]. Our results suggested that natural elements, such as the sound of rain, visuals of forests, and ambient tactile cues, are particularly effective in creating a relaxing multisensory experience. Such stimuli foster deeper relaxation by immersing users in familiar, calming environments that reflect their preferences and feel cohesive [27]. Effective multisensory experiences require crossmodal correspondence where stimuli work together, forming a coherent sensory experience.

To exemplify multisensory experiences in VR the *Rage Room* integrates multisensory elements to amplify the release of stress. Users hear realistic sounds of their interaction synchronized with the visual effects. Haptic feedback in controllers mimics the tactile sensation of impacts, supported by a high-performance physics engine capable of real-time collision detection and dynamic object response to ensure realistic manipulation and interaction. On the other hand, *Outdoor Exploration* synchronizes natural sounds with corresponding visual cues (e.g., rain sounds paired with falling rain visuals), working together to create a calm and immersive environment. This experience relies on the integration of real-time, physics-based rendering to accurately simulate and depict natural environments. Designing multisensory experiences with cohesive stimuli improves immersion and relaxation for VR relaxation applications.

Overall, system architectures for VR should synchronize sensory streams (e.g., visuals, audio, haptics) using real-time event-driven pipelines to ensure coherence and minimize sensory conflicts.

5.2 Balancing Embodied Interaction: Movement Versus Stillness

Relaxation techniques vary significantly in their level of physical engagement [17]. Techniques such as meditation and yoga are generally low in movement, encouraging stillness and introspection; they promote mindfulness, support relaxation, and mental well-being by allowing the mind to focus and remove distractions [21]. In contrast, movement-based relaxation, such as simulated running and walking, enables physical expression as a form of stress release [15]. Our results suggest that within VR, we could mimic those techniques and take advantage of the virtual part of the world to provide both types of experience, as most of the novice users related VR with movements rather than stillness.

In the proposed scenarios, the *Rage Room* supports movement-based relaxation by offering physically engaging activities such as smashing, throwing, and destroying objects. However, the scenario transitions into a calming cooldown phase with minimal movement, balancing activity and stillness. The *Outdoor Exploration* scenario blends both approaches by allowing users to move through the environment at their own pace and/or engage with the environment actively or simply observe the scenery in a meditative state. Overall, VR applications should support both movement-intensive and stillness-oriented relaxation modes.

This shows that VR software should provide flexibility to switch between high-movement and meditative modes, which includes a management system that optimizes the gesture recognition only when needed, and they could also control passive interaction using physiological feedback. Considering that modern VR systems integrate multimodal tracking of the hands, head, and body, software design should leverage these capabilities to adapt interaction modes dynamically, ensuring a seamless and responsive experience that supports both active engagement and calm reflection.

5.3 The Role of Feelings in Personalization

Personalization emerged as a critical factor in user satisfaction with VR experiences [10], where the relaxation topic has also been explored. Our study revealed that relaxation is highly subjective, with varied user preferences for environments and activities. To promote relaxation, VR applications should incorporate personalization options that allow users to select the types and intensities of relaxation activities that best serve their needs. For example, offering a customization interface where users can choose from various relaxation modes, including creative, interactive, or purely observational, could provide a flexible experience that accommodates different emotional and sensory preferences [20]. On the other hand, with the use of wearables and/or another type of analysis, by integrating data-driven or AI technology, we can predict the level of stress/relaxation [26], and personalize the experience in real-time using data from those sensors.

To exemplify this, in the *Rage Room*, users can customize their environment by selecting objects to destroy (e.g., plates, electronic devices, or books) and adjusting the intensity of sensory elements like sound effects and visual feedback. They can also choose background music to match their mood, from calming tracks to energetic beats. In contrast, in the *Outdoor Exploration*, users can adjust the weather (e.g., sunny, rainy), season (e.g., spring, winter), and timeline of the environment. They can also tailor auditory elements, such as nature sounds or background music, to enhance their sense of immersion and relaxation. For both scenarios, we envision that dynamic personalization could be used in real-time but informed data from wearables to enhance the experience. Overall, VR applications should provide a personalization mechanism that either manually or automatically adapts to the user's preferences.

Architecturally, this would require modular plug-ins capable of ingesting biosensor data (e.g., heart rate variability, EEG) and adapting system parameters via a personalization engine, supporting closed-loop feedback systems for user experience optimization.

6 Conclusion

This study explored how novice users experience VR relaxation activities and how user-centered design methods can inform early stages of software engineering for immersive systems. Our findings translate into high-level system requirements such as supporting multisensory stimuli, balancing dynamic and passive embodied interaction, and embedding adaptive personalization mechanisms. These requirements go beyond traditional functional requirements, showing the importance of involving the users in the VR experience so they can provide more details and features beyond functionality.

We proposed two functional VR scenarios: *Rage Room* and *Outdoor Exploration*, that serve as illustrative examples of how those features can inform specific prototypes. Although the scenarios were not validated through full usability testing, they provide grounded use-case prototypes for iterative development cycles, allowing developers to scaffold future feature sets based on user-centered insights. Future work should implement and evaluate these scenarios within functioning VR prototypes.

Embedding user-centered design methodologies into the software engineering lifecycle offers a powerful strategy for developing emerging technologies that are more responsive, inclusive, and aligned with real user needs.

Acknowledgments. We thank our participants for their valuable feedback. The human subject research was approved by the Institutional Review Board at Chapman University with IRB number: IRB-22-250. This research was partially funded by the Research Startup Funds of Dr. Franceli Cibrian and Dr. Trudi Qi and undergraduate research grants at the Fowler School of Engineering at Chapman University.

References

1. Andrunyk, V., Kalka, N., Shestakevych, T.: Virtual reality in art therapy for children with autism. In: MoMLeT+ DS, pp. 514–525 (2023)
2. Ashtari, N., Bunt, A., McGrenere, J., Nebeling, M., Chilana, P.K.: Creating augmented and virtual reality applications: current practices, challenges, and opportunities. In: Proceedings of the 2020 CHI Conference on Human Factors in Computing Systems, pp. 1–13 (2020)

3. Bennett, M., Christensen, K.: Use of virtual reality (VR) as a clinical tool for management of self-perceived anxiety in college students. J. High. Educ. Theory Pract. **24**(1) (2024). https://doi.org/10.33423/jhetp.v24i1.6761
4. Chauvergne, E., Hachet, M., Prouzeau, A.: User onboarding in virtual reality: an investigation of current practices. In: Proceedings of the 2023 CHI Conference on Human Factors in Computing Systems, pp. 1–15 (2023)
5. Dozio, N., et al.: A design methodology for affective virtual reality. Int. J. Hum. Comput. Stud. **162**, 102791 (2022)
6. Gabrielli, S., et al.: Co-design of a virtual reality multiplayer adventure game for adolescents with autism spectrum disorder: mixed methods study. JMIR Serious Games **11**(1), e51719 (2023)
7. Gao, T., Zhang, T., Zhu, L., Gao, Y., Qiu, L.: Exploring psychophysiological restoration and individual preference in the different environments based on virtual reality. Int. J. Environ. Res. Public Health **16**(17), 3102 (2019). https://doi.org/10.3390/ijerph16173102
8. Gentile, A., Ficarra, S., Thomas, E., Bianco, A., Nordstrom, A.: Nature through virtual reality as a stress-reduction tool: a systematic review. Int. J. Stress Manag. (2023)
9. Haeyen, S., Jans, N., Heijman, J.: The use of VR tilt brush in art and psychomotor therapy: an innovative perspective. Arts Psychother. **76**, 101855 (2021). https://doi.org/10.1016/j.aip.2021.101855
10. Jung, H.W., et al.: Personalized virtual reality exposure for panic disorder and agoraphobia: a preliminary neurophysiological study. Comprehensive Psychiatry **129**, 152447 (2024). https://doi.org/10.1016/j.comppsych.2023.152447. https://www.sciencedirect.com/science/article/pii/S0010440X23000846
11. Karre, S.A., Pareek, V., Mittal, R., Reddy, R.: A role based model template for specifying virtual reality software. In: Proceedings of the 37th IEEE/ACM International Conference on Automated Software Engineering, pp. 1–5 (2022)
12. Karre, S.A., Reddy, Y.R.: Model-based approach for specifying requirements of virtual reality software products. Front. Virtual Reality **5**, 1471579 (2024)
13. Karre, S.A., Reddy, Y.R., Mittal, R.: Re methods for virtual reality software product development: a mapping study. ACM Trans. Softw. Eng. Methodol. **33**(4), 1–31 (2024)
14. Kay, T., Raswan, M., Camarillo-Abad, H.M., Qi, T.D., Cibrian, F.L.: Using virtual reality to foster creativity for co-design a new self-expression and relaxation virtual environment for students. In: Proceedings of the 15th Conference on Creativity and Cognition, pp. 365–367 (2023)
15. Keating, L.E., et al.: Effects of a 12-week running programme in youth and adults with complex mood disorders. BMJ Open Sport Exercise Med. **4**(1), e000314 (2018). https://doi.org/10.1136/bmjsem-2017-000314
16. Marougkas, A., Troussas, C., Krouska, A., Sgouropoulou, C.: How personalized and effective is immersive virtual reality in education? A systematic literature review for the last decade. Multimed. Tools Appl. **83**(6), 18185–18233 (2024)
17. Matzer, F., Nagele, E., Lerch, N., Vajda, C., Fazekas, C.: Combining walking and relaxation for stress reduction-a randomized cross-over trial in healthy adults. Stress. Health **34**(2), 266–277 (2017). https://doi.org/10.1002/smi.2781
18. McGarry, S., Brown, A., Gardner, M., Plowright, C., Skou, R., Thompson, C.: Immersive virtual reality: an effective strategy for reducing stress in young adults. Br. J. Occup. Ther. **86**(8), 030802262311656 (2023). https://doi.org/10.1177/03080226231165644

19. Naylor, M., Ridout, B., Campbell, A.: A scoping review identifying the need for quality research on the use of virtual reality in workplace settings for stress management. Cyberpsychol. Behav. Soc. Netw. **23**(8), 506–518 (2020). https://doi.org/10.1089/cyber.2019.0287
20. Pardini, S., et al.: The role of personalization in the user experience, preferences and engagement with virtual reality environments for relaxation. Int. J. Environ. Res. Public Health **19** (2022). https://api.semanticscholar.org/CorpusID:249699971
21. Park, S.H., Han, K.S.: Blood pressure response to meditation and yoga: a systematic review and meta-analysis. J. Alternative Complementary Med. **23**(9), 685–695 (2017). https://doi.org/10.1089/acm.2016.0234
22. Qi, T.D., Boyd, L., Fitzpatrick, S., Raswan, M., Cibrian, F.L.: Towards a virtual reality visualization of hand-object interactions to support remote physical therapy. In: International Conference on Ubiquitous Computing and Ambient Intelligence, pp. 136–147. Springer, Cham (2023)
23. Riches, S., Azevedo, L., Bird, L., Pisani, S., Valmaggia, L.: Virtual reality relaxation for the general population: a systematic review. Soc. Psychiatry Psychiatr. Epidemiol. **56**(10), 1707–1727 (2021). https://doi.org/10.1007/s00127-021-02110-z
24. Seabrook, E., et al.: Understanding how virtual reality can support mindfulness practice: Mixed methods study. J. Med. Internet Res. **22**(3), e16106 (2020). https://doi.org/10.2196/16106. https://www.jmir.org/2020/3/e16106/
25. Shen, B., Tan, W., Guo, J., Cai, H., Wang, B., Zhuo, S.: A study on design requirement development and satisfaction for future virtual world systems. Future Internet **12**(7), 112 (2020)
26. Sim, S.H., Paranjpe, T., Roberts, N., Zhao, M.: Exploring edge machine learning-based stress prediction using wearable devices. In: 2022 21st IEEE International Conference on Machine Learning and Applications (ICMLA) (2022). https://doi.org/10.1109/icmla55696.2022.00203
27. Song, I., Baek, K., Kim, C., Song, C.: Effects of nature sounds on the attention and physiological and psychological relaxation. Urban Forestry Urban Greening **86**, 127987 (2023). https://doi.org/10.1016/j.ufug.2023.127987
28. Stephen, C., Kunnumpurath, B.: Virtual reality tilt brush for creativity: an experimental study among architecture students. Nanotechnol. Perceptions **20**(S11) (2024). https://doi.org/10.62441/nano-ntp.v20is11.53
29. Tan, J., Kannis-Dymand, L., Jones, C.: Examining the potential of VR program tilt brush in reducing anxiety. Virtual Reality **27**(4), 3379–3391 (2023)
30. Téllez, A.M., Castro, L.A., Tentori, M.: Developing and evaluating a virtual reality videogame using biofeedback for stress management in sports. Interact. Comput. **35**(2), 407–420 (2023)
31. Thalen, J.P., van der Voort, M.C.: User centred methods for gathering VR design tool requirements. In: Proceedings of the 17th Eurographics conference on Virtual Environments & Third Joint Virtual Reality, pp. 75–81 (2011)
32. Valtchanov, D., Barton, K.R., Ellard, C.: Restorative effects of virtual nature settings. Cyberpsychol. Behav. Soc. Netw. **13**(5), 503–512 (2010). https://doi.org/10.1089/cyber.2009.0308
33. Wang, X., Shi, Y., Zhang, B., Chiang, Y.: The influence of forest resting environments on stress using virtual reality. Int. J. Environ. Res. Public Health **16**(18), 3263 (2019)
34. Wang, Z., et al.: Effects of restorative environment and presence on anxiety and depression based on interactive virtual reality scenarios. Int. J. Environ. Res. Public Health **19**(13), 7878 (2022). https://doi.org/10.3390/ijerph19137878

35. Wilding, R., et al.: Introducing virtual reality to older adults: a qualitative analysis of a co-design innovation with care staff. Arch. Gerontol. Geriatr. **125**, 105505 (2024)

Can Large Language Models be Used as an Alternative for Human Annotation: A Case Study of Emotion Classification

Nek Dil Khan[1], Maram Fahaad Almufareh[2(✉)], Javed Ali Khan[3], Jianqiang Li[1(✉)], Arif Ali Khan[5], and Mamoona Humayun[4]

[1] Faculty of Information Technology, Beijing University of Technology, Beijing 100124, China
nekdilkhan@emails.bjut.edu.cn, lijianqiang@bjut.edu.cn
[2] Department of Information Systems, College of Computer and Information Sciences, Jouf University, Sakaka, Saudi Arabia
mfalmufareh@ju.edu.sa
[3] Department of Computer Science, Faculty of Physics, Engineering and Computer Science, University of Hertfordshire, Hatfield, UK
j.a.khan@herts.ac.uk
[4] Department of Computing, School of Arts Humanities and Social Sciences, University of Roehampton, London SW15 5PJ, UK
Mamoona.Humayun@roehampton.ac.uk
[5] M3S Empirical Software Engineering Research Unit, University of Oulu, Oulu, Finland
Arif.khan@oulu.fi

Abstract. For market-based software evolution, user feedback has become a primary source utilized by various machine learning (ML) algorithms to identify insightful information. However, it heavily employs human subjects to complete such experimental tasks, particularly for data annotation. It is reported in software engineering (SE) literature that human subjects are challenging to find, prone to errors, and can have a second guess in identifying the correct annotation type, resulting in possible bias. In contrast, large language models (LLMs) have recently demonstrated comparatively equal or better performances in various complex SE tasks, making them a good alternative for data annotation tasks. For this purpose, the proposed approach investigated and experimented with the performance of LLMs, particularly ChatGPT, to annotate end-user feedback for ML classification tasks. We experimented with two datasets, i.e., human and ChatGPT API annotated, to explore whether ChatGPT can be used as an alternative to human annotators when preparing labeled datasets for ML experiments. For this purpose, we identify the efficacy of various deep learning (DL) classifiers in detecting associated emotions, including anger, confusion, distrust, sadness, disappointment, frustration, disgust, and fear, with end-user reviews. We obtained satisfactory results with BILSTM, GRU, CNN, LSTM, BiGRU, and RNN algorithms using the ChatGPT-generated dataset compared to the human-annotated data set. We obtained an average accuracy of 92%,

S. Hussain et al. (Eds.): SEET 2025, CCIS 2725, pp. 400–416, 2026.
https://doi.org/10.1007/978-3-032-08977-9_25

92%, 91%, 90%, 91%, and 91% compared to the manually annotated data set, 75%, 75%, 79%,48%, 73%, and 85%, with CNN, LSTM, BILSTM, GRU, BiGRU, and RNN Classifiers, respectively. The study results show that LLMs can be an alternative source for annotating datasets for ML classification experiments. However, the results need to be validated by human experts for improved generalizability and trust.

Keywords: Large Language Model(LLMs) · Emotion classification · Chat-GPT · Human Annotations · User Feedback Analysis

1 Introduction

The rapid advancement of ML techniques has shown their increasing application in SE tasks, including examining end-user feedback for software development [12]. With the explosion of end-user-generated feedback on platforms like the Google Play Store, Amazon App Store, and various social media channels, feedback from end-users has become an essential resource for improving software functionalities, particularly for market-driven software apps [15]. These end-user reviews often contain important information about customer needs, software issues [20], feature requests [10,17], and other essentials for ensuring software quality and user satisfaction [21,30]. However, analyzing large volumes of feedback is challenging and resource-intensive, often requiring human annotators to label data accurately, which may raise bias and inconsistencies [11,19].

Many recent studies in SE literature have emphasized the importance of containing end-user feedback in the software development life cycle [5,12,15]. Tools and techniques such as sentiment analysis, opinion mining, and emotion detection derive insights from user reviews [18]. However, most existing approaches rely heavily on manual data annotation, which is time-consuming and tends to make mistakes due to subjective variations [6]. Annotating large datasets for sentiment classification tasks is particularly challenging when users express complex emotions or mixed sentiments in their feedback [7,18]. Therefore, an efficient and scalable alternative annotation process is necessary compared to human annotators to reduce human biases and automate it with comparatively less or no human intervention.

Recently, LLMs have achieved significant success in automating various software engineering activities [14]. From bug detection to requirement generation and code summarization, LLMs show their potential to revolutionize the field. Similarly, LLMs have been successfully implemented in automating various requirements-related activities [27]. For example, Lubos et al., [26], assess the capabilities of LLM (Llama 2) to evaluate NL software requirements for various quality attributes. Following this, Khan et al., [19] utilize chatGPT as a negotiator to settle disputes by annotating end-user feedback for various emotion types. While Nasution and Onan [28] utilized ChatGPT to annotate textual data from various low-resource languages for various natural language processing (NLP) tasks and compared the results with those of human experts. Considering the success of LLMs in automating various complex NLP and software engineering-related tasks by surpassing humans, it can be considered to investigate the performance of ChatGPT in annotating end-user feedback from the Amazon store to various emotion types and comparing the performance to human-annotated datasets by exposing it to various DL classifiers.

In our proposed approach, we utilized the ChatGPT API as a possible alternative source to annotate end-user comments with various emotion types. The manual identification of associated emotions in end-user reviews is challenging, time-consuming, and prone to potential biases due to the human coders involved in the annotation process. This led us to investigate whether ChatGPT can be a dependable substitute for human annotators in creating labeled datasets for ML experiments. To test this hypothesis, we used two datasets, one annotated by humans and the other by ChatGPT using the ChatGPT API. We then compared the performance of several DL classifiers in detecting a wide range of emotions using both datasets. Our focus on accuracy, precision, recall, and F-measure ensured a comprehensive evaluation of these emotions. The results unequivocally demonstrate the reliability of ChatGPT-generated annotations, which perform comparably better than human-annotated datasets, thereby strengthening the case for LLMs as a valuable alternative for automating the data annotation process in SE applications. The key contributions are:

- We utilized ChatGPT to annotate user reviews as an alternative to human annotators for generating labeled datasets for ML tasks, seeking to minimize bias and increase efficiency.
- We evaluated different DL classifiers, including GRU, BiGRU, CNN, LSTM, BILSTM and RNN, on human and ChatGPT annotated datasets to assess the effectiveness of LLM-generated annotations in detecting emotions.
- ChatGPT as an alternative annotation tool yields better classification performance of DL models, with accuracies surpassing human annotated datasets.

2 Related Work

SE continuously evolves by incorporating emerging state-of-the-art techniques and tools into software evolution. Below, we discuss recent developments in software evolution.

2.1 Large Language Model(LLMs) in Software Engineering

Researchers recently started using LLMs to automate various SE activities [14], including requirements engineering (RE) [16]. LLMs are a helpful alternative in automating and improving different RE activities. For example, Lubos et al., [26] used LLM to evaluate the quality characteristics of software requirements, including appropriate, complete, conforming, correct, feasible, necessary, singular, unambiguous, and verifiable in natural language requirements. Ren et al. [29] proposed an LLM-based approach to elicit and model requirements by analyzing end-user reviews, identifying topics with Latent Dirichlet Allocation, and using customized LLM prompts. Similarly, Khan et al., [19] utilized LLM to annotate end-user feedback from Amazon store into various emotion types. In contrast, we are interested in evaluating the performances of existing fine-tuned DL classifiers in identifying the quality of ChatGPT annotation compared to human annotation.

2.2 User Feedback for Software Improvement

End-user reviews play a crucial role in the evolution of software, enhancing its quality and boosting user satisfaction by promptly integrating feedback from users. Crowd-based requirements engineering (CrowdRE) has significantly changed the traditional RE processes by providing reach to diverse stakeholders distributed across the globe [8]. End-user reports valuable information related to software evolution, including new features, issues, and non-functional requirements across various social media platforms such as app stores, X (Twitter), Amazon Store, specialized crowdRE platforms, and User forums [15]. Similarly, Lin et al. conducted a detailed study on the importance of opinion mining and sentiment analysis by processing end-user reviews for software development and evolution [25]. Hassan et al., [12], conducted a detailed mapping study to identify the most prominent and successful machine and DL classifiers and data sources for improved software evolution. Hou et al. analyze customer feedback, emphasizing key elements in end-user research for product evolution [13]. Khan et al. proposed a CrowdRE approach using argumentation to analyze Reddit forum feedback for better software evolution [17]. Kurtanovic and Maalej identify rationale information from end-user reviews for improved software decision-making [23]. These studies stress end-user feedback as a crucial software engineering quality improvement tool.

2.3 Opinion Mining in Software Reviews

In SE, sentiment analysis (opinion mining) is essential, and app reviews are a rich source of user opinions [10]. Mining these opinions involves identifying user sentiment about discussed topics [9], features [10], issues [18], or software qualities [1]. These opinions can help software engineers understand how users perceive their app [10], discover end-users' opinions about specific features and remedies to resolve these issues [4], and factors affecting sales and downloads of software applications [24]. Understanding end-user opinions is important information that developers must pursue to achieve satisfaction [2].

3 Proposed Research Approach

This section outlines the proposed approach, which consists of two parts. Firstly, we develop the research questions that we intend to explore. As a second step, we go into more detail about the suggested DL-based approach. The research steps are described below.

3.1 Background

In the previous study [20], the authors focused on analyzing low-rated software applicants by mining user reviews to identify frequently occurring issues. The study provided valuable insight into software bugs and issues. However, it was limited to categorizing negative feedback without considering other types of user responses. Building on the foundation, the authors of another study [19] leverage LLMs, specifically Chat-GPT, as an annotator in the analysis of low-rated software applications through the mining of end-user reviews. The idea behind this approach was to identify the emotions intertwined with the negative feedback, focusing on specific emotion types such as anger, confusion, disappointment, distrust, disgust, frustration, fear and sadness. The study has utilized ChatGPT to help it construct annotated datasets and relied on DL classifiers to recognize the respective emotions out of feedback provided by end users. The experiment demonstrated that ChatGPT is a promising tool for annotating user feedback data. In contrast, the proposed work aims to compare the results of various DL algorithms on a manually annotated and ChatGPT-annotated dataset for emotion classification. While manual annotations are prone to human bias, inconsistencies, and inefficiency, ChatGPT offers a scalable, consistent, and faster solution. This study aims to validate ChatGPT's effectiveness in automating emotion detection while maintaining high accuracy and efficiency, providing a promising alternative for large-scale feedback analysis.

3.2 Proposed Research Questions

With the proposed approach, we aim to examine ChatGPT's performance in annotating end-user feedback in ML experiments. In the CrowdRE literature, annotating end-user reviews for software evolution is challenging, time-consuming, and resource-intensive [20,30]. However, LLMs have been successfully employed to automate various SE activities. Therefore, we aim to investigate whether ChatGPT-based annotation can be considered an alternative to human annotation in terms of accuracy, precision, recall, and F-measure. To address this purpose, we propose the following research questions.

RQ1. Does LLM help in automating the human annotation process?

RQ2. How efficiently do distant DL algorithms identify user emotion types from human and ChatGPT-annotated data sets?

3.3 Research Methodology

The proposed approach for examining the performance of ChatGPT in annotating end-user reviews is illustrated in Fig. 1. There are six primary steps in the research methodology: First, we adopted two datasets of user reviews for low-rated software applications in the Amazon software store [19]. The datasets are annotated with various continuously occurring emotion types, including anger, confusion, disgust, disappointment, distrust, frustration, fear, and sadness, utilizing the ChatGPT API and human experts. To compare and evaluate the performances of ChatGPT and human-annotated datasets, we performed a series of experimental steps, following step 1, as shown in Fig. 1. We preprocessed both the ChatGPT and human-annotated datasets by removing punctuation and digits, and lemmatizing words to their base forms. After text cleaning, the feedback text is tokenized and converted into integer sequences appropriate for DL models, with padding used to maintain uniform sequence lengths. After preprocessing, in step 3, data balancing approaches, i.e., under and oversampling, are employed to guarantee equitable representation for each emotional category while mitigating biases of DL classifiers that skew towards the majority classes. To better generalize the DL results for ChatGPT and human annotated results, we tweak various hyperparameter tuning for the DL classifiers in step 4. This includes optimizing the loss function, tweaking dropout to remove overfitting, etc. Next, the cross-validation approach trains and validates the DL classifiers for generalized results. Finally, a comprehensive comparative and evaluative study is conducted by determining average accuracies, analyzing confusion matrices, and generating detailed classification reports, which furnish insights into each model's capabilities and reliability on both datasets, to assess the efficacy of ChatGPT as a possible automated alternative source for data annotation.

4 Experimental Setup

We shortlisted potential classifiers for DL experiments based on their performance on text data. We selected CNN, LSTM, BiLSTM, GRU, BiGRU, and RNN DL classifiers based on their superior performance in identifying associated requirements-related information [6,20]. Furthermore, we followed the same experimental steps for the human and ChatGPT annotated datasets. The experiment is described below:

4.1 Reviews Dataset

The datasets used in the proposed approach are adopted from our previously published work [19]. Each dataset comprises 11,800 end-user feedback reviews from the Amazon App Store against low-rated software apps. Two annotators who are expert in software annotation tasks were involved in the human annotation process. To ensure the reliability and consistency of the human annotations, a detailed set of annotation guidelines was followed, which was developed based on a grounded theory approach described in prior work [19]. Inter-annotator reliability metrics, such as Cohen's Kappa, were also calculated to ensure high agreement among the annotators. ChatGPT and human experts annotate the end-user reviews in the datasets with frequently occurring emotion types, including anger, confusion, distrust, disgust, disappointment, fear, frustration, and sadness. The proposed approach aims to explore an alternative annotation source compared to human annotators. For this purpose, we seek to identify the suitability of

ChatGPT by analyzing the performance of various DL classifiers on human and ChatGPT-annotated datasets in terms of precision, accuracy, F-measure, recall, and confusion matrices.

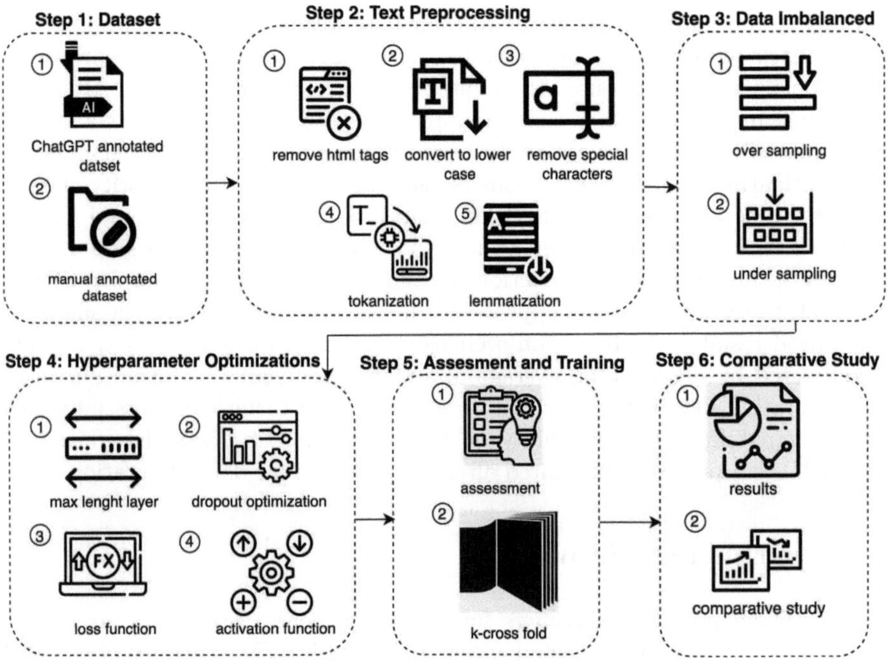

Fig. 1. Proposed research methodology overview.

4.2 Preprocessing

We performed several key pre-processing steps to organize the intake data for the DL experiments. First, HTML tags in crowd-user reviews were removed to maintain text purity. After that, end-user comments with URLs were removed. Lowercase text was used to standardize and analyze all material. Textual documents were stripped of special characters, punctuation, alphanumeric words, and brackets to reduce data noise. Additionally, text lemmatization was used to reduce dataset words to their root forms. These pre-processing steps have proven successful in better generalizing and improving DL algorithm performance [19,20]. For example, the reviews were tokenized, padded for uniform length, and lemmatized to standardize the data for DL models. The emotion labels in the dataset were encoded as categorical variables, preparing the data for model training and ensuring accurate classification results.

4.3 Feature Engineering

To better assess and compare the performances of DL classifiers on ChatGPT and experts' annotated datasets, fine-tuning their hyperparameters is required. In CrowdRE literature, feature engineering has been reported as a major component of DL experiments for improved and generalized results. For this purpose, we employed a grid search algorithm to determine the optimized values for the DL classifiers. For example, to identify an optimized "output_dim" value for the DL classifier, the grid search algorithm was experimented with 16, 32, 64, and 100 values, resulting in better accuracy with the "100" value. Similarly, the grid search algorithm results in better accuracy with a 0.001 learning rate than 0.01, 0.03, and 0.1. Table 1 indicates that a Max Features value of 2000 is optimal for limiting extraneous features, preventing overfitting, and prioritizing critical features for faster training and an improved classifier. We set maxlen to 100 for consistent text input, remembering efficiency, and DL model performance. Padding input words with zeros allows the DL classifier to examine end-user feedback in the variable-length ASA storage. The "maxlen" function of the DL classifier determines the maximum length of the padding. Data were fed into 10 epochs, ensuring that DL classifiers learned from the entire data set, generalized well, and converged to a steady training loss. A grid search algorithm enhances classifier performance and generalization by using 64 dense layers. DL algorithms lose generality when they overfit their data when training and testing. To avoid overfitting, researchers recommend dropout, regularization, or classifier complexity reduction [20,30]. Classifiers fared better with dropout layers than regularization and model complexity with different overfitting algorithms. A 0.2 dropout rate improved the proposed approach classification results. The 100-dimensional Embedding Layer was created. Adam optimized gradient descent better than SGD and RMSProp. Additionally, DL classifiers yield better classification accuracy with a categorical cross-entropy loss function. The softmax activation function in the output layer provided the final class probabilities.

Table 1. Hyperparameters for DL classifiers

Hyperparameter	Value
Max Features	2000
Learning Rate	0.001
Epochs	10
Max Length (maxlen)	100
Dense Layer	64
Dropout	0.2
Loss Function	Categorical Crossentropy
Embedding Dimension	100
Activation Function	Softmax
Optimizer	Adam

4.4 Data Imbalance

Managing imbalanced datasets is essential for supervised classification. Both ChatGPT and manual annotations exhibit imbalances in annotation classes. Only 0.64% of end-user comments were classified as sadness, whereas 40.5% were frustrated by ChatGPT. Similarly, frustration is 27.9%, and distrust is 6.0% in the manual dataset. Such imbalances can cause DL classifiers to favor the majority and ignore the minority. We used two standard balancing methods: oversampling and undersampling. These methods enable model and minority forecast accuracy. Oversampling balances data by duplicating minority class examples [3], while under-sampling reduces majority class samples [22]. We examined these approaches using ROC and precision-recall curves to find the optimum approach. Figures 2(a) show the CNN model ROC, and Fig. 2(b) displays the LSTM model ROC curve with ChatGPT annotations. We also obtained similar curves for the human-annotated dataset. Results indicate that oversampling is more effective than undersampling, which can result in lost data [20].

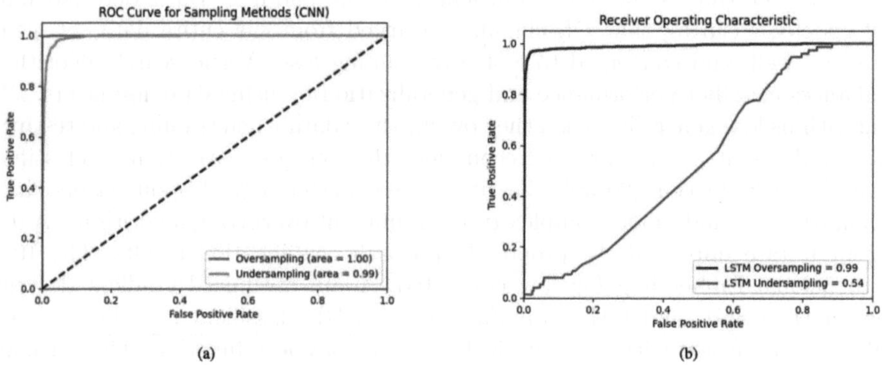

Fig. 2. Oversampling and undersampling ROC curves for CNN (a) and LSTM (b) models for ChatGPT annotated datasets.

4.5 Training and Assessment of the DL Algorithms

For the proposed method, we used stratified ten-fold cross-validation for both datasets. We train DL classifiers using nine-fold techniques. We validate the algorithm using one-fold cross-validation. We rotate the training and testing folds ten times to test and train the proposed technique. A lot of research has been done on the stratified K-fold cross-validation method for training and validating DL classifiers [18,19,30]. Precision (P), recall (R), and F1-score metrics were used to evaluate and compare supervised DL methods.

5 Comparative Study/Results

The comparative results of distant DL algorithms on manually annotated and ChatGPT-annotated datasets to identify end-user emotion types are summarized in Table 2. The outcomes show that different DL classifiers are more confident in the ChatGPT dataset because it has better precision, recall, and F-measure results than the human-annotated dataset. This performance disparity suggests that human experts' subjective interpretations of end-user feedback may introduce label noise or discrepancies. In contrast, ChatGPT adheres to uniform guidelines for annotating feedback, resulting in fewer edge cases and more reliable tagging. The CNN classifier outperforms LSTM, BiLSTM, GRU, BiGRU, and RNN in terms of its optimal features. Table 2 shows that, on the ChatGPT dataset, classifiers had an average accuracy of 92%, 92%, 91%, 90%, 91%, and 91%, but only 75%, 75%, 79%, 48%, 73%, and 85% on the manually annotated dataset. In 'Anger', the CNN model had 96% precision and 96% recall on ChatGPT. In 'Disgust', the ChatGPT LSTM model had 97% precision, 98% recall, and 97% F1-score, compared to 73%, 70%, and 71% on the manually annotated dataset. On ChatGPT, the GRU model detected 'Sadness' with 93% precision, 89% recall, and 91% F-measure, significantly better than on the manually annotated dataset. DL models routinely show improved metrics on ChatGPT data for emotions, including "confusion", "disappointment", and "distrust", supporting the benefits of machine-generated annotations in reducing variability and improving model training.

In summary, the DL classifiers perform comparatively better with the ChatGPT annotated dataset, which encourages possible automation of the data annotation process. Additionally, it addresses the challenges of identifying suitable annotation experts, resolving conflicts, and minimizing potential bias. To make the results more general, Figs. 4(a) and (b) show how well CNN and LSTM classifiers work for training and validating data that has been annotated with Chat-

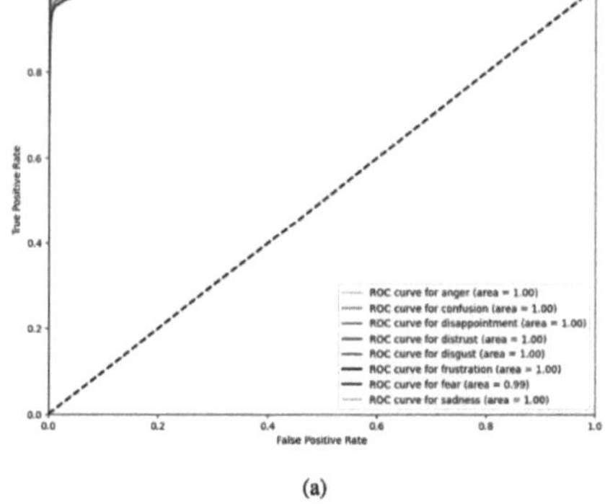

Fig. 3. ROC curves of CNN ChatGPT and LSTM classifiers for ChatGPT Annotated data set

Table 2. Results comparison of ChatGPT and manually annotated datasets.

Labeled Tags	DL Algorithms	Precision ChatGPT/Manual	Recall ChatGPT/Manual	F-Measure ChatGPT/Manual
Anger	CNN Model	0.96/0.84	0.96/0.93	0.96/0.88
	LSTM Model	0.84/0.82	0.89/0.72	0.86/0.77
	BiLSTM Model	0.82/0.70	0.87/0.84	0.85/0.76
	GRU Model	0.96/0.36	0.92/0.62	0.94/0.46
	BiGRU Model	0.94/0.86	0.96/0.87	0.95/0.86
	RNN Model	0.80/0.83	0.56/0.93	0.66/0.87
Confusion	CNN Model	0.99/0.90	0.99/0.94	0.99/0.92
	LSTM Model	0.97/0.84	0.97/0.93	0.97/0.88
	BiLSTM Model	0.95/0.78	0.98/0.94	0.97/0.85
	GRU Model	0.97/0.55	0.99/0.77	0.98/0.64
	BiGRU Model	0.99/0.84	0.99/0.95	0.99/0.90
	RNN Model	0.93/0.82	0.95/0.94	0.94/0.88
Disappointment	CNN Model	0.95/0.93	0.96/0.82	0.96/0.87
	LSTM Model	0.83/0.72	0.76/0.78	0.79/0.75
	BiLSTM Model	0.83/0.78	0.74/0.70	0.78/0.74
	GRU Model	0.95/0.47	0.90/0.34	0.92/0.39
	BiGRU Model	0.95/0.85	0.95/0.83	0.95/0.84
	RNN Model	0.67/0.88	0.54/0.83	0.60/0.85
Disgust	CNN Model	0.99/0.88	0.99/0.95	0.99/0.91
	LSTM Model	0.86/0.73	0.98/0.70	0.91/0.71
	BiLSTM Model	0.92/0.68	0.93/0.75	0.92/0.72
	GRU Model	0.97/0.55	0.98/0.75	0.97/0.63
	BiGRU Model	0.99/0.86	0.99/0.95	0.99/0.90
	RNN Model	0.72/0.87	0.95/0.88	0.82/0.87
Distrust	CNN Model	0.97/0.87	0.98/0.89	0.98/0.88
	LSTM Model	0.97/0.85	0.99/0.90	0.98/0.87
	BiLSTM Model	0.97/0.87	0.99/0.90	0.98/0.88
	GRU Model	0.91/0.44	0.99/0.60	0.95/0.51
	BiGRU Model	0.96/0.89	0.98/0.83	0.97/0.86
	RNN Model	0.89/0.89	0.98/0.96	0.92/0.92
Frustration	CNN Model	0.99/0.88	0.99/0.82	0.99/0.85
	LSTM Model	0.83/0.66	0.70/0.60	0.76/0.63
	BiLSTM Model	0.76/0.68	0.74/0.56	0.75/0.62
	GRU Model	0.98/0.32	0.99/0.36	0.99/0.34
	BiGRU Model	0.98/0.79	0.99/0.82	0.99/0.81
	RNN Model	0.59/0.87	0.54/0.69	0.57/0.77
Fear	CNN Model	0.96/0.80	0.94/0.79	0.95/0.80
	LSTM Model	0.99/0.69	0.99/0.59	0.99/0.64
	BiLSTM Model	0.99/0.72	0.99/0.43	0.99/0.54
	GRU Model	0.93/0.43	0.89/0.04	0.91/0.08
	BiGRU Model	0.95/0.83	0.90/0.72	0.92/0.77
	RNN Model	0.92/0.88	0.99/0.79	0.96/0.83
Sadness	CNN Model	0.99/1.00	0.99/0.94	0.99/0.97
	LSTM Model	0.98/0.70	0.99/0.80	0.99/0.75
	BiLSTM Model	0.98/0.69	0.99/0.77	0.99/0.73
	GRU Model	0.99/0.98	0.97/0.18	0.98/0.30
	BiGRU Model	0.99/0.99	0.98/0.95	0.99/0.97
	RNN Model	0.93/0.98	0.97/0.99	0.95/0.99

Cross-validation with stratified K-fold (Split Size = 10)

DL Classifiers	Accuracy ChatGPT/Manual
CNN Model	0.92/0.75
LSTM Model	0.92/0.75
BiLSTM Model	0.91/0.79
GRU Model	0.90/0.48
BiGRU Model	0.91/0.73
RNN Model	0.91/0.85

GPT. Each DL model performs similarly on manually annotated data. Additionally, ROC curves for CNN classifiers are shown in Fig. 3(a) for the ChatGPT-annotated dataset and Fig. 3(b) for the LSTM classifier. Classifiers use these ROC curves to categorize end-user feedback for various moods, highlighting the edges of ChatGPT annotations. To build the ROC curve for a multiple-class challenge, we minimized it to a binary classification problem with Class 0 (anger) and Classes 1, 2, 3,4,5,6, and 7 (confusion, disappointment, distrust, disgust, frustration, fear, and sadness). The CNN anger classifier correctly identified crowd-user comments' wrath emotions, resulting in the True Positive Rate (FPR). The False Positive Rate (FPR) represents angry crowd-user feedback that represents anger, confusion, disappointment, distrust, disgust, frustration, fear, and sadness.

Furthermore, Figs. 5 (a, b) show the CNN model confusion matrix for ChatGPT and manually annotated datasets. Row tags show basic classes; column labels are CNN model-predicted classes. The confusion matrix categorizes correct and incorrect predictions into categorization classes to assess DL algorithms' emotional categorization of end-user comments. The fine-tuned DL classifiers outperformed the manually annotated end-user emotions dataset compared to the ChatGPT annotated dataset. Manual annotation can be time-consuming and confusing because annotators may misinterpret end-user feedback. DL classifier annotations are more reliable when ChatGPT finds hidden inferences between end-user reviews and emotion types using LLMs. CNN classifiers outperform other DL methods in classifying end-user reviews into emotion types on ChatGPT and manually annotated datasets. Thus, the CNN model with optimized textual features best classifies feedback-related end-user emotions. Due to its superior performance over manual annotation, experimental results recommend ChatGPT for software engineering dataset annotation. It boosts classification accuracy and cuts annotation time.

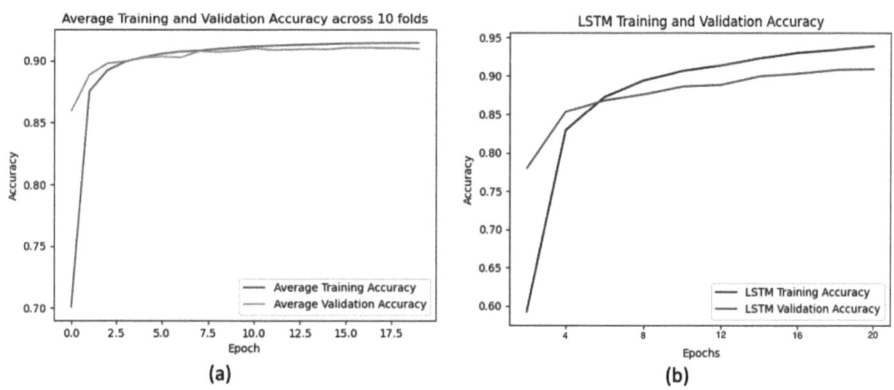

Fig. 4. Training and validation accuracy of CNN and LSTM classifiers for the ChatGPT-annotated dataset.

6 Discussion

The study's findings persuasively advocate for the use of Generative AI, specifically ChatGPT, to automate the process of human annotation in software engineering, particularly in RE. The results show that ChatGPT performs better than human annotators in classifying emotions in end-user feedback, as measured by accuracy, precision, recall, F-measure, and consistency. This aligns with the increasing body of studies supporting the integration of LLM into software development practices [14,19]. Human annotation often suffers from subjectivity, inconsistency, and the potential for bias [20], which can lead to inaccuracies in identifying and classifying emotions from end-user reviews. In contrast, ChatGPT provides a more efficient and neutral alternative by systematically classifying emotions from large datasets with high precision, achieving an average accuracy of 90% across various DL classifiers. This accelerates the annotation process, offering greater reliability and scalability, making it a promising solution for automating user review annotation. Additionally, using ChatGPT to summarize complex feedback helps developers focus on key issues, enhancing their ability to make data-driven decisions and address user concerns more efficiently. However, the results need to be validated with the human experts for improved generalizability.

In addition to automating the annotation process, the study also explored how well various DL classifiers can identify emotion types from both human-annotated and ChatGPT-annotated datasets. The comparison showed a clear advantage for ChatGPT-annotated datasets. LLM can be considered an alternative annotation source that improves the data quality used for ML tasks. Specifically, classifiers such as CNN, LSTM, and BILSTM performed significantly better with ChatGPT-generated datasets, showcasing their capacity to accurately detect subtle emotions like sadness, anger, and confusion. The high performance of ChatGPT-annotated data demonstrates its potential to serve as a reliable substitute for human annotators, offering an alternative for dataset preparation in large-scale ML projects. However, it is essential to acknowledge that while ChatGPT's performance is better in annotating end-user feedback compared to human annotators, based on improved accuracy and other evaluation metrics, its reliability is still subject to validation by human experts. Additionally, its application in different domains or with different datasets may yield varying results. Overall, the findings suggest that ChatGPT has the potential to revolutionize the emotion classification process, leading to more efficient, accurate, and scalable approaches to understanding end-user feedback and improving software quality.

Applicability for Software Requirements Engineers: The proposed approach using Chat-GPT for emotion classification from user feedback can significantly support software requirement engineers in improving software quality. Automating the annotation of reviews enables engineers to quickly identify critical areas of improvement based on feedback and user sentiment. It would allow for prioritizing bug fixes and feature enhancements based on user dissatisfaction,

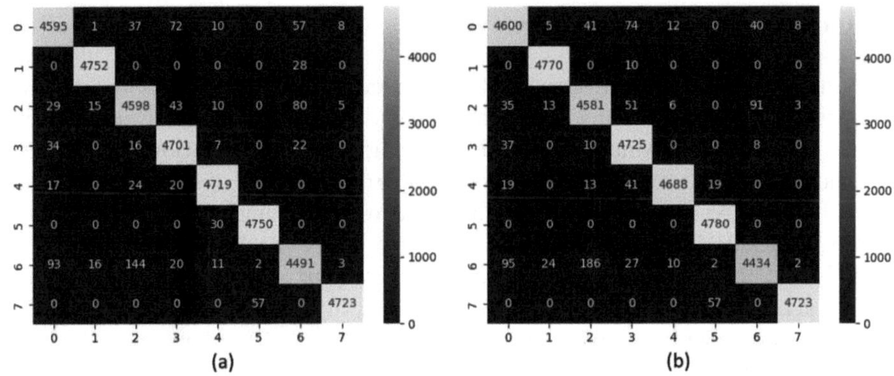

Fig. 5. Confusion matrix for CNN (a) and LSTM(b) classifiers for ChatGPT annotated dataset for emotion classes: 0 = anger, 1 = confusion, 2 = disappointment, 3 = distrust, 4 = disgust, 5 = frustration, 6 = fear, 7 = sadness.

ensuring that the most impactful issues are addressed first. Additionally, the automation and scalability of Chat-GPT enable the integration of this approach into user feedback, facilitating faster iterations and continuous improvements.

Threats to Validity: A significant threat to validity in employing ChatGPT for annotations is hallucination, where the model may produce incorrect or fabricated details that are not present in the original text. However, the threat can be overcome by efficiently optimizing with prompt engineering [19]. Additionally, it can be mitigated by human experts validating the annotations and by improving the model with more specific training data. Additionally, the implementation of ChatGPT as an annotation tool may vary, especially with different types of datasets, such as those involving more complicated or less structured end-user feedback. Furthermore, the reliance on specific DL learning models for evaluation may skew the results. It's crucial to acknowledge that other models not included in the study could potentially yield different results. This transparency about the study's limitations reassures the audience of the research's integrity and helps contextualize the findings for future research. Additionally, we only experimented with ChatGPT, overlooking the performance of other LLMs in annotating end-user feedback.

Furthermore, the performance of Chat-GPT in emotion classification can be affected by the presence of informal language, slang, and sarcasm in user feedback. While ChatGPT is more effective than traditional models in handling informal language and slang, sarcasm remains a challenge due to its reliance on deep contextual understanding. Both Chat-GPT and human annotators may struggle with misinterpreting sarcastic expressions.

7 Conclusion and Future Work

This analysis enhances data-driven RE by leveraging user feedback to improve software. We proposed using LLM, specifically ChatGPT, to analyze negative reviews of low-rated Amazon apps, identifying bugs and emotions like anger, confusion, disappointment, distrust, disgust, frustration, fear and sadness. Our method surpassed human annotation approaches, achieving an average accuracy of 92%, 92%, 91%, 90%, 91%, and 91% with CNN, LSTM, BILSTM, GRU, BiGRU, and RNN classifiers, respectively. In contrast, the manually annotated dataset achieved an accuracy of 75%, 75%, 79%, 48%, 73%, and 85% with the same classifiers. This accuracy is crucial for developers and retailers looking to improve software based on customer feedback. Future studies offer exciting opportunities, including collecting more diverse user reviews across Amazon software ratings and categories to validate the scalability of our approach. This scalability is a key strength, ensuring its applicability to various software products and user feedback. Previous research indicates that a deeper understanding of user requirements and emotions is possible. Additionally, the potential for real-time software updates based on research findings could enable continuous improvements, boosting user satisfaction and software quality. We also plan to expand the system to other LLMs, like Llama 2 and Gemini, to evaluate their effectiveness in annotating end-user feedback.

Data Availability and Replication:. Access to data sets and replication information is provided through this link (https://github.com/nekdil566/experimental_work/tree/main).

References

1. Bakiu, E., Guzman, E.: Which feature is unusable? Detecting usability and user experience issues from user reviews. In: 2017 IEEE 25th International Requirements Engineering Conference Workshops (REW), pp. 182–187. IEEE (2017)
2. Buse, R.P., Zimmermann, T.: Information needs for software development analytics. In: 2012 34th International Conference on Software Engineering (ICSE), pp. 987–996. IEEE (2012)
3. Chawla, N.V., Bowyer, K.W., Hall, L.O., Kegelmeyer, W.P.: Smote: synthetic minority over-sampling technique. J. Artif. Intell. Res. (2002)
4. Dąbrowski, J., Letier, E., Perini, A., Susi, A.: Finding and analyzing app reviews related to specific features: a research preview. In: Knauss, E., Goedicke, M. (eds.) REFSQ 2019. LNCS, vol. 11412, pp. 183–189. Springer, Cham (2019). https://doi.org/10.1007/978-3-030-15538-4_14
5. Dabrowski, J., Letier, E., Perini, A., Susi, A.: Analysing app reviews for software engineering: a systematic literature review. Empir. Softw. Eng. **27**(2), 1–63 (2022)
6. Fatima, E., Kanwal, H., Khan, J.A., Khan, N.D.: An exploratory and automated study of sarcasm detection and classification in app stores using fine-tuned deep learning classifiers. Autom. Softw. Eng. **31**(2), 69 (2024)
7. Gao, C., Zeng, J., Lyu, M.R., King, I.: Online app review analysis for identifying emerging issues. In: Proceedings of the 40th International Conference on Software Engineering, pp. 48–58 (2018)

8. Groen, E.C., et al.: The crowd in requirements engineering: the landscape and challenges. IEEE Softw. **34**(2), 44–52 (2017)
9. Gu, X., Kim, S.: What parts of your apps are loved by users?(t). In: 2015 30th IEEE/ACM International Conference on Automated Software Engineering (ASE), pp. 760–770. IEEE (2015)
10. Guzman, E., Maalej, W.: How do users like this feature? A fine grained sentiment analysis of app reviews. In: 2014 IEEE 22nd International Requirements Engineering Conference (RE), pp. 153–162. IEEE (2014)
11. Haering, M., Stanik, C., Maalej, W.: Automatically matching bug reports with related app reviews. In: 2021 IEEE/ACM 43rd International Conference on Software Engineering (ICSE), pp. 970–981. IEEE (2021)
12. Hassan, S., Li, Q., Aurangzeb, K., Yasin, A., Khan, J.A., Anwar, M.S.: A systematic mapping to investigate the application of machine learning techniques in requirement engineering activities. CAAI Trans. Intell. Technol. (2024)
13. Hou, T., Yannou, B., Leroy, Y., Poirson, E.: Mining customer product reviews for product development: a summarization process. Expert Syst. Appl. **132**, 141–150 (2019)
14. Hou, X., et al.: Large language models for software engineering: a systematic literature review. arXiv preprint arXiv:2308.10620 (2023)
15. Khan, J.A., Liu, L., Wen, L., Ali, R.: Crowd intelligence in requirements engineering: current status and future directions. In: International Working Conference on Requirements Engineering: Foundation for Software Quality, pp. 245–261 (2019)
16. Khan, J.A., Qayyum, S., Dar, H.S.: Large language model for requirements engineering: a systematic literature review. PREPRINT (Version 1) available at Research Square (2025). https://doi.org/10.21203/rs.3.rs-5589929/v1
17. Khan, J.A., Xie, Y., Liu, L., Wen, L.: Analysis of requirements-related arguments in user forums. In: 2019 IEEE 27th International Requirements Engineering Conference (RE), pp. 63–74. IEEE (2019)
18. Khan, N.D., et al.: How do crowd-users express their opinions against software applications in social media? A fine-grained classification approach. IEEE Access (2024)
19. Khan, N.D., Khan, J.A., Li, J., Ullah, T., Zhao, Q.: Leveraging large language model chatgpt for enhanced understanding of end-user emotions in social media feedbacks. Expert Syst. Appl. 125524 (2024)
20. Khan, N.D., Khan, J.A., Li, J., Ullah, T., Zhao, Q.: Mining software insights: uncovering the frequently occurring issues in low-rating software applications. PeerJ Comput. Sci. **10**, e2115 (2024)
21. Kifetew, F.M., Perini, A., Susi, A., Siena, A., Muñante, D., Morales-Ramirez, I.: Automating user-feedback driven requirements prioritization. Inf. Softw. Technol. **138**, 106635 (2021)
22. Kotsiantis, S., Kanellopoulos, D., Pintelas, P.: Handling imbalanced datasets: a review. GESTS Int. Trans. Comput. Sci. Eng. **30**, 25–36 (2006). Synthetic Oversampling of Instances Using Clustering
23. Kurtanović, Z., Maalej, W.: On user rationale in software engineering. Requirements Eng. **23**(3), 357–379 (2018). https://doi.org/10.1007/s00766-018-0293-2
24. Liang, T.P., Li, X., Yang, C.T., Wang, M.: What in consumer reviews affects the sales of mobile apps: a multifacet sentiment analysis approach. Int. J. Electron. Commer. **20**(2), 236–260 (2015)
25. Lin, B., Cassee, N., Serebrenik, A., Bavota, G., Novielli, N., Lanza, M.: Opinion mining for software development: a systematic literature review. ACM Trans. Softw. Eng. Methodol. (TOSEM) **31**(3), 1–41 (2022)

26. Lubos, S., et al.: Leveraging LLMs for the quality assurance of software requirements. In: Requirements Engineering Conference (RE), pp. 389–397. IEEE (2024)
27. Marques, N., Silva, R.R., Bernardino, J.: Using chatgpt in software requirements engineering: a comprehensive review. Future Internet **16**(6), 180 (2024)
28. Nasution, A.H., Onan, A.: Chatgpt label: comparing the quality of human-generated and LLM-generated annotations in low-resource language NLP tasks. IEEE Access (2024)
29. Ren, S., Nakagawa, H., Tsuchiya, T.: Combining prompts with examples to enhance LLM-based requirement elicitation. In: COMPSAC, pp. 1376–1381. IEEE (2024)
30. Ullah, T., Khan, J.A., Khan, N.D., Yasin, A., Arshad, H.: Exploring and mining rationale information for low-rating software applications. Soft Comput. (2023)

A Quantum Ising Model for Solving Sudoku Puzzles

Wen-Li Wang[1(✉)], Mei-Huei Tang[2], Shahid Hussain[1], and Kevin Wang[1]

[1] Penn State University Behrend, Erie 16563, PA, USA
wxw18@psu.edu
[2] Gannon University, Erie 16541, PA, USA

Abstract. Quantum algorithms are good at solving combinatorial situations, a challenge faced by many NP-hard and NP-complete optimization problems. In general, each non-polynomial (NP) problem has its own characteristics and requires special attention. Despite this fact, one hard problem can naturally be deduced from others and the approaches of solving one may be helpful to solve others. Therefore, this study develops a three-dimensional quantum Ising model to solve the NP-Complete Sudoku puzzle games, based on the widely adopted approach of optimizing Hamiltonian energy to model NP-hard Ising spin glasses. This developed paradigm can benefit software practitioners to solve more NP problems. In our proposed methodology, mathematical foundations are first formulated based on the couplings of atomic spins to model the puzzle rules and constraints. Next, quantum modeling is discussed to demonstrate the construction of observable operators from Pauli gates to compute the expectation values of plausible quantum states for the puzzle. Finally, individual quantum algorithms are integrated to become a Sudoku solver. The solver is investigated through the execution of quantum approximate optimization algorithm (QAOA) combined with the constrained optimization by linear approximation (COBYLA) optimizer provided in the IBM Qiskit SDK. A code snippet for one of the puzzle rules is presented to verify the outcome of the developed quantum circuits.

Keywords: Ising Models · Quantum · Hamiltonian Energy · QAOA · COBYLA

1 Introduction

A Sudoku puzzle requires a non-polynomial (NP) algorithm to solve it and is known as an NP-complete problem [1]. The game is a grid puzzle with 9×9 cells that can be decomposed into 9 non-intersected 3×3 boxes, with one box highlighted in red as shown in Fig. 1. Besides the precondition of having preset values in certain cells, the player needs to fill in an integer between 1 and 9 to those empty cells. One rule of the game is to fill each row with integers from 1 to 9 without a duplicate. A similar rule is applied to each column and box to have unique integers from 1 to 9 without any number repetition. For example, in the sample puzzle of Fig. 1, the top row, left-most column, and the upper-left corner box all require four empty cells to be filled in. Under the circumstances of those preset values, the top row can only take values of 1, 3, 5, and 6 in some permutation for the cells to prevent a rule violation.

S. Hussain et al. (Eds.): SEET 2025, CCIS 2725, pp. 417–429, 2026.
https://doi.org/10.1007/978-3-032-08977-9_26

Several solvers have been developed to solve this popular puzzle game, such as applying an algorithmic approach [2], taking advantage of evolutionary programming [3], or incorporating artificial intelligence [4]. Without loss of generality, the development of this quantum solver for Sudoku will consider the game as a grid of $n \times n$ cells to accommodate small and big size puzzles as well. In this regard, there will be n non-intersected $\sqrt{n} \times \sqrt{n}$ boxes in the grid, where $\sqrt{n} \in \mathbb{Z}$.

7		8	9		2	4		
	4			5				
5	2		3		1			7
9	8							5
		3	5		7	1		
4							7	2
3			8		6		9	4
				9			2	
		4	2		3	5		6

Fig. 1. A sample Sudoku puzzle

Quantum algorithms are known to demonstrate good proficiency in solving combinatorial problems. For example, Shor's algorithm [5] performs prime factorization of large numbers efficiently. Other NP optimization problems, such as Max-Cut and Traveling-Salesperson problems (TSP) [6, 7], also benefit from the parallel computation power of quantum computing (QC). One NP-hard problem that has attracted great interest is the Ising spin glass problem [8] that finds the ground states for a spin glass system through the optimization of Hamiltonian energy. By converting the problem into a quantum version, the optimization process can apply algorithms like QAOA [9] and quantum annealing [8, 10] as well as optimizers like COBYLA [11] to compute the minimal eigen value of a constructed matrix to attain the solution. This Ising modeling approach serves as the foundation of this study to solve Sudoku games. The rules and constraints are formulated based on the values of Ising spins. Subsequent steps of modeling are transformed into a quantum circuit with Pauli gates [12]. Finally, the optimization process for minimizing the Hamiltonian energy is applied to find the solution.

In this paper, Sect. 2 lists the major related work. The rules and constraints for Sudoku are formulated in Sect. 3. Section 4 conducts quantum modeling that converts formulas to observable operators, computes the expectation values of quantum states, and shows the optimization process. The conclusions are given in Sect. 5.

2 Related Work

There have been broad interests in applying QAOA and AQO to solve NP-hard and NP-complete problems [9, 13, 14]. The idea is to build a device that can run such algorithms [15–17], if a problem of interest can be modeled by Hamiltonian energy and written as the quantum version of an Ising spin glass. As named after physicists Ernst Ising and Wilhelm Lenz [18], Ising spin glasses are known to be NP-hard problems for classical computers [19], and the models are constructed as glasses that consist of discrete variables. These variables represent the magnetic dipole moments of atomic spins with positive couplings and negative couplings. These values can be used to compute the energy of an Ising model by a Hamiltonian function [20–22] through interaction and the external magnetic field. Figure 2 shows an example of a two-dimensional Ising model. For the linked cells or elements, a positive coupling (+1) with an up arrow leads to a change in the same direction, while a negative coupling (–1) with a down arrow leads to an opposite direction. The Max-Cut problem [6] has been a widely demonstrated example adopting the Ising model, because it is typical to apply deduction from one NP problem to other NP problems and the Hamiltonian energy function may be formulated by a quantum version of an Ising spin glass. This study adopts the same principles. Our approach tackles the rules and constraints of Sudoku puzzle games to formulate Hamiltonian energy equations and construct quantum Ising models. The optimal solution can then be computed to find the minimum eigenvalue by utilizing the parallel computation power of QC.

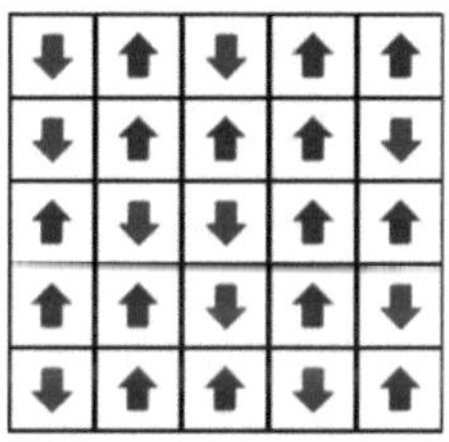

Fig. 2. A sample two-dimensional Ising model

3 Methodology

This section details our methodology to construct Ising spin glasses and denotes the equations to solve Sudoku puzzle games. Typically, a classical Ising model can be written as a Hamiltonian function H of a set of m spins with their values $s_k = \pm 1$, as shown in Eq. (1). This equation shows a quadratic function with spinning inputs s_k for H, where J_{ij} and h_i are real numbers. The value of J_{ij} is the interaction between two elements i and j, while h_i is the external magnetic field.

$$H(s_1, s_2, \ldots, s_m) = -\sum_{i<j} J_{ij} s_i s_j - \sum_{i=1}^{m} h_i s_i \tag{1}$$

For a generalized $n \times n$ Sudoku puzzle, each cell can accept a value ranging from 1 to n. To construct an Ising model, a simple approach is to model the puzzle with $m = n^3$ spin variables $s_k = \pm 1$, $1 \le k \le m$, to address the range of values for all the cells or elements. In this case, it is a three-dimensional Ising model. For the convenience of model construction, we define binary variables $x_{(i,j,v)}$, $1 \le i, j, k \le n$, to indicate whether it is true or false for cell at row i and column j to contain value v. The tuple (i, j, v) of a binary variable corresponds to the index of spin variable s_k, where $k = (i - 1) \times n^2 +$

$(j-1) \times n + v$, as shown in Eq. (2). For each binary variable, the corresponding values of –1 and 1 for a spin will yield a 1 (true) and 0 (false), respectively.

$$x_{(i,j,v)} = \frac{1 - s_k}{2} \tag{2}$$

Resembling Eq. (1), an Ising model formulated as a Hamiltonian function H can be constructed by modeling subfunctions individually and then summing them up together. In this regard, the developed model for Sudoku will consist of five subfunctions, as shown in Eq. (3). To find the solution, the goal is to minimize the Hamiltonian energy to yield ground state energy of getting $H = 0$, like solving an optimization problem. Details of the subfunctions are formulated and described in the subsequent sections.

$$H = H_1 + H_2 + H_3 + H_4 + H_5 \tag{3}$$

3.1 The Cell Rule

Equation (4) denotes the formula of H_1, which is the energy subfunction for all cells with each one being filled with one unique integer value between 1 and n. Regarding the binary variable $x_{(i,j,v)}$, the possible value v for a cell at a specified row and column can range from 1 to n. It is important to see a cell having exactly one value for v to get $x_{(i,j,v)} = 1$ and the other values for v to get $x_{(i,j,v)} = 0$. Otherwise, there is a conflict because a cell should not have multiple values coexist. The Ising model with $H_1 = 0$ assures that every cell has just one unique integer value v that can be $x_{(i,j,v)} = 1$. In this case, each cell regardless of its location is supposed to have the summation of binary variables $x_{(i,j,v)}$ for all its possible v values to be equal to 1. The solution is for equation H1 to yield a result 0 for the complete set of cells in the puzzle. Otherwise, the computed square of the difference will be greater than 0, i.e., not a solution.

$$H_1 = \sum_{i=1}^{n}\sum_{j=1}^{n}\left(1 - \sum_{v=1}^{n} x_{(i,j,v)}\right)^2 \tag{4}$$

3.2 The Row Rule

The row rule of the game is to ensure that each row has all distinctive integers from 1 to n to be covered exactly once without a repetition. Equation (5) formulates the energy subfunction H_2 for this rule. For the summation portion within the square, the change of variable j is to visit every column cell on a row i. Under the situation of a specific value v, if there is exactly one occurrence of v on that row, the summation will be equal to 1 and the result of $(v - v \times 1)^2$ will become 0. For $H_2 = 0$, this means that all cells in every row cover all unique integer values in the range exactly once in an arbitrary order without having a duplicate.

$$H_2 = \sum_{i=1}^{n}\sum_{v=1}^{n}\left(v - v\left(\sum_{j=1}^{n} x_{(i,j,v)}\right)\right)^2 \tag{5}$$

3.3 The Column Rule

Similarly, another rule of the game is to ensure that each column has all distinctive integers from 1 to n in the range to be covered without getting a duplicate. Like Eq. (5), the energy subfunction H_3 in Eq. (6) swaps the positions of the two summations for variables i and j. This means for a given column j, the consideration is shifted to variable i regarding every row cell on that column. Likewise, if there is exactly one occurrence of v on that column, the summation will be equal to 1 and the result of $(v - v \times 1)^2$ will be equal to 0. Therefore, $H_3 = 0$ implies that all cells in each column j cover those distinctive v values exactly once without a duplicate or a strict order.

$$H_3 = \sum_{j=1}^{n} \sum_{v=1}^{n} \left(v - v \left(\sum_{i=1}^{n} x_{(i,j,v)} \right) \right)^2 \tag{6}$$

3.4 The Box Rule

The other similar rule is not to regulate the entire rows or columns but the boxes. It is important to ensure that each of the n boxes of the puzzle covers all integers from 1 to n without a repetition as well. For a $n \times n$ Sudoku puzzle, the width and height of a box is equal to $\sqrt{n}$. The same concept of Eqs. (5) and (6) can be applied. The major difference is to decompose both the rows and columns into $\sqrt{n}$ chunks. The original variables i and j for the indices on rows and columns are substituted by two new variables a and b. Both variables only range from 0 to $\sqrt{n} - 1$ to address $\sqrt{n}$ chunks. For each box, the summations computed inside the square function of Eq. (7) consider all the cells in the box. Hence, if there is exactly one occurrence of v inside the box, the summation is equal to 1 and the result of $(v - v \times 1)^2$ will be 0. The energy subfunction H_4 manages all the n boxes. When $H_4 = 0$, all cells in each box cover distinctive v values exactly once without a duplicate or being in a fixed order.

$$H_4 = \sum_{a=0}^{\sqrt{n}-1} \sum_{b=0}^{\sqrt{n}-1} \sum_{v=1}^{n} \left(v - v \left(\sum_{i=1+a\sqrt{n}}^{(1+a)\sqrt{n}} \sum_{j=1+b\sqrt{n}}^{(1+b)\sqrt{n}} x_{(i,j,v)} \right) \right)^2 \tag{7}$$

3.5 The Preset Value Constraint

A typical Sudoku puzzle is ideal to have only one single solution. For that reason, it is typical to see the design of a puzzle to have preset values in certain cells to accomplish that. Therefore, these values are necessary to be considered during the construction of the Ising model. Let C be a set of m cells with a preset decimal value, i.e., $C = \{c_1, c_2, \ldots, c_m\}$. Adhered to the format of our defined binary variables $x_{(i,j,v)}$, each cell element is represented by a tuple to be $c_\phi = (i^\phi, j^\phi, v^\phi)$, $1 \leq \phi \leq m$, indicating a preset decimal value v^ϕ at row i^ϕ and column j^ϕ. Equation (8) formulates energy subfunction H_5 to tackle all the preset values of elements in C. Unlike Eqs. (5), (6) and (7), the modeling only needs to consider the cells in set C instead of all the cells in the puzzle. Therefore, the summation for $c_\phi \in C$ only needs to process $|C| = m$ cells. For each cell $c_\phi = (i^\phi, j^\phi, v^\phi)$, the tuple facilities the checking of the set of n binary variables $x_{(i,j,v)}$ at the location of row i^ϕ and column j^ϕ to see whether v^ϕ and v have the same value. In respect to Eq. (4), the goal for a cell is that one and only one of its n binary variables should be equal to 1. For the preset value constraint, not only must exactly one binary variable for summation in the square of Eq. (4) be equal to 1, but also that value v must be equal to v^ϕ so that $(v^\phi - v)^2 = 0$. In consequence, the Hamiltonian energy for the outcome of $H_5 = 0$ reflects that all preset values are correctly modeled.

$$H_5 = \sum_{c \in C} \left(v - \left(\sum_{v=1}^{n} v \cdot x_{(i,j,v)} \right) \right)^2 \tag{8}$$

4 Quantum Modeling

For QC, the inputs for the constructed quantum circuits are qubits, with each being a vector not a regular scalar value. Hence, the quantum version of the Hamiltonian function H_Q is modeled as shown in Eq. (9). In the equation, q_k^z for $1 \le k \le m$ is a 2×2 Pauli matrix such as a Pauli I, X, Y, or Z gate [21]. For the Sudoku puzzle problem, the set of q_k^z are built using I and Z gates, and the identity matrix I is simply skipped in the notation during construction of quantum circuits. Since our constructed Ising model in Section III requires n^3 spins, the H_Q needs $m = n^3$ qubits for the Hamiltonian function H to solve a Sudoku puzzle.

$$H_Q = H\left(q_1^z, q_2^z, \ldots, q_m^z\right) \tag{9}$$

Today, the number of qubits available on quantum computers is not yet abundant and to perform quantum simulation in classical computers is slow in performance and high in memory consumption. Therefore, the discussion of H_Q below mainly focuses on the key points using a simple example for illustration. This small case study equips two cells in a row and each cell has a range of values from 1 to 2 to cut down the need of many qubits. Consequently, the range for a cell can be modeled by two binary variables, and the entire scenario can be modeled by a total of four qubits to demonstrate and explain the subsequent modeling steps in detail.

Starting with Eq. (4), a cell should have only one of its n binary variables equal to 1. To model the case, there will be two binary variables $x_{(i,j,v)}$ needed for each cell. The quantum observable Q [23] of the Ising model can thus be built from four Pauli Z gates to tackle the scalar values 1 and –1 of spin variables s_k in Eq. (2). Adhered to Eq. (9), the Z gates are subscripted with an index number k, denoted as Z_k for the kth qubit, to correspond to the individual indices of the spin variables s_k, as shown below.

$$\begin{aligned} Q &= \sum_{j=1}^{2} \left(1 - \sum_{v=1}^{2} x_{(1,j,v)} \right)^2 \\ &= \left(1 - \left(\frac{1 - Z_1}{2} + \frac{1 - Z_2}{2} \right) \right)^2 + \left(1 - \left(\frac{1 - Z_3}{2} + \frac{1 - Z_4}{2} \right) \right)^2 \end{aligned}$$

$$= 1 + 0.5Z_1Z_2 + 0.5Z_3Z_4$$

The quantum Hamiltonian subfunction H_1 is equivalent to the expectation value $<Q>$ computed as $<\Psi|Q|\Psi>$ for the quantum state Ψ. The following demonstrates the computation details for one chosen quantum state $\Psi = |0001>$ of four qubits, and the other quantum states can be computed accordingly. Table 1 lists the outcomes of the sixteen different states of Ψ, in which $|0101>$, $|0110>$, $|1001>$ and $|1010>$ are four plausible solutions with $H_1 = 0$.

$$\begin{aligned}
<\Psi|Q|\Psi> &= <1000|1 + 0.5Z_1Z_2 + 0.5Z_3Z_4|0001> \\
&= 1 + 0.5(<00|Z_1Z_2|00>) + 0.5(<10|Z_3Z_4|01>) \\
&= 1 + 0.5(<0|Z_1|0>)(<0|Z_2|0>) + 0.5(<0|Z_3|0>)(<1|Z_4|1>) \\
&= 1 + 0.5 \times 1 \times 1 + 0.5 \times 1 \times -1 = 1,
\end{aligned}$$

where $<0|Z|0>$ and $<1|Z|1>$ are derived as below, regardless of the qubit indices.

$$<0|Z|0> = (10)\begin{pmatrix} 1 & 0 \\ 0 & -1 \end{pmatrix}\begin{pmatrix} 1 \\ 0 \end{pmatrix} = 1 \text{ and } <1|Z|1> = (01)\begin{pmatrix} 1 & 0 \\ 0 & -1 \end{pmatrix}\begin{pmatrix} 0 \\ 1 \end{pmatrix} = -1.$$

By Eq. (5), the discussed example needs to conform to the rule that both cells have different values without a duplicate. Since each cell has two binary variables to represent its value, it is important to ensure that only one of the cells has the first binary variable equal to 1, so that the summation of first binary variables from both cells is equal to 1. The same applies to the second binary variables to get a sum of 1 for both cells. The following modeling result shows the derived quantum circuits from four Pauli Z gates. The outcome of $v - v \times 1 = 0$ will cover each plausible value of v exactly once. Table 2 displays the outcomes of the sixteen different states of Ψ, in which $|0101>$, $|0110>$, $|1001>$ and $|1010>$ are acceptable solutions with $H_2 = 0$.

$$Q = \sum_{v=1}^{2}\left(v - v\left(\sum_{j=1}^{2} x_{(1,j,v)}\right)\right)^2$$

$$= \left(1 - 1\left(\frac{1-Z_1}{2} + \frac{1-Z_3}{2}\right)\right)^2 + \left(2 - 2\left(\frac{1-Z_2}{2} + \frac{1-Z_4}{2}\right)\right)^2$$

$$= 2.5 + 0.5Z_1Z_3 + 2Z_2Z_4$$

The simplicity of this two-cell case study makes Eqs. (6) and (7) unnecessary so their modeling steps are skipped. For a typical Sudoku puzzle, they will be modeled in a similar manner to Eq. (5) for other qubits by updating the qubit indices.

The Eq. (8) addresses the preset values for cells. With just two cells in the discussed example, we assume the first cell has a preset value 2 for illustration, i.e., $|C| = 1$ and $(i^\phi, j^\phi, v^\phi) = (1, 1, 2)$ with $\phi = 1$. Under this situation, a solution will need the first qubit to be 0 and the second qubit to be 1. For the third and fourth qubits, we "don't care" because their values can be arbitrary to be 0 or 1. Table 3 shows the computation results according to the following derived quantum circuits with four feasible solutions.

$$Q = \sum_{c \in C}\left(v - \left(\sum_{v=1}^{2} v \cdot x_{(i,j,v)}\right)\right)^2 = \left(2 - \left(1 \times \frac{1 - Z_1}{2} + 2 \times \frac{1 - Z_2}{2}\right)\right)^2$$
$$= 1.5 + 0.5Z_1 + Z_2 + Z_1Z_2$$

Table 1. Highlighted solutions have exactly one binary variable being 1 for each cell.

Ψ	$H_1 = <Q> = <\Psi \vert Q \vert \Psi>$
$\vert 0000>$	$1 + 0.5 \times 1 \times 1 + 0.5 \times 1 \times 1 = 2$
$\vert 0001>$	$1 + 0.5 \times 1 \times 1 + 0.5 \times 1 \times -1 = 1$
$\vert 0010>$	$1 + 0.5 \times 1 \times 1 + 0.5 \times -1 \times 1 = 1$
$\vert 0011>$	$1 + 0.5 \times 1 \times 1 + 0.5 \times -1 \times -1 = 2$
$\vert 0100>$	$1 + 0.5 \times 1 \times -1 + 0.5 \times 1 \times 1 = 1$
$\vert 0101>$	$1 + 0.5 \times 1 \times -1 + 0.5 \times 1 \times -1 = 0$
$\vert 0110>$	$1 + 0.5 \times 1 \times -1 + 0.5 \times -1 \times 1 = 0$
$\vert 0111>$	$1 + 0.5 \times 1 \times -1 + 0.5 \times -1 \times -1 = 1$
$\vert 1000>$	$1 + 0.5 \times -1 \times 1 + 0.5 \times 1 \times 1 = 1$
$\vert 1001>$	$1 + 0.5 \times -1 \times 1 + 0.5 \times 1 \times -1 = 0$
$\vert 1010>$	$1 + 0.5 \times -1 \times 1 + 0.5 \times -1 \times 1 = 0$
$\vert 1011>$	$1 + 0.5 \times -1 \times 1 + 0.5 \times -1 \times -1 = 1$
$\vert 1100>$	$1 + 0.5 \times -1 \times -1 + 0.5 \times 1 \times 1 = 2$
$\vert 1101>$	$1 + 0.5 \times -1 \times -1 + 0.5 \times 1 \times -1 = 1$
$\vert 1110>$	$1 + 0.5 \times -1 \times -1 + 0.5 \times -1 \times 1 = 1$
$\vert 1111>$	$1 + 0.5 \times -1 \times -1 + 0.5 \times -1 \times -1 = 2$

Table 2. Highlighted solutions have all distinctive values covered by the cells.

Ψ	$H_2 = <Q> = <\Psi \vert Q \vert \Psi>$
$\vert 0000>$	$2.5 + 0.5 \times 1 \times 1 + 2 \times 1 \times 1 = 5$
$\vert 0001>$	$2.5 + 0.5 \times 1 \times 1 + 2 \times 1 \times -1 = 1$
$\vert 0010>$	$2.5 + 0.5 \times 1 \times -1 + 2 \times 1 \times 1 = 4$
$\vert 0011>$	$2.5 + 0.5 \times 1 \times -1 + 2 \times 1 \times -1 = 0$
$\vert 0100>$	$2.5 + 0.5 \times 1 \times 1 + 2 \times -1 \times 1 = 1$
$\vert 0101>$	$2.5 + 0.5 \times 1 \times 1 + 2 \times -1 \times -1 = 5$

(continued)

Table 2. (*continued*)

Ψ	$H_2 = \langle Q \rangle = \langle \Psi \vert Q \vert \Psi \rangle$
|0110>	$2.5 + 0.5 \times 1 \times -1 + 2 \times -1 \times 1 = 0$
|0111>	$2.5 + 0.5 \times 1 \times -1 + 2 \times -1 \times -1 = 4$
|1000>	$2.5 + 0.5 \times -1 \times 1 + 2 \times 1 \times 1 = 4$
|1001>	$2.5 + 0.5 \times -1 \times 1 + 2 \times 1 \times -1 = 0$
|1010>	$2.5 + 0.5 \times -1 \times -1 + 2 \times 1 \times 1 = 5$
|1011>	$2.5 + 0.5 \times -1 \times -1 + 2 \times 1 \times -1 = 1$
|1100>	$2.5 + 0.5 \times -1 \times 1 + 2 \times -1 \times 1 = 0$
|1101>	$2.5 + 0.5 \times -1 \times 1 + 2 \times -1 \times -1 = 4$
|1110>	$2.5 + 0.5 \times -1 \times -1 + 2 \times -1 \times 1 = 1$
|1111>	$2.5 + 0.5 \times -1 \times -1 + 2 \times -1 \times -1 = 5$

Table 3. Highlighted solutions match with the preset value 2 for the first cell.

Ψ	$H_5 = \langle Q \rangle = \langle \Psi \vert Q \vert \Psi \rangle$
|0000 >	$1.5 + 0.5 \times 1 + 1 + 1 \times 1 = 4$
|0001 >	$1.5 + 0.5 \times 1 + 1 + 1 \times 1 = 4$
|0010 >	$1.5 + 0.5 \times 1 + 1 + 1 \times 1 = 4$
|0011 >	$1.5 + 0.5 \times 1 + 1 + 1 \times 1 = 4$
|0100 >	$1.5 + 0.5 \times 1 + -1 + 1 \times -1 = 0$
|0101 >	$1.5 + 0.5 \times 1 + -1 + 1 \times -1 = 0$
|0110 >	$1.5 + 0.5 \times 1 + -1 + 1 \times -1 = 0$
|0111 >	$1.5 + 0.5 \times 1 + -1 + 1 \times -1 = 0$
|1000 >	$1.5 + 0.5 \times -1 + 1 + -1 \times 1 = 1$
|1001 >	$1.5 + 0.5 \times -1 + 1 + -1 \times 1 = 1$
|1010 >	$1.5 + 0.5 \times -1 + 1 + -1 \times 1 = 1$
|1011 >	$1.5 + 0.5 \times -1 + 1 + -1 \times 1 = 1$
|1100 >	$1.5 + 0.5 \times -1 + -1 + -1 \times -1 = 1$
|1101 >	$1.5 + 0.5 \times -1 + -1 + -1 \times -1 = 1$
|1110 >	$1.5 + 0.5 \times -1 + -1 + -1 \times -1 = 1$
|1111 >	$1.5 + 0.5 \times -1 + -1 + -1 \times -1 = 1$

Table 4: The highlighted solution meets the rules of all three subfunctions.

Ψ	$H_Q = H(q_1^z, q_2^z, q_3^z, q_4^z) = H_1 + H_2 + H_5$
$\|0000>$	$2+5+4=11$
$\|0001>$	$1+1+4=6$
$\|0010>$	$1+4+4=9$
$\|0011>$	$2+0+4=6$
$\|0100>$	$1+1+0=2$
$\|0101>$	$0+5+0=5$
$\|0110>$	$0+0+0=0$
$\|0111>$	$1+4+0=4$
$\|1000>$	$1+4+1=6$
$\|1001>$	$0+0+1=1$
$\|1010>$	$0+5+1=6$
$\|1011>$	$1+1+1=3$
$\|1100>$	$2+0+1=3$
$\|1101>$	$1+4+1=6$
$\|1110>$	$1+1+1=3$
$\|1111>$	$2+5+1=8$

By Eq. (9), we have $H_Q = H(q_1^z, q_2^z, q_3^z, q_4^z) = H_1 + H_2 + H_5$. The subfunctions H_3 and H_4 were excluded due to the simplicity of the case but without loss of generality. Table 4 shows the summed results and highlights the solution $|0110>$ that fulfills H_1, H_2, and H_5 subfunctions simultaneously with $H_Q = 0$. This solution implies $x_{(1,1,1)} = 0$, $x_{(1,1,2)} = 1$, $x_{(1,2,1)} = 1$, and $x_{(1,2,2)} = 0$, i.e., cell values are 2 and 1, respectively and distinctively.

For verification, additional scenarios are evaluated to find solutions utilizing the IBM Qiskit SDK [24]. The quantum Pauli gates are grouped together into a list to create a matrix operator based on the number of qubits. The optimization process uses the QAOA algorithm [9] combined with the COBYLA optimizer [11] to compute the minimum eigenvalue for the matrix. Each solution is then verified with the expected result of the scenario. Subject to limited memory space of our classical computer, all simulated scenarios are within 16 qubits because the matrix size has grown to $2^{16} \times 2^{16}$. A snippet of Python code for the previously modeled H_5 is provided below. The shift value 1.5 is a constant and ignored during the process of searching for the minimum eigen value. It is added back afterwards to derive a 0 for the final expectation value.

```
pauli_list = [("Z",[1],0.5),("Z",[2],1),("ZZ",[1, 2],1)]
op = SparsePauliOp.from_sparse_list(pauli_list, num_qubits=4)
qaoa = QAOA(sampler=Sampler(), optimizer=COBYLA(), reps=1)
result = qaoa.compute_minimum_eigenvalue(op)
print(result.best_measurement)
```

5 Conclusions

We have developed a generalized quantum Sudoku solver using the modeling approach of Ising spin glasses. For a puzzle with $n \times n$ cells, each cell value can range from 1 to n. Therefore, this solver is a three-dimensional Ising model that incorporates n^3 qubits to model the puzzle rules and constraints. The formulation is based on the couplings of atomic spins like modeling spin glasses. The rules and constraints are tackled individually and the separately developed observable operators of Pauli gates circuits for Sudoku are integrated to construct the complete quantum Ising model. The solver is verified with extra scenarios in addition to the illustration example. For each scenario, the optimization process takes advantage of the QAOA algorithm combined with the COBYLA optimizer to compute the minimum eigenvalue that identifies the lowest Hamiltonian energy for a solution.

The Ising model is powerful to solve NP problems but can be computationally inefficient for complex systems due to the exponential growth of quantum states. If the model construction requires a complete graph to tackle sparse interactions, the circumstances become undesirable, especially for a big model. Therefore, it is important to reduce the number of spins or quantum qubits needed when possible. Our future work is to model the cell values by bits instead of decimal values. This will not only allow a broad range of values to be covered through only a few bits but also can save computation time without checking the situation of different values coexisting in a cell. This can be particularly useful and efficient if there are only certain numbers that need to be explored in a widespread range when solving combinatorial problems.

References

1. Yato, T., Seta, T.: Complexity and completeness of finding another solution and its application to puzzles. IEICE Trans. Fundamentals of Electron. Commun. Comput. Sci. **E86-A**(5), 1052–1060 (2003)

2. Simons H.: Sudoku as a constraint problem. In: CP Workshop on Modeling and Reformulating Constraint Satisfaction Problems, pp. 13–27 (2005)
3. Wang, W-L., Loker, D., Tang, M.-H.: A swarm intelligent Sudoku solver. In: Proceedings of 19th Artificial Neural Network in Engineering Conference (ANNIE), pp. 269–274, St. Louis, Missouri (2009)
4. Hathidara, A., Pandey, L.: Neuro-symbolic Sudoku solver. In: ACM KDD Workshop on Knowledge-Infused Learning (KiL), Long Beach, California (2023)
5. Shor, P.: Polynomial-time algorithms for prime factorization and discrete logarithms on a quantum computer. In: Proceedings of the 35th Annual Symposium on Foundations of Computer Science, Santa Fe, New Mexico (1994)
6. Corli, S., Dragoni, D., Proietti, M., Dispenza, M., Cavazzoni, C., Prati, E.: A max k-cut implementation for QAOA in the measurement based quantum computing formalism. In: IEEE International Conference on Quantum Computing and Engineering (QCE), pp. 284–285, Bellevue, Washington (2023)
7. Sharma, A., Deshpande N., Ghos, S.: An efficient quantum algorithm for the traveling salesman problem. Cryptology ePrint Archive. https://eprint.iacr.org/2024/626. Last accessed 21 July 2025
8. Kadowaki, T., Nishimori, H.: Quantum annealing in the transverse Ising model. Phys. Rev. E **58**(5), 5355–5363 (1998)
9. Zhou, L., Wang, S., Choi, S., Pichler, H., Lukin, M.: Quantum approximate optimization algorithm: performance, mechanism, and implementation on near-term devices. Am. Phys. Soc. (APS) J. Phys. Rev. **10**(2) (2020)
10. Hen, I., Spedalieri, F.M.: Quantum annealing for constrained optimization. Am. Phys. Soc. (APS) J. Phys. Rev. **5**(3) (2016)
11. Powell, M.: A direct search optimization method that models the objective and constraint functions by linear interpolation. In: Gomez, S., Hennart, J.P. (eds.) Advances in Optimization and Numerical Analysis. Mathematics and its Applications, vol. 275, pp. 51–67. Springer, Dordrecht (1994)
12. Barenco, A., et al.: Elementary gates for quantum computation. Phys. Rev. A **52**(5), 3457–3467 (1995)
13. Farhi, E., Goldstone, J., Gutmann, S., Lapan, J., Lundgren, A., Preda, D.: A quantum adiabatic evolution algorithm applied to random instances of an NP-complete problem. Science **292**(5516), 472–475 (2001)
14. Das, A., Chakrabarti, B.: Colloquium: quantum annealing and analog quantum computation. Rev. Mod. Phys. **80**(3), 1061–1081 (2008)
15. Boixo, S., Albash, T., Spedalieri, F., Chancellor, N., Lidar, D.: Experimental signature of programmable quantum annealing. Nat. Commun. **4**, 2067 (2013)
16. Boixo, S., et al.: Evidence for quantum annealing with more than one hundred qubits. Nat. Phys. **10**, 218–224 (2014)
17. Johnson, M., et al.: Quantum annealing with manufactured spins. Nature **473**, 194–198 (2011)
18. Niss, M.: History of the Lenz-Ising model 1965–1971: the role of a simple model in understanding critical phenomena. Arch. Hist. Exact Sci. **65**, 625–658 (2011)
19. Barahona, F.: On the computational complexity of Ising spin glass models. J. Phys. A: Math. Gen. **15**(10), 3241 (1982)
20. Skotiniotis, M., Sekatski, P., Dür, W.: Quantum metrology for the Ising Hamiltonian with transverse magnetic field. New J. Phys. **17**(7), 073032 (2015)
21. Lucas, A.: Ising formulations of many NP problems. Frontiers in Physics 2(5), (2014)
22. Haythorpe, M.: Reducing the generalised Sudoku problem to the Hamiltonian cycle problem. AKCE Int. J. Graphs Comb. **13**(3), 272–282 (2016)

23. Shlosberg, A., Jena, A., Mukhopadhyay, P., Haase, J., Leditzky, F., Dellantonio, L.: Adaptive estimation of quantum observables. Quantum **7**, 906 (2023)
24. Javadi-Abhari, A., et al.: Quantum computing with {Q}iskit. https://arxiv.org/abs/2405.08810. Last accessed 21 July 2025

Women's Role in Software Engineering - An Empirical Study

Mahima Sachan(✉), Mayank Maurya, Akash Kumar Singh, Mohammed Faizaan Lnu, Syed Mohammed Sami Abedi, and Muhammad Abdul Basit Ur Rahim

Department of Computer Engineering and Computer Science, California State University, Long Beach, USA
{mahima.sachan01,mayank.maurya01,akash.singh01,mohammed.lnu01, syed.abedi01}@student.csulb.edu, muhammad.abdulbasiturrahim@csulb.edu

Abstract. Women remain underrepresented in senior software engineering roles, despite increasing diversity initiatives. This study investigates the structural, cultural, and organizational factors influencing women's career trajectories in the software industry. Using a mixed-methods approach, we analyze data from 72 detailed surveys across various career stages. Our findings reveal a critical "mid-career cliff," where representation, advancement prospects, and organizational support sharply decline. Quantitative data highlights role segregation and persistent challenges in worklife balance, while qualitative responses emphasize recognition gaps and limited leadership pathways. The study concludes with targeted recommendations—ranging from internal sponsorship programs to transparent promotion criteria—designed to improve retention and equity beyond entry-level hiring. The questionnaire used to conduct this survey can be found here.

1 Introduction

The software industry has expanded exponentially over the past two decades, yet women occupy only about a quarter of computing roles worldwide [12]. Evidence from innovation economics demonstrates that such demographic skew constrains problem-solving capacity and economic output [13]. Although targeted initiatives—from mentorship networks to inclusive recruiting—have become common, their macro-level impact remains modest.

Research consistently documents a precipitous decline in women's representation after the first few years of professional experience, a phenomenon often dubbed the "leaky pipeline" [15]. Intersectional analyses further show that women of colour, LGBTQ+ women and caregivers face compounded exit pressures [9]. Yet organisational data rarely pinpoint the precise career junctures or mechanisms through which attrition accelerates inside technical tracks.

To interrogate these junctures, we deployed a multi-dimensional instrument titled *Women in Software Engineering: Experiences, Challenges, and*

S. Hussain et al. (Eds.): SEET 2025, CCIS 2725, pp. 430–445, 2026.
https://doi.org/10.1007/978-3-032-08977-9_27

Opportunities. The questionnaire integrated multiple-choice, Likert and open-response items across eleven thematic blocks—including role assignment, leadership access, worklife balance and remote-work effects—allowing us to blend quantitative cross-tabulations with qualitative thematic analysis. Respondents were purposively sampled via professional networks, women-in-tech forums and university mailing lists.

Our analysis confirms that women enter the profession in healthy numbers but rapidly lose both peer parity and perceived organisational support between the third and tenth year of tenure. Exposure to mixed-gender teams shrinks by forty percentage points, skepticism about technical-leadership encouragement resurges to 28%, and the belief that worklife-balance hurdles fall disproportionately on women spikes to 78%. Qualitative narratives attribute this compound bottleneck to inflexible on-call norms, opaque promotion criteria and a dearth of senior female role models, setting the stage for the theory and recommendations that follow.

2 Methodology

2.1 Survey Design

The survey instrument titled "Women in Software Engineering: Experiences, Challenges, and Opportunities" comprises 11 thematic sections, each targeting a specific domain related to women's experiences in the software industry. The questionnaire includes a combination of multiple-choice, Likert-scale, checkbox (select-all-that-apply), and open-ended questions. Each section is mapped to a distinct thematic concern—ranging from roles and technical skills to organizational support and intersectionality. The survey was designed to balance quantitative structure with opportunities for qualitative insight, allowing participants to elaborate on their individual perspectives and experiences.

2.2 Target Population and Sampling

The target population includes women currently or previously employed in software engineering roles, as well as those pursuing related academic or training pathways (e.g., computer science students, bootcamp participants). While the survey primarily targets women, it also welcomes input from allies or others in tech with insights into gender dynamics. The sampling approach is non-probabilistic and purposive, distributed via academic networks, professional communities, LinkedIn groups, women-in-tech forums, and university mailing lists. This approach aims to capture a broad spectrum of perspectives from diverse roles, industries, and geographic locations.

2.2.1 Respondent Demographics

To contextualize our findings, we present a breakdown of the survey respondents based on key demographic factors:

Years of Experience: Respondents span a wide range of experience levels. A significant number reported 0–2 years and 3–5 years of experience, while a notable portion also represented the 6–10 and 11+ year brackets. This distribution supports cohort comparisons across early-career, mid-career, and veteran stages.

Organization Type: Participants were drawn from diverse work environments including large tech companies, medium-sized enterprises, freelance/independent roles, and startups. This variation adds depth to the organizational analysis of support structures and workplace culture (Figs. 1 and 2).

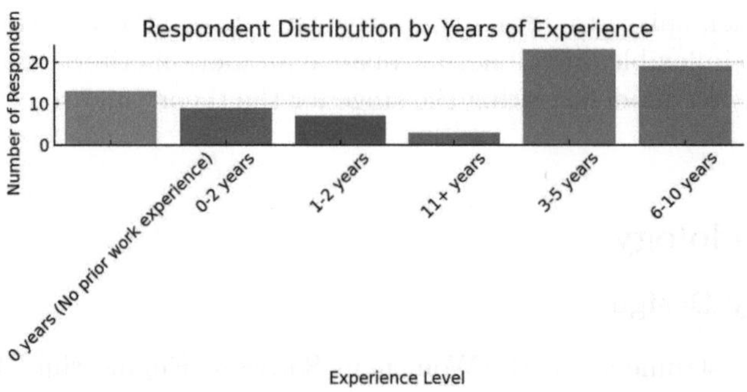

Fig. 1. Respondent Distribution by Years of Experience

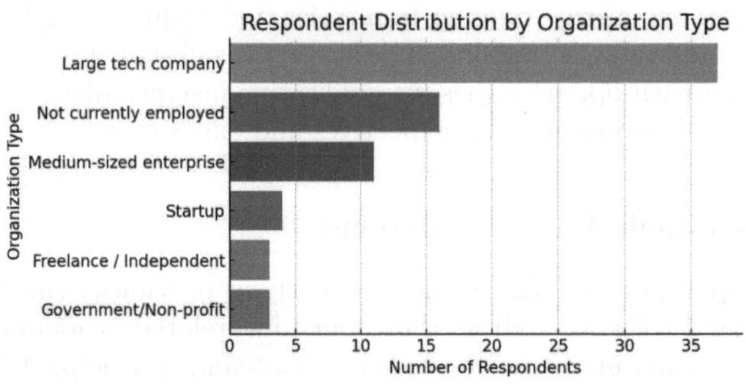

Fig. 2. Respondent Distribution by Organization Type

Note: Although the survey targeted a broad audience, most responses originated from U.S.-based professionals. This U.S.-centric distribution is considered when interpreting generalizability.

2.3 Data Analysis Plan

The collected data will undergo both quantitative and qualitative analysis. Quantitative responses (e.g., role distributions, skill rankings, recognition ratings) will be analyzed using descriptive statistics such as frequencies, percentages, and cross-tabulations. Key comparisons—such as between organization types or years of experience—will be explored to detect trends. For qualitative responses (open-ended questions), thematic analysis will be applied to identify recurring narratives and insights, particularly around challenges, support structures, and career enablers. Visualization techniques (e.g., bar charts, word clouds) will be used where appropriate to enhance interpretation.

3 Literature Review

3.1 Demographics and Background

Survey Questions Addressed: Current role, years of experience, organization type, team gender composition, perceived changes in women's representation.

Understanding the demographic distribution is essential to trace patterns in participation and progression. While multiple studies confirm that women remain underrepresented in senior technical and leadership roles [15], they often fail to distinguish how these disparities evolve across different career stages. This lack of temporal nuance makes it difficult to isolate when and why attrition accelerates. Additionally, although research like [12] highlights positive trends driven by diversity initiatives, it rarely evaluates the depth or sustainability of these efforts. By capturing variables such as years of experience and team gender composition, our study seeks to bridge this gap—probing not just whether diversity exists, but how it translates (or fails to translate) into inclusion and advancement.

3.2 Roles, Preferences, and Skills

Survey Questions Addressed: Common roles, valuable technical skills, encouragement toward leadership, and success attributes.

This section draws from literature examining occupational segregation in software engineering. While many studies report that women are disproportionately channeled into roles such as front-end development, QA, or UX—fields often perceived as less technical [16]—the causes of this segregation remain contested. Some scholars attribute it to organizational bias, while others point to self-selection influenced by early exposure and mentorship patterns. However, few studies explore whether such role distribution is driven by constrained opportunity or actual preference, leaving a critical gap in understanding agency versus structural limitation. Furthermore, while research highlights the importance of leadership encouragement, proactive sponsorship, and visible role models [7], it often lacks data on whether these efforts result in tangible advancement. Our survey also investigates perceptions of skill value, probing whether soft skills like resilience and communication—frequently cited as important [6]—are equally recognized and rewarded compared to technical competencies, a distinction often overlooked in existing studies.

3.3 Barriers and Challenges

Survey Questions Addressed: Major challenges, gender-based promotion bias, assignment to non-technical roles, recognition for technical work.

This section investigates the structural and interpersonal barriers women face in software engineering. While numerous studies confirm that gender bias in hiring and promotions persists [2], there is limited consensus on how overt or covert these biases are in modern workplaces. Some research emphasizes systemic exclusion from core development tasks or diversion into support roles [14], yet others argue that such patterns are diminishing due to increasing awareness and process reforms. However, few studies rigorously examine whether these reforms are effective beyond surface-level metrics. Additionally, although recognition disparity—where women's technical contributions are undervalued—has been widely documented [8], prior work often overlooks how this invisibility intersects with race, seniority, or work setting (e.g., remote vs. in-person). By capturing both quantitative trends and qualitative narratives, our study addresses these underexplored dimensions and offers a more layered understanding of how structural and interpersonal barriers manifest across different career stages.

3.4 Organizational Support and Inclusion

Survey Questions Addressed: Existence and types of support programs, effectiveness of diversity efforts, suggestions for improvement.

While formal support structures such as mentorship and leadership development programs are frequently cited as key drivers of retention and job satisfaction [1], the literature remains divided on their long-term effectiveness. Some studies highlight that mentorship often lacks the strategic impact of sponsorship, especially when not tied to promotion pathways or performance evaluations. Moreover, although many organizations publicly promote inclusion programs, research indicates that these efforts often suffer from inconsistent execution, limited accountability, or unclear success metrics [11]. Few studies provide concrete evaluations of which specific interventions—such as ERGs, coaching, or upskilling tracks—actually drive advancement. By collecting both frequency and perceived impact of various support initiatives, our survey fills this evaluative gap and surfaces practitioner-informed recommendations for meaningful organizational reform.

3.5 Work-Life Balance and Career Growth

Survey Questions Addressed: Work-life balance impact, effect of flexible arrangements, available career paths, factors influencing retention.

Worklife balance remains a persistent challenge in the tech industry, particularly for women navigating caregiving responsibilities and cultural expectations [5]. While workplace flexibility is often promoted as a retention tool, existing research presents mixed results—some studies associate it with improved morale and retention, while others warn it may inadvertently reduce visibility, access to stretch projects, or informal mentorship opportunities. Despite the proliferation of flexible work policies, there is limited evidence on whether they translate into sustained career growth or merely serve as short-term retention fixes. Prior work also tends to generalize flexibility's impact, without distinguishing outcomes across role types or career stages. By directly probing organizational practices and their perceived effects on advancement, our study seeks to clarify which interventions are genuinely enabling progression versus those that risk reinforcing gendered career ceilings [10].

3.6 Personal Perspectives

Survey Questions Addressed: Female mentorship, contribution ratings, unique perspectives, future gender equity, single most helpful change.

Personal experiences offer essential qualitative depth, revealing patterns and perceptions often missed in purely quantitative analyses. While mentorship is frequently associated with increased confidence and persistence among women in tech [3], studies rarely distinguish between passive mentorship and active sponsorship, the latter being more strongly correlated with career advancement. Similarly, although recognition is acknowledged as vital for morale and retention, prior research often assumes its presence without exploring how recognition is distributed—or withheld—across gender lines. Existing literature also tends to treat the value of women's perspectives in tech as a given, without rigorously analyzing how those perspectives are integrated into team decision-making or innovation processes. By asking participants to reflect on unique contributions, critical support structures, and their single most helpful change, our study addresses these gaps and surfaces actionable insights grounded in lived experience.

3.7 Remote Work Effects

Survey Questions Addressed: Effects on work experience, mentorship, work-life balance, long-term gender equity.

Remote work has significantly reshaped the tech landscape, offering flexibility and autonomy that many women cite as beneficial [4]. However, its impact on gender equity remains contested. While some studies praise remote work for lowering entry barriers and accommodating caregiving responsibilities, others highlight emerging concerns—such as diminished visibility, reduced access to informal mentorship, and exclusion from high-impact projects. Notably, most existing literature stops short of examining how these trade-offs vary across career stages, technical roles, or organizational cultures. Moreover, the long-term consequences of remote arrangements on promotion trajectories and leadership representation remain underexplored. By capturing respondents' nuanced views on remote work's benefits and limitations, our survey contributes empirical clarity to a topic often framed in binary terms and informs the design of more equitable hybrid work structures.

4 Ablation Study

Our working theory posits: "Supportive structures are moving the needle on representation, but subtle sorting and life-load pressures are still keeping women on the periphery of core technical power and senior decision-making".

4.1 Analysis of Contributing Factors

Factor 1: Structural Supports and Representation. Most respondents in Fig. 3 indicate that the share of women has increased in recent years. Companies are implementing programs specifically designed for women, with diversity and inclusion efforts rated as somewhat or very effective Fig. 4a. Flexible work arrangements are overwhelmingly credited with helping retain women in tech Fig. 4b.

This evidence suggests a tangible payoff from policy-level interventions, including parent-friendly flexibility, Employee Resource Groups (ERGs), mentoring programs, and targeted recruiting efforts.

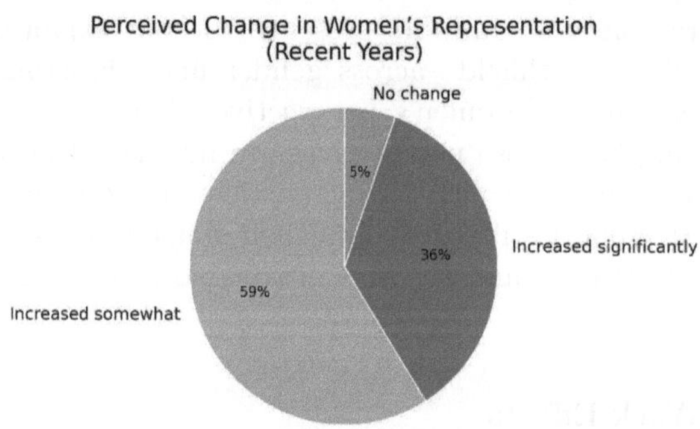

Fig. 3. Perceived change in women's representation in software engineering during recent years.

Factor 2: Role Distribution and Technical Tracks. The multi-select role distribution data reveals a heavy concentration of women in frontend development, UX/UI, quality assurance, and data analysis, with notably thinner representation in backend development, AI/ML, and cybersecurity positions Fig. 5.

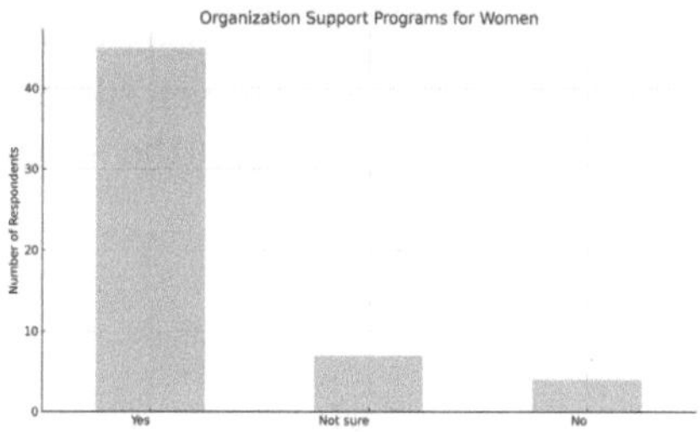

(a) Organizations with programs or initiatives that support women.

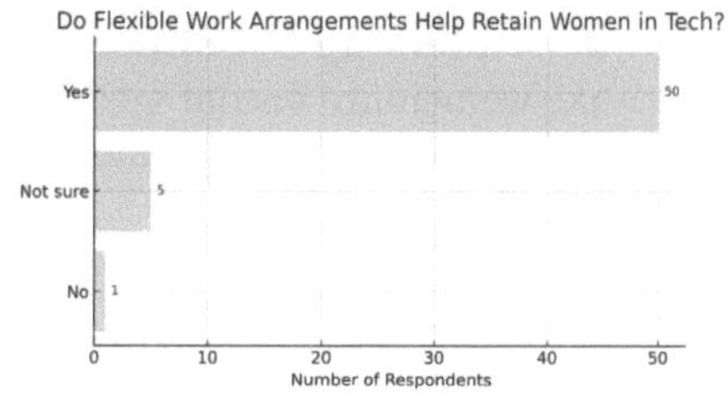

(b) Responses to "Do flexible work arrangements help retain women in tech roles?"

Fig. 4. Organizational supports and flexible work effectiveness.

This pattern suggests persistent gender sorting: women are welcomed into the industry but often channeled into roles perceived as user-facing, quality-oriented, or "applied"—areas that historically carry less political capital within engineering organizations.

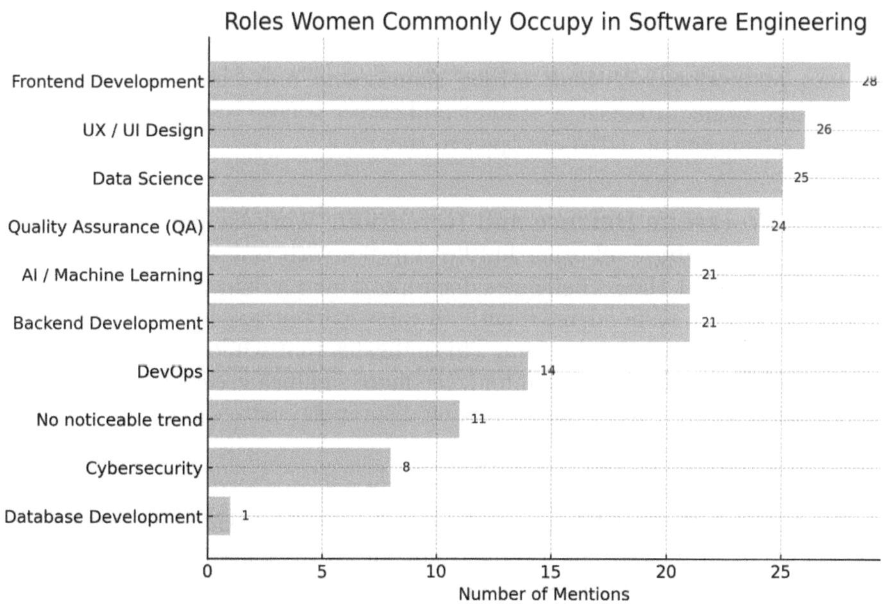

Fig. 5. Roles that women most frequently occupy in software engineering, based on survey respondents.

Factor 3: Leadership Pipeline Challenges. A large majority of respondents report that women are encouraged toward leadership roles Fig. 6a, yet "limited visibility in leadership" ranks among the top challenges identified in the survey Fig. 6b.

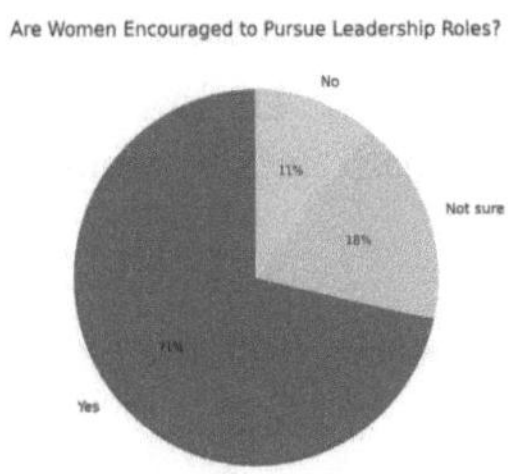

(a) Are women encouraged to pursue leadership roles?

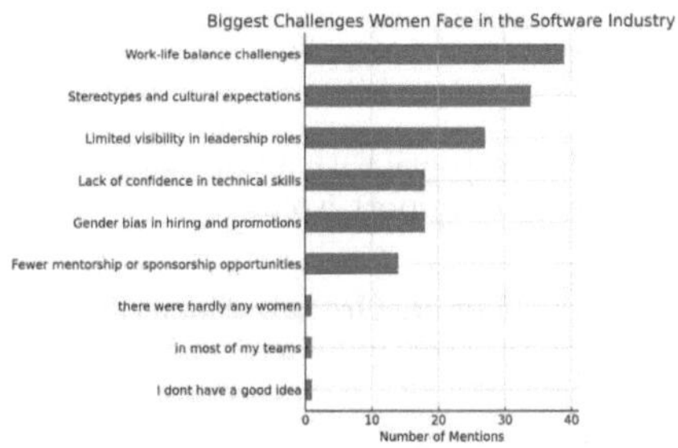

(b) Biggest challenges women report facing in software engineering.

Fig. 6. Encouragement for pursuing leadership roles and experienced challenges.

The data suggests that formal encouragement does not automatically translate into promotions. Without strong sponsorship and bias-proof evaluation mechanisms, women frequently stall at mid-career stages—even when explicitly told that advancement paths are open to them.

Factor 4: Work-Life Balance and Retention. Work-life balance challenges consistently rank above all other hurdles Fig. 6b, with respondents overwhelmingly reporting that these challenges disproportionately affect women Fig. 7.

Simultaneously, respondents identify flexible work arrangements as the single most effective retention mechanism. This indicates that while many women possess the technical capabilities required, the more significant challenge lies in sustaining career progression while managing disproportionate caregiving responsibilities or cultural expectations.

Factor 5: Evolution of Bias in Advancement. Approximately one-third of respondents report experiencing gender-based headwinds in career advancement, though reports of "frequent" bias represent a smaller subset Fig. 8.

This pattern aligns with a shift from blatant discrimination to more subtle, accumulative disadvantages, such as fewer stretch assignments, exclusion from informal networks, or evaluation criteria that reward confidence displays that are often penalized when exhibited by women.

Factor 6: Remote Work Amplifier. Survey data on remote work shows a dichotomy in its effects on gender equity in technical fields. Approximately 56%

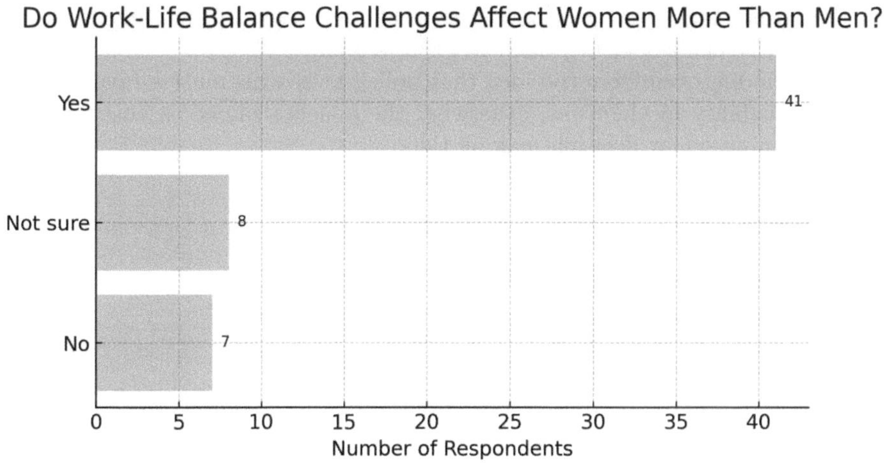

Fig. 7. Survey response to "Do work-life balance challenges affect women more than men in software engineering?"

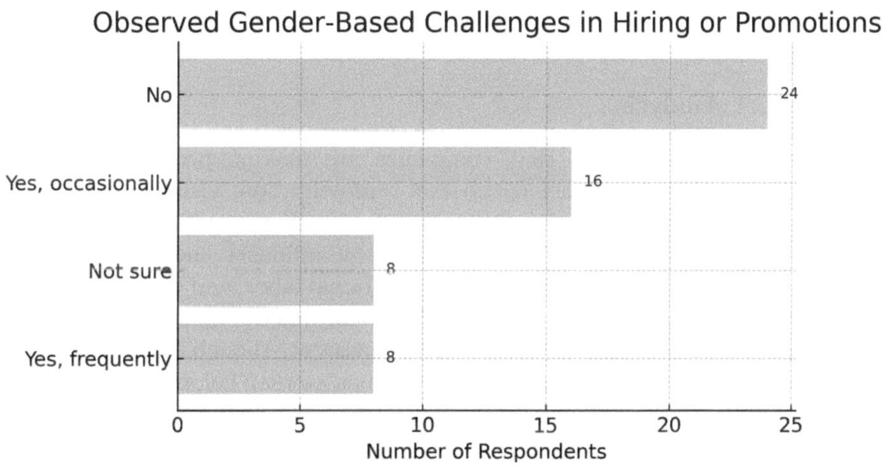

Fig. 8. Responses to "Have you observed or experienced gender-based challenges in hiring or promotions?"

of respondents believe remote work improves gender equity Fig. 9b, confirming that flexible, location-agnostic policies are perceived as another supportive structure lifting initial representation—consistent with Factors 1 and 4.

However, there is a notable split regarding mentorship visibility in remote settings: 24% report it becomes easier while 21% find it harder Fig. 9a. This division suggests that without deliberate scaffolding, remote work can re-create subtle sorting and invisible-labor traps. Women who work remotely risk missing the ad-hoc sponsorship opportunities that traditionally fuel advancement, paralleling the challenges identified in Factors 3 and 5.

These findings reinforce the idea that policy-level wins must be paired with anti-bias visibility mechanisms; otherwise, the benefits gained at entry plateau before reaching senior decision-making tiers.

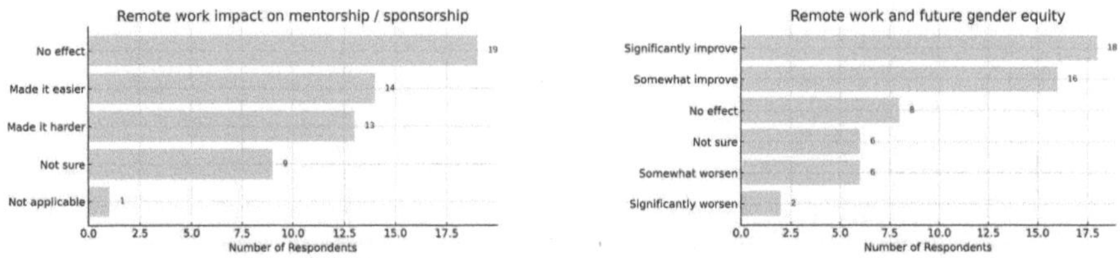

(a) Mentorship / sponsorship

(b) Future gender equity

Fig. 9. Respondent views on how remote work affects mentorship opportunities and long-term gender equity.

4.2 Cohort Analysis

Our ablation study reveals that companies are making progress on initial inclusion—evidenced by higher entry-level representation, visible support programs, and flexible work options. However, once inside the organization, women are often steered into roles with limited strategic influence and face a life-load tax—the cumulative burden of caregiving, emotional labor, and logistical responsibilities that disproportionately affects them and quietly stalls career momentum. When these pressures intersect with persistent, though subtle, biases in evaluation and promotion processes, many women plateau before reaching senior technical or executive positions.

The most pronounced organizational support appears during the junior-to-mid career stages; however, the largest disparities—such as visibility of bias and diversion into non-technical roles—re-emerge among veteran professionals. This suggests that attempts to advance into top technical or executive tiers often encounter renewed resistance, along with increased demands for invisible labor—unrecognized tasks like mentoring, coordination, or emotional support that, while essential, are rarely rewarded in promotion criteria.

Table 1 distills the trends depicted in Fig. 10, providing a concise numerical summary of the cohort-level patterns illustrated by the graphs.

5 Recommendations

Based on our findings from the ablation study, we propose a set of actionable recommendations for organizations seeking to improve gender representation

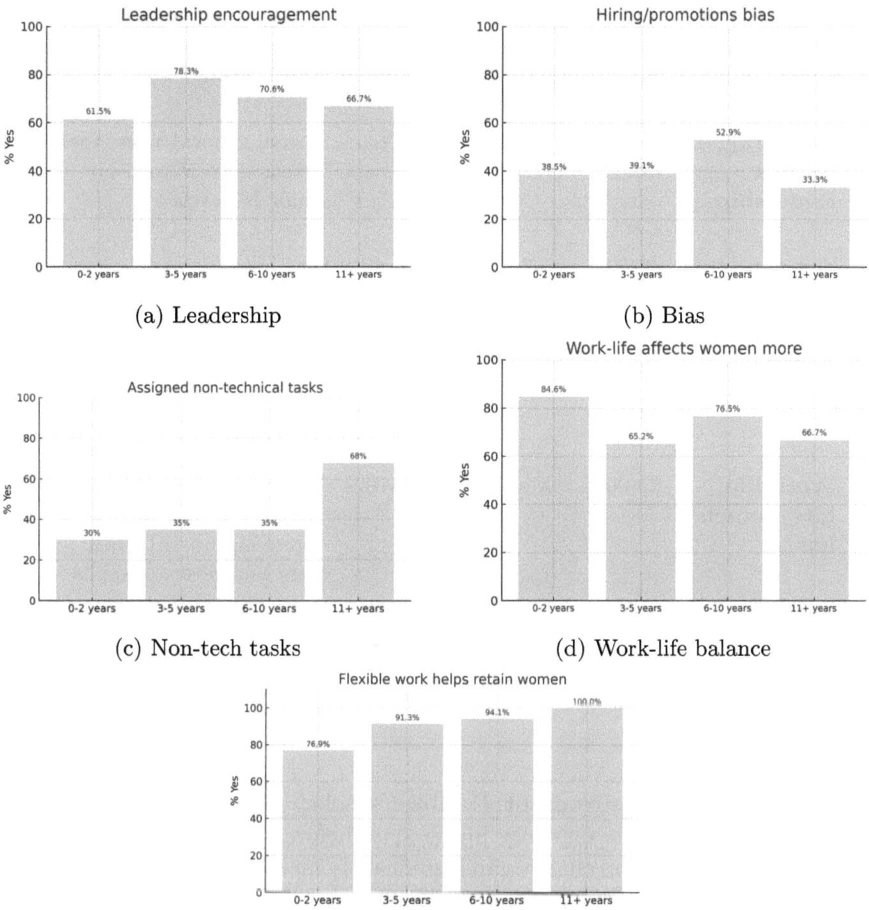

(a) Leadership (b) Bias

(c) Non-tech tasks (d) Work-life balance

(e) Flexible work

Fig. 10. Percentage answering "Yes" across experience brackets for five key perceptions.

and advancement in technical roles. These recommendations are categorized into two groups: (1) immediately implementable interventions requiring minimal resources, and (2) high-impact initiatives requiring more substantial investment but potentially yielding transformative results.

5.1 Readily Implementable Interventions

We identify several measures that organizations can deploy with minimal resource allocation or process disruption:

Table 1. Career Stage Comparison of Key Indicators

Feature	Early-career	Mid-career	Veteran	Implication
Encouraged toward leadership	Builds from ~50% to ~80%	Plateau ~70-80%	~65%	Formal support rises, then softens once women hit senior IC levels
See gender bias in advancement	40-50% say "Yes"	~35-40%	Spikes to ~50%	Bias becomes visible again when vying for director/staff elevations
Assigned non-tech work	30%	Mid-30%	65-70% (spike in 11+ group)	Long-tenured women still get diverted to coordination/glue work
Work-life hits women harder	85-90%	Mid-60%	~65-70%	The load is worst right as careers start (child-bearing + proving worth), then eases but never disappears
Flexible work helps retention	85-90%	90-95%	~100%	Universally popular; the more career capital women have, the more essential flexibility becomes

- **Internal hiring requirement**: Establish a policy requiring at least one qualified woman candidate on every hiring slate before it is considered complete. This simple procedural change can significantly increase the pipeline of female talent without adding complexity to the recruitment process.
- **Flexible-first scheduling norm**: Implement core-hours blocks (e.g., 10:00–15:00) for meetings and collaboration, while supporting asynchronous work outside these hours. Publishing usage metrics of flexible policies across all genders can reduce stigmatization of their uptake.
- **Role prestige neutralization**: Publish transparent role-level pay bands and scope definitions to ensure equivalence between traditionally gendered technical domains (e.g., ensuring "frontend L5" carries the same compensation and promotion criteria as "backend L5").
- **Promotion visibility initiative**: Create a quarterly feature in company all-hands meetings that highlights newly promoted women engineers, their projects, and the sponsors who supported their advancement.
- **Meeting structure reforms**: Establish meeting-free days (e.g., Wednesdays) and implement a rotation system for meeting facilitation and note-taking duties to prevent the disproportionate assignment of "glue work" to women.

- **Communication boundaries**: Set clear expectations regarding after-hours communication, restricting non-emergency messages after established working hours, with enforcement facilitated by communication platform analytics.
- **Transparent opportunity allocation**: Create an internal "gig board" where high-impact projects are advertised openly rather than assigned through closed-door selections, thereby democratizing access to career-advancing opportunities.
- **Post-promotion cycle equity check**: Implement routine analysis of promotion outcomes through fairness metrics (e.g., gender parity in success rates, time-in-level comparisons). Flag and review decisions when disparities exceed a predetermined threshold (e.g., 5% points).

5.2 High-Impact Strategic Investments

The following recommendations require more substantial resource allocation, planning, and organizational commitment, but evidence suggests they may yield significant improvements in retention and advancement of women in technical roles:

- **Technical rotation program**: Establish structured 6-month rotational opportunities into infrastructure, security, or machine learning teams for volunteers—funded and evaluated as equivalent to product delivery work. This intervention directly addresses the channeling of women into "front-of-house" roles by providing supported pathways into core technical domains.
- **Targeted technical upskilling**: Implement reimbursement programs specifically for certifications in lower-representation technical domains (e.g., Kubernetes, deep-learning frameworks, security specializations), creating incentives for women to develop expertise in these areas.
- **Formalized sponsorship system**: Require each director-level and above leader to actively sponsor at least two women annually, with this sponsorship activity tracked and evaluated in performance reviews. Research consistently demonstrates the impact of sponsorship (versus mentorship alone) on career advancement.
- **Promotion panel diversity requirement**: Mandate the inclusion of at least one senior woman engineer from outside the candidate's direct reporting line on every senior individual contributor or management promotion review panel, introducing perspective diversity into evaluation processes.
- **Principal Engineer shadowing initiative**: Create a structured program enabling mid-career women to shadow staff/principal engineers during architecture reviews for one release cycle, paired with an active sponsor rather than merely a passive mentor.
- **Executive accountability measures**: Establish and publish two organization-wide objectives and key results (OKRs): (1) senior individual contributor and leadership representation targets, and (2) stretch-project gender parity metrics. Link executive compensation incentives to achievement of both measures.

Organizations should consider implementing a combination of readily accessible interventions alongside more resource-intensive strategic investments based on their specific context and resources.

6 Conclusion

Our study identifies a pronounced mid-career bottleneck for women in software engineering between years 3–10 of professional experience. The proportion of women on gender-balanced teams drops from 57% at entry level to 17% by mid-career, while work-life balance concerns rise to 78% agreement. Despite improvements in entry-level representation through flexible work arrangements and diversity initiatives, women continue to be channeled away from core technical roles and senior decision-making positions.

We term this phenomenon the "mid-career cliff"—characterized by reduced peer parity, resurgent leadership pathway skepticism, and amplified work-life pressures. These findings suggest that policy interventions focused exclusively on entry-level recruitment are insufficient. Organizations must implement targeted strategies addressing mid-career retention and advancement, including transparent promotion criteria, equitable opportunity allocation, and formalized sponsorship systems.

References

1. Ashcraft, A., Eger, B., Friend, K.: Solving the equation: the variables for women's success in engineering and computing (2016). https://www.aauw.org/resources/research/solving-the-equation/, aAUW Report
2. Corbett, C., Hill, C.: Solving the equation: the variables for women's success in engineering and computing (2015). https://www.aauw.org/resources/research/solving-the-equation/, American Association of University Women (AAUW)
3. Denner, J., Werner, L., Ortiz-Young, S.: Women's perspectives on mentoring in computing. In: Proceedings of the 45th ACM Technical Symposium on Computer Science Education (SIGCSE), pp. 657–662 (2014)
4. Gartner: The impact of remote work on women in tech (2021). https://www.gartner.com/en/articles/the-impact-of-remote-work-on-women-in-tech
5. Hewlett, S., Luce, C.B.: Off-ramps and on-ramps: keeping talented women on the road to success. Harvard Business Review (2005)
6. Hewlett, S., Luce, C.B., Sherbin, P., Sumberg, K.: The Athena factor: reversing the brain drain in science, engineering, and technology (2008), Harvard Business Review Research Report
7. Ibarra, H., Carter, N., Silva, C.: Why men still get more promotions than women. Harvard Business Review (2010)
8. Kaplan, A., Donovan, S., Moulton, M.: The state of women in tech (2020). https://www.womenwhotech.com/resources/state-women-tech-2020, women Who Tech
9. Kapor Center: The leaky tech pipeline: A comprehensive framework for understanding and addressing the lack of diversity across the tech ecosystem (2018). https://www.kaporcenter.org/the-leaky-tech-pipeline/

10. Kerr, E., London, P., Mahajan, K.: The keys to retaining tech talent (2019). https://www2.deloitte.com/us/en/insights/focus/technology-and-the-future-of-work/retaining-tech-talent.html, deloitte Insights
11. McKinsey & Company: Women in the workplace 2023 (2023). https://www.mckinsey.com/featured-insights/diversity-and-inclusion/women-in-the-workplace, in partnership with LeanIn.Org
12. NCWIT: Women in tech: The facts (2020). https://www.ncwit.org/resources/women-tech-facts. Accessed 14 Apr 2025
13. Page, S.E.: The Difference: How the Power of Diversity Creates Better Groups, Firms, Schools, and Societies. Princeton University Press (2007)
14. Shih, M.: Positive stigma: examining resilience and empowerment in overcoming stigma. Ann. Am. Acad. Pol. Soc. Sci. **591**(1), 175–185 (2004)
15. Simard, C.: Climbing the technical ladder: obstacles and solutions for mid-level women in technology (2008). https://anitab.org/wp-content/uploads/2013/12/Climbing_the_Technical_Ladder.pdf, anita Borg Institute Report
16. Wang, Q., Maaren, M.V., Patil, H.: Biases in assignment of software roles. IEEE Trans. Softw. Eng. **47**(6), 1191–1206 (2021)

Mammo-Find: An LLM-Based Multi-channel Tool for Recommending Public Mammogram Datasets

Raiyan Jahangir(✉) and Vladimir Filkov

University of California, Davis, CA, USA
{rjahangir,vfilkov}@ucdavis.edu

Abstract. Breast cancer is a leading cause of mortality among women, requiring early detection and diagnosis. Researchers are developing increasingly sophisticated AI models to predict breast cancer risk, assisting radiologists in screening. However, to learn effectively, the models require large amounts of data that can be difficult to source from a single location. Although there are various public mammogram breast cancer datasets, they differ in terms of data quality and format and cover diverse demographic, geographic, and outcome distributions. Thus, including them in a new AI model development is a challenge. In this study, we introduce Mammo-Find, an LLM agent-based tool for the discovery of public mammogram datasets using a multichannel user interface (text and visual). Mammo-Find has knowledge of 22 mammogram datasets and uses different LLMs and Retrieval-Augmented Generation (RAG) techniques. LLM responses are given as text and as a knowledge graph. This study highlights the feasibility of LLMs as agents for interacting with datasets, which can help reduce search time and ease the work of medical researchers.

Keywords: LLM · RAG · Multi-channel · Mammogram

1 Introduction

Breast cancer has been one of the leading causes of death in women worldwide [2]. 30% of all new cancer cases in women every year are breast cancer [1]. Due to its severity, physicians and scientists continually seek more effective and efficient methods to detect and diagnose it. Since cancer treatment is costly and unpredictable, health professionals recommend regular breast screening to detect cancerous tumors. One of the most prominent technologies used to detect breast cancer is mammography, which uses radiographs to identify abnormalities in breast tissue and thus to detect breast cancer [36]. Radiologists examine these images for abnormal findings by observing the breast tissue and its composition. Based on mammograms and other studies, they can choose a severity score called the Breast Imaging Reporting and Data System (BIRADS) score, which ranges from 0 to 6 [9]. Finally, radiologists write reports that include all the findings and suggestions for follow-up actions.

S. Hussain et al. (Eds.): SEET 2025, CCIS 2725, pp. 446–463, 2026.
https://doi.org/10.1007/978-3-032-08977-9_28

With the emergence of Artificial Intelligence (AI) [14,15], researchers have been exploring various ways to utilize AI in healthcare, simplifying tasks for healthcare professionals [13,16,17]. Similarly, the incorporation of AI into the detection and diagnosis of breast cancer has been an active area of research [38]. Recently, Large Language Models (LLMs) with their ability to generate human-like text have become the state-of-the-art in generative AI [7]. These models are increasingly being incorporated into medical research and clinical practice [43], including for the screening and diagnosis of breast cancer [42]. Radiologists are also leveraging the power of AI to detect, diagnose, and treat breast cancers, as well as to calculate risk factors from mammogram images.

However, large amounts of data are necessary to refine AI or LLM models so that they can perform effective cancer detection or screening tasks. Although there are various public mammogram breast cancer datasets, they differ in terms of data quality and format and cover diverse demographic, geographic, and outcome distributions. Thus, including them in a new AI model development is a challenging task. Thus, researchers who develop and/or optimize mammogram screening algorithms may find it challenging to identify suitable datasets for their work. Medical data in general, such as mammograms, requires institutional approval [19,30], which can be a time-consuming procedure.

Publicly available data sets [29,32] come in a variety of different formats and data types, for example, the number of images may vary and may be inconsistent with the metadata, and clinical data and reports may or may not be present. These cases may make the datasets suitable only for certain research tasks. Thus, a researcher would have to find public datasets and then search through them one by one to find out which dataset is suitable for their research purpose, which is tedious and time-consuming.

With the rise of LLMs and specifically ChatGPT [3], researchers can turn to them to search for related datasets. However, they generate answers that can be a combination of real, hallucinated, and non-relevant information, so out-of-the-box is not a reliable tool for this task. Other tools include curated websites that serve as a one-stop shop for data repositories, such as the National Cancer Institute and the National Institute of Health. A notable tool is Google Dataset Search, developed by Google [5], which provides links to various available datasets. However, most of those datasets are in text format, and the details and contents of the datasets are not consistently mentioned, making it difficult to extract the information. Previous research has shown that people can perceive information faster when it is presented visually [39] or in a multichannel method of text and visualization. None of the above tools has any answers for downstream pipelines for clinical and translational tasks.

1.1 Goals

Despite showing immense potential in multiple tasks, the utilization of LLMs in recommending mammogram datasets in a multichannel setting remains largely unexplored. Our goals in this paper are to:

- Compile a comprehensive knowledge base of public mammogram datasets and relevant research articles and structure them to facilitate efficient, accurate, and context-sensitive queries.
- Develop a multichannel UI enabling user interaction with visual tools, conversational agents, and direct queries.
- Enable natural, human-like interactions by using a RAG architecture to handle complex, context-sensitive, and provide users with context-aware responses that leverage the full breadth of the knowledge base.
- Offer personalized dataset recommendations for research tasks based on user input without hallucinations.

There has not been any considerable work done previously that has adopted a multi-channel approach (text+visualization) to suggest appropriate medical datasets to the researchers. Some similar work includes developing a dataset similarity visualizer by Skoda et al. [41]. They made a tool called ODIN (Open Dataset INspector) that has a knowledge graph from which the tool calculates dataset similarity to determine whether two datasets are similar or not. Kao et al. [20] developed a novel analysis tool for visualization of ODD (Open Data Deidentification). Their tool detects whether openly available datasets have personally identifiable information or not. Moreover, a study by Vazquez [44] shows that LLMs have been used for the generation of graphs and charts. However, their usage in graph visualization is still new and remains largely unexplored. Therefore, to our knowledge, this study is the first that develop an LLM-based medical data set recommendation tool using a multichannel method.

2 Related Work

LLMs have been used as aids in almost all health domains, including breast cancer. Haver et al. [12] explored the ability of ChatGPT to predict cancer BIRADS from mammogram images. Pesapane et al. [34] explored the capability of ChatGPT in zero-shot mode to generate mammogram reports from mammogram images. They found that GPT-4 correctly identified 53.3% of the cases while showing fluctuating accuracy in finding microcalcifications and masses. Piao et al. [35] compared the performance of three different LLMs in answering medical questions related to breast cancer. Their experiments showed that ChatGPT excelled among the other three models in answering questions, answering 66.7% comprehensively and 10% correct but inadequate answers. Cao et al. [6] developed MammoVLM, a Vision-Language Model (VLM) for diagnostic assistance in mammography. The model was developed by modifying and fine-tuning GLM-4 9B, an open-source LLM, and provides diagnostic reports based on mammogram images, using unimodal and multimodal contrastive learning strategies. Ghosh et al. [11] proposed MammoClip, a VLM developed by fine-tuning a CLIP model. The MammoClip takes multimodal input in the form of images and reports. Then it uses a novel feature attribution method to highlight abnormal findings in mammogram images. It also classifies the presence or absence of cancer in the breasts. Jain et al. [18] proposed a multimodal breast cancer detection VLM framework that takes mammogram images and clinical history as input and outputs the presence or absence of cancer in the image.

Despite these efforts, LLMs have not yet been effective in recommending mammogram datasets. Our work is focused on developing a tool that utilizes the LLMs to generate suggestions for new researchers in selecting suitable datasets for their research, in a multichannel method.

3 Methodology

Our methodology workflow is shown in Fig. 1. The boxes with dashed lines are further detailed in subsequent figures. We break down the methodology into a number of subsections.

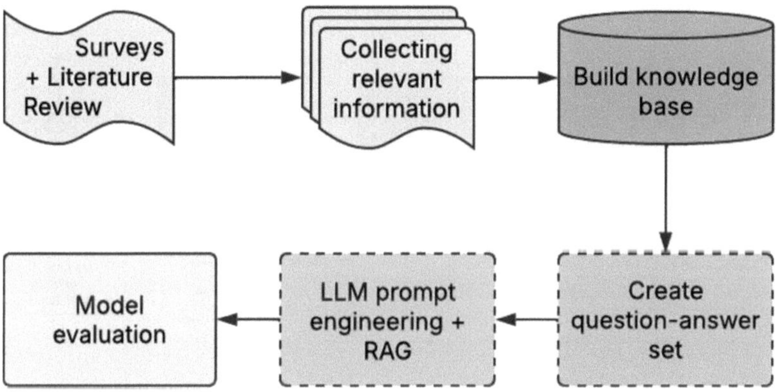

Fig. 1. The methodology of thc study

3.1 Collection of Dataset Articles

The initial search for information was carried out with the keywords "Mammograms" and "Breast Cancer" on Google Scholar, PhysioNet [28], PubMed [45], Kaggle, and Figshare [40]. A comprehensive literature review was conducted on the resulting articles and datasets, published between 1994 and 2024. We thus obtained 20 datasets with articles and 2 datasets without articles, for a total of 22 datasets. From the datasets, relevant information was extracted, including the number of mammogram images, image types, file formats, dataset size, source location, accessibility, publication year, and potential research tasks. Datasets were cross-referenced with published research to ensure accuracy and reliability while assessing their suitability for various research tasks. The findings were documented in a structured database to allow easy access and retrieval for research purposes.

3.2 Building the Knowledge Graph

We built a knowledge graph for each of the 22 datasets. A Retrieval Augmented Generation (RAG) [22] architecture was used to allow interaction with the knowledge base. We used Ollama [24] and Langchain [26] to convert the information extracted from the datasets into embeddings, which were then indexed into ChromaDB [47], a vector database. We use the Nomic-Embed-Text transformer [31] to convert the texts into embeddings. The general structure of the RAG pipeline is shown in Fig. 2.

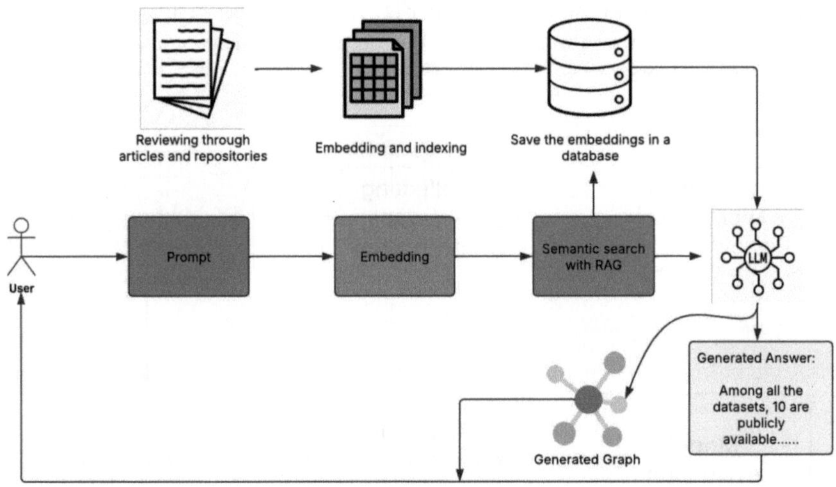

Fig. 2. The architecture of our RAG pipeline

3.3 Preparing the Data for LLM Training

We started by identifying the types of questions that users ask when searching for datasets on platforms such as Kaggle, Google Dataset Search, and PhysioNet. We conducted extensive reviews of these resources and analyzed authentic user discussions. We enhanced these findings with direct human feedback from domain experts that comprises radiologists and potential users, such as researchers, data scientists, and Ph.D. students who are working in this field, to ensure that the questions truly reflected real-world information needs. We categorized the questions into 11 different types based on description, task, availability, size, time, format, clinical data, associated articles, geographic origin, comparative, and filter. Based on these categories, we compiled a set of 216 questions, with each question paired with a manually recorded answer derived from the datasets, ensuring that every answer was accurate, complete, and reflective of the current properties of the dataset. Throughout the process, every step was carefully observed to ensure that the answers were taken from real interactions. The question-answer pairs are given in the supplementary information section.

3.4 LLM Prompting for Dataset Recommendations

Prompt engineering is a process of crafting instructions for LLMs to generate the desired output [25]. For our work, we implemented the zero-shot and few-shot learning strategy. Zero-shot learning is a prompt engineering technique in which LLMs are simply given a prompt, question, or instruction to which to answer [37]. No examples are provided. In few-shot learning, a few examples of question-answer pairs are provided along with the prompt to the LLM from which it infers to generate a response similar to those in the examples. In our study, we passed 10 examples to the LLM as part of the few-shot learning, each example a question-answer pair. A sample of both zero-shot and few-shot prompts is given below:

Zero Shot Framework:
You are an AI assistant that provides information about mammogram datasets. You will answer them from the relevant document to ensure the response is precise, medically relevant, and well-organized.

Relevant information from the document: {*Information fetched by RAG*}

Question: {*The question asked by the user*}

Few Shot Framework:
You are an AI assistant that provides information about mammogram datasets. You will answer them from the relevant document to ensure the response is precise, medically relevant, and well-organized.

Here are some provided questions and how to answer them:
"question": "What is the largest mammogram dataset available?",
"answer": "The largest mammogram dataset available is the EMory BrEast Imaging Dataset (EMBED)."

"question": "What is the most common format of mammogram datasets?",
"answer": "The most common format of mammogram datasets is DICOM."

"question": "List me all the publicly available mammogram datasets.",
"answer": "The datasets that are publicly available are: DDSM, CBIS-DDSM, RBIS-DDSM, Inbreast, Vindr-Mammo, MIAS, RSNA, CMMD, KAU-BCMD, BCS-DBT, and DMID."

"question": "Give me a comparison between EMBED and DMID dataset.",
"answer": "The EMBED dataset is the largest mammogram dataset available, with 3.4 million images, while the DMID dataset is the most recent, published in 2024, with only 510 images. The EMBED dataset has racially

diverse data with mammogram images, clinical data, and metadata, while the DMID dataset contains mammogram images, metadata, and radiological reports."

"question": "Tell something about EMBED dataset.",
"answer": "Stands for EMory BrEast imaging Dataset. This dataset contains 3,383,659 screening and diagnostic mammogram images from 115,910 patients. Among these, 20% of the total 2D and C-view dataset is available for research use. This 20% contains a total of 480,606 DICOM images, a total of 676,009 PNG images (20%), and a total of 34,004 spot magnified images. It also has 4 files of clinical data and metadata."

"question": "What type of task can I perform with the EMBED dataset?",
"answer": "Breast Cancer Detection, Breast Cancer Risk Prediction, Mammographic Report Generation, Breast Cancer Type Classification, Breast Tumor Classification, Tumor Localization, Breast Density Estimation, Synthetic Data Generation"

"question": "Is the DDSM dataset available?",
"answer": "Yes, the DDSM dataset is publicly available at http://www.eng.usf.edu/cvprg/Mammography/Database.html and a mini version is available at https://www.kaggle.com/datasets/skooch/ddsm-mammography"

"question": "Which datasets were collected from the USA?",
"answer": "EMBED, DREAM, DDSM, CBIS-DDSM, RBIS-DDSM, RSNA, BCS-DBT, LLNL datasets were collected from the USA."

Relevant information from the document: {*Information fetched by RAG*}

Question: {*The question asked by the user*}

We selected 5 instruction type LLMs: *Llama3.2-3B*, *Mistral Nemo*, *Deepseek-R1 7B*, *Medllama2*, and *Tiny Llama*. We chose instruction-based LLMs as these models are explicitly trained to respond to instructions, aligning with user intent, consistency in responses, and better handling of step-by-step reasoning. We also considered hardware constraints and context windows of the model before selection. We trained all models with zero-shot and few-shot learning and recorded their performance.

We ensured that the LLMs infer all answers based on the knowledge graph by implementing the Retrieval Augmented Generation (RAG) mechanism. The temperature hyperparameter was set to 0 to minimize creativity and hallucinations.

3.5 Visual Depiction of Response

Our goal was to allow multiple ways, i.e., multi-channel interaction with the information provided by the LLM. In addition to a text interaction, we also developed a graphical view of the responses. To create the graphical view, we instructed the LLM to extract the meaningful terms from the response and create a JSON object consisting of nodes and edges, where nodes represent important terms from the response and the edges represent the semantic workflow between the nodes. To visually represent the nodes, we used the JavaScript Vis library, which is an interactive network graph that can be rendered on web pages. The prompt used to generate the network graph is given below:

Prompt for Graph Generation

Extract the most important keywords, key phrases, or ideas from the following text. Do not just split sentences; extract the concepts that capture the meaning. Then output a mindmap as a JSON object with two arrays: 'nodes' and 'edges'. Do not output anything other than a JSON object. No extra words outside the JSON object.

The 'nodes' array should include: - A central node with id "root" and a label representing the main idea in 1-3 words (use shape "box" and color "#ffd700"). - For each key phrase, add a node with a unique id ("node_0", "node_1", ...) and the label set to the phrase. - The other nodes may also be connected if they are related. Use shape "box" and color "#87CEEB" for these nodes. The 'edges' array should include an edge from the central node "root" to each key phrase node. Output only valid JSON. During describing datasets, try to make nodes out of the total number of images in the dataset, filetypes, datatypes, country of origin, special properties, and so on. For comparative analysis, you may make separate root nodes for each dataset with their features and feature values as other nodes, or you may connect the dataset name nodes with a main root node. The other nodes may be connected to feature nodes.

Example JSON format:

{
"nodes": [
{"id": "root", "label": "Main Idea", "shape": "box", "color": "#ffd700"},
{"id": "node_0", "label": "key phrase 1", "shape": "box",
"color": "#87CEEB"}, ...],
"edges": [
{"from": "root", "to": "node_0", "color": "#898980", "weight": 1},
...]
}

3.6 UI Setup

A web interface was developed to allow users to interact with the tool. The website consists of two sections divided vertically. A snapshot of the website is shown in Fig. 3. As seen from the figure, the left side consists of a canvas-like option where the generated graph network is visualized. There is a drop-down list to choose the layout of the graph. The layout consists of different hierarchical views, a circular view, and a grid view. The right side consists of the chat box, where users can talk with the LLMs. There are also two drop-down lists here to choose the LLM model with which the user wants to talk and which prompt method the model should follow to generate the response.

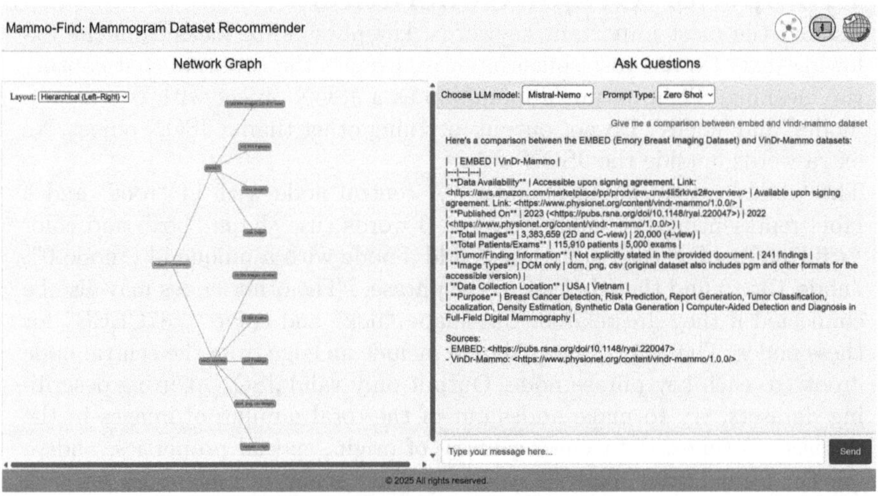

Fig. 3. A snapshot of the UI of the Mammo-Find tool

3.7 Model Evaluation

We used 4 LLM evaluation metrics: BLEU, ROUGE-L, BERTScore, and METEOR. The BERTScore yields 3 subscores: BERT_Precision, BERT_Recall, and BERT_F1-score. BLEU stands for Bilingual Evaluation Understudy. It is the geometric mean of n-gram precisions up to 4-grams. It is a widely used metric for automatically evaluating the quality of machine-translated text by comparing it to human-translated references, measuring the degree of similarity between the two [33]. ROUGE-L stands for Recall-Oriented Understudy for Gisting Evaluation. It measures the longest matching sequence of words using the Longest Common Subsequence algorithm [23]. BERTScore measures the semantic meaning between two sentences or paragraphs [46]. METEOR stands for Metric for Evaluation of Translation with Explicit Ordering [21]. It is another semantic metric used to evaluate LLMs, considering word order and synonyms. In addition to the evaluation metrics, we also assessed the LLM response with soundness and precision. Soundness refers to the quality of being well-founded, sensible, or valid and does not have any contradiction [10]. Precision refers to accuracy and exactness in the use of language [27]. We measured these parameters by letting some users try reading out and understanding the responses. We also used the same technique for evaluating the generated network graph. The users observed the network graph along with the response, and they provided their opinion on how sound, precise, and useful the response was.

3.8 Use Case Study

We also carried out 3 use case studies. For the first use case, we asked a question to the model and got the response and the network graph. We saved the response and the network graph. For the second use case, we let a user provide the LLM with their questions. Based on the question provided, the LLM generated the response and the network graph. Then we compared whether the answer in response, the answer in the graph, and the answer in the knowledge base semantically match or not. For the third use case, we took an article that has used the EMBED dataset [19]. Donnelly et al. [8] developed the deep learning model AsymMirai, which works as a breast cancer risk predictor. Their reason for choosing the EMBED dataset is that it is the largest racially diverse mammogram dataset through 2024, along with containing a very large amount of clinical information. With this dataset, their model learned to predict cancer risk from mammogram images comprising diverse racial backgrounds. We took this information and asked our model to suggest an appropriate dataset to check if the model also provided the same response.

4 Results and Discussions

Tables 1 and 2 show the LLM performance in zero-shot and few-shot, respectively. For zero-shot, from Table 1 we see that *mistral nemo* dominated the other models in all evaluation metrics. For few-shot learning, *llama3.2* performed better across the board (Table 2). The better performance is with the few-shot learning strategy, but the performance difference is small. This is likely because the question-answer set fed to the models had high variability, and thus, a 10-question-answer set was not sufficient for the models to get better than zero-shot.

It is also notable from the tables that the BERT_Precision, BERT_Recall, and BERT_F1-scores are all very high (more than 0.86) compared to the BLEU, ROUGE-L, and METEOR. This is likely because the latter focuses more on the order of similar words as opposed to the semantic meaning of the word, which is the focus of the former. For example, the sentence "*EMBED Stands for EMory BrEast imaging Dataset. This dataset contains 3,383,659 screening and diagnostic mammogram images from 115,910 patients.*" is semantically the same to the generated sentence "*The EMBED (EMory BrEast imaging Dataset) is a large-scale mammographic dataset containing 3,383,659 screening and diagnostic mammogram images from 115,910 patients.*". However, as the words inside are ordered differently, the BLEU, ROUGE-L, and METEOR scores are lower. Despite this, the ROUGE-L and METEOR scores are above 0.4, which is considered satisfactory for natural language processing [4]. However, the BLEU values are much lower (0.1 or lower). This could be because BLEU is more focused on the quality of machine translation from one human language to another and is likely not the appropriate evaluation parameter in this case.

Table 1. LLM performance on zero-shot

Model	BLEU	ROUGE-L	BERT_Precision	BERT_Recall	BERT_F1-score	METEOR
llama3.2-3b	0.08397	0.32605	0.83849	0.90067	0.86761	0.45175
mistral-nemo	**0.10644**	**0.41202**	**0.86194**	**0.9076**	**0.88327**	**0.49353**
deepseek-r1-7b	0.01261	0.06549	0.77437	0.85301	0.81146	0.17182
medllama2	0.06916	0.2981	0.85028	0.89227	0.87003	0.41209
tinyllama	0.0269	0.20641	0.82936	0.87527	0.85107	0.31119

Table 2. LLM performance on few-shot

Model	BLEU	ROUGE-L	BERT_Precision	BERT_Recall	BERT_F1-score	METEOR
llama3.2-3b	**0.13494**	**0.41471**	**0.86394**	**0.91319**	**0.88706**	**0.52822**
mistral-nemo	0.0554	0.34451	0.8509	0.89244	0.87024	0.42596
deepseek-r1-7b	0.00999	0.06253	0.77398	0.8482	0.80902	0.16305
medllama2	0.06203	0.30883	0.85805	0.88761	0.8719	0.41033
tinyllama	0.02547	0.19534	0.82539	0.8689	0.84597	0.31214

4.1 Use Case Analysis

The use case analysis was carried out on the basis of the soundness and precision of the LLM response and its visualization by human users. When the model was provided with a query *"Tell something about the EMBED dataset."*, the LLM generated a network graph that is shown in Fig. 4. The response of the model is also shown below. If the graph and the response are observed, it is seen that they are describing the same information, but in a multichannel way. The words and phrases that are most meaningful to the sentence are depicted as nodes in the graph network.

Information about the EMBED (EMory BrEast imaging Dataset) mammogram dataset:

- **Name:** EMBED

- **Contents:** Contains 3,383,659 screening and diagnostic mammogram images from 115,910 patients.

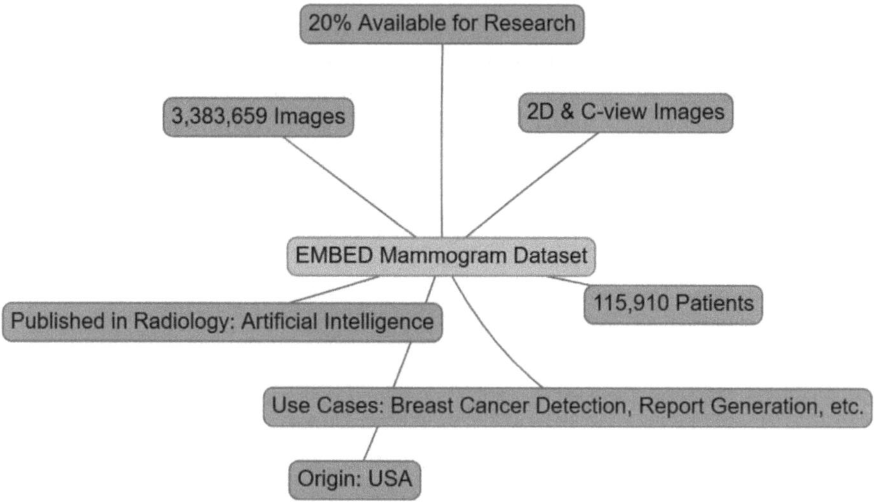

Fig. 4. Visualization of LLM response on "Tell something about the EMBED dataset".

- **Image Types:** Includes both 2D and C-view images.

- **Availability for Research:** 20% of the total dataset is available for research use upon signing an agreement. You can access it via AWS Marketplace at
<https://aws.amazon.com/marketplace/pp/prodview-unw4li5rkivs2#overview>.

- **Publication:** The dataset was published in an article titled "The EMory BrEast imaging Dataset (EMBED): A Racially Diverse, Granular Dataset of 3.4 Million Screening and Diagnostic Mammographic Images" on Radiology: Artificial Intelligence in 2023
(<https://pubs.rsna.org/doi/10.1148/ryai.220047>).

- **Use Cases:** Suitable for tasks such as breast cancer detection, risk prediction, mammographic report generation, breast cancer type classification, tumor localization, breast density estimation, and synthetic data generation.

- **Origin:** Collected from the USA.

Dataset Breakdown:
- Total Images: 3,383,659
- Total Patients: 115,910

For our second use-case, the user asked the question *"I need a dataset which has a large number of images and also needs a lot of racial diversity. Which dataset should I choose?"*. The LLM response is shown below, and the generated network graph is shown in Fig. 5.

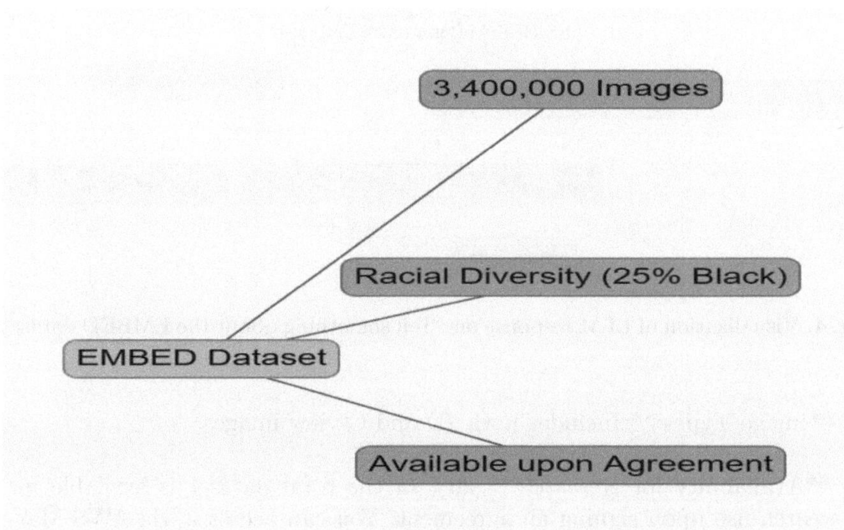

Fig. 5. Visualization of LLM response on user question

Question: I need a dataset that has a large number of images, and I also need a lot of racial diversity. Which dataset should I choose?

Answer: Based on your requirements, the EMory BrEast imaging Dataset (EMBED) would be an excellent choice. Here's why:

- **Large Number of Images**: EMBED contains 3.4 million diagnostic and screening mammographic images, making it one of the largest publicly available datasets. - **Racial Diversity**: EMBED is designed to be racially diverse, including a significant number of images from black women (around 25%), which is not common in many other datasets. This diversity helps address biases that may exist in other datasets.
- **Data Availability**: The data set is available upon signing an agreement and can be accessed via the provided link.

You can find more information on EMBED in the associated article: [The EMory BrEast imaging data set (EMBED): A Racially Diverse,

> Granular Dataset of 3.4 Million Screening and Diagnostic Mammographic Images](https://pubs.rsna.org/doi/10.1148/ryai.220047)

For our third use-case study, we also got a match. The article in question used the EMBED dataset. Our models also suggested the same answer. The question and its answer are provided below.

> **Question:** I want to develop a model for breast cancer risk prediction from mammogram images of people of different races. Which dataset do you suggest I use?
>
> **Answer:** Based on your requirements, I would recommend using the EMory BrEast imaging Dataset (EMBED). Here's why: 1. **Diversity**: EMBED is racially diverse, containing mammographic images from 115,910 patients across various races. 2. **Quantity and Quality**: With over 3.3 million screening and diagnostic mammogram images, it has a large and representative sample size. 3. **Availability for Research**: 20% of the total dataset (including both 2D and C-view images) is available for research use upon signing an agreement. 4. **Relevant Tasks**: EMBED can be used for Breast Cancer Risk Prediction, which aligns with your goal. Here are some details about accessing the data: - Data Availability: Available upon signing an agreement. - Data Link: Available at https://aws.amazon.com/marketplace/pp/prodview-unw4li5rkivs2#overview - Associated Article: The EMory BrEast imaging Dataset (EMBED): A Racially Diverse, Granular Dataset of 3.4 Million Screening and Diagnostic Mammographic Images. Published in 2023. Available at https://pubs.rsna.org/doi/10.1148/ryai.220047. Although other data sets, such as DREAM, have diverse images, they may not be as large or suitable for risk prediction specifically. Therefore, EMBED seems to be the most suitable option for your purpose.

5 Threats to Validity

Construct Validity. Only 22 mammogram datasets were gathered, so the sample may not fully represent the diversity of available data and other data that are not accessible. Additionally, our tool does not automatically scrape/update. New data needs to be manually uploaded by the user.

Internal Validity. Our models produce results based only on in-context prompts provided to them. No fine-tuning was performed. Therefore, no weight updates, parameter adjustments, or learning is taking place. We used zero and few-shot learning but did not explore other advanced prompting techniques such as chain-of-thought (CoT) and tree-of-thought (ToT). Since LLMs rely on prompts, changes in the words and meaning of the prompts may result in different results.

External Validity. Because of the limitations of the hardware and graphics processing units, we were unable to use larger and more powerful models in this work. We demonstrated our work only on mammogram datasets. We did not explore other medical datasets.

6 Conclusion and Future Work

This work demonstrated that LLMs can be plausibly used for matching mammogram datasets to downstream tasks of clinical and translational pipelines in a multichannel UI environment. Our results demonstrated the capability of the models with zero and few-shot learning to provide multichannel dataset recommendations. This work can pave the way for LLMs to be used for other dataset recommendations and help researchers save time when searching for appropriate datasets for their hypotheses.

Future studies could focus on fine-tuning models and try other advanced prompting techniques. This work can be expanded to other medical datasets in addition to the mammogram dataset. Larger models could be used on devices with more powerful specifications. Lastly, the system could be made dynamic to allow newer dataset information to be added automatically.

7 Supplementary Information

The question-answer pairs are available here. The codes are available on Github. An earlier frontend-only demo version of the tool is available here.

References

1. Arnold, M., et al.: Current and future burden of breast cancer: global statistics for 2020 and 2040. Breast **66**, 15–23 (2022)
2. Azamjah, N., Soltan-Zadeh, Y., Zayeri, F.: Global trend of breast cancer mortality rate: a 25-year study. Asian Pac. J. Cancer Prevent.: APJCP **20**(7), 2015 (2019)
3. Biswas, S.S.: Role of chat GPT in public health. Ann. Biomed. Eng. **51**(5), 868–869 (2023)
4. Blagec, K., Dorffner, G., Moradi, M., Ott, S., Samwald, M.: A global analysis of metrics used for measuring performance in natural language processing. arXiv preprint arXiv:2204.11574 (2022)
5. Brickley, D., Burgess, M., Noy, N.: Google dataset search: building a search engine for datasets in an open web ecosystem. In: The World Wide Web Conference, pp. 1365–1375 (2019)
6. Cao, Z., Deng, Z., Ma, J., Hu, J., Ma, L.: MammoVLM: a generative large vision-language model for mammography-related diagnostic assistance. Inf. Fusion 102998 (2025)
7. De Angelis, L., et al.: ChatGPT and the rise of large language models: the new AI-driven infodemic threat in public health. Front. Public Health **11**, 1166120 (2023)

8. Donnelly, J., et al.: AsymMirai: interpretable mammography-based deep learning model for 1-5-year breast cancer risk prediction. Radiology **310**(3), e232780 (2024)
9. D'Orsi, C., Bassett, L., Feig, S.: Breast Imaging Reporting and Data System (BI-RADS). Oxford University Press, New York (2018)
10. Fan, L., Tang, C., Yang, W., Zhou, H.S.: Two halves make a whole: how to reconcile soundness and robustness in watermarking for large language models. Cryptology ePrint Archive (2024)
11. Ghosh, S., Poynton, C.B., Visweswaran, S., Batmanghelich, K.: Mammo-CLIP: a vision language foundation model to enhance data efficiency and robustness in mammography. In: Linguraru, M.G., et al. (eds.) MICCAI 2024. LNCS, vol. 15012, pp. 632–642. Springer, Cham (2024). https://doi.org/10.1007/978-3-031-72390-2_59
12. Haver, H.L., Yi, P.H., Jeudy, J., Bahl, M.: Use of chatGPT to assign BI-RADS assessment categories to breast imaging reports. Am. J. Roentgenol. **223**(3), e2431093 (2024)
13. Jahangir, R., Islam, M.N., Islam, M.S., Islam, M.M.: ECG-based heart arrhythmia classification using feature engineering and a hybrid stacked machine learning. BMC Cardiovasc. Disord. **25**(1), 260 (2025)
14. Jahangir, R., Mohim, N.S., Khan, N.I., Akhtaruzzaman, M., Islam, M.N.: Proposing novel recurrent neural network architectures for infant cry detection in domestic context. In: 2023 IEEE 11th Region 10 Humanitarian Technology Conference (R10-HTC), pp. 7–12. IEEE (2023)
15. Jahangir, R., et al.: Development of a smart infant monitoring system for working mothers. In: 2023 IEEE 11th Region 10 Humanitarian Technology Conference (R10-HTC), pp. 37–42. IEEE (2023)
16. Jahangir, R., Sakib, T., Haque, R., Kamal, M.: A performance analysis of brain tumor classification from MRI images using vision transformers and CNN-based classifiers. In: 2023 26th International Conference on Computer and Information Technology (ICCIT), pp. 1–6. IEEE (2023)
17. Jahangir, R., Sakib, T., Juboraj, M.F.U.A., Feroz, S.B., Sharar, M.M.I.: Brain tumor classification on MRI images with big transfer and vision transformer: Comparative study. In: 2023 IEEE 9th International Women in Engineering (WIE) Conference on Electrical and Computer Engineering (WIECON-ECE), pp. 46–51. IEEE (2023)
18. Jain, K., Bansal, A., Rangarajan, K., Arora, C.: MMBCD: multimodal breast cancer detection from mammograms with clinical history. In: Linguraru, M.G., et al. (eds.) MICCAI 2024. LNCS, vol. 15001, pp. 144–154. Springer, Cham (2024). https://doi.org/10.1007/978-3-031-72378-0_14
19. Jeong, J.J., et al.: The emory breast imaging dataset (embed): a racially diverse, granular dataset of 3.4 million screening and diagnostic mammographic images. Radiol.: Artif. Intell. **5**(1), e220047 (2023)
20. Kao, C.H., Hsieh, C.H., Chu, Y.F., Kuang, Y.T., Yang, C.K.: Using data visualization technique to detect sensitive information re-identification problem of real open dataset. J. Syst. Architect. **80**, 85–91 (2017)
21. Lavie, A., Denkowski, M.J.: The meteor metric for automatic evaluation of machine translation. Mach. Transl. **23**, 105–115 (2009)
22. Lewis, P., et al.: Retrieval-augmented generation for knowledge-intensive NLP tasks. Adv. Neural. Inf. Process. Syst. **33**, 9459–9474 (2020)
23. Lin, C.Y.: ROUGE: a package for automatic evaluation of summaries. In: Text Summarization Branches Out, pp. 74–81 (2004)

24. Marcondes, F.S., Gala, A., Magalhães, R., de Britto, F.P., Durães, D., Novais, P.: Using ollama. In: Marcondes, F.S., Gala, A., Magalhães, R., de Britto, F.P., Durães, D., Novais, P. (eds.) Natural Language Analytics with Generative Large-Language Models: A Practical Approach with Ollama and Open-Source LLMs. SpringerBriefs in Computer Science, pp. 23–35. Springer (2025) . https://doi.org/10.1007/978-3-031-76631-2_3
25. Marvin, G., Hellen, N., Jjingo, D., Nakatumba-Nabende, J.: Prompt engineering in large language models. In: Jacob, I.J., Piramuthu, S., Falkowski-Gilski, P. (eds.) ICDICI 2023. Algorithms for Intelligent Systems, pp. 387–402. Springer, Singapore (2023). https://doi.org/10.1007/978-981-99-7962-2_30
26. Mavroudis, V.: Langchain (2024)
27. Menditto, A., Patriarca, M., Magnusson, B.: Understanding the meaning of accuracy, trueness and precision. Accred. Qual. Assur. **12**, 45–47 (2007)
28. Moody, G.B.: PhysioNet. In: Encyclopedia of Computational Neuroscience, pp. 2806–2808. Springer, Heidelberg (2022)
29. Moreira, I.C., Amaral, I., Domingues, I., Cardoso, A., Cardoso, M.J., Cardoso, J.S.: INbreast: toward a full-field digital mammographic database. Acad. Radiol. **19**(2), 236–248 (2012)
30. Nguyen, H.T., et al.: VinDr-Mammo: a large-scale benchmark dataset for computer-aided diagnosis in full-field digital mammography. Sci. Data **10**(1), 277 (2023)
31. Nussbaum, Z., Morris, J.X., Duderstadt, B., Mulyar, A.: Nomic embed: training a reproducible long context text embedder. arXiv preprint arXiv:2402.01613 (2024)
32. Oza, P., et al.: Digital mammography dataset for breast cancer diagnosis research (DMID) with breast mass segmentation analysis. Biomed. Eng. Lett. **14**(2), 317–330 (2024)
33. Papineni, K., Roukos, S., Ward, T., Zhu, W.J.: BLEU: a method for automatic evaluation of machine translation. In: Proceedings of the 40th Annual Meeting of the Association for Computational Linguistics, pp. 311–318 (2002)
34. Pesapane, F., et al.: A preliminary investigation into the potential, pitfalls, and limitations of large language models for mammography interpretation. Discov. Oncol. **16**(1), 233 (2025)
35. Piao, Y., Chen, H., Wu, S., Li, X., Li, Z., Yang, D.: Assessing the performance of large language models (LLMs) in answering medical questions regarding breast cancer in the chinese context. Digit. Health **10**, 20552076241284772 (2024)
36. Pisano, E.D., Yaffe, M.J.: Digital mammography. Radiology **234**(2), 353–362 (2005)
37. Russe, M.F., Reisert, M., Bamberg, F., Rau, A.: Improving the use of LLMs in radiology through prompt engineering: from precision prompts to zero-shot learning. In: RöFo-Fortschritte auf dem Gebiet der Röntgenstrahlen und der bildgebenden Verfahren, vol. 186. Georg Thieme Verlag KG (2024)
38. Shah, S.M., Khan, R.A., Arif, S., Sajid, U.: Artificial intelligence for breast cancer analysis: trends & directions. Comput. Biol. Med. **142**, 105221 (2022)
39. Shneiderman, B.: The eyes have it: a task by data type taxonomy for information visualizations. In: The Craft of Information Visualization, pp. 364–371. Elsevier (2003)
40. Singh, J.: Figshare. J. Pharmacol. Pharmacotherap. **2**(2), 138 (2011)
41. Škoda, P., Matějík, J., Skopal, T.: Visualizer of dataset similarity using knowledge graph. In: Satoh, S., et al. (eds.) SISAP 2020. LNCS, vol. 12440, pp. 371–378. Springer, Cham (2020). https://doi.org/10.1007/978-3-030-60936-8_29

42. Sorin, V., et al.: Utilizing large language models in breast cancer management: systematic review. J. Cancer Res. Clin. Oncol. **150**(3), 140 (2024)
43. Thirunavukarasu, A.J., Ting, D.S.J., Elangovan, K., Gutierrez, L., Tan, T.F., Ting, D.S.W.: Large language models in medicine. Nat. Med. **29**(8), 1930–1940 (2023)
44. Vázquez, P.P.: Are LLMs ready for visualization? In: 2024 IEEE 17th Pacific Visualization Conference (PacificVis), pp. 343–352. IEEE (2024)
45. White, J.: PubMed 2.0. Med. Reference Serv. Q. **39**(4), 382–387 (2020)
46. Zhang, T., Kishore, V., Wu, F., Weinberger, K.Q., Artzi, Y.: BERTScore: evaluating text generation with BERT. arXiv preprint arXiv:1904.09675 (2019)
47. Şorecău, M., Şorecău, E.: An alternative application to chatGPT that uses reliable sources to enhance the learning process. In: International Conference Knowledge-Based Organization, vol. 29, pp. 113–119 (2023)

Exploring Manifold-Based Clustering Techniques for Enhanced Inductive Thematic Analysis

Jesus A. Beltran[1(✉)], Hanna Mofid[2], Harita Parikh[1], Jaydeep Gondaliya[1], Diego Guzman[2], Jenil Shah[1], Lizbeth Escobedo[3], and Franceli Cibrian[4]

[1] California State University, Los Angeles, USA
{abeltr99,hparikh5,jgondal,jshah25}@calstatela.edu
[2] University of California, Irvine, USA
{hmofid,guzmand7}@uci.edu
[3] Dalhousie University, Halifax, NS, Canada
lizbeth.escobedo@dal.ca
[4] Fowler School of Engineering, Chapman University, Orange, USA
fcibrian@chapman.edu

Abstract. In this paper, we introduce Augmented Thematic Analysis with Large Language Models (ATA-LLM), a novel framework that integrates manifold learning algorithms and clustering techniques to support inductive thematic analysis. This qualitative method, widely used in software engineering, is essential for uncovering patterns and understanding human factors and software requirements. Traditional thematic analysis involves data coding, theme identification, and the interpretation of complex narratives, making it a labor-intensive and time-consuming process. Recent advances in large language models (LLMs) offer promising opportunities; however, it remains unclear how comparable these approaches are to traditional human thematic analysis. To address this gap, we evaluated ATA-LLM using a validated qualitative dataset and compared the outcomes against human-coded analysis. Our findings indicate that within the ATA-LLM framework, DenseMAP and UMAP effectively preserve both local and global structures of high-dimensional data, resulting in more coherent and meaningful themes than other techniques. These results highlight the potential of ATA-LLM to enhance the rigor, consistency, and efficiency of inductive thematic analysis.

Keywords: Inductive Thematic Analysis · Large Language Models · Clustering

1 Introduction

Thematic Analysis (TA) is a method used in software engineering to analyze qualitative data and uncover patterns related to technical practices and human-centered aspects of software development [21,36]. TA is beneficial for understanding complex phenomena and uncovering software requirements [21,36]. TA involves systematically reviewing textual data (often collected from interviews,

S. Hussain et al. (Eds.): SEET 2025, CCIS 2725, pp. 464–480, 2026.
https://doi.org/10.1007/978-3-032-08977-9_29

focus groups, observations, or open-ended surveys) and identifying "codes" that represent thoughts, ideas, or attitudes. Those codes are iteratively grouped into broader categories or higher-level "themes" that help understand insights into social, technical, and organizational processes [46].

Depending on the research or team goals, TA can follow either a deductive or inductive approach [7]. Deductive TA starts with a predefined framework or theory, while inductive TA allows themes to emerge from the data without prior assumptions. Inductive TA typically involves six phases: (1) familiarization with the data, (2) generating initial codes, (3) identifying candidate themes, (4) reviewing themes, (5) defining and naming themes, and (6) producing the final analysis and themes [6]. Although TA provides an in-depth understanding, it tends to be labor-intensive and time-consuming, and the interpretative nature of TA requires human involvement and teamwork to ensure the validity of the findings [7]. The burden could be intensified with a large amount of data.

Recent progress in generative Large Language Models (LLMs) offers a promising avenue for addressing challenges and enhancing thematic analysis techniques due to their advanced comprehension capabilities in software engineering [11,26]. Some of the potential advantages are: increase efficiency and scalability [37,50]; augmenting human cognitive and reasoning abilities by leveraging LLMs to reduce cognitive load and enable deeper text analysis [26]; identifying novel themes and patterns, especially in large and complex text corpora [37].

LLMs' methods aim to identify recurring patterns in text data [26]. They rely on representing the data in numerical form. Using text embeddings, a manifold learning technique, and a clustering algorithm, underlying themes are revealed. The current research trajectory in integrating LLMs with qualitative analysis has focused primarily on deductive analysis [10,51]. Initial strides have also been taken to explore the application of LLMs to inductive analysis, indicating the viability of utilizing these models to support thematic analysis [12]. However, it is unclear how comparable these approaches are to the original human-coded analysis. In this sense, our research question is as follows:

Which combination of manifold learning and clustering techniques most effectively supports inductive thematic analysis of semi-structured interview data in comparison with human-coded analysis?

To answer this question, this paper presents a systematic empirical comparison of leading manifold learning algorithms combined with clustering techniques within the context of inductive thematic analysis included in Augmented Thematic Analysis with Large Language Model (ATA-LLM), a framework designed to leverage the capabilities of LLMs to enhance thematic coding, pattern recognition, and insight generation while maintaining the interpretive depth and reliability of human analysis. Our findings show that within the ATA-LLM framework, DenseMAP and UMAP, two non-linear dimensionality reduction algorithms that preserve both local and global structures of high-dimensional data, capturing semantic relationships, generated more coherent and meaningful themes than other techniques. These results highlight the potential of ATA-LLM to enhance the rigor, consistency, and efficiency of inductive thematic analysis.

2 Background and Related Work

2.1 The Role of Thematic Analysis in Software Engineering

Qualitative methods have been used to gain deep insights into how people think, feel, and behave. In software engineering, these methods are increasingly recognized as essential for understanding the complex, human-centered dimensions of software development processes and practices [15,48]. Among the most frequently used qualitative methods in software engineering are Grounded Theory [20] and Thematic Analysis (TA) [28], both of which enable software engineers to derive rich, contextualized insights from textual data, mostly from interviews and observations [1,13].

Software engineers have adopted and adapted qualitative methods over the past two decades. For instance, Seaman and Easterbrook et al. found that software engineering used qualitative analysis to analyze interviews, ethnography, and participant observation [16,48]. Later work focused on developing adaptations of those techniques, but focused on the context of software systems engineering. For example, Runeson et al. provided detailed methodological guidance on case study research [42,43]. Sharp et al. explored the role of ethnographic methods in understanding software teams and organizational settings [49]. More recently, Hoda has proposed a socio-technical adaptation of Grounded Theory tailored to software engineering challenges, emphasizing the importance of aligning methods with the unique socio-technical realities of software development [21,22]. In a similar manner, Lenberg et al. [28] argue that such adaptations represent a critical step forward in legitimizing and strengthening the use of qualitative research in software engineering.

Despite these advances, there is still uncertainty about whether existing methodological guidelines are sufficient to fully support the application of qualitative methods in software engineering practice [47]. This question has become especially urgent with the rise of AI-enabled tools for qualitative data analysis [3,22]. As Seaman observes, these emerging technologies offer "rich opportunities to test and explore the boundaries of what is possible and wise" in qualitative research [47]. However, integrating AI tools into rigorous, theory-driven analysis remains an open challenge, requiring new guidance specific to the epistemological and practical demands of the software engineering discipline.

2.2 Integrating AI Into Thematic Analysis

The use of AI to support TA has increased, particularly given the improvements of algorithms in natural language processing (NLP) and LLMs. Early work combined manual coding with tools like LIWC, which quantifies word categories across text to support interpretation [35,39]. Gauthier et al. [18] introduced a toolkit to aid in data visualization and filtering during thematic analysis, though it lacked automated theme identification.

LLMs are now applied primarily in deductive thematic analysis—linking predefined codes to qualitative data. Studies show promising results: Xiao et al. [51]

achieved moderate agreement between GPT-3 and human coders (Cohen's K = 0.61), and Chew et al. [10] reported even higher agreement (above 0.76) with GPT-3.5. Exploration into inductive thematic analysis using LLMs is still in the early stages. De Coster et al. [12] demonstrated that GPT-3.5 can approximate Braun and Clarke's six-step framework, generating themes from data; however, further validation is needed. The quality of AI-generated themes is evaluated using metrics such as inter-coder agreement (e.g., Cohen's Kappa), precision, recall, F1-score, and topic coherence measures like NPMI and UCI scores [11, 19,25]. However, human validation remains crucial for assessing interpretability, accuracy, and ethical considerations [34,50].

Despite promising advances, AI-assisted thematic analysis still faces critical technical challenges, particularly in managing and interpreting the high-dimensional text embeddings produced by LLMs. These embeddings are foundational for identifying and clustering semantically similar data segments, yet their complexity can hinder analysis and theme discovery without proper preprocessing. To address this, our work explores two key components essential for scaling and refining AI-driven thematic analysis in software engineering: (1) high-dimensional data representation and dimensionality reduction techniques to improve interpretability, and (2) clustering algorithms to support robust, inductive theme identification. The following sections detail our methodological approach and empirical evaluation of these techniques.

2.3 High-Dimensional Data Representation and Dimensional Reduction Algorithms for Thematic Analysis

Thematic analysis using AI techniques increasingly relies on transforming qualitative textual data into numerical representations, most commonly through text embeddings generated by LLMs, which enables clustering and finding patterns across text ("themes"). These embeddings, often high-dimensional, encode semantic and contextual meaning but pose interpretability and computational challenges. As a result, dimensionality reduction techniques are employed to enhance computational efficiency while preserving semantic integrity in qualitative research [38]. Principal Component Analysis (PCA) has been widely used to reduce embedding dimensions while maintaining variance in textual themes, as seen in studies applying LLM-based thematic profiling [24].

Similarly, Uniform Manifold Approximation and Projection (UMAP) has demonstrated effectiveness in non-linear feature reduction, enabling researchers to visualize and cluster emergent themes from LLM-generated embeddings [17]. The integration of t-SNE (t-Distributed Stochastic Neighbor Embedding) has also been noted in studies that seek to improve interpretability when mapping high-dimensional textual data into low-dimensional spaces for qualitative coding validation [19]. Furthermore, sentence embeddings derived from transformer models such as BERT and GPT-4 have been subjected to cosine similarity-based clustering, refining theme extraction through vector space modeling [12,25]. One of the notable approaches is the use of BERT-based embeddings, where text is converted into 768-dimensional dense vectors that encapsulate both word semantics and context [8]. In the study "BERT-Based Deep Embedded Clustering for Topic Modeling" [8], BERT embeddings were combined with Deep Embedded Clustering (DEC) and Improved Deep Embedded Clustering (IDEC) to reduce dimensionality and optimize the clustering process simultaneously. This approach preserves semantic coherence and improves theme identification in high-dimensional data. The study "Opinion Text Clustering Using Manifold Learning Based on Sentiment and Semantics Analysis" [23] employed Doc2Vec embeddings to convert opinion texts into 300-dimensional vectors. To overcome the curse of dimensionality, the ISOMAP manifold learning algorithm was applied to reduce the text representations while preserving the semantic structure [23]. Overall, these methods enhance computational efficiency and data visualization, but challenges remain in selecting optimal reduction parameters that maintain thematic consistency without information loss.

2.4 Clustering Algorithm for Thematic Analysis

Applying clustering algorithms in TA has significantly advanced with the integration of LLMs, enabling efficient organization of text-based data into meaningful themes [11]. Traditional hierarchical clustering methods, such as agglomerative clustering, have been employed to structure qualitative data by merging semantically similar text segments iteratively [24]. Meanwhile, K-Means clustering, widely used in NLP tasks, has demonstrated efficacy in grouping LLM-generated embeddings into distinct thematic clusters, particularly when combined with word embeddings from transformer models like BERT and GPT-4 [25]. Studies exploring DBSCAN (Density-Based Spatial Clustering of Applications with Noise) have highlighted its ability to identify outlier topics and rare themes, offering a robust framework for analyzing highly variable qualitative datasets [19,26].

More recent advancements involve topic modeling approaches, such as Latent Dirichlet Allocation (LDA) and Structural Topic Modeling (STM), which enable probabilistic clustering of text into coherent topics for further manual refinement [12,17]. Additionally, cosine similarity-based clustering has been leveraged in thematic analysis to compute semantic distances between textual embeddings, facilitating automated theme detection with high interpretability [45]. The use of Deep Embedded Clustering (DEC) and Improved DEC (IDEC) in BERT-based clustering [8] allows for direct clustering in the low-dimensional latent space. Similarly, K-Means clustering applied to ISOMAP-reduced embeddings [23] effectively groups texts based on sentiment and semantics. This body of work shows that clustering methods improve efficiency in theme extraction and organization; however, challenges persist in optimizing the number of clusters and refining model interpretability to ensure thematic coherence in qualitative research.

Overall, thematic analysis is widely used in software engineering, however, its manual implementation remains time-consuming and cognitively demanding. Recent applications of LLMs have focused mainly on deductive coding. To our knowledge, there is limited validation and comparison with a human-coded system, especially for inductive coding. Although techniques like UMAP and DenseMAP offer promise to be used in qualitative analysis, their integration into inductive thematic analysis has not been explored. This paper addresses this gap by introducing and evaluating ATA-LLM, a framework that combines LLMs, dimensionality reduction, and clustering to enhance the coherence, efficiency, and interpretability of inductive thematic analysis in software engineering.

3 Methodology

We conducted a study to evaluate the outcome of the ATA-LLM compared to a human-generated codebook. We used an open dataset from the Researching Students' Information Choices (RSIC) study [9], which we used as a ground truth. ATA-LLM generates a codebook using five steps (see Fig. 1). First, each transcript excerpt and its surrounding context are converted into open codes. Second, the open code set is reduced to keep the unique code or those with low semantic similarity. Third, the dimensionality of embedding is reduced. Then, the resulting embeddings are clustered to organize unique open code into potential organic themes. Lastly, a theme is generated using LLM for each cluster.

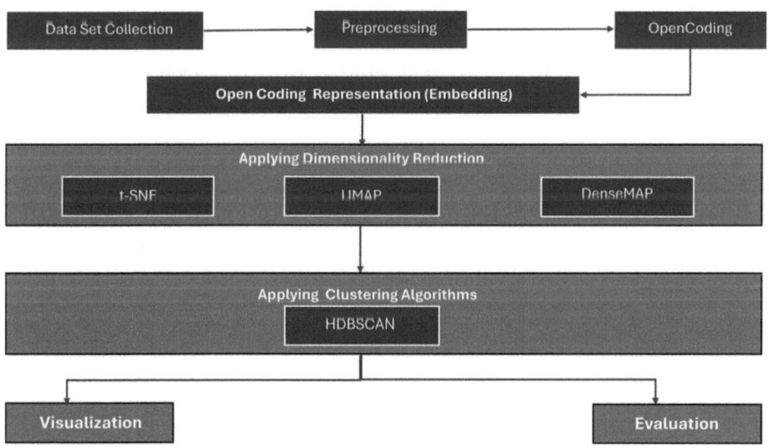

Fig. 1. The overall scheme of the Augmented Thematic Analysis - Large Language Model (ATA-LLM) approach.

3.1 Dataset: Transcripts and Codebook

The dataset [9], from the Researching Students' Information Choices (RSIC) study, examines how students assess and select online information sources. Research in the dataset aims to understand students' decision-making processes when evaluating the credibility and relevance of digital resources during a science-related research task. It includes qualitative and quantitative data, providing insights into how students from different educational levels interact with search engine results. The dataset comprises 1,201 questionnaire responses, 175 interview transcripts, 175 simulation task decisions, and 175 think-aloud transcripts. Data was collected from participants across six educational stages: elementary school, middle school, high school, community college, undergraduate, and graduate levels. The study setting included simulated online searches designed to replicate real-world research behaviors.

This dataset's key component is providing a codebook (i.e., the set of codes, categories, relationships, definitions, and examples [44]). This codebook is traditionally used to enhance consistency in analysis, supporting methodological transparency and reproducibility [40].

3.2 Preprocessing: Open Code Generation and Embedding

In ATA-LLM, the preprocessing phase begins by segmenting interview transcripts into chunks that include each sentence and its surrounding context. For each segment, a pre-trained LLM is prompted to generate open codes, i.e., short phrases (typically 1 to 4 words) that capture the core meaning of the text. These open codes serve as the foundational units for thematic analysis. Figure 2 illustrates the prompt used for open code generation. Each open code is then transformed into an embedding, a high-dimensional vector representation, such that semantically similar codes are positioned closer together in the embedding space. The code generation process was guided by a research question similar to that used in [9], ensuring consistency across the dataset.

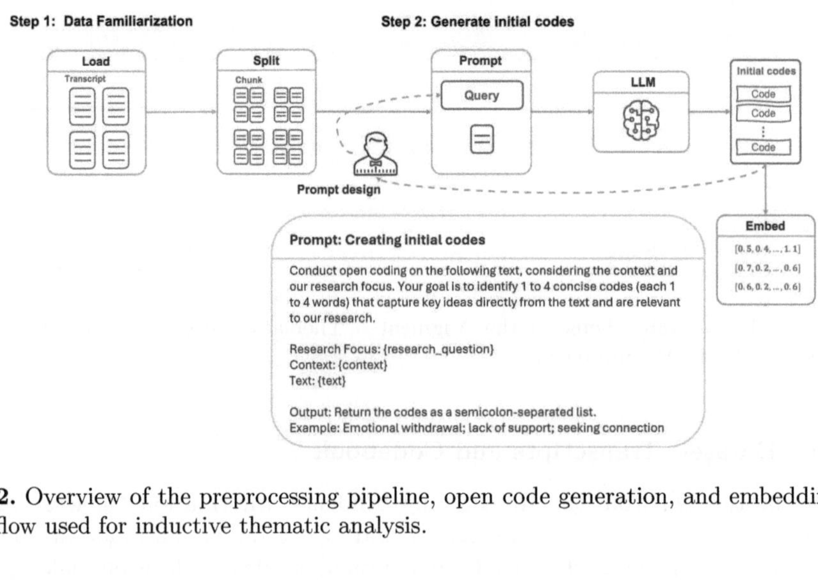

Fig. 2. Overview of the preprocessing pipeline, open code generation, and embedding workflow used for inductive thematic analysis.

3.3 Open Code Embedding Dimensionality Reduction

Open-code embeddings are represented in high dimensionality. For instance, in the embedding model 'text-embedding-ada-002', each text segment is mapped to a 1536-dimensional vector. Organizing code into meaningful groups to identify patterns can be difficult in high-dimensional spaces due to the curse of dimensionality [5]. For this reason, we apply three well-known manifold algorithms to reduce the dimensionality of each open-code embedding. The methods include:

- UMAP (Uniform Manifold Approximation and Projection) [32]
- DenseMAP [33]
- t-SNE (t-Distributed Stochastic Neighbor Embedding) [29]

3.4 Theme Identification Through Clustering Algorithms

After generating the open codes, the next step is to group them based on similarity. These grouped codes will form potential themes, which can vary in shape and size. Given the properties of these groups, we have chosen to use the clustering algorithm, HDBSCAN (Hierarchical Density-Based Spatial Clustering of Applications with Noise) [31]. This unsupervised machine learning model effectively identifies meaningful clusters with varying densities while filtering out noise.

Then, a potential theme for each cluster was inferred via GPT-4o-mini. We constructed our prompt by providing only the initial code per cluster:

Prompt: Themes inferred.

You are a qualitative researcher. You are helping me write a potential theme or category for initial codes.
Write a potential category name or topic using the following list of topics.
INITIAL CODES:{codes} THEME TITLE:"

3.5 Evaluation Criteria

The evaluation criteria include unsupervised and supervised metrics, which help determine the optimal combination of the dimensionality reduction algorithm and the clustering algorithm for thematic analysis.

The unsupervised metrics help evaluate the theme clustering quality when a human-annotated codebook is unavailable. For this purpose, we employ the silhouette score (S) [41] to evaluate cluster separation, topic coherence (TC) [27] to measure the semantic similarity of the top open codes within each theme, and topic diversity (TD) [14] to quantify the uniqueness of code vocabularies across the model.

The supervised metrics allow us to evaluate the themes generated by the ATA-LLM with a human-annotated codebook. For this purpose, we employ a similar approach to [30], in which we embed both the human-annotated codebook and the ATA-LLM-generated themes into a shared semantic space using the embedding model. Then, we compute the average pairwise cosine similarity between aligned themes. The measure range is [0, 1], where 1 indicates a perfect similarity.

4 Experiments and Results

4.1 Parameter Settings and Hyperparameter Optimization

Each manifold and clustering algorithm has symbolic and numeric parameters. To find the best configuration over the hyperparameter search space Θ, we model this problem as a black-box optimization problem in which, given a specific pipeline configuration in ATA-LLM ($\theta \in \Theta$), we evaluate the quality using the following utility function U:

$$U(\theta) = \lambda_1 TC(\theta) + \lambda_2 TD(\theta) + \lambda_3 S(\theta)$$

where λ_1, λ_2, and λ_3 are weights used in the utility function to set the preference over metrics TC, TD, and S. In our experiments, we used $\lambda_1 = 0.3$, $\lambda_2 = 0.6$, and $\lambda_3 = 0.1$, respectively. Then, the tuning problem can be stated as:

$$\theta^* = \arg\max_{\theta \in \Theta} U(\theta)$$

To solve this tuning problem efficiently, we employed the open-source framework Optuna [2], which supports the search for hyperparameters by using Bayesian optimization. Table 1 presents the hyperparameters and their corresponding values. Over 200 trials were conducted to find the best hyperparameter configuration.

4.2 Results

Using the optimal hyperparameters found by Optuna (see Table 2), we evaluated each configuration based on three metrics: topic coherence (TC), topic diversity (TD), and silhouette score (S). The results are presented in Table 3. From Table 3, we can observe that UMAP and DenseMAP have high topic coherence ($TC = 0.893$), indicating a strong consistency in the themes generated. Conversely, the combination of t-SNE and HDBSCAN demonstrates the highest topic diversity ($TD = 0.975$). Overall, all three manifold algorithms demonstrate a competitive topic diversity score, suggesting that ATA-LLM can effectively name themes using varied vocabulary within clusters. Concerning the silhouette score (S), which evaluates cluster separation, DenseMAP receives the highest rating ($S = 0.152$).

Table 1. Hyperparameters used in Optuna optimization [2].

Algorithm	Hyperparameter	Hyperparameter values
Dimensional Reduction Algorithm		
UMAP	n_neighbors	$[5, 50]$
	min_dist	$[0.0, 0.5]$
	metric	cosine
DenseMAP	n_neighbors	$[5, 50]$
	min_dist	$[0.0, 0.5]$
	dens_lambda	$[0.1, 0.3]$
tSNE	perplexity	$[5, 50]$
	learning_rate	auto
Clustering Algorithm		
HDBSCAN	min_cluster_size	$[5, 100]$
	min_samples	$[5, 20]$
	cluster_selection_epsilon	$[0.1, 1.0]$

Table 2. Best hyperparameter configuration identified by Optuna [2]

Algorithm	Hyperparameter	Hyperparameter values
UMAP	n_neighbors	21
	min_dist	0.10
HDBSCAN	min_cluster_size	23
	min_samples	10
	cluster_selection_epsilon	0.229
DenseMAP	n_neighbors	14
	min_dist	0.25
	dens_lambda	2.79
HDBSCAN	min_cluster_size	15
	min_samples	3
	cluster_selection_epsilon	0.331
tSNE	perplexity	11
HDBSCAN	min_cluster_size	44
	min_samples	17
	cluster_selection_epsilon	0.919

Table 3. Comparison of metrics across different dimensionality reduction and clustering configurations for thematic analysis.

Metric	UMAP + HDBSCAN	DenseMAP + HDBSCAN	t-SNE + HDBSCAN
TC	**0.893**	**0.893**	0.817
TD	0.935	0.925	**0.975**
S	0.140	**0.152**	−0.046

Open Code Embedding Dimensionality Reduction. Our ATA-LLM framework identified 4,536 initial codes from semi-structured interviews [9]. To capture the semantic relationships among these codes, we generated 1,536-dimensional embedding vectors for each code (see Sect. 3.2). We then applied three manifold learning algorithms for dimensionality reduction.

Figure 3 presents the reduced embeddings of a sample set of six open codes. Notably, the codes "pubmed search" and "created by librarian" consistently appear nearby across all three manifold algorithms, suggesting substantial semantic similarity. In contrast, we also observe several initial codes positioned far from the dense cloud of points. We hypothesize that these outliers either represent semantically unique codes, lack sufficient transcript data to support them, or align with other initial codes.

Grouping Codes Into Themes: We employed the unsupervised clustering technique HDBSCAN [31] to identify distinct thematic groups within the initial codes. Each code was treated as mutually exclusive (i.e., they only belong to one category). To improve the quality of the clusters, we pre-processed the data by removing outlying codes that HDBSCAN identified. This approach is similar to affinity diagramming, where ideas are organized into groups, although some outlier ideas should not be forced into categories.

Figure 4 shows the cluster assignments produced by HDBSCAN [31] for each manifold learning algorithm: UMAP, DenseMAP, and t-SNE. Across all three methods, HDBSCAN consistently identifies four well-separated clusters, providing a clear structure for theme inference. In addition, Fig. 4 shows the potential theme for each cluster, inferred using GPT-4o-mini. Notably, UMAP and DenseMAP are highly comparable thematic results, with three out of four inferred themes that align closely. Both algorithms share two of four themes with t-SNE (see Table 4).

Table 4. Similar thematic labels identified across UMAP, DenseMAP, and t-SNE projections

UMAP	DenseMAP	t-SNE
Evaluating Credibility and Uncertainty in Online Research Sources	Challenges of Online Information Sourcing in Research Tasks	Evaluation and Credibility of Online Sources
Citation Management Confusion and Tools	Evaluation and Preference for Reference Management Tools	Citation Management and Tool Utilization
Perceptions of Wikipedia's Credibility and Reliability as a Source	Reliability and Credibility of Wikipedia as a Source	

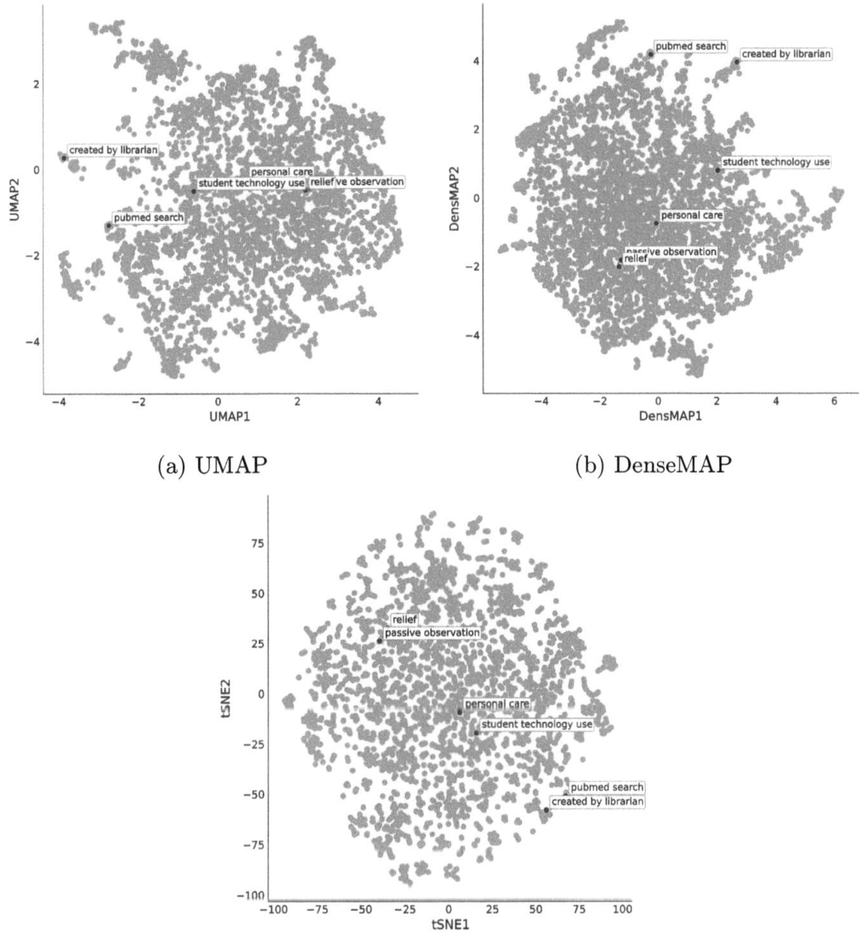

(a) UMAP

(b) DenseMAP

(c) t-SNE

Fig. 3. Dimensionality reduction of open code embeddings from the dataset in [9] using three different manifold learning algorithms. Blue dots represent a random sample of open codes, where spatial proximity indicates semantic similarity. (Color figure online)

Evaluation Between Human and ATA-LLM-Generated Themes. To evaluate the similarity between the themes generated by the ATA-LLM and a human-annotated codebook, we employ a similar approach to [30], in which we embed both the human-annotated codebook and the ATA-LLM-generated themes into a shared semantic space using an embedding model. We then compute the average pairwise cosine similarity between aligned themes. The measure ranges from 0 to 1, where 1 indicates a perfect similarity.

The human-annotated codebook in [9] presents one theme and four levels of subthemes: Theme (I, II, III), Subtheme (A, B, C), Subtheme (1, 2, 3), Subtheme

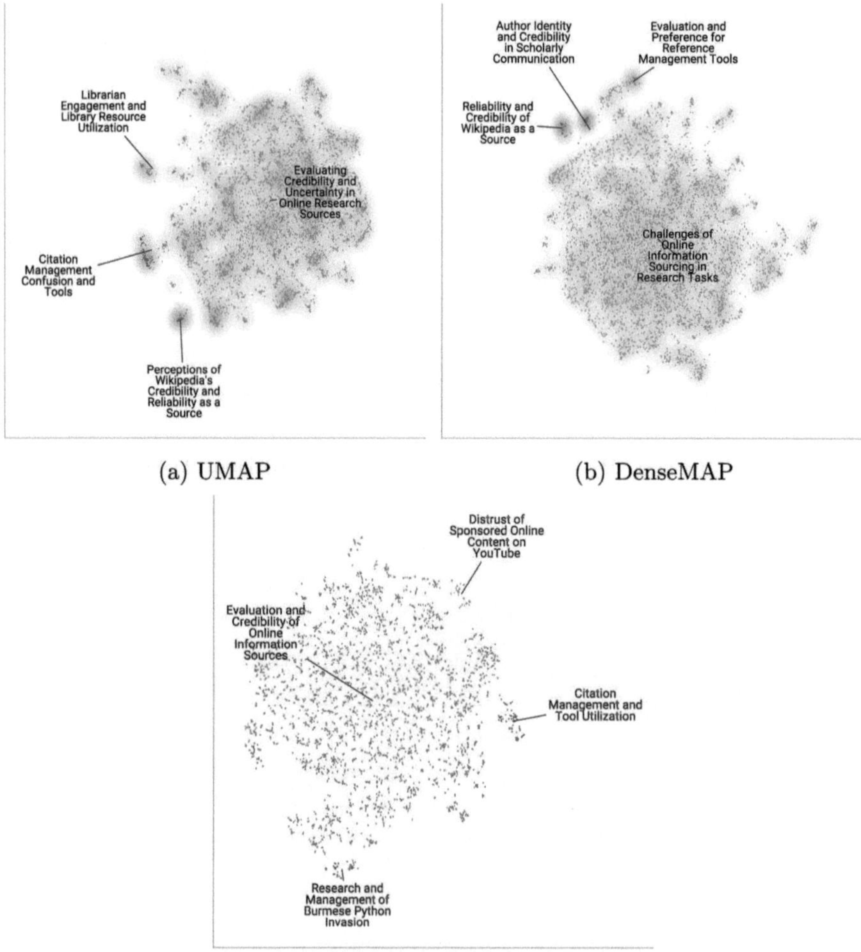

(a) UMAP (b) DenseMAP

(c) t-SNE

Fig. 4. Theme Identification through Clustering Algorithms.

(a, b, c), Subtheme (i, ii, iii). For this reason, we compute the average cosine similarity between human-generated themes and those generated by our three different approaches for each level.

The subtheme level (A, B, C) in the human-annotated codebook [9] exhibited the highest average cosine similarity. DenseMAP produces the highest average score at this level, with a similarity of 0.77. Similarly, UMAP and t-SNE show a similarity score of 0.76.

Overall, all three manifold learning approaches demonstrated reliable performance across subtheme granularities, with DenseMAP providing slightly more stable scores across all theme structures.

5 Conclusions, Limitations, and Future Perspectives

This study evaluated the effectiveness of integrating manifold learning algorithms with HDBSCAN to support inductive thematic analysis using LLMs. Our findings show that DenseMAP [33] combined with HDBSCAN [31] offers a more substantial alignment with human-coded themes. We selected these techniques to capture semantically coherent and contextually meaningful themes. In contrast, some manifold learning algorithms, such as t-SNE, failed to preserve the nuance of qualitative data, ultimately oversimplifying or distorting the semantic relationships among codes. These limitations are consistent with previous findings that t-SNE can distort global structure and exaggerate local patterns, making it less reliable for interpretable clustering tasks [29].

A key insight from our study is the importance of balancing automation with human supervision. While specific sections of the ATA-LLM pipeline, such as the open code embedding (see Sect. 3.3) and dimensionality reduction, can be automated without significantly compromising interpretability. However, other stages, such as open coding and theme identification, benefit substantially from human-in-the-loop involvement to ensure contextual accuracy and to mitigate potential biases. Integrating domain expertise at these stages allows for more contextually accurate theme refinement, such as merging semantically similar clusters or splitting broad clusters into more meaningful subthemes. Moreover, incorporating human feedback into the LLM-based coding process helps ensure that the resulting themes align with the underlying research questions and analytical objectives. Our comparative analysis also reveals that LLM-driven approaches frequently generate codes and themes with uniform granularity. In contrast, human coders adjust the level of abstraction according to context and interpretive judgment. Supporting user control over granularity and consistency can improve the usability and trustworthiness of AI-assisted thematic analysis tools.

Some limitations of our study include that our evaluation is based on a single dataset, one datatype, and tested with only one large language model (GPT-4o-mini). These constraints may limit generalizability, and we acknowledge that performance will likely vary across domains, datasets, and model types. Nonetheless, we view this case study as a foundation for designing future AI-based tools that ethically and transparently support inductive qualitative analysis.

Ethical considerations must be central in the development of these types of tools. It is known that LLMs are trained on large, generalized corpora that may encode biases [4], which may influence how themes are identified and interpreted. Therefore, to increase trust in AI-assisted qualitative analysis, we advocate for augmented approaches that prioritize human judgment and emphasize transparency and reproducibility. This can also bridge the gap between qualitative and quantitative research communities by showing how rigorous and replicable qualitative methods can benefit from AI support. Educators must also prepare students to use these AI tools ethically by building a deep understanding of their potential and limitations among students.

Future work should explore human-in-the-loop AI-assisted tools that can serve as collaborative partners, enabling scalable, interpretable, and ethically grounded thematic analysis. Such tools should aim to preserve the richness of human insight while leveraging the efficiency and scalability of machine learning.

References

1. Adolph, S., Kruchten, P., Hall, W.: Reconciling perspectives: a grounded theory of how people manage the process of software development. J. Syst. Softw. **85**(6), 1269–1286 (2012)
2. Akiba, T., Sano, S., Yanase, T., Ohta, T., Koyama, M.: Optuna: a next-generation hyperparameter optimization framework. In: Proceedings of the 25th ACM SIGKDD International Conference on Knowledge Discovery and Data Mining (2019)
3. Bano, M., Hoda, R., Zowghi, D., Treude, C.: Large language models for qualitative research in software engineering: exploring opportunities and challenges. Autom. Softw. Eng. **31**(1), 8 (2024)
4. Bender, E.M., Gebru, T., McMillan-Major, A., Shmitchell, S.: On the dangers of stochastic parrots: can language models be too big?. In: Proceedings of the 2021 ACM Conference on Fairness, Accountability, and Transparency, pp. 610–623 (2021)
5. Beyer, K., Goldstein, J., Ramakrishnan, R., Shaft, U.: When is "nearest neighbor" meaningful? In: Beeri, C., Buneman, P. (eds.) ICDT 1999. LNCS, vol. 1540, pp. 217–235. Springer, Heidelberg (1999). https://doi.org/10.1007/3-540-49257-7_15
6. Braun, V., Clarke, V.: Using thematic analysis in psychology. Qual. Res. Psychol. **3**(2), 77 (2006)
7. Braun, V., Clarke, V.: Toward good practice in thematic analysis: avoiding common problems and be (com)ing a knowing researcher. Int. J. Transgender Health **24**(1), 1–6 (2023)
8. Cahyadi, D.J., Murfi, H., Satria, Y., Abdullah, S., Widyaningsih, Y.: BERT-based deep embedded clustering for topic modeling. In: 2024 International Conference on Computer, Control, Informatics and its Applications (IC3INA), pp. 331–336. IEEE (2024)
9. Cataldo, T., et al.: Researching students' information choices (RSIC): determining identity and judging credibility in digital spaces (2023)
10. Chew, R., Bollenbacher, J., Wenger, M., Speer, J., Kim, A.: LLM-assisted content analysis: using large language models to support deductive coding. arXiv preprint arXiv:2306.14924 (2023)
11. Dai, S.C., Xiong, A., Ku, L.W.: LLM-in-the-loop: leveraging large language model for thematic analysis. arXiv preprint arXiv:2310.15100 (2023)
12. De Paoli, S.: Performing an inductive thematic analysis of semi-structured interviews with a large language model: an exploration and provocation on the limits of the approach. Soc. Sci. Comput. Rev. 08944393231220483 (2023)
13. DeFranco, J.F., Laplante, P.A.: A content analysis process for qualitative software engineering research. Innov. Syst. Softw. Eng. 129–141 (2017). https://doi.org/10.1007/s11334-017-0287-0
14. Dieng, A.B., Ruiz, F.J., Blei, D.M.: Topic modeling in embedding spaces. Trans. Assoc. Comput. Linguist. **8**, 439–453 (2020)

15. Dittrich, Y., John, M., Singer, J., Tessem, B.: Editorial for the special issue on qualitative software engineering research. Inf. Softw. Technol. **49**(6), 531–539 (2007)
16. Easterbrook, S., Singer, J., Storey, M.A., Damian, D.: Selecting empirical methods for software engineering research. In: Guide to Advanced Empirical Software Engineering, pp. 285–311 (2008)
17. Gamieldien, Y., Case, J.M., Katz, A.: Advancing qualitative analysis: an exploration of the potential of generative AI and NLP in thematic coding. Available at SSRN 4487768 (2023)
18. Gauthier, R.P., Wallace, J.R.: The computational thematic analysis toolkit. In: Proceedings of the ACM on Human-Computer Interaction, vol. 6, no. GROUP, pp. 1–15 (2022)
19. Ghahremanlou, L., et al.: Automating thematic analysis: how LLMs analyze controversial topics. Microsoft J. Appl. Sci. **21**, 69–87 (2024)
20. Glaser, B., Strauss, A.: Discovery of Grounded Theory: Strategies for Qualitative Research. Routledge (2017)
21. Hoda, R.: Socio-technical grounded theory for software engineering. IEEE Trans. Softw. Eng. **48**(10), 3808–3832 (2021)
22. Hoda, R.: Qualitative Research with Socio-Technical Grounded Theory. Springer, Cham (2024)
23. Jahanbakhsh Gudakahriz, S., Eftekhari Moghadam, A.M., Mahmoudi, F.: Opinion texts clustering using manifold learning based on sentiment and semantics analysis. Sci. Program. **2021**(1), 7842631 (2021)
24. Johnson, D.R., Green, A.E., van Hell, J.G., Beaty, R.E.: Creativity in context: thematic profile analysis reveals the explanatory power of themes and culture in creative ideas (2024)
25. Katz, A., Fleming, G.C., Main, J.: Thematic analysis with open-source generative AI and machine learning: a new method for inductive qualitative codebook development. arXiv preprint arXiv:2410.03721 (2024)
26. Khan, A.H., et al.: Automating thematic analysis: how LLMs analyse controversial topics. arXiv preprint arXiv:2405.06919 (2024)
27. Lau, J.H., Newman, D., Baldwin, T.: Machine reading tea leaves: automatically evaluating topic coherence and topic model quality. In: Proceedings of the 14th Conference of the European Chapter of the Association for Computational Linguistics, pp. 530–539 (2014)
28. Lenberg, P., Feldt, R., Gren, L., Wallgren Tengberg, L.G., Tidefors, I., Graziotin, D.: Qualitative software engineering research: reflections and guidelines. J. Softw.: Evol. Process **36**(6), e2607 (2024)
29. Van der Maaten, L., Hinton, G.: Visualizing data using t-SNE. J. Mach. Learn. Res. **9**(11) (2008)
30. Mathis, W.S., Zhao, S., Pratt, N., Weleff, J., De Paoli, S.: Inductive thematic analysis of healthcare qualitative interviews using open-source large language models: how does it compare to traditional methods? Comput. Methods Programs Biomed. **255**, 108356 (2024)
31. McInnes, L., Healy, J., Astels, S., et al.: HDBSCAN: hierarchical density based clustering. J. Open Sour. Softw. **2**(11), 205 (2017)
32. McInnes, L., Healy, J., Melville, J.: UMAP: uniform manifold approximation and projection for dimension reduction. arXiv preprint arXiv:1802.03426 (2018)
33. Narayan, A., Berger, B., Cho, H.: Density-preserving data visualization unveils dynamic patterns of single-cell transcriptomic variability. bioRxiv, pp. 2020–05 (2020)

34. Parker, M.J., Anderson, C., Stone, C., Oh, Y.: A large language model approach to educational survey feedback analysis. Int. J. Artif. Intell. Educ. 1–38 (2024)
35. Pennebaker, J.W., Boyd, R.L., Jordan, K., Blackburn, K.: The development and psychometric properties of LIWC2015. Technical report (2015)
36. Rahman, T., Nwokeji, J., Matovu, R., Frezza, S., Sugnanam, H., Pisolkar, A.: Analyzing competences in software testing: combining thematic analysis with natural language processing (NLP). In: 2021 IEEE Frontiers in Education Conference (FIE), pp. 1–9. IEEE (2021)
37. Raza, M.Z., et al.: LLM-TA: an LLM-enhanced thematic analysis pipeline for transcripts from parents of children with congenital heart disease. arXiv preprint arXiv:2502.01620 (2025)
38. Reddy, G.T., et al.: Analysis of dimensionality reduction techniques on big data. IEEE Access **8**, 54776–54788 (2020)
39. Renz, S.M., Carrington, J.M., Badger, T.A.: Two strategies for qualitative content analysis: an intramethod approach to triangulation. Qual. Health Res. **28**(5), 824–831 (2018)
40. Roberts, K., Dowell, A., Nie, J.B.: Attempting rigour and replicability in thematic analysis of qualitative research data; a case study of codebook development. BMC Med. Res. Methodol. **19**(1), 1–8 (2019)
41. Rousseeuw, P.J.: Silhouettes: a graphical aid to the interpretation and validation of cluster analysis. J. Comput. Appl. Math. **20**, 53–65 (1987)
42. Runeson, P., Höst, M.: Guidelines for conducting and reporting case study research in software engineering. Empir. Softw. Eng. **14**, 131–164 (2009)
43. Runeson, P., Host, M., Rainer, A., Regnell, B.: Case Study Research in Software Engineering: Guidelines and Examples. Wiley (2012)
44. Ryan, G.W., Bernard, H.R.: Data management and analysis methods. In: Denzin, N.D., Lincoln, Y.S. (eds.) Handbook of Qualitative Research, 2nd edn., pp. 769–803 (2000)
45. Sabbaghan, S.: Exploring the synergy of human and AI-driven approaches in thematic analysis for qualitative educational research. J. Appl. Learn. Teach. **7**(2) (2024)
46. Saldaña, J.: The coding manual for qualitative researchers (2021)
47. Seaman, C., Hoda, R., Feldt, R.: Qualitative research methods in software engineering: past, present, and future. IEEE Trans. Softw. Eng. (2025)
48. Seaman, C.B.: Qualitative methods in empirical studies of software engineering. IEEE Trans. Softw. Eng. **25**(4), 557–572 (1999)
49. Sharp, H., Dittrich, Y., De Souza, C.R.: The role of ethnographic studies in empirical software engineering. IEEE Trans. Softw. Eng. **42**(8), 786–804 (2016)
50. Singh, S.H., Jiang, K., Bhasin, K., Sabharwal, A., Moukaddam, N., Patel, A.B.: Racer: an LLM-powered methodology for scalable analysis of semi-structured mental health interviews. arXiv preprint arXiv:2402.02656 (2024)
51. Xiao, Z., Yuan, X., Liao, Q.V., Abdelghani, R., Oudeyer, P.Y.: Supporting qualitative analysis with large language models: combining codebook with GPT-3 for deductive coding. In: Companion Proceedings of the 28th International Conference on Intelligent User Interfaces, pp. 75–78 (2023)

Detailed Cryptanalysis of "Privacy-Preserving Quantum Federated Learning via Gradient Hiding"

Zafar Iqbal[1], Syed Zohaib Hassan[1(✉)], Jie Zhao[2], and Shafiya Mubeen Umme[3]

[1] COMSATS University Islamabad, Sahiwal Campus, Islamabad, Pakistan
roy_zafar@cuisahiwal.edu.pk, syedzohaibhassan302@gmail.com

[2] Department of Computer Science and Software Engineering, Penn State Behrend, Erie, PA, USA
jkz5273@psu.edu

[3] Department of Computer Engineering and Computer Science, California State University, Long Beach, CA, USA
ShafiyaMubeen.Umme01@student.csulb.edu

Abstract. Quantum Federated Learning (QFL) has crystallized as a formidable paradigm that aspires to reconcile distributed intelligence with uncompromised privacy. Notably, the protocol articulated by Changhao Li et al. [1], which harnesses gradient concealment through Blind Quantum Bipartite Correlators and GHZ-entangled states, epitomizes this ambition. However, its ostensible guarantees remain largely untested against sophisticated adversarial models capable of subverting quantum safeguards. In this study, we undertake a rigorous cryptographic dissection of the protocol, constructing formal threat models encompassing twelve distinct attack vectors, from phase manipulation and amplitude distortion to entanglement erosion and replay amplification. Through meticulous mathematical scrutiny, we demonstrate that these vectors can precipitate the disclosure of private gradients and compromise aggregation fidelity. To remediate these deficiencies, we propose a cohesive set of countermeasures, including randomized phase obfuscation, authenticated quantum encodings, and temporal binding strategies. These contributions collectively advance a resilient architectural framework, charting a credible path toward quantum-secure federated learning in adversarial settings.

Keywords: Quantum Federated Learning · Secure Inner-Product Estimation · GHZ Entanglement · Gradient Hiding · Cryptanalysis · Phase Manipulation · Quantum Attacks · Quantum Privacy · Blind Quantum Bipartite Correlators (BQBC) · Secure Aggregation · Post-Quantum Security · Replay Attack · Entanglement Leakage · Quantum DoS

S. Hussain et al. (Eds.): SEET 2025, CCIS 2725, pp. 481–499, 2026.
https://doi.org/10.1007/978-3-032-08977-9_30

1 Introduction

The convergence of quantum computing and distributed machine learning has catalyzed the development of novel frameworks that aspire to reconcile collaborative intelligence with rigorous privacy guarantees. Within this evolving landscape, Quantum Federated Learning (QFL) has garnered particular attention as a conceptual and technological advance capable of mitigating inference attacks that threaten conventional federated paradigms. By encoding gradient information into quantum states endowed with superposition and entanglement, QFL protocols endeavor to obscure sensitive local contributions during aggregation. Among the most notable of these efforts, the protocol proposed by Changhao Li et al. [1] delineates a gradient concealment mechanism premised upon Blind Quantum Bipartite Correlators in conjunction with GHZ-entangled architectures. While this construction represents a compelling departure from classical cryptographic primitives, its purported resilience remains largely speculative in the absence of exhaustive adversarial scrutiny.

Recognizing this deficiency, the present study is situated at the intersection of cryptographic analysis and quantum information security. It seeks to illuminate the latent vulnerabilities inherent in gradient-hiding QFL schemes by articulating a comprehensive threat model encompassing a diverse spectrum of attack vectors. To this end, we formulate the following research questions to guide our inquiry:

1. What classes of adversarial strategies can systematically compromise the confidentiality and integrity of aggregated quantum gradients?
2. How can these threats be formally characterized and quantified within an operational federated learning environment?
3. Which defensive countermeasures can be devised to counteract such attacks while preserving protocol scalability and efficiency?

To address these questions, we advance a detailed mathematical framework through which twelve distinct attack modalities are modeled and evaluated, ranging from phase manipulation and amplitude distortion to entanglement erosion and replay amplification. The following sections present the notation, foundational assumptions, and formal definitions that underpin this investigation and set the stage for the ensuing cryptographic analysis.

In federated learning, a global model $\mathcal{M}$ is collaboratively trained across m distributed clients, $\{C_1, C_2, \ldots, C_m\}$, each possessing local data $\mathcal{D}_i$ [1,8]. The objective is to minimize a global loss function $L(\theta)$, where θ represents the model parameters:

As shown in Eq. 1, this formulation defines the global optimization objective, where the server aims to minimize the weighted sum of individual client loss functions across all participants.

$$\theta^* = \arg\min_{\theta} \sum_{i=1}^{m} w_i L_i(\theta) \tag{1}$$

Equation 2 enforces the normalization constraint on the weights assigned to each client, ensuring that all contributions collectively sum to unity.

$$w_i \geq 0, \sum_{i=1}^{m} w_i = 1. \tag{2}$$

Quantum federated learning introduces quantum states to encode local gradients $\nabla L_i(\theta)$, leveraging properties such as entanglement and superposition for enhanced security and scalability. A client C_i encodes its gradient into a quantum phase ϕ_i:

$$\phi_i = w_i \nabla L_i(\theta), \tag{3}$$

which is transmitted to the server for aggregation:

$$\Phi = \sum_{i=1}^{m} \phi_i. \tag{4}$$

Equation 3 describes the process by which each client encodes its local gradient information into a quantum phase prior to transmission. As expressed in Eq. 4, the server aggregates all received quantum phases into a single value to compute the global gradient update.

The server uses Φ to update the global model $\mathcal{M}$ according to a gradient descent rule:

$$\theta^{(t+1)} = \theta^{(t)} - \eta\Phi, \tag{5}$$

where η is the learning rate.

As illustrated in Fig. 1, our cryptanalysis workflow comprises five stages from protocol selection to recommendations.

Equation 5 specifies the iterative gradient descent update rule applied to the model parameters using the aggregated quantum phase.

Two protocols are proposed to ensure the privacy of ϕ_i and the integrity of Φ: **1. Secure Inner-Product Estimation Protocol:** Aggregates gradients ϕ_i using Blind Quantum Bipartite Correlators (BQBC). **2. Incremental Learning Protocol**: Utilizes GreenbergerHorneZeilinger (GHZ) entangled states to compute Φ securely [1].

Key Contributions: This paper makes the following contributions:

- It provides the first in-depth cryptanalysis of the quantum federated learning protocols proposed by Changhao Li et al. [1], focusing on both secure inner-product estimation and incremental learning protocols.
- We formally model and evaluate twelve potential attacks, including phase manipulation, quantum state tomography, and entanglement leakage, all with rigorous mathematical justification.
- We propose lightweight, cryptographically grounded countermeasures such as quantum state authentication, time-stamped encoding, and entanglement witness verification to mitigate identified vulnerabilities.
- Our work serves as a foundational security analysis to inform future designs of quantum-resilient federated learning systems.

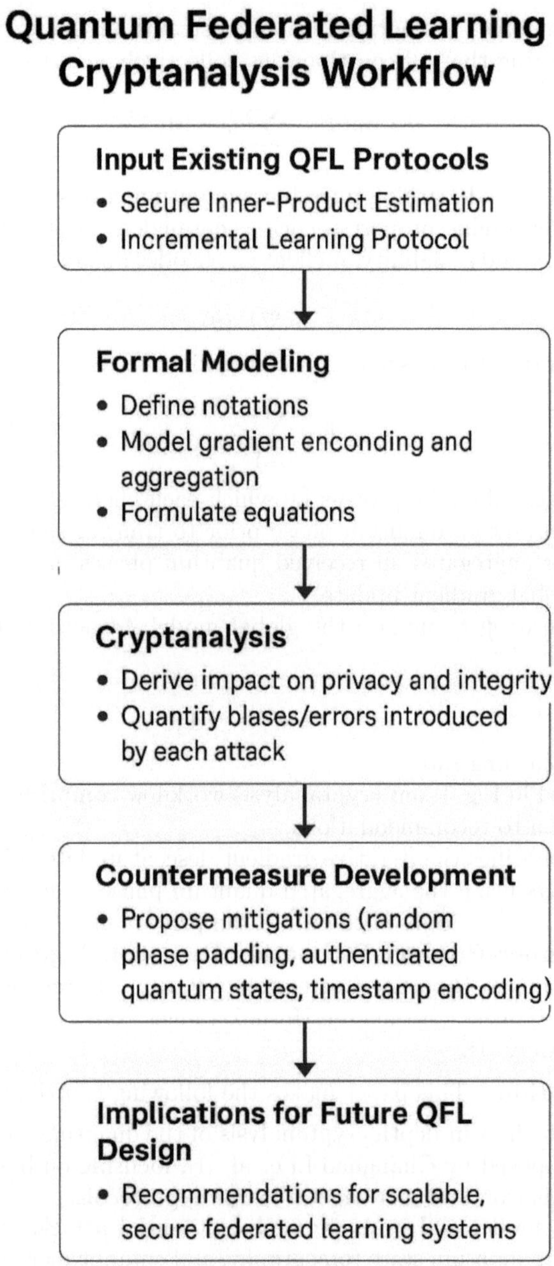

Fig. 1. Workflow of the cryptanalysis methodology adopted to evaluate gradient-hiding quantum federated learning protocols.

1.1 Challenges in Privacy Preservation

The primary challenge is protecting ϕ_i from adversaries who may attempt to reconstruct $\nabla L_i(\theta)$ or tamper with Φ. Key adversarial actions include: - **Phase Manipulation**: Introducing an additional phase ϵ, biasing Φ:

$$\Phi' = \Phi + m\epsilon.$$

- **Gradient Inversion**: Exploiting the relationship $\nabla L_i(\theta) = \frac{\phi_i}{w_i}$ to recover private gradients. - **Entanglement Manipulation**: Collapsing the entanglement structure of GHZ states:

$$|\psi\rangle = \frac{1}{\sqrt{2}} \left(|0\rangle^{\otimes(m+1)} + e^{i\Phi} |1\rangle^{\otimes(m+1)} \right).$$

1.2 Objectives

The proposed protocols aim to achieve: **1. Privacy Preservation**: Preventing the disclosure of individual gradients $\nabla L_i(\theta)$ while allowing the server to compute Φ. **2. Robustness Against Attacks**: Securing Φ from adversarial tampering, including: - Noise injection $\eta_i \sim \mathcal{N}(0, \sigma^2)$, - Replay attacks $\Phi' = \Phi + (k-1)\phi_i$, - Side-channel attacks leveraging timing or photon leakage. **3. Scalability**: Ensuring the protocols operate efficiently as $m \to \infty$ [6].

1.3 Notations and Assumptions

- w_i: Weight assigned to client C_i, satisfying $\sum_{i=1}^{m} w_i = 1$. - ϕ_i: Quantum phase encoding the gradient of C_i, $\phi_i = w_i \nabla L_i(\theta)$. - Φ: Aggregated phase, $\Phi = \sum_{i=1}^{m} \phi_i$. - $|\psi\rangle$: Quantum state used for encoding gradients, depending on the protocol [2,4]:

$$|\psi\rangle = \frac{1}{\sqrt{m}} \sum_{i=1}^{m} e^{i\phi_i} |i\rangle. \tag{6}$$

Equation 6 formalizes the quantum state representation that encodes individual client contributions within a superposed state.

This paper provides a comprehensive cryptanalysis of these protocols, identifying potential vulnerabilities and proposing mathematical countermeasures to enhance their security and privacy guarantees (Table 1).

Table 1. Symbols and Notations

Symbol	Description
$\mathcal{M}$	Global model in federated learning
$\mathcal{D}_i$	Local dataset of the i-th client
$L(\theta)$	Global loss function, where θ represents model parameters
$L_i(\theta)$	Local loss function for the i-th client
$\nabla L_i(\theta)$	Gradient of the local loss function for client i
θ	Model parameters to be optimized
w_i	Weight of client C_i, satisfying $\sum_{i=1}^{m} w_i = 1$
ϕ_i	Quantum phase encoding the gradient of C_i, $\phi_i = w_i \nabla L_i(\theta)$
Φ	Aggregated phase, $\Phi = \sum_{i=1}^{m} \phi_i$
η_i	Random noise introduced by clients for obfuscation
ϵ	Adversarial phase shift introduced by the server
$\|\psi\rangle$	Quantum state encoding gradients: $\|\psi\rangle = \frac{1}{\sqrt{m}} \sum_{i=1}^{m} e^{i\phi_i} \|i\rangle$
$\|\psi_{\text{decoy}}\rangle$	Decoy quantum state used to detect adversarial tampering: $\|\psi_{\text{decoy}}\rangle = \frac{1}{\sqrt{2}}(\|0\rangle + \|1\rangle)$
$\|\psi_{\text{auth}}\rangle$	Authenticated quantum state, combining the encoded state and its hash: $\|\psi_{\text{auth}}\rangle = \|\psi\rangle \otimes \|H(\phi_i)\rangle$
$H(\cdot)$	Cryptographic hash function
$\mathcal{S}$	Subset of clients considered during entanglement manipulation
$\Phi_{\mathcal{S}}$	Partial aggregated phase of the subset $\mathcal{S}$, $\Phi_{\mathcal{S}} = \sum_{i \in \mathcal{S}} \phi_i$
$\|\psi_{\text{noise}}\rangle$	Random noise state introduced during a Denial-of-Service attack
F	Fidelity between the expected and received quantum states: $F = \langle \psi_{\text{expected}} \| \psi_{\text{received}} \rangle$
t	Timestamp used for encoding quantum states to prevent replay attacks
r	Redundancy factor for encoding quantum states
δ_i	Perturbation introduced by an adversary in differential phase attacks
σ^2	Variance of noise in side-channel or gradient obfuscation
W	Entanglement witness operator, used to verify the integrity of quantum entanglement: $W = I - \|\psi\rangle\langle\psi\|$
$\mathcal{V}$	Valid set of gradients verified in zero-knowledge proofs

2 "Privacy-Preserving Quantum Federated Learning via Gradient Hiding" Proposed Protocols by Changhao Li et al.

2.1 Secure Inner-Product Estimation Protocol

Protocol Summary
Each client C_i encodes its gradient $\nabla L_i(\theta)$ into a phase:

$$\phi_i = w_i \nabla L_i(\theta),$$

where w_i is the weight of client i, and θ represents the model parameters. The server aggregates the encoded phases:

$$\Phi = \sum_{i=1}^{m} \phi_i = \sum_{i=1}^{m} w_i \nabla L_i(\theta).$$

2.2 Potential Attacks

Attack 1: Phase Manipulation by the Server
The server introduces a controlled phase shift ϵ, modifying the encoded phase:

$$\phi_i' = \phi_i + \epsilon.$$

The modified quantum state becomes:

$$|\psi'\rangle = \frac{1}{\sqrt{m}} \sum_{i=1}^{m} e^{i(\phi_i+\epsilon)} |i\rangle.$$

The aggregated phase retrieved by the server is:

$$\Phi' = \sum_{i=1}^{m} (\phi_i + \epsilon) = \Phi + \ m\epsilon.$$

Mathematical Justification: For $m = 100$ clients and $\epsilon = 0.001$, the total bias is:

$$\Delta\Phi = m\epsilon = 0.1. \tag{7}$$

As depicted in Eq. 7, this expression quantifies the cumulative bias introduced when the server manipulates the phase by a constant offset.

Attack 2: Amplitude Manipulation
The server modifies the amplitude distribution c_i of the state instead of using the uniform distribution $c_i = 1/\sqrt{m}$:

$$|\psi\rangle = \sum_{i=1}^{m} c_i e^{i\phi_i} |i\rangle, \quad c_i = \sqrt{p_i}, \quad \sum_{i=1}^{m} p_i = 1.$$

The aggregated phase becomes:

$$\Phi' = \sum_{i=1}^{m} p_i \phi_i = \sum_{i=1}^{m} p_i w_i \nabla L_i(\theta),$$

where $p_i \neq 1/m$.

Example: Let $p_1 = 0.5, p_2 = 0.25,$ and $p_i = \frac{0.25}{m-2}$ for $i > 2$. Then:

$$\Phi' = 0.5 w_1 \nabla L_1(\theta) + 0.25 w_2 \nabla L_2(\theta) + \frac{0.25}{m-2} \sum_{i=3}^{m} w_i \nabla L_i(\theta).$$

Attack 3: Gradient Inversion

The server attempts to reconstruct individual gradients $\nabla L_i(\theta)$ from the aggregated phase. Given w_i, the server solves:

$$\nabla L_i(\theta) = \frac{\phi_i}{w_i}.$$

If the server has access to Φ and partial knowledge of w_i, it isolates ϕ_i as:

$$\phi_i = \Phi - \sum_{j \neq i} \phi_j.$$

Attack 4: Quantum State Tomography Attack

Description

The adversary applies quantum state tomography to reconstruct the encoded client states $|\psi_i\rangle$, where:

$$|\psi_i\rangle = e^{i\phi_i}|i\rangle, \quad \phi_i = w_i \nabla L_i(\theta).$$

Attack Strategy

1. The adversary collects N identical copies of $|\psi_i\rangle$.
2. Using tomography algorithms, the adversary estimates ϕ_i with high precision.

Mathematical Analysis

The reconstruction error ϵ scales as:

$$\epsilon \sim O\left(\frac{1}{\sqrt{N}}\right). \tag{8}$$

For $N = 10^6$, the error becomes:

$$\epsilon \sim 10^{-3}.$$

Thus, the adversary can reconstruct $\phi_i \approx w_i \nabla L_i(\theta)$.

Equation 8 indicates the scaling relationship between the number of measurement samples and the reconstruction error achievable via quantum state tomography.

Attack 5: Quantum Channel Eavesdropping Attack
Description

An adversary intercepts quantum states $|\psi_i\rangle$ during transmission over quantum channels, extracting gradient information.

Attack Strategy

1. **Intercept-Resend Attack:** The adversary measures $|\psi_i\rangle = e^{i\phi_i}|i\rangle$ in the computational basis.
2. After measurement, the adversary resends a fabricated state $|\psi_i'\rangle = e^{i\phi_i'}|i\rangle$.

Mathematical Analysis

If $\phi_i' = \phi_i + \eta_i$, the total bias in Φ' is:

$$\Delta\Phi = \sum_{i=1}^{m} \eta_i.$$

Assuming $\eta_i \sim \mathcal{U}(-\pi, \pi)$, the variance of the bias is:

$$\mathrm{Var}(\Delta\Phi) = m \cdot \frac{\pi^2}{3}. \tag{9}$$

According to Eq. 9, the variance of the aggregated phase bias grows linearly with the number of clients under random noise injection during eavesdropping.

Attack 6: Side-Channel Attack on Quantum Hardware
Description

The adversary exploits side-channel vulnerabilities in quantum hardware, such as photon leakage or timing variations, to infer encoded client gradients.

Attack Strategy

1. Monitor physical side-channel data, such as:
   - Photon intensity during gradient encoding.
   - Timing variations between $|0\rangle$ and $|1\rangle$.
2. Correlate observed data with expected quantum operations to estimate ϕ_i.

Mathematical Analysis

Modeling the side-channel noise as δ_i, the observed phase becomes:

$$\phi_i^{\mathrm{obs}} = \phi_i + \delta_i.$$

For $\delta_i \sim \mathcal{N}(0, \sigma^2)$, the variance of ϕ_i^{obs} is:

$$\mathrm{Var}(\phi_i^{\mathrm{obs}}) = \frac{\sigma^2}{N},$$

where N is the number of side-channel samples.

7. Differential Phase Attack
Description
An adversary injects controlled perturbations δ_i into client phases ϕ_i to analyze the server's aggregation mechanism.

Attack Strategy

1. Inject perturbation $\phi_i' = \phi_i + \delta_i, \quad \delta_i \sim \mathcal{U}(-\epsilon, \epsilon)$.
2. Observe changes in the aggregated phase:

$$\Delta\Phi = \Phi' - \Phi = \sum_{i=1}^{m} \delta_i.$$

Mathematical Analysis
For $\delta_i \sim \mathcal{U}(-\epsilon, \epsilon)$, the variance of $\Delta\Phi$ is (Table 2):

$$\text{Var}(\Delta\Phi) = m \cdot \frac{\epsilon^2}{3}.$$

Table 2. Cryptanalysis of Secure Inner-Product Estimation Protocol

Attack Name	Description	Cryptographic Implications
Phase Manipulation	Server introduces a phase shift ϵ, biasing the aggregated phase Φ.	$\Phi' = \Phi + m\epsilon$. For $m = 100, \epsilon = 0.001$, $\Delta\Phi = 0.1$
Amplitude Manipulation	Server alters the amplitude distribution c_i of quantum states, favoring certain clients.	$\Phi' = \sum_{i=1}^{m} p_i\phi_i$, where $p_i \neq 1/m$. Example biases Φ' toward p_1
Gradient Inversion	Server reconstructs individual gradients $\nabla L_i(\theta)$ using partial knowledge of w_i.	$\nabla L_i(\theta) = \frac{\phi_i}{w_i}$. Isolation of ϕ_i enables gradient recovery
Quantum State Tomography	Adversary reconstructs $\|\psi_i\rangle = e^{i\phi_i}\|i\rangle$ using N identical copies.	Reconstruction error scales as $\epsilon \sim O(1/\sqrt{N})$. For $N = 10^6$, $\epsilon \sim 10^{-3}$
Quantum Channel Eavesdropping	Adversary intercepts $\|\psi_i\rangle$, introducing random noise η_i.	Bias $\Delta\Phi = \sum_{i=1}^{m} \eta_i$. Variance $\text{Var}(\Delta\Phi) = m \cdot \pi^2/3$
Side-Channel Attack	Exploits hardware noise (e.g., photon leakage) to infer ϕ_i.	Observed phase: $\phi_i^{\text{obs}} = \phi_i + \delta_i$. Variance $\text{Var}(\phi_i^{\text{obs}}) = \frac{\sigma^2}{N}$
Differential Phase Attack	Perturbs ϕ_i with controlled noise δ_i.	Variance $\text{Var}(\Delta\Phi) = m \cdot \epsilon^2/3$, where $\delta_i \sim \mathcal{U}(-\epsilon, \epsilon)$.

3 Incremental Learning Protocol

3.1 Protocol Summary

This protocol uses global entanglement through GHZ states. Each client encodes its gradient $\nabla L_i(\theta)$ into the phase of the entangled state:

$$|\psi\rangle = \frac{1}{\sqrt{2}} \left(|0\rangle^{\otimes m+1} + e^{i\Phi}|1\rangle^{\otimes m+1}\right), \tag{10}$$

where $\Phi = \sum_{i=1}^{m} w_i \nabla L_i(\theta)$.

Equation 10 defines the entangled GHZ quantum state used to encode the collective phase across all clients participating in the incremental learning protocol.

3.2 Potential Attacks

Attack 1: Entanglement Manipulation
A malicious server entangles only a subset $\mathcal{S} \subseteq \{1, \ldots, m\}$, excluding others. The modified state is:

$$|\psi'\rangle = \frac{1}{\sqrt{2}} \left(|0\rangle^{\otimes|\mathcal{S}|} + e^{i\Phi_{\mathcal{S}}} |1\rangle^{\otimes|\mathcal{S}|} \right),$$

where $\Phi_{\mathcal{S}} = \sum_{i \in \mathcal{S}} w_i \nabla L_i(\theta)$.

Attack 2: Malicious Client Contribution
A dishonest client C_k injects noise η_k into its gradient:

$$\nabla L'_k(\theta) = \nabla L_k(\theta) + \eta_k.$$

The aggregated phase becomes:

$$\Phi' = \Phi + w_k \eta_k.$$

If $\eta_k \sim \mathcal{N}(0, \sigma^2)$, the variance of Φ' is:

$$\mathrm{Var}(\Phi') = \mathrm{Var}(\Phi) + w_k^2 \sigma^2.$$

Attack 3: Entanglement Leakage Attack
Description
The adversary exploits partial measurement of the globally entangled GHZ state:

$$|\psi\rangle = \frac{1}{\sqrt{2}} \left(|0\rangle^{\otimes(m+1)} + e^{i\Phi} |1\rangle^{\otimes(m+1)} \right),$$

where $\Phi = \sum_{i=1}^{m} w_i \nabla L_i(\theta)$.

Attack Strategy

1. The server (or adversary) measures k qubits in the computational basis ($|0\rangle$ or $|1\rangle$).
2. The GHZ state collapses, reducing coherence in the remaining $(m - k + 1)$ qubits.

Mathematical Impact
Post-measurement, the quantum state becomes:

$$|\psi'\rangle = \frac{1}{\sqrt{2}}\left(|0\rangle^{\otimes(m-k+1)} + e^{i\Phi}|1\rangle^{\otimes(m-k+1)}\right). \tag{11}$$

The adversary can approximate:

$$\Phi_k = \sum_{i=1}^{k} w_i \nabla L_i(\theta),$$

leaking partial gradient information.

As illustrated in Eq. 11, partial measurement of the GHZ state reduces the entanglement, resulting in a collapsed quantum state with diminished coherence.

Attack 4: Quantum Denial-of-Service (DoS) Attack
Description
An adversary disrupts quantum communication by injecting noise into transmitted quantum states.

1. The adversary introduces random quantum states:

$$|\psi_{\text{noise}}\rangle = \sum_{j=1}^{n} c_j e^{i\phi_j}|j\rangle,$$

where c_j and ϕ_j are randomly generated.
2. These states combine with legitimate client states, corrupting the aggregated phase.

Mathematical Analysis
The combined state is:

$$|\psi'\rangle = |\psi\rangle + |\psi_{\text{noise}}\rangle.$$

The corrupted aggregated phase becomes:

$$\Phi' = \Phi + \sum_{j=1}^{n} c_j \phi_j.$$

For $n \gg m$, noise dominates, rendering Φ' unreliable.

Attack:5 Replay Attack
Description
An adversary reuses previously captured quantum states $|\psi_i\rangle$ to mislead the server.

1. The adversary intercepts $|\psi_i\rangle = e^{i\phi_i}|i\rangle$ during a valid session.
2. The adversary resends $|\psi_i\rangle$ multiple times to amplify ϕ_i's contribution.

Mathematical Analysis
If $|\psi_i\rangle$ is replayed k times, the aggregated phase becomes:

$$\Phi' = \Phi + (k-1)\phi_i. \tag{12}$$

For $k = 5$, the contribution of ϕ_i is amplified by 400%, skewing the gradient. Equation 12 demonstrates how replaying a captured quantum state multiple times amplifies the contribution of a single client's phase to the aggregated value (Table 3).

Table 3. Cryptanalysis of Incremental Learning Protocol

Attack Name	Description	Cryptographic Implications
Entanglement Manipulation	Server reduces entanglement to a subset $\mathcal{S} \subseteq \{1, \ldots, m\}$, leaking partial gradients.	Reduced state: $|\psi'\rangle = \frac{1}{\sqrt{2}}\left(|0\rangle^{\otimes|\mathcal{S}|} + e^{i\Phi_\mathcal{S}}|1\rangle^{\otimes|\mathcal{S}|}\right)$
Malicious Client Contribution	Client injects noise η_k into $\nabla L_k(\theta)$, biasing Φ.	Aggregated phase: $\Phi' = \Phi + w_k\eta_k$. Variance: $\mathrm{Var}(\Phi') = \mathrm{Var}(\Phi) + w_k^2\sigma^2$
Entanglement Leakage	Server measures k qubits in GHZ state, collapsing entanglement and leaking partial gradients.	Post-measurement state: $|\psi'\rangle = \frac{1}{\sqrt{2}}\left(|0\rangle^{\otimes(m-k+1)} + e^{i\Phi}|1\rangle^{\otimes(m-k+1)}\right)$
Quantum Denial-of-Service	Adversary injects random quantum states $|\psi_{\text{noise}}\rangle$ to corrupt aggregation.	Corrupted phase: $\Phi' = \Phi + \sum_{j=1}^{n} c_j\phi_j$. For $n \gg m$, noise dominates
Replay Attack	Adversary reuses $|\psi_i\rangle$ to amplify ϕ_i, skewing Φ.	Amplified phase: $\Phi' = \Phi + (k-1)\phi_i$. For $k = 5$, ϕ_i's contribution increases by 400%.

4 Countermeasures for Cryptanalysis of Privacy-Preserving Quantum Federated Learning Protocols

4.1 Secure Inner-Product Estimation Protocol

4.1.1 Phase Manipulation

Problem: An adversary introduces a phase shift ϵ, biasing the aggregated phase:

$$\Phi' = \Phi + m\epsilon.$$

Countermeasure: *Random Phase Padding*
Each client C_i adds a random padding $\eta_i \sim \mathcal{U}(-\pi, \pi)$:

$$\phi_i' = \phi_i + \eta_i, \quad \phi_i = w_i \nabla L_i(\theta).$$

The server corrects the aggregated phase:

$$\Phi_{\text{corrected}} = \Phi' - \sum_{i=1}^{m} \eta_i.$$

4.1.2 1.2 Amplitude Manipulation

Problem: The server modifies the amplitude c_i of quantum states:

$$|\psi\rangle = \sum_{i=1}^{m} c_i e^{i\phi_i}|i\rangle, \quad c_i = \sqrt{p_i}, \sum_{i=1}^{m} p_i = 1.$$

Countermeasure: *Quantum State Authentication*
Clients encode ϕ_i into authenticated quantum states:

$$|\psi_i\rangle_{\text{auth}} = |\psi_i\rangle \otimes |H(\phi_i)\rangle, \tag{13}$$

where $H(\phi_i)$ is the hash of ϕ_i. Tampering with c_i is detected during verification. Equation 13 describes the construction of an authenticated quantum state by appending a cryptographic hash, thereby enabling integrity verification.

4.1.3 Gradient Inversion

Problem: The server computes $\nabla L_i(\theta)$ by isolating ϕ_i:

$$\nabla L_i(\theta) = \frac{\phi_i}{w_i}.$$

Countermeasure: *Obfuscation of Gradients*

Clients introduce noise $\epsilon_i \sim \mathcal{N}(0, \sigma^2)$:

$$\phi_i' = w_i(\nabla L_i(\theta) + \epsilon_i).$$

The aggregated phase becomes:

$$\Phi' = \Phi + \sum_{i=1}^{m} w_i \epsilon_i.$$

The noise is removed during verification.

4.1.4 Quantum State Tomography

Problem: An adversary reconstructs $|\psi_i\rangle = e^{i\phi_i}|i\rangle$ using multiple copies.

Countermeasure: *State Redundancy*
Each client encodes ϕ_i into r redundant states:

$$|\psi_i\rangle = \bigotimes_{k=1}^{r} e^{i\phi_i}|k\rangle.$$

Partial tampering does not reveal ϕ_i.

4.1.5 Quantum Channel Eavesdropping

Problem: An adversary intercepts $|\psi_i\rangle$ and introduces noise η_i:

$$\Delta\Phi = \sum_{i=1}^{m} \eta_i.$$

Countermeasure: *Quantum Key Distribution (QKD)*
Secure quantum channels using QKD protocols. An interception collapses the quantum state:

$$|\psi_i\rangle \to |i\rangle.$$

4.1.6 Differential Phase Attack

Problem: The adversary perturbs ϕ_i with $\delta_i \sim \mathcal{U}(-\epsilon, \epsilon)$:

$$\Phi' = \Phi + \sum_{i=1}^{m} \delta_i.$$

Countermeasure: *Phase Randomization*
Encode ϕ_i as a time-dependent function:

$$\phi_i' = f(\phi_i, t), \quad f(\phi_i, t) = \phi_i + H(t), \tag{14}$$

where $H(t)$ is a hash of the timestamp t. According to Eq. 14, incorporating a timestamp-dependent hash into the phase encoding mitigates replay attacks by rendering outdated states invalid.

5 Incremental Learning Protocol

5.1 Entanglement Manipulation

Problem: The server reduces entanglement to a subset $\mathcal{S}$:

$$|\psi'\rangle = \frac{1}{\sqrt{2}}\left(|0\rangle^{\otimes|\mathcal{S}|} + e^{i\Phi_{\mathcal{S}}}|1\rangle^{\otimes|\mathcal{S}|}\right).$$

Countermeasure: *Entanglement Witness Verification*
Verify the GHZ state using:

$$W = I - |\psi\rangle\langle\psi|,$$

where $|\psi\rangle$ is the expected GHZ state.

5.2 Malicious Client Contribution

Problem: A client injects noise η_k into $\nabla L_k(\theta)$:

$$\Phi' = \Phi + w_k \eta_k.$$

Countermeasure: *Zero-Knowledge Proofs*
Clients provide a zero-knowledge proof to verify:

$$\nabla L_k(\theta) \in \mathcal{V},$$

where $\mathcal{V}$ is the set of valid gradients.

5.3 Quantum Denial-of-Service (DoS)

Problem: An adversary injects noise states $|\psi_{\text{noise}}\rangle$:

$$|\psi'\rangle = |\psi\rangle + |\psi_{\text{noise}}\rangle.$$

Countermeasure: *Decoy State Insertion*
Insert decoy states $|\psi_{\text{decoy}}\rangle = |+\rangle$:

$$|\psi_{\text{decoy}}\rangle = \frac{1}{\sqrt{2}}(|0\rangle + |1\rangle).$$

Detect tampering by testing fidelity:

$$F = \langle\psi_{\text{expected}}|\psi_{\text{received}}\rangle.$$

5.4 Replay Attack

Problem: The adversary reuses $|\psi_i\rangle$, amplifying ϕ_i:

$$\Phi' = \Phi + (k-1)\phi_i.$$

Countermeasure: *Time-Stamped Encoding*
Encode each quantum state with a timestamp t:

$$|\psi_i\rangle = e^{i(\phi_i + t)}|i\rangle.$$

Outdated states are invalid if $t < t_{\text{current}}$.

6 Conclusion

In this work, we performed an in-depth cryptanalysis of the protocols proposed in *"Privacy-preserving quantum federated learning via gradient hiding"*, evaluating their security under various adversarial models. Our analysis focused on two protocols: the **Secure Inner-Product Estimation Protocol** and the **Incremental Learning Protocol**, each utilizing quantum states $|\psi\rangle$ to encode client gradients $\phi_i = w_i \nabla L_i(\theta)$, where w_i and $\nabla L_i(\theta)$ denote the client weight and gradient, respectively.

1. **Vulnerability to Phase Manipulation:** An adversary introducing a phase shift ϵ biases the aggregated phase:

$$\Phi' = \Phi + m\epsilon, \quad \Phi = \sum_{i=1}^{m} \phi_i.$$

2. **Amplitude Manipulation and Gradient Inversion:** The server's manipulation of quantum states $|\psi\rangle = \sum_{i=1}^{m} c_i e^{i\phi_i}|i\rangle$ results in biased aggregation Φ'. Additionally, the server can isolate ϕ_i using:

$$\nabla L_i(\theta) = \frac{\phi_i}{w_i}.$$

3. **Quantum State Tomography and Side-Channel Exploitation:** By reconstructing quantum states $|\psi_i\rangle = e^{i\phi_i}|i\rangle$ or leveraging noise δ_i, an adversary can infer private information:

$$\phi_i^{\text{obs}} = \phi_i + \delta_i, \quad \delta_i \sim \mathcal{N}(0, \sigma^2).$$

4. **Entanglement Manipulation in GHZ States:** Partial measurement of entangled states $|\psi\rangle = \frac{1}{\sqrt{2}}\left(|0\rangle^{\otimes m+1} + e^{i\Phi}|1\rangle^{\otimes m+1}\right)$ leaks:

$$\Phi_{\mathcal{S}} = \sum_{i \in \mathcal{S}} \phi_i, \quad \mathcal{S} \subseteq \{1, \ldots, m\}.$$

5. **Replay Attacks and DoS Vulnerabilities:** Adversaries amplifying ϕ_i via replays or injecting noise states $|\psi_{\text{noise}}\rangle$ disrupt the aggregation:

$$\Phi' = \Phi + (k-1)\phi_i, \quad \text{or} \quad \Phi' = \Phi + \sum_{j=1}^{n} c_j \phi_j.$$

Our cryptanalysis demonstrates that the proposed protocols, while leveraging quantum properties for gradient encoding and aggregation, remain vulnerable to adversarial actions under certain conditions. These vulnerabilities directly compromise: **1. Privacy of $\nabla L_i(\theta)$:** The inference of gradients ϕ_i reveals private client data. **2. Integrity of Φ:** Biases in the aggregated phase Φ lead to inaccurate global model updates:

$$\theta^{(t+1)} = \theta^{(t)} - \eta\Phi,$$

where η is the learning rate.

To address these vulnerabilities, we proposed countermeasures such as random phase padding $\phi_i' = \phi_i + \eta_i$, authenticated quantum states $|\psi_{\text{auth}}\rangle = |\psi\rangle \otimes |H(\phi_i)\rangle$, and timestamped encoding $\phi_i' = \phi_i + H(t)$. These solutions, rigorously evaluated, provide enhanced security against phase manipulation, gradient inversion, entanglement leakage, and replay attacks. Future work should explore scalable implementations of these countermeasures, ensuring the robustness of quantum federated learning protocols as $m \to \infty$.

6.1 Prospective Experimental Validation

This study presents a rigorous cryptographic analysis of gradient-hiding quantum federated learning protocols without incorporating empirical simulation results. In future work, the attack scenarios and mitigation techniques delineated herein could be systematically validated using quantum circuit simulation environments, including Qiskit, Cirq, and PyQuil. These platforms facilitate the emulation of quantum phase encoding, aggregation, and entanglement mechanisms under controlled parameters. By configuring simulated adversarial modules capable of injecting calibrated phase distortions, executing partial measurements, or orchestrating replay attacks, researchers can empirically assess the practical impact of each threat vector. Furthermore, countermeasures such as random phase obfuscation, authenticated state encoding, and temporal binding can be benchmarked by quantifying reconstruction fidelity, error rates, and convergence deviations across iterative simulation runs. This experimental validation framework would complement the formal proofs and reinforce confidence in the protocol's resilience under realistic deployment conditions.

References

1. Li, C., Zhang, Y., Wang, X., Li, Y., Li, Z.: Privacy-preserving quantum federated learning via gradient hiding. Quantum Sci. Technol. **9**(3), 035028 (2024). https://doi.org/10.1088/2058-9565/acf84e
2. Shor, P.W.: Polynomial-time algorithms for prime factorization and discrete logarithms on a quantum computer. SIAM J. Comput. **26**(5), 1484–1509 (1997). https://doi.org/10.1137/S0097539795293172
3. Nielsen, M.A., Chuang, I.L.: Quantum Computation and Quantum Information, 10th edn. Cambridge University Press, Cambridge (2010)
4. Bennett, C.H., Brassard, G.: Quantum cryptography: public key distribution and coin tossing. In: Proceedings of IEEE International Conference on Computers, Systems, and Signal Processing, Bangalore, India, pp. 175–179 (1984)
5. Lo, H.-K., Curty, M., Qi, B.: Measurement-device-independent quantum key distribution. Phys. Rev. Lett. **108**(13), 130503 (2012). https://doi.org/10.1103/PhysRevLett.108.130503
6. Preskill, J.: Quantum computing in the NISQ era and beyond. Quantum **2**, 79 (2018). https://doi.org/10.22331/q-2018-08-06-79

7. Dunjko, T., Briegel, H.J.: Machine learning and artificial intelligence in the quantum domain: a review of recent progress. Rep. Prog. Phys. **81**(7), 074001 (2018). https://doi.org/10.1088/1361-6633/aab406
8. Gottesman, D.: Stabilizer codes and quantum error correction. Ph.D. dissertation, California Institute of Technology, Pasadena, CA, USA (1997). arXiv:quant-ph/9705052

A Systematic Mapping Study on Toolchain Support for Quantum Computing as a Service

Maryam Tavassoli Sabzevari(✉)

M3S Research Unit, University of Oulu, 90014 Oulu, Finland
maryam.tavassolisabzevari@oulu.fi

Abstract. Context: Quantum computing (QC) is reshaping multiple disciplines by enabling computational capabilities that surpass those of classical systems. However, realizing QC's potential requires not only access to quantum hardware but also significant domain expertise. Platforms, libraries, and frameworks that offer Quantum Computing as a Service (QCaaS) aim to overcome these barriers by abstracting quantum-specific complexities and enhancing accessibility for a broader range of users.

Motivation: The rapid growth of QCaaS platforms and tools underscores the need for a structured and comprehensive understanding of their design properties, functional capabilities, and practical limitations. Critical aspects such as scalability, usability, and maintainability require systematic investigation to support evidence-based decision-making and to guide the development of more effective and sustainable QCaaS ecosystems.

Aim: This paper presents preliminary findings from an ongoing systematic mapping study (SMS) that aims to identify, categorize, and synthesize existing toolchains supporting QCaaS. Nine tools were analyzed, selected through a structured search strategy applied across five major digital libraries. These tools were evaluated based on five key characteristics: source code availability, input type, output type, level of automation, and type of evaluation. Results indicate that most tools are open source, support high-level input formats, produce simulated outputs, employ semi-automated processes, and are evaluated through explicit empirical methods. These findings offer an early yet insightful overview of the QCaaS tooling landscape and establish a foundation for further analysis. The extended version of this study will additionally examine architectural concerns (e.g., core components, design principles) and the key challenges involved in the adoption and integration of QCaaS toolchains.

Keywords: Quantum computing · Quantum computing as a service · Quantum service · Quantum framework · Quantum tool · Quantum library · Quantum toolchain

S. Hussain et al. (Eds.): SEET 2025, CCIS 2725, pp. 500–516, 2026.
https://doi.org/10.1007/978-3-032-08977-9_31

1 Introduction

Quantum computing (QC) is increasingly recognized as a transformative technology with promising applications across diverse domains, including cybersecurity, robotics, finance, and healthcare. Its potential has also been demonstrated in emerging areas such as agriculture and environmental science [2]. This growing relevance has captured substantial industrial interest, with leading technology firms, such as IBM [9], Google [6], and Microsoft [14], investing heavily in QC research and development. In parallel, major governmental initiatives, most notably the European Quantum Technologies Flagship, have been launched to accelerate quantum advancement and adoption[1].

As with classical computing, there is a critical need for robust quantum software systems to operationalize quantum hardware and fully exploit the potential of quantum information processing [11]. However, quantum software development introduces unique complexities arising from quantum mechanical phenomena such as superposition and entanglement [8]. To address these challenges, the emerging discipline of quantum software engineering (QSE) [23,24,30] aims to adapt conventional software engineering practices for quantum application development. Despite its promise, QSE faces several barriers, including the inherent difficulty of quantum programming and the continued reliance on classical servers for quantum circuit compilation, largely due to the lack of quantum data storage technologies [16].

To mitigate these challenges, an increasing number of platforms and frameworks now offer quantum resources via Quantum Computing as a Service (QCaaS). QCaaS facilitates access to quantum computing by abstracting hardware complexities and delivering services that lower the technical barrier for developers and researchers.

Although QCaaS has gained considerable momentum, systematic analyses of the toolchains and frameworks providing it remain limited. Gaining a structured understanding of their architectural principles, functional capabilities, and usage-related challenges is critical to advancing QCaaS development and enabling its integration into QSE practices.

Specifically, the extended version of this study first provides an overview of how current toolchains and their architectural designs abstract quantum-specific complexities—particularly superposition collapse and entanglement correlations—from the developer's perspective [7]. Second, it identifies architectural, usability, scalability, and security limitations that continue to hinder broader adoption of QCaaS [15].

This paper reports preliminary findings from a systematic mapping study (SMS) of QCaaS toolchains. We examine nine representative tools and frameworks, analyzing their source code availability, input and output types, automation levels, and evaluation strategies in relation to Research Question 1 (RQ1). The SMS follows the five-stage methodology proposed by Petersen et al. [22], comprising planning, study identification, data extraction, data analysis, and

[1] https://tinyurl.com/mr4bxmv5.

results reporting. In this paper, we detail the SMS schema and present early insights obtained through the analysis of the nine selected toolchains.

In future work, through an extended systematic mapping study, we aim to address all three research questions (RQ1, RQ1.1, and RQ2) by broadening our analysis beyond the preliminary findings presented in this paper. The extended study will explore architectural aspects—such as design principles; core and management components; support for quantum application development; enterprise backend integration; scalability; security; telemetry; vendor agnosticism; and user interfaces—as well as the practical challenges associated with the adoption and use of QCaaS tools. These efforts are intended to inform both the academic community and industry stakeholders in the design and deployment of next-generation QCaaS platforms.

2 Background

This section outlines the foundational concepts necessary to understand the context and scope of this study. The first subsection introduces the principles of quantum computing (QC), followed by an overview of Quantum Computing as a Service (QCaaS). The final subsection presents the key concepts and challenges of Quantum Software Engineering (QSE), which form the basis for this work.

2.1 Quantum Computing

The term *quantum* in "quantum computing" refers to the principles of quantum mechanics that enable systems to perform computationally intensive operations [17,30]. In physics, a quantum represents the smallest discrete unit of a physical property and typically refers to atomic or subatomic particles, such as electrons, neutrons, and photons. Quantum computing (QC) leverages these principles to process information and execute certain computational tasks at speeds that surpass those of conventional computing systems. Unlike classical computers, which evaluate possibilities sequentially, quantum computers can explore multiple possibilities simultaneously. QC is particularly well-suited for problems such as optimization, simulation, cryptography, data analysis, and molecular modeling [3,13,30].

The fundamental difference between classical and quantum computers lies in their basic unit of information. Classical computers operate on *bits*, which can represent either 0 or 1. In contrast, quantum computers utilize *qubits*, which can exist in a superposition of both states simultaneously. Mathematically, a qubit is expressed as:

$$|\psi\rangle = x|0\rangle + y|1\rangle \tag{1}$$

where $|\psi\rangle$ denotes the quantum state of the qubit, $|0\rangle$ and $|1\rangle$ are the computational basis states, and x and y are complex-valued probability amplitudes. This linear combination represents a superposition, allowing the qubit to exist in both states simultaneously until measurement collapses it to one. The amplitudes x and y must satisfy the normalization condition:

$$|x|^2 + |y|^2 = 1 \tag{2}$$

This condition ensures that the total probability of observing the qubit in either $|0\rangle$ or $|1\rangle$ upon measurement is equal to one.

Superposition is a defining feature of quantum mechanics and the foundation for quantum computational parallelism. For example, while a classical register of n bits can represent only one of 2^n possible states at a time, a quantum register with n qubits can exist in a superposition of all 2^n states simultaneously, enabling massively parallel computation.

Another key characteristic is *entanglement*, a phenomenon where two or more quantum systems become strongly correlated such that the state of one cannot be described independently of the others. Notably, entanglement is not constrained by physical distance: measurements on one entangled system can instantaneously influence the state of the other [30]. Together, superposition and entanglement empower quantum computers to solve particular classes of problems far more efficiently than their classical counterparts.

2.2 Quantum Computing as a Service

In the computing paradigm, an evolutionary model called Service-oriented Computing (SOC) uses services as the fundamental elements for computing and developing applications [20]. A key concept in SOC is Service-oriented Architecture (SOA), an architectural style in which business and IT systems are designed in terms of services with well-defined interfaces and outcomes. A service is a logical representation of a set of activities with specified outcomes, is self contained, and may be composed of other services. However, consumers of the service need not be aware of its internal structure [10].

In the quantum computing domain, companies providing quantum resources utilize this concept in a model known as Quantum Computing as a Service (QCaaS). This approach enables providers to offer quantum computing capabilities to a broader audience, democratizing access to quantum resources and fostering their adoption [15].

QCaaS platforms abstract the complexities of quantum hardware and deliver development environments, execution backends, and simulators as on-demand services. Examples include IBM Quantum Experience, Amazon Braket, and Azure Quantum. These platforms differ significantly in their supported quantum technologies, programming languages, and interaction models. This heterogeneity poses integration and usability challenges, especially for software engineers seeking to build reliable quantum applications. As such, a structured investigation of existing QCaaS platforms is needed to understand how they support software engineering tasks and contribute to the broader goals of quantum software development.

2.3 Quantum Software Engineering

The development of quantum applications presents unique challenges due to the fundamental physical and mathematical properties of quantum systems, including superposition, entanglement, state decoherence, measurement constraints, and low qubit fidelity [8]. To address these complexities, the field of Quantum Software Engineering (QSE) has emerged, aiming to adapt classical software engineering principles and practices to quantum software development [23,24,30].

A central theme in QSE is the design of hybrid architectures that integrate classical and quantum components [23,30]. In such architectures, computationally intensive tasks are offloaded to quantum processors, while classical systems handle orchestration and auxiliary tasks [25]. This division leverages the strengths of both paradigms: the robustness of classical computing and the exponential parallelism of quantum processing [27,28].

However, hybridization introduces new engineering challenges. Developers must address issues such as algorithm partitioning, classical–quantum communication, system integration, and the scalability of hybrid solutions [1,12,26]. These challenges call for both technical solutions and methodological frameworks tailored to the unique lifecycle of quantum software systems.

This study presents preliminary results from an investigation of nine tools and frameworks that deliver QCaaS, focusing on key characteristics such as source code availability, input and output formats, level of automation, and evaluation approaches. These findings partially address the existing gap in understanding QCaaS support for quantum software development. The future comprehensive systematic mapping study will explore the intersection of QCaaS and QSE by systematically classifying and analyzing these tools. Special attention will be given to their architectural characteristics, functional capabilities, and the challenges associated with their use, contributing to the design of more accessible, scalable, and effective quantum software platforms.

3 Related Work

This section reviews prior systematic mapping studies (SMS), systematic literature reviews (SLRs), and traditional reviews in the domains of quantum computing, quantum computing as a service (QCaaS), and quantum software engineering (QSE).

Several systematic studies have investigated quantum computing from various perspectives. Peral-García et al. [21] conducted an SLR on quantum machine learning algorithms published between 2017 and 2023, focusing on their classification and applications. However, their study primarily emphasized algorithmic aspects and did not consider QCaaS platforms or toolchains. Similarly, Gill et al. [5] proposed a taxonomy and systematic review of quantum computing literature, highlighting theoretical frameworks and open research challenges, but lacking a focus on practical QCaaS implementations. Khan et al. [11] explored quantum software architecture, covering design patterns and architectural processes. While relevant to QSE, their work does not explicitly address QCaaS tools or usability concerns.

Nimbe et al. [18] provided a systematic review of quantum computing models, analyzing their advantages and limitations without specific reference to QCaaS. Osaba et al. [19] examined the application of quantum computing in routing problems, offering a domain-specific perspective that did not consider broader toolchain or platform issues.

Despite the contributions of these studies, significant gaps remain in the literature concerning QCaaS. None of the reviewed works specifically investigate tools, frameworks, or platforms offering QCaaS capabilities, nor do they address cross-cutting concerns such as usability, scalability, or automation.

This systematic mapping study aims to partially address this gap by analyzing nine tools that deliver QCaaS. We identify their key characteristics, including source code availability, input and output types, automation level, and evaluation approach. In future work, we will extend this analysis into a comprehensive mapping study focused on architectural elements, functional capabilities, and the engineering challenges of QCaaS platforms. Our goal is to provide actionable insights to support the development of more usable, scalable, and effective QCaaS ecosystems.

4 Research Method

This study adopts a Systematic Mapping Study (SMS) methodology, following the guidelines proposed by Petersen et al. [22], as illustrated in Fig. 1. SMS was selected over Multivocal Literature Reviews (MLRs) due to its exclusive reliance on peer-reviewed literature, which ensures methodological rigor and reliability in identifying and analyzing tools and frameworks for Quantum Computing as a Service (QCaaS). Although MLRs incorporate grey literature and may offer broader contextual insights, the rapidly evolving and academically driven nature of quantum computing necessitates a focus on validated and foundational studies. This decision is further supported by the fact that quantum computing research is primarily disseminated through scholarly publications.

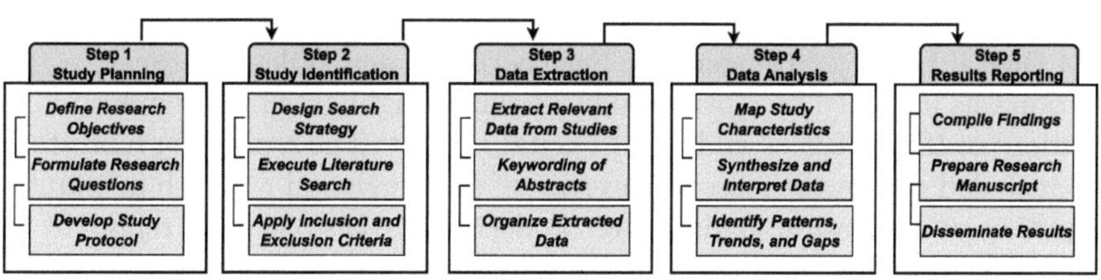

Fig. 1. The research methodology

4.1 Study Planning

The first phase of planning involved defining the research objectives. This SMS aims to present preliminary findings from the analysis of toolchains that deliver QCaaS, with a specific focus on their structural and design-related characteristics. In subsequent work, we intend to conduct a comprehensive SMS that will investigate in greater depth the architectural features and challenges associated with QCaaS toolchains. The findings from both phases aim to support researchers and developers in more effectively leveraging quantum computing resources and addressing limitations in current toolchain designs.

The second planning phase involved formulating research questions aligned with the objectives of both the preliminary and future comprehensive studies. Table 1 presents the research questions along with their corresponding rationale.

Table 1. Research questions of this SMS and their rationale.

RQ	Research Question	Rationale
RQ1	What are the existing tools and frameworks that support quantum computing as a service?	To identify the tools and frameworks enabling QCaaS, focusing on their availability, usage, and purpose. This will provide a comprehensive understanding of the diversity and scope of existing solutions, helping to situate their role within the field of quantum computing
RQ1.1	What are the technical features and implementations of the identified tools and frameworks?	To explore the technical aspects, such as design and architecture, of the identified QCaaS tools and frameworks in detail
RQ2	What challenges are associated with the use of available QCaaS tools and frameworks?	To identify and analyze the key challenges and limitations of adopting QCaaS, providing insights for improving toolchains and addressing research gaps

The final planning phase focused on developing the study protocol, which defined the search strategy, inclusion and exclusion criteria, and the data extraction process.

4.2 Study Identification

The literature search was conducted across five major repositories: IEEE Xplore, ACM Digital Library, SpringerLink, ScienceDirect, and Wiley InterScience. This selection was informed by a prior study [4], which highlighted the significant contributions of IEEE Xplore and ACM Digital Library. The remaining repositories were included due to their broad coverage of peer-reviewed research in quantum computing and software engineering. Collectively, these sources represent the primary venues where studies on QCaaS are most likely to appear.

The search strings were designed to align with the objectives of both the current study and its subsequent extended phase. Core terms such as "quantum computing" and "service*" were included in all queries, with synonyms like "as a service" used to broaden coverage. Additional keywords—"tools," "frameworks," "open source," and "challenges"—were added to capture studies relevant to tool support and usage-related concerns. A complementary string also included the term "software" to further refine the scope. Together, these strings support the identification of literature relevant to RQ1 (tools and frameworks) and RQ2 (usage challenges). Table 2 provides the exact search strings applied across the selected repositories.

Table 2. Search strings used in this systematic mapping study.

#	Search String
1	(quantum computing) AND (service* OR "as a service") AND (tool* OR framework* OR "open source" OR "challenge*")
2	(quantum computing) AND (software) AND (service* OR "as a service") AND (tool* OR framework* OR "open source")

Inclusion and Exclusion Criteria. The inclusion and exclusion criteria were developed in accordance with the guidelines of Petersen et al. [22] and adapted to meet the specific objectives of this study. As outlined in Table 3, these criteria were designed to ensure the selection of high-quality, relevant, and primary research. In particular, the focus is on peer-reviewed studies that discuss toolchains enabling QCaaS or examine the challenges associated with their adoption and use.

Table 3. Criteria for screening and qualitative assessment of selected studies with justifications.

Criteria	Justification
S1 – The study does not discuss any solution or proposal for quantum computing as a service	To ensure that the study focuses on QCaaS-related tools and frameworks rather than unrelated topics
S2 – The study is not reported in English	Non-English studies are excluded to ensure consistent and reliable analysis, as language barriers may hinder accurate interpretation
S3 – The study is a duplicate study. Duplicate studies are studies with overlapping contents, e.g., a conference paper extended as a journal article	To avoid redundancy and ensure only the most complete and detailed version of a study is included
S4 – The study is a secondary study/survey paper	Secondary studies are excluded to focus on primary contributions, ensuring originality in the findings
Q1 – Study objectives and contributions are clear	Clear objectives and contributions indicate the study's relevance and value to the SMS
Q2 – Research method to conduct the study is reported	A well-reported method ensures the study's validity and reproducibility
Q3 – Design and/or implementation details of the solution are provided	Design and implementation details are critical for understanding the functionality of tools and frameworks
Q4 – Study limitations and needs for future research are discussed	Discussion of limitations and future research needs demonstrates the study's depth and contribution to the field

4.3 Data Extraction

Data extraction was carried out to systematically collect structured characteristics from the selected primary studies, particularly those describing tools and frameworks developed for QCaaS. These characteristics align with the objectives of RQ1, which focuses on the features of such tools and frameworks.

To enhance consistency and reduce manual effort, a large language model (GPT) was used to assist with both the initial data extraction and subsequent categorization. The results were thoroughly reviewed and validated by the authors to ensure reliability. This semi-automated approach—combining machine-assisted processing with human oversight—enhances methodological transparency and supports reproducibility.

The extracted features are organized to address each of the research questions. This paper focuses on RQ1, while RQ1.1 and RQ2 will be addressed in the forthcoming comprehensive SMS.

Existing Tools and Frameworks Overview (RQ1). For each identified toolchain that provides QCaaS, detailed information is extracted to build a structured understanding of its core characteristics. The extracted features include general information—namely, the name of the tool and its stated purpose—which provides contextual insight into the tool's scope, target users, and functionality. The source type is classified as either open-source (OS) or closed-source (CS), indicating the level of accessibility and modifiability. Open-source tools grant users permission to study, modify, and reuse the code, while closed-source tools restrict access to the underlying implementation.

The input instruction type refers to the format of instructions the tool accepts for executing logic. Input types include high-level (HL) instructions, which offer abstraction and ease of use; quantum instructions (QI), which directly define quantum circuits at a lower level; and mathematical variables (MV), where inputs are specified using symbolic or algebraic representations.

Output types describe the kinds of results generated by the tool, including quantum source code (QSC), quantum algorithms (QA), and simulation findings (SF). In addition, some tools provide performance metrics such as gate fidelity and error rates, as well as operational indicators like system health reports and usage logs.

The automation level captures the extent to which manual intervention is reduced during operation, with tools categorized as fully automated (FA), semi-automated (SA), or non-automated (NA). Finally, the evaluation type indicates whether the tool has undergone performance validation, distinguishing between explicit evaluation (EX), which involves complete and systematic benchmarking or testing, and implicit evaluation (IM), which refers to informal or partial assessments.

These elements form the basis for a structured classification and comparison of QCaaS toolchains, directly supporting the objectives of RQ1.

Technical Features and Implementations (RQ1.1). To analyze the internal structure and technical design of each identified QCaaS toolchain, a set of architectural and development characteristics will be extracted in the subsequent phase of this study. These include design principles, which refer to the foundational software engineering strategies guiding the toolchain's architecture, and technological foundations, which encompass the tools, frameworks, programming languages, development methodologies, and libraries employed during implementation.

Architectural features will also be analyzed to understand how each toolchain is organized and operates, as well as how its components interact. This includes identifying a core or backbone component responsible for coordinating communication between modules and serving as a central integration point. In addition, the manager component will be examined as the unit that orchestrates the execution and deployment of quantum applications. The degree of support for quantum application development will be assessed, including the availability of debugging tools, test environments, or simulation frameworks.

Further elements of interest include integration capabilities with enterprise backends—such as cloud orchestration, asynchronous processing, load balancing, and high availability—as well as built-in mechanisms for security and scalability to ensure safe and efficient operation under varying workloads. The availability of telemetry systems will also be reviewed to evaluate runtime monitoring and compatibility with both quantum hardware and simulators.

The study will examine whether the platform provides a vendor-agnostic abstraction layer to support interoperability across different quantum providers by translating workflows or source code between backend technologies. Finally, user interface and dashboard functionalities will be evaluated to determine the extent of visual support available for managing tasks, configuring workflows, and interpreting results.

These elements will collectively provide a robust basis for characterizing the technical architecture of QCaaS toolchains and will enable a meaningful comparison across different implementations.

Challenges (RQ2). In the forthcoming systematic mapping study, we will extract and analyze evidence from selected primary studies to investigate the challenges associated with the use of QCaaS tools and frameworks. These challenges will be categorized to reveal recurring barriers and constraints documented in the literature.

The identified challenges may relate to adoption, implementation, or practical usage. Common issues may include usability limitations, performance bottlenecks—such as execution latency or reliability concerns—and restricted access to quantum hardware or limited system stability. These challenges will be systematically extracted, coded, and grouped thematically to enable a comprehensive understanding of the obstacles currently limiting the effectiveness and scalability of QCaaS toolchains.

4.4 Data Analysis

The data analysis phase involves synthesizing the extracted information to derive meaningful insights. Frequency analysis is used to summarize the distribution of tool features and evaluation characteristics. These statistics provide a quantitative overview of the QCaaS research landscape and support the identification of broader trends.

5 Results and Discussion

This section presents the results of analyzing nine tools to address the first research question regarding the key features of existing QCaaS tools and frameworks. The remaining two research questions, which explore architectural characteristics and challenges associated with tool usage, will be addressed in future work as part of a comprehensive SMS.

5.1 Existing Tools and Frameworks Overview (RQ1)

Before completing the final analysis of the dataset, a preliminary review of the currently selected studies was conducted to further emphasize the necessity of this mapping study.

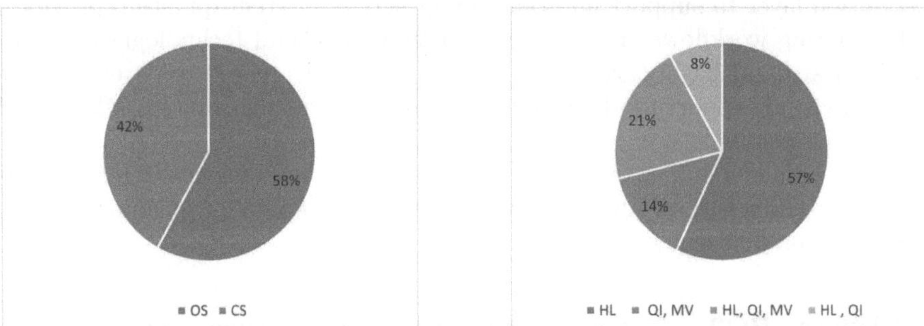

(a) Source type (b) Input

Fig. 2. Source type and input support

In terms of general features observed thus far, as illustrated in Fig. 2, the majority of the currently available toolchains are open-source, enabling users, particularly researchers, to contribute to ongoing advancements in the field. Three types of input are observed across the tools: high-level (HL) instructions, quantum instructions (QI), and mathematical variables (MV). More than half of the tools accept high-level input, allowing developers to interact with quantum computing systems with relatively minimal effort.

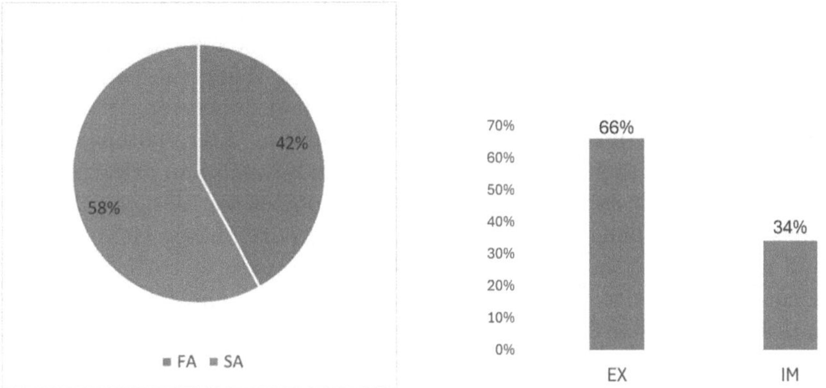

(a) Automation level (b) Evaluation type

Fig. 3. Automation level and evaluation type of QCaaS tools

However, as shown in Fig. 3, less than half of the analyzed toolchains offer full automation versus semi-automation, which may pose limitations for usability and broader adoption. On a more promising note, 66% of the tools have undergone explicit evaluation, suggesting increasing maturity in performance assessment practices. Regarding tool outputs, simulation findings appear most frequently, followed by quantum source code, as shown in Fig. 4. This indicates a strong focus on virtual experimentation and quantum program generation in current QCaaS toolchains.

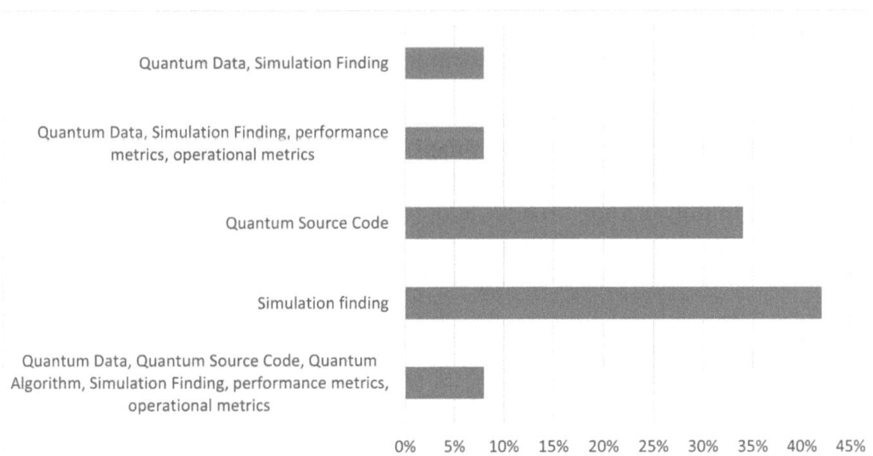

Fig. 4. Output types among analyzed QCaaS tools

These early insights underscore the need for a structured and comprehensive mapping effort. The final dataset will be used to validate and expand upon these observations during the formal analysis phase. While the current stage focuses on descriptive categorization across individual dimensions, it does not yet incorporate comparative analysis, such as evaluating interrelations between input formats, output types, automation levels, and evaluation strategies. Furthermore, an in-depth examination of toolchain objectives, design principles, and usage-related challenges is also deferred to the next phase. These comparative and architectural analyses may reveal systemic gaps or correlations that can inform more effective toolchain design and selection. These aspects will be systematically addressed through RQ1.1 and RQ2 in the extended study.

6 Expected Contributions and Implications

This study provides a preliminary analysis of the design and distinguishing features of platforms, libraries, and toolkits that offer Quantum Computing as a Service (QCaaS). While the current results focus on general toolchain characteristics, future work will extend this study into a comprehensive SMS that includes architectural aspects and challenges associated with QCaaS adoption and implementation.

The findings are expected to support two primary audiences:

- **Researchers and developers:** The results may inform the design, evaluation, and enhancement of QCaaS toolchains by offering an evidence-based overview of currently available solutions within the quantum software engineering domain.
- **Practitioners and end-users:** The synthesized findings may guide more informed decisions when selecting QCaaS platforms, especially in relation to technical needs, development constraints, and usability goals.

By systematically organizing the QCaaS toolchain landscape, this study aims to contribute to the advancement of quantum software engineering. The preliminary results promote better alignment between toolchain developers and users and lay the groundwork for broader adoption of QCaaS platforms.

The full contributions and implications of this research will be established through the final version of the systematic mapping study.

7 Threats to Validity

According to Wohlin et al. [29], threats to validity may arise throughout the review process and can impact the overall reliability of a study. This section outlines two key types of validity threats—construct validity and internal validity—and describes the strategies employed to minimize their influence.

Construct Validity Construct validity relates to how well the study design reflects the concepts it intends to investigate. In this study, potential threats include the incompleteness of search strings, the varying types of platforms or tools offering quantum computing as a service, and the potential impact of these issues on study identification.

To mitigate these risks, we expanded our search strategy to include synonyms for "service," such as "as a service", and various expressions representing toolchains, including "framework" and "open source." These additions broadened the search scope and enriched the dataset. Furthermore, the application of clearly defined inclusion and exclusion criteria, combined with a structured three-stage screening process (title, abstract, and full-text), enhanced both the precision and consistency of the study selection process.

Internal Validity Several potential threats to internal validity were identified and addressed in this study. One major concern was data extraction consistency, which was mitigated through the use of standardized data extraction forms to ensure uniformity across all reviewed studies. Researcher bias was also considered; this was addressed by implementing predefined protocols throughout the study selection and extraction phases.

To minimize selection bias, we utilized multiple scientific databases and designed the search strategy to ensure broad and comprehensive coverage. In addition, we considered the risk of publication bias, wherein studies reporting significant or positive results are more likely to be published than those with null or negative outcomes. To counter this, we carefully reviewed all included studies, regardless of outcome, to reduce the potential impact of such bias.

Regarding the potential inadequacy in the volume of primary studies, we broadened the scope to include relevant book chapters and articles available in public archives, which were identified via Google Scholar. To further ensure methodological reliability, four researchers independently reviewed the selected studies to confirm their alignment with the predefined study protocol.

8 Conclusion and Future Work

This study reports the preliminary results of a systematic mapping study focused on tools, frameworks, and platforms that provide Quantum Computing as a Service (QCaaS). Based on the analysis of nine QCaaS toolchains, we identified key trends in design and implementation practices. Specifically, 58% of the analyzed tools were open-source, reflecting a community-driven effort in the domain. However, only 8% of the tools supported both high-level (HL) and quantum instructions (QI) as input formats, indicating limited support for abstraction and flexibility in user interaction. Furthermore, just 42% of the tools offered full automation, revealing substantial opportunities for enhancing usability and integration. Encouragingly, 63% of the tools underwent explicit evaluation, indicating increasing maturity in assessment and validation practices.

By addressing the first research question, this study provides an early yet insightful overview of the current state of QCaaS toolchains and highlights critical areas for future investigation. These findings are expected to support both researchers seeking evidence-based insights into QCaaS technologies and practitioners aiming to identify suitable platforms for adoption.

As part of a two-phase systematic mapping effort, this foundational study sets the stage for deeper analysis of architectural aspects and usage-related challenges. Building upon these findings, future work will extend this study into a comprehensive systematic mapping effort to address RQ1.1 and RQ2. The next phase will focus on characterizing architectural elements—such as design principles, orchestration mechanisms, and interoperability layers—as well as identifying the practical challenges associated with the use of QCaaS platforms. By systematically mapping usability, scalability, and integration barriers, the study aims to bridge critical gaps in the current QCaaS landscape.

Together, the results of this two-phase mapping study aim to provide actionable insights for researchers designing next-generation quantum software toolchains and for practitioners seeking to adopt QCaaS solutions. Ultimately, this work contributes to advancing the field of quantum software engineering by supporting evidence-based tool development and informed decision-making.

Acknowledgments. The author acknowledges the financial support provided by FAST, the Finnish Software Engineering Doctoral Research Network, funded by the Ministry of Education and Culture, Finland. We would also like to thank Aleya Siddika, Muhammad Javed, and Husnain Waleed, three Master's students who contributed during the early stages of this work as summer interns. Finally, we acknowledge the use of large language models as writing aids to enhance the clarity and linguistic quality of this manuscript.

References

1. Ahmad, A., et al.: Engineering software systems for quantum computing as a service: a mapping study. arXiv preprint arXiv:2303.14713 (2023)
2. Aithal, P.: Advances and new research opportunities in quantum computing technology by integrating it with other ICCT underlying technologies. Int. J. Case Stud. Bus. IT Educ. (IJCSBE) **7**(3), 314–358 (2023)
3. Bova, F., Goldfarb, A., Melko, R.G.: Commercial applications of quantum computing. EPJ Quantum Technol. **8**(1), 1–13 (2021). https://doi.org/10.1140/epjqt/s40507-021-00091-1
4. Chen, L., Babar, M.A., Zhang, H.: Towards an evidence-based understanding of electronic data sources. In: Proceedings of the 14th International Conference on Evaluation and Assessment in Software Engineering, EASE 2010, pp. 135–138. BCS Learning & Development Ltd., Swindon, GBR (2010)
5. Gill, S.S., et al.: Quantum computing: a taxonomy, systematic review and future directions. Softw.: Pract. Exp. **52**(1), 66–114 (2022). https://doi.org/10.1002/spe.3039
6. Google: Google. Cirq. (2022). https://quantumai.google/cirq/google/concepts
7. Hevia, J.L., Peterssen, G., Piattini, M.: Quantumpath: a quantum software development platform. Softw.: Pract. Exp. **52**(6), 1517–1530 (2022). https://doi.org/10.1002/spe.3064
8. Horodecki, R., Horodecki, P., Horodecki, M., Horodecki, K.: Quantum entanglement. Rev. Mod. Phys. **81**(2), 865 (2009). https://doi.org/10.1103/RevModPhys.81.865

9. IBM: Qiskit is the open-source toolkit for useful quantum (2021). https://qiskit.org/
10. ISO/IEC: Information technology—reference architecture for service oriented architecture (soa ra)—part 3: Service oriented architecture ontology (2016). https://www.iso.org/standard/63106.html, iSO/IEC Standard 18384-3
11. Khan, A.A., et al.: Software architecture for quantum computing systems: a systematic review. J. Syst. Softw. **201**, 111682 (2023). https://doi.org/10.1016/j.jss.2023.111682
12. Lubinski, T., et al.: Advancing hybrid quantum–classical computation with real-time execution. Front. Phys. **10**, 940293 (2022). https://doi.org/10.48550/ARXIV.2206.12950
13. McArdle, S., Endo, S., Aspuru-Guzik, A., Benjamin, S.C., Yuan, X.: Quantum computational chemistry. Rev. Mod. Phys. **92**(1), 015003 (2020). https://doi.org/10.1103/RevModPhys.92.015003
14. Microsoft: Q# and the quantum development kit (2021). https://azure.microsoft.com/en-us/resources/development-kit/quantum-computing
15. Moguel, E., Rojo, J., Valencia, D., Berrocal, J., Garcia-Alonso, J., Murillo, J.M.: Quantum service-oriented computing: current landscape and challenges. Softw. Qual. J. **30**(4), 983–1002 (2022). https://doi.org/10.1007/s11219-022-09589-y
16. Nguyen, H.T., Usman, M., Buyya, R.: QFaaS: a serverless function-as-a-service framework for quantum computing. Futur. Gener. Comput. Syst. **154**, 281–300 (2024). https://doi.org/10.1016/j.future.2024.01.018
17. Nielsen, M.A., Chuang, I.L.: Quantum Computation and Quantum Information. Cambridge University Press, Cambridge (2010)
18. Nimbe, P., Weyori, B.A., Adekoya, A.F.: Models in quantum computing: a systematic review. Quantum Inf. Process. **20**(2), 1–61 (2021). https://doi.org/10.1007/s11128-021-03021-3
19. Osaba, E., Villar-Rodriguez, E., Oregi, I.: A systematic literature review of quantum computing for routing problems. IEEE Access **10**, 55805–55817 (2022). https://doi.org/10.1109/ACCESS.2022.3177790
20. Papazoglou, M.P., Georgakopoulos, D.: Introduction: service-oriented computing. Commun. ACM **46**(10), 24–28 (2003)
21. Peral-García, D., Cruz-Benito, J., García-Peñalvo, F.J.: Systematic literature review: quantum machine learning and its applications. Comput. Sci. Rev. **51**, 100619 (2024). https://doi.org/10.1016/j.cosrev.2024.100619
22. Petersen, K., Feldt, R., Mujtaba, S., Mattsson, M.: Systematic mapping studies in software engineering. In: 12th international Conference on Evaluation and Assessment in Software Engineering (EASE). BCS Learning & Development (2008)
23. Piattini, M., et al.: The Talavera manifesto for quantum software engineering and programming. In: QANSWER, pp. 1–5 (2020)
24. Piattini, M., Serrano, M., Perez-Castillo, R., Petersen, G., Hevia, J.L.: Toward a quantum software engineering. IT Prof. **23**(1), 62–66 (2021). https://doi.org/10.1109/MITP.2020.3019522
25. Ramouthar, R., Seker, H.: Hybrid quantum algorithms and quantum software development frameworks. ScienceOpen Preprints (2023). https://doi.org/10.14293/PR2199.000298.v1
26. Weder, B., Barzen, J., Leymann, F., Vietz, D.: Quantum software development lifecycle. In: Quantum Software Engineering, pp. 61–83. Springer, Cham (2022). https://doi.org/10.1007/978-3-031-05324-5_4

27. Weder, B., Barzen, J., Leymann, F., Zimmermann, M.: Hybrid quantum applications need two orchestrations in superposition: a software architecture perspective. In: 2021 IEEE International Conference on Web Services (ICWS), pp. 1–13. IEEE (2021). https://doi.org/10.1109/ICWS53863.2021.00015
28. Weder, B., Breitenbücher, U., Leymann, F., Wild, K.: Integrating quantum computing into workflow modeling and execution. In: 2020 IEEE/ACM 13th International Conference on Utility and Cloud Computing (UCC), pp. 279–291. IEEE (2020). https://doi.org/10.1109/UCC48980.2020.00046
29. Wohlin, C., et al.: Experimentation in Software Engineering, vol. 236. Springer, Cham (2012)
30. Zhao, J.: Quantum software engineering: landscapes and horizons. arXiv preprint arXiv:2007.07047 (2020)

A Scalable Software-Hardware Co-design FPGA Platform for Floating-Point Operations

Cameron D. DiSomma[1], Dania Susanne Mosuli[1], Hailu Xu[2], and Xiaokun Yang[1](✉)

[1] University of Houston Clear Lake, 2700 Bay Area Blvd., Houston, TX 77058, USA
yangxia@uhcl.edu
[2] California State University, Long Beach, 1250 Bellflower Blvd., Long Beach, CA 90840, USA

Abstract. This paper presents a scalable software-hardware co-design platform to demonstrate floating point (FP) operations in scientific computing. The system-on-chip (SoC) architecture is built on the AMD-Xilinx Python Productivity for Zynq (PYNQ) framework, integrating an ARM Cortex-A9 MPCore with the AMD/Xilinx Zynq-based PYNQ field-programmable gate array (FPGA). As a case study, the platform presents the implementation of a trigonometric function, one of the FP operations from the *OpenFPU* design library executed on the FPGA and controlled by software through Jupyter Notebooks. The framework is designed to be scalable and extensible, supporting a wide range of FP operations and hardware accelerators, including FP adders and multipliers, Fourier transforms, matrix processing, and linear algebra computations. The evaluation results show a significant acceleration to the FP operations over the specialized hardware design on the FPGA.

Keywords: floating-point operations · FPGA · machine learning · scientific computing

1 Introduction

Floating-point (FP) operators, such as linear algebra and trigonometric functions, are crucial building blocks for hardware accelerator designs in the areas of machine learning [1,2], scientific computing [3], and audio/video processing [4,5]. Custom hardware design in such an area can significantly improve computational speed and power efficiency. For example, the *dot* product, which involves the accumulation of element-wise multiplications, is widely used in hardware accelerators for a range of mathematical applications, such as multilayer perceptron neural networks, general matrix-matrix multiplication (GEMM), and Fourier transforms [6]. Trigonometric functions are also frequently used to accelerate simulations in physics and chemistry, such as to model wave motion in sound, light, and electromagnetic wave propagation [7]. However, interfacing

S. Hussain et al. (Eds.): SEET 2025, CCIS 2725, pp. 517–528, 2026.
https://doi.org/10.1007/978-3-032-08977-9_32

between software control and hardware design platforms remains a major challenge due to the multidisciplinary knowledge and skills required. Software teams often lack experience with hardware design platforms such as field-programmable gate arrays (FPGAs) and application-specific integrated circuits (ASICs), while hardware teams may struggle to implement the necessary software interfaces required for software-hardware co-design systems.

In this context, this paper presents a scalable software-hardware co-design platform using the Python Productivity for Zynq (PYNQ) framework – an open-source development environment built around AMD/Xilinx Zynq FPGAs [8]. The platform enables software execution on the processing system (PS), an embedded ARM processor, while hardware design is implemented on the programmable logic (PL) side of the FPGA. The PS-PL interface is automatically constructed using an AMBA AXI-based wrapper system that integrates the ARM core with user-designed hardware accelerators [9], establishing a true system-on-chip (SoC) platform. High-level control is provided through Jupyter Notebooks, allowing the entire system to be managed from the software side.

This paper demonstrates and validates the proposed platform using hardware generation for trigonometric functions as a case study. The platform is scalable and can be extended to support a wide range of FP operations such as *dots* products and Fourier transforms. The main contributions of this paper are as follows.

- A scalable and reusable software-hardware co-design platform for FP operations, supporting applications in scientific computing and machine learning;
- An automatic AXI-based interface that bridges the gap between software and hardware development, enabling controllable demonstrations on traditional programmable logic FPGAs;
- A comprehensive evaluation result to demonstrate the hardware acceleration using the co-design platform;
- An open-source framework that can be reused and extended for future large-scale designs and demonstrations.

The organization of this paper is as follows. Section 2 introduces the *OpenFPU* hardware design library. Section 3 describes the software-hardware co-design platform based on the PYNQ FPGA. Section 4 details the implementation of hardware and software components, while Sect. 5 presents the experimental results and evaluation. Section 6 provides concluding remarks and outlines the direction for future work.

2 Overview of *OpenFPU* Hardware Library

This section introduces floating-point operations using the proposed software-hardware co-design platform. In digital system design, an FP number is commonly represented following the IEEE 754 standard, which is widely used for FP arithmetic. For example, a single precision FP number, shown in Fig. 1, can be represented using 32 bits divided into three sections: sign (S), exponent (E), and mantissa (M), also known as significand. The MSB denotes the sign bit, which indicates whether the number is positive (zero) or negative (one). The subsequent eight bits represent the exponent, which is biased by 127 as per the IEEE 754 standard. This bias implies that to determine the actual power of two, one needs to subtract 127 from the exponent. The remaining 23 bits make up the mantissa, representing the fraction that forms the significant digits of the number.

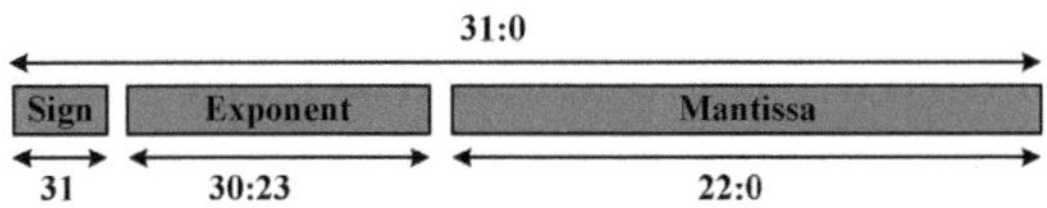

Fig. 1. IEEE 754 Format for Floating-Point Number.

Based on the IEEE 754 format, an open source hardware design library named *OpenFPU* is developed using the Chisel hardware construction language [10,11]. Chisel [12], which is embedded in Scala, facilitates the development of Verilog/SystemVerilog code generators instead of static register transfer level (RTL) designs. It supports highly parameterized designs, allowing configurable precision levels (half-, single-, double-, and quad-precision), latency (in clock cycles), pipeline depth (to optimize maximum operational frequency), and iteration control.

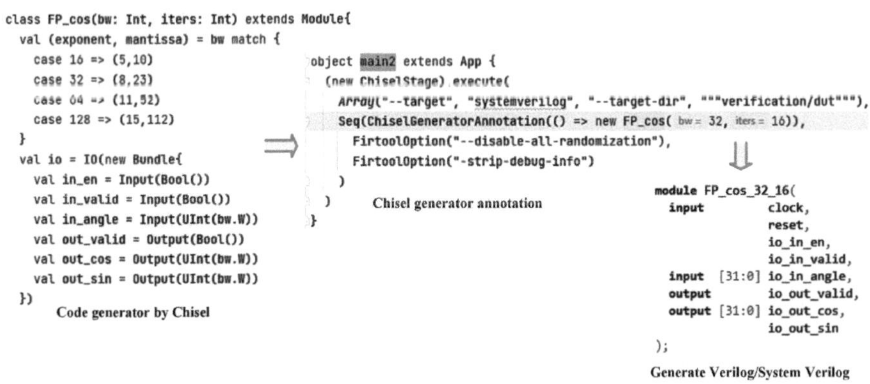

Fig. 2. Chisel-Verilog Design Flow

For example, Fig. 2 shows the Chisel implementation of a FP *cosine* trigonometric function. This design exposes two key parameters for Verilog generation: bit width (*bw*) and iteration rounds using the *CORDIC* algorithm [13]. A larger bit width improves the numerical accuracy, while increased iteration rounds enhance the accuracy of the overall trigonometric function. The input/output bundle is also parameterized based on the specified bit width. Verilog code can be generated using the *ChiselGeneratorAnnotation* method, as illustrated in Figure. In the example, the bit width is set to 32 bits and the iteration rounds are set to 16 to achieve high accuracy. After executing the generation method, the Verilog code can be generated with 32-bit parameterized precisions. Similarly, the *OpenFPU* library offers parameterized implementations of various floating-point units (FPUs) needed by a wide array of applications, including FP adders, multipliers, subtractors, dividers, reciprocals, exponential functions, etc.

3 Software-Hardware Co-Design Architecture

Unlike traditional FPGAs designed solely for digital logic implementation, the PYNQ-Z2 platform is built around the Xilinx Zynq-7000 system-on-chip (SoC), which integrates a dual-core ARM Cortex-A9 MPCore as the processing system (PS). This architecture enables seamless software control and interfacing through the PS, while leveraging the programmable logic (PL) for hardware acceleration including a variety of FP operations. The PYNQ-Z2 FPGA consists of approximately 85,000 logic cells usable as look-up tables (LUTs) and flip-flops, 512 KB of L2 cache, 256 KB of on-chip memory, and multiple peripheral interfaces such as UART, I^2C, and GPIO for diverse applications. All these hardware resources can be used to map the FP operations designed in register-transfer level descriptions using Verilog, and the PS interfacing enables the higher level control through the ARM MPCore.

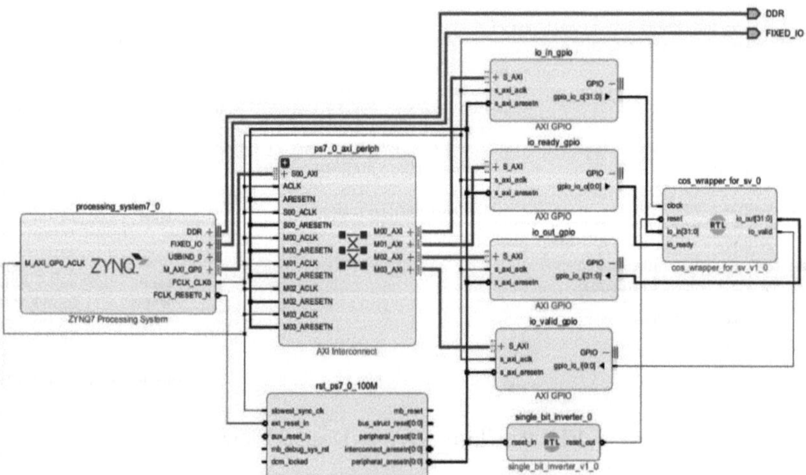

Fig. 3. PS-PL Co-Design Wrapper for the Software-Hardware Co-Design Platform

Using the PYNQ FPGA, Fig. 3 illustrates the implementation of the software-hardware co-design platform, also known as the PS-PL (Processing System -

Programmable logic) co-design system on chip (SoC). The SoC architecture integrates a Zynq core, which functions as the CPU, and a hardware wrapper labeled "RTL" in the figure, representing the hardware implementation of various FP operations. Additional intellectual property (IP) of the design is instantiated using the AMD-Xilinx Vivado toolchain to interface the Zynq processing system with RTL-based hardware modules. Specifically, an AMBA AXI bus is used to bridge communication between the PS and the PL. In what follows, AXI-based GPIO peripherals are instantiated to connect the ARM core to the FP hardware modules. This configuration allows data to be transmitted from software to hardware through the AXI-GPIO interface. Data read/write operations are handled via hardware interfaces that link the GPIOs to the RTL-based FP computation units, thereby enabling seamless communication between the software and hardware layers.

At the software layer, the PYNQ FPGA runs a standalone Linux kernel and supports network access through a local area network (LAN). A key advantage of the PYNQ-Z2 board over traditional FPGA platforms is its ability to run Jupyter Notebook directly through the Linux kernel. This allows users to control the PS using standard Python libraries, enabling high-level software-hardware co-design and rapid prototyping. As illustrated in Fig. 4, a bitstream file (e.g., "bit_file.bit") implemented from the FP design can be imported into the FPGA using the *Overlay* function in Jupyter Notebook. Once loaded, the hardware design encapsulated in the bitstream can be interfaced and controlled through the Python-based software layer, completing the co-design workflow.

```
In [1]: from pynq import Overlay
        overlay = Overlay("./bit_file.bit")
```

Fig. 4. Overlay Instantiation in Jupyter Notebook

4 Project Implementation

This section presents the hardware and software implementations developed using a suite of design tools. A trigonometric function is used as a case study to validate the functionality of the software-hardware co-design platform. However, the system is extensible and can be adapted to support the full range of FP operations described in Sect. 2.

4.1 Hardware Implementation

The industry-standard FPGA design flow is followed for hardware implementation, including Verilog design/generation, functional simulation/verification, synthesis & implementation, and performance evaluation. A key distinction in

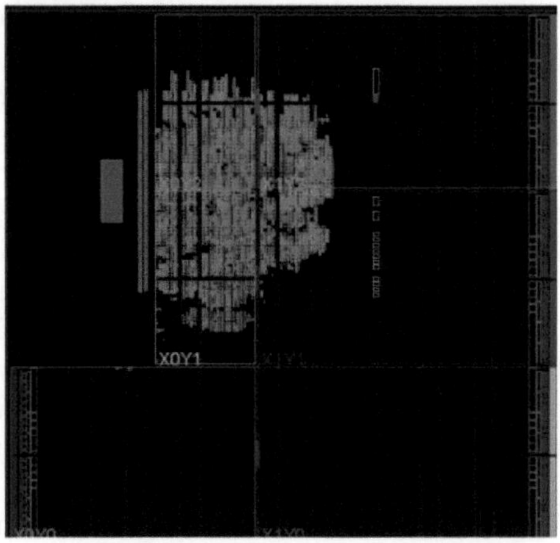

Fig. 5. Hardware Design Layout

this workflow is that the Verilog design for FP operations is generated using code generators from the *OpenFPU* library. This library offers flexibility and productivity by enabling the automated generation of various FP designs, allowing trade-offs among area, speed, and power. For example, configuring the trigonometric function with the highest bit width (128-bit) yields the highest numerical accuracy but also incurs the largest area and power cost. Similarly, increasing the number of iterations in the CORDIC algorithm improves accuracy at the expense of area and power. With the *OpenFPU* library, users can easily configure and generate multiple design variants in Chisel, tailored to different hardware performance requirements. Furthermore, higher-level numerical hardware modules, such as *dot*-product and matrix-matrix operations, can be constructed by composing these FP operators.

After generating the Verilog design, functional verification is performed using Siemens-Mentor Graphics ModelSim [14]. FP operators are implemented in a pipelined fashion, enabling streaming inputs and outputs to be observed during simulation. Hardware synthesis & implementation are conducted using AMD/Xilinx Vivado [15]. Figure 5 shows the synthesized & implemented layout, represented as a schematic netlist. The netlist illustrates all the logic connections and reveals the total footprint of the design on the FPGA fabric.

This completes the block design as an SoC to be synthesized and placed onto the FPGA fabric by exporting the bitstream file, the tcl script, and the hardware handoff file. These files are uploaded to PYNQ Z2 to be used to create a custom overlay to interface with our design on the FPGA board. Figure 6 illustrates the hardware implementation on the PYNQ FPGA platform. The software portion is introduced in the following section.

Fig. 6. Hardware Implementation on PYNQ FPGA Platform

4.2 Software Implementation

With the bitstream files imported from Vivado into Jupyter Notebook, the custom overlay can be created using the commands seen in Fig. 7. Now that the custom overlay has been created and verified, the drivers for the GPIO ports can be initialized and named so that the data can be accessed between software and hardware. Using Python, a FP angle array can be easily created that contains 100 points from $-\pi$ to π. This angle array will be used to write into the GPIO and, by extension, inputted into the *cosine* module. Another corresponding FP data array will be used to collect the 100 FP data outputs of the *cosine* module that are the results of $cos(-\pi)$ to $cos(\pi)$.

```
In [ ]: write_out = overlay.ip_dict['io_in_gpio']
        read_in = overlay.ip_dict['io_out_gpio']
        write_ready = overlay.ip_dict['io_ready_gpio']
        read_valid = overlay.ip_dict['io_valid_gpio']

        write_data_out = AxiGPIO(write_out).channel1
        read_data_in = AxiGPIO(read_in).channel1
        write_ready_out = AxiGPIO(write_ready).channel1
        read_valid_out = AxiGPIO(read_valid).channel1

        mask = 0xffffffff
        write_ready_out.write(0x1, mask)
```

Fig. 7. Software Implementation on Jupiter Notebook

Jupyter Notebook, with the library *matplotlib*, is utilized further to create a waveform for combining the two 100 data point arrays into a single wave. This wave is plotted as Θ versus *cosine* to visually compare the input versus output of the *cosine* design module. The waveform shows the different accuracies of the different designs of *cosine* modules in terms of iteration rounds and precisions, which is illustrated in the following section.

5 Experimental Results

This section evaluates the design performance of the Verilog code on the PYNC FPGA built with 28 nm technology. Additionally, the output can support -1.0 to 1.0 for *sine*and *consine* functions, and $-2\pi/2$ to $2\pi/2$ for the arctangent function.

5.1 Accuracy Evaluation on Proposed Platform

Using the code generators, the trigonometric functions can be parameterized by precision, iteration count, and pipeline depth. Precision and iteration settings directly affect computational accuracy, while pipeline depth primarily influences the achievable maximum operating frequency.

Table 1 presents the design precision, measured as the percentage of error, across various precision levels and their highest iteration numbers. As expected, the 128-bit implementation achieves the highest accuracy, while the 16-bit design yields the lowest. In particular, the single-precision (32-bit) implementation reduces the error to below 1%, demonstrating the optimal trade-off between accuracy and hardware cost for a wide range of numerical applications. For applications that prioritize low cost and low power, approximate designs using 16-bit precision may still be viable, with error percentages ranging from 1% to 15%. Overall, accuracy improves with increasing bit width, as higher precision enables a more accurate representation of numerical inputs and operations, thereby reducing quantization and rounding errors.

Table 1. Error Percentage Across Different Precisions for Trigonometric Functions.

Designs	16-bit	32-bit	64-bit	128-bit
Sin	1.0–15%	0.1–0.7%	0.1–0.3%	0%
Cos	1.0–15%	0.1–0.7%	0.1–0.3%	0%
Arctan	1.0–18%	0%	0%	0%

Figure 8 further shows the output of the *cosine* function using 16-bit and 32-bit hardware designs. The 16-bit version shows rough edges, indicating noticeable errors due to limited precision. This lower accuracy makes the 16-bit design better suited for low-power or cost-sensitive applications where small errors are acceptable. However, the 32-bit version creates a smooth curve that closely matches the true cosine function, showing that it has enough precision for tasks that require accurate results, such as scientific computing or machine learning. This comparison shows the trade-off between using fewer hardware resources and achieving better accuracy, highlighting the importance of higher precision for designs that need reliable computation.

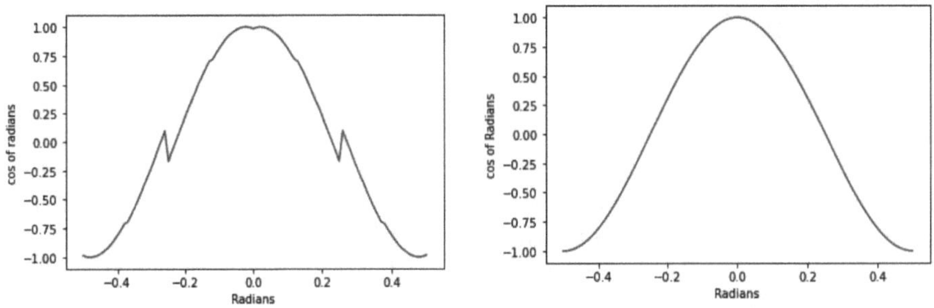

Fig. 8. Waveform of 16-bit cos architecture | Waveform of 32-bit cos architecture

5.2 Performance Evaluation on Proposed Platform

In the previous subsection, the precision was evaluated with respect to the precision and the number of iteration rounds. In this subsection, the focus shifts to the evaluation of hardware acceleration, primarily based on different pipeline depths (*pd*). Table 2 presents the evaluation results, including maximum operating frequency (MOF), latency measured in clock cycles (CCs), power consumption, and resource utilization in terms of look-up tables (LUTs) and flip-flops (FFs).

Table 2. Hardware Performance Evaluation on Various Pipeline Depths.

pd	MOF (MHz)	Latency (CCs)	D-Power (mW)	LUTs	FFs
4	22.68	24	191	9,621	994
8	45.50	28	136	8,106	1,506
16	53.86	36	111	7,312	2,528
32	54.69	52	107	6,981	4,545

The achievable MOFs are summarized in the second column in MHz. By configuring the reference clock T_{ref}, the MOF can be estimated using the equation $MOF = \frac{1}{T_{ref} - WNS}$, where WNS can be obtained through implementation to represent the worst negative slack time [11]. MOF serves as one of the most important performance metrics in the hardware design of digital systems. In general, deeper pipelining leads to higher MOF due to reduced critical path delays, which can be demonstrated in the second column results. Note that the slack time is evaluated based on the target FPGA board. Different FPGAs may have very different evaluation results for the MOF.

The latency, measured in clock cycles, is summarized in the third column. The implementation of *cosine* with the highest pipeline depth requires the most clock cycles between the input angle θ and the resulting output $cos(\theta)$. However, since the design is implemented as a streaming pipeline, this increase in latency does not significantly affect the throughput of streaming input and output across the hardware. By multiplying the MOF by four bytes or one word, the bandwidth of the single precision operation *cosine* reaches 218.76 MBps, demonstrating the significant hardware acceleration achieved through specialized hardware design on FPGAs.

The dynamic power consumption, presented in the fourth column, shows that the design with the highest pipeline depth consumes more dynamic power, primarily due to increased signal toggling across I/Os and logic elements. The last two columns summarize the utilization of hardware resources in terms of LUTs and FFs. As expected, higher pipeline depths require more layers of registers, resulting in increased usage of FFs. In contrast, LUT usage exhibits the opposite trend: the design with the lowest pipeline depth (4 stages) consumes the most LUTs. This suggests that deeper pipelining helps distribute logic more efficiently, thereby reducing LUT utilization at the cost of additional registers.

5.3 Assessment of Jupyter Notebook as Firmware

The key contribution of the FPGA design platform is its ability to accelerate computation-intensive applications such as scientific computing and machine learning. Additionally, the software interface enables higher-level control over hardware accelerator designs, providing flexibility and ease of integration and evaluation. However, this software interaction can introduce latency, potentially limiting the overall system acceleration due to software bottlenecks. Therefore, in this subsection, the latency introduced by the Jupyter Notebook is evaluated as a firmware overhead.

Table 3. Results of Increased Latency due to Jupyter Notebook

cases	16-bw (mS)	32-bw (mS)
1W-0R	0.98	1.01
2W-0R	1.46	1.49
4W-0R	2.33	2.45
1W-1R	1.43	1.53
2W-1R	1.92	1.94
4W-1R	2.85	2.89

Table 3 presents the latency evaluation results for using Linux and Jupyter Notebook to run embedded programs on the PYNQ Z2 FPGA [8]. Each test case represents a specific combination of write and read operations between the software and the SoC. For example, the case labeled $1W$–$0R$ indicates a single write operation and no read, with observed latencies of 0.98 ms for the 16 bit (16 bw) design and 1.01 ms for the 32 bit width. The most extensive operation, $4W$–$1R$, involves four writes and one read, taking 2.85 ms for the 16 bit design and 2.89 ms for the 32 bit design.

Although Jupyter Notebook significantly improves accessibility—particularly for software developers without a hardware or firmware background—it introduces substantial latency in the millisecond range, which is orders of magnitude higher than the microsecond-level latency of hardware accelerators. This overhead stems from the interpreted nature of Python running atop the Linux kernel and communicating with the PL through GPIO interfaces. Future work will focus on reducing this latency by optimizing data transfer mechanisms and integrating on-chip memory interfaces to replace low-speed GPIOs.

6 Conclusion

This paper presents an extensible software-hardware co-design FPGA platform that integrates high-level control via Jupyter Notebook with low-level hardware accelerator designs with AXI and GPIO interfaces. The platform supports the demonstration of various FP operations, including addition, multiplication, subtraction, division, and exponential functions, as well as trigonometric functions such as *sine*, *cosine*, and *arctan*. The successful implementation and verification of the trigonometric modules validate both the functionality and accuracy of the platform, establishing a foundation for further expansion to more complex numerical hardware acceleration.

7 Future Works

This project demonstrates the scalability and extensibility of the proposed platform for a wide range of FP applications in scientific computing and machine learning. However, it also exposes limitations in interfacing bandwidth due to low-speed GPIO and the latency overhead introduced by Jupyter Notebook. To address these challenges, a potential future enhancement involves utilizing on-chip SRAM to preload FP data in bulk. This data can then be transmitted to and from the hardware accelerators via the high-throughput SRAM interface, with results subsequently retrieved through the Jupyter Notebook. By handling all data transfers internally within the hardware, this approach significantly reduces latency and minimizes communication bottlenecks caused by the software layer. With this SRAM-augmented platform, future work will focus on extending support for more complex mathematical operations and integrating the system into larger-scale hardware acceleration pipelines, including Fourier transforms, sigmoid neuron computations, and matrix-matrix operations.

References

1. Madineni, M.C., Vega, M., Yang, X.: Parameterizable design on convolutional neural networks using chisel hardware construction language. MDPI Micromachines **14**(3), 531 (2023). https://doi.org/10.3390/mi14030531
2. Westby, I., Yang, X., Liu, T., Xu, H.: Exploring FPGA acceleration on a multilayer perceptron neural network for digit recognition. J. Supercomput. 1–18 (2021). https://doi.org/10.1007/S11227-021-03849-7
3. Vega, M., Yang, X., Shalf, J., Popovici, D.T.: Towards a flexible hardware implementation for mixed-radix fourier transforms. In: 2023 IEEE High Performance Extreme Computing Conference (HPEC), pp. 1–7. IEEE (2023). https://doi.org/10.1109/HPEC58863.2023.10363540
4. Vaca, K., Gajjar, A., Yang, X.: Real-time automatic music transcription (AMT) with Zynq FPGA. In: Proceedings of the 2019 IEEE Computer Society Annual Symposium VLSI (ISVLSI), Miami, FL, USA, pp. 378–384 (2019)
5. Yang, X., Zhang, Y., Wu, L.: A scalable image/video processing platform with open source design and verification environment. In: Proceedings of the 20th International Symposium Quality Electronic Design (ISQED), Santa Clara, CA, USA, pp. 110–116 (2019)
6. Reed, A.L., Yang, X.: Lightweight neural network architectures for resource-limited devices. In: Proceedings of the IEEE/ACM 23rd International Symposium Quality Electronic Design (ISQED), Santa Clara, CA, USA, pp. 1–7 (2022)
7. Wong, P., Mosuli, D.S., Zhang, X., Yang, X.: Hardware generation on trigonometric functions. In: Proceedings of the 2024 IEEE International Conference on Big Data (BigData), Washington, DC, USA, pp. 7571–7576 (2024). https://doi.org/10.1109/BigData62323.2024.10825243
8. AMD. PYNQ: Python Productivity for AMD Adaptive Computing Platforms (2024). https://www.pynq.io/. Accessed 10 Apr 2025
9. ARM. AMBA AXI Protocol Specification, Axis, Sunnyvale, CA, USA (2003)
10. Shalf, J., Yang, X., Popovici, D.A.T., Vega, M.: OpenFPU: OpenSource hardware generators for scientific computing. In: Advanced Computation: HPC - Design & Methods, Version 1.0 (2024). Repository Link: Coming soon
11. Yang, X.: Integrated Circuit Design: IC Design Flow and Project-Based Learning. CRC Press – Taylor & Francis Group (2024). ISBN 978-1-032-03079-1. Online. ISBN 978-1-003-18708-0
12. UC Berkeley, EECS. Chisel: Constructing Hardware in a Scala Embedded Language (2022). https://www.chisel-lang.org/. Software. Accessed 9 Mar 2024
13. Volder, J.E.: The Cordic trigonometric computing technique. IRE Trans. Electron. Comput. **EC-8**(3), 330–334 (1959)
14. Siemens Digital Industries Software. Siemens ModelSim® (2022). Software. https://www.mentor.com/products/fpga/modelsim. Accessed 9 Mar 2024
15. Xilinx, Inc.: Xilinx Vivado® (2023). Software. https://www.xilinx.com/products/design-tools/vivado.html. Accessed 9 Mar 2024

AI-Powered Engine Component Identifier for Vehicle Maintenance

Aron Cruz, Yalong Wu, and Xiaokun Yang(✉)

University of Houston Clear Lake, 2700 Bay Area Blvd., TX 77058, USA
yangxia@uhcl.edu

Abstract. This paper presents an artificial intelligence (AI)-enabled system for identifying engine components, aimed at assisting car owners in recognizing parts within the engine bay. Using object detection and segmentation models, the system accurately identifies critical components and augments them with interactive overlays that provide labels, tooltips, and maintenance guidance. The overarching objective is to establish the algorithmic foundation for future hardware implementation, with the long-term goal of improving automotive maintenance efficiency through the development of a dedicated application-specific diagnostic and maintenance integrated circuit.

Keywords: artificial intelligence · integrated circuit design · machine learning

1 Introduction

Maintaining a vehicle's engine can be a significant challenge for many car owners, especially those without mechanical experience. Recent advances in artificial intelligence (AI)—including multilayer perceptron (MLP) neural networks for digit recognition [1], convolutional neural networks (CNN) for word segmentation [2], and object detection models such as YOLO (You Only Look Once) [3]—have demonstrated broad applicability across a wide range of domains. In the context of automotive diagnostics and component recognition, models such as Faster R-CNN and Mask R-CNN have shown strong performance in real-time object detection and segmentation [4,5]. Despite these advances, relatively few studies have focused on engine component identification and diagnostics specifically tailored for consumer use. Projects such as CarNet [6] have shown promise in recognizing car models and parts from images; however, a notable gap remains in translating these technologies into interactive and user-friendly systems designed for everyday users with limited technical expertise.

Therefore, this paper presents an AI-powered engine component identification system for vehicle maintenance, allowing automated interpretation of complex visual data. Specifically, it introduces a comprehensive software-centric solution that analyzes a photograph of the engine bay of a vehicle, automatically identifies key components, and provides users with interactive visual guidance.

S. Hussain et al. (Eds.): SEET 2025, CCIS 2725, pp. 529–537, 2026.
https://doi.org/10.1007/978-3-032-08977-9_33

By incorporating vehicle-specific information, such as model, make, and year, the system also connects users to compatible replacement parts from online retailers. This approach allows car owners to take greater control of routine maintenance and repairs, effectively transforming a simple photo into a personalized, actionable tool for vehicle care. The main contributions of this paper are as follows.

- A comprehensive workflow for an AI-powered engine component identification system is proposed, integrating data collection, model training, and interactive interface design;
- A set of performance evaluation metrics is introduced to assess detection accuracy, processing speed, component coverage, and the effectiveness of user interaction.
- The proposed system is scalable and extensible, allowing for future enhancements and broader applications such as vehicle diagnostics, automated maintenance recommendations, and integration with augmented reality interfaces.
- A solid algorithmic model for the future hardware implementation of the AI model in the application-specific integrated circuit.

The organization of this paper is as follows. Section 2 outlines the proposed system and design flow. Section 3 describes the software-centric design platform implemented using GPU acceleration. Section 4 presents the experimental results and evaluation. Section 5 provides concluding remarks and Sect. 6 discusses directions for future work using the hardware platform and *OpenFPU* chip design library.

2 Proposed AI-Powered System

To develop an effective AI-powered system for the identification of engine components, a structured design methodology and workflow are essential. This section illustrates a modular approach that integrates computer vision, deep learning, and user interface design to construct a platform capable of recognizing engine components from user-submitted images. The workflow is organized into four primary stages: (1) data collection and annotation, (2) model training and evaluation, (3) interactive user interface design, and (4) integration with vehicle-specific databases. Each stage builds on the previous one, ensuring a seamless progression from data acquisition to intelligent component recognition and personalized user interaction.

Specifically, the overall system workflow is illustrated in Fig. 1. The pipeline begins with image upload and preprocessing, followed by inference using a trained AI model. Post-processing is then applied to generate interactive visual overlays and to link identified components to relevant replacement parts and maintenance recommendations. Both the front- and back-end processes are detailed in the following subsections.

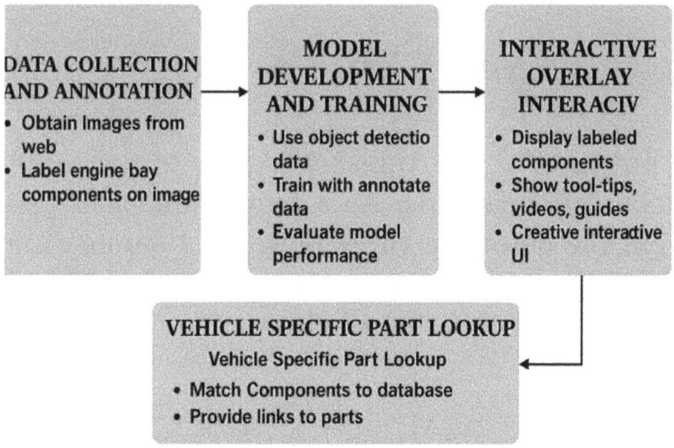

Fig. 1. Workflow for the proposed AI-powered engine component identification system.

2.1 Data Collection and Annotation

Since there is no publicly available dataset that provides detailed annotation of individual engine components, a custom dataset is developed. Images are sourced from public web repositories, automotive forums on-line, and original equipment manufacturer (OEM) service manuals [7]. Each image will be manually annotated using labeling tools such as CVAT or Roboflow [8] to identify and label key engine components such as air filter, battery, alternator, and engine. Metadata including vehicle make, model, and year will be recorded when available, supporting future part matching functionality.

2.2 Model Development and Training

Deep learning models are utilized to identify and segment components within engine bay images. Object detection architectures such as YOLO [3] and segmentation models such as Mask R-CNN [5] are investigated and evaluated for this task. Training is carried out using the PyTorch [9] framework, with data augmentation techniques applied to improve the accuracy of the model.

In addition, the performance of the model is evaluated using standard metrics such as the mean average precision (mAP) [10] and the intersection over the union (IoU) on a validation set. Specifically, mAP is a widely used evaluation metric in object detection and information retrieval tasks. It provides quality estimation by averaging the precision values at different thresholds. The average precision, denoted by AP, for a single class is defined as the area under the precision-recall curve:

$$AP = \int_0^1 P(R)\, dR \tag{1}$$

Here, $P(R)$ is the precision as a function of recall R. Using Eq. 1, it can evaluate the trade-off between precision and recall over different thresholds. In the approximate evaluation, this integral can be rewritten as:

$$AP = \sum_{k=1}^{n}(R_k - R_{k-1}) \cdot P_k \tag{2}$$

where P_k is the precision at the threshold k, R_k is the recall at threshold k, and n is the number of thresholds. As a finite number of precision and recall points derived from the detection thresholds, Eq. 1 summarizes the area under the precision-recall curve using a stepwise approximation. Given C classes, mAP is computed as the mean of APs for all classes:

$$\text{mAP} = \frac{1}{C}\sum_{c=1}^{C} AP_c \tag{3}$$

where AP_c is the Average Precision for class c. Detection accuracy is a key performance metric for evaluating the proposed system, as it directly reflects the system's ability to correctly identify engine components from input images. High detection accuracy ensures reliable assistance for end users, particularly in real-world automotive maintenance scenarios.

Another critical performance evaluation metric is detection latency and power efficiency. In real-world vehicle maintenance applications, it is essential to deploy an inference model that is both energy-efficient and low-latency. As the central design goal of this vision paper, the computationally intensive components of the system will be investigated, hardcoded, and offloaded onto an application-specific integrated circuit (ASIC). To support this objective, cost-effective chip design techniques will be employed, including mixed-precision floating-point (FP) operations within neural units, approximate computing for deep learning models, and low-overhead architectural strategies to optimize data movement between software and hardware interfaces. This hardware acceleration approach is expected to significantly improve the inference speed while reducing the overall power consumption of the system.

2.3 Interactive Overlay Interface

A key feature of the system is its ability to display detected components through an interactive overlay on the uploaded image. This is implemented using web technologies such as *HTML* Canvas and JavaScript. The overlay consists of bounding boxes or segmentation masks, tooltip labels, and brief maintenance tips for each component. This interface enables users, especially non-experts, to visually identify engine parts and better understand their function and condition.

2.4 Vehicle Specific Part Lookup

To assist users in replacing identified components, the system incorporates a database matching feature that links detected parts to compatible replacements. By entering the vehicle's make, model, and year, users can receive links to online retailers such as *RockAuto*, *NAPA* or *AutoZone*. In the future, this feature can be automated through API integration or VIN decoding services to improve ease of use and accuracy.

3 Project Implementation

This section presents the implementation of the project on software platforms, providing a future vision for hardware implementation in Sect. 6. As a vision paper, the current focus is on software-based implementation for training and inference using GPU platforms. Basically, it follows a software-centric pipeline, built in Python using PyTorch [9] as the main deep learning framework. All training and inference are performed on a standard personal device equipped with a NVIDIA GeForce series GPU [11].

The data set is composed of engine bay images manually collected from public Web sources such as auto-repair forums, instructional YouTube videos, and manufacturer service documentation. These images are labeled using tools such as CVAT and RoboFlow [8], with a focus on identifying common engine components such as battery, air filter, alternator, and radiator. Training is conducted using CNNs, particular object detection models like YOLO and Mask R-CNN once trained, the inference process involves the following steps:

- Input preprocessing including resizing and normalization
- Inference via trained detection model
- Output generation with bounding boxes or segmentation masks
- Rendering of interactive overlays and tool-tips on user interface
- Matching detected parts to vehicle specific components based on user-inputted make, model, and year.

The architecture will remain modular to facilitate future porting to platforms for real-time deployment in consumer applications. Furthermore, future work will investigate hardware-based inference acceleration through ASIC design tailored for targeted use cases. For additional details on this long-term vision, including a hypothesis of achieving greater than 50× acceleration with comparable accuracy, pre-validated on the software platform, please refer to Sect. 6.

4 Experimental Results

This section presents preliminary experimental results of object detection in an engine bay using software-based platforms. The model is designed to identify and label at least ten common engine components - such as the battery, air filter, alternator, engine block, and radiator - across various vehicle types. As illustrated in Fig. 2, the proposed early stage system demonstrates the ability to accurately detect and annotate key engine components using an object detection model, with labels overlaid directly on the image to enhance user clarity.

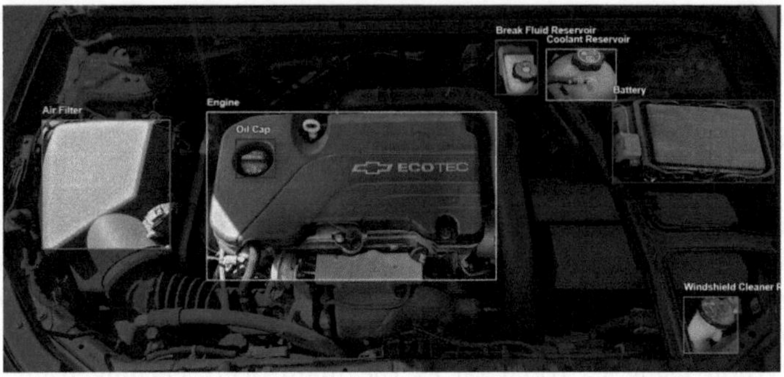

Fig. 2. AI-enabled system output showing labeled engine components on an uploaded engine bay image.

For future work, performance evaluation metrics and expected outcomes are defined as follows:

- **Detection Accuracy**: The performance of object detection of the system will be evaluated using standard metrics such as mAP [10] and Intersection over Union (IoU). While the software platform primarily determines the accuracy of the proposed algorithmic models, the hardware implementation focuses on balancing accuracy with design constraints related to area, speed, and power consumption. In general, higher accuracy can be achieved at the expense of increased hardware resource usage, highlighting the trade-off between performance and implementation cost.
- **Processing Speed**: Inference latency on software platforms will be measured using a typical consumer-grade personal computer to assess responsiveness and usability in real-world scenarios. These results will serve as a baseline for estimating the potential speedup achievable through future ASIC-based implementations. In general, the most latency-critical computational modules will be identified and hardcoded onto hardware accelerators to significantly enhance overall system performance.

5 Conclusion

This paper presents an AI-embedded system for the identification of engine components to support vehicle maintenance. The project is in its early stage research phase and focuses on developing a deep learning model capable of recognizing various types and components of engines. The primary research objectives are to evaluate the accuracy and inference speed of the model. In addition, the paper explores speculative ideas and forward-looking perspectives that have the potential to guide future research directions in dedicated chip design for intelligent automotive diagnostics and maintenance automation.

6 Future Vision

The proposed software platform serves as a foundational step towards future hardware implementation, with the ultimate goal of significantly improving the efficiency in automotive maintenance through the development of a dedicated diagnostic and maintenance ASIC. Once the deep learning model is validated in the software environment, its computationally intensive components can be mathematically abstracted into basic building blocks of linear algebra, such as multiply-accumulate (MAC) units and matrix-matrix or matrix-vector operations. These building blocks can, in turn, be decomposed into fundamental FP operations, including addition, multiplication, subtraction, division, exponential functions, and many more. This decomposition facilitates the construction of the inference model by leveraging reusable hardware design intellectual properties (IPs) to implement an equivalent algorithmic architecture in hardware. Previous research has demonstrated the effectiveness of this design methodology in the construction of CNN and MLP neural networks using basic FP operators on field-programmable gate array (FPGA) platforms [12,13].

In contrast, in this paper the open source hardware design library *OpenFPU* [14,15], developed using the Chisel hardware construction language [16], will be used to build the hardware back-end. Chisel, embedded in Scala, facilitates the development of highly parameterized Verilog/SystemVerilog code generators instead of static register-transfer-level (RTL) designs. It offers two key advantages: (1) it follows a software-style design paradigm that links naturally with software-based algorithmic models, and (2) it supports configurable and reusable hardware modules, such as various precisions and latency, in contrast to the rigid descriptions used in traditional hardware description languages such as Verilog and SystemVerilog.

```
class FFT_SingleRadix(N:Int, r: Int, w: Int, bw: Int) extends Module{
  val io = IO(new Bundle() {
    val in = Input(Vec(N, new ComplexNum(bw)))
    val in_ready = Input(Bool())
    val out_validate = Output(Bool())
    val out = Output(Vec(N, new ComplexNum(bw)))
  })
```

Fig. 3. Code Generator of FP FFT using Chisel.

For example, Fig. 3 shows a previous hardware design for the Fourier transform implemented in Chisel. This design exposes four key parameters for Verilog generation: the Fourier transform size (N), radix (r), streaming width (w), and bit width or precision (bw). Increasing the streaming width improves hardware resource efficiency, while expanding the bit width enhances numerical precision. The input/output bundles are also parameterized on the basis of the selected bit width. Once the generator is developed, the Verilog code can be produced using the *ChiselGeneratorAnnotation* method. Previous research [17] has demonstrated the substantial potential of chip-based architectures to accelerate Fourier transform computations using 16nm TSMC technology. This novel approach achieved exceptional results, outperforming the NVIDIA H100 by 50× in both performance per area and energy efficiency per FLOP (floating-point operation). A similar level of acceleration is hypothesized for deep learning inference models implemented on dedicated hardware platforms, representing a key component of future vision.

References

1. Reed, A.L., Yang, X.: Lightweight neural network architectures for resource-limited devices. In: Proceedings of the IEEE/ACM 23rd International Symposium on Quality Electronic Design (ISQED 2022), pp. 1–7. Santa Clara (2022)
2. He, H., Yang, X., Wu, L., Wang, G.: Iterated dilated convolutional neural networks for word segmentation. Neural Netw. World **30**(5), 333–346 (2020)
3. Redmon, J., Farhadi, A.: YOLOv3: An Incremental Improvement. arXiv preprint, arXiv:1804.02767 (2018)
4. Ren, S., He, K., Girshick, R., Sun, J.: Faster R-CNN: towards real-time object detection with region proposal networks. Adv. Neural Inf. Process. Syst. (2015)
5. He, K., Gkioxari, G., Dollár, P., Girshick, R.: Mask R-CNN. In: Proceedings of the IEEE International Conference on Computer Vision (ICCV) (2017)
6. Krause, J., Stark, M., Deng, J., Fei-Fei, L.: 3D Object representations for fine-grained categorization. In: Proceedings of the IEEE International Conference on Computer Vision (ICCV) Workshops, pp. 554–561 (2013)
7. Oem Factory Shop Manuals. OEM Auto Repair Manuals - Factory Repair Service Manuals. https://www.themotorbookstore.com/factory-manuals.html, Accessed 02 May 2025
8. RoboFlow. Computer vision tools for developers and enterprises. Roboflow. https://roboflow.com/, Accessed 12 Mar 2025
9. GeeksforGeeks. What is pytorch?, GeeksforGeeks. https://www.geeksforgeeks.org/getting-started-with-pytorch/, Accessed 08 Feb 2025
10. Ye, Y., Zhang, T., Lu, R.: Margin and average precision loss calibration for long-tail object detection. In: 2024 9th International Conference on Computer and Communication Systems (ICCCS), pp. 26–32, Xi'an (2024)
11. NVIDIA Corporation. NVIDIA GeForce Graphics Cards. https://www.nvidia.com/en-us/geforce/, Accessed 9 May 2025
12. Madineni, M.C., Vega, M., Yang, X.: Parameterizable design on convolutional neural networks using chisel hardware construction language. MDPI Micromach. **14**(3), 531 (2023)
13. Westby, I., Yang, X., Liu, T., Xu, H.: Exploring FPGA acceleration on a multi-layer perceptron neural network for digit recognition. J. Supercomput., 1–18 (2021)
14. Shalf, J., Yang, X., Popovici, D.A.T., Vega, M.: OpenSource hardware generators for scientific computing. Advanced Computation: HPC - Design & Methods, Version 1.0. (2024)
15. Yang, X.: Integrated circuit design: IC design flow and project-based learning. CRC Press – Taylor & Francis Group (2024). ISBN: 978-1-032-03079-1: ISBN 978-1-003-18708-0

16. UC Berkeley, EECS. Chisel: Constructing Hardware in a Scala Embedded Language 2022. Software. https://www.chisel-lang.org/, Accessed 9 Mar 2024.
17. Vega, M., Yang, X., Shalf, J., Popovici, D.T.: OpenSource hardware generators for scientific computing. In: 2023 IEEE High Performance Extreme Computing Conference (HPEC), pp. 1–7. IEEE (2023). https://doi.org/10.1109/HPEC58863.2023.10363540

Short Research Paper (SRP)

Lightweight and Generalizable Glioma Grading Using Hyperdimensional Computing

Mehjabeen Tasnim, Justin Morris, and Sreedevi Gutta(✉)

California State University San Marcos, San Marcos, USA
sgutta@csusm.edu

Abstract. Glioma grading plays a crucial role in determining treatment strategies and patient outcomes. Traditional machine learning models, while effective, often require extensive hyperparameter tuning and high computational resources, limiting their generalizability. In this study, we explore Hyperdimensional Computing (HDC) as a lightweight and efficient alternative for glioma grade classification. To enhance interpretability, SHapley Additive exPlanations (SHAP) analysis was applied, identifying key features that contributed to model predictions. Experimental results demonstrated that HDC achieved competitive performance while significantly reducing training time and inference latency compared to machine learning models. Moreover, HDC has shown better generalizability, requiring minimal hyperparameter tuning. The findings suggest that HDC is a promising approach for real-time and resource-efficient glioma grading.

Keywords: Glioma Grading · Hyperdimensional Computing · SHAP · Feature Selection · Lightweight Models · Generalizability

1 Introduction

A brain tumor is an abnormal and uncontrolled growth of cells within the brain or its surrounding tissues in the central nervous system (CNS) [1]. The most common malignant brain tumor in adults is glioma and are categorized into four grades (I–IV) [1–3]. Low-grade gliomas (LGG, grades I–II) are less aggressive, whereas high-grade gliomas (HGG, grades III–IV) are more aggressive and associated with poor survival rates despite treatments such as chemotherapy and radiation therapy [4]. It is important to determine an accurate grade for appropriate treatment planning. The current gold-standard way to determine glioma grade is through biopsy, which are invasive, expensive, time-consuming, and pose risks to patients [5]. Thus, there is a need for a non-invasive and accurate method to determine glioma grade.

Prior research has explored extracting radiomic features from Magnetic Resonance Imaging (MRI) scans and then using machine learning algorithms, such as support vector machine, decision trees for glioma grade prediction [6–8]. However, these models require extensive hyperparameter tuning, limiting their generalizability.

This study investigates Hyperdimensional Computing (HDC), a lightweight model that predicts glioma grade without extensive tuning. To identify key predictive features, we apply SHapley Additive exPlanations (SHAP) analysis. We further utilized

S. Hussain et al. (Eds.): SEET 2025, CCIS 2725, pp. 541–550, 2026.
https://doi.org/10.1007/978-3-032-08977-9_34

the insights from SHAP to enhance HDC's performance. By integrating feature analysis with HDC, this research aims to establish a generalizable framework for accurate glioma grading.

2 Imaging Data Description

The dataset used in this work is from the Brain Tumor Segmentation 2020 (BraTS'20) challenge. The dataset consists of multi-institutional clinically acquired pre-operative multimodal MRI scans [9–11]. The dataset includes a total of 369 patients, with 293 high-grade glioma (HGG) and 76 low-grade glioma (LGG) cases. For each patient, the following scans were collected: native (T1), post-contrast T1-weighted (T1CE), T2-weighted (T2), and T2 Fluid Attenuated Inversion Recovery (T2-FLAIR) [12]. Each scan provides unique information about the tumor [13]. The dataset was provided after co-registration, skull-stripping, and manual segmentation of tumors by expert radiologists [12].

3 Methodology

In this section, we first describe the pre-processing steps, followed by the machine learning, HDC, and SHAP algorithms.

3.1 Pre-processing

The following pre-processing steps were applied in preparation of data for ML and HDC algorithms. First, radiomic features were extracted from MRI scans using the PyRadiomics toolbox [14]. The extracted radiomic features play a crucial role in glioma grade prediction by quantifying tumor characteristics from multimodal MRI scans. These features can be broadly categorized into first-order statistical features, which capture intensity-based properties such as mean, variance, skewness, and kurtosis; texture features, derived from gray-level co-occurrence matrix (GLCM), gray-level run-length matrix (GLRLM), and gray-level dependence matrix (GLDM), which describe spatial relationships and heterogeneity within the tumor region; and higher-order features, obtained through wavelet or Laplacian of Gaussian (LoG) transformations to enhance fine-grained patterns. A total of 428 features were extracted for each patient.

Next, to facilitate robust evaluation and prevent data leakage, a patient-level train-test split in the ratio of 80:20 was implemented. Stratified sampling ensured the proportional representation of HGG and LGG cases across the training and testing cohorts. Next, feature scaling was performed on both training and testing sets to make it easier for the model training. The MinMax scaling was utilized to map features within the [0,1] range. This step improved model performance, particularly for techniques sensitive to feature magnitudes, such as gradient-boosting models.

Note that the dataset has inherent class imbalance, particularly the underrepresentation of LGG cases. To account for the class imbalance, the Synthetic Minority Oversampling Technique (SMOTE) was applied only the training set. This technique generated synthetic LGG samples, ensuring a balanced training set and mitigating bias toward the majority class. By enhancing class representation, this approach improved model generalizability and predictive accuracy across both glioma grades. The pre-processed radiomic features were further used by ML and HDC algorithms as described in the next section.

3.2 Machine Learning Models

The following machine learning models were trained on the radiomic features for prediction of glioma grade.

Support Vector Machine (SVM):

SVM is a supervised learning algorithm that has gained significant popularity for its effectiveness in classification tasks [15]. At its core, SVM identifies an optimal hyperplane that separates classes within a high-dimensional space, ensuring the largest possible margin between data points of differing classes [15]. This capability makes SVM particularly well-suited for datasets where clear boundaries between classes may be challenging to discern. During the model training, we tuned the following hyperparameters: the regularization parameter (C), which balances the trade-off between maximizing the margin and minimizing classification error; the kernel type, which transforms the data into a higher-dimensional space using functions like linear, polynomial, or radial basis function.

Decision Tree (DT):

DT is a powerful machine learning model that operates by recursively splitting data based on feature thresholds, forming a tree-like structure [16]. Each split aims to maximize information gain, resulting in a series of decisions that predict outcomes at the leaf nodes. As one of the simplest models in machine learning, DT serves as an excellent baseline for performance comparisons. Despite its simplicity, DT's interpretability and effectiveness in capturing basic patterns make it a valuable tool. During the model training, we tuned the maximum depth (max_depth) of the tree and the minimum number of samples required to create a split (min_samples_split) to prevent overfitting.

Random Forest (RF):

RF is an ensemble learning method renowned for its robustness and versatility in classification tasks. Unlike single decision trees, which may be prone to overfitting, RF constructs multiple trees during training, each using a random subset of features [17]. The diversity among these trees leads to more generalized and reliable predictions, as the model aggregates outputs from all trees to make final classifications. For this work, the following key hyperparameters were fine-tuned to enhance RF's performance: the number of trees (n_estimators), which determines the forest's size; the maximum depth (max_depth), controlling the complexity of individual trees; and the minimum number of samples required to split a node (min_samples_split).

Gradient Boosting (GB):

GB is another powerful ensemble learning method, distinguished by its sequential approach to model building [18]. Unlike RF, which trains trees independently, GB builds trees iteratively, with each new tree correcting errors made by its predecessors. This gradual refinement process minimizes the model's loss function, leading to improved performance over time. The following hyperparameters were tuned in GB: the learning rate, which controls the contribution of each tree to the final model and thus affects the pace of learning; the subsample parameter, specifying the fraction of data used to train each tree, which helps prevent overfitting; and the maximum depth (max_depth) of the trees, which was tuned to balance expressiveness with generalization.

3.3 Hyperdimensional Computing

Hyperdimensional Computing (HDC) represents a cutting-edge approach inspired by brain-like computing principles [19]. Unlike traditional models, HDC encodes data into high-dimensional vectors, known as hypervectors, which can represent complex information in a distributed and error-tolerant manner. This method's simplicity lies in its reliance on basic operations, such as addition and multiplication, making it computationally efficient while maintaining robustness against noise. For glioma grade classification, ID-level encoding was employed to translate features into hypervectors, capturing essential characteristics in a manner resilient to variability and sparsity in the data [20]. HDC's ability to work well with complex medical data makes it a promising option for tasks that require both performance and speed [21]. This study integrates radiomic feature extraction, data preprocessing, SHAP-based feature selection, and HDC to develop a lightweight, interpretable, and generalizable system for accurate glioma grade classification.

3.4 Feature Importance Analysis

In machine learning models applied to medical diagnosis, understanding which features drive the model's predictions is critical for clinical trust and validation. In this study, we employed SHapley Additive exPlanations (SHAP) to quantify the contribution of individual radiomic features to model decisions. SHAP offers a theoretically grounded, model-agnostic framework for interpreting complex models by assigning each feature an importance value based on its marginal contribution to prediction outcomes.

This analysis served two key purposes:

1. To gain insight into which radiomic features (e.g., intensity and texture descriptors from different MRI modalities) were most influential in distinguishing high-grade from low-grade gliomas.
2. To inform feature selection for the HDC model by isolating the top 40 most informative features, thus improving both interpretability and predictive performance.

The SHAP-based interpretability pipeline is central to our proposed approach, enabling a transition from black-box predictions to clinically meaningful insights and lightweight model design.

4 Results and Discussion

This section presents the classification performance of machine learning and HDC models for glioma grade prediction. Additionally, it includes feature analysis and a comparison of the computational time of the models.

4.1 Classification Performance

The performance of six classifiers: Support Vector Machine (SVM), Decision Tree (DT), Random Forest (RF), Gradient Boosting (GB), and HDC (without SHAP and with SHAP) was assessed on both training and testing datasets using key performance metrics, including accuracy, precision, recall, and F1-score. During model training, hyperparameter tuning was executed through five-fold cross-validation, with the F1-score designated as the principal evaluation metric.

Tables 1 and 2 show the performance of ML and HDC models on training and on an independent testing set respectively. As can be seen from the results, SVM, Random Forest, and Gradient Boosting exhibit high F1-scores in training (~99.3%, ~99.6%, ~96.9%) but drop significantly in testing (~90.13%, ~91.07%, ~86.79%). This suggests potential overfitting, where these models perform exceptionally well on the training set but generalize poorly on unseen test data. The Decision Tree model has the lowest performance among all models, with 85.09% F1-score on training data and a further drop to 79.94% on test data. This indicates that a simple Decision Tree struggles to capture complex patterns in glioma grading.

Table 1. Performance comparison of different machine learning models and Hyperdimensional Computing (HDC) models on the training dataset. Metrics reported include Accuracy (A), Precision (P), Recall (R), and F1-score (F1). The HDC model incorporating SHAP-based feature selection outperforms the standard HDC model, demonstrating improved predictive capability.

Model	A	P	R	F1
SVM	99.32	99.33	99.32	99.32
Decision Tree	85.42	84.88	85.42	85.09
Random Forest	99.66	99.67	99.66	99.65
Gradient Boosting	96.95	96.97	96.95	96.96
HDC (without SHAP)	87.46	87.54	87.46	87.50
HDC (with SHAP)	94.92	94.85	94.92	94.87

HDC (without SHAP) has an F1-score of 87.50 in training but drops to 78.16 in testing, suggesting that the model generalizes better than some traditional ML models but still has room for improvement. HDC (with SHAP) shows a significant improvement, achieving 94.87 in training and 90.42 in testing. The gap is smaller compared to traditional ML models, indicating better generalization. The inclusion of SHAP-enhanced features in HDC (with SHAP) led to an increase in F1-score from 78.16 to 90.42 on the test set, proving the effectiveness of SHAP in improving feature selection and model interpretability. The HDC model with SHAP achieves comparable test performance to SVM (90.13) and Random Forest (91.07) while maintaining better generalization (smaller train-test gap).

Table 2. Performance comparison of different machine learning models and Hyperdimensional Computing (HDC) models on the testing dataset. Metrics reported include Accuracy (A), Precision (P), Recall (R), and F1-score (F1). The noticeable drop in performance for SVM and Random Forest suggests potential overfitting. HDC with SHAP achieves competitive performance compared to SVM and Random Forest while maintaining better generalizability.

Model	A	P	R	F1
SVM	90.54	90.19	90.54	90.13
Decision Tree	81.08	79.40	81.80	79.94
Random Forest	91.89	92.64	91.89	91.07
Gradient Boosting	86.49	87.25	86.49	86.79
HDC (without SHAP)	77.03	79.99	77.03	78.16
HDC (with SHAP)	90.54	90.34	90.54	90.42

4.2 Feature Analysis

Figure 1 illustrates the feature importance ranking derived from the SHAP analysis for glioma grade prediction. The most influential feature identified is T1CE_firstorder_Skewness, indicating its strong contribution to the classification model. This feature captures the asymmetry in intensity distribution within the contrast-enhanced T1-weighted MRI scans. Other highly ranked features include T1CE_glcm_Idmn and T2_glcm_Imc2, which belong to the Gray Level Co-occurrence Matrix (GLCM) category, highlighting the importance of texture-based features in glioma classification. Additionally, T1_glcm_RunEntropy and T2_glcm_LargeDependenceHighGrayLevelEmphasis further emphasize the significance of textural heterogeneity in tumor characterization. The features extracted from multiple MRI modalities contribute to the model performance, reinforcing the necessity of multimodal imaging in glioma grading. The dominance of texture and intensity-based features suggests that variations in tumor heterogeneity and enhancement patterns play a pivotal role in classification.

These insights from SHAP analysis were used to rank and select the top 40 most influential radiomic features based on their contribution to glioma grade prediction, as determined from Random Forest and Gradient Boosting models. These selected features were then used to retrain the HDC model, replacing the full 428-feature set. This targeted feature reduction not only eliminated noisy or redundant inputs but also preserved the most discriminative information, leading to improved classification accuracy and reduced model complexity. SHAP significantly enhanced the HDC model's performance by providing interpretable and data-driven feature selection, which improved generalizability and ensured the model's robustness across varying data samples, highlighting its central role in building an efficient and interpretable glioma grading framework.

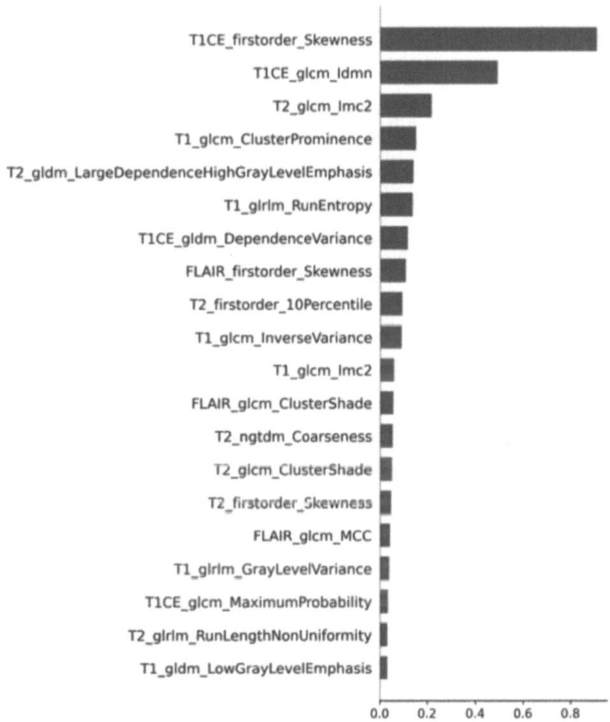

Fig. 1. Feature importance ranking for glioma grade prediction using SHAP analysis. The bar plot highlights the most influential radiomic features extracted from MRI scans. T1CE_firstorder_Skewness is identified as the most significant feature, followed by T1CE _glcm_Idmn and T2_glcm_Imc2, emphasizing the importance of intensity and texture-based characteristics. Features from multiple MRI sequences contribute to the classification, reinforcing the role of multimodal imaging in glioma grading.

4.3 Computational Performance Analysis

Table 3 presents the training time and per-patient inference time for various ML and HDC models for glioma grade prediction. The experiments were conducted on an Intel Core i7 CPU, with 16 GB of RAM, and 512 GB SSD storage. It can be observed that among traditional ML models, Random Forest has the highest training time (869.20 s), followed by SVM (172.72 s) and Gradient Boosting (132.95 s). Decision Tree, in contrast, is the most efficient among these models, requiring only 30.31 s for training. In terms of per-patient inference time, all models perform rapid predictions. Decision Tree achieves the fastest per-patient inference time (0.000024 s), while Random Forest is the slowest (0.000335 s), likely due to its ensemble nature.

The HDC models demonstrate exceptional efficiency, with HDC (without SHAP) requiring only 0.0354 s for training, significantly outperforming conventional methods. Incorporating SHAP slightly increases training time to 0.0511s, but the improvement in feature selection may justify this minimal overhead. In terms of per-patient inference, HDC remains highly competitive, with 0.000187 s (without SHAP) and 0.000209 s (with SHAP), making it a computationally attractive alternative for real-time glioma classification. The exceptional efficiency of the HDC models, both with and without SHAP, can be attributed to the simplicity of the HDC training process. Unlike traditional machine learning algorithms that require iterative optimization, gradient descent, or complex ensemble learning, HDC relies on high-dimensional vector operations such as binding, bundling, and majority voting, all of which are computationally lightweight and do not involve backpropagation. Moreover, the use of binary or integer-based hypervectors reduces memory and computational overhead. When SHAP is incorporated, although feature selection is done beforehand using more computationally intensive models (RF and GB), the final HDC training itself still involves only a small subset (top 40) of features, further reducing the dimensionality and contributing to the model's rapid training time.

Table 3. Computational Efficiency of Machine Learning and HDC Models. Training time (in seconds) refers to the total time required to train each model. Testing time per patient (in seconds) indicates the time needed to classify a single patient's data. Lower training and inference times indicate higher computational efficiency.

Model	Training Time (s)	Testing Time Per Patient (s)
SVM	172.72	0.000292
Decision Tree	30.31	0.000024
Random Forest	869.20	0.000335
Gradient Boosting	132.95	0.000137
HDC (without SHAP)	0.0354	0.000187
HDC (with SHAP)	0.0511	0.000209

5 Conclusion

This study explored the use of HDC for glioma grade classification using radiomic features extracted from MRI scans. While traditional ML models such as SVM, Random Forest, and Gradient Boosting demonstrated strong classification performance, they required extensive hyperparameter tuning and significant computational resources.

In contrast, HDC provided a lightweight and efficient alternative, achieving competitive performance with minimal training time and rapid inference. Additionally, SHAP-based feature analysis was integrated into the HDC framework, improving model interpretability and enhancing predictive accuracy. The results demonstrated that incorporating SHAP-selected features led to improved performance, reinforcing the importance of feature selection in glioma classification tasks. Furthermore, computational efficiency analysis revealed that HDC models significantly outperformed conventional machine learning methods in terms of training speed and per-patient inference time, making them well-suited for real-time and resource-constrained environments. These findings highlight the potential of HDC as a lightweight and generalizable approach for glioma grading.

References

1. Bakas, S., et al.: Advancing the cancer genome atlas glioma MRI collections with expert segmentation labels and radiomic features. Sci. Data **4**(1), 1–3 (2017)
2. Yathirajam, S.S., Gutta, S.: Efficient glioma grade prediction using learned features extracted from convolutional neural networks. J. Med. Artif. Intell. **30**, 7 (2024)
3. Wen, P.Y., Kesari, S.: Malignant gliomas in adults. N. Engl. J. Med. **359**(5), 492–507 (2008)
4. Gutta, S., Acharya, J., Shiroishi, M.S., Hwang, D., Nayak, K.S.: Improved glioma grading using deep convolutional neural networks. Am. J. Neuroradiol. **42**(2), 233–239 (2021)
5. Jackson, R.J., et al.: Limitations of stereotactic biopsy in the initial management of gliomas. Neuro Oncol. **3**(3), 193–200 (2001)
6. Tian, Q., et al.: Radiomics strategy for glioma grading using texture features from multiparametric MRI. J. Magn. Reson. Imaging **48**(6), 1518–1528 (2018)
7. Ullah F, Nadeem M, Abrar M, Amin F, Salam A, Alabrah A, AlSalman H. Evolutionary model for brain cancer-grading and classification. IEEE Access. 2023 Nov 7
8. Yang, Y., et al.: Glioma grading on conventional MR images: a deep learning study with transfer learning. Front. Neurosci. **15**(12), 804 (2018)
9. Menze, B.H., et al.: The multimodal brain tumor image segmentation benchmark (BRATS). IEEE Trans. Med. Imaging **34**(10), 1993–2024 (2014)
10. Bakas, S., et al.: Identifying the best machine learning algorithms for brain tumor segmentation, progression assessment, and overall survival prediction in the BRATS challenge (2018). arXiv preprint arXiv:1811.02629.
11. Skogen, K., Schulz, A., Dormagen, J.B., Ganeshan, B., Helseth, E., Server, A.: Diagnostic performance of texture analysis on MRI in grading cerebral gliomas. Eur. J. Radiol. **85**(4), 824–829 (2016)
12. Yathirajam, S.S., Gutta, S.: Improved glioma grade prediction with mean image transformation. In: International Conference on Artificial Intelligence in Medicine (pp. 90–94). Cham, Springer Nature Switzerland (2024)
13. Awan, A.A.: An introduction to SHAP values and machine learning interpretability (2023). Datacamp.com
14. Van Griethuysen, J.J.M., et al.: Computational radiomics system to decode the radiographic phenotype. Cancer Res. **77**(21), e104–e107 (2017). https://doi.org/10.1158/0008-5472.CAN-17-0339
15. Guido, R., Ferrisi, S., Lofaro, D., Conforti, D.: An overview on the advancements of support vector machine models in healthcare applications: a review. Information **15**(4), 235 (2024)
16. De Ville, B.: Decision trees. Wiley Interdis. Rev. Comput. Stat. **5**(6), 448–455 (2013)

17. Breiman, L.: Random forests. Mach. Learn. **45**, 5–32 (2001)
18. Bentéjac, C., Csörgő, A., Martínez-Muñoz, G.: A comparative analysis of gradient boosting algorithms. Artif. Intell. Rev. **54**, 1937–1967 (2021)
19. Amrouch, H., et al.: Brain-inspired hyperdimensional computing for ultra-efficient edge ai. In: 2022 International Conference on Hardware/Software Codesign and System Synthesis (CODES+ ISSS), (pp. 25–34). IEEE (2022)
20. Ponzina, F., Rosing, T.: MicroHD: an accuracy-driven optimization of hyperdimensional computing algorithms for TinyML systems (2024). arXiv preprint arXiv:2404.00039
21. Thomas, A., Dasgupta, S., Rosing, T.: A theoretical perspective on hyperdimensional computing. J. Artif. Intell. Res. **72**, 215–249 (2021)

muRelBench: MicroBenchmarking for Zonotope Domains

Kenny Ballou[1(✉)] and Elena Sherman[2]

[1] California State University San Marcos, San Marcos, USA
kballou@csusm.edu
[2] Boise State University, Boise, USA
elenasherman@boisestate.edu

Abstract. We present `muRelBench`, a framework for synthetic benchmarks for weakly-relational abstract domains and their operations. This extensible microbenchmarking framework enables researchers to experimentally evaluate proposed algorithms for numerical abstract domains, such as closure, least-upper bound, and forget, enabling them to quickly prototype and validate performance improvements before considering more intensive experimentation. Additionally, the framework provides mechanisms for checking correctness properties for each of the benchmarks to ensure correctness within the synthetic benchmarks.

Keywords: Weakly-Relational Abstract Domains · Zonotopes · Benchmarks · Tests

1 Introduction

Zonotopes [9], relational numerical abstract domains, are widely used in program and system verification using static analysis and model-checking techniques and, recently, found their way into the verification of neural networks [11]. To reason about their computations, verifiers manipulate abstract domains through a predefined set of operations, e.g., Least-Upper Bound (LUB), closure, or forget operators [15]. Such manipulations of abstract states commonly dominate the computation time of a verifier. Consequently, there has been extensive research on improving the efficiency of operations over Zonotopes such as closure [1,3,7,15,18].

While new algorithms provide their complexity estimates, empirically evaluating their runtimes remains crucial to comprehensively assessing their impact. Commonly, such evaluations are performed in the context of a verifier and its target, e.g., a data-flow analyzer using Zones [13,14] over a set of programs. However, depending on program structure and semantics [2], one may or may not detect the effect of the new operation over the abstract domain. As such, the question shifts to whether the set of programs are representative or the implementation of the new algorithm is inefficient and requires additional tuning. Because of the complexity of Zonotope states, it is difficult to assess whether a

S. Hussain et al. (Eds.): SEET 2025, CCIS 2725, pp. 551–559, 2026.
https://doi.org/10.1007/978-3-032-08977-9_35

verifier produces states with properties that a novel operation algorithm sufficiently takes advantage.

This problem is known to other research communities such as software engineering and compiler optimization community, which they solve by establishing microbenchmarking frameworks [12]. Microbenchmarking isolates the effects of a specific technique such as a certain optimization on syntactically generated code with desired features. In this work, we introduce `muRelBench`[1], an extensible microbenchmarking framework for Zonotopes that is built on top of the `JMH` [16,17] profiling tool for Java programs. `muRelBench` eliminates verifier and program dependencies and focuses on specific operations of parameterized Zonotope states.

For a given type of Zonotope domain, Z and its operation *ops*, `muRelBench` takes as input a set of predefined parameters for each characteristic of the corresponding Z typed abstract domain. Then the framework exhaustively generates abstract states corresponding to each element of the Cartesian product of those parameters and applies *ops* and correctness checks, if any, within the `JMH` context. Upon the completion of experiments, `muRelBench` writes the runtime results for each abstract domain to a variety of output formats, including Comma-Separated Values (CSV) files or `JSON` files, which researchers can use for further analysis and evaluation.

In its current version, generation of abstract states is parameterized by the number of variables and variable connectivity for the Octagons(Z) [15]. Thus, synthetically generated matrices that encode Octagon states vary in their size and variable relation *density*. `muRelBench` implements two closure operations (*ops*): Full Transitive Closure (using Floyd-Warshall all pairs shortest path [5]) and Chawdhary [3] incremental closure. However, as we describe in the next section, `muRelBench` can be easily extended to different Z and *ops* types.

This microbenchmarking framework has the following three key features: (1) dynamic generation of parameterized abstract states, (2) application of user defined operations on them, and (3) checks to user-defined properties, e.g., pre/-post conditions on Zonotope states before and after executing operations. We believe that `muRelBench` will help rapid prototyping of abstract operations and evaluating the efficiency of existing implementations.

In the next Sect. 2, we describe framework details and explain how the framework generates different abstract states. To demonstrate the usefulness of `muRelBench`, in Sect. 3, we present a case study on runtime data of two closure operators on Octagon states. We conclude the paper with future work on `muRelBench`.

2 `muRelBench` Framework

Figure 1 provides an overview of `muRelBench`'s components. In the dashed, rounded rectangle are user-defined components of an abstract domain type Z,

[1] Available on GitHub: https://github.com/fmsea/muRelBench.

operations, e.g., *ops*1, and property checks of the state after *ops*1 modifies the abstract state. These bindings are defined at compile-time. A *state generator* component takes generation parameters N and D—number of variables and density of the synthetic difference bounded matrix (DBM), respectively, and Z type, and randomly (up to the seed) generates $N \times D$ abstract states.

The *Benchmarking* component takes the generated states and applies *ops*1 state operation and checks the results with *check*1. The component also takes the runtime parameters for `JMH` that defines what type or runtime data to collect and how many times to repeat the experiments. Upon completion, the data is written to the console and, optionally, to an output file.

The framework is implemented in Java and uses interfaces and abstract classes to provide extension points for user-defined components. `JMH` provides a strong foundation for constructing and executing profiling benchmarks whilst minimizing confounding runtime variables such as Java Virtual Machine (JVM) startup, Just-in-Time (JIT) warmup, and Garbage Collection (GC) pauses. Specifically, `muRelBench` defaults to *three* warmup iterations before executing *five* experimental iterations for each benchmark. This way, the code under bench has a chance to JIT compile. We do not specifically tackle the notorious issue of CPU boosting and other dynamic scaling policies that generally plague benchmarks.

The framework currently has extension for Octagon abstract domain, i.e., $Z = Octagon$. The implementation encodes Octagon constraints, which are constraints of the form: $\pm x \pm y \leq c$, where $x, y \in V$ where V is the set of program variables and $c \in \mathbb{I}$, where $\mathbb{I}$ is one of $\mathbb{R}$, $\mathbb{Q}$, or $\mathbb{Z}$. Octagons are encoded as a 2-dimensional matrix, e.g., DBM [6] in the `OctagonDifferenceBoundedMatrix` class.

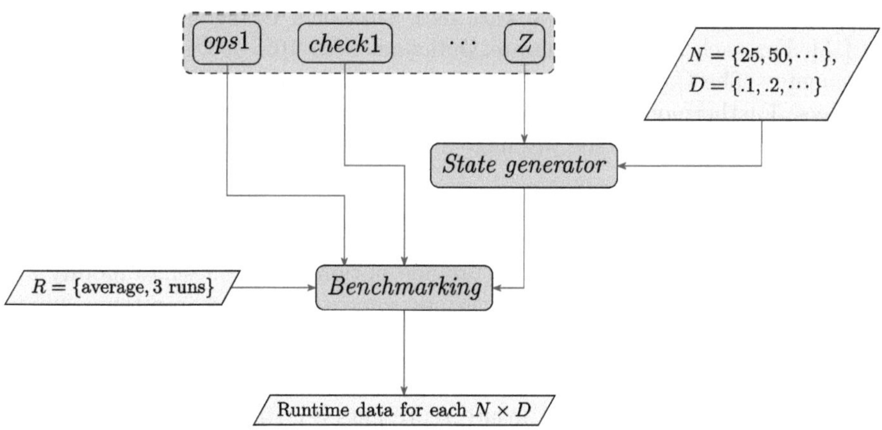

Fig. 1. Component diagram of `muRelBench`, specifying the framework's and user-defined components.

To extend operations over Octagons, users would provide extensions to `OctagonDifferenceBoundedMatrix`, overriding various operations with their implementation they wish to test. Furthermore, users provide additional instances of `*Bench`, e.g., `JoinBench`. Similar to `JUnit` [4], the naming follows convention: `muRelBench` automatically includes classes containing the `Bench` suffix.

User Extension Beyond Octagons. It is reasonably straightforward to extend `muRelBench` with additional abstract domains. A user must provide three additional classes: the abstract container type for the domain, e.g., `ZoneDBM` to add Zones [13]; a builder for the new abstract type; and finally, a *state* type which provides a container for the different parameterization sets for `JMH`.

3 Octagons and Closure Operation Case Study

Benchmark Set Up. We examine the benefits of `muRelBench` in a case study. The framework randomly generates Octagons, varying the *density* of relations between variables to create a continuum of synthetic instances. This density progression roughly correlates to the different instances of Octagons from real programs. That is, early in analysis, variables have a tendency to have few relations as only few program statements are explored. In the middle of analysis, after exploring several assignment statements, variables become tightly coupled with one another. Finally, after several fixed point iterations and widening operations, islands of connectivity emerge [7,8,19]. Furthermore, we also vary the number of variables of the synthetic Octagons to account for different programs sizes.

For this case study, we generate Octagons with 25, 50, and 100 program variables, i.e., 50, 100, and 200 variables using the Octagon variable encoding [15]. For each size, we generate Octagons with 10%–90% density, in 10% increments. The Cartesian product of these parameters results in 27 Octagon instances. Furthermore, while other tools such as `Apron` [10] can also generate random, synthetic Octagons, we make a point to only generate *consistent* synthetic Octagons.

Using `JMH`, we default to 3 "warmup" iterations and 5 experimental iterations for each benchmark. Thus, for a single benchmark, the operation under test executes 216 times. However, we do provide options for the user to modify and otherwise specify their own desired warmup and experimental iterations, among other options available via `JMH`.

Case Study. In this case study, we chose to evaluate different closure algorithms for Octagon abstract domain. Closure represents a critical operation for static program analysis and abstract interpretation because it provides critical functions: normalization for equality comparisons for data-flow analysis (DFA) [1] and precision benefits for other domain operations such as LUB [14].

Canonicalizing or normalizing Octagon states is a necessary operation because an octagonal bounded region can be represented by infinitely many different Octagons. The closure operation normalizes an Octagon by making explicit implicit edges and minimizing edge weights between variables within the Octagons. In the simplest case, this amounts to computing the all-pairs shortest-path problem for the directed, weighted graph used to represent the Octagon.

There exist several algorithms for computing the all-pairs-shortest-path problem for weighted-directed graphs such as Floyd-Warshall and Bellman-Ford algorithms [5]. While these algorithms are relatively simple and straightforward to implement, their cost can be excessive. Floyd-Warshall, for example has cubic time complexity, $\Theta(n^3)$, where n is the number of variables in the abstract Octagon state.

Chawdhary et al. [3] proposed an incremental closure algorithm for Octagons which uses code motion and hoisting to minimize the number of comparisons required to incrementally close an Octagon. Thus, they were able to reduce the incremental closure, a modified Floyd-Warshall, to $O(20n^2 - 4n)$.

Table 1. Small programs used to demonstrate performance characteristics of using different closure algorithms.

Closure	Program	Mean (ms)	σ
Floyd-Warshall	Fibonacci	144	32.2
	Loop	46.8	3.1
Chawdhary	Fibonacci	117	5.1
	Loop	49.6	10.3

Clearly, these two algorithms should have a different runtime growth with the increased number of variables. We first examined their result in the context of DFA on two small programs to see if any differences can be detected. Table 1 shows the results of the full-closure algorithm Floyd-Warshall and the Chawdhary et al.'s incremental closure. The data is averaged over five executions and includes the mean runtime for each along with their standard deviation, σ. As the data shows, the results are not entirely conclusive since on the `Loop` program, Floyd-Warshall performed better while Chawdhary runs faster on `Fibonacci`. When we analyzed the properties of the two programs, we discovered that `Fibonacci` algorithm had a maximum of six variables with density of 72% and `Loop` program had two variables with no density, which is purely interval.

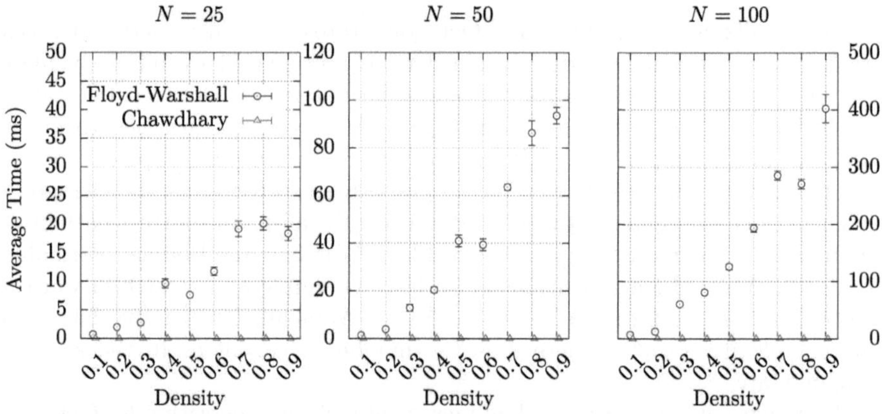

Fig. 2. Plots of microbenchmark results of closure operations, each subplot varies the number of variables, each sample varies the connectivity of program variables.

Plots in Fig. 2 show the results of the comparison of the two closure algorithm on benchmarks that `muRelBench` generates and runs. Each plot presents runtime data for different values of N while varying in density of connections between variables. Using this detailed data, we can discern clear differences between the two algorithms under comparison. Specifically, when the density is small, in each variable instance, the two algorithms seem to perform similarly. However, as soon as the density starts to climb above 30%, the incremental algorithm of Chawdhary et al. clearly computes closure operations more efficiently than that of Floyd-Warshall. Furthermore, variable density shows a significant impact on the runtime for Floyd-Warshall compared to Chawdhary et al.'s, which remains constant.

While it is expected to see a vast performance gap between full closure and incremental closure, we can zoom into the incremental approach and examine two different incremental approaches to closure. Figure 3 shows similar set of plots between the Chawdhary et al. incremental closure algorithm and an incremental closure algorithm similar to the original proposed by Miné [14]. Aside from some expected statistical noise for the small variable size, $N = 25$, these two closure algorithms perform nearly identically. Furthermore, density does not appear to significantly contribute to the runtime of the incremental algorithms under consideration, as was the case for full closure.

It may be tempting to use small programs to quickly validate new algorithm performance, however, such small programs often do not demonstrate realized benefit, as shown in Table 1. The results shown in Fig 2 more acutely capture the performance differences between full closure and an incremental closure. The results of the benchmark would thus encourage further experimentation. However, the results from Fig 3 encourage further algorithmic refinements before more intensive experimental study. That is, using a tool like `muRelBench` can save

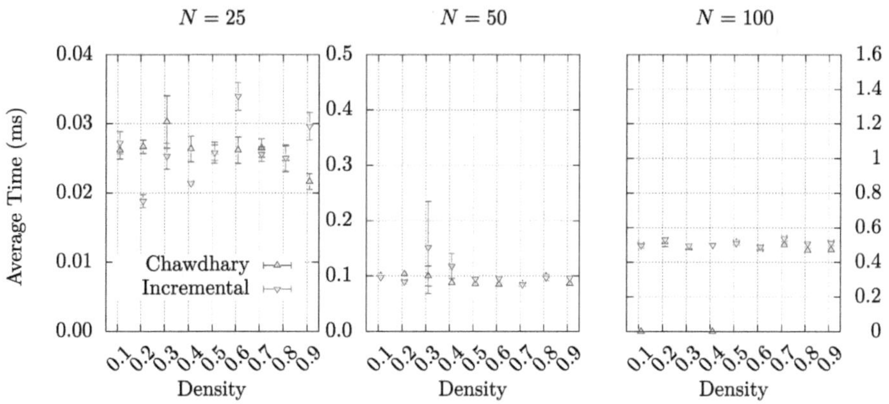

Fig. 3. Plots of microbenchmark results for incremental closure operations. Each subplot again varies by number of variables, each sample varies by connectivity of the program variables.

time and focus efforts by having a smaller but appropriate set of benchmarks to validate algorithmic improvements[2].

4 Conclusion and Future Work

In this paper, we present the `muRelBench` benchmarking framework to the abstract interpretation research community. This framework offers standardized and uniform support for comparing various operations within Zonotope abstract domains. When developing new algorithms or new abstract domains, a standard set of benchmarks and a common framework to easily test them helps convince the community of their value.

Our framework of generated benchmarks invites many improvements and future work to better situate it for the research community and software engineers at large. For example, we invite contributions of additional algorithms to be added to the suite, so others can use the results in their comparisons. Additionally, more parameters could provide a wider surface area of study for different Zonotope operations.

Acknowledgments. The work reported here was partially supported by the U.S. National Science Foundation under award CCF-19-42044.

[2] The current set of benchmarks were run using GitHub Actions on a default Ubuntu 24.04 Linux-2 instance, which currently only takes approximately 30 min.

References

1. Ballou, K., Sherman, E.: Incremental transitive closure for zonal abstract domain. In: Deshmukh, J.V., Havelund, K., Perez, I. (eds.) NFM 2022. LNCS, vol. 13260, pp. 800–808. Springer, Cham (2022). https://doi.org/10.1007/978-3-031-06773-0_43
2. Brunner, R., Dyer, R., Paquin, M., Sherman, E.: Paclab: a program analysis collaboratory. In: Proceedings of the 28th ACM Joint Meeting on European Software Engineering Conference and Symposium on the Foundations of Software Engineering, ESEC/FSE 2020. ACM (2020). https://doi.org/10.1145/3368089.3417936
3. Chawdhary, A., Robbins, E., King, A.: Incrementally closing octagons. Formal Methods Syst. Design **54**(2), 232–277 (2018). https://doi.org/10.1007/s10703-017-0314-7
4. Contributors, M.: Junit (2024). https://junit.org/
5. Cormen, T., Leiserson, C., Rivest, R., Stein, C.: Introduction to Algorithms. Computer science. McGraw-Hill (2009). https://doi.org/10.1.1.708.9446, https://books.google.com/books?id=aefUBQAAQBAJ
6. Dill, D.L.: Timing assumptions and verification of finite-state concurrent systems. In: Sifakis, J. (ed.) CAV 1989. LNCS, vol. 407, pp. 197–212. Springer, Heidelberg (1990). https://doi.org/10.1007/3-540-52148-8_17
7. Gange, G., Ma, Z., Navas, J.A., Schachte, P., Søndergaard, H., Stuckey, P.J.: A fresh look at zones and octagons. ACM Trans. Programm. Lang. Syst. **43**(3), 1–51 (2021). https://doi.org/10.1145/3457885
8. Gange, G., Navas, J.A., Schachte, P., Søndergaard, H., Stuckey, P.J.: Exploiting sparsity in difference-bound matrices. In: Rival, X. (ed.) SAS 2016. LNCS, vol. 9837, pp. 189–211. Springer, Heidelberg (2016). https://doi.org/10.1007/978-3-662-53413-7_10
9. Ghorbal, K., Goubault, E., Putot, S.: The zonotope abstract domain Taylor1+. In: Bouajjani, A., Maler, O. (eds.) CAV 2009. LNCS, vol. 5643, pp. 627–633. Springer, Heidelberg (2009). https://doi.org/10.1007/978-3-642-02658-4_47
10. Jeannet, B., Miné, A.: Apron: a library of numerical abstract domains for static analysis. In: Bouajjani, A., Maler, O. (eds.) CAV 2009. LNCS, vol. 5643, pp. 661–667. Springer, Heidelberg (2009). https://doi.org/10.1007/978-3-642-02658-4_52
11. Jordan, M., Hayase, J., Dimakis, A., Oh, S.: Zonotope domains for Lagrangian neural network verification. Adv. Neural. Inf. Process. Syst. **35**, 8400–8413 (2022)
12. Laaber, C., Leitner, P.: An evaluation of open-source software microbenchmark suites for continuous performance assessment. In: Proceedings of the 15th International Conference on Mining Software Repositories, ICSE 2018. ACM (2018). https://doi.org/10.1145/3196398.3196407
13. Miné, A.: A new numerical abstract domain based on difference-bound matrices. In: Danvy, O., Filinski, A. (eds.) PADO 2001. LNCS, vol. 2053, pp. 155–172. Springer, Heidelberg (2001). https://doi.org/10.1007/3-540-44978-7_10
14. Miné, A.: Weakly relational numerical abstract domains (2004). https://pastel.archives-ouvertes.fr/tel-00136630
15. Miné, A.: The octagon abstract domain. Higher-Order Symb. Comput. **19**(1), 31–100 (2006). https://doi.org/10.1007/s10990-006-8609-1
16. Oracle: JMH (2024). https://openjdk.org/projects/code-tools/jmh/

17. Oracle: openjdk/jmh (2024). https://github.com/openjdk/jmh
18. Schwarz, M., Seidl, H.: Octagons revisited. In: Hermenegildo, M.V., Morales, J.F. (eds) SAS 2023. LNCS, vol. 14284, pp. 485–507. Springer, Cham (2023). https://doi.org/10.1007/978-3-031-44245-2_21
19. Singh, G., Püschel, M., Vechev, M.: Making numerical program analysis fast. ACM SIGPLAN Not. **50**(6), 303–313 (2015). https://doi.org/10.1145/2813885.2738000

A Lightweight Machine Learning Pipeline for Crypto Forecasting: A Capstone Case Study in Software Engineering Education

Lucas Norpchen, Omar Garcia, Koby Winkler, Jose Temblador, and Benyamin Ahmadnia(✉)

Department of Computer Science, California State University, Dominguez Hills, Carson, USA
bahmadniayebosari@csudh.edu

Abstract. This paper presents a reproducible Machine Learning (ML) pipeline designed for short-term cryptocurrency price prediction using multimodal data sources. The system integrates minute-level OHLCV data from Kraken with pre-scored Reddit sentiment, both resampled to hourly resolution and aligned to create a six-hour-ahead binary classification task. Twelve lagged hours of sentiment and price signals are appended to construct the feature set. Four classifiers–Support Vector Machine (SVM), Random Forest (RF), Extreme Gradient Boosting (XGB), and a majority-vote ensemble–are trained and evaluated using a walk-forward validation scheme. The results in the final test window show that the SVM produces the highest overall accuracy (52.05%), while the ensemble model achieves the best F1 score and recall (86.36%) in the minority "rise" class. Feature importance analysis indicates that historical price data dominate sentiment inputs, although all models benefit modestly from the added social signal. Although precision remains modest, high recall on upward trends highlights practical value for momentum-sensitive and risk-aware trading scenarios. Beyond modeling, this paper serves as a pedagogical tool in a senior software engineering course, emphasizing reproducibility, pipeline modularity, latency profiling, and data-centric system design. The fully automated Python framework, from ZIP extraction to model benchmarking, is openly available to support future enhancements, instructional use, and community-driven research.

Keywords: Cryptocurrency forecasting · Reddit sentiment · Multimodal features

1 Introduction

Cryptocurrency markets are characterized by sharp sentiment-driven price changes that challenge short-term forecasting models and complicate risk-aware decision making [2]. Social media platforms such as Reddit and X^{TM} (formerly

S. Hussain et al. (Eds.): SEET 2025, CCIS 2725, pp. 560–567, 2026.
https://doi.org/10.1007/978-3-032-08977-9_36

Twitter) have emerged as influential drivers of investor sentiment, offering real-time insights that can augment traditional financial indicators [3,4]. Although prior work suggests that crowd sentiment can contribute predictive value, the effectiveness of lightweight, interpretable models in capturing these signals, particularly under latency constraints, remains underexplored [5,6].

This paper presents a reproducible Machine Learning (ML) pipeline for the prediction of the direction of movement of the six-hour intraday on Bitcoin and Ethereum. The system integrates Kraken minute-level OHLCV price data with Reddit sentiment scores per hour using the VADER lexicon. Both data streams are aligned, resampled to hourly cadence, and enriched with twelve lagged hours of historical sentiment and price. The resulting multimodal matrix is normalized and split chronologically into training, validation, and test sets through a walk-forward protocol. Four classifiers–Support Vector Machine (SVM), Random Forest (RF), Extreme Gradient Boosting (XGBoost), and a simple majority vote ensemble. Feature-gain analysis further clarifies the relative importance of sentiment versus price history in model predictions.

Beyond its forecasting objective, this paper was conducted as a semester-long capstone in a senior software engineering course, where cryptocurrency prediction served as a unifying theme for building modular and reproducible ML systems. Student teams designed and version controlled the entire pipeline in Git, implementing hourly resampling, lag-feature generation, and walk-forward evaluation in a single automated workflow. Continuous integration hooks were used to track latency in single-CPU inference, forcing trade-offs between model complexity and real-time performance. Deliverables included unit-tested preprocessing modules, Bayesian hyperparameter tuning notebooks, and containerized dashboards with explainable outputs based on experience with reproducibility, data drift, and maintainability. The system remains lightweight enough for undergraduate replication while supporting ongoing faculty-led research extensions.

2 Related Work

Recent research on cryptocurrency forecasting has increasingly leveraged multimodal learning, combining technical indicators with crowd sentiment to improve short-horizon price prediction. One of the most advanced contributions is the "Multi-Source Hard and Soft Information Fusion" framework [1], which integrates three heterogeneous data streams: order-book microstructure data, OHLCV-derived technical indicators and Telegram-based sentiment. Their method performs hard vote at the feature level and soft Bayesian fusion at the decision level, achieving an F1 score of 0.74 in minute-level Bitcoin data, outperforming the baselines of standalone Long-Short-Term Memory (LSTM) and Convolutional Neural Network (CNN) by 6 to 9% points. This work demonstrates that sentiment signals can complement price-based features and that structured fusion can enhance predictive robustness.

Simpler two-source pipelines have also shown value. [2] correlated Twitter sentiment with GARCH volatility, while [3] used Reddit polarity scores from the VADER lexicon to boost XGBoost classifiers. Transformer-based sentiment encoding has only recently been introduced: [4] showed that FinBERT-enhanced BiLSTM models achieved a 4-percent improvement over lexicon methods on Ethereum. In terms of classifier selection, SVMs remain favored for their interpretability and speed in high-frequency domains [5], while tree-based ensembles such as XGBoost and LightGBM continue to set the top benchmarks on tabular and financial data [6].

Although these studies contribute valuable information, they often emphasize performance gains without addressing reproducibility, latency profiling, or software engineering practices. Many prior pipelines are proprietary, lack version control artifacts, or omit deployment considerations.

Our work diverges from those of [1] and similar fusion-heavy systems in three key ways. First, we limit the predictive stack to lightweight, interpretable classifiers (SVM and XGBoost), explicitly targeting sub-100 ms inference latency to meet real-time deployment constraints. Second, we adopt a streamlined, two-source design, combining Kraken market data with Reddit sentiment, processed through a fully open-source and script-driven workflow. This modularity supports reproducibility and extensibility, both pedagogically and for applied research. Third, we validate using an expanding walk-forward protocol, preserving temporal causality and reflecting real-world deployment timelines better than static test splits. These design decisions produce a transparent software pipeline that isolates the incremental utility of social sentiment while maintaining accessibility for classroom replication and community-driven research.

3 Methodology

This section details the end-to-end workflow used to develop, train, and evaluate a reproducible ML pipeline for short-term cryptocurrency forecasting. The methodology is divided into three main components: 1) data acquisition and preprocessing, 2) software engineering practices that ensure modularity and reproducibility, and 3) model training, validation, and latency-aware evaluation. Each stage is designed to support lightweight experimentation, rapid iteration, and instructional reuse in an educational or applied research setting.

3.1 Data Acquisition and Preprocessing

Minute-level OHLCV records for Bitcoin and Ethereum were downloaded from Kraken's public archives (January 2021 - April 2025) and stored in compressed ZIP format. A custom Python routine inflates and concatenates the data into a single `pandas` DataFrame. Hourly Reddit sentiment files pre-scored using the VADER sentiment analyzer [7] provide polarity values in the range $[-1, 1]$. Both data streams are converted to Coordinated Universal Time (UTC), downsampled to hourly resolution, and joined by timestamp. Missing sentiment or price rows (fewer than 0.2%) are forward-filled or discarded.

To capture temporal context, twelve lagged hours of both sentiment and close price are appended (i.e., `sentiment_prev_1h_12h`, `close_prev_1h_12h`). The close price is shifted six hours into the future, and the binary label `rise_6h` is assigned 1 if the future close exceeds the current value. All features are normalized using a z-score transformation ($\mu = 0$, $\sigma = 1$). The dataset is chronologically partitioned into 70% training, 15% validation, and 15% testing using an expanding walk-forward protocol to avoid look-ahead bias.

3.2 Software Engineering Practices

The pipeline adheres to professional software engineering standards. All source code, configuration files, and notebooks are version-controlled in a public GitHub repository. GitHub Actions automates continuous integration, triggers unit tests, and lint upon each pull request. The system is organized into modular, function-per-stage scripts (e.g., data ingestion, preprocessing, model training), allowing independent module replacement. Runtime parameters–including API keys, time horizons, and resampling intervals–are externalized in human-readable YAML configuration files.

The students followed a lightweight agile process throughout the development. Weekly issues defined goals; feature branches were merged via peer-reviewed pull requests that enforced documentation, testing, and maintainability. The result is a reproducible and extensible ML workflow suitable for both instructional and research settings.

3.3 Modeling and Training Procedure

We evaluate two low-latency and interpretable classifiers suitable for real-time deployment:

- SVM with an RBF kernel. The predictors are normalized as previously described. Hyperparameters $C \in [10^{-3}, 10^{3}]$ and $\gamma \in [10^{-4}, 10^{4}]$ are tuned using Bayesian optimization with an expected improvement acquisition function over 30 trials. The class imbalance (~70% fall vs. 30% rise) is mitigated by applying the inverse class weighting.
- XGBoost uses raw (unscaled) features and a binary logistic objective. Hyperparameters include the number of trees ($n_{\text{estimators}} = 100$–$800$), maximum depth (3–10), learning rate (0.01–0.3), subsample ratio (0.5–1.0), and column sample ratio (0.5–1.0). Early stopping halts training if validation loss does not improve after 30 rounds.

Both models are trained using an expanding walk-forward regime: At each iteration t, the model is trained on all data up to t, validated on the next 15% slice, and tested on a disjoint 15% window. Metrics include accuracy, precision, recall, macro, and weighted F1 score, averaged across folds. Confidence intervals are computed using blocked bootstrap sampling to address temporal autocorrelation.

Latency was profiled over 1,000 random inputs on an Intel® i7 CPU (2.8 GHz, 16 GB RAM). Inference times averaged 62 ms (SVM) and 74 ms (XGBoost), with no instance exceeding the 100 ms latency threshold, satisfying the requirements for real-time dashboard integration. All experiments were carried out using Python 3.13 with `scikit-learn` 1.4.1 and `xgboost` 2.0.

4 Results and Discussion

Table 1 reports the aggregate and class-wise performance metrics for all four classifiers, averaged over the final walk-forward test window (≈15% of the timeline, $n = 71$). Among the models, SVM achieved the highest overall test accuracy (52.05%), followed by XGBoost (47.95%), the ensemble (46.58%), and Random Forest (41.10%).

Table 1. Test-Window Performance (P = Precision, R = Recall)

Metric	SVM	Random Forest	XGBoost	Ensemble
Validation Accuracy	0.6111	0.5278	0.6111	–
Test Accuracy	0.5205	0.4110	0.4795	0.4658
Precision (Class 1)	0.3617	0.3220	0.3333	0.3455
Recall (Class 1)	0.7727	0.8636	0.7273	0.8636
F1 Score (Class 1)	0.4928	0.4691	0.4571	0.4935

When evaluating performance in the minority "rise" class, the ensemble classifier yielded the highest F1 score (0.4935), balancing a dataset-leading recall (0.8636, tied with Random Forest) against a precision of 0.346. Random Forest, while equally strong in recall (0.8636), produced lower precision (0.322), making it a suitable choice for use cases that prioritize recall over false-positive control. SVM posted the highest macro F1 score due to its relatively strong precision in class 1, despite a lower recall.

XGBoost offered the best balance between predictive performance and latency (mean inference time: 74 ms), confirming its viability for real-time dashboard integration. All models maintained the above recall 70% for upward movements, a desirable trait in momentum-sensitive forecasting. However, class-1 precision across models remained limited (0.322–0.364), highlighting a persistent "false-rise" issue. This limitation underscores the need for richer feature engineering and potentially better-calibrated sentiment sources.

To further interpret the behavior of the model, Fig. 1 shows the importance of gain-based characteristics for the XGBoost classifier. Price-derived lag features overwhelmingly dominate predictive power, particularly the most recent lag hours. However, reddit sentiment features contribute a measurable gain, especially at shorter temporal offsets, validating their inclusion as complementary signals.

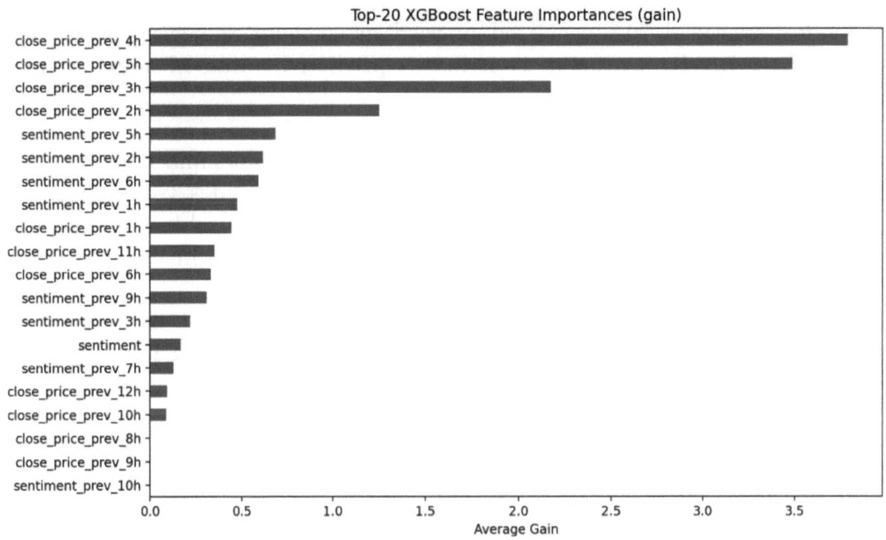

Fig. 1. XGBoost gain-based feature importance. Lagged close-price features dominate, while shorter-lag sentiment features contribute measurable gain.

Beyond classification metrics, these results illustrate the benefit of a reproducible modular pipeline that supports rapid experimentation between model types and tradeoff strategies. The pipeline's low-latency design and explainability components make it suitable not only for educational deployment but also for practical use in financial forecasting systems.

Error analysis revealed that the majority false positives in the "rise" class occurred during periods of sentiment spikes not matched by market behavior. For instance, on March 7, 2024, the high Reddit polarity on Ethereum corresponded to regulatory speculation that did not materialize in price movement. Additionally, sentiment features with lags that exceeded 8 h contributed noise rather than signal, likely due to topic drift. These findings suggest future models could benefit from sentiment freshness metrics or relevance filtering based on recent post-context.

5 Conclusions and Future Work

This paper presents a reproducible, end-to-end software pipeline for short-horizon cryptocurrency price forecasting that integrates Kraken OHLCV market data with hourly Reddit sentiment. The system includes automated data extraction, timestamp-aligned multimodal fusion, YAML-based configuration, and latency-constrained walk-forward evaluation. Four lightweight classifiers were benchmarked: SVM achieved the highest overall accuracy (52.05%), the ensemble recorded the best F1-score, and Random Forest offered the highest recall (86.36%), while XGBoost balanced predictive strength and latency (74 ms).

All models exceeded 70% recall on upward movements, indicating that even lexicon-based Reddit sentiment contributes predictive value without compromising real-time responsiveness.

The project was conducted in a senior software engineering course and serves as a pedagogically grounded case study in modular, testable, and latency-aware ML system design. The fully containerized codebase includes version control, unit tests, continuous integration workflows, and a configurable `config.yaml` providing an extensible foundation for instructional reuse and future research in software engineering education.

In addition to its technical contributions, the project was evaluated for its pedagogical effectiveness. 24 students participated in the semester-long capstone, working in agile teams with peer-reviewed pull requests and CI-enforced quality gates. Post-project surveys (n = 21, 87.5% response rate) indicated improved confidence in software engineering tools and practices, with mean Likert scores of 4.6/5 for Git workflows, 4.7/5 for reproducible pipeline design and 4.4/5 for data-centric system architecture. Instructors observed that students wrote more modular and better-tested code compared to previous cohorts, with median unit test pass rates exceeding 95%. These findings support the effectiveness of the pipeline as a reusable instructional framework.

We acknowledge that Reddit sentiment is susceptible to manipulation through bots, sarcasm, and coordinated pump-and-dump campaigns, which the VADER lexicon may not reliably detect. As a result, polarity scores could embed misleading signals or bias-model outputs. To mitigate this risk, we recommend integrating a human-in-the-loop validation layer and limiting automated exposure through strict position sizing. Future extensions may incorporate anomaly detection techniques, trustworthiness scores for users, or post-history credibility filtering to improve sentiment reliability. Further work may also explore integrating toxicity filters or trustworthiness heuristics to strengthen sentiment robustness in adversarial or noisy environments. All datasets, model parameters, and attribution plots are publicly released to encourage independent auditing, replication, and further study of both performance and fairness implications.

Although the present use case is centered on cryptocurrency markets, the underlying design is generalized to other instructional domains such as real-time monitoring in IoT, anomaly detection in cybersecurity, and time-series analysis in the system log. The modular architecture and YAML-configured parameters allow educators to easily swap alternative data sources and tasks. We plan to release a templated GitHub Classroom repository and an autograding-compatible workflow to facilitate adoption across institutions.

This study currently focuses on a single social source (Reddit), excludes order book microstructure and blockchain-level metrics, and evaluates only a six-hour prediction horizon. Future work will extend the system to incorporate multi-platform sentiment (e.g., X/Twitter, Telegram), on-chain features, and sequence-aware architectures such as Temporal Convolutional Networks and Transformers. The fully open-source, containerized implementation offers a replicable and extensible foundation for educators, researchers, and practitioners exploring data-centric AI systems in volatile financial domains.

Acknowledgments. The authors would like to thank the Department of Computer Science and the College of Natural and Behavioral Sciences at CSUDH for their support.

Disclosure of Interests. The authors have no competing interests to declare that are relevant to the content of this article.

References

1. Dashtaki, S.M., Chagahi, M.H., Moshiri, B., Piran, M.J.: Multi-source hard and soft information fusion approach for accurate cryptocurrency price movement prediction (2024)
2. Pagnottoni, M., Dimpfl, T.: Price jumps on bitcoin markets. Econ. Lett. **191** (2020)
3. Feng, W., Zhang, Y., He, D.: Can social media predict cryptocurrency returns? Evidence from Reddit. In: Proceedings of the IEEE International Conference on Blockchain (ICBC) (2021)
4. Sun, S., Li, J., Zhu, Q.: Transformer-enhanced sentiment for crypto forecasting. Expert Syst. Appl. **224** (2023)
5. Mallqui, R., Ferreira, R.: Predicting the direction of bitcoin price using machine learning. Appl. Soft Comput. **75** (2019)
6. Livieris, N., et al.: An ensemble learning strategy for intraday bitcoin price prediction. Neurocomputing **425** (2021)
7. Hutto, C.J., Gilbert, E.: VADER: a parsimonious rule-based model for sentiment analysis of social media text. ICWSM (2014)

Solving Prime Factorization Using Quantum Ising Model

Wen-Li Wang[1(✉)], Mei-Huei Tang[2], Shahid Hussain[1], and Kevin Wang[1]

[1] Penn State University Behrend, Erie 16563, PA, USA
wxw18@psu.edu
[2] Gannon University, Erie 16541, PA, USA

Abstract. Quantum algorithms demonstrate good proficiency in solving combinatorial problems, a challenge faced by many optimization and cryptographic systems. Prime factorization is one of the hard problems and an efficient solver can significantly benefit those systems. In this regard, Shor's algorithm utilizing quantum Fourier Transform has been proven to factor numbers exponentially faster than classical methods. However, it relies on finding the period of a function, which can sometimes be a challenging task. This study proposes another idea without that dependency to solve prime factorization through the construction of a quantum Ising model. The goal is to optimize or minimize Hamiltonian energy like the widely adopted approach of modeling NP-hard Ising spin glasses. This developed paradigm can benefit software practitioners to solve more and bigger scale combinatorial problems. Our methodology is a procedure of three steps. Step one formulates mathematical formulas based on the couplings of atomic Ising spins to model the range and product of numerical values. The second step accounts for the input value to construct observable operators that form a large matrix for quantum modeling through Pauli gates. The final step identifies the prime factors by computing the minimum eigenvalue of the matrix. This approach is validated through the execution of quantum approximate optimization algorithm (QAOA) combined with the constrained optimization by linear approximation (COBYLA) optimizer available in the IBM Qiskit SDK. Experimental results are presented to verify the degree of correctness.

Keywords: Ising · Quantum · Hamiltonian · Prime Factors · QAOA · COBYLA

1 Introduction

Prime factorization is a fundamental concept in number theory and has practical applications on cryptography, data compression, and so on. The objective of factorization is to decompose a number into its prime factors and algorithms for classical computers have been developed to support the applications. A simple algorithm is the traditional trial division that finds the prime factors of a number by continuously dividing the original number by prime factors until the remainder is equal to 1. The most advanced and efficient algorithm is the General Number Field Sieve (GNFS) [1].

S. Hussain et al. (Eds.): SEET 2025, CCIS 2725, pp. 568–574, 2026.
https://doi.org/10.1007/978-3-032-08977-9_37

Today, quantum algorithms that take advantage of the parallel computation power of quantum computers for prime factorization are available [2]. Among them, the most well-known and innovative quantum algorithm is Shor's algorithm [3]. It demonstrates good proficiency in performing prime factorization of large numbers by taking advantage of quantum Fourier Transform [4] to find the period of a function. The algorithm can run exponentially faster than classical methods, but the difficulty is in the challenge of finding the period of any arbitrary functions and reducing the need for the number of qubits. In this regard, a scalable version in [5] conserves the usage of qubits through an iterative approach.

In [2], an Ising model approach was introduced and related work on prime factorization was surveyed. There is no need for the approach to find the period of a function, but it requires more qubits than Shor's algorithm to handle the same size input value. In that article, the equations focused on one instance without being generalized and modeled into quantum gates. This hinders the prevalence of the approach to software practitioners. The objective of this study is to incorporate the same model but generalize factorization formulas, limit qubit usage no more than Shor's, perform modeling into quantum gates, and introduce range concepts to identify prime numbers during the search of prime factors.

Our approach conforms to the paradigm of modeling the Ising spin glass problem [6] that finds the ground states for a spin glass system through the optimization of Hamiltonian energy. By converting the problem into a quantum version, the optimization process can apply algorithms like QAOA [7] and quantum annealing [6, 8] as well as optimizers like COBYLA [9] to compute the minimal eigen value of a constructed matrix to attain the solution. The prime values and their ranges are formulated based on the values of Ising spins. Subsequent steps of modeling are transformed into a quantum circuit with Pauli gates [10]. Finally, the optimization process for minimizing the Hamiltonian energy is applied to find the solution.

In this paper, Sect. 2 formulates prime values and the factorization problem. Quantum modeling to build observable operators from Pauli gates is conducted in Sect. 3. Section 4 shows experimental results, and Sect. 5 concludes the work.

2 Methodology

Ising spin glasses, named after Ernst Ising and Wilhelm Lenz [11], are models constructed as glasses that consist of discrete variables. These variables represent the magnetic dipole moments of atomic spins with positive couplings (+1) for the up arrows and negative couplings (−1) for the down arrows. Figure 1 shows a one-dimensional Ising model used in our methodology. The values of the variables are used to compute the energy of an Ising model formulated by a Hamiltonian function [12, 13] through interaction and the external magnetic field. The optimal solution is then to find the minimum eigenvalue of a matrix, utilizing the parallel quantum computing (QC) power.

The following describes our approach to construct the Ising models and denote the equations to solve the prime factorization problem. Basically, a classical Ising model can be written as a Hamiltonian function H of a set of m spins with their values $s_k = \pm 1$, as shown in Eq. (1). This quadratic function has spinning inputs s_k for H, where J_{ij} is

Fig. 1. A sample one-dimensional Ising model

the interaction between two elements i and j, while h_i is the external magnetic field.

$$H(s_1, s_2, \ldots, s_m) = -\sum_{i<j} J_{ij} s_i s_j - \sum_{i=1}^{m} h_i s_i \tag{1}$$

To factorize a numeric value v of n bits into a product of two prime numbers, a prime factor can likely go up to n bits, i.e., a total of $m = 2n$ spin variables $s_k = \pm 1, 1 \leq k \leq m$, to address the ranges of the two primes. For model construction, we define binary variables x_k to be true or false for a bit of a prime factor as 1 and 0. As formulated in Eq. (2), the spin values of –1 and 1 will yield a 1 (true) and 0 (false), respectively.

$$x_k = \frac{1 - s_k}{2}, 1 \leq k \leq m \tag{2}$$

A Hamiltonian function H of Eq. (1) can be constructed from subfunctions individually and then summed up together. Our model for prime factorization consists of two subfunctions, as shown in Eq. (3). The goal is to minimize the entire Hamiltonian energy to yield the ground state energy of $H = 0$, as discussed in the subsections below.

$$H = H_A + H_B \tag{3}$$

2.1 The Multiplication Constraint

Equation (4) denotes the formula of H_A, which is the energy subfunction regarding the product of two factors to yield the n-bit input value v. Coefficient A is a positive real number that can be used to control the weight of this subfunction. The two internal summation functions convert the binary values into decimal values for the two factors, respectively. If the product of the two factors is equal to v, we have $H_A = 0$ meaning a satisfied result for the subfunction. Otherwise, the squared result will make H_A greater than 0 as no solution is found.

$$H_A = A\left(v - \left(\sum_{i=1}^{n} 2^{i-1} \cdot x_i\right)\left(\sum_{j=n+1}^{m} 2^{j-n-1} \cdot x_j\right)\right)^2 \tag{4}$$

2.2 The Range Constraint

The range constraint is to ensure that values 0 and 1 are excluded to be a prime factor, because the smallest prime value is 2. Equation (5) formulates the energy subfunction of H_B. Like Eq. (4), coefficient B is a positive real number to control the weight of this subfunction. For H_B, the idea is straightforward. The two out-of-range values 0 and 1 all have upper bits equal to 0 and the lowest bit value can vary. Therefore, as long as one of the upper bits of a potential factor is 1, the multiplication result will yield a 0 for it can be accepted in the range. The product is equal to 1 only when all the upper bits have a value of 0, i.e., the factor is not within the range and should be excluded. When both factors are not out of the range, we have $H_B = 0$, meaning the values of the two factors are likely to be a candidate solution.

$$H_B = B\left(\prod_{i=2}^{n}(1 - x_i) + \prod_{j=n+2}^{m}(1 - x_j)\right) \tag{5}$$

3 Quantum Modeling

For QC, inputs are qubits, i.e., vectors not scalar values. Hence, the quantum version of the Hamiltonian function H_Q is modeled as shown in Eq. (6), in which q_k^z for $1 \leq k \leq m$ is a 2×2 Pauli matrix that can be a Pauli I, X, Y, or Z gate [21]. For the prime factorization problem, the set of q_k^z can be built using Z gates with identity matrix I being skipped in the notation. Since our Ising model requires $2n$ spins, the H_Q needs $m = 2n$ qubits for the Hamiltonian function H to solve prime factorization.

$$H_Q = H\left(q_1^z, q_2^z, \ldots, q_m^z\right) \tag{6}$$

The same example of $11 \times 13 = 143$, i.e., $n = 8$ as discussed in [2], is adopted for illustration on quantum modeling. The total number of qubits required is $m = 2 \times 8 = 16$, i.e., 8 for each factor. For simplicity, the coefficients of both A and B are set to be 1 without affecting the solution result. By Eq. (4), the quantum observable Q [14] of the Ising model is built from the Pauli Z gates to tackle the scalar values 1 and –1 of spin variables s_k in Eq. (2). In the following, gate Z_k subscripted with an index number k corresponds to the binary variable x_k of the same index. Subject to limited space, only nine computation results out of a total of 1369 terms are listed.

$$\begin{aligned}
Q &= 1 \cdot \left(143 - \left(\sum_{i=1}^{8} 2^{i-1}\left(\tfrac{1-Z_i}{2}\right)\right)\left(\sum_{j=9}^{16} 2^{j-9}\left(\tfrac{1-Z_j}{2}\right)\right)\right)^2 \\
&= 467020967.75 - 2750748.75Z_1 + \ldots - 3.5209584E8Z_{16} \\
&+21717.5Z_1Z_2 + 43435Z_1Z_3 + \ldots + 8.895488E7Z_{15}Z_{16} \\
&+\ldots+ \\
&+1Z_1Z_2Z_9Z_{10} + 2Z_1Z_2Z_8Z_{10} + \ldots + 1.6777216E7Z_7Z_8Z_{15}Z_{16}
\end{aligned}$$

The quantum Hamiltonian subfunction H_A is equivalent to the expectation value $<Q>$ computed as $<\Psi|Q|\Psi>$ for the quantum state Ψ. For this observable Q, only the four 16-qubit quantum states in Table 1 yield an expectation value $<Q>$ to be equal to 0. The other (2^{16}–4) states will all get a Hamiltonian energy result greater than 0.

Table 1. Four quantum states with $H_A = 0$

Ψ	$H_A = \langle Q \rangle = \langle \Psi \vert Q \vert \Psi \rangle$	Prime Factor 1	Prime Factor 2
$\vert 0000000110001111\rangle$	0	1	143
$\vert 1000111100000001\rangle$	0	143	1
$\vert 0000101100001101\rangle$	0	11	13
$\vert 0000110100001011\rangle$	0	13	11

By Eq. (5), the range constraint further excludes the consideration of values 0 and 1 as a legitimate prime factor. For the observable operator Q, we have

$$
\begin{aligned}
Q &= 1 \cdot \left(\prod_{i=2}^{8} (1 - x_i) + \prod_{j=10}^{16} (1 - x_j) \right) \\
&= 0.015625 + 0.0078125 Z_2 + \ldots + 0.0078125 Z_{16} \\
&+ 0.0078125 Z_2 Z_3 + 0.0078125 Z_2 Z_4 + \ldots + 0.0078125 Z_{15} Z_{16} \\
&+ \ldots + \\
&+ 0.0078125 Z_2 Z_3 Z_4 Z_5 + \ldots + 0.0078125 Z_{13} Z_{14} Z_{15} Z_{16} \\
&+ 0.0078125 Z_2 Z_3 Z_4 Z_5 Z_6 Z_7 Z_8 + \ldots + 0.0078125 Z_9 Z_{10} Z_{11} Z_{12} Z_{13} Z_{14} Z_{15}
\end{aligned}
$$

Due to limited space, only 10 out of a total of 255 terms are listed. By Eqs. (3) and (6), we have $H_Q = H\left(q_1^z, q_2^z, \ldots, q_{16}^z\right) = H_A + H_B$. Table 2 shows the combined results with two solutions left to have $H_Q = 0$. The first two quantum states in Table 1 are excluded, because one of the factors has all upper bits equal to 0.

Table 2. Two quantum states with $H_Q = H_A + H_B = 0$

Ψ	$H_Q = H_A + H_B$	Prime Factor 1	Prime Factor 2
$\vert 0000101100001101\rangle$	0	11	13
$\vert 0000110100001011\rangle$	0	13	11

4 Experimental Results

Experiments were conducted to evaluate different input scenarios using the IBM Qiskit SDK on a PC with Intel Core i7-7700K CPU. The prime factorization process exploits the QAOA algorithm [7] combined with the COBYLA optimizer [9] to compute the minimum eigenvalue of the matrix for solution. Table 3 lists the exercised scenarios and their computation time under the simulator. A snippet of Python code is also included below. The pauli_list includes a list of Z gates with indices and coefficients, such as [("Z", [1], 0.5), …, ("ZZ",[3, 4],1)].

```
op = SparsePauliOp.from_sparse_list(pauli_list, num_qubits=16)
qaoa = QAOA(sampler=Sampler(), optimizer=COBYLA(), reps=1)
result = qaoa.compute_minimum_eigenvalue(op)
print(result.best_measurement)
```

Table 3. Inputs and Qiskit simulator performance on prime factorization

Input Value	Prime Factor 1	Prime Factor 2	Performance
1,040,399	1019	1021	147.13 s
59,989	251	239	18.07 s
2,257	61	37	7.71 s
143	11	13	1.43 s

5 Conclusions

A new quantum Ising model for prime factorization is successfully developed. For an input value of n bits, it requires about $2n$ qubits like Shor's algorithm. The equations are formulated based on the couplings of atomic spins like modeling spin glasses. The multiplication and range constraints are handled as separate observable operators and then combined to find solutions. Experiments are conducted to exercise larger input values for factorization and the process takes advantage of QAOA algorithm and COBYLA optimizer to compute the minimum eigenvalue of the constructed matrix from quantum Pauli gates. The result yields the lowest Hamiltonian energy as the solution. Our methodology generalizes the mathematical formulas, conserves qubit usage, performs quantum modeling into gates, and introduces the range concept to ignore values 0 and 1 as a prime factor.

References

1. Lenstra, A., Lenstra, H., Manasse, M., Pollard, J.: The number field sieve. In: Proceedings of the 22nd Annual ACM Symposium on Theory of Computing, Baltimore, Maryland (1990)
2. Wang, B., Hu, F., Yao, H., Wang, C.: Prime factorization algorithm based on parameter optimization of Ising model. Sci. Rep. **10**, 7106 (2020)
3. Shor, P.: Polynomial-time algorithms for prime factorization and discrete logarithms on a quantum computer. In: Proceedings of the 35th Annual Symposium on Foundations of Computer Science, Santa Fe, New Mexico (1994)
4. Coppersmith, D.: An approximate Fourier Transform useful in quantum factoring. IBM Res. Rep. (1994). https://arxiv.org/abs/quant-ph/0201067. Last accessed 21 July 2025
5. Martín-López, E., Laing, A., Lawson, T., Alvarez, R., Zhou, X.-Q., O'Brien, J.: Experimental realization of Shor's quantum factoring algorithm using Qubit recycling. Nat. Photonics **6**, 773–776 (2012)

6. Kadowaki, T., Nishimori, H.: Quantum annealing in the transverse Ising model. Phys. Rev. E **58**(5), 5355–5363 (1998)
7. Zhou, L., Wang, S.-T., Choi, S., Pichler, H., Lukin, M.: Quantum approximate optimization algorithm: performance, mechanism, and implementation on near-term devices. Am. Phys. Soc. (APS) J. Phys. Rev. **10**(2) (2020)
8. Hen, I., Spedalieri, F.M.: Quantum annealing for constrained optimization. Am. Phys. Soc. (APS) J. Phys. Rev. **5**(3) (2016)
9. Powell, M.: A direct search optimization method that models the objective and constraint functions by linear interpolation. In: Gomez, S., Hennart, J.P. (eds.) Advances in Optimization and Numerical Analysis. Mathematics and its Applications, vol. 275, pp. 51–67. Springer, Dordrecht (1994)
10. Barenco, A., et al.: Elementary gates for quantum computation. Phys. Rev. A **52**(5), 3457–3467 (1995)
11. Niss, M.: History of the Lenz-Ising model 1965–1971: the role of a simple model in understanding critical phenomena. Arch. Hist. Exact Sci. **65**, 625–658 (2011)
12. Skotiniotis, M., Sekatski, P., Dür, W.: Quantum metrology for the Ising Hamiltonian with transverse magnetic field. New J. Phys. **17**(7), 073032 (2015)
13. Lucas, A.: Ising formulations of many NP problems. Front. Phys. **2**(5) (2014)
14. Shlosberg, A., Jena, A., Mukhopadhyay, P., Haase, J., Leditzky, F., Dellantonio, L.: Adaptive estimation of quantum observables. Quantum **7**, 906 (2023)

Comparative Fine-Tuning of GPT-2 on Question Answering and Dialogue Datasets for Medical Text Generation

Caleb Nhkum[1], Mohammad Masudur Rahman[2], Tanvir Ahmed[3], and Md. Faisal Kabir[1](✉)

[1] Penn State Harrisburg, Middletown, PA 17057, USA
{czn5226,mpk5904}@psu.edu

[2] School of Computing and Informatics, University of Louisiana at Lafayette, Lafayette, LA, USA
mohammad.rahman3@louisiana.edu

[3] School of Computer and Cyber Sciences, Augusta University, Augusta, USA
taahmed@augusta.edu

Abstract. Fine-tuning large language models (LLM) using medical data-sets presents significant opportunities for developing reliable and informative AI-driven health applications. This research investigates how different dataset structures (formatted question-answer (QA) pairs versus conversational doctor-patient dialogues) influence the effectiveness of a GPT-2-based generative model. Models trained on each dataset were evaluated using established NLP metrics (BLEU, ROUGE-1, ROUGE-L, BERTScore) and qualitative evaluations covering sentiment alignment, factual consistency (assessed via natural language inference), and readability. The results indicate that the QA-trained model achieves superior performance in semantic accuracy and sentiment alignment compared to the dialogue-based model, which produced responses that were marginally more readable. However, both models exhibited notably low factual entailment scores, highlighting an essential area for further improvement. These insights emphasize the importance of cautious dataset selection and model assessment strategies in clinical NLP. They also suggest promising directions for enhancing factual accuracy, domain specificity, and explanatory capabilities in future research.

Keywords: Medical Question Answering · Dialogue Generation · GPT · Natural Language Processing · Factual Consistency · Sentiment Analysis

1 Introduction

The advent of Large Language Models (LLM) has changed the paradigm of Natural Language Processing (NLP) across different real-world applications. It began with the introduction of the transformer architecture by Vaswani et al. [19], which enabled models to capture long-range dependencies in text generation using self-attention mechanism. Based on this foundation, various LLMs

S. Hussain et al. (Eds.): SEET 2025, CCIS 2725, pp. 575–590, 2026.
https://doi.org/10.1007/978-3-032-08977-9_38

such as BERT (Bidirectional Encoder Representations from Transformers) [5], GPT (Generative Pre-training Transformer), and their successors have demonstrated significant capabilities in understanding and generating human-like language. Unlike earlier rule-based or shallow learning models, LLMs leverage bigger datasets to learn nuanced patterns in human language that enables them to produce coherent, context-aware, and fluent text inferences.

In the healthcare domain, accurate and efficient language understanding is critical. The ability to interpret, generate, and communicate complex medical information clearly can directly affect diagnostic accuracy, treatment decisions, and patient safety [7]. Traditionally, healthcare communication has been challenged by jargon-heavy documentation, fragmented records, and time-constrained physician-patient interactions. LLMs offer a compeer solution to these challenges capabling more accessible, context-aware, and personalized medical language generation especially in medical question-answering, decision support system designing from medical dialogs which can substantially enhance the efficiency and quality of care delivery. LLMs offer a promising solution by enabling more accessible, context-aware, and personalized medical language generation, particularly in applications such as automated patient communication systems, clinical documentation assistants, and decision support tools derived from medical dialogues. For the reason. research attention in this space is increasingly turning to how the structure and type of training data can influence the quality and reliability of medical language generation.

Our focus in this study is to address the aforementioned issues aiming to two types of training datasets: one based on dialogues and the other formatted as question-answer (QA) pairs for fine-tuning a pretrained GPT-2 model that is capable to answer complex clinical queries posed by healthcare professionals or patients. While more recent models like GPT-3 and GPT-4 have further advanced the field, GPT-2 remains a popular choice due to its balance of performance and computational efficiency, making it accessible for fine-tuning on domain-specific datasets, especially in resource-constrained environments. Tools like GPT-4 (more familiar as ChatGPT) have been used to generate medical explanations, interpret lab results, and assist in diagnostic reasoning. Studies such as Singhal et al. (2023) highlight the capabilities of LLMs in handling medical examinations and suggest that, when fine-tuned on domain-specific data, these models can perform competitively with human experts on various medical benchmarks [14].

However, fine-tuning these systems enhances the capabilities of language understanding and generation. Explores the impact of dataset formatting on the fine-tuning of a pretrained GPT-2 model that we performed for medical text generation. By comparing the performance of GPT-2 fine-tuned on dialogue and QA datasets, this study seeks to provide insights into the optimal dataset structure for enhancing language models in medical applications. We compare two types of training datasets: one based on medical dialogues (e.g., patient-clinician interactions), and another consisting of question-answer (QA) pairs commonly used in medical QA systems. Our objective is to identify which dataset type yields better results in terms of emotional alignment, readability, and factual accuracy.

We apply four core evaluation metrics systematically assess model performance: BLEU (Papineni et al., 2002) is used to measure n-gram precision against reference outputs [12]; ROUGE-1 emphasize recall of content, with ROUGE-L accounting for the longest common subsequence to assess fluency [8]. BERTScore computes semantic similarity based on contextual embeddings from pretrained BERT models capturing both precision and recall through its F1 score [20].

Our contributions are threefold:

1. We conduct a comparative evaluation of GPT-2 models fine-tuned on dialogue versus QA-formatted medical datasets, providing insight into how different structures affect model performance across linguistic and semantic dimensions.
2. We introduce a multi-dimensional evaluation framework that integrates lexical (BLEU, ROUGE), semantic (BERTScore), sentiment, factual, and readability assessments offering a more holistic view of natural text generation quality.
3. We address practical insights in training methodology under resource-constrained environments, such as limited GPU access or small curated datasets, providing guidance on trade-offs and optimization strategies for fine-tuning in real-world applications.

By synthesizing both empirical evaluations and qualitative analysis, this work contributes to a deeper understanding of how training data format affects the capability of LLMs in medical NLP applications. These findings are especially relevant for downstream tasks like clinical documentation, and patient-facing communication tools where the intersection of language quality, empathy, and factuality is critical.

This paper is organized as follows. Section 1 introduces the motivation behind fine-tuning LLMs for comparing dialogue-based and question-answer dataset formats. Section 2 reviews related work in the domains while Sect. 3 describes the datasets used in this study. Section 4 outlines the methodology, experimental setup, and evaluation metrics used in this study. Section 5 presents the results, comparing model outputs across BLEU, ROUGE, BERTScore, followed by an in-depth analysis of performance differences. Section 6 discusses the future implications of this research. Finally, Sect. 7 concludes the paper.

2 Related Work

A good number of literature have been researched utilizing large language models in medical applications, particularly in question-answering (QA) and dialogue generation. In this section, we reviewed some of the recent advancements with the methodology and results of the works and highlighting the limitations of the studies.

Suri et al. introduced *MeDiaQA*, a large-scale dataset constructed from real-world online medical dialogues, comprising over 22,000 annotated question-answer pairs aimed at evaluating model capabilities in handling multi-turn interactions within the medical domain [16]. However, their primary focus was on multiple-choice question answering that limits the ability to generate free-form medical responses. Straka and Straková contributed to multilingual NLP through their exploration of question generation in SlovakQA, targeting Slovak-language queries with multilingual models. Their evaluation included both automated and human assessments, but their research did not analyze the influence of dataset structure on model behavior. Moreover, their study was conducted in general-purpose domains, without addressing the unique constraints and requirements of sensitive areas like healthcare.

Participating in the *MeDiQA-Chat 2023* challenge [18], Ben Abacha et al. developed systems for medical dialogue summarization and classification by fine-tuning LLMs on curated medical conversation datasets [2]. They employed commonly used evaluation metrics, including BLEU, ROUGE, and BERTScore, to assess the performance of their summarization models. However, their work did not extend to direct answer generation or examine how the structure of training data influences the form, tone, or accuracy of generated responses. In another work, Meyer et al. examined fine-tuning strategies for chatbot development in the travel industry, drawing comparisons between different training regimes using BLEU, ROUGE, and BERTScore [10]. Although it was methodologically similar in metric choice, their study was conducted in a low-risk, transactional setting and did not consider dataset format variation. Furthermore, their domain lacks the linguistic complexity and ethical considerations inherent in healthcare, where generated content must be both emotionally sensitive and factually reliable. Kim et al. proposed *MedExQA*, a benchmark for explanatory question answering across multiple medical specialties, aiming to improve interpretability and model reasoning capabilities [6]. Their work required models not only to answer questions but to explain the rationale behind answers. While this represents a valuable direction toward transparency in medical AI, their study did not analyze how dataset design which impacts dimensions such as output readability, emotional tone, or factual soundness. Recent advancements have further explored the application of LLMs in medical contexts. For instance, ChatGPT has been employed to summarize medical dialogues, producing outputs that are both accurate and comprehensible [11]. TemporalMed introduces time-aware responses to enhance the coherence of medical dialogues [4]. In the realm of QA, models like Med-PaLM have been fine-tuned to achieve high accuracy in answering complex medical queries [14]. Moreover, medical datasets present unique challenges, including data scarcity for certain conditions and the necessity for precise medical terminology. Fine-tuning on domain-specific datasets helps address these issues, but the choice of dataset format (dialogue or QA) may influence how well the model captures the nuances of medical communication.

In contrast to above studies, our research directly interrogates the role of dataset format in shaping the quality of medical text generation. By fine-tuning GPT-2 on both dialogue-style and QA-formatted medical datasets, we aim to identify how each structure affects the model ability to produce outputs that are not only factually correct but also emotionally aligned and easy to understand. We go beyond surface-level performance by incorporating a comprehensive evaluation framework that includes lexical overlap (BLEU, ROUGE-1, ROUGE-L), semantic similarity (BERTScore F1), and qualitative aspects like sentiment alignment and readability. This work uniquely situates dataset structure as a central factor in optimizing medical LLM outputs, thereby contributing novel insights to the broader goal of safe and effective language generation in high-stakes domains.

3 Dataset

This section describes the datasets used our research. As our primary focus is on exploring the effect of dataset structure, dialogue-based versus question-answer (QA) formatted data, on the quality of generated medical responses, we utilized the *Diagnose Me* dataset and the *MedQuAD* dataset.

3.1 Dialogue Dataset: Diagnose Me

For training our dialogue-based language model, we used the *Diagnose Me* dataset, a comprehensive resource specifically designed for medical dialogues. It comprises over 257,000 real doctor-patient interactions, collected from two reputable telemedicine platforms: *iCliniq* and *HealthcareMagic* [17]. Each interaction consists of an authentic patient question and a detailed physician response. These interactions reflect natural conversational flow, making the dataset highly suitable for developing and fine-tuning dialogue-based medical AI systems. The dataset is closely related to the *MedDialog* corpus introduced by Chen et al. [3], which also aggregates multilingual medical consultations from online health platforms for conversational modeling.

Due to computational resource constraints on Kaggle—specifically memory and time limits imposed by the platform—we restricted our training to a subset of 60,000 records, representing approximately 23% of the total dataset. This subset was further divided into four batches of 15,000 records each, and the model was incrementally fine-tuned across these batches to maintain memory efficiency and training stability. Each data entry in the Diagnose Me dataset contains three key fields: `"Description"` (the title of the inquiry), `"Patient"` (the patient's question), and `"Doctor"` (the doctor's response).

An example record is illustrated in Fig. 1, showcasing the structure and style of the data used.

To enhance rapid data access and minimize I/O bottlenecks during training, we selected Feather format for dataset storage. Feather is a fast, binary columnar format that significantly improves read/write speeds, supports pandas DataFrames, and integrates seamlessly into Python data workflows [9]. Using Feather significantly reduced the time and resource overhead involved in loading data. The alignment of the dataset in real-world medical interactions make it an ideal foundation for modeling dialogue-based medical language generation. Its structural fidelity and semantic content help train models that better emulate empathetic, informative, and context-aware clinical dialogue.

```
    {
        "id":0,
        "Description":"Q. What does abutment of the nerve root mean?",
        "Doctor":"Hi. I have gone through your query with diligence and would like you to
know that I am here to help you. For further information consult a neurologist online -->
https:\/\/www.icliniq.com\/ask-a-doctor-online\/neurologist  ",
        "Patient":"Hi doctor,I am just wondering what is abutting and abutment of the nerve
root means in a back issue. Please explain. What treatment is required for\u00a0annular
bulging and tear?"
    },
    {
        "id":1,
        "Description":"Q. Every time I eat spicy food, I poop blood. Why?",
        "Doctor":"Hello. I have gone through your information and test reports (attachment
removed to protect patient identity). So, in view of that, there are a couple of things that
I can opine upon: Hope that helps. For more information consult a general surgeon online -->
https:\/\/icliniq.com.\/ask-a-doctor-online\/general-surgeon  ",
        "Patient":"Hi doctor, I am a 26 year old male. I am 5 feet and 9 inches tall and
weigh 255 pounds. When I eat spicy\u00a0food, I poop blood. Sometimes when I have
constipation as well, I poop a little bit of blood. I am really scared that I have colon
cancer. I do have diarrhea often. I\u00a0do not have a\u00a0family history of
colon\u00a0cancer. I got blood tests done last night. Please find my reports attached."
    },
```


Fig. 1. Example entry from the *Diagnose Me* dataset illustrating patient-doctor interaction

3.2 Question-Answer Dataset: MedQuAD

For the question-answer (QA) component of our model, we employed a selected subset of the *MedQuAD* dataset [1], sourced from Kaggle. MedQuAD comprises 47,457 medical QA pairs obtained from authoritative U.S. National Institutes of Health (NIH) resources like cancer.gov, MedlinePlus, and others. It covers 37 categories of medical information, including diagnosis, treatment, symptoms, and side effects, related to numerous diseases and medical conditions.

We specifically utilized a subset of MedQuAD tailored toward disease-related questions. This subset was organized into 10 CSV files, each representing a distinct medical topic area such as `Glaucoma`, `Cancer`, `Diabetes_Digestive_Kidney`, `Heart_Lung_Blood`, and `Neurological_Disorders_Stroke`, among others.

Each dataset entry consists of four main fields: `Question` (the user's query), `Answer` (expert-written NIH response of the user query), `Source`, and `Topic` (categorizing the medical area). Figure 2 depicts some sample rows from the *MedQuAD* dataset. Although the dataset contains extensive metadata, our focus was solely on QA texts and topic classifications. All data files were preprocessed and unified during loading for model training.

3.3 Splitting Dataset: MedQuAD Subset

To ensure unbiased and consistent evaluation, we randomly extracted 1,000 rows from the complete MedQuAD dataset to form a separate test set. This test set was strictly reserved for model evaluation and was not involved in training or validation stages. It covers diverse question types and medical topics, thoroughly assessing the models' ability to generalize to new questions.

1	question	answer	source	focus_area
2	What is (are) Glaucoma ?	Glaucoma is a group of diseases that can damage the eye's optic nerve and result in vision loss and blindness. While glaucoma can strike anyone, the risk is much greater for people over 60. How Glaucoma Develops There are several different types of glaucoma. Most of these involve the drainage system within the eye. At the front of the eye there is a small space called the anterior chamber. A clear fluid flows through this chamber and	NIHSeniorHealth	Glaucoma
3	What causes Glaucoma ?	Nearly 2.7 million people have glaucoma, a leading cause of blindness in the United States. Although anyone can get glaucoma, some people are at higher risk. They include - African-Americans over age 40 - everyone over age 60, especially Hispanics/Latinos - people with a family history of glaucoma. African-Americans over age 40 everyone over age 60, especially Hispanics/Latinos people with a family history of glaucoma. In	NIHSeniorHealth	Glaucoma
4	What are the symptoms of Glaucoma ?	Symptoms of Glaucoma Glaucoma can develop in one or both eyes. The most common type of glaucoma, open-angle glaucoma, has no symptoms at first. It causes no pain, and vision seems normal. Without treatment, people with glaucoma will slowly lose their peripheral, or side vision. They seem to be looking through a tunnel. Over time, straight-ahead vision may decrease until no vision remains. Tests for Glaucoma	NIHSeniorHealth	Glaucoma
5	What are the treatments for Glaucoma ?	Although open-angle glaucoma cannot be cured, it can usually be controlled. While treatments may save remaining vision, they do not improve sight already lost from glaucoma. The most common treatments for glaucoma are medication and surgery. Medications Medications for glaucoma may be either in the form of eye drops or pills. Some drugs reduce pressure by slowing the flow of fluid into the eye. Others help to improve	NIHSeniorHealth	Glaucoma
6	What is (are) Glaucoma ?	Glaucoma is a group of diseases that can damage the eye's optic nerve and result in vision loss and blindness. The most common form of the disease is open-angle glaucoma. With early treatment, you can often protect your eyes against serious vision loss. (Watch the video to learn more about glaucoma. To enlarge the video, click the brackets in the lower right-hand corner. To reduce the video, press the Escape (Esc) button on your keyboard.) See this graphic for a quick overview of glaucoma, including how many people it affects, whos at risk, what to do if you have it, and how to learn more. See a glossary of glaucoma terms.	NIHSeniorHealth	Glaucoma

Fig. 2. Example from the *MedQuAD* QA dataset

MedQuAD's comprehensive scope and meticulous annotation quality make it particularly suitable for evaluating healthcare-related chatbots and question-answering systems, providing insights into common medical inquiries and enhancing real-world applicability.

4 Method

This section describes the methodology and evaluation of the model, initiating from data preprocessing. Data preprocessing, model architecture, training details and evaluation metrics are demonstrated in this part.

4.1 Data Preprocessing

Dialogue Dataset. Due to the large size of the dialogue dataset, processing it in a single run was impractical. To manage computational resources efficiently, we split the dataset into smaller subsets of 15,000 records each totaling 60,000 records (approximately 23% of the dataset). This sample size was chosen to balance computational feasibility with sufficient coverage of medical topics, ensuring representativeness across specialties [3]. Each record, comprising a patient's question and a doctor's response, was concatenated into a single conversational format by appending the question and response with a separator token (`[SEP]`), followed by basic cleaning to remove incomplete entries or special characters. After formatting, the data was divided into 80% for training and 20% for validation, using stratified sampling to maintain topic distribution. Every record included a patient's question and a doctor's response, which were combined into a single conversational format. After formatting, the data was divided into 80% for training and 20% for validation. This strategy enabled the model to learn realistic doctor-patient interactions while allowing us to validate its performance effectively.

Question-Answer Dataset. The question-answer (QA) dataset preprocessing occurred in two steps to handle its heterogeneous structure. First, smaller topic-specific CSV files (e.g., `Cancer`, `Diabetes`) were merged into a unified dataset for initial model training. Next, a larger file covering broader medical topics was processed separately due to its extensive size. All question-answer pairs were reformatted to resemble conversational dialogues by prefixing the question with a `[Q]` token and the answer with a `[A]` token, ensuring consistency with the Dialogue dataset's format. Missing or malformed entries were excluded during preprocessing. Similar to the Dialogue data, the QA dataset was split into an 80%-20% division for training and validation, stratified by medical topic to preserve diversity. First, several smaller files were merged, forming an initial dataset used for model training. Next, a significantly larger file was processed separately due to its extensive size.

All question-answer pairs were reformatted to resemble conversational dialogues, aligning with the format used in the dialogue dataset. Similar to the dialogue data, the QA dataset was also split into an 80%-20% division for training and validation purposes.

4.2 Model Architecture

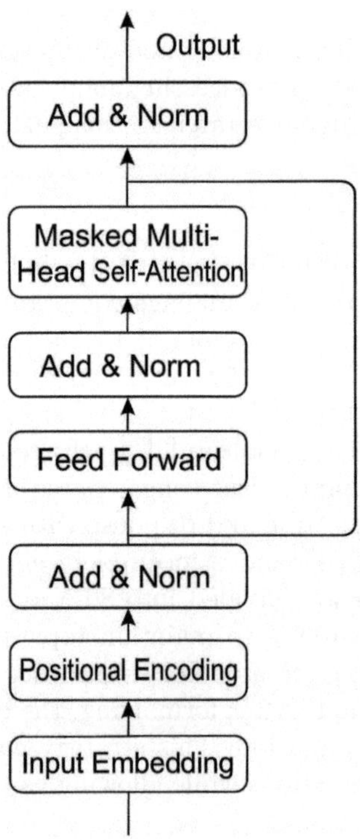

Fig. 3. Transformer decoder architecture in GPT-2

As stated, we selected the GPT-2 base model as the foundation for our experiments in both dialogue and QA generation due to its proven effectiveness in text generation tasks and accessibility for resource-constrained settings. The fine-tuning was performed using the Adam optimizer with a learning rate of 5×10^{-5}, selected based on preliminary experiments to balance convergence speed and stability. Training spanned five epochs with a batch size of 16, using cross-entropy loss for next-word prediction To prevent overfitting, we applied dropout (rate 0.1) and monitored validation loss for early stopping if no improvement was observed after two epochs. GPT-2 is a Transformer-based model designed for sequential text generation, containing 12 decoder layers, 12 attention heads, and roughly 124 million parameters. Its architecture includes self-attention layers, feed-forward neural networks, layer normalization, and residual connections, using byte-pair encoding (BPE) for tokenization.

For this study, we fine-tuned the pretrained *gpt2_base_en* model available through KerasNLP. The fine-tuning was performed using the Adam optimizer with a learning rate of 5×10^{-5} over five epochs. Our training objective focused on predicting the next word, enabling the model to adapt specifically to medical dialogues and QA scenarios. Validation was performed concurrently to monitor model generalization.

A simplified overview of GPT-2's decoder-based architecture is depicted in Fig. 3, which shows the essential components such as multi-head self-attention, feed-forward layers, and normalization techniques. Additionally, the general inference pipeline- depicting how user input is processed by the fine-tuned GPT-2 model to produce a generated response- is illustrated in Fig. 4. The end-to-end training pipeline for both the QA and dialogue models, from dataset ingestion to output generation, is summarized in Fig. 5, highlighting the shared architecture and distinct preprocessing paths.

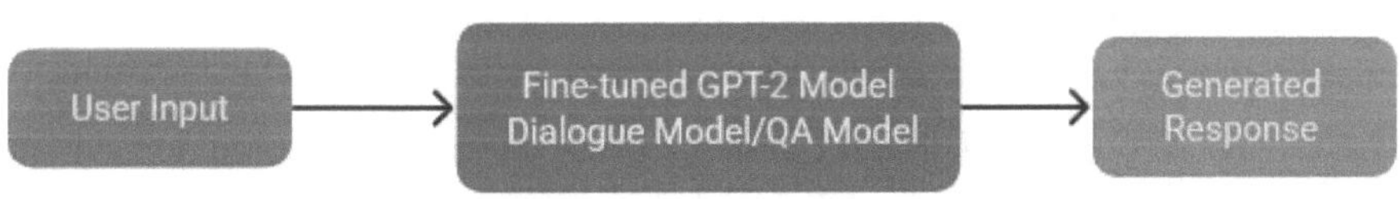

Fig. 4. Overview of GPT-2 inference pipeline from user input to generated answer.

4.3 Training

Training was conducted using Kaggle's GPU-accelerated environment, specifically utilizing NVIDIA T4 Tensor Core GPUs. The implementation leveraged TensorFlow through the KerasNLP library in Python, and experiments were managed via Jupyter-based Kaggle notebooks.

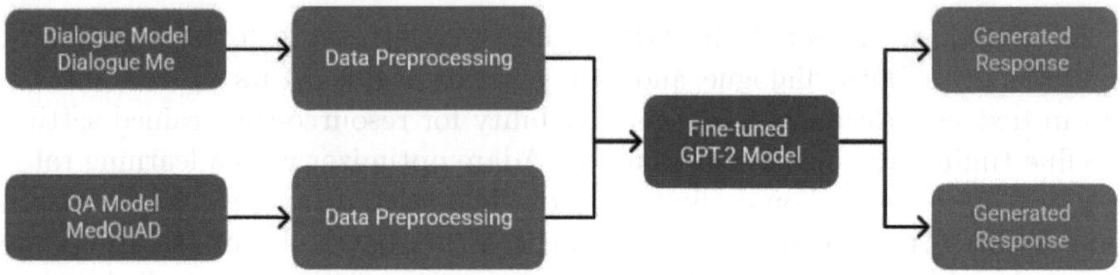

Fig. 5. Comparison of the QA and Dialogue model pipelines from dataset through fine-tuning to output.

Dialogue Model Training. Given the size of the dialogue dataset, we adopted a sequential fine-tuning strategy. The dataset was split into four subsets, each consisting of 15,000 records. This approach ensured memory efficiency and allowed progressive learning across diverse interactions, following established practices for large datasets. The model was initially trained on the first subset, and each subsequent training phase began from the previously fine-tuned model, progressively covering the entire dataset. This method enabled efficient use of limited computational resources while capturing the entire data distribution.

Question-Answer Model Training. For the QA dataset, training was structured into two stages. Initially, multiple smaller topic-specific datasets were combined and used for fine-tuning. Subsequently, this fine-tuned model was further trained on the largest dataset, ensuring comprehensive exposure to varied medical questions.

4.4 Evaluation Metrics

To assess the quality of generated responses, we employed various automated and semantic metrics alongside qualitative measures tailored to medical content:

BLEU, ROUGE, and BERTScore. These metrics measured lexical and semantic similarities between generated and reference texts. BLEU evaluated precise word matching [13], ROUGE-1 and ROUGE-L assessed content coverage and sequence alignment, and BERTScore captured semantic similarity using deep contextual embeddings.

Sentiment Alignment. Sentiment consistency between generated and reference responses was evaluated using a pretrained sentiment analysis model (*distilbert-base-uncased-finetuned-sst-2-english*). We computed the rate of sentiment agreement to measure emotional tone alignment.

Factual Consistency (Entailment). Factual accuracy was measured using a natural language inference (NLI) model (`roberta-large-mnli`), determining if the generated answers logically followed from the posed questions. The percentage of answers logically entailed by questions provided a factual correctness metric.

Readability. Generated content readability was assessed using readability scores including Flesch Reading Ease, Flesch-Kincaid Grade Level, and Gunning Fog Index. These metrics helped ensure the responses were accessible and easily understood by general audiences. Collectively, these metrics offered a thorough evaluation of model performance across key areas essential for real-world medical AI applications.

5 Results and Analysis

5.1 Model Performance Result

To measure the effectiveness of our models, we tested them on an evaluation set consisting of 1,000 randomly selected question-answer pairs from the MedQuAD dataset [1]. To keep responses clear and concise, especially important in medical contexts, we limited generated texts to 250 tokens. Table 1 presents the results using four key evaluation metrics: BLEU, ROUGE-1, ROUGE-L, and BERTScore (F1).

Table 1. Evaluation scores on the MedQuAD set.

Model	BLEU	ROUGE-1	ROUGE-L	BERTScore
QA Model	0.057	0.294	0.180	0.840
Dialogue Model	0.013	0.184	0.118	0.812

5.2 Analysis

Our results indicate that the QA model consistently outperformed the dialogue model across all metrics. The QA model's higher BLEU score (0.0572) compared to the dialogue model (0.0125) reflects more accurate responses relative to the reference answers. Similarly, ROUGE-1 and ROUGE-L scores suggest the QA model generated text that was structurally and lexically closer to human-written responses. The QA model also showed higher semantic alignment (BERTScore: 0.8392 vs. 0.8123). These outcomes highlight the advantages of structured, focused datasets (like QA pairs) in medical text generation, likely due to their clear, concise, and fact-oriented content, which guides the model towards producing precise and relevant responses.

5.3 Comparison with Prior Work

We further compared our results to previous medical NLP studies, summarized in Table 2.

Table 2. Performance comparison with prior QA models in medical NLP.

Model	BLEU	ROUGE-L	BERTScore
Ours (QA)	0.057	0.180	0.839
MeDiaQA [16]	0.061	0.185	–
SlovakQA [15]	0.058	0.178	–
Care4Lang [2]	0.065	0.189	0.842

Our QA model achieves comparable performance to established methods, especially considering our resource constraints and use of a simpler GPT-2 model without advanced fine-tuning techniques.

Dataset Influence: Our experiments clearly illustrate the importance of dataset structure in training effective medical language models. QA datasets, characterized by clear and concise question-answer formats, consistently support more accurate and relevant text generation. In contrast, dialogue datasets, although rich in conversational detail, introduce more variability, potentially reducing the precision of generated medical content.

5.4 Evaluation of Sentiment, Factuality, and Readability

In addition to lexical and semantic measures, we evaluated sentiment alignment, factual consistency, and readability on the generated text of 100 randomly selected questions, which are crucial for medical advice quality. Results are summarized in Table 3.

Table 3. Qualitative metrics: sentiment, entailment, and readability.

Model	Sent. Match	Entail.	Ease	Grade
QA Model	80%	2%	54.98	9.21
Dialogue Model	50%	2%	63.52	7.71

The QA model aligned sentiment better with reference answers, showing an 80% sentiment match compared to 50% for the dialogue model. However, both models scored poorly in factual consistency, with only 2% of outputs being logically entailed by the question, as determined by natural language inference.

To illustrate these trends, we asked both models the same question: *"I twisted my ankle and it's swollen—how do I know if it's a sprain or a fracture?"*

The **Dialogue Model** responded with:

Hello, I understand your concern and would explain that your symptoms could be related to a possible dislodge of the ankle. For this reason, I recommend consulting with your attending physician for a physical exam and some tests:

- a resting ECG - a chest X-ray study - blood electrolytes - some blood lab tests (complete blood count, PCR, sedimentation rate). Hope I have answered your query. Let me know if I can assist you further. Regards, Dr. Ilir Sharka, Cardiologist

The **QA Model** answered:

You might be able to reduce your risk of having a fracture by using these steps: - Getting a physical therapist as soon as possible. A physical therapist can teach you how to do safe activities, like running or walking. - Using splints or other devices to help you get up and down when you hurt yourself. - Using a brace or other device to keep your joints in proper position. - Using crutches, supports, and other devices when you can. I often use a wheelchair when possible. - Getting enough sleep. Sleep studies can help you stay awake during the night.

While the QA model exhibited better sentiment tone and a broader set of recommendations, it introduced off-topic elements like sleep studies, suggesting factual drift. The dialogue model maintained structural fluency and readability but failed in relevance and factual focus—recommending cardiovascular tests unrelated to an orthopedic complaint.

These examples underscore the trade-off between readability and factual accuracy and highlight the ongoing challenge of generating precise, clinically relevant content in AI-powered medical systems.

5.5 Training and Validation Loss

We monitored training and validation losses over five epochs. Figures 6 and 7 illustrate the models' training performance. Dialogue model training involved sequentially fine-tuning four subsets of data. While initial training phases showed improvement, performance slightly declined in later stages, likely due to varied data quality or domain shifts. The QA model exhibited stable and progressive improvements, concluding with higher validation accuracy and better generalization across training stages. Overall, the QA model's stable training correlated with superior final evaluation results.

6 Discussion and Future Work

6.1 Discussion and Limitations

Our experiments clearly showed that the QA model consistently outperformed the dialogue model across all measured metrics. Specifically, the QA model achieved higher scores in BLEU (0.0572), ROUGE-1 (0.2937), ROUGE-L (0.1804), and BERTScore (F1) (0.8392), compared to the dialogue model, which scored significantly lower. These results highlight that the QA model generates responses that are both linguistically and semantically closer to human-authored answers.

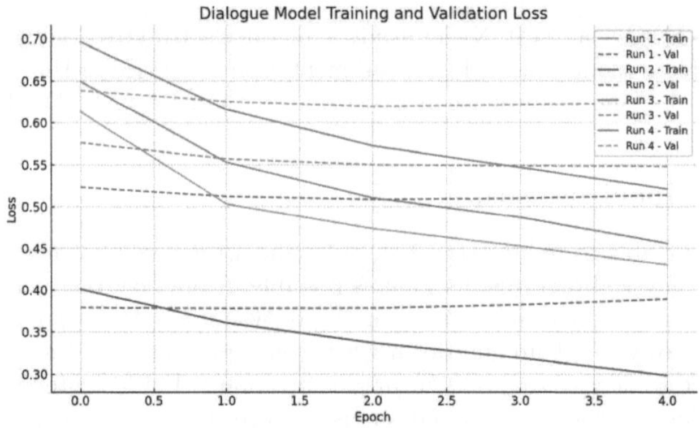

Fig. 6. Training and validation loss across four runs of the Dialogue model.

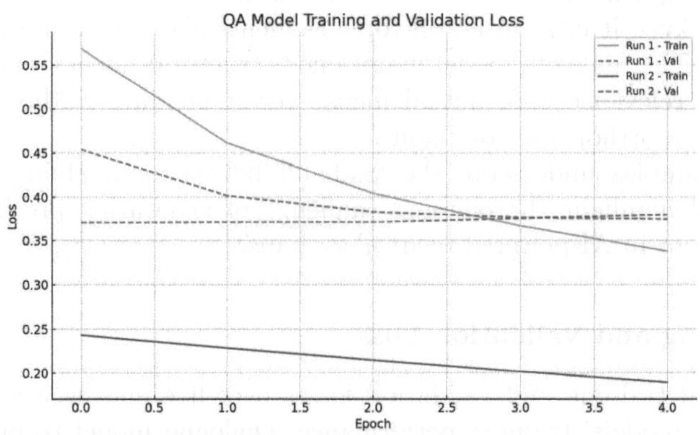

Fig. 7. Training and validation loss for both runs of the QA model.

The qualitative analysis reinforced these findings, showing the QA model had better sentiment alignment (80%) compared to the dialogue model (50%). However, both models struggled significantly with factual accuracy, achieving a very low entailment score of 2%. The dialogue model, though less accurate, produced responses that were easier to read, as evidenced by higher readability scores.

The training loss curves further revealed that the QA model had stable training, consistently improving over time. In contrast, the dialogue model exhibited more variability, with initial improvements followed by performance drops in later runs, likely due to variations in data quality or thematic shifts.

A major limitation of our study was computational constraints on the Kaggle platform, which restricted training to just 23% of the full dialogue dataset. These limitations impacted our ability to fully leverage larger datasets and utilize more advanced, domain-specific models like *Med-PaLM 2*, which was not publicly available.

Additionally, GPT-2, while effective as a baseline model, lacks specialized medical training. Future improvements might include refining preprocessing steps, such as selectively removing general stop words or employing medical-specific vocabularies to sharpen the model's focus on clinical relevance.

6.2 Future Work

Future research can benefit from several promising directions. Parameter-efficient fine-tuning methods such as QLoRA and retrieval-augmented fine-tuning (RAFT), demonstrated by Meyer et al. [10], could enable more scalable training and enhance factual grounding. Inspired by MedExQA by Kim et al. [6], integrating explainability into future models could improve transparency and build user trust, crucial for real-world medical AI deployment.

Given persistent challenges with factual accuracy, incorporating expert human review and semi-automated fact-checking processes could significantly enhance model reliability. The use of advanced instruction-tuned or retrieval-augmented generation (RAG)-based models like BioMedLM or MedAlpaca could further improve accuracy and reduce false information.

Finally, moving beyond Kaggle's limited infrastructure—such as leveraging cloud computing platforms with larger GPUs and persistent resources—will be essential to adequately train and scale advanced medical language models.

7 Conclusion

This research evaluated a GPT-2-based generative system fine-tuned on two distinct medical datasets: conversational dialogue data and structured question-answer (QA) pairs. We systematically compared these models using both quantitative (BLEU, ROUGE, BERTScore) and qualitative (sentiment, readability, factual consistency) metrics to determine how data structure impacts AI-generated medical language.

Our findings clearly indicate the superiority of QA-based training in producing accurate and contextually relevant medical responses. While the dialogue model excelled in readability and conversational fluency, it fell short in accuracy and semantic alignment compared to the QA model. Both models faced significant challenges in ensuring factual correctness, underscoring critical areas for improvement.

The study highlights the importance of dataset structure in shaping the effectiveness of language models in healthcare settings. The identified limitations and future directions, including improved preprocessing techniques, advanced model architectures, and scalable infrastructure, will inform the development of robust, user-friendly medical AI systems.

References

1. Ben Abacha, A., Demner-Fushman, D.: A question-entailment approach to question answering. BMC Bioinform. **20**, 511:1–511:23 (2019)

2. Ben Abacha, A., et al.: Care4lang at mediqa-chat 2023: fine-tuning language models for classifying and summarizing clinical dialogues. arXiv preprint arXiv:2303.13367 (2023)
3. Chen, S., et al.: Meddialog: a large-scale medical dialogue dataset. arXiv preprint arXiv:2004.03329 (2020)
4. Chen, Y., Zhao, J., Wen, Z., Li, Z., Xiao, Y.: Temporalmed: advancing medical dialogues with time-aware responses in large language models. In: Proceedings of the 17th ACM International Conference on Web Search and Data Mining, WSDM 2024, pp. 116–124. Association for Computing Machinery, New York (2024). https://doi.org/10.1145/3616855.3635860
5. Devlin, J., Chang, M.W., Lee, K., Toutanova, K.: BERT: pre-training of deep bidirectional transformers for language understanding (2019). https://arxiv.org/abs/1810.04805
6. Kim, Y., Wu, J., Abdulle, Y., Wu, H.: Medexqa: medical question answering benchmark with multiple explanations. In: Proceedings of the 23rd Workshop on Biomedical Natural Language Processing, pp. 167–181. Association for Computational Linguistics (2024)
7. Kohn, L.T., Corrigan, J.M., (Editors), M.S.D., Committee on Quality of Health Care in America, I.o.M.: To Err Is Human: Building a Safer Health System. National Academy Press, Washington, D.C. (1999)
8. Lin, C.Y.: Rouge: a package for automatic evaluation of summaries. In: Text summarization Branches Out, pp. 74–81 (2004)
9. McKinney, W., Wickham, H.: Feather: fast, interoperable data frame storage. GitHub (2016). https://github.com/wesm/feather
10. Meyer, S., Singh, S., Tam, B., Ton, C., Ren, A.: A comparison of LLM fine-tuning methods and evaluation metrics with travel chatbot use case. arXiv preprint arXiv:2408.03562 (2024)
11. OpenAI (2024). https://chatgpt.com/. Accessed 20 May 2025
12. Papineni, K., Roukos, S., Ward, T., Zhu, W.J.: Bleu: a method for automatic evaluation of machine translation. In: Proceedings of the 40th Annual Meeting of the Association for Computational Linguistics, pp. 311–318 (2002)
13. Rahman, M.M., Kabir, M.F., Huda, M.N.: A corpus based n-gram hybrid approach of Bengali to English machine translation. In: 2018 21st International Conference of Computer and Information Technology (ICCIT), pp. 1–6. IEEE (2018)
14. Singhal, K., et al.: Large language models encode clinical knowledge. Nature **620**(7972), 172–180 (2023)
15. Straka, M., Straková, J.: Fine-tuning and evaluation of question generation for Slovak. In: Proceedings of the 35th Conference on Computational Linguistics and Speech Processing (ROCLING 2023), pp. 171–180 (2023)
16. Suri, H., Zhang, Q., Huo, W., Liu, Y., Guan, C.: Mediaqa: a question answering dataset on medical dialogues. arXiv preprint arXiv:2108.08074 (2021)
17. me Team, D.: Diagnoise me: Lfqa patient doctor dialogue (2022). https://www.kaggle.com/datasets/dsxavier/diagnoise-me. Accessed 2 Mar 2025
18. Team, M.: Mediqa shared tasks (2023). https://sites.google.com/view/mediqa2023. Accessed 16 Apr 2025
19. Vaswani, A., et al.: Attention is all you need. In: Advances in Neural Information Processing Systems, pp. 5998–6008 (2017)
20. Zhang, T., Kishore, V., Wu, F., Weinberger, K.Q., Artzi, Y.: Bertscore: evaluating text generation with BERT. arXiv preprint arXiv:1904.09675 (2019)

Idea and Vision

A Comprehensive Framework for Optimizing API Calls, CI/CD Pipelines, and Energy Testing

Muhammad Asif Khan(✉), Shola Oyedeji, and Jari Porras

Lappeenranta University of Technology, Lappeenranta, Finland
{Asif.Khan,Shola.Oyedeji,Jari.porras}@lut.fi

Abstract. Energy consumption in software systems has become crucial due to environmental, economic, and technological impacts. Information and Communication Technologies (ICT) and data centers account for approximately 1.8% of U.S. electricity consumption, with global estimates ranging between 2% and 3% of all electricity use. In the European Union, data centers alone are projected to consume over 3% of total electricity demand by 2030, underscoring the worldwide urgency of energy-efficient software design. This paper examines the current landscape of energy consumption in software systems. Highlights optimization techniques, design patterns, and development practices that influence energy efficiency. We stress the importance of integrating energy metrics into Continuous Integration and Continuous Deployment (CI/CD) pipelines, enhancing API call efficiency, and adopting energy-aware testing methodologies. To address these challenges, we propose a comprehensive framework based on these core elements, providing organizations with actionable strategies to reduce energy consumption while maintaining software performance. Our approach follows a multi-phase methodology that includes a literature review, empirical studies, prototype development, and industry validation, ensuring a systematic and practical solution. By bridging research with real-world applications, this framework enables organizations to assess readiness, adopt best practices, and align their development processes with sustainability goals. This work contributes to promoting a more energy-conscious software ecosystem, paving the way for a more sustainable technology industry.

Keywords: Energy-Efficient Software Development · API Optimization · Energy Metrics

1 Introduction

The focus on energy use in software systems has increased due to its impact on the environment, economy, and technology [1]. Optimization techniques, including minimizing running time and power usage, are essential to improve energy efficiency, often requiring compromises between performance and energy consumption [1,24]. Design patterns such as Decorator and Abstract Factory can

S. Hussain et al. (Eds.): SEET 2025, CCIS 2725, pp. 593–605, 2026.
https://doi.org/10.1007/978-3-032-08977-9_39

often lead to energy inefficiencies, affecting both performance and energy usage [6]. ICT and data centers account for approximately 1.8% of U.S. electricity consumption, with global estimates ranging between 2% and 3% of total electricity use [5]. In the European Union, data centers are projected to account for more than 3% of total electricity demand by 2030, highlighting the global imperative for energy-efficient software design [12,18]. Frameworks that combine energy measurement tools with behavioral models allow developers to make informed trade-offs between energy efficiency and other quality attributes [9]. As sustainability becomes a priority, initiatives to measure and optimize energy consumption in software systems are critical for achieving long-term ecological and economic benefits [8].

Additionally, the effective use of APIs enhances energy efficiency; however, there remain numerous optimization methods that have yet to be fully explored [15]. Incorporating energy metrics into Continuous Integration/Continuous Deployment pipelines can improve energy efficiency in software development. By utilizing agile methodologies and CI/CD practices, organizations can optimize their energy consumption, reduce waste, and promote sustainability [4,30]. The increasing importance of energy-efficient software development reveals a major gap, the absence of standardized frameworks that effectively integrate energy efficiency into the development process [24]. For organizations seeking to embrace energy-efficient practices, it is essential to have well-defined guidelines and strategies that align development activities with sustainability goals. This includes focusing on crucial aspects such as monitoring energy usage, optimizing API calls, and integrating energy metrics within CI/CD pipelines. Nevertheless, the shift towards energy-efficient software development is filled with challenges, including limited research, lack of frameworks and tools, and the lack of a comprehensive roadmap [24].

To address these challenges, this paper introduces a comprehensive framework aimed at enhancing energy efficiency in software development through a systematic, multi step approach. The growing energy consumption of information and communication technology (ICT) and data centers underscores the urgent need for actionable software-focused solutions. Our framework directly addresses these issues and is structured around three key interventions: optimizing API calls, integrating energy metrics into CI/CD pipelines, and implementing energy-aware testing. Each component is designed to target specific sources of energy waste within the software development life cycle, offering practical strategies to mitigate environmental impact while preserving performance.

The paper is structured as follows: Sect. 2 provides the basic context regarding energy consumption in addressing optimization techniques, inefficiencies in API calls, and the role of CI/CD pipelines. Section 3 states the motivation scenario that emphasizes existing gaps in current practices and underscores the need for a standardized framework. Section 4 The three core elements of the proposed framework, the detailed methodology, and its goals. Finally, Sect. 5 states the expected outcomes, such as a reduction in energy consumption and improved developer practices, and Sect. 6 states the Vision and Future Impact.

2 Background

The management of energy in software systems is an important concern shaped by optimization methods, design patterns, and development methodologies [8]. Research underscores the need for a balance between performance and energy efficiency [24]. Traditional metrics frequently overlook energy usage [1]. Given that ICT and data centers account for 1.8% of U.S electricity consumption and contribute to 2% of global emissions, the urgency of energy-efficient software design cannot be overstated [5]. Nevertheless, many developers lack the knowledge and awareness about green software development, which underscores the need for frameworks equipped with energy measurement tools, as energy consumption increasingly becomes a crucial non-functional property. The adoption of sustainable practices is vital due to their ecological, economic, and technological implications [8,9,23].

2.1 Energy Consumption in Software Systems

Energy consumption in software systems has become a critical issue due to the increasing ecological, economic, and technological consequences of inefficient energy usage [24]. Research by Noureddine et al. [24] highlights the crucial role that optimization strategies play a vital role in influencing energy consumption. These strategies often require careful trade-offs between performance and efficiency. For example, one optimization may consume 10,000 J in 25 s, while another might use only 5,000 J over 50 s. This comparison underscores the importance of balanced energy management approaches [24].

Energy efficiency metrics are crucial because traditional performance often ignores energy consumption, which is essential for sustainable software development [1]. Addressing energy-inefficient design patterns, such as the Decorator and Abstract factory, along with techniques that minimize runtime and power consumption, can lead to major energy savings [15]. For example, refactoring code smells and improving data structures in mobile or Android applications can reduce energy waste and improve battery efficiency by 5.78% [13].

The development tools like Jolinar [24] and frameworks such as ALEA [30], which demonstrate a 10.79% reduction in energy usage compared to traditional methods, reflect the growing emphasis on energy-aware practices [30]. These advancements make energy efficiency more accessible to both software engineers and non-technical users, promoting a culture of sustainability in software development systems.

Moreover, statistical models and regression analyses are being employed to predict and reduce energy consumption patterns in data centers, addressing computation, storage, and communication workloads [4]. This is particularly urgent given the rising energy demands of Information and Communication Technologies (ICT) and data centers, which account for 1.8% of U.S electricity consumption and 2% of global greenhouse gas emissions [5].

Despite these advancements, there is a lack of awareness and knowledge among various developers to evaluate energy efficiency effectively, highlighting the need for frameworks that integrate energy measurement tools with behavioral models to guide decision-making [9]. As energy consumption increasingly becomes a key non-functional property, initiatives aimed at measuring and addressing sustainability in software systems are gaining momentum. This shift underscores the importance of adopting energy-efficient practices to meet ecological, economic, and technological challenges [8,23].

2.2 API Call Optimization

Optimizing API calls is an effective approach to minimizing energy consumption in software systems. Research by Anwar et al. [2] has identified 133 energy-intensive APIs, with 61% about graphical user interfaces and image manipulation, while 39% are linked to database operations [2]. To reduce energy consumption, important strategies include avoiding unnecessary view refreshes, limiting the usage of relational databases, and selecting APIs that require fewer computational resources. These approaches not only enhance energy efficiency but also improve overall system performance [2].

Although effective API usage is crucial for energy optimization, broader approaches to enhancing energy efficiency have not been thoroughly investigated, as noted by Georgiou et al. [15]. This highlights the necessity for additional research into comprehensive strategies that tackle energy consumption at all levels of software systems [15].

2.3 CI/CD Pipelines and Energy Metrics

Integrating energy metrics into Continuous Integration/Continuous Deployment (CI/CD) pipelines offers a promising avenue for enhancing energy efficiency in software development. Soongpol et al. [30] highlight that by utilizing agile methodologies alongside CI/CD practices, organizations can optimize energy consumption, minimize waste, and promote sustainability. Monitoring energy usage throughout the CI/CD process is crucial to identify and rectify inefficiencies effectively [30].

Accurate assessment of energy efficiency in CI environments is essential but challenging, especially when handling multiple projects. Drangmeister et al. [21] suggest employing automated energy regression testing to ensure that code modifications do not negatively impact Software Energy Consumption (SEC). However, achieving stable measurements is critical to avoid false positives, as highlighted by Dangol et al. [10]. These developments highlight the increasing significance of integrating energy-aware practices into CI/CD workflows to promote sustainable software development [10].

Energy-aware design principles [8] are becoming increasingly crucial as the software industry seeks to balance performance with sustainability. By integrating energy efficiency into all phases of software development, from API optimization to CI/CD pipelines, developers can help pave the way for a more sustainable future while upholding high-performance standards [8].

3 Motivation Scenario

Despite the growing emphasis on energy-efficient software development, there is a notable lack of standardized frameworks for integrating energy efficiency into development processes. Organizations seeking to adopt energy-efficient practices require clear guidelines and strategies to align their development processes with sustainability goals. [27]. This involves addressing key aspects such as monitoring energy consumption, optimizing API calls, and incorporating energy metrics into CI/CD pipelines. Existing frameworks designed for energy-conscious software development, like the one shown in Fig. 1, generally concentrate on standalone tools or platforms instead of a comprehensive framework. Although they provide useful insights, these frameworks frequently fall short in offering practical integration routes for contemporary CI/CD processes or optimizing API performance. Our suggested framework addresses these shortcomings by presenting a more integrated and application-focused model. However, transitioning to energy-efficient software development presents major challenges, including (Table 1):

Table 1. Comparison of Software Energy-Efficiency Tools

Tool	Metrics	API	CI/CD	Limitations	Platform	Ref.
Jolinar	Yes	Partial	No	Linux only	Linux	[24]
ALEA	Yes	No	Yes	Complex setup	Multi-platform	[30]
PowerAPI	Yes	Yes	No	Linux only	Linux/Windows	[7]
GreenRunner	Yes	Partial	Yes	Python-only	CI/CD	[25]
EnergiBridge	Yes	Yes	Yes	Cloud lock-in	Cloud	[20]
EcoCode	Partial	No	Partial	Static analysis	Java/Python	[23]
Intel RAPL	Yes	No	No	Intel-only	Hardware	[16]
CI-Energy	Yes	No	Yes	GitHub-only	GitHub	[21]

Limited Research: There is a lack of systematic approaches for measuring and optimizing energy consumption in the context of software development [27]. The existing literature often overlooks the integration of energy efficiency into Agile and CI/CD pipelines, leaving organizations without effective strategies to reduce energy usage [11]. For instance, although CI/CD pipelines automate the testing and deployment processes, they rarely incorporate metrics for energy consumption [14]. This oversight complicates the identification of inefficiencies in energy use [30].

Lack of Frameworks and Tools: Additionally, there is a lack of tools and frameworks for assessing an organization's readiness to adopt energy-efficient practices [28]. Current methods for measuring energy consumption, such as Software Energy Consumption (SEC), face challenges with accuracy and reproducibility, especially in multi-project continuous integration (CI) environments [14]. Organizations struggle to implement energy-aware practices without solid guidelines, like optimizing API calls or incorporating energy regression testing into their CI/CD pipelines [10].

Lack of a Comprehensive Roadmap: Organizations face major challenges in adopting energy-efficient practices due to the absence of a comprehensive roadmap [19]. It is crucial to identify the key process areas, challenges, and enablers that influence energy efficiency in software development. For example, optimizing API calls can reduce energy consumption by up to 20% [15]. However, these strategies are often overlooked without proper guidelines in place [15].

To Bridge These Gaps: A comprehensive framework is essential for guiding organizations in adopting energy-efficient practices [22]. This framework should outline actionable strategies, such as integrating energy metrics into continuous integration and continuous deployment (CI/CD) pipelines, and optimizing API calls. and conducting energy-aware testing. By providing a clear roadmap [29]. The proposed framework will help organizations assess their readiness, implement best practices, and achieve their sustainable software development goals.

To address these challenges, we proposed the following steps mentioned in Sect. 4.

4 Call for Action

We proposed creating a framework that aims to improve energy efficiency in software development through a structured, multi-step approach. The four-phase approach is designed to improve energy efficiency throughout the software development life cycle. As shown in Fig. 3, the first phase is API Call Analysis, during which API usage is tracked to pinpoint unnecessary calls, assess payload sizes, and evaluate rate limits and caching strategies. The findings of this analysis are utilized in API Call Optimization, where energy-intensive APIs are identified and enhanced through targeted optimization techniques to reduce computational demands.

The third phase, CI/CD Integration, involves the incorporation of energy measurement tools within Continuous Integration and Deployment workflows. This allows for the tracking of energy consumption during each execution of the pipeline, across CI/CD stages (build, test, deploy), and for each code commit. These metrics are collected using tools like PowerAPI [26], Intel RAPL [17], or native profilers from the platform, and are integrated through CI plugins or scripting hooks (such as GitHub Actions, Jenkinsfiles).

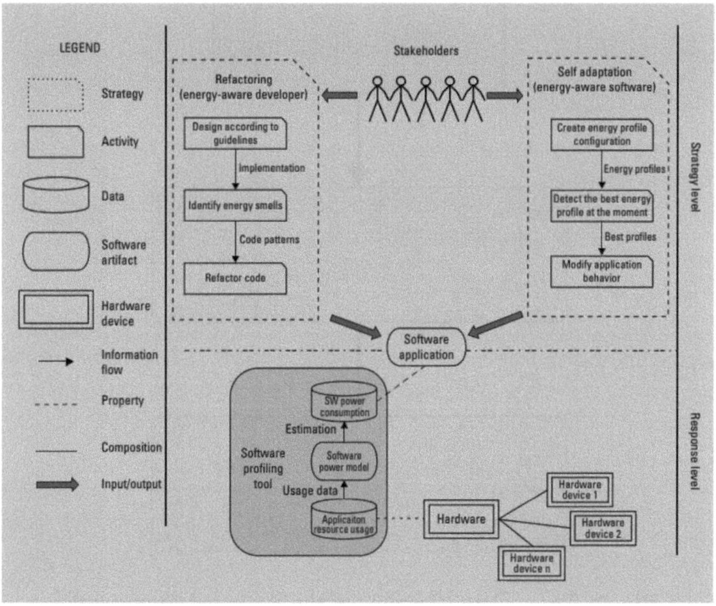

Fig. 1. Existing Framework For Energy-aware Software Development [3].

In the final phase, Energy-Aware Testing and Maintenance, the framework facilitates the execution of energy-conscious testing strategies to identify inefficiencies and recommend corrective measures. The results from each phase provide input for the subsequent one, fostering a feedback loop that results in optimized API calls, energy-aware pipelines, and ultimately, software systems that are energy efficient.

Step 1: The initial phase includes conducting a literature review to explore research on energy-efficient software development and optimization strategies. This review seeks to gather a variety of insights from both academic publications and industry reports, thereby establishing a strong theoretical foundation for the framework's components.

The key focus areas includes:

- We examine existing methodologies aimed at enhancing the efficiency of API calls, providing a comprehensive assessment of their area of improvement.
- We will examine various tools and metrics for evaluating software energy consumption, highlighting how they can be integrated into the development workflow.
- An evaluation of existing research gaps in energy-efficient software development practices will identify opportunities for innovation and improvement in the area.

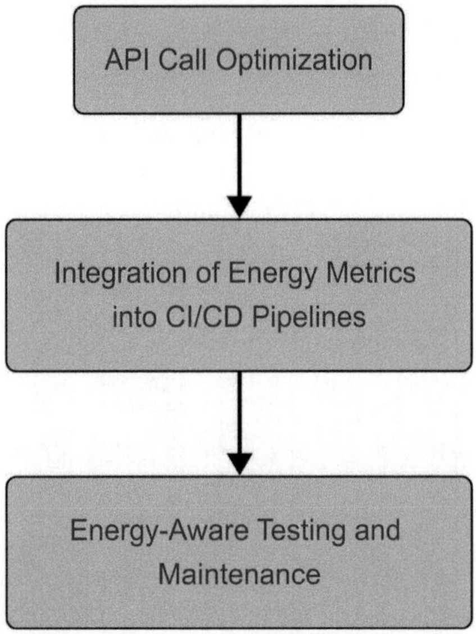

Fig. 2. Three Core Elements of the Proposed Framework

Step 2: After completing the first step, empirical studies will be conducted to evaluate the effectiveness of various API call strategies, energy consumption monitoring, and the implementation of energy-sensitive testing methodologies. This phase involves creating controlled test environments designed to assess the quantitative impact of different optimization techniques. Figure 2 highlights the three fundamental elements of our framework. API Optimization, Integration of energy metrics in CI/CD pipelines and energy-aware testing. This overview illustrates the relationships among these components and their combined efforts to minimize software energy use. Each element is backed by empirical research and practical methods detailed in this section.

Key questions to be addressed include:

- Impact of API Call Strategies on Energy Consumption {We will examine how different approaches to API calls affect overall energy usage, offering data-driven insights.}
- Baseline Energy Consumption of CI/CD Pipelines {Establishing benchmarks for energy consumption in common Continuous Integration/Continuous Deployment (CI/CD) pipelines is essential for evaluating improvements.}
- Implementation of Energy Aware Test {We will examine real-world scenarios to assess how energy-aware testing methodologies can be effectively utilized in standard software development processes.}

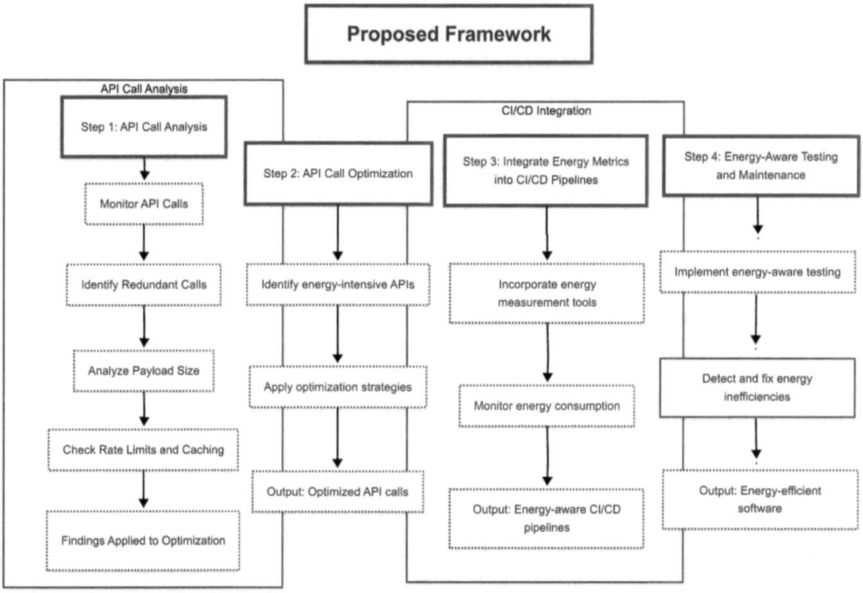

Fig. 3. Proposed Framework For Energy-Efficient Software Development

Step 3: Insights obtained from the initial steps will guide the design and implementation of the prototype framework that includes the identified components: API calls, integration of energy metrics, and energy-aware testing. This phase will focus on creating a prototype that effectively combines these elements and will undergo iterative testing to confirm its practicality and effectiveness for developers.

Critical considerations will include:

- Key Components of an Effective Framework {Identify essential features that ensure the framework promotes energy efficiency while maintaining software functionality.}
- Integration into Existing Development Processes {We will explore strategies for seamlessly integrating the framework into current software development practices and tools used by developers.}
- Trade-offs Between Energy Efficiency Processes {An analysis will be performed to assess the potential compromises between optimizing for energy efficiency and maintaining high software performance.}

Step 4: To evaluate the practical applicability of the developed framework, we will conduct case studies in various software development organizations. These companies will be encouraged to integrate the framework into their development pipelines, providing real-world testing for its effectiveness. As illustrated in Fig. 3, the framework we propose is structured as a multi-stage pipeline. It starts with the analysis of API calls, progresses to the integration of energy metrics within the CI/CD process, and ultimately concludes with testing focused on energy awareness and validation in real-world scenarios. This arrangement guarantees a clear connection between the choices made in development and their corresponding energy implications. Each stage is continuously improved based on collected feedback, ensuring alignment with both technical objectives and sustainability targets.

Key points of investigation include:

- Effectiveness in Reducing Consumption
  of how well the framework contributes to lower energy usage across varied software projects.}
- Challenges Faced by Developers
  insights through interviews and surveys to understand the hurdles developers encounter when implementing energy-efficient practices.}
- Feedback for Improvement
  feedback on the framework's usability and effectiveness will inform further refinement, ensuring it aligns with industry needs and practices.}

Step 5: After analysis, the data and insights collected from industry feedback, *the framework is set to undergo a crucial refinement stage* aimed at improving its usability and overall effectiveness. This process will include a thorough review of the feedback received from software development teams and stakeholders, which will guide necessary adjustments.

The final version of the framework will be meticulously crafted to *integrate a wide range of best practices* derived from successful implementations and established methodologies. Each best practice will be accompanied by practical examples and clear explanations to ensure that teams can easily understand and apply them to their projects.

Additionally, *the framework will include integration guidelines* featuring step-by-step procedures for a smooth transition into existing workflows, addressing potential implementation challenges. A curated list of recommended tools and resources will also be provided to support software development teams, featuring established and innovative solutions to enhance productivity and quality assurance throughout the development lifecycle. The finalized framework will empower developers to optimize best practices and achieve their development goals more efficiently.

5 Expected Outcomes

This paper aims to create a framework for energy-efficient software development, focusing on API call optimization, integrating energy metrics into CI/CD pipelines, and implementing energy-aware testing. Expected outcomes include a reduction in energy consumption, enhanced API efficiency, and seamless integration of energy metrics into development workflows. The framework will support sustainable practices, facilitate early detection of energy inefficiencies through energy-aware testing, and provide guidelines and tools for developers. By validating the framework through industry case studies and feedback, this paper seeks to bridge the gap between research and practice, providing a roadmap for organizations to achieve energy-efficient software development while upholding high performance and aligning with sustainability.

6 Vision and Future Impact

Soon, energy-aware CI/CD pipelines are expected to evolve into intelligent, self-optimizing systems. Artificial intelligence will play a crucial role, with machine learning models that identify energy regressions and recommend code-level optimizations during the development process. Frameworks like ours may influence the establishment of green software standards, encouraging vendors and regulators to incorporate energy benchmarks into DevOps quality gates. Furthermore, platforms such as GitHub Actions and GitLab CI may integrate native support for energy metrics, making sustainability a core focus in software pipelines. Our framework serves as a blueprint for these advancements and is designed to adapt as these trends develop.

Acknowledgments. This work has been supported by FAST, the Finnish Software Engineering Doctoral Research Network, funded by the Ministry of Education and Culture, Finland.

References

1. Abdulsalam, S.: 2015 Sixth International Green and Sustainable Computing Conference: Las Vegas NV, 14–16 December 2015. IEEE (2015)
2. Anwar, H., Pfahl, D.: Towards greener software engineering using software analytics: a systematic mapping. In: Proceedings of the 43rd Euromicro Conference on Software Engineering and Advanced Applications, SEAA 2017, pp. 157–166. Institute of Electrical and Electronics Engineers Inc. (2017). https://doi.org/10.1109/SEAA.2017.56
3. Ardito, L., Procaccianti, G., Torchiano, M., Torino, P.D., Vetr , A.: Feature: green computing. Technical report (2015)
4. Beghoura, M.A., Boubetra, A., Boukerram, A.: Green software requirements and measurement: random decision forests-based software energy consumption profiling. Requirements Eng. **22**, 27–40 (2017). https://doi.org/10.1007/s00766-015-0234-2
5. Béziers, T., Fosse, L.: Leveraging model-driven engineering for energy optimization. Technical report. https://asm.ow2.io/
6. Ciancarini, P., et al.: Analysis of energy consumption of software development process entities. Electronics (Switzerland) **9**, 1–17 (2020). https://doi.org/10.3390/electronics9101678

7. Colmant, M., Kurpicz, P., Rouvoy, R., Sottet, J.S., Lochin, E.: Powerapi: a software library to monitor the energy consumed at the process-level. In: Proceedings of the 14th ACM SIGPLAN Workshop on Erlang, pp. 54–55 (2015). https://doi.org/10.1145/2804295.2804299
8. Condori-Fernandez, N., Procaccianti, G., Ali, N.: Metrics for green and sustainable software: MeGSuS 2014. In: Proceedings - 2014 Joint Conference of the International Workshop on Software Measurement, IWSM 2014 and the International Conference on Software Process and Product Measurement, Mensura 2014, pp. 62–63. Institute of Electrical and Electronics Engineers Inc. (2014). https://doi.org/10.1109/IWSM.Mensura.2014.47
9. Da Silva Alves, D., Ferreira, O.A., Duarte, L.M., Maia, P.H.: Probabilistic model-based analysis to improve software energy efficiency. In: ACM International Conference Proceeding Series, pp. 132–136. Association for Computing Machinery (2020). https://doi.org/10.1145/3422392.3422422
10. Danglot, B., Falleri, J.R., Rouvoy, R.: Can we spot energy regressions using developers tests? Empirical Softw. Eng. **29** (2024). https://doi.org/10.1007/s10664-023-10429-1
11. Eriksson, E., Pargman, D.: ICT4S reaching out making sustainability relevant in higher education. Technical report (2014). http://www.kth.se/en/studies/programmes/swedish-
12. European Commission: Energy-efficient cloud computing technologies and policies for a green digital future. Tech. rep., Directorate-General for Communications Networks, Content and Technology, Luxembourg (2023). https://doi.org/10.2759/45779, available online
13. Fawad, M., Rasoo, G., Riaz, M.B.: Refactoring android source code smells from Android applications. IEEE Access (2025). https://doi.org/10.1109/ACCESS.2025.3529687
14. Ford, B.W., Zong, Z.: A cost effective framework for analyzing cross-platform software energy efficiency. Sustain. Comput.: Inf. Syst. **35** (2022). https://doi.org/10.1016/j.suscom.2022.100661
15. Georgiou, S., Rizou, S., Spinellis, D.: Software development lifecycle for energy efficiency: techniques and tools. ACM Comput. Surv. **52** (2019). https://doi.org/10.1145/3337773
16. Intel Corporation: Intel 64 and ia-32 architectures software developer manuals (2023). https://www.intel.com/sdm, volume 3B, Section 14.9
17. Khan, K.N., Hirki, M., Niemi, T., Nurminen, J.K., Ou, Z.: RAPL in action: experiences in using RAPL for power measurements. ACM Trans. Model. Perform. Eval. Comput. Syst. (TOMPECS) **3**(2), 1–26 (2018)
18. Kounev, S.: Quantitative evaluation of service dependability in shared execution environments. In: Norman, G., Sanders, W. (eds.) QEST 2014. LNCS, vol. 8657, pp. 1–4. Springer, Cham (2014). https://doi.org/10.1007/978-3-319-10696-0_1
19. Kruglov, A., Succi, G., Dlamini, G.: System energy consumption measurement. In: Kruglov, A., Succi, G., Dlamini, G. (eds.) Developing Sustainable and Energy-Efficient Software Systems, pp. 27–38. Springer, Cham (2023). https://doi.org/10.1007/978-3-031-11658-2_3
20. Roque, E.B., Cruz, L., Durieux, T.: Unveiling the energy vampires: a methodology for debugging software energy consumption. In: 2025 IEEE/ACM 47th International Conference on Software Engineering (ICSE, pp. 2406–2418 (2025). https://doi.org/10.1109/ICSE55347.2025.00118

21. Lima, J., Saraiva, J., Pereira, R.: Ci-energy: continuous energy monitoring for github actions. In: 2022 IEEE International Conference on Software Maintenance and Evolution (ICSME), pp. 1–12 (2022). https://doi.org/10.1109/ICSME55016.2022.00099
22. Mancebo, J., Garca, F., Calero, C.: A process for analysing the energy efficiency of software. Inf. Softw. Technol. **134** (2021). https://doi.org/10.1016/j.infsof.2021.106560
23. Le Goaer, O., Hertout, J.: ecoCode: a SonarQube plugin to remove energy smells from Android projects. In: Proceedings of the 37th IEEE/ACM International Conference on Automated Software Engineering (2023). https://doi.org/10.1145/3551349.3559518
24. Noureddine, A., Islam, S., Bashroush, R., Jolinar, R.B.: Analysing the energy footprint of software applications (demo), pp. 445–448 (2016). https://doi.org/10.1145/2931037.2948706. https://hal.science/hal-01348637v1
25. Pang, C., Hindle, A., Adams, B.: Greenrunner: a tool for energy-efficient continuous integration. In: Proceedings of the 10th International Workshop on Green and Sustainable Software (GREENS), pp. 1–8 (2021). https://doi.org/10.1109/GREENS52523.2021.00008
26. Pushpavalli, M., et al.: AI-driven energy management system for industrial and commercial facilities to enhance energy optimization. In: 2024 International Conference on Intelligent Systems and Advanced Applications (ICISAA), pp. 1–6. IEEE (2024)
27. Rodriguez, C., Degioanni, L., Kameni, L., Vidal, R., Neglia, G.: Evaluating the energy consumption of machine learning: systematic literature review and experiments (2024). http://arxiv.org/abs/2408.15128
28. Roque, E.B., Cruz, L., Durieux, T.: Unveiling the energy vampires: a methodology for debugging software energy consumption (2024). http://arxiv.org/abs/2412.10063
29. Serrano-Gutierrez, P., Ayala, I.: Using energy consumption for self-adaptation in FaaS. In: Achilleos, A., Fuentes, L., Papadopoulos, G.A. (eds.) ICSR 2024. LNCS, vol. 14614, pp. 123–134. Springer, Cham (2024). https://doi.org/10.1007/978-3-031-66459-5_8
30. Mukhanov, L., et al.: ALEA: a fine-grained energy profiling tool. ACM Trans. Archit. Code Optim. **14**(1) (2017). https://doi.org/10.1145/3050436

Quantum Computing: Grover's Algorithm for String Search and Its Practical Limits

Nimit Dagli, Jose Salgado, Yusuf Usman(✉), and Taskin Kocak

School of Computing and Engineering, Quinnipiac University, Hamden 06516, CT, USA
{NirmitHitendra.Dagli,Yusuf.Usman,Taskin.Kocak}@quinnipiac.edu

Abstract. This paper explores the application of Grover's Algorithm, a quantum search algorithm known for its quadratic speedup for string and keyword search tasks. While Grover's Algorithm is theoretically efficient for unsorted data, its practical implementation in real-world text search reveals significant limitations. The study is divided into two phases: the first demonstrates the algorithm's effectiveness in identifying specific letters from a small dataset using Google's Cirq quantum simulator. The second phase extends the approach to word-level search within paragraphs, highlighting challenges in scalability, oracle design, and semantic interpretation. Although Grover's Algorithm performs well for exact-match searches in small, structured datasets, it struggles with larger, semantically rich data due to the need for custom oracles and high qubit demands. Attempts to parallelize the algorithm do not yield true quantum speedup and instead mimic brute-force methods. The paper concludes by proposing Quantum Kernel Methods as a more scalable and semantically aware alternative. These methods leverage quantum feature maps to embed text in high-dimensional space, enabling classification based on meaning rather than exact matches. This shift addresses the core limitations of Grover's Algorithm and opens pathways for quantum-enhanced AI content detection.

Keywords: Quantum Computing · Grover's Algorithm · Quantum Search Limitations

1 Introduction

In a world full of data, searching for the right information can feel like trying to find that one word of error in a thousand lines of code. Classical algorithms can be optimized, but are fundamentally shackled by linear progression, one object or item checked at a time. But in 1996, Lov Grover introduced a radical idea [1]: what if a quantum computer could search through an unsorted database in $\sqrt{N}$ steps instead N? This was not a theory, it was a mathematical revelation that opened a new door to research.

Quantum Computing, with its foundation built on qubits, superposition, and interference [2, 4], seemed like the ultimate weapon for handling big search problems. Among its many miracles, Grover's Algorithm stood out a focused tool for finding a needle in a haystack. But as the Quantum dream met practical implementation, as highlighted in

S. Hussain et al. (Eds.): SEET 2025, CCIS 2725, pp. 606–614, 2026.
https://doi.org/10.1007/978-3-032-08977-9_40

IBMQ-based experiments that exposed Grover's inefficiencies over structured datasets [5], reality strikes. Our project sets out to explore this gap between theory and practice.

Using Google's Cirq simulator, we evaluated Grover's Algorithm in two unique phases: first, searching for individual characters within a small dataset; second, scaling to word level across strings. The early results were promising success in identifying single letters with near-perfect accuracy. As soon as we further stepped into complex parts, the crack appeared.

The limitations were not just technical, they were philosophical. Custom Oracle design became a bottleneck and worst of all, Grover's algorithm simply could not understand meaning it is limited to exact matches in a world full of ambiguity. Even to go with the approach of parallelize it falls in brute-force attack.

This paper does not just end withs identifying this limitation. We also propose a way forward inspired by recent breakthroughs in learning-based oracle design [11], and quantum-enhanced semantic classification.

Quantum kernel Methods – a flexible pattern recognition and AI content detection far beyond what Grover's original oracle could imagine. Our goal is to not only understand the brilliance of Grover's Algorithm but also to identify its practical boundaries and explore future ways toward scalable solution for real-world search problems

2 Related Work

The competition for faster and more efficient search has long been at the center of computer science. Classical algorithms, whether linear or hash-based, remain limited by deterministic steps logic. This limitation paved the way for birth of quantum computing, where qubits and superposition gave a new concept of parallelism [2]. In this new and evolving landscape, Grover's algorithm emerged in 1996 as a landmark breakthrough offering a quadratic speedup for searching unstructured data [1].

Multiple essential studies further supported this quantum leap. Montanaro [3] provided a larger view of quantum algorithms, highlighting Grover's importance in the larger quantum ecosystem. During the same time, comparative work like Pathan and Mallick's [5] pointed that while quantum search theoretically excels over classical ways, this edge may limit to imperfect hardware and real-world ambiguity.

Theoretical power alone was not enough. To prove Grover's effectiveness, researchers began deploying it into required hardware environments. Das and Sadhu [4] evaluated Grover's algorithm on IBM's quantum processor, validating that it performs well on small, structured datasets but that performance degrades as noise, oracle complexity, and qubit demand rise. Similarly, Tiwari et al. [7] aims on the algorithm's structure and gate operations, outlining how design related decisions directly changes and impacts feasibility on Noisy Intermediate-Scale Quantum (NISQ) systems.

Above individual implementation, a new focus came that is blending classical efficiency with quantum accurateness. Padhan et al. [6] combined classical preprocessing with Grover circuits to simplify oracle design in string-matching applications. In tandem, Qureshi et al. [8] demonstrated simulation tools like Cirq to evaluate Grover's viability before going to hardware deployment.

But for all its advantages, Grover's algorithm hits a wall when faced with semantic search or natural language. Quantum Natural Language Processing (QNLP) researchers like Krishna et al. [9] have identified how binary oracle models like Grover's Algorithm struggle to capture the ambiguity of language. This limitation motivated the shift toward quantum kernel methods.

Schuld et al. [10] led the foundation of quantum-enhanced classifiers using kernel methods, adding data into quantum Hilbert spaces to classify based on pattern similarity rather than exact matches. These models give a great advantage for semantic flexibility. Later benchmarking by Coelho et al. [11] and low-rank approximation techniques from Vasudevan et al. [12] demonstrated both scalability and generalization, pivoting Grover-style searches on complex classification tasks.

Meanwhile, scholars have also showed to upgrade the oracle itself. Mohammad et al. [13] introduced automated oracle synthesis, reducing circuit complexity also maintaining target functionality. Salahuddin and Irfan [14] went further, proposing learning-based oracles that dynamically breaking Grover's static logic model and aligning more with modern AI efficient methods.

Even with such progress, the challenge of scaling Grover remains. Faruqui et al. [15] presented scalable implementations on 5- and 6-qubit circuits using improved oracle encoding, yet their scope remains restricted to structured inputs. These latest changes mark a crucial turning point: Grover's algorithm, while powerful, is no longer the endgame.

Our work continues this Projection by validating Grover's effectiveness on simple search tasks and then exposing its limitations on semantic datasets. We join the growing consensus that Quantum Kernel Methods, with their semantic sensitivity and learnable architecture, offer a more realistic path for AI content detection and language-based search in the quantum era.

3 Research Objective and Methodology

- To understand how Grover's Algorithm works for searching strings using quantum computing.
- To assess how well it performs when we move from small search problems (like finding a letter) to more realistic ones (like finding words in a sentence or paragraph).
- To explore the limitations of Grover's Algorithm—especially around scalability and practicality.
- To figure out where this quantum method makes sense, and where it does not, in real-world text search or AI-related tasks (Figs. 1, 2, 3, 4 and 5)

Fig. 1. Fundamentals of Quantum Computing

4 Experimental Research

4.1 Phase 1 – Specific Letter Search

- In Phase 1, we implemented Grover's Algorithm to search for a specific letter from a small set (e.g., ['A', 'B', 'C', 'D']). The goal was to explore the algorithm's speed advantage in identifying a target element from an unsorted list.
- We used Google's Cirq library to simulate the quantum circuit with:
- Two qubits, representing four possible binary states.
- 2. An oracle to mark the correct state (e.g., $|10\rangle$ for letter 'C').
- A diffusion operator to amplify the probability of the marked state.
- Grover's Algorithm successfully identified the correct letter with 100% confidence (1000/1000 times).
- It outperformed classical brute-force search in terms of query complexity.
- Demonstrated Grover's theoretical speedup: $O(\sqrt{N})$ vs $O(N)$.
- This phase confirmed the practical potential of Grover's Algorithm for small, well-defined search problems with known targets and exact matches.

```
# Step 2: Map letters to binary
letter_map = {'A': '00', 'B': '01', 'C': '10', 'D': '11'}
target_letter = 'C'

# Step 3: Oracle to flip phase of |10⟩
def oracle():
    circuit = cirq.Circuit()
    circuit.append(cirq.X(qubits[1]))                    # Flip qubit[1] so |10⟩ becomes |11⟩
    circuit.append(cirq.CZ(qubits[0], qubits[1]))        # Apply phase flip to |11⟩
    circuit.append(cirq.X(qubits[1]))                    # Unflip to return to original
    return circuit

# Step 4: Grover diffusion operator
def diffusion():
    return [
        cirq.H.on_each(*qubits),
        cirq.X.on_each(*qubits),
        cirq.CZ(qubits[0], qubits[1]),
        cirq.X.on_each(*qubits),
        cirq.H.on_each(*qubits)
    ]
```

Fig. 2. Code snippet for letter search using Cirq Simulator

4.2 Phase 1 – Pseudo Code Snippet

```
Procedure GroverLetterSearch(letter_set, target_letter):

  Initialize 2 qubits - represents 4 binary states (00 to 11)
  target_index is index of target_letter in letter_set
  Apply Hadamard gates to all qubits and create equal superposition

  Define Oracle(target_index):
    Flip the phase of the state corresponding to target_index

  Define DiffusionOperator():
    The average amplitude

  Apply Oracle(target_index)
  Apply DiffusionOperator()

  Measure qubits
  Return measured state and map binary to corresponding letter
```

```
print("🔍 Grover's Algorithm Result for finding letter 'C':")
for outcome, count in sorted(counts.items()):
    bits = format(outcome, '02b')
    letter = list(letter_map.keys())[list(letter_map.values()).index(bits)]
    print(f"Letter '{letter}' (|{bits}⟩): {count} times")

🔍 Grover's Algorithm Result for finding letter 'C':
Letter 'C' (|10⟩): 1000 times

In [5]:
print("\n🧠 Classical Search for letter 'C' in ['A', 'B', 'C', 'D']:")
letters = ['A', 'B', 'C', 'D']
for i, letter in enumerate(letters):
    if letter == target_letter:
        print(f"✅ Found '{letter}' at index {i} using O(N) brute-force search")
        break

🧠 Classical Search for letter 'C' in ['A', 'B', 'C', 'D']:
✅ Found 'C' at index 2 using O(N) brute-force search
```

Fig. 3. Output of letter search for both classical search and Grover's Algorithm'

4.3 Phase 2 – Specific Word Search

The second phase of the research extended Grover's Algorithm beyond basic letter search to simulate **word search within a paragraph**. The approach involved:

- Dividing a paragraph into small fixed-length chunks (e.g., four words)
- Encoding these chunks using **two qubits** to represent 4-word positions
- Applying **Grover's Algorithm** to amplify the correct word's binary position
- The target word was converted to binary based on its index in the chunk, and the quantum oracle was designed to flip its phase.
- The diffusion operator then amplified this state. When simulated, Grover's Algorithm successfully returned the correct word with high probability—validating its theoretical advantage for small-scale, exact-match search.

```
[12] # Simulated 4-word paragraph chunk
     words = ['data', 'quantum', 'classical', 'search']
     target_word = 'quantum'
     target_index = words.index(target_word)
     target_bin = format(target_index, '02b')

     # Define qubits (2 qubits for 4 words)
     qubits = [cirq.LineQubit(i) for i in range(2)]
```

Fig. 4. Code snippet for letter word using Cirq Simulator

4.4 Phase 2 – Pseudo Code Snippet

```
Procedure GroverWordSearch(paragraph, target_word):
  Divide paragraph into fixed-length chunks (e.g., 4 words per chunk)

  For each chunk:
    Encode word positions using 2 qubits (for 4-word chunks)
    target_index is position of target_word in current chunk
    Apply Hadamard gates and create superposition of positions

    Define Oracle(target_index):
      Flip the phase of the state at target_index

    Apply Oracle(target_index)
    Apply DiffusionOperator()

    Measure qubits
    If measurement matches target_index:
      Return "Target word found in chunk"
```

```
# Parse results
counts = result.histogram(key="result")
print("🔍 Simulated Word Search using Grover's Algorithm:")
for outcome, count in sorted(counts.items()):
    bin_str = format(outcome, '02b')
    word = words[int(bin_str, 2)]
    print(f"Word '{word}' (|{bin_str}⟩): {count} times")
```

```
🔍 Simulated Word Search using Grover's Algorithm:
Word 'quantum' (|01⟩): 1000 times
```

Fig. 5. Output for word search using Cirq Simulator

4.5 Why not just Use Parallelism with Grover's Algorithm?

At first, it seemed logical to scale Grover's Algorithm by splitting a paragraph into smaller chunks and running the search in parallel. Why Parallel Grover Falls Short.

- Still Needs Custom Oracles: - Each chunk requires its own oracle, adding overhead and complexity.
- No Semantic Understanding: - Grover works for exact matches only—it cannot detect AI rewording or paraphrased text.
- No Real Quantum Speedup: - Parallel runs $\neq$ better performance. Running Grover per chunk behaves like brute-force (O($\sqrt{}$n $\times$ chunks)).
- High Resource Demand: - Multiple instances mean multiple circuits and high qubit load—not feasible on today's hardware.

4.6 Toward a Better Solution: Quantum Kernel Methods

Instead of searching for exact words, Quantum Kernel Methods classify content based on meaning and pattern, they:

- Use quantum feature maps to embed text in high-dimensional space
- Measure semantic similarity, not just equality
- Enable AI vs human content detection with real-world performance.

5 Threats and Validity

While the proposed framework shows the strengths and limitations of Grover's Algorithm in quantum string and word search tasks, there are few factors may impact the results.

- Simulation vs. Real Quantum Hardware
  All experiments in this study were conducted using Google's Cirq simulator, which assumes ideal, noise-free execution. Although real quantum devices, current NISQ hardware suffer from gate errors, decoherence, and readout inaccuracies.
- Manual Oracle Design
  Each oracle used in our experiments was manually constructed for known search targets. While this approach is useable for testing small-scale problems, it does not scale well to large, real-world datasets. Designing oracles for arbitrary or semantically complex queries remains a major open challenge.
- Dataset and Problem Scope
  The practical use case focused on limited character sets and short paragraph chunks, with controlled input data. This constraint limits the evaluation of Grover's algorithm on diverse, noisy, or high-dimensional natural language datasets particularly those encountered in AI-generated content analysis.
- Lack of Semantic Representation
  Grover's algorithm inherently performs exact-match search. It cannot capture semantic similarity, paraphrasing, or contextual patterns. This limits its utility in modern NLP tasks where meaning matters more than string identity.
- Qubit and Circuit Constraints
  The number of qubits and depth of circuits were constrained to fit within simulator limits. Real-world applications such as document-level search or multi-level classification — would require significantly more quantum resources, which are not yet practical on today's hardware.

6 Conclusion

Grover's Algorithm, while great theoretically powerful, proves impactful only in structure use cases. Our experiment using Google's Cirq simulator shows its perfect accuracy for simple letter and word. However, the point we want to scale towards semantically hard or complex inputs such as paragraph or AI-generated content limitation becomes undeniable. The requirement of custom oracles, the exponential growth in circuit and hard binary structure of oracle itself shows the Grover approach struggle in real world application. Also attempts to parallelize Grover's logic resulted in classical brute force behavior. To address this, we shift to **Quantum Kernel Methods**, which allow for the encoding of text into high-dimensional Hilbert spaces, enabling classification based not on string match, but on semantic similarity. They offer better scalability, compatibility with hybrid quantum-classical models, and practical ways in AI tasks like text generation detection or contextual search. In conclusion, while Grover's Algorithm has educational and theoretical value, its real-world applications are bounded in limits. Future work will explore the integration of kernel-based quantum methods with learning-based oracle generation to achieve success for both efficiency and flexibility in quantum-enhanced natural language processing.

References

1. Grover, L.K.: A Fast Quantum Mechanical Algorithm for Database Search. In Proceedings of the Twenty-Eighth Annual ACM Symposium on Theory of Computing (pp. 212–219). ACM (1996)
2. Nielsen, M.A., Chuang, I.L.: Quantum Computation and Quantum Information. Cambridge University Press (2010)
3. Montanaro, A.: Quantum algorithms: an overview. npj Quantum Inf. **2**, 15023 (2016)
4. Das, K., Sadhu, A.: Experimental study on the quantum search algorithm over structured datasets using IBMQ experience. J. King Saud Univ. Comput. Inf. Sci. **34**(6), 6441–6452 (2022)
5. Pathan, M., Mallick, M.: Comparison of quantum and classical algorithm in searching a number in a database case. Procedia Comput. Sci. **185**, 152–159 (2021)
6. Padhan, R., Sahu, N., Panda, G.: Bridging classical and quantum string matching. Quantum Rep. **3**(2), 237–251 (2021)
7. Tiwari, S., Das, M.: Grover's algorithm: a practical perspective. J. Quantum Appl. **8**(1), 101–110 (2023)
8. Qureshi, M., Singh, R.: Simulation of quantum circuits using QSim and Cirq. Int. J. Quantum Comput. **5**(4), 201–210 (2023)
9. Krishna, V., Shukla, A.: Quantum Natural Language Processing: Challenges and Opportunities. ACM Comput. Surv. **55**(3), 45 (2022)
10. Schuld, M., Bocharov, A., Svore, K.M., Wiebe, N.: Circuit-centric quantum classifiers. Phys. Rev. A **101**(3), 032308 (2020)
11. Coelho, C.S., et al.: Quantum kernel methods under scrutiny: a benchmarking study. Quantum Mach. Learn. J. **2**(2), 112–130 (2023)
12. Vasudevan, A., et al.: Parameterized quantum circuits with quantum kernels for machine learning. IEEE Trans. Quantum Eng. **4**, 220–231 (2023)
13. Mohammad, T., Gupta, P.: Automated quantum oracle synthesis with a minimal number of qubits. Algorithms **16**(5), 243 (2023)
14. Salahuddin, M., Irfan, M.: Grover's search with learning oracle for constrained binary optimization. Quantum Inf. Process. **21**, 189 (2022)
15. Faruqui, A., Raina, A.: A scalable 5,6-Qubit Grover's quantum search model. Quantum Eng. Lett. **3**(1), 77–89 (2024)

Open-Source LLMs for Technical Q&A: Lessons from StackExchange

Zeerak Babar, Nafiz Imtiaz Khan(✉), Muhammad Hassnain, and Vladimir Filkov

University of California at Davis, Davis, CA, USA
{zebabar,nikhan,mhassnain,vfilkov}@ucdavis.edu

Abstract. In the rapidly evolving domain of software engineering (SE), Large Language Models (LLMs) are increasingly leveraged to automate developer support. Open source LLMs have grown competitive with proprietary models such as GPT-4 and Claude-3, without the associated financial and accessibility constraints. This study investigates whether state of the art open source LLMs including Solar-10.7B, CodeLlama-7B, Mistral-7B, Qwen2-7B, StarCoder2-7B, and LLaMA3-8B can generate responses to technical queries that align with those crafted by human experts. Leveraging retrieval augmented generation (RAG) and targeted fine tuning, we evaluate these models across critical performance dimensions, such as semantic alignment and contextual fluency. Our results show that Solar-10.7B, particularly when paired with RAG and fine tuning, most closely replicates expert level responses, offering a scalable and cost effective alternative to commercial models. This vision paper highlights the potential of open-source LLMs to enable robust and accessible AI-powered developer assistance in software engineering.

Keywords: Large Language Models (LLMs) · Open Source Models · Retrieval-Augmented Generation (RAG) · Technical Queries · StackExchange

1 Introduction

Large Language Models (LLMs) are built on complex architectures and trained on extensive datasets, enabling them to generate human-like text that can answer questions, write essays, summarize content, and engage in conversations [49]. Furthermore, by using tailored prompts, the output can be adjusted to mimic the behavior of specific demographic profiles. As a result, the advent of LLMs offers a valuable opportunity to simulate software developers, addressing traditional challenges associated with recruiting human developers for coding assistance/research purposes.

In the current environment of ever-increasing expectations, software developers are starting to rely on LLMs to obtain immediate and insightful answers to software development-related questions and solve technical challenges [10,21].

S. Hussain et al. (Eds.): SEET 2025, CCIS 2725, pp. 615–626, 2026.
https://doi.org/10.1007/978-3-032-08977-9_41

For instance, the study by Oishwee et al. [32] analyzed whether ChatGPT can answer Android permission-related questions. The authors analyzed 1,008 Stack-Overflow questions and their accepted answers, finding that 50% of ChatGPT-generated responses aligned with those accepted by developers. In another study, Gerosa et al. [16] proposed leveraging LLMs to generate synthetic qualitative data, suggesting that AI could potentially replace human participants in software engineering research. However, they caution that ethical concerns, model biases, and authenticity issues remain significant challenges. Separately, Haque [17] argues that LLMs are not only reshaping software development but also redefining the developer's role. While challenges persist, LLMs present unprecedented opportunities for innovation and collaboration, making early adoption essential for remaining competitive in this rapidly evolving field.

While LLMs are widely used by developers and researchers, most current research focuses on proprietary LLMs like `ChatGPT`, `Gemini` and `Claude-3` [28, 44]. These models, although powerful, come with high financial costs, often making them inaccessible to many developers and researchers. In this scenario, Open-source LLMs, which can be run locally and are free to use, offer a promising alternative for broader accessibility.

A Retrieval-Augmented Generation (RAG) [15] framework could further enhance LLM-generated responses by supplying relevant contextual information alongside user queries. However, no previous studies have explored how the RAG framework can be implemented, what type of context should be provided for individual user queries, or the effectiveness of the RAG framework in this specific task. Additionally, fine-tuning LLMs [11] may improve their ability to answer developer questions accurately, yet no studies have explored the combined effects of fine-tuning and the RAG framework in this context.

Moreover, although some research has examined question-answering platforms like `StackOverflow` [12] and `Reddit` [36], there has been no focused analysis of the broader community network `StackExchange` [12], which consists of 183 Q&A sites [12], including `StackOverflow`, `Super User`, and `Game Development`. The platform includes 60 technical sites out of a total of 183, such as `Data Science`, `Web Development`, and `Information Security`. The vast majority of contributors to these technical sites are developers, sharing their expertise and solving coding-related problems [40].

Focusing on the research gaps, we have developed three research questions:

> **RQ$_1$**: Can local LLMs Effectively Answer Technical Questions in a Base Setting?
> **RQ$_2$** : To what extent does the RAG framework enhance LLM response quality by incorporating additional contextual information?
> **RQ$_3$**: Can Fine-Tuning Within the RAG Framework Further Improve Model Performance?

The study is structured to address the research questions outlined above, specifically examining whether free, open source models can provide developers with equally valuable insights.

2 Study Methodology

2.1 Data Collection

For collecting data, we identified StackExchange [4] data source containing developer-posed questions alongside human responses. Rather than directly scraping data from this platform, we leveraged the publicly available StackExchange Data Dump [5], a downloadable archive that provides snapshots of the platform's content at specific intervals. This dataset includes various elements such as questions, answers, comments, user profiles, and tags, structured in formats like `XML`. Spanning from May 2014 to December 2023, the gathered dataset comprises 73,560 posts and 81,283 comments contributed by 54,037 distinct authors. Out of 73,560 posts, we randomly collected 41,000 posts and divided them into three subsets: 1) *Testing Dataset*: 1,000 samples used exclusively for testing; 2) *RAG Database*: 20,000 samples for the RAG framework; and 3) *Training Dataset*: 20,000 samples for fine-tuning the selected LLM model.

2.2 Data Synthesis

The `StackExchange` dataset underwent pre-processing to ensure data quality. First, each post included multiple comments as potential solutions to developer queries. Using the `AcceptedAnswer` tag, we identified the most relevant human response, selecting only posts with an accepted answer to create a reliable question-answer dataset for comparison with LLM responses. Next, we removed unnecessary HTML tags from posts and comments to maintain a clean text format for analysis.

2.3 Selecting the LLM Models

In this study, we required models capable of generating both natural language and code, suitable for question-answering tasks grounded in technical software engineering contexts. Based on prior work in code-related question-answering [23, 27,38], we selected a set of high-performing, open-source language models with approximately 7–10 billion parameters. Our selection prioritized models that support general-purpose instruction following, code generation, and contextual reasoning-making them viable candidates for integration into RAG pipelines. The selected models are briefly described below:

Mistral-7B: `Mistral-7B` is a 7-billion-parameter dense transformer model developed by Mistral-AI [2,20]. Known for its competitive performance across reasoning and generation tasks, it remains efficient and accurate despite its relatively compact size. We use the "Mistral-7B Instruct" variant, which is fine-tuned for instruction-following and conversational use cases [1].

Solar-10.7B: `Solar-10.7B` is a 10.7-billion-parameter model that balances performance across both code and text generation tasks. Prior studies have shown its strength in semantic reasoning and synthesis, making it a top choice for coding-related QA [23].

CodeLlama-7B: `CodeLlama-7B` is an open-source model specialized for code-related tasks. Developed by Meta, it provides strong support for multi-language programming and accurate code synthesis [38]. While optimized for code generation, it is also capable of producing well-structured natural language responses.

Qwen2-7B: `Qwen2-7B`, developed by Alibaba, is a general-purpose transformer with strong multilingual and reasoning capabilities [29]. It performs competitively across standard NLP benchmarks and is particularly well-suited for retrieval-augmented tasks due to its robustness in context-grounded generation.

StarCoder2-7B: `StarCoder2-7B`, jointly developed by Hugging Face and ServiceNow, is trained on permissively licensed code and instruction datasets. While it excels at code generation, it also supports high-quality natural language output, making it suitable for technical QA workflows involving both modalities [30].

LLaMA-3 8B: `LLaMA-3 8B` delivers state-of-the-art performance for its size. Its instruction-tuned variant demonstrates notable improvements in coherence and factual accuracy [47].

These chosen models represent the most recent and widely adopted 7-10B range open-source models with strong instruction-following capabilities. Fine-tuning was selectively applied to the best-performing model due to resource constraints and its superior baseline performance.

2.4 Prompt Design

A well-defined prompt is essential for an LLM to generate high-quality responses [46]. The prompt guides the LLM to align the query with context, ensuring clarity, relevance, and integration of technical details. In this study, we used a vanilla prompting technique for all experiments, outlined as follows:

Listing 1.1. Prompt Template

```
You are a helpful assistant with expertise in coding and
    technical topics. Use the following context to answer
    the question as accurately as possible, especially
    focusing on technical details and code examples if
    relevant.
Context:<<CONTEXT>>
Question:<<QUESTION>>
Provide a helpful and accurate answer, focusing on coding
    and technical topics.
```

2.5 Experimental Design

Base Configuration. The base setting involves providing only the query to the model and eliciting responses from models. To obtain responses, we have used a tool named `Ollama` [3], which enables the local execution of open-source models. Each of the questions of the dataset is passed to the LLM models as a prompt, and the obtained responses are recorded in local machine.

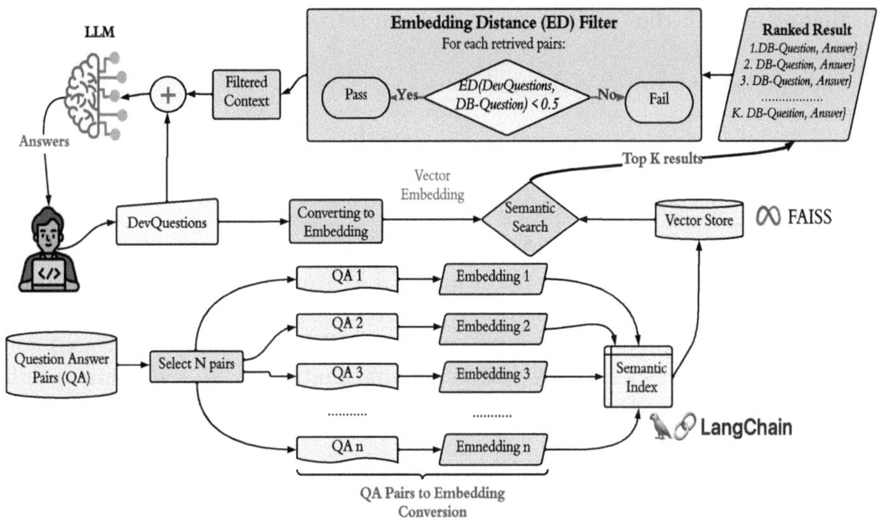

Fig. 1. Architecture of the proposed RAG pipeline

RAG Configuration. We set up an RAG pipeline to supply additional context to the LLM with each question. The proposed RAG architecture, shown in Fig. 1, includes interconnected components that efficiently retrieve and utilize contextual information from a vector database.

Initially, each of the question-answer pairs is converted into documents. The purpose of this transformation is to prepare the data for vectorization. Next, each of the documents is converted into embeddings. For embedding generation, `all-MiniLM-L6-v2` sentence transformer model has been used [39], which is based on the `MiniLM` architecture and is designed to balance performance and speed [42]. The design considerations make the model suitable for tasks such as semantic search, clustering, and classification [42].

Next, the pipeline leverages `LangChain` [25] to build semantic indexes for each embedding, facilitating efficient retrieval and ranking of information based on meaning and context, rather than relying solely on keyword matching [33]. These embeddings, along with their semantic indexes, are stored in `FAISS` [31], which is a high-performance vector database tailored for similarity search.

When a user submits a query, it is converted into an embedding using the sentence transformer model (`all-MiniLM-L6-v2`). The pipeline performs a semantic search within the vector database using this embedded query, retrieving the most relevant indexes (n = 5). The plain text of these indexes is then appended to the user's query and sent to the model. Since some retrieved contexts may be irrelevant, we evaluate the similarity between the query ($\mathbf{q}$) and the retrieved indexes ($\mathbf{d}$) using an embedding distance evaluator [24]. This evaluator calculates a relevance score to ensure only relevant question-answer pairs are included. If $S(\mathbf{q}, \mathbf{d}) > 0.5$, the context is excluded, as a higher similarity score suggests misalignment with the original query and the retrieved content from the vector database.

The similarity score S is defined as:

$$S(\mathbf{q}, \mathbf{d}) = \frac{\mathbf{q} \cdot \mathbf{d}}{\|\mathbf{q}\| \|\mathbf{d}\|}$$

Fine-Tuned Model with RAG Configuration. In this configuration, we fine-tuned the model (the best-performing LLM from the *Base* and *RAG* configurations) and used it within the RAG architecture. The fine-tuned model improves the generative component, while the RAG framework ensures contextually relevant responses by retrieving information from a domain-specific knowledge base. The model fine-tuning process is outlined in Subsect. 2.6.

Experimental Consideration. In our study, all experiments were conducted with a constant model temperature ($temp = 0$). Temperature is a hyper-parameter that controls the randomness of an LLM's output [37]. A lower temperature makes responses more deterministic and focused, while a higher temperature increases randomness and creativity. Other hyper-parameters, such as *top_p*, *top_k*, *min_p*, and *repeat_penalty*, were kept at their default values.

2.6 Fine-Tuning LLM

The fine-tuning process, along with the selected hyperparameters, is illustrated in Fig. 2. We employed the Low-Rank Adaptation (`LoRA`) [19] technique to fine-tune the best-performing model on 20,000 question-answer pairs, using the test set (n=1,000) as the validation set. The fine-tuning parameters included a batch size of 8, `AdamW` [13] as the optimizer, a learning rate of 2.5e-5, and 500 training steps. The `q_proj` layer was specifically fine-tuned, and early stopping [34] was applied as the stopping criterion to ensure optimal performance. Furthermore, we utilized 4-bit quantization combined with a mixed-precision configuration using `bfloat16`. This setup significantly minimized the model's memory footprint without compromising its performance.

2.7 Evaluating the Responses of LLMs

We selected three quantitative evaluation metrics based on prior literature [22]. These metrics allow assessment of the LLM-generated responses using gold annotations as references. The selected metrics include one text-similarity-based metric (*Cosine Similarity*) and two semantic-based metrics (*BERTScore* and *METEOR*). Semantic-based metrics analyze meaning and context, emphasizing coherence and relevance [18], whereas similarity-based metrics focus primarily on lexical overlap or statistical similarity between texts [14]. Although no fixed threshold universally defines good performance, recent studies from top-ranked venues suggest that a *BERTScore* above 0.5, a *Cosine Similarity* score above 0.3, and a *METEOR* score above 0.5 are indicative of strong performance [6–8, 41].

Cosine Similarity. It calculates the cosine of the angle between two vectors to assess similarity, quantifying the semantic closeness between human and LLM-generated responses [35].

BERTScore. It uses embeddings from pre-trained BERT models to measure semantic similarity between machine-generated and reference text, comparing cosine similarity of embeddings to quantify alignment in meaning and context with human-written references [48].

METEOR Score. It stands for Metric for Evaluation of Translation with Explicit Ordering, which assesses both lexical and semantic similarity, incorporating synonymy, stemming, and word order for a nuanced alignment between generated content and human references [9].

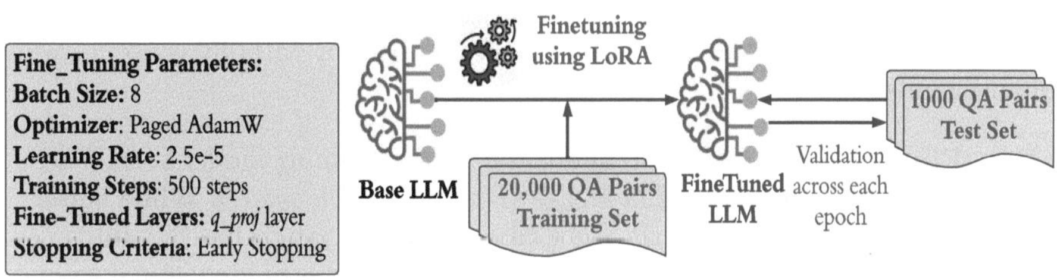

Fig. 2. Overview of the fine-tuning process, along with the selected hyper-parameters

3 Results and Discussion

The results of the experiments of this study are shown in Table 1. This section answers the questions of the stated RQs and discusses the implications of the results.

RQ1: Can local LLMs Effectively Answer Technical Questions in a Base Setting?

To address RQ1, base-setting experiments were conducted across a set of local models. Among all evaluated models, *Solar-10.7B* consistently outperformed others, achieving the highest `Cosine Similarity` (0.56) and `BERTScore` (0.54) in the base configuration. Its superior alignment with human-authored answers highlights its capability in understanding and replicating technical semantics effectively.

Other models such as *LLaMA-3 8B* (0.55 cosine, 0.53 BERT) and *CodeLlama-7B* (0.54 cosine, 0.54 BERT) followed closely behind, indicating strong but slightly less reliable performance. *Qwen2-7B* and *StarCoder2-7B* also showed competitive results.

Mistral-7B, on the other hand, underperformed in the base setting, especially with a `Cosine Similarity` of 0.32 and a notably lower `BERTScore` of 0.41. This

Table 1. Comprehensive overview of the performance of local language models across three configurations: Base Setting, RAG Configuration, and RAG and Fine-Tuned Configuration. In the RAG+Fine-Tuned configuration, "X" indicates that a particular model was not fine-tuned.

Models	Base Setting			RAG Architecture			RAG+Fine-Tuned Model		
	Cosine-Similarity	BERT	METEOR	Cosine-Similarity	BERT	METEOR	Cosine-Similarity	BERT	METEOR
CodeLlama-7B	0.54	0.54	0.22	0.54	0.55	0.25	X	X	X
Solar-10.7B	0.56	0.54	0.23	0.64	0.59	0.31	0.65	0.63	0.61
Mistral-7B	0.32	0.41	0.11	0.57	0.55	0.26	X	X	X
StarCoder2-7B	0.50	0.52	0.20	0.58	0.56	0.28	X	X	X
Qwen2-7B	0.53	0.53	0.22	0.60	0.57	0.29	X	X	X
LLaMA 3 8B	0.55	0.53	0.23	0.61	0.58	0.30	X	X	X

suggests limited effectiveness in capturing the semantic intent of the technical responses.

Across all models, `METEOR` scores remained relatively low in the base setting (ranging from 0.11 to 0.23), pointing to ongoing challenges in achieving fluent and well-structured natural language generation without context-aware enhancements.

> **RQ$_1$ Findings:** *Solar-10.7B* remains the top-performing model in the base setting, closely followed by *LLaMA-3 8B* and *CodeLlama-7B*. While newer 7B models like *Qwen2-7B* and *StarCoder2-7B* show promising capabilities, low `METEOR` scores across the board highlight limitations in linguistic fluency that could benefit from contextual or architectural augmentation.

RQ2: To what extent does the RAG framework enhance LLM response quality by incorporating additional contextual information? To explore RQ2, we evaluated the effectiveness of integrating a RAG framework in enhancing response quality. As shown in Table 1, all evaluated models demonstrated performance improvements in the **RAG Architecture** configuration, benefiting from access to relevant contextual information.

Solar-10.7B exhibited the most substantial gains, with its `Cosine Similarity` increasing from 0.56 to 0.64 and `BERTScore` rising to 0.59. These results indicate stronger semantic alignment and better preservation of the intended meaning in technical responses. The `METEOR` score also improved notably, reaching 0.31, suggesting enhanced fluency and coherence under the RAG framework.

Other models, including *LLaMA-3 8B* (0.61 cosine, 0.58 BERT), *Qwen2-7B* (0.60 cosine, 0.57 BERT), and *StarCoder2-7B* (0.58 cosine, 0.56 BERT), also showed meaningful improvements compared to their base performance. *Mistral-7B*, despite having the weakest base scores, experienced a sharp increase in `Cosine Similarity` from 0.32 to 0.57 under RAG, highlighting RAG's corrective effect on underperforming models.

RQ$_2$ Findings: The RAG framework significantly improves performance across all models by enriching responses with relevant contextual content. *Solar-10.7B* benefits the most, while even weaker models like *Mistral-7B* see large relative gains, underscoring RAGŠs potential to enhance both semantic fidelity and linguistic fluency.

RQ3: Can Fine-Tuning Within the RAG Framework Further Improve Model Performance?

We fine-tuned the *Solar-10.7B* model, which we found as the best performed LLM from base and RAG configurations. Alike other settings, fine-tuning under the RAG framework showed substantial improvements. Fine-tuning resulted in increased `BERTScore` and `METEOR`, enhancing the model's ability to generate responses with both semantic richness and fluency. While `Cosine Similarity` showed minor changes from the RAG-only setting, the gains in `BERTScore` and `METEOR` indicate that fine-tuning refines the model's response quality.

RQ$_3$ Findings: The RAG framework with a fine-tuned model yields additional performance gains, indicating that their integration enhances the quality and relevance of the generated insights, leading to more accurate and contextually appropriate results.

4 Threats to Validity

Our study has several limitations that highlight directions for future work. First, the dataset size for different experiments was relatively small. Future studies could improve reliability by using larger datasets. Second, we analyzed only six LLM models within a limited parameter range; expanding to a wider variety, especially larger models, could offer deeper insights into model performance. Third, we used a basic prompting technique, without advanced in-context approaches like `Chain-of-Thought` [43], `Tree-of-Thought` [45], or `n-shot prompting` [26]. Future research exploring these techniques may enhance model reasoning and response quality.

5 Conclusion

This study examined the viability of using locally deployed, fine-tuned LLMs as alternatives to proprietary models for SE tasks. By addressing three research questions, we assessed six open source models in different configurations: a base setting, a RAG framework, and fine-tuning within RAG. Our results show that *Solar-10.7B*, a locally deployed model, aligned well with human responses, especially with RAG and fine-tuning, excelling in technical inquiries on Stack-Exchange. RAG integration enhanced performance, while fine-tuning further improved contextual fluency. This vision paper demonstrates that open-source LLMs, optimized with RAG and fine-tuning, present a promising, cost-effective alternative for SE tasks.

Acknowledgement. This research was supported by the National Science Foundation under Grant No. 2020751, as well as by the Alfred P. Sloan Foundation through the OSPO for UC initiative (Award No. 2024-22424).

References

1. Mistral-7b instruct v0.2 on hugging face. https://huggingface.co/mistralai/Mistral-7B-Instruct-v0.2. Accessed 08 Nov 2024
2. Mistral AI. https://mistral.ai/. Accessed 08 Nov 2024
3. Ollama. https://ollama.com/. Accessed 08 Nov 2024
4. Stack exchange - where developers learn, share, & build careers. https://stackexchange.com/. Accessed 08 Nov 2024
5. Stack exchange archive on the internet archive. https://archive.org/details/stackexchange. Accessed 08 Nov 2024
6. Ahmed, T., Bird, C., Devanbu, P., Chakraborty, S.: Studying LLM performance on closed-and open-source data. arXiv preprint arXiv:2402.15100 (2024)
7. Ahmed, T., Pai, K.S., Devanbu, P., Barr, E.: Automatic semantic augmentation of language model prompts (for code summarization). In: Proceedings of the IEEE/ACM 46th International Conference on Software Engineering, pp. 1–13 (2024)
8. Al-Kaswan, A., Ahmed, T., Izadi, M., Sawant, A.A., Devanbu, P., van Deursen, A.: Extending source code pre-trained language models to summarise decompiled binaries. In: 2023 IEEE International Conference on Software Analysis, Evolution and Reengineering (SANER), pp. 260–271. IEEE (2023)
9. Banerjee, S., Lavie, A.: Meteor: an automatic metric for MT evaluation with improved correlation with human judgments. In: Proceedings of the ACL Workshop on Intrinsic and Extrinsic Evaluation Measures for Machine Translation and/or Summarization, pp. 65–72 (2005)
10. Chen, X., Gao, C., Chen, C., Zhang, G., Liu, Y.: An empirical study on challenges for LLM developers. arXiv preprint arXiv:2408.05002 (2024)
11. Dodge, J., Ilharco, G., Schwartz, R., Farhadi, A., Hajishirzi, H., Smith, N.: Fine-tuning pretrained language models: weight initializations, data orders, and early stopping. arXiv preprint arXiv:2002.06305 (2020)
12. Exchange, S.: Stack exchange. https://stackexchange.com/. Accessed 09 Nov 2024
13. Face, H.: Adamw optimizer (2025). https://huggingface.co/docs/bitsandbytes/en/reference/optim/adamw. Accessed 17 Jan 2025
14. Finnie, G., Sun, Z.: Similarity and metrics in case-based reasoning. Int. J. Intell. Syst. **17**(3), 273–287 (2002)
15. Gao, Y., et al.: Retrieval-augmented generation for large language models: a survey. arXiv preprint arXiv:2312.10997 (2023)
16. Gerosa, M., Trinkenreich, B., Steinmacher, I., Sarma, A.: Can AI serve as a substitute for human subjects in software engineering research? Autom. Softw. Eng. **31**(1), 13 (2024)
17. Haque, M.A.: LLMs: a game-changer for software engineers? arXiv preprint arXiv:2411.00932 (2024)
18. Hu, B., Kalfoglou, Y., Alani, H., Dupplaw, D., Lewis, P., Shadbolt, N.: Semantic metrics. In: Staab, S., Svátek, V. (eds.) EKAW 2006. LNCS (LNAI), vol. 4248, pp. 166–181. Springer, Heidelberg (2006). https://doi.org/10.1007/11891451_17

19. Hu, E.J., et al.: Lora: low-rank adaptation of large language models. arXiv preprint arXiv:2106.09685 (2021)
20. Jiang, A.Q., et al.: Mistral 7b. arXiv preprint arXiv:2310.06825 (2023)
21. Jin, H., Huang, L., Cai, H., Yan, J., Li, B., Chen, H.: From LLMs to LLM-based agents for software engineering: a survey of current, challenges and future. arXiv preprint arXiv:2408.02479 (2024)
22. Khan, N.I., Filkov, V.: Evidencebot: a privacy-preserving, customizable rag-based tool for enhancing large language model interactions. In: FSE Companion 2025: Proceedings of the 33rd ACM International Conference on the Foundations of Software Engineering (2025)
23. Kim, D., et al.: Solar 10.7 b: scaling large language models with simple yet effective depth up-scaling. arXiv preprint arXiv:2312.15166 (2023)
24. LangChain: Embedding distance evaluation (2024). https://python.langchain.com/v0.1/docs/guides/productionization/evaluation/string/embedding_distance/
25. LangChain: Langchain - building applications with LLMs (2024). https://www.langchain.com/. Accessed 06 Sept 2024
26. Lee, U., et al.: Few-shot is enough: exploring chatgpt prompt engineering method for automatic question generation in English education. Educ. Inf. Technol. **29**(9), 11483–11515 (2024)
27. Li, L., He, X., Wang, H., Wang, L., He, L.: How do humans write code? Large models do it the same way too. arXiv preprint arXiv:2402.15729 (2024)
28. Liang, J.T., et al.: Can GPT-4 replicate empirical software engineering research? Proc. ACM Softw. Eng. **1**(FSE), 1330–1353 (2024)
29. Liu, W., et al.: Optimizing few-shot learning: from static to adaptive in qwen2-7b. In: Amazon KDD Cup 2024 Workshop (2024)
30. Lozhkov, A., et al.: Starcoder 2 and the stack v2: The next generation. arXiv preprint arXiv:2402.19173 (2024)
31. Meta AI: Faiss: Facebook AI similarity search. https://ai.meta.com/tools/faiss/. Accessed 28 Nov 2024
32. Oishwee, S.J., Stakhanova, N., Codabux, Z.: Large language model vs. stack overflow in addressing Android permission related challenges. In: 2024 IEEE/ACM 21st International Conference on Mining Software Repositories (MSR), pp. 373–383. IEEE (2024)
33. Papadimitriou, C.H., Tamaki, H., Raghavan, P., Vempala, S.: Latent semantic indexing: a probabilistic analysis. In: Proceedings of the Seventeenth ACM SIGACT-SIGMOD-SIGART Symposium on Principles of Database Systems, pp. 159–168 (1998)
34. Prechelt, L.: Early stopping - but when? In: Orr, G.B., Müller, K.-R. (eds.) Neural Networks: Tricks of the Trade. LNCS, vol. 1524, pp. 55–69. Springer, Heidelberg (1998). https://doi.org/10.1007/3-540-49430-8_3
35. Rahutomo, F., Kitasuka, T., Aritsugi, M., et al.: Semantic cosine similarity. In: The 7th International Student Conference on Advanced Science and Technology ICAST, vol. 4, p. 1. University of Seoul South Korea (2012)
36. Reddit: Reddit. https://www.reddit.com/?rdt=40286. Accessed 09 Nov 2024
37. Renze, M., Guven, E.: The effect of sampling temperature on problem solving in large language models. arXiv preprint arXiv:2402.05201 (2024)
38. Roziere, B., et al.: Code llama: open foundation models for code. arXiv preprint arXiv:2308.12950 (2023)
39. Sentence-Transformers: all-minilm-l6-v2 on hugging face. https://huggingface.co/sentence-transformers/all-MiniLM-L6-v2. Accessed 08 Nov 2024

40. Tahir, A., Dietrich, J., Counsell, S., Licorish, S., Yamashita, A.: A large scale study on how developers discuss code smells and anti-pattern in stack exchange sites. Inf. Softw. Technol. **125**, 106333 (2020)
41. Virk, Y., Devanbu, P., Ahmed, T.: Enhancing trust in LLM-generated code summaries with calibrated confidence scores. arXiv preprint arXiv:2404.19318 (2024)
42. Wang, W., Wei, F., Dong, L., Bao, H., Yang, N., Zhou, M.: Minilm: deep self-attention distillation for task-agnostic compression of pre-trained transformers. Adv. Neural. Inf. Process. Syst. **33**, 5776–5788 (2020)
43. Wei, J., et al.: Chain-of-thought prompting elicits reasoning in large language models. Adv. Neural. Inf. Process. Syst. **35**, 24824–24837 (2022)
44. Xiao, T., Treude, C., Hata, H., Matsumoto, K.: DevGPT: studying developer-chatgpt conversations. In: 2024 IEEE/ACM 21st International Conference on Mining Software Repositories (MSR), pp. 227–230. IEEE (2024)
45. Yao, S., et al.: Tree of thoughts: deliberate problem solving with large language models. In: Advances in Neural Information Processing Systems, vol. 36 (2024)
46. Zamfirescu-Pereira, J., Wong, R.Y., Hartmann, B., Yang, Q.: Why Johnny can't prompt: how non-AI experts try (and fail) to design LLM prompts. In: Proceedings of the 2023 CHI Conference on Human Factors in Computing Systems, pp. 1–21 (2023)
47. Zhang, D., Huang, X., Zhou, D., Li, Y., Ouyang, W.: Accessing GPT-4 level mathematical olympiad solutions via Monte Carlo tree self-refine with llama-3 8b. arXiv preprint arXiv:2406.07394 (2024)
48. Zhang, T., Kishore, V., Wu, F., Weinberger, K.Q., Artzi, Y.: Bertscore: evaluating text generation with BERT. arXiv preprint arXiv:1904.09675 (2019)
49. Zhao, W.X., et al.: A survey of large language models. arXiv preprint arXiv:2303.18223 (2023)

Student Research Competition (SRC)

Analyzing and Visualizing Software Quality of Code in GitHub Repositories Using AST-Based Metrics

Dipen Rathod(✉)

Department of Software Engineering, Pennsylvania State University World Campus, University Park, PA, USA
dar6078@psu.edu

Abstract. Context: High code quality is essential in software development, as it directly impacts readability, maintainability, reliability, security, and efficiency. Quality assessment becomes increasingly important as projects grow more complex and new developers are added. **Problem**: Tracking and maintaining code quality in growing projects with multiple contributors poses significant challenges, especially for development teams with limited resources. **Method**: This paper introduces a Python-based tool that automatically retrieves, analyzes, and visualizes software quality metrics for Python code files in user-selected GitHub repositories. Using Abstract Syntax Tree (AST) analysis, the tool calculates Halstead, Traditional, and Object-Oriented metrics on a per-file basis and supports visualizing these values across commits and pull requests. **Result**: The tool accurately calculates Halstead, LOC, Length of Identifier, and Cyclomatic Complexity metrics, with the results verified using manual calculations. However, the tool produces incorrect metric results for Fan-in, Fan-out, and inheritance-related OO metrics due to the lack of multi-file analysis. **Conclusion**: The tool's ability to automate metric calculation, store results, visualize results, and integrate into GitHub workflows helps developers monitor code quality trends over time. Though currently limited to per-file analysis, the tool provides a foundation for continuous quality assessment, with the next step for adding multi-file analysis support discussed.

Keywords: Software metrics · Design metrics · Halstead metrics · Traditional metrics · Object-Oriented metrics · Code quality · Abstract Syntax Trees · Python AST analysis · GitHub

1 Introduction

Software quality metrics serve as quantitative indicators of various aspects of software quality, offering insights into characteristics such as maintainability, complexity, defect likelihood, and adherence to design principles. These metrics play a crucial role in the software development lifecycle by providing objective measures that help teams identify potential issues, prioritize refactoring efforts, and track quality improvements over time.

Prior research has introduced several metric suites that address different aspects of software quality. The Metrics for Object-Oriented Design (MOOD) suite [1] focuses

S. Hussain et al. (Eds.): SEET 2025, CCIS 2725, pp. 629–648, 2026.
https://doi.org/10.1007/978-3-032-08977-9_42

on encapsulation, inheritance, polymorphism, and coupling at the system level. The Quality Model for Object-Oriented Design (QMOOD) [2] extends this by linking design properties to quality attributes. The Chidamber and Kemerer (CK) metrics suite [3] offers metrics specific to object-oriented programming, while Halstead metrics [4] provide a language-independent way to measure program complexity based on operators and operands.

Despite the established value of these metrics, small development teams often lack the resources to implement comprehensive metric tracking solutions. While enterprise-grade tools like SonarQube provide robust static analysis capabilities, they require significant setup effort and may not integrate smoothly into existing workflows. Similarly, tools like Radon [8] offer Python-specific analysis but typically provide only point-in-time measurements rather than tracking quality evolution over time.

This paper proposes a Python-based tool that addresses these limitations by:

- Automatically retrieving and analyzing GitHub-hosted [14] Python code
- Calculating key software quality metrics using Abstract Syntax Tree (AST) analysis on a per-file basis
- Tracking quality changes over time across different commits and branches
- Offering visual insights into software evolution through interactive graphs
- Providing pull request analysis to assess potential quality impacts before merging

The proposed approach enables development teams to incorporate quality monitoring into their workflows with minimal overhead while gaining valuable insights into their projects' evolution.

1.1 Abstract Syntax Tree (AST)

An Abstract Syntax Tree (AST) represents a program in tree form while omitting unnecessary syntactic details, such as punctuation marks [16].

Table 1 shows a comparison between a Python code snippet and its AST.

To calculate metrics, the abstract syntax tree is traversed, and when visiting a node relevant to a metric, its attributes are used to obtain information used in metric calculation.

Details of each node of a Python program's AST can be found in the official documentation [9].

1.2 Halstead Metrics and Python

This section provides the formulae used for the Halstead Metrics suite and the limitations of this suite with the Python Programming Language. For an in-depth understanding of this metrics suite, please refer to citations [4].

Halstead Metrics uses the total number of unique operators ($n1$), unique operands ($n2$), total operators ($N1$), and total operands ($N2$) [4].

These four integer values can be used to calculate the following metrics:

$$\text{Program Vocabulary} = \text{n1} + \text{n2} \tag{1}$$

$$\text{Program Length} = \text{N1} + \text{N2} \tag{2}$$

$$\text{Estimated Program Length} = \text{n1} * \log_2(\text{n1}) + \text{n2} * \log_2(\text{n2}) \tag{3}$$

$$\text{Volume} = \text{Program Length} * \log_2(\text{Program Vocabulary}) \tag{4}$$

$$\text{Difficulty} = (\text{n1}/2) + (\text{N2}/\text{n2}) \tag{5}$$

$$\text{Effort} = \text{Difficulty} * \text{Volume} \tag{6}$$

Table 1. Python code and its AST

<table>
<tr><th>Code</th><th>AST</th></tr>
<tr><td><pre>
def Hello(i=0):
  print("Hello World: ", i)
Hello(1)
</pre></td><td><pre>
Module(
 body=[
  FunctionDef(
   name='Hello',
   args=arguments(
    posonlyargs=[],
    args=[
     arg(arg='i')],
    kwonlyargs=[],
    kw_defaults=[],
    defaults=[
     Constant(value=0)]),
   body=[
    Expr(
     value=Call(

func=Name(id='print',
ctx=Load()),
      args=[
       Con-
stant(value='Hello World:
'),
       Name(id='i',
ctx=Load())],
      keywords=[]))],
   decorator_list=[],
   type_params=[]),
  Expr(
   value=Call(
    func=Name(id='Hello',
ctx=Load()),
    args=[
     Constant(value=1)],
    keywords=[]))],
 type_ignores=[])
</pre></td></tr>
</table>

Limitations of Halstead Metrics with the Python Programming Language. The Halstead metrics suite does not explicitly define what constitutes an operator or operand in Python. Consequently, different tools used to calculate the Halstead metrics may produce different results. The Python AST nodes counted as either operator or operand in this tool are:

- **Operator:** For, While, IfExp, If, Return, Pass, Break, Continue, Subscript, Slice, ListComp, SetComp, DictComp, GeneratorExp, Call, Attribute, Yield, YieldFrom, Raise, Assert, TypeAlias, Try, TryStar, ExceptHandler, With, UnaryOp, BinOp, BoolOp, Compare, Assign, AnnAssign, AugAssign, Delete, Match, ClassDef, FunctionDef
- **Operand:** Name, Constant, JoinedStr.

1.3 Traditional Metrics and Python

Traditional metrics offer useful insights into code quality, though they are less commonly emphasized than object-oriented metrics [10].

The tool supports the following Traditional metrics at present:

- Lines Of Code (LOC)
- Fan-in and Fan-out coupling metrics – Number of incoming and outgoing method calls to and from a method
- (Average) Length of Identifier
- Cyclomatic Complexity [11]

1.4 Object-Oriented (OO) Metrics and Python

For detailed information about OO Metrics, please refer to works [1–3].

Python can be considered an object-oriented language, but it is more appropriate to call it a multi-paradigm language. Not all Python programs use object-oriented programming concepts, such as classes and inheritance, to work. Therefore, it should be noted that the OO metrics results may be empty for some tested files. Nonetheless, supporting OO metrics remains valuable, as many Python programs continue to utilize object-oriented design principles.

The tool supports the following OO metrics at present:

- Weighted Methods Per Class (WMC) - Number of methods defined in a class [3]
- Number of Children (NOC) - Number of immediate subclasses of a class [3]
- Depth of Inheritance Tree (DIT) - Longest inheritance path from a class to the root class.

2 Related Work

Several tools and techniques exist for assessing software quality, each with its strengths and limitations:

Static Analysis Tools. Solutions such as SonarQube [5] and Pylint [6] provide comprehensive static code analysis and suggest improvements based on predefined rules. While powerful, these tools often focus on code smells and potential bugs rather than tracking quality metrics over time.

Code Review Systems. GitHub's built-in review system allows manual quality checks and facilitates discussion around code changes. However, this approach relies heavily on reviewer expertise and availability, potentially leading to inconsistent quality assessments.

AI-Powered Assistants. Tools like GitHub Copilot [7] offer AI-driven code suggestions that may improve quality, but they do not track quality trends explicitly or provide historical context for quality-related decisions.

Metric-Specific Tools. Radon [8] and similar Python-specific tools calculate metrics like cyclomatic complexity and Halstead metrics, but typically provide only snapshot analyses rather than temporal tracking.

Designite [17] is a paid example that supports metrics such as fan-in and fan-out. It also integrates into the CI pipeline. It was excluded from the comparison due to its licensing restrictions.

Unlike these approaches, the proposed tool is free and focuses on tracking code quality changes over time, offering historical analysis and comparison features that are often missing in existing solutions.

3 Proposed Methodology

3.1 Overview

The methodology employs static analysis using Abstract Syntax Trees (ASTs) to extract quality metrics from Python source code. ASTs provide a structured representation of code that facilitates accurate metric calculation while abstracting away syntax details [9].

The process is split into two phases:

- Phase 1: Retrieving code files and calculating metrics
- Phase 2: Serving the calculated metrics via a dashboard

Phase 1: Retrieving Code Files and Calculating Metrics. Two server programs are used to retrieve the code files from the selected GitHub repositories. The PyGitHub (V3) [15] API is used to retrieve the code files from the repositories. These servers check for new and updated files in user-defined intervals.

Main Branch Metric Server:

1. Retrieve the access token and the list of repositories of interest from the associated config file
2. Generate an AST of all Python code files present in the main branch of the repositories of interest
3. Calculate the Halstead metrics, OO metrics, and Traditional metrics using the generated ASTs
4. Store the metrics as JSON files locally and in the respective repositories online
5. Rerun logic when the time interval is complete

Pull-Requests Metrics Server:

1. Retrieve the access token and the list of repositories of interest from the associated config file
2. Generate an AST of all Python code files present in the **open pull requests** of the repositories of interest
3. Calculate the Halstead metrics, OO metrics, and Traditional metrics using the generated ASTs
4. Store the metrics as JSON files locally and in the respective repositories online
5. Rerun logic when the time interval is complete

Previously processed commits and pull requests should be skipped to avoid unnecessary computation.

Figure 1 illustrates the working of the two server files.

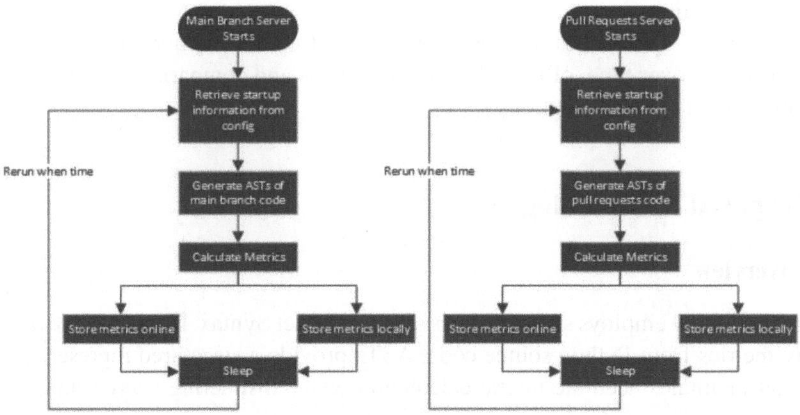

Fig. 1. Ideal working flow of the server programs

Phase 2: Serving the Calculated Metrics via a Dashboard. A multi-page web application provides the following features:

- **Login Page:** Users enter the repository name for which they want to visualize pre-calculated metrics, and their GitHub token acts as a 'password'
- **Halstead metrics page:** A page where users can select the file and its associated Halstead metrics for plotting
- **Object-oriented metrics page:** A page where users can select the file and its associated Object-oriented metrics for plotting
- **Traditional metrics page:** A page where users can select the file and its associated Traditional metrics for plotting

The web app has been developed using Plotly-Dash [13]. Plotly-Dash was selected arbitrarily; however, any framework supporting Plotly charts can be used.

Note: Some metrics must have been calculated and stored in appropriate directories. The server programs need not be active.

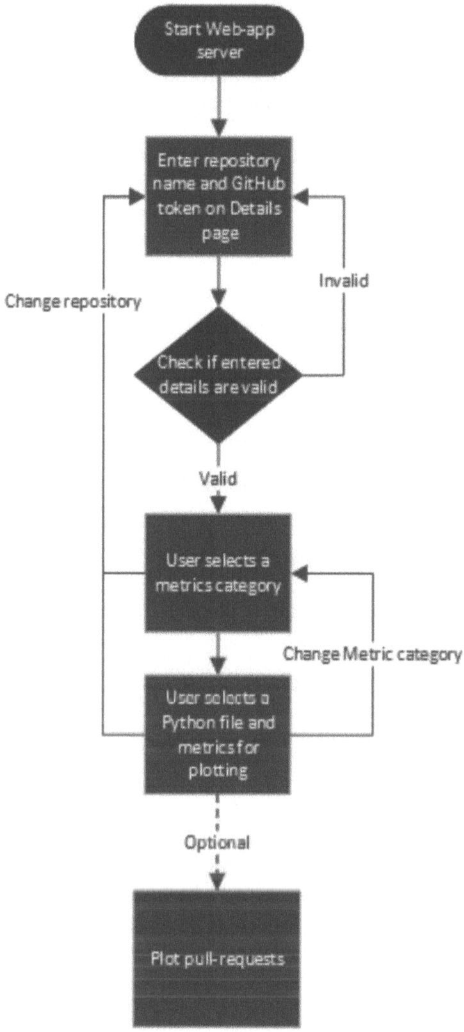

Fig. 2. User interaction with the web app

Figure 2 illustrates the ideal user interaction with the webpage.

3.2 Integration into GitHub Workflow

This section describes how the tool works when new files are added to the main branch or when new open pull requests are available.

- The two server programs check for new files in the main branch and new open pull requests at user-defined intervals. For testing, this interval is 0.017 h (approximately 1 min).

- The newly calculated metrics are added to the existing JSON files for each repository. If any JSON files do not exist, they are recreated.
- The graphs on the webpage are updated automatically at predefined intervals. A user may manually refresh the graphs if they like.

This integration enables continuous quality monitoring without requiring developers to adopt new workflows or platforms.

4 Experimental Setup

The tool is evaluated based on two primary goals:

1. Expected application behavior: All supporting features work
2. Correct Metrics calculation: All calculated metrics (Halstead, Object-oriented, and Traditional) are correct and stored appropriately.

Link to the tool: https://github.com/dipenarathod/Python-Code-Quality-Visualizer.

4.1 Expected Application Behavior

Although metrics calculation is the highest priority, it is also necessary to check that the following work is as expected:

- Server programs (retrieve code files from the repository and store calculations as JSON files)
- JSON to Pandas [12] data frames conversion
- Plotting functionality
- Web dashboard

The dipenarathod/desktop-tutorial repository (https://github.com/dipenarathod/desktop-tutorial) was used to test the application's behavior. It has various Python code files added over time, with open pull requests over a year old.

4.2 Correct Metrics Calculation

It is necessary to check whether the metric values calculated by the tool match the manually calculated values.

The repository dipenarathod/Metrics-Research_Python-Code-Files (https://github.com/dipenarathod/Metrics-Research_Python-Code-Files) is used to verify calculations.

There are a few Python code files in this repository that use OOP concepts such as classes and inheritance, which will help when calculating Object-oriented metrics. The programs here are also short, making manual calculations for metrics like Lines of code manageable.

5 Calculation Logic

The tool is designed for individual file analysis. While calculating metrics for a file, other files in the repository are ignored. Multi-file analysis is not supported.

5.1 Halstead Metrics

Classification of nodes into operators and operands was made based on the criteria defined in Sect. 1.2. Please note that the criteria themselves can't make the calculation logic clear. Nodes not categorized may be traversed to calculate the number of operators and operands. For example, the Argument AST node needs to be traversed to get to some operands. Similarly, calls and attributes need to be chained and built as a string for function calls, which are considered operators.

Function parameters are treated as operands to better reflect the method's complexity.

The programmer may alter what is considered an operator, operand, or how one is constructed by tailoring the appropriate AST node visitor classes. The visitor classes and calculation logic are available in HalsteadMetricsClasses.py.

The metrics dictionary has a flat structure because all calculated values are real numbers.

5.2 Traditional Metrics

The LOC metric ignores comment lines, including docstrings, during calculations. It focuses on Python code statements.

The Length of Identifier metric considers built-in keywords for its calculations. For example, self and __init__ are considered valid identifiers.

Fan-in is calculated based on how many times any function is called in a code file. Therefore, built-in functions, such as range(), also have an associated Fan-in count. A call to the parent's class constructor will give the parent's class init function a fan-in value.

Fan-out is calculated using the number of method calls from inside the method definition. 'super()' is not counted as a function call by itself because it is always accompanied by a method call from the super (parent) class. Calls to built-in functions, such as range(), are counted as function calls. This design choice was made to avoid the assumption that in-built function definitions will not change over time.

Cyclomatic Complexity, or CC, is measured using the definition laid out in [11]. CC is calculated on a per-method basis to restrict the count of connected components to 1.

Fan-in, Fan-out, and CC have a nested metrics result structure as they are calculated on a per-method basis rather than the Python code file.

5.3 Object-Oriented (OO) Metrics

All OO metrics have a nested structure because there may be multiple classes defined in the same code file.

WMC is the number of methods defined in a class. It is achieved by counting the function definition nodes in a class.

Any defined class in Python has a DIT value of at least 1. The calculated value may increase when a class inherits from another class in the same code file.

The NOC metric is 0 for all defined classes unless a class defined is used as a parent for another class in the same code file.

6 Results

6.1 Results of Goal 1 – Expected Application Behavior

This section shares screenshots of different pages from the web application. The metrics were calculated using the server programs discussed in Sect. 3.1. The screenshots aim to show the reader how various metrics are plotted. Metrics in JSON file format can be found in the repository (Fig. 3):

- 'metrics' folder contains the main branch code metrics
- 'pull_request_metrics' folder contains the open pull request metrics

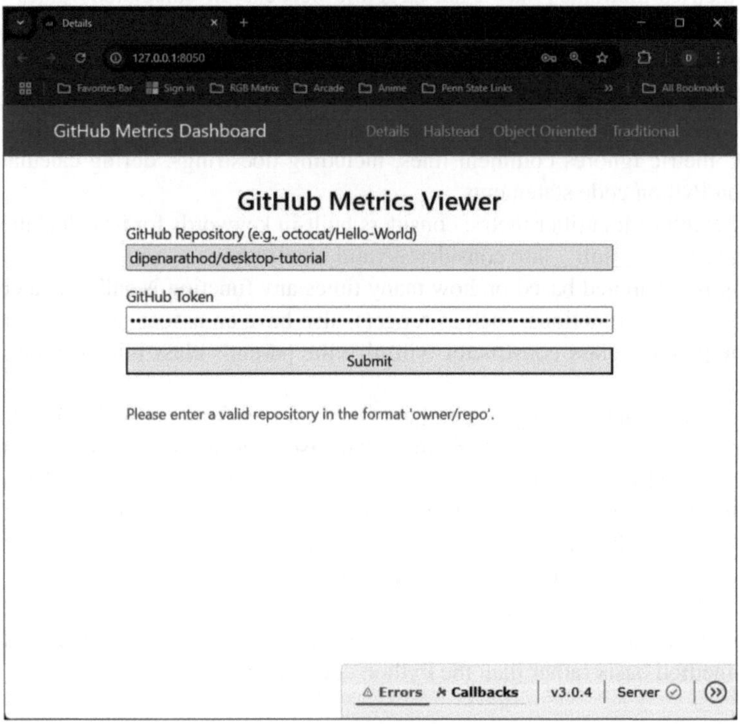

Fig. 3. Details (login) page to select the repository and enter the GitHub token

In Fig. 4, some Halstead metrics for Test1.py are plotted. The metrics plotted are **Program Vocabulary** (visible) and **Estimated Program Length**. Test1.py has open pull requests, so enabling PR overlay shows additional data.

The user can plot multiple graphs for Halstead metrics for the same code file simultaneously.

In Fig. 5, Traditional metrics for Test1.py are plotted. The **LOC** and **Length of Identifier** metrics are plotted**.** Test1.py has open pull requests, so enabling PR overlay shows additional data.

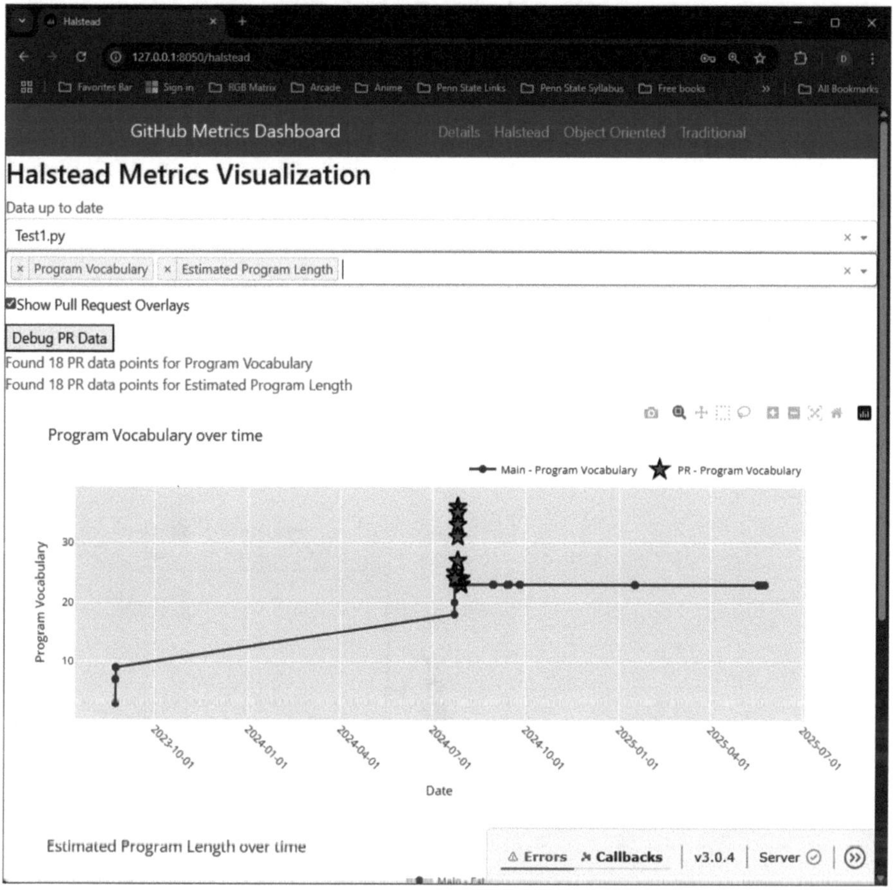

Fig. 4. Halstead page with metrics plotted for Test.py (PR overlay enabled)

Like Halstead metrics plotting, the user can plot multiple graphs for traditional metrics for the same code file simultaneously.

The app is functioning as expected, signaling that the supporting functionality of the tool is ready for use.

In Fig. 6, OO metrics for the file TestClasses.py are plotted. The metrics plotted are **WMC_B** (weighted methods per class for class B) and **DIT_A** (depth of inheritance tree for class A). Classes A and B are present in TestClasses.py. Since no open pull requests exist for TestClasses.py, none are plotted.

Multiple OO metrics can be plotted simultaneously on a per-code-file basis.

6.2 Results of Goal 2 – Correct Metrics Calculation

This section compares the metric values calculated by the tool with the expected value. Results from Radon are used when possible.

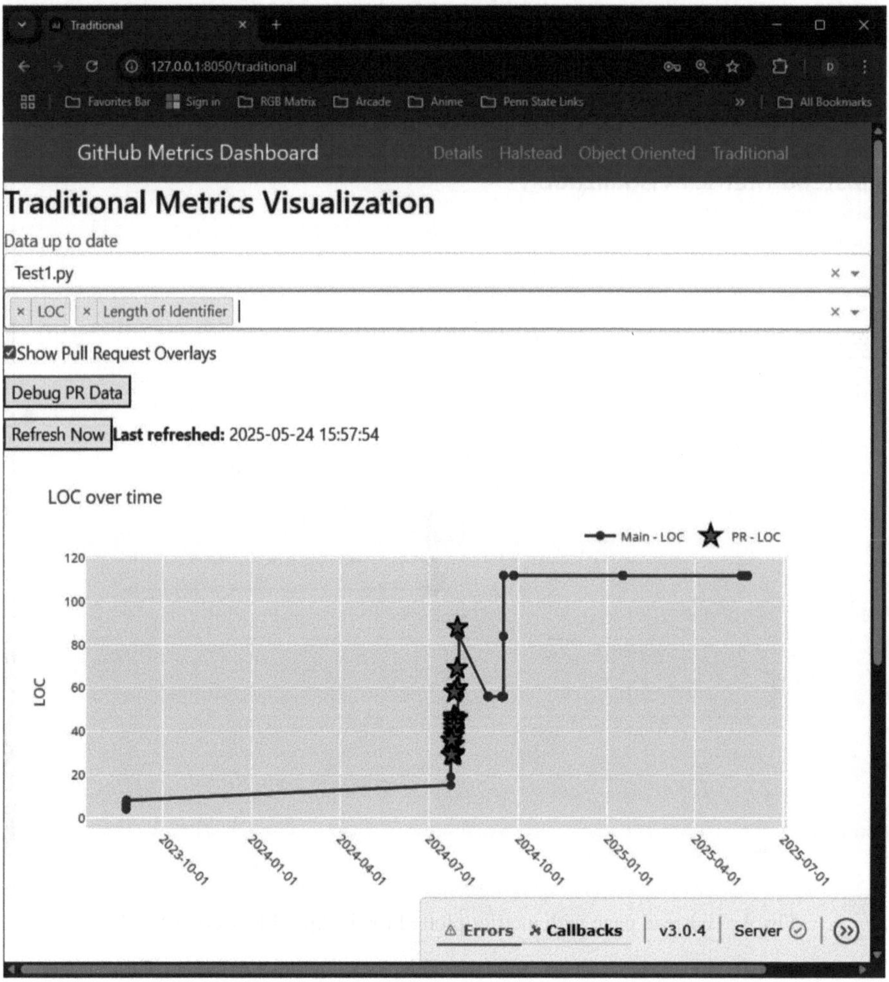

Fig. 5. Traditional Metrics page for Test1.py (PR overlay enabled)

The results from this section can be used to expose any shortcomings in the tool's logic, making it clearer where future work is necessary.

As discussed in Sect. 5, this tool calculates metrics on a per-file basis. To show what the result may have been if multi-file analysis were supported, a multi-file analysis column has been added where relevant. The values in this column are manually calculated.

The files inspected are:

- Shape_Rectangle.py
- Square.py

The manual calculations can be found in the repository as scanned PDFs.

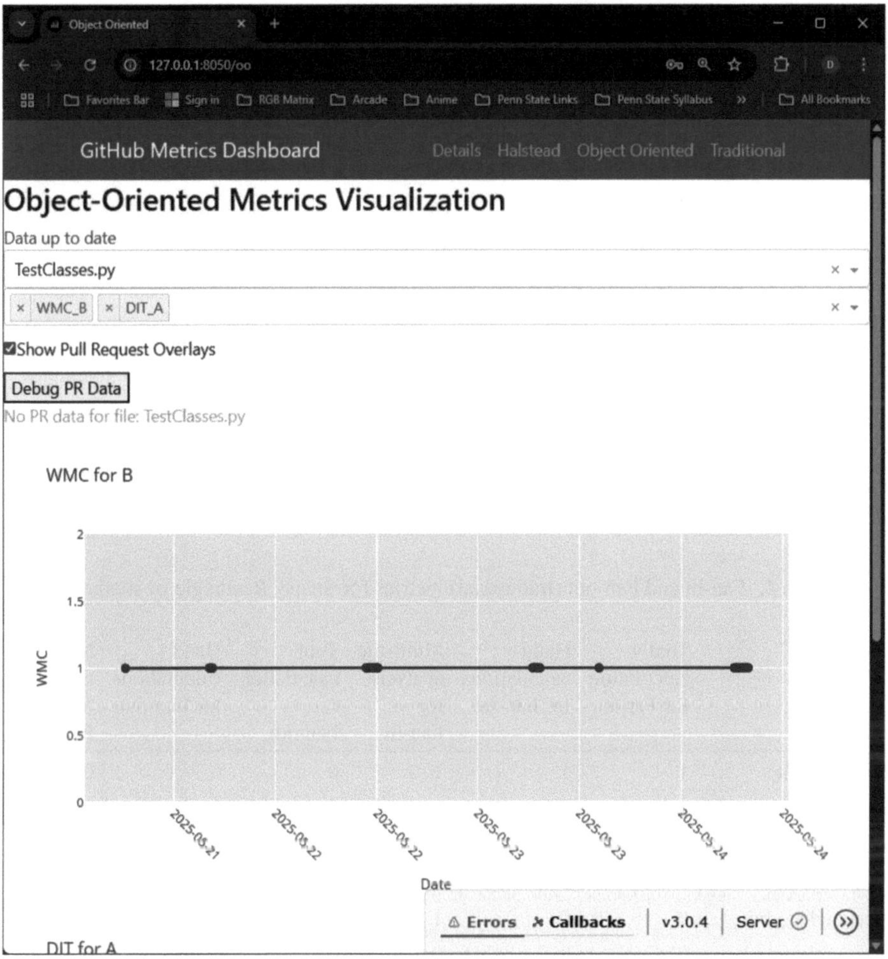

Fig. 6. OO Metrics page for TestClasses.py (PR overlay enabled)

For Halstead metrics, only unique operators ($n1$), unique operands ($n2$), total operators ($N1$), and total operands ($N2$) are calculated because the Halstead metrics suite depends on these four values, as discussed in Sect. 1.2.

'X' means the value was not calculated or thought to be irrelevant. Any other interpretation of 'X' is discussed when necessary.

Metrics Results for Shape_Rectangle.py

Halstead Metrics

Traditional Metrics – LOC and Length of Identifier

Traditional Metrics – Fan-in and Fan-out

Traditional Metrics – Cyclomatic Complexity

OO Metrics – Class Shape

OO Metrics – Class Rectangle

Table 2. Halstead metrics result for Shape_Rectangle.py

	Tool's calculations	Hand-calculations	Radon
n1	8	8	2
N1	35	35	6
n2	16	16	3
N2	31	31	6

Table 3. LOC and Length of Identifier metrics for Shape_Rectangle.py

	Tool's calculations	Hand-calculations	Radon
LOC	18	18	18
Length of Identifier	5.2	5.2	(Not supported)

Table 4. Fan-in and Fan-out (traditional) metrics for Shape_Rectangle.py methods

	Tool's calculation for Fan-in	Hand calculations for Fan-in	Multi-file analysis for Fan-in	Tool calculation for Fan-out	Hand calculations for Fan-out	Multi-file analysis for Fan-out
Shape.__init__	1	1	1	0	0	0
Shape.area	1	1	1	0	0	0
Shape.perimeter	1	1	1	0	0	0
Shape.describe	0	0	0	2	2	2
Rectangle.__init__	0	0	1	1	1	1
Rectangle.area	0	0	0	0	0	0
Rectangle.perimeter	0	0	0	0	0	0

Metrics Results for Square.py

Halstead Metrics

Traditional Metrics – LOC and Length of Identifier

Traditional Metrics – Fan-in and Fan-out

Traditional Metrics – Cyclomatic Complexity

OO Metrics – Class Square

OO Metrics – Class Rectangle

Discussion on Halstead Metrics Results and Calculation Logic. The Halstead metrics results obtained from the tool and manual calculations are identical.

The results from Radon differ significantly from those of the tool, likely due to differences in how each defines operators and operands. As mentioned in Sect. 1.2, there is no official definition for what an operator and an operand in Python are.

Table 5. Cyclomatic Complexity for Shape_Rectangle.py methods

	Tool's calculation for CC	Hand calculations for CC	Radon
Shape.__init__	1	1	1
Shape.area	1	1	1
Shape.perimeter	1	1	1
Shape.describe	1	1	1
Rectangle.__init__	1	1	1
Rectangle.area	1	1	1
Rectangle.perimeter	1	1	1

Table 6. OO metrics for class Shape from Shape_Rectangle.py

	Tool's calculations	Hand-calculations	Multi-file analysis
WMC	4	4	4
NOC	1	1	1
DIT	1	1	1

Table 7. OO metrics for class Rectangle from Shape_Rectangle.py

	Tool's calculations	Hand-calculations	Multi-file analysis
WMC	3	3	3
NOC	X	0	1
DIT	2	2	2

Table 8. Halstead Metrics for Square.py

	Tool's calculations	Hand-calculations	Radon
n1	11	11	3
N1	20	20	3
n2	15	15	4
N2	22	22	6

Table 9. LOC and Length of Identifier metrics for Square.py

	Tool's calculations	Hand-calculations	Radon
LOC	18	18	18
Length of Identifier	5.2	5.2	(Not supported)

Table 10. Fan-in and Fan-out metrics for Square.py

	Tool's calculation for Fan-in	Hand calculations for Fan-in	Multi-file analysis for Fan-in	Tool calculation for Fan-out	Hand calculations for Fan-out	Multi-file analysis for Fan-out
Square.__init__	0	0	0	2	2	2
range	1	X	X	X	X	X
Rectangle.__init__	1	1	1	X	X	X

Table 11. Cyclomatic Complexity for Square.py methods

	Tool's calculation for CC	Hand calculations for CC	Radon
Square.__init__	4	4	4

Table 12. OO metrics for class Square from Square.py

	Tool's calculations	Hand-calculations	Multi-file analysis
WMC	1	1	1
NOC	0	0	0
DIT	2	2	3

Table 13. OO metrics for class Rectangle from Square.py

	Tool's calculations	Hand-calculations	Multi-file analysis
WMC	X	X	X
NOC	1	1	1
DIT	1	X	2

The higher result from the tool could have various interpretations:

- The calculation is inflated due to poor node choices. All programs will have higher Halstead metrics results
- A simple program hides more complexity and dependency than anticipated

Discussion on Traditional Metrics Results. The LOC, Length of Identifier, and CC metrics results were as expected. The LOC and CC results matched Radon's.

The fan-in and fan-out metrics from Tables 4 and 10 showed that without multi-file analysis, these metrics cannot show the full picture.

The class Rectangle's __init__ method is called from class Square. Both these classes are defined in separate files: Shape_Rectangle.py and Square.py, respectively.

Modifying the Rectangle's init method may inadvertently affect dependent classes such as Square. Showing there is a link between the two methods spread across classes will give the real picture. According to the results from Table 4, Rectangle's init method is used nowhere, which is not the case.

Fan-out is complementary to Fan-in and can show how dependent a function is on other methods. One improvement possible here is to ignore/delete metrics entries for built-in functions. For example, range() will contribute to the fan-out of a user-defined function but will be removed from the fan-in metrics result (hence the X in the row for 'range' in Table 10).

Discussion on Object-Oriented (OO) Metrics Results. The WMC results for all classes were as expected. WMC for classes whose methods were called in another code file was not calculated, as denoted by 'X' in Table 13 for the Rectangle class. Rectangle was defined in Shape_Rectangle.py and used in Square.py.

The NOC and DIT metrics failed to show the complete picture due to the lack of multi-file analysis.

Referring to Table 7, the tool did not calculate the NOC metric for the Rectangle class, hence the X, because no class in Shape_Rectangle.py inherited from Rectangle. But class Square from Square.py does inherit from Rectangle. In Table 13, we can see that the Rectangle class has a NOC value of 1. Without a multi-file import-aware analysis, the tool cannot determine whether the Rectangle classes are identical.

The DIT metric was incorrect for all classes, except the base class, due to the lack of multi-file analysis.

The inheritance hierarchy is Shape - > Rectangle - > Square.

The DIT for class Square in Table 12 is incorrect. It is 2, when it should be 3. The analysis does not include the Shape class in its calculation. Similarly, the DIT result for Rectangle in Table 13 was 1. Ideally, it should not be calculated, but even then, the DIT result should be 2. The tool is not factoring the Shape class from Shape_Rectangle.py.

7 Limitations and Future Work

While the tool provides a reliable, file-level analysis of software metrics and offers clear visualizations for Halstead, traditional, and object-oriented metrics, several key limitations remain, particularly in supporting modern, modular Python codebases.

7.1 Lack of Multi-File Analysis

The most notable limitation is the absence of multi-file analysis. In real-world applications, class hierarchies, function calls, and data flows often span multiple files. Metrics such as Depth of Inheritance Tree (DIT), Number of Children (NOC), Fan-in, and Fan-out are currently calculated in isolation, which may result in underreporting and misrepresentation when dependencies exist across modules.

Future Work. To support multi-file analysis, the tool could be extended with a module-aware parsing system that resolves imports, identifies symbol origins across files, and builds a comprehensive code graph on a per-commit basis. These enhancements would allow the tool to compute cross-file relationships and reflect a more complete picture of software quality.

7.2 Visualization Refinements and Thresholding

As projects grow, the sheer volume of metric data can make visualizations noisy or difficult to interpret. While nested structures and filtering help, further refinement is possible.

Future Work. Enhancements such as metric thresholding, customizable views, or anomaly detection using historical trends can improve interpretability. These features would make the dashboard more scalable for large repositories and long-term monitoring.

7.3 Additional Language Support

The tool only works with Python code files. Many other popular languages, such as C, C++, and Java, are left out.

Future Work. The tool demonstrates that ASTs are effective in calculating code quality metrics. If metrics calculator classes that return results in the same format are developed for other languages, this tool will evolve to be more inclusive of more code bases.

The implications of these limitations are significant for practical application. Without addressing these issues, the tool's utility for large-scale projects may be compromised, particularly when analyzing complex object-oriented codebases. Additionally, the lack of threshold configuration may lead to information overload for users, making it difficult to identify truly problematic trends in the metric data.

8 Conclusion

This paper presented a lightweight tool for tracking and visualizing software quality metrics in GitHub-hosted Python projects. By leveraging Abstract Syntax Tree analysis and integrating with the GitHub API, the tool provides developers with valuable insights into code quality evolution across commits and pull requests.

The primary contributions of this work include:

- A methodology for automatically extracting quality metrics from Python source code using AST analysis
- A visualization approach that tracks metric evolution over time and across different branches
- Integration with GitHub workflows to facilitate quality assessment during code reviews

By providing developers with a clear view of quality trends, the tool enables more informed decisions about code improvements and refactoring priorities. This approach is particularly valuable for small teams that may lack the resources for more comprehensive quality management systems.

The current implementation allows Halstead, Traditional, and OO metrics to be calculated and visualized. However, the lack of multi-file analysis does not allow the user to get insights into how code files depend on each other.

Future research will focus on supporting multi-file analysis, expanding the range of supported metrics, implementing filter techniques, and validating the tool's effectiveness through user studies. Additionally, implementing machine learning techniques to identify potential quality issues based on historical patterns represents a promising direction for extending this work.

References

1. Abreu, F., Carapuça, R.: Object-oriented software engineering: measuring and controlling the development process. In: Proceedings of the 4th International Conference on Software Quality (1994). https://www.researchgate.net/publication/2253619_Object-Oriented_Software_Engineering_Measuring_and_Controlling_the_Development_Process
2. Bansiya, J., Davis, C.G.: A hierarchical model for object-oriented design quality assessment. IEEE Trans. Software Eng. **28**(1), 4–17 (2002). https://doi.org/10.1109/32.979986
3. Chidamber, S.R., Kemerer, C.F.: A metrics suite for object oriented design. IEEE Trans. Software Eng. **20**(6), 476–493 (1994). https://doi.org/10.1145/117954.117970
4. Halstead, M.H.: Elements of Software Science. Elsevier North-Holland, New York (1977)
5. SonarSource. SonarQube. https://www.sonarqube.org
6. Python Code Quality Authority: Pylint. https://pylint.org
7. GitHub. GitHub Copilot. https://github.com/features/copilot
8. Lacchia, M.: Radon: code metrics in Python. https://radon.readthedocs.io/en/latest/
9. Python Software Foundation. AST - Abstract Syntax Trees. https://docs.python.org/3/library/ast.html
10. Radjenović, D., et al.: Software fault prediction metrics: a systematic literature review. Inf. Softw. Technol. **55**(8), 1397–1418 (2013). https://doi.org/10.1016/j.infsof.2013.02.009
11. McCabe, T.J.: A complexity measure. IEEE Trans. Softw. Eng. **SE-2**(4), 308–320 (1976). https://doi.org/10.1109/TSE.1976.233837
12. The pandas development team. pandas-dev/pandas: Pandas (2024). https://zenodo.org/records/10957263
13. Plotly Technologies Inc.: Plotly: The interactive graphing library for Python. https://plot.ly/. [Accessed: 8 Sep 2024]

14. GitHub, Inc.: GitHub. https://github.com/
15. PyGithub. PyGithub/PyGithub: typed interactions with the GitHub API V3. https://github.com/PyGithub/PyGithub
16. Jones. Abstract Syntax Tree Implementation idioms (2021). https://hillside.net/plop/plop2003/Papers/Jones-ImplementingASTs.pdf
17. Designite - Designite (Python). https://www.designite-tools.com/products-dpy

ASSIST: AI Soccer Statistics and Information Systems Technology

A Computer Vision Approach to Player Tracking and Game Analysis

Ian Weiss(✉) and Oscar Morales-Ponce

California State University, Long Beach, Long Beach, CA 90815, USA
igweiss8@gmail.com

Abstract. We present a machine-learning-based system for automated soccer analytics, leveraging computer vision techniques to detect players, differentiate teams, determine ball possession, and generate graphical representations of player movement and influence. Traditional sports analytics rely on manual observation, which is time-consuming and prone to human error. To address this, a You Only Look Once (YOLO) based object detection model was created for identifying players, referees, and the ball, coupled with a multiple-object tracking (MOT) algorithm to maintain detection continuity across frames. For team differentiation, a novel method utilizing SigLIP embeddings, UMAP dimensionality reduction, and K-Means clustering ensures robust classification, even in the presence of variations in lighting and jersey colors. Additionally, a statistical analysis framework was developed to calculate ball possession between the teams. To enhance tactical insights, the system generates graphical outputs, including radar views, Voronoi diagrams, and heat maps, providing an intuitive visualization of game dynamics. Experimental results demonstrate an average team classification confidence of 87.54% across test videos, with ball detection accuracy varying based on occlusions and camera perspectives.

Keywords: Computer Vision · Machine Learning

1 Introduction

The integration of machine learning and computer vision in sports analytics has significantly enhanced the ability to analyze player performance, tactical information, and game statistics. Soccer, as one of the most popular sports worldwide, presents a unique opportunity for the application of these technologies. Traditional methods of game analysis rely on manual observation and statistical tracking, which are often time-consuming and prone to human error. Automated systems provide a data-driven approach, enabling faster and more accurate assessments.

This paper explores the development and implementation of a machine learning-based system for soccer analytics. The system is designed to automatically process pre-recorded game footage by detecting individual players and the

S. Hussain et al. (Eds.): SEET 2025, CCIS 2725, pp. 649–669, 2026.
https://doi.org/10.1007/978-3-032-08977-9_43

ball, tracking player movement, identifying possession statistics, and generating graphical outputs for enhanced tactical analysis. Using machine learning techniques such as the You Only Look Once (YOLO) object detection model and multiple-object tracking (MOT) methods, the system aims to provide a scalable and efficient solution for automated sports analytics.

We address several key challenges in automated soccer analysis. First, the detection and tracking of players and the ball must be robust against varying lighting conditions, occlusions, and rapid movements. Second, team differentiation requires accurate classification of players despite similar jersey colors, which is accomplished through embedding techniques and clustering methods. Other detections, such as referees, needed to be addressed. Finally, the system must generate meaningful statistical insights, such as possession analysis and heat maps, to enhance post-game review and strategic decision-making.

The primary research objective of this study was to determine whether computer vision techniques can be effectively utilized to automatically detect, track, and classify key events and player movements in professional soccer matches to enhance performance analysis and tactical evaluation.

1.1 Contributions

Our contribution in this paper is the implementation of an automated player and ball detection system using a YOLO-based computer vision model. This system enables real-time identification of players, referees, and the ball with high accuracy. Additionally, an object-tracking algorithm was developed to maintain the identity of detected objects across multiple frames, improving motion analysis and enabling precise player movement tracking. To differentiate teams, a novel approach was introduced using SigLIP embeddings, UMAP dimensionality reduction, and K-Means clustering, resulting in an average team classification confidence of 0.8754.

Beyond detection and tracking, the system generates detailed statistical and graphical analyses of soccer matches. The possession analysis algorithm estimates team ball control by computing the closest player to the ball in each frame. Furthermore, the system produces visual outputs such as radar views, Voronoi diagrams, and heat maps, which provide insight into player positioning and influence on the field.

1.2 Organization of the Paper

This manuscript is organized as follows. Section 2 discusses related works in automated sports analytics, highlighting existing research in the machine learning field. Section 3 presents the design and implementation of the proposed system, detailing the methodologies used for object detection, tracking, and team differentiation. Section 4 explores the applications of the developed system, focusing on statistical analysis, graphical representations, and testing procedures. Section 5 presents the results obtained from running the system on test datasets, including performance evaluations and accuracy metrics. Finally, Sect. 6

concludes with a discussion on the significance of the contributions, limitations of the current approach, and potential directions for future research.

2 Related Works

The intersection of sports and technology is not a new concept. As the implementation of machine learning in sports analytics continues to evolve, several studies have explored the use of machine learning in soccer applications. One team of researchers used machine learning to assist in injury prevention. Using GPS data obtained from team training sessions, along with machine learning techniques, such as decision trees, a model was made to help predict the likelihood of player injuries [11]. Other studies have used machine learning to perform outcome prediction on soccer games [5]. The study successfully created accurate prediction models by leveraging k-nearest neighbors algorithms and neural networks for better results.

These studies help demonstrate the effectiveness of machine learning and technology in modern sports. However, there is a lack of studies focused on sports automation, team determination, and statistical analysis. This paper aims to bridge that gap by developing a machine learning-based system for the automated extraction of key game insights from recorded soccer matches. The game insights could later be used for player development and tactical analysis.

While some studies have tackled automated player detection, most have focused on controlled environments rather than real-world match footage. One study introduced a genetic algorithm-based approach for detecting and labeling players in broadcast soccer videos [7]. This achieved highly accurate results, but the algorithm relied on user input and highly contrasting colors. Many of the innovative procedures from this study were considered during the development of the ASSIST system. Another exploration of machine learning was used for player positioning, utilizing spatial-temporal models to analyze team formations [8]. The findings were not used in the current ASSIST implementation but can be considered for further exploration into tactical analysis programs.

The foundation for automated object detection is well explored, with You Only Look Once (YOLO) being one of the most commonly used detection algorithms. A team of researchers introduced YOLO as a real-time object detection model capable of detecting multiple objects within a single frame [10]. Unlike traditional object detection methods that use region-based proposals, YOLO processes entire images at once, significantly improving speed and efficiency. YOLO has been widely adopted in applications that must detect multiple objects simultaneously, and it can be coupled with multiple-object tracking (MOT) for results that correspond to multiple input frames.

Recent studies have attempted to improve MOT in soccer, particularly for player tracking and ball movement prediction. A team of researchers introduced SoccerNet-Tracking, a large-scale MOT dataset and benchmark for soccer videos [6]. Their research highlights the importance of high-quality labeled datasets for training robust tracking models, which directly applies to this paper's methodology.

One of the most challenging aspects of automated sports systems is team discrimination, which involves determining to which team a player belongs. One study proposed an associative embedding method to classify players by team, combining color-based characteristics and deep-learning embeddings [9]. Using dimensionality reductions and clustering, the researchers achieved efficient team determination in fast-paced sports scenarios. This research guided how I handled team discrimination in dynamic situations such as varying lighting and occlusion events.

This paper contributes to the growing body of automated sports analytics research by developing a machine learning-based system that extracts key game insights from recorded match footage. Building on existing player detection and tracking research, this study provides a novel system for MOT and team differentiation that could improve player performance evaluation and tactical decision-making.

3 Design and Implementation

This chapter details the development of the computer vision-based soccer analytics system. The system leverages a YOLO-based detection model, multiple object tracking (MOT), and a novel team classification method. The methodologies and algorithms presented form the foundation for accurate player tracking and statistical analysis.

3.1 Detecting Objects

To start the development of the computer vision model, the detection of objects in a video needed to be solved. The You Only Look Once (YOLO) computer vision model was used as it can be easily imported and applied to computer vision tasks. A basic, pre-trained YOLOv8 model was provided by a user on *roboflow universe* [3]. This model was trained on 298 images of soccer games with all players, referees, and the ball being labeled. All images and test videos for this model come from the Kaggle Bundesliga data shootout competition [1]. Using this model, a Python-based computer vision application was created that attempts to identify players, referees, and the ball on individual frames. This application leverages the supervision, cv2, and roboflow Python libraries to make a comprehensive computer vision system.

As shown in Fig. 1, the application was altered to display the classification of objects along with the confidence level of each classification. This system served as a basis for the remainder of the implementation and was used as the detection model for all frames.

Fig. 1. Initial Computer Vision Model

3.2 Tracking Objects

The next step in development was to track the various objects between frames. Using the supervision Python library, objects could be identified in each frame and tracked across frames by temporarily keeping the location value of each object in the previous frame. Each detected object was given a detection identification number and current detection box coordinates in 'top left and bottom right corner' (xyxy) format. This location was then saved along with the ID in a key-value hash table for constant-time lookup for future use. In the next frame, all detected objects would be compared to the previously stored location values, and if the new location is within a threshold, then the system will determine the detection to be of the same object. This implementation runs in $O(n^2)$, but by designing a more advanced algorithm that uses Voronoi diagrams, it can likely be reduced to $O(n \log n)$ runtime [4]. The following formulas provide a mathematical representation of this algorithm.

Let τ be the maximum distance threshold, and let

$$L[t] = (x[t]_{\text{min}}, y[t]_{\text{max}}, x[t]_{\text{max}}, y[t]_{\text{min}})$$

be the location of the object detection box at time t. Define the distance

$$d(L[t+1], L[t])$$

as the Euclidean distance between their center points:

$$d(L[t+1], L[t]) = \sqrt{(x_c[t+1] - x_c[t])^2 + (y_c[t+1] - y_c[t])^2}$$

where

$$x_c[t] = \frac{x[t]_{\text{min}} + x[t]_{\text{max}}}{2} \quad y_c[t] = \frac{y[t]_{\text{min}} + y[t]_{\text{max}}}{2}$$

and similarly for $L[t+1]$. If $d(L[t+1], L[t]) < \tau$, then the detection is determined to be the same object. The model displaying the detection IDs is shown in Fig. 2.

Fig. 2. Computer Vision Model with Tracking

3.3 Team Differentiation

One of the most significant challenges to overcome was team differentiation. Many techniques were considered to accomplish this task.

Initially, implementation involved Hue, Saturation, and Value (HSV) filtering on the player's torsos. This involved creating an HSV mask of the two most common colors of the players. To do this, the detection model was run on one of every 30 frames for the length of the video. These detections were then automatically cropped to where the torso was likely found, and an HSV value of the center point was then taken. All of the HSV values were checked for similarities, and the two most common colors were determined to be the team colors. These team colors were then used as a mask on all future detections to find which color had the most similar pixels to a detection.

This method worked in many cases, but did not perform with the desired consistency. The functionality was severely limited by occlusions such as shadows and concentrated light, which would dull the color. Ultimately, another solution was required.

Algorithm 1 *createClassifier*: Create Team Classifier Object

---

Input
playerCrops : list
Output
clusterModel : Team Classification Cluster Object
Vars
data : list

for *crop* in *playerCrops* **do**
  data.append(SigLIP.embed(*crop*))
end for
projections = UMAP.reduce(*data*)
clusterModel = KMEANS.cluster(*projections*)
return *clusterModel*

As shown in Algorithm 1, the final solution involved similar techniques but relied on SigLIP embeddings, UMAP dimensionality reduction, and K-Means clustering. Before using the computer vision model, player crops were used to create a database for team identification. These crops were then embedded using a SigLIP vector of length 768, which represents each player's appearance as a numerical representation in 768-dimensional space. Similar-looking players had embeddings that were close to each other. Since 768 dimensions are too high for efficient clustering, the UMAP (Uniform Manifold Approximation and Projection) library was used to project these embeddings down to three-dimensional space while preserving their structural relationships. Once in 3D space, K-Means clustering was applied to group the player embeddings into two clusters, each representing a team. K-Means works by identifying two centroids and assigning each player's embedding to the nearest centroid, effectively classifying players into their respective teams.

When the computer vision model was run, player detections were put through the same processing techniques. Crops were taken from all player detections. The crops were then processed by the same embedding and reduction algorithms to turn them into projections. This time, instead of creating a K-means cluster, the projections were plotted in three-dimensional space, and the team was determined to be the closest preexisting K-means cluster. This process is detailed in Algorithm 2.

Algorithm 2 *classifyTeams*: Perform Team Classification

Input
playerCrops, *playerDetections* : list
clusterModel : Team Classification Cluster Object
Output
team1Detections, *team2Detections* : list
Vars
data : list

for *crop* in *playerCrops* **do**
  data.append(SigLIP.embed(*crop*))
end for
projections = UMAP.reduce(*data*)
team1Detections, *team2Detections* = *clusterModel*.predict(*projections*, *playerDetections*)
return *team1Detections*, *team2Detections*

Soccer goalies are required to wear a different color jersey from the rest of their team and the opposition team. To determine the team to which the goalie belonged, the goalie's location was compared to the centroid of both teams. The goalie's team was determined to be the closest centroid.

Let $G = (x_{\min}, y_{\min}, x_{\max}, y_{\max})$ be the location of the goalie detection box.

Let $P_1 = \{x1_{i_{\min}}, y1_{i_{\min}}, x1_{i_{\max}}, y1_{i_{\max}})\}_{i=1}^{N_1}$ be the set of locations for all N_1 players on Team 1.

Let $P_2 = \{(x2_{j_{\min}}, y2_{j_{\min}}, x2_{j_{\max}}, y2_{j_{\max}})\}_{j=1}^{N_2}$ be the set of locations for all N_2 players on Team 2.

Compute the centroid of Team 1 as the average position of all players:

$$C_1 = \left(\frac{1}{N_1}\sum_{i=1}^{N_1} x1_{i_{\min}}, \frac{1}{N_1}\sum_{i=1}^{N_1} y1_{i_{\min}}, \frac{1}{N_1}\sum_{i=1}^{N_1} x1_{i_{\max}}, \frac{1}{N_1}\sum_{i=1}^{N_1} y1_{i_{\max}}\right).$$

Compute the centroid of Team 2 as the average position of all players:

$$C_2 = \left(\frac{1}{N_2}\sum_{j=1}^{N_2} x2_{j_{\min}}, \frac{1}{N_2}\sum_{j=1}^{N_2} y2_{j_{\min}}, \frac{1}{N_2}\sum_{j=1}^{N_2} x2_{j_{\max}}, \frac{1}{N_2}\sum_{j=1}^{N_2} y2_{j_{\max}}\right).$$

A diagram to help visualize this methodology for team centroid calculation is shown in Fig. 3.

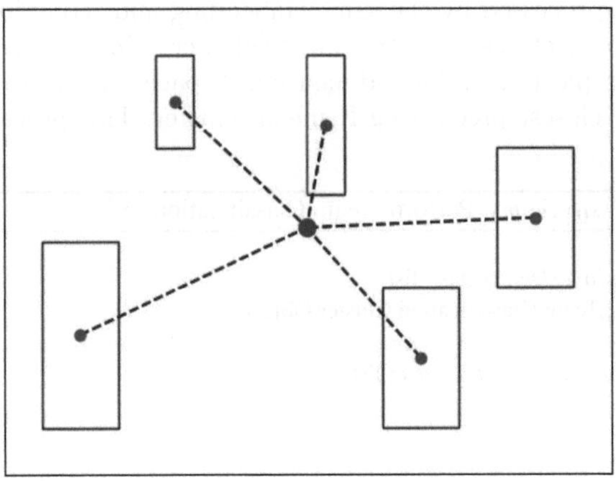

Fig. 3. Team Centroid Diagram

Compute the goalie's center position:

$$C_G = \left(\frac{x_{\min} + x_{\max}}{2}, \frac{y_{\min} + y_{\max}}{2}, \frac{x_{\min} + x_{\max}}{2}, \frac{y_{\min} + y_{\max}}{2}\right).$$

Compute the Euclidean distances from the goalie to each team centroid:

$$d_1 = \sqrt{(C_{G,x_{\min}} - C_{1,x_{\min}})^2 + (C_{G,y_{\min}} - C_{1,y_{\min}})^2 + (C_{G,x_{\max}} - C_{1,x_{\max}})^2 + (C_{G,y_{\max}} - C_{1,y_{\max}})^2}.$$

$$d_2 = \sqrt{(C_{G,x_{\min}} - C_{2,x_{\min}})^2 + (C_{G,y_{\min}} - C_{2,y_{\min}})^2 + (C_{G,x_{\max}} - C_{2,x_{\max}})^2 + (C_{G,y_{\max}} - C_{2,y_{\max}})^2}.$$

If $d_1 < d_2$, then we can deduce the goalie's team assignment to be team 1. These algorithms provided highly accurate results; an example output is shown in Fig. 4.

Fig. 4. Computer Vision Model with Team Differentiation

4 Applications

This chapter explores the applications of the developed system in soccer analytics, demonstrating how extracted data can provide meaningful insights into game dynamics. It discusses statistical analysis techniques, such as ball possession estimation, and the generation of graphical outputs, including radar views, Voronoi diagrams, and heat maps to visualize player positioning and game influence. These applications provide insight into the practical value of the system for game analysis, coaching strategies, and performance evaluation.

4.1 Statistical Analysis

One application that was explored involved using the computer vision model for statistical analysis. One statistic that is common in soccer games is team ball possession. We designed the model to automatically detect the time in possession for both teams. Algorithm 3 shows how the model determined the closest player to the ball and the team to which the player belonged. The closest player could be computed by determining an estimated position of each player's feet and the Euclidean distance to the center point of the ball. To simplify foot position estimation, the location of each foot was set at a point one-quarter of the detection box's total width inward from each bottom corner. An example of this estimation is shown in Fig. 5.

Fig. 5. Player Foot Estimation

The following equations were used to estimate the locations of each player's feet and calculate the distance to the ball.

Let $P = (x_{\min}, y_{\max}, x_{\max}, y_{\min})$ be the location of the player detection box at time t.

Let $B = (x_{\min}, y_{\max}, x_{\max}, y_{\min})$ be the location of the ball detection box at time t.

Define the player's first foot position as: $F_1 = (x_{\min} + \frac{1}{4}(x_{\max} - x_{\min}), y_{\max})$.

Define the player's second foot position as: $F_2 = (x_{\max} - \frac{1}{4}(x_{\max} - x_{\min}), y_{\max})$.

Define the ball's center position as: $C_B = \left(\frac{x'_{min}+x'_{max}}{2}, \frac{y'_{min}+y'_{max}}{2}\right)$.

Compute the Euclidean distance from the first foot to the ball:

$$d_1 = \sqrt{(F_{1,x} - C_{B,x})^2 + (F_{1,y} - C_{B,y})^2}$$

Compute the Euclidean distance from the second foot to the ball:

$$d_2 = \sqrt{(F_{2,x} - C_{B,x})^2 + (F_{2,y} - C_{B,y})^2}$$

Determine the closest foot: $d_{min} = \min(d_1, d_2)$.

Algorithm 3 *findPossession*: Find the Team with Possession of the Ball

```
Input
  team1Detections, team2Detections, ballDetections : list
Output
  closestTeam : String
Vars
  closestPlayer : Detection Object
  allPlayerDetections : list


closestTeam = None
maxDistance = 60 //furthest away in pixels that possession is considered to occur
minDistance = ∞
allPlayerDetections = team1Detections + team2Detections
// Find the closest player's foot to the ball to determine possession
for player in allPlayerDetections do
  ballCenter =findCenter(ballDetections[0]) // assume most confident ball detection is the ball
  foot1 = findFoot1(player)
  foot2 = findFoot2(player)
  distance = calculateDistance(foot1, foot2, ballCenter)
  if distance < minDistance and distance < maxDistance then
    minDistance = distance
    closestPlayer = player
    closestTeam = closestPlayer.team
  end if
end for
return = closestTeam
```

While this implementation contains a slight margin of error due to the use of estimations, such as the player's foot location, it provides a computationally efficient way of determining possession. Another simplification is introduced with a distance threshold. To determine whether a team had possession, a maximum distance threshold was implemented. The ball needed to be within sixty pixels of the closest player's foot to be considered within that player's possession. The threshold was determined by analyzing the average distance of the ball in frames where the ball appeared visually close to a player. Since the frames were selected by a human, the threshold is subject to human error and would need to be refined for future implementations.

After computing the closest player to the ball, the ball was determined to belong in one of 3 categories: Team 1 Possession, Team 2 Possession, or No Possession. Since the ball was not detected in every frame due to occlusions, as discussed in the Results section, these frames were omitted from possession calculations. The team possession statistics were calculated with the following equations: Let P_1 be the number of frames in which Team 1 is in possession. Let P_2 be the number of frames in which Team 2 is in possession.

Team 1 Possession (%) $= \frac{P_1}{P_1+P_2} \times 100.$

Team 2 Possession (%) $= \frac{P_2}{P_1+P_2} \times 100.$

To display possession, a purple dot marked the foot and ball locations with the closest Euclidean distance. A purple triangle indicates the player with possession. An example of this output is shown in Fig. 6.

Fig. 6. Computer Vision Model with Possession Detection

4.2 Graphical Outputs

Multiple two-dimensional (2D) representations were created to demonstrate further applications of the computer vision model. Algorithm 4 depicts how radar (bird's-eye view), Voronoi diagram, and heat map views were created. An example of these views is shown in Fig. 7. A separate, pre-trained machine learning model was used to detect key points such as the corners of the field, penalty box, and center circle on a soccer field [2]. These detected key points serve as reference points for calculating a homography matrix, which corrects for camera distortion and allows for perspective transformation.

The radar view was used as the basis for all remaining 2D representations. Using the homography matrix, all detected objects can be accurately projected onto a 2D plane representing the soccer field. The detected key points in the video frame act as anchor points, mapping real-world field positions to the image coordinates. This transformation ensures that all objects maintain their spatial relationships as they would appear in a bird's-eye view of the field, enabling further analysis and visualization.

Algorithm 4 *generate2DViews*: Draws Radar, Voronoi, and Heat Map Views

Input
allDetections : list
fieldModel : Field Keypoint Detection Model
frame : Video Frame
Output
Vars
ballDetections, playersDetections, refereesDetections : list

```
ballDetections, playersDetections, refereesDetections = split(allDetections)
// Detect key points on the field
fieldResult = fieldModel.inferField(frame)
keyPoints = extractKeyPoints(fieldResult)
// Filter high-confidence key points for projection
filter = keyPoints.confidence > 0.5
frameReference = keyPoints.xy[filter]
fieldReference = CONFIG.vertices[filter]
// Apply camera distortion correction
transformer = ViewTransformer(frameReference, fieldReference)
// Project objects onto the field
fieldBall = transform(transformer, ballDetections)
fieldPlayers = transform(transformer, playersDetections)
fieldReferees = transform(transformer, refereesDetections)
// Generate and overlay Multiple Graphical Views
drawRadar(fieldBall, fieldPlayers, playersDetections, fieldReferees)
drawVoronoi(fieldPlayers, playersDetections)
drawHeatmap(fieldBall, fieldPlayers, playersDetections)
```

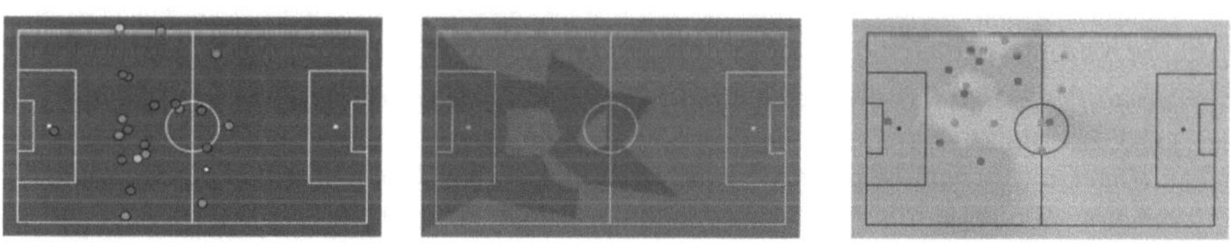

(a) Radar View (b) Voronoi View (c) Heatmap View

Fig. 7. Collection of 2D Computer Vision Outputs

Voronoi diagrams were generated by computing the Euclidean distance of each pixel on the 2D field to the nearest detected player position. This produced a 2D influence map, where each pixel was assigned the color of the closest player's team. This creates a visual representation of each team's control over that part of the field. To enhance visualization, a heat map effect was also created by blending and smoothing the transitions between the control areas of each team. These representations provide an intuitive way to analyze match control by highlighting regions where each team is most concentrated on the field.

4.3 Testing Procedure

The completed computer vision model was evaluated on five videos, each consisting of 750 frames. The model was run on the same hardware for each trial. Each of the five videos introduced different scenarios and challenges, such as varying camera distance, challenging lighting, similar team colors, more ball occlusions, and player speeds.

For each video input, the following were created: an annotated version of the video with object detections, a possession analysis, a radar view video, a Voronoi diagram video, and a heat map diagram video. All outputs were created simultaneously and used the same detections. Algorithm 5 depicts an overview of this process.

Algorithm 5 Complete Soccer Video Analysis

```
allCrops : list
videoFrames : list
// Collect crops from many frames throughout the video, then create the team classifier
for frame in videoFrames do
  crops = extractCrops(frame)
  allCrops += crops
end for
teamClassifier = createClassifier(allCrops)
for frame in videoFrames do
  detections = model.detect(frame)
  playerDetections, ballDetections, refDetections = separate(detections)
  playerCrops = extractCrops(frame)
  team1Detections,team2Detections = classifyTeams(teamClassifier, playerCrops, playerDetections)
  team1Detections,team2Detections = resolveGoalies(playerDetections, team1Detections, team2Detections)
  teamInPossession = findPossession(ballDetections, team1Detections, team2Detections)
  calcPossession(teamInPossession)
  allDetections = ballDetections + team1Detections + team2Detections + refDetections
  annotatedFrame = superVision.annotateFrame(allDetections)
  annotatedVideo.write(annotatedFrame) // Repeated for the annotated frames, radar, Voronoi, and heat map
  generate2DViews(allDetections, fieldModel, frame)
end for
```

5 Results

This chapter presents the results obtained from testing the system in multiple videos of soccer games, evaluating its accuracy and effectiveness in detecting players, tracking objects, and differentiating teams. It analyzes the performance of the team classification algorithm, the accuracy of ball detection under varying conditions, and the reliability of the statistical insights generated. The findings demonstrate the strengths of the ASSIST system while identifying areas for further refinement and optimization.

5.1 Visual Outputs

The main results generated were the visual components. Each input video was processed into four distinct output video representations. The detections from each frame of the input video were applied to the corresponding frame in each output video. As a result, all four output videos remain synchronized, allowing for easy comparison by viewing the same frame number across all videos. An example of this simultaneous view is shown in Fig. 8.

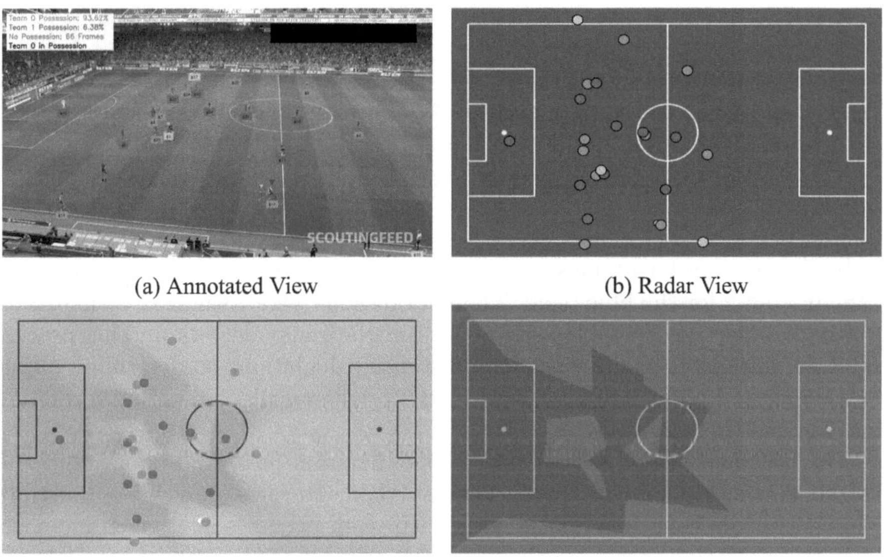

(a) Annotated View (b) Radar View

(c) Heatmap View (d) Voronoi View

Fig. 8. Various Views of Computer Vision Output from the Same Frame

The annotated view in Fig. 8a provides a detailed visual representation of the soccer game by drawing detection boxes around players and the ball, distinguishing between teams, and tracking which team has ball possession. This video output can be used to automatically compute key statistical data, such as team possession times. Additionally, using the same object tracking, the model could be used to analyze average player positions, estimate player speeds, and measure ball speed. Beyond these metrics, the annotated view could be used for the creation of 2D representations, pass tracking, and movement pattern analysis, offering deeper insights into team strategies and player performance.

The two-dimensional radar view in Fig. 8b provides a top-down perspective of the soccer game. This visualization has several potential applications, including generating training materials that allow coaches to analyze player positioning and movement. Additionally, it could serve as a match preview tool for websites or search engines, allowing them to display live game data without streaming the actual video feed. Another significant use case is strategic analysis, such as team formation detection, as demonstrated in Fig. 9.

(a) Annotated Frame for Formation Analysis (b) Radar View of Formation Analysis

Fig. 9. Formation Analysis Example from Matching Frames

In Fig. 9b, the formations were manually identified as 3-3-3-1 for the pink team and 5-3-2 for the blue team. These formations were visualized by manually drawing connecting lines between players in the radar detection. This process could be automated using Euclidean distance calculations to determine player positioning and team structure, with vectors dynamically generating formation lines for real-time analysis.

The heatmap in Fig. 8c and the Voronoi diagram in Fig. 8d offer additional insights for tactical analysis by coaches and commentators. These views illustrate field control, showing how much space each team occupies at a given moment. Such representations provide valuable insights into a team's playing style, defensive organization, and attacking tendencies, making them possible tools for both coaching and in-depth match analysis. Individual players can also be trained by tracking their position and movement, and how it affects each team's match control.

5.2 Model Analysis

While running the computer vision simulation on the input videos, data was collected on the model's confidence for ball detection and team differentiation. The ball detection proved to be frequently variable and highly subject to occlusions. Due to this, the moving average of the ball detection confidence was computed with and without frames that included occlusions. Occlusions were determined to be any frame in which no ball was detected; these frames resulted in a ball confidence of 0. Examples of occlusions include frames in which the ball detection box overlaps with player detection boxes - as shown in Fig. 10, when the ball cannot be detected on the background, when players or objects block the camera's line of sight to the ball, or when the ball moves too quickly - as shown in Fig. 11, and other scenarios.

Fig. 10. Occlusion Due to Overlapping Detection Boxes

Fig. 11. Occlusion Due to Ball Speed

Test Video 1 represents a best-case scenario for the model. The ball was detected in the large majority of the frames, and therefore, the moving averages with and without the ball are similar. The overall average ball confidence without occlusions was 0.6460 and 0.5341 with occlusions. This indicates that the ball was detected with a relatively high confidence level throughout the test video. The moving averages are plotted in Fig. 12.

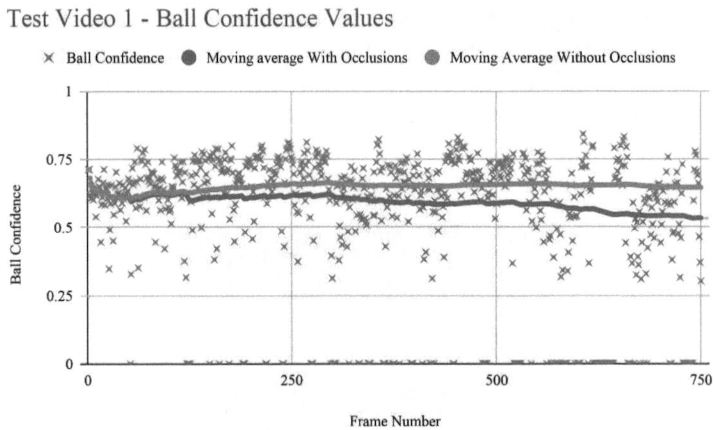

Fig. 12. Test Video 1 - Ball Confidence Values

Test Video 3 provides a more average representation of the model. This video included a larger number of frames with occlusions. This leads the moving averages to have a larger difference. The overall average ball confidence without occlusions was 0.6037 and 0.3469 with occlusions. This video had more occlusions, mostly due to frames where players are standing in front of the ball. Figure 13 displays the computed values.

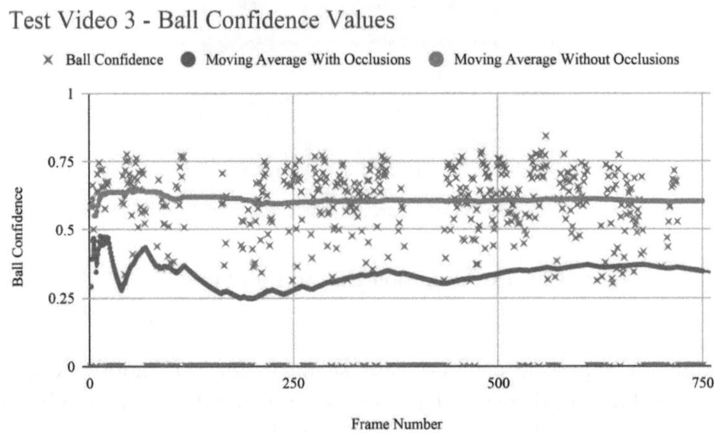

Fig. 13. Test Video 3 - Ball Confidence Values

Test Video 2 represents the worst case for the detection model. As shown in Fig. 14, the ball was not detected for the majority of frames due to the camera being on the far side of the field from where the play was taking place. The ball was not able to be detected for the first 75 frames of the video, and therefore, the moving average including occlusions was very low. The overall average ball confidence without occlusions was 0.5877 and 0.1716 with occlusions. This shows that when the model can find the ball, it proves to be relatively confident, but the occlusion frames play a drastic role in the model's limitations.

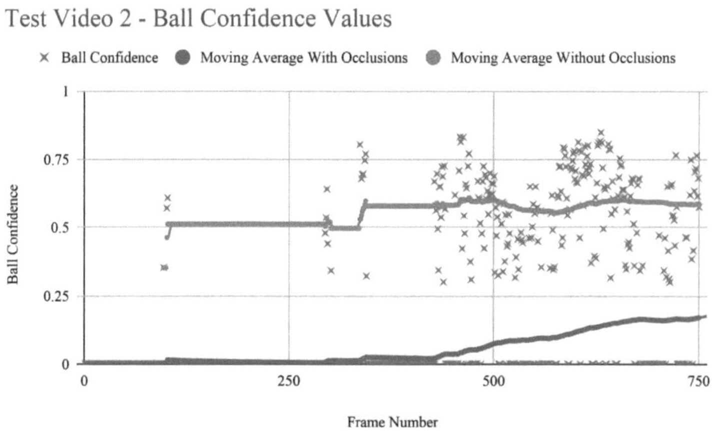

Fig. 14. Test Video 2 - Ball Confidence Values

Unlike ball detection, team differentiation demonstrated consistently high confidence across all five test videos. The model achieved an average confidence score of 0.8754, with each video exceeding 0.84. This suggests that the team classification algorithm remained robust, even in challenging conditions such as varying lighting. The overall results are shown in Fig. 15.

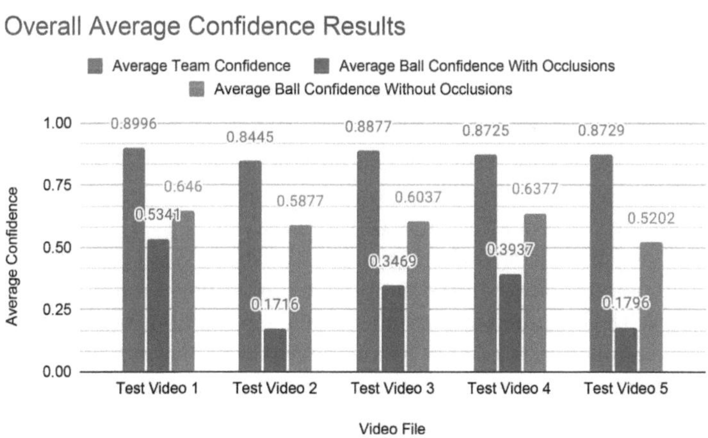

Fig. 15. Overall Confidence Results across all Frames

6 Conclusion

This paper presented a machine learning-based approach to soccer analytics, leveraging computer vision techniques to calculate meaningful statistics and generate valuable visual representations. By implementing object detection, player tracking, and team identification, the system automatically calculated ball possession, generated comprehensive visual representations, as well as monitored team influence on the field. The results demonstrated that computer vision, when integrated with machine learning, can provide valuable insights into player performance and team strategies, offering an automated and scalable alternative to traditional manual soccer analysis.

6.1 Limitations and Further Studies

Although this approach demonstrated promising results, several limitations were identified that present opportunities for future improvement.

One key challenge was the accuracy of ball detection, which was affected by occlusions, rapid movements, and proximity to the camera. These factors occasionally led to inconsistencies in tracking. A potential enhancement involves implementing real-time tracking techniques that reference the ball's previous location in each new frame. By narrowing the search area to a cropped region around the last known position, the model could reduce unnecessary computations and improve detection confidence. This targeted approach would allow the system to maintain more consistent tracking, even under difficult conditions.

Similarly, while the team differentiation algorithm proved effective, it relied on computationally intensive methods that could be optimized for greater efficiency. One potential improvement is the introduction of majority vote-based classifications. Since each player is already being tracked across frames with a unique detection ID, the model could maintain a running record of team assignments over a defined window - such as 100 frames - until a team classification surpasses a 75% majority threshold. Once this threshold is met, the player's team assignment could be permanently stored, eliminating the need to rerun the classification algorithm in every frame. Additionally, if a player becomes occluded, the system could identify the missing detection ID and reassign it to the most likely corresponding player upon reappearance, ensuring continuity in tracking even after a temporary loss of visibility.

Despite these limitations, this research contributes to advancing the rapidly evolving field of automated sports analytics by providing a foundation for further exploration. With continued improvements in deep learning and computer vision, the potential applications of this technology extend beyond player analysis to real-time strategy recommendations, automated match analysis, and enhanced fan engagement. Future work can build upon this framework to create more robust, adaptable, and intelligent systems for sports analysis.

References

1. Dfl - bundesliga data shootout — kaggle, kaggle. https://www.kaggle.com/competitions/dfl-bundesliga-data-shootout. Accessed 20 Mar 2025
2. football-field-detection computer vision project, roboflow. https://universe.roboflow.com/roboflow-jvuqo/football-field-detection-f07vi. Accessed 25 Mar 2025
3. football-players-detection object detection dataset, roboflow. https://universe.roboflow.com/roboflow-jvuqo/football-players-detection-3zvbc/dataset/12. Accessed 10 Mar 2025
4. Berg, M.d., Overmars, M., Kreveld, M.v., Cheong, O.: Computational Geometry: Algorithms and Applications, 3rd edn. Springer, Berlin, Germany (2008). https://doi.org/10.1007/978-3-540-77974-2
5. Berrar, D., Lopes, P., Dubitzky, W.: A data- and knowledge-driven framework for developing machine learning models to predict soccer match outcomes. Mach. Learn. **113**(10), 8165–8204 (2024)
6. Cioppa, A., et al.: Soccernet-tracking: multiple object tracking dataset and benchmark in soccer videos. In: 2022 IEEE/CVF Conference on Computer Vision and Pattern Recognition Workshops (CVPRW), pp. 3490–3501. IEEE Computer Society, Los Alamitos, CA, USA (2022). https://doi.org/10.1109/CVPRW56347.2022.00393, https://doi.ieeecomputersociety.org/10.1109/CVPRW56347.2022.00393
7. Davoodifar, G., Gholizade, M., Rahmanimanesh, M., Haghshenas, R., Soltanizadeh, H.: Automatic player detection and labeling in broadcast soccer video using genetic algorithm. Model. Simul. Electr. Electron. Eng. **2**(3), 25–37 (2022) https://doi.org/10.22075/mseee.2023.27826.1105, https://mseee.semnan.ac.ir/article_8206.html
8. Di Giacomo, U., Mercaldo, F., Santone, A., Capobianco, G.: Machine learning on soccer player positions. Int. J. Decis. Support Syst. Technol. **14**(1), 1–19 (2022)
9. Istasse, M., Moreau, J., De Vleeschouwer, C.: Associative embedding for team discrimination. In: Proceedings of the IEEE/CVF Conference on Computer Vision and Pattern Recognition (CVPR) Workshops (June 2019)
10. Redmon, J., Divvala, S., Girshick, R., Farhadi, A.: You only look once: unified, real-time object detection. In: 2016 IEEE Conference on Computer Vision and Pattern Recognition (CVPR), pp. 779–788. IEEE Computer Society, Los Alamitos, CA, USA (2016). https://doi.org/10.1109/CVPR.2016.91, https://doi.ieeecomputersociety.org/10.1109/CVPR.2016.91
11. Rossi, A., Pappalardo, L., Cintia, P., Iaia, F.M., Fernàndez, J., Medina, D.: Effective injury forecasting in soccer with gps training data and machine learning. PLoS ONE **13**(7), e0201264–e0201264 (2018)

Holistic Risk Management for Next-Gen Technologies Using AI and Governance Standards

Samuel Oakes(✉)

Sacred Heart University, Fairfield, CT 06825, USA
oakess2@mail.sacredheart.edu

Abstract. Emerging technologies like AI, blockchain, and quantum computing drive innovation but introduce systemic risks that outpace traditional governance frameworks. While standards such as ISO/IEC 27001, NIST Cybersecurity Framework (CSF), and FAIR provide foundational controls, they lack mechanisms for real-time, adaptive risk assessment in dynamic environments. This paper bridges this gap by proposing an AI-driven risk management platform that synthesizes governance, risk, and compliance (GRC) principles with a 22-dimension weighted scoring rubric. Deployed as a Dockerized container, the model evaluates organizational risk across technical, strategic, and operational domains-from cloud security posture to talent readiness-and generates large language model (LLM)-tailored mitigation strategies. A case study of a cybersecurity startup demonstrates the platform's efficacy, yielding a normalized risk score of 70.71/100 and actionable recommendations aligned with NIST CSF and ISO 27001 controls. By automating risk quantification, benchmarking against industry standards, and prioritizing ethical integration, this approach enables organizations to adopt emerging technologies responsibly without stifling innovation. The results highlight how AI-augmented governance can sharmonize security, compliance, and agility in an era of exponential technological change, synthesizing with current established frameworks to build upon and improve risk mnagement to align with emerging technologies.

Keywords: Emerging Technology · Risk Management · Cybersecurity Governance · Artificial Intelligence · Blockchain · Quantum Computing

1 Introduction

The advancement of emerging technologies—particularly artificial intelligence (AI), blockchain, and quantum computing—has accelerated innovation across industries, offering solutions to major societal challenges and improving operational efficiency. However, these same technologies also introduce significant, under-governed risks that, if not effectively managed, can cause more harm than good. From deep learning systems functioning as opaque "black boxes" to decentralized blockchain architectures that compromise data provenance, the traditional boundaries of risk management are being strained beyond their original design.

S. Hussain et al. (Eds.): SEET 2025, CCIS 2725, pp. 670–679, 2026.
https://doi.org/10.1007/978-3-032-08977-9_44

Ensuring that the risks associated with the integration of innovative technologies are identified, measured, and mitigated is critical to unlocking their potential benefits while protecting essential sectors such as healthcare, energy, and finance. This paper seeks to analyze and close the gap in effectively managing these risks in an environment where technological capabilities are evolving faster than regulatory or governance frameworks can adapt.

2 Background and Literature Review

Emerging technologies such as artificial intelligence (AI), blockchain, robotic automation, and quantum computing offer significant opportunities for economic advancement and societal benefit. However, these technologies also create novel risks that challenge conventional governance models, as well as a lack of oversight in exchange for more innovation, requiring us to improve upon existing frameworks and ensuring proper implementation for adaptable, interdisciplinary, and resilient risk management systems.

2.1 Defining Emerging Technology Risks

Emerging technology risks are defined by their complexity, uncertainty, and potential for systemic impact. Unlike traditional IT risks, which are often technical and isolated, these new risks are multidimensional—encompassing privacy, ethics, legal compliance, infrastructure resilience, and societal trust. Aljarrah et al. categorize these risks into systemic, operational, and regulatory layers, emphasizing the growing need for transparent and explainable systems in AI and blockchain infrastructures [4].

AI technologies, in particular, present governance challenges due to their autonomous behavior, difficulty in interpretability, and susceptibility to adversarial manipulation. Similarly, blockchain systems introduce trustless architectures that can undermine traditional oversight mechanisms and complicate data provenance and compliance audits [2]. Big data environments exacerbate these issues by increasing exposure to data leakage, bias, and cyber intrusion, especially in sectors where sensitive personal or biometric data is involved [16, 20].

Wearable devices, IoT endpoints, and robotic process automation (RPA) expand the attack surface for cyber threats. For example, in the context of wearable tech used in sports, real-time geolocation and biometric monitoring systems have been shown to lack encryption and risk management protocols, thereby exposing users to surveillance and data misuse [22]. These examples underscore the importance of embedding governance into design and policy at the earliest stages of technology adoption.

2.2 Existing Frameworks and Limitations

Several established frameworks guide organizations in managing cyber risk and information assurance. These include the NIST Risk Management Framework (RMF), ISO/IEC 27001 for Information Security Management Systems, COBIT 2019 for IT governance, and ISO 31000 for enterprise risk management [5]. However, these standards are frequently criticized for their lack of flexibility, difficulty in scaling across different industries, and minimal applicability to non-traditional architectures such as AI-driven platforms or decentralized blockchain networks.

NIST SP 800-37 Rev. 2 updates the RMF to include a "Prepare" step that addresses organizational context and business alignment. However, it remains primarily applicable to static system boundaries and lacks explicit mechanisms for evaluating real-time, adaptive risks introduced by machine learning or cloud-native systems [5]. ISO/IEC 27001 provides strong baseline controls for confidentiality, integrity, and availability, yet fails to address explainability, lifecycle monitoring, and the ethical use of AI or blockchain [6]. Similarly, COBIT 2019 emphasizes strategic alignment between IT and business objectives but offers limited operational guidance for managing predictive or behavioral risks unique to AI [7].

De Smet and Mayer's systematic review reveals that integration between IT governance and security risk management is one of the weakest links in current practice. Risk is often treated as an afterthought rather than a proactive pillar in system design, and risk officers are excluded from critical decision-making roles [8]. Further analysis by Grob et al. supports this view, showing that most commercial IT risk tools lack simulation, coordination, and real-time alerting functions, rendering them ineffective for dynamic threat environments [9].

Recent approaches such as the AIRMan framework and the 4D-ISS lifecycle model aim to address these limitations. AIRMan integrates AI-specific governance using ISO 31000 principles and contextual risk treatment methods tailored to evolving regulatory frameworks like the EU AI Act [14]. Similarly, 4D-ISS introduces continuous reassessment and feedback across the Define, Design, Deploy, and Drive phases of information system development, offering a more agile alternative to legacy frameworks [10]. Despite these innovations, adoption remains uneven. Many organizations, particularly SMEs, still lack the internal capacity, tools, and strategic support to implement integrated, continuous, and context-aware risk governance.

3 Strategic Gaps and Framework Evolution

3.1 Governance Misalignment and Cultural Disconnects

Effective risk management for emerging technologies is hindered by misalignment between cybersecurity strategies and enterprise risk management (ERM). Alzoubi et al. highlight how frameworks like 4D-ISS enable real-time feedback loops and lifecycle tracking to better align IT security with evolving strategic risks [13]. However, without executive sponsorship and cultural adaptation, integration fails. This is echoed by Takamura et al., who argue that GRC failures stem more from lack of organizational ownership and communication than from technological constraints [2].

Boards and C-suites often see cybersecurity as a compliance issue rather than a business enabler. Resiliency studies demonstrate that strategic foresight and the alignment of cybersecurity with ERM significantly improve risk posture, but uptake remains inconsistent across industries [12].

3.2 Big Data, IoT, and Automation: Security Risk Governance

The era of big data and automation has revolutionized how organizations manage operations and extract insights, but it has simultaneously created complex cybersecurity and governance challenges. Big data ecosystems strain conventional governance, necessitating hybrid approaches that blend ISO/IEC 27001 with national legislation to ensure compliance and resilience [2].

Automation solutions have enhanced detection capabilities, but as Jakimoski notes, most enterprises still rely on manually triggered risk alerts, delaying mitigation and increasing incident severity [3]. The inclusion of AI in governance processes—such as anomaly detection, threat modeling, and policy enforcement—provides improved outcomes but requires proper training and oversight. Kanban-based models, like those studied by Dorca et al., prove valuable in increasing visibility, communication, and task ownership in cybersecurity teams, thus shortening risk response cycles and bridging governance-execution gaps [11].

3.3 Sector-Specific Risk Trends and Case Applications

Healthcare and critical infrastructure sectors face unique risk landscapes. The wearable tech industry in sports, for example, is highly vulnerable to identity theft and data leaks due to lack of encryption and proper governance controls [22]. In robotic process automation (RPA), rapid deployment without secure configurations has led to regulatory breaches and operational failures, particularly in finance and telecom [9].

Similarly, energy and public sector use cases demonstrate that blockchain's decentralized trust model can undermine centralized governance norms. Luo et al. propose blockchain-based governance to enhance traceability, but acknowledge risks involving immutable data, privacy, and lack of enforceability. AI-specific risk models like AIRMan and governance guidelines like the EU AI Act offer forward-looking frameworks. Yet, they require industry adaptation and clearer legal backing to operationalize principles like transparency, accountability, and bias reduction [20].

4 AI-Driven Risk Assessment Model

This section describes how our 22-dimension scoring rubric feeds into an end-to-end AI assessment platform, how we evaluate its outputs, and how the solution is containerized and demonstrated via a case study. This tool aims to provide tailored AI insight based on industry, technical expertise and business alignment of an enterprise to provide a risk assessment and help prepare to integrate any emerging technologies into a business while mitigating the risk landscape.

4.1 Scoring Rubric

(See Table 1).

Each dimension is scored $s_i \in$ according to the detail and positivity of the user's response. The overall risk score is computed and normalized to a 0–100 scale: Overall Score $= (\sum_i w_i \cdot s_i \div \sum_i w_i) \times 10$.

Table 1. Scoring Rubric for Emerging-Tech Risk Assessment

Risk Dimension	Weight	Max Score	Rationale for Weighting
Business Strategy Alignment	0.06	10	Strategic alignment is foundational
Market Position & Competitive Advantage	0.05	10	Market impact is important but not always critical
Financial Impact & Investment	0.05	10	Financial readiness is key for adoption
Regulatory Compliance	0.05	10	Compliance is a must in regulated industries
Organizational Readiness	0.05	10	Change management and skills are crucial
Asset Visibility	0.04	10	Knowing assets is a baseline for security
Data Sensitivity & Classification	0.05	10	Data is often the main target of attacks
Access Management	0.05	10	IAM is a common attack vector
Network Security Posture	0.04	10	Network is a key defense layer
Cloud Security	0.05	10	Cloud is increasingly critical
Third-Party Risk	0.05	10	Supply chain attacks are rising
Incident Detection & Response	0.05	10	Response capability limits impact
Security Awareness Training	0.04	10	Human error is a major risk
Governance, Risk & Compliance (GRC)	0.05	10	Governance underpins all controls
Secure Development (SDLC)	0.04	10	Secure code is essential for tech organizations
Business Continuity & Resilience	0.04	10	Outages can be catastrophic
Security Monitoring & Logging	0.04	10	Visibility is key for detection
Risk Quantification & Reporting	0.03	10	Communicating risk is important for buyin
Application Security	0.04	10	Apps are a common breach vector
Emerging Technology Adoption	0.03	10	New tech brings new risks
Innovation Culture	0.04	10	Innovation drives competitive advantage
Talent Management	0.05	10	Skills gaps are a top risk for new technologies

4.2 Performance Metrics and Evaluation

Because the rubric is rule-based (not statistical), we assess effectiveness through:

- Manual review of rubric outputs across diverse synthetic and real company profiles
- Expert validation of LLM-generated recommendations for relevance and actionability
- Comparative alignment with industry frameworks such as NIST CSF, ISO/IEC 27001, and FAIR

4.3 System Architecture and Deployment

The AI assessment pipeline comprises:

1. Ingest company profile via a REST API
2. Run the 22-dimension rubric evaluator (api.py) to obtain a score vector
3. Feed the vector and metadata into an LLM to generate tailored mitigation recommendations
4. Aggregate numeric scores and narrative advice into a unified risk report

Deployment is containerized in Docker for portability and security:

- Base image: python:3.11-slim
- Dependencies pinned in requirements.txt
- Dockerfile exposes port 5000 and launches api.py
- Security hardening: least-privilege user, resource limits, CI/CD vulnerability scans, and restricted network policies

5 Case Study: Sample Company Profile and Output

Profile for a cybersecurity startup with minimal controls and early AI + cloud adoption:

- Industry: Cybersecurity
- Size: Startup
- Tech Adoption: Early Adopter
- Security Controls: Minimal, ad hoc
- Risk Posture: Brief, evolving
- Emerging Technologies: AI, Cloud

Sample Output:

- Overall Weighted Score: 70.71 / 100
- Top Risks (Score / Max): o Asset Visibility (4 / 10) o Incident Detection & Response (3 / 10) o Organizational Readiness (5 / 10)
- Recommendations:

  o Implement a formal risk assessment process for emerging technology adoption.
  o Develop a comprehensive security framework aligned with industry standards.

- Resources:

  o NIST Cybersecurity Framework (nist.gov/cyberframework)
  o ISO/IEC 27001 Information Security Management (iso.org/isoiec-27001-informationsecurity.html)

This case study demonstrates how our holistic AI platform leverages the weighted rubric to deliver both a quantitative risk score and actionable guidance.

6 Toward Effective Risk Management: Principles and Recommendations

6.1 Integrative Governance by Design

As reinforced by IRGC's framework, governance must be adaptive and participatory to manage ambiguous, uncertain risks. Risk must be governed not only through standards but through multi-stakeholder decision-making and pre-assessment mechanisms [17]. Unified GRC models, as discussed by Aljarrah et al. and Jakimoski, emphasize integrating AI governance, cybersecurity, and operational strategy via feedback loops and crossfunctional decision trees [5, 6].

6.2 Continuous Learning and Strategic Foresight

Risk management should be embedded as a continuous process. Strategic foresight practices that align cybersecurity and ERM ensure early identification of high-impact risks. Training risk professionals to use predictive analytics, incident forensics, and AI validation models is vital [3].

6.3 Measured Onboarding and Gradual Integration

Emerging technologies should not be rushed into production. As this paper argues, "we don't need to reinvent the wheel." Instead, applying proven controls while gradually onboarding new systems with sandbox testing and phasebased authorization minimizes risk. Systems should not access mission-critical data until compliance, security, and reliability are independently verified [12].

7 Case Studies

7.1 Healthcare and Wearable Technologies

The healthcare sector has experienced a surge in wearable technologies used for real-time health monitoring, but this innovation comes with substantial risk. Wearable devices used in sports and clinical monitoring often lack robust encryption and governance structures. A study on wearable technology in sports revealed that the absence of security protocols such as anonymization and access control exposes users to identity theft, unauthorized surveillance, and misuse of sensitive biometric data [22].

7.2 Robotic Process Automation in Finance

Robotic Process Automation (RPA) has been adopted extensively in financial services for process optimization. However, rapid implementation without proper oversight has led to regulatory breaches, audit failures, and the exploitation of process vulnerabilities. One case demonstrated how poorly configured bots bypassed critical compliance checks, leading to unreported financial discrepancies. Risk governance in this space must evolve to monitor RPA behavior in real time and to integrate audit trails directly into workflows [9].

7.3 Blockchain in Energy and Public Sector

Blockchain's immutable and decentralized design offers strong data traceability, but its deployment in government and energy sectors has revealed a lack of enforceability for smart contracts and data immutability concerns. For instance, energy projects using blockchain for asset tracking struggled to comply with privacy laws, as the technology could not accommodate regulatory requirements for data deletion or modification [19].

7.4 AI in Critical Infrastructure

The application of AI in public safety, utility control, and defense operations raises ethical and operational challenges. The AIRMan framework was designed to address these issues through stakeholder-driven risk governance and adaptive monitoring [14]. However, many institutions lack the technical maturity or legal structure to enforce AI accountability, leading to inconsistent implementation and increased systemic exposure.

8 Recommendations

8.1 Design Governance into the Technology Lifecycle

Risk governance should be embedded at every stage of the technology lifecycle—from system design and development to deployment and decommissioning. Adopting lifecycle-based models such as 4D-ISS or AIRMan can enable real-time decision-making and dynamic risk reassessment [13].

8.2 Incentivize Cross-Functional Integration

Risk should not be siloed in IT or compliance departments. Organizations must foster cross-functional alignment through executive sponsorship, stakeholder training, and cultural adaptation. Frameworks like MAVEN demonstrate that enterprise-wide engagement improves GRC outcomes and speeds up response times [18].

8.3 Adopt Sector-Specific Risk Postures

Each industry faces unique regulatory, ethical, and operational threats. Risk frameworks should be tailored to sectoral needs, with specialized protocols for sectors like healthcare (e.g., HIPAA compliance), finance (e.g., SOX, GLBA), and energy (e.g., NERC CIP).

8.4 Enable Regulatory Sandboxes and Pilot Testing

Organizations should adopt sandboxing approaches to test emerging technologies in controlled environments. These pilots can identify unforeseen risks, allow for stakeholder feedback, and create a feedback loop for continuous governance improvement.

8.5 Invest in Automation and AI-Augmented Oversight

Human oversight remains critical, but automated tools are essential to scale governance in dynamic environments. Workflow automation, predictive analytics, and anomaly detection systems must be integrated into GRC platforms to maintain real-time visibility and compliance [3].

9 Conclusion

Emerging technologies promise transformative benefits but also introduce substantial, multifaceted risks that challenge existing governance and risk management models. This paper has reviewed existing literature and identified significant strategic, technical, and cultural gaps in contemporary approaches. Effective governance in this rapidly evolving technological landscape requires adaptive frameworks that integrate seamlessly with organizational strategy, incorporate continuous learning, and promote strategic foresight. Additionally, governance structures must be tailored to specific industry contexts, addressing unique sectoral challenges proactively. Organizations can achieve an optimal balance between innovation and resilience by embedding robust cybersecurity and comprehensive risk management practices deeply into their operational frameworks and organizational culture. Leveraging advanced AI-driven assessment tools and adopting measured onboarding strategies ensure that emerging technologies can be responsibly deployed, maximizing their potential benefits while effectively mitigating associated risks. Ultimately, a proactive, integrated, and human-centric approach will position organizations not only to manage current and future challenges but also to capitalize sustainably on technological advancements.

References

1. Wang, X., Bai, X., Luo, W., Wang, Y.: Research on big data security and privacy risk governance. In: 2021 International Conference on Big Data, AI and Risk Management (ICBAR), pp. 1–7. IEEE (2021)
2. Jakimoski, K.: Automation improvement in cyber risk management. In: 2023 International Conference on Info Systems and Cyber Resilience, pp. 37–44. IEEE (2023)
3. Aljarrah, S., et al.: On the comparative analysis of trends in cybersecurity risk assessment, governance, and compliance frameworks. In: 2024 International Jordanian Cybersecurity Conf. (IJCC), pp. 1–11. IEEE (2024)
4. National Institute of Standards and Technology (NIST): Risk Management Framework for Information Systems and Organizations. NIST SP 800-37 Rev. 2 (2018)
5. International Organization for Standardization: ISO/IEC 27001:2022 Information Security, Cybersecurity and Privacy Protection—ISMS (2022)
6. ISACA: COBIT 2019 Framework: Governance and Management Objectives. ISACA, Rolling Meadows, IL (2019)
7. De Smet, D., Mayer, N.: Integration of IT governance and security risk management: a systematic literature review. In: i-Society 2016, pp. 1–7. IEEE (2016)
8. Boodai, R., Alessa, H., Alanazi, A.: An approach to address risk management challenges focused on IT governance. In: 2022 IEEE Conference on Cybersecurity and Resilience, pp. 180–188. IEEE (2022)

9. Grob, H.L., Strauch, G., Buddendick, C.: Applications for IT-risk management: requirements and practical evaluation. In: ARES 2008, pp. 758–765. IEEE (2008)
10. Dorca, V., et al.: Agile approach with kanban in information security risk management. In: 2016 International Conference on Electrical and Electronics Engineering (ISEEE), pp. 1–6. IEEE (2016)
11. Yuan, W., Wang, H., Zhang, J., Qi, W.: Research on risk control system ITG-HRCM in IT governance. In: ITME 2012, pp. 1005–1010. IEEE (2012)
12. Alzoubi, Y., et al.: A new approach of information system security governance: the 4D-ISS model. In: 2023 International Conference on Cybersecurity Trends (CYTR), pp. 51–59. IEEE (2023)
13. Jakimoski, K.: AIRMan: an artificial intelligence risk management system. In: 2022 International Conference on Info Tech Security and Automation, pp. 22–30. IEEE (2022)
14. Dorca, V., et al.: Agile kanban integration for risk management teams. In: ISEEE 2016, pp. 20–26. IEEE (2016)
15. IEEE Standards Association: IEEE Std 2145-2023 – Standard for Blockchain Governance and DLT Systems. IEEE, Piscataway, NJ (2023)
16. International Risk Governance Center (IRGC): Guidelines for Emerging Risk Governance. EPFL, Lausanne (2017)
17. Takamura, E., et al.: MAVEN information security governance, risk management, and compliance: lessons learned. In: IEEE Aerospace Conference 2014, pp. 1–10. IEEE (2014)
18. Luo, W., Bai, X., Wang, X.: Improve governance system level and apply blockchain for strategic transformation. In: 2022 International Conference on Blockchain & Data Sharing, pp. 12–20. IEEE (2022)
19. European Commission: Proposal for a Regulation Laying Down Harmonised Rules on Artificial Intelligence (AI Act), COM/2021/206 Final. Brussels (2021)
20. ISO/IEC: ISO/IEC 42001:2023 Artificial Intelligence Management System Standard. ISO, Geneva (2023)
21. Laveti, S.: Risk Management: Understanding Security Risks in Emerging Technologies. Medium. https://medium.com/@laveti/risk-management-understanding-security-risks-in-emerging-technologies-0fb43b88762e. Accessed 08 May 2025
22. IDC Research: Worldwide Security Spending Guide, 2023 Forecast. IDC. https://www.idc.com. Accessed 08 May 2025

Timed I/O Automata for Searching in Dynamic Environments with Humanoid Robots

Fozhan Babaeiyan Ghamsari(✉), Stephen Martinez, Soroush Mirzaee, and Oscar Morales Ponce

California State University, Long Beach, Long Beach, CA 90840, USA
{fozhan.babaeiyanghamsari01,soroush.mirzaee01}@student.csulb.edu, oscar.moralesponce@csulb.edu

Abstract. We explore the use of timed I/O automata for the searching problem in navigating and searching dynamic environments with humanoid robots. An operator gives commands to the robot to search and look for a ball. Then, the robot starts browsing its environment in search of the specified object. We designed timed input/output automata to perform tasks such as object detection, searching, and speech commands and implemented them in the Nao robot. The proposed framework is easy to implement and our experiments confirm that it is effective for timed-critical robotic tasks such as Search and Rescue applications.

Keywords: Search and Rescue · Timed Input Output Automata · Humanoid Robots

1 Introduction

Recent natural disasters—such as wildfires and earthquakes in California-highlight the urgent need for effective search and rescue (SAR) operations in dangerous environments. In these situations, quickly finding victims and hazards while keeping human rescuers safe is critical [8]. However, disaster zones are often unpredictable, cluttered, and constantly changing, making it difficult for robots to operate.

In this work, we focus on implementing autonomous robotic behaviors using the Timed Input/Output Automata (TIOA) framework. TIOA is a formalism specifically designed to describe time-critical systems with clearly defined input and output actions. It supports modular development and compositional verification, allowing developers to define individual behaviors and then compose them into larger, synchronized systems [12]. Unlike traditional FSMs, which capture only discrete states and transitions, TIOA incorporates temporal constraints directly into its structure, enabling the specification of real-time guarantees.

We apply TIOA to model core robot functions such as object detection, speech command processing, and timed state transitions in searching operations. The framework supports deterministic transitions (e.g., `Idleness`, `Searching`,

S. Hussain et al. (Eds.): SEET 2025, CCIS 2725, pp. 680–696, 2026.
https://doi.org/10.1007/978-3-032-08977-9_45

`Approaching`, `Grabbing`) while incorporating time-bounded execution to ensure responsiveness and system liveness. In unpredictable environments, this is especially critical: for instance, if a robot fails to detect a target within a specified timeout, TIOA ensures a fallback to broader exploration (e.g., random walk).

The system architecture includes a real-time publish-subscribe mechanism for managing asynchronous input, such as speech recognition and visual data. This supports concurrency and modular integration while minimizing delays or conflicts across subsystems. Our implementation validates how these TIOA-driven components can operate synchronously or asynchronously under bounded delays, enabling robust decision-making.

This work investigates the following questions:

- **RQ1:** How do timing constraints enforced by TIOA enhance the responsiveness and reliability of search operations, particularly when the robot lacks prior knowledge about the environment?
- **RQ2:** Can TIOA improve coordination among multiple robots, especially in environments where communication and perception are limited?
- **RQ3:** What are the trade-offs of using a TIOA-driven framework compared to probabilistic or machine learning-based control for multimodal sensor integration?

By grounding our system in TIOA, we offer a formal model capable of managing real-time decisions, synchronizing robotic components, and scaling toward fault-tolerant multi-agent coordination. In contrast to prior systems that layered timing behaviors on top of FSMs, our approach uses TIOA as the foundational model of computation.

Organization. The remainder of this paper is structured as follows: Sect. 3 presents the modeling framework using TIOA. Section 4 describes the system architecture, behavioral diagrams, and timing structure. Section 6 details the experimental setup and results. Section 7 considers broader implications including safety and ethics. We conclude in Sect. 8 and outline future directions including scaling and learning-based extensions.

2 Related Work

This section surveys previous research across four interrelated domains: (1) robotic systems in search and rescue (SAR), (2) multi-robot coordination and swarm robotics, (3) AI techniques in perception and autonomy, and (4) formal models-particularly finite state machines (FSMs) and timed automata-applied to robotics.

Robots have long been envisioned as tools for operating in environments too dangerous or inaccessible for humans. Early efforts in SAR robotics demonstrated the potential of ground-based robots, such as those used in the response to the 9/11 World Trade Center disaster [6], and aerial platforms, including UAVs designed for wilderness rescue operations [9]. Robotic response units deployed during the Fukushima nuclear incident provided further evidence that autonomous systems can enhance situational awareness and reduce risk to human responders [13].

Despite these successes, many SAR systems rely heavily on predefined routines or centralized architectures, which limit adaptability in dynamic or unknown environments. Emerging frameworks, like those proposed in [7], offer robust alternatives through decentralized, fault-tolerant, and self-coordinating robot teams capable of operating with minimal environmental assumptions.

Multi-robot systems (MRS) offer scalability and redundancy, both of which are essential for SAR tasks such as area coverage, object search, and victim retrieval. A growing body of work focuses on distributed control strategies that allow robots to self-assign tasks, avoid redundancy, and dynamically adapt to failures or communication loss [3,5]. Swarm robotics, inspired by biological systems, emphasizes simple, scalable behaviors that emerge from local interactions, enabling systems to handle large-scale exploration and search efficiently.

The Synchronous Robotic Framework (SyRoF) [2] exemplifies this philosophy by offering a platform for undergraduate students to implement time-synchronized cooperative algorithms using a high-level programming interface. SyRoF is particularly notable for its use of a real-time publish-subscribe system, transparent membership tracking, and synchronization protocols grounded in the Timed I/O Automata (TIOA) model. These features enable robust common knowledge sharing and coordinated action execution, even in the presence of partial communication failures.

Recent developments in artificial intelligence have significantly advanced robotic capabilities in navigation, perception, and interaction. Approaches such as deep reinforcement learning, visual SLAM, and convolutional neural networks (CNNs) for object detection (e.g., YOLO) have been increasingly employed to support autonomous operation [10]. These methods enable robots to interpret noisy sensor data, adapt to novel environments, and improve performance over time.

However, the integration of these AI systems into safety-critical SAR tasks poses several challenges. Models trained in simulation often struggle with generalization to real-world domains. Additionally, perception algorithms may inherit dataset biases, leading to reduced performance under certain lighting, weather, or acoustic conditions [4]. These shortcomings motivate hybrid systems that integrate AI perception with deterministic FSM and TIOA-based control, ensuring robust baseline behavior even when perception fails.

Finite State Machines (FSMs) have been a foundational model for designing reactive robotic behaviors due to their interpretability, modularity, and deterministic nature. In our approach, we utilize Searching and Idleness as key states in FSMs to model robot behavior. FSMs define system states (e.g., `Idleness`, `Searching`, `Approaching`) and transitions based on input events or internal conditions. Hierarchical FSMs and statecharts [11] further support complex behaviors through layered abstraction.

Timed automata, introduced by Alur and Dill [1], add real-time semantics by incorporating clock variables and temporal guards on transitions. These models have proven effective for specifying and verifying real-time systems. The

Timed I/O Automata (TIOA) extension [12] builds on this by explicitly modeling inputs, outputs, and composition—making it particularly well-suited for robotic systems operating in uncertain environments.

Recent work has demonstrated the practical benefits of applying TIOA to multi-robot coordination. For instance, in [7], TIOA is used to formally describe and implement a distributed protocol for collaborative box-pushing, in which robots must coordinate their actions despite lacking global localization or synchronized headings. The authors show that the algorithm remains correct under failures, and validate it experimentally using SyRoF. These results highlight the potential of TIOA to model not just reactive systems, but also cooperative and fault-tolerant behavior.

Collectively, these strands of research point to an important convergence: combining formal control models like FSM and TIOA with distributed coordination protocols and robust perception systems. Our work builds on these insights by proposing a TIOA-guided FSM framework that is compatible with real-time, reactive, and partially observable environments. This approach bridges the gap between theoretical guarantees and practical performance, aiming to enhance robotic autonomy in high-stakes SAR scenarios.

3 Model

This work employs TIOA to model robot behaviors for search and rescue operations. TIOA enforce time constraints for critical tasks and a modular framework for defining discrete robot behaviors. This combination addresses key challenges in search and rescue, including real-time responsiveness, adaptability to dynamic environments, and ease of integration across heterogeneous robot platforms.

3.1 Timed Input/Output Automaton in Robotics

Timed Input/Output Automata provide a structured framework for systems governed by timing constraints. They ensure precise control over robot behavior in time-critical scenarios by enforcing deadlines on state transitions. For instance, a robot transitions from the *Scan* state to the *Wander* state if no object is detected within a predefined time limit (e.g., 10 s).

In multi-robot coordination, Input/Output synchronize tasks such as shared resource usage or obstacle avoidance to prevent conflicts. This ensures timely task execution while maintaining robustness in dynamic environments. Formally, a Input/Output can be represented as:

$$A = (S, \Sigma, \delta, s_0, F, C, I)$$

where:

- S: Finite set of states (e.g., Idleness, Searching, Grabbing).
- Σ: Set of input symbols (e.g., CD, OB, TO).
- $\delta : S \times \Sigma \times C \rightarrow S$: Transition function.

- s_0: Initial state (Idle).
- F: Set of final states (e.g., Completion).
- C: Set of clocks (e.g., time elapsed since entering a state).
- $I(s)$: Invariant conditions for each state s.

3.2 Timed Input/Output Automata for Behavior Modeling

While timed automata handle temporal constraints, Finite state machines provide a high-level abstraction of the robot's behavioral structure. FSMs define discrete states and transitions, enabling robots to respond dynamically to environmental inputs. Figure 1 illustrates the primary FSM for the robot, encompassing states. Each state in the FSM corresponds to a distinct robotic activity, such as listening for a command, scanning the environment, approaching a detected object, or attempting to grasp it. Transitions between states are triggered by sensor events or user inputs, making the system reactive to both internal and external stimuli.

The FSM begins in an `Idleness` state, during which the robot awaits voice commands. Upon receiving a valid command, it transitions to a `Speaking` state for interpretation and subsequently enters task-specific states like `Searching` or `Grabbing`. This modular approach facilitates code clarity and fault isolation - individual states can be developed and debugged independently.

Moreover, FSMs are crucial for encoding behavior under physical constraints. For example, because the NAO robot is non-holonomic (i.e., it cannot move freely in all directions), the FSM incorporates logic to handle turning and alignment maneuvers carefully during transitions between `Searching` and `Approaching`. Head movements, walking direction, and turn angles are adjusted dynamically to account for mechanical limitations.

To better manage task complexity, we adopt a hierarchical FSM architecture. High-level states such as `Searching` are decomposed into sub-states like `Scanning` and `Wandering`. The `Scanning` sub-state rotates the robot's head to detect objects in its immediate field of view. If no object is detected after a timeout period (controlled by the timed automaton), the system transitions to `Wandering`, wherein the robot walks forward or rotates its body to expand the search area. This hierarchical structure enables scalability and reuse of behaviors across tasks.

Timed transitions between these sub-states ensure that the robot avoids indefinite stalling in any given mode. For instance, the `Scanning` state is bounded by a 10-second timeout; upon expiration, the automaton forces a transition to `Wandering`. Similarly, obstacle encounters in the `Approaching` state redirect the robot into an `Avoidance` state, which itself contains logic for dynamic re-routing.

3.3 Modeling Multi-robot Interaction and Task Reallocation

Although the present implementation is demonstrated using a single NAO robot, the model is designed to support multiple robots operating in a shared environment. In such settings, the FSM and timed automaton models can be extended to enable inter-robot communication and coordination. For example, two robots can use shared topics and timers to allocate tasks dynamically: if one robot fails to reach an object due to obstacles, another robot can take over after a timeout period.

Synchronization between robots is planned to be achieved with a synchronizer component. We envision the synchronizer as a self-stabilizing service that will synchronize the states of the robots. Timed transitions can ensure that handoffs or recovery mechanisms occur predictably. This aspect lays the groundwork for swarm-based or collaborative SAR systems where coordination is paramount.

While global synchronization is commonly proposed in multi-robot systems, our architecture does not require a global time reference for coordinated behavior. Instead, we adopt a thread-based execution model, where each robot runs concurrent TIOA threads that independently handle tasks such as object detection, movement, and recovery. This ensures that transitions are non-blocking and tasks can be executed asynchronously without central coordination.

In prior work, Balaji et al. [2] demonstrated that multi-robot coordination can be achieved without strict global time synchronization using a membership and synchronizer protocol based on stream consensus. Their framework, SyROF, guarantees cooperative behavior with bounded disagreement even in the presence of message loss. This protocol allows each robot to execute maneuvers concurrently while maintaining a shared operational mode, enabling robust synchronization without requiring a global time variable.

Therefore, we do not explicitly introduce a second time variable in our model, as the existing publish-subscribe threads and local invariants suffice for responsive, fault-tolerant behavior across multiple robots.

3.4 FSM Formalization

Finite State Machines are similar to Timed Input Output Automata but they do not include time constraints. For simplicity, we use FSMs when time constraints are not a necessity in the model. The finite state machine for robot behavior is formally defined as:

$$FSM = (S, \Sigma, \delta, s_0, F)$$

where:

- S: States of the FSM.
- $\Sigma\}$: Set of triggers and events.
- $\delta : S \times \Sigma \rightarrow S$: Transition function.
- Initial state.
- Final or accepting states.

4 Design

This section outlines the architectural and algorithmic design of the humanoid robot's behavior control system. We describe how the system components are structured around a Timed Input/Output Automaton (TIOA) model and how this model governs both high-level task flow and low-level timing constraints. Subsections include an overview of robot architecture, TIOA design, speech command integration, hierarchical state transitions, and the implementation of time-bound control.

4.1 Robotic Architecture

The system is built around a humanoid robot platform (SoftBank NAO) equipped with vision and speech interfaces. The robot's onboard camera and microphone serve as the primary input sensors, while its motors (for locomotion and head movement) and speaker act as output actuators. The overall architecture is modular: we separate perception, control, and actuation into distinct components that interact through a Timed Input/Output Automaton (TIOA) framework. This mapping between components and automaton elements ensures consistency with the formal model discussed in Sect. 3. Input actions represent sensory data or user commands, and output actions correspond to robot behaviors such as movement or speech.

Figure 1 shows the primary FSM for core robot behaviors. Meanwhile, Table 1 details abbreviations and their meanings and Table 4 summarizes the hierarchical Search FSM transitions.

- **Speech Recognition (SR)**: Interprets user commands and translates them into FSM inputs.
- **Object Detection (OB)**: Processes video streams to identify target objects using HSV filtering.
- **Motorized Movement (MM)**: Controls head and body movement for scanning, walking, and grasping.
- **Communication Protocols**: Employs a publish-subscribe model using ROS for modular and scalable data sharing.

4.2 Timed I/O Automata Integration

The robot's core behavior is governed by a finite state machine (FSM) augmented with timed transitions as defined in our TIOA model. Figures 1 and 3 illustrate the overall behavioral structure. Each FSM state encapsulates a specific robot activity (e.g., `Searching`, `Approaching`, `Grabbing`), while transitions are triggered by sensor events, speech inputs, or timeouts enforced via internal timers.

To ensure deterministic responses and prevent indefinite blocking, states like `Scan` or `Search` include timed invariants. If the robot fails to detect an object in a fixed time, the automaton transitions to the next state (e.g., from `Search` to `Wander`). This timed behavior is aligned with the model formalism in Sect. 3 and guarantees liveness.

The following diagram (Fig. 1) shows the top-level TIOA.

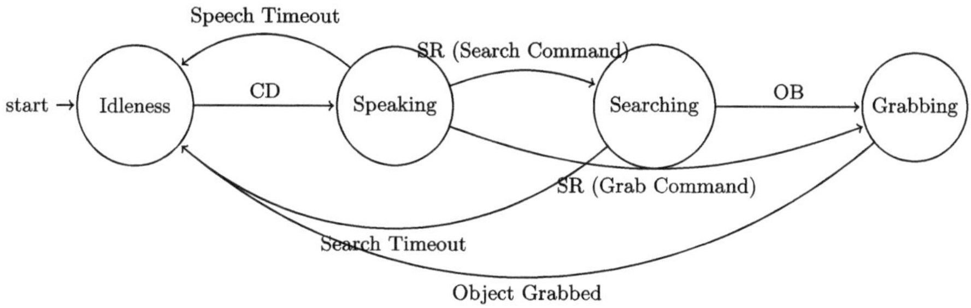

Fig. 1. TIOA for core behaviors of the NAO robot, including states like Idleness, Speaking, Searching, and Grabbing. Transitions represent triggers such as detected commands (CD) or object events (OB). Detailed explanations are provided in Table 1.

Table 1. TIOA Abbreviations and Description; see Sect. 5.2 for more details.

Abbreviation	Action	State	Meaning
CD	Command Detected	Idleness	Detects user command
OB	Object Found	Searching	Ball detected

4.3 Speech Command Integration

The speech recognition subsystem allows real-time human interaction with the robot. When specific voice commands are recognized (e.g., "Find the ball"), corresponding input symbols are generated in the TIOA. These inputs trigger defined transitions consistent with the TIOA framework, enabling command-responsive behavior.

Commands such as "Look left" or "Stop tracking" are directly mapped to states. If the robot is currently in `Idleness`, a recognized command like "Find the ball" will cause an immediate state transition to `Searching`, along with an audible acknowledgment.

Table 2 shows the mapping between recognized speech and states. Each command is implemented as a deterministic transition input, ensuring consistency across repeated interactions.

Table 2. Mapping of Verbal Commands to States.

Verbal Command	Mapped State
"Find the ball"	Listening
"Track the ball"	Processing
"Stop tracking"	Idleness
"Look left"	Executing
"Look right"	Executing
"Look up"	Executing
"Look down"	Executing

The speech recognition process is governed by a finite state machine (FSM) to handle voice commands dynamically and efficiently. Figure 2 outlines the states and transitions, while Table 3 summarizes the states and transitions.

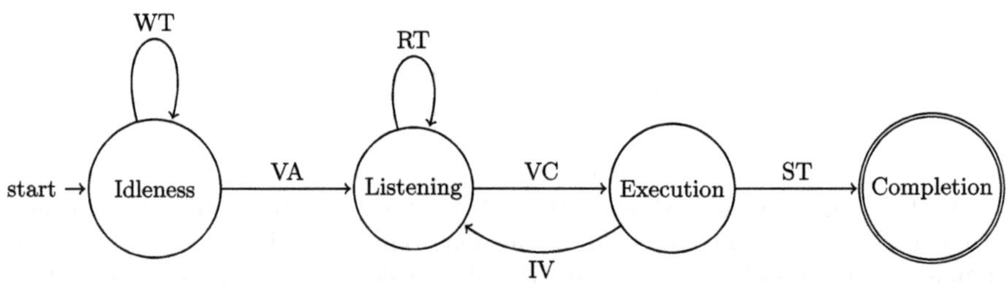

Fig. 2. FSM for speech recognition process. Abbreviations are detailed in Table 3.

Table 3. Abbreviations and detailed descriptions for the speech recognition FSM transitions.

Abbreviation	Trigger/Event	From State	To State	Description
WT	Wait Timer	Idleness	Idleness	Robot remains idle until activation
VA	Voice Activation	Idleness	Listening	Activation of the speech recognition system
IV	Invalid Command	Processing	Error	Command is processed but found to be invalid
VC	Valid Command	Processing	Executing	Command is validated and execution begins
ST	Successful Task	Executing	Done	Task is completed successfully
RT	Retry	Error	Listening	Returns to listening after an error

4.4 Search and Go

The Search and Go behavior uses a hierarchical TIOA with sub-states such as `Scanning`, `Wandering`, and `Approaching`. The TIOA progresses based on object detections and environmental conditions. Time-bounded transitions ensure timely state changes even when no new sensor data arrives.

For example, if an object is not detected within the `Scanning` state's time-out window, the state transitions to `Wandering` to relocate the robot. Upon successful detection (`OD`), the TIOA proceeds to `Approaching`. If an obstacle is encountered (`OB`), the TIOA diverts to `Avoidance`, with a bypass path defined for safe reentry into `Approaching`.

The formal structure of this FSM is depicted in Fig. 3, and the associated transitions are detailed in Table 4.

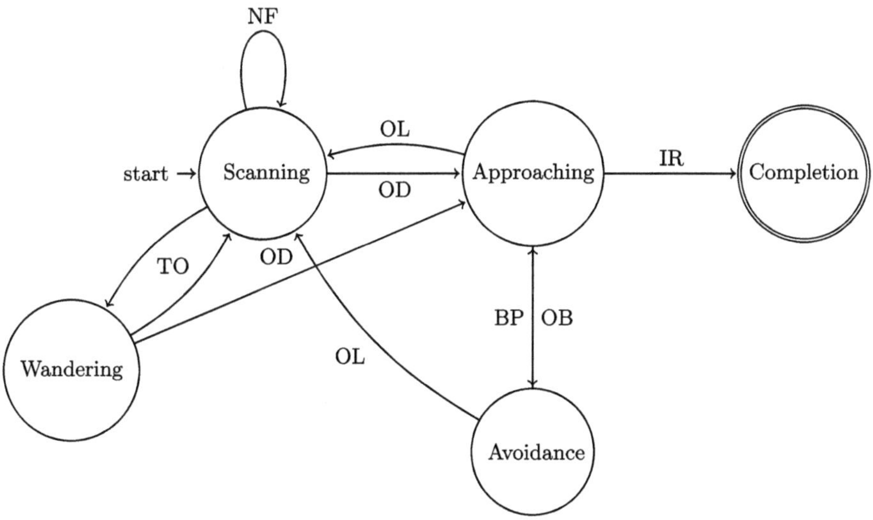

Fig. 3. FSM for the Search and Go process with concise transitions. Abbreviations are detailed in Table 4.

Table 4. Abbreviations and detailed descriptions for the Search and Go TIOA transitions.

Abbreviation	Trigger/Event	From State	To State	Description
NF	Object Not Found	Scan	Scan	Continuous scanning for an object
TO	Timeout	Scan/Wander	Wander/Scan	Transitions due to no object detected within the time limit
OD	Object Detected	Scan/Wander	Approaching	Begins approaching the detected object
OB	Obstacle Detected	Approaching	Avoid	Executes obstacle avoidance maneuvers
OL	Object Lost	Approach/Avoid	Scan	Returns to scanning after losing the object
IR	In Range	Approaching	Reached	Successfully reaches the object
BP	Bypass Completed	Avoid	Approaching	Resumes approaching after bypassing an obstacle

4.5 Timed Transitions and Search Strategy

Timed transitions play a central role in preventing robot stalling and enforcing progress in searching behavior. Each state in the TIOA that involves scanning or waiting for external input includes an invariant condition specifying a maximum allowable time (e.g., 10 s). These timers are implemented using local clock variables in the TIOA model.

The robot follows a structured searching cycle: beginning in `Search-Left`, timing out to `Search-Right`, and eventually moving to `Walk` if no detection occurs. This loop increases spatial coverage incrementally. Upon receiving a valid sensor event like `BallDetected`, the TIOA immediately transitions to `Reached`, interrupting the timed loop and confirming the detection.

This use of timed transitions ensures that every state has a defined lifespan, supporting both reactivity and reliability in dynamic environments. The resulting behavior adheres to the formal constraints of the TIOA model while remaining adaptable through voice command inputs and asynchronous sensory data.

The robot's walking speed was empirically measured to be approximately 0.14 m/s on flat indoor terrain. Given this, the 10-second timeout in the `Scanning` or `Approaching` state corresponds to a navigational coverage radius of roughly 1.4 m, sufficient for indoor SAR environments with minimal obstruction.

5 Implementation

This section describes the concrete realization of our proposed TIOA-based framework on the NAO robot. We detail the software components, sensor integrations, and behavioral implementations that correspond to each state. The modular system architecture ensures that each TIOA transition has a direct mapping to physical actions, sensor triggers, or timer-based events.

5.1 NAO Capabilities

The NAO robot provides several hardware and software features critical for autonomous search and interaction.

- **Speech Recognition (SR)**: The robot uses an onboard microphone array and speech recognition software to process verbal commands such as "search for the ball" and "stop." Commands are mapped to TIOA states, enabling dynamic transitions. Preprocessing includes noise filtering for improved recognition in noisy environments.
- **Object Detection (OB)**: The RGB camera enables robust detection of objects based on their HSV color properties. Detection algorithms use Haar Cascade classifiers for object identification and can process video frames in real time. The module publishes detection results to a designated ROS topic for TIOA consumption.

- **Motorized Movement (MM):** The robot's motorized joints support precise movements, including:
  - Head Rotation: For scanning the environment during the Searching state.
  - Walking: Dynamically adjusting speed and trajectory during the Approaching state.
  - Arm Manipulation: Coordinating pre-programmed actions for grasping objects in the Grabbing state.
- **Communication and Coordination (CC):** The ROS-based publish-subscribe architecture enables seamless communication between modules. Detection events, commands, and error feedback are exchanged via specific topics.

5.2 Implementation of TIOA States

Each state, as described in our model, is implemented through coordinated service calls and state-specific routines. Below, we describe the functionality and transition logic for each major state.

- **Idleness State:** In this state, the robot remains stationary and passively listens for voice input. It continuously monitors the speech recognition system for known command phrases. Upon detecting a valid command, an event is published that triggers a transition to the `Speech` state.
- **Speech State:** Once a command is detected, the robot enters the speech state to validate and interpret the verbal input. The recognized command is mapped to an FSM action (e.g., `Find Ball`, `Stop Tracking`) and published to the FSM. Valid commands initiate transitions to task-specific states like `Searching` or `Grabbing`.
- **Searching State:** In the searching state, the robot performs head movements to scan its surroundings. The `balldetection.py` module processes HSV-filtered video frames to detect the target object. If no object is found within a predefined timeout, the TIOA transitions to `Wandering`. If a detection occurs, the TIOA transitions to `Approaching`.
- **Approaching State:** Here, the robot uses the relative coordinates of the detected object to align and walk toward it. Movement commands are issued using `setWalkTargetVelocity`, and real-time feedback adjusts trajectory as necessary. If the object is lost or an obstacle is detected, the TIOA moves to `Scanning` or `Avoidance`, respectively.
- **Grabbing State:** Upon reaching the target, the robot attempts to grasp it using a predefined sequence of arm motions. If the grab fails, the system loops back to the `Searching` state to retry the task or reposition.
- **Avoidance State:** When an obstacle is encountered during approach, the robot temporarily enters the avoidance state. Here, trajectory planning modules compute an alternate path. Once the obstacle is bypassed, the TIOA transitions back to `Approaching`.

Communication and Thread Synchronization: All modules operate within a publish-subscribe framework implemented via ROS. Each module listens to and publishes on FSM-relevant topics. Thread synchronization ensures atomic updates during transitions, and timers enforce temporal constraints consistent with the automaton's invariants.

System Initialization: Upon startup, the NAO robot initializes all sensory modules, TIOA threads, and state flags. The control system starts in `Idleness`, with modules ready to respond to user commands and sensor inputs. Each TIOA transition from this point onward is driven by external events or time-based guards defined in the TIOA model.

6 Experiments

This section evaluates the practical performance of the proposed TIOA-guided framework on the NAO robot. The experiments were designed to assess the robot's ability to autonomously detect, search for, and react to objects in a dynamic indoor environment, while maintaining robust state transitions and timing constraints. We describe the experimental setup, procedures, evaluation metrics, and results, and conclude with key observations.

Setup: Experiments were conducted in a controlled indoor environment that simulated simplified search-and-rescue conditions. The test area featured a flat, obstacle-free floor with uniform overhead lighting to minimize visual noise. A green ball—selected for its distinct HSV color properties—was placed randomly within a two-meter radius from the robot's starting position at the beginning of each trial.

The robot platform used was the SoftBank NAO V6, equipped with vision and speech recognition systems. All necessary modules were initialized via ROS, and the TIOA began execution in the `Idleness` state. Each experiment ran for up to 60 s or until the robot successfully detected and approached the target object.

Procedure: Each trial began with the robot standing in the `Idleness` state, waiting for user input. Upon receiving the spoken command "find the ball," the robot transitioned into the `Searching` state and initiated head-scanning behavior. If an object was detected, the system transitioned to the `Approaching` state to begin locomotion toward the target. If detection did not occur within a predefined interval, the robot moved into the `Wandering` state before cycling back to `Searching`. This loop was governed by the timed transitions defined in the automaton. A trial concluded when the object was reached or a timeout limit was exceeded.

Multiple trials were conducted with different ball placements and minor background variations to test robustness under slight environmental changes.

6.1 Metrics

System performance was evaluated based on four criteria: detection accuracy, response time, speech recognition accuracy, and TIOA consistency.

Detection accuracy measured the proportion of trials in which the robot successfully located the target within the time window. Response time referred to the time elapsed between the reception of the voice command and the detection (or timeout). Speech recognition accuracy was evaluated by measuring correct interpretation rates of user commands under both quiet and moderately noisy conditions. FSM consistency assessed whether the robot's state transitions conformed to the expected TIOA model, ensuring that no undefined or erroneous transitions occurred during runtime.

6.2 Results

Preliminary results indicate that the system operated reliably under the tested conditions. In all trials, the TIOA executed transitions according to the expected temporal and logical model, with no deviation from the designed state sequences. The object detection component performed well under uniform lighting conditions, although its reliability decreased in lower light or when the background color closely matched the target object.

Speech recognition yielded high accuracy in quiet environments but was prone to degradation when background noise was introduced. Despite this, the TIOA maintained stability, and timed transitions such as those from `Scan` to `Wander` effectively prevented deadlock or stalling behavior.

It should be noted that these findings are based on a limited number of trials. Additional experiments under varied lighting, acoustic, and spatial conditions are needed to establish quantitative benchmarks for detection rate, average response time, and recovery from error states. As such, the current results are qualitative and serve as validation of system stability and architectural soundness, rather than statistical performance claims.

6.3 Observations

A number of practical insights were gathered during testing. The object detection module, while functional, exhibited false positives in cluttered environments or when bright reflections were present. This suggests the need for more sophisticated filtering or classifier calibration. The TIOA-based framework, on the other hand, proved resilient to incomplete or noisy input: when detection failed, the robot appropriately defaulted to scanning or movement behaviors based on the internal timing logic.

Latency in speech recognition occasionally delayed transitions, but the model continued to operate within its designed temporal bounds, highlighting the importance of integrating timeout guards. Overall, the use of a formal automaton model made it easier to debug and verify the system, as each state and transition could be directly traced to implementation modules.

These experiments affirm the feasibility of using timed I/O automata as a reliable control structure in robotic systems. Future work will extend this framework to multi-robot scenarios and more complex environments to further validate its scalability and robustness.

7 Discussion

The deployment of autonomous humanoid robots in real-world scenarios such as search and rescue introduces not only engineering challenges but also critical ethical, safety, and social considerations. These concerns must be proactively addressed to ensure responsible development and deployment.

One of the primary ethical issues is **privacy**. Robots equipped with cameras and microphones inherently carry the risk of capturing sensitive or personally identifiable information from victims or bystanders. To mitigate this, we propose implementing data governance protocols that include anonymization, encryption during transmission, and automatic deletion of non-essential data post-mission. These practices align with modern standards of digital ethics and data protection.

Equally important is the issue of **reliability and accountability**. In time-sensitive and high-risk environments, it is essential that robotic systems operate deterministically and transparently. Our system logs all transitions, sensor inputs, and decision events, creating an audit trail that can be analyzed for post-deployment reviews. This not only improves future iterations of the system but also enables a framework for assigning accountability in case of failure or malfunction.

Another important concern is **algorithmic bias**, particularly in the robot's perception systems. Object detection algorithms may perform unevenly across lighting conditions or object colors, and speech recognition may struggle with accents, dialects, or ambient noise. These limitations could lead to unequal performance across populations or scenarios. Future versions of our system will incorporate more diverse datasets and domain adaptation techniques to enhance generalization and mitigate such biases.

From an operational standpoint, **safety protocols** are vital. Our robot incorporates mechanisms for collision avoidance, fail-safe behaviors, and energy-efficient locomotion. These are enforced at the TIOA level through dedicated states like `Avoid` and through temporal constraints that prevent prolonged exposure to risky states. For example, if an object is lost or not detected for an extended period, the robot resets its behavior to a known safe scanning mode.

As we consider scaling to multi-robot systems, new ethical considerations emerge around **coordination and fairness**. In such environments, task allocation must be handled in a way that avoids redundancy, prevents starvation of resources, and ensures balanced workload distribution. Our proposed extension of the TIOA framework to multi-agent settings will incorporate synchronized clocks and shared events to manage cooperative behavior while preserving each robot's autonomy. Additionally, data sharing between robots must maintain privacy and minimize communication overload.

Environmental concerns also factor into deployment discussions. The manufacture and operation of robotic systems in disaster zones should adhere to principles of sustainability. Our future designs emphasize the use of recyclable and modular components to reduce electronic waste and enable long-term serviceability. Minimizing ecological disruption during operation is also a goal, which will be addressed by constraining robot movement to predefined safe zones and optimizing path planning algorithms for minimal energy expenditure.

Lastly, equitable deployment is a guiding principle in this work. Robotics technologies should not be restricted to affluent regions or institutions. By using low-cost, open-source platforms and providing training and support for rescue personnel globally, we aim to lower the barrier to adoption and promote inclusive access to life-saving technology.

Overall, the combination of ethical foresight, system-level safety design, and responsible deployment strategies positions our framework not only as a technological contribution but also as a step toward principled and sustainable robotics for real-world impact.

8 Conclusion

This paper presents a formal framework for programming humanoid robots to perform autonomous search tasks in dynamic and partially unknown environments. Using Timed Input/Output Automata (TIOA) as our foundational model, we encode both the timing semantics and state-based behaviors required for robust real-time decision-making. The modular structure of TIOA enables compositional design, verifiable transitions, and scalability to more complex scenarios.

We implemented and validated this framework on a SoftBank NAO robot, integrating visual object detection, speech command recognition, and motion control within a time-bounded control architecture. The use of timed transitions allowed the robot to recover from perception delays and continue its search mission without stalling. The system responded reliably to real-time commands and operated predictably across a variety of test conditions.

Preliminary experiments demonstrated that TIOA provides a solid foundation for managing sensor noise, controlling timed behaviors, and supporting concurrent input modalities. Although our evaluation was limited to a single robot in a controlled indoor setting, the underlying design generalizes to multi-robot systems and more complex environments.

Future work includes scaling the system for cooperative multi-robot search, incorporating adaptive learning modules for environment-specific tuning, and conducting field trials in real-world disaster response scenarios. We also plan to investigate formal performance guarantees-such as time-to-detection bounds and failure recovery correctness-using model checking or runtime verification techniques.

Ultimately, this work lays the groundwork for reliable, explainable, and ethically responsible robotic systems capable of supporting high-stakes tasks in uncertain and dynamic environments.

References

1. Alur, R., Dill, D.L.: A theory of timed automata. Theor. Comput. Sci. **126**(2), 183–235 (1994)
2. Balaji, N.H., Kilaru, J., Morales-Ponce, O.: Synchronous robotic framework. In: 2020 16th International Conference on Distributed Computing in Sensor Systems (DCOSS), pp. 333–337. IEEE (2020)
3. Brambilla, M., Ferrante, E., Birattari, M., Dorigo, M.: Swarm robotics: a review from the swarm engineering perspective. Swarm Intell. **7**(1), 1–41 (2013). https://doi.org/10.1007/s11721-012-0075-2
4. Buolamwini, J., Gebru, T.: Gender shades: intersectional accuracy disparities in commercial gender classification. In: Proceedings of the Conference on Fairness, Accountability and Transparency (FAT*). Proceedings of Machine Learning Research, vol. 81, pp. 1–15 (2018)
5. Cao, Y.U., Fukunaga, A.S., Kahng, A.B., Meng, F.: Cooperative mobile robotics: antecedents and directions. Auton. Robot. **4**(1), 7–27 (1997)
6. Casper, J., Murphy, R.R.: Human–robot interactions during the robot-assisted urban search and rescue response at the world trade center. IEEE Trans. Syst. Man Cybern. Part B **33**(3), 367–385 (2003). https://doi.org/10.1109/TSMCB.2003.811794
7. Castorena, M., Doan, N., Gillmore, B., Lahn, J., Lorenzen, J., Morales-Ponce, O.: Overweight object transportation with a set of collaborative robots. In: 2020 16th International Conference on Distributed Computing in Sensor Systems (DCOSS), pp. 320–327. IEEE (2020)
8. Davids, A.: Urban search and rescue robots: from tragedy to technology. IEEE Intell. Syst. **17**(2), 81–83 (2002)
9. Goodrich, M.A., Cooper, J.L., Adams, J.A., Humphrey, C., Zeeman, R.S., Buss, B.G.: Using a mini-UAV to support wilderness search and rescue practices for human–robot teaming. In: Proceedings of the IEEE International Workshop on Safety, Security and Rescue Robotics (SSRR). Rome, Italy (September 2007)
10. Goodrich, M.A., Schultz, A.C.: Human-robot interaction: a survey. Found. Trends Hum.-Comput. Interact. **1**(3), 203–275 (2007)
11. Harel, D.: Statecharts: a visual formalism for complex systems. Sci. Comput. Program. **8**(3), 231–274 (1987)
12. Kaynar, D.K., Lynch, N.A., Segala, R., Vaandrager, F.W.: Timed I/O Automata: a mathematical framework for modeling and analyzing real-time systems. In: Proceedings of the 24th IEEE International Real-Time Systems Symposium (RTSS), pp. 166–177 (2003)
13. Queralta, J.P., et al.: Collaborative multi-robot search and rescue: planning, coordination, perception, and active vision (2020). https://doi.org/10.1109/ACCESS.2020.3030190

An Analysis of Worldwide Language Networks and Cultural Clustering

Fozhan Babaeiyan Ghamsari(✉), Anh Le(✉), Claudia Rawson, Lesly Castellanos, Salvador Sandoval, Richie Prak, and Oscar Morales Ponce

California State University, Long Beach, Long Beach, CA 90840, USA
{fozhan.babaeiyanghamsari01,anh.le02}@student.csulb.edu,
oscar.moralesponce@csulb.edu

Abstract. This study explores the global structure of multilingual interactions through the lens of network analysis, aiming to determine whether language relationships are more accurately captured by decentralized networks than by models centered on a single dominant language. Using three complementary datasets—OpenSubtitles movie translations, Wikipedia interlanguage links, and spoken-at-home data from the World Values Survey—we construct weighted language networks and apply community detection, centrality metrics, and clustering analysis. Across all datasets, we observe consistent patterns of linguistic clustering that align with historical alliances, colonial legacies, and migration flows. While English consistently emerges as a central hub, regional clusters such as those in Eastern Europe, Latin America, and Southeast Asia demonstrate substantial structural autonomy. These findings suggest that multilingual network models offer a more faithful representation of linguistic and cultural dynamics than monolingual hierarchies, highlighting the value of graph-based approaches in studying global language systems.

Keywords: Language networks · Community detection · PageRank · Cultural clustering · Multilingual data

1 Introduction

Language is more than a tool for communication–it is a carrier of culture, memory, identity, and power. As globalization accelerates cross-cultural exchange, understanding how languages interact across societies becomes critical for mapping human connection and cultural influence.

Traditional studies of global language dynamics often focus on dominant languages–such as English, Mandarin, or Spanish–as singular vectors of influence. However, this approach risks oversimplifying the complex and multilingual nature of real-world communication. A more holistic view considers languages

F. B. Ghamsari—Equal contribution.
A. Le—Equal contribution.

S. Hussain et al. (Eds.): SEET 2025, CCIS 2725, pp. 697–715, 2026.
https://doi.org/10.1007/978-3-032-08977-9_46

not in isolation, but as part of dynamic, interconnected networks shaped by history, politics, media, and migration.

In this study, we ask: Can multilingual language networks offer a more accurate and culturally grounded model of global linguistic relationships than models centered on a single universal language? To explore this, we introduce the concept of a *World Language Network* (WLN)–a network model where languages are nodes and translation, co-usage, or content-sharing relationships form weighted edges. We hypothesize that these networks naturally cluster in ways that reflect geopolitical alliances, colonial histories, and regional proximity.

To test this, we analyze three distinct datasets:

- **OpenSubtitles:** subtitle translation frequencies between 94 languages, capturing media-driven language interaction;
- **Wikipedia Interlanguage Links:** hyperlinks between language editions, reflecting digital knowledge connectivity;
- **World Values Survey (WVS):** spoken-at-home language data across 66 countries, providing insight into real-world linguistic presence.

Using graph-based techniques–community detection (Louvain clustering), centrality analysis (PageRank, betweenness, weighted degree), and network visualization–we examine which languages function as hubs or bridges, how languages group into communities, and what cultural patterns emerge from their structure.

Our results suggest that while English consistently plays a central role, multilingual clusters rooted in colonial legacies, migration corridors, and regional identity persist. These findings highlight the value of network models in revealing the cultural geography of language on a global scale.

2 Related Work

Languages are not isolated entities but part of evolving systems shaped by communication, history, and power. Network-based approaches have become essential for modeling the global structure of these linguistic systems. Prior research has consistently shown that language interactions–whether through translation, knowledge-sharing, or everyday use–tend to form clusters shaped by cultural, geographic, and political forces.

Ronen et al. [8] laid the groundwork by constructing a global language network from Wikipedia, book translations, and Twitter. They found that languages cluster by historical relationships such as colonization and regional proximity. This early work established that language networks do not reflect global equality but instead reproduce geopolitical and cultural hierarchies.

Building on this, Johansson and Lindberg [6] analyzed Wikipedia interlanguage links and revealed how editorial practices–especially bot-generated content–distort connectivity in certain language editions. Despite these anomalies, they confirmed that interlanguage networks still reflect meaningful cultural and historical proximity among major languages.

To understand how people bridge languages in practice, Esmaeilialiabadi et al. [3] examined translation demand using Google Translate queries. Their network analysis showed that translation flows are not random but closely aligned with colonial legacies, economic ties, and regional communication needs. Languages like English, French, and Spanish emerged as global pivots.

Other researchers have expanded this perspective using demographic or media-based data. Gurevich et al. [4] introduced a cross-country language connectivity index based on shared official and spoken languages. Their findings revealed clusters of countries aligned along linguistic families and colonial histories. Similarly, Dueñas and Mandel [2] found that even the spread of YouTube music videos follows linguistic and regional pathways, suggesting that language remains a key conduit of cultural diffusion–even in globally accessible media.

This cultural clustering effect is also visible in the flow of misinformation. Quelle et al. [7] found that most false claims stay confined within a single language cluster and rarely cross into linguistically distant groups. Even when content spreads globally, it often does so along linguistic and historical lines.

These studies frequently rely on clustering methods such as the Louvain algorithm [1] to detect community structures within language networks. The availability of multilingual corpora like OpenSubtitles [9] has made it easier to build large-scale language graphs based on real communication data. Hale [5] further highlighted the multilingual reality of the web, showing that many users access or contribute content across multiple languages, reinforcing the importance of studying interconnected language systems.

While these studies each explore meaningful facets of the global language network, they are typically limited to one platform or dataset–Wikipedia, Google, YouTube, or fact-checking archives. In contrast, our study integrates three complementary datasets–subtitle translations, Wikipedia interlanguage links, and spoken-at-home survey data–to examine whether consistent patterns of linguistic clustering emerge across media, digital, and demographic layers. This triangulated approach offers a more comprehensive view of how language reflects, reinforces, and transcends cultural boundaries.

3 Methodology

3.1 Data Sources

To model multilingual relationships, we draw from three large-scale datasets that capture language interaction across different domains:

1. Movie Subtitles (OpenSubtitles). The OpenSubtitles corpus contains aligned subtitle pairs across 94 languages. We use translation pair counts from the 2024 release, collected via the OPUS API, to build a weighted graph-a network where each connection (edge) between two languages is assigned a numerical value representing the number of translated sentence pairs between them. This dataset captures cultural exchange through media consumption.

Limitations and Biases: The OpenSubtitles dataset reflects the global film and television industry, resulting in overrepresentation of languages with large international media markets-such as English, Spanish, French, and Portuguese-Brazil-and underrepresentation of many minority or regional languages. Subtitle quality varies, with contributions from professionals, amateurs, and machine translations, which may affect the reliability of translation counts. Metadata inconsistencies, missing or duplicate files, and ambiguous language codes can also impact data accuracy. The dataset is skewed toward recent and popular media, with older or niche productions less represented. Edges are weighted by translation volume, which may reflect industry practices or fan activity rather than organic language interaction. For **visualization clarity only**, our network graphs focus on the most connected languages, potentially understating smaller languages in figures, though not in the underlying analysis. All network construction and quantitative analysis use the full, original alignment count data. Thus, our results reflect translation activity present in OpenSubtitles and should be interpreted within the context of media-driven language interaction, not as a complete representation of global linguistic diversity.

2. Wikipedia Interlanguage Links. We extracted interlanguage link data from the top 20 Wikipedia editions by article count, using language edition SQL dumps. Each edge in this network corresponds to a hyperlink from one language's article to its counterpart in another language, capturing cross-lingual knowledge connectivity. The final network is directed-a network where each connection has a direction, indicating a one-way relationship from one language to another-and weighted by link frequency (the number of times articles in one language edition link to another).

Limitations and Biases: The Wikipedia interlanguage link network is shaped by both editorial practices and automated bot activity, leading to overrepresentation of certain language editions (such as Cebuano and Waray) that have high article counts and interlanguage links due to automated content creation, rather than organic community growth. This can inflate connectivity and centrality for those languages, potentially distorting network structure and cluster detection. The network is constructed from the top 20 Wikipedia editions by article count, which means smaller or less active language editions-and thus many minority or under-documented languages-are excluded. Interlanguage links are not always reciprocal, and some editions link out more than they receive, affecting measures like in-degree, out-degree, and PageRank. Edges are weighted by the number of interlanguage links, reflecting editorial and bot activity rather than real-world linguistic or cultural proximity. For **visualization clarity**, network graphs highlight the most connected languages and strongest links, making complex patterns more accessible in large networks. All network construction and quantitative analysis use the full, original interlanguage link data. Results reflect the editorial and digital knowledge connectivity present in Wikipedia and should be interpreted within the context of platform-driven language interaction, not as a complete representation of global linguistic diversity or real-world language use.

3. Spoken-at-Home Languages (World Values Survey). We used Wave 7 of the World Values Survey (WVS), which includes responses from 66 countries. We extracted question Q272: "What language do you normally speak at home?" This data was used to construct a bipartite network-a network with two types of nodes (countries and languages), where edges only connect nodes of different types-with edge weights corresponding to the proportion of respondents per country.

Limitations and Biases: The WVS dataset covers only 66 countries, so many regions and languages-especially indigenous or minority ones-are missing. Some responses are grouped as "Unlisted Language" or "Other," reducing the visibility of linguistic diversity. Sample sizes vary by country, so smaller languages may not appear. The survey asks for the language "normally" spoken at home, which may not reflect all multilingual households. For **visualization clarity only**, we display in our bipartite graph and heatmap only languages spoken by more than 5% of a country's population. This threshold does not affect our data analysis or findings, but simply makes the figures easier to interpret. All network analysis uses the full, original survey data. Thus, our results reflect the surveyed populations and not the entire world. The full list of surveyed countries and reported languages is available in the official World Values Survey Wave 7 codebook and methodology documentation (see Section "Language spoken at home (Q272)" and country/language code lists) [10].

A summary of key dataset limitations is provided in Table 1.

Table 1. Summary of Key Limitations for Each Dataset

Dataset	Main Limitations
OpenSubtitles	Overrepresents major media languages; underrepresents minority/regional languages; variable subtitle quality; metadata inconsistencies; recent/popular media skew; edge weights reflect translation volume, not organic interaction.
Wikipedia Interlanguage Links	Editorial and bot-driven bias; inflated article/link counts for some editions; excludes smaller/minority languages; link asymmetry; edge weights reflect editorial activity, not real-world proximity.
World Values Survey (WVS)	Only 66 countries; many regions/languages missing; "Unlisted Language"/"Other" reduces diversity visibility; sample size variation; self-reporting bias; only home language captured.

3.2 Graph Construction and Analysis

Each dataset was transformed into a weighted network:

- **Subtitle Network:** Undirected graph-a network where connections between languages have no direction, indicating a mutual relationship-where edges are weighted by the number of aligned subtitle translations between them.

- **Wikipedia Network:** Directed graph where nodes are language editions and edges are weighted by the number of interlanguage links.
- **Spoken Language Network:** Bipartite graph (country-language) projected into a co-occurrence language-language graph, where two languages are connected if they are both spoken in the same country, and the edge weight represents how frequently this co-usage occurs. Formally, if in country c the proportions of speakers of languages u and v are $p_{c,u}$ and $p_{c,v}$, then the projected $u-v$ edge weight is incremented by $p_{c,u} \times p_{c,v}$.

For instance, in Nigeria 80 % of respondents speak English at home and 20 % speak Yoruba, so our projection algorithm connects English—Yoruba with weight 0.20 for that country. All networks were analyzed using Python's NetworkX and visualized with Matplotlib and Gephi.

3.3 Network Metrics and Community Detection

To analyze language prominence and connectivity, we applied three standard centrality metrics, now defined with full mathematical rigor:

$$\mathrm{WD}(v) = \sum_{u \in N(v)} w_{uv},$$

$$\mathrm{BC}(v) = \sum_{\substack{s,t \in V \\ s \neq v \neq t}} \frac{\sigma_{st}(v)}{\sigma_{st}},$$

$$\mathrm{PR}(v) = \frac{1-d}{N} + d \sum_{u \in N(v)} \frac{\mathrm{PR}(u)}{\deg^{+}(u)},$$

where

- V is the set of all nodes and $N = |V|$ its size,
- w_{uv} is the weight of the edge between u and v,
- σ_{st} is the total number of shortest paths from s to t, and $\sigma_{st}(v)$ the number of those passing through v,
- $\deg^{+}(u)$ denotes the out-degree of u in directed graphs,
- $d = 0.85$ is the standard PageRank damping factor.

- **Weighted Degree (WD):** The total sum of edge-weights incident on node v, measuring how strongly v is connected to all others. English tops the subtitle network with the highest WD, reflecting over 500 million aligned subtitle lines with other languages.
- **Betweenness Centrality (BC):** The fraction of all shortest-path routes between any two nodes that pass through v, capturing how often v acts as a "bridge." Spanish ranks second in BC in the subtitle network, showing it frequently links other language pairs.

- **PageRank (PR):** A random-walk—based score combining the quantity and quality of incoming links, where each neighbor u passes on a fraction $1/\deg^{+}(u)$ of its own PR to v. In the Wikipedia interlanguage graph, English achieves the highest PR score, underlining its role as the primary hub for interlanguage links.

To identify regional or cultural clusters, we applied the Louvain algorithm for community detection-an unsupervised method that groups languages into clusters (communities) so that languages within the same group are more densely connected to each other than to those outside the group. The algorithm seeks to maximize a value called modularity, which quantifies the strength of the division into communities.

4 Results and Analysis

4.1 Limitations and Caveats

Although we triangulate three datasets, each has biases that may shape our findings. OpenSubtitles over-represents blockbuster languages and undercounts oral/minority tongues. Wikipedia interlanguage links are inflated by bot-generated editions (e.g. Cebuano, Waray) and exclude low-activity languages. The WVS survey covers only 66 countries, omitting many regions and capturing only primary home languages. These biases likely amplify global hubs (English, French) and understate peripheral or under-documented languages. Moreover, because the WVS covers only 66 countries and OpenSubtitles relies on media from major film-producing regions, entire regions (e.g., many Pacific Island nations, some sub-Saharan countries) are omitted, which could skew cluster detection away from those linguistic groups.

Having defined our metrics and methods, we first examine media-driven interactions via the OpenSubtitles corpus.

4.2 Subtitle Translation Network (OpenSubtitles)

To assess whether decentralized networks capture cultural proximity, we begin with subtitle translations. The subtitle translation network (Fig. 1) exhibits a heavy-tailed distribution: most language pairs exchange under 500 K lines, but the top corridors exceed 80 M lines. The median alignment count is 140 K lines, whereas the mean is 6.1 M—reflecting a few extremely high-volume pairs (Table 2).

Table 2 shows that English—Portuguese (Brazil) leads with 115 M lines, followed by English—Spanish (105 M) and English—Romanian (100 M). Figure 2 then maps these volumes onto a network: English sits at the center, connecting strongly to all major languages.

Applying Louvain clustering (Figs. 4a, 4b and 4c) reveals three robust communities. Cluster 0 (dark blue) is a global media core around English and other high-traffic languages (historical: colonialism; economic: global trade). Cluster 1 (light blue) groups Western and Slavic European languages (EU ties; commerce). Cluster 2 (orange) contains Scandinavian languages, reflecting deep historical and political bonds.

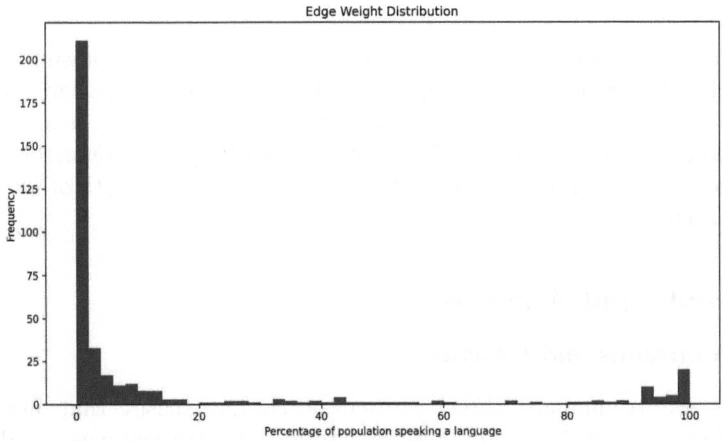

Fig. 1. Edge weight distribution (log scale). A few translation pairs dominate the network, showing a heavy-tailed distribution.

Figure 1 illustrates a strongly right-skewed distribution. Most translation pairs have low volumes, while a small number exchange extremely high volumes. The median line count per language pair is approximately 140,000, but the mean exceeds 6 million due to a handful of very strong links. Only a small subset of edges surpasses 10 million lines, forming the network's long tail. This distribution is visualized in Fig. 1.

Table 2. Top 5 Subtitle Translation Pair Volumes (in millions of lines)

Language Pair	Lines (M)
English–Portuguese (Brazil)	115
English–Spanish	105
English–Romanian	100
English–Arabic	88
English–French	84

As shown in Fig. 2, English functions as the central hub, connected to nearly all major languages (Table 3).

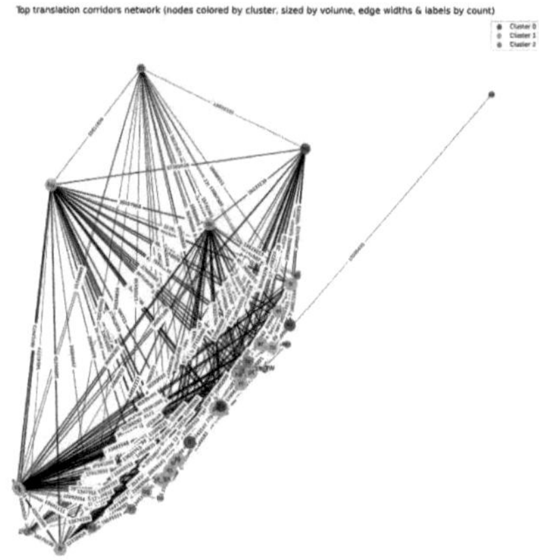

Fig. 2. Top translation corridors in the subtitle network. Nodes are sized by weighted degree and colored by Louvain cluster. Edges are weighted by subtitle alignment volume.

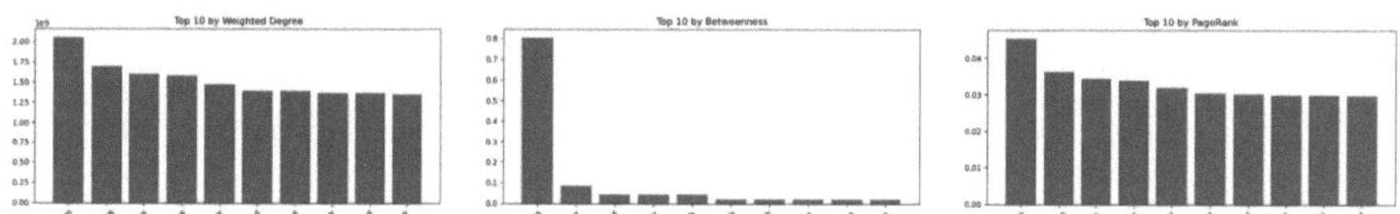

(a) Weighted Degree (b) Betweenness (c) PageRank

Fig. 3. Top 10 languages ranked by centrality metrics.

Figure 3 summarizes key centrality metrics. English scores highest in all three—PageRank, betweenness, and weighted degree—reinforcing its role as a translation bridge. Portuguese (Brazil) and Romanian also exhibit surprisingly high centrality, likely due to regional subtitling practices and the influence of diaspora communities.

The clustering structure is further illustrated in Figs. 4a–4c

- **Cluster 0 (dark blue):** A global cluster centered on English and other high-traffic languages. *Historical ties: colonialism; economic ties: global trade; cultural ties: media distribution (e.g., Hollywood).*
- **Cluster 1 (light blue):** Western and Slavic European languages with strong mutual connections. *Political ties: EU membership; economic ties: European commerce.*

Table 3. Top 10 Languages by Centrality Metrics

Language	Weighted Degree Rank	Betweenness Rank	PageRank Rank
English	1	1	1
Portuguese (BR)	2	3	4
Romanian	3	5	7
Spanish	4	2	2
Arabic	5	4	5
French	6	6	3
German	7	9	6
Russian	8	7	8
Hindi	9	8	9
Mandarin Chinese	10	10	10

- **Cluster 2 (orange):** Scandinavian languages with dense internal connections. *Political legacy: Union of Kalmar; modern institutions: Nordic Council.*

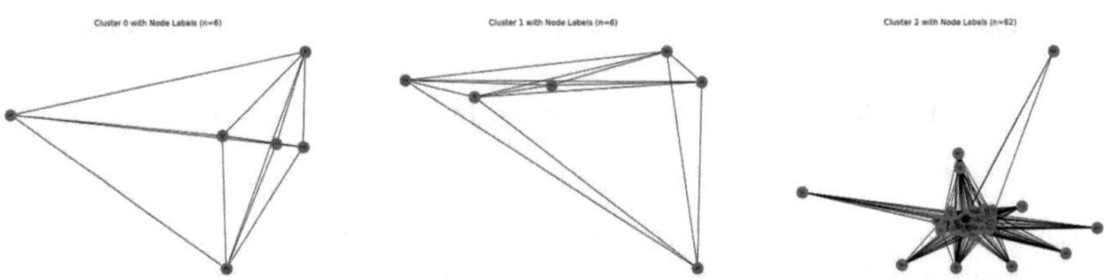

(a) High-traffic global languages (b) Western and Slavic European languages (c) Scandinavian languages

Fig. 4. Louvain clusters in the subtitle network.

These results confirm that multilingual networks are structured by cultural, political, and economic histories. Despite English's global dominance, regionally coherent clusters persist—suggesting that network-based language modeling can reveal both global centrality and localized cohesion.

We then shift to digital knowledge networks by analyzing Wikipedia interlanguage links.

4.3 Wikipedia Interlanguage Link Network

To test if editorial link patterns echo the same clusters, we next analyze interlanguage links. The Wikipedia interlanguage network models how knowledge is shared across language editions. In this directed, weighted graph, nodes represent Wikipedia language editions, and an edge from language A to B indicates the number of articles in A that link to their equivalents in B.

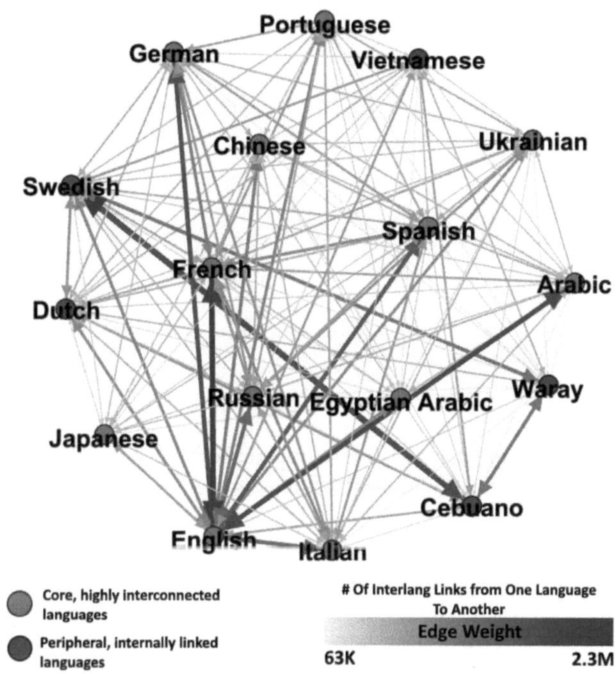

Fig. 5. Wikipedia interlanguage network. Node size corresponds to in-degree; edge thickness indicates link volume. Node color shows Louvain cluster.

Figure 5 shows that English is the largest and most linked language edition, receiving links from nearly all other editions. This reflects its role as a central source of knowledge on the platform. French, Spanish, and German also appear as strong hubs with high mutual link exchange.

The resulting language co-occurrence network is visualized in Fig. 9. Louvain clustering reveals several distinct communities:

- A **core global cluster** (green) includes English, French, Spanish, German, and Russian—well-developed editions with many mutual links.
- A **peripheral cluster** (purple) includes languages like Cebuano, Waray, and Dutch. These editions are inflated by automated article creation (e.g., bots), which increases article count but not mutual connectivity.

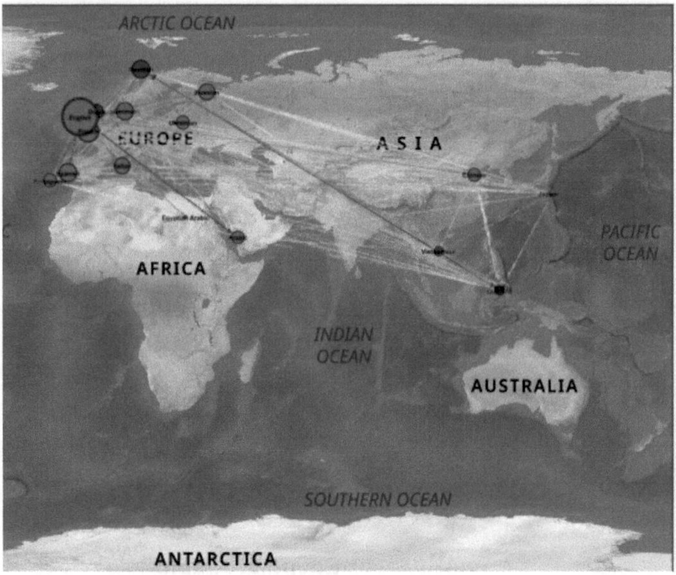

Fig. 6. Wikipedia interlanguage network mapped geographically. Stronger links appear between culturally or regionally aligned languages.

In Fig. 6, when the same network is geographically overlaid, regional proximities align with higher interlanguage connectivity. For instance, strong linkages are visible between Spanish, Portuguese, and Catalan; and between Germanic languages such as German, Dutch, and Swedish.

These patterns reflect not only linguistic similarity but also political and historical relationships. For example, English and French both act as hubs for many African and Southeast Asian language editions due to colonial history and institutional partnerships.

Compared to the subtitle network, the Wikipedia network reflects more editorial and infrastructural asymmetries. Bot-driven editions distort standard network measures like degree and clustering. Nevertheless, community detection still reveals cultural blocks shaped by both language family and content strategy.

This network reinforces the observation that global language systems are not strictly hierarchical. While English remains central, the presence of mutually reinforcing regional hubs illustrates the decentralized structure of digital knowledge production.

Finally, we ground our study in real-world usage by projecting spoken-at-home survey responses into a language co-occurrence network.

4.4 Spoken Language Network (World Values Survey)

To see if everyday speech aligns with these patterns, we then project survey data into a co-occurrence graph. The spoken language network constructed from the

World Values Survey (WVS) captures ground-level linguistic distributions across 66 countries. Each respondent answered question Q272, 'What language do you usually speak at home?', offering a direct insight into the use of the household language, regardless of media exposure or institutional status.

A bipartite network was built connecting countries to languages, with edge weights corresponding to the percentage of survey respondents who reported speaking a particular language. For readability, Fig. 7 filters out edges where fewer than 5% of a country's population speaks a language.

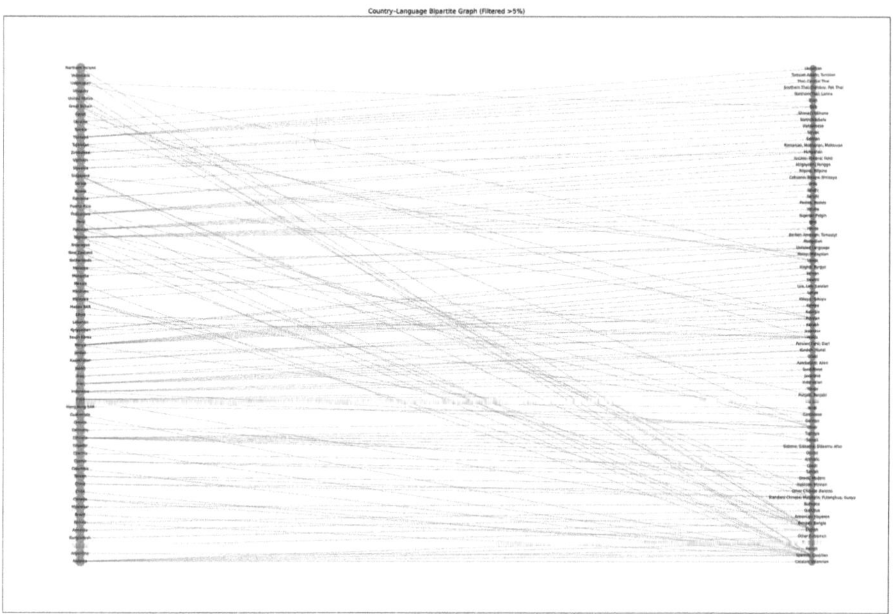

Fig. 7. Country–Language Bipartite Graph (filtered for usage > 5%). Countries are shown in blue, languages in orange. (Color figure online)

As shown in Fig. 7, many countries link to a single language, such as Bengali in Bangladesh or Arabic in Egypt, indicating national linguistic homogeneity. In contrast, countries such as India, Nigeria, and the Philippines link to multiple languages, revealing rich internal linguistic diversity and multilingualism shaped by colonial history, ethnicity, and migration.

To further analyze language prominence, we visualized the edge weight distribution (Fig. 8). The histogram shows how frequently different language percentages appear across countries. The distribution is heavily right-skewed: while a few country–language pairs reach 100% usage, the majority fall below 10%, representing minority or regional languages.

We then projected the bipartite network into a language–language graph. Two languages are connected if they co-occur in the same country, with edge

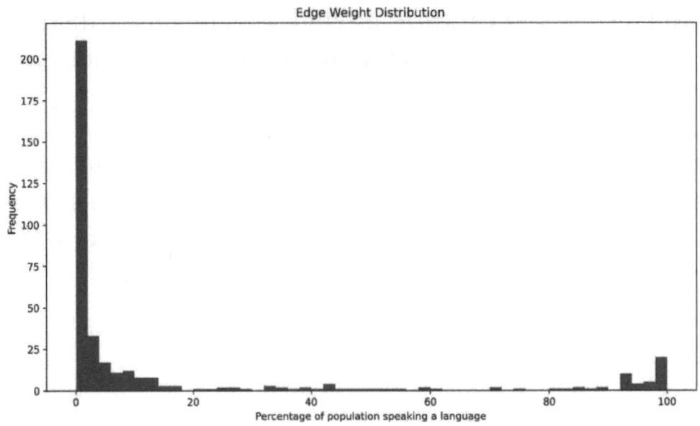

Fig. 8. Edge Weight Distribution: Percent of population speaking a language in each country. Most connections represent small language populations.

weights proportional to shared speaker populations. Louvain community detection was applied to reveal network communities (Fig. 9).

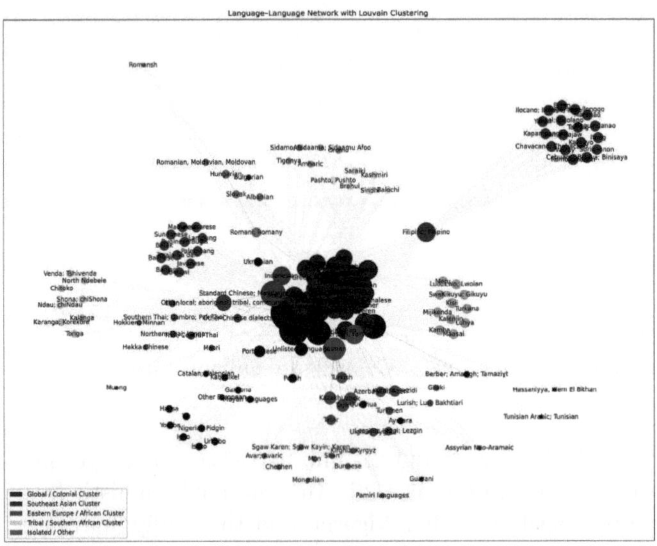

Fig. 9. Language–Language Network with Louvain Clustering. Node size indicates weighted degree; node color shows cluster membership.

The Louvain algorithm revealed distinct language clusters:

- **Global / Colonial Cluster (purple)**: Includes English, Arabic, French, Urdu, and Hindi—languages spread through colonization, migration, and trade.

- **Southeast Asian Cluster (blue)**: Javanese, Cebuano, Tagalog, and other languages from Indonesia and the Philippines.
- **Eastern European / African Cluster (green)**: Russian, Slovak, Ukrainian, Swahili, Luo—languages tied through regional or political alignment.
- **Tribal / Southern African Cluster (yellow)**: Tshivenda, Tonga, Shona, Chitoko—indigenous African languages with strong national ties.
- **Isolated / Other (gray)**: Peripheral or low-co-occurrence languages, such as Romansh or Assyrian Neo-Aramaic.

At the center of the network lies a dense cluster of globally spoken languages, with English as the most prominent hub. It connects directly to Spanish, Arabic, Hindi, and Mandarin, underscoring its bridging role across diverse language groups. Surrounding this core are several regional clusters: a Romance group (French, Spanish, Portuguese, Italian), a Slavic cluster (Russian, Ukrainian), and a Southeast Asian cluster (Tagalog, Cebuano, Filipino).

Central Asian languages such as Kazakh, Uzbek, and Kurdish also group together, reflecting geographic and cultural proximity. Interestingly, Bulgarian appears close to Slovak and Hungarian geographically but is structurally clustered with Russian and Romanian due to stronger co-use patterns. Arabic appears within the European cluster-likely influenced by modern migration trends that have increased Arabic usage in Europe.

Smaller, less globally dominant languages are still represented. Some link to regional hubs, while others connect directly to English, highlighting the diverse and interconnected nature of home language usage.

To visualize the intensity of language use, we constructed a heatmap of the top 30 global languages across all countries (Fig. 10).

This heatmap reveals clear national dominances: Spanish across Latin America, Arabic in North Africa and the Middle East, and English's scattered presence across regions. Countries like India and South Africa display multiple active languages, confirming multilingual realities observed in the bipartite structure.

Overall, the spoken language network reveals both expected and surprising connections between languages, shaped by population distribution, history, and migration. The structure complements findings from other networks and underscores the value of network analysis in modeling real-world linguistic diversity.

4.5 Cross-Network Synthesis and Cultural Patterns

Across all three networks—subtitles, Wikipedia links, and spoken-at-home data—we observe a consistent tendency for languages to cluster according to historical, cultural, and geopolitical factors. These clusters are not artifacts of any one medium or dataset, but appear repeatedly in different linguistic contexts: mass media, digital encyclopedias, and everyday communication.

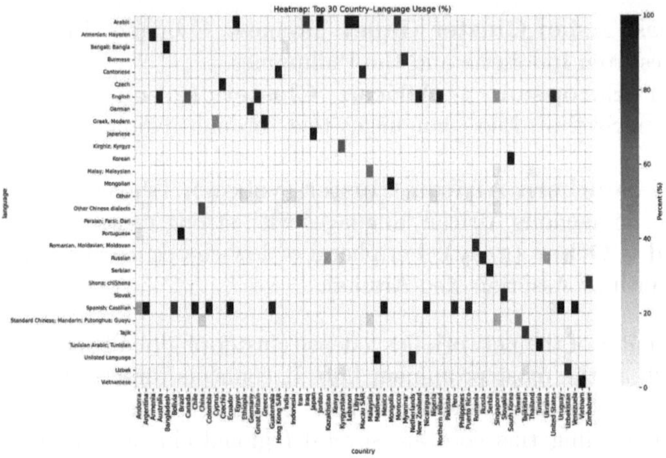

Fig. 10. Heatmap: Top 30 Spoken Languages Across Countries (WVS Q272). Darker shades represent higher usage percentages.

English. consistently emerges as the most central node across all networks, acting as a global linguistic bridge. However, its dominance is not uniform. In the spoken-at-home network, for example, English often shares space with regional languages, suggesting that cultural presence does not always translate into grassroots usage.

Regional Clusters. also reappear across all layers:

- A *Scandinavian cluster* (e.g., Swedish, Danish, Norwegian) is tightly connected in subtitles and Wikipedia, reflecting historical and political cooperation.
- *Western European and Slavic languages* form overlapping communities, often shaped by EU membership, cross-border media, and educational exchange.
- A *global colonial cluster* includes English, French, Arabic, and Portuguese, often reflecting former empire languages used for administration, trade, or migration.

Interestingly, some languages exhibit strong centrality in one network but not others. For instance, Romanian has high translation volume in the subtitle network but plays a less prominent role in Wikipedia or WVS data. This highlights how platform-specific dynamics—such as media subtitling norms—can shape network topology.

Overall, the convergence of structure across these independent networks suggests that language relationships are deeply embedded in global cultural systems. A network-based model not only captures central hubs but also reveals enduring regional cohesion. Our findings underscore the value of triangulating diverse datasets to reveal the multi-layered geography of global language interaction.

5 Discussion

Our three-layered analysis shows both convergence and divergence across media, editorial, and self-report networks. English remains the dominant hub everywhere, but platform idiosyncrasies matter: Romanian ranks highly in subtitles (due to strong fan-sub communities) but not in Wikipedia or WVS. Likewise, bot-inflated Wikipedias form their own cluster that disappears in survey data. This suggests that real-world language proximity is best captured by combining data sources: a single network risks over- or under-emphasizing certain languages.

For application in multilingual AI or cultural policy, our results highlight the need to weight data sources appropriately or to develop ensemble network models that correct for each platform's bias.

6 Conclusion and Future Work

This study introduced a multi-layered approach to analyzing global language relationships through the lens of network science. By constructing and comparing language networks derived from subtitle translations, Wikipedia interlanguage links, and spoken-at-home data, we identified consistent patterns of cultural clustering, regional cohesion, and linguistic centrality.

Across all datasets, English consistently emerged as a global bridge language, while other colonial or regionally dominant languages-such as Spanish, Arabic, French, and Portuguese-formed secondary hubs. Importantly, community detection revealed recurring clusters that reflect historical, political, and cultural alignments, such as Scandinavian cooperation, post-colonial linguistic blocs, and multilingual cross-border regions in Europe and Asia.

Our results demonstrate that a single "universal language" cannot fully capture the diversity of global linguistic systems. Instead, multilingual network models better reflect how languages function in parallel-shaping, preserving, and transmitting culture across digital, institutional, and everyday contexts.

Looking ahead, there are several directions that future research could explore. One avenue is to incorporate additional platforms such as social media (e.g., Twitter, Reddit, YouTube) or multilingual news corpora to observe how real-time language interaction differs from formal content like Wikipedia or survey responses. Another extension could focus on temporal dynamics-measuring how language clusters evolve over time in response to geopolitical change, migration, or digital media trends. Future work could incorporate additional platforms (social media, news corpora) and explore temporal dynamics to broaden our view of multilingual interaction.

Finally, this type of cross-network linguistic modeling could inform the development of more equitable and culturally aware multilingual AI systems, including translation tools, voice interfaces, and search algorithms. As global communication continues to grow, so does the need for computational methods that reflect not just linguistic frequency, but linguistic context, history, and cultural proximity (Table 4).

Table 4. Summary of Author Contributions

Name	Contributions
Fozhan Babaeiyan Ghamsari	Co-first author; full data collection, analysis, and visualization of OpenSubtitles translation data; supported full paper development; poster construction; prepared and delivered the conference presentation.
Anh Le	Co-first author; full analysis of spoken-at-home language data (processing, visualization, interpretation); led and finalized manuscript revisions based on peer review, addressing limitations, bias, and clarifying metrics across all three datasets.
Claudia Rawson	Pre-paper development support; early project framing and identification of datasets for spoken-at-home analysis.
Lesly Castellanos Ibanez	Pre-paper development support; assisted OpenSubtitles dataset analysis; researched cultural and political factors for cluster interpretation.
Salvador Sandoval	Pre-paper development support; led Wikipedia data collection, analysis, and data visualization.
Richie Prak	Pre-paper development support; assisted Wikipedia data collection and analysis.
Oscar Morales Ponce	Supervised the project; provided guidance throughout all stages; reviewed manuscript drafts and revisions.

References

1. Blondel, V.D., Guillaume, J.L., Lambiotte, R., Lefebvre, E.: Fast unfolding of communities in large networks. J. Stat. Mech: Theory Exp. **2008**(10), P10008 (2008)
2. Dueñas, M., Mandel, A.: The structure of global cultural networks: evidence from the diffusion of music videos. PLoS ONE **18**(11), e0294149 (2023)
3. Esmaeilialiabadi, D., Avşar, B., Yousefnezhad, R., Aliabadi, E.E.: Investigating global language networks using google search queries. Expert Syst. Appl. **121**, 66–77 (2019)
4. Gurevich, T., Herman, P.R., Toubal, F., et al.: A dataset on linguistic connectivity across and within countries. Sci. Data **12**, 542 (2025)
5. Hale, S.A.: Global connectivity and multilinguals on the web. Inf. Commun. Soc. **17**(4), 405–421 (2014)
6. Johansson, S., Lindberg, Y.: Wikipedia as a virtual learning site and a multilingual language site. In: Ahlqvist, S., Olsson, M. (eds.) Virtual Sites as Learning Spaces, pp. 181–204. Springer, Cham (2019). https://www.diva-portal.org/smash/get/diva2:1426913/FULLTEXT01.pdf
7. Quelle, D., Cheng, C.Y., Bovet, A., et al.: Lost in translation: using global fact-checks to measure multilingual misinformation prevalence, spread, and evolution. EPJ Data Sci. **14**(22) (2025)

8. Ronen, S., Gonçalves, B., Hu, K.Z., Vespignani, A., Pinker, S., Hidalgo, C.A.: Links that speak: The global language network and its association with global fame. In: Proceedings of the National Academy of Sciences. vol. 111, pp. E5616–E5622. National Academy of Sciences (2014)
9. Tiedemann, J.: Parallel data, tools and interfaces in opus. Proceedings of LREC, pp. 2214–2218 (2012)
10. World Values Survey Association: World Values Survey Wave 7 (2017–2022): Codebook and Methodology (2022). Available at: https://www.worldvaluessurvey.org/WVSDocumentationWV7.jsp

Artificial Intelligence Applications in Software Development: A Bibliometric Approach

Syn Nguyen(✉) and Manohar Valabi

Department of Computer Engineering and Computer Science,
California State University, Long Beach, Long Beach, USA
{Syn.Nguyen01,Manohar.Vallabi01}@student.csulb.edu

Abstract. This study presents a bibliometric analysis of Artificial Intelligence (AI) applications in software development, focusing on literature published from 2014 to 2025. Drawing on data from Scopus and Web of Science, we use quantitative citation analysis and network visualization (via VOSviewer) to identify research trends, influential contributors, and thematic clusters in the field. Five major research themes emerge—ranging from machine learning in the software development life cycle to large language models (LLMs) in agile frameworks and convolutional neural networks (CNNs) for software testing. Results show a marked increase in AI-related publications after 2018, with strong academic interest in automation, defect prediction, and process optimization. Despite this momentum, persistent challenges remain in areas such as model interpretability, data bias, and integration into existing development workflows. We highlight research gaps and propose future directions, including the need for standardized AI integration frameworks and qualitative assessments of tool adoption in real-world settings. This analysis provides a structured foundation for future research on the evolving role of AI in software engineering.

1 Introduction

Artificial Intelligence has become an integral component of modern software engineering, fundamentally transforming how software is designed, developed, and maintained. Incorporating AI techniques into software process models—structured frameworks that guide development phases such as requirements engineering, coding, testing, and maintenance—has enabled notable improvements in automation, optimization, and decision-making [1,2]. Techniques such as machine learning, deep learning, and large language models are increasingly used in software testing, defect prediction, and agile project management, reshaping conventional development workflows [2].

Although prior reviews have examined AI's role in software engineering broadly [1,2], few have focused specifically on how AI integrates into software process models. Moreover, most existing bibliometric studies have relied solely

S. Hussain et al. (Eds.): SEET 2025, CCIS 2725, pp. 716–732, 2026.
https://doi.org/10.1007/978-3-032-08977-9_47

on citation metrics, often overlooking network-based insights such as keyword co-occurrence, thematic clustering, and research collaboration patterns [3,4]. As a result, there is a lack of structured, quantitative understanding of how research in this domain has evolved, which areas are receiving the most attention, and what challenges remain unresolved.

To address this gap, the present study conducts a bibliometric analysis of AI applications in software development, with a focus on integration within software process models. Drawing from two major academic databases—Scopus and Web of Science—we analyze publications from 2014 to 2025 using both citation analysis and network visualization techniques [5,6]. This dual approach allows us to identify key research trends, map collaborations, and extract thematic clusters from keyword co-occurrences. Our objectives are fourfold:

1. Identify key research trends in AI-driven software process models.
2. Map research collaborations and highlight influential authors and publications.
3. Analyze thematic clusters in AI applications for software development.
4. Highlight persistent challenges, including issues of model interpretability, scalability, and ethical considerations [7].

By situating AI within the structured context of software engineering workflows, this study offers a comprehensive overview of the field's evolution. It contributes both a quantitative landscape of scholarly activity and a roadmap for future research, aiming to support informed progress in the integration of AI into real-world software engineering practices.

The remainder of this paper is structured as follows: Sect. 2 details the data collection process while Sect. 3 highlights the bibliometric methodology. Section 4 presents the quantitative findings, while Sect. 5 explores network analysis results. Section 6 discusses key insights, implications, and limitations. Finally, Sect. 7 concludes the study and suggests future research directions.

2 Data Collection

This study conducted a bibliometric analysis using two major academic databases: Scopus and Web of Science. Web of Science is widely recognized for its comprehensive coverage of STEM disciplines [6], making it a solid foundation for analyzing trends in artificial intelligence and software process models. Scopus, with its broad indexing of peer-reviewed literature and the largest database of abstracts [9], complements Web of Science by offering a balanced view across subject areas. Together, these databases provide a robust basis for an in-depth examination of the challenges and developments in AI-integrated software process models.

The query construction for this article involved the following steps:

1. **Initial Search**: Searched in Scopus and Web of Science, with AI-discipline terms (machine learning, AI system, neural network) in the titles, abstracts, and keywords.

2. **Boolean Filtering**: Used the "AND" operator to combine AI terms with software process terms (e.g., software process model, software development life cycle, agile development).
3. **Challenge Focus**: Refined the search further using keywords such as challenges, difficulties, and issues.
4. **Time Frame**: Restricted results to publications from 2014 to 2025.
5. **Document Type and Language**: Excluded book chapters and non-English works, retaining only peer-reviewed journal articles in English.

The complete filtering process is illustrated in the figure below Fig. 1.

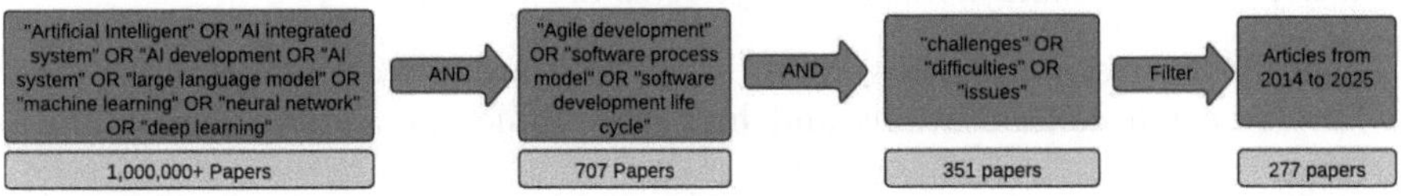

Fig. 1. Articles Filtering Process.

3 Bibliometric Approach

Bibliometric analysis is a powerful method for quantitatively assessing the structure and evolution of a research field. As defined by Donthu et al. (2021, as cited in [3]), it evaluates key scientific indicators such as citations, co-citations, publication trends, author productivity, and journal impact across disciplines. This approach enables a comprehensive view of how interest and activity in a particular area develop over time.

In the context of this study, an initial keyword search for "artificial intelligence" yielded over 500,000 results in Scopus and over 80,000 in Web of Science. Similarly, "software process model" produced tens of thousands of results, reinforcing the significance and timeliness of this intersection. Bibliometric analysis proves particularly effective for investigating such rapidly evolving domains, where traditional content analysis would struggle to scale [4].

To capture both breadth and depth, we adopt the framework proposed by Ozturk et al. (2024), which integrates both quantitative citation analysis and network-based coupling analysis. This dual approach enables the identification of research impact and scholarly influence, while also uncovering relationships among publications, concepts, and research clusters. In doing so, we provide a richer, multi-dimensional view of how artificial intelligence is shaping software development practices [3,4]

Quantitative Analysis. Quantitative analysis in bibliometric research focuses on measuring key scientific outputs, including publications, authorship, and journal influence. This approach helps evaluate the scope, impact, and relevance of research trends over time [3,4]. In this study, we first examine the distribution of publications related to AI-system challenges from 2014 to 2025 to understand the field's evolution.

Following the methodology of Fahimnia et al. (2015) [8] (as cited by [4]), we incorporate additional metrics such as total citation counts and publication frequency to assess scholarly impact. As [9] notes, citation counts serve not only as indicators of a paper's influence but also as a form of academic validation. For this analysis, citation data was collected exclusively from Scopus and Web of Science.

To process and analyze the raw bibliometric data, we utilized BibExcel. This software extracts and organizes information related to citations, co-citations, and co-authorship. BibExcel also supports compatibility with visualization tools such as Gephi and VOSviewer, enabling effective representation of bibliometric networks [4]. Additionally, Canva and Lucidchart were used to design supplementary figures and diagrams to enhance visual clarity and understanding.

Network Analysis. While quantitative analysis measures the impact and relevance of publications and authors, network analysis uncovers the relationships among them by visualizing patterns of co-authorship, keyword co-occurrence, and citation linkages [3,10]. In this study, we applied network analysis to examine how keywords cluster across AI-related software development literature and to better understand the interconnections between topics, authors, and research themes.

We focused on keyword co-occurrence analysis, which groups frequently co-occurring terms into clusters. Each cluster reflects a thematic area within the field, with the size of the cluster indicating its relative prominence. This method is especially valuable in identifying shared concepts and overlapping challenges in AI system development. We also analyzed co-citation patterns to explore how often certain publications are cited together, revealing topic similarity and academic influence across studies [3,10].

To perform this analysis, we used VOSviewer—an established tool developed by Nees Jan van Eck and Ludo Waltman—for constructing and visualizing bibliometric maps. VOSviewer supports the generation of keyword clusters and co-citation networks, making it ideal for uncovering structural relationships in large datasets [6]. We combined cleaned datasets from Scopus and Web of Science and generated networks from the text-based metadata. The resulting keyword co-occurrence network is presented in Fig. 5, and the overall process is illustrated in Fig. 2.

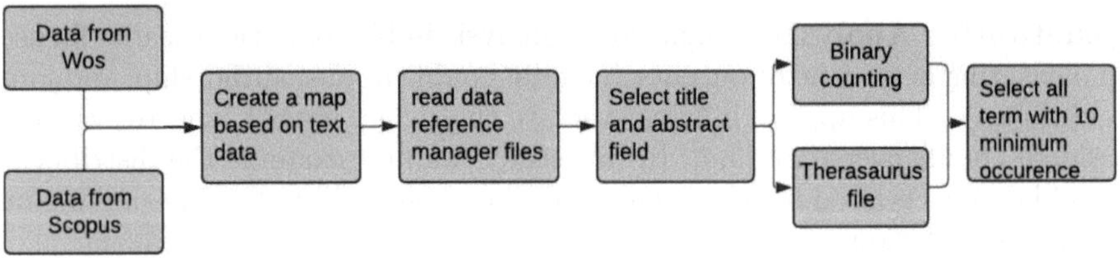

Fig. 2. Visualizing Word Occurrence Network Process.

4 Quantitative Analysis Results

A total of 277 relevant articles were analyzed, revealing a clear upward trend in research focused on AI in software process models and their associated challenges. As shown in Fig. 3. The earliest publications in this domain appeared in 2014, with just four articles. These initial works focused on 3 topics such as agile software development, model-driven engineering, and cyber defenses. In the context of agile practices, early limitations were primarily organizational—centered around communication and collaboration barriers—which hindered widespread adoption [11,12].

Since 2018, the number of publications has risen sharply, reflecting growing academic and industrial interest in the integration of AI within software engineering workflows. Notably, 2024 saw a publication volume nearly double that of the previous year and over 19 times greater than that of 2014.

Figure 4 highlights the top 10 most cited articles in this field, each of which applies AI techniques—such as machine learning, deep learning, or reinforcement learning—to domain-specific challenges. These include optimizing solid waste management systems [13], analog and mixed-signal circuits design [14], and enhancing agile development of network services [15], etc. These highly cited studies also address critical aspects of the software lifecycle, such as testing, maintainability, and performance optimization.

Table 1 presents the journals and conferences with the highest number of publications in the field of AI-integrated software development. Collectively, these venues account for just over 11% of all articles reviewed. The journal with the highest contribution is Lecture Notes in Networks and Systems with 11 publications, followed by Lecture Notes in Computer Science (including subseries in AI and Bioinformatics) with 7 publications. Conferences such as the International Conference on Software Engineering, Communications in Computer and Information Science, and the ACM International Conference Proceeding Series each contributed 5 papers.

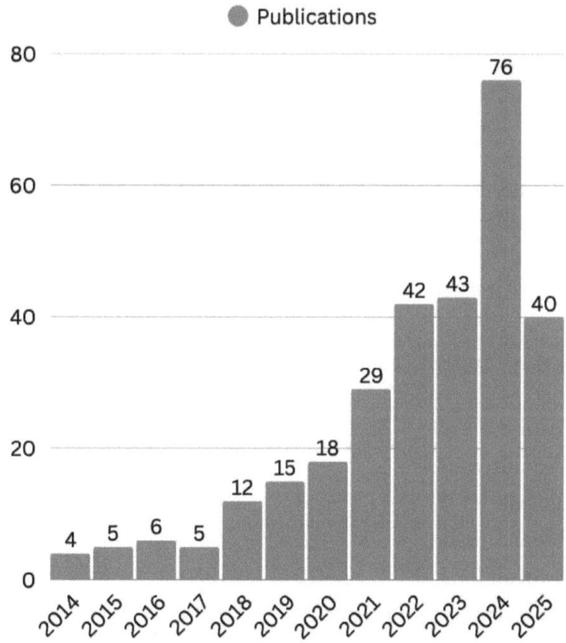

Fig. 3. Publications over time highlighting challenges in AI-based system.

While some of these venues, particularly the Lecture Notes series, are categorized as conference proceedings, they are peer-reviewed and indexed in Scopus and Web of Science, and are widely used in technical domains for disseminating emerging research.

Table 1. Most active journals and conference in AI-based system.

Journals	Count
Lecture Notes In Networks And Systems	11
Lecture Notes In Computer Science Including Subseries Lecture Notes In Artificial Intelligence And Lecture Notes In Bioinformatics	7
Proceedings International Conference on Software Engineering	5
Communications In Computer And Information Science	5
ACM International Conference Proceeding Series	5

Table 2 highlights the most prolific and highly cited authors in the domain. Authors are ranked by the number of publications, with Malhotra, R. leading with 4 articles focused on software development life cycles and AI integration. Bansal, C. follows with 3 publications, while the remaining listed scholars each contributed 2 publications. Notably, over 190 authors in the dataset have contributed just one paper.

The table also reflects the citation impact of each author. Abrahamsson, P. stands out with over 4,600 citations in areas related to AI and software engineering. Diez, Isabel De la Torre, with 4,326 citations, focuses on health informatics and computer science. Malhotra, R. (2,211 citations) and Awotunde, J.B. (1,618 citations) have significantly contributed to defect prediction, neural networks, and AI-based software solutions. Collectively, these authors represent key contributors to the advancement of AI in the software development field.

Table 2. Publications per Author and Author's Citation

Author	Count	Cited by Publication
Malholtra, R.	4	2,211
Bansal, C.	3	436
Abrahamsson, P.	2	4,696
Awotunde, J.B.	2	1,618
Diez, Isabel De la Torre	2	4,326
Zakeri-Nasrabadi, M.	2	97
Vakkuri, V.	2	204
Shetty, M.	2	38
Rao, N.	2	65
Ragone, A.	2	839

Table 3 presents the top countries contributing to AI-integrated software development research. Collectively, the top 10 countries account for approximately 74% of all publications. India leads with 53 articles, followed by the United States (39), China (29), and Germany (15). Other contributors include Spain, Canada, Australia, Malaysia, Brazil, and Turkey.

Notably, some institutions and corporations emerged as particularly active in the field. Delhi Technological University (India), Microsoft Corporation, and Cisco Systems (United States) were among the most prolific contributors. These organizations have supported foundational and applied research across multiple AI application domains.

Table 3. Publication per Country

Country	Count
India	53
United States	39
China	29
Germany	15
Spain	10
Canada	9
Australia	9
Malaysia	7
Brazil	6
Turkey	5

Figure 4 highlights the top 10 most cited articles in the dataset, showcasing their influence on the field. The most cited work is by Abdallah et al. (2020), with 194 citations, which explores the application of AI in improving solid waste management. Settaluri et al. (2020) follows with 119 citations for their work on AutoCkt—a machine learning-based framework for optimizing analog and mixed-signal circuit design.

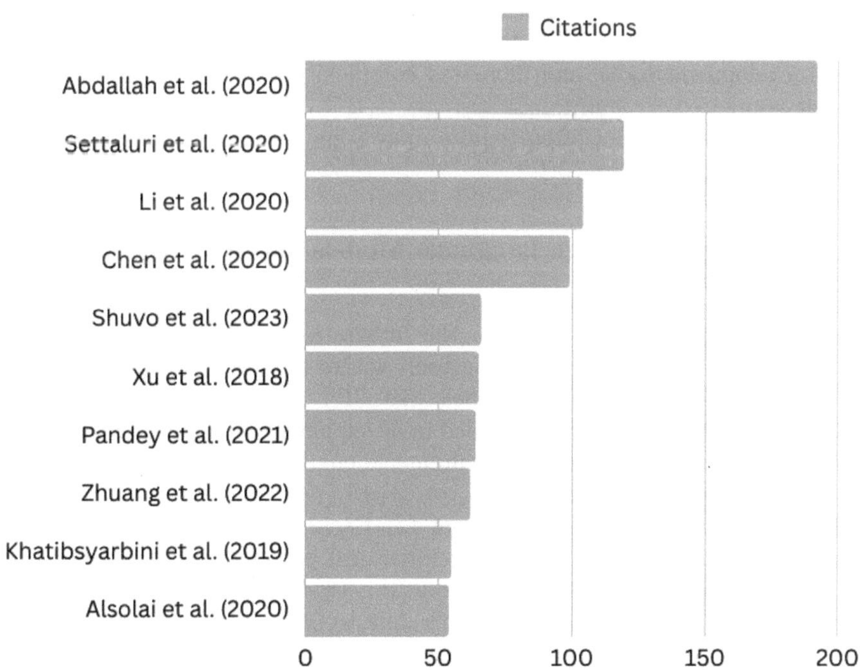

Fig. 4. Top 10 Articles Based on Citation.

These highly cited publications reflect foundational contributions that have informed subsequent research in both applied and theoretical areas of AI-driven software development. Interestingly, half of these top 10 articles were published in 2020, a year that appears to mark a spike in high-impact publications.

5 Network Analysis Results

The keyword co-occurrence network generated using VOSviewer, shown in Fig. 5, revealed five thematic clusters. The red cluster was the most dominant, focusing on machine learning applications in the software development life cycle. Other clusters captured topics such as natural language processing, agile frameworks, software testing, and deep learning. A summary of cluster descriptions and representative keywords is provided in Table 4

5.1 Applied Machine Learning in the Software Development Life Cycle

The red cluster centers on applying machine learning techniques—including support vector machines, decision trees, random forests, and artificial neural networks—to various phases of the software development life cycle. Optimization algorithms such as genetic algorithms and simulated annealing are used for improving defect prediction, while ant colony optimization aids in software requirement selection. Cuckoo search is applied in test case generation [1].

However, challenges remain. Issues like model interpretability, lack of appropriate development tools, and increased complexity make AI integration more difficult compared to traditional systems [1, 17]. These systems can produce unpredictable results and often require more sophisticated validation and testing strategies.

5.2 Integration of Large Language Models and NLP in Software Development

The green cluster Fig. 5 centers on the integration of Large Language Models and Natural Language Processing tools within modern software engineering workflows. With the advent of models like GPT-4, Claude 3, and DeepSeek, LLMs are now being actively embedded in development pipelines—extending far beyond code generation to affect requirements engineering, architectural design, and software quality assurance.

Recent studies highlight the use of LLM)s in two primary areas: design-support tasks—such as generating architectural patterns or microservice recommendations from textual requirements [16]—and vulnerability-aware testing, where models like GPT-4 can generate unit tests that witness security flaws and validate fixes across software versions [17]. LLMs and natural NLPtechniques have also been employed to bridge human and machine language, thereby improving software requirements quality through capabilities such as code clone detection, code completion, generation, and summarization [18,19]. Beyond these use cases, LLMs are now routinely applied in code documentation, architectural reconstruction, and prompt-driven exploration of design trade-offs, signaling their expanding role across multiple stages of the software development lifecycle [17,20].

However, significant challenges remain for developers and researchers when implementing LLMs and NLP techniques in software engineering. One key concern is the introduction of vulnerabilities without clear insight into their type or location, making mitigation difficult [21]. Additionally, biases in the training data and the provenance of that data can undermine the reliability and trustworthiness of both the models and the engineering processes they support [18,19,21]. Beyond these concerns, broader issues persist in the areas of reliability, explainability, and architectural alignment. LLMs may hallucinate architectural recommendations that are not grounded in actual requirements or that violate established design principles [16,20]. Furthermore, their outputs often lack systematic evaluation against non-functional quality attributes such as maintainability, scalability, and modifiability—limiting their applicability in high-assurance or production-level architectural tasks [16].

5.3 Agile Development Frameworks and AI Applications

The blue cluster in the Fig. 5 revolves around utilizing artificial intelligence to enhance agile development, and the challenges of applying such AI applications. Additionally, agile methodologies and frameworks were used to optimize AI systems. Relevant keywords are "agile development", "framework", "development", "methodology", and "architecture".

Researchers have found to be optimizing agile development using machine learning applications. For instance, [22] introduced a novel deep learning model, Long-Deep Recurrent Neural Network (LD-RNN), to optimize the user story point estimation, hence, enhancing the accuracy in agile contexts. Not only that, scholars also utilized a hybrid learning model (HI-HL) with deep belief network (DBN) and artificial neural network (ANN) for software effort, and complexity estimation [23].

Additionally, agile methodologies can be effective when building software and hardware (SW/HW) codesigns ML systems due to the iterative approach and constant feedback loops [24,25]. For instance, [25] customized their own agile methodology, utilizing design space exploration (DSE), and cross-layer optimization specifically for machine learning systems. Ultimately, enhancing the efficiency of neural processing unit (NPU) designs, and improving the reliability and security of the system. Another example would be [26] introduced CFEACT, a coarse-grained reconfigurable arrays (CGRAs) based framework, that enabled agile development for flexibility and iterative approach. Due to that, a twofold improvement in area-delay product for CNN was observed while the performance of the transformer was two times higher.

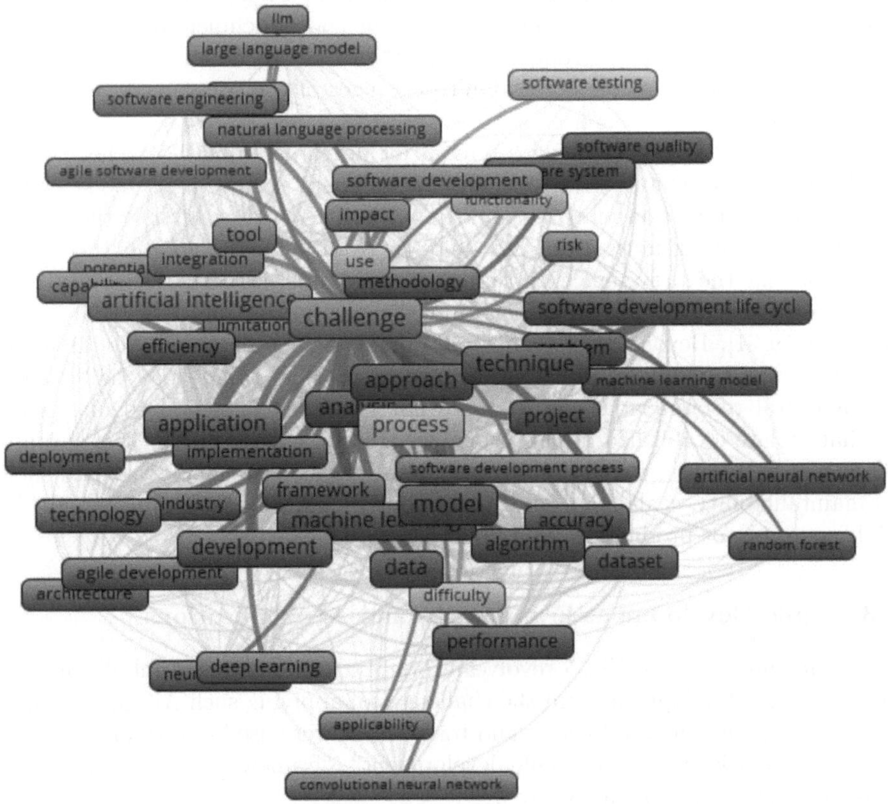

Fig. 5. Keyword occurrence network. (Color figure online)

Table 4. Cluster Descriptions and Keywords.

Red Cluster	Green Cluster	Blue Cluster	Yellow Cluster	Purple Cluster
Applied machine learning in the software development life cycle	The integration of Large language model, and natural language processing in software development	Agile development framework, and methodology in artificial intelligence applications	Software testing process: use, functionality, and difficulties	Deep learning, and convolutional neural network applications in the software development process
Model technique machine learning software development life cycle	Integration natural language processing large language model software development	Agile development framework methodology artificial intelligence	Software testing process use functionality difficulties	Deep learning convolutional neural network applications software development process

5.4 Deep Learning, and CNN in the Software Development

The purple cluster and yellow cluster Fig. 5 focus on utilizing deep learning and CNN to enhance multiple phases of software development life cycle, requirements analysis [2], code analysis, threat detection [27], and testing [28]. The relevant keywords are "deep learning", "convolutional neural network", "software testing", "use", "process" and "software development process".

However, applying deep learning and CNN in the software development process can cause a multitude of challenges. For instance, acquiring a large, and high quality dataset to build an effective deep-learning system can be difficult. Data with high bias can hurt the performance of the model [7,28]. Next, complex computations demand expensive hardware and consume high power. It can also be extremely difficult to interpret the model, making it hard to debug and explain their decisions [7,27,28]. Lastly, there were also the problem of scalability and integration into the existing workflows [7,27].

6 Discussion

6.1 Interpretation of Findings

The results from both the quantitative and network analyses demonstrate a significant rise in scholarly attention to AI's integration within software engineering, particularly after 2018. This surge corresponds with technological advancements in machine learning, deep learning, and large language models, which have transitioned from theoretical interest to practical implementation in various software development stages.

Cluster. Thematic cluster analysis reveals four major research trajectories, each contributing unique but sometimes overlapping insights into how AI is being embedded in the software lifecycle. While these clusters indicate progress, they also expose meaningful research gaps and unresolved tensions in the field.

Applied Machine Learning in Software Development Life Cycle (Red Cluster): This cluster shows the dominance of classical machine learning techniques—support vector machines, decision trees, random forests—in tasks such as defect prediction, testing, and requirement analysis. The widespread application of optimization methods (e.g., genetic algorithms, simulated annealing) signals a push toward automation and predictive accuracy. However, much of this research focuses on algorithmic novelty or benchmark performance, with limited attention to long-term maintainability, tool usability, or integration into actual software pipelines. Moreover, conflicting findings on model interpretability and transferability across domains suggest a need for more robust, generalizable ML pipelines.

Integration of LLMs and NLP in Software Development (Green Cluster): The rise of LLMs and NLP techniques has extended AI support into earlier phases of the software development lifecycle, including requirements translation, code summarization, and automated code generation. These tools promise to enhance developer productivity and reduce the burden of documentation. However, existing studies often neglect—or only superficially address—critical risks such as data bias, model hallucination, and lack of explainability, particularly in safety-critical or regulated environments. Although humanAI collaboration holds significant potential, there remains a scarcity of empirical studies validating LLM outputs in industrial contexts. Future research must investigate trust dynamics, accountability frameworks, and robust evaluation mechanisms to enable safe and effective real-world adoption.

AI Applications in Agile Development (Blue Cluster): This cluster highlights the intersection of AI and agile methodologies, where machine learning models are used to enhance story point estimation, sprint planning, and co-design workflows. These efforts reflect a deeper integration of AI into team-based, iterative development practices. However, the field lacks standardized evaluation criteria for measuring the success of AI-augmented agile workflows. Furthermore, scalability remains an open issue: models trained in controlled environments often struggle when deployed across diverse teams, domains, and project sizes. Research should pivot toward frameworks that support cross-team generalizability and dynamic adaptation of AI tools.

Deep Learning and CNN Applications in the SDLC (Purple & Yellow Clusters): The application of CNN and other deep learning architectures is increasingly prevalent in software quality assurance, anomaly detection, and traceability analysis. These models enable early detection of code defects and vulnerabilities. However, their reliance on large, curated datasets and high compute power raises barriers to accessibility—particularly for small and medium-sized enterprises. Additionally, the opaque nature of deep models presents explainability challenges that hinder their adoption in domains requiring traceable decision-making. Research in this area would benefit from hybrid models combining symbolic reasoning with deep learning to strike a balance between accuracy and interpretability.

Cross-Cluster Observations and Gaps. Although the clusters are distinct, several cross-cutting challenges emerge. First, there is limited research on the socio-technical integration of AI into existing development workflows—how developers actually interact with these tools, what metrics they trust, and what friction points arise. Second, the lack of standardized benchmarks across studies makes it difficult to compare efficacy and generalizability. Third, there is minimal longitudinal evidence on the sustainability and evolution of AI tools once deployed. Most studies stop at proof-of-concept or academic evaluation stages.

6.2 Limitation and Furtherwork

This study offers a comprehensive bibliometric mapping AI's role in software development, but several limitations should be acknowledged. First, the dataset includes only articles indexed in Scopus and Web of Science. Key insights from other repositories such as IEEE Xplore, ACM DL, and arXiv—particularly conference papers and preprints—may have been excluded.

Second, while the network and citation analyses reveal structural patterns, the study does not incorporate performance metrics such as precision, recall, or adoption rates to compare the effectiveness of different AI methods. A future meta-analysis that includes these variables would provide richer quantitative depth. [4].

Third, the absence of practitioner validation limits the study's industrial relevance. Developer surveys, case studies, or interviews could help assess whether the academic trends identified here reflect real-world challenges and tool adoption. Fourth, this analysis concludes in early 2025 and may not fully capture breakthroughs in generative AI tools like GPT-4, Gemini, or Claude 3, which are rapidly influencing development practices.

Finally, the study does not propose a new theoretical framework or taxonomy. However, by identifying and labeling coherent research clusters, it provides a foundation for future conceptual models that explain AI's layered integration across the software lifecycle.

7 Conclusion

This study conducted a comprehensive bibliometric analysis to examine how Artificial Intelligence has been applied within software development processes over the past decade. Focusing specifically on the integration of AI into software process models, we analyzed 253 peer-reviewed publications from 2014 to 2025 sourced from Scopus and Web of Science. By combining quantitative citation metrics with network-based analyses using VOSviewer, we identified dominant research trends, influential contributors, and thematic clusters that define the evolving landscape of AI-enhanced software engineering.

Our findings reveal a significant increase in AI-related research post-2018, with five prominent clusters emerging: applied machine learning in the software development life cycle, natural language processing and large language model integration, AI-supported agile development, software testing and quality assurance, and deep learning techniques such as CNN. These clusters reflect growing interest in AI's role across a broad spectrum of development activities—from automation and estimation to anomaly detection and testing. Notably, we observe that much of this work remains at the academic or proof-of-concept stage, with limited validation in real-world development environments.

Despite the field's rapid expansion, several challenges persist. Issues such as model interpretability, training data quality, computational resource requirements, and tool integration into existing workflows continue to limit the practical adoption of AI in software engineering. Moreover, the lack of standardized benchmarks and evaluation frameworks hinders comparability and generalizability across studies. Our analysis also highlights a scarcity of empirical studies assessing AI's impact on developer productivity, software quality, or organizational outcomes in industrial contexts.

To address these gaps, future research should pursue several directions. First, integrating practitioner feedback through case studies, surveys, or longitudinal field experiments will be essential to validate the utility and adoption of AI tools in real-world settings. Second, the development of standardized frameworks for evaluating AI-assisted methods in software engineering—especially in agile, DevOps, and CI/CD environments—will enable more consistent assessment and benchmarking. Third, combining bibliometric approaches with qualitative and empirical investigations can provide a more nuanced understanding of both the promises and limitations of AI in software practice.

By offering a structured, data-driven overview of how AI is influencing software development research, this study provides a foundational map for scholars and practitioners alike. As the field continues to evolve—particularly with the advent of generative AI and human-AI collaboration—ongoing bibliometric monitoring and critical analysis will be crucial in guiding responsible, effective integration of AI into software engineering.

References

1. Durrani, U.K., et al.: A decade of progress: a systematic literature review on the integration of AI in software engineering phases and activities (2013–2023). IEEE Access **12**, 171185–171204 (2024). https://doi.org/10.1109/ACCESS.2024.3488904
2. Shafiq, S., et al.: A literature review of using machine learning in software development life cycle stages. IEEE Access **9**, 140896–140920 (2021). https://doi.org/10.1109/ACCESS.2021.3119746
3. Ozturk, O., Kocaman, R., Kanbach, D.K.: How to design bibliometric research: an overview and a framework proposal. Rev. Managerial Sci. **18**, 3333–3361 (2024). https://link.springer.com/article/10.1007/s11846-024-00738-0#:~:text=Bibliometric%20analysis%20enables%20having%20a,the%20focus%20of%20the%20field
4. Rejeb, A., Rejeb, K., Simske, S.J., Treiblmaier, H.: Blockchain technologies in logistics and supply chain management: a bibliometric review. Logistics **5**, 72 (2021). https://www.researchgate.net/publication/355195259_Blockchain_Technologies_in_Logistics_and_Supply_Chain_Management_A_Bibliometric_Review/citation/download
5. Viera, E.S., Gomes, J.A.N.F.: A comparison of scopus and web of science for a typical university. Scientometrics **81**, 587–600 (2008). https://doi.org/10.1007/s11192-009-2178-0
6. van Eck, N.J., Waltman, L.: Software survey: vosviewer, a computer program for bibliometric mapping. Scientometrics **84**, 523–538 (2010). https://doi.org/10.1007/s11192-009-0146-3
7. Falcini, F., Lami, G.: Deep learning in automotive: challenges and opportunities. In: Mas, A., Mesquida, A., O'Connor, R.V., Rout, T., Dorling, A. (eds.) SPICE 2017. CCIS, vol. 770, pp. 279–288. Springer, Cham (2017). https://doi.org/10.1007/978-3-319-67383-7_21
8. Fahimnia, B., Sarkis, J., Davarzani, H.: Green supply chain management: a review and bibliometric analysis. Int. J. Prod. Econ. **162**, 101–114 (2015). https://doi.org/10.1016/j.ijpe.2015.01.003

9. Velho, L.: The "meaning" of citation in the context of a scientifically peripheral country. Scientometrics **9**, 71–89 (1986). https://doi.org/10.1007/BF02016609
10. Zupic, I., Cater, T.: Bibliometric methods in management and organization. Organ. Res. Methods **18**, 429–472 (2015). https://journals.sagepub.com/doi/10.1177/1094428114562629
11. Lakshminarayana, K.: Agile methods, organizational culture and agility: some insights. In: Proceedings of the 8th International Workshop on Cooperative and Human Aspects of Software Engineering (CHASE 2014), pp. 40–47 (2014). https://dl.acm.org/doi/10.1145/2593702.2593708
12. Kropp, M., et al.: Teaching and learning agile collaboration. In: 2014 IEEE 27th Conference on Software Engineering Education and Training, CSEE and T 2014 - Proceedings, pp. 139–148. IEEE Computer Society (2014)
13. Abdallah, M., et al.: Artificial intelligence applications in solid waste management: a systematic research review. Waste Manage. **109**, 231–246 (2020). https://doi.org/10.1016/j.wasman.2020.04.057
14. Settaluri, K., et al.: Autockt: deep reinforcement learning of analog circuit designs. In: Proceedings of the 2020 Design, Automation and Test in Europe Conference and Exhibition, DATE 2020, pp. 490–495 (2020). https://doi.org/10.23919/DATE48585.2020.9116200
15. Li, W., et al.: Blockchain-based data security for artificial intelligence applications in 6g networks. IEEE Network **34**, 31–37 (2020). https://doi.org/10.1109/MNET.021.1900629
16. Esposito, M., et al.: Generative AI for software architecture: applications, challenges, and future directions. arXiv preprint arXiv:2503.13310 (2025)
17. Antal, G., et al.: Leveraging GPT-4 for vulnerability-witnessing unit test generation. In: Proceedings of the 29th International Conference on Evaluation and Assessment in Software Engineering (EASE) (2025, to appear). https://arxiv.org/abs/2506.11559
18. Necula, S.-C., Dumitriu, F., Greavu-Serban, V.: A systematic literature review on using natural language processing in software requirements engineering. In: Department of Accounting, Business Information Systems and Statistics, Faculty of Economics and Business Administration, Alexandru Ioan Cuza University of Iasi, 700506 Iasi, Romania (2024). https://doi.org/10.3390/electronics13112055
19. Imgrund, E., et al.: Broken promises: measuring confounding effects in learning-based vulnerability discovery. In: AISec 2023: Proceedings of the 16th ACM Workshop on Artificial Intelligence and Security, pp. 149–160 (2023). https://doi.org/10.1145/3605764.3623915
20. Saad, M., et al.: Senai: towards software engineering native generative artificial intelligence. In: Proceedings of the ACM Conference. ACM (2025). https://arxiv.org/abs/2503.15282
21. Kalouptsoglou, I., et al.: Vulnerability classification on source code using text mining and deep learning techniques. In: 2024 IEEE 24th International Conference on Software Quality, Reliability, and Security Companion (QRS-C), pp. 47–56 (2024). https://doi.org/10.1109/QRS-C63300.2024.00017
22. Mittal, H.K., Arsalan, M., Garg, P.: A novel deep learning model for effective story point estimation in agile software development. In: 2024 International Conference on Emerging Innovations and Advanced Computing (INNOCOMP), pp. 404–410 (2024). https://doi.org/10.1109/INNOCOMP63224.2024.00073
23. Gupta, N., Mahapatra, R.: Automated software effort estimation for agile development system by heuristically improved hybrid learning. Concurr. Comput.: Pract. Exp. **34** (2022). https://doi.org/10.1002/cpe.7267

24. Wu, B., et al.: Industry-track: towards agile design of neural processing unit. In: 2022 International Conference on Hardware/Software Codesign and System Synthesis (CODES+ISSS), pp. 17–20 (2022). https://doi.org/10.1109/CODES-ISSS55005.2022.00015
25. Dave, S., et al.: Special session: towards an agile design methodology for efficient, reliable, and secure ml systems. In: 2022 IEEE 40th VLSI Test Symposium (VTS), pp. 1–14 (2022). https://doi.org/10.1109/VTS52500.2021.9794253
26. Mao, Y., et al.: CFEACT: a CGRA-based framework enabling agile CNN and transformer accelerator design. In: 2024 34th International Conference on Field-Programmable Logic and Applications (FPL), pp. 213–219 (2024). https://doi.org/10.1109/FPL64840.2024.00037
27. Yulianto, S., Ngo, G.N.C.: Enhancing devsecops pipelines with AI-driven threat detection and response. In: 2024 International Conference on ICT for Smart Society (ICISS), pp. 1–8 (2024). https://doi.org/10.1109/ICISS62896.2024.10751269
28. Ahammad, A., El Bajta, M., Radgui, M.: Automated software testing using machine learning: a systematic mapping study. In: 2024 10th International Conference on Optimization and Applications (ICOA), pp. 1–6 (2024). https://doi.org/10.1109/ICOA62581.2024.10754031

Fairness Testing: Review of the Relevance and Methodologies of Ensuring Software Fairness

Ilmaan Zia(✉), Ankit Raj, and Jonathan Dabu

California State University, Long Beach, CA 90840, USA
{Ilmaan.Zia01,Ankit.Raj01,Jonathan.Dabu01}@student.csulb.edu

Abstract. The quality of software is becoming vital as it becomes more pervasive in human's daily operations. Today's software is employed differently than in the past because of automation, machine learning advancements, and the availability of copious quantities of data, all of which allow the program to make more independent judgments. The concept of fairness in software engineering refers to the different approaches used to address the problem of bias to ensure zero discrimination while using the software in question. Testing in software engineering that specifically examines a system's fairness is known as "fairness testing". It can also be defined as the process of revealing imperfections that can lead to some friction between the needed and existing fairness conditions, in a software system. As part of this process, it is common practice to test for bias based on demographics like color and gender to make sure the system is not prejudiced in any way. In the construction of any system that might have significant consequences for people's lives, testing for fairness is a crucial stage that can assist guarantee the system is fair and impartial in its decision making. Unfortunately, throughout the software development life cycle, fairness is not prioritized or even considered. There have been many instances of unfair software appearing. Using algorithms, Amazon.com, Inc. decided in 2016 which areas of the United States would get free same-day delivery. At times when every other community around it was participating, the algorithms decided against include minority areas. The same kind of software is now being utilized to assign suspects with risk assessment ratings. At each level of the criminal justice process, from determining guilt to setting bond amounts to sentence, these scores are used to guide judgments about who may be released free. This paper looks into some of the important methodologies that can be used for fairness testing in software engineering, and come up with a survey on fairness while using software systems.

Keywords: Fairness · fairness testing · methodology · ASTRAEA · Genetic Algorithm · Deep Learning · Statistical Fairness Testing · Collaborative Governance · causal inference

S. Hussain et al. (Eds.): SEET 2025, CCIS 2725, pp. 733–759, 2026.
https://doi.org/10.1007/978-3-032-08977-9_48

1 Introduction

Due to societal biases in areas like credit scoring, hiring, and criminal justice, fairness in ML software systems has become a major social concern. Researchers have been working to correctly define fairness inside ML models for many years in an effort to make future AI algorithms impartial and independent from human bias.

In our research, the term fairness refers to any software system flaw that results in a discrepancy between the actual and necessary fairness criteria. Such flaws may result from a person's characteristics, including age, sex, occupation, and race. For instance, the German Credit Data set tends to give male applicants a better credit score than female applicants. Additionally, a male applicant with a low anticipated credit score is more likely to really have a high credit score. This discrimination is immoral, and it puts women at a disadvantage when applying for loans.

Fairness is one of the most controversial topics in the ML and AI landscape and Software Engineering in general, coming from the realization of how models trained with data could pick up on biases in that data and possibly even amplify existing biases. The concept of fairness is difficult to capture precisely. Over thousands of years, philosophers have discussed what decisions are fair, and over hundreds of years, societies have attempted to regulate certain (different) notions of fairness into law. In the machine learning community, there is plenty of discussion of different measures of fairness and how to change the machine-learning pipeline to optimize the model for such fairness measures. When building a product with machine-learning components, fairness needs to be discussed throughout all phases of the development process and during operations, which includes both ML and non-ML parts of the system. Such discussions are often necessarily political in nature—for instance, it includes negotiating among many stakeholders what notion of fairness is relevant for the product (and complies with the law) while navigating various trade-offs and conflicting preferences involved. As with other responsible engineering properties, fairness is clearly not just a model-level concern but requires reasoning about the entire system and how the system interacts with users and the rest of the world.

As the world becomes more automated, the fairness level of these computer algorithms can decide whether the information and data produced become beneficial or detrimental to society. This issue has sparked many software engineers and computer scientists to reconsider the ethics behind said technology and correct its behavior where necessary to promote fair and equal outputs. This paper discusses this process which is considered today to be a branch of software fairness development and research called "fairness testing."

Fairness testing is a meticulous, qualitative, and socio-technical valuation of an Artificial Intelligence or Machine Learning model and dataset based on careful inputs that may produce inadvertent outputs, creating or perpetuating unfair bias against historically marginalized groups in society. [1] The testing proceeds to ensure the examination of an algorithm's ability to influence human behavior and decide whether it is biased thus avoiding predictive bias. It also identifies any vulnerabilities or inconsistencies in public data sets and assesses whether there are violations in the safety and security of society. In this paper, we analyze various distinct methodologies.

2 Background

The definitions of fairness that are most often used are presented in this section. We examine results from each of the five basic definition, which are further divided into individual and group fairness type.

2.1 Definition of Fairness

The fairness definition establishes the fairness requirement that software systems must meet. This has been discussed and suggested before.

Table 1. Fairness Definitions

Name	Definition	Type
Conditional Statistical Parity	Predicted Outcome	Group
Predictive Parity	Predicted and Actual Outcome	Group
Balance For Positive Class	Predicted Probabilities and Actual Outcome	Group
Fairness Through Unawareness	Similarity-Based	Individual
Counterfactual Fairness	Casual Reasoning	Individual

We introduce the definitions generally used and adopted (Table 1) and divide them into two types: group type and individual type. Predicted outcomes centers around different segment dispersions of subjects. Predicted and actual outcomes thinks about the predicted outcome for various segment dispersions of the subject and the actual outcome. Predicted probabilities and actual outcomes thinks about the actual outcome and the predicted likelihood of the score. Similarity-based definitions help try not to minimize over inhumane characteristics of the subject. Casual reasoning definitions assist with making a diagram and show the connection among credits and their impact on result, which are utilized to give techniques to gauge impacts of delicate characteristics and construct calculations that guarantee a decent degree of segregation because of their qualities [2].

Group Fairness. We introduce three common individual fairness from three categories of definitions in group fairness. We will use the German Credit data to visualize examples of each definition where female and male should have equal opportunity.

Predicted Outcome (Conditional Statistical Parity) [3]. Definitions emphasize the expected result for diverse topic demographic distributions. They stand for the purest and most natural understanding of fairness. If individuals in the protected and unprotected groups have an equal chance of being placed in the class that is expected to be positive. In addition, allows other factors to legitimately influence the result. If individuals in the protected and unprotected groups have an equal chance of belonging to the positive predicted class, this criteria is met. For example, male and female applicants should have equal probability of attaining good credit.

Predicted and Actual Outcome (Predictive Parity) [4]. Definitions compare the actual outcome recorded in the dataset to the expected outcome for various demographic distributions of the system software algorithm topic. The positive predictive values for protected and unprotected groups are equivalent. Specifically, the percentage of positive instances out of all positive cases projected that were accurately classified as positive. Precision is the term used to describe the likelihood that a topic with a positive predictive value will fall into the positive class. For example, the likelihood that an application with a strong forecasted credit score would really have a good credit score should be the same for both male and female candidates.

Predicted Probabilities and Actual Outcome (Balance For Positive Class) [5]. Definitions take into account both the actual result and the calculated probability score. Both protected and unprotected groups' subjects who make up positive classes have comparable average projected probability scores. For example, Male and female applicants with strong real credit scores should receive the same anticipated value of likelihood from the software system algorithm.

Individual Fairness. We provide two common fairness for individual fairness within two categories.

Similarity-based (Fairness Through Unawareness) [6]. With the exception of the particular sensitive property, definitions basically disregard all characteristics of the categorized topic. Sensitive characteristics aren't expressly considered when making decisions. All similar individuals with just a gender difference share the same characteristics. For instance, the software system algorithm does not employ gender-related characteristics, therefore judgments cannot be based on these features. Similar applicants with the same qualities should receive the same classification decision.

Casual Reasoning (Counterfactual Fairness) [7]. Definitions presuppose a casual graph that is directed and acyclic with nodes denoting applicant qualities and edges denoting connections between the attributes. A collection of structural equations, which are then utilized to give ways to assess the impacts of sensitive characteristics and develop algorithms that assure tolerable level of discrimination owing to these qualities, specifically represent the relationships between attributes and their influence on result. If the projected result in a casual graph does not depend on a descendent of the protected characteristic, then the graph is counterfactually fair.

2.2 Definition of Fairness Testing

Fairness as a concept is defined as the state, condition, or quality of being fair. Looking at this through the lens and perspective of software, fairness testing as a whole can be defined as the process or method of ensuring fairness in software through checking for, detecting, and flagging instances of discrimination. There are a wide range of definitions when it comes to fairness in algorithms [8]. Each methodology specifies its own set of requirements when it comes to fairness as well and what constitutes as discrimination. A catalog of fairness definitions and guidelines for when each definition is something that should be strived for in the study of fair software [9]. In order to do this, software engineers must understand the context of these requirements, get critical questions answered, raise any concerns, clear up any assumptions, and understand any accompanying implications. In fairness testing, discrimination ends up as a value that is calculated. If a piece of software or algorithm exceeds a certain value, it is considered biased in the category that was being tested.

2.3 Importance and Relevance of Fairness Testing

Software has had an immeasurable impact on the advancement of our society, shaping human life in a myriad of ways. From the programs utilized in hospitals to the applications artists create their art in, software is ever present in an immense capacity. Being so ubiquitous and having such a huge importance on people and the world, software must uphold humanity's own ethics and executive fairness.

The concept of fairness, defined as being free from bias, dishonesty, or injustice, is one whose extent of being upheld varies in particular countries and differs per institution, for example the workplace or court systems. These establishments might not always be fair, with biases running rampant in a multitude of its processes. For example, workplaces might pay women less and courts may be more likely to find people of certain races guilty. Regardless, fairness is something that we strive for in our society.

As aforementioned, software plays a role in a wide range of aspects of human life, even taking on human-related tasks such as hiring, credit assessment, criminal justice, and disease detection [1]. Software, while not human itself, must also uphold the principle of fairness when administering its services to humans, especially for such critical tasks that affect our lives in such important ways. After all, humans are unique in their appearance, how they identify and present gender-wise, cultural backgrounds (race and ethnicity), beliefs, and experiences. Software must account for diversity in humans, but software does often err. Software has limitations and its own biases (Fig. 1).

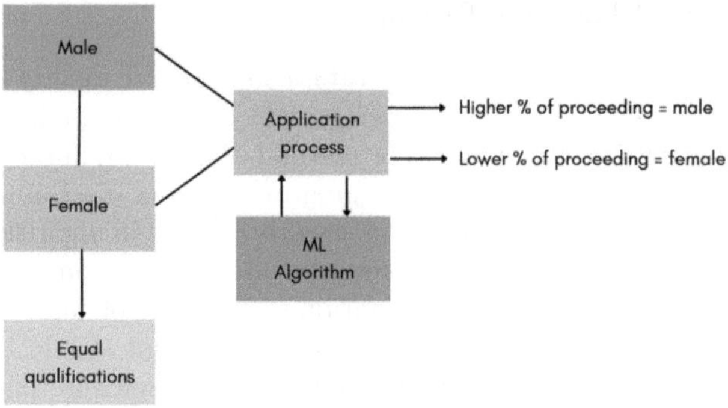

Fig. 1. Gender Bias in Application Process

The presence of bias in software that plays an imperative role in human life can cause more serious consequences. An exemplification of this would be software that helps predict health outcomes so institutions such as hospitals and public health departments can plan for care, whether it's through budgeting or allocating resources. A more specific case of this is when a commercial prediction algorithm showed significant racial bias in predicting outcomes [10]. The algorithm had a bias of using health costs as a proxy for health needs. Black patients had lower health costs and were defined as having the same level of risk as white people. In reality, black patients had more health needs. Establishments might have planned for care in a different way, leaving out black patients which is consequential.

Another example of software bias causing consequence includes socioeconomic bias in software regarding education. More specifically in 2020, A-Level students in the UK were awarded grades generated by calculation through use of a biased algorithm [11]. The algorithm was biased in having favored students attending private and independent schools and hitting students from disadvantaged backgrounds harder. This case shows how software bias can affect the educational standing of students (Fig. 2).

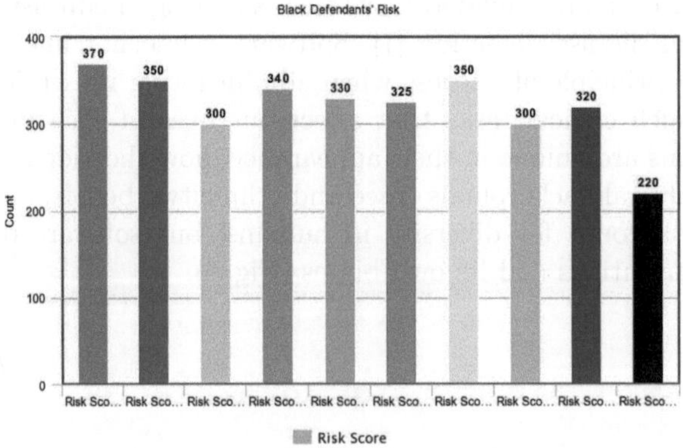

Fig. 2. Black Defendants' Risk Scores

One last example is software that is being used to generate risk-assessment scores for suspected criminals being "particularly likely to falsely flag black defendants as future criminals, wrongly labeling them this way at almost twice the rate as white defendants; white defendants were mislabeled as low risk more often than black defendants" [12]. This case shows how software bias can affect the incineration rates of minorities and protected groups. As seen in these examples, these "fairness bugs" may bring ramifications that are unethical, specifically being highly disadvantageous underrepresented groups.

Software must be tested for its own biases and be taught how to avoid making decisions based on them. Thus, software fairness testing is an essential topic in the world of development. Those in the field know this and its prevalence as a subject of study shows its relevance (Fig. 3).

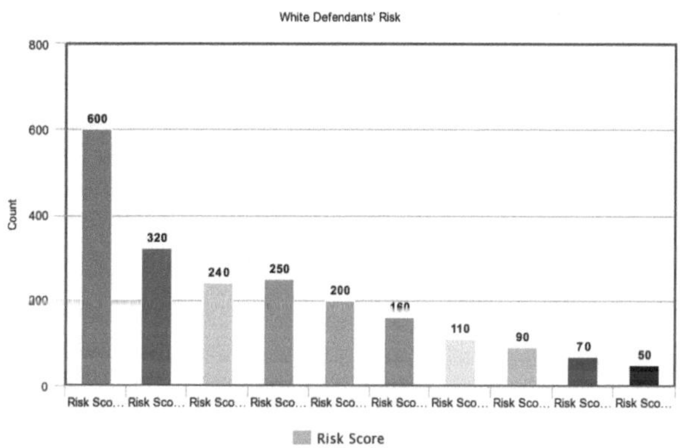

Fig. 3. White Defendants' Risk Scores

2.4 Fairness Testing Trade-Offs

While finding the right metrics to modify fairness values, as they provide different advantages and disadvantages. It's not productive to have a classifier that equalizes both calibration and odds, as it would satisfy multiple notions of fairness simultaneously. What is important is making all factors of changing fairness values in isolation. Tuning different parameters while taking social issues into effect could lead to false positive errors on one demographic, while increasing false negative errors on the other demographic, which can be harmful for both odds in a group. Thus, we need to find different combinations of parameters that would be fair in both standpoints.

We propose a measure-and-trade framework with two variants: By measuring fairness in terms of social issues, we expect the most bias-free model to be one where all weights are equalized. Pessach highlighted a trade-off between fairness and accuracy, citing various studies. The ideal state would be a model that has a high fairness without compromising the accuracy when taking a dataset. [13] A more aggressive trade-off would be one that does not have many false negatives and the model is accurate.

The Fairness Trade-off framework has received a lot of interest within academia. However, the only metric is fairness, which was established from meta-analysis studies on media and social influence. A measure of fairness based on individual differences (such as sensitivity to unfairness) might be useful in different applications in an attempt to optimize fairness against other criteria such as performance or accuracy.

In Machine reading comprehension, this framework could be applied to the difference between a document and a verbatim transcript. It could also be applied to understanding related passages in a book or different versions of a document.

3 Contrastive Fairness

In order to guarantee the fairness of machine learning algorithms, counterfactual fairness codified the use of causal inference. While many real-life concerns about fairness relate to how two people are handled and whether the difference in the choice for them was fair, the criteria are population-based. Why was this decision made for a certain person as opposed to another? [14] These are all contrasting instances of individual fairness that need the incorporation of other factors.

3.1 Methodology

The fairness for the two people over the entire choice space should first be established. Second, even if the decision-making process is fair, for the decision to make sense, it must be given a more significant probability score by the predictor for one person than the alternative decision. However, it must be given a lower probability score for the other person. Finally, one must ensure that even if the protected variable values of the two people were to be the same counterfactually, the initial decision would still be more valuable than the prime decision for the first individual, and the prime decision would be more valuable than the initial decision for the second.

$$\begin{aligned} P(\hat{Y}_{Ai \leftarrow a_i}(U_i) = d|X_i = x_i, A_i = a_i) = \\ P(\hat{Y}_{Ai \leftarrow a_i'}(U_i) = d|X_i = x_i, A_i = a_i) \end{aligned} \tag{1}$$

$$\begin{aligned} P(\hat{Y}_{Aj \leftarrow a_j}(U_j) = d|X_j = x_j, A_j = a_j) = \\ P(\hat{Y}_{Aj \leftarrow a_j'}(U_j) = d|X_j = x_j, A_j = a_j) \end{aligned} \tag{2}$$

$$\begin{aligned} P(\hat{Y}(U_i) = d|X_i = x_i, A_i = a_i) > \\ P(\hat{Y}_A(U_i) = d'|X_i = x_i, A_i = a_i) \end{aligned} \tag{3}$$

$$\begin{aligned} P(\hat{Y}(U_j) = d'|X_j = x_j, A_j = a_j) > \\ P(\hat{Y}_A(U_j) = d|X_j = x_j, A_j = a_j) \end{aligned} \tag{4}$$

$$P(\hat{Y}_{Ai\leftarrow a_j}(U_i) = d|X_i = x_i, A_i = a_i) > \\ P(\hat{Y}_{Ai\leftarrow a_j}(U_i) = d'|X_i = x_i, A_i = a_i) \tag{5}$$

$$P(\hat{Y}_{Aj\leftarrow a_i}(U_j) = d'|X_j = x_j, A_j = a_j) > \\ P(\hat{Y}_{Aj\leftarrow a_i}(U_j) = d|X_j = x_j, A_j = a_j) \tag{6}$$

By satisfying these equations, one may infer that the choice comparison between these two individuals is fair. You must make additional assumptions when comparing the choices of two people. Not only must the decision-making procedures be impartial for each individual, but the choice differences also needs to make sense, as shown by the probability values produced by the predictor.

4 Linear-Regression Based Training Data Debugging (LTDD)

4.1 Methodology

Debugging feature values in training data is necessary to produce unbiased features for a linear regression model. For instance, to retrieve as much valuable and unbiased information as possible, determine which characteristics and which portions of them are biased and eliminate the biased portions. Analyze the relationship between sensitive and non-sensitive characteristics. For the sensitive characteristics, create a linear regression model using the non-sensitive features. Three steps of LTDD's can be used to do this [15].

1. Estimate the biased components of the biased characteristics. You assess the correlation between the sensitive features in the training dataset for each non-sensitive feature.
2. From the training samples, remove the biased components. You run the operators for any training sample to remove bias. deleting the sensitive feature and, by eliminating the association, updating the values of the non-sensitive feature. Then, using the updated and objective training dataset, you create a fair machine learning program.
3. The testing samples should get the same modification. To make the testing sample match the ML program, you apply the same revisions to the dimension and distribution of the training data. Consider removing the sensitive feature and making changes to the other characteristics based on the estimates derived from the training samples. The label is then predicted using the ML system.

4.2 Results

It is possible to significantly increase the fairness of the original ML program and somewhat decrease its performance when using LTDD to enhance the fairness of ML software. Comparing LTDD performance to baselines for cutting-edge fairness algorithms like fairway, reweighing, and disparate impact remover reveals that LTDD outperforms baselines in terms of improving fairness indicators while exhibiting performance harm that is less than or equivalent to baselines. While assuring that the overall favorable rate is near to the original amount and doesn't require extra societal resources, LTDD enhances the fairness indicators when applied to realistic settings.

5 Adversarial Sampling

5.1 Methodology

Two phases—a global generation phase and a local generation phase—of Adversarial Discrimination Finder (ADF) sample generation process [16]. The objective is to extract from the original dataset those discriminating samples close to the decision border, which are subsequently used as the seed data for the local generation stage. By repeatedly perturbing in the direction of the decision boundary, ADF first locates the discriminating samples close to the decision boundary. In the local generation phase, it makes sense to generate more selective samples since they are more likely to be found close to the seed data. ADF takes new gradient-based samples in order to look for nearby

5.2 Results

The ADF algorithm surpassed the standard approaches for locating discriminating samples. Comparing ADF to AEQUITAS for tabular data reveals that it searches 9.6 times as much input area, creates 25 times as many discriminating samples, and achieves more than double the success rate. When given the same time constraint as SG, ADF searches 6.6 times the input space, creates 6.5 discriminating samples, and has a somewhat better success rate. Effective direction is offered by gradient during both global and local generation. For text data, ADF creates samples that are 2.68 times more discriminative and, on average, have a success rate that is 9.01% higher than random perturbation. The discriminating samples produced by ADF resemble the original samples. When creating discriminating samples, ADF performs ok. Gradient-guided perturbation application has a modest time overhead, which is especially pronounced for RNN. With an average improvement of 57.2% on tabular datasets and 60.2% on text datasets, the discriminating samples produced by ADF are helpful to enhance the fairness of the DL models through retraining. The experiment on 22 benchmarks of 5 datasets demonstrates that ADF can provide correct discriminating samples in a timely manner.

6 Black Box Fairness Testing

An approach for creating test cases called "black box fairness" looks for instances of individual prejudice in machine learning algorithms [17]. It combines the idea of symbolic evaluation, which consistently provides test input for every program, with local explanation, which uses a linear and understandable model to approximation the execution route in the model. Its nature as a black box gives it an added benefit. The two main components of the search strategy are global search and local search.

6.1 Global Search

Path coverage is taken care of via global search, which also aids in the discovery of an initial set of discriminating inputs. To do that, you employ symbolic execution with a seed data set, take into account approximations included in the local model, and wisely use the confidence associated with the path constraints received from the local model. Additionally, local search looks for increasingly biased inputs. It builds on the adversarial robustness trait by starting with the initial set of accessible discriminating pathways and producing additional inputs for the close-by execution paths. This methodically performs local explanation. The results of the experimental assessments unmistakably demonstrate that the strategy outperforms all currently available instruments.

6.2 Symbolic Testing

The efficacy of symbolic testing of machine learning models is excellent. For four well-known benchmarks—German gender, German age, adult race, and adult sex—the average efficacy falls from 45.4% to 25.2% when the local symbolic search option is disabled. Given that it has a high rate of efficacy, it is certain to pave the way for a number of endeavors (mentioned below) in the future.

Generic Framework. The global search approach is not just a tool to address individual discrimination, but also a general way to evaluate any black-box ML model [18].

Local Model Generation. The LIME local model generator, which is a key component of this black-box fairness testing methodology. In terms of how well systematic exploration works, the approximation that the local model causes does have a part to play. Ultimately, you can research ways to create a local model for exploration that is more successful and efficient [19].

Model Path. Neuron activation may be used to accurately specify route while testing neural networks [20].

Global Approximation. In order to extract an interpretable section of the model, local approximation is utilized [21]. That choice seems to fit with the on-demand exploration method, which does not call for complete model re-engineering. Additionally, there is no need for training data while creating local models. Finally, if training data is available, you may study the global approximation approach to build.

Adversarial Robustness. There exists many white-box approaches addressing the problem for finding adversaries [22]. Down the road, you may look at whether such methods can be used in black-box testing to catch individual prejudice [23].

Hybrid Search Strategy. The algorithm favors seed data over global search and local search over global search. Another course of action that may be taken later is to discover an interleaved approach [24].

Individual Discrimination and De-biasing. Once a model detects a certain distinction, you want to determine what caused it, especially by mapping it to the training set of data. It is therefore feasible to de-bias the model by either eliminating or correctly perturbing the training data instances once you have identified the training data instance and its characteristics responsible for bias.

7 ASTRAEA

7.1 Background

ASTRAEA is conceptualized, designed, and implemented as the first grammar-based methodology to test, diagnose and improve Natural Language Processing (NLP) system fairness. As the first approach to utilize grammars to systematically to generate discriminatory inputs via metamorphic relations, it automatically discovers and diagnoses fairness violations.

In addition to having desirable features such as being 1) lightweight, 2) easily integrated in the software development pipeline for continuous testing, and 3) resilient to change, ASTRAEA is also highly extensible. The grammars ASTRAEA leverages cover a variety of NLP tasks such as sentiment analysis and mask language modeling as accounts for biases including gender, religion and occupation. ASTRAEA can also be used to test and diagnose both individual and group fairness violations.

This methodology has had two major challenges in its development: the need to formalize the fairness criteria for a set of test sentences in a way that open and responsive to automated software testing and the facilitation of the generation of a large number of discriminatory inputs.

7.2 Grammar-Based Method

ASTRAEA uses grammar-based input generation. The software explores the input grammar at random to generate an initial test input. Mutations in the grammar are then used for the generation of equivalent test inputs. Afterward, the token in the input is mutated. Following that, metamorphic relations are then defined and applied to analyze equivalent test inputs for software fairness. ASTRAEA accounts for diagnostic intuition by evaluating failing test cases. This diagnostic information is used to further optimize the test generation process.

Two-Phase Approach. In regards to individual fairness, the test generation process consists of two phases: random test generation and probabilistic test generation. In the RAND phase, the probabilities of choosing alternatives in production rules from the Grammar is equal for all alternatives. In the PROB phase probabilities associated with the alternatives of the production rules are computed.

In the diagnosis stage, error rate calculated through median absolute deviation is used to detect anomalous tokens. Tokens with absolute anomaly indices greater than two are considered anomalies. The occurrences of the tokens in the generated tests is recorded. The number of occurrences reflects fairness violations. Error rates are then computed for each token. ASTRAEA also tests for group fairness violations in a similar fashion where all tokens with absolute anomaly indices above two are considered to exhibit a violation of group fairness.

ASTRAEA can be used for specific gender biases in occupations, for example he/she pronouns against roles such as farmers and CEOs. In a NeuralCoref example, sentences containing "CEO" showed a 98% error rate. This means that in 98% of the sentences, "CEO" was in reference to "he" and not "she".

ASTRAEA is a two-phase approach. The first phase includes the random exploration of grammar production rules to generate a large number of input sentences. For any two sentences that only differ in the sensitive attributes, ASTRAEA detects a fairness violation. In the second phase, ASTRAEA analyzes those fairness violations that were discovered in the first phase and isolates input features that are mostly and directly responsible for fairness violations.

Distinction. Even with a separate line of inquiry into data debiasing, ASTRAEA's automated test creation is still a desired feature. This is due to the fact that the final NLP model, although taking data debiasing techniques into account, may still display bias, and ASTRAEA checks for such breaches. Moreover, compared to manually crafted testing data for evaluating fairness problems, ASTRAEA's automated technique of test creation offers flexibility for testing NLP models [25].

ASTRAEA is distinct from other studies in fairness testing because of the special formalization it employs to ensure justice in natural language processing systems. Existing inputs on testing NLP systems either investigate prediction mistakes at random or need seed inputs for test creation, in contrast to the guided fairness testing technique included in ASTRAEA [26]. The current seed-input based test generating technique is time-consuming and needs thousands of seed inputs. Not only does this imply bias from the seeds themselves, but it also requires a lot more time and effort than ASTRAEA's method of building grammars [27]. Also, no other method offers diagnostic and rigorous retraining of NLP systems to enhance their fairness; ASTRAEA is the only one of its kind [28].

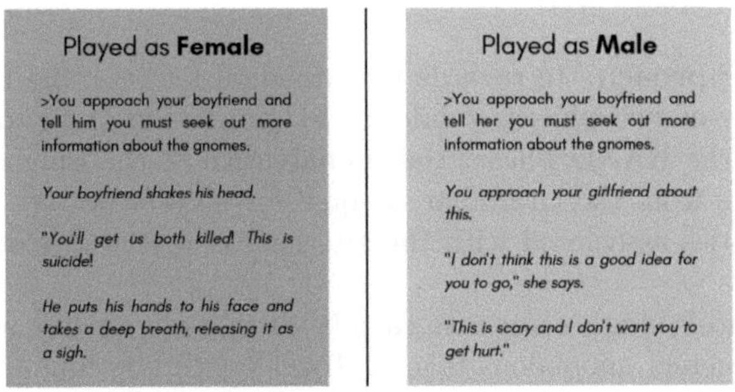

Fig. 4. Black Defendants' Risk Scores

7.3 Natural Language Processing

It is clear that software utilizes the English language to its fullest affect when making decisions and producing outputs. Unfortunately these scenarios usually mean that the software itself is also susceptible to creating an innate bias towards certain words. For example in an AI game created, the term "woman" is seen in a negative light when it created a story from it's series of inputs as shown in Fig. 4 [29]. Thus, the test inputs in language processing is put in stage and conveys it's importance in the fairness testing model.

To create test inputs, ASTRAEA uses a grammar and then applies mutations to that grammar to create comparable test inputs. The program then uses metamorphic correlations to assess the fairness of its test inputs. Moreover, ASTRAEA uses diagnostic information to enhance the test creation process by analyzing (failed) test cases for diagnostic insight. This methodology is important for ensuring fairness in natural language processing (NLP) systems. NLP systems are considered in this case because of their widespread use and the moral questions that result from such use. Hovy and Spruit have emphasized the social effect of NLP systems, particularly how such systems influence equitable chances for society groups and individuals [30]. The fairness of a machine learning model may be investigated by providing it with a list of potentially discriminatory features, such as a person's gender and profession. In order to make the model more software-fair, ASTRAEA creates tests that systematically add to the training data depending on the outcomes of the diagnostic. It is the first grammar-based method for thoroughly testing, diagnosing, and improving the fairness of NLP models. Even with a separate line of inquiry into data debiasing, ASTRAEA's automated test creation is still a desired feature. This is due to the fact that the final NLP model, although taking data debiasing techniques into account, may still display bias, and ASTRAEA checks for such breaches. Moreover, compared to manually crafted testing data for evaluating fairness problems, ASTRAEA's automated technique of test creation offers flexibility for testing NLP models [31].

8 Identifying and Modifying Hyperparameters that Affect Fairness

Because of socially critical data-driven datasets, researchers utilize various off-the-shelf machine learning libraries with various parameters to account for fairness. Fairness-aware Configuration of Machine Learning Libraries [32] utilized ways to prevent biases within ML algorithms. The use of hyperparameters, restricting the search space of attributes, can make the scope specific for trained models.

To impose fairness requirements towards the ML algorithms, they define a true positive rate and a false positive rate. With that, they change the average odd difference, along with the equal opportunity difference. The TPR will be studied and checked if it was changed whatsoever. Their proposals utilize a dynamic search algorithm to find hyperparameters that could suppress or amplify biases. In this algorithm, bias can be amplified by increasing the number of parameters and decreasing either the number of features or the number of training examples. The best configuration is found by searching up to several hundred different configurations.

To overcome the biases within the dataset, they also choose hyperparameters to reduce overfitting. Multiple configuration search is also executed to find the best configuration that reduces overfitting while maintaining accuracy. In this approach, they minimize bias while not sacrificing precision. Tuning the hyperparameters shows that it significantly affects fairness. They did a global analysis of over 180 machine learning models and it shows their configurations can systematically amplify or suppress biases.

Some limitations that could be that they could not fully eliminate all the fairness issues with their approach. Because it's a dynamic analysis, they rely on existing data within their dataset, which cannot always find notable hyperparameters within their dataset.

Their approach can be broadened to different ML problems and be adjusted for various types of biases. The negative effect on precision is very low for the configurations. This configuration can potentially reduce the classification errors in a public dataset, improving public datasets. As stated, they focused on general applications across a wide range of methods, models and bias types. Bias-reducing hyperparameter configurations have a significant effect on fairness and accuracy, but at a very small cost, which indicates that this work could be used as a regular part of standard machine learning research practice.

Future work could include their application to more datasets across different domains, validating their results with cross validation and benchmark datasets. Their fairness configuration approach can be broadened to other bias types beyond the two they focused on in this paper, reducing the negative effects on precision even further.

8.1 Need of Fairness Testing Within Industry

Holstein [33] conducted a study with various industry practitioners focusing on the need for Fairness Testing with the industry. They noticed that while most models utilize a "bias in, bias out" framing, fairness testing has taken an emphasis on algorithmic methods to mitigate bias. Instead of modifying the dataset, the algorithms with fine tuning hyperparameters have been focused on.

They have outlined various methods that can be used as components of a fairness test strategy. The authors also note that it would be nice if there were a standard framework to compare different methods which would not only allow comparability but also be applicable in a variety of domains. The authors look to the literature and frame several issues that they believe are important for fairness testing: The idea is that algorithmic techniques are the most robust against bias and therefore should be the focus of fairness testing.

The majority of fairness test methods rely on a bias in/bias out framework. In this framework, the test procedure first performs the hidden training set and then checks for a bias. When biases are detected and their effects are corrected, the model is run on the testing data to check for more bias. If no more biases are found, the model is deemed to be fair. A challenge posed could be the need for more holistic auditing methods. Auditors could look at the model's characteristics and make sure that there are not hidden biases in the model. In addition, a thorough audit may need to stress test the model.

9 Fairness Testing Through Genetic Algorithms, Causal Inference, and Sum Product Networks

Machine learning fairness testing must be done in consideration of both classification and regression-based machine learning. While classification-based machine learning is much easier to determine variable sensitive attributes that might result in bias predictions, the same cannot be easily said for regression-based machine learning [34]. Regression would need to measure differences in outcome and attribute them to a sensitive variable and fairness testing would have to identify if that outcome is biased. Then it could narrow down whether a variable had an effect on that bias. Additionally, different fairness testing measures may result in more biased predictions when testing as bias might not be fully representative or captured in an incorrect context [34].

Another consideration should be whether the fairness testing is done during preprocessing, inside the black box model, or after the outputs are spit out. In essence, solutions look to solve in the "pre-processing" phase, "in-process" phase, or the "post-process" phase [35]. ExpGA and Sum Product Networks (SPN) covers fairness testing during the pre-processing phase, and SBFT (Search-Based Fairness Testing) acts in the post-process phase as well as AuFair.

Fairness testing approaches can sometimes suffer from lack of variable data involving sensitive attributes, which different approaches using genetic algorithms can cover. The approaches with genetic algorithms generate data before use by the machine learning algorithm and benchmark the results to accurately determine whether changes need to be made in terms of fairness adjustment.

9.1 Search-Based Fairness Testing

One such approach to fairness testing using genetic algorithms is SBFT (Search-Based Fairness Testing). This is a fairness testing solution that uses a genetic algorithm on a machine learning model meant for regression. Although the paper only tested the novelty of this solution under a specific scenario (emergency wait times) the paper concluded good results from this approach [34]. Instead of looking to generate better discriminatory inputs, SBFT focuses on testing the test inputs to measure fairness. Taking test inputs and finding those with the largest fairness degrees in order to create offspring from them and using them in the next evaluation of test inputs. The fairness degree would be the maximum difference between any outputs given identical inputs given only differences in a sensitive attribute, with a larger number correlating to more bias within the model [34]. In order to test these inputs further, the values of the sensitive target variables are mutated in order to see if further changes appear. It also relies on a caching system in order to improve speed and allow the algorithm more flexibility when dealing with sensitive attributes that are non-binary. Once SBFT has its initial set of test inputs and checks for the fairness degree and finds the test inputs with the highest fitness, the inputs are then subject to crossover, mutation, and selection to create a new generation of inputs. These new inputs will have varying attributes except for any protected variables which will remain the same. This makes SBFT one of the simpler approaches to fairness testing, but if expanded upon could be used in a variety of scenarios.

9.2 Augmented Fairness

Another strategy that employed genetic algorithms is AuFair, short for Augmented Fairness, which is another model strategy for achieving fairness in machine learning models and their outcomes. AuFair focuses on post-processing and binary classification models and scenarios. Its goal is to create an augment to the decision making of the model and employ a type of genetic algorithm framework called Nondominated Sorting Genetic Algorithm II (NSGA-II) in order to optimize the augment [35]. The solutions it comes to will have good levels of both fairness and error, after using the genetic algorithm to produce and find the most fit solutions. Another function AuFair uses is FPGrowth. FPGrowth is a rule mining algorithm meant to create candidate rule sets that the main AuFair algorithm can use. AuFair also has a budget constraint set on it. AuFair must first create true labels itself because it deals with black box models. Once it's queried and found suitable labels it will execute generating a new population and attempt to minimize unfairness for the augment.

9.3 Explanation Guided Genetic Algorithm

Another approach is ExpGA, which is a genetic algorithm implementation of explanation fairness testing. The main goal of ExpGA is to generate higher quality samples of discriminatory samples to be used the by whichever black box machine learning model needs them. ExpGA is compatible with any black box model because it doesn't require intimate knowledge of how it works and only needs to be able to modify the samples being input into the black box model. The reason for this is due to the use of an interpretable method that can identify samples that are valuable based on a scoring system. The interpretable method will try to rank important features that would explain an output based on a given input. ExgGA is thus able to add more discriminatory samples to a model while using interpretable methods to try to identify those discriminatory samples in the outputs in order implement fairness testing of a black box model [36].

A knowledge graph is necessary whether the dataset is a text-based dataset or a tabular dataset. The preprocessing phase ExpGA will need to identify potential sensitives words that can generate discriminatory samples. A knowledge graph is used as a basis for finding sensitive words or attributes of a dataset such as gender, race, or religion in both text-based datasets and tabular datasets [36]. It should be noted that knowledge graphs have more importance in a text-based database as it will need to sift through far more sensitive words, and understand context in the dataset's sentences or other structures.

After the preprocessing phase ExpGA applies the genetic algorithm on the selected seed samples of discriminatory samples found in the preprocessing phase. The genetic algorithm will first construct an initial population and then select the highest quality seeds based on a fitness function value ranking. Afterwards crossover and mutation is applied to the samples and retested as discriminatory samples. The fitness function has to be careful about the amount of samples it approves because it runs into the problem of quantity of samples vs quality of samples, which makes a middleground the best. A large enough size of samples that each sample will rank high enough to be a discriminatory factor. This is the basis for generating discriminatory samples for the model to use as a new dataset in combination with the original one.

When compared to more mainstream solutions such as AEQUITAS, ADF, and SG ExpGA is higher in efficiency, higher in effectiveness, and model-agnostic. Three models were used to experiment and test the differences between ExpGA, AEQUITAS, ADF, and SG. The paper reported that between ExpGA, AEQUITAS, ADF, and SG the TSN (total sample number) reported by ExpGA was much higher than each of the other approaches. ExpGA also had the advantage when it came to DSS (discriminatory samples per second). When measuring SUR (success rate), the success rate for generating discriminatory samples, ExpGA and the other toolkits were comparable, but when all solutions were given additional time ExpGA would eventually outcompete them. It should be noted that the paper does acknowledge that ExpGA performs better on tabular datasets rather than text datasets [36].

9.4 Causal Inference

Another area to explore is inference with respect to machine learning. There's going to be a focus on causal inference and inference in relation to tractable probability models, both in relation to machine learning fairness. In one area is the use of causal inference to explore contrastive fairness in machine learning models. Contrastive fairness is a method of determining fairness in machine learning models that is different from counterfactual fairness. While counterfactual fairness uses causal inference to measure population based data, contrastive fairness evaluates the fairness between two individuals and their attributes.

Causal inference is an important component to measure contrastive fairness. Causal inference methods consist of many structural causal models (SCM). SCMs consist of causal diagrams, which are directed acyclic graphs, structural equations, and intervention logic. In essence the causal diagrams represent attributes of a sample input, whether classified as part of a protected attribute, a latent attribute, or an observed attribute. Each of these attributes are observed and input to structural equations and intervention logic is then applied to these equations to get probabilities that a certain observed attribute is output given a certain condition. In this way this method of contrastive fairness can be used to evaluate a model's fairness decisions and whether there is potential bias within the model. It should also be noted that implementing contrastive fairness means that not only must the decisions made be fair to both parties, but that the decision needs to be reasonable in a given context [14]. Considering this was an experimental approach to machine learning fairness there were still plenty of areas unexplored in the research and it only provided a theoretical and mathematical foundation for future research into contrastive fairness in machine learning.

9.5 Sum Product Networks

While the framework of contrastive fairness is more experimental, the use of tractable probability models has more data to explore. This is also a statistical approach to the problem, much like the earlier paper on contrastive fairness. However it is pointed out that using counterfactual fairness as a metric is often difficult to use due to lack of definitive information on some of the data within the datasets, making the approach less feasible. The paper on SPNs argues that the counterfactual approach is less than ideal [37]. It argues in favor of tractable models because tractable models in machine learning can provide insight into the decision making process and offer explanations for potentially biased outcomes in machine learning models. Tractable solutions to fairness focus on Sum Product Networks (SPNs) without necessarily needing directed graphs or information that's not obtainable for the counterfactual probability equations.

Sum Product Networks are pitched as a potential solution for machine learning models that is applied in the preprocessing phase before learning. SPNs are arithmetic circuits that essentially act in a way similar to a network. SPNs will take an inference query and generate a probability that all its leaf nodes will be able to accept a set of values simultaneously. Using the SPN would mean being able to compute inference queries which are normally difficult to do due to the intractability of inferences. Further SPNs can efficiently compute computational probabilities to find probabilities for protected attributes in relationship to other background attributes and results given by the machine learning model. The results of the tests using SPNs found that on both fair and "unfair" data (data that did not account for any fairness testing measures) the difference in accuracy was marginal. There were no large changes to accuracy as a result of using SPNs to boost fairness of the model, regardless of model implementation [37].

10 Fairness Testing Using Deep Reinforcement Learning

Machine learning models are used for major decision making systems for classifying and predicting. In statistics and machine learning, it is important to have fairness testing of models, especially for a model that is used for discriminatory purposes. An unfair decision could lead to a variety of issues including discriminative profiling and discrimination in hiring decisions.

Given a dataset, reinforcement learning is applied on machine learning models. A certain state within the complex environment will take an appropriate action depending on the environment and is rewarded for said action. Reinforcement learning is an important computation that is used in machine learning. It is a type of deep learning that improves itself by making decisions and having feedback on them (reward or penalty based on the event). It also uses these rewards to learn from example data that it hasn't been trained with.

Deep learning models are believed to be fair in the noise level segmentation problem, which is demonstrated by reducing bias when the training data set is irregularly distributed. There are two important levels of fairness in a deep learning model: (1) non-discriminatory fairness, where the model performs well for all classes using equal weight and does not have a class-specific deficiency, and (2) non-normative fairness, where the model performs well for all classes without having a class dependence. With this being stated, Reinforcement Learning is a type of deep learning that often involves a neural network with many layers which has the ability to make decisions based off the network's previous experiences.

In this study, the use of deep neural networks were incorporated into the reinforcement learning paradigm. This is used to test the discriminatory fairness in the noise level segmentation problem. In an adversarial environment, the two network models, the one with a human-oriented model for generating actions, and the other with a machine-oriented model for visualizing actions, are tested. Both are utilizing reinforcement learning for Black-Box fairness testing. The results show that unfairness of various machine learning models are reduced when the discriminative power of human-model deep networks is increased. The study also highlights that, when compared to human-model deep learning, a machine model can learn to generate actions more reliably within the limited set of actions for each class.

Black Box fairness testing was applied, utilizing the study's proposed methodology called Deep Q-Network. Through reinforcement learning, the policy of calculating fairness score is iteratively updated over time. The main questions that were posed by the study were how efficient was the given output after the reward functional model, along with how does the parameters within the models in the dataset influence said effectiveness.

Comparing this state of the art methodology, it outperforms greatly compared to Aequitas and SG, other fairness testing models when comparing to the G-Ratio and G-Rate.

11 Managing Fairness Discrepancies Within Federated Learning Models

Federated learning is a new and developing type of machine learning technique that does model training focusing on decentralized datasets. It is able to produce better results whether you're doing reinforcement learning, supervised learning, or unsupervised learning. The most significant benefits are that it doesn't require any changes to how we think about the world. Federated learning has been developed to work within a decentralized system of datasets and data. This kind of data is not centrally housed, but rather distributed across different parties who all contribute to improve itself.

Because of the decentralized nature of these datasets, it can lead to some discrepancies within fairness. It becomes an issue to prevent biases. Bias is a type of issue that can arise in learning algorithms. It is typically expressed as negative when talking about issues in programs and algorithms. Federated learning has been developed to find solutions to this and other issues. They were built to combat issues that would arise within a decentralized system.

Federated learning is different from other types of machine learning in that it doesn't require a lot of data to actually train. The way this works is by cutting off some of the unnecessary training processes, so you don't need as much data as you would normally. It's able to do this by making sure that all the learning algorithms used are trained on some sort of different technique. This means that all the algorithms are able to use the same data, but they're not able to share information about how they use it.

This is much like how a node would share information with other nodes over a decentralized network of data. This means that the decision trees used by machine learning algorithms cannot be transferred between different datasets without being changed. It's also different in that it doesn't require that what comes out of the algorithm is always wrong or whatever data you're using for training is always correct. In its initial stages, it's able to test on both training and test datasets to just see how it will perform on new data.

The biggest benefit of this is that one can take advantage of algorithms from multiple parties simply by including trust in their operating procedures. These procedures are being used by all the parties involved to ensure that each party is considered a fair subset of the problem. For example, if you wanted to test your algorithm over a distributed network, you would need to make sure that the data was created in such a way that all parties could be considered equal parts of the dataset. The decentralized nature of this data means that you don't need to trust anybody with it. They automatically have some sort of trust in one another simply because each other owner has their own data to use in testing their algorithm. This would mean that one can take advantage of algorithms from multiple parties simply by including trust in their operating procedures.

FairFed: Cross-Device Fair Federated Learning [38] proposes a method in 3 sequential stages, to enable and provision the Federated Learning environment, to manage, monitor, and interpret the model statistics, and finally to manage the fairness scores among them. The main objective is to find out whether the proposed method can be used for fairness testing in terms of managing bias. The experimental results showed that our proposed method has a good performance for fairness testing, and the algorithm yielded fair results on all the different datasets used in this study. Testing FairFed, the model proposed, the use of a Deep Neural Network can increase the accuracy after changing the biases affecting the fairness testing.

12 Design and Approach

Fairness testing today has come a long way and has pushed many researchers to create various ways in tackling the diverse biases generated from data and modern society. Though several of these methodologies have introduced their own optimal way of executing fairness testing, the main ideal revolving around this task still remains and are incorporated in the design and techniques utilized by these methodologies.

12.1 Statistical Fairness Testing

Utilizing statistical approaches for the purpose of analyzing and evaluating the fairness of a software system is what this methodology entails. This may involve comparing the results of various groups of users to detect possible discrepancies, examining the data created by the system to discover potential biases, and running simulations to assess the fairness of the platform under a variety of different conditions. This may be helpful in identifying possible problems with the system or algorithm, which then enables modifications to be made in order to guarantee that all users are treated in a fair and equal manner [39]. This is of utmost significance in the areas of artificial intelligence and machine learning, as algorithms may sometimes display bias depending on the data that was used to train them. Software developers may assure the fairness and unbiasedness of their systems and algorithms by carrying out statistical fairness testing.

12.2 User-Centered Design

Users and other stakeholders are brought into the design and development process via the usage of this technique. It is predicated on the notion that the user's viewpoint ought to be a primary concern in the process of conception and development, and that the system ought to be created to be useable, accessible, and helpful to the user in some capacity or another. User-centered design may be used to the process of ensuring that the developed software does not discriminate against any users based on their characteristics, including those with disabilities and those of various ethnicities, genders, and ages, among other factors. In order to ensure that the software is accessible to all users, it is necessary to first undertake research about their requirements and skills. In order to make sure the program is useful for a wide range of people and doesn't have any negative effects on any subset of its users, it should be put through rigorous testing.

12.3 Algorithmic Accountability

The term "algorithmic accountability" describes the concept that software engineers and algorithm designers should be held liable for any unfair or biased outcomes caused by their creations. The usage of algorithms in decision-making processes is on the rise in fields like artificial intelligence and machine learning, making this idea crucial to software engineering. Testing algorithms for fairness is a common practice in software engineering. To prevent bias, it is common practice to test an algorithm on data from a wide range of demographics, including people of various ethnicities, genders, and socioeconomic statuses [40]. One of the main goals of algorithmic accountability is to guarantee that persons in charge of designing and executing algorithms are held to account for any potential bias or unfairness in their designs. Methods for ensuring that algorithms are developed and used fairly and impartially include frequent audits and testing, as well as the creation of regulations and standards. Software developers may aid in making sure that algorithms are utilized fairly and without bias if they advocate for algorithmic accountability [41].

12.4 Transparency and Explainability

For a system or algorithm to be transparent, it must be able to explain how it arrived at its conclusions and what considerations it considered. Users are better able to spot biases or other problems in the system when they have insight into its inner workings and decision-making processes. The capacity of a system or algorithm to offer clear and intelligible explanations for its choices is known as explainability. This helps users understand the reasoning behind the system's judgments and, in turn, spot any biases or problems that may exist.

To verify that systems and algorithms are not biased or discriminating, fairness testing in software engineering relies heavily on transparency and explainability. These systems may be better examined for possible biases and concerns if they provide clear and intelligible explanations and information about the process of decision-making they use.

12.5 Collaborative Governance

Collaborative governance refers to the process of including numerous stakeholders in determining the bias and fairness of a software system throughout its evaluation. People within the development team, specialists in the field, and even potential end users might all be a part of this. Collaborative governance seeks to ensure that the fairness of a software system is evaluated from a range of viewpoints, minimizing the possibility of bias and allowing for a more thorough assessment of the system's fairness, by incorporating multiple points of view and expertise in the testing process. This method also promotes openness and accountability in testing by encouraging dialogue and teamwork amongst all parties involved [42]. In order to guarantee that the final software system is fair and impartial, collaborative governance may assist to detect and solve any fairness challenges at an early stage in the process of development.

13 Conclusion

In recent years, software technologies have been utilized to fulfill specific needs or perform tasks prescribed by users in an efficient and effective manner. Among these technologies are Artificial Intelligence (AI) and Machine Learning (ML) which have long been regarded as potential sources of business innovation for their efficiency and streamlining of workflows. But AI has not just been about improving menial and laborious tasks, it has also been widely adopted into social-critical, human-related tasks, such as hiring, credit assessment, criminal justice, and disease detection. Although leaving such decisions to an algorithm developed by specific inputs and instruction may result in an unbiased and practical outcome in a technical space, it can also create consequential and improper results in terms of societal standards and biases. This concept introduced by a learning model generating user inputs and attempting to establish a decision from an algorithm or algorithms while conducting various attempts in correcting any possible biases and stereotypes is called "fairness".

This paper defines the methodologies and relevance of software fairness testing by introducing the concept of fairness in the development process of a software product and the implications of the results it produces. This paper conveys the possible discrimination and injustice an algorithm may demonstrate and how software developers and researchers develop a testing-based method called "fairness testing" for measuring if and how much software discriminates, focusing on causality in discriminatory behavior. Evidence of software discrimination has been found in modern software systems that recommend criminal sentences, grant access to financial products, and determine who is allowed to participate in promotions. We introduce various methodologies in this paper or fairness testing to mitigate the effects resulting from the ethical issues produced by software classification and decision-making, among them are the Grammar-based approach (ASTRAEA), the Genetic Algorithm approach, the Machine Deep Learning approach, and many others. These fairness testing methodologies, each with their own unique approach to ensuring fairness, constitute the current perspective of research focus, trends, promising directions, as well as widely-adopted datasets and open source tools for fairness testing.

References

1. Chen, Z., Zhang, J.M., Hort, M., Sarro, F., Harman, M.: Fairness testing: a comprehensive survey and analysis of trends. arXiv preprint arXiv:2207.10223 (2022)
2. Verma, S., Rubin, J.: Fairness definitions explained. In: 2018 IEEE/ACM International Workshop on Software Fairness (Fairware), pp. 1–7. IEEE (2018)
3. Ritov, Y., Sun, Y., Zhao, R.: On conditional parity as a notion of non-discrimination in machine learning. arXiv preprint arXiv:1706.08519 (2017)
4. Zeng, X., Dobriban, E., Cheng, G.: Fair bayes-optimal classifiers under predictive parity. arXiv preprint arXiv:2205.07182 (2022)
5. Yan, S., Kao, H., Ferrara, E.: Fair class balancing: enhancing model fairness without observing sensitive attributes. In: Proceedings of the 29th ACM International Conference on Information & Knowledge Management, pp. 1715–1724 (2020)
6. Chen, J., Kallus, N., Mao, X., Svacha, G., Udell, M.: Fairness under unawareness: assessing disparity when protected class is unobserved. In: Proceedings of the Conference on Fairness, Accountability, and Transparency, pp. 339–348 (2019)
7. Kusner, M.J., Loftus, J., Russell, C., Silva, R.: Counterfactual fairness. In: Advances in Neural Information Processing Systems, vol. 30 (2017)
8. Narayanan, A.: Translation tutorial: 21 fairness definitions and their politics. In: Proceedings of the Conference on Fairness Accountability Transparency, New York, USA, vol. 1170, p. 3 (2018)
9. Brun, Y., Meliou, A.: Software fairness. In: Proceedings of the 2018 26th ACM Joint Meeting on European Software Engineering Conference and Symposium on the Foundations of Software Engineering, pp. 754–759 (2018)
10. Vokinger, K.N., Feuerriegel, S., Kesselheim, A.S.: Mitigating bias in machine learning for medicine. Commun. Med. **1**(1), 1–3 (2021)
11. Smith, H.: Algorithmic bias: should students pay the price? AI Soc. **35**(4), 1077–1078 (2020). https://doi.org/10.1007/s00146-020-01054-3
12. Angwin, J., Larson, J., Kirchner, L.: Machine bias: risk assessments in criminal sentencing
13. Pessach, D., Shmueli, E.: A review on fairness in machine learning. ACM Comput. Surv. (CSUR) **55**(3), 1–44 (2022)
14. Chakraborti, T., Patra, A., Noble, J.A.: Contrastive fairness in machine learning. IEEE Lett. Comput. Soc. **3**(2), 38–41 (2020)

15. Li, Y., et al.: Training data debugging for the fairness of machine learning software. In: Proceedings of the 44th International Conference on Software Engineering, pp. 2215–2227 (2022)
16. Zhang, P., et al.: Automatic fairness testing of neural classifiers through adversarial sampling. IEEE Trans. Softw. Eng. (2021)
17. Aggarwal, A., Lohia, P., Nagar, S., Dey, K., Saha, D.: Black box fairness testing of machine learning models. In: Proceedings of the 2019 27th ACM Joint Meeting on European Software Engineering Conference and Symposium on the Foundations of Software Engineering, pp. 625–635 (2019)
18. Arusoaie, A., Lucanu, D., Rusu, V.: A generic framework for symbolic execution. In: Erwig, M., Paige, R.F., Van Wyk, E. (eds.) SLE 2013. LNCS, vol. 8225, pp. 281–301. Springer, Cham (2013). https://doi.org/10.1007/978-3-319-02654-1_16
19. Nilsson, U., Lübcke, J.: Constraint logic programming for local and symbolic model-checking. In: Lloyd, J., et al. (eds.) CL 2000. LNCS (LNAI), vol. 1861, pp. 384–398. Springer, Heidelberg (2000). https://doi.org/10.1007/3-540-44957-4_26
20. Collingbourne, P., Cadar, C., Kelly, P.H.J.: Symbolic testing of OpenCL code. In: Eder, K., Lourenço, J., Shehory, O. (eds.) HVC 2011. LNCS, vol. 7261, pp. 203–218. Springer, Heidelberg (2012). https://doi.org/10.1007/978-3-642-34188-5_18
21. Baars, A., et al.: Symbolic search-based testing. In: 2011 26th IEEE/ACM International Conference on Automated Software Engineering (ASE 2011), pp. 53–62. IEEE (2011)
22. Shao, D., Khurshid, S., Perry, D.E.: Whispec: white-box testing of libraries using declarative specifications. In: Proceedings of the 2007 Symposium on Library-Centric Software Design, pp. 11–20 (2007)
23. Dey, S., Dasgupta, P., Chakrabarti, P.P.: Symdnn: simple & effective adversarial robustness for embedded systems. In: Proceedings of the IEEE/CVF Conference on Computer Vision and Pattern Recognition, pp. 3599–3609 (2022)
24. Mayan, J.A., Ravi, T.: Test case optimization using hybrid search technique. In: Proceedings of the 2014 International Conference on Interdisciplinary Advances in Applied Computing, pp. 1–7 (2014)
25. Zhao, J., Wang, T., Yatskar, M., Ordonez, V., Chang, K.-W.: Gender bias in coreference resolution: evaluation and debiasing methods. arXiv preprint arXiv:1804.06876 (2018)
26. Udeshi, S., Arora, P., Chattopadhyay, S.: Automated directed fairness testing. In: Proceedings of the 33rd ACM/IEEE International Conference on Automated Software Engineering, pp. 98–108 (2018)
27. Ribeiro, M.T., Wu, T., Guestrin, C., Singh, S.: Beyond accuracy: behavioral testing of NLP models with checklist. arXiv preprint arXiv:2005.04118 (2020)
28. Ma, P., Wang, S., Liu, J.: Metamorphic testing and certified mitigation of fairness violations in NLP models. In: IJCAI, pp. 458–465 (2020)
29. Product fairness testing for developers. https://developers.google.com/codelabs/product-fairness-testing
30. Hovy, D., Spruit, S.L.: The social impact of natural language processing. In: Proceedings of the 54th Annual Meeting of the Association for Computational Linguistics (Volume 2: Short Papers), pp. 591–598 (2016)
31. Sun, T., et al.: Mitigating gender bias in natural language processing: literature review. arXiv preprint arXiv:1906.08976 (2019)
32. Tizpaz-Niari, S., Kumar, A., Tan, G., Trivedi, A.: Fairness-aware configuration of machine learning libraries. arXiv preprint arXiv:2202.06196 (2022)

33. Holstein, K., Wortman Vaughan, J., Daumé, H., III., Dudik, M., Wallach, H.: Improving fairness in machine learning systems: what do industry practitioners need? In: Proceedings of the 2019 CHI Conference on Human Factors in Computing Systems, pp. 1–16 (2019)
34. Perera, A., et al.: Search-based fairness testing for regression-based machine learning systems. Empir. Softw. Eng. **27**(3), 1–36 (2022). https://doi.org/10.1007/s10664-022-10116-7
35. Wang, T., Saar-Tsechansky, M.: Augmented fairness: An interpretable model augmenting decision-makers' fairness. arXiv preprint arXiv:2011.08398 (2020)
36. Fan, M., Wei, W., Jin, W., Yang, Z., Liu, T.: Explanation-guided fairness testing through genetic algorithm. arXiv preprint arXiv:2205.08335 (2022)
37. Varley, M., Belle, V.: Fairness in machine learning with tractable models. Knowl.-Based Syst. **215**, 106715 (2021)
38. ur Rehman, M.H., Dirir, A.M., Salah, K., Svetinovic, D.: Fairfed: cross-device fair federated learning. In: 2020 IEEE Applied Imagery Pattern Recognition Workshop (AIPR), pp. 1–7. IEEE (2020)
39. Zhang, L., Zhang, Y., Zhang, M.: Efficient white-box fairness testing through gradient search. In: Proceedings of the 30th ACM SIGSOFT International Symposium on Software Testing and Analysis, pp. 103–114 (2021)
40. Galhotra, S., Brun, Y., Meliou, A.: Fairness testing: testing software for discrimination. In: Proceedings of the 2017 11th Joint Meeting on Foundations of Software Engineering, pp. 498–510 (2017)
41. Khademi, A., Lee, S., Foley, D., Honavar, V.: Fairness in algorithmic decision making: an excursion through the lens of causality (2019)
42. Lang, A., Bresch, C.: Collaborative governance in program implementation: the development of e-relocation notification in the swiss canton of Zurich. Int. J. Public Adm. **43**(12), 1083–1095 (2020)
43. Soremekun, E., Udeshi, S.S., Chattopadhyay, S.: Astraea: grammar-based fairness testing. IEEE Trans. Softw. Eng. (2022)
44. Zhang, P., et al.: White-box fairness testing through adversarial sampling. In: Proceedings of the ACM/IEEE 42nd International Conference on Software Engineering, pp. 949–960 (2020)
45. Soremekun, E., Papadakis, M., Cordy, M., Traon, Y.L.: Software fairness: an analysis and survey. arXiv preprint arXiv:2205.08809 (2022)
46. Xie, W., Wu, P.: Fairness testing of machine learning models using deep reinforcement learning. In: 2020 IEEE 19th International Conference on Trust, Security and Privacy in Computing and Communications (TrustCom), pp. 121–128. IEEE (2020)
47. Friedler, S.A., Scheidegger, C., Venkatasubramanian, S., Choudhary, S., Hamilton, E.P., Roth, D.: A comparative study of fairness-enhancing interventions in machine learning. In: Proceedings of the Conference on Fairness, Accountability, and Transparency, pp. 329–338 (2019)

Author Index

S. Hussain et al. (Eds.): SEET 2025, CCIS 2725, pp. 761–763, 2026.
https://doi.org/10.1007/978-3-032-08977-9

MIX
Papier aus verantwortungsvollen Quellen
Paper from responsible sources
FSC® C105338

If you have any concerns about our products,
you can contact us on
ProductSafety@springernature.com

In case Publisher is established outside the EU,
the EU authorized representative is:
Springer Nature Customer Service Center GmbH
Europaplatz 3, 69115 Heidelberg, Germany

Printed by Libri Plureos GmbH
in Hamburg, Germany